We accepted 67 full papers, 13 short papers and 6 PHD Showcase papers from 283 submissions to the General Tracks of the conference (acceptance rate 30%). For the 61 workshops we accepted 350 full papers, 29 short papers and 2 PHD Showcase papers. We would like to express our appreciations for the workshops chairs and co-chairs for their hard work and dedication.

The success of the ICCSA series in general, and of ICCSA 2023 in particular, vitally depends on the support of many people: authors, presenters, participants, keynote speakers, workshop chairs, session chairs, organizing committee members, student volunteers, Program Committee members, Advisory Committee members, International Liaison chairs, reviewers and others in various roles. We take this opportunity to wholehartedly thank them all.

We also wish to thank our publisher, Springer, for their acceptance to publish the proceedings, for sponsoring part of the best papers awards and for their kind assistance and cooperation during the editing process.

We cordially invite you to visit the ICCSA website https://iccsa.org where you can find all the relevant information about this interesting and exciting event.

July 2023

Osvaldo Gervasi
David Taniar
Bernady O. Apduhan

Preface

These two volumes (LNCS volumes 13956–13957) consist of the peer-reviewed papers from the 2023 International Conference on Computational Science and Its Applications (ICCSA 2023) which took place during July 3–6, 2023. In addition, the peer-reviewed papers of the 61 Workshops, the Workshops proceedings, are published in a separate set consisting of nine volumes (LNCS 14104–14112).

The conference was finally held in person after the difficult period of the Covid-19 pandemic in the wonderful city of Athens, in the cosy facilities of the National Technical University. Our experience during the pandemic period allowed us to enable virtual participation also this year for those who were unable to attend the event, due to logistical, political and economic problems, by adopting a technological infrastructure based on open source software (jitsi + riot), and a commercial cloud infrastructure.

ICCSA 2023 was another successful event in the International Conference on Computational Science and Its Applications (ICCSA) series, previously held as a hybrid event (with one third of registered authors attending in person) in Malaga, Spain (2022), Cagliari, Italy (hybrid with few participants in person in 2021 and completely online in 2020), whilst earlier editions took place in Saint Petersburg, Russia (2019), Melbourne, Australia (2018), Trieste, Italy (2017), Beijing, China (2016), Banff, Canada (2015), Guimaraes, Portugal (2014), Ho Chi Minh City, Vietnam (2013), Salvador, Brazil (2012), Santander, Spain (2011), Fukuoka, Japan (2010), Suwon, South Korea (2009), Perugia, Italy (2008), Kuala Lumpur, Malaysia (2007), Glasgow, UK (2006), Singapore (2005), Assisi, Italy (2004), Montreal, Canada (2003), and (as ICCS) Amsterdam, The Netherlands (2002) and San Francisco, USA (2001).

Computational Science is the main pillar of most of the present research, industrial and commercial applications, and plays a unique role in exploiting ICT innovative technologies, and the ICCSA series have been providing a venue to researchers and industry practitioners to discuss new ideas, to share complex problems and their solutions, and to shape new trends in Computational Science. As the conference mirrors society from a scientific point of view, this year's undoubtedly dominant theme was the machine learning and artificial intelligence and their applications in the most diverse economic and industrial fields.

The ICCSA 2023 conference is structured in 6 general tracks covering the fields of computational science and its applications: Computational Methods, Algorithms and Scientific Applications – High Performance Computing and Networks – Geometric Modeling, Graphics and Visualization – Advanced and Emerging Applications – Information Systems and Technologies – Urban and Regional Planning. In addition, the conference consisted of 61 workshops, focusing on very topical issues of importance to science, technology and society: from new mathematical approaches for solving complex computational systems, to information and knowledge in the Internet of Things, new statistical and optimization methods, several Artificial Intelligence approaches, sustainability issues, smart cities and related technologies.

Editors
Osvaldo Gervasi (iD)
University of Perugia
Perugia, Italy

David Taniar (iD)
Monash University
Clayton, VIC, Australia

Ana Cristina Braga (iD)
University of Minho
Braga, Portugal

Anastasia Stratigea (iD)
National Technical University of Athens
Athens, Greece

Beniamino Murgante (iD)
University of Basilicata
Potenza, Italy

Bernady O. Apduhan
Kyushu Sangyo University
Fukuoka, Japan

Chiara Garau (iD)
University of Cagliari
Cagliari, Italy

ISSN 0302-9743   ISSN 1611-3349 (electronic)
Lecture Notes in Computer Science
ISBN 978-3-031-36804-2   ISBN 978-3-031-36805-9 (eBook)
https://doi.org/10.1007/978-3-031-36805-9

This Springer imprint is published by the registered company Springer Nature Switzerland AG
The registered company address is: Gewerbestrasse 11, 6330 Cham, Switzerland

Osvaldo Gervasi · Beniamino Murgante ·
David Taniar · Bernady O. Apduhan ·
Ana Cristina Braga · Chiara Garau ·
Anastasia Stratigea
Editors

Computational Science and Its Applications – ICCSA 2023

23rd International Conference
Athens, Greece, July 3–6, 2023
Proceedings, Part I

Springer

The series Lecture Notes in Computer Science (LNCS), including its subseries Lecture Notes in Artificial Intelligence (LNAI) and Lecture Notes in Bioinformatics (LNBI), has established itself as a medium for the publication of new developments in computer science and information technology research, teaching, and education.

LNCS enjoys close cooperation with the computer science R & D community, the series counts many renowned academics among its volume editors and paper authors, and collaborates with prestigious societies. Its mission is to serve this international community by providing an invaluable service, mainly focused on the publication of conference and workshop proceedings and postproceedings. LNCS commenced publication in 1973.

Lecture Notes in Computer Science   13956

Founding Editors

Gerhard Goos
Juris Hartmanis

Welcome Message from Organizers

After the 2021 ICCSA in Cagliari, Italy and the 2022 ICCSA in Malaga, Spain, ICCSA continued its successful scientific endeavours in 2023, hosted again in the Mediterranean neighbourhood. This time, ICCSA 2023 moved a bit more to the east of the Mediterranean Region and was held in the metropolitan city of Athens, the capital of Greece and a vibrant urban environment endowed with a prominent cultural heritage that dates back to the ancient years. As a matter of fact, Athens is one of the oldest cities in the world, and the cradle of democracy. The city has a history of over 3,000 years and, according to the myth, it took its name from Athena, the Goddess of Wisdom and daughter of Zeus.

ICCSA 2023 took place in a secure environment, relieved from the immense stress of the COVID-19 pandemic. This gave us the chance to have a safe and vivid, in-person participation which, combined with the very active engagement of the ICCSA 2023 scientific community, set the ground for highly motivating discussions and interactions as to the latest developments of computer science and its applications in the real world for improving quality of life.

The National Technical University of Athens (NTUA), one of the most prestigious Greek academic institutions, had the honour of hosting ICCSA 2023. The Local Organizing Committee really feels the burden and responsibility of such a demanding task; and puts in all the necessary energy in order to meet participants' expectations and establish a friendly, creative and inspiring, scientific and social/cultural environment that allows for new ideas and perspectives to flourish.

Since all ICCSA participants, either informatics-oriented or application-driven, realize the tremendous steps and evolution of computer science during the last few decades and the huge potential these offer to cope with the enormous challenges of humanity in a globalized, 'wired' and highly competitive world, the expectations from ICCSA 2023 were set high in order for a successful matching between computer science progress and communities' aspirations to be attained, i.e., a progress that serves real, place- and people-based needs and can pave the way towards a visionary, smart, sustainable, resilient and inclusive future for both the current and the next generation.

On behalf of the Local Organizing Committee, I would like to sincerely thank all of you who have contributed to ICCSA 2023 and I cordially welcome you to my 'home', NTUA.

On behalf of the Local Organizing Committee.

Anastasia Stratigea

Organization

ICCSA 2023 was organized by the National Technical University of Athens (Greece), the University of the Aegean (Greece), the University of Perugia (Italy), the University of Basilicata (Italy), Monash University (Australia), Kyushu Sangyo University (Japan), the University of Minho (Portugal). The conference was supported by two NTUA Schools, namely the School of Rural, Surveying and Geoinformatics Engineering and the School of Electrical and Computer Engineering.

Honorary General Chairs

Norio Shiratori   Chuo University, Japan
Kenneth C. J. Tan   Sardina Systems, UK

General Chairs

Osvaldo Gervasi   University of Perugia, Italy
Anastasia Stratigea   National Technical University of Athens, Greece
Bernady O. Apduhan   Kyushu Sangyo University, Japan

Program Committee Chairs

Beniamino Murgante   University of Basilicata, Italy
Dimitris Kavroudakis   University of the Aegean, Greece
Ana Maria A. C. Rocha   University of Minho, Portugal
David Taniar   Monash University, Australia

International Advisory Committee

Jemal Abawajy   Deakin University, Australia
Dharma P. Agarwal   University of Cincinnati, USA
Rajkumar Buyya   Melbourne University, Australia
Claudia Bauzer Medeiros University of Campinas, Brazil
Manfred M. Fisher   Vienna University of Economics and Business, Austria
Marina L. Gavrilova   University of Calgary, Canada

| Sumi Helal | University of Florida, USA and University of Lancaster, UK |
| Yee Leung | Chinese University of Hong Kong, China |

International Liaison Chairs

Ivan Blečić	University of Cagliari, Italy
Giuseppe Borruso	University of Trieste, Italy
Elise De Donker	Western Michigan University, USA
Maria Irene Falcão	University of Minho, Portugal
Inmaculada Garcia Fernandez	University of Malaga, Spain
Eligius Hendrix	University of Malaga, Spain
Robert C. H. Hsu	Chung Hua University, Taiwan
Tai-Hoon Kim	Beijing Jaotong University, China
Vladimir Korkhov	Saint Petersburg University, Russia
Takashi Naka	Kyushu Sangyo University, Japan
Rafael D. C. Santos	National Institute for Space Research, Brazil
Maribel Yasmina Santos	University of Minho, Portugal
Elena Stankova	Saint Petersburg University, Russia

Workshop and Session Organizing Chairs

| Beniamino Murgante | University of Basilicata, Italy |
| Chiara Garau | University of Cagliari, Italy |

Award Chair

| Wenny Rahayu | La Trobe University, Australia |

Publicity Committee Chairs

Elmer Dadios	De La Salle University, Philippines
Nataliia Kulabukhova	Saint Petersburg University, Russia
Daisuke Takahashi	Tsukuba University, Japan
Shangwang Wang	Beijing University of Posts and Telecommunications, China

Local Organizing Committee Chairs

Anastasia Stratigea	National Technical University of Athens, Greece
Dimitris Kavroudakis	University of the Aegean, Greece
Charalambos Ioannidis	National Technical University of Athens, Greece
Nectarios Koziris	National Technical University of Athens, Greece
Efthymios Bakogiannis	National Technical University of Athens, Greece
Yiota Theodora	National Technical University of Athens, Greece
Dimitris Fotakis	National Technical University of Athens, Greece
Apostolos Lagarias	National Technical University of Athens, Greece
Akrivi Leka	National Technical University of Athens, Greece
Dionisia Koutsi	National Technical University of Athens, Greece
Alkistis Dalkavouki	National Technical University of Athens, Greece
Maria Panagiotopoulou	National Technical University of Athens, Greece
Angeliki Papazoglou	National Technical University of Athens, Greece
Natalia Tsigarda	National Technical University of Athens, Greece
Konstantinos Athanasopoulos	National Technical University of Athens, Greece
Ioannis Xatziioannou	National Technical University of Athens, Greece
Vasiliki Krommyda	National Technical University of Athens, Greece
Panayiotis Patsilinakos	National Technical University of Athens, Greece
Sofia Kassiou	National Technical University of Athens, Greece

Technology Chair

Damiano Perri	University of Florence, Italy

Program Committee

Vera Afreixo	University of Aveiro, Portugal
Filipe Alvelos	University of Minho, Portugal
Hartmut Asche	University of Potsdam, Germany
Ginevra Balletto	University of Cagliari, Italy
Michela Bertolotto	University College Dublin, Ireland
Sandro Bimonte	CEMAGREF, TSCF, France
Rod Blais	University of Calgary, Canada
Ivan Blečić	University of Sassari, Italy
Giuseppe Borruso	University of Trieste, Italy
Ana Cristina Braga	University of Minho, Portugal
Massimo Cafaro	University of Salento, Italy
Yves Caniou	Lyon University, France

Ermanno Cardelli	University of Perugia, Italy
José A. Cardoso e Cunha	Universidade Nova de Lisboa, Portugal
Rui Cardoso	University of Beira Interior, Portugal
Leocadio G. Casado	University of Almeria, Spain
Carlo Cattani	University of Salerno, Italy
Mete Celik	Erciyes University, Turkey
Maria Cerreta	University of Naples "Federico II", Italy
Hyunseung Choo	Sungkyunkwan University, Korea
Rachel Chieng-Sing Lee	Sunway University, Malaysia
Min Young Chung	Sungkyunkwan University, Korea
Florbela Maria da Cruz Domingues Correia	Polytechnic Institute of Viana do Castelo, Portugal
Gilberto Corso Pereira	Federal University of Bahia, Brazil
Alessandro Costantini	INFN, Italy
Carla Dal Sasso Freitas	Universidade Federal do Rio Grande do Sul, Brazil
Pradesh Debba	The Council for Scientific and Industrial Research (CSIR), South Africa
Hendrik Decker	Instituto Tecnológico de Informática, Spain
Robertas Damaševičius	Kausan University of Technology, Lithuania
Frank Devai	London South Bank University, UK
Rodolphe Devillers	Memorial University of Newfoundland, Canada
Joana Matos Dias	University of Coimbra, Portugal
Paolino Di Felice	University of L'Aquila, Italy
Prabu Dorairaj	NetApp, India/USA
Noelia Faginas Lago	University of Perugia, Italy
M. Irene Falcao	University of Minho, Portugal
Cherry Liu Fang	U.S. DOE Ames Laboratory, USA
Florbela P. Fernandes	Polytechnic Institute of Bragança, Portugal
Jose-Jesus Fernandez	National Centre for Biotechnology, CSIS, Spain
Paula Odete Fernandes	Polytechnic Institute of Bragança, Portugal
Adelaide de Fátima Baptista Valente Freitas	University of Aveiro, Portugal
Manuel Carlos Figueiredo	University of Minho, Portugal
Maria Celia Furtado Rocha	PRODEB–PósCultura/UFBA, Brazil
Chiara Garau	University of Cagliari, Italy
Paulino Jose Garcia Nieto	University of Oviedo, Spain
Raffaele Garrisi	Polizia di Stato, Italy
Jerome Gensel	LSR-IMAG, France
Maria Giaoutzi	National Technical University, Athens, Greece
Arminda Manuela Andrade Pereira Gonçalves	University of Minho, Portugal

Louiza de Macedo Mourelle	State University of Rio de Janeiro, Brazil
Nadia Nedjah	State University of Rio de Janeiro, Brazil
Laszlo Neumann	University of Girona, Spain
Kok-Leong Ong	Deakin University, Australia
Belen Palop	Universidad de Valladolid, Spain
Marcin Paprzycki	Polish Academy of Sciences, Poland
Eric Pardede	La Trobe University, Australia
Kwangjin Park	Wonkwang University, Korea
Ana Isabel Pereira	Polytechnic Institute of Bragança, Portugal
Massimiliano Petri	University of Pisa, Italy
Telmo Pinto	University of Coimbra, Portugal
Maurizio Pollino	Italian National Agency for New Technologies, Energy and Sustainable Economic Development, Italy
Alenka Poplin	University of Hamburg, Germany
Vidyasagar Potdar	Curtin University of Technology, Australia
David C. Prosperi	Florida Atlantic University, USA
Wenny Rahayu	La Trobe University, Australia
Jerzy Respondek	Silesian University of Technology Poland
Humberto Rocha	INESC-Coimbra, Portugal
Jon Rokne	University of Calgary, Canada
Octavio Roncero	CSIC, Spain
Maytham Safar	Kuwait University, Kuwait
Chiara Saracino	A.O. Ospedale Niguarda Ca' Granda - Milano, Italy
Marco Paulo Seabra dos Reis	University of Coimbra, Portugal
Jie Shen	University of Michigan, USA
Qi Shi	Liverpool John Moores University, UK
Dale Shires	U.S. Army Research Laboratory, USA
Inês Soares	University of Coimbra, Portugal
Elena Stankova	St. Petersburg University, Russia
Takuo Suganuma	Tohoku University, Japan
Eufemia Tarantino	Polytechnic of Bari, Italy
Sergio Tasso	University of Perugia, Italy
Ana Paula Teixeira	University of Trás-os-Montes and Alto Douro, Portugal
M. Filomena Teodoro	Portuguese Naval Academy and University of Lisbon, Portugal
Parimala Thulasiraman	University of Manitoba, Canada
Carmelo Torre	Polytechnic of Bari, Italy
Javier Martinez Torres	Centro Universitario de la Defensa Zaragoza, Spain

Giuseppe A. Trunfio	University of Sassari, Italy
Pablo Vanegas	University of Cuenca, Equador
Marco Vizzari	University of Perugia, Italy
Varun Vohra	Merck Inc., USA
Koichi Wada	University of Tsukuba, Japan
Krzysztof Walkowiak	Wroclaw University of Technology, Poland
Zequn Wang	Intelligent Automation Inc, USA
Robert Weibel	University of Zurich, Switzerland
Frank Westad	Norwegian University of Science and Technology, Norway
Roland Wismüller	Universität Siegen, Germany
Mudasser Wyne	SOET National University, USA
Chung-Huang Yang	National Kaohsiung Normal University, Taiwan
Xin-She Yang	National Physical Laboratory, UK
Salim Zabir	France Telecom Japan Co., Japan
Haifeng Zhao	University of California, Davis, USA
Fabiana Zollo	University of Venice "Cà Foscari", Italy
Albert Y. Zomaya	University of Sydney, Australia

Workshop Organizers

Advanced Data Science Techniques with Applications in Industry and Environmental Sustainability (ATELIERS 2023)

Dario Torregrossa	Goodyear, Luxemburg
Antonino Marvuglia	Luxembourg Institute of Science and Technology, Luxemburg
Valeria Borodin	École des Mines de Saint-Étienne, Luxemburg
Mohamed Laib	Luxembourg Institute of Science and Technology, Luxemburg

Advances in Artificial Intelligence Learning Technologies: Blended Learning, STEM, Computational Thinking and Coding (AAILT 2023)

Alfredo Milani	University of Perugia, Italy
Valentina Franzoni	University of Perugia, Italy
Sergio Tasso	University of Perugia, Italy

Advanced Processes of Mathematics and Computing Models in Complex Computational Systems (ACMC 2023)

Yeliz Karaca   University of Massachusetts Chan Medical
                                School and Massachusetts Institute of
                                Technology, USA
Dumitru Baleanu   Cankaya University, Turkey
Osvaldo Gervasi   University of Perugia, Italy
Yudong Zhang   University of Leicester, UK
Majaz Moonis   University of Massachusetts Medical School,
                                USA

Artificial Intelligence Supported Medical Data Examination (AIM 2023)

David Taniar   Monash University, Australia
Seifedine Kadry   Noroff University College, Norway
Venkatesan Rajinikanth   Saveetha School of Engineering, India

Advanced and Innovative Web Apps (AIWA 2023)

Damiano Perri   University of Perugia, Italy
Osvaldo Gervasi   University of Perugia, Italy

Assessing Urban Sustainability (ASUS 2023)

Elena Todella   Polytechnic of Turin, Italy
Marika Gaballo   Polytechnic of Turin, Italy
Beatrice Mecca   Polytechnic of Turin, Italy

Advances in Web Based Learning (AWBL 2023)

Birol Ciloglugil   Ege University, Turkey
Mustafa Inceoglu   Ege University, Turkey

Blockchain and Distributed Ledgers: Technologies and Applications (BDLTA 2023)

Vladimir Korkhov	Saint Petersburg State University, Russia
Elena Stankova	Saint Petersburg State University, Russia
Nataliia Kulabukhova	Saint Petersburg State University, Russia

Bio and Neuro Inspired Computing and Applications (BIONCA 2023)

Nadia Nedjah	State University of Rio De Janeiro, Brazil
Luiza De Macedo Mourelle	State University of Rio De Janeiro, Brazil

Choices and Actions for Human Scale Cities: Decision Support Systems (CAHSC–DSS 2023)

Giovanna Acampa	University of Florence and University of Enna Kore, Italy
Fabrizio Finucci	Roma Tre University, Italy
Luca S. Dacci	Polytechnic of Turin, Italy

Computational and Applied Mathematics (CAM 2023)

Maria Irene Falcao	University of Minho, Portugal
Fernando Miranda	University of Minho, Portugal

Computational and Applied Statistics (CAS 2023)

Ana Cristina Braga	University of Minho, Portugal

Cyber Intelligence and Applications (CIA 2023)

Gianni Dangelo	University of Salerno, Italy
Francesco Palmieri	University of Salerno, Italy
Massimo Ficco	University of Salerno, Italy

Conversations South-North on Climate Change Adaptation Towards Smarter and More Sustainable Cities (CLAPS 2023)

Chiara Garau	University of Cagliari, Italy
Cristina Trois	University of kwaZulu-Natal, South Africa
Claudia Loggia	University of kwaZulu-Natal, South Africa
John Östh	Faculty of Technology, Art and Design, Norway
Mauro Coni	University of Cagliari, Italy
Alessio Satta	MedSea Foundation, Italy

Computational Mathematics, Statistics and Information Management (CMSIM 2023)

Maria Filomena Teodoro	University of Lisbon and Portuguese Naval Academy, Portugal
Marina A. P. Andrade	University Institute of Lisbon, Portugal

Computational Optimization and Applications (COA 2023)

Ana Maria A. C. Rocha	University of Minho, Portugal
Humberto Rocha	University of Coimbra, Portugal

Computational Astrochemistry (CompAstro 2023)

Marzio Rosi	University of Perugia, Italy
Nadia Balucani	University of Perugia, Italy
Cecilia Ceccarelli	University of Grenoble Alpes and Institute for Planetary Sciences and Astrophysics, France
Stefano Falcinelli	University of Perugia, Italy

Computational Methods for Porous Geomaterials (CompPor 2023)

Vadim Lisitsa	Russian Academy of Science, Russia
Evgeniy Romenski	Russian Academy of Science, Russia

Workshop on Computational Science and HPC (CSHPC 2023)

Elise De Doncker	Western Michigan University, USA
Fukuko Yuasa	High Energy Accelerator Research Organization, Japan
Hideo Matsufuru	High Energy Accelerator Research Organization, Japan

Cities, Technologies and Planning (CTP 2023)

Giuseppe Borruso	University of Trieste, Italy
Beniamino Murgante	University of Basilicata, Italy
Malgorzata Hanzl	Lodz University of Technology, Poland
Anastasia Stratigea	National Technical University of Athens, Greece
Ljiljana Zivkovic	Republic Geodetic Authority, Serbia
Ginevra Balletto	University of Cagliari, Italy

Gender Equity/Equality in Transport and Mobility (DELIA 2023)

Tiziana Campisi	University of Enna Kore, Italy
Ines Charradi	Sousse University, Tunisia
Alexandros Nikitas	University of Huddersfield, UK
Kh Md Nahiduzzaman	University of British Columbia, Canada
Andreas Nikiforiadis	Aristotle University of Thessaloniki, Greece
Socrates Basbas	Aristotle University of Thessaloniki, Greece

International Workshop on Defense Technology and Security (DTS 2023)

Yeonseung Ryu	Myongji University, South Korea

Integrated Methods for the Ecosystem-Services Accounting in Urban Decision Process (Ecourbn 2023)

Maria Rosaria Guarini	Sapienza University of Rome, Italy
Francesco Sica	Sapienza University of Rome, Italy
Francesco Tajani	Sapienza University of Rome, Italy

Carmelo Maria Torre	Polytechnic University of Bari, Italy
Pierluigi Morano	Polytechnic University of Bari, Italy
Rossana Ranieri	Sapienza Università di Roma, Italy

Evaluating Inner Areas Potentials (EIAP 2023)

Diana Rolando	Politechnic of Turin, Italy
Manuela Rebaudengo	Politechnic of Turin, Italy
Alice Barreca	Politechnic of Turin, Italy
Giorgia Malavasi	Politechnic of Turin, Italy
Umberto Mecca	Politechnic of Turin, Italy

Sustainable Mobility Last Mile Logistic (ELLIOT 2023)

Tiziana Campisi	University of Enna Kore, Italy
Socrates Basbas	Aristotle University of Thessaloniki, Greece
Grigorios Fountas	Aristotle University of Thessaloniki, Greece
Paraskevas Nikolaou	University of Cyprus, Cyprus
Drazenko Glavic	University of Belgrade, Serbia
Antonio Russo	University of Enna Kore, Italy

Econometrics and Multidimensional Evaluation of Urban Environment (EMEUE 2023)

Maria Cerreta	University of Naples Federico II, Italy
Carmelo Maria Torre	Politechnic of Bari, Italy
Pierluigi Morano	Polytechnic of Bari, Italy
Debora Anelli	Polytechnic of Bari, Italy
Francesco Tajani	Sapienza University of Rome, Italy
Simona Panaro	University of Sussex, UK

Ecosystem Services in Spatial Planning for Resilient Urban and Rural Areas (ESSP 2023)

Sabrina Lai	University of Cagliari, Italy
Francesco Scorza	University of Basilicata, Italy
Corrado Zoppi	University of Cagliari, Italy

Gerardo Carpentieri   University of Naples Federico II, Italy
Floriana Zucaro   University of Naples Federico II, Italy
Ana Clara Mourão Moura   Federal University of Minas Gerais, Brazil

Ethical AI Applications for a Human-Centered Cyber Society (EthicAI 2023)

Valentina Franzoni   University of Perugia, Italy
Alfredo Milani   University of Perugia, Italy
Jordi Vallverdu   University Autonoma Barcelona, Spain
Roberto Capobianco   Sapienza University of Rome, Italy

13th International Workshop on Future Computing System Technologies and Applications (FiSTA 2023)

Bernady Apduhan   Kyushu Sangyo University, Japan
Rafael Santos   National Institute for Space Research, Brazil

Collaborative Planning and Designing for the Future with Geospatial Applications (GeoCollab 2023)

Alenka Poplin   Iowa State University, USA
Rosanna Rivero   University of Georgia, USA
Michele Campagna   University of Cagliari, Italy
Ana Clara Mourão Moura   Federal University of Minas Gerais, Brazil

Geomatics in Agriculture and Forestry: New Advances and Perspectives (GeoForAgr 2023)

Maurizio Pollino   Italian National Agency for New Technologies, Energy and Sustainable Economic Development, Italy
Giuseppe Modica   University of Reggio Calabria, Italy
Marco Vizzari   University of Perugia, Italy
Salvatore Praticò   University of Reggio Calabria, Italy

Geographical Analysis, Urban Modeling, Spatial Statistics (Geog-An-Mod 2023)

Giuseppe Borruso   University of Trieste, Italy
Beniamino Murgante   University of Basilicata, Italy
Harmut Asche   Hasso-Plattner-Institut für Digital Engineering
                            Ggmbh, Germany

Geomatics for Resource Monitoring and Management (GRMM 2023)

Alessandra Capolupo   Polytechnic of Bari, Italy
Eufemia Tarantino   Polytechnic of Bari, Italy
Enrico Borgogno Mondino   University of Turin, Italy

International Workshop on Information and Knowledge in the Internet of Things (IKIT 2023)

Teresa Guarda   Peninsula State University of Santa Elena,
                             Ecuador
Modestos Stavrakis   University of the Aegean, Greece

International Workshop on Collective, Massive and Evolutionary Systems (IWCES 2023)

Alfredo Milani   University of Perugia, Italy
Rajdeep Niyogi   Indian Institute of Technology, India
Valentina Franzoni   University of Perugia, Italy

Multidimensional Evolutionary Evaluations for Transformative Approaches (MEETA 2023)

Maria Cerreta   University of Naples Federico II, Italy
Giuliano Poli   University of Naples Federico II, Italy
Ludovica Larocca   University of Naples Federico II, Italy
Chiara Mazzarella   University of Naples Federico II, Italy

Stefania Regalbuto	University of Naples Federico II, Italy
Maria Somma	University of Naples Federico II, Italy

Building Multi-dimensional Models for Assessing Complex Environmental Systems (MES 2023)

Marta Dell'Ovo	Politechnic of Milan, Italy
Vanessa Assumma	University of Bologna, Italy
Caterina Caprioli	Politechnic of Turin, Italy
Giulia Datola	Politechnic of Turin, Italy
Federico Dellanna	Politechnic of Turin, Italy
Marco Rossitti	Politechnic of Milan, Italy

Metropolitan City Lab (Metro_City_Lab 2023)

Ginevra Balletto	University of Cagliari, Italy
Luigi Mundula	University for Foreigners of Perugia, Italy
Giuseppe Borruso	University of Trieste, Italy
Jacopo Torriti	University of Reading, UK
Isabella Ligia	Metropolitan City of Cagliari, Italy

Mathematical Methods for Image Processing and Understanding (MMIPU 2023)

Ivan Gerace	University of Perugia, Italy
Gianluca Vinti	University of Perugia, Italy
Arianna Travaglini	University of Florence, Italy

Models and Indicators for Assessing and Measuring the Urban Settlement Development in the View of ZERO Net Land Take by 2050 (MOVEto0 2023)

Lucia Saganeiti	University of L'Aquila, Italy
Lorena Fiorini	University of L'Aquila, Italy
Angela Pilogallo	University of L'Aquila, Italy
Alessandro Marucci	University of L'Aquila, Italy
Francesco Zullo	University of L'Aquila, Italy

Modelling Post-Covid Cities (MPCC 2023)

Giuseppe Borruso	University of Trieste, Italy
Beniamino Murgante	University of Basilicata, Italy
Ginevra Balletto	University of Cagliari, Italy
Lucia Saganeiti	University of L'Aquila, Italy
Marco Dettori	University of Sassari, Italy

3rd Workshop on Privacy in the Cloud/Edge/IoT World (PCEIoT 2023)

Michele Mastroianni	University of Salerno, Italy
Lelio Campanile	University of Campania Luigi Vanvitelli, Italy
Mauro Iacono	University of Campania Luigi Vanvitelli, Italy

Port City Interface: Land Use, Logistic and Rear Port Area Planning (PORTUNO 2023)

Tiziana Campisi	University of Enna Kore, Italy
Socrates Basbas	Aristotle University of Thessaloniki, Greece
Efstathios Bouhouras	Aristotle University of Thessaloniki, Greece
Giovanni Tesoriere	University of Enna Kore, Italy
Elena Cocuzza	University of Catania, Italy
Gianfranco Fancello	University of Cagliari, Italy

Scientific Computing Infrastructure (SCI 2023)

Elena Stankova	St. Petersburg State University, Russia
Vladimir Korkhov	St. Petersburg University, Russia

Supply Chains, IoT, and Smart Technologies (SCIS 2023)

Ha Jin Hwang	Sunway University, South Korea
Hangkon Kim	Daegu Catholic University, South Korea
Jan Seruga	Australian Catholic University, Australia

Spatial Cognition in Urban and Regional Planning Under Risk (SCOPUR23)

Domenico Camarda   Polytechnic of Bari, Italy
Giulia Mastrodonato   Polytechnic of Bari, Italy
Stefania Santoro   Polytechnic of Bari, Italy
Maria Rosaria Stufano Melone   Polytechnic of Bari, Italy
Mauro Patano   Polytechnic of Bari, Italy

Socio-Economic and Environmental Models for Land Use Management (SEMLUM 2023)

Debora Anelli   Polytechnic of Bari, Italy
Pierluigi Morano   Polytechnic of Bari, Italy
Benedetto Manganelli   University of Basilicata, Italy
Francesco Tajani   Sapienza University of Rome, Italy
Marco Locurcio   Polytechnic of Bari, Italy
Felicia Di Liddo   Polytechnic of Bari, Italy

Ports of the Future - Smartness and Sustainability (SmartPorts 2023)

Ginevra Balletto   University of Cagliari, Italy
Gianfranco Fancello   University of Cagliari, Italy
Patrizia Serra   University of Cagliari, Italy
Agostino Bruzzone   University of Genoa, Italy
Alberto Camarero   Politechnic of Madrid, Spain
Thierry Vanelslander   University of Antwerp, Belgium

Smart Transport and Logistics - Smart Supply Chains (SmarTransLog 2023)

Giuseppe Borruso   University of Trieste, Italy
Marco Mazzarino   University of Venice, Italy
Marcello Tadini   University of Eastern Piedmont, Italy
Luigi Mundula   University for Foreigners of Perugia, Italy
Mara Ladu   University of Cagliari, Italy
Maria del Mar Munoz Leonisio   University of Cadiz, Spain

Smart Tourism (SmartTourism 2023)

Giuseppe Borruso	University of Trieste, Italy
Silvia Battino	University of Sassari, Italy
Ainhoa Amaro Garcia	University of Alcala and University of Las Palmas, Spain
Francesca Krasna	University of Trieste, Italy
Ginevra Balletto	University of Cagliari, Italy
Maria del Mar Munoz Leonisio	University of Cadiz, Spain

Sustainability Performance Assessment: Models, Approaches, and Applications Toward Interdisciplinary and Integrated Solutions (SPA 2023)

Sabrina Lai	University of Cagliari, Italy
Francesco Scorza	University of Basilicata, Italy
Jolanta Dvarioniene	Kaunas University of Technology, Lithuania
Valentin Grecu	Lucian Blaga University of Sibiu, Romania
Georgia Pozoukidou	Aristotle University of Thessaloniki, Greece

Spatial Energy Planning, City and Urban Heritage (Spatial_Energy_City 2023)

Ginevra Balletto	University of Cagliari, Italy
Mara Ladu	University of Cagliari, Italy
Emilio Ghiani	University of Cagliari, Italy
Roberto De Lotto	University of Pavia, Italy
Roberto Gerundo	University of Salerno, Italy

Specifics of Smart Cities Development in Europe (SPEED 2023)

Chiara Garau	University of Cagliari, Italy
Katarína Vitálišová	Matej Bel University, Slovakia
Paolo Nesi	University of Florence, Italy
Anna Vaňová	Matej Bel University, Slovakia
Kamila Borsekova	Matej Bel University, Slovakia
Paola Zamperlin	University of Pisa, Italy

Smart, Safe and Health Cities (SSHC 2023)

Chiara Garau	University of Cagliari, Italy
Gerardo Carpentieri	University of Naples Federico II, Italy
Floriana Zucaro	University of Naples Federico II, Italy
Aynaz Lotfata	Chicago State University, USA
Alfonso Annunziata	University of Basilicata, Italy
Diego Altafini	University of Pisa, Italy

Smart and Sustainable Island Communities (SSIC_2023)

Chiara Garau	University of Cagliari, Italy
Anastasia Stratigea	National Technical University of Athens, Greece
Yiota Theodora	National Technical University of Athens, Greece
Giulia Desogus	University of Cagliari, Italy

Theoretical and Computational Chemistry and Its Applications (TCCMA 2023)

Noelia Faginas-Lago	University of Perugia, Italy
Andrea Lombardi	University of Perugia, Italy

Transport Infrastructures for Smart Cities (TISC 2023)

Francesca Maltinti	University of Cagliari, Italy
Mauro Coni	University of Cagliari, Italy
Francesco Pinna	University of Cagliari, Italy
Chiara Garau	University of Cagliari, Italy
Nicoletta Rassu	University of Cagliari, Italy
James Rombi	University of Cagliari, Italy

Urban Regeneration: Innovative Tools and Evaluation Model (URITEM 2023)

Fabrizio Battisti	University of Florence, Italy
Giovanna Acampa	University of Florence and University of Enna Kore, Italy
Orazio Campo	La Sapienza University of Rome, Italy

Urban Space Accessibility and Mobilities (USAM 2023)

Chiara Garau	University of Cagliari, Italy
Matteo Ignaccolo	University of Catania, Italy
Michela Tiboni	University of Brescia, Italy
Francesco Pinna	University of Cagliari, Italy
Silvia Rossetti	University of Parma, Italy
Vincenza Torrisi	University of Catania, Italy
Ilaria Delponte	University of Genoa, Italy

Virtual Reality and Augmented Reality and Applications (VRA 2023)

Osvaldo Gervasi	University of Perugia, Italy
Damiano Perri	University of Florence, Italy
Marco Simonetti	University of Florence, Italy
Sergio Tasso	University of Perugia, Italy

Workshop on Advanced and Computational Methods for Earth Science Applications (WACM4ES 2023)

Luca Piroddi	University of Malta, Malta
Sebastiano Damico	University of Malta, Malta
Marilena Cozzolino	Università del Molise, Italy
Adam Gauci	University of Malta, Italy
Giuseppina Vacca	University of Cagliari, Italy
Chiara Garau	University of Cagliari, Italy

Sponsoring Organizations

ICCSA 2023 would not have been possible without the tremendous support of many organizations and institutions, for which all organizers and participants of ICCSA 2023 express their sincere gratitude:

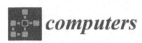

Springer Nature Switzerland AG, Switzerland
(https://www.springer.com)

Computers Open Access Journal
(https://www.mdpi.com/journal/computers)

National Technical University of Athens, Greece
(https://www.ntua.gr/)

University of the Aegean, Greece
(https://www.aegean.edu/)

University of Perugia, Italy
(https://www.unipg.it)

University of Basilicata, Italy
(http://www.unibas.it)

 Monash University, Australia
(https://www.monash.edu/)

 Kyushu Sangyo University, Japan
(https://www.kyusan-u.ac.jp/)

 University of Minho, Portugal
(https://www.uminho.pt/)

Referees

Francesca Abastante   Turin Polytechnic, Italy
Giovanna Acampa   University of Enna Kore, Italy
Adewole Adewumi   Algonquin College, Canada
Vera Afreixo   University of Aveiro, Portugal
Riad Aggoune   Luxembourg Institute of Science and Technology,
                               Luxembourg
Akshat Agrawal   Amity University Haryana, India
Waseem Ahmad   National Institute of Technology Karnataka, India
Oylum Alatlı   Ege University, Turkey
Abraham Alfa   Federal University of Technology Minna, Nigeria
Diego Altafini   University of Pisa, Italy
Filipe Alvelos   University of Minho, Portugal
Marina Alexandra Pedro Andrade University Institute of Lisbon, Portugal
Debora Anelli   Polytechnic University of Bari, Italy
Mariarosaria Angrisano   Pegaso University, Italy
Alfonso Annunziata   University of Cagliari, Italy
Magarò Antonio   Sapienza University of Rome, Italy
Bernady Apduhan   Kyushu Sangyo University, Japan
Jonathan Apeh   Covenant University, Nigeria
Daniela Ascenzi   University of Trento, Italy
Vanessa Assumma   University of Bologna, Italy
Maria Fernanda Augusto   Bitrum Research Center, Spain
Marco Baioletti   University of Perugia, Italy

Ginevra Balletto	University of Cagliari, Italy
Carlos Balsa	Polytechnic Institute of Bragança, Portugal
Benedetto Barabino	University of Brescia, Italy
Simona Barbaro	University of Palermo, Italy
Sebastiano Barbieri	Turin Polytechnic, Italy
Kousik Barik	University of Alcala, Spain
Alice Barreca	Turin Polytechnic, Italy
Socrates Basbas	Aristotle University of Thessaloniki, Greece
Rosaria Battarra	National Research Council, Italy
Silvia Battino	University of Sassari, Italy
Fabrizio Battisti	University of Florence, Italy
Yaroslav Bazaikin	Jan Evangelista Purkyne University, Czech Republic
Ranjan Kumar Behera	Indian Institute of Information Technology, India
Simone Belli	Complutense University of Madrid, Spain
Oscar Bellini	Polytechnic University of Milan, Italy
Giulio Biondi	University of Perugia, Italy
Adriano Bisello	Eurac Research, Italy
Semen Bochkov	Ulyanovsk State Technical University, Russia
Alexander Bogdanov	St. Petersburg State University, Russia
Letizia Bollini	Free University of Bozen, Italy
Giuseppe Borruso	University of Trieste, Italy
Marilisa Botte	University of Naples Federico II, Italy
Ana Cristina Braga	University of Minho, Portugal
Frederico Branco	University of Trás-os-Montes and Alto Douro, Portugal
Jorge Buele	Indoamérica Technological University, Ecuador
Datzania Lizeth Burgos	Peninsula State University of Santa Elena, Ecuador
Isabel Cacao	University of Aveiro, Portugal
Francesco Calabrò	Mediterranea University of Reggio Calabria, Italy
Rogerio Calazan	Institute of Sea Studies Almirante Paulo Moreira, Brazil
Lelio Campanile	University of Campania Luigi Vanvitelli, Italy
Tiziana Campisi	University of Enna Kore, Italy
Orazio Campo	University of Rome La Sapienza, Italy
Caterina Caprioli	Turin Polytechnic, Italy
Gerardo Carpentieri	University of Naples Federico II, Italy
Martina Carra	University of Brescia, Italy
Barbara Caselli	University of Parma, Italy
Danny Casprini	Politechnic of Milan, Italy

Omar Fernando Castellanos Balleteros	Peninsula State University of Santa Elena, Ecuador
Arcangelo Castiglione	University of Salerno, Italy
Giulio Cavana	Turin Polytechnic, Italy
Maria Cerreta	University of Naples Federico II, Italy
Sabarathinam Chockalingam	Institute for Energy Technology, Norway
Luis Enrique Chuquimarca Jimenez	Peninsula State University of Santa Elena, Ecuador
Birol Ciloglugil	Ege University, Turkey
Elena Cocuzza	Univesity of Catania, Italy
Emanuele Colica	University of Malta, Malta
Mauro Coni	University of Cagliari, Italy
Simone Corrado	University of Basilicata, Italy
Elisete Correia	University of Trás-os-Montes and Alto Douro, Portugal
Florbela Correia	Polytechnic Institute Viana do Castelo, Portugal
Paulo Cortez	University of Minho, Portugal
Martina Corti	Politechnic of Milan, Italy
Lino Costa	Universidade do Minho, Portugal
Cecília Maria Vasconcelos Costa e Castro	University of Minho, Portugal
Alfredo Cuzzocrea	University of Calabria, Italy
Sebastiano D'amico	University of Malta, Malta
Maria Danese	National Research Council, Italy
Gianni Dangelo	University of Salerno, Italy
Ana Daniel	Aveiro University, Portugal
Giulia Datola	Politechnic of Milan, Italy
Regina De Almeida	University of Trás-os-Montes and Alto Douro, Portugal
Maria Stella De Biase	University of Campania Luigi Vanvitelli, Italy
Elise De Doncker	Western Michigan University, USA
Luiza De Macedo Mourelle	State University of Rio de Janeiro, Brazil
Itamir De Morais Barroca Filho	Federal University of Rio Grande do Norte, Brazil
Pierfrancesco De Paola	University of Naples Federico II, Italy
Francesco De Pascale	University of Turin, Italy
Manuela De Ruggiero	University of Calabria, Italy
Alexander Degtyarev	St. Petersburg State University, Russia
Federico Dellanna	Turin Polytechnic, Italy
Marta Dellovo	Politechnic of Milan, Italy
Bashir Derradji	Sfax University, Tunisia
Giulia Desogus	University of Cagliari, Italy
Frank Devai	London South Bank University, UK

Piero Di Bonito	University of Campania Luigi Vanvitelli, Italy
Chiara Di Dato	University of L'Aquila, Italy
Michele Di Giovanni	University of Campania Luigi Vanvitelli, Italy
Felicia Di Liddo	Polytechnic University of Bari, Italy
Joana Dias	University of Coimbra, Portugal
Luigi Dolores	University of Salerno, Italy
Marco Donatelli	Università of Insubria, Italy
Aziz Dursun	Virginia Tech University, USA
Jaroslav Dvořak	Klaipeda University, Lithuania
Wolfgang Erb	University of Padova, Italy
Maurizio Francesco Errigo	University of Enna Kore, Italy
Noelia Faginas-Lago	University of Perugia, Italy
Maria Irene Falcao	University of Minho, Portugal
Stefano Falcinelli	University of Perugia, Italy
Grazia Fattoruso	Italian National Agency for New Technologies, Energy and Sustainable Economic Development, Italy
Sara Favargiotti	University of Trento, Italy
Marcin Feltynowski	University of Lodz, Poland
António Fernandes	Polytechnic Institute of Bragança, Portugal
Florbela P. Fernandes	Polytechnic Institute of Bragança, Portugal
Paula Odete Fernandes	Polytechnic Institute of Bragança, Portugal
Luis Fernandez-Sanz	University of Alcala, Spain
Maria Eugenia Ferrao	University of Beira Interior and University of Lisbon, Portugal
Luís Ferrás	University of Minho, Portugal
Angela Ferreira	Polytechnic Institute of Bragança, Portugal
Maddalena Ferretti	Politechnic of Marche, Italy
Manuel Carlos Figueiredo	University of Minho, Portugal
Fabrizio Finucci	Roma Tre University, Italy
Ugo Fiore	University Pathenope of Naples, Italy
Lorena Fiorini	University of L'Aquila, Italy
Valentina Franzoni	Perugia University, Italy
Adelaide Freitas	University of Aveiro, Portugal
Kirill Gadylshin	Russian Academy of Sciences, Russia
Andrea Gallo	University of Trieste, Italy
Luciano Galone	University of Malta, Malta
Chiara Garau	University of Cagliari, Italy
Ernesto Garcia Para	Universidad del País Vasco, Spain
Rachele Vanessa Gatto	Università della Basilicata, Italy
Marina Gavrilova	University of Calgary, Canada
Georgios Georgiadis	Aristotle University of Thessaloniki, Greece

Ivan Gerace	University of Perugia, Italy
Osvaldo Gervasi	University of Perugia, Italy
Alfonso Giancotti	Sapienza University of Rome, Italy
Andrea Gioia	Politechnic of Bari, Italy
Giacomo Giorgi	University of Perugia, Italy
Salvatore Giuffrida	Università di Catania, Italy
A. Manuela Gonçalves	University of Minho, Portugal
Angela Gorgoglione	University of the Republic, Uruguay
Yusuke Gotoh	Okayama University, Japan
Mariolina Grasso	University of Enna Kore, Italy
Silvana Grillo	University of Cagliari, Italy
Teresa Guarda	Universidad Estatal Peninsula de Santa Elena, Ecuador
Eduardo Guerra	Free University of Bozen-Bolzano, Italy
Carmen Guida	University of Napoli Federico II, Italy
Kemal Güven Gülen	Namık Kemal University, Turkey
Malgorzata Hanzl	Technical University of Lodz, Poland
Peter Hegedus	University of Szeged, Hungary
Syeda Sumbul Hossain	Daffodil International University, Bangladesh
Mustafa Inceoglu	Ege University, Turkey
Federica Isola	University of Cagliari, Italy
Seifedine Kadry	Noroff University College, Norway
Yeliz Karaca	University of Massachusetts Chan Medical School and Massachusetts Institute of Technology, USA
Harun Karsli	Bolu Abant Izzet Baysal University, Turkey
Tayana Khachkova	Russian Academy of Sciences, Russia
Manju Khari	Jawaharlal Nehru University, India
Vladimir Korkhov	Saint Petersburg State University, Russia
Dionisia Koutsi	National Technical University of Athens, Greece
Tomonori Kouya	Shizuoka Institute of Science and Technology, Japan
Nataliia Kulabukhova	Saint Petersburg State University, Russia
Anisha Kumari	National Institute of Technology, India
Ludovica La Rocca	University of Napoli Federico II, Italy
Mara Ladu	University of Cagliari, Italy
Sabrina Lai	University of Cagliari, Italy
Mohamed Laib	Luxembourg Institute of Science and Technology, Luxembourg
Giuseppe Francesco Cesare Lama	University of Napoli Federico II, Italy
Isabella Maria Lami	Turin Polytechnic, Italy
Chien Sing Lee	Sunway University, Malaysia

Filipe Mota Pinto	Polytechnic Institute of Leiria, Portugal
Maria Mourao	Polytechnic Institute of Viana do Castelo, Portugal
Eugenio Muccio	University of Naples Federico II, Italy
Beniamino Murgante	University of Basilicata, Italy
Rocco Murro	Sapienza University of Rome, Italy
Giuseppe Musolino	Mediterranean University of Reggio Calabria, Italy
Nadia Nedjah	State University of Rio de Janeiro, Brazil
Juraj Nemec	Masaryk University, Czech Republic
Andreas Nikiforiadis	Aristotle University of Thessaloniki, Greece
Silvio Nocera	IUAV University of Venice, Italy
Roseline Ogundokun	Kaunas University of Technology, Lithuania
Emma Okewu	University of Alcala, Spain
Serena Olcuire	Sapienza University of Rome, Italy
Irene Oliveira	University Trás-os-Montes and Alto Douro, Portugal
Samson Oruma	Ostfold University College, Norway
Antonio Pala	University of Cagliari, Italy
Maria Panagiotopoulou	National Technical University of Athens, Greece
Simona Panaro	University of Sussex Business School, UK
Jay Pancham	Durban University of Technology, South Africa
Eric Pardede	La Trobe University, Australia
Hyun Kyoo Park	Ministry of National Defense, South Korea
Damiano Perri	University of Florence, Italy
Quoc Trung Pham	Ho Chi Minh City University of Technology, Vietnam
Claudio Piferi	University of Florence, Italy
Angela Pilogallo	University of L'Aquila, Italy
Francesco Pinna	University of Cagliari, Italy
Telmo Pinto	University of Coimbra, Portugal
Luca Piroddi	University of Malta, Malta
Francesco Pittau	Politechnic of Milan, Italy
Giuliano Poli	Università Federico II di Napoli, Italy
Maurizio Pollino	Italian National Agency for New Technologies, Energy and Sustainable Economic Development, Italy
Vijay Prakash	University of Malta, Malta
Salvatore Praticò	Mediterranean University of Reggio Calabria, Italy
Carlotta Quagliolo	Turin Polytechnic, Italy
Garrisi Raffaele	Operations Center for Cyber Security, Italy
Mariapia Raimondo	Università della Campania Luigi Vanvitelli, Italy

Bruna Ramos	Universidade Lusíada Norte, Portugal
Nicoletta Rassu	University of Cagliari, Italy
Roberta Ravanelli	University of Roma La Sapienza, Italy
Pier Francesco Recchi	University of Naples Federico II, Italy
Stefania Regalbuto	University of Naples Federico II, Italy
Rommel Regis	Saint Joseph's University, USA
Marco Reis	University of Coimbra, Portugal
Jerzy Respondek	Silesian University of Technology, Poland
Isabel Ribeiro	Polytechnic Institut of Bragança, Portugal
Albert Rimola	Autonomous University of Barcelona, Spain
Corrado Rindone	Mediterranean University of Reggio Calabria, Italy
Maria Rocco	Roma Tre University, Italy
Ana Maria A. C. Rocha	University of Minho, Portugal
Fabio Rocha	Universidade Federal de Sergipe, Brazil
Humberto Rocha	University of Coimbra, Portugal
Maria Clara Rocha	Politechnic Institut of Coimbra, Portual
Carlos Rodrigues	Polytechnic Institut of Bragança, Portugal
Diana Rolando	Turin Polytechnic, Italy
James Rombi	University of Cagliari, Italy
Evgeniy Romenskiy	Russian Academy of Sciences, Russia
Marzio Rosi	University of Perugia, Italy
Silvia Rossetti	University of Parma, Italy
Marco Rossitti	Politechnic of Milan, Italy
Antonio Russo	University of Enna, Italy
Insoo Ryu	MoaSoftware, South Korea
Yeonseung Ryu	Myongji University, South Korea
Lucia Saganeiti	University of L'Aquila, Italy
Valentina Santarsiero	University of Basilicata, Italy
Luigi Santopietro	University of Basilicata, Italy
Rafael Santos	National Institute for Space Research, Brazil
Valentino Santucci	University for Foreigners of Perugia, Italy
Alessandra Saponieri	University of Salento, Italy
Mattia Scalas	Turin Polytechnic, Italy
Francesco Scorza	University of Basilicata, Italy
Ester Scotto Di Perta	University of Napoli Federico II, Italy
Nicoletta Setola	University of Florence, Italy
Ricardo Severino	University of Minho, Portugal
Angela Silva	Polytechnic Institut of Viana do Castelo, Portugal
Carina Silva	Polytechnic of Lisbon, Portugal
Marco Simonetti	University of Florence, Italy
Sergey Solovyev	Russian Academy of Sciences, Russia

Maria Somma	University of Naples Federico II, Italy
Changgeun Son	Ministry of National Defense, South Korea
Alberico Sonnessa	Polytechnic of Bari, Italy
Inês Sousa	University of Minho, Portugal
Lisete Sousa	University of Lisbon, Portugal
Elena Stankova	Saint-Petersburg State University, Russia
Modestos Stavrakis	University of the Aegean, Greece
Flavio Stochino	University of Cagliari, Italy
Anastasia Stratigea	National Technical University of Athens, Greece
Yue Sun	European XFEL GmbH, Germany
Anthony Suppa	Turin Polytechnic, Italy
David Taniar	Monash University, Australia
Rodrigo Tapia McClung	Centre for Research in Geospatial Information Sciences, Mexico
Tarek Teba	University of Portsmouth, UK
Ana Paula Teixeira	University of Trás-os-Montes and Alto Douro, Portugal
Tengku Adil Tengku Izhar	Technological University MARA, Malaysia
Maria Filomena Teodoro	University of Lisbon and Portuguese Naval Academy, Portugal
Yiota Theodora	National Technical University of Athens, Greece
Elena Todella	Turin Polytechnic, Italy
Graça Tomaz	Polytechnic Institut of Guarda, Portugal
Anna Tonazzini	National Research Council, Italy
Dario Torregrossa	Goodyear, Luxembourg
Francesca Torrieri	University of Naples Federico II, Italy
Vincenza Torrisi	University of Catania, Italy
Nikola Tosic	Polytechnic University of Catalonia, Spain
Vincenzo Totaro	Polytechnic University of Bari, Italy
Arianna Travaglini	University of Florence, Italy
António Trigo	Polytechnic of Coimbra, Portugal
Giuseppe A. Trunfio	University of Sassari, Italy
Toshihiro Uchibayashi	Kyushu University, Japan
Piero Ugliengo	University of Torino, Italy
Jordi Vallverdu	University Autonoma Barcelona, Spain
Gianmarco Vanuzzo	University of Perugia, Italy
Dmitry Vasyunin	T-Systems, Russia
Laura Verde	University of Campania Luigi Vanvitelli, Italy
Giulio Vignoli	University of Cagliari, Italy
Gianluca Vinti	University of Perugia, Italy
Katarína Vitálišová	Matej Bel University, Slovak Republic
Daniel Mark Vitiello	University of Cagliari

Marco Vizzari	University of Perugia, Italy
Manuel Yañez	Autonomous University of Madrid, Spain
Fenghui Yao	Tennessee State University, USA
Fukuko Yuasa	High Energy Accelerator Research Organization, Japan
Milliam Maxime Zekeng Ndadji	University of Dschang, Cameroon
Ljiljana Zivkovic	Republic Geodetic Authority, Serbia
Camila Zyngier	IBMEC-BH, Brazil

Plenary Lectures

A Multiscale Planning Concept for Sustainable Metropolitan Development

Pierre Frankhauser

Théma, Université de Franche-Comté, 32, rue Mégevand, 20030 Besançon, France
pierre.frankhauser@univ-fcomte.fr

Keywords: Sustainable metropolitan development · Multiscale approach · Urban modelling

Urban sprawl has often been pointed out as having an important negative impact on environment and climate. Residential zones have grown up in what were initially rural areas, located far from employment areas and often lacking shopping opportunities, public services and public transportation. Hence urban sprawl increased car-traffic flows, generating pollution and increasing energy consumption. New road axes consume considerable space and weaken biodiversity by reducing and cutting natural areas. A return to "compact cities" or "dense cities" has often been contemplated as the most efficient way to limit urban sprawl. However, the real impact of density on car use is less clear-cut (Daneshpour and Shakibamanesh 2011). Let us emphasize that moreover climate change will increase the risk of heat islands on an intra-urban scale. This prompts a more nuanced reflection on how urban fabrics should be structured.

Moreover, urban planning cannot ignore social demand. Lower land prices in rural areas, often put forward by economists, is not the only reason of urban sprawl. The quality of the residential environment comes into play, too, through features like noise, pollution, landscape quality, density etc. Schwanen et al. (2004) observe for the Netherlands that households preferring a quiet residential environment and individual housing with a garden will not accept densification, which might even lead them to move to lower-density rural areas even farther away from jobs and shopping amenities. Many scholars emphasize the importance of green amenities for residential environments and report the importance of easy access to leisure areas (Guo and Bhat 2002). Vegetation in the residential environment has an important impact on health and well-being (Lafortezza et al. 2009).

We present here the Fractalopolis concept which we developed in the frame of several research projects and which aims reconciling environmental and social issues (Bonin et al., 2020; Frankhauser 2021; Frankhauser et al. 2018). This concept introduces a multiscale approach based on multifractal geometry for conceiving spatial development for metropolitan areas. For taking into account social demand we refer to the fundamental work of Max-Neef et al. (1991) based on Maslow's work about basic human needs. He introduces the concept of satisfiers assigned to meet the basic needs of "Subsistence, Protection, Affection, Understanding, Participation, Idleness, Creation, Identity and Freedom". Satisfiers thus become the link between the needs of everyone and society and may depend on the cultural context. We consider their importance, their location and their accessibility and we rank the needs according to their importance for individuals or households. In order to enjoy a good quality of life and to shorten trips and to reduce automobile use, it seems important for satisfiers of daily needs to be easily accessible. Hence, we consider the purchase rate when reflecting on the implementation of shops which is reminiscent of central place theory.

The second important feature is taking care of environment and biodiversity by avoiding fragmentation of green space (Ekren and Arslan 2022) which must benefit, moreover, of a good accessibility, as pointed out. These areas must, too, ply the role of cooling areas ensuring ventilation of urbanized areas (Kuttler et al. 1998).

For integrating these different objectives, we propose a concept for developing spatial configurations of metropolitan areas designed which is based on multifractal geometry. It allows combining different issues across a large range of scales in a coherent way. These issues include:

- providing easy access to a large array of amenities to meet social demand;
- promoting the use of public transportation and soft modes instead of automobile use;
- preserving biodiversity and improving the local climate.

The concept distinguishes development zones localized in the vicinity of a nested and hierarchized system of public transport axes. The highest ranked center offers all types of amenities, whereas lower ranked centers lack the highest ranked amenities. The lowest ranked centers just offer the amenities for daily needs. A coding system allows distinguishing the centers according to their rank.

Each subset of central places is in some sense autonomous, since they are not linked by transportation axes to subcenters of the same order. This allows to preserve a linked system of green corridors penetrating the development zones across scales avoiding the fragmentation of green areas and ensuring a good accessibility to recreational areas.

The spatial model is completed by a population distribution model which globally follows the same hierarchical logic. However, we weakened the strong fractal order what allows to conceive a more or less polycentric spatial system.

We can adapt the theoretical concept easily to real world situation without changing the underlying multiscale logic. A decision support system has been developed allowing to simulate development scenarios and to evaluate them. The evaluation procedure is based on fuzzy evaluation of distance acceptance for accessing to the different types of amenities according to the ranking of needs. We used for evaluation data issued from a great set of French planning documents like Master plans. We show an example how the software package can be used concretely.

References

Bonin, O., et al.: Projet SOFT sobriété énergétique par les formes urbaines et le transport (Research Report No. 1717C0003; p. 214). ADEME (2020)

Daneshpour, A., Shakibamanesh, A.: Compact city; dose it create an obligatory context for urban sustainability? Int. J. Archit. Eng. Urban Plann. 21(2), 110–118 (2011)

Ekren, E., Arslan, M.: Functions of greenways as an ecologically-based planning strategy. In: Çakır, M., Tuğluer, M., Fırat Örs, P.: Architectural Sciences and Ecology, pp. 134–156. Iksad Publications (2022)

Frankhauser, P.: Fractalopolis—a fractal concept for the sustainable development of metropolitan areas. In: Sajous, P., Bertelle, C. (eds.) Complex Systems, Smart Territories and Mobility, pp. 15–50. Springer, Cham (2021). https://doi.org/10.1007/978-3-030-59302-5_2

Frankhauser, P., Tannier, C., Vuidel, G., Houot, H.: An integrated multifractal modelling to urban and regional planning. Comput. Environ. Urban Syst. 67(1), 132–146 (2018). https://doi.org/10.1016/j.compenvurbsys.2017.09.011

Guo, J., Bhat, C.: Residential location modeling: accommodating sociodemographic, school quality and accessibility effects. University of Texas, Austin (2002)

Kuttler, W., Dütemeyer, D., Barlag, A.-B.: Influence of regional and local winds on urban ventilation in Cologne, Germany. Meteorologische Zeitschrift, 77–87 (1998) https://doi.org/10.1127/metz/7/1998/77

Lafortezza, R., Carrus, G., Sanesi, G., Davies, C.: Benefits and well-being perceived by people visiting green spaces in periods of heat stress. Urban For. Urban Green. 8(2), 97–108 (2009)

Max-Neef, M. A., Elizalde, A., Hopenhayn, M.: Human scale development: conception, application and further reflections. The Apex Press (1991)

Schwanen, T., Dijst, M., Dieleman, F. M.: Policies for urban form and their impact on travel: The Netherlands experience. Urban Stud. 41(3), 579–603 (2004)

Graph Drawing and Network Visualization – An Overview – (Keynote Speech)

Giuseppe Liotta

Dipartimento di Ingegneria, Università degli Studi di Perugia, Italy
giuseppe.liotta@unipg.it

Abstract. Graph Drawing and Network visualization supports the exploration, analysis, and communication of relational data arising in a variety of application domains: from bioinformatics to software engineering, from social media to cyber-security, from data bases to powergrid systems. Aim of this keynote speech is to introduce this thriving research area, highlighting some of its basic approaches and pointing to some promising research directions.

1 Introduction

Graph Drawing and Network Visualization is at the intersection of different disciplines and it combines topics that traditionally belong to theoretical computer science with methods and approaches that characterize more applied disciplines. Namely, it can be related to Graph Algorithms, Geometric Graph Theory and Geometric computing, Combinatorial Optimization, Experimental Analysis, User Studies, System Design and Development, and Human Computer Interaction. This combination of theory and practice is well reflected in the flagship conference of the area, the *International Symposium on Graph Drawing and Network Visualization*, that has two tracks, one focusing on combinatorial and algorithmic aspects and the other on the design of network visualization systems and interfaces. The conference is now at its 31st edition; a full list of the symposia and their proceedings, published by Springer in the LNCS series can be found at the URL: http://www.graphdrawing.org/.

Aim of this short paper is to outline the content of my Keynote Speech at ICCSA 2023, which will be referred to as the "Talk" in the rest of the paper. The talk will introduce the field of Graph Drawing and Network Visualization to a broad audience, with the goal to not only present some key methodological and technological aspects, but also point to some unexplored or partially explored research directions. The rest of this short paper briefly outlines the content of the talk and provides some references that can be a starting point for researchers interested in working on Graph Drawing and Network Visualization.

2   Why Visualize Networks?

Back in 1973 the famous statistician Francis Anscombe, gave a convincing example of why visualization is fundamental component of data analysis. The example is known as the *Anscombe's quartet* [3] and it consists of four sets of 11 points each that are almost identical in terms of the basic statistic properties of their x– and y– coordinates. Namely the mean values and the variance of x and y are exactly the same in the four sets, while the correlation of x and y and the linear regression are the same up to the second decimal. In spite of this statistical similarity, the data look very different when displayed in the Euclidean plane which leads to the conclusion that they correspond to significantly different phenomena. Figure 1 reports the four sets of Anscombe's quartet. After fifty years, with the arrival of AI-based technologies and the need of explaining and interpreting machine-driven suggestions before making strategic decision, the lesson of Anscombe's quartet has not just kept but even increased its relevance.

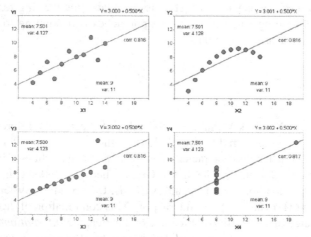

Fig. 1. The four point sets in Anscombe's quartet [3]; the figure also reports statistical values of the x and y variables.

As a matter of fact, nowadays the need of visualization systems goes beyond the verification of the accuracy of some statistical analysis on a set of scattered data. Recent technological advances have generated torrents of data that area relational in nature and typically modeled as networks: the nodes of the networks store the features of the data and the edges of the networks describe the semantic relationships between the data features. Such networked data sets (whose algebraic underlying structure is a called graph in discrete mathematics) arise in a variety of application domains including, for example, Systems Biology, Social Network Analysis, Software Engineering, Networking, Data Bases, Homeland Security, and Business Intelligence. In these (and many other) contexts, systems that support the visual analysis of networks and graphs play a central role in critical decision making processes. These are human-in-the-loop processes where the continuous interaction between humans (decision makers) and data mining or optimization algorithms (AI/ML components) supports the data exploration, the development of verifiable theories about the data, and the extraction of new knowledge that is used to make strategic choices. A seminal book by Keim et al. [33] schematically represents the human-in-the-loop approach to making sense of networked data sets as in Fig. 2. See also [46–49].

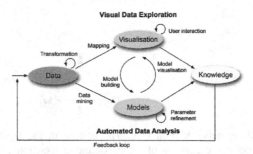

Fig. 2. Sense-making/knowledge generation loop. This conceptual interaction model between human analysts and network visualization system is at the basis of network visual analytics system design [33].

To make a concrete application example of the analysis of a network by interacting with its visualization, consider the problem of contrasting financial crimes such as money laundering or tax evasion. These crimes are based on relevant volumes of financial transactions to conceal the identity, the source, or the destination of illegally gained money. Also, the adopted patterns to pursue the illegal goals continuously change to conceal the crimes. Therefore, contrasting them requires special investigation units which must analyze very large and highly dynamic data sets and discover relationships between different subjects to untangle complex fraudulent plots. The investigative cycle begins with data collection and filtering; it is then followed by modeling the data as a social network (also called *financial activity network* in this context) to which different data mining and data analytic methods are applied, including graph pattern matching, social network analysis, machine learning, and information diffusion. By the network visualization system detectives can interactively explore the data, gain insight and make new hypotheses about possible criminal activities, verify the hypotheses by asking the system to provide more details about specific portions of the network, refine previous outputs, and eventually gain new knowledge. Figure 3 illustrates a small financial activity network where, by means of the interaction between an officer of the Italian Revenue Agency and the MALDIVE system described in [10] a fraudulent pattern has been identified. Precisely, the tax officer has encoded a risky relational scheme among taxpayers into a suspicious graph pattern; in response, the system has made a search in the taxpayer network and it has returned one such pattern. See, e.g., [9, 11, 14, 18, 38] for more papers and references about visual analytic applications to contrasting financial crimes.

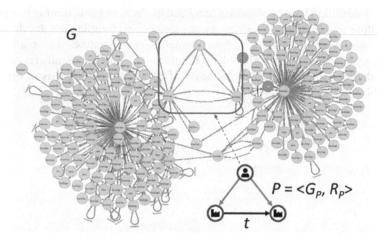

Fig. 3. A financial activity network from [10]. The pattern in the figure represents a Sup-pliesFromAssociated scheme, consisting of an economic transaction and two shareholding relationships.

3   Facets of Graph Drawing and Network Visualization

The Talk overviews some of the fundamental facets that characterize the research in Graph Drawing and Network Visualization. Namely:

- Graph drawing metaphors: Depending on the application context, different metaphors can be used to represent a relational data set modeled as a graph. The talk will briefly recall the matrix representation, the space filling representation, the contact representation, and the node-link representation which is, by far, the most commonly used (see, e.g., [43]).
- Interaction paradigms: Different interaction paradigms have different impacts on the sense-making process of the user about the visualized network. The Talk will go through the full-view, top-down, bottom-up, incremental, and narrative paradigms. Pros and cons will be highlighted for each approach, also by means of examples and applications. The discussion of the top-down interaction paradigm will also consider the hybrid visualization models (see, e.g., [2, 24, 26, 28, 39]) while the discussion about the incremental paradigm will focus on research about graph storyplans (see, e.g., [4, 6, 7]).
- Graph drawing algorithms: Three main algorithmic approaches will be reviewed, namely the force-directed, the layered), and the planarization-based approach; see, e.g., [5]. We shall also make some remarks about FPT algorithms for graph drawing (see, e.g., [8, 19, 20, 25, 27, 40, 53]) and about how the optimization challenges vary when it is assumed that the input has or does not have a fixed combinatorial embedding (see, e.g., [12, 13, 16, 17, 23]).
- Experimental analysis and user-studies: The Talk will mostly compare two models to define and experimentally validate those optimization goals that define a "readable"

network visualization, i.e. a visualization that in a given application context can easily convey the structure of a relational data set so to guarantee efficiency both in its visual exploration and in the elaboration of new knowledge. Special focus will be given to a set emerging optimization goals related to edge crossings that are currently investigated in the graph drawing and network visualization community unedr the name of "graph drawing beyond planarity" (see, e.g., [1, 15, 29, 35]).

The talk shall also point to some promising research directions, including: (i) Extend the body of papers devoted to user-studies that compare the impact of different graph drawing metaphors on the user perception. (ii) Extend the study of interaction paradigms to extended reality environments (see, e.g., [21, 30, 36, 37]); (iii) Engineer the FPT algorithms for graph drawing and experimentally compare their performances with exact or approximate solutions; and (iv) Develop new algorithmic fameworks in the context of graph drawing beyond planarity.

We conclude this short paper with pointers to publication venues and key references that can be browsed by researchers interested in the fascinating field of Graph Drawing and Network Visualization.

4 Pointers to Publication venues and Key References

A limited list of conferences where Graph Drawing and Network Visualization papers are regularly part of the program includes *IEEE VIS, EuroVis, SoCG, ISAAC, ACM-SIAM SODA, WADS,* and *WG*. Among the many journals where several Graph Drawing and Network Visualization papers have appeared during the last three decades we recall *IEEE Transactions on Visualization and Computer Graphs, SIAM Journal of Computing, Computer Graphics Forum, Journal of Computer and System Sciences, Algorithmica, Journal of Graph Algorithms and Applications, Theoretical Computer Science, Information Sciences, Discrete and Computational Geometry, Computational Geometry: Theory and Applications, ACM Computing Surveys,* and *Computer Science Review*. A limited list of books, surveys, or papers that contain interesting algorithmic challenges on Graph Drawing and Network Visualization include [5, 15, 22, 29, 31–35, 41–45, 50–52].

References

1. Angelini, P., et al.: Simple k-planar graphs are simple (k+1)-quasiplanar. J. Comb. Theory, Ser. B, **142**, 1–35 (2020)
2. Angori, L., Didimo, W., Montecchiani, F., Pagliuca, D., Tappini, A.: Hybrid graph visualizations with chordlink: Algorithms, experiments, and applications. IEEE Trans. Vis. Comput. Graph. **28**(2), 1288–1300 (2022)
3. Anscombe, F.J.: Graphs in statistical analysis. Am. Stat. **27**(1), 17–21 (1973)
4. Di Battista, G., et al.: Small point-sets supporting graph stories. In: Angelini, P., von Hanxleden, R. (eds.) Graph Drawing and Network Visualization. GD 2022, LNCS, vol. 13764, pp. 289–303. Springer, Cham (2022). https://doi.org/10.1007/978-3-031-22203-0_21

5. Battista, G.D., Eades, P., Tamassia, R., Tollis, I.G.: Graph Drawing: Algorithms for the Visualization of Graphs. Prentice-Hall, Hoboken (1999)
6. Binucci, C., et al.: On the complexity of the storyplan problem. In: Angelini, P., von Hanxleden, R. (eds.) Graph Drawing and Network Visualization. GD 2022. LNCS, vol. 13764, pp. 304–318. Springer, Cham (2023). https://doi.org/10.1007/978-3-031-22203-0_22
7. Borrazzo, M., Lozzo, G.D., Battista, G.D., Frati, F., Patrignani, M.: Graph stories in small area. J. Graph Algorithms Appl. **24**(3), 269–292 (2020)
8. Chaplick, S., Giacomo, E.D., Frati, F., Ganian, R., Raftopoulou, C.N., Simonov, K.: Parameterized algorithms for upward planarity. In: Goaoc, X., Kerber, M. (eds.) 38th International Symposium on Computational Geometry, SoCG 2022, June 7–10, 2022, Berlin, Germany, LIPIcs, vol. 224, pp. 26:1–26:16. Schloss Dagstuhl - Leibniz-Zentrum für Informatik (2022)
9. Didimo, W., Giamminonni, L., Liotta, G., Montecchiani, F., Pagliuca, D.: A visual analytics system to support tax evasion discovery. Decis. Support Syst. **110**, 71–83 (2018)
10. Didimo, W., Grilli, L., Liotta, G., Menconi, L., Montecchiani, F., Pagliuca, D.: Combining network visualization and data mining for tax risk assessment. IEEE Access **8**, 16073–16086 (2020)
11. Didimo, W., Grilli, L., Liotta, G., Montecchiani, F., Pagliuca, D.: Visual querying and analysis of temporal fiscal networks. Inf. Sci. **505**, 406–421 (2019)
12. W. Didimo, M. Kaufmann, G. Liotta, and G. Ortali. Didimo, W., Kaufmann, M., Liotta, G., Ortali, G.: Rectilinear planarity testing of plane series-parallel graphs in linear time. In: Auber, D., Valtr, P. (eds.) Graph Drawing and Network Visualization. GD 2020. LNCS, vol. 12590, pp. 436–449. Springer, Cham (2020). https://doi.org/10.1007/978-3-030-68766-3_34
13. Didimo, W., Kaufmann, M., Liotta, G., Ortali, G.: Rectilinear planarity of partial 2-trees. In: Angelini, P., von Hanxleden, R. (eds.) Graph Drawing and Network Visualization. GD 2022. LNCS, vol. 13764, pp. 157–172. Springer, Cham (2023). https://doi.org/10.1007/978-3-031-22203-0_12
14. Didimo, W., Liotta, G., Montecchiani, F.: Network visualization for financial crime detection. J. Vis. Lang. Comput. **25**(4), 433–451 (2014)
15. Didimo, W., Liotta, G., Montecchiani, F.: A survey on graph drawing beyond planarity. ACM Comput. Surv. **52**(1), 4:1–4:37 (2019)
16. Didimo, W., Liotta, G., Ortali, G., Patrignani, M.: Optimal orthogonal drawings of planar 3-graphs in linear time. In: Chawla, S. (ed.) Proceedings of the 2020 ACM-SIAM Symposium on Discrete Algorithms, SODA 2020, Salt Lake City, UT, USA, January 5–8, 2020, pp. 806–825. SIAM (2020)
17. Didimo, W., Liotta, G., Patrignani, M.: HV-planarity: algorithms and complexity. J. Comput. Syst. Sci. **99**, 72–90 (2019)
18. Dilla, W.N., Raschke, R.L.: Data visualization for fraud detection: practice implications and a call for future research. Int. J. Acc. Inf. Syst. **16**, 1–22 (2015)
19. Dujmovic, V., et al.: A fixed-parameter approach to 2-layer planarization. Algorithmica **45**(2), 159–182 (2006)
20. Dujmovic, V., et al.: On the parameterized complexity of layered graph drawing. Algorithmica **52**(2), 267–292 (2008)

21. Dwyer, T., et al.: Immersive analytics: an introduction. In: Marriott, K., et al. (eds.) Immersive Analytics, LNCS, vol. 11190, pp. 1–23. Springer, Cham (2018)
22. Filipov, V., Arleo, A., Miksch, S.: Are we there yet? a roadmap of network visualization from surveys to task taxonomies. Computer Graphics Forum (2023, on print)
23. Garg, A., Tamassia, R.: On the computational complexity of upward and rectilinear planarity testing. SIAM J. Comput. **31**(2), 601–625 (2001)
24. Di Giacomo, E., Didimo, W., Montecchiani, F., Tappini, A.: A user study on hybrid graph visualizations. In: Purchase, H.C., Rutter, I. (eds.) Graph Drawing and Network Visualization. GD 2021. LNCS, vol. 12868, pp. 21–38. Springer, Cham (2021). https://doi.org/10.1007/978-3-030-92931-2_2
25. Giacomo, E.D., Giordano, F., Liotta, G.: Upward topological book embeddings of dags. SIAM J. Discret. Math. **25**(2), 479–489 (2011)
26. Giacomo, E.D., Lenhart, W.J., Liotta, G., Randolph, T.W., Tappini, A.: (k, p)-planarity: a relaxation of hybrid planarity. Theor. Comput. Sci. **896**, 19–30 (2021)
27. Giacomo, E.D., Liotta, G., Montecchiani, F.: Orthogonal planarity testing of bounded treewidth graphs. J. Comput. Syst. Sci. **125**, 129–148 (2022)
28. Giacomo, E.D., Liotta, G., Patrignani, M., Rutter, I., Tappini, A.: Nodetrix planarity testing with small clusters. Algorithmica **81**(9), 3464–3493 (2019)
29. Hong, S., Tokuyama, T. (eds.) Beyond Planar Graphs. Springer, Singapore (2020). https://doi.org/10.1007/978-981-15-6533-5
30. Joos, L., Jaeger-Honz, S., Schreiber, F., Keim, D.A., Klein, K.: Visual comparison of networks in VR. IEEE Trans. Vis. Comput. Graph. **28**(11), 3651–3661 (2022)
31. Jünger, M., Mutzel, P. (eds.) Graph Drawing Software. Springer, Berlin (2004). https://doi.org/10.1007/978-3-642-18638-7
32. Kaufmann, M., Wagner, D. (eds.): Drawing Graphs, Methods and Models (the book grow out of a Dagstuhl Seminar, April 1999), LNCS, vol. 2025. Springer, Berlin (2001). https://doi.org/10.1007/3-540-44969-8
33. Keim, D.A., Kohlhammer, J., Ellis, G.P., Mansmann, F.: Mastering the Information Age - Solving Problems with Visual Analytics. Eurographics Association, Saarbrücken (2010)
34. Keim, D.A., Mansmann, F., Stoffel, A., Ziegler, H.: Visual analytics. In: Liu, L., Özsu, M.T. (eds.) Encyclopedia of Database Systems, 2nd edn. Springer, Berlin (2018)
35. Kobourov, S.G., Liotta, G., Montecchiani, F.: An annotated bibliography on 1-planarity. Comput. Sci. Rev. **25**, 49–67 (2017)
36. Kraus, M., et al.: Immersive analytics with abstract 3D visualizations: a survey. Comput. Graph. Forum **41**(1), 201–229 (2022)
37. Kwon, O., Muelder, C., Lee, K., Ma, K.: A study of layout, rendering, and interaction methods for immersive graph visualization. IEEE Trans. Vis. Comput. Graph. **22**(7), 1802–1815 (2016)
38. Leite, R.A., Gschwandtner, T., Miksch, S., Gstrein, E., Kuntner, J.: NEVA: visual analytics to identify fraudulent networks. Comput. Graph. Forum **39**(6), 344–359 (2020)

39. Liotta, G., Rutter, I., Tappini, A.: Simultaneous FPQ-ordering and hybrid planarity testing. Theor. Comput. Sci. **874**, 59–79 (2021)
40. Liotta, G., Rutter, I., Tappini, A.: Parameterized complexity of graph planarity with restricted cyclic orders. J. Comput. Syst. Sci. **135**, 125–144 (2023)
41. Ma, K.: Pushing visualization research frontiers: essential topics not addressed by machine learning. IEEE Comput. Graphics Appl. **43**(1), 97–102 (2023)
42. McGee, F., et al.: Visual Analysis of Multilayer Networks. Synthesis Lectures on Visualization. Morgan & Claypool Publishers, San Rafael (2021)
43. Munzner, T.: Visualization Analysis and Design. A.K. Peters visualization series. A K Peters (2014)
44. Nishizeki, T., Rahman, M.S.: Planar Graph Drawing, vol. 12. World Scientific, Singapore (2004)
45. Nobre, C., Meyer, M.D., Streit, M., Lex, A.: The state of the art in visualizing multivariate networks. Comput. Graph. Forum **38**(3), 807–832 (2019)
46. Sacha, D.: Knowledge generation in visual analytics: Integrating human and machine intelligence for exploration of big data. In: Apel, S., et al. (eds.) Ausgezeichnete Informatikdissertationen 2018, LNI, vol. D-19, pp. 211–220. GI (2018)
47. Sacha, D., et al.: What you see is what you can change: human-centered machine learning by interactive visualization. Neurocomputing **268**, 164–175 (2017)
48. Sacha, D., Senaratne, H., Kwon, B.C., Ellis, G.P., Keim, D.A.: The role of uncertainty, awareness, and trust in visual analytics. IEEE Trans. Vis. Comput. Graph. **22**(1), 240–249 (2016)
49. Sacha, D., Stoffel, A., Stoffel, F., Kwon, B.C., Ellis, G.P., Keim, D.A.: Knowledge generation model for visual analytics. IEEE Trans. Vis. Comput. Graph. **20**(12), 1604–1613 (2014)
50. Tamassia, R.: Graph drawing. In: Sack, J., Urrutia, J. (eds.) Handbook of Computational Geometry, pp. 937–971. North Holland/Elsevier, Amsterdam (2000)
51. Tamassia, R. (ed.) Handbook on Graph Drawing and Visualization. Chapman and Hall/CRC, Boca Raton (2013)
52. Tamassia, R., Liotta, G.: Graph drawing. In: Goodman, J.E., O'Rourke, J. (eds.) Handbook of Discrete and Computational Geometry, 2nd edn., pp. 1163–1185. Chapman and Hall/CRC, Boca Raton (2004)
53. Zehavi, M.: Parameterized analysis and crossing minimization problems. Comput. Sci. Rev. **45**, 100490 (2022)

Understanding Non-Covalent Interactions in Biological Processes through QM/MM-EDA Dynamic Simulations

Marcos Mandado

Department of Physical Chemistry, University of Vigo, Lagoas-Marcosende s/n, 36310
Vigo, Spain
mandado@uvigo.es

Molecular dynamic simulations in biological environments such as proteins, DNA or lipids involves a large number of atoms, so classical models based on widely parametrized force fields are employed instead of more accurate quantum methods, whose high computational requirements preclude their application. The parametrization of appropriate force fields for classical molecular dynamics relies on the precise knowledge of the non-covalent inter and intramolecular interactions responsible for very important aspects, such as macromolecular arrangements, cell membrane permeation, ion solvation, etc. This implies, among other things, knowledge of the nature of the interaction, which may be governed by electrostatic, repulsion or dispersion forces. In order to know the balance between different forces, quantum calculations are frequently performed on simplified molecular models and the data obtained from these calculations are used to parametrize the force fields employed in classical simulations. These parameters are, among others, atomic charges, permanent electric dipole moments and atomic polarizabilities. However, it sometimes happens that the molecular models used for the quantum calculations are too simple and the results obtained can differ greatly from those of the extended system. As an alternative to classical and quantum methods, hybrid quantum/classical schemes (QM/MM) can be introduced, where the extended system is neither truncated nor simplified, but only the most important region is treated quantum mechanically.

In this presentation, molecular dynamic simulations and calculations with hybrid schemes are first introduced in a simple way for a broad and multidisciplinary audience. Then, a method developed in our group to investigate intermolecular interactions using hybrid quantum/classical schemes (QM/MM-EDA) is presented and some applications to the study of dynamic processes of ion solvation and membrane permeation are discussed [1–3]. Special attention is paid to the implementation details of the method in the EDA-NCI software [4].

References

1. Cárdenas, G., Pérez-Barcia, A., Mandado, M., Nogueira, J.J.: Phys. Chem. Chem. Phys. **23**, 20533 (2021)
2. Pérez-Barcia, A., Cárdenas, G., Nogueira, J.J., Mandado, M.: J. Chem. Inf. Model. **63**, 882 (2023)

3. Alvarado, R., Cárdenas, G., Nogueira, J.J., Ramos-Berdullas, N., Mandado, M.: Membranes **13**, 28 (2023)
4. Mandado, M., Van Alsenoy, C.: EDA-NCI: A program to perform energy decomposition analysis of non-covalent interactions. https://github.com/marcos-mandado/ EDA-NCI

Contents – Part I

High Performance Computing and Networks

Information Systems and Technologies

Contents – Part II

Urban and Regional Planning

PHD Showcase Papers

Short Papers

Computational Methods, Algorithms and Scientific Applications

Review on Nuclear Thermal Propulsion Analysis of Fuel Element and Simulation Methods

César A. Cárdenas R.[1](✉), Carlos Andrés Collazos Morales[2](✉),
Juan Carlos Amaya[3], Fabian C. Castro[4], César E. Mora[5],
Ramón E. R. Gonzalez[6], José L. Simancas-García[7],
and Farid A. Meléndez Pertuz[7]

[1] Department of Aerospace Engineering, Virginia Polytechnic Institute and State
University, Blacksburg, VA, USA
cesarac1975@vt.edu
[2] Grupo de Ciencias Básicas y Laboratorios, Universidad Manuela Beltrán,
Bogotá D.C., Colombia
carlos.collazos@docentes.umb.edu.co
[3] Departamento de Ingeniería Mecatrónica, Universidad Manuela Beltrán,
Bogotá D.C., Colombia
[4] Vicerrectoria de investigación, Universidad Manuela Beltrán,
Bogotá D.C., Colombia
[5] Centro de Investigación en Ciencia Aplicada y Tecnología Avanzada, Instituto
Politécnico Nacional, Ciudad de México, Mexico
[6] Universidade Federal Rural de Pernanbuco, Recife, Brazil
[7] Department of Computer Science and Electronics,Universidad de la Costa,
Barranquilla, Colombia

Abstract. This paper is mainly focused on reviewing different approaches for nuclear thermal propulsion analysis of fuel elements used for this matter. Mathematical models, simulation options and code generation that have been applied using computational tools such as OpenFOAM and other resources are considered. Additionally, experimental data from the Nuclear Engine for Rocket Vehicle Application (NERVA) is included in this paper. Nuclear thermal propulsion is known as one of the most important choice of propulsion technologies for coming manned missions to different interplanetary destinations. Systems based on Nuclear Thermal Propulsion (NTP) could improve vehicle returning and reduce missions risks. It can be done through travel time reduction and payload capacity improvement in comparison to for instance chemical propulsion systems. Nowadays developments of these systems are based on low enriched uranium fuels and this review work is focused on such fuel systems.

O. Gervasi et al. (Eds.): ICCSA 2023, LNCS 13956, pp. 3–18, 2023.
https://doi.org/10.1007/978-3-031-36805-9_1

1   Introduction

1.1   Fundamentals of Nuclear Propulsion

This type of rocket propulsion has some advantages and disadvantages. An important drawback is that the exhaust gasses are radioactive. On the other hand, the engine design is simple and can be started, stopped or restarted. This fact make these types of engines more suitable over other such as chemical rocket engines. Also, a nuclear rocket engine can produce bigger impulse and the energy resource to be able to start it is generated by itself. One of the first nuclear engines was developed during the ROVER program. Its initial basic concept was based on a graphite reactor loaded with highly-enriched uranium. In addition, hydrogen was used as propellant as well as coolant. Then, hydrogen was passed through fuel elements. This high temperature gas was discharged out of a nozzle creating thrust. Commonly, high performance is required for a high temperature gas. So, materials that can support long periods at these conditions are needed. As these kinds of propulsion engines started to evolve, fuel elements and nozzle configurations began to change as well. The program mentioned earlier was divided in four different sections, NERVA, KIWI, RIFT and PHOEBUS. The original idea of the NERVA project was to construct a 200000–250000 lb of thrust engine. Later, this NERVA reactor design changed the PHOEBUS model and other additional techniques were applied for testing purposes. Although at the beginning of the 70s this program was cancelled, it showed the benefits of the space technology advancements. The FE elements implemented in the 60s in different nuclear propulsion reactors such as the KIWI, PHOBEUS contained a graphite matrix. A set of coolant channels were coated with NbC or 2rC for carbon protection. Moreover, during those trials, mass losses were noted and this fact had an important effect on the neutronic features of the core reactor. At that time the development of novel fuel elements that could operate at high temperatures was started [6, 12, 19, 23, 30].

Nomenclature

NTP Abbreviations

NERVA Nuclear Engine for Rocket Vehicle Application
LEU low-enriched uranium
NTP Nuclear Thermal Propulsion
NRX Nuclear Rocket Experiment
HEU High-enriched uranium
LEU low-enriched uranium
OpenFOAM Symbols

k Turbulent Kinetic Energy
P Fluid Pressure
U Fluid Speed
T Temperature
ρ Density
ϵ Turbulent Dissipation

So, Nuclear thermal propulsion (NTP) is one of the most suitable technologies taken into inconsideration for space agencies such as NASA for long term or deep missions to space. It looks like the main source of energy is fission to be able to heat a fluid, particularly hydrogen which allows to get very high temperatures. Also, it permits to obtain a larger specific impulse (Isp) compared to chemical rockets. It is well known that most relevant performance variables of a rocket engine are Isp, thrust, and thrust to weight ratio. It is important to point out the importance of the temperature of gas that enters a nozzle in which the higher the temperature the higher Isp. The trust of the type of system is primarily driven by the pressure of the chamber, expansion nozzle and nozzle mass flow. Some studies state that common thrust and Isp values can vary from 10–100 klbf and 800–1000 s. One of the biggest programs for the development of NTP systems was the Nuclear Engine for Rocket Vehicle Applications (NERVA). During this program many technical information and experimental data were generated. Approximately, 20 reactor models were designed, manufactured, and tested. All NERVA designs are based on highly enriched uranium (HEU) fuel systems. The majority of these nuclear rockets designed under this program utilized graphite based, extruded hexagonal fuel elements in which nineteen coolant channels were included. Although many significant advancements were achieved during the NERVA program, there is a lot of research and development required to meet the future objectives of space agencies as NASA. It is important to note that the biggest challenge would be to change to low-enriched uranium (LEU) fuel systems. The initial research projects related to NTP systems were mainly experimental with different engines tested pointed earlier (Kiwi, Phoebus, Pewee, NERVA NRX). In the Phoebus case, its design was then modified by NERVA NRX series and other techniques were applied to carry out the first flight system to evaluate. The NERVA NRX-A6 was certainly the last uranium-fueled reactor that was tested. This program was cancelled because a lack of funding from government [5,7,16,26–28,35].

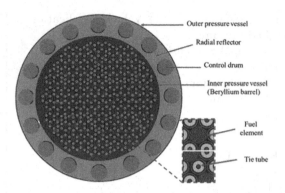

Fig. 1. NERVA configuration core, from [45]

However, these reactor programs could show that they are feasible with a high efficiency for the advancement of technologies for space propulsion. Highly-enriched uranium (HEU) was used in early NTP system designs which is not currently recommended regarding security and governing matters. Nowadays, designs are focused on high-efficiency engines based on low enriched uranium fuel (LEU). To be able to accomplish high specific impulse as well as thrust to weight values, these recent LEU developments would need geometry changes and length and configuration of the core. These adjustments might bring some doubts related to some parameters relations such as heat transfer that were studied within the NERVA program. Several specific Reynolds numbers were set for the large data obtained. However, it may not be totally used in recently developed designs. Likewise, the doubts mentioned earlier could be reduced by setting new experimental works that are expensive and are not available yet [45]. Hence, it is necessary to complete these costly experiments by using modeling and computational tools for simulation. Some of the research works covered in this review employed for instance Finite Volume Methods (FVMs) that seems to be a very suitable numerical method for NTP modeling. Also, these approaches have been used for many years for thermal hydraulic analysis based upon code generation [16,20].

For instance, the KLAXON code was one the first computational models utilized for NTP studies. Despite this, this methodology relied on just a 1D model. Then, another work implemented a 3D numerical method for simulations of a NERVA-type engine through a computational fluid dynamics code known as UNIC. In this simulation a CHT (Conjugate Heat Transfer) solver was applied [8]. This research proved that there is an important capacity of modeling a NTP through Finite Volume Methods. A very well - known computational source is OpenFOAM. It is a open-source finite volume method code to resolve problems regarding chemical reactions, turbulence, and heat transfer phenomena. In addition, OpenFOAM is used for many nuclear usages. A very significant option is GeN-Foam which is a OpenFOAM based solver. It can execute different simulations for cores of reactors [13,14]. This review work is focused on OpenFOAM applications in which CHT approaches are used. The simulations conditions established are similar to the preliminary experimental tasks. The NRX-A6 trial reports provide initial data and results of measurements that were taken for OpenFOAM validation. In this current review, a detailed description of geometry configuration, thermal analysis and other variables is given. This simulation and analysis method can be a source solution to assist other codes such as THERMO [38]. Moreover, OpenFOAM and THERMO results are compared.

2   Nuclear Thermal Core Description

At the beginning of the 1960s, there used to be a lack of information regarding the properties and manufacturing techniques of materials used for NRE core (zirconium, uranium carbides, and zirconium hydride). However, a well-known fact is that a fuel based on UC-ZrC and UC-NbC with nearly can supply the hydrogen heating until 3.000 K. Hence, later studies found that the right progress is the consideration of materials with heating melting points such s uranium, zirconium and monocarbide. A typical nuclear core is made of fuel elements with cooling channels in which a high pressure fluid (hydrogen) flows. Normally, fuel elements (FE) are hexagonal-shaped with a composite matrix (U, ZrC). During previous research works, coolant channels were coated with ZrC in order to avoid reactions of the carbon contained in the matrix with the hydrogen. On the other hand, a Nuclear Reactor Engine (NTR) has turbopumps that are in charge of pressurizing the hydrogen and other components such as the nuclear reactor and nozzle. Also, the fuel core has tie tubes that are responsible of getting additional thermal energy to drive the pumps. In addition, high temperatures are reached by the fluid as it passes across the cooling channels and then increases in the converging-diverging nozzle. Core temperatures can get up to 2500 K which is very close to the maximum temperature of the hydrogen. Regarding pressure, a common usual NTR core can be about 3 MPa. However, some experimental devices are able to run at even higher pressures. A summary of operating conditions for a typical NTR NERVA engine is given. A schematic is displayed in Fig. 2. Within the experiments carried out during the NERVA program, the one known as the NRX-A6 trial is certainly the best documented. The NRX-A6 core has different clusters that contain six fuel elements. These are around an unfueled element in the center. Thermocouples are located in the unfueled elements. An important matter to point is the fact that to design a high performance NTR engine will need a good comprehension of these tricky processes as well as core material developments that are able to support high temperatures and flow rates of hydrogen [2,3,11,22,29,33,43].

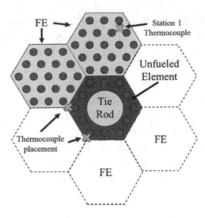

Fig. 2. Cluster of fuel elements for NERVA, from [45]

3 Mathematical Model Simulation Methods and Codes

Recently, OpenFOAM's CHT (Conjugate Heat Transfer) is the method employed as heat transfer model for graphite-based fuel elements. Also, the results obtained are compared to experimental data given by the NRX-A6 technical reports. In addition, a wide array of numerical methods have been developed. Some of them are still being developed because of several functioning limitations [8,21, 31,41]. For nuclear reactor analysis, an implementation of multiphysics coupling approaches are mainly involved. The neutronics/thermal (N/TH) is the most used and is being extensively-researched. The coupling solutions for the neutron transport equation solution can be divided into tight and loose. Tight is related to new computations code and loose are solved individually or decoupled. Coupling is achieved when information is exchanged by the boundary condition between them. Also loose coupling is also classified as internal and external coupling [4,15,24,37]. OpenFOAM (Open Field Operation And Manipulation) is a open free source C++ toolbox. OpenFOAM is based on a large library that provides several core functionalities such as discretization of partial differential equations, meshing, linear equations solutions, turbulence models and others. The users can develop resources to solve differential equations as well as new boundary conditions. This computational tool also offers solvers for specific problems, tools for meshing and pre and post-processing procedures. OpenFOAM mostly runs in parallel. In order to run an application, an OpenFOAM case should be set up. A case is just a directory that contains all the required files to be able to run a particular case. In Fig. 1 the basic structure of a case is shown. Each folder has a specific task. The *constant* directory has the mesh in the *polyMesh* subdirectory and the configuration files contain physical properties. In the *system* directory all the information about the solution process is found. It has mostly the following files:

– *controlDict*

– fvSchemes
– fvSolution

The first one defines control parameters to run a case. It includes solver, starting/ending times and time steps. The *fvSchemes* is employed to choose a discretization scheme. *fvSolution* manages the linear equation solvers and algorithms of solution. In addition, the directories of time have single data for all fields such as pressure p or velocity U. Initial conditions are commonly established in the *0* time directory.

3.1   Semi-Implicit Method for Pressure Linked Equations (SIMPLE)

SIMPLE algorithm is a extensively iterative strategy for solution of the Navier-Stokes equations. It is basically a estimation-and-adjustment approach to calculate pressure. It begins by assuming a pressure field $p*$. It is then changed in the iteration procedure with pressure modifications p'. Hence, the field of pressure can be got from:

$$p = p * + p' \tag{1}$$

Some similar corrections are done to velocities as follows:

$$u = u * + u' \tag{2}$$
$$v = v * + v' \tag{3}$$
$$w = w * + w' \tag{4}$$

The velocity changes are computed from the pressure adjustments by taking a velocity change formula. This is obtained from the discretized equation of momentum in which some terms are omitted. There are two steps to perform when this algorithm is applied. The first one is the solutions of momentum equations for the new "starred" velocities. If the pressure field is not adjusted, the velocity field will not fulfill the equation of continuity. The main goal of the SIMPLE algorithm is to fix the pressure field in the iteration process in such a way that the velocity field can closely meet the equation of continuity. To be able to do so, the changes of pressure have to be done in some way. So, to accomplish this, a pressure change equation is acquired from the equation of continuity with some modifications. In the second step, these pressure adjustments equation is solved and a new pressure field is computed (Eq. 1). After that, the velocity fields are updated by using velocity changes formulas. The last step is to find the solution of other differential equations for other variables such as temperature, turbulence. New iterations are needed until convergence is got and no additional pressure adjustments are required [17, 18, 34, 36, 46].

3.2   Conjugate Heat Transfer (CHT) Model

The Conjugated heat transfer method is when there are two or more thermal subdomains which are connected. Likewise, heat transfer differential equations are solved. These equations are linked by conjugate conditions on the interfaces of the subdomain. This condition is normally about requiring temperature continuity and heat flow. It is important to specify that in subdomains of solid kind, the heat equation is the only one that is solved. However, in fluid subdomain cases the equations, the Navier-Stokes equations and the energy equation have to be resolved. A couple of numerical approaches are considered within this methodology. One of them is to find the solution of the equations in all subdomains. The other one is utilize iterations to solve the differential equations in the subdomains individually. Boundary conditions are set for the subdomains and these are updated after a subdomain is solved. Iterations continue until solutions for all subdomains converge [10, 27, 39, 42]. The OpenFOAM CHT solver taken indicated as *chtMultiRegionSimpleFoam* is a steady-state solver that can model turbulence of compressible flows by using the SIMPLE algorithm. Since this solver has a multiregion skill, it is used to mesh each region or subdomain. Hence, the recent studies have employed this option to be able to model for instance the heat transfer or fluid mechanics of the propellant and subdomains of solid fuel. Also, an interface for boundary conditions called *turbulentTemperatureCoupledBaffleMixed* is used by the CHT solver to combine fluid and solid regions. The following are the governing equations:

$$\lambda_1 \nabla_\perp T_1 = \lambda_2 \nabla_\perp T_2 \tag{5}$$

where λ denotes the thermal conductivity and T is the interface temperature. The suffixes 1 and 2 are the domains placed at the boundary of the interface. $\nabla_\perp$ is the gradient operator. Then, the heat flow q_s can be determined as follows:

$$q_s \approx \frac{T_s - T_i}{\nabla_i} \lambda_i(T_s) \tag{6}$$

where $\lambda_i(T_s), T_s, T_i)$ and ∇_i are the thermal conductivity, temperature of the interface, temperature of the first cell and the normal distance from the domain ($i = 1$ or 2). Additionally, the surface temperature is computed as follows:

$$T_s = \frac{\frac{\lambda_1}{\nabla_1} T_1 + \frac{\lambda_2}{\nabla_2} T_2}{\frac{\lambda_1}{\nabla_1} + \frac{\lambda_2}{\nabla_2}} \tag{7}$$

where the values of thermal conductivity λ_1 and λ_2 are calculated in both domains (1 and 2) considering thermodynamic properties combined with the model of turbulence. The following is a short description of the CHT solver:

Read fluid fields and solid fields;
while t < tMax **do**
    for all all fluid regions **do**
        Solve the equation of momentum;
        Solve the equation of energy and update thermophysical characteristics;
        Solve the equation of pressure and adjust velocities;
        Solve the equations of turbulence;

end for
for all solid regions **do**
　 Solve the equation of energy and update thermophysical characteristics;;
　end for
　t++;
end while

Firstly, a reading of all fields is done for all regions. After, the differential equations are solved at each time interval for all fluid regions and solid regions. The solution procedure begins by collecting initial fields and resolving equation of momentum for velocities. Then, the energy equation is solved and the thermophysical attributes are updated based upon the new temperature and pressure field of the former time step. Besides, the pressure equation should be solved and velocities are corrected in order to meet the equation of continuity equation by employing the recent field of pressure. Finally, the turbulence equations are computed for a fluid region the turbulence viscosity is updated. Regarding solid regions, just the energy equation is solved. The several regions are joined by boundary conditions. Once a equation is solved, the respective region boundary conditions are upgraded.

3.3　Generalized Nuclear Foam - GeN-Foam

For many years, simulation of nuclear reactor transient behaviour has been dependant on coupling of diverse codes for diffusion of neutron and thermal hydraulics (1D). In addition, recent research works on nuclear reactors analysis have used different codes that are focused on porous medium. One of these approaches is the GeN-Foam which can be applied to fuel elements as well as core of nuclear reactors. An advantage that can be pointed is the capacity to handle the porous medium equations are returned to the regular Navier-Stokes equations. Furthermore, another benefit is the possibility to be used with unstructured mesh configurations. It also has a wide range of applications and different mesh details (coarse or fine). Likewise, the possibility to solve different physics variables is included as well [14, 36]. This solver contains four main sub-solvers elements: thermal-hydraulics, thermalmechanics, neutronics and a 1D sub-solver which tests temperatures in fuel. All of them use an unstructured mesh that is an importance difference compared to other codes which just operate with structured meshes. All sub-solvers have the capacity of parallel computing. For equations discretization issues, a finite-volume method is implemented and the algebraic equations obtained are resolved by applying OpenFOAM linear iterative solvers.

3.4　Thermal Hydraulics Equations

One of the main objectives of GeN-Foam option is to study the complete core of a nuclear reactor. It has been seen that a standard turbulence modeling such as RANS (Reynolds averaged Navier-Stokes) has a high computational cost. So, an alternative is to deal with these kind of arrangements as porous media. The resulting equations of mass, momentum and energy in this type of media are:

$$\frac{\partial \gamma \rho}{\partial t} + \nabla \cdot (\gamma \rho \mathbf{u}) = 0 \tag{8}$$

$$\frac{\partial \gamma \rho \mathbf{u}}{\partial t} + \nabla \cdot (\gamma \rho \mathbf{u} \otimes \mathbf{u}) = \nabla \cdot (\mu_T \nabla \mathbf{u}) - \nabla \gamma p + p_i \nabla \gamma + \gamma \mathbf{F_g} + \gamma \mathbf{F_{ss}} \tag{9}$$

$$\frac{\partial \gamma \rho \mathbf{e}}{\partial t} + \nabla . (\mathbf{u} \gamma (\rho e + p)) = \nabla \cdot (\gamma k_T \nabla T) + \gamma \mathbf{F_{ss}} \cdot \mathbf{u} + \gamma \dot{Q}_{ss} \tag{10}$$

where $\mathbf{F_{ss}}$ represents the drag force on the fluid carried out by the sub-scales layouts. $\dot{Q}_{ss}$ is the volumetric heat transferred during the interaction of the fluid and the sub-scale layout.

3.5   Thermal Mechanics Equations

It is a solver provided by OpenFOAM commonly known as *solidDisplacement-Foam*. It is used to check core structure deformations due to induced temperatures. The following displacement equation D_f is solved:

$$\mathbf{v}_f \cdot \nabla \cdot D_f = \alpha (T - T_r ef) \tag{11}$$

where $\mathbf{v}_f$ is axial direction and α is an expansion coefficient [9,32,40,44,47].

3.5.1   Turbulence Model The most common model taken for turbulence flow modeling and simulation is the $k - \epsilon$ one. It can work with different Reynolds numbers. The last research studies have used high R_e values. This model is very suitable when flow paths do not have curvatures or are all straight. An important issue is that eddy viscosity is considered as scalar. Nevertheless, this assumption may be true just for regions in which the fluid is completely developed. On the contrary, when near walls is not certainly valid. Therefore, some additional analysis is needed for near-wall when the $k - \epsilon$ approach is applied. To be able to deal with these possible concerns some additional OpenFOAM functions are also taken into consideration (*epsilonWallFunction* and *kqRWallFunction*) [1].

3.5.2   OpenFOAM Mesh Structure The OpenFOAM mesh type used for fuel elements modeling is hybrid. It is made of hexahedron and tetrahedron cells (structured and unstructured). The structured mesh is placed close to the solid-fluid region (Fig. 3). On the other hand, the unstructured one is employed in the other domains (coolant and solid). Regarding quality of the mesh, finite volume methods (FVM) normally require high - quality meshes. These can be structured or non- structured. A non-orthogonality approach can be used to correct issues that may generate inaccurate solutions [25,31,45].

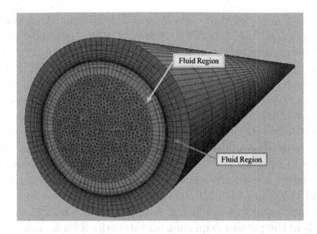

Fig. 3. OpenFOAM geometry for validation, from [45]

4 Summary

There is a wide range of methods that can be implemented for nuclear reactor analysis. For instance, some of them involve either neutronics or thermal-hydraulics coupling and even some deterministic models. Therefore, different solution methods for the neutron transport equations can be used. It seems that the THERMO technique is no totally reliable when applied to new designs. It may have some limitations for thermal hydraulic computations. On the contrary, OpenFOAM shows much better results since it does not depend on heat transfer interactions as the CHT solver is applied. A simple comparison between OpenFOAM and THERMO is done for validation work purposes by using data mapping of the outcomes got from [45] after post-processing (Figs. 5 and 6). Regarding the experimental tasks realized in the same study (Fig. 4), an analysis is performed between some experimental data and OpenFOAM. THERMO results are not included in this data mapping approach. Some good approximations are seen particularly in the exit temperature of the propellant. In this case is noted that THERMO can not provide a reasonable temperature approximation. In the axial mean temperature a right correspondence is observed. In [18] another important comparison is analysed among three distinctive coupling methodologies (OpenFOAM, RMC and Monte Carlo). In addition, other variables that may get an important variation are the fuel temperature, fuel distribution over the core within the reactor, deformation of the core due to change in temperature and power change. A new solver named thermalMechanicsFoam is employed to solve thermal expansion and heat conduction analysis in the core. On the other hand, RCM is applied for simulation of reactor core and its neutron transport features. The RCM and OpenFOAM strategies provide results which are very adequate with no significant differences and accurate for coupling computations. Other solving approaches such as Monte Carlo and 3D Thermal Hidraulic codes (3D TH) are even more precise nowadays. However, more research and validations studies would be required since there are still some computational restrictions and troubles with code improvements. Likewise, Picard and JFNK methods also need more research to be able to validate their performance and accuracy. Currently, most numerical simulation works apply the Picard system for coupling due to its higher reliability. Despite this, it has some low computational capability. Some additional methods have been added to be able to upgrade the low computational issue. For multiphysics coupling simulations the main solution method that could be considered in the near future is the JFKN approach. This solving option offers a high-efficiency performance. An interesting novel model based on OpenFOAM in which 1D, 2D or 3D domains are not really necessary to solve the governing equations. Hence, it is important to notice some advantages for the residuals of the pressure equation and iterations for several applications of interest. For future work this code development will be added to the GeN-Foam system for validation and examination.

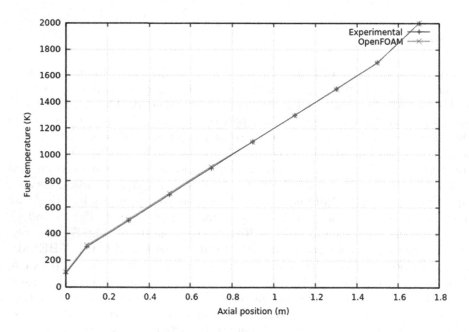

Fig. 4. Numerical and experimental comparison, from [45]

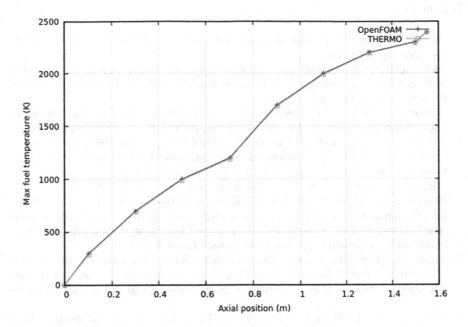

Fig. 5. Code comparison/Fuel maximum temperature), from [45]

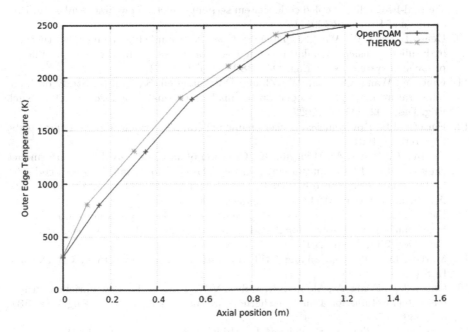

Fig. 6. Code comparison (Fuel outer edge temperature), from [45]

References

1. CFD Direct. 2015–2020. OpenFOAM v5 User Guide (2020). https://cfd.direct/openfoam/user-guide-v5/
2. Akyuzlu, K.M.: Numerical study of high-temperature and high-velocity gaseous hydrogen flow in a cooling channel of a nuclear thermal rocket core. J. Nucl. Eng. Radiat. Sci. **1**(4) (2015)
3. Aufiero, M., Fratoni, M.: Development of multiphysics tools for fluoride-cooled high-temperature reactors. In: Proceedings of PHYSOR, pp. 2116–2127 (2016)
4. Aufiero, M., Fiorina, C., Laureau, A., Rubiolo, P., Valtavirta, V.: Serpent-OpenFOAM coupling in transient mode: simulation of a Godiva prompt critical burst. In: Proceedings of M&C+ SNA+ MC, pp. 19–23 (2015)
5. Ballard, R.: Nuclear thermal propulsion update. Technical report (2019)
6. Benensky, K., Collins, R., Duchek, M., Holmes, L., Harnack, C., Abrams, J.: Reactor subsystem trades for a near-term nuclear thermal propulsion flight demonstration mission. In: Proceedings of Nuclear and Emerging Technologies for Space Applications, Oak Ridge National Laboratory (April 2020)
7. Braun, R., Myers, R., Bragg-Sitton, S.: Space nuclear propulsion for human mars exploration. NASEM Space Nuclear Propulsion Technologies Committee Report. Washington, DC: National Academies of Sciences, Engineering and Medicine (2021)
8. Cheng, G., Ito, Y., Ross, D., Chen, Y.-S., Wang, T.-S.: Numerical simulations of single flow element in a nuclear thermal thrust chamber. In: 39th AIAA Thermophysics Conference, p. 4143 (2007)
9. Daeubler, M., Jimenez, J., Sanches, V.: Development of a high-fidelity Monte Carlo thermal-hydraulics coupled code system serpent/subchanflow-first results. In: Proceedings of PHYSOR (2014)
10. Deng, J., Zeng, W., Wang, J., Ding, S., Chai, X.: Coupled neutronics and thermal-hydraulics transient simulation of a gas-cooled reactor in the aircraft nuclear propulsion system. Nucl. Eng. Des. **389**, 111674 (2022)
11. Fang, Y., Wang, C., Tian, W., Zhang, D., Guanghui, S., Qiu, S.: Study on high-temperature hydrogen dissociation for nuclear thermal propulsion reactor. Nucl. Eng. Des. **392**, 111753 (2022)
12. Finseth, J.L.: Rover nuclear rocket engine program: Overview of rover engine tests. final report (1991)
13. Fiorina, C., Pautz, A., Mikityuk, K.: Creation of an OpenFOAM fuel performance class based on FRED and integration into the GeN-foam multi-physics code. In: International Conference on Nuclear Engineering, vol. 51456, p. V003T02A027. American Society of Mechanical Engineers (2018)
14. Fiorina, C., Clifford, I., Aufiero, M., Mikityuk, K.: Gen-foam: a novel openfoam® based multi-physics solver for 2d/3d transient analysis of nuclear reactors. Nucl. Eng. Des. **294**, 24–37 (2015)
15. Marcos, I.G.: Thermal mixing CHT simulations with OpenFOAM: URANS and LES (2013)
16. Gates, J.T., Denig, A., Ahmed, R., Mehta, V.K., Kotlyar, D.: Low-enriched cermet-based fuel options for a nuclear thermal propulsion engine. Nucl. Eng. Des. **331**, 313–330 (2018)
17. Grande, L., Villamere, B., Allison, L., Mikhael, S., Rodriguez-Prado, A., Pioro, I.: Thermal aspects of uranium carbide and uranium dicarbide fuels in supercritical water-cooled nuclear reactors. J. Eng. Gas Turbines Power **133**(2), 022901 (2011)

18. Guo, Y., Li, Z., Huang, S., Liu, M., Wang, K.: A new neutronics-thermal-mechanics multi-physics coupling method for heat pipe cooled reactor based on RMC and OpenFOAM. Prog. Nucl. Energy **139**, 103842 (2021)

19. Gustafson, J.L.: Space nuclear propulsion fuel and moderator development plan conceptual testing reference design. Nucl. Technol. **207**(6), 882–884 (2021)

20. Hall, M.L., Rider, W.J., Cappiello, M.W.: Thermohydraulic modeling of nuclear thermal rockets: the KLAXON code. Technical report, Los Alamos National Lab., NM (United States) (1992)

21. Han, Z., Zhang, J., Wang, M., Tian, W., Qiu, S., Su, G.H.: A modified system analysis code for thermo-hydraulic calculation of hydrogen in a nuclear thermal propulsion (NTP) system. Ann. Nucl. Energy **164**, 108632 (2021)

22. Holman, R., Pierce, B.: Development of NERVA reactor for space nuclear propulsion. In: 22nd Joint Propulsion Conference, p. 1582 (1986)

23. Houts, M.G.: Advanced exploration with nuclear thermal propulsion. In: Tennessee Valley Interstellar Workshop (TVIW) Symposium on The Power of Synergy, number MSFC-E-DAA-TN62268 (2018)

24. Johnson, A.E., Kotlyar, D., Terlizzi, S., Ridley, G.: serpenttools: a Python package for expediting analysis with serpent. Nucl. Sci. Eng. **194**(11), 1016–1024 (2020)

25. Kim, H.T., Chang, S.-M., Son, Y.W.: Unsteady simulation of a full-scale CANDU-6 moderator with OpenFOAM. Energies **12**(2), 330 (2019)

26. Krecicki, M., Kotlyar, D.: Low enriched nuclear thermal propulsion neutronic, thermal hydraulic, and system design space analysis. Nucl. Eng. Des. **363**, 110605 (2020)

27. Krecicki, M.A.: Neutronic, thermal hydraulic, and system design space analysis of a low enriched nuclear thermal propulsion engine. Ph.D. thesis, Georgia Institute of Technology (2019)

28. Los Alamos National Laboratory. NUCLEAR ROCKETS: To Mars and Beyond (2020). https://www.lanl.gov/science/NSS/issue1_2011/story4.shtml

29. Lanin, A.: Nuclear rocket engine reactor. Nuclear Rocket Engine Reactor: 170 (2013)

30. Lyon, L.L.: Performance of (U, Zr)C-graphite (composite) and of (U, Zr)C (carbide) fuel elements in the Nuclear Furnace 1 test reactor. Technical report, Los Alamos Scientific Lab., N. Mex. (USA) (1973)

31. Moraes, A., Lage, P., Cunha, G., da Silva, L.F.L.R.: Analysis of the non-orthogonality correction of finite volume discretization on unstructured meshes. In: Proceedings of the 22nd International Congress of Mechanical Engineering, Ribeirão Preto, Brazil, pp. 3–7 (2013)

32. Mousseau, V.A.: Accurate solution of the nonlinear partial differential equations from thermal hydraulics: thermal hydraulics. Nucl. Technol. **158**(1), 26–35 (2007)

33. Pempie, P., de l'Espace, R.-P.: History of the nuclear thermal rocket propulsion. In: AAAF 6th International Symposium Propulsion for Space Transportation, vol. 9 (2002)

34. Perotti, S.: Thermo-mechanical analysis of heat pipe cooled reactor for space applications with OpenFOAM (2022)

35. Petitgenet, V., et al.: A coupled approach to the design space exploration of nuclear thermal propulsion systems. In: AIAA Propulsion and Energy 2020 Forum, p. 3846 (2020)

36. Radman, S., Fiorina, C., Pautz, A.: Development of a novel two-phase flow solver for nuclear reactor analysis: algorithms, verification and implementation in Open-FOAM. Nucl. Eng. Des. **379**, 111178 (2021)

37. Romano, P.K., Forget, B.: The OpenMC Monte Carlo particle transport code. Ann. Nucl. Energy **51**, 274–281 (2013)
38. Shaposhnik, Y., Shwageraus, E., Elias, E.: Thermal-Hydraulic Feedbackmodule for BGCore System. Ben Gurion University of the Negev (2008)
39. Slaby, J.G.: Heat-Transfer Coefficients for Hydrogen Flowing Through Parallel Hexagonal Passages at Surface Temperatures to 2275 K, vol. 4959. National Aeronautics and Space Administration (1968)
40. Stewart, M.: Thermal, fluid, and neutronic analysis of the GCD LEU nuclear thermal propulsion core. In: AIAA Propulsion and Energy 2019 Forum, p. 3944 (2019)
41. Tuominen, R., et al.: Coupling serpent and OpenFOAM for neutronics-CFD multiphysics calculations. Master's thesis (2015)
42. Tuominen, R., Valtavirta, V., Peltola, J., Leppänen, J.: Coupling serpent and OpenFOAM for neutronics-CFD multi-physics calculations. In: International Conference on the Physics of Reactors, PHYSOR 2016: Unifying Theory and Experiments in the 21st Century, pp. 255–269. American Nuclear Society (ANS) (2016)
43. Walton, J.T.: Program ELM: a tool for rapid thermal-hydraulic analysis of solidcore nuclear rocket fuel elements (1992)
44. Wang, J., Krecicki, M., Kotlyar, D.: Initial comparison of reduced and higher order thermal hydraulic solvers for nuclear thermal propulsion fuel element design. In: Proceedings of Nuclear and Emerging Technologies for Space Applications, Oak Ridge National Laboratory (April 2020)
45. Wang, J.C., Kotlyar, D.: High-resolution thermal analysis of nuclear thermal propulsion fuel element using OpenFOAM. Nucl. Eng. Des. **372**, 110957 (2021)
46. Wang, J.C.: Coarse-mesh-based Reduced-order Package for Multiphysics Simulation of Nuclear Thermal Propulsion Reactor Core. Ph.D. thesis, Georgia Institute of Technology (2021)
47. Wang, J., Wang, Q., Ding, M.: Review on neutronic/thermal-hydraulic coupling simulation methods for nuclear reactor analysis. Ann. Nucl. Energy **137**, 107165 (2020)

Modified Differential Evolution Algorithm Applied to Economic Load Dispatch Problems

Gabriella Lopes Andrade[1], Claudio Schepke[2(✉)], Natiele Lucca[2], and João Plinio Juchem Neto[3]

[1] School of Technology, Pontifical Catholic University of Rio Grande do Sul (PUCRS), Porto Alegre, RS, Brazil
gabriella.andrade@edu.pucrs.br
[2] Laboratory of Advances Studies in Computation, Federal University of Pampa (UNIPAMPA), Alegrete, RS, Brazil
{claudioschepke,natielelucca.aluno}@unipampa.edu.br
[3] Department of Economics and International Relations, Federal University of Rio Grande do Sul (UFRGS), Porto Alegre, RS, Brazil
plinio.juchem@ufrgs.br

Abstract. This paper proposes a modification of the Differential Evolution (DE) algorithm to solve the problem of Economic Load Dispatch (ELD). DE is an algorithm based on the theory of natural selection of species, where the fittest are more likely to survive. In the original DE, each possible solution to the target problem composes an initial population. This population evolved through genetic operators of mutation, selection, and crossover of individuals. In each iteration of the DE, the newly generated population replaces and discards the old population input. At the end of execution, the DE should return the best solution found. The Modification of the Differential Evolution (MDE) present in this paper considers that, in the selection stage, the ablest individual will replace the old one in the current population instead of being inserted in the new sample. To verify the performance of the MDE about the original DE, we solve a set of test functions to obtain the global minimum and different instances of the ELD. Both algorithms were effective in minimizing the three least-dimensional functions. Our results showed that DE proved more effective than MDE in minimizing the set of higher dimensional test functions, presenting a solution up to 99.99% better. However, none of the algorithms managed to obtain the optimal solution. In the ELD resolution, where it is to find the production level of each thermoelectric generating unit, satisfying the total system demand at the lowest cost, MDE was more effective than DE in all cases, finding a solution up to 1.10% better, solving the constraints of the problem. In addition, the computation time reduction of MDE concerning DE was up to 95.98%. Therefore, we confirm the efficiency of the proposed modification over the original DE version.

Keywords: Economic Load Dispatch · Modified Differential Evolution · Differential Evolution · Optimization

O. Gervasi et al. (Eds.): ICCSA 2023, LNCS 13956, pp. 19–37, 2023.
https://doi.org/10.1007/978-3-031-36805-9_2

1   Introduction

Many engineering problems are challenging or impossible to solve using classical mathematical optimization methods. These occur due to the difficulty in formulating the modelling or the mathematical effort required to solve it because they are non-linear, non-differentiable, or discontinuous [10]. Thus, bio-inspired algorithms based on populations are widely applied to solve this problem type.

Bio-inspired algorithms use a constructive method to obtain an initial population. From the initial population, applying local and global search techniques optimize population solutions. Among the most prominent classes of bio-inspired algorithms is Evolutionary Computing [10]. Algorithms belonging to the Evolutionary Computing class use rules of the natural selection theory, where individuals that best adapt to the environment are more likely to survive.

This paper proposes changes in the Differential Evolution (DE) algorithm [13], which belongs to the class of Evolutionary Computing algorithms. We present a Modification to the DE algorithm (MDE) to make it more efficient. In the original DE, the initial population advances to the evolutionary process, which consists of applying the genetic operators of mutation and crossover and the selection of individuals for insertion in the new input. At each iteration, a newly generated population replaces the old discarded one. In the end, the DE returns the best solution found. In MDE, instead of inserting the fittest individual in the new population, it replaces the old one in the current population. In this way, the population is updated in the greedy selection step and not replaced at the end of the iteration.

The target problem of this work is the Economic Load Dispatch (ELD) [7]. The purpose of the ELD is to scale the outputs of the power generation units of a thermoelectric plant to meet the consumer load demand at a minimum operation cost, which satisfies all the operating restrictions of the generating units and the restrictions of equality and inequality imposed [10]. Due to the increased demand for electricity in recent years and the scarcity of water resources [2], thermoelectric plants are of paramount importance for the contribution of the supply of electricity demand [14]. However, the fuel used for energy generation by thermoelectric plants presents a high cost. Soon, the importance of using ELD in optimizing the operation of energy systems is justified. In addition, with the resolution of the ELD, we will be able to verify the performance of the MDE compared to the original DE.

The **objective** of this paper is to propose a modification of the classical Differential Evolution algorithm to solve Economic Load Dispatch problems. The **contributions** of the paper are:

– Implementation of the Differential Evolution method and the proposed modification in Matlab;
– Application and comparison of methods in problems of the Economic Dispatch of a load of different sizes;
– Verification of the performance of methods about other methods already used in the literature to solve the Economic Dispatch.

The organization of this paper is into seven sections. Section 2 presents a general description of the ELD problem with the main restrictions applied to it. Section 3 discusses the DE heuristic. Section 4 points to the modifications of the DE, resulting in the proposed MDE heuristic. Section 5 shows aspects of methodology, like implementation and parameters for the executions. Section 6 details the results obtained through the execution of the DE and MDE heuristics to solve ELD. Section 7 presents the conclusion of this paper and future works.

2 Economic Load Dispatch Problem Description

Economic Load Dispatch (ELD) is a non-linear mathematical problem considered a sub-problem of the Unit Commitment (UC) [4,7]. The problem consists of allocating the total demand among generating units to minimize the total cost of production [8]. In addition, it must satisfy the system load demand, spinning reserve capacity, and practical operation constraints of generators such as valve-point effects, ramp rate limit, and prohibited operating zone [7,9].

This paper considers thermal sources (biomass, natural gas, coal, nuclear) to generate electricity. The generating units offer different production costs from the energy source used to produce the electricity [8]. In this way, ELD is an optimization problem in which the objective function to determine the total cost of electricity generation satisfies an equality problem and inequality of the problem [10].

2.1 Objective Function

In our ELD problem, we want to find the generation level of each thermoelectric power-generating unit that satisfies the total demand of the system at a minimum cost [10]. Considering a set of thermal groups with n generating units, the total fuel cost F to minimize the sum of the contributions from the generating units is given by the following equation:

$$\min C(P) = \sum_{i=1}^{n} C_i(P_i) \tag{1}$$

In this equation, C_i is the operating cost for the generating unit i (in \$/h), and P_i (in MW) is the power supplied by this unit. The operating cost C_i of each generating unit can be expressed as a function of the output power P_i through the following equation [7,10]:

$$\sum_{i=1}^{n} C_i(P_i) = \sum_{i=1}^{n} \alpha_i + \beta_i P_i + \gamma_i P_i^2 \tag{2}$$

Where the variables α_i, β_i and γ_i are restrictions on the characteristics of the generating unit i [10].

In the basic ELD, the supplied power must satisfy the power balance. That is, the sum of the contributions from the generating units must meet the total demand of the system P_D [8]. The following equation defines the power balance:

$$\sum_{i=1}^{n} P_i = P_D \tag{3}$$

Where P_D is the constant load power demanded. Furthermore, in the basic DE, transmission losses are not considered ($P_L = 0$).

According to [10], the objective function (2) must be modified to contemplate not only the load distribution with low cost in the generating units but also to satisfy the equality constraint of the system. Thus, we have the following objective function:

$$\sum_{i=1}^{n} F_i(P_i) + \phi \left(abs \left(\sum_{i=1}^{n} P_i - P_D \right) \right) \tag{4}$$

In this equation, ϕ is the penalty factor for solutions that do not meet the equilibrium in the power balance, which is a positive constant [10].

2.2 Practical Operation Constraints of Generator

The ELD problem generally has practical operation constraints of generating units. These restrictions are the balance of power and transmission losses, minimum and maximum limits of power operation by generating units, valve points, ramp limits, and prohibited operating zones [7].

Power Balance Constraint. The totality of generated power by the thermal units should be equal to the sum of the total system demand (P_D) and the total transmission network losses (P_L), according to the following equation:

$$\sum_{i=1}^{n} P_i = P_D + P_L \tag{5}$$

Where P_D is a constant value and P_L is a function of unit power outputs that uses the B coefficients according to the Kron equation [7]:

$$P_L = \sum_{i=1}^{n} \sum_{j=1}^{n} B_{ij} P_i P_j + \sum_{i=1}^{n} B_{0i} P_i + B_{00} \tag{6}$$

Where B_{ij} is the i-th element of the loss coefficient matrix, B_{0i} is the i-th element of the loss coefficient vector, and B_{00} is the loss coefficient constant [10].

The objective function (2) must be modified to contemplate not only the low-cost load distribution in the generating units, but also to satisfy the equality constraint of the system. Thus, we have the following objective function:

$$\sum_{i=1}^{n} F_i(P_i) + \phi \left(abs \left(\sum_{i=1}^{n} P_i - P_D - P_L \right) \right) \tag{7}$$

In this equation, ϕ is the penalty factor for solutions that do not meet the equilibrium in the load balance, which is a positive constant [10].

Power Output Limits. The power P_i (in MW) of each generating unit i must be within its minimum and maximum limits. The restriction on the power P_i is given by the following inequality:

$$P_i^{min} \leq P_i \leq P_i^{max} \tag{8}$$

Where P_i^{min} and P_i^{max} are, respectively, the minimum and maximum operating outputs of the generating unit i (in MW) [10]. According to [8], when power limit constraints are considered, along with power balance constraints and transmission losses, the classification of the DE problem is classic.

Valve Point. The modelling of the objective function of the ELD is as a quadratic polynomial. The effect of valve points in the form of a rectified sinusoidal function is by adding to the quadratic cost function. This ripple effect occurs when each valve in a turbine starts to open [15]. The description of sinusoidal components is in the following way:

$$F_i(P_i) = \alpha_i P_i^2 + \beta_i P_i + \gamma_i + \sigma |e_i \times \sin[f_i \times (P_i^{min} - P_i)]| \tag{9}$$

Where σ is equal to 1 if valve points exist, otherwise σ is setting to zero, e_i the coefficient due to the effect of valve points, P_i^{min} is the minimum output limit on the power P_i (in MW) generated [4,9].

Prohibited Zones. The operating prohibited zones divide the operating limits into several regions. In addition to considering the minimum and maximum operating limits, we will have intermediate limits representing the restriction of operating prohibited zones. In practice, it is difficult to determine the shape of the input-output curve close to the prohibited zones, either by carrying out machine performance tests or through operational records [4,7]. Thus, the best way to deal with the problem is to adjust the output of the P_i generation to avoid the unit operation in the prohibited zones [7]. The possible mathematical description of operating zones for an energy-generating unit i is as follows:

$$\begin{aligned} P_i^{min} &\leq P_i \leq P_{i,1}^l \\ P_{i,j-1}^u &\leq P_i \leq P_{i,j}^l, \ j = 2, 3, \ldots, n_i \\ P_{i,n_i}^u &\leq P_i \leq P_i^{max} \end{aligned} \tag{10}$$

Where $P_{i,j}^l$ and $P_{i,j}^u$ are the lower and upper limits of the prohibited operating zone j of the generating unit i [7,9].

Ramp Limits. The adjustment of the generator output could not be instantly in practice. Therefore, the restricting the operating range of all generating units is by their ramp limits to force it to operate continuously between two adjacent specific operating periods [7]. The inequality restrictions due to ramp-rate limits for unit generation changes are given by:

– As the generation grows:

$$P_i - P_i^0 \leq UR_i \tag{11}$$

– As the generation decreases:

$$P_i - P_i^0 \leq DR_i \tag{12}$$

Where P_i is the current output power of the generating unit i at time t; P_i^0 is the previous output power of the generating unit at time $t-1$; UR_i and DR_i (in MW) are respectively the ascent and descent restrictions of generator i [7,9]. The inclusion of ramp rate limits in Eq. 11 and Eq. 12 modifies the output power limits, as can be seen in the following Equation [9]:

$$\max(P_i^{min}, P_i^0 - DR_i) \leq P_i \leq \min(P_i^{max}, P_i^0 + UR_i) \tag{13}$$

3   Differential Evolution

The Differential Evolution algorithm is a direct parallel search method based on the theory of species evolution [12]. In DE, each possible solution of the target problem composes the initial population, which is evaluated and applied to the evolution process, which consists of mutating individuals with a certain probability, crossing the mutant individual with the current individual generating a new individual, and selecting the fittest individuals.

3.1   Algorithm

Algorithm 1 illustrates DE's behaviour. The algorithm returns the best solution upon satisfying the stopping criterion (by the number of iterations or solutions quality). Initially, three parameters are defined: the population size (NP), the disturbance factor (F), and the probability of crossing over (CR). These parameters will remain the same throughout the [13] optimization process. According to [12], the most used values for F and CR must respect the following restrictions: $F \in [0; 1,2]$ and $CR \in [0; 1]$. The generation of the initial population is after defining the parameters, which is composed of NP possible solutions for the target problem. Considering a target problem with D dimensions, each x_i solution is a D-dimensional vector, where the generation of each position is randomly performed from the following equation:

$$x_{i,G} = x_{i,G}^{min} + rand(0,1)(x_{i,G}^{max} - x_{i,G}^{min}); \tag{14}$$

Where min and max are the lower and upper bounds of the parameter G (1, ..., D) of the solution x_i and $rand(0,1)$ generates a number between $[0,1]$ [12].

Algorithm 1: Differential Evolution Algorithm

Input: NP, F, CR
Output: *Best Solution Found*
1 Generates initial population;
2 Evaluates all individuals from the initial population;
3 **while** *Stop method is not satisfied* **do**
4   **for** *each individual in the population* **do**
5   Selects an individual from the population;
6   Performs mutation in the selected individual;
7   Crosses the current individual with the mutant in a certain probability;
8   Evaluates the generated descendant;
9   Performs the greedy selection;
10   **end**
11   Replaces the old population with the new one;
12 **end**
13 **return** *Best Solution Found*

Behind the generation of the initial population, it is necessary to calculate the value of the objective function for each x_i of the population NP, where the value of each position i of the vector $x_{i,G}$ is given as a parameter of the objective function. If the target problem is a maximization problem, the best individual will be the one that produces the large solution. If it is a minimization problem, the best individual will be the one that produces the smallest solution.

After the evaluation of the population, the application of the evolutionary process occurs. The fundamental idea behind DE is a scheme for generating vectors of experimental parameters. In this way, the evolutionary process generates new parameter vectors by adding a weighted difference vector between two individuals to a third individual of the population [13]. The performance of this process is by the mutation and crossover genetic operators.

3.2   Mutation and Crossover Operators

The mutation is responsible for modifying a vector through the weighted difference between two individuals in the population. For each $x_{i,G}$ belonging to the population NP, the generation of an experimental vector $v_{i,G+1}$ is done.

After finishing the mutation process, the crossover occurs, which is the exchange of attributes among the individuals of the population and the mutant vectors to create a new modified vector [13]. The performed crossover increases the diversity of the parameters of the perturbed vectors. It occurs with a certain probability [12]. There are different ways to mutate the DE vector and two crossover modes. The following DE notation: $/x/y/z$ defines mutation and crossover, where x specifies whether to choose a random vector to mutate (*rand*) or the vector that produces the best solution (*best*), y defines the number of weighted differences used for the perturbation, and z specifies whether the perform type of crossover will be binomial (*bin*) or exponential (*exp*).

4 Modified Differential Evolution

This paper proposes a modification to the original DE algorithm. We aim to optimize it and improve the quality of the solutions found. In the original DE, a new population is generated at each iteration, replacing the old discarded one. This process performs a copy of the current population at the beginning of the evolutionary process. The update of this copy is according to the greedy selection step. That is, the insertion of the fittest individuals occurs into the new population. The new population replaces the old one after all individuals have gone through the evolution process [12].

The population update is after the greedy selection step in the proposed modification. If the solution of the new individual $v_{i,G+1}$ is better than the solution of the current $x_{i,G}$, the replacement of the individual $x_{i,G}$ will be immediately in the population. Otherwise, it kept the current individual. Therefore, there will be no need to create a new population at each iteration. In this way, we will increase the possibility of improving the solution of a given individual.

Algorithm 2 shows the Modified Differential Evolution (MDE). Initially, the definition of parameters NP, F, and CR occurs according to the restrictions imposed by [12]. The generation and evaluation of the initial population are then performed, where the individual who obtains the smallest solution will be the fittest.

The application of the evolutionary process to the population is after the evaluation, which involves the selection of a random individual to the mutation and crossover genetic operators. Crossover occurs with a certain probability. Soon after, an individual is generated and evaluated, and then performs the greedy selection and the updating of the population. In the end, the MDE algorithm should return the best solution found.

Algorithm 2: Modified Differential Evolution Algorithm - Pseudo-code

---

   Input: NP, F, CR
   Output: *Better Solution Found*
1 Generates initial population;
2 Evaluates all individuals in the initial population;
3 **while** *The stopping criterion is not met* **do**
4   **for** *each individual in the population* **do**
5   Selects an individual from the population;
6   Performs mutation on the selected individual;
7   Performs the Crossing of the current individual with the mutant;
8   Evaluates the generated descendant;
9   Performs the greedy selection;
10   Updates the population;
11   **end**
12 **end**
13 **return** *Best Solution Found*

---

5   Methodology

We will solve the ELD by considering systems of different sizes and constraints to verify how the DE and MDE[1] heuristics behave. One of the issues in solving the ELD is how the algorithm handles the equality and inequality constraints of the problem [9]. The address of five constraints must be power balance, operating limits, forbidden zones, ramp limits, and valve points. We used the penalty factor ϕ, according to Eq. 7, to satisfy the power balance restriction [10]. In this way, the objective function contemplates not only the load distribution, with low cost in the generating units but also satisfies the power balance constraint.

To satisfy the restriction of the operating limits on the power P_i generated by each generating unit i (in MW), the value of P_i is adjusted when it exceeds the limits. The power P_i is scared to the nearest to the limit. The performance adjustment is by adopting the following strategy:

$$P_i = \begin{cases} P_i^{min}, \text{ se } & P_i < P_i^{min}, \\ P_i^{max}, \text{ se } & P_i > P_i^{max} \end{cases} \tag{15}$$

Where P_i^{min} and P_i^{max} are, respectively, the minimum and maximum operating outputs of the generating unit i (in MW) [10].

The power value P_i that is in the j-th zone of prohibited operation must be readjusted to the closest limit of this zone to satisfy the restriction of prohibited zones, as follows:

$$P_i = \begin{cases} P_{i,j}^l, \text{ se } & P_{i,j}^l \leq P_i \leq (P_{i,j}^l + P_{i,j}^u)/2, \\ P_{i,j}^u, \text{ se } & (P_{i,j}^l + P_{i,j}^u)/2 \leq P_i \leq P_{i,j}^u \end{cases} \tag{16}$$

Where $P_{i,j}^l$ and $P_{i,j}^u$ are respectively the lower and upper limits of the prohibited operating zone j of the generating unit i [7,9].

The restriction inclusion of ramp rate limits modifies the output power limits as seen in Eq. 13 [9]. Therefore, we deal with the constraints of operating limits and ramp limits simultaneously, adopting the following strategy:

$$P_i = \begin{cases} \max(P_i^{min}, P_i^0 - DR_i), \text{ se } & P_i \leq \max(P_i^{min}, P_i^0 - DR_i) \\ \min(P_i^{max}, P_i^0 + UR_i), \text{ se } & P_i \geq \min(P_i^{max}, P_i^0 + UR_i) \\ P_i & \text{other cases.} \end{cases} \tag{17}$$

Rectified sinusoidal components must be added to the objective function (Eq. 2), as can be seen in Eq. 9 to satisfy the valve point restriction.

We implemented the DE and MDE algorithms in the Matlab programming language. The executions running on a microcomputer with an Intel i5-7200U processor with two physical cores (four logical cores) of 2.5 GHz frequency, 4 GB DDR4 RAM, and Windows operating system version 10 of 64-bit.

To verify the performance of the MDE to the original DE, we solved two cases of the Economic Load Dispatch problem: Classic DE with a system of 15 generating units (Subsect. 5.1) and Non-Convex DE with 15 generating units (Subsect. 5.2).

---

[1] Available at: https://github.com/gabriella-andrade/DifferentialEvolution.

5.1 Classic Economic Load Dispatch with 15 Generating Units

The ELD with 15 thermoelectric energy generating units considers power balance restrictions, transmission losses, and each generating unit operating between minimum and maximum operating levels. It is a classic problem if it considers only these restrictions, being just nonlinear [8]. The classic ELD with 15 generating units can be mathematically described as the following nonlinear constrained optimization problem [7].

$$\min F = \sum_{i=1}^{15} F_i(P_i)$$

$$\text{s.a} \ \sum_{i=1}^{15} P_i = P_D + P_L, \tag{18}$$

$$P_i^{min} \leq P_i \leq P_i^{max}, i = 1, \ldots, 15$$

For this system, the total power demand is $P_D = 2{,}630$ MW [5]. The penalty factor was $\phi = 50$ to satisfy the power balance constraint [5]. The values of the minimum (P_i^{min}) and maximum (P_i^{max}) limits of each of the i ($i \in \{1, 2, \ldots, 15\}$) generating units, in addition to the parameters α_i, β_i and γ_i, which can be consulted in the Table 1 [7]. The values of the loss coefficients B_{ij}, B_{0i} and B_{00} are in the Eq. 19, Eq. 20, and Eq. 21.

$$B_{ij} = 10^{-3} \times \begin{bmatrix}
1.4 & 1.2 & 0.7 & -0.1 & -0.3 & -0.1 & -0.1 & -0.1 & -0.3 & 0.5 & -0.3 & -0.2 & 0.4 & 0.3 & -0.1 \\
1.2 & 1.5 & 1.3 & 0.0 & -0.5 & -0.2 & 0.0 & 0.1 & -0.2 & -0.4 & -0.4 & 0.0 & 0.4 & 1.0 & -0.2 \\
0.7 & 1.3 & 7.6 & -0.1 & -1.3 & -0.9 & -0.1 & , & 0.0 & -0.8 & -1.2 & -1.7 & -0.0 & -2.6 & 11.1 & -2.8 \\
-0.1 & 0.0 & -0.1 & -3.4 & , & -0.7 & -0.4 & -1.1 & 5.0 & -2.9 & -3.2 & -1.1 & -0.0 & 0.1 & 0.1 & -2.6 \\
-0.3 & -0.5 & -1.3 & -0.7 & 9.0 & 1.4 & -0.3 & -1.2 & -1.0 & -1.3 & 0.7 & -0.2 & -0.2 & -2.4 & -0.3 \\
-0.1 & -0.2 & -0.9 & -0.4 & 1.4 & 1.6 & -0.0 & -0.6 & -0.5 & -0.8 & 1,1 & -0,1 & -0.2 & -1.7 & 0.3 \\
-0.1 & 0.0 & -0.1 & 1.1 & -0.3 & -0.0 & 1.5 & , & 1,7 & 1.5 & 0.9 & -0,5 & 0.7 & -0.0 & -0.2 & -0,8 \\
-0,1 & 0,1 & 0,0 & 5.0 & -1.2 & -0.6 & 1.7 & 16.8 & 8,2 & 7.9 & -2,3 & -3.6 & 0.1 & 0.5 & -7.8 \\
-0.3 & -0.2 & -0.8 & 2.9 & , & -1.0 & -0.5 & 1.5 & 8,2 & 12.9 & 11.6 & -2.1 & -2,5 & 0.7 & -1.2 & -7.2 \\
-0.5 & -0.4 & -1.2 & 3.2 & , & -1.3 & -0.8 & 0.9 & 7.9 & 11.6 & 20.0 & -2.7 & -3,4 & 0,9 & -1,1 & -8,8 \\
-0.3 & -0.4 & -1.7 & -1.1 & 0.7 & 1.1 & -0.5 & -2.3 & -2.1 & -2.7 & 14.0 & 0.1 & 0.4 & -3.8 & 16,8 \\
-0.2 & -0.0 & -0.0 & -0.0 & -0.2 & -0.1 & 0.7 & -3.6 & , & -2.5 & -3,4 & 0.1 & 5.4 & , & -0.1 & -0.4 & 2.8 \\
0.4 & 0.4 & -2.6 & 0.1 & -0.2 & -0.2 & -0.0 & , & 0.1 & 0.7 & 0.9 & 0.4 & -0.1 & 10.3 & -10.1 & 2.8 \\
0.3 & 1.0 & 11,1 & , & 0.1 & -2.4 & -1.7 & -0.2 & 0.5 & -1.2 & -1.1 & -3.8 & -0,4 & -10.1 & 57.8 & -9.4 \\
-0.1 & -0.2 & -2.8 & -2.6 & -0.3 & 0.3 & -0.8 & -7.8 & -7.2 & -8.8 & 16.8 & 2.8 & 2.8 & -9.4 & 128.3
\end{bmatrix}$$

$$\tag{19}$$

$$B_{0i} = 10^{-3} \times [-0.1 \ -0.2 \ 2.8 \ -0.1 \ 0.1 \ -0.3 \ -0.2 \ -0.2 \ 0,6 \ 3.9 \ -1.7 \ -0.0 \ -3.2 \ 6.7 \ -6.4]$$

$$\tag{20}$$

$$B_{00} = 0.0055 \tag{21}$$

As parameters of the DE and MDE algorithms, we used a population NP of 75 individuals, and [13] indicate that NP must be between $5 \times D$ and $10 \times D$, where D is the dimension of the problem, with $D = 15$ in this case. The disturbance factor F and the crossing probability CR must respect the following conditions: $F \in [0; 1,2]$ and $CR \in [0; 1]$. According to [13], for good results, F should be from 0.5 up to 1.0, and CR can start at 0.1 to the crossover probability.

Table 1. Input data from the 15 Thermoelectric Energy Generating Units of the Economic Dispatch Problem

Unit	P_i^{min}	P_i^{max}	α_i ($)	β_i ($/MW)	γ_i ($/MW^2)
1	150	455	671	10.1	0.000299
2	150	455	574	10.2	0.000183
3	20	130	374	8.8	0.001126
4	20	130	374	8.8	0.001126
5	150	470	461	10.4	0.000205
6	135	460	630	10.1	0.000301
7	135	465	548	9.8	0.000364
8	60	300	227	11.2	0.000338
9	25	162	173	11.2	0.000807
10	25	160	175	10.7	0.001203
11	20	80	186	10.2	0.003586
12	20	80	230	9.9	0.005513
13	25	85	225	13.1	0.000371
14	15	55	309	12.1	0.001929
15	15	55	323	12.4	0.004487

In this way, we vary the value of F from 0.5 to 1 and CR from 0.1 to 1. We use the mutation $DE/rand/1/bin$, where $rand$ determines a randomly chosen vector to mutate, 1 determines the value of weighted differences used for the perturbation, and bin specifies a binomial crossover.

Based on the results of [5], the stopping criterion used for both algorithms was the percentage relative error in the last 500 iterations of the algorithm. We check if the error for tolerance is less than 10^{-6} in this stopping criterion. In addition, we perform 20 runs for each configuration of both algorithms with a random initial population. We compare the results obtained by the DE and MDE methods to verify the performance of the MDE to the original DE. Furthermore, we compared the results obtained with those of other methods in the literature.

5.2 Non-Convex Economic Load Dispatch with 15 Generating Units

The non-convex ELD with 15 generating units can be mathematically described as a constrained non-linear, discontinuous, and non-convex optimization problem [7]. There are constraints regarding prohibited operating zones and ramp limits in the non-convex ELD with 15 generating units. This problem is challenging due to a non-convex decision space of 192 convex subspaces [9]. Therefore, the outputs of the generators have a high degree of nonlinearities and discontinuities as characteristics [7]:

Table 2. Data from the 15 Thermoelectric Energy Generating Units of the Non-Convex Economic Load Dispatch

Unit	UR_i	DR_i	P_i^0	Forbidden Zones (MW)
1	80	120	400	-
2	80	120	300	[185 225] [305 335] [420 450]
3	130	130	105	-
4	130	130	100	-
5	80	120	90	[180 200] [305 335] [390 420]
6	80	120	400	[230 255] [365 395] [430 455]
7	80	120	350	-
8	65	100	95	-
9	60	100	105	-
10	60	100	110	-
11	80	80	60	-
12	80	80	40	[30 40] [55 65]
13	80	80	30	-
14	55	55	20	-
15	55	55	20	-

$$\min F = \sum_{i=1}^{15} F_i(P_i)$$

$$\text{s.a} \sum_{i=1}^{15} P_i = P_D + P_L,$$

$$P_i^{min} \leq P_i \leq P_i^{max}, i = 1, \ldots, 15 \tag{22}$$

$$P_{i,j-1}^u \leq P_i \leq P_{i,j}^l, j = 2, \ldots, n_i$$

$$P_{i,n_i}^u \leq P_i \leq P_i^{max}$$

$$max(P_i^{min}, P_i^0 - DR_i \leq P_i \leq min(P_i^{max}, P_i^0 + UR_i)$$

For this system, the total power demand is $P_D = 2{,}630$ MW [5]. To satisfy the power balance constraint, the penalty factor was $\phi = 50$ [5]. The values of the minimum (P_i^{min}) and maximum (P_i^{max}) limits of each of the i ($i \in \{1, 2, \ldots, 15\}$) generating units, in addition to the parameters α_i, β_i and γ_i, which can be consulted in the Table 2 [7]. The values of the loss coefficients B_{ij}, B_{0i} and B_{00} are in the Eq. 19, Eq. 20, and Eq. 21.

Based on the results obtained by [9], the stopping criterion used for both algorithms was the maximum number of the objective function (FEs) evaluation. To control the stopping criterion FEs, we use a variable called $fitc$, incremented in each time of the evaluation of the objective function. The algorithm ends its execution when the value of $fitc$ is the value of FEs. Conform [9], the number of FEs was defined as 6×10^4. We ran 20 executions for each DE and MDE configuration, and in each execution the solution of the problem was with a random initial solution.

6   Results

In this section, we present the evaluation of MDE in relation to DE heuristic, considering the classic (Subsect. 6.1) and non-convex economic dispatch (Subsect. 6.2). In both cases, we use 15 thermoelectric power-generating units that satisfy the total demand of the system. We also compare both implementations with find results in the literature to other optimization algorithms. At the end, we show the execution time of DE and MDE.

6.1   Classic Economic Load Dispatch with 15 Generating Units

We seek the best solutions for each DE and MDE configuration, considering that the penalty factor F was varied from 0.5 to 1.0 and the crossing probability CR ranged from 0.1 to 1.0. For the DE, the best solution was 32,763.74$/h with F equal to 1 and CR equal to 0.2. For MDE, the best solution was 32,548.78 $/h with F equal to 1 and CR equal to 0.8. The best solution found by MDE is 0.66% smaller than the one found by DE. Therefore, the modification performed in the DE achieved the best result.

We compare the performance of the best solution found by the DE and MDE algorithms with the results of [5] to verify the performance of the implemented heuristics. [5] proposed three methods to solve the classic ELD with 15 units: Particle Swarm Optimization (PSO), Firefly Algorithm (FA), and the Lagrange Multiplier Method (LMM). PSO is an algorithm based on a population composed of individuals capable of interacting with each other and the environment, changing direction and speed to find the location in the search space that leads to the best [6] solution. The FA associates the light of fireflies with the objective function. Therefore, the more intense the light of the firefly, or its brightness, the better the [16] solution. LMM is a classic mathematical optimization method [11]. In comparison with the results obtained by PSO and FA and with the solution obtained via LMM, we verify the performance of the implemented heuristics. The parameters used in the execution of PSO and FA and the results used in the comparison are at [5].

Table 5 show the statistics of the total costs ($/h) for the ELD problem found by the PSO, FA, DE, and MDE algorithms. It presents the lowest cost ($/h) found, the highest cost ($/h), the average cost ($/h) of the 20 executions performed, the standard deviation of this average, and the coefficient of variation. Observing Table 5, we see that the algorithm that led to the best solution was the MDE, obtaining a minimum cost of 32,548.78 $/h. The solution obtained by MDE is approximately 1.10% smaller than the solution obtained by PSO, 0.01% smaller than the FA solution, and 0.66% smaller than the DE.

We compared the results obtained through the DE and MDE methods with the results obtained by 25 algorithms from the [9] literature to verify the performance of the implemented heuristics. Table 3 shows the lowest cost ($/h), the highest cost ($/h), the average cost ($/h), and the standard deviation of this average. Solutions not evaluated have the value marked as NA. We highlighted

Table 3. Total Costs ($/h) found by PSO [5], FA [5], ABC [1], DE, and MDE algorithms in solving the classic ELD problem with 15 generating units.

Method	Min. Cost ($/h)	Max. Cost ($/h)	Average Cost ($/h)	Std. Deviation	Var. Coefficient
PSO	32912.00	33313.11	33108.61	109.95	0.33%
FA	32551.70	32686.94	32584.91	40.08	0.12%
ABC	32894.05	33375.11	33112.15	112.30	0.33%
DE	32763.74	33134.21	33009.36	76.57	0.23%
MDE	**32548.78**	32608.87	32564.79	17.33	0.05%

Table 4. Min, max, and average costs of each method

Method	Min. Cost ($/h)	Max. Cost ($/h)	Average Cost ($/h)	Standard Deviation
PSO	32858.00	33331.00	33039.00	NA
GA	33113.00	33337.00	33228.00	NA
AIS	32854.00	32892.00	32873.25	10.81
MTS	32716.87	32796.15	32767.21	3.65
TSA	32762.12	32942.71	32822.84	60.59
SA	32786.40	33028.95	32869.51	112.32
APSO	32742.78	NA	32976.68	133.93
SA-PSO	32708.00	32789.00	32732.00	18.03
PC PSO	32775.36	NA	NA	NA
SOH-PSO	32751.00	32945.00	32878.00	NA
DSPSO-TSA	32715.06	32730.39	32724.63	8.40
MDE	32704.90	32711.50	32708.10	NA
CTPSO	32704.45	32704.45	32704.45	0.00
CSPSO	32704.45	32704.45	32704.45	0.00
COPSO	32704.45	32704.45	32704.45	0.00
CCPSO	32704.45	32704.45	32704.45	0.00
MPSO	32738.42	NA	NA	NA
ABC	32707.85	32708.27	32707.95	NA
FA	32704.50	33175.00	32856.10	141.17
SWT-PSO	32704.45	NA	NA	NA
MsEBBO	32692.40	32692.40	32692.40	0.00
SQPSO	32704.57	32711.62	32707.08	NA
IA EDP	32698.20	32823.78	32750.22	9.30
IODPSO-G	32692.39	32692.39	32692.39	0.00
IODPSO-L	32692.39	32692.39	32692.39	0.00
DE	32804.11	33076.68	32996.08	75.84
MDE	32706.66	32719.72	32709.76	4.22

DE and MDE solutions in bold. Observing Table 3, we see that the DE and MDE algorithms failed to obtain the best result compared to the literature.

Observing the standard deviation values in Table 4, we verify that the PSO algorithm presents the large variability of solutions between one execution and another. However, as the coefficient of variation for the PSO is 0.33%, the variability can be considered small. Therefore, all algorithms present a low variability of solutions found, where the data set present low dispersion since all coefficients of variation are below 0.34% about the mean.

The computational cost of each algorithm is shown in Table 4 and measured by the total number of iterations executed. We measure the computational cost from the total number of iterations executed. Table 4 presents the minimum number of iterations, the maximum and average of the iterations performed, the standard deviation of this average, and the coefficient of variation. Observing Table 4, we see that the MDE algorithm, which presents the best solution for the DE, performs an average of iterations approximately 2.90 times greater than the original DE and 1.15 times greater than the PSO. Although the average computational cost of the MDE is higher than that of the DE and PSO algorithms, the MDE manages to obtain the lowest cost (\$/h) for the DE problem. Therefore, for the stopping criterion used, the DE and PSO algorithms cannot converge to the best solution. An alternative to these algorithms would be to use a different stopping criterion, such as the maximum number of the objective function evaluations [9].

In relation to the FA algorithm, the MDE performs an average of iterations approximately 3.5 times small. Therefore, the MDE method can find the best solution with less computational effort in relation to the FA, which is the most expensive algorithm.

Observing the standard deviation values presented in Table 4, we verify that the variability of the number of iterations between one execution and another is significantly greater for the FA algorithm than other algorithms. However, both algorithms have large variability since the value of the coefficient of variation is more than 25%. It means that the number of iterations required until convergence varies from one to the next run. Therefore, the dispersion of the data to the mean is large.

6.2 Non-Convex Economic Load Dispatch with 15 Generating Units

In order to make a comparison with the results found in the literature, we used a population NP of 40 individuals [9] as parameters for the DE and MDE. As in the previous test case, the disturbance factor F was varied from 0.5 to 1 and the crossing probability CR was varied from 0.1 to 1. Therefore, it can select parameters that lead to the best result. As in the previous test case, we used the mutation $DE/rand/1/bin$. It is the most general and used mutation form [3]. The conduction of results evaluations are to verify the performance of the MDE to the original DE. Furthermore, we compared the results obtained by the DE and MDE methods with those obtained by other methods in the literature.

Considering that the penalty factor F ranges from 0.5 to 1.0 and the crossing probability CR ranged from 0.1 to 1.0 the best solution obtained by each algorithm is in bold highlight. For DE, the best solution of 32,804.11 \$/h considers F equal to 1 and CR equal to 0.9. For MDE, the best solution was 32,706.66 \$/h with F equal to 1 and CR equal to 0.8. The best solution found by MDE is

Table 5. Comparison of Different Methods in Solving Non-Convex DE with 15 Generating Units

Method	Min Cost ($/h)	Max Cost ($/h)	Average Cost ($/h)	Std. Deviation
PSO	32,858.00	33,331.00	33,039.00	NA
GA	33,113.00	33,337.00	33,228.00	NA
AIS	32,854.00	32,892.00	32,873.25	10.81
MTS	32,716.87	32,796.15	32,767.21	3.65
TSA	32,762.12	32,942.71	32,822.84	60.59
SA	32,786.40	33,028.95	32,869.51	112.32
APSO	32,742.78	NA	32,976.68	133.93
SA-PSO	32,708.00	32,789.00	32,732.00	18.03
PC PSO	32,775.36	NA	NA	NA
SOH-PSO	32,751.00	32,945.00	32,878.00	NA
DSPSO-TSA	32,715.06	32,730.39	32,724.63	8.40
MDE	32,704.90	32,711.50	32,708.10	NA
CTPSO	32,704.45	32,704.45	32,704.45	0.00
CSPSO	32,704.45	32,704.45	32,704.45	0.00
COPSO	32,704.45	32,704.45	32,704.45	0.00
CCPSO	32,704.45	32,704.45	32,704.45	0.00
MPSO	32,738.42	NA	NA	NA
ABC	32,707.85	32,708.27	32,707.95	NA
FA	32,704.50	33,175.00	32,856.10	141.17
SWT-PSO	32,704.45	NA	NA	NA
MsEBBO	32,692.40	32,692.40	32,692.40	0.00
SQPSO	32,704.57	32,711.62	32,707.08	NA
AI EDP	32,698.20	32,823.78	32,750.22	9.30
IODPSO-G	32,692.39	32,692.39	32,692.39	0.00
IODPSO-L	32,692.39	32,692.39	32,692.39	0.00
DE	**32,804.11**	**33,076.68**	**32,996.08**	**75,84**
MDE	**32,706.66**	**32,719.72**	**32,709.76**	**4,22**

0.30% smaller than the one found by DE. Therefore, the modification performed in the DE algorithm enables to find the best result, proving to be more effective.

We compared the results obtained through the DE and MDE methods with the results obtained by 25 algorithms from the [9] literature to verify the performance of the implemented heuristics. Table 5 shows the lowest cost ($/h), the highest cost ($/h), the average cost ($/h), and the standard deviation of this average. We marked as NA the values of solutions not evaluated. Solutions from DE and MDE are in bold highlights. Observing Table 5, we see that the DE and MDE algorithms failed to obtain the best result compared to the literature.

The DE obtained the best solution compared only to the PSO, GA, and AIS methods. It is up to 0.93% better. The MDE obtained the best solution against the PSO, GA, AIS, MTS, TSA, SA, APSO, SA-PSO, PC PSO, SOH-PSO, DSPSO-TA, MPSO, and ABC methods, being up to 1.23% better as can be seen in Table 5. The best solution of 32,692.39 \$/h for this case was obtained using the IODPSO-G and IODPSO-L methods implemented by [9], which are PSO variants. To the best solution obtained by the literature, the solutions obtained by the DE and MDE methods are 0.34% and 0.04% worse, respectively.

We analyze the computation time of the DE and MDE algorithms to verify the efficiency of the modification performed to the original version. This comparison did not carry out with the other methods in the literature because they ran in different architectures. The computational cost was evaluated by the average execution time (in seconds) of the 20 executions. We see that the average cost of DE is 23.31 s, and the MDE had 0.93 s. Therefore, although the MDE does not obtain the best solution concerning the literature, this method is quite efficient to the original DE, presenting a reduction in the average execution time of 95.98%.

7   Conclusion and Future Works

This article presented a Modification of the Differential Evolution algorithm (MDE), which belongs to the class of Evolutionary Computation algorithms. In the original Differential Evolution (DE) algorithm, each possible solution to the target problem represents an individual in the population. The population suffers from genetic operators of mutation, crossover, and greedy selection. At each iteration, a newly generated population replaces the discarded old one. The step of greedy selection is responsible for choosing the fittest elements and inserting them into the new population. In the proposed MDE, we modify the selection step. Instead of inserting the fittest individual into the new population, the old one gives place to the fittest elements in the current population. In this way, the population is updated in the greedy selection stage and not replaced at the end of the iteration.

We apply the algorithms to an Economic Load Dispatch problem to find the generation level of each thermoelectric energy generating unit that satisfies the total demand of the system at a minimum cost and to satisfy the problem constraints. Furthermore, we saw that restrictions such as forbidden zones, ramp limits, and valve points make the problem non-convex and hard to solve by classical optimization methods.

We solve the ELD problem by considering different sizes and restrictions to verify the performance of the algorithms applied to different scenarios. Initially, we solved the ELD problem with 15 thermoelectric energy generating units, considering the classic constraints of power balance, transmission line losses, and minimum and maximum operating limits for each one. Our results showed that the MDE algorithm obtained the lowest cost (\$/h) for the ELD compared to the other optimization algorithms. The best solution found by MDE is up to 1.10% better than DE and other heuristics in the literature. Therefore, we concluded that the MDE is the most effective method concerning others algorithms. In addition, we conclude that solving the DE via LMM becomes costly due to the great system of nonlinear equations and the initial effort in formulating the problem and manually inserting the system in Matlab. Therefore, the DE using an optimization heuristic is more efficient to be solved.

We solve an ELD problem with 15 units, which in addition to considering the classic constraints of the issue, also considers forbidden zones and ramp limits. The restriction of forbidden zones results in a non-convex decision space and is difficult to be solved by classical methods. Our results showed that the MDE algorithm obtained the lowest cost (\$/h) if compared to the DE, being 0.30% better. Compared to other methods in the literature, MDE failed to obtain the best solution, presenting a result up to 0.043% worse.

In future works, we intend to solve the Economic Dispatch Problem by considering another instance of the problem. We want to use the specifications of a thermoelectric power plant. Soon, we will be able to verify if the performance of the MDE concerning the DE is maintained. Furthermore, we intend to implement a version of MDE combined with another optimization algorithm like PSO because hybrid versions have shown very effective results in the literature.

References

1. Andrade, G.L.: Algoritmo evolução diferencial modificado aplicado ao problema do despacho econômico de carga. Master thesis, Federal University of Pampa, Alegrete (2020)
2. BEN: Balanço energético nacional 2018: Ano base 2017/empresa de pesquisa energética. Technical report, EPE, Rio de Janeiro (2018)
3. De Carvalho, L., Morais, M.d.F., Ceolho, L.d.S., Da Rocha, R.P., Beline, E.L.: Evolução diferencial: Características dos métodos de solução para programação em ambientes flow shop permutacional. In: Anais do XXXVI Encontro Nacional de Engenharia de Produção. ABEPRO, João Pessoa, PB (2016)
4. De Oliveira, K.W.R.C.B., Nascimento Jr., N.T., Saavedra, O.R.: Uma abordagem via estratégias evolutivas para o despacho econômico considerando restrições de geração. IEEE Latin America Trans. **6**(1), 42–50 (2008)
5. Dos Santos, J.O., Kapelinski, K., dos Santos, E.M., Juchem Neto, J.P.: Resolução de um problema de despacho econômico de carga utilizando enxames de partículas e vaga-lumes. Proc. Ser. Braz. Soc. Comput. Appl. Math. **6**(1) (2018)
6. Eberhart, R., Kennedy, J.: A new optimizer using particle swarm theory. In: 1995 Proceedings of the 6th International Symposium on Micro Machine and Human Science, MHS 1995, pp. 39–43. IEEE (1995)
7. Gaing, Z.L.: Particle swarm optimization to solving the economic dispatch considering the generator constraints. IEEE Trans. Power Syst. **18**(3), 1187–1195 (2003)
8. Gomez-Exposito, A., Conejo, A.J., Canizares, C.: Electric Energy Systems: Analysis and Operation. CRC Press (2009)
9. Qin, Q., Cheng, S., Chu, X., Lei, X., Shi, Y.: Solving non-convex/non-smooth economic load dispatch problems via an enhanced particle swarm optimization. Appl. Soft Comput. **59**, 229–242 (2017)
10. Serapião, A.B.d.S.: Fundamentos de otimização por inteligência de enxames: uma visão geral. Sba: Controle & Automação Sociedade Brasileira de Automatica **20**(3), 271–304 (2009)

11. Simon, C.P., Blume, L.: Matemática para Economistas. Bookman, Porto Alegre - RS (2004)
12. Storn, R., Price, K.: Differential evolution - a simple and efficient heuristic for global optimization over continuous spaces. J. Global Optim. 11, 341–359 (1997)
13. Storn, R., Price, K.: Differential evolution-a simple and efficient adaptive scheme for global optimization over continuous spaces. ICSI, Berkeley (1995)
14. Tolmasquim, M.T.: Energia termelétrica: gás natural, biomassa, carvão e nuclear. Rio de Janeiro: EPE (2016)
15. Walters, D.C., Sheble, G.B.: Genetic algorithm solution of economic dispatch with valve point loading. IEEE Trans. Power Syst. 8(3), 1325–1332 (1993)
16. Yang, X.S., Hosseini, S.S.S., Gandomi, A.H.: Firefly algorithm for solving non-convex economic dispatch problems with valve loading effect. Appl. Soft Comput. 12(3), 1180–1186 (2012)

An Evaluation of Direct and Indirect Memory Accesses in Fluid Flow Simulator

Stiw Harrison Herrera Taipe[1(✉)], Thiago Teixeira[1], Weber Ribeiro[1],
Andre Carneiro[1], Marcio R. Borges[1], Carla Osthoff[1], F. L. Cabral[1],
and S. L. Gonzaga de Oliveira[2]

[1] National Laboratory for Scientific Computing (LNCC), MCTIC,
Av. Getulio Vargas, 333 - Quitandinha, Petrópolis, RJ 25651-076, Brazil
{stiw,tteixeira,webergdr,andrerc,mrborges,osthoff,fcabral}@lncc.br
[2] Universidade Federal de São Paulo (UNIFESP), Av. Cesare Monsueto Giulio
Lattes, 1201 - Eugênio de Melo, São José dos Campos - SP,
São José dos Campos, SP 12247-014, Brazil
sanderson.oliveira@unifesp.br
https://www.gov.br/lncc/pt-br, https://www.unifesp.br/

Abstract. In petroleum reservoir simulations, the level of detail incorporated into the geologic model typically exceeds the capabilities of traditional flow simulators. In this sense, such simulations demand new high-performance computing techniques to deal with a large amount of data allocation and the high computational cost of computing the behavior of the fluids in the porous media. This paper presents optimizations performed on a code that implements an explicit numerical scheme to provide an approximate solution to the governing differential equation for water saturation in a two-phase flow problem with heterogeneous permeability and porosity fields. The experiments were performed on the SDumont Supercomputer using 2nd Generation Intel®Xeon®Scalable Processors (formerly Cascade Lake architecture). The paper employs a direct memory data access scheme to reduce the execution times of the numerical method. The article analyzes the performance gain using direct memory access related to indirect access memory. The results show that the optimizations implemented in the numerical code remarkably reduce the execution time of the simulations.

Keywords: Transport in Porous Media · Biphasic Flow · Data Structure · Performance

1 Introduction

Numerical simulations of gas and oil reservoirs use mathematical models to describe the physical processes of fluid flows in a porous medium. Natural porous media, such as aquifers and reservoirs, present a high degree of heterogeneities

Supported by organization LNCC/SEPAD.

in their petrophysical properties (porosity, permeability, etc.). These hetero-geneities extend from the pore scale to the field scale, and governing equations incorporate them for flow problems based on geostatistical models [2,6,9,10].

The variability and complex connectivity of the petrophysical properties affect the subsurface flow and transport behavior, and simulations of realistic problems must include these characteristics [11]. For simulations in this field of research, one needs to discretize huge domains in meshes that employ very refined polytopes. Consequently, one faces a very demanding computational problem that needs high-performance computing to be approximately solved.

The geometric representation of the reservoirs, which can present complex shapes, stimulates the adoption of irregular meshes in their discretization. On the other hand, despite less fidelity to geometric representation, applying regular grids to discretize the domains allows more simplified and faster calculations. Additionally, the resolution of the problem investigated in this study is highly scalable. Thus, it is possible to compensate for the loss of precision by increasing the number of polytopes in the mesh. The scalability of the code also allows us to refine the mesh until reaching reasonable accuracy of the solution, thus compensating for the considerable numerical diffusion present in first-order upwind schemes. Furthermore, one can incorporate a hyperbolic conservation nature law to design better approximate code solutions [26]. In future it will be very interesting to see the comparison them on another architectures.

Domain decomposition techniques divide a domain into subdomains. Thus, one can use Message Passing Interface (MPI) to calculate them in parallel [25]. The number of domain divisions depends on computational and communication costs. The higher the computational cost of the method, the greater the number of possible domain partitions. The higher the communication cost generated by the method stencil, the lower the number of subdomain partitions. In a previous paper [11], we presented a domain decomposition technique implementation based on block decomposition [18]. Specifically, we used the scheme to test different vertical and horizontal cross-sections to evaluate the best block decomposition given a certain number of processes. The scheme presented satisfactory performance.

Frequently, in numerical method codes for two-phase fluids flow in porous media, lines in the input file consist of the finite component and its neighbors [5]. Thus, when loading the file, the project needed another data structure to reference the location of the neighbors, resulting in an indirect access memory scheme [5]. The results from a previous publication [27] showed that, after the domain technique implementation, the computational environment performance bottleneck was, not surprisingly, the memory access time due to the indirect memory access in the data structure.

The present paper employs a data structure to provide direct memory access for the numerical fluid-flow method aiming to reduce memory access time and, consequently, improve code performance. We organized the manuscript as follows. In Sect. 2, we present related work. Afterward, in Sect. 3, we describe the mathematical model. In Sect. 3, the paper shows the approaches of the new data structure strategy. In Sect. 4, we describe the tests performed. Finally, in Sect. 5, the conclusion and future work are presented.

2   Contextualization and Related Work

One can classify memory access into three types: direct, indirect, and semi-direct. One uses indirect access in applications that access irregular meshes and present unsatisfactory performance in data access due to the high cache miss rate. Semi-direct access occurs when a part of the data is available directly in the array, whereas the application accesses another part through a function. This form can reduce the cache miss or help in finding the necessary data [15]. Herschlag et al. [12] compared these forms of data access. Clearly, the data structure and the mode to access data are critical for the performance of an application. Memory access can vary depending on the purpose of the application. Although direct access shows better results than the other accesses, semi-direct access can be more advantageous depending on the number of variables used in the calculations. The difference between these accesses is how the process accesses data. In direct access, the application accesses data directly in the array without using an index to inform the memory region where the data is. This form of access presents better performance when avoiding cache misses. However, it may not be feasible in irregular meshes, where it is not trivial to identify which data to use without employing a function to fetch data. In indirect access, the application uses a procedure to identify the location of the data (e.g., [8,17,21]. Although necessary in some applications, this type of access can generate a cache miss. Semi-direct access occurs when part of the data is available directly in the array, and the application needs to fetch only portion of the data through a function. This form of access can reduce the cache miss and help in the search for the data (e.g., [15]).

Domain decomposition techniques divide a domain into subdomains. Thus, they can be calculated in parallel using Message Passing Interface (MPI). The number of domain divisions depends on computational and communication costs. The higher the computational cost of the method, the greater the number of possible domain partitions.

Previous work [11] employed the domain decomposition method to split the 3-D reservoir onto n sub-domains that are solved using each Message Passing Interface (MPI) process. The paper analyzed the performance of the domain decomposition strategies and identified communication bottlenecks as the mesh size and the number of computational nodes increased. Results show that the optimizations implemented in the numerical code remarkably reduced the execution time of the simulations.

In the context of three-dimensional meshes, Shashkov and Steinberg [22] and Silvester and Ferrari [23] describe how to work with oil reservoir domains using regular meshes. In this scenario, the application access each control volume using only the indices (i, j, k) of a three-dimensional matrix (e.g., [4,28]). The idea is to solve the partial differential equation by discretizing the computational domain through a Cartesian mesh.

3   Numerical Fluid-Flow Simulator Data Structure

The fluid flow simulator used in this work consists of two primary modules [3]: the velocity transport modules. They are responsible for solving the system of nonlinear partial differential equations. Furthermore, the modules consider the pressure, Darcy velocity, and water saturation [26]. This paper adopted the IMPES methodology (implicit in pressure and explicit in saturation) to solve the decoupled systems of partial differential equations [1,3,26]. Briefly, the simulation uses two numerical methods. They interact with each other, as illustrated in Fig. 1. The importance of working with subsystems instead of operating with the complete system of partial differential equations is to make it possible to use suitable numerical methods for each one.

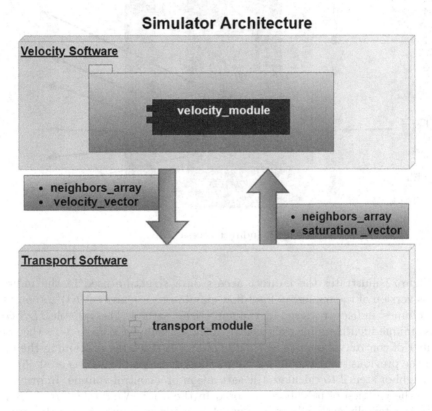

Fig. 1. Simulator architecture with velocity and transport modules

The numerical fluid flow simulator uses data from the computational grid with information on the parameters and domains of the reservoir. The velocity and transport modules perform the computations using the respective initial and boundary conditions [3]. Initially, the velocity module uses a finite element method to find the velocity field. Subsequently, the module sends the results to the transport module through an array that contains information about the velocities and locations of neighboring volumes of each control volume. Then the transport module receives this information to find the water saturation. The transport module sends back the new results to the velocity module to start a new iteration. This paper evaluates the performance of the transport module to reduce the execution time for data collection.

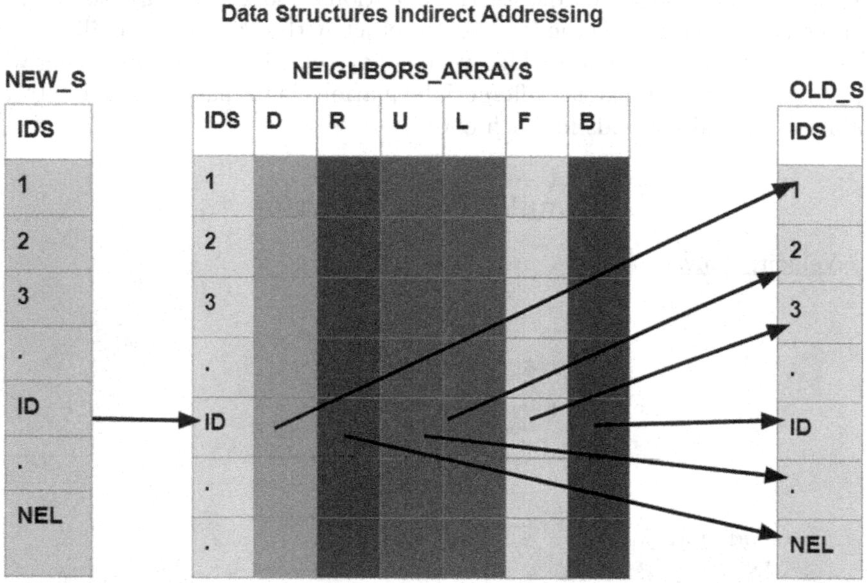

Fig. 2. Indirect access array.

Figure 2 illustrates the indirect access data structure used in the indirect access version of the numerical fluid-flow simulator. The array NEW_S contains the volumes' indices traversed by the numerical method. The variable IDS contains unique identifiers for each control volume, numbered from 1 to the total number of control volumes (NEL), and OLD_S is the array containing the data from the previous step. The numerical method developed by correa et al. [5] uses a 6-neighbor stencil to calculate the saturation of a control volume. Information about the location of neighbors is stored in the array $NEIGHBOR\_ARRAY$, which is a two-dimensional array in which the first column contains the volume identifiers and the remaining columns D, R, U, L, F, and B are the abbreviations of down, right, up, left, front and back, respectively, and contain the data identifiers of the neighbors. At each iteration, the numerical method runs through the identifiers of each volume. Additionally, the numerical method uses the array $NEIGHBOR\_ARRAY$ to locate the identifiers of the neighbors, which, in turn, point to the data in the computer vector OLD_S, generating a high cache miss rate.

Algorithm 1. Numerical method with indirect access array.

---

input : $S_{old1} \ldots S_{oldN}$, **MVIZ**

output: $S_{new1} \ldots S_{newN}$ (saturation array)

Function Numerical Method($S[\,]$):

    for $EL \leftarrow 1$ *to* $NUMEL$ **do**

        $NEW\_S(EL) \leftarrow OLD\_S(EL)$

        $-(DT/DX) * V_{xp}(EL) * (OLD\_S(EL) - OLD\_S(\mathbf{MVIZ}(EL, 4)))$

        $-(DT/DX) * V_{xm}(EL) * (OLD\_S(\mathbf{MVIZ}(EL, 2)) - OLD\_S(EL))$

        $-(DT/DY) * V_{yp}(EL) * (OLD\_S(EL) - OLD\_S(\mathbf{MVIZ}(EL, 5)))$

        $-(DT/DY) * V_{ym}(EL) * (OLD\_S(\mathbf{MVIZ}(EL, 6)) - OLD\_S(EL))$

        $-(DT/DZ) * V_{zp}(EL) * (OLD\_S(EL) - OLD\_S(\mathbf{MVIZ}(EL, 1)))$

        $-(DT/DZ) * V_{zm}(EL) * (OLD\_S(\mathbf{MVIZ}(EL, 3)) - OLD\_S(EL))$

    end

    return NEW_S

Algorithm (1) presents only one loop varying the iterator from 1 to the total number of control volumes. The algorithm updates each polytope of the array NEW_S. Each control volume of the array NEW_S points to a location in the array **MVIZ**. In turn, the array **MVIZ** references the respective saturation array OLD_S of each neighbor volume of the control volume and $V_{xp}, V_{xm}, V_{yp}, V_{ym}, V_{zp}, V_{zm}$ are the velocity vectors of each control volumes.

Figure 2 illustrates the data access. When updating the saturation of a position of the array NEW_S, it is necessary to access the data of the saturation of two neighbor volumes using the array **MVIZ**. The matrix **MVIZ** contains locations of two neighbor control volumes that reference for positions of data in the array OLD_S, generating a high cache miss rate. It is possible to reduce this high cache miss rate using an adequate data structure, as used in this paper.

The direct access data structure used in the direct access version of the numerical method fluid-flow simulator uses a three-dimensional matrix that contains the NEW_S saturation data, and a three-dimensional matrix that contains the saturation data from the previous step OLD_S.

At each iteration, the numerical method developed in Correa and Borges work [5] uses a 6-neighbor stencil to calculate the saturation of a control volume. When searching for the saturation of a control volume of the matrix NEW_S, the method accesses the saturation data of two neighbor volumes through positions $(i\text{-}1,j,k), (i\text{+}1,j,k), (i,j\text{-}1,k), (i,j\text{+}1,k), (i,j,k\text{-}1), (i,j,k\text{+}1)$ of the matrix OLD_S, which are located contiguously in memory, reducing the cache miss rate.

Algorithm 2. Numerical method with direct access array.

input : $MSEW, MSOLD$

output: $MSNEW$ (saturation array)

Function Numerical Method($S[\ ]$):

    for $K \leftarrow 1$ *to* NZ do

        for $J \leftarrow 1$ *to* NY do

            for $I \leftarrow 1$ *to* NX do

$$MSNEW(I, J, K) \leftarrow MSOLD(I, J, K)$$
$$-(DT/DX) * V_{xm}(I, J, K) * (MSOLD(I, J, K) - MSOLD(I-1, J, K))$$
$$-(DT/DX) * V_{xp}(I, J, K) * (MSOLD(I+1, J, K) - MSOLD(I, J, K))$$
$$-(DT/DY) * V_{ym}(I, J, K) * (MSOLD(I, J, K) - MSOLD(I, J-1, K))$$
$$-(DT/DY) * V_{yp}(I, J, K) * (MSOLD(I, J+1, K) - MSOLD(I, J, K))$$
$$-(DT/DZ) * V_{zm}(I, J, K) * (MSOLD(I, J, K) - MSOLD(I, J, K-1))$$
$$-(DT/DZ) * V_{zp}(I, J, K) * (MSOLD(I, J, K+1) - MSOLD(I, J, K))$$

            end

        end

    end

    return $MSNEW$

Algorithm (2) shows the direct access approach. Algorithm 1 traverses the three-dimensional matrix and accesses the volume's neighbors directly, which are located in positions $(i\text{-}1,j,k), (i\text{+}1,j,k), (i,j\text{-}1,k), (i,j\text{+}1,k), (i,j,k\text{-}1), (i,j,k\text{+}1)$.

4 Results and Analysis

In this section, we evaluate the performance of the numerical fluid-flow simulator using the direct access data structure compared with the indirect access structure. The tests carried out in this study were conducted on the SDumont supercomputer, using two different architectures of nodes. The Cascade Lake architecture features two Intel® Xeon® Gold 6252 CPU (24 cores) processors running at 2.10 GHz and 384 GB of main memory. The Ivy Bridge architecture features two Intel® Xeon® E5-2695v2 Ivy Bridge (12c) processors running at 2.4 GHz and 64 GB of main memory. The nodes communicate between the processors through the INTEL® UPI channel, and we disabled the hyper-threading function.

As the present study evaluates the performance of MPI messages, we disabled the I/O operations and executed only the transport module. Thus, we disabled the velocity module and kept the input parameters constant. For the experiments presented in this study, we used a matrix containing $300 \times 300 \times 300$ control volumes using $NX = 300$, $NY = 300$, $NZ = 300$, and $NEL = 27,000,000$.

As shown in previous work [11], the present paper uses the domain decomposition technique called block decomposition [18]. Specifically, it used the scheme to test different vertical and horizontal cross-sections to evaluate the best block decomposition given a certain number of processes, which presents better performance.

This experiment used SDumont Supercomputer computational nodes for the Cascade Lake node architecture and the Ivy Bridge. The time measured for each test corresponds to an average of thirty runs.

Figure 3 presents the simulator execution time for 10, 24, 48, 96, and 150 MPI processes. The blue line represents computing load-balanced MPI processes domain decomposition for indirect access for Cascade Lake computer architecture node. The red line represents computing and communication load-balanced MPI processes domain decomposition for direct access Cascade Lake. The orange line represents computing load-balanced MPI processes domain decomposition for the indirect access Ivy Bridge computer architecture node. The green line represents computing and communication load-balanced MPI processes domain decomposition for direct access to Ivy Bridge.

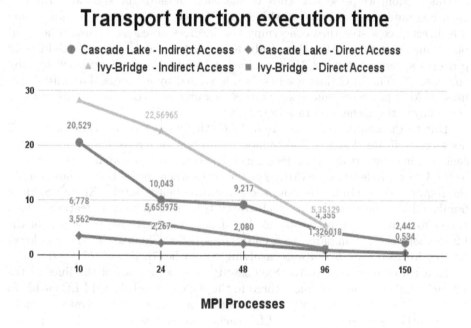

Fig. 3. Transport function execution time in the SDumont supercomputer.

As the number of MPI processes increases, the execution time gap between indirect and direct accesses decreases in both architectures. The main reason is that, for a fixed mesh size, as we increase the number of MPI processes, each MPI subdomain's volume decreases, reducing the number of cache misses on each core until a point there are no more cache misses at the last level cache. Still, the impact is more substantial on the Ivy Bridge architecture. The main reason is unsurprisingly the cache architecture.

We used the Intel® VTune Profiler tool to analyze the hardware events available on Intel® processors by a unit called the Performance Monitoring Unit (PMU), which counts various events that occur during execution and makes them available for profiling tools [24]. The events used are related to cache hit and miss counts generated by instructions (Intel® Xeon® Cascade Lake Gold 6252) and microinstructions (Intel® Xeon® E5-2695v2 Ivy Bridge).

In Sect. 4.1, we present the analysis that shows the reduction of cache miss rates of the algorithm with direct access compared to the algorithm with indirect access. In the Sect. 4.2, we show the comparison of the behavior of the simulator between Intel® Xeon® Cascade Lake Gold 6252 and Intel® Xeon processors textsuperscript® E5-2695v2 Ivy Bridge.

4.1   VTUNE Analysis: Cache Miss Evaluation

In this section, we present a study of the cache miss of the simulator running on a computational machine of the Santos Dumont supercomputer and using the direct access structure concerning the indirect access structure. The computational system used in this study features two Intel® Xeon® Gold 6252 processors, each containing 24 cores. Each L1 and L2 cache is accessed by only one core [7]. The LLC (last-level cache), is shared by all cores. The initial test uses 10 MPI processes, and each process executes in a core. With this test, we can analyze the cache miss rate in the LLC.

Due to the non-inclusive nature of LLC, the absence of a cache line in LLC does not indicate that the line cannot be present in any of the cores' private caches. Thus, the architecture design uses a snoop filter to search the cache lines in the L2 or mid-level cache (MLC) of the cores when the LLC does not contain the required data. On CPUs from the generation before Intel® Xeon® Skylake family CPUs, the shared LLC itself solves this task. With this feature, which allows for a reduction in the size of the LLC and an increase in the size of the L2 memory cache, compared to architectures before Skylake-SP, there is lower latency in read/write operations involving the cache [7].

In architectures prior to the Skylake-SP architecture, all of the lines in the L2 cache for each core were also stored in the inclusive and shared LLC cache. In Skylake-SP and Cascade Lake, each physical core has a 1 MB private L2 cache and all other cores share a larger LLC cache that can reach 38.5 MB (typically 1.375 MB/core). All lines stored in the L2 cache for each core may not be present in the non-inclusive and shared LLC cache. A larger L2 cache increases the hit ratio from the L2 cache, which results in lower memory latency and reduced demand on the LLC cache [7]. Nodes with these architectures comprise the SDumont supercomputer [16]. We collected some hardware events associated with memory usage employing the Intel® VTune Profiler tool.

Table 1. Instructions for collecting events in the Cascade Lake architecture.

Collect Cache miss events in Cascade Lake architecture	
L1 MISS COUNT	$MEM\_LOAD\_RETIRED.L1\_MISS\_PS$
L2 MISS COUNT	$MEM\_LOAD\_RETIRED.L2\_MISS\_PS$
LLC MISS COUNT	$MEM\_LOAD\_RETIRED.LLC\_MISS\_PS$

Table 1 shows the hardware events available in the Cascade Lake processor microarchitecture, which have load instructions terminated with at least one micro-operation that has generated faults in L1, L2, and LLC. Table 2 shows the collected results.

Table 2. Vtune analysis on one node with 10 processes.

Description	indirect access	direct access	Indirect/Direct ratio
L1 Miss Count	5808374246	1028930867	5.645
L2 Miss Count	3015415943	341943556	8.818
LLC Miss Count	2864200480	272019040	10.529
Transport time (s)	20,529	3,562	5,764

Table 2 exhibits that the cache miss count of L1 (L2) for indirect access is 5.6 (8.8) times higher than direct access. The results of the experiments show that the algorithm with direct access is 5.7x times more efficient than the code with indirect access.

Table 3. Vtune analysis on one node with 24 processes.

Description	indirect access	direct access	Indirect/Direct ratio
L1 Miss Count	5672670175	1002030060	5.661
L2 Miss Count	3362811788	365603489	9.198
LLC Miss Count	3392237440	200014000	16.960
Transport	10.043	2.267	4.431

Table 3 shows cache miss count using 24 processes, i.e., the number of physical cores of a processor of a computational node. Concerning the values of the Table 2, which shows tests with 10 MPI processes, the proportion remains constant for the L1 cache, and there is an increase of approximately 5% for the L2 cache and an increase of approximately 60% for LLC. This impact does not occur in the reduction of the execution time.

Table 4. Vtune analysis on one node with 48 processes.

Description	indirect access	direct access	Indirect/Direct ratio
L1 Miss Count	6129683885	1002030060	6.117
L2 Miss Count	3644880207	365603489	9.969
LLC Miss Count	3296230720	72005040	45.778
Transport Time	9.217	2.080	4.432

Table 4 shows the cache miss count for 48 processes, i.e., the number of physical cores of two processors of the computational node. Concerning Table 3, with tests with 24 MPI processes, there was an increase of approximately 5% for the L1 cache. Additionally, the proportion remains constant for the L2 cache, and one observes a growth of around 300% for the LLC. However, a similar impact did not occur in the reduction of the execution time.

Table 5. Vtune analysis on two nodes with 96 processes.

Description	indirect access	direct access	Indirect/Direct ratio
L1 Miss Count	7789333673	2180665418	3.572
L2 Miss Count	3813300914	591448304	6.447
LLC Miss Count	2880201600	0	–
Transport Time	4.355	0.990	4.397

Table 5 shows a cache miss count for 96 processes, i.e., the physical cores of two processors of two computing nodes. Concerning Table 5, which shows the results with 48 MPI processes, there is a decrease of approximately 40% for the L1 cache, a reduction of approximately 30% for the L2 cache, and miss cache does not happen in LLC. However, a similar impact does not occur in proportion to the decrease in execution time.

Table 6. Vtune analysis on four nodes with 150 processes.

Description	indirect access	direct access	Indirect/Direct ratio
L1 Miss Count	13018290537	1870256106	4.107
L2 Miss Count	6153633441	765821510	3.670
LLC Miss Count	0	0	–
Transport Time	2.373	0.534	4.442

Table 6 shows a cache miss count for 150 processes related to the execution in four computer systems, with 38 processes in two nodes and 27 processes in the other two nodes. This division was necessary so that it was possible to divide the mesh into 150 processes. Concerning Table 4, which shows tests with the execution of 96 MPI processes, there is an increase of approximately 20% for the L1 cache, a decrease of about 45% for the L2 cache, and cache miss did not happen in LLC. However, a similar impact did not occur in proportion to the decrease in execution time.

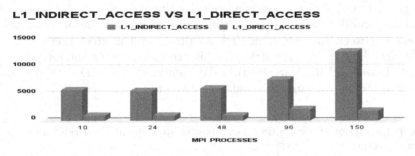

(a) Cache miss in L1

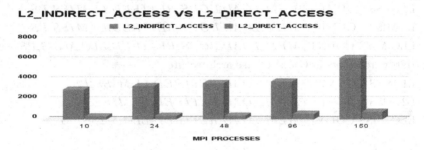

(b) Cache miss in L2

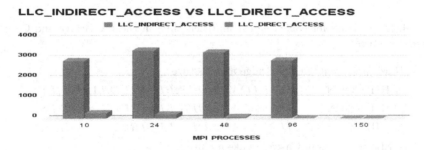

(c) Cache miss in LLC

Fig. 4. Cache miss evaluation.

Figure 4 shows plots that relate the cache miss rate as a function of the number of processes, which varies from 10 to 150, for the simulator executed with indirect access relative to direct access. Figure (a), (b), and (c) represents the cache miss rates for the L1, L2, and LLC memory caches. In the plots, the values are much higher for the simulator with indirect access.

4.2   Cache Miss and Cache Hit Evaluations on Intel® Xeon® E5-2695v2 Ivy Bridge and Intel® Xeon® Cascade Lake Gold 6252

In this section, we present numerical experiments to verify that the performance gains generated by direct access concerning indirect access are still more accentuated in a pre-Skylake generation architecture. The investigation evaluates the difference between the execution time for direct and indirect accesses for the Intel® Xeon® E5-2695v2 Ivy Bridge architecture concerning the Intel® Xeon® Cascade Lake Gold 6252 architecture. We analyzed the code with the Intel® Vtune [24] tool to validate the simulator on the two architectures.

Table 7. Instructions for collecting events (cache miss) in the Ivy-Bridge and Cascade Lake architecture.

Hardware events in Ivy-Bridge architecture	
L1 MISS COUNT	$MEM\_LOAD\_UOPS\_RETIRED.L1\_MISS\_PS$
L2 MISS COUNT	$MEM\_LOAD\_UOPS\_RETIRED.L2\_MISS\_PS$
LLC MISS COUNT	$MEM\_LOAD\_UOPS\_RETIRED.LLC\_MISS\_PS$
Hardware events in Cascade Lake architecture	
L1 MISS COUNT	$MEM\_LOAD\_RETIRED.L1\_MISS\_PS$
L2 MISS COUNT	$MEM\_LOAD\_RETIRED.L2\_MISS\_PS$
LLC MISS COUNT	$MEM\_LOAD\_RETIRED.LLC\_MISS\_PS$

Table 7 shows the hardware events that report how many microinstructions of load generated cache miss in L1, L2, and LLC.

Table 8. Instructions for collecting events (cache hit) in the Ivy-Bridge and Cascade Lake architecture.

Hardware events in Ivy-Bridge architecture	
L1 HIT COUNT	$MEM\_LOAD\_UOPS\_RETIRED.L1\_HIT\_PS$
L2 HIT COUNT	$MEM\_LOAD\_UOPS\_RETIRED.L2\_HIT\_PS$
LLC HIT COUNT	$MEM\_LOAD\_UOPS\_RETIRED.LLC\_HIT\_PS$
Hardware events in Cascade Lake architecture	
L1 HIT COUNT	$MEM\_LOAD\_RETIRED.L1\_HIT\_PS$
L2 HIT COUNT	$MEM\_LOAD\_RETIRED.L2\_HIT\_PS$
LLC HIT COUNT	$MEM\_LOAD\_RETIRED.LLC\_HIT\_PS$

Table 8 informs the hardware events used to collect the number of load microinstructions that will not generate any miss cache in L1, L2, and LLC.

The cache miss counts and the cache hit counts for L1, L2, and LLC in the Ivy-Bridge architecture was collected so that it was possible to calculate the miss/hit ratio. Table 9 shows the ratio for the two versions of the method, i.e., using direct and indirect accesses. The last line shows that the version with direct access is approximately four times faster than the version with indirect access. The indirect/direct ratio of the miss/hit ratio is always greater than one for the three cache levels, evidencing that the version with direct access presents less cache error concerning the hits when compared to the implementation with indirect access.

Table 9. Vtune analysis on one node with 10 processes using Ivy-Bridge architecture.

Vtune analysis on intel® Ivy-Bridge architecture			
Description	indirect access	direct access	Indirect/Direct ratio
L1 Miss Count/L1 Hit Count	0.018	0.017	**1.069**
L2 Miss Count/L2 Hit Count	2.835	1.243	**2.280**
LLC Miss Count/LLC Hit Count	1.557	0.953	**1.634**
Transport time(seg)	28.151	6.778	**4.152**

The cache miss count and the cache hit count for the L1 and L2 memory caches of the Ivy-Bridge architecture were collected Table in 9, so that it would be possible to calculate the miss/hit ratio, which gives us the cache miss rate concerning the hit rate.

Table 10. Vtune analysis on one node with 10 processes using Intel® Xeon® Cascade Lake Gold 6252.

Vtune analysis on intel® Xeon® Cascade Lake Gold 6252 architecture			
Description	indirect access	direct access	Indirect/Direct ratio
L1 Miss Count/ L1 Hit Count	0.008	0.000	**13.320**
L2 Miss Count/L2 Hit Count	1.099	0.492	**2.232**
Transport time(seg)	20.529	3.562	**5.764**

Table 10 shows the ratio for the two implementations of the simulator, i.e., using direct and indirect memory-access. The last line shows that the version with direct access is approximately 5.8 times faster than the version with indirect access. The indirect/direct ratio of the miss/hit ratio is always greater than 1 for the two cache levels, evidencing that the version with direct access presents less cache error concerning the hits compared with the implementation employing indirect access.

Table 11 shows a ratio for Ivy Bridge/Cascade Lake of the percentages of the cache miss concerning the cache hits for levels L1 and L2. All the numbers are higher than 1 for both direct and indirect accesses versions. The Table emphasizes the value for the L1 level of the implementation with direct access (26.091), suggesting that this version takes more advantage of the cache hierarchy than the version with indirect access in the Cascade Lake processor architecture, which

Table 11. Ratio of Ivy Bridge/Cascade Lake of the cache miss rate concerning cache hit rate for L1 and L2 memory caches.

Description	indirect access	direct access
L1	2.094	**26.091**
L2	2.579	2.525

reflects in the execution times. The direct access version is approximately 5.8 times faster on Cascade Lake (see Table 10). Furthermore, it is around four times faster on Ivy Bridge (Table 9), confirming what we mentioned in Sect. 4.1.

5   Conclusions and Future Works

Adopting the direct access data structure strategy improved the performance and scalability of the numerical fluid-flow simulator concerning using an indirect access data structure for distributed memory architectures. We presented a Vtune cache miss analysis. The analysis showed that the main reason for the results was not surprisingly the low cache miss rate when using the direct access data structure. We also showed that the impact of decreasing the number of cache misses is even more substantial for previous Intel® Xeon® Gold 6252 processors architectures that present inclusive cache LLC.

The experiments presented in this paper shows that by implementing direct access data, we can further improve the execution time of the numerical fluid-flow simulator that uses the optimized domain decomposition technique presented in previous work [11].

We intend to improve the communication between MPI processes using advanced techniques, such as the adaptive MPI, based on a previous investigation [13] to provide further scalability to the present study. Moreover, the present study is part of a research effort to develop a computational environment for academic studies to provide scalability to the new numerical methods developed in the oil and gas field. We are developing a scalable code written in the Fortran language to approach the solution of the advection problem using the well-known first-order finite volume method upwind [14]. We also plan to implement numerical methods of higher order in the code, as recommended in previous publications [3,5].

As can be seen in the Algorithm 1, from the direct access data structure, the calculation of each control volume of the three-dimensional matrix is carried out through the path of the indices (i, j, k) of the saturation matrix. In future work, we intend to evaluate the strategies developed by Respondek [19] to increase the locality of access to data in the saturation matrix. We also want to develop research to evaluate the performance of the code for vectorization instructions such as Intel(AVX) and develop studies for other processor architectures such as the ARM architecture [20].

Authorship Statement. The authors confirm that they are the sole liable persons responsible for the authorship of this work, and that all material that has been herein included as part of the present paper is either the property (and authorship) of the authors or has the permission of the owners to be included here.

Acknowledgement. The authors acknowledge the National Laboratory for Scientific Computing (LNCC/MCTI, Brazil) for providing HPC resources for the SDumont supercomputer. The use of HPC resources contributed significantly to the research results reported in this paper. URL: http://sdumont.lncc.br. This study was financed in part by the *Coordenação de Aperfeiçoamento de Pessoal de Nível Superior* - Brasil (CAPES) Finance Code 001.

References

1. Abreu, E.C.d., et al.: Modelagem e simulação computacional de escoamentos trifásicos em reservatórios de petróleo heterogêneos. Ph.D. thesis, Universidade do Estado do Rio de Janeiro (2007)
2. Borges, M., Furtado, F., Pereira, F., Souto, H.A.: Scaling analysis for the tracer flow problem in self-similar permeability fields. Multiscale Model. Simul. **7**(3), 1130–1147 (2009)
3. Carneiro, I.B., Borges, M.R., Malta, S.M.C.: Aplicação de métodos de alta ordem na resolução de problemas bifásicos. Proc. Ser. Braz. Soc. Comput. Appl. Math. **6**(2) (2018)
4. Causon, D., Mingham, C.: Introductory Finite Difference Methods for PDEs. Bookboon (2010)
5. Correa, M., Borges, M.: A semi-discrete central scheme for scalar hyperbolic conservation laws with heterogeneous storage coefficient and its application to porous media flow. Int. J. Numer. Meth. Fluids **73**(3), 205–224 (2013)
6. Dagan, G.: Flow and Transport in Porous Formations. Springer, Heidelberg (2012). https://doi.org/10.1007/978-3-642-75015-1
7. Mulnix, D.L.: Intel®Xeon®processor scalable family technical overview (2017). https://www.intel.com/content/www/us/en/developer/articles/technical/xeon-processor-scalable-family-technical-overview.html
8. Dupuis, A., Chopard, B.: Lattice gas: an efficient and reusable parallel library based on a graph partitioning technique. In: Sloot, P., Bubak, M., Hoekstra, A., Hertzberger, B. (eds.) HPCN-Europe 1999. LNCS, vol. 1593, pp. 319–328. Springer, Heidelberg (1999). https://doi.org/10.1007/BFb0100593
9. Durlofsky, L.J.: Numerical calculation of equivalent grid block permeability tensors for heterogeneous porous media. Water Resour. Res. **27**(5), 699–708 (1991)
10. Gelhar, L.W., Axness, C.L.: Three-dimensional stochastic analysis of macrodispersion in aquifers. Water Resour. Res. **19**(1), 161–180 (1983)
11. Herrera, S., et al.: Optimizations in an numerical method code for two-phase fluids flow in porous media using the sDumont supercomputer. In: CILAMCE 2021-PANACM 2021 Proceedings of the XLII Ibero-Latin-American Congress on Computational Methods in Engineering and III Pan-American Congress on Computational Mechanics, ABMEC-IACM Rio de Janeiro, Brazil, 9–12 November 2021. CILAMCE (2021)
12. Herschlag, G., Lee, S., Vetter, J.S., Randles, A.: GPU data access on complex geometries for D3Q19 lattice Boltzmann method. In: 2018 IEEE International Parallel and Distributed Processing Symposium (IPDPS), pp. 825–834. IEEE (2018)

13. Huang, C., Lawlor, O., Kalé, L.V.: Adaptive MPI. In: Rauchwerger, L. (ed.) LCPC 2003. LNCS, vol. 2958, pp. 306–322. Springer, Heidelberg (2004). https://doi.org/ 10.1007/978-3-540-24644-2_20

14. LeVeque, R.J.: Finite Difference Methods for Ordinary and Partial Differential Equations: Steady-State and Time-Dependent Problems. SIAM (2007)

15. Martys, N.S., Hagedorn, J.G.: Multiscale modeling of fluid transport in heterogeneous materials using discrete Boltzmann methods. Mater. Struct. **35**, 650–658 (2002)

16. Osthoff, C., et al.: A arquitetura do supercomputador sDumont e os desafios da pesquisa brasileira na área de computação de alto desempenho. In: Anais da XI Escola Regional de Alto Desempenho de São Paulo, pp. 1–5. SBC (2020)

17. Pan, C., Prins, J.F., Miller, C.T.: A high-performance lattice Boltzmann implementation to model flow in porous media. Comput. Phys. Commun. **158**(2), 89–105 (2004)

18. Parashar, M., Yotov, I.: An environment for parallel multi-block, multi-resolution reservoir simulations. In: Proceedings of the 11th International Conference on Parallel and Distributed Computing Systems (PDCS 98), Chicago, IL, International Society for Computers and their Applications (ISCA), pp. 230–235 (1998)

19. Respondek, J.: Matrix black box algorithms - a survey. Bull. Pol. Acad. Sci. Tech. Sci. **70**(2), e140535 (2022)

20. Ryzhyk, L.: The Arm architecture. Chicago University, Illinois, EUA (2006)

21. Schulz, M., Krafczyk, M., Tölke, J., Rank, E.: Parallelization strategies and efficiency of CFD computations in complex geometries using lattice Boltzmann methods on high-performance computers. In: High Performance Scientific and Engineering Computing: proceedings of the 3rd International FORTWIHR Conference on HPSEC, Erlangen, 12–14 March 2001, vol. 21, pp. 115–122. Springer, Heidelberg (2002). https://doi.org/10.1007/978-3-642-55919-8_13

22. Shashkov, M.: Conservative Finite-Difference Methods on General Grids, vol. 6. CRC Press (1995)

23. Silvester, P.P., Ferrari, R.L.: Finite Elements for Electrical Engineers. Cambridge University Press (1996)

24. Intel Corporation Site: performance monitoring events supported by Intel performance monitoring units (PMUs). https://perfmon-events.intel.com/

25. Message Passing Interface Forum: MPI: a message passing interface. In: Proceedings of the 1993 ACM/IEEE Conference on Supercomputing, pp. 878–883 (1993)

26. Tuane, V.L.: Simulação Numérica tridimensional de escoamento em reservátorios de petróleo Heterogêneos. Master's thesis, LNCC/MCT, Petrópolis, RJ, Brasil (2012)

27. Tuszyński, J., Löhner, R.: Parallelizing the construction of indirect access arrays for shared-memory machines. Commun. Numer. Meth. Eng. **14**(8), 773–781 (1998)

28. Vázquez-Cendón, M.E.: Solving Hyperbolic Equations with Finite Volume Methods. U, vol. 90. Springer, Cham (2015). https://doi.org/10.1007/978-3-319-14784-0

Design and Implementation of Wind-Powered Charging System to Improve Electric Motorcycle Autonomy

Luis Felipe Changoluisa[1] and Mireya Zapata[2(✉)] (iD)

[1] Departamento de Ciencias de la Energía y Mecánica, Universidad de las Fuerzas Armadas ESPE, Latacunga, Ecuador
[2] Centro de Investigación en Mecatrónica y Sistemas Interactivos - MIST, Universidad Indoamérica, Av. Machala y Sabanilla, Quito 170103, Ecuador
mireyazapata@uti.edu.ec

Abstract. The careless use of fossil fuels for decades has had a negative effect on the environment, which has led to addressing climate change as one of the greatest challenges of our time. Electric mobility is an option to reduce CO_2 emissions, but its main disadvantage is its limited range. As well, one alternative for reducing global warming is to use clean energy. In this sense, wind energy is one alternative to clean energy sources, because it does not produce greenhouse gas emissions or air pollutants that contribute to climate change and air pollution. It is also abundant and increasingly cost-effective, making it an attractive option for electricity generation. In this paper, we propose a charging system that harnesses gusts of wind hitting the front of an electric motorcycle and converts their kinetic energy into mechanical energy to produce alternating current through a three-phase generator connected to a propeller system. This research seeks to develop a wind generator that is installed on the front of an electric motorcycle to generate electricity, which is stored in an auxiliary lead acid battery. A Computational Fluid Dynamic (CFD) simulation was performed to visualize the behaviour of the propeller system when exposed to a wind flow. The optimised prototype was implemented using 3D printing, along with the fabrication of metal parts to support the structure. As a result, it was feasible to create alternating current using the suggested prototype, achieving an increase of motorcycle autonomy by 5 to 10%.

The blade system managed to generate an acceptable amount of current, operating in wind regimes higher than 5 m/s, which implies good efficiency in power generation. Finally, the prototype has a better performance in straight tracks where high speeds can be reached and consequently a better efficiency in power generation.

Keywords: Wind energy · propeller system · wind generator

1 Introduction

Climate change is one of the greatest challenges of our time, but it is important to mention the indiscriminate use of fossil fuels that has been occurring for decades, with negative effects on the environment. The continuous progress in the development of new

O. Gervasi et al. (Eds.): ICCSA 2023, LNCS 13956, pp. 55–66, 2023.
https://doi.org/10.1007/978-3-031-36805-9_4

technologies in the automotive industry has made it possible to transform the energy propulsion system and adapt it to the new needs of using clean energy, which is expected to reduce environmental pollution.

The development of mankind has always been largely determined by the use of different forms of energy according to the needs and availability of each time and place. From the very beginning, the main resources were based on the use of renewable energies in the form of biomass, wind, water and sun. Used mainly as a fuel source, these elements should be considered as the energy base for human development [1].

According to [2] mentions that the massive use of fossil fuels has led to a significant increase of greenhouse gases (GHG), mainly CO_2, in the atmosphere of our planet. The accumulation of these gases has made climate change a reality. This phenomenon implies not only a rise in global temperature and sea level, but also a significant increase in the intensity and frequency of extreme weather events.

The year 2020 was disruptive in terms of transportation. In the midst of the COVID-19 health, economic and social crisis, sustainable mobility has become even more relevant as a central element for improving the quality of life and the resilience of cities in the face of unprecedented events, in Latin America and the Caribbean various elements of public policy are adapted to the needs of a new product and service such as electric mobility. For 2020, several countries in the region have set more ambitious climate targets to avoid a global average temperature increase of more than 1.5 degrees Celsius [3].

According to [4], a wind generator for vehicles is based on the use of the air that enters through the front grille of a vehicle when it is moving to produce electrical energy and provide it with greater autonomy. When the vehicle is moving, the air hits the blades, generating a movement that is transmitted to the rotor shaft, which starts the generators that produce electrical energy that is used to recharge the battery set of vehicles that move with electrical energy [5]. The electric car is currently presented as the alternative of the future in terms of urban transportation and brings, as a fundamental consequence, the reduction of environmental pollution in large cities [6]. An electric vehicle (EV) has zero emissions of polluting gases because it relies on batteries to power its engine and does not burn fuel inside. It also requires less polluting fluids such as oil and coolant.

Renewable energy is gaining popularity because it is more economical and efficient than conventional energy sources. New green energy technologies, such as wind energy, are mainly used to maintain environmental sustainability. This study analyzed the asymmetric relationship between wind energy and ecological footprint in the top 10 wind energy consuming countries [7]. Climate change mitigation is a major societal challenge, and renewable energy is a central element in the transition to a low-carbon society. However, the growth of the renewable energy sector has altered landscapes and land-use dynamics, leading to new land-use conflicts [8].

The global installed capacity of wind power, both onshore and offshore, increased from 7.5 GW in 1997 to 743 GW in 2020. In line with this increase in capacity, knowledge of wind energy and its impacts has improved and a number of reviews have been conducted on the subject [9]. With the help of renewable energy, the carbon footprint can definitely be reduced. Wind energy is a renewable energy source because it does not run out when it is used. The utilization of wind energy through a wind turbine and its excellent conversion efficiency makes the construction of a wind generator feasible [10].

Clean energy resources will be further utilized to enhance sustainability and sustainable development. Efficient technologies for energy production, storage, and use will reduce gas emissions and improve the global economy. Despite the fact that 30% of electricity is produced from wind energy, the connection of wind farms to medium and large power grids still creates problems of instability and intermittency [11]. Researchers [12] mention that the electric vehicle stores energy and uses it when the need for mobility arises, therefore it does not consume energy from the grid at the time of use. The aerodynamic profile has a fundamental importance in the wind generator. In this section, the effects produced by the wind on each surface or airfoil are studied in depth and the forces acting on the entire blade are studied [13].

The electric generator represents the simplicity of an electric motor, where the permanent magnet produces a magnetic flux with a small mass, the magnets are made of samarian and neodymium [14]. The traditional motorcycle brake generates kinetic energy, which is converted into heat. This process is in perfect harmony with the principle of energy conservation. Thus, the motorcycle dissipates part of its kinetic energy in the form of heat during braking, thanks to the friction generated between the brake disk and the brake pads [15]. The existence of charging infrastructure is a key factor in supporting the large-scale deployment of EVs. If there is no network to charge vehicles everywhere, there will be no place for EVs [16]. A battery charger is a device used to provide current or voltage that is stored at the same time. The charging current depends on the technology and capacity of the battery that the electric motorcycle is equipped with [17]. An electric motor controller is used for signal processing and power management, while the processor is activated, allows the motor to start or stop, and enables the electronic components that receive direct commands from the user. It is also equipped with various protection functions, such as those used against voltage drops or overcurrents [18].

1.1 Design and Calculate

The design process can be divided into several key elements, each of which is essential to the proper functioning of the prototype, and some of which are detailed because they are the fundamental basis for the construction of the prototype. The rotor-generator prototype to be designed consists mainly of a horizontal axis motor connected to wind energy collecting blades. After reviewing the necessary information and defining the necessary requirements to obtain the wind load system (see Fig. 1).

The operating phases of the rotor-generator type charging system. This illustration highlights the importance of exploiting the renewable energies present in the environment, in this case the wind energy present in the gusts of wind that hit the front of the electric motorcycle, generating a kinetic force that is received by a system of blades connected to a three-phase generator (see Fig. 2).

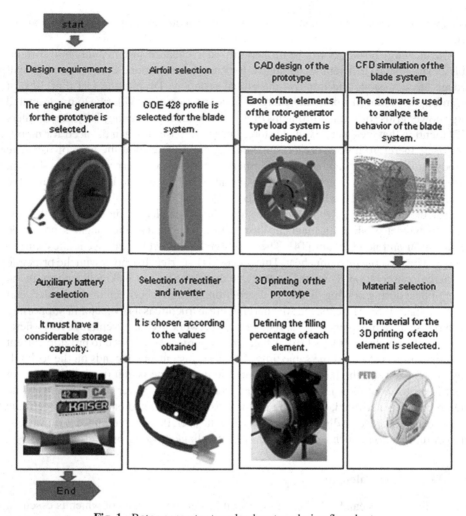

Fig. 1. Rotor-generator type load system design flowchart.

Design Considerations

The prototype to be developed must meet the following general characteristics for proper operation:

– Components must be made of lightweight, durable, commercially available materials that allow for proper fabrication and assembly.
– Avoid the use of mechanical transmission between the rotor and the generator to minimize energy conversion losses.
– The suitable construction of the prototype will allow field testing on the given route, easy to install and light, while providing rigidity, stability to counteract the effects of excessive vibration.

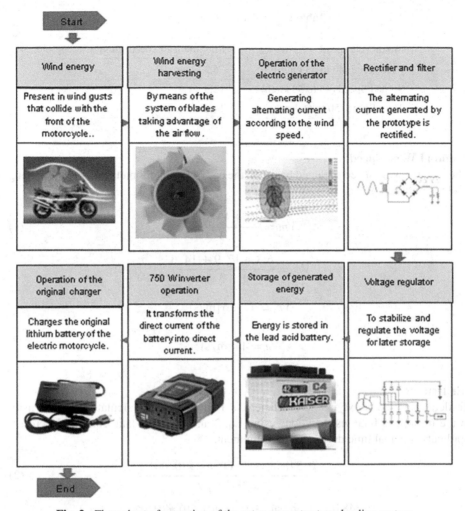

Fig. 2. Flow chart of operation of the rotor-generator type loading system.

– It should be easy to transport and position so that it can be installed on the front of the electric motorcycle.

Evaluation of Available Wind

In order to evaluate the feasibility of using wind as an energy source, it is necessary to know its characteristics, since wind is an unstable and uncertain resource, therefore, through the use of an anemometer we proceed to obtain the velocities at the site of the initial tests (Table 1).

Table 1. Tabulation of wind speeds

Motorcycle speed	Maximum air speed (m/s)
First Speed (40 to 45 km/h)	6,3
Second Speed (45 to 50 km/h)	12,9
Third Speed (50 to 60 km/h)	14,6

Nominal Wind Speed

The average wind speed obtained based on the use of the anemometer during the driving cycle is obtained by Eq. 1.

$$Vm = \frac{V_1 + V_2 + V_3}{3} \tag{1}$$

$$Vm = \frac{6.3 + 12,9 + 14,6}{3}$$

$$Vm = 11,26 \, [m/s]$$

$$Vn = 11 \, [m/s]$$

Air Density

To determine the aerodynamic coefficient, it is important to calculate the air density at the initial and final test locations using Eq. 2 and the time data from the Microsoft application in real time during test development.

$$\rho = \frac{0,34848p - 0,009h_T * (0,061t)}{273,15 + t} \tag{2}$$

$$\rho = \frac{0,34848(1026\text{mbar}) - 0,009(0,59) * (0,061 * 13\,°C)}{273,15 + 13°C}$$

$$\rho = 1,2495 \, [kg/m^3]$$

Wind Force

When the wind hits the blade system, it generates a force determined by Eq. 3.

$$P\,viento = \frac{1}{2} * \rho * v^2 \tag{3}$$

$$P\,viento = \frac{1}{2} * 1,2495 * 11,26^2$$

$$P\,viento = 79,21 \, [Pa]$$

Centrifugal Force

The centrifugal force is due to the rotation of the blade system and is calculated by Eq. 4.

$$F_c = m * R * w^2 \tag{4}$$

$$F_c = 0.025\text{kg} * 0,05\,\text{m} * 180,16^2$$

$$F_c = 40[\text{N}]$$

$$w = \frac{\gamma * v}{R} \tag{5}$$

$$w = \frac{0,8 * 11,26}{0,05}$$

$$w = 180,16\,[\text{rad/s}]$$

Wind Flow Measurement

To measure the flow rate, the area (Eq. 6) of the prototype exposed to the gusts of wind is determined, and this result is multiplied by the average wind speed when the motorcycle is in operation to obtain the flow rate.

$$A = \pi * r^2 \tag{6}$$

$$A = \pi * (0,106)^2$$

$$A = 0,035\,[\text{m}^2]$$

With this, the wind flow can be determined in the prototype using Eq. 7.

$$Q = Vm * A \tag{7}$$

$$Q = 11,26\frac{\text{m}}{\text{s}} * 0,035\,\text{m}^2$$

$$Q = 0,39\,[\text{m}^3/\text{s}]$$

Blade Design

The blades are one of the most important components of the prototype, as they are responsible for capturing the kinetic energy of the wind. For this aerodynamic profile to be used is one of the most important design of the most important design aspects to achieve optimal performance. Optimal performance. The blades convert the linear motion of the wind into a rotary motion into rotary motion and transmit it to the generator.

Aerodynamic Profile

The GOE 428 AIRFOIL airfoil was chosen because this type of airfoil is recommended for wind turbine applications such as this design. It is one of the most widely used airfoils in aerodynamics. This airfoil conforms to aerodynamic tests and therefore expresses its geometry in percentages that adapt to different blade thicknesses and widths in the XY plane (see Fig. 3).

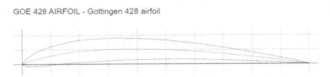

GOE 428 AIRFOIL - Gottingen 428 airfoil

Fig. 3. GOE 428 profile selected for prototype

CAD Analysis of the Blade System

Through these analyses, it is possible to visualize the behavior of the blade system when exposed to constant air flows. The maximum and minimum speeds supported by the entire system are known and the location where the pressure exerted by the wind is concentrated is visualized.

Dynamic Analysis of the Blade System

This simulation allows visualization of the behavior of the blade system when exposed to an airflow at both the inlet and outlet. Nylon plastic material was chosen because it has similar characteristics to PETG material. This simulation observes the trajectories of the air flow to see where there is a higher concentration of flow, the inlet and outlet of the flow as it passes through the blade system, and the way the flow meets the entire system(see Fig. 4) (Fig. 5).

Analysis of the Prototype at Medium Speed

Due to the type of geometry of the prototype and the 9 blades that make up the whole system, the simulation shows that the largest amount of air is concentrated in the middle part, a rectilinear amount of air enters, hits the blade system and generates air distortion at the outlet. As a result, the geometry of the blades is optimal for the best capture of wind gusts (see Fig. 6) (Fig. 7).

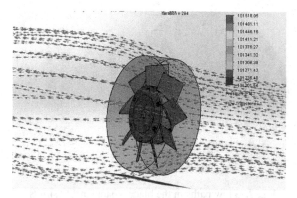

Fig. 4. Dynamic analysis of the blade system

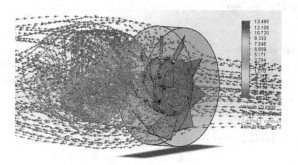

Fig. 5. Flow paths in the blade system

Fig. 6. Analysis of the blade system at an average speed of 11.24 m/s

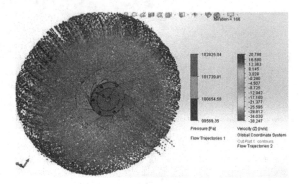

Fig. 7. Flow paths in the blade system at 11.24 m/s

1.2 Results and Discussion

Dynamic Analysis Results

The CFD simulation of the prototype at rest made it possible to visualize its operation and the speed values it reaches in a dynamic state. Table 2 shows results obtained from dynamic simulation.

Table 2. Results obtained from dynamic simulation

Variables to analyze	Values
Pressure	101201.54 [**Pa**]–101516.05 [**Pa**]
Speed	0.223 [m/s]–19.314 [m/s]
Temperature	293.14 °K–293.28 °K (19.99 °C–20.13 °C)
Air density	1.20 [kg/m^3]–1.21 [kg/m^3]
Reference pressure	101325.00 [Pa]

Results of the Analysis at Average Speed

By means of CFD simulation, when the prototype is exposed to an average speed of 11.24 m/s, it was possible to visualize its operation and the speed values it reaches during its operation (Table 3).

Table 3. Analysis results at an average speed

Variables to analyze	Values
Pressure	99569.35 [**Pa**]–102655.31 [**Pa**]
Speed	0.160 [m/s]–63.995 [m/s]
Temperature	293.03 °K–295.27 °K (19.88 °C–22.12 °C)
Air density	1.18 [kg/m^3]–1.22 [kg/m^3]
Reference pressure	101325.00 [Pa]

1.3 Conclusions

In this part of the research, the CFD simulation of the blade system was developed in the dynamic state of the vehicle and when exposed to an average wind speed, with which the value of pressures, minimum speeds and maximum speeds at which the prototype works were obtained. Next, a test protocol and a driving cycle were developed on the route defined within the university.

The reason for choosing Computational Fluid Dynamics (CFD) simulation is to obtain the behavior of the blade system during operation and also to visualize the flow paths at a given average velocity.

Within the CAD simulation software, the flow simulation tool was used to obtain results of pressures and speeds at which the blade system can operate, considering the type of fluid, the atmospheric pressure, and the wind force of 11.24 m/s when the electric motorcycle reaches an average speed. The CFD simulation of the prototype showed some aspects to consider regarding the importance of an optimal aerodynamic design of the blade system and its behavior when exposed to a given wind speed.

For the development of this prototype a CFD simulation was performed to visualize the behavior of the propeller system when exposed to a wind flow, also an optimal design of the entire prototype was performed to later manufacture them by 3D printing.

The blade system managed to generate an acceptable amount of current, operating in wind regimes higher than 5 m/s, which implies a good efficiency in power generation. The prototype has a better performance in straight tracks where high speeds can be reached and consequently a better efficiency in power generation.

CFD simulation was used from the conceptual phase of this project to determine the feasibility of the propeller system for the wind generator, and through this simulation it was determined that the shape of the propeller system was the most appropriate for proper use of wind energy.

References

1. Perez, R.: Renewable Energy Plants; Electricity Generation with Renewable energies. Pearson Education, Madrid (2009)
2. Martinez, J.: Motorized mobility, environmental impact, alternatives and future perspectives. Scielos Public Health (2018)

3. Máñez, G.: Electric Mobility; Advances in Latin America and the Caribbean. UNEP, Panama (2021)
4. Spanish Patent and Trademark Office. SPTO. Retrieved from Eolic generator for vehicles (2011)
5. Manero, J.R.: Spain Patent no. ES1074375U (2010)
6. Molero, E., Pozo, A.: The Electric Vehicle and its Charging Infrastructure. MARCOMBO S.A, Barcelona (2013)
7. Chen, M., Huang, W., Alib, S.: Asymmetric linkages between wind energy and ecological sustainability: evidence from quantile estimation. Environ. Dev (2023). https://doi.org/10.1016/j.envdev.2022.100798
8. Frantal, B., Frolovab, M., Liñan, J.: Conceptualizing the patterns of land use conflicts in wind energy development: towards a typology and implications for practice. Energy Res. Soc. Sci. (2023). https://doi.org/10.1016/j.erss.2022.102907
9. Kinani, K., Meunier, S., Vido, L.: Interdisciplinary analysis of wind energy - a focus on France. Sustain. Energy Technol. Assess. (2023). https://doi.org/10.1016/j.seta.2022.102944
10. Yawharaa, B., Amein, M., Panda, S.: A numerical study of the effect of building height and shape on amount of wind energy available on the roof (2022). https://doi.org/10.1016/j.matpr.2022.12.071
11. Barhoumi, M., Salah, M., Okonkwo, C.: Techno-economic optimization of wind energy based hydrogen refueling station case study Salalah city Oman. Int. J. Hydrogen Energy (2022).https://doi.org/10.1016/j.ijhydene.2022.12.148
12. Rodríguez, P., Chacón, J.: Electric Vehicle Guide II. Graphics Arias Montano, S.A, Madrid (2015)
13. Ramirez, A.: Design of Blades, Rotor and Transmission of a 500 W Horizontal Axis Wind Generator. Undergraduate thesis. Technological Institute of Pachuca (2019)
14. Minguela, I.: Electrical and electronic design of an electric motorcycle. Undergraduate thesis. University of Valladolid (2016)
15. Guizien, V.: Development of a controller for electric motorcycle. Undergraduate thesis. Comillas Pontifical University (2018)
16. Guillen, F.: Electric Vehicle Guide. Graphics Arias Montano, S.A, Madrid (2009)
17. Grijalva, F.: Analyze the efficiency of an electric motorcycle in the city of Quito. Undergraduate thesis. UTE (2014)
18. Bastidas, C., Cabrera, D.: Conversion of an internal combustion motorcycle to electric with solar energy supply and with electric energy charge. Undergraduate thesis. WAIT (2014)

Computational Studies Unveiling the Mechanism of Action of Selected Pt-, Te-, Au-, Rh-, Ru-Based Drugs

Iogann Tolbatov[1]([⊠]) [iD] and Alessandro Marrone[2] [iD]

[1] Institute of Chemical Research of Catalonia (ICIQ), The Barcelona Institute of Science and Technology, av. Paisos Catalans 16, 43007 Tarragona, Spain
tolbatov.i@gmail.com
[2] Dipartimento di Farmacia, Università "G d'Annunzio" di Chieti-Pescara, via dei Vestini 31, Chieti, Italy

Abstract. Modern medicinal chemistry is unimaginable without the employment of metallodrugs, which form a crucial source of novel anticancer, antiviral, antibacterial, and antiparasitic agents. The wide variety of molecular geometries, availability of several oxidation states, redox properties are ascribable to the presence of a metal center that can be exploited in the design of bioactive metal scaffolds with various modes of action, different selectivities, and activation mechanisms. This minireview focuses on an abridged account of the computational studies of the mechanism of action of selected Pt-, Te-, Au-, Rh-, Ru-based drugs, carried out in our group. This account is specifically focused on how the molecular geometry and the reactivity with the biological milieu may influence the modus operandi of these metal scaffolds.

1 Introduction

The unique characteristics for metallodrugs, such as wide range of coordination geometries and numbers, and attainability of various redox states, make them essential components of the toolbox of modern medicine [1, 2]. Furthermore, it is possible to synthesize novel derivative complexes on the basis of existing metal scaffolds via modification of ligands, thus finely regulating the electronic, steric, and electrostatic properties of the metallodrug [3].

After the cytotoxicity of cisplatin has been discovered, a plethora of metallodrugs based on other transition metals have been synthesized and studied [4]. The synthesis of novel scaffolds is guided by the necessity to circumvent the heavy toxic effects, which are, unfortunately, the intrinsic drawbacks of the medications based on metals due to the widespread reactivity of these complexes with biomolecular targets the inherent promiscuity of these complexes. The development of complexes with improved therapeutic profiles is gained by fine-tuning the reactivity of the metal-based pharmacophore via modulating its carrier ligands, i.e. those which stay bound to the metal center after its activation, or its labile ligands, the cleavage of which occurs during the activation.

O. Gervasi et al. (Eds.): ICCSA 2023, LNCS 13956, pp. 67–81, 2023.
https://doi.org/10.1007/978-3-031-36805-9_5

Another valuable strategy is assembling active ligands and metal scaffolds, thus developing dual-acting drugs. This method allows to program the release of the therapeutically active ligands after the metallodrug coordinates to its biomolecular target, thus providing the effective scheme of delivery of medicinal agents. The above mentioned characterictics depict the reasons behind the success of metallodrugs in the fields of anticancer, antiparasitic, antibacterial, and antiviral agents [5–7].

The role of computational chemistry in the bioinorganic drug design is constantly expanding, driven by the growing hardware and software capabilities [8]. Calculations can be now addressed to accurately describe the mode of action of metallodrugs, thus being essential for their rational development. Density functional theory (DFT) provides for an accurate and robust computational paradigm for investigation of metallodrugs. DFT allows the accurate description of the major features describing the pharmaceutical profile of a metal scaffold: (1) its activation, which is essential before the biomolecular target is reached, (2) the undertaken ligand exchange scheme yielding its binding to a biomolecular target, and (3) the ability of metallodrugs to attack multiple targets [9].

This minireview features multiple computational investigations carried out in our group, unveiling the *modus operandi* of Pt-, Te-, Au-, Rh-, Ru-based drugs. The computational studies on the Pt-based arsenoplatin as well as diRh- and diRu-based paddlewheel metallodrugs shed light on the interaction of these metallodrugs with their biomolecular targets, by spotlighting the most likely protein binding sites. The investigation on the Te-based AS101 exemplified the importance of hydrolytic activation and, more specifically, how this feature may impact the biological activity of this species. The study of the Au-based auranofin and its acetylcysteine-based derivative evidenced how the strength of metal-ligand bonds may be pivotal in the mechanism of action of metallodrugs, and provided corroboration to the experimental data demonstrating the different mode of action of these two Au-based complexes.

2   Pt-Based Antitumour Metallodrug: Arsenoplatin

Arsenoplatin-1(AP-1) is a metallodrug that features both the square-planar Pt(II) and the arsenic trioxide bound to it (Fig. 1) [10]. This complex has demonstrated elevated antitumor effects against a multitude of cancers [10, 11]. Nevertheless, the biomolecular basis for the action of this drug is not disclosed yet [12, 13]. A recent study has shown that this metallodrug is able to form the adducts with the DNA of MDA-MB-231 cancer cell line [10]. It was reported that the coordination of DNA via its Pt center induces the collapse of the arsenic center and concomitant release of the cytotoxic $As(OH)_2$ portion. The major target of arsenoplatin is expected to be the guanine nucleobase, which makes this Pt-based scaffold different from other Pt-based complexes which target adenine [14]. At variance from cisplatin, AP-1 attacks DNA nucleobases in its non-aquated form due to the high activation energy of aquation. Therefore, it was shown recently that in bovine pancreatic ribonuclease (RNase A) and hen egg white lysozyme (HEWL) AP-1 may bind at histidine residues, through the the the Pt center coordination [10]. This is strikingly different from the protein binding profiles of cisplatin and carboplatin, which were found to preferentially target the Met side chains in RNase A [15]. This distinction is attributed to the As-Pt bond and to the trans effect of As on the reactivity of Pt center. In order to get a clearer picture of the selectivity of AP-1, our group has studied its reactions with the side chains of histidine, methionine, cysteine, and selenocysteine residues by means of DFT [16]. These protein side chains were modelled with their nucleophilic groups, (imidazole, CH_3S^-, HS^-, and HSe^- for His, Met, Cys, and Sec residues) attached to ethyl (Fig. 1). The computational investigation of thermodynamics revealed that the exchange reactions of AP-1 with only neutral histidine and anionic cysteine and selenocysteine are favourable. Indeed, the reaction energy values for Cys^- and Sec^- are -16.2 and -15.5 kcal/mol, whereas only slight exergonicity is observed for His, the reaction energy being -0.8 kcal/mol. On the other hand, the barriers within the range 15–19 kcal/mol are consistent with fast reactions.

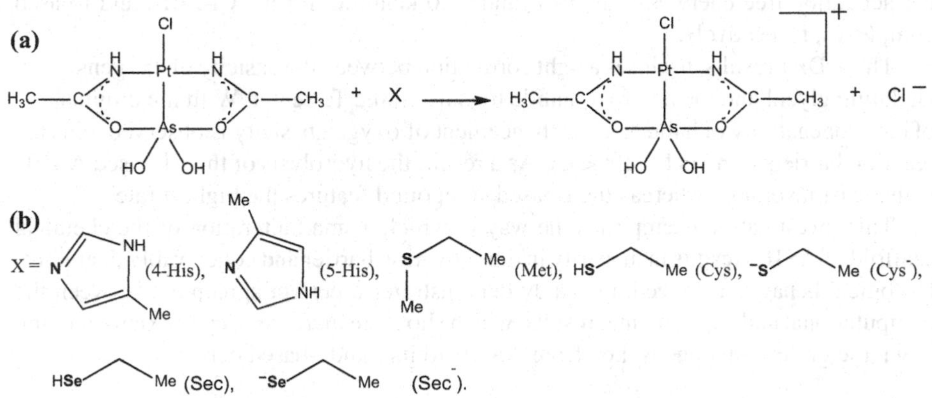

Fig. 1. Studied reaction of AP-1 (a) with the protein residue side chains (b).

3   Te-Based Antitumour Metallodrug: AS101

Not only transition metals but also most metalloids – chemical elements the properties of which include both features of metals and nonmetals – are xenobiotics that can be employed in the synthesis of complexes with extraordinary therapeutic activity [17]. Ammonium trichloro dioxoethylene-O,O' tellurate (AS101, Fig. 2) is the first Te-based complex that has entered the clinical phase of development, which demonstrates immunomodulatory activity and is used against a plethora of diseases, including chemotherapy-induced thrombocytopenia, acute myeloid leukemia, HIV, psoriasis, and dermatitis [18, 19]. AS101 targets thiol-containing biomolecules, for example, cysteine proteases [20]. This scaffold has also found an application in the development of organotelluranes via the substitution of its chloride ligands with various halides [21].

There is a general consensus that AS101 needs to be activated via the aquation in order to yield the species $TeOCl_3^-$ which in turn attacks the thiols [22]. This mechanism suggests the crucial role of the aquation in the mode of action of this metalloid-based drug. In order to study the effect of various ligands on the aquation of AS101, its bromido- and iodido-based derivatives were synthesized, and their reactivity was studied via a joint experimental-theoretical approach [23]. It was demonstrated that the aquation of AS101 became more likely with moving down in the halogens' group.

Hydrolysis of AS101 and its bromide and iodide derivatives includes two attacks of the water molecules which result in the glycol detachment and formation of $TeX_3(OH)_2$, with X = Cl, Br, or I (Fig. 2), followed by dehydration which yields the product TeX_3O^-. The DFT study has shown that the reaction free energies of the aquation were quite high, i.e., 13.0, 9.9, 9.4 kcal/mol for Cl, Br, and I, respectively. Nevertheless, the reaction rate determining barriers were 23.8, 21.9, and 20.5 kcal/mol for Cl, Br, and I, thus consistent with kinetically viable reactions. Taking into account the 20-fold excess of water in experimental conditions and assuming the second-order reaction (v = k[reactant][H_2O]), the activation barrier estimates were further refined by −1.7 kcal/mol, thus yielding the activation free energies 20.5, 19.7, and 17.0 kcal/mol for the Cl-, Br-, and I-based complexes, respectively.

These DFT results discloses a tight correlation between the basicity of oxygens of the chelating glycol and the nature of halide ligands on the Te center. With the diminishing of electronegativity of halides, the enhancement of oxygen basicity is observed, thus the reaction barriers trend is I < Br < Cl. As a result, the hydrolysis of the Cl-based AS101 is the least favorable, whereas the I-based compound features the highest rate.

This investigation exemplifies the way in which a small alteration of the chemical scaffold of AS101 results in disparity in the activation barrier and conceivably distinctive biological behaviour. Indeed, the study demonstrates a perfect agreement between the computational and experimental results, which show the increase of cytotoxicity moving down the group of halogens, i.e., from AS101 to its iodide-based derivative.

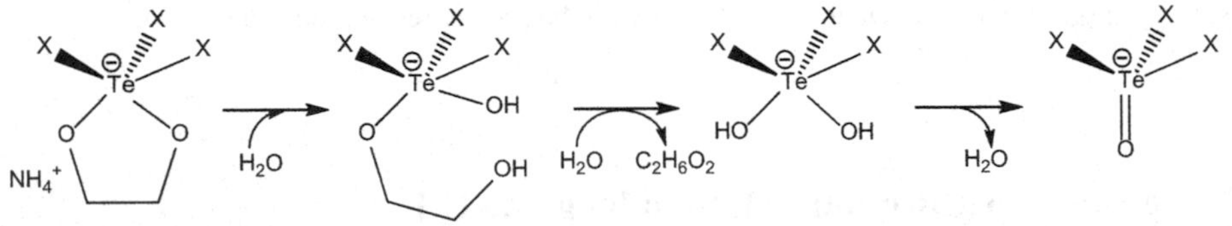

Fig. 2. Hydrolysis of AS101 (X = Cl) and its halide derivatives (X = Br, I).

4 Au-Based Metallodrug: Auranofin

Gold-based complexes have been employed in medicine for many centuries due to their unique antirheumatic, anticancer and anti-infective properties [24–26]. Recently, gold complexes have drawn the attention of medicinal chemists as perspective agents against bacterial infections in the framework of drug repurposing strategy [27]. Auranofin (1-thio-β-D-glucopyranosatotriethylphosphine gold-2,3,4,6-tetraacetate, AF, Fig. 3) is the most known Au(I)-based compound [28]. Its repurposing as an antibacterial drug eventuated exceptionally auspicious [29].

AF has been found out to be efficacious against Gram-positive strains, yet demonstrating inferior activity against Gram-negative bacteria [30, 31]. Nevertheless, the accurate understanding of its *modus operandi* on a biomolecular level is largely missing.

There is a general consensus that its gold center targets thiol- and selenol-containing proteins, thus impeding their crucial cellular functions [32]. Indeed, gold-based complexes were proven to proficiently inhibiting the thiol-redox balance via hampering the activity of thioredoxin reductase. Other presumed pharmacological targets of AF were DNA, procariotic cell wall, and bacterial protein biosynthesis machinery [32]. In 2009, on the basis of an investigation of AF activity against the oral bacterium *Treponema denticola,* it was proposed that AF inhibits the selenium metabolism, thus impeding the production of selenoproteins due to the subtracted accessibility of Se indispensable for the production of essential bacterial proteins [33]. Indeed, multiple computational studies also demonstrated the selectivity of AF toward selenocysteine [32]. On the other hand, the marginal inhibition of Gram-negative bacteria is probably caused by the impermeability of the outer membrane [34].

The general consensus is that the $[Au(PEt_3)]^+$ cation forming after the activation of auranofin, i.e. the detachment of thiosugar in the aqueous/biological milieu, is the true pharmacophore [35]. Taking into account this activation mechanism, the substitution of thiosugar, which is non-crucial from the pharmacological point of view, with other ligands is a viable approach to the synthesis of novel auranofin analogues.

In a recent study, an AF derivative was synthesized with the acetylcysteine ligand linearly attached to the gold(I) center (AF-AcCys, Fig. 3) and its antibacterial effects were investigated [36]. Biological experiments comparing the antibacterial activity of AF-AcCys and AF included the inhibition of *S. aureus,* in which both drugs demonstrated the same efficacy, and the application against *S. epidermidis,* in which AF-AcCys showed an abrupt activity drop. With the aim of elucidating the impact of the ligand replacement, we performed the DFT calculations of the energies required for the breaking of the bond between Au and its ligands in AF and AF-AcCys. It was shown that the Au-S bond in AF-AcCys (bond dissociation enthalpy of 51.8 kcal/mol) is slightly more stable in comparison with the Au-thiosugar bond in AF (49.8 kcal/mol). The Mulliken charges analysis corroborated that the stronger Au-S bond in Au-AcCys emerges from the greater electrostatic character of the bond as compared to the same bond in AF. Hence, calculations showed that the activation profiles of AF-thiosugar and AF-AcCys are similar, yielding comparable amounts of released active species $[AuP(Et)_3]^+$. Thus, the lower lipophilicity of AF-AcCys, rather than the slight difference in Au–S bond enthalpies, may better account for the diverse antimicrobic activity of this AF analogue, i.e., active on *S. aureus* and much less active on *S. epidermidis* [34].

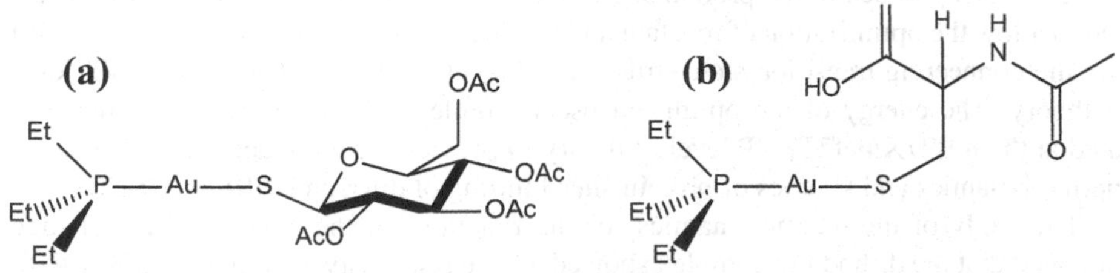

Fig. 3. Structures of auranofin (a) and its acetylcysteine analogue (b).

5 DiRh- and diRu-Based Paddlewheel Metallodrugs

Dirhodium and diruthenium complexes with the general formula $[M_2(O_2CR)_4]L_2$ (M = Rh, Ru; R = CH_3^-, $CH_3CH_2^-$, etc., L = solvent molecule or anionic ligand) have been long known in the field of metal-complex-mediated catalysis, nevertheless, their appreciable cytotoxicity drew the attention of the medicinal chemists [37, 38]. Despite similar structure incorporating four carboxylate bridging ligands positioned in a lentern-like fashion around the axial dimetallic center, the paddlewheel complexes based on Rh and Ru atoms demonstrate different patterns of reactivity.

The dirhodium paddlewheel complex is efficient versus various cancer lines, namely, Ehrlich-Lettre ascites carcinoma [38], L1210 tumors [39], sarcoma 180 [37], and P388 leukemia [37]. However, the basis of its biomolecular action remains largely undisclosed. It is assumed that it attacks amino acids [40, 41], peptides [42, 43], proteins [44, 45], single- and double-stranded DNA [37]. Rh compounds form adducts with proteins by means of direct coordination of metal center [46, 47] or non-covalent interaction between Rh ligands and protein residues, i.e., dative anchoring [45]. Experiments reveal that the $[Rh_2(\mu\text{-}O_2CCH_3)_4]$ complex binds selectively to side chains of protein residues Asn, Asp, His, Lys, as well as the C-terminal carboxylate [45, 48].

Ru-based complex $[Ru_2(\mu\text{-}O_2CCH_3)_4Cl]$ possesses a (II,III) mixed valence type defined by the availability of three uncoupled electrons [49]. While this compound exists in the form of polymer incorporating bimetallic members bridged by chlorides in solid state, the monomeric structure emerges in solution, yielding either $[Ru_2(\mu\text{-}O_2CCH_3)_4(H_2O)Cl]$ or $[Ru_2(\mu\text{-}O_2CCH_3)_4(H_2O)_2]^+$ complexes [50]. Experimental evidence on selectivity of these complexes in biological milieu is largely non-existent, except for its interactions with proteins [44, 45, 48]. The crystallographic data demonstrated the formation of adducts of these Ru-based complexes and aspartate side chains [51].

Several recent computational studies performed by our group investigated the selectivity of paddlewheel bimetallic complexes $[Rh_2(\mu\text{-}O_2CCH_3)_4(H_2O)_2]$, $[Ru_2(\mu\text{-}O_2CCH_3)_4(H_2O)Cl]$, and its hydroxo form $[Ru_2(\mu\text{-}O_2CCH_3)_4(OH)Cl]^-$ for binding to various protein residue side chains and protein terminals: Arg, Asn, Asp, Asp$^-$, C-term, C-term$^-$, Cys, Cys$^-$, His, Lys, Met, N-term, Sec, Sec$^-$ (paddlewheel complexes at Fig. 4, models of side chains Figs. 1 and 4) [52, 53]. DFT calculations were employed for studies of thermodynamics and kinetics of the ligand exchange reactions at axial sites of the paddlewheel scaffolds. In particular, the pseudo-molecular model was adopted to model the approach of the protein site to the diRu and diRh paddlewheel complexes and to allow the optimization of reactant and product adducts (RA and PA, respectively) and the connecting transition state structures (TS) at the PCM/ωB97X/def2SVP level of theory. The energy of the optimized pseudo-molecular models was then recalculated at the ωB97X/def2TZVP level of theory to provide for more accurate estimate of thermodynamics and kinetics of protein sites binding of diRu and diRh complexes.

The study of the thermodynamics for the reactions of the axial ligand exchange indicated that the dirhodium complex showed a little selectivity, reacting favorably with all the studied protein side chains. It was concluded that the main targets of this scaffold in physiological conditions are Asp$^-$, C-term$^-$, His, and Sec$^-$, based on the calculated Gibbs free energies and the experimental factors such as their most probable protonation states and likely degree of their solvent-accessibility. The same selectivity is demonstrated by the diruthenium complex in case when the axial water is substituted. Nevertheless, the exchange of Cl plays a major role at higher pH, when the basic side chains (Arg, Lys, His) are deprotonated, thus becoming the likely targets of the Ru(II)Ru(III) scaffold upon the chloride cleavage.

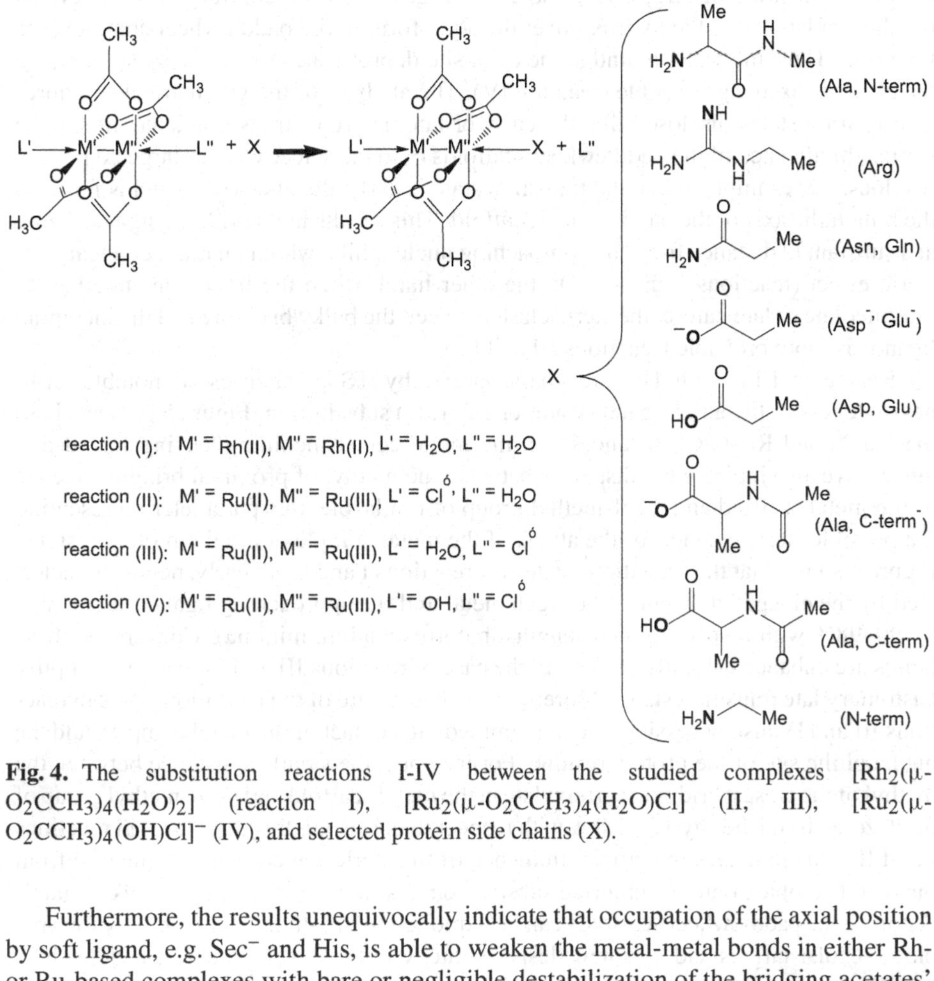

reaction (I):   M' = Rh(II), M" = Rh(II), L' = H_2O, L" = H_2O

reaction (II): M' = Ru(II), M" = Ru(III), L' = Cl⁻, L" = H_2O

reaction (III): M' = Ru(II), M" = Ru(III), L' = H_2O, L" = Cl⁻

reaction (IV): M' = Ru(II), M" = Ru(III), L' = OH⁻, L" = Cl⁻

Fig. 4. The substitution reactions I-IV between the studied complexes [Rh₂(μ-O₂CCH₃)₄(H₂O)₂] (reaction I), [Ru₂(μ-O₂CCH₃)₄(H₂O)Cl] (II, III), [Ru₂(μ-O₂CCH₃)₄(OH)Cl]⁻ (IV), and selected protein side chains (X).

Furthermore, the results unequivocally indicate that occupation of the axial position by soft ligand, e.g. Sec⁻ and His, is able to weaken the metal-metal bonds in either Rh- or Ru-based complexes with bare or negligible destabilization of the bridging acetates' coordination. Taking into account that the principal impact was observed in Ru-based paddlewheel complexes, it was observed that these scaffolds are more likely to yield two monometallic parts, therefore disrupting the μ-coordination of carboxylate ligands. Furthermore, the availability of several neighbour nucleophiles in the protein may produce a synergetic effect via the multiple binding to the metals – a sort of chelate-effect; such a concerted effort would weaken the stability greatly. Hence, there exists a robust thermodynamic stimulus to the bimetallic complex disruption if several coordination sites are situated in the same region of the biomolecular target, i.e. in proximity one from another, indicating that the preferred targets of these complexes are the tiled regions, whereas the effects of other parameters, such as the pH, the solvent's nature, the composition of the bulk, may be less significant.

Computational investigation of the reaction kinetics showed that the acidic milieu assists the reactions including the substitution of water at the axial position (reactions I and II), providing the thermodynamic control for these reactions, thus shifting the selectivity in favor of Arg, Cys$^-$, and Sec$^-$ (Fig. 4). On the contrary, at the elevated pH the availability of the hydroxo over the aquo form in the paddlewheel complexes is favoured. Thus, the water bound at the axial site deprotonates to a hydroxide, inducing the chloride exchange feasible (reaction IV). The analysis of the geometrical structures of transition states disclosed that the early or late nature of transition state affects the sterical hindrance of the paddlewheel scaffolds onto the selectivity for targeted protein residues. For example, when the transition state is early, the attacked ligand is far from the bimetallic axis of the paddlewheel scaffold. This results in its bridging ligands being at a substantial distance from the approaching nucleophile, which guarantees a marginal steric effect (reactions I and II). On the other hand, when the transition state has an intermediate or late nature, the steric clash between the bulky bridging and the incoming ligands is more probable (reactions III and IV).

Reactions I-IV with His are characterized by TS geometries of notable earliness/lateness of the axial ligand (water or chloride) substitution. Figure 5 presents both the Ru–N and Ru–O/Cl distances, i.e. the metal center-incoming/leaving ligand distances. We also indicate the distances between the methyl of proximal bridging acetate of the metal scaffold and the 4-methyl group of imidazole, this parameter representing the possible steric contact for the attack of the metal complex onto the protein residue. Figure 5 shows that the transitions states for reactions I and II are early, being characterized by the elongated distances between metal and the approaching ligand (augmented by 90–98% with respect to their lengths in corresponding minima). Conversely, these bonds are enhanced slightly (1–7%) in the case of reactions III and IV which exemplify customary late transition states. Moreover, the late nature of the transition states in reactions III and IV also necessitates a more immediate contact of the metal complex and the nucleophilic site of the protein residue. For instance, the smallest distance between the methyl of the closest bridging carboxylate in the metal scaffold and the 4-methyl group of imidazole diminishes by 1.7–2.0 Å with respect to corresponding structures in reactions I and II. This indicates the crucial influence of the steric impediment originating from the metal complex onto the chloride substitution. As shown recently [54], bulky ligands decoring the paddlewheel scaffolds can be exploited to fine-tune their reactivity towards biomolecular targets and as a new design strategy in the development of paddlewheel metallodrugs.

It is demonstrated that the reaction IV featuring the presence of hydroxo complex should be considered as the most advantageous. Indeed, the complex [Ru$_2$(µ-O$_2$CR)$_4$(OH)Cl]$^-$ reveals a substantial selectivity toward Lys, Cys$^-$, and Sec$^-$ and an intrinsic susceptibility to produce early TS structures in the reaction with the protein residue side chains caused by the steric obstruction originating from availability of bulky bridging ligands.

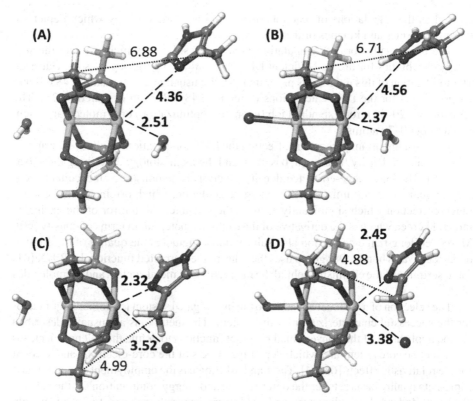

Fig. 5. Transition state geometries for the substitution reactions of the studied metal complexes with His: (A) $[Rh_2(\mu\text{-}O_2CCH_3)_4(H_2O)_2]$ (reaction I), (B, C) $[Ru_2(\mu\text{-}O_2CCH_3)_4(H_2O)Cl]$ (reactions II and III), (D) $[Ru_2(\mu\text{-}O_2CCH_3)_4(OH)Cl]^-$ (reaction IV). Dashed lines denote the distances between metals and approaching/leaving ligands, these values are **bold**. Dotted lines shows the distances between the 4-methyl group of imidazole and the closest C atom of the carboxylate methyl group. Colour scheme: Rh (cyan), Ru (faded orange), Cl (green), O (red), C (carbon), H (white). All distances in Å. (Color figure online)

The combination of these effects, i.e., (1) acidic pH, (2) accessibility of Lys, Cys⁻, and Sec⁻ residues, and (3) the presence of steric constraints from the equatorial ligands, may result in the augmented selectivity of $[Ru_2(\mu\text{-}O_2CR)_4(OH)Cl]^-$ for thioredoxin reductase overexpressed in cancer cells.

6 Computational Perspective

DFT is broadly utilized in the domain of bioinorganic and organometallic chemistry [55–57]. Its employment permits the mechanistic description of the processes important for understanding the *modus operandi* of metallodrugs, such as metallodrug activation, its selectivity toward various biomolecular targets. This is done by means of optimizations of geometries of constituents of the investigated system, i.e., metallodrug and its targets, as well as the calculations of reaction energy and activation energy which depict the thermodynamics and kinetics of the process.

There exist a plethora of computational chemistry software which provides the necessary capabilities for fast and efficient DFT calculations. Our group uses the Gaussian 16 modification of this ubiquitous program [58]. We usually use the memory 48 GB and 24 processors for the DFT calculations (%mem = 48 GB, %nprocshared = 24). The CPU time is 20–30 h for a standard job (geometry optimization) on a molecular system containing 60–70 atoms.

The most important parameters affecting the DFT computation results are the appropriate choice of density functional, basis set, and the methodology describing the solvation [59]. The long-range-corrected density functionals demonstrate an excellent accuracy in geometrical optimization and energy calculation, which originates in the long-range correction which significantly reduces the self-interaction error of the exchange integral kernel, which is the derivative of the exchange potential in terms of density [60]. Moreover, long-range correction also substantially augments the quality of description of van der Waals bonds. Our group uses the long-range-corrected functional ωB97X [61] for description of the chemistry behind the interactions of metal centers and biomolecules [62].

The selection of a basis set adequate to the investigated system is another major factor for the successful characterization of the system. The metal ions are usually described via the application of the conventional basis set functions to define the valence electrons and effective core potentials, which depict the effects of the core-electrons and account for the relativistic effects [63, 64]. The standard choice is the employment of double- and triple-zeta quality basis sets for the optimization and energy computation for the valence electrons. Indeed, bond distances and angles are generally reputed to be adequately described via the use of double-zeta basis sets. Therefore, the use of smaller basis sets in geometry optimization runs also improves the localization of minimum and saddle points of the potential energy surface, e.g. by easing the employment of optimization algorithms based on the analytical Hessian. On the other hand, the electronic energies of the optimized structures can be significantly improved by the use of larger basis sets allowing a more accurate description of the electron density distribution within the molecular system.

The studies performed in our group and presented in the present minireview allow us to draw important conclusions on the effects of various parameters for the computation. The investigations of the reactivity of arsenoplatin as well as the diRh- and diRu-paddlewheel complexes with the protein residue side chains underline the importance of adoption of the smaller models for the biomolecular systems. Without such a facilitation, it is impossible to portray the biomolecular system usually consisting of bulky constituents. The simplified models of the protein side chains that we use are limited by size, yet they are an optimum choice for including the electronic and steric effects originating from the nucleophilic part of the protein side chains.

The investigation of the hydrolysis of the Te-based scaffold AS101 demonstrates the importance of the detailed mechanistic understanding of the very first reaction many metallodrugs may undergo in the physiological milieu, i.e., the hydrolytic activation. This study has shown that alteration of Cl ligands in the native AS101 scaffold to the halides Br and I substantially modifies the behaviours of the drug by augmenting its activation rate. This is an excellent example of how the theoretical approach can interpret the impact of metal ligands changes to the speed of its transformation in the active form, thus affecting its pharmacochemical profile.

The DFT analysis of the strengths of the metal ligand bonds in auranofin and its acetylcysteine-based derivative has shown that the particular selection of the softer ligands for Au, a transition metal center of an intermediate yet slightly soft nature, permits to stabilize the bond to the point that it changes biological activity of the metal scaffold.

These theoretical data may be particularly useful in the design of AF analogues that need to be promptly activated in the site of administration.

The DFT-optimized geometrical structures of transition states in the diRh- and diRu-paddlewheel complexes demonstrated the effects of the bulky equatorial ligands in these lantern-shaped complexes on their selectivity. It was shown that the presence of the late transition state results into the steric clash between the bridging ligands and the entering nucleophile, thus increasing the barrier for this type of reactions, resulting into unfavourable kinetics. Moreover, it was shown that the acidic pH leads to the deprotonation of the axially bound water in the Ru-based complex, thus substantially strengthening its bond to the bimetallic unit and making the cleavage of Cl more favourable. It yields a better selectivity toward the thiols and selenols, typical targets for anticancer drugs.

7 Conclusions

Metallodrugs constitute an invaluable reserve of novel therapeutical agents against cancer, parasitic, viral, and bacterial infections. Their capability to produce various geometries originates in the unique features of transition metals, i.e., ability to assume a wide range of oxidation states and various electronic configurations. Moreover, the addition of electron-donating/withdrawing ligands allows to modulate the electrophilicity of metal centers, whereas the incorporation of bulky or electrically charged ligands allows the fine-tuning of their steric features and the strength of the metal-ligand bonds. These modifications permit to calibrate the selectivity of metal centers which tend to exhibit a substantial promiscuity versus various biological nucleophiles.

This minireview showcases several computational studies on the reactivity of Pt-, Te-, Au-, Rh-, Ru-based metallodrugs in the biological milieu, performed by our group. This short account emphasizes particularly the effects of the structure of these metal complexes and their environment. Indeed, all of the described investigations serve as the valuable examples of the consequences of the particular geometrical structure and specific choice of the ligands onto the selectivity of metal scaffold. On the other hand, the studies on the hydrolytic activation of AS101 and the reactivity of the paddlewheel complexes in the acidic pH corroborate the crucial effects of the milieu in which the metallodrug is administered onto its reactivity.

It is shown that the DFT computations permit to accurately characterize the behavior of metallodrug in physiological conditions. The computational description of the *modus operandi* of a metal complex is a valuable tool *per se* or as a part of a joint experimental-theoretical approach. It allows to carefully define its activation mechanism, its selectivity toward various biomolecular targets, and the possible effects of modification of its structure on its behavior. That is why the *in silico* studies are an essential tool in the apparatus of modern bioinorganic chemistry.

References

1. Mjos, K.D., Orvig, C.: Metallodrugs in medicinal inorganic chemistry. Chem. Rev. **114**(8), 4540–4563 (2014). https://doi.org/10.1021/cr400460s
2. Anthony, E.J., Bolitho, E.M., Bridgewater, H.E., Carter, O.W., Donnelly, J.M., Imberti, C., et al.: Metallodrugs are unique: opportunities and challenges of discovery and development. Chem. Sci. **11**(48), 12888–12917 (2020). https://doi.org/10.1039/D0SC04082G
3. Yousuf, I., Bashir, M., Arjmand, F., Tabassum, S.: Advancement of metal compounds as therapeutic and diagnostic metallodrugs: current frontiers and future perspectives. Coord. Chem. Rev. **445**, 214104 (2021). https://doi.org/10.1016/j.ccr.2021.214104
4. Zaki, M., Arjmand, F., Tabassum, S.: Current and future potential of metallo drugs: revisiting DNA-binding of metal containing molecules and their diverse mechanism of action. Inorg. Chim. Acta **444**, 1–22 (2016). https://doi.org/10.1016/j.ica.2016.01.006
5. Navarro, M., Gabbiani, C., Messori, L., Gambino, D.: Metal-based drugs for malaria, trypanosomiasis and leishmaniasis: recent achievements and perspectives. Drug Discov. Today **15**(23–24), 1070–1078 (2010). https://doi.org/10.1016/j.drudis.2010.10.005
6. Riddell, I., Lippard, S.J., Brabec, V., Kasparkova, J., Menon, V., Farrell, N.P., et al.: Metallodrugs: development and action of anticancer agents, vol. 18. Walter de Gruyter GmbH & Co KG, Wustermark (2018)
7. Cirri, D., Marzo, T., Tolbatov, I., Marrone, A., Saladini, F., Vicenti, I., et al.: In vitro anti-SARS-CoV-2 activity of selected metal compounds and potential molecular basis for their actions based on computational study. Biomolecules **11**(12), 1858 (2021). https://doi.org/10.3390/biom11121858
8. Tolbatov, I., Marrone, A., Paciotti, R., Re, N., Coletti, C.: Multilayered modelling of the metallation of biological targets. In: Gervasi, O., et al. (eds.) ICCSA 2021. LNCS, vol. 12958, pp. 398–412. Springer, Cham (2021). https://doi.org/10.1007/978-3-030-87016-4_30
9. Lee, R.F., Menin, L., Patiny, L., Ortiz, D., Dyson, P.J.: Versatile tool for the analysis of metal–protein interactions reveals the promiscuity of metallodrug–protein interactions. Anal. Chem. **89**(22), 11985–11989 (2017). https://doi.org/10.1021/acs.analchem.7b02211
10. Miodragović, Đ., et al.: Arsenoplatin-1 is a dual pharmacophore anticancer agent. J. Am. Chem. Soc. **141**(16), 6453–6457 (2019). https://doi.org/10.1021/jacs.8b13681
11. Miodragović, Đ.U., Quentzel, J.A., Kurutz, J.W., Stern, C.L., Ahn, R.W., Kandela, I., et al.: Robust structure and reactivity of aqueous arsenous acid–platinum (II) anticancer complexes. Angew. Chem. Int. Ed. **52**(41), 10749–10752 (2013). https://doi.org/10.1002/anie.201303251
12. Miodragović, Đ., Swindell, E.P., Waxali, Z.S., Bogachkov, A., O'Halloran, T.V.: Beyond cisplatin: Combination therapy with arsenic trioxide. Inorg. Chim. Acta 119030 (2019). https://doi.org/10.1016/j.ica.2019.119030
13. Parise, A., Russo, N., Marino, T.: The platination mechanism of RNase a by arsenoplatin: Insight from the theoretical study. Inorg. Chem. Front. **8**(7), 1795–1803 (2021). https://doi.org/10.1039/d0qi01165g
14. Marino, T., Parise, A., Russo, N.: The role of arsenic in the hydrolysis and DNA metalation processes in an arsenous acid–platinum (II) anticancer complex. Phys. Chem. Chem. Phys. **19**(2), 1328–1334 (2017). https://doi.org/10.1039/c6cp06179f
15. Messori, L., Merlino, A.: Cisplatin binding to proteins: molecular structure of the ribonuclease a adduct. Inorg. Chem. **53**(8), 3929–3931 (2014). https://doi.org/10.1021/ic500360f

16. Tolbatov, I., Cirri, D., Tarchi, M., Marzo, T., Coletti, C., Marrone, A., et al.: Reactions of arsenoplatin-1 with protein targets: a combined experimental and theoretical study. Inorg. Chem. **61**(7), 3240–3248 (2022). https://doi.org/10.1021/acs.inorgchem.1c03732
17. Sekhon, B.S.: Metalloid compounds as drugs. Res. Pharm. Sci. **8**, 145–158 (2013)
18. Halpert, G., Sredni, B.: The effect of the novel tellurium compound AS101 on autoimmune diseases. Autoimmun. Rev. **13**(12), 1230–1235 (2014). https://doi.org/10.1016/j.autrev.2014. 08.003
19. Ling, D., Liu, B., Jawad, S., Thompson, I.A., Nagineni, C.N., Dailey, J., et al.: The tellurium redox immunomodulating compound AS101 inhibits IL-1β-activated inflammation in the human retinal pigment epithelium. Br. J. Ophthalmol. **97**, 934–938 (2013). https://doi.org/10. 1136/bjophthalmol-2012-301962
20. Albeck, A., Weitman, H., Sredni, B., Albeck, M.: Tellurium compounds: selective inhibition of cysteine proteases and model reaction with thiols. Inorg. Chem. **37**, 1704–1712 (1998). https://doi.org/10.1021/IC971456T
21. Princival, C.R., Archilha, M.V.L.R., Dos Santos, A.A., Franco, M.P., Braga, A.A.C., Rodrigues-Oliveira, A.F., et al.: Stability study of hypervalent tellurium compounds in aqueous solutions. ACS Omega **2**, 4431–4439 (2017). https://doi.org/10.1021/acsomega.7b0 0628
22. Layani-Bazar, A., Skornick, I., Berrebi, A., Pauker, M.H., Noy, E., Silberman, A., et al.: Redox modulation of adjacent thiols in vla-4 by as101 converts myeloid leukemia cells from a drug-resistant to drug-sensitive state. Cancer Res. **74**, 3092–3103 (2014). https://doi.org/ 10.1158/0008-5472.can-13-2159
23. Chiaverini, L., Cirri, D., Tolbatov, I., Corsi, F., Piano, I., Marrone, A., et al.: Medicinal hypervalent tellurium prodrugs bearing different ligands: a comparative study of the chemical profiles of AS101 and its halido replaced analogues. Int. J. Mol. Sci. **23**(14), 7505 (2022). https://doi.org/10.3390/ijms23147505
24. Messori, L., Marcon, G.: Gold complexes in the treatment of rheumatoid arthritis. Met. Ions Biol. Syst. **41**, 279–304 (2004)
25. Navarro, M.: Gold complexes as potential anti-parasitic agents. Coord. Chem. Rev. **253**(11–12), 1619–1626 (2009). https://doi.org/10.1016/j.ccr.2008.12.003
26. Casini, A., Sun, R.W.Y., Ott, I.: Medicinal chemistry of gold anticancer metallodrugs. In: Metallo-Drugs: Development and Action of Anticancer Agents, vol. 18, pp. 199–217 (2018)
27. Tolbatov, I., Marrone, A.: Auranofin targeting the NDM-1 beta-lactamase: computational insights into the electronic configuration and quasi-tetrahedral coordination of gold ions. Pharmaceutics **15**(3), 985 (2023). https://doi.org/10.3390/pharmaceutics15030985
28. Yamashita, M.: Auranofin: Past to Present, and repurposing. Int. Immunopharmacol. **101**, 108272 (2021). https://doi.org/10.1016/j.intimp.2021.108272
29. Roder, C., Thomson, M.J.: Auranofin: repurposing an old drug for a golden new age. Drugs R&D **15**(1), 13–20 (2015). https://doi.org/10.1007/s40268-015-0083-y
30. Thangamani, S., Mohammad, H., Abushahba, M.F.N., Sobreira, T.J.P., Hedrick, V.E., Paul, L.N., et al.: Antibacterial activity and mechanism of action of auranofin against multi-drug resistant bacterial pathogens. Sci. Rep. **6**, 22571 (2016). https://doi.org/10.1038/srep22571
31. Thangamani, S., Mohammad, H., Abushahba, M.F.N., Sobreira, T.J.P., Seleem, M.N.: Repurposing auranofin for the treatment of cutaneous staphylococcal infections. Int. J. Antimicrob. Agents **47**, 195–201 (2016). https://doi.org/10.1016/j.ijantimicag.2015.12.016
32. Tolbatov, I., Marrone, A., Coletti, C., Re, N.: Computational studies of Au (I) and Au (III) anticancer metallodrugs: a survey. Molecules **26**(24), 7600 (2021). https://doi.org/10.3390/ molecules26247600
33. Jackson-Rosario, S., Self, W.T.: Inhibition of selenium metabolism in the oral pathogen treponema denticola. J. Bacteriol. **191**, 4035–4040 (2009). https://doi.org/10.1128/jb.001 64-09

34. Marzo, T., Cirri, D., Pollini, S., Prato, M., Fallani, S., Cassetta, M.I., et al.: Auranofin and its analogues show potent antimicrobial activity against multidrug-resistant pathogens: structure-activity relationships. ChemMedChem **13**, 2448–2454 (2018). https://doi.org/10.1002/cmdc.201800498
35. Gamberi, T., Pratesi, A., Messori, L., Massai, L.: Proteomics as a tool to disclose the cellular and molecular mechanisms of selected anticancer gold compounds. Coord. Chem. Rev. **438**, 213905 (2021). https://doi.org/10.1016/j.ccr.2021.213905
36. Chiaverini, L., Pratesi, A., Cirri, D., Nardinocchi, A., Tolbatov, I., Marrone, A., et al.: Anti-staphylococcal activity of the auranofin analogue bearing acetylcysteine in place of the thio-sugar: an experimental and theoretical investigation. Molecules **27**(8), 2578 (2022). https://doi.org/10.3390/molecules27082578
37. Katsaros, N., Anagnostopoulou, A.: Rhodium and its compounds as potential agents in cancer treatment. Crit. Rev. Oncol. Hematol. **42**(3), 297–308 (2002). https://doi.org/10.1016/s1040-8428(01)00222-0
38. Nothenberg, M.S., Zyngier, S.B., Giesbrecht, A.M., Gambardella, M.T.P., Santos, R.H.A., Kimura, E., et al.: Biological activity and crystallographic study of a rhodium propionate-metronidazole adduct. J. Braz. Chem. Soc. **5**(1), 23–29 (1994)
39. Howard, R.A., Kimball, A.P., Bear, J.L.: Mechanism of action of tetra-μ-carboxylatodirhodium (II) in L1210 tumor suspension culture. Cancer Res. **39**(7.1), 2568–2573 (1979)
40. Enriquez Garcia, A., Jalilehvand, F., Niksirat, P.: Reactions of $Rh_2(CH_3COO)_4$ with thiols and thiolates: a structural study. J. Synchrotron Radiat. **26**(2), 450–461 (2019). https://doi.org/10.1107/s160057751900033x
41. Enriquez Garcia, A., Jalilehvand, F., Niksirat, P., Gelfand, B.S.: Methionine binding to dirhodium (II) tetraacetate. Inorg. Chem. **57**(20), 12787–12799 (2018). https://doi.org/10.1021/acs.inorgchem.8b01979
42. Popp, B.V., Chen, Z., Ball, Z.T.: Sequence-specific inhibition of a designed metallopeptide catalyst. Chem. Comm. **48**(60), 7492–7494 (2012). https://doi.org/10.1039/c2cc33808d
43. Zaykov, A.N., Ball, Z.T.: A general synthesis of dirhodium metallopeptides as MDM2 ligands. Chem. Comm. **47**(39), 10927–10929 (2011). https://doi.org/10.1039/c1cc13169a
44. Loreto, D., Esposito, A., Demitri, N., Guaragna, A., Merlino, A.: Digging into protein met-alation differences triggered by fluorine containing-dirhodium tetracarboxylate analogues. Dalton Trans. **51**(18), 7294–7304 (2022). https://doi.org/10.1039/D2DT00873D
45. Loreto, D., Merlino, A.: The interaction of rhodium compounds with proteins: a structural overview. Coord. Chem. Rev. **442**, 213999 (2021). https://doi.org/10.1016/j.ccr.2021.213999
46. Laureanti, J.A., Buchko, G.W., Katipamula, S., Su, Q., Linehan, J.C., Zadvornyy, O.A., et al.: Protein scaffold activates catalytic CO2 hydrogenation by a rhodium bis (diphosphine) complex. ACS Catal. **9**(1), 620–625 (2018). https://doi.org/10.1021/acscatal.8b02615
47. Panella, L., Broos, J., Jin, J., Fraaije, M.W., Janssen, D.B., Jeronimus-Stratingh, M., et al.: Merging homogeneous catalysis with biocatalysis; papain as hydrogenation catalyst. Chem. Comm. **45**, 5656–5658 (2005). https://doi.org/10.1039/B512138H
48. Ferraro, G., Pratesi, A., Messori, L., Merlino, A.: Protein interactions of dirhodium tetraac-etate: a structural study. Dalton Trans. **49**(8), 2412–2416 (2020). https://doi.org/10.1039/C9DT04819G
49. Aquino, M.A.: Recent developments in the synthesis and properties of diruthenium tetracar-boxylates. Coord. Chem. Rev. **248**(11–12), 1025–1045 (2004). https://doi.org/10.1016/j.ccr.2004.06.016
50. Santos, R.L., van Eldik, R., de Oliveira Silva, D.: Thermodynamics of axial substitution and kinetics of reactions with amino acids for the paddlewheel complex tetrakis (acetato) chloridodiruthenium (II, III). Inorg. Chem. **51**(12), 6615–6625 (2012). https://doi.org/10.1021/ic300168t

51. Messori, L., Marzo, T., Sanches, R.N.F., de Oliveira Silva, D., Merlino, A.: Unusual structural features in the lysozyme derivative of the tetrakis (acetato) chloridodiruthenium (II, III) complex. Angew. Chem. Int. Ed. 53(24), 6172–6175 (2014). doi: https://doi.org/10.1002/anie.201403337

52. Tolbatov, I., Marrone, A.: Reaction of dirhodium and diruthenium paddlewheel tetraacetate complexes with nucleophilic protein sites: a computational study. Inorg. Chim. Acta 530, 120684 (2021). https://doi.org/10.1016/j.ica.2021.120684

53. Tolbatov, I., Marrone, A.: Kinetics of reactions of dirhodium and diruthenium paddlewheel tetraacetate complexes with nucleophilic protein sites: computational insights. Inorg. Chem. 61(41), 16421–16429 (2022). https://doi.org/10.1021/acs.inorgchem.2c02516

54. Tolbatov, I., Barresi, E., Taliani, S., La Mendola, D., Marzo, T., Marrone, A.: Diruthenium (II, III) paddlewheel complexes: effects of bridging and axial ligands on anticancer properties. Inorg. Chem. Front. 10(8), 2226–2238 (2023). https://doi.org/10.1039/D3QI00157A

55. Tolbatov, I., Storchi, L., Marrone, A.: Structural reshaping of the zinc-finger domain of the SARS-CoV-2 nsp13 protein using bismuth (III) ions: a multilevel computational study. Inorg. Chem. 61(39), 15664–15677 (2022). https://doi.org/10.1021/acs.inorgchem.2c02685

56. Ritacco, I., Russo, N., Sicilia, E.: DFT investigation of the mechanism of action of organoiridium (III) complexes as anticancer agents. Inorg. Chem. 54(22), 10801–10810 (2015). https://doi.org/10.1021/acs.inorgchem.5b01832

57. Todisco, S., Latronico, M., Gallo, V., Re, N., Marrone, A., Tolbatov, I., et al.: Double addition of phenylacetylene onto the mixed bridge phosphinito–phosphanido Pt (I) complex [(PHCy$_2$)Pt(μ-PCy$_2$){κ^2P, O-μ-P(O)Cy$_2$}Pt(PHCy$_2$)](Pt–Pt). Dalton Trans. 49(20), 6776–6789 (2020). https://doi.org/10.1039/D0DT00923G

58. Frisch, M.J., Trucks, G.W., Schlegel, H.B., Scuseria, G.E., Robb, M.A., Cheeseman, J.R., et al.: Gaussian 16 Revision C. Gaussian Inc.m Wallingford, CT, USA (2016)

59. Tolbatov, I., Marrone, A.: Computational strategies to model the interaction and the reactivity of biologically-relevant transition metal complexes. Inorg. Chim. Acta 530, 120686 (2022). https://doi.org/10.1016/j.ica.2021.120686

60. Tsuneda, T., Hirao, K.: Long-range correction for density functional theory. Wiley Interdiscip. Rev. Comput. Mol. Sci. 4(4), 375–390 (2014). https://doi.org/10.1002/wcms.1178

61. Chai, J.D., Head-Gordon, M.: Long-range corrected hybrid density functionals with damped atom–atom dispersion corrections. Phys. Chem. Chem. Phys. 10(44), 6615–6620 (2008). https://doi.org/10.1039/B810189B

62. Tolbatov, I., Marrone, A.: Reactivity of N-heterocyclic carbene half-sandwich Ru-, Os-, Rh-, and Ir-based complexes with cysteine and selenocysteine: a computational study. Inorg. Chem. 61(1), 746–754 (2021). https://doi.org/10.1021/acs.inorgchem.1c03608

63. Dolg, M.: Effective core potentials. In: Grotendorst, J. (Ed.), Modern Methods and Algorithms of Quantum Chemistry, Second Edition, John von Neumann Institute for Computing, Julich, NIC Series, Vol. 3, pp. 507–540 (2000)

64. Paciotti, R., Tolbatov, I., Marrone, A., Storchi, L., Re, N., Coletti, C.: Computational investigations of bioinorganic complexes: the case of calcium, gold and platinum ions. In: AIP Conference Proceedings, vol. 2186, no. 1, pp. 030011:1–4. AIP Publishing LLC (2019). https://doi.org/10.1063/1.5137922

Formulations for the Split Delivery Capacitated Profitable Tour Problem

Marvin Caspar$^{(\boxtimes)}$ (ID), Daniel Schermer (ID), and Oliver Wendt (ID)

Business Information Systems and Operations Research (BISOR), University of
Kaiserslautern-Landau, Postfach 3049, 67653 Kaiserslautern, Germany
{marvin.caspar,daniel.schermer,wendt}@wiwi.uni-kl.de
https://wiwi.rptu.de/fgs/bisor

Abstract. In this paper, we study the *Split Delivery Capacitated Profitable Tour Problem* (SDCPTP) that extends the profitable tour problem by a fleet of vehicles and the possibility of split deliveries. In the SDCPTP, the objective is to select a subset of requests and find for each vehicle a feasible tour such that the prize collected by fulfilling the selected requests net of the cost of delivery is maximized. We propose three mixed-integer linear programming formulations for modeling the SDCPTP. These formulations differ primarily in their treatment of the subtour elimination constraints within the branch-and-cut algorithm. The first of these formulations is applicable to the more general asymmetric case, whereas the other two are computationally more efficient in presence of symmetric variants of the problem. Using benchmark instances from the literature, we provide a detailed numerical study that demonstrates the effectiveness of a state-of-the-art solver in tackling these models. For managerial insights, we perform a sensitivity analysis on the SDCPTP with respect to the number of vehicles and requests as well as the benefits of enabling split delivery.

Keywords: Mixed-Integer Linear Programming · Branch-and-Cut Algorithm · Capacitated Profitable Tour Problem · Split Delivery

1 Introduction

The *Traveling Salesman Problem* (TSP) is one of the most well-known combinatorial optimization problems that has driven the advancement of branch-and-cut algorithms for several decades [15]. Many practical problems can be expressed in terms of a TSP, and therefore it comes as no surprise that many variants of the problem exist. For example, in the context of scheduling and routing, an important generalization of the problem relaxes the standard assumption that every vertex must be visited exactly once (see, e. g., [8,16,18]). Instead, the vertices are viewed as requests that yield a *prize* (i. e., a reward) that is gained for fulfilling a given demand; and it falls to the decision maker to determine which requests to accept and in which order to process them. From the standpoint of operations

© The Author(s), under exclusive license to Springer Nature Switzerland AG 2023
O. Gervasi et al. (Eds.): ICCSA 2023, LNCS 13956, pp. 82–98, 2023.
https://doi.org/10.1007/978-3-031-36805-9_6

research, this trade-off is known in the literature as *Traveling Salesman Problem with Profits* (TSPPs) (refer to [18]) or, in the case of multiple vehicles, *Vehicle Routing Problem with Profits* (VRPPs) (refer to [27]). In VRPPs, a standard assumption is that each demand must be fulfilled by at most one vehicle. However, especially in the fields of transportation and logistics, where demands may exceed the capacity of a single vehicle, there are many applications in which it becomes beneficial or even necessary to fulfill a demand by more than one vehicle. Such applications include, e. g., the distribution of livestock feed [24], waste management [7], routing helicopters for crew exchanges [25], or watering services [30]. In the literature, the assumption that a demand may be fulfilled by more than one vehicle is known as *split delivery*, which can make logistics more efficient and therefore also more sustainable. However, as addressed in [5] (and as we will see in more detail in Sect. 2), there is a scientific gap concerning the investigation of split delivery in the context of VRPPs.

In order to address this scientific gap, we study the *Split Delivery Capacitated Profitable Tour Problem* (SDCPTP), which is a variant of VRPPs (see [27]). In the SDCPTP, we are given a fleet of homogenous vehicles with a limited capacity and a set of requests. Each request is associated with a prize that is gained only if the corresponding demand is fully satisfied. The objective is to select a subset of requests and find a feasible tour for each vehicle (that visits some of the selected requests exactly once and then returns to the depot) such that the prize collected by fulfilling these requests net of the cost of delivery is maximized. By the nature of split delivery, accepted requests may be fulfilled jointly, i. e., by more than one vehicle.

In our paper, we make the following contributions. After a brief literature review, we provide three *Mixed-Integer Linear Programming* (MILP) formulations for the SDCPTP. These formulations differ primarily in their treatment of the subtour elimination constraints within the branch-and-cut algorithm. In particular, whereas the first of these formulations is applicable to the more general asymmetric case, the other two are computationally more efficient in presence of symmetric variants of the problem, which are commonly studied in the literature. Using these formulations, we provide a detailed numerical study that demonstrates the effectiveness of a state-of-the-art solver in tackling these models. For managerial insights, we perform a sensitivity analysis on the SDCPTP with respect to the number of vehicles and requests as well as the benefits of enabling split delivery.

The remainder of this paper is organized as follows. We begin with a brief overview of the related literature in Sect. 2. In particular, we discuss the foundations of the SDCPTP in more detail, i. e., the *Profitable Tour Problem* (PTP) and split delivery in the context of routing problems. Afterwards, in Sect. 3, we begin with a concise problem definition of the SDCPTP and provide the MILP formulations. In Sect. 4 we discuss the computational experiments and their numerical results. Finally, with Sect. 5, we draw concluding remarks on our work and discuss further research implications.

2   Related Literature

In what follows, we briefly address PTP problems in Sect. 2.1. Afterwards, in Sect. 2.2, we outline relevant works of routing problems with split delivery.

2.1   Profitable Tour Problems

Routing problems with profits are a family of problems in which each request is associated with a prize (i. e., a reward) that is gained only if the demand that is associated with that request is satisfied; and the arcs, that connect accepted requests in a feasible tour, are associated with a cost (see [18]). Within this family of problems, the essential characteristic is that it becomes necessary to trade off the cumulative prize against the cost that is incurred by traversing arcs. In general, we can differentiate three main variants of TSPPs:

- In the *Prize-Collecting TSP* (see [8,16]) there is a lower bound on the cumulative prize that must be collected. The objective then becomes to minimize the total travel costs while respecting the prize limit.
- In contrast, in the *Orienteering Problem* (refer to [28]) there is an upper bound on the costs (e. g., the length of the tour). Here, the objective is to maximize the collected prize by a tour that does not exceed the cost limit.
- In the *Profitable Tour Problem* (PTP) there is neither a lower bound on the total prize nor an upper bound on the costs. Instead, the objective consists in maximizing the profit, i. e., the cumulative prize net of the costs (see [16]).

For the purpose of this paper, we restrict ourselves to the PTP in what follows, as the inherent trade-off in that problem is of particular interest for a variety of routing and scheduling problems (see [27] and references therein). Furthermore, the PTP is also worthwhile because it relates to fundamental problems such as the elementary shortest path problem with resource constraints (refer to [22]). While most existing literature on the PTP does not consider a fleet of vehicles (for further references, see [27]), generalizations of the problem have become increasingly common in recent years.

In particular, the *Capacitated* PTP (CPTP) was introduced in [6] as a generalization of the PTP, in which we are given a capacitated fleet of vehicles. The authors introduced a branch-and-price algorithm, a variable neighborhood search algorithm, and two tabu search algorithms for solving the problem and their computational experiments show that the heuristic procedures often find the same optimal solutions as the exact method. Later, in [4], an improved branch-and-price algorithm is proposed that includes a modified branching rule and further acceleration techniques, to speed up the pricing problem. This enabled the authors to find optimal solutions to several benchmark instances that were previously unsolved. Apart from these fundamental works, there exist various extensions to the CPTP such as the introduction of time windows [26] or electric vehicles [13]. The latter variant has also been refined through the inclusion of multi-periods with recharge services and mandatory stops [14].

Further variants of the PTP include time-dependent travel times and resource constraints [23] or stochastic variants of the problem [1], in which accepted requests show up only with a given probability during the execution of the tour.

2.2   Split Delivery in Routing Problems

The assumption that a request may be fulfilled by more than one vehicle is known as *Split Delivery* (SD). The *Split Delivery Vehicle Routing Problem* (SDVRP) was first introduced by [17] and has been extensively analyzed in the last three decades. In particular, several worst-case analyses and empirical studies have shown that considerable savings can occur when split delivery is allowed [27]. Furthermore, several exact and heuristic algorithms have been proposed to effectively solve the SDVRP and its variants (refer to [27] and references therein). Such variants include, e. g., the inclusion of time windows [19], minimum delivery amounts [20], or three-dimensional loading constraints [11].

Naturally, SD may also be beneficial in the context of routing problems with profits, as this allows for more flexibility when it comes to fulfilling demands. To the best of our knowledge, [2, 3, 5, 29] are the only contributions that consider SD within routing problems with profits. In [3] the authors investigate the *Split Delivery Capacitated Team Orienteering Problem* (SDCTOP) with the option of *Incomplete Service* (IS), i. e., the assumption that requests may only be partially served. Apart from theoretical contributions that analyze the maximum possible profit, the authors also propose a branch-and-price approach as well as a variable neighborhood search and tabu search heuristic and verify their effectiveness on benchmark instances for the SDCTOP and SDCTOP-IS. A detailed study in [2] revealed that the combination of IS and SD does not significantly increase the profits in the CTOP compared to only allowing either IS or SD. Furthermore, the experiments show that the largest increase in profits in the SDCTOP and the SDCTOP-IS is observed when the average demand exceeds half the vehicle capacity. In [5], a branch-and-price algorithm and a hybrid heuristic based on tabu search are used to solve four different sets of instances for the CTOP and SDCTOP. It was shown that, depending on the instances, the hybrid heuristic could be significantly more effective than branch-and-price in terms of computation time. In [29], the *SDCTOP with Minimum Delivery Amounts* (SDCTOP-MDA) is discussed, and in a worst-case analysis correlations between the CTOP and the SDCTOP-MDA are analyzed.

In general, these works demonstrate that the option of SD has been intensively studied in the context of team orienteering problems. However, to the best of our knowledge and as stated in [5], there is no literature on the CPTP that investigates SD. This provides further motivation for the SDCPTP presented in the following section.

3   Problem Definition and Mathematical Programming Formulations

In this section, we begin with a concise problem definition of the SDCPTP in Sect. 3.1. Afterwards, in Sect. 3.2, we present three mathematical programming formulations for the problem.

3.1   Problem Definition

Let $G(V, A)$ be a complete graph, where $V = \{0, 1, \ldots, |N|\}$ is the set of vertices and $A = \{(i, j) \mid i, j \in V(i \neq j)\}$ is the set of arcs. The vertex $0 \in V$ represents the depot and $N = \{1, \ldots, |N|\} = V \setminus \{0\}$ represents a set of requests. Each request $i \in N$ is associated with a prize $p_i \in \mathbb{R}_{>0}$ (i.e., a reward) that is only obtained if the corresponding demand $d_i \in \mathbb{N}$ is completely satisfied. A non-negative travel cost $c_{i,j}$ is associated with each arc $(i, j) \in A$ and we assume that the triangle inequality holds for these values. We say that the problem is symmetric only if $c_{i,j} = c_{j,i}$ holds for all $(i, j) \in A$. In the SDCPTP, we are given a fleet K of homogenous vehicles, each with a maximum capacity C. The tour of each vehicle $k \in K$ starts and ends at the depot and, in contrast to the CPTP, each request $i \in N$ may be served by more than one vehicle. The objective is to find feasible tours for the fleet such that the cumulative prize net of the cost of delivery is maximized. Figure 1 illustrates the problem.

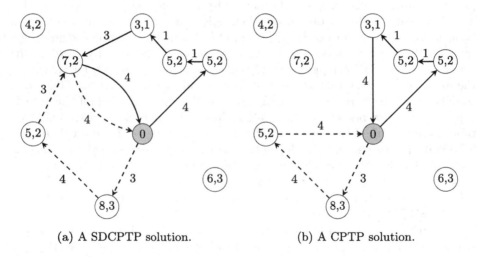

(a) A SDCPTP solution.   (b) A CPTP solution.

Fig. 1. An illustration of optimal SDCPTP (a) and CPTP (b) solutions on a problem with $|N| = 8$ requests and a fleet of two vehicles, each with a capacity of $C = 6$. The depot is labelled with 0 and the remaining vertices are labelled with a tuple (p_i, d_i). The tours are indicated by the solid and dashed arcs, respectively, and the costs $c_{i,j}$ are shown next to each arc. A single request receives a split delivery in (a), increasing the profit by 1 unit compared to (b).

3.2   Mathematical Programming Formulations

In this section, we propose three novel MILP formulations for the SDCPTP. The first model follows up on the work in [5] and the other two models draw some inspiration from [22]. In general, all of these formulations are three-index vehicle flow formulations that differ primarily in their treatment of the subtour elimination constraints within the branch-and-cut algorithm. Whereas the first of these formulations is applicable to the more general asymmetric case, the other two are only suitable in presence of symmetric variants of the problem, which are commonly studied in the literature. At the end of this section, we will also demonstrate how these formulations can be adjusted to model the CPTP, i. e., for special cases where split delivery is not allowed. The common notation for the models is summarized in Table 1.

Table 1. Common notation for the MILP models in Sect. 3.2.

N	Set of requests $N = \{1, ..., \|N\|\}$
V	Set of all vertices $V = \{0, ..., \|N\|\}$
A	Set of arcs in the complete graph $A = \{(i,j) \mid i, j \in V(i \neq j)\}$
K	Set of vehicles $K = \{1, ..., \|K\|\}$
C	Maximum capacity of each vehicle $k \in K$
p_i	Prize associated with request $i \in N$
d_i	Demand associated with request $i \in N$
$c_{i,j}$	Travel cost between two vertices $(i, j) \in A$
$x_{i,j,k}$	Binary variable, equals 1 iff arc $(i, j) \in A$ is part of the tour of vehicle $k \in K$
z_i	Binary variable, equals 1 iff request $i \in N$ is accepted
$y_{i,k}$	Binary variable, equals 1 iff request $i \in N$ is the only request that is served by vehicle $k \in K$. Iff $y_{0,k} = 1$ then vehicle k remains idle at the depot
$h_{i,k}$	Binary variable, equals 1 iff request $i \in N$ is visited by vehicle $k \in K$
$q_{i,k}$	Integer decision variable, indicates the quantity delivered to $i \in N$ by $k \in K$

The first MILP model for the SDCPTP is (1)–(11) (referred to as SDCPTP1 in what follows):

$$\max \quad \sum_{i \in N} p_i \cdot z_i - \sum_{k \in K} \sum_{i \in V} \sum_{\substack{j \in V \\ j \neq i}} c_{i,j} \cdot x_{i,j,k} \tag{1}$$

$$\sum_{j \in N} x_{0,j,k} \leq 1 \quad \forall k \in K \tag{2}$$

$$\sum_{\substack{j \in V \\ i \neq j}} x_{i,j,k} = \sum_{\substack{j \in V \\ i \neq j}} x_{j,i,k} \quad \forall i \in V, k \in K \tag{3}$$

$$\sum_{\substack{i \in V \\ j \neq j}} \sum_{j \in V} x_{i,j,k} \leq (|N| + 1) \cdot \sum_{j \in N} x_{0,j,k} \quad \forall k \in K \tag{4}$$

$$\sum_{k \in K} q_{i,k} = d_i \cdot z_i \quad \forall i \in N \tag{5}$$

$$\sum_{i \in N} q_{i,k} \leq C \quad \forall k \in K \tag{6}$$

$$\sum_{\substack{j \in V \\ i \neq j}} x_{i,j,k} \leq q_{i,k} \leq C \cdot \sum_{\substack{j \in V \\ i \neq j}} x_{i,j,k} \quad \forall i \in N, k \in K \tag{7}$$

$$\sum_{\substack{i \in S \\ i \neq j}} \sum_{j \in S} x_{i,j,k} \leq |S| - 1 \quad \forall S \subseteq N \, (|S| \geq 2), k \in K \tag{8}$$

$$z_i \in \{0, 1\} \quad \forall i \in N \tag{9}$$

$$x_{i,j,k} \in \{0, 1\} \quad \forall i, j \in V \, (i \neq j), k \in K \tag{10}$$

$$q_{i,k} \in \mathbb{N}_0 \quad \forall i \in N, k \in K \tag{11}$$

The objective function (1) maximizes the difference between the prize gained from accepted requests and the transportation costs. The latter are determined by the total length of all tours. Constraints (2) impose that each vehicle k may leave the depot at most once and conservation of flow for each vehicle k at each vertex i is guaranteed by constraints (3). Constraints (4) are valid inequalities that express that at most $(|N|+1)$ arcs can be selected to form a feasible tour for each vehicle k if and only if vehicle k leaves the depot. In principle, these valid inequalities are not required for correctly formulating the problem; however, preliminary experiments have shown that they are quite effective in strengthening the linear relaxation of the formulation. For all requests i, constraints (5) ensure that, in case the request is accepted (i. e., $z_i = 1$), the cumulative delivered quantities $q_{i,k}$ must match the demand d_i. The capacity constraints (6) limit the total delivered quantity of each vehicle k to be at most C. Constraints (7) guarantee the consistency between the variables $q_{i,k}$ and $x_{i,j,k}$. For every vehicle k and every subset of requests $S \subseteq N$, the subtour elimination constraints are given by (8). More precisely, these constraints guarantee connectivity to the depot and they are based on the *Danzig-Fulkerson-Johnson* (DFJ) subtour elimination constraints (refer to [15]). Finally, (9)–(11) formalize the domains of the decision variables. As [5] note, the integrality requirement in (11) may be relaxed if all demands d_i and the vehicle capacity C are integer-valued, as optimal solutions would still exhibit integral values for $q_{i,k}$ in such cases.

The second MILP model for the SDCPTP is (12)–(26) (referred to as SDCPTP2 in what follows). In contrast to SDCPTP1, the three-indexed variables $x_{i,j,k}$ in this model represent undirected edges. Therefore, the SDCPTP2 is limited to symmetric problems. However, as we will see in Sect. 4, this gives the formulation a computational advantage in presence of symmetric problems, which are commonly studied in the literature.

$$\max \quad \sum_{i \in N} p_i \cdot z_i - \sum_{k \in K} \sum_{i \in V} \sum_{\substack{j \in V \\ i < j}} c_{i,j} \cdot x_{i,j,k} - \sum_{k \in K} \sum_{j \in N} 2 \cdot c_{0,j} \cdot y_{j,k} \tag{12}$$

$$x_{i,j,k} = x_{j,i,k} \quad \forall i,j \in V \, (i < j), k \in K \tag{13}$$

$$\sum_{i \in V} 2 \cdot y_{i,k} + \sum_{j \in N} x_{0,j,k} = 2 \quad \forall k \in K \tag{14}$$

$$2 \cdot y_{i,k} + \sum_{\substack{j \in V \\ i \neq j}} x_{i,j,k} = 2 \cdot h_{i,k} \quad \forall i \in N, k \in K \tag{15}$$

$$\sum_{i \in V} \sum_{\substack{j \in V \\ i \neq j}} x_{i,j,k} \leq 2 \cdot (|N| + 1) \cdot \left(1 - \sum_{i \in V} y_{i,k}\right) \quad \forall k \in K \tag{16}$$

$$\sum_{k \in K} h_{i,k} \leq z_i \cdot |K| \quad \forall i \in N \tag{17}$$

$$\sum_{k \in K} q_{i,k} = d_i \cdot z_i \quad \forall i \in N \tag{18}$$

$$\sum_{i \in N} q_{i,k} \leq C \quad \forall k \in K \tag{19}$$

$$h_{i,k} \leq q_{i,k} \leq h_{i,k} \cdot C \quad \forall i \in N, k \in K \tag{20}$$

$$\sum_{i \in S} \sum_{\substack{j \in S \\ i < j}} x_{i,j,k} \leq |S| - 1 \quad \forall S \subseteq N \, (|S| \geq 2), k \in K \tag{21}$$

$$z_i \in \{0,1\} \quad \forall i \in N \tag{22}$$

$$y_{i,k} \in \{0,1\} \quad \forall i \in V, k \in K \tag{23}$$

$$h_{i,k} \in \{0,1\} \quad \forall i \in N, k \in K \tag{24}$$

$$x_{i,j,k} \in \{0,1\} \quad \forall i,j \in V \, (i \neq j), k \in K \tag{25}$$

$$q_{i,k} \in \mathbb{N}_0 \quad \forall i \in N, k \in K \tag{26}$$

The objective function (12) is analogous to (1) with the difference that the variables $y_{i,k}$ are included. Constraints (13) enforce the symmetry of the decision variables $x_{i,j,k}$. The equations in (14) guarantee that every vehicle k leaves the depot exactly once to start a tour that serves two or more customers (exactly two $x_{0,j,k}$ have value 1), serves a single customer (exactly one $y_{i,k}, i \neq 0$ has value 1), or remains idle at the depot ($y_{0,k} = 1$). For each customer i that is visited by vehicle k, constraints (15) force $h_{i,k}$ to take value 1. Constraints (16) are valid inequalities that are structurally identical to those presented for SDCPTP1 in (4). They express that at most $(|N| + 1)$ edges can be selected to form a feasible tour for each vehicle k if and only if that vehicle does neither serve a single customer nor remain idle at the depot (i. e., all $y_{i,k}$ have value 0). Constraints (17) force z_i to take value 1 if at least one vehicle visits request i and constraints (18) assure that the delivered quantities match the demand for each accepted request.

Consistency between the variables $q_{i,k}$ and $h_{i,k}$ is ensured by constraints (20). Analogously to the SDCPTP1 formulation, for every vehicle and every subset of requests, the subtour elimination constraints are given by (21). Finally, the domains of the variables are defined by (22)–(26). Note that the considerations that apply to (11) also apply to (26).

Another representation of subtour elimination constraints, which to the best of our knowledge was first presented in [10] for a prize-collecting TSP, can also be applied to the SDCPTP. Let us define $\delta(S \subseteq N) := \{(i,j) \mid i \in S, j \in V \setminus S\}$. Then, the third MILP formulation of the SDCPTP (referred to as SDCPTP3 in what follows) is given by (12)–(26) with the only difference that the subtour elimination constraints (21) are substituted for the following constraints (27):

$$\sum_{(i,j)\in\delta(S)} x_{i,j,k} \geq 2 \cdot h_{i,k} \quad \forall S \subseteq N, i \in S, k \in K \tag{27}$$

The subtour elimination constraints (27) guarantee that, for each request i in every subset of requests ($S \subseteq N$), iff i is served (i. e., $h_{i,k} = 1$) there must be at least two edges that connect vertices in S to the remaining vertices in $V \setminus S$, such that connectivity to the depot is enforced and no subtours occur. As in constraints (8) in SDCPTP1 and (21) in SDCPTP2, note that the number of these constraints grows exponentially with the number of requests. This implies that these constraints should be generated dynamically in the branch-and-cut framework (see Sect. 4).

Disallowing SD in these formulations is straightforward. In SDCPTP1, it becomes necessary to extend the model by constraints (28):

$$\sum_{k\in K}\sum_{\substack{j\in N \\ i\neq j}} x_{i,j,k} \leq z_i \quad \forall i \in N \tag{28}$$

And in SDCPTP2 or SDCPTP3 it suffices to replace constraints (17) with (29):

$$\sum_{k\in K} h_{i,k} \leq z_i \quad \forall i \in N \tag{29}$$

4 Computational Experiments and Numerical Results

In this section, we describe our computational experiments and discuss their numerical results. All experiments were performed on a shared compute cluster equipped with Intel Xeon Gold 6126 processors. For our experiments, we used 4 cores and 16 GB of RAM. We implemented the MILP models with Python 3.9 and used the branch-and-cut solver Gurobi Optimizer 10.0 [21] with a time limit of 3600 s using 4 threads. The subtour elimination constraints are implemented as lazy constraints, i. e., at every node of the branch-and-cut tree that yields an integer-feasible solution, we examine if there exist any subtours. If this is the case, we identify the smallest subset of vertices S that constitutes a subtour and apply the corresponding constraint (8), (21), or (27) for that subset.

The remainder of this section is structured as follows. We begin in Sect. 4.1 with a description of the problem instances. Afterwards, in Sect. 4.2, we discuss the numerical results.

4.1 Instance Generation

We base our experiments on two sets of instances. The first set was originally proposed for the CPTP in [6], where the authors adapted 10 instances from the well-known benchmark set for the vehicle routing problem in [12]. In these proposed CPTP instances, there are between 50 to 199 requests $|N|$ (each of which is associated with a demand and a prize) on a complete graph, a fleet size $|K| \in \{2, 3, 4\}$, and vehicle capacity $C \in \{50, 75, 100\}$. All of these instances were optimally solved for the CPTP in [6]; therefore, it is interesting to investigate the same instances from the perspective of the SDCPTP.

The second set of instances are motivated by the experiments in [5], where the SDCTOP has been studied. In that paper, the authors observed that SD typically only has a marginal impact if the customer demands are small w.r.t. the capacity (which applies to the first set of instances discussed above). To investigate if this observation also holds for the SDCPTP, we generate the second set based on the methodology in [9,17]. In particular, the demands are drawn uniformly at random from the interval $[\eta \cdot C, \nu \cdot C]$. Following [5], we consider the following eleven pairs of values for (η, ν): $(0.01, 0.1)$, $(0.1, 0.3)$, $(0.1, 0.5)$, $(0.1, 0.7)$, $(0.1, 0.9)$, $(0.3, 0.5)$, $(0.3, 0.7)$, $(0.3, 0.9)$, $(0.5, 0.7)$, $(0.5, 0.9)$, $(0.7, 0.9)$.

4.2 Experimental Results

As the SDCPTP contains the capacitated vehicle routing problem as a special case, the problem is NP-hard (refer to [27]). Therefore, finding optimal solutions to larger instances quickly becomes intractable. However, we can still solve small test instances optimally in a reasonable time, and compare the efficiency of SDCPTP1 to 3 (refer to Sect. 3.2).

Table 2 illustrates the numerical results on the first set of test instances. The first column displays the instance and the corresponding optimal CPTP solution z^* (taken from [6]) is shown in the second column. For SDCPTP1 to 3, the objective value z of the best feasible solution that was found is reported. If the solver proved z to be optimal, we report the runtime t in seconds; otherwise, we report the remaining *Mixed-Integer Programming* (MIP) gap g after $3600\,\mathrm{s}$ as a percentage value. For each row, the smallest runtime or MIP gap (in case none of the formulations returned the optimal solution) is displayed in bold. Additionally, the best SDCPTP solution is highlighted in bold (z') and this value is used to calculate the improvement w.r.t. z^*, i.e., the potential benefit of enabling split delivery. These percentages are calculated as $\frac{z'-z^*}{z^*}$, where z' is the best feasible solution found by SDCPTP1 to 3.

Table 2. Numerical results for the first set of instances (based on [6]).

Instance	CPTP	SDCPTP1		SDCPTP2		SDCPTP3		Imp.
$(|N|, C, |K|)$	z^*	z	t or g	z	t or g	z	t or g	(%)
6 (50,50,2)	33.88	**38.72**	45.5 s	**38.72**	**1.8 s**	**38.72**	1.8 s	14.3
6 (50,75,2)	72.28	**72.28**	170.2 s	**72.28**	4.3 s	**72.28**	**2.7 s**	0.0
6 (50,100,2)	100.27	**100.27**	961.2 s	**100.27**	9.0 s	**100.27**	**5.5 s**	0.0
6 (50,50,3)	40.95	**48.62**	35.8%	**48.62**	23.4 s	**48.62**	**17.2 s**	18.7
6 (50,75,3)	92.32	91.68	29.1%	**92.32**	106.0 s	**92.32**	**36.3 s**	0.0
6 (50,100,3)	134.72	133.65	23.9%	**134.72**	239.1 s	**134.72**	**42.0 s**	0.0
6 (50,50,4)	45.43	**50.50**	105.0%	**50.50**	2506 s	**50.50**	**1295 s**	11.2
6 (50,75,4)	99.37	90.55	79.7%	**109.01**	2594 s	**109.01**	**379.6 s**	9.7
6 (50,100,4)	153.30	136.05	60.9%	**154.59**	**10.9%**	**154.59**	2216 s	0.8
7 (75,50,2)	49.18	**50.13**	82.5 s	**50.13**	4.2 s	**50.13**	**4.2 s**	1.9
7 (75,75,2)	92.44	**95.90**	192.4 s	**95.90**	4.6 s	**95.90**	**4.0 s**	3.7
7 (75,100,2)	132.70	**133.20**	2211 s	**133.20**	24.9 s	**133.20**	**15.0 s**	0.4
7 (75,50,3)	69.94	73.23	21.5%	**73.67**	43.9 s	**73.67**	**41.4 s**	5.3
7 (75,75,3)	131.12	**135.51**	15.1%	**135.51**	149.8 s	**135.51**	**106.1 s**	3.4
7 (75,100,3)	185.25	179.44	25.8%	**187.37**	2328 s	**187.37**	**458.7 s**	1.1
7 (75,50,4)	90.65	**96.16**	39.0%	**96.16**	594.8 s	**96.16**	**387.9 s**	6.1
7 (75,75,4)	158.11	163.26	36.5%	164.70	10.6%	**167.14**	**4.0%**	5.7
7 (75,100,4)	233.40	213.37	42.3%	232.91	13.3%	**234.86**	**7.0%**	0.6
3 (100,50,2)	57.75	**57.75**	2237 s	**57.75**	**8.1 s**	**57.75**	14.1 s	0.0
3 (100,75,2)	106.15	**109.01**	19.9%	**109.01**	61.3 s	**109.01**	**26.5 s**	2.7
3 (100,100,2)	158.21	**168.15**	10.5%	162.20	161.6 s	162.20	**50.0 s**	6.3
3 (100,50,3)	80.82	76.36	66.4%	**80.82**	461.1 s	**80.82**	**164.3 s**	0.0
3 (100,75,3)	147.55	124.28	66.1%	**151.63**	**10.9%**	**151.63**	1679 s	2.8
3 (100,100,3)	218.63	187.87	45.1%	**222.62**	6.3%	**222.62**	**1.0%**	1.8
3 (100,50,4)	100.36	74.72	130.8%	99.45	24.8%	**100.36**	**9.5%**	0.0
3 (100,75,4)	185.27	133.53	96.1%	**181.41**	22.8%	179.07	**20.8%**	−2.1
3 (100,100,4)	255.33	195.91	74.9%	254.92	**20.8%**	**268.33**	11.9%	5.1
8 (100,50,2)	57.75	**57.75**	2104 s	**57.75**	**7.9 s**	**57.75**	13.9 s	0.0
8 (100,75,2)	106.15	108.88	20.3%	**109.01**	68.5 s	**109.01**	**29.5 s**	2.7
8 (100,100,2)	158.21	**168.15**	10.6%	162.20	178.3 s	162.20	**54.7 s**	6.3
8 (100,50,3)	80.82	76.36	66.5%	**80.82**	467.8 s	**80.82**	**167.2 s**	0.0
8 (100,75,3)	147.55	124.28	66.1%	**151.63**	**10.7%**	**151.63**	1596 s	2.8
8 (100,100,3)	218.63	175.59	55.3%	**222.62**	6.3%	**222.62**	**1.2%**	1.8
8 (100,50,4)	100.36	74.72	130.7%	99.45	24.5%	**100.36**	**9.1%**	0.0
8 (100,75,4)	185.27	133.53	96.2%	**181.41**	22.8%	179.07	**20.9%**	−2.1

(*continued*)

Table 2. (*continued*)

Instance	CPTP	SDCPTP1		SDCPTP2		SDCPTP3		Imp.
($|N|, C, |K|$)	z^*	z	t or g	z	t or g	z	t or g	(%)
8 (100,100,4)	268.34	195.91	74.9%	254.92	20.8%	**268.33**	11.9%	−0.0
14 (100,50,2)	43.26	**43.26**	501.1 s	**43.26**	11.7 s	43.26	5.7 s	0.0
14 (100,75,2)	77.09	75.76	33.7%	**77.09**	1798 s	77.09	222.6 s	0.0
14 (100,100,2)	125.29	112.34	41.9%	**125.29**	3076 s	125.29	203.5 s	0.0
14 (100,50,3)	59.43	**59.43**	41.3%	**59.43**	559.1 s	59.43	105.1 s	0.0
14 (100,75,3)	112.56	66.36	160.8%	**112.81**	16.3%	112.81	2531 s	0.2
14 (100,100,3)	182.31	159.44	59.5%	176.25	22.7%	**182.31**	3.5%	0.0
14 (100,50,4)	68.63	14.69	785.8%	**68.63**	33.2%	68.63	8.4%	0.0
14 (100,75,4)	139.88	44.75	423.2%	99.24	105.0%	**137.21**	19.7%	−1.9
14 (100,100,4)	237.68	50.73	558.1%	204.54	52.0%	**237.68**	5.6%	0.0
Avg. ($n \le 100$)	124.32	106.05	81.1%	123.93	9.7%	126.27	3.0%	2.4
13 (120,50,2)	64.12	**69.77**	1773 s	**69.77**	40.4 s	69.77	43.2 s	8.8
13 (120,75,2)	110.12	102.79	26.1%	**110.62**	444.9 s	110.62	133.1 s	0.5
13 (120,100,2)	145.75	80.47	119.9%	**145.75**	7.4%	145.75	3.6%	0.0
13 (120,50,3)	87.25	38.57	217.4%	**91.04**	8.9%	91.04	1492 s	4.3
13 (120,75,3)	139.37	**108.17**	79.5%	62.24	186.7%	97.09	67.3%	−22.4
13 (120,100,3)	181.63	99.22	161.3%	**141.00**	74.5%	100.70	125.2%	−22.4
13 (120,50,4)	104.18	45.13	270.7%	46.98	208.4%	**65.75**	99.5%	−36.9
13 (120,75,4)	161.62	47.12	438.5%	**109.52**	116.3%	52.77	306.3%	−32.2
13 (120,100,4)	200.62	75.12	343.6%	115.58	178.3%	**133.50**	117.4%	−33.5
9 (150,50,2)	65.03	**66.13**	1532 s	**66.13**	29.9 s	66.13	30.2 s	1.7
9 (150,75,2)	117.66	110.58	16.6%	**117.66**	93.2 s	117.66	57.6 s	0.0
9 (150,100,2)	161.23	147.70	24.8%	**161.23**	5.4%	161.23	1058 s	0.0
9 (150,50,3)	96.16	70.77	75.8%	**98.41**	448.0 s	98.41	178.3 s	2.3
9 (150,75,3)	160.96	101.57	99.9%	**161.20**	12.5%	161.20	6.8%	0.1
9 (150,100,3)	230.49	129.65	114.5%	195.89	34.3%	**228.33**	9.8%	−0.9
9 (150,50,4)	121.35	42.66	296.8%	**125.71**	12.2%	125.71	6.7%	3.6
9 (150,75,4)	204.25	80.04	241.1%	182.54	37.3%	**186.41**	28.7%	−8.7
9 (150,100,4)	290.54	128.23	188.3%	**260.24**	35.0%	203.52	65.9%	−10.4
15 (150,50,2)	64.98	**66.96**	6.5%	**66.96**	56.5 s	66.96	33.3 s	3.0
15 (150,75,2)	120.93	115.54	20.0%	**120.93**	549.1 s	120.93	183.0 s	0.0
15 (150,100,2)	169.71	162.49	21.6%	**171.05**	5.6%	171.05	1858 s	0.8
15 (150,50,3)	96.42	82.41	63.2%	**98.63**	5.5%	98.63	509.7 s	2.3
15 (150,75,3)	174.58	116.57	84.6%	162.94	21.8%	**171.05**	8.3%	−2.0
15 (150,100,3)	244.08	173.50	66.9%	228.69	21.3%	**247.78**	6.6%	1.5
15 (150,50,4)	124.02	91.73	96.6%	119.38	29.7%	**124.61**	17.4%	0.5
15 (150,75,4)	219.22	150.39	87.0%	**194.20**	36.6%	189.58	35.1%	−11.4

(*continued*)

Table 2. (*continued*)

Instance	CPTP	SDCPTP1		SDCPTP2		SDCPTP3		Imp.
($|N|, C, |K|$)	z^*	z	t or g	z	t or g	z	t or g	(%)
15 (150,100,4)	308.07	206.45	83.0%	244.39	49.0%	**255.14**	**37.7%**	−17.2
10 (199,50,2)	70.87	**70.87**	21.5%	**70.87**	123.6 s	**70.87**	**111.3 s**	0.0
10 (199,75,2)	124.85	119.45	26.7%	**124.85**	**432.6 s**	**124.85**	442.0 s	0.0
10 (199,100,2)	171.24	157.89	31.7%	169.04	10.1%	**171.24**	**3.6%**	0.0
10 (199,50,3)	103.79	72.94	105.7%	**104.46**	10.8%	**104.46**	**3.2%**	0.6
10 (199,75,3)	177.90	103.24	128.3%	**167.06**	24.0%	161.20	**22.1%**	−6.1
10 (199,100,3)	250.18	183.66	72.7%	**238.36**	21.8%	233.41	**18.9%**	−4.7
10 (199,50,4)	134.81	40.95	397.7%	132.96	24.8%	**134.66**	**17.3%**	−0.1
10 (199,75,4)	229.27	114.98	172.4%	**225.81**	**24.9%**	199.74	33.3%	−1.5
10 (199,100,4)	324.02	169.11	147.2%	230.74	70.9%	**262.36**	**42.8%**	−19.0
16 (199,50,2)	66.81	**69.96**	13.9%	**69.96**	110.5 s	**69.96**	**74.8 s**	4.7
16 (199,75,2)	123.38	120.11	21.4%	**125.37**	540.9 s	**125.37**	**371.1 s**	1.6
16 (199,100,2)	177.23	154.01	34.1%	176.28	**5.4%**	**177.23**	2243 s	0.0
16 (199,50,3)	99.70	88.12	64.9%	101.35	11.4%	**101.63**	**6.8%**	1.9
16 (199,75,3)	179.55	107.34	116.4%	156.69	32.3%	**176.16**	**11.0%**	−1.9
16 (199,100,3)	258.07	156.81	98.3%	245.20	18.1%	**248.03**	**14.1%**	−3.9
16 (199,50,4)	131.37	60.73	231.1%	**133.01**	21.3%	130.36	**18.9%**	1.2
16 (199,75,4)	235.03	133.40	130.2%	**207.68**	**34.0%**	195.38	38.3%	−11.6
16 (199,100,4)	336.24	136.90	201.1%	**285.73**	**34.9%**	273.65	37.4%	−15.0
Avg. ($n \leq 199$)	143.92	106.03	99.0%	135.68	20.7%	136.71	14.9%	−1.3

The results in Table 2 demonstrate that SDCPTP1 has the worst performance overall. In particular, SDCPTP2 or 3 either find optimal solutions faster or yield a lower MIP gap than SDCPTP1 on instances that remain unsolved after 3600 s. This shows that (in presence of these symmetric test instances) the symmetric formulations are much more efficient. Comparing SDCPTP2 to SDCPTP3, the former achieves better performance (by finding optimal solutions faster or returning lower MIP gaps after runtime) in only 12 out of 90 cases. Concerning the benefits of split delivery, for the instances with up to 100 requests, an average improvement of 2.4% is observed. However, when we also consider instances with more than 100 requests, we have negative improvements of −1.3% on average. This is explained by the fact that the MIP gaps after runtime are often large; and the feasible solutions found for the SDCPTP are still worse than the optimal CPTP solutions. Regarding the improvements, [5] already observed that the demands may be too small w. r. t. the vehicle capacity in these instances and thus, split delivery has no significant impact.

The numerical results of our experiments on the second set, where the ratio of demand to capacity is larger, are displayed in Table 3. As in the previous table, we compare the solutions of the SDCPTP after 3600 s of computation time with the corresponding optimal solution of the CPTP. For these instances, there are no existing optimal solutions, which are important to highlight the benefits of split delivery. Therefore, we resorted to the following method for generating reference values. We used SDCPTP3 and integrated constraints (29) to disable SD. We then solved each instance for 48 h on 24 cores (using 24 threads) with sufficient RAM in our Intel Xeon Gold 6126 compute cluster. This allowed us to find all optimal CPTP solutions except for a few cases that are explicitly highlighted in Table 3.

Table 3. Numerical results for the second set of instances (based on [5]).

Instance	CPTP	SDCPTP1		SDCPTP2		SDCPTP3		Imp.
$(|N|, C, |K|)$	z^*	z	t or g	z	t or g	z	t or g	(%)
6 ($|N| = 50, C = 160, |K| = 10$)								
(0.01, 0.1)	270.04	246.84	24.2%	**270.04**	2.8%	**270.04**	**2.2%**	0.0
(0.1, 0.3)	1143.09[1]	65.60	2049%	**1113.57**	**17.1%**	1055.67	23.9%	−3.7
(0.1, 0.5)	1363.44[1]	1315.11	28.9%	**1386.67**	**13.6%**	1380.10	13.8%	2.5
(0.1, 0.7)	1370.32[1]	763.62	125%	1416.16	12.4%	**1444.18**	**9.4%**	5.4
(0.1, 0.9)	1425.15	1456.32	31.7%	1531.04	14.3%	**1550.11**	**11.7%**	8.8
(0.3, 0.5)	1299.91	1261.59	43.6%	1455.84	16.6%	**1469.63**	**14.9%**	13.1
(0.3, 0.7)	1351.07	489.22	261%	**1377.94**	15.0%	1375.26	**13.4%**	2.0
(0.3, 0.9)	1583.81	1657.35	19.3%	1704.94	8.3%	**1717.53**	**6.1%**	8.4
(0.5, 0.7)	1107.72	1673.19	19.2%	**1698.54**	**8.4%**	1684.44	8.5%	52.1
(0.5, 0.9)	1369.87	1707.55	14.0%	**1714.62**	**5.2%**	1706.67	5.5%	25.2
(0.7, 0.9)	1432.22	1651.31	22.9%	1686.67	9.3%	**1712.68**	**7.1%**	19.6
7 ($|N| = 75, C = 140, |K| = 8$)								
(0.01, 0.1)	198.45	0.00	1302%	228.35	10.1%	**234.89**	**5.6%**	18.4
(0.1, 0.3)	879.92[2]	395.08	187%	**838.50**	**27.8%**	581.04	82.7%	−4.7
(0.1, 0.5)	1051.10[2]	908.20	43.5%	**1076.38**	13.7%	1074.45	**10.1%**	2.4
(0.1, 0.7)	1102.18[2]	871.46	50.7%	1144.17	8.8%	**1160.22**	**5.8%**	5.3
(0.1, 0.9)	1050.50	1069.98	25.3%	**1136.04**	7.9%	1132.08	**6.5%**	8.1
(0.3, 0.5)	1041.70	1064.12	26.9%	1152.12	9.5%	**1155.28**	**8.4%**	10.9
(0.3, 0.7)	1034.43	1005.61	35.1%	1080.50	17.3%	**1094.14**	**12.9%**	5.8
(0.3, 0.9)	1106.43	1207.11	14.3%	1241.53	4.0%	**1248.28**	**2.5%**	12.8
(0.5, 0.7)	761.38	1154.29	15.9%	1172.06	7.3%	**1178.23**	**4.7%**	54.7
(0.5, 0.9)	917.96	1151.68	20.3%	**1203.31**	4.7%	**1203.31**	**3.8%**	31.1
(0.7, 0.9)	1048.90	1225.84	12.5%	**1235.12**	2.5%	**1235.12**	**2.1%**	17.8
Avg.	1086.80	1015.50	198%	1221.10	11.1%	1211.97	11.9%	13.5

[1] These MIP gaps are up to 5.28% after 48 h of computation.
[2] The MIP gap is 12.2% after 48 h of computation.

In Table 3, even though the average MIP gaps for SDCPTP2 and 3 are more than 11% on average, we can observe that split delivery can drastically increase the objective value for such instances, where there is a high ratio of demand to vehicle capacity. For 2 of the 22 instances, improvements of more than 50% are possible through split delivery and the overall average is 13.5%. Within the 3600 s of computation time, we can see that with an increasing ratio of demand to vehicle capacity, the MIP gaps become smaller in relative terms for all three formulations. As was the case for the first set of test instances, it is once again evident that SDCPTP1 can not compete with SDCPTP2 or SDCPTP3. Regarding the latter formulations, SDCPTP3 provides better solutions than SDCPTP2 in 14 out of 22 cases (see Table 3).

Regarding the experiments as a whole and with respect to Tables 2 and 3, it can be concluded that in some cases with high MIP gaps, SDCPTP2 can perform slightly better than SDCPTP3 in terms of the feasible solution found after 3600 s of computation time. However, for small problem instances, with up to 75 requests and 10 vehicles, both formulations SDCPTP2 and SDCPTP3 typically lead to satisfactory solutions within 3600 s of computation time. Thus with our experimental results and as [5] already stated for the CTOP, the main advantages of split deliveries for the CPTP are also obtained in instances with high request demands, especially when demands exceed half of the vehicle capacity.

5   Conclusion and Future Research

In this paper, we investigated the SDCPTP that extends the profitable tour problem by a fleet of vehicles and the possibility of split deliveries. We began with a brief overview of routing problems with profits and split delivery in vehicle routing in Sect. 2. In particular, that section demonstrated that there is a scientific gap in studying split delivery in the context of profitable tour problems. To address this gap, we proposed three novel MILP formulations for the SDCPTP in Sect. 3. All of these formulations are three-index vehicle flow formulations that differ primarily in their treatment of the subtour elimination constraints within the branch-and-cut algorithm. Afterwards, in Sect. 4, we performed a computational study that consisted of solving the three different MILP formulations with a state-of-the-art solver on different instances from the literature. Our numerical results showed that there is a significant difference in performance when using these formulations. Whereas the performance of SDCPTP1 was comparatively poor, the second and third formulation showed promising results. While SDCPTP3 performed the best overall in our experiments, there are some cases where the SDCPTP2 can perform better. These cases concern especially those with a high ratio of request demand to vehicle capacity. On such instances, it became clear that split delivery can significantly improve the solution.

Based on this paper, there are several future research directions. While SDCPTP2 and SDCPTP3 showed promising performance, attempting to solve the SDCPTP optimally with an off-the-shelf solver quickly becomes intractable on larger instances. Therefore, apart from exact branch-and-price procedures for the SDCPTP, heuristic methods should be investigated for the problem. As mentioned above, it would also be worthwhile to investigate cases where demand can exceed vehicle capacity, making split delivery indispensable. Moreover, in the context of practical applications, where requests might not be deterministic, it would be worthwhile to consider stochastic variants of the SDCPTP.

References

1. Angelelli, E., Mansini, R., Rizzi, R.: The probabilistic profitable tour problem under a specific graph structure. arXiv preprint arXiv:2204.07378 (2022)
2. Archetti, C., Bianchessi, N., Speranza, M.G.: The capacitated team orienteering problem with incomplete service. Optim. Lett. **7**(7), 1405–1417 (2013)
3. Archetti, C., Bianchessi, N., Speranza, M.G., Hertz, A.: Incomplete service and split deliveries in a routing problem with profits. Networks **63**(2), 135–145 (2014)
4. Archetti, C., Bianchessi, N., Speranza, M.G.: Optimal solutions for routing problems with profits. Discret. Appl. Math. **161**(4–5), 547–557 (2013)
5. Archetti, C., Bianchessi, N., Speranza, M.G., Hertz, A.: The split delivery capacitated team orienteering problem. Networks **63**(1), 16–33 (2014)
6. Archetti, C., Feillet, D., Hertz, A., Speranza, M.G.: The capacitated team orienteering and profitable tour problems. J. Oper. Res. Soc. **60**(6), 831–842 (2009)
7. Archetti, C., Speranza, M.G.: Vehicle routing in the 1-skip collection problem. J. Oper. Res. Soc. **55**(7), 717–727 (2004)
8. Balas, E.: The prize collecting traveling salesman problem. Networks **19**(6), 621–636 (1989)
9. Belenguer, J.M., Martinez, M., Mota, E.: A lower bound for the split delivery vehicle routing problem. Oper. Res. **48**(5), 801–810 (2000)
10. Bienstock, D., Goemans, M.X., Simchi-Levi, D., Williamson, D.: A note on the prize collecting traveling salesman problem. Math. Program. **59**(1), 413–420 (1993)
11. Bortfeldt, A., Yi, J.: The split delivery vehicle routing problem with three-dimensional loading constraints. Eur. J. Oper. Res. **282**(2), 545–558 (2020)
12. Christofides, N.: The vehicle routing problem. In: Combinatorial Optimization (1979)
13. Cortés-Murcia, D.L., Afsar, H.M., Prodhon, C.: A branch and price algorithm for the electric capacitated profitable tour problem with mandatory stops. IFAC-PapersOnLine **52**(13), 1572–1577 (2019)
14. Cortés-Murcia, D.L., Afsar, H.M., Prodhon, C.: Multi-period profitable tour problem with electric vehicles and mandatory stops. Int. J. Sustain. Transp. **17**, 1–17 (2022)
15. Dantzig, G., Fulkerson, R., Johnson, S.: Solution of a large-scale traveling-salesman problem. J. Oper. Res. Soc. Am. **2**(4), 393–410 (1954)
16. Dell'Amico, M., Maffioli, F., Värbrand, P.: On prize-collecting tours and the asymmetric travelling salesman problem. Int. Trans. Oper. Res. **2**(3), 297–308 (1995)
17. Dror, M., Trudeau, P.: Savings by split delivery routing. Transp. Sci. **23**(2), 141–145 (1989)
18. Feillet, D., Dejax, P., Gendreau, M.: Traveling salesman problems with profits. Transp. Sci. **39**(2), 188–205 (2005)
19. Frizzell, P.W., Giffin, J.W.: The split delivery vehicle scheduling problem with time windows and grid network distances. Comput. Oper. Res. **22**(6), 655–667 (1995)

20. Gulczynski, D., Golden, B., Wasil, E.: The split delivery vehicle routing problem with minimum delivery amounts. Transp. Res. Part E Logist. Transp. Rev. **46**(5), 612–626 (2010)
21. Gurobi Optimization, LLC.: Gurobi Optimizer Reference Manual (2023)
22. Jepsen, M.K., Petersen, B., Spoorendonk, S., Pisinger, D.: A branch-and-cut algorithm for the capacitated profitable tour problem. Discret. Optim. **14**, 78–96 (2014)
23. Lera-Romero, G., Miranda-Bront, J.J.: A branch and cut algorithm for the time-dependent profitable tour problem with resource constraints. Eur. J. Oper. Res. **289**(3), 879–896 (2021)
24. Mullaseril, P.A., Dror, M., Leung, J.: Split-delivery routeing heuristics in livestock feed distribution. J. Oper. Res. Soc. **48**(2), 107–116 (1997)
25. Sierksma, G., Tijssen, G.A.: Routing helicopters for crew exchanges on off-shore locations. Ann. Oper. Res. **76**, 261–286 (1998)
26. Sun, P., Veelenturf, L.P., Dabia, S., Van Woensel, T.: The time-dependent capacitated profitable tour problem with time windows and precedence constraints. Eur. J. Oper. Res. **264**(3), 1058–1073 (2018)
27. Toth, P., Vigo, D. (eds.): Vehicle Routing: Problems, Methods, and Applications. Society for Industrial and Applied Mathematics (SIAM) (2014)
28. Tsiligirides, T.: Heuristic methods applied to orienteering. J. Oper. Res. Soc. **35**(9), 797–809 (1984)
29. Wang, X., Golden, B., Gulczynski, D.: A worst-case analysis for the split delivery capacitated team orienteering problem with minimum delivery amounts. Optim. Lett. **8**(8), 2349–2356 (2014)
30. Yu, M., Jin, X., Zhang, Z., Qin, H., Lai, Q.: The split-delivery mixed capacitated arc-routing problem: applications and a forest-based tabu search approach. Transp. Res. Part E Logist. Transp. Rev. **132**, 141–162 (2019)

Multidimensional Scattered Time-varying Scattered Data Meshless Interpolation for Sensor Networks

Vaclav Skala$^{(\boxtimes)}$ [ID]

Faculty of Applied Sciences, Department of Computer Science,
University of West Bohemia, 301 00 Pilsen, Czech Republic
skala@kiv.zcu.cz
https://www.vaclavskala.eu/

Abstract. Interpolation and approximation of scattered scalar and vector data is a part of a solution of many engineering problems. The methods are based mostly on some triangulation of the data domain, usually limited to 2D or 3D data, followed by an interpolation or an approximation to obtain a smooth result. This contribution presents a meshless approach based on the Radial Basis Functions (RBF). It is nearly dimensionless and it enables interpolation of time varying data, i.e. interpolation of scattered spatio-temporal varying data, i.e. interpolation in space-time domain without "time-frames". The meshless methods for scattered spatio-temporal data can be used for interpolation, approximation and evaluation of data acquired from buoys, sensor networks, sensors for tsunami, chemical and radiation detectors, ships and submarines detection, weather forecast, 3D vector fields compression and visualization, etc.

Keywords: Meshless method · meshfree method · Radial Basis Functions · scattered data · time-varying data · approximation · interpolation · sensor network · military application · tsunami detection · weather forecast · 3D vector fields · radiation situation · chemical situation

1 Introduction

Data interpolation and approximation is a frequent task in many areas. Usually the interpolation is used for data sets $h_i = f(\mathbf{x_i})$, where h_i is a value at $\mathbf{x_i} \in \Omega$, where Ω is the data domain in E^d and $d = 2, 3$ mostly. The data domain is somehow tessellated, but not necessarily by the Delaunay triangulation(DT). The values h_i might be scalar or vector values, e.g. a wind velocity (v_x, v_y, v_z). In the case of spatio-temporal data, the "framing" is implicitly expected with the fixed known correspondence of points Petrik [33,34]. It leads to spatio-temporal meshes with the fixed connectivity of points in frames t_i and t_{i+1}, if the domain

---

Research partially supported by the University of West Bohemia - Institutional research support.

O. Gervasi et al. (Eds.): ICCSA 2023, LNCS 13956, pp. 99–112, 2023.
https://doi.org/10.1007/978-3-031-36805-9_7

tessellation is used. It should be noted that if the spatial domain $\Omega \in E^3$ then in the spatio-temporal case a tessellation for E^4 is to be used.

A usual tessellation technique is the Delaunay triangulation(DT).[1]. However, the computational complexity is $O(n^{\lceil d/2+1 \rceil})$, i.e. $O(n^2)$ for $d = 2$, $O(n^3)$ for $d = 3, 4$, see Smolik [44], WiKi [52]. Also, due to numerical robustness issues, the complexity of the DT implementation grows significantly with the dimensionality. The smoothness of the final interpolation of the h_i values is a fundamental requirement, which is not an easy task if triangular or tetrahedral meshes are used to represent the data domain. This approach can be used in the spatio-temporal case, when the data are "framed" for the given "time-slice" t_i and with fixed and known connectivity of points, see Petrik [33, 35].

However, there are many areas when an interpolation of scattered spatio-temporal "non-framed" data are required, e.g. sensor networks, floating buoys with sensors on sea, when data sources are not constantly on-line and sending data occasionally only, e.g. tsunami detection, ships and submarine identification. Such sensors are connected only shortly. It leads to energy savings and hard detection of those.

2   Spatio-temporal Data Classification

Interpolation and approximation is usually made for the "ordered" data domains, e.g. rectangular, triangular and tetrahedral meshes, etc. In the CAD systems, the parametric space is used for interpolation, e.g. for parametric curves and surfaces. The data domain can be classified as:

– ordered
   • structured
      * regular, e.g. a rectangular mesh where all elements have same size, triangular meshes with a constant vertex valency,
      * irregular, e.g. a rectangular mesh, but elements have different size triangular meshes with non-constant vertex valencies,
   • unstructured, e.g. general triangular or tetrahedral meshes,
– unordered
   • clustered - points form clusters in the data domain,
   • scattered - points are scattered across the domain, generally.

Table 1. Classification of spatio-temporal data sets

		Temporal property	
		Static	Dynamic
Spatial property	Static	$h = f(\mathbf{x})$	$h = f(\mathbf{x}, t)$
	Dynamic	$h = f(\mathbf{x}(t))$	$h = f(\mathbf{x}(t), t)$

---

[1] For non DT tessellation, see Smolik [45].

The domain data can also be classified as static or dynamic in space and time, see Table 1. It can be seen that the case $h = f(\mathbf{x}(t), t)$ represents interpolation of a scalar value h on the d-dimensional domain of $\mathbf{x}(t) \in \Omega(t)$, where the position $\mathbf{x}(t)$ is changing within time t. It should be noted that the $\Omega(t)$ is not constant in time, generally.

Now, the case of the scattered spatio-temporal domain is dynamic in both, i.e. $h(t) = f(\mathbf{x}(t), t)$, can be classified further as:

- framed in time - points lie on a hyperplane $\rho \in E^d$ for the given time slice t_i,
- framed in space - all points for the given slice in the given E^d space are given (limited to the (x, t) case, i.e. $x \in R^1$),
- unframed in space and time - just an unordered "heap of points" scattered in space-time.

Also, the points in the Ω domain might also be with known mutual point correspondences, i.e. a geometrical trajectory of a point can be reconstructed, e.g. using the buoys ID, or without any similar information, i.e. the buoys ID is not available. In the following, a general approach to interpolation is described and the radial basis functions (RBF) are used for interpolation.

3   Radial Basis Functions

The Radial Basis Functions (RBF) interpolation is based on the mutual distances of points in the data domain Ω, see Hardy [18,19], Schaback [37], Fasshauer [14], Wendland [50,51], Franke [16], Iske [20], Floater [15], Wu [54], Belytschko [6], etc. RBFs are also used in many applications, e.g. Biancolini [7], Cuomo [11], Sarra [36] and Zhang [55].

The RBF interpolation is given in the form:

$$h(\mathbf{x}) = \sum_{j=1}^{N} \lambda_j \varphi \| \mathbf{x} - \mathbf{x}_j \|) = \sum_{j=1}^{N} \lambda_j \varphi(r_j) \tag{1}$$

where r_j is the distance from a point $\mathbf{x}$ to the point $\mathbf{x}_j$. As the parameter r of the function $\varphi(r)$ is a distance of two points in the d-dimensional space, the interpolation is non-separable by a dimension. The RBF function $\varphi(r)$ will be described in detailed later on.

For each point, $\mathbf{x}_i$ the interpolating function has to have the value h_i. It leads to a system of linear equations:

$$h(\mathbf{x}_i) = \sum_{j=1}^{N} \lambda_j \varphi(\| \mathbf{x}_i - \mathbf{x}_j \|) = \sum_{j=1}^{N} \lambda_j \varphi(r_{ij}) \tag{2}$$

where λ_j are unknown weights for each radial basis function, N is the number of given points and $\varphi(r)$ is the radial basis function itself.

The Eq. 2 can be written if the matrix form as:

$$\mathbf{A}\boldsymbol{\lambda} = \mathbf{h} \tag{3}$$

or using $\varphi_{ij} = \varphi(r_{ij})$ as:

$$\begin{bmatrix} \varphi_{11} & \cdots & \varphi_{1j} & \cdots & \varphi_{1N} \\ \vdots & \ddots & \vdots & \ddots & \vdots \\ \varphi_{i1} & \cdots & \varphi_{ij} & \cdots & \varphi_{iN} \\ \vdots & \ddots & \vdots & \ddots & \vdots \\ \varphi_{N1} & \cdots & \varphi_{Nj} & \cdots & \varphi_{NN} \end{bmatrix} \begin{bmatrix} \lambda_1 \\ \vdots \\ \lambda_i \\ \vdots \\ \lambda_N \end{bmatrix} = \begin{bmatrix} h_1 \\ \vdots \\ h_i \\ \vdots \\ h_N \end{bmatrix} \tag{4}$$

The interpolated value at a point $\mathbf{x}$ is computed using the Eq. 1. However, due to numerical robustness and stability, additional polynomial conditions are usually added Fasshauer [14], Skala [39,40].

It can be seen, that the size of the matrix is nearly independent of the dimension and matrix size is $\approx (N \times N)$ only.[2]

In the case of an additional polynomial $P_k(\mathbf{x}_i)$ of a degree k, we obtain:

$$h(\mathbf{x}_i) = \sum_{j=1}^{N} \lambda_j \varphi(||\mathbf{x}_i - \mathbf{x}_j||) + P_k(\mathbf{x}_i) \tag{5}$$

In the case of a bilinear polynomial $P_1(x, y)$:

$$P_1(x, y) = a_0 + a_1 x + a_2 y + a_3 xy \tag{6}$$

the additional orthogonal conditions are to be used:

$$\sum_{j=1}^{N} \lambda_j = 0 \quad \sum_{j=1}^{N} \lambda_j x_j = 0 \quad \sum_{j=1}^{N} \lambda_j y_j = 0 \quad \sum_{j=1}^{N} \lambda_j x_j y_j = 0 \tag{7}$$

Then the RBF interpolation with the additional orthogonal conditions can be rewritten as in a more compact way:

$$\begin{bmatrix} \mathbf{A} & \mathbf{P} \\ \mathbf{P^T} & \mathbf{0} \end{bmatrix} \begin{bmatrix} \boldsymbol{\lambda} \\ \mathbf{a} \end{bmatrix} = \begin{bmatrix} \mathbf{h} \\ \mathbf{0} \end{bmatrix} \tag{8}$$

where the matrix $\mathbf{P}$ represents the polynomial, $\boldsymbol{\lambda}$ is the vector of the RBF weights, the vector $\mathbf{a}$ contains resulting the polynomial coefficients and $\mathbf{h}$ are given values at the given points. The matrix $\mathbf{P^T}$ represents the additional orthogonal conditions, see Eq. 7. From the geometrical point of view, the polynomial $P_k(\mathbf{x})$ actually represents a rough approximation of the given data.

It should be noted that if the polynomial $P_k(\mathbf{x})$ is used:

− the RBF interpolation is not invariant to rotation and translation,
− interpolation, i.e. $\boldsymbol{\lambda}$ and $\mathbf{a}$, depends on physical units used for the vector $\mathbf{x}$,
− it might be actually counterproductive in the case of large range of domain data Jäger [21], Skala [39,40].

It can be seen that the RBF interpolation leads to a linear system of equations $\mathbf{Ax} = \mathbf{b}$.

---

[2] In the case of high N using block matrices might help in solving large systems of linear equations, see Majdisova [28] - a system of $6.7 \ 10^6$ points was solved.

3.1   Distance

The $r_{ij} = \|\mathbf{x}_i - \mathbf{x}_j\|$ is the distance between points $\mathbf{x}_i$ and $\mathbf{x}_j$, i.e. in the case of:

– spatial data (time independent) - usually the Euclidean norm is used: [3]

$$r_{ij} = \|\mathbf{x}_i - \mathbf{x}_j\| = \sqrt{\sum_{k=1}^{d} (^k x_i - {}^k x_j)^2} \tag{9}$$

where $^k x_i$ means the kth element of the vector $\mathbf{x}_i$,
– spatio-temporal data (time varying)

$$r_{ij} = \|(\mathbf{x}, t)_i - (\mathbf{x}, t)_j\| = \sqrt{\sum_{k=1}^{d} (^k x_i - {}^k x_j)^2 + \beta^2 (t_i - t_j)^2} \tag{10}$$

where $^k x_i$ means the kth element of the vector $\mathbf{x}_i$.
The coefficient β has physical unit $[m/s]$ and reflects the speed of the physical phenomena, e.g. speed of sound in water, speed of light, etc.

Another possibility is to use the $\varphi(r)$ RBF with a multiplicative exponential time term as:

$$\phi(r(t), t) = \varphi(r)\, e^{-kt} \qquad \text{or} \qquad \phi(r(t), t) = \varphi(r)\, e^{(-k_1 t^2 - k_2 t)}$$

where k, k_1 and k_2 are some positive constants, see Ku [23].
It should be noted, that if the points $\mathbf{x}$ are not static, i.e. $\mathbf{x} = \mathbf{x}(t)$ then the mutual distances of points are not constant, i.e. $r = r(t)$.
The above-mentioned radial basis functions are used for interpolation and approximation, solution of ordinary differential equations (ODE) and partial differential equations (PDE), etc.

3.2   Squared Normalized RBF

Normalized RBF is another modification of the "standard" RBF. The Normalized RBF (N-RBF) is given in the form:

$$h(\mathbf{x}) = \frac{\sum_{j=1}^{N} \lambda_j \varphi \|\mathbf{x} - \mathbf{x}_j\|)}{\sum_{j=1}^{N} \varphi \|\mathbf{x} - \mathbf{x}_j\|} = \frac{\sum_{j=1}^{N} \lambda_j \varphi(r_j)}{\sum_{j=1}^{N} \varphi(r_j)} \tag{11}$$

where r_j is the distance from a point $\mathbf{x}$ to the point $\mathbf{x}_j$.
The N-RBF are used especially in the RBF neural networks applications, see WiKi [53].

---

[3] The distance defined as $\|.\|_1$ is used in fuzzy approach, see Perfilieva [32].

However, some functions $\varphi(r)$ used for the interpolation and approximation are not strictly positive, e.g. $r^2 \ln(r)$ (Thin-Plate Spline - TPS) [4], which is negative on the interval $(0,1)$, the Euclidean norm should be used for robustness of computation, see Eq. 12.

The Squared Normalized RBF (SN-RBF) is given in the form:

$$h(\mathbf{x}) = \frac{\sum_{j=1}^{N} \lambda_j \varphi(\|\mathbf{x} - \mathbf{x}_j\|)}{\sqrt{\sum_{j=1}^{N} \varphi^2(\|\mathbf{x} - \mathbf{x}_j\|)}} = \frac{\sum_{j=1}^{N} \lambda_j \varphi(r_j)}{\sqrt{\sum_{j=1}^{N} \varphi^2(r_j)}} \tag{12}$$

This is actually the Euclidean normalization of each row of the matrix $\mathbf{A}$ in Eq. 4.

$$\sum_{j=1}^{N} \lambda_j \varphi(\|\mathbf{x}_i - \mathbf{x}_j\|) = h(\mathbf{x}) \sqrt{\sum_{j=1}^{N} \varphi^2(r_{ij})} \quad i = 1, \dots, N \tag{13}$$

where $r_{ij} = \|\mathbf{x}_i - \mathbf{x}_j\|$.

It should be noted, that $O(N^2)$ division operations are replaced by $O(N)$ multiplications; the given values $h(\mathbf{x}_i)$ are just multiplied by the values $\sqrt{\sum_{j=1}^{N} \varphi^2(r_{ij})}$. It leads to higher robustness of computation for high N.

In the case of interpolation a polynomial of a degree k $P_k(\mathbf{x})$ can be added:

$$h(\mathbf{x}) = \frac{\sum_{j=1}^{N} \lambda_j \varphi\|\mathbf{x} - \mathbf{x}_j\|)}{\sqrt{\sum_{j=1}^{N} \varphi^2(r_j)}} + P_k(\mathbf{x}) \tag{14}$$

and some orthogonal conditions have to be added as well, see Eq. 7.

The polynomial $P_k(\mathbf{x})$ improves the conditionality of the matrix $\mathbf{A}$, see Eq. 3, and also roughly approximate the given data. The Eq. 14 can be modified similarly as the Eq. 13 to:

$$\sum_{j=1}^{N} \lambda_j \varphi\|\mathbf{x}_i - \mathbf{x}_j\|) + P_k(\mathbf{x}_i)\sqrt{\sum_{j=1}^{N} \varphi^2(r_{ij})} = h(\mathbf{x}_i)\sqrt{\sum_{j=1}^{N} \varphi^2(r_{ij})} \quad i = 1, \dots, N \tag{15}$$

As the $q_i = \sqrt{\sum_{j=1}^{N} \varphi^2(r_{ij})}$ is constant for the ith row $(i = 1, \dots, N)$ in the Eq. 4, the Eq. 15 can be simplified to:

$$\sum_{j=1}^{N} \lambda_j \varphi\|\mathbf{x}_i - \mathbf{x}_j\|) + q_i P_k(\mathbf{x}_i) = q_i h(\mathbf{x}_i) \quad i = 1, \dots, N \tag{16}$$

---

[4] It should be noted that $r^2 \log(r) = \frac{1}{2} r^2 \log(r^2)$, i.e. actually no $\sqrt{r^2}$ computation is needed, only the values of the weights λ_j are doubled.

and in the matrix for the SN-RBF interpolation has form:

$$
\begin{bmatrix}
\varphi_{11} & \cdots & \varphi_{1N} & q_1 & q_1 x_1 & q_1 y_1 & q_1 x_1 y_1 \\
\vdots & \ddots & \vdots & 1 & \vdots & \vdots & \vdots \\
\varphi_{N1} & \cdots & \varphi_{NN} & q_N & q_N x_N & q_N y_N & q_N x_n y_N \\
1 & 1 & 1 & 0 & 0 & 0 & 0 \\
x_1 & \cdots & x_N & 0 & 0 & 0 & 0 \\
y_1 & \cdots & y_N & 0 & 0 & 0 & 0 \\
x_1 y_1 & \cdots & x_N y_N & 0 & 0 & 0 & 0
\end{bmatrix}
\begin{bmatrix}
\lambda_1 \\ \vdots \\ \lambda_N \\ a_0 \\ a_1 \\ a_2 \\ a_3
\end{bmatrix}
=
\begin{bmatrix}
q_1 h_1 \\ \vdots \\ q_N h_N \\ 0 \\ 0 \\ 0 \\ 0
\end{bmatrix}
\tag{17}
$$

or in a more compact way:

$$
\begin{bmatrix} \mathbf{A} & \mathbf{QP} \\ \mathbf{P^T} & \mathbf{0} \end{bmatrix}
\begin{bmatrix} \boldsymbol{\lambda} \\ \mathbf{a} \end{bmatrix}
=
\begin{bmatrix} \mathbf{Qh} \\ \mathbf{0} \end{bmatrix}
\tag{18}
$$

where $\mathbf{Q} = diag[q_1, \ldots, q_N]$ is a diagonal matrix and $q_i > 0$, $i = 1, \ldots, N$ in the case of SN-RBFs.

However, in the approximation case, i.e. the matrix $\mathbf{A}$ is $(N \times M), N > M$, the polynomial part has to be handled differently and the Least Square Method (LSE) cannot be used directly, see Skala [42], Majdisova [26,29,30].

4   RBF Functions

There are several radial basis functions Fasshauer [14], Buhmann [8],Majdisova [28,29] and Smolik [46]. The RBFs can be divided into two major groups:

- "global" RBFs having global influence, e.g.
  - Polyharmonic spline:
    $$\varphi(r) = r^k, \quad k = 1, 3, 5, \ldots$$
    $$\varphi(r) = r^k \ln r, \quad k = 2, 4, 6, \ldots$$
  - Thin plate spline [TPS](a special polyharmonic spline): $\varphi(r) = r^2 \ln r$, [5]
  - Gaussian: $\varphi(r) = e^{-\alpha r^2}$
  - Multiquadric: $\sqrt{1 + \alpha r^2}$
  - Inverse quadratic: $\frac{1}{1 + \alpha r^2}$
  - Inverse multiquadratic: $\frac{1}{\sqrt{1 + \alpha r^2}}$

  where $\alpha > 0$ is a shape parameter, $r \in < 0, \infty)$.
  The RBF matrix is usually full and the matrix can be very ill conditioned.
- "local" RBFs - Compactly Supported RBF (CS-RBF) have a non-zero positive value on the interval $< 0, 1)$ only. The RBF matrix is usually sparse and it depends on the shape parameter α. Some function examples are listed in Table 2.

There are other RBFs used, e.g. the "bumb CS-RBF" based on Gaussian:

$$
\varphi(r) = \begin{cases} e^{-\frac{1}{1-r^2}} & r \in < 0, 1) \\ 0 & r \geq 1 \end{cases}
$$

---

[5] In the actual implementation $\varphi(r) = r^2 \ln r^2$ should be used as $r^2 \ln r^2 = 2\, r^2 \ln r$. The λ weights are doubled and $\sqrt{\cdot}$ operation is not needed.

Buhmann [8] proposed CS-RBF in the form:

$$\varphi(r) = \begin{cases} \frac{1}{3} + r^2 - \frac{4}{3}r^3 + 2r^2 \log r & r \in <0,1) \\ 0 & r \geq 1 \end{cases}$$

and Manandro [31] proposed two new rational CS-RBF classes.

Table 2. Wendland's Compactly Supported RBF (CS-RBF) $(x)_+$ means, that the value of the expression is zero for $r \geq 1$

ID	RBF	Function	ID	RBF	Function
1	$\varphi_{1,0}$	$(1-r)_+$	2	$\varphi_{1,1}$	$(1-r)_+^3(3r+1)$
3	$\varphi_{1,2}$	$(1-r)_+^5(8r^2+5r+1)$	4	$\varphi_{3,0}$	$(1-r)_+^2$
5	$\varphi_{3,1}$	$(1-r)_+^4(4r+1)$	6	$\varphi_{3,2}$	$(1-r)_+^6(35r^2+18r+3)$
7	$\varphi_{3,3}$	$(1-r)_+^8(32r^3+25r^2+8r+3)$	8	$\varphi_{5,0}$	$(1-r)_+^3$
9	$\varphi_{5,1}$	$(1-r)_+^3(5r+1)$	10	$\varphi_{5,2}$	$(1-r)_+^7(16r^2+7r+1)$

5   RBF Interpolation Example

For demonstration of the RBF spatio-temporal scattered data interpolation properties, the Rainfall data of the Peninsular Malaysia from the Malaysian Meteorology Department in 2007 [4] were taken. The data are static from the spatial point of view and dynamic from the temporal one.

5.1   Algorithm Based on Triangulation and Timmer Patches

One possible approach is to make the domain tessellation, then subdivide the mesh and then smooth it. Ali [4] used Delaunay triangulation on 25 major mete-orological stations positions and used cubic Timmer triangular patches, see Ali [2,3,5], for the triangular surface representation and interpolation. The Ali's algorithm is presented by Algorithm 1 and the final triangular surface is presented in Table 3.

It should be noticed, that additional operations are need in order to obtain a smooth surface over the triangular mesh generated by the Ali's algorithm.

In the following, a solution based on the RBF interpolation is presented.

5.2   RBF Interpolation

The RBF approach leads to smooth surface automatically, however, interpolation on borders might not be reliable. Examples of the data interpolation are presented in figures in Table 4[6].

---

[6] The SN-RBF with the Gauss function and bilinear polynomial was used; parameters $\alpha = 0.255$ and $\beta = 1$ in Eq. 10.

Table 3. Tessellation of the Peninsular Malaysia and Triangular surface generated by Ali's algorithm for May-2007; courtesy Ali [4]

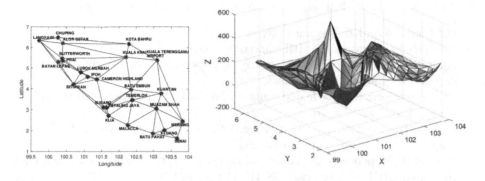

Algorithm 1. Ali's Construction scattered data interpolation algorithm

---

1: Input: Data points
2: Triangulate the domain by using Delaunay triangulation.
3: Specify the derivatives at the data points using [17] then assign Timmer ordinates values for each triangular patch.
4: Generate the triangular patches of the surfaces by using cubic Timmer triangular patches.
5: Output: Surface reconstruction.

Table 4. Interpolation of the Rainfall data at Peninsular Malaysia in 2007; the polygon represents a convex hull of the meteorological stations positions

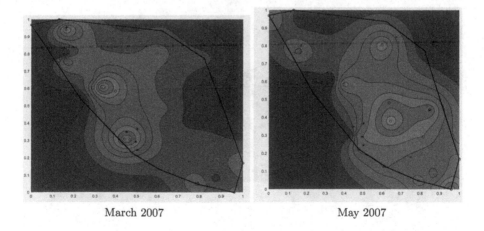

March 2007   May 2007

The 3D views of the Rainfall interpolated data are presented in Fig. 1 and Fig. 2. It should be noted that the α shape parameter has to be set *reasonably*[7].

In general, the RBF interpolation benefits from the following properties:

- the final interpolation is naturally smooth,
- if CS-RBFs are used, the RBF matrix is sparse,
- computational complexity is nearly independent of the dimensionality, depends on the number of points,
- an explicit formal analytical formula of the final interpolation is obtained, see Eq. 12, Eq. 14 and Eq. 15,
- if the RBF function $\varphi(r)$ is positive definite, iterative methods for solving linear system of equations can be used,
- the SN-RBF increases the numerical stability as it actually normalizes each row of the RBF matrix Skala [38,41], Cervenka [10],
- as a solution of linear system of equations is equivalent to the outer product (extended cross product) use, the standard symbolic operations can be used for further processing *without need of the numerical evaluation*,
- the block matrix decomposition might be used in the case of large data, see Majdisova [27,28],
- the domain decomposition can be applied, which leads to faster computation, see Smolik [46–48].

It should be noted, that the RBFs are also used in solution of partial differential equations (PDEs) or surface reconstruction of the acquired data Carr [9], Drake [13] Cuomo [11,12] and Macedo [24,25].

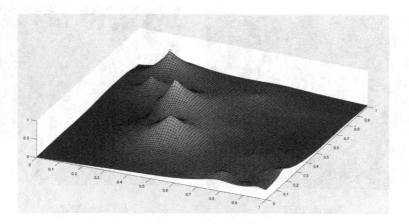

Fig. 1. Interpolation of the Rainfall data March 2007 the Gauss function used, shape parameter $\alpha = 0.255$

---

[7] There are several suboptimal shape parameters, see Afiatdoust [1], Skala [43], Kara-georghis [22] and Wang [49].

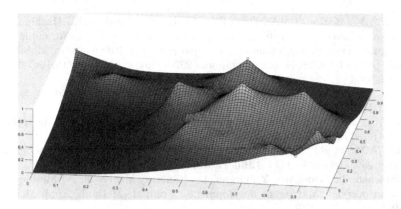

Fig. 2. Interpolation of the Rainfall data May 2007 the Gauss function used, shape parameter $\alpha = 0.2550$

6 Conclusion

This contribution briefly presents a new form of normalized RBF, the Squared Normalized RBF SN-RBF, for the spatio-temporal data and a perspective of use in sensor networks, when sensors do not have a fixed position and data are not synchronized in time, i.e. in the time-slots. The proposed SN-RBF formulation leads to better RBF matrix conditionality, too.

The presented SN-RBF interpolation method is especially convenient for scattered spatio-temporal interpolation of data cases, e.g. when the sensors are transmitting data only in the case, when physical phenomena reach values outside the expected range and/or changing their positions, e.g. surveillance sensors in the sea, etc.

Future work is to be targeted to analysis of the β parameter setting and its sensitivity, to the TPS $(r^2 \ln r)$ function applicability for large data sets, conditionality of the resulting RBF matrices and to methods for visualization of spatio-temporal data for 2D+T and 3D+T data as they cannot be visualized using methods like contour plots or 3D projections.

Acknowledgments. The author thanks to colleagues at the Shandong University(Jinan) and Zhejiang University(Hangzhou) China, University of West Bohemia, Pilsen for their critical comments, discussions, especially to colleagues Michal Smolik, Zuzana Majdisova, Martin Cervenka, Mariia Martynova and Jan Kasak for producing some images and for numerical verification.

References

1. Afiatdoust, F., Esmaeilbeigi, M.: Optimal variable shape parameters using genetic algorithm for radial basis function approximation. Ain Shams Eng. J. **6**, 639–647 (2015)

2. Ali, F.A.M., Karim, S.A.A., Dass, S.C., Skala, V., Hasan, M.K., Hashim, I.: Efficient visualization of scattered energy distribution data by using cubic timmer triangular patches. In: Sulaiman, S.A. (ed.) Energy Efficiency in Mobility Systems, pp. 145–180. Springer, Singapore (2020). https://doi.org/10.1007/978-981-15-0102-9_8

3. Ali, F., et al.: New cubic timmer triangular patches with c1 and g1 continuity. Jurnal Teknologi **81**(6), 1–11 (2019)

4. Ali, F., et al.: Construction of cubic timmer triangular patches and its application in scattered data interpolation. Mathematics **8**, 159 (2020)

5. Ali, F.A.M., et al.: Visualizing the energy of scattered data by using cubic timmer triangular patches. J. Phys. **1366**(1), 012098 (2019)

6. Belytschko, T., Krongauz, Y., Organ, D., Fleming, M., Krysl, P.: Meshless methods: an overview and recent developments. Comput. Methods Appl. Mech. Eng. **139**(1–4), 3–47 (1996)

7. Biancolini, M.E.: Fast Radial Basis Functions for Engineering Applications, 1st edn. Springer, Heidelberg (2017). https://doi.org/10.1007/978-3-319-75011-8

8. Buhmann, M.: On quasi-interpolation with radial basis functions. J. Approx. Theory **72**(1), 103–130 (1993)

9. Carr, J., et al.: Reconstruction and representation of 3d objects with radial basis functions. In: Proceedings of the 28th Annual Conference on Computer Graphics and Interactive Techniques, SIGGRAPH 2001, pp. 67–76 (2001)

10. Červenka, M., Skala, V.: Conditionality analysis of the radial basis function matrix. In: Gervasi, O., Murgante, B., Misra, S., Garau, C., Blečić, I., Taniar, D., Apduhan, B.O., Rocha, A.M.A.C., Tarantino, E., Torre, C.M., Karaca, Y. (eds.) ICCSA 2020. LNCS, vol. 12250, pp. 30–43. Springer, Cham (2020). https://doi.org/10.1007/978-3-030-58802-1_3

11. Cuomo, S., Galletti, A., Giunta, G., Marcellino, L.: Reconstruction of implicit curves and surfaces via rbf interpolation. Appl. Numer. Math. **116**, 157–171 (2017)

12. Cuomo, S., Galletti, A., Giunta, G., Starace, A.: Surface reconstruction from scattered point via rbf interpolation on gpu. In: 2013 Federated Conference on Computer Science and Information Systems, FedCSIS 2013, pp. 433–440 (2013)

13. Drake, K.P., Fuselier, E.J., Wright, G.B.: Implicit surface reconstruction with a curl-free radial basis function partition of unity method (2021)

14. Fasshauer, G.: Meshfree Approximation Methods with Matlab, 1st edn. World Scientific, Singapore (2007)

15. Floater, M.S., Iske, A.: Multistep scattered data interpolation using compactly supported radial basis functions. J. Comput. Appl. Math. **73**(1–2), 65–78 (1996)

16. Franke, R.: A critical comparison of some methods for interpolation of scattered data. Technical report. Naval Postgraduate School Monterey, CA (1979)

17. Goodman, T., Said, H., Chang, L.: Local derivative estimation for scattered data interpolation. Appl. Math. Comput. **68**(1), 41–50 (1995)

18. Hardy, R.L.: Multiquadric equations of topography and other irregular surfaces. J. Geophys. Res. **76**, 1905–1915 (1971)

19. Hardy, R.L.: Theory and applications of the multiquadric-biharmonic method 20 years of discovery 1968–1988. Comput. Math. Appl. **19**, 163–208 (1990)

20. Iske, A.: Multiresolution Methods in Scattered Data Modelling, vol. 37. Springer, Heidelberg (2004). https://doi.org/10.1007/978-3-642-18754-4

21. Jäger, J.: Advances in radial and spherical basis function interpolation. PhD thesis, Justus-Liebig-Universität, Otto-Behaghel-Str. 8, 35394 Gießen. PhD Thesis (2018)

22. Karageorghis, A., Tryfonos, P.: Shape parameter estimation in RBF function approximation. Int. J. Comput. Methods Exp. Meas. **7**, 246–259 (2019)

23. Ku, C.-Y., Hong, L.-D., Liu, C.-Y., Xiao, J.-E.: Space-time polyharmonic radial polynomial basis functions for modeling saturated and unsaturated flows. Eng. Comput. (2021)
24. Macedo, I., Gois, J., Velho, L.: Hermite interpolation of implicit surfaces with radial basis functions. In: Proceedings of SIBGRAPI 2009–22nd Brazilian Symposium on Computer Graphics and Image Processing, pp. 1–8 (2009)
25. Macedo, I., Gois, J., Velho, L.: Hermite radial basis functions implicits. Comput. Graph. Forum 30(1), 27–42 (2011)
26. Majdisova, Z., Skala, V.: A new radial basis function approximation with reproduction. In: CGVCVIP 2016, pp. 215–222 (2016)
27. Majdisova, Z., Skala, V.: A radial basis function approximation for large datasets. In: SIGRAD 2016, pp. 9–14 (2016)
28. Majdisova, Z., Skala, V.: Big geo data surface approximation using radial basis functions: a comparative study. Comput. Geosci. 109, 51–58 (2017)
29. Majdisova, Z., Skala, V.: Radial basis function approximations: comparison and applications. Appl. Math. Model. 51, 728–743 (2017)
30. Majdisova, Z., Skala, V., Smolik, M.: Algorithm for placement of reference points and choice of an appropriate variable shape parameter for the RBF approximation. Integr. Comput. Aided Eng. 27, 1–15 (2020)
31. Menandro, F.: Two new classes of compactly supported radial basis functions for approximation of discrete and continuous data. Eng. Rep. 1, e12028:1–30 (2019)
32. Perfilieva, I., Vlasanek, P., Wrublova, M.: Fuzzy Transform for Image Reconstruction, pp. 615–620. World Scientific, Singapore (2012)
33. Petrik, S., Skala, V.: Iso-contouring in time-varying meshes. In: SCCG 2007: 23rd Spring Conference on Computer Graphics, pp. 175–182 (2007)
34. Petrik, S., Skala, V.: Z-diamonds: a fast iso-surface extraction algorithm for dynamic meshes. MCCSIS 2007(3), 67–74 (2007)
35. Petrik, S., Skala, V.: Space and time efficient isosurface extraction. Comput. Graph. (Pergamon) 32(6), 704–710 (2008)
36. Sarra, S.A., Sturgill, D.: A random variable shape parameter strategy for radial basis function approximation methods. Eng. Anal. Bound. Elements 33, 1239–1245 (2009)
37. Schaback, R.: Optimal geometric hermite interpolation of curves, mathematical methods for curves and surfaces. ii. Innov. Appl. Math., 417–428 (1998)
38. Skala, V.: High dimensional and large span data least square error: numerical stability and conditionality. Int. J. Appl. Phys. Math. 7(3), 148–156 (2017)
39. Skala, V.: RBF interpolation with CSRBF of large data sets. Proceedia Comput. Sci. 108, 2433–2437 (2017)
40. Skala, V.: RBF interpolation and approximation of large span data sets. In: MCSI 2017 - Corfu, pp. 212–218. IEEE (2018)
41. Skala, V.: Conditionality of linear systems of equation and matrices using projective geometric algebra. In: Gervasi, O., Murgante, B., Misra, S., Garau, C., Blečić, I., Taniar, D., Apduhan, B.O., Rocha, A.M.A.C., Tarantino, E., Torre, C.M., Karaca, Y. (eds.) ICCSA 2020. LNCS, vol. 12250, pp. 3–17. Springer, Cham (2020). https://doi.org/10.1007/978-3-030-58802-1_1
42. Skala, V., Kansa, E.: Why is the least square error method dangerous? Computacion y Sistemas 25(1), 149–151 (2021)
43. Skala, V., Karim, S.A.A., Zabran, M.: Radial basis function approximation optimal shape parameters estimation. In: Krzhizhanovskaya, V.V., et al. (eds.) ICCS 2020. LNCS, vol. 12142, pp. 309–317. Springer, Cham (2020). https://doi.org/10.1007/978-3-030-50433-5_24

44. Smolik, M., Skala, V.: Fast parallel triangulation algorithm of large data sets in E^2 and E^3 for in-core and out-core memory processing. In: Murgante, B., et al. (eds.) ICCSA 2014. LNCS, vol. 8580, pp. 301–314. Springer, Cham (2014). https://doi.org/10.1007/978-3-319-09129-7_23

45. Smolik, M., Skala, V., In-core and out-core memory fast parallel triangulation algorithm for large data sets in E2 and E3. In: ACM SIGGRAPH,: Posters. SIGGRAPH 2014 (2014)

46. Smolik, M., Skala, V.: Large scattered data interpolation with radial basis functions and space subdivision. Integr. Comput. Aided Eng. **25**, 49–62 (2018)

47. Smolik, M., Skala, V.: Efficient simple large scattered 3D vector fields radial basis function approximation using space subdivision. In: Computational Science and Its Application, ICSSA 2019 proceedings, pp. 337–350 (2019)

48. Smolik, M., Skala, V.: Efficient speed-up of radial basis functions approximation and interpolation formula evaluation. In: Gervasi, O., et al. (eds.) ICCSA 2020. LNCS, vol. 12249, pp. 165–176. Springer, Cham (2020). https://doi.org/10.1007/978-3-030-58799-4_12

49. Wang, J., Liu, G.: On the optimal shape parameters of radial basis functions used for 2-d meshless methods. Comput. Methods Appl. Mech. Eng. **191**, 2611–2630 (2002)

50. Wendland, H.: Piecewise polynomial, positive definite and compactly supported radial functions of minimal degree. Adv. Comput. Math. **4**(1), 389–396 (1995)

51. Wendland, H.: Scattered Data Approximation. Cambridge University Press, Cambridge (2004)

52. Wikipedia contributors. Delaunay triangulation – Wikipedia, the free encyclopedia (2022). Accessed 9 June 2022

53. Wikipedia contributors. Radial basis function network – Wikipedia, the free encyclopedia (2022). Accessed 22 June 2022

54. Wu, Z.: Compactly supported positive definite radial functions. Adv. Comput. Math. **4**(1), 283–292 (1995)

55. Zhang, X., Song, K.Z., Lu, M.W., Liu, X.: Meshless methods based on collocation with radial basis functions. Comput. Mech. **26**, 333–343 (2000)

CFD Prediction of Wind Turbine Blade Compressible Aerodynamics

A. Mezzacapo⦾, M. C. Vitulano⦾, A. D. Tomasso⦾, and G. De Stefano$^{(\boxtimes)}$⦾

Engineering Department, University of Campania Luigi Vanvitelli,
Aversa 81031, Italy
giuliano.destefano@unicampania.it

Abstract. Computational fluid dynamics (CFD) analysis is carried out to evaluate the compressible aerodynamics of a large horizontal axis wind turbine blade. The mean turbulent flow around the rotating blade is simulated by adopting the unsteady Reynolds-averaged Navier-Stokes modelling approach, where the governing equations are solved by means of a finite volume-based numerical method, supplied with a two-equation eddy-viscosity turbulence model. The present CFD model using an open-source code for computational wind engineering applications was verified to have significant practical potential by making a comparison with a reference steady solution.

Keywords: Computational Wind Engineering · Compressible Flow · Turbine Blade Aerodynamics · Open Source Software

1   Introduction

To meet the global energy demands, the size of wind turbines (WT) is getting larger and larger, in order to maximize power generation. This holds, in particular, for offshore systems that can be installed in deep water locations, where very large rotors are able to generate higher power due to high wind speeds. Therefore, the trend of adopting very large rotor diameters and high tip-speeds has brought about a renovated interest in the aerodynamic design of wind turbine blades, where significant compressibility effects have to be taken into account [1,2]. In fact, the aerodynamic design of large wind turbines represents a very challenging task, calling for deep innovations in the scaled-up design methodology [3].

Computational fluid dynamics (CFD) analysis is heavily used as a base method for analyzing WT designs [4], with the Reynolds-averaged Navier-Stokes (RANS) modeling approach being usually followed [5]. In the computational wind engineering (CWE) domain, however, past compressible studies were mostly conducted for airfoil flows, e.g. [6]. Concerning previous three-dimensional simulations, as either the WT sizes were not large enough, or the tip speeds were not high enough, much more research is needed for better investigating the aerodynamic properties of these novel systems, including compressibility effects.

O. Gervasi et al. (Eds.): ICCSA 2023, LNCS 13956, pp. 113–125, 2023.
https://doi.org/10.1007/978-3-031-36805-9_8

Table 1. IEA-15-240-RWT: relevant parameters.

Parameter	Value
Power	15 MW
Rotor diameter	240 m
Rotor speed	7.56 rpm
Maximum tip speed	95 m/s
Hub height	150 m
Wind speed	10.6 m/s

Table 2. IEA-15-240-RWT: blade geometric parameters.

Parameter	Value
Blade length	117 m
Root diameter	5.20 m
Root cylinder length	2.34 m
Max chord	5.77 m
Max chord spanwise position	27.2 m
Tip prebend	4.0 m

This study deals with the three-dimensional model of a horizontal axis wind turbine (HAWT) that represents the most common design for modern large machines. The blade under investigation belongs to the IEA Wind 15 MW offshore reference wind turbine (RWT) that was recently released [7]. Specifically, the model data for the present work were originally developed within the International Energy Agency (IEA) Wind Task 37 on wind energy systems engineering [8]. Some key parameters of this three-bladed machine, which is referred to as IEA-15-240-RWT, are given in Table 1. It represents a standard design model that can be used for concept studies, like the present one, as the wind energy industry progresses toward larger systems. Given the blade length and the maximum tip speed, the compressible regime is indeed approached.

The main goal of the present work is the computational evaluation of the compressible aerodynamics for the single blade of the above RWT, using open-source CFD software that is available to the industrial researchers. Differently from similar works, where compressibility corrections were employed, the compressibility effects are directly simulated. Specifically, the mean turbulent flow past the rotating blade is predicted by using the open-source code OpenFOAM, employing the finite volume (FV) discretization approach, supplied with an unsteady RANS turbulence modeling procedure.

The rest of this paper is organized as follows. In Sect. 2, the overall CFD model is introduced, including details about the blade geometry, the computational domain, the turbulence closure, and the numerical method. The results of the simulations are made known and discussed in Sect. 3. Finally, some concluding remarks are drawn in Sect. 4.

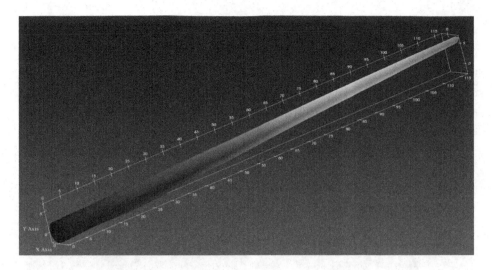

Fig. 1. Computational geometry of the RWT blade.

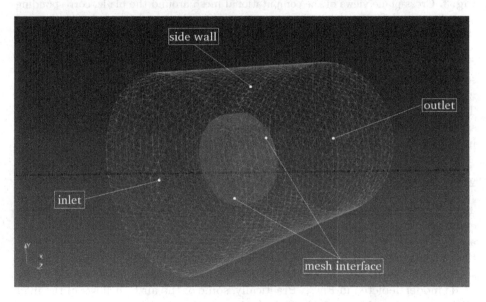

Fig. 2. Sketch of the computational domain: rotating mesh, represented by the inner cylinder including the blade, along with the outer stationary mesh.

2   CFD Model

2.1   Case Study

The computer-aided design (CAD) geometry of the IEA-15-240-RWT blade model was taken from [8], where it is publicly available. Some relevant geometric parameters of this model are summarized in Table 2. The DTU FFA-W3

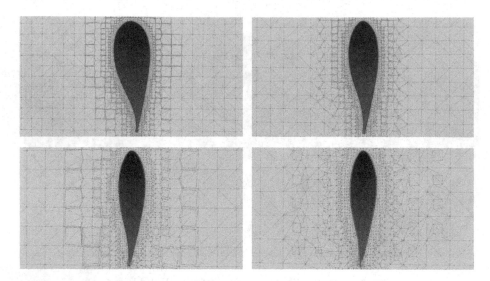

Fig. 3. Cross-plane views of the computational mesh around the blade, corresponding to sections at 40% (top left), 60% (top right), 80% (bottom left), and 90% (bottom right) of its length.

series of airfoils was used in the blade design. These well-documented airfoils were also used in the IEA Wind/DTU 10 MW offshore RWT [4], for instance. The blade rotates around the horizontal X axis with constant angular velocity, say Ω. Figure 1 shows the CAD geometry, with the rotating blade occupying the instantaneous position along the Z axis direction.

2.2   Computational Domain

The computational domain was constructed by employing two nested coaxial cylinders, with the cylinder axis being horizontal. The inner cylinder, which has a length of 60 m and a radius of 150 m, rotates together with the blade, while the outer one, which has a length of 1050 m and a radius of 350 m, remains stationary. The inner part of the computational domain is created around the blade model depicted in Fig. 1. Practically, some of the air that flows in the inlet of the outer domain passes through the inner rotating domain.

Two different meshes are constructed, independently, for the two above subdomains. Since the inner cylinder mesh rotates with respect to the outer cylinder one, the interface between the two sliding meshes is handled by a special boundary condition referred to as arbitrary mesh interface (AMI). The present work follows a similar approach adopted in past studies for the CFD simulation of smaller turbines [9].

The computational domain is sketched in Fig. 2, which shows the rotating mesh, represented by the inner cylinder including the blade, along with the outer stationary mesh. Note that these ones are not the true meshes, but coarser ones used for illustration only. In fact, the results presented in the following were obtained using an overall mesh consisting of about 5 million FV cells. The mesh was suitably refined in the space region close to the blade surface, including the near wake. For illustration, in Fig. 3, the cross-plane views of the FV mesh are shown at four different stations along the blade, namely at 40%, 60%, 80%, and 90% of its length.

Table 3. Types of boundary conditions for mean flow variables.

Boundary	Velocity	Pressure	Temperature
Inlet	fixedValue	zeroGradient	fixedValue
Outlet	inletOutlet	inletOutlet	inletOutlet
Side wall	slip	zeroGradient	zeroGradient
Blade	movingWallVelocity	zeroGradient	zeroGradient
AMIs	cyclicAMI	cyclicAMI	cyclicAMI

Table 4. Types of boundary conditions for turbulence variables.

Boundary	Kinetic-energy k	Specific dissipation ω
Inlet	fixedValue	fixedValue
Outlet	inletOutlet	inletOutlet
Side wall	fixedValue	fixedValue
Blade	kqRWallFunction	omegaWallFunction
AMIs	cyclicAMI	cyclicAMI

2.3   Unsteady RANS Model

The mean compressible flow around the blade was described by the unsteady RANS governing equations. These equations, which are not reported here for brevity, can be found in [5], for instance. The governing equations were supplied with suitable boundary conditions for the mean velocity, pressure, and temperature, as summarized in Table 3. The ambient temperature and pressure levels were set to standard values that are $T_\infty = 293\ K$ and $p_\infty = 101325\ Pa$, respectively. The freestream conditions corresponded to a uniform horizontal wind with constant velocity that was $U_\infty = 10.59\ m/s$. The latter was imposed at the inlet, along with the zero gradient boundary condition for the mean pressure field. Note that the blade surface was assumed as an adiabatic rotating wall with the constant angular velocity $\Omega = 0.79\ rad/s$. These operating conditions correspond to the theoretical parameters of the IEA-15-240-RWT model that are

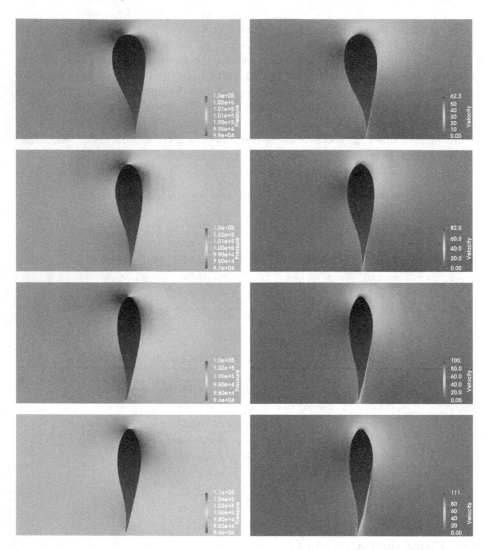

Fig. 4. Contour maps of pressure (left) and velocity modulus (right) around the blade, for four different cross-sections, corresponding to 40% , 60%, 80%, and 90% of its length (from top to bottom).

given in Table 1. Also, slip wall boundary conditions were used at the side wall of the virtual wind tunnel, while the no-slip boundary condition was imposed on the blade surface.

As is usual for industrial aerodynamics applications, eddy viscosity-based diffusion was introduced into the mean flow equations to mimic the effects of

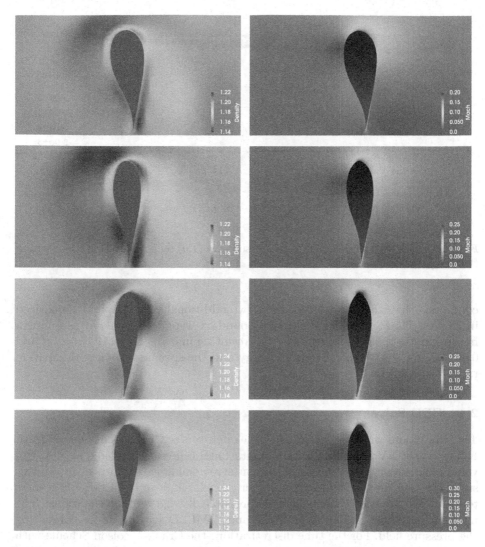

Fig. 5. Contour maps of density (left) and flow Mach number (right) around the blade, for four different cross-sections, corresponding to 40% , 60%, 80%, and 90% of its length (from top to bottom).

turbulence [10, 11]. In this work, the k–ω SST two-equation turbulence model [12] was employed, where two additional evolution equations for the turbulent kinetic energy k and the specific turbulent dissipation rate ω are solved to determine the instantaneous pointwise eddy-viscosity parameter. Note that this model is commonly used for computational wind engineering applications [6]. The boundary

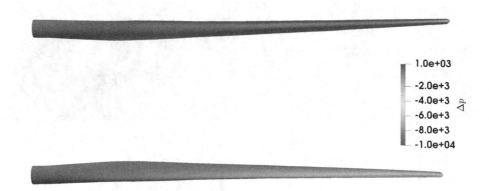

Fig. 6. Surface distribution of relative pressure Δp (Pa) on pressure (top) and suction (bottom) sides of the blade.

conditions that were imposed for these two additional variables are summarized in Table 4. The fixed values at the inlet boundary were determined by assuming a freestream turbulence intensity of 0.1%, resulting in being 1.11×10^{-4} m^2/s^2 and 0.45 s^{-1}, for the turbulent kinetic energy and the specific turbulent dissipation ratio, respectively.

2.4 CFD Solver

The simulations were conducted using the open-source CFD toolkit OpenFOAM. Following the FV approach, each computational cell was considered as a control volume, where discrete versions of the conservation laws are imposed [13]. In this study, we use the *rhoPimpleFoam* solver, which employs the PIMPLE scheme to solve the transient, turbulent compressible flow governing equations. The numerical method combines the PISO and SIMPLE algorithms for computing the pressure field. For the time discretization, the Crank-Nicolson Scheme with an off-centering coefficient of 0.33 was used. The second-order linear upwind scheme was used for pressure, momentum and turbulence variables. To achieve a good convergence rate, the convergence criterion and the under-relaxation factors were properly tuned. Moreover, for all other flow variables, the smoothSolver with the symmetric Gauss-Seidel smoother was used. The adaptive time-step size was determined by setting the maximum Courant number of 0.5 for the transient calculation.

3   Results

The predicted mean flow around the blade is illustrated in Fig. 4, where the contour maps of mean pressure and velocity modulus are reported for four different cross-sections, corresponding to 40%, 60%, 80%, and 90% of the blade length. The corresponding contour maps of density and flow Mach number are depicted in Fig. 5. As was expected, the density variations are significant, as the local flow conditions approach the compressibile regime. This effect is more pronounced at high distance form the rotation axis, due to the high relative wind velocity. Moreover, the highest deviation from the ambient air density, which was chosen as $\rho_\infty = 1.22\ kg/m^3$, occurs on the suction side of the blade. This is

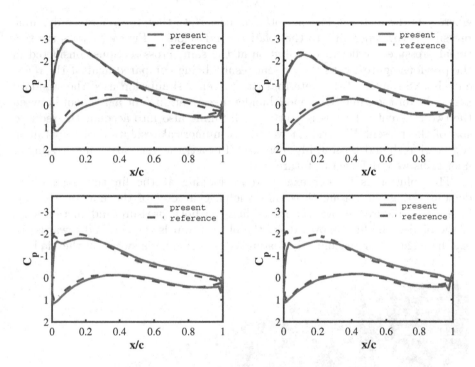

Fig. 7. Sectional pressure coefficient distribution for four different blade cross-sections at 40% (top left), 60% (top right), 80% (bottom left), and 90% (bottom right) span, compared to reference data.

Fig. 8. Limiting streamlines on pressure (top) and suction (bottom) sides of the blade.

clearly demonstrated by looking at the Mach number contours. Apparently, the flow region with large Mach number increases, along with the maximum value of this parameter, with the cross-section station moving towards the blade tip. The location of the maximum Mach number, for each blade section, is close to the leading edge, where the air speed increases due to the high expansion. Furthermore, the relative surface pressure $\Delta p = p - p_\infty$ on the blade is drawn in Fig. 6, for both suction and pressure sides.

From a quantitative point of view, the pressure distribution on the blade surface was examined by estimating the sectional pressure coefficient that is defined by:

$$C_p = \frac{\Delta p}{\frac{1}{2}\rho_\infty \left(U_\infty^2 + \Omega^2 r^2\right)} \tag{1}$$

where r is the distance for the rotation axis. Note that the reference dynamic pressure is corresponding to the relative wind velocity. Figure 7 shows the sectional pressure coefficient distribution at the same cross-sections considered in the previous figures, with the present results being compared against the reference RANS solution [14]. Note that the reference simulation used the standard k-ϵ model for the same RWT model under investigation. The agreement between the two different solutions is pretty good, taking also into account the reduced size of the present FV grid. However, the numerical resolution of the trailing edge region should be suitably increased. In fact, the generation and testing of finer grids were deferred to future work.

The solution is further examined by looking at the limiting streamlines demonstrating the strong three-dimensional character of the flow on the turbine blade. Figure 8 shows the streamlines on both pressure and suction sides of the blade. The fluid moves down the blade towards the tip, and towards the leading edge. After reaching the leading edge region, it is swept off the blade in

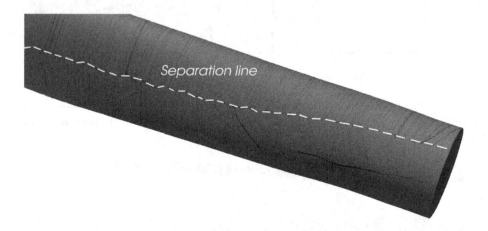

Fig. 9. Separated flow visualization on the suction side, near the blade root (right bottom corner).

the separation shear layer. The separation line on the suction side of the blade is visualized in Fig. 9, where the flow is demonstrated to be highly separated in the blade root region. In fact, this separation line becomes less pronounced moving along the blade towards the tip.

Finally, the WT blade performance is examined by looking at the predicted thrust that is the force experienced by the turbine in the direction parallel to airflow. After the initial transient, the thrust reaches an approximate value of 2.5 MN, which slightly differs from the reference value of 2.2 MN [14]. Note that the present unsteady simulation used a fully three-dimensional computational domain, whereas the reference steady solution was obtained for one third of this domain, while employing peridodic boundary conditions in the azimuthal direction.

4   Conclusions and Perspectives

The present study has to be intended as the proof-of-concept, namely, the preliminary development of a CFD prediction tool using the OpenFOAM software for studying the compressible aerodynamics of a modern wind turbine. The CFD analysis of a 15 MW wind turbine blade model was performed under normal operating conditions. The observed characteristics were in acceptable agreement, both qualitatively and quantitatively, with the data available from a steady flow simulation of the same turbine model. This work paves the way for directly investigating the effects of compressibility on the blade aerodynamics of relevance to modern type large scale wind turbine rotors, using open source software. This research shows that it is possible to successfully simulate the compressible aerodynamics of these systems using the unsteady compressible RANS approach, instead of using compressibility corrections. However, the present CFD model needs further improvement to be effectively used for the aerodynamic design of the whole three-blade rotor.

As to future perspectives, there remains the possibility of developing more sophisticated computational models for this particular wind engineering application, pursuing higher levels of accuracy. For instance, the wavelet-based adaptive multiscale approach for aerodynamic turbulent flows is subject of ongoing research [15, 16]. This innovative methodology exploits the wavelet transform to dynamically and automatically adjust the grid resolution to the local flow conditions [17, 18]. Wavelet-based adaptive unsteady RANS modelling procedures that have been recently developed [19, 20] will be explored in this context, even considering the possibility of supersonic flow on near-future large wind turbines [21]. Finally, the use of higher-fidelity scale-resolving simulation methods, such as wall-modeled hybrid RANS-LES [22], will be subject of future investigation.

References

1. Yan, C., Archer, C.L.: Assessing compressibility effects on the performance of large horizontal-axis wind turbines. Appl. Energy **212**, 33–45 (2018)
2. Sørensen, J.N.; Bertagnolio, F.; Jost, E.; Lutz, T. Aerodynamic effects of compressibility for wind turbines at high tip speeds. J. Phys.: Conf. Ser. **1037**, 022003 (2018)
3. Sørensen, J.N.: Aerodynamic aspects of wind energy conversion. Annu. Rev. Fluid Mech. **43**, 427–448 (2011)
4. Madsen, M.H.A., Zahle, F., Sørensen, N.N., Martins, J.R.R.A.: Multipoint high-fidelity CFD-based aerodynamic shape optimization of a 10 MW wind turbine. Wind Energ. Sci. **4**, 163–192 (2019)
5. Wilcox, D.C.: Turbulence Modeling for CFD, 3rd edn. DCW Industries Inc, La Canada CA (2006)
6. Hossain, M.A., Ziaul, H., Kommalapati, R.R., Khan, S.: Numeric investigation of compressible flow over NREL Phase VI airfoil. Int. J. Eng. Res. Technol. **2**, 2 (2013)
7. Gaertner, E.; Rinker, J.; Sethuraman, L. et al. Definition of the IEA 15-Megawatt Offshore Reference Wind Turbine, NREL/TP-75698, International Energy Laboratory (2020)
8. IEA Wind Task 37 Model data for the 15 MW offshore reference wind turbine. https://github.com/IEAWindTask37/IEA-15-240-RWT Accessed 03 Jan 2023
9. Song, X., Perot, J.B.: CFD Simulation of the NREL Phase VI Rotor. Wind Eng. **39**, 299–310 (2015)
10. De Stefano, G., Natale, N., Reina, G.P., Piccolo, A.: Computational evaluation of aerodynamic loading on retractable landing-gears. Aerospace **7**, 68 (2020)
11. Natale, N., Salomone, T., De Stefano, G., Piccolo, A.: Computational evaluation of control surfaces aerodynamics for a mid-range commercial aircraft. Aerospace **7**, 139 (2020)
12. Menter, F.R.: Two-equation eddy-viscosity turbulence models for engineering applications. AIAA J. **32**, 1598–1605 (1994)
13. Denaro, F.M., De Stefano, G.: A new development of the dynamic procedure in large-eddy simulation based on a finite volume integral approach. Theor. Comput. Fluid Dyn. **25**, 315–355 (2011)
14. Cao, J., et al.: Study of air compressibility effects on the aerodynamic performance of the IEA-15 MW offshore wind turbine. Energy Conv. Manag. **282**, 116883 (2023)
15. De Stefano, G., Dymkoski, E., Vasilyev, O.V.: Localized dynamic kinetic-energy model for compressible wavelet-based adaptive large-eddy simulation. Phys. Rev. Fluids **7**, 054604 (2022)
16. De Stefano, G.: Wavelet-based adaptive large-eddy simulation of supersonic channel flow with different thermal boundary conditions. Phys. Fluids **35**, 035138 (2023)
17. De Stefano, G., Brown-Dymkoski, E., Vasilyev, O.V.: Wavelet-based adaptive large-eddy simulation of supersonic channel flow. J. Fluid Mech. **901**, A13 (2020)
18. Ge, X., De Stefano, G., Hussaini, M.Y., Vasilyev, O.V.: Wavelet-based adaptive eddy-resolving methods for modeling and simulation of complex wall-bounded compressible turbulent flows. Fluids **6**, 331 (2021)
19. Ge, X., Vasilyev, O.V., De Stefano, G., Hussaini, M.Y.: Wavelet-based adaptive unsteady Reynolds-averaged Navier-Stokes computations of wall-bounded internal and external compressible turbulent flows. In: Proceedings of the 2018 AIAA Aerospace Sciences Meeting, Kissimmee, Florida, January (2018)

20. Ge, X., Vasilyev, O.V., De Stefano, G., Hussaini, M.Y.: Wavelet-based adaptive unsteady Reynolds-averaged Navier-Stokes simulations of wall-bounded compressible turbulent flows. AIAA J. **58**, 1529–1549 (2020)
21. De Tavernier, D.; von Terzi, D. The emergence of supersonic flow on wind turbines. J. Phys.: Conf. Ser. **2265**, 042068 (2022)
22. Salomone, T., Piomelli, U., De Stefano, G.: Wall-modeled and hybrid large-eddy simulations of the flow over roughness strips. Fluids **8**, 10 (2023)

Fast CUDA Geomagnetic Map Builder

Delia Spridon$^{(\boxtimes)}$ ⓘ, Adrian Marius Deaconu ⓘ, and Laura Ciupala ⓘ

Department of Mathematics and Computer Science, Transilvania University, Brasov,
BV 0500036, Romania
{delia.cuza,a.deaconu,laura.ciupala}@unitbv.ro

Abstract. In this paper, we use kriging techniques and inverse distance weighting (IDW) to generate geomagnetic maps in Romania. Kriging is a method of spatial interpolation that calculates unknown values based on statistical analysis of the correlation of known values in space. On the other hand, IDW estimates unknown values using a weighted average of nearby known values. Both methods are used in geophysics to interpolate Earth's magnetic field measurements in areas where no data is available, to fill gaps in existing data, or to generate maps for regions without discrete information. Each method has its advantages and limitations, and the selection of the appropriate method is dependent on factors such as the distribution of known data points and the properties of the underlying geophysical process. In this study, we used these interpolation methods to produce reliable and accurate maps of the Earth's magnetic field over a large spatial area. To speed up the computations and take advantage of the impresive computational power of GPUs, we used CUDA to parallelize the interpolation computations. The use of GPU programming for geomagnetic data interpolation has the potential to provide significant performance advantages, allowing us to analyze large datasets promptly and accurately.

Keywords: CUDA · IDW · kriging · geomagnetism

1 Introduction

Interpolation methods for geomagnetic data are used to estimate magnetic field values at locations where measurements are not available [1]. There are several interpolation methods that have been used for this purpose, each with its own strengths and weaknesses. Some of the interpolation methods for geomagnetic data are kriging, spline interpolation, radial basis functions, IDW, Artificial Neural Networks(ANN).

Kriging is a geostatistical interpolation method that can be used for interpolating discrete geomagnetic data using a variogram to model the spatial correlation of the data and estimates the values at unsampled locations using a weighted average of nearby measurements. Kriging is particularly effective for estimating data values in areas with high spatial variability.

O. Gervasi et al. (Eds.): ICCSA 2023, LNCS 13956, pp. 126–138, 2023.
https://doi.org/10.1007/978-3-031-36805-9_9

Spline interpolation is a non-parametric interpolation method that uses a mathematical function to fit a curve to the data. This method is particularly useful for data that has a smooth spatial variation.

Radial Basis Functions interpolation is a method that uses a set of radial basis functions to interpolate data values at unsampled locations and is particularly effective for data that has a strong directional dependence.

Inverse Distance Weighting (IDW) is a simple interpolation method that estimates values at unsampled locations based on the weighted average of nearby measurements. This method assumes that data values influence decreases with distance from known measurements by assigning higher weights to closer measurements. IDW is particularly useful for estimating values in areas with low spatial variability.

Artificial Neural Networks (ANNs) are machine learning models that can be used to interpolate data [2]. ANNs can learn complex spatial relationships in the data and are particularly useful for estimating values in areas with non-linear spatial variations.

Overall, the choice of interpolation method depends on the characteristics of the data and the specific research question being addressed. The interpolation methods for geomagnetic data continues to evolve, with new methods and approaches being developed and tested.

In this paper, we use kriging and IDW interpolation methods to obtain geomagnetic maps for Romania. The algorithms for this methods are also parallelised by using CUDA arhitecture on GPUs in order to obtain fast, high resolution geomagnetic maps for the studied area. The accuracy of the obtained maps are compared for the two interpolation methods, also the algorithms are analysed taking into account the execution time and the speed-up.

1.1 Geomagnetic Data

Geomagnetic data is the information gathered about the Earth's magnetic field. Geomagnetic data can be collected using a range of methods, including magnetic surveys conducted from aircraft, ships, or ground-based instruments [3, 4]. Geomagnetic maps are graphical representations of this data that show variations in the strength and direction of the magnetic field at different locations on the Earth's surface [5]. Geomagnetic data and maps are used in a wide range of scientific, industrial, and commercial applications, from understanding the Earth's structure to identifying potential mineral and energy resources.

Geomagnetic data are essential for understanding the structure and dynamics of the Earth's interior [6]. The magnetic field is generated by the motion of molten iron in the Earth's outer core, and variations in the field can provide insights into the structure and behavior of the region [7]. For example, changes in the strength and direction of the magnetic field can indicate the presence of geological structures such as faults, magma chambers, and mineral deposits [8].

Geomagnetic data are also used to study the Earth's upper atmosphere and its interaction with the solar wind. The magnetic field acts as a shield, deflecting high-energy particles from the sun and protecting the Earth's atmosphere from erosion [9]. However, the magnetic field is not uniform, and variations in its strength and direction can result in the formation of regions known as the Van Allen radiation belts, where charged particles are trapped and can cause damage to spacecrafts and satellites.

Geomagnetic data are also used in navigation and surveying. The magnetic field provides a reference for compasses and can be used to determine the orientation and position of objects on the Earth's surface. This information is used in a range of applications, from mapping and surveying to navigation and mineral exploration [4].

Geomagnetic maps are graphical representations of the Earth's magnetic field. They show variations in the strength and direction of the field at different locations on the Earth's surface, and can be used to identify geological structures, mineral deposits, and other features [5].

Geomagnetic maps are used in a range of applications, including mineral exploration, where variations in the magnetic field can indicate the presence of mineral deposits. For example, the Sudbury Basin in Canada is a large geological structure that contains a rich deposit of nickel, copper, and other minerals [10]. The basin is marked by a large magnetic anomaly, which was identified using magnetic surveys and helped to guide the exploration and development of the deposit.

Geomagnetic maps are also used in environmental monitoring, where changes in the magnetic field can indicate the presence of pollutants or other contaminants. For example, magnetic surveys have been used to map the extent of oil spills and other environmental disasters, providing valuable information for cleanup and mitigation efforts.

Geomagnetic maps are also used in geophysical research, where they can provide insights into the structure and behavior of the Earth's interior. For example, magnetic anomalies in the oceanic crust have been used to study the process of seafloor spreading and the formation of new oceanic crust.

Geomagnetic data and maps are essential tools for understanding the Earth's magnetic field and its diverse applications. Geomagnetic data provides insights into the structure and dynamics of the Earth's interior, while geomagnetic maps are used for navigation, geological mapping, and scientific research. Geomagnetic data and maps have practical applications in industry and commercial ventures, particularly in mineral exploration, energy development, and navigation.

1.2   Inverse Distance Weight

Inverse distance weighting (IDW) is a widespread adopted interpolation algorithm used to estimate values at unsampled locations based on measured values at nearby sample locations. The algorithm assumes that the values being estimated are a function of distance from the sample locations and that values closer to the sample locations have a greater influence on the estimated value than those farther away.

The basic idea behind IDW is to calculate a weighted average of the measured values at the sample locations, with the weights being proportional to the inverse of the distance between the unsampled location and each sample location. The weights are usually normalized so that they sum to one. The estimated value at the unsampled location is then the weighted average of the measured values. The IDW algorithm can be expressed mathematically as follows:

Let $V(u)$ be the estimated value at the unsampled location u, $V(i)$ be the measured value at the ith sample location, located at coordinates $(x(i), y(i))$, and let $l(i)$ be the distance between the unsampled location and the ith sample location. Then, the estimated value at the unsampled location can be calculated using the following formula:

$$V(u) = (\sum_{i=1}^{k} [w(i) \cdot V(i)]) / (\sum_{i=1}^{k} w(i)) \tag{1}$$

where $w(i) = 1/l(i)^p$, p is a positive exponent that controls the rate at which the weights decrease with distance and k is the total number of sample locations.

There are different ways to choose the value of the exponent p, but the most common values are 2 (inverse square distance weighting) and 3 (inverse cube distance weighting). IDW is a simple and computationally efficient algorithm, but it has some limitations. One of the main limitations is that it assumes that the values being estimated are a function of distance only, and it does not take into account other factors that may influence the values, such as topography, soil type, or land use. Another limitation is that it may produce unrealistic estimates at locations far from the sample locations, especially when the sample locations are unevenly distributed.

Despite its limitations, IDW is widely used in various fields, including geology, environmental science, and geography. It is often used as a baseline method for comparison with other interpolation algorithms, and it is also used for simple applications where high accuracy is not required.

1.3   Kriging

Kriging is a spatial interpolation algorithm that estimates unknown values at unobserved locations based on spatial correlation among observed values. It was first introduced by D. G. Krige in the 1950s s [11] and has since become a popular method for spatial prediction in geostatistics.

The basic idea behind kriging is to estimate the unknown value $z(u)$ at an unsampled location u based on a weighted average of the observed values $z(x_i)$ at nearby sampled locations x_i. The weights are chosen to minimize the prediction error and are determined based on the spatial correlation structure of the data. The kriging weights are obtained by solving a system of linear equations that express the spatial autocovariance function of the data.

The kriging predictor for the unknown value $z(u)$ is given by:

$$z(u) = \sum w_i z(x_i)$$

where w_i are the kriging weights and $z(x_i)$ are the observed values at sampled locations x_i. The kriging weights are obtained by solving the following system of equations:

$$Cw = \lambda$$

where C is the spatial autocovariance matrix between the observed values at sampled locations x_i, w is the vector of kriging weights, and λ is a Lagrange multiplier that enforces the unbiasedness condition on the predictor.

The kriging algorithm can be extended to incorporate additional information, such as trend and measurement error, by modifying the kriging system of equations. There are several variants of kriging, including ordinary kriging, simple kriging, and universal kriging, each with different assumptions about the underlying spatial correlation structure.

Kriging has been widely applied in many fields, including geology, hydrology, ecology, and environmental sciences. It has proven to be a powerful tool for spatial prediction and uncertainty quantification [12,13].

1.4 GPU Programming

Graphics Processing Units (GPUs) are specialized hardware designed to perform complex mathematical computations in parallel, making them an ideal platform for high-performance computing (HPC) applications. Originally designed for graphics rendering, GPUs have been adapted for a variety of scientific, engineering, and financial applications that require large-scale parallelism. In order to take full advantage of GPUs, developers need to have a good understanding of GPU programming and frameworks such as CUDA (Compute Unified Device Architecture). GPU programming involves writing code that runs on both the CPU (central processing unit) and GPU. The CPU is responsible for managing the overall system and launching the GPU kernels, while the GPU is responsible for executing the computations in parallel. CUDA is a parallel computing platform and programming model that enables developers to write code in a language such as C or C++ and then compile and run it on NVIDIA GPUs.

CUDA provides several key features that make GPU programming more accessible to developers. First, it provides a compiler that translates CPU code into GPU code. This compiler also optimizes the code to take advantage of the GPU's architecture and capabilities. Second, CUDA provides a set of libraries that implement common functionality, such as linear algebra, signal processing, and image processing. These libraries are optimized for the GPU, and they can significantly improve the performance of GPU applications [14].

One of the most important concepts in CUDA programming is the kernel. A kernel is a function that executes on the GPU and is designed to perform a specific computation in parallel. Kernels are written in C or C++, and they use CUDA-specific language extensions to access GPU-specific functionality, such as shared memory and thread synchronization. CUDA kernels are executed on a grid of thread blocks, with each block containing multiple threads. The CUDA runtime manages the execution of the kernel across multiple blocks and threads, and it provides mechanisms for thread synchronization and memory management.

One of the main advantages of using CUDA for GPU programming is its ability to achieve significant speedups compared to traditional CPU-based implementations. This is because GPUs have a massively parallel architecture that allows them to execute thousands of threads simultaneously. For example, a GPU with 1,000 processing cores can execute 1,000 threads in parallel, while a CPU with 8 cores can only execute 8 threads in parallel. The increased parallelism of GPUs enables developers to perform computationally intensive tasks much faster than on a CPU. CUDA is widely used in many fields such as scientific computing, machine learning, image processing, and finance. In scientific computing, CUDA is used for performing simulations and modeling of complex physical systems such as fluid dynamics, astrophysics, and climate modeling. In machine learning, CUDA is used to train deep neural networks and perform large-scale data analytics. In image processing, CUDA is used for real-time video processing, image segmentation, and feature detection. In finance, CUDA is used for performing complex financial simulations and risk analysis.

CUDA is supported on a wide range of NVIDIA GPUs, including those in desktops, workstations, and servers. It is also supported on a variety of operating systems, including Windows, Linux, and macOS. NVIDIA provides a comprehensive set of documentation and resources for developers interested in learning CUDA, including online tutorials, sample code, and user forums.

GPU programming has become an essential skill for developers in many fields due to the significant performance gains it offers. CUDA is a popular programming framework that enables developers to leverage the power of NVIDIA GPUs for general-purpose computing tasks. CUDA provides a comprehensive set of programming tools and libraries, and its parallel computing model enables developers to achieve significant speedups compared to traditional CPU-based implementations. With the increasing demand for high-performance computing in various fields, CUDA programming is expected to play an increasingly important role in the future.

Few recent researches show the advantages that CUDA can bring when is used for parallelizing interpolation methods. Thus, in [15], researchers proposed a CUDA-based parallel algorithm for IDW interpolation on big data sets and the results showed that the CUDA-based algorithm outperformed the traditional CPU-based algorithm in terms of computation time and accuracy. An other example is presented in [16], where researchers proposed a CUDA-based parallel algorithm for Kriging interpolation and concluded that the CUDA-based algorithm achieved significant speedups compared to the traditional CPU-based algorithm, especially for large-scale data sets. In [17], researchers proposed a CUDA-based framework for IDW and Kriging interpolation and showed also the time performance and accuracy improvement.

2   Methods

The aim of our paper is to obtain a geomagnetic map for Romania, by using IDW
and kriging interpolation methods.The geomagnetic data were obtained from
Romanian geomagnetic stations and with help of Physics Toolbox Sensor Suite
app in more than 1300 GPS positions spreaded all over the country. The data
was gather using Citizen Science action from Researchers Night 2018–2019 Handle with Science European project, financed from H2020, GA no. 818795/2018.
The implemented algorithms were tested on a system with Intel(R) Core(TM)
i7-10750H CPU @ 2.60GHz 2.59 GHz, 16.0 GB RAM, NVIDIA GeForce RTX
2060 GPU and Windows 10 Pro operating system. These interpolation methods were accelerated by using CUDA programming for obtaining high resolution
geomagnetic maps in real time. This tool could be used for example for monitoring geomagnetic modifications of a large area in order to identify the changes
that could take place in Earth's structure or for identifying regions with certain
magnetic properties.

The IDW algorithm pseudocode is presented below [18]:

Algorithm 1. IDW algorithm

$dy \leftarrow \frac{y_{max} - y_{min}}{n}$

$dx \leftarrow \frac{x_{max} - x_{min}}{m}$

$y \leftarrow y_{min}$

for $i \leftarrow 1$ to n **do**

    $x \leftarrow x_{min}$

    for $j \leftarrow 1$ to m **do**

        $g_{ij} \leftarrow v(x, y)$

        $x \leftarrow x + dx$

    end for

    $y \leftarrow y + dy$

end for

---

where g_{ij} are the points of a 2D grid of $m \times n$ interpolated values, $m, n \in N^*$ for
a rectangular region given by coordinates $x_{min}, x_{max}, y_{min}, y_{max} \in R, (x_{min} <
x_{max}, y_{min} < y_{max})$. To obtain the IDW estimated value by using Eq. 1, the
distance between two points was calculated using the formula for distance on
Earth.

To use CUDA for IDW, we first need to parallelize the algorithm. In IDW,
we need to calculate the distance between the unsampled points and each of the
sampled points. This distance calculation can be parallelized by assigning each
GPU thread to a single unsampled point and calculating the distances to all
sampled points.

Once we have calculated the distances, we need to calculate the weights for
each sampled point based on its distance from the unsampled point. This weight
calculation can also be parallelized by assigning each GPU thread to a single
sampled point and calculating its weight for all unsampled points.

Finally, we can use the calculated weights to interpolate the values at the unsampled points. This interpolation step can also be parallelized by assigning each GPU thread to a single unsampled point and calculating its value based on the weighted average of the sampled point values.

The kriging algorithm was implemented following the next 4 steps:

Step 1. Calculation of semivariance points (Algorithm 2))
Step 2. Calculation of semivariance coefficients using least squares method [19]
Step 3. Calculation of interpolation weights (Algorithm 3)
Step 4. Calculation of interpolated values (Algorithm 4)

For parallelizing kriging algoritm using CUDA, multiple steps are necessary: the variogram calculation, the kriging matrix calculation, and the kriging weight calculation.

The variogram calculation involves computing the semivariance between all pairs of sampled points. This step can be parallelized by assigning each GPU thread to a single pair of sampled points and calculating their semivariance.

The kriging matrix calculation involves inverting a matrix that depends on the semivariances between the sampled points.

Finally, the kriging weight calculation involves computing the weights for each sampled point based on its distance and spatial correlation with the unsampled point. This step can be parallelized by assigning each GPU thread to a single unsampled point and calculating its weights for all sampled points.

3   Results and Discussions

The studied region is between 21° lon E and 29° lon E and between 41° lat N and 49° lat N. The obtained grids have 400×400, 800×800, 1200×1200 and 1600×1600 resolutions, so each grid point have approximatelly 2 km, 1 km, 0.75 km and, respectivelly, 0.5 km. In Fig. 1 and Fig. 2, 1 km resolution geomagnetic maps for Romania region obtained by IDW and, respectively, kriging interpolation are presented.

The accuracy of the results are presented in Table 1. Mean difference between interpolated and real value, standard deviation, median value and maximum difference are presented for each studied resolution, for both interpolation methods. The error was obtained eliminating one point at a time and calculating the difference between the interpolated value and the real value measured at each specific point. The results showed better accuracy for kriging interpolation method, for all studied resolution. For example, if for IWD the median value of error is between 4.476 and 4.895 μT, depending on resolution, for kriging method this value is between 2.871 and 3.687 μT. Moreover, in Fig. 3, the lower values of geomagnetic field mean error for kriging method can be observed.

In Table 2, the execution times on CPU and GPU, and the speed-up for the CUDA imeplemented algorithms are shown. As could be seen, the complex calculus from kriging method leads to an increased execution time for all resolutions, comparing with IDW (Fig. 4). The speed up obtained for IDW implementation is very high and it increases with the grid resolution, up to 104 times for

Algorithm 2. Calculation of semivariance points

▷ Input:
▷   Maximum distance between points: maxdist = 100 km
▷   Tolerance: toler = 2
▷   np = number of sample points
▷ P_i = coordinates of sample point i (i=0, np-1)
▷ v_i = value at sample point i (i=0, np-1)
▷ Ouput:
▷   ns = number of semivariance points
▷   ns = maxdist/toler
▷ s_k = semivariance values (k=0, ns-1)
▷ w_k = weights (k=0, ns-1)
for $i \leftarrow 0$ to $ns - 1$ **do**
   $s_k \leftarrow 0$
   $w_k \leftarrow 0$
end for
for $i \leftarrow 0$ to $np - 2$ **do**
   for $j \leftarrow i + 1$ to $np - 1$ **do**
      $d \leftarrow dist(P_i, P_j)$
      if $d < a + toler$ **then**
         $k \leftarrow \frac{d}{toler}$
         $s_k \leftarrow s_k + \left(v_i - v_j\right)^2$
         $w_k \leftarrow w_k + 1$
      end if
   end for
end for
for $i \leftarrow 0$ to $ns - 1$ **do**
   if $w_k > 0$ **then**
      $s_k = \frac{s_k}{2w_k}$
   end if
end for
$Sw \leftarrow \sum_{k=0}^{n_s} w_k$
for $i \leftarrow 0$ to $ns - 1$ **do**   ▷ normalization of weights "w"
   $w_k \leftarrow \frac{w_k}{Sw}$
end for

Table 1. The interpolation methods accuracy.

Interpolation method	Resolution	Median error (μT)	Maximum error (μT)	Mean error (μT)	Standard deviation
IDW	400 × 400	4.895	9.21	3.600	0.275
	800 × 800	4.550	9.271	3.137	0.289
	1200 × 1200	4.495	9.268	3.065	0.254
	1600 × 1600	4.476	9.274	2.941	0.247
Kriging	400 × 400	3.687	7.21	3.102	0.312
	800 × 800	3.551	7.02	2.542	0.271
	1200 × 1200	3.215	6.82	2.14	0.252
	1600 × 1600	2.871	6.01	1.92	0.248

Algorithm 3. Calculation of semivariance coefficients using least squares method

---

▷ Input:

▷   Maximum distance between points: maxdist = 100 km

▷   np = number of sample points

▷ P_i = coordinates of sample point i (i=0, np-1)

▷ v_i = value at sample point i (i=0, np-1)

▷ Ouput:

▷ W_k = kriging interpolation weights (k=0, ns-1)

$np_2 \leftarrow 0$

for $i \leftarrow 0$ to $np - 1$ **do**

    for $k \leftarrow 0$ to $np - 1$ **do**

        if $i \neq k$ **then**

            $d \leftarrow dist(P_i, P_k)$

            if $d < maxdist$ **then**

                $Calculate semivariance \sigma^1_{np2} using d$

                $P2_{np2} \leftarrow P_i$

                $np_2 \leftarrow np_2 + 1$

            end if

        end if

    end for

    for $k \leftarrow 0$ to $np_2 - 1$ **do**

        for $l \leftarrow 0$ to $np_2 - 1$ **do**

            $h \leftarrow dist(P2_k, P2_l)$

            Calculate semivariance $\sigma^2_{k,l} = \sigma^2_{l,k}$ using h

        end for

    end for

    Solve the linear system of equations $\sigma^2_w W = \sigma^1$

    to calculate the weights $W_k(k = 0, np_2 - 1)$

end for

Algorithm 4. Calculation of interpolated values

▷ Input:

▷   nq = number of interpolated points

▷   Qi = coordinates of interpolated point i (i=0,nq-1)

▷   np = number of sample points

▷   vi = value at sample point i (i=0,np-1)

▷ Ouput:

▷   ui = interpolated value at point Qi (i=0,nq-1)

for $i \leftarrow 0$ to $nq - 1$ **do**

    Find the sample points at distance less than maxdist from Q_i

    u_i = interpolated value of the nearby values using the weights W

end for

1600×1600 grid. Eventhough, the speed up for kriging is not as high as for IDW (Fig. 5), for the highest studied resolution the execution time when running on GPU decreased 10 times comparing with CPU.

Fig. 1. Geomagnetic map obtained by IDW

Fig. 2. Geomagnetic map obtained by kriging

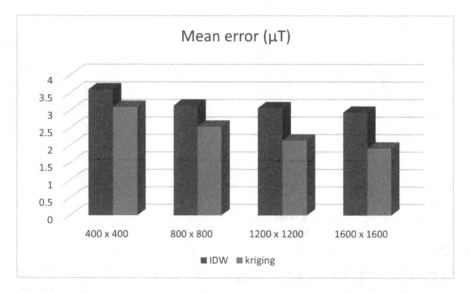

Fig. 3. Geomagnetic field mean error comparison between IDW and kriging

Table 2. The execution times and algorithms speedup on CUDA.

Interpolation method	Resolution	Execution time on CPU (s)	Execution time on GPU (s)	Speed-up
IDW	400×400	13.7	0.355	38.6
	800×800	54. 1	0.724	74.4
	1200×1200	121.7	1.265	96.2
	1600×1600	212.8	2.044	104.1
Kriging	400×400	49.4	11.9	4.15
	800×800	190.5	33.0	5.77
	1200×1200	440.9	53.0	8.32
	1600×1600	757.1	72.4	10.45

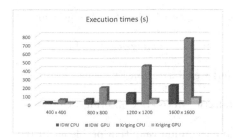

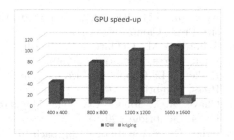

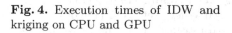

Fig. 4. Execution times of IDW and kriging on CPU and GPU

Fig. 5. GPU speed-up comparison between IDW and kriging

4 Conclusions and Perspectives

To conclude, both IDW and kriging interpolation methods could be used for obtaining high resolution geomagnetic maps. Using IDW algorithm, maps are obtained in a shorted execution time, but the accuracy of the obtained data is lower than the one obtined using kriging method. Both algorithms can be accelerated by CUDA programming, the speed-up for IDW being up to 10 times higher then the speed-up for kriging algorithm. By employing memory management techniques, the performance of CUDA implementation of interpolation algorithms can be improved, and better speedup could be achieved.

The use of CUDA for IDW and kriging interpolation has been used to improve the computational efficiency and accuracy of these techniques. This study demonstrates the potential of CUDA-based parallel algorithms and frameworks for improving the scalability and performance of IDW and Kriging interpolation on large-scale data sets. These results are expected to have practical implications for many other fields that rely on interpolation techniques, such as geology, meteorology, or environmental science.

References

1. Li, J., Oldenburg, D.W.: A comparison of interpolation methods for geomagnetic data. Geophys. J. Int. **181**(3), 1549–1560 (2010)
2. Rasmussen, C.E., Williams, C.K.I.: Gaussian Processes for Machine Learning. MIT Press, Cambridge (2006)
3. Blakely, R.J.: Potential Theory in Gravity and Magnetic Applications. Cambridge University Press, Cambridge (1996)
4. Campbell, W.H.: Introduction to Geomagnetic Fields. Cambridge University Press, Cambridge (1996)
5. Thébault, E., Finlay, C.C., Beggan, C.D., et al.: International geomagnetic reference field: the 12th generation. Earth Planets Space **67**(1), 79 (2015)
6. McElhinny, M.W., McFadden, P.L.: Paleomagnetism: Continents and Oceans. Academic Press, Cambridge (2000)

7. Kivelson, M.G., Russell, C.T.: Introduction to Space Physics. Cambridge University Press, Cambridge (2017)
8. Telford, W.M., Geldart, L.P., Sheriff, R.E.: Applied Geophysics. Cambridge University Press, Cambridge (1990)
9. Parker, R.L.: Geophysical Inverse Theory and Regularization Problems. Academic Press, Cambridge (2013)
10. Chave, A.D., Jones, A.G.: The Magnetotelluric Method. Cambridge University Press, Cambridge (2012)
11. Krige, D.G.: A statistical approach to some basic mine valuation problems on the Witwatersrand. J. South. Afr. Inst. Mining Metall. **52**(6), 119–139 (1951)
12. Cressie, N.: Statistics for Spatial Data, revised Wiley, New York (1993)
13. Journel, A.G., Huijbregts, C.J.: Mining Geostatistics. Academic Press, London (1978)
14. NVIDIA. CUDA C Programming Guide. https://docs.nvidia.com/cuda/cuda-c-programming-guide/index
15. Liu, Q., Hu, C., Tian, Y.: Parallel implementation of IDW interpolation algorithm based on CUDA. J. Appl. Geophys. **189**, 104332 (2021)
16. Gao, S., Cao, J., Yang, J.: Parallel implementation of kriging interpolation based on CUDA. J. Comput. Appl. Math. **370**, 112665 (2020)
17. Ji, X., Wu, H., Wang, J.: A CUDA-based framework for IDW and Kriging interpolation. Int. J. Geogr. Inf. Sci. **34**(8), 1572–1587 (2020)
18. Ciupala, L., Deaconu, A., Spridon, D.: IDW map builder and statistics of air pollution in Brasov. Bull. Transilvania Univ. Brasov **1**(63), 247–256 (2021)
19. Oliver, M.A., Webster, R.: A tutorial guide to geostatistics: computing and modelling variograms and kriging. Catena **113**, 56–69 (2014)

A Compact-RBF-FD Scheme for Valuing Financial Derivatives Based on Short-Rate Models

Nawdha Thakoor[✉][ID]

Department of Mathematics, University of Mauritius, Moka, Mauritius
n.thakoor@uom.ac.mu

Abstract. Modelling the term structure of interest rate is of crucial importance nowadays since during times of financial crisis, governments tend to adopt monetary policies which usually result in changes in interest rates. Therefore, it is more realistic to assume that interest rates fluctuate, even over a short time period. Numerous models have been proposed in financial engineering, to describe the stochastic dynamics of interest rates. Interest rate options are among the most liquid options that trade in derivative markets. Due to the enormous size of these markets, there is a need to develop fast and accurate numerical methods for pricing these financial derivatives. In comparison to equity derivatives where a lot of research efforts have been devoted to developing sophisticated methods, research in the area of numerical valuation of interest rate options has been quite sparse. In this paper, we propose a compact localised radial basis function method for pricing interest rate derivatives when exact solutions are not available, as in the case of European and American options on bonds. It is shown numerically that fourth-order accurate results are obtained for American bond options and the proposed method does not suffer from mispricing for long maturity problems or when the short-term rate is high.

Keywords: Stochastic interest rates · Bonds and bond options · Compact radial basis functions method

1 Introduction

A distinguishing feature of short-rate models is the need for the models to exhibit mean reversion and the volatility being dependent on the interest rate. Various stochastic models for the evolution of interest rates have been proposed, but due to the complexities of mean reversion and non-constant volatility, one-factor models are still popular among practitioners although sophisticated multi-factor models have been proposed. Following the introduction of the popular Vasicek [24] and Cox-Ingersoll-Ross (CIR) [8] models, diffusion processes have been often used in finance to model the evolution of interest rates. Recently, an interest rate model embedding the interest rate process with a non-stationary

© The Author(s), under exclusive license to Springer Nature Switzerland AG 2023
O. Gervasi et al. (Eds.): ICCSA 2023, LNCS 13956, pp. 139–151, 2023.
https://doi.org/10.1007/978-3-031-36805-9_10

mean was developed by Al-Zoubi [1] and it was empirically shown that imposing a non-stationary mean in the Vasicek model is very efficient and leads to considerable amelioration in the root-mean-square error. Ascione et al. [2] introduced the Heston-CIR Lévy model for the Forex market and the jump-extended CIR model was considered in [4,16].

The models of Vasicek and Cox-Ingersoll-Ross admit analytical solutions for bond prices and European style derivatives. A comparison of different approaches for the valuation bond and options on bonds under these models can be found in [12]. However Chan, Karoyli, Longstaff and Sanders (CKLS) [5] have shown that a more general form for the stochastic differential equation may have a greater ability in capturing the dynamics of the interest rate. For such cases, analytical solutions are not available and numerical approaches are necessary for computing approximations to bond and bond-option prices.

Costabile and Massabó [7] also considered the pricing of interest rate derivatives for the square root diffusion process using their approximating binomial and trinomial tree method. Tian [22] mentioned that a problem arises when $4\kappa\theta < \sigma^2$, while implementing a discrete model by defining the transition probabilities on transformed processes which has a drift that explodes when the process reaches zero. However, Costabile and Massabó [7] showed that no such problem arises using their transformed process since the moment-matching condition is defined with respect to the drift of the original process. Choi and Wirjanto [6] proposed an analytical approximation formula for pricing bonds under the CKLS model. The authors mentioned in their paper that as time to maturity or the initial interest rate increases, the method leads to mispricing.

While there exists many numerical techniques such as lattice methods or second-order finite difference methods for pricing interest rate derivatives [7,14, 17], meshless methods have recently gained popularity for pricing equity derivatives and they are highly efficient. We proposed 5-point localised RBF methods for pricing real estate derivatives using Gaussian basis functions in Narsoo et al. [13], 3-point localised RBF method using multiquadrics basis for pricing equity derivatives under the Stochastic-Alpha-Beta-Rho model in Thakoor [18] and regime-switching stochastic volatility models with jumps was considered in Tour et al. [23]. More recently, a sixth-order non-uniform method was proposed in Thakoor [21]. In this work we propose a compact radial basis function method for pricing bonds, European and American bond options with fourth order accuracy under the generalised CKLS model. Localised radial basis function based on finite difference (RBF-FD) approximations for the discretisation of the spatial derivatives are first derived following [3,20] and these are then adapted to the high-order compact method of [15]. We demonstrate numerically that the method is fast, highly accurate and does not suffer from mispricing problems which is common for long maturity problems.

The organisation of this paper is as follows. In §2 we give a review of the CKLS model and the analytical solution for bond pricing under the Vasicek and CIR models. In §3, the compact RBF scheme is derived and in §4 we present some numerical results to show the merits of the proposed method. Finally §5 contains the conclusion of this work.

2   The CKLS Model

Chan, Karoyli, Longstaff and Sanders [5] proposed a generalised framework for short rate models under which several popular models can be considered as special cases. Let r be the riskless interest rate which is considered to be stochastic. The CKLS model assumes that r satisfies the stochastic differential equation

$$dr = a(b - r)dt + \sigma r^\gamma dW_t, \qquad (1)$$

where a is known as the reversion rate about the long run mean b, σ is the diffusion volatility and γ is the nesting parameter. Recently, Kubilius and Medžiūnas [11] investigated the fractional generalization of the CKLS model. Special cases in the CKLS term structure models are the Vasicek model which corresponds to $\gamma = 0$ and the Cox-Ingersoll-Ross (CIR) model [8] for which $\gamma = 1/2$. Only these two models admit closed-form expressions for bond and options on bond prices and for other values of the parameter γ, numerical evaluation of the prices are required.

A zero-coupon bond is the most basic interest rate derivative which promises a payment of a face value at maturity date T. If we let $B(r_0, T)$ denote the time-zero value of a zero coupon bond, then under the risk-neutral measure $\mathbb{Q}$,

$$B(r_0, T) = \mathbb{E}^{\mathbb{Q}} \left[\exp \left(- \int_0^T r(s)\, ds \right) \right].$$

Under the measure $\mathbb{Q}$, the market price of risk is zero and $B(r_0, \tau)$ is the solution of the pde

$$\frac{\partial B}{\partial \tau} = \frac{1}{2}\sigma^2 r^{2\gamma} \frac{\partial^2 B}{\partial r^2} + a(b - r)\frac{\partial B}{\partial r} - rB, \qquad (2)$$

where $\tau = T - t$, $0 \leq \tau \leq T$ $B(r_0, 0) = FV$ as the initial condition, where FV denote the bond's face value.

Let $T_O < T$ be the date on which a European option on a zero-coupon bond can be exercised and $\tau^* \in [0, T_O]$ bethe bond option's time to maturity and K be the strike price, then the value $B(r, \tau^*)$ of a European call bond option satisfies

$$\frac{\partial B}{\partial \tau^*} = \frac{1}{2}\sigma^2 r^{2\gamma} \frac{\partial^2 B}{\partial r^2} + a(b - r)\frac{\partial B}{\partial r} - rB, \qquad (3)$$

with initial condition $B(r, 0) = \max[B(r, T - T_O) - K, 0]$.

For American options on a zero-coupon bond, there is an unknown optimal exercise interest rate $r^*(\tau^*)$ at τ^*, which is the smallest interest rate value at which it becomes optimal to exercise the option.

Applying the operator splitting method [10] for solving the linear complementarity problem for American options on bonds [25], we add a penalty term, λ and the value $B_{Am}(r, \tau^*)$ of an American call option on bond satisfies

$$\frac{\partial B_{Am}}{\partial \tau^*} - \mathcal{L}_r B_{Am} - \lambda = 0, \quad \lambda \geq 0, \qquad (4)$$

where the spatial operator $\mathcal{L}$ is given by

$$\mathcal{L}_r = \frac{1}{2}\sigma^2 r^{2\gamma}\frac{\partial^2}{\partial r^2} + a(b-r)\frac{\partial}{\partial r} - r,$$

subject to

$$B_{Am}(r, 0) = \max\left(B(r, 0) - K, 0\right), \quad r \geq 0,$$
$$B_{Am}(r, \tau^*) \geq \max\left(B(r, \tau^*) - K, 0\right), \quad 0 < r < r^*(\tau^*), 0 \leq \tau^* < T_O,$$
$$\left[\frac{\partial B_{Am}}{\partial \tau} - \mathcal{L}_r B_{Am} = \lambda\right] \wedge \left[B_{Am}(r, \tau^*) - \max\left(B(r, \tau^*) - K, 0\right)\right].$$

2.1   Analytical Solution for Bonds

The Vasicek and CIR models admit analytical solutions for the bond price $B(r, t, T)$ in the form

$$B(r, t, T) = X(t, T)e^{-r(t)Y(t, T)}. \tag{5}$$

For the Vasicek model, $X(t, T)$ and $Y(t, T)$ are given by

$$Y(t, T) = \frac{1}{a}\left(1 - e^{-a(T-t)}\right),$$
$$X(t, T) = \exp\left(\left(b - \frac{\sigma^2}{2a^2}\right)(Y(t, T) - T + t) - \frac{\sigma^2}{4a}Y^2(t, T)\right).$$

For the Cox-Ingersoll-Ross square root diffusion model, we have

$$X(t, T) = \left(\frac{2\sqrt{2\sigma^2 + a^2}e^{(\sqrt{2\sigma^2+a^2}+a)(T-t)/2}}{2\sqrt{2\sigma^2 + a^2} + (\sqrt{2\sigma^2 + a^2} + a)\left(e^{\sqrt{2\sigma^2+a^2}(T-t)} - 1\right)}\right)^{2ab/\sigma^2},$$

$$Y(t, T) = \frac{2\left(e^{\sqrt{2\sigma^2+a^2}(T-t)} - 1\right)}{2\sqrt{2\sigma^2 + a^2} + (\sqrt{2\sigma^2 + a^2} + a)\left(e^{\sqrt{2\sigma^2+a^2}(T-t)} - 1\right)}.$$

3   Compact-RBF Method

To develop the Compact RBF scheme for the CKLS pde (2), we first truncate the spatial domain to $[r_{\mathrm{rmin}}, r_{\mathrm{rmax}}]$ and we consider a grid in the r-direction with uniform mesh spacing $h = (r_{\mathrm{rmax}} - r_{\mathrm{rmin}})/M$ with $r_m = r_{\mathrm{min}}+mh$, $0 \leq m \leq M$. We then re-write (2) in the form

$$B_\tau = \frac{1}{2}\sigma^2 r^{2\gamma}B_{rr} + a(b-r)B_r - rB. \tag{6}$$

The derivative terms B_{rr} and B_r in (6) are approximated using a 3-node RBF-FD approximations [3, 20] in the form

$$B_r(r_m, \tau) \approx \sum_{i=-1}^{1} \alpha_i^{(1)} B(r_m + ih, \tau),$$

$$B_{rr}(r_m, \tau) \approx \sum_{i=-1}^{1} \alpha_i^{(2)} B(r_m + ih, \tau),$$

for $1 \leq m \leq M - 1$ and the coefficients $\alpha_i^{(1)}$ and $\alpha_i^{(2)}$ are obtained by solving

$$\phi_j'(r_m) = \sum_{i=-1}^{1} \alpha_i^{(1)} \phi_j(r_m + ih) \quad \text{for} \quad -1 \leq j \leq 1,$$

and

$$\phi_j''(r_m) = \sum_{i=-1}^{1} \alpha_i^{(2)} \phi_j(r_m + jh) \quad \text{for} \quad -1 \leq j \leq 1,$$

where ϕ is the multiquadrics basis function with shape parameter c given by

$$\phi_j(r_m) = \sqrt{c^2 + (r_m - r_{m+j})^2},$$

with

$$\phi_j'(r_m) = \frac{r_m - r_{m+j}}{\sqrt{c^2 + (r_m - r_{m+j})^2}},$$

$$\phi_j''(r_m) = \frac{c^2}{(c^2 + (r_m - r_{m+j})^2)^{3/2}}.$$

In the limit $c \gg h$, the coefficients $\alpha_i^{(1)}$ and $\alpha_i^{(2)}$ are given as

$$\alpha_{\pm 1}^{(1)} = \frac{1}{2h} \left(1 + \frac{h^2}{2c^2} - \frac{9h^4}{8c^4} \right)$$

$$\alpha_0^{(1)} = 0,$$

$$\alpha_{\pm 1}^{(2)} = \frac{1}{h^2} \left(1 + \frac{h^2}{c^2} - \frac{15h^4}{8c^4} \right),$$

$$\alpha_0^{(2)} = -\frac{2}{h^2} \left(1 + \frac{h^2}{c^2} - \frac{3h^4}{2c^4} \right).$$

Then letting

$$\delta_r B_m \approx \frac{1}{2h} \left(1 + \frac{h^2}{2c^2} - \frac{9h^4}{8c^4} \right) (B_{m+1} - B_{m-1}),$$

and

$$\delta_r^2 B_m \approx \frac{1}{h^2}\left(1 + \frac{h^2}{c^2} - \frac{15h^4}{8c^4}\right)(B_{m+1} - B_{m-1}) - \frac{2}{h^2}\left(1 + \frac{h^2}{c^2} - \frac{3h^4}{2c^4}\right)B_m,$$

and replacing in (6) gives the second-order approximation scheme

$$(B_\tau)_m = \frac{1}{2}\sigma^2 r_m^{2\gamma}\delta_r^2 B_m + a(b - r_m)\delta_r B_m - r_m B_m - T_m, \qquad (7)$$

where T_m is the truncation error given by

$$T_m = \frac{h^2}{12c^4}\left[2c^2 a(b - r_m)\left(3\,(B_r)_m + c^2\,(B_{rr})_m\right)\right.$$

$$\left. + \frac{1}{2}\sigma^2\left(r^{2\gamma}\right)_m\left(-9B_m + 12c^2\,(B_{rr})_m + c^4\,(B_{rrrr})_m\right)\right] + \mathcal{O}(h^4). \quad (8)$$

Differentiating the pde (6) twice gives

$$\sigma^2\,(B_{rrr})_m = 2r^{-2\gamma-1}\left(r_m(B_{r\tau})_m + \left(ar_m^2 - abr_m - \gamma\sigma^2 r_m^{2\gamma}\right)(B_{rr})_m\right.$$
$$\left. + \left(ar_m + r_m^2\right)(B_r)_m\right),$$

$$\sigma^2\,(B_{rrrr})_m = 2r^{-2\gamma-2}\left[r_m(B_{rr\tau})_m + \left(ar_m^3 - abr_m^2 - 2\gamma\sigma^2 r_m^{2\gamma+1}\right)(B_{rrr})_m\right.$$
$$\left. + \left(2ar_m^2 + r_m^3 + \gamma\sigma^2 r_m^{2\gamma} - 2\gamma^2\sigma^2 r_m^{2\gamma}\right)(B_{rr})_m + 2r_m^2\,(B_r)_m\right].$$

Replacing the third and fourth order derivatives in terms of lower derivatives in (8) gives the scheme

$$\left(I + \left(\frac{h^2}{12}r_m^{2-2\gamma}D_{rr}\right)\right.$$

$$\left. + \frac{h^2 r_m^{-4\gamma}}{6\sigma^2}\left(-a(b-r_m)(r_m^2 - 2r_m^{2\gamma}) - 2\gamma\sigma^2 r_m^{2\gamma+1}\right)D_r\right)(B_\tau)_m$$

$$= \rho_m D_{rr} B_m + \vartheta_m D_r B_m + \zeta_m B_m, \quad (9)$$

where $I \in \mathbb{R}^{(M+1)\times(M+1)}$ denotes the sparse identity matrix, $D_r, D_{rr} \in \mathbb{R}^{(M+1)\times(M+1)}$ are sparse tridiagonal matrices given by

$$D_r = \text{tridiag}\left[\alpha_{-1}^{(1)},\, 0,\, \alpha_1^{(1)}\right],$$
$$D_{rr} = \text{tridiag}\left[\alpha_{-1}^{(2)},\, \alpha_0^{(2)},\, \alpha_1^{(2)}\right],$$

and

$$\rho_m = \frac{1}{12}\left(\frac{2a^2\,h^2(b - r_m)^2\left(r_m^2 - 2r_m^{2\gamma}\right)r_m^{-4\gamma}}{\sigma^2}\right.$$

$$+ \frac{2ah^2\left(r_m^{2-2\gamma}(3b\gamma - 3\gamma r_m + r_m) + 2\gamma(r_m - b)\right)}{r_m}$$

$$\left. + h^2\left(\frac{6\sigma^2 r_m^2}{c^2} + \gamma(2\gamma + 1)\sigma^2 + r_m^{3-2\gamma}\right) - 6\sigma^2 r_m^2\right),$$

$$\vartheta_m = \frac{r_m^{-4\gamma}}{6c^2\sigma^2} \left[-a^2c^2\,h^2(b-r_m)\left(r_m^2 - 2r_m^{2\gamma}\right) - c^2(2\gamma-1)h^2\sigma^2 r_m^{2\gamma+2} \right.$$
$$+a\left(-bc^2\left(h^2\left(r_m^3 - 2r_m^{2\gamma+1}\right) + 6\sigma^2 r_m^{4\gamma}\right) + 3bh^2\sigma^2 r_m^{4\gamma} \right.$$
$$\left. \left. +c^2 r_m\left(h^2\left(-2\gamma\sigma^2 r_m^{2\gamma} - 2r_m^{2\gamma+1} + r_m^3\right) + 6\sigma^2 r_m^{4\gamma}\right) - 3\,h^2\sigma^2 r_m^{4\gamma+1}\right)\right],$$

and

$$\zeta_m = \frac{1}{24}\left(-\frac{4ah^2(b-r_m)\left(r_m^2 - 2r_m^{2\gamma}\right)r_m^{-4\gamma}}{\sigma^2} - \frac{9\,h^2\sigma^2 r_m^2}{c^4} + 8r_m\left(3 - \gamma h^2 r_m^{-2\gamma}\right)\right).$$

At the left and right boundaries, we use RBF-FD one-sided approximations and the first and last of the matrices D_r and D_{rr} are replaced by the one sided coefficients as follows

$$D_r(1,1:3) = \left[-\frac{3}{2h}\left(1 - \frac{h^2}{c^2}\right), \frac{4}{2h}\left(1 - \frac{h^2}{c^2}\right), -\frac{1}{2h}\left(1 - \frac{h^2}{c^2}\right)\right],$$
$$D_r(M+1, M-1:M+1) = -\text{flip}[D_r(1,1:3)],$$
$$D_{rr}(1,1:4) = \left[\frac{2}{h^2}\left(1 - \frac{41h^2}{4c^2}\right), -\frac{5}{h^2}\left(1 - \frac{101h^2}{10c^2}\right)\right.$$
$$\left. \frac{4}{h^2}\left(1 - \frac{79h^2}{8c^2}\right), -\frac{1}{h^2}\left(1 - \frac{19h^2}{2c^2}\right)\right],$$
$$D_{rr}(M+1, M-2:M+1) = \text{flip}[D_{rr}(1,1:4)].$$

The semi-discrete scheme (9) can then be written in the form

$$PB'(\tau) = QB(\tau) \quad \text{for} \quad 0 \le \tau \le T, \tag{10}$$

where $P, Q \in \mathbb{R}^{(M+1)\times(M+1)}$ are the resulting matrix from the left hand side and right hand side of Eq. (9) respectively.

For the time discretisation, let $\Delta\tau = T/N$ and $\tau_n = n\Delta\tau$ for $0 \le n \le N$ and let the vector of bond prices be denoted by $B^n = [B_0^n, B_1^n, B_2^n, \ldots, B_M^n]$. Using an implicit Euler scheme we require the solution of

$$(P - \Delta\tau Q)\,B^{n+1} = PB^n, \quad 0 \le n \le N-1, \tag{11}$$

with initial condition $B^0 = [B_0^0, B_1^0, \ldots, B_M^0]^T$. The accuracy is further enhanced with an $s = 6$ stage extrapolation as in [9,19] with $N = 20$ initial time steps.

4   Numerical Results

In this section we present some numerical results to validate the accuracy of the compact RBF method. In all our numerical examples, we use $r_{\min} = 0$ and $r_{\max} = 1$ except for the Vasicek model we use $r_{\min} = -0.5$ and $r_{\max} = 1$ since the interest can go negative in the latter case. The face value (FV) of the bond is taken as 100. The accuracy of the Compact RBF scheme is first established for the case of $\gamma = 0$ corresponding to the Vasicek interest rate model which

Table 1. Bonds prices under the Vasicek model.

M	RBF-3pt				C-RBF			
	Price	Error	Rate	Cpu(s)	Price	Error	Rate	Cpu(s)
20	97.379268	2.0e-4	–	0.009	97.379413	7.4e-5	–	0.006
40	97.379433	5.0e-5	2.000	0.011	97.379494	6.1e-6	3.616	0.075
80	97.379474	1.0e-5	2.000	0.032	97.379487	3.5e-7	4.105	0.105
160	97.379484	3.0e-6	2.000	0.084	97.379488	2.3e-8	3.907	0.224
320	97.379487	9.0e-7	2.000	0.181	97.379488	1.7e-9	3.778	0.468
Exact	97.3794875586436							

$T = 0.5$, $a = 0.5$, $b = 0.08$, $\sigma = 0.1$, $r_0 = 0.05$

admits analytical bond prices. Consider the pricing of a zero-coupon bond with a principal of 100 and a short time to maturity of 0.5 year. Numerical results given by the solution of the pde (11) when $a = 0.5$, $b = 0.08$ and $\sigma = 0.1$ are given in Table 1. The initial value of the short rate is taken as $r_0 = 0.05$.

Comparison with the exact solution shows that a three-node localised radial basis function method (RBF-3point) yields the expected second order convergence prices while the Compact-RBF method (C-RBF) is able to yield fourth-order accurate results.

Consider a short-maturity bond under the CIR model using the Compact-RBF method. Comparison is drawn against the exact analytical solution and the analytical approximation of Choi and Wirjanto and the results are reported in Table 2. For this short maturity problem, we observe close agreement between all the different methods.

Table 2. Bonds prices for $\gamma = \frac{1}{2}$ for a short maturity problem.

M	C-RBF				Choi-Wirjanto Approx.	
	Price	Error	Rate	Cpu(s)	Price	Error
20	97.363491948	1.8e-5	–	0.002	97.363475825303	2.0e-6
40	97.363474897	1.1e-6	4.085	0.056		
80	97.363473893	6.4e-8	4.060	0.097		
160	97.363473832	3.0e-9	4.421	0.162		
320	97.363473829	7.3e-11	5.359	0.326		
Exact	97.363473829394					

$T = 0.5$, $a = 0.5$, $b = 0.08$, $\sigma = 0.1$, $r_0 = 0.05$

We next consider the case of a longer maturity bond under the CIR model and comparison is done against the Choi-Wirjanto Approximation [6] and the Box methods of Sorwar et al. [14]. In the previous example it was observed that for the shorter maturity problem, the Choi-Wirjanto approximation yielded a solution with an error of 10^{-6} while for this longer maturity problem of $T = 5$ years, the solution is less accurate with an error of 10^{-2} as shown in Table 3. A similar accuracy is observed for the Box methods by Sorwar et al. [14]. In contrast, the pde methods, that is the RBF-3point and the C-RBF methods are still very accurate with second and fourth order convergence.

Table 3. Bonds prices under the CIR model for a longer maturity problem.

$T = 5$, $a = 0.5$, $b = 0.08$, $\sigma = 0.1$, $r_0 = 0.05$

	RBF-3pt				C-RBF			
M	Price	Error	Rate	Cpu(s)	Price	Error	Rate	Cpu(s)
20	71.036123	1.8e-4	–	0.002	71.038108	1.7e-4	–	0.006
40	71.037552	3.9e-4	2.233	0.004	71.037947	8.9e-6	4.261	0.056
80	71.037840	9.8e-5	1.981	0.009	71.037938	6.1e-7	3.867	0.096
160	71.037913	2.4e-5	2.000	0.010	71.037938	4.3e-8	3.810	0.168
320	71.037932	6.1e-6	2.000	0.029	71.037938	3.1e-9	3.803	0.322
	Choi-Wirjanto Approx.				Box Methods			
	Price	Error			Time Steps	Price	Error	
	71.074008366	3.6e-2			300	71.0614	2.3e-2	
					500	71.0603	2.2e-2	
					1000	71.0595	2.2e-2	
Exact	71.0379377726464							

The observations made from the results in Table 3 are further illustrated in Fig. 1 where it is shown that for small maturity problems, all the methods agree closely with the exact solution. As maturity increases, the Choi-Wirjanto approximation leads to mispricing while the C-RBF method is still in good agreement with the exact solution even for the very long maturity case of $T = 30$ years. Having established the accuracy of the C-RBF method, we also report on computed bond prices for different values of the parameter $\gamma = \{0.2, 0.4, 0.6, 0.8, 1\}$ for which analytical expressions are not available in Table 4.

Table 4. Bonds prices under the general CKLS model.

$T = 5$, $a = 0.5$, $b = 0.08$, $\sigma = 0.1$, $r_0 = 0.05$

	γ				
Method	0.2	0.4	0.6	0.8	1.0
RBF-3	71.80179	71.18419	70.95074	70.86919	70.84145
C-RBF	71.80162	71.18419	70.95074	70.86919	70.84145

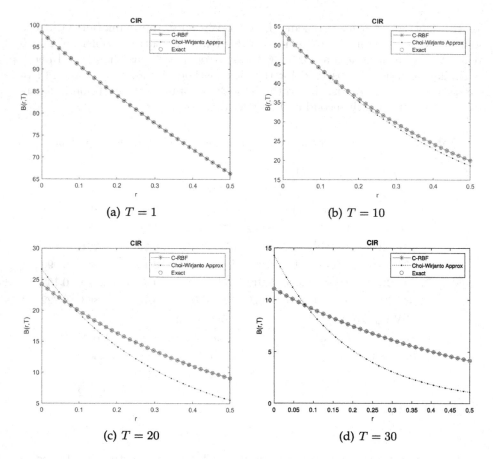

Fig. 1. Mispricing With Choi-Wirjanto approximations for parameters $a = 0.5$, $b = 0.08$, $\sigma = 0.1$.

4.1   Bond Options

We now consider two European call options with maturities $T_O = 2$ and $T_O = 5$ years and strike price $E = 35$ on a $T = 10$-year zero-coupon bond. The other parameters are chosen as $a = 0.5$, $b = 0.08$, $\sigma = 0.1$ and $r_0 = 0.08$. The bond prices and errors computed by the RBF-3point and Compact RBF methods for the case of the CIR model are given in Table 5. The European bond option prices are shown to be converging with smooth fourth-order convergence rate with the C-RBF method.

Given the high accuracy of the C-RBF method, in Table 6 we report the prices of European bond option for different values of the parameter γ for which no analytical solutions are known.

In this final numerical example, an American put option with a maturity of $T_O = 5$ years with strike price $E = 55$ on a bond with maturity $T = 10$ is priced. Table 7 gives the option prices and the corresponding errors. Since it is

Table 5. European call bond options under CIR.

$K = 35$, $T = 10$, $a = 0.5$, $b = 0.08$, $r_0 = 0.08$, $\sigma = 0.1$						
		RBF-3pt			C-RBF		
	M	Price	Error	Rate	Price	Error	Rate
$T_O = 5$	20	21.8789823	1.2e-3	–	21.8780248	2.2e-3	–
	40	21.8799699	2.2e-4	2.438	21.8800599	1.3e-4	4.021
	80	21.8801380	5.6e-5	2.010	21.8801855	7.9e-6	4.073
	160	21.8801795	1.4e-5	1.985	21.8801940	4.8e-7	4.049
	320	21.8801900	3.5e-6	1.990	21.8801935	3.0e-8	4.017
Exact		21.880193482973					
$T_O = 2$	20	15.5834337	2.9e-3	–	15.5837021	2.6e-3	–
	40	15.5856776	6.3e-4	2.194	15.5861313	1.7e-4	3.906
	80	15.5861491	1.6e-4	2.009	15.5862946	1.0e-5	4.069
	160	15.5862658	3.9e-5	1.993	15.5863056	6.5e-7	3.994
	320	15.5862951	9.8e-6	1.997	15.5863049	4.0e-8	4.021
Exact		15.5863049533542					

Table 6. European call bond options under general CKLS

T_O	$\gamma = 0.2$	$\gamma = 0.4$	$\gamma = 0.6$	$\gamma = 0.8$
5	23.150081	22.135136	21.721509	21.563779
2	17.077626	15.885238	15.400344	15.215627

Table 7. American put bond options for $T = 10$ and $T_O = 5$.

$E = 55$, $a = 0.5$, $b = 0.08$, $\sigma = 0.1$, $r_0 = 0.08$				
American Put Options ($\gamma = 0.5$)				
M	Price	Error	Rate	Cpu(s)
20	9.5754748	2.8e-3	–	0.011
40	9.5728934	2.0e-4	3.805	0.019
80	9.5727064	1.2e-5	4.065	0.053
160	9.5726936	9.3e-7	3.684	0.128
320	9.5726944	5.9e-8	3.983	0.245
Ref Values	9.57269450			
γ	0.2	0.4	0.6	0.8
160	8.027698	9.263475	9.764938	9.955800

well known that for American bond options there are no analytical formulas, the reference values are computed on a refined mesh of $M = 1280$ spatial steps. Similar conclusions as in the previous examples can be reached where the C-RBF is observed to yield fourth-order accurate results. We also report on the prices of some American put bond options for $\gamma = \{0.2, 0.4, 0.6, 0.8\}$.

5 Conclusion

We propose a high-order compact localised radial basis function method for pricing interest rate derivatives under the CKLS model. Fourth-order accurate results are obtained for bonds, European and American bond options and it is also shown the method does not suffer from mispricing problems when maturity increases. The methodology can be extended to the pricing of contingent claims under two-factor interest rate models.

Acknowledgements. The author sincerely acknowledges the financial support under the award number ID-2019-14 for a high-performance laptop from the Higher Education Commission, Mauritius, that was used for the numerical computations in Matlab.

References

1. Al-Zoubi, H.A.: Bond and option prices with permanent shocks. J. Empir. Finan. **53**, 272–290 (2019). https://doi.org/10.1016/j.jempfin.2019.07.010
2. Ascione, G., Mehrdoust, F., Orlando, G., Samimi, O.: Foreign exchange options on Heston-CIR model under Lévy process framework. Appl. Math. Comput. **446**, 127851 (2023). https://doi.org/10.1016/j.amc.2023.127851
3. Bayona, M., Moscoso, M., Carretero, M., Kindelan, M.: RBF-FD formulas and convergence properties. J. Comput. Phys. **229**, 8281–8295 (2010). https://doi.org/10.1016/j.jcp.2010.07.008
4. Chalmers, G.D., Higham, D.J.: First and second moment reversion for a discretized square root process with jumps. J. Differ. Equ. Appl. **16**, 143–156 (2010). https://doi.org/10.1080/10236190802705719
5. Chan, K.C., Karolyi, G.A., Longstaff, F.A., Sanders, A.B.: An empirical comparison of alternative models of the short-term interest rate. J. Finan. **1**, 1209–1227 (1992). https://doi.org/10.1111/j.1540-6261.1992.tb04011.x
6. Choi, Y., Wirjanto, T.S.: An analytic approximation formula for pricing zero-coupon bonds. Finan. Res. Lett. **4**, 116–126 (2007). https://doi.org/10.1016/j.frl.2007.02.001
7. Costabile, M., Massabó, I.: A simplified approach to approximate diffusion processes widely used in finance. J. Deriv. **17**, 65–85 (2010). https://doi.org/10.3905/jod.2010.17.3.065
8. Cox, J.C., Ingersoll, J.E., Ross, S.A.: A theory of the term structure of interest rates. Econometrica **53**, 385–407 (1985). https://doi.org/10.2307/1911242
9. Deuflhard, P.: Recent progress in extrapolation methods for ordinary differential equations. SIAM Rev. **27**, 505–534 (1985). https://www.jstor.org/stable/2031057
10. Ikonen, S., Toivanen, J.: Operator splitting methods for American option pricing. Appl. Math. Lett. **17**, 809–814 (2004). https://doi.org/10.1016/j.aml.2004.06.010
11. Kubilius, K., Medžiūnas, A.: Positive solutions of the fractional SDEs with non-Lipschitz diffusion coefficient. Mathematics **9** (2021). https://doi.org/10.3390/math9010018

12. Larguinho, M., Dias, J.C., Braumann, C.A.: Valuation of bond options under the CIR model: some computational remarks. In: Pacheco, A., Santos, R., do Rosário Oliveira, M., Paulino, C.D. (eds.) New Advances in Statistical Modeling and Applications. STAS, pp. 125–133. Springer, Cham (2014). https://doi.org/10.1007/978-3-319-05323-3_12
13. Narsoo, J., Thakoor, N., Tangman, Y.D., Bhuruth, M.: High-order Gaussian RBF-FD methods for real estate index derivatives with stochastic volatility. Eng. Anal. Bound. Elements **146**, 869–879 (2023). https://doi.org/10.1016/j.enganabound.2022.11.015
14. Sorwar, G., Barone-Adesi, G., Allegretto, W.: Valuation of derivatives based on single-factor interest rate models. Glob. Finan. J. **18**, 251–269 (2007). https://doi.org/10.1016/j.gfj.2006.04.005
15. Spotz, W.F., Carey, G.F.: Extension of high-order compact schemes to time-dependent problems. Numer. Methods Part. Diff. Equ. **6**, 657–672 (2001)
16. Tan, J., Chen, Y., Men, W., Guo, Y.: Positivity and convergence of the balanced implicit method for the nonlinear jump-extended CIR model. Math. Comput. Simul. **182**, 195–210 (2021). https://doi.org/10.1016/j.matcom.2020.10.024
17. Tangman, D.Y., Thakoor, N., Dookhitram, K., Bhuruth, M.: Fast approximations of bond option prices under CKLS models. Finan. Res. Lett. **8**, 206–212 (2011)
18. Thakoor, N.: Localised radial basis functions for no-arbitrage pricing of options under Stochastic-Alpha-Beta-Rho dynamics. ANZIAM J. **63**, 203–227 (2021). https://doi.org/10.1017/S1446181121000237
19. Thakoor, N., Tangman, D.Y., Bhuruth, M.: Efficient and high accuracy pricing of barrier options under the CEV diffusion. J. Comput. Appl. Math. **259**, 182–193 (2014). https://doi.org/10.1016/j.cam.2013.05.009
20. Thakoor, N., Tangman, D.Y., Bhuruth, M.: RBF-FD schemes for option valuation under models with price-dependent and stochastic volatility. Eng. Anal. Bound. Elements **92**, 207–217 (2018). https://doi.org/10.1016/j.enganabound.2017.11.003
21. Thakoor, N.: A sixth-order CEV option valuation algorithm on non-uniform spatial grids. In: Gervasi, O., Murgante, B., Misra, S., Rocha, A.M.A.C., Garau, C. (eds.) Computational Science and Its Applications - ICCSA 2022 Workshops, pp. 435–449. Springer, Cham (2022). https://doi.org/10.1007/978-3-031-10536-4_29
22. Tian, Y.: A reexamination of lattice procedures for interest rate-contingent claims. Adv. Fut. Opt. Res. **7**, 87–111 (1994). https://ssrn.com/abstract=5877
23. Tour, G., Thakoor, N., Tangman, D.Y., Bhuruth, M.: A high-order RBF-FD method for option pricing under regime-switching stochastic volatility models with jumps. J. Comput. Sci. **35**, 25–43 (2019). https://doi.org/10.1016/j.jocs.2019.05.007
24. Vasicek, O.: An equilibrium characterization of the term structure. J. Finan. Econ. **5**, 177–188 (1977). https://doi.org/10.1016/0304-405X(77)90016-2
25. Zhou, H.J., Yiu, K.F.C., Li, L.K.: Evaluating American put options on zero-coupon bonds by a penalty method. J. Comput. Appl. Math. **235**, 3921–3931 (2011). https://doi.org/10.1016/j.cam.2011.01.038

Heuristics for the de Bruijn Graph Sequence Mapping Problem

Lucas B. Rocha[✉][iD], Said Sadique Adi[iD], and Eloi Araujo[iD]

Faculdade de Computação, Universidade Federal de Mato Grosso do Sul, Campo Grande, MS, Brazil
lucas.lb.rocha@gmail.com, {said.sadique,francisco.araujo}@ufms.br

Abstract. In computational biology, mapping a sequence s onto a sequence graph G is a significant challenge. One possible approach to addressing this problem is to identify a walk p in G that spells a sequence which is most similar to s. This problem is known as the Graph Sequence Mapping Problem (GSMP). In this paper, we study an alternative problem formulation, namely the De Bruijn Graph Sequence Mapping Problem (BSMP), which can be stated as follows: given a sequence s and a De Bruijn graph G_k (where $k \geq 2$), find a walk p in G_k that spells a sequence which is most similar to s according to a distance metric. We present both exact algorithms and approximate distance heuristics for solving this problem, using edit distance as a criterion for measuring similarity.

Keywords: Edit distance · De Bruijn Graph · Mapping · Sequences

1 Introduction

A very relevant task in computational biology is to map a sequence onto another for comparison purposes. Typically, one sequence is compared to a reference sequence, which is considered a high-quality sequence representing a set of sequences [9,10]. On the other hand, the reference sequence is biased as it represents only a limited set of sequences and it is unable to account for all possible variations. One way to overcome this bias is to represent multiple sequences as another robust structure [6], such as the sequence graph or De Bruijn graph [7,13,14].

The *sequence graph* is a graph such that each node is labeled with one or more characters and the *simple sequence graph* is one where each node is labeled with exactly one character [7]. In the *De Bruijn graph* [13,14] of order k, each node is labeled with a distinct sequence of length k and there is an arc from one node to another if and only if there is an overlap of length $k - 1$ from the suffix of the first to the prefix of second.

Informally, a walk p in a graph G is a sequence of connected nodes by arcs. Given a sequence graph G, a walk p in G can spell a sequence s' by concatenating

Supported by CAPES and UFMS.

the characters associated with each node of p. The *Graph Sequence Mapping Problem* – GSMP consists of finding a walk p in a sequence graph G that spells a sequence as similar as possible to a given sequence s.

The GSMP, restricted to simple sequence graph, was first addressed by Manber and Wu that propose an algorithm to find an approximated pattern in a hypertext [16]. Akutsu proposes a polynomial time algorithm for exact mappings when hypertext is represented by a tree [15]. Park and Kim propose a polynomial time algorithm when the hypertext is represented by a directed acyclic graph [11].

One of the first articles that addresses GSMP in more details was written by Amir *et. al.* in the article entitled *Pattern Matching in Hypertext* [1]. Navarro improved the results of this article and detailed these improvements in the article entitled *Improved Approximate Pattern Matching on Hypertext* [8]. For the approximate mapping, Amir *et. al.* were the first authors in the literature who identified an asymmetry in the location of the changes, showing the importance of understanding whether changes happen only in the pattern, only in the hypertext or in both. Considering the asymmetry identified by Amir *et. al.*, the GSMP allows three variants:

1. allows changes only in the pattern when mapping the pattern in hypertext;
2. allows changes only in the hypertext when mapping the pattern in hypertext;
3. allows changes in the pattern and hypertext when mapping the pattern in hypertext.

For variant 1, Amir *et. al.* proposed an algorithm that runs in $O(|V|+m\cdot|A|)$ time which was improved by Navarro to run in $O(m(|V|+|A|))$ time. Here, $|V|$ is the number of nodes in the graph, $|A|$ is the number of arcs, and m is the length of the mapped pattern. For variants 2 and 3, Amir *et. al.* proved that the respective problems are NP-complete considering the Hamming and edit distance when the alphabet Σ has $|\Sigma| \geq |V|$.

More recently, the GSMP restricted to simple sequence graph was addressed in the article entitled *Aligning Sequences to General Graphs in $O(|V| + m \cdot |A|)$ time* [12]. In this work, Rautiainen and Marschall propose an algorithm for the variant 1 that runs in $O(|A|\cdot m+|V|\cdot m\cdot\log(|A|\cdot m))$ time, which we refer to as the GSMP algorithm. Additionally, they also propose a more efficient version of the algorithm that returns only the distance in $O(|V|+m\cdot|A|)$ time, which we refer to as the GSMP$_d$ algorithm. In the work entitled *On the Complexity of Sequence-to-Graph Alignment* [3], Jain *et. al* propose a correction in the algorithm proposed by Rautiainen and Marschall. They also prove that the variants 2 and 3 are NP-complete when the alphabet Σ has $|\Sigma| \geq 2$.

The first time the GSMP was addressed using a De Bruijn graph as input was in the article entitled *Read Mapping on De Bruijn Graphs* [2]. In this work, Limasset *et. al.* propose the following problem, called here *De Bruijn Graph Sequence Mapping Problem* – BSMP: given a De Bruijn graph G_k and a sequence s, the goal is to find a path p in G_k such that the sequence s' spelled by p have at most d differences between s and s' with $d \in \mathbb{N}$. The BSMP was proved to be NP-complete considering the Hamming distance, leading to the development of a seed-and-extended heuristic by the mentioned authors. Note that for the BSMP it does not make sense to talk about the three variants mentioned above since there are no node repetitions.

Recently, the BSMP was addressed for walks in the article entitled *On the Hardness of Sequence Alignment on De Bruijn Graphs* [4]. Aluru *et. al.* proved that the problem is NP-complete when the changes occur in the graph and they proved that there is no algorithm faster than $O(|A| \cdot m)$ for De Bruijn graphs when we have changes only occur in s in which $|A|$ is a number of arcs and m is the length of s.

Given the practical importance of the graph sequence mapping problem and the extensive use of De Bruijn graphs in the representation of sequencing data, the main focus of this work lies on a comprehensive study of the sequence mapping problem on De Bruijn graphs restricted to changes in the sequence. The main results of this study include an exact algorithm for the task of finding a walk p in a De Bruijn Graph G_k that best spells a sequence s under the edit distance and the development of three heuristics for the same problem which are much more efficient both in memory and time than the proposed algorithm.

This work is organized as follows: in Sect. 2, we describe the basic concepts we use throughout this work. In Sect. 3 we present the main contributions of this paper that are approaches for the BSMP: one adaptation of the GSMP algorithm and we call it here De Bruijn Sequence Mapping Tool – BMT, one adaptation of the GSMP$_d$ algorithm and we call it here BMT$_d$, one heuristic using BMT, two heuristics using seed-and-extend and one heuristic using BMT$_d$. In Sect. 4 we perform experiments. Finally, in Sect. 5 we discuss the results and perspectives.

2   Preliminaries

In this section, we describe some necessary concepts such as computational definitions and problem definition that are used in this paper.

2.1   Sequence, Distance and Graphs

Let Σ be an **alphabet** with a finite number of characters. We denote a sequence (or string) s over Σ by $s[1]s[2] \ldots s[n]$ in which each character $s[i] \in \Sigma$. We say that the **length** of s, denoted by $|s|$, is n and that s is a n-**length** sequence. We say that the sequence $s[i]s[i+1] \ldots s[j]$ is a **substring** of s and we denote it by $s[i, j]$. A substring of s with length k is a k-length sequence and also called k-**mer** of s. For $1 \leq j \leq n$ in which $n = |s|$, a substring $s[1, j]$ is called a **prefix** of s and a substring $s[j, n]$ is called a **suffix** of s.

Given five sequences s, t, x, w, z, we define st the **concatenation** of s and t and this concatenation contains all the characters of s followed by the characters of t. If s and t are n- and m-length sequences respectively, st is a $(n+m)$-length sequence. If $s = xw$ (x is a prefix and w is a suffix of s) and $t = wv$ (w is a prefix and z is a suffix of t), we say the substring w is an **overlap** of s and t.

The **Hamming distance** d_h of two n-length sequences s and t is defined as

$$d_h(s,t) = \sum_{i=1}^{n} s[i] \overset{?}{=} t[i],$$

where $s[i] \overset{?}{=} t[i]$ is equal to 1 if $s[i] \neq t[i]$, and 0 otherwise. In this context, we also say that s and t have $d_h(s,t)$ differences.

The **edit distance** is the minimum number of edit operations (insertion, deletion and substitution) required to transform one sequence onto another. Formally, the edit distance $d_e(s,t)$ between s and t, such that $n = |s|$ and $m = |t|$, is defined as

$$d_e(s,t) = \begin{cases} n+m & \text{if } n = 0 \text{ or } m = 0, \\ \min \begin{cases} d_e(s[1,n], t[1,m-1]) + 1 \\ d_e(s[1,n-1], t[1,m]) + 1 \\ d_e(s[1,n-1], t[1,m-1]) + s[n] \overset{?}{=} t[m] \end{cases} & \text{otherwise,} \end{cases}$$

where $s[n] \overset{?}{=} t[m]$ is equal to 1 if $s[n] \neq t[m]$, and 0 otherwise.

A **graph** is an ordered pair (V, A) of two sets in which V is a set of elements called **nodes** (of the graph) and A is a set of ordered pairs of nodes, called **arcs** (of the graph). Given a graph G, a **walk** in G is a sequence of nodes $p = v_1, \ldots, v_k$, such that for each pair v_i, v_{i+1} of nodes in p there is a arc $(v_i, v_{i+1}) \in A$. A **path** in G is a walk with no repeated nodes. Given a walk $p = v_1, \ldots, v_k$, $|p| = k - 1$ is the **length** of p. For graphs with costs associated with their arcs, the **cost** of a walk p is the sum of the cost of all arcs of all consecutive pairs of nodes (v_i, v_{i+1}) in p. A **shortest path** from v_1 to v_k is one whose cost is minimum (a path of **minimum cost**).

A **sequence graph** is a graph (V, A) with a sequence of characters, built on an alphabet Σ, associated with each of its nodes. A **simple sequence graph** is a graph in which each node is labeled with only one character. Given a set $S = \{r_1, \ldots, r_m\}$ of sequences and an integer $k \geq 2$, a **De Bruijn graph** is a graph $G_k = (V, A)$ such that:

- $V = \{d \in \Sigma^k |$ such that d is a substring of length k (k-mer) of $r \in S$ and d labels only one node$\}$;
- $A = \{(d, d')|$ the suffix of length $k - 1$ of d is a prefix of $d'\}$.

In this paper, informally for readability, we consider the node label as node. Given a walk $p = v_1, v_2, \ldots, v_n$ in a De Bruijn graph G_k, the **sequence spelled** by p is the sequence $v_1 v_2[k] \ldots v_n[k]$, given by the concatenation of the k-mer v_1 with the last character of each k-mer $v_2, \ldots, v_n$. For a walk $p = v_1, v_2, \ldots, v_n$ in a simple sequence graph G, the sequence spelled by p is $v_1 v_2 \ldots v_n$. A **mapping** of a sequence s onto a simple sequence graph or a De Bruijn graph G is a walk p in G whose editing cost between s and the sequence spelled by p is minimum.

Given the definitions above, we state the following problem for simple ssequence graphs (GSMP) and for De Bruijn graphs (BSMP) when we have changes only in the sequence, respectively:

*Problem 1 (**Graph Sequence Mapping Problem** – GSMP).* Given a m-sequence s and a simple sequence graph G, find a mapping of s onto G.

*Problem 2 (**De Bruijn Graph Sequence Mapping Problem** – BSMP).* Given a m-sequence s and a De Bruijn graph of order k, G_k, find a mapping of s onto G_k.

When the changes are allowed only in the sequence, we have a polynomial time algorithm proposed firstly by Amir *et. al* and Navarro [1,8] and adapted afterward by Rautiainen and Marschall [12], that solve it. For the BSMP, considering paths, Limasset *et. al* [2] proved that the problem is NP-complete. More recently, for walks, Aluru *et. al* [4] proved that there is no algorithm faster than $O(|A| \cdot |s|)$ when only changes in the sequence are allowed, in which $|A|$ is a number of arcs and $|s|$ is the $|s|$-length.

Given that the results of our work are strongly based on the Rauatiainen and Marschall algorithm, we show next how it works, starting with the definition of a multilayer graph. Given a n-sequence s and a simple sequence graph $G = (V = \{v_1, \ldots, v_m\}, A)$, the **multilayer graph** $G' = (V', A')$ is a graph obtained from G and s with weight $\sigma(e) \in \{0,1\}$ for each $e \in A'$. Informally, each layer do G' is a "copy" of G. More precisely, the node set V' is $(V \cup \{v_0\} \times \{1, 2, \ldots, n\}) \cup \{u, w\}$ and arc set is $A' = S \cup T \cup L \cup D \cup I$ where

1. $S = \{(u, (v_j, 1)) : 0 \le j \le m\}$ with

$$\sigma(s, (v_j, 1)) = \begin{cases} 1 \text{ if } j = 0; \\ 0 \text{ otherwise}; \end{cases}$$

2. $T = \{((v_j, n), w) : 0 \le j \le m\}$, with

$$\sigma((v_j, n), w) = 0;$$

3. $L = \{((v_j, i), (v_h, i)) : 1 \le i \le n \wedge (v_j, v_h) \in A\}$, with

$$\sigma((v_j, i), (v_h, i)) = 1;$$

4. $D = \{((v_j, i), (v_h, i')) : 1 \le i < i' \le n \wedge v_j = v_h \wedge i + 1 = i'\}$, with

$$\sigma((v_j, i), (v_h, i')) = 1;$$

5. $I = \{((v_j, i-1), (v_h, i))((v_0, i-1), (v_0, i)) : h \ne 0, 1 < i \le n, (v_j, v_h) \in A \text{ or } j = 0\}$, with

$$\sigma((v_j, i-1), (v_h, i)) = v_h \overset{?}{=} s[i] \text{ and } \sigma((v_0, i-1), (v_0, i)) = 1.$$

The $s[n] \overset{?}{=} t[m]$ is equal to 1 if $s[n] \ne t[m]$, and 0 otherwise. Nodes u, w, (v_0, j) are called *source, target* and *dummy* nodes respectively. Multilayer graph is proposed by Rautiainen and Marschall [12] to solve GSMP by finding a shortest path from u to w in G' through a dynamic programming algorithm. Figure 1 shows an example of multilayer graph obtained from a sequence and a simple sequence graph.

Rautiainen and Marschall Algorithm. Given the definition of the multilayer graph, the solution proposed by Rautiainen and Marschall to map s onto simple sequence graph G consists of building the multilayer graph G' for s and G and to find a shortest path (path of minimum cost) in G' from u to v. An example of a mapping based on this solution is shown in Fig. 1. For this same example, a possible solution is the walk $w = v_1, v_2, v_3, v_4$ in the simple sequence graph G, spelled by the path $p = u, (v_1, 1), (v_2, 2), (v_3, 2), (v_4, 3), v$ in G'. The sequence spelled by w corresponds to ACGT, whose distance to the example sequence $s =$ ACT is 1.

In the paper entitled by *Aligning Sequences to General Graphs in $O(|V| + m \cdot |A|)$ time* [12], the authors propose the algorithm detailed above that return both the mapping and the distance between the two sequences involved in $O(|A| \cdot m + |V| \cdot m \cdot \log(|A| \cdot m))$ time, and we call it here the GSMP algorithm. In the same paper, the authors also propose a more efficient version of the algorithm that returns only the distance in $O(|V| + m \cdot |A|)$ time and we call it here the $GSMP_d$ algorithm, in which A and V is a set of arcs and nodes, respectively and m is a length of mapped sequence s. The details of this algorithm is omitted, but its main idea is to compute the distance $\min d_e(s, s')$ over all spelled sequence s' of all walks p in simple sequence graph G and for this the authors propose an algorithm that considers only two rows of the multilayer graph in each processing step, that is, for $i = 1, \ldots, m-1$, the algorithm builds rows i and $i+1$, processes the two rows, deletes row i, advances with i and repeats the process until finished.

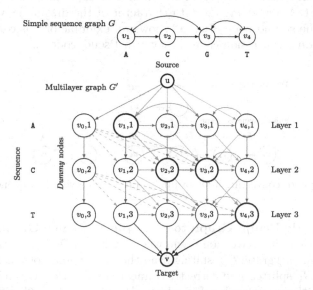

Fig. 1. Example of mapping the sequence $s =$ ACT in the simple sequence graph G. The weight of the red, blue, and green arcs are the insertion, deletion, and substitution weights, respectively. [3,12]. (Color figure online)

3   Approaches for the de Bruijn Graph Sequence Mapping Problem

In this section, we provide a detailed overview of different approaches to solve the De Bruijn Graph Sequence Mapping Problem – BSMP. First, we introduce an adaptation of the GSMP algorithm (applicable to GSMP$_d$) that allow it to run with De Bruijn graphs. Then, we present three heuristics for the BSMP, all of which aim to find the mapping between the sequence and the graph. Two of these heuristics use the seed-and-extend strategy and one uses GSMP algorithm. Finally, we introduce a heuristic for the BSMP that only finds the distance using the GSMP$_d$ algorithm.

3.1   An Algorithm for the de Bruijn Graph Sequence Mapping Problem

The algorithm proposed here for the BSMP follows the same idea as the GSMP algorithm, but with an additional preprocessing step that converts the input De Bruijn graph into a simple sequence graph. Given a De Bruijn graph G_k, it can be converted to a simple sequence graph following two steps: first, each node v of the G_k is splitted into k nodes $v_1 \ldots v_k$ labeled with $v_1 = v[1], \ldots, v_k = v[k]$; in a second step, an arc is inserted for each pair of consecutive nodes resulting from the split of a node of G_k, and for each pair of adjacent nodes of this graph, an arc is inserted connecting the k-th character of the first node with the k-th character of the second node. Figure 2 shows an example of this conversion and the corresponding conversion code is shown in Pseudocode 1.

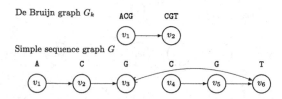

Fig. 2. Example of converting a De bruijn graph G_k to a simple sequence graph G.

Converting a de Bruijn Graph to a Simple Sequence Graph Works. It is easy to see that the conversion is equivalent. Given a De Bruijn graph G_k and the simple sequence graph G resulting from the conversion, note that G contains all k-mers of G_k splitted and correctly connected with arcs. Given $p = v_1 \ldots v_n$ a walk in G_k, there is a walk qp' in which $p' = v'_1, \ldots, v'_n$ in G and, as a result of splitted, before v'_1 a path $q = u_1, \ldots, u_{k-1}$ with $u_{k-1} = v'_1$, so

$$p = v_1, v_2, \ldots, v_n$$
$$= u_1, \ldots, v'_1, v'_2, \ldots, v'_n$$
$$= qp'$$

Pseudocode 1. *convertGraph*

Input: a De Bruin graph G_k and k value.
Output: a simple sequence graph $G = (V, A)$.
 1: $V, A \leftarrow \emptyset$
 2: **for** each k-mer $q \in G_k$ **do**
 3:     **for** $i = 1$ to $k - 1$ **do**
 4:         $V \leftarrow V \cup q[i], q[i+1]$ ▷ $q[i]$ and $q[i+1]$ represents two new nodes in G
 5:         $A \leftarrow A \cup (q[i], q[i+1])$ ▷ $(q[i], q[i+1])$ represents a new arc in G
 6:     **for** each adjacent k-mer q' to q in G_k **do**
 7:         $A \leftarrow A \cup (q[k], q'[k])$ ▷ $(q[k], q'[k])$ represents a new arc in G
 8: **return** (V, A)

---

it is easy to see that the path $q = u_1, \ldots, v_1'$ spells the same sequence as the node v_1, and each character is spelled equivalently in $v_2[k] = v_2', \ldots, v_n[k] = v_n'$. Therefore p and qp' spell the same sequences.

Given the simple sequence graph G resulting from the conversion detailed above, a solution to the BSMP can be achieved running the GSMP (or the GSMP$_d$) algorithm taking G as input. We call this algorithm, made up of the conversion step and running of the GSMP (or the GSMP$_d$) algorithm, the De Bruijn sequence Mapping Tool – BMT (or BMT$_d$).

Given a sequence s, a De Bruijn graph $G_k = (V, A)$, the simple sequence graph $G = (V', A')$ obtained from G_k and the multilayer graph M obtained from s and G, the time complexity of our approach BMT is

$$O(|V| \cdot k) + O(|s| \cdot (|V'| + |A'|)) + O(|A'| \cdot |s| + |V'| \cdot |s| \cdot \log(|A'| \cdot |s|))$$

in which $O(|V| \cdot k)$ is to convert a De Bruijn G_k into to a simple sequence graph G, $O(|s| \cdot (|V'| + |A'|))$ is to build M, and $O(|A'| \cdot |s| + |V'| \cdot |s| \cdot \log(|A'| \cdot |s|))$ to run GSMP algorithm.

The main problem of the BMT is in the construction of the multilayer graph. In real cases a De Bruijn graph can have thousands of k-mers, for example, for k=32 we have $|\Sigma|^{32}$ possible k-mers in which $|\Sigma|$ is the number of characters in the alphabet and the mapped sequences usually have lengths greater than 10000. When we build the multilayer graph, we have a copy of a De Bruijn graph converted into the simple sequence graph for each character of the sequence s and it is easily unfeasible to store so many graphs. For this reason, heuristics that reduce the size of the multilayer graph are welcome and may allow mapping in real cases. For our approach BMT$_d$ the time complexity is

$$O(|V| \cdot k) + O(|V'| + |s| \cdot |A'|)$$

in which $O(|V| \cdot k)$ is to convert a De Bruijn G_k into to a simple sequence graph G and $O(|V'| + |s| \cdot |A'|)$ to run GSMP$_d$ algorithm.

BMT$_d$, unlike BMT, is able to run real cases because the tool does not need to store the entire multilayer graph in memory, but the main problem is that we must update all the arcs when we are building a new row of the multilayer graph and that is its bottleneck in time. To resolve this question we propose a heuristic that improves your time considerably.

3.2 Heuristics

Heuristic 1. Given a sequence s and a De Bruijn graph G_k, the idea of our first heuristic for the BSMP, called here BMT_{h1}, is to anchor some k-mers of the sequence s into the graph and use the BMT to map only the substrings of s that could not be anchored. In more details, the first step of the BMT_{h1} is to look for all the k-mers in s that are present in G_k, that we call **anchors**. Note that, after this step, we can have several substrings of s built by k-mers of the sequence that are not in G_k, that we call **gaps**. For each one of these gaps bordered by two anchors, the heuristic use the BMT to find a walk that, starting at the anchor immediately to the left of the gap and ending at anchor immediately to the right of the gap, best fill it. Figure 3 and 4 shows an example of how BMT_{h1} proceeds, in the first step (Fig. 3) we determine all anchors and in the second step (Fig. 4) we determine, with BMT, the best walks between two anchors The wavy lines are the walks (found with the BMT algorithm) that best fill each gap (starting at the first anchor and ending at the second anchor).

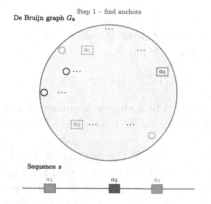 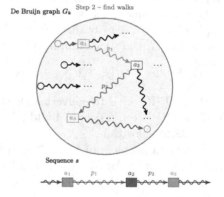

Fig. 3. First step – each square is an anchor found in G_k.

Fig. 4. Second step – The wavy lines between the anchors are the best walks found between them with BMT algorithm.

We show in Pseudocode 2 the steps that BMT_{h1} follows and we show in Pseudocode 3 the steps that **findAnchors** follows. **FindAnchors** returns a sequence of anchors H, and for each consecutive anchors $a, a' \in H$ the BMT_{h1} uses BMT to find the best walk from a to a'.

Experimental results show that it is costly to consider the entire De Bruijn graph in each call of BMT in Heuristic 2. For this reason, BMT_{h1} considers only a subset of $V(G_k)$ in the search for a best walk between two consecutive anchors: considering that the gap has size N, only nodes that are $0.5 \cdot N$ distant, in terms

---

Pseudocode 2. BMT$_{h1}$

Input: a sequence s and a De Bruin graph G_k.
Output: the best walk p that covers the sequence s.
  1: $H \leftarrow$ **findAnchors**(G_k, s) $\triangleright$ find k-mers present in both s and G_k
  2: $p_{temp}, p_{best} \leftarrow \emptyset$
  3: **for** each pair of consecutive anchors $a, a' \in H$ **do**
  4:      $q \leftarrow$ substring of s between a and a'
  5:      $p \leftarrow$ BMT(G_k, q, a, a') $\triangleright$ find the best walk from a to a'
  6:      **if** p is found **then** $p_{temp} \leftarrow p_{temp} \cdot p$
  7:      **if** p is not found **then**
  8:          **if** len$(p_{temp}) \geq$ len(p_{best}) **then**
  9:              $p_{best} \leftarrow p_{temp}$
10:        $p_{temp} \leftarrow \emptyset$
11: **return** p_{best}

Pseudocode 3. *findAnchors*

Input: a sequence s, a De Bruin graph G_k and the k value.
Output: a sequence of anchors (k-mers in G_k and s) H.
  1: **for** $i = 1$ to $|s| - (k - 1)$ **do**
  2:      $q \leftarrow s[i, i + k]$ $\triangleright$ q is a k-mer in s
  3:      **if** $q \in G_k$ **then** $H \leftarrow H, q$
  4: **return** H

---

of their arcs, from the source and target nodes are considered. Considering this constraint, the heuristic is able to process larger instances, but the resulting walk may not be able to cover the entire sequence since BMT may not find a walk from the source and the target nodes. In this case, we consider as the final answer the longest mapping. The main advantage of BMT$_{h1}$ over BMT is the amount of memory used. For the BMT we have to build a multilayer graph considering the whole sequence and the whole De Bruijn graph, whereas for the BMT$_{h1}$ we build the multilayer graph for the substring of the gaps and consider only a subgraph of G_k. For the BMT$_{h1}$ we can find the anchors in constant time and it takes $O(|s| - k)$ to find all the anchors of s. Given N anchors found, the time complexity is $O(N \cdot (|A'| \cdot |s| + |V'| \cdot |s| \cdot \log(|A'| \cdot |s|)))$.

We also developed the BMT$_{h1_d}$ using the same idea as BMT$_{h1}$. The BMT$_{h1_d}$ anchor some k-mers of the sequence s into the graph and use the BMT$_d$ to find the distance of the best walk. In more details, the first step of the BMT$_{h1_d}$ is to look for all the anchors (k-mers) in s that are present in G_k. Note that, after this step, we can also have several gaps. For each one of these gaps bordered by two anchors, the heuristic use the BMT$_d$ to find the distance of the best walk, starting at the anchor immediately to the left of the gap and ending at anchor immediately to the right of the gap. Here BMT$_{h1_d}$ also consider only a subset of $V(G_k)$ in the search for distance of the best walk between two consecutive anchors and the BMT$_{h1_d}$ consider as the final answer the approximated distance of the longest mapping. The BMT_d is capable of processing large inputs, but it takes a long time to run and the main advantage of BMT_{h1_d} over BMT_d is in runtime because we run BMT_d only for gaps and it is advantageous. For the BMT_{h1_d} we can find the anchors in constant time and it takes $O(|s| - k)$ to find all the anchors of s. Given N anchors found, the time complexity is $O(N \cdot ((|V| \cdot k) + (|V'| + |s| \cdot |A'|)))$.

In order to improve the performance of BMT_{h1} and BMT_{h1_d}, we develop two versions of it called BMT_{h1_b} and $BMT_{h1_{db}}$ for BMT_{h1} and BMT_{h1_d} respectively. In this new versions, we build De Bruijn graphs with the Bifrost – a tool that allows to build De Bruijn graphs efficiently and run algorithms like Breadth-First Search and dijkstra on these graphs [9]. A relevant point of using Bifrost in BMT_{h1_b} and $BMT_{h1_{db}}$ is that Bifrost has its own way of efficiently creating the De Bruijn graph and its own interpretation of k-mers, in general, the amount of anchors between our tools with and without Bifrost can vary and this has an impact on the final answer. We can observe this impact in tests when looking at the difference between the responses of BMT_{h1_d} and $BMT_{h1_{db}}$, and between BMT_{h1} and BMT_{h1_b}.

Heuristic 2. Another way to perform the mapping of a sequence in a De Bruijn graph is using the seed-and-extend approach, which consists of, given a set of seeds (substrings of) in the query sequence, to extend each of them in both directions (left and right) while comparing their subsequent characters with the characters of a subject sequence. These extensions proceed until a number of differences be found in this comparison process. This idea is used by us in the development of a new heuristic to the BSMP, called here BMT_{h2}, that consists of the following steps: (1) find all anchors (seeds) in the sequence s (subject sequence); (2) try to extend all the anchors to the right comparing the subsequent characters with the characters (query sequence) spelled by a walk in the De Bruijn graph starting in the anchor node until one difference be found; (3) return the walk that induces the largest extension of s. In order to allow substitutions in the sequence s, for each anchor to be extended, we evaluate the possibility of changing its last character and, with this, to find a better walk in the graph starting on a new modified anchor node. If during the extension we reach another anchor, we continue the extension and this new anchor is part of the solution. Considering that we can have several extensions, the resulting walk may not be able to cover the entire sequence since BMT_{h2} may not find a walk during the extension. In this case, we consider as the final answer the longest mapping.

Figure 5 and 6 shows an example of how BMT_{h2} proceeds, in the first step (Fig. 5) we determine all anchors and in the second and third step (Fig. 6) we determine, with extend, the best walk between two anchors and return it. The wavy lines are the walks, and the green walk is the best walk (starting at the new modified anchor node and ending at the second anchor). For the BMT_{h2} we can find the anchors in constant time and it takes $O(|s| - k)$ to find all the anchors of s. Given N anchors found and an alphabet $|\Sigma| = M$, the time complexity is

$O(|N| \cdot (M \cdot |A|))$ to extend all anchors in which $|A|$ is the number of arcs in the De Bruijn graph.

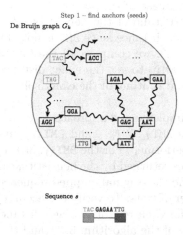

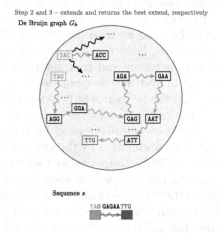

Fig. 5. Step 1 – square orange and purple are anchors found in G_k. (Color figure online)

Fig. 6. Step 2 – extends by changing the last character, for this example, it is best to change (in s) TAC to TAG and extend from the new anchor. Step 3 – return the best extend.

Heuristic 3. In order to improve the BMT_{h2} coverage, we develop a new heuristic that allows substitution and deletion in the mapped sequence, called here BMT_{h3}, that consists the same steps of the BMT_{h2}, but if during the extension step we fail to extend for any walks, we remove $k - 1$ characters from the anchor and repeat the extension process. For the BMT_{h3} we can find the anchors in constant time and it takes $O(|s| - k)$ to find all the anchors of s. Given N anchors found and an alphabet $|\Sigma| = M$, the time complexity is $O(|N| \cdot (M \cdot (|s| - (k - 1)) \cdot |A|))$ to extend all anchors in which $|A|$ is the number of arcs in the De Bruijn graph and $|s| - (k - 1)$ is a number of deletions.

Note that in heuristic 2 we only perform substitution operations and in heuristic 3 we perform substitution and deletion operations in the sequence. All implementations are available on github: github.com/LucasBarbosaRocha.

4   Experiments and Results

In order to evaluate our approaches, the accuracy and performance of the proposed heuristics were assessed by a number of experiments on random(ou quasi-random) data. All the experiments were performed on a computer with processor Intel(R) Xeon(R) CPU E5-2620 2.00GHz with 24 CPUs and 62 GB of RAM. Our dataset includes more than 20 De Bruijn Graphs, build on short reads (100bp on average) of DNA sequences of Escherichia coli (set A) and Escherichia fergusonii (set B) organisms and more than 100 long reads (5000 bp on average) of Escherichia coli (set C) organisms to be mapped in the graph. All of these sequences were obtained from the GenBank[1] database of the NCBI.

In Sect. 4.1, we compare the accuracy and runtime of the heuristics BMT_{h1} and BMT_{h1_b} and we used the BMT_d to get the exact distance since BMT is not able of processing large numbers of k-mers. In Sect. 4.2, we compare all the four in terms of accuracy and runtime using again the BMT_d to get the exact distance. Finally, In Sect. 4.3, we compare the accuracy and runtime of the exact solution BMT_d and the heuristics BMT_{h1_d} and $BMT_{h1_{db}}$.

To calculate the average of distances of the implemented approaches, we add up all the distances obtained by the heuristics BMT_d, BMT_{h1_d} and $BMT_{h1_{db}}$ and divide this summation by the number of tests performed. For the BMT_{h1}, BMT_{h1_b}, BMT_{h2} and BMT_{h3} heuristics, we take the sequences returned by the heuristics, calculate the edit distance between each of them and the original mapped sequence, add uo these distances and divide by the number of tests. To verify the accuracy of the results, we checked in the next sections for each row on average distance tables the difference between the exact distance of the algorithm BMT_d and that one of each heuristic.

4.1   Tests to Obtain Mapping - Heuristic 1

To run the tests of this section, we use the De Bruijn graph with varying number of k-mers built by Set A and we take sequences of length between 2381 and 6225 from Set C. The heuristics return the string spelled by the best walk found and we calculate the edit distance between the original string and the spelled string and compare it to the exact distance returned by the BMT_d. In these tests, the number of anchors lies between 0 and 2015 and we can see how using the Bifrost tool on BMT_{h1_b} brought the distance closer to BMT_d than BMT_{h1}.

The average distances and running runtime obtained in this round of tests are shown on Table 1 and Table 2, respectively. The charts for the calculate average distances and running time are shown on Fig. 7 and Fig. 8, respectively. Different from our heuristics, the BMT was not able to manage the vast majority of test cases. In our analyses, BMT managed to process small test cases for long reads with a length close to 1000 and a De Bruijn graph with approximately 2000 k-mers. We were able to use BMT and 3 out of 100 tests, and this fact attests the applicability of our approaches. We can see in Table 1 that the heuristics are able to perform the mapping in relation to BMT and we can see in Table 2 that the distance obtained by the heuristics are not so far away from the exact cost obtained by BMT_d.

4.2   Tests to Obtain Mapping - All Heuristics

To run the tests of this section, we use De Bruijn graphs with a varying amount of k-mers built by Set B and we take sequences of length between 2381 and 6225

---
[1] https://www.ncbi.nlm.nih.gov/genbank/.

Table 1. Average distances and accuracy: tests with length of long reads between 2381 and 6225.

k	Qty. k-mers in G_k	Average distances			Accuracy	
		BMT_d	BMT_{h1_b}	BMT_{h1}	BMT_{h1_b}	BMT_{h1}
10	78661	1746,4	3046,8	5623,0	1,7	3,2
15	86214	2416,3	5197,5	6255,8	2,2	2,6

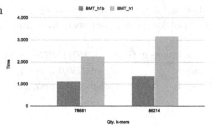

Fig. 7. Average distances: chart for Table 1.

Table 2. Average time (seconds): tests with length of long reads between 2381 and 6225.

k	Qty. k-mers in G_k	BMT_{h1}	BMT_{h1_b}
10	78661	2250,0	1125,0
15	86214	3160,3	1365,0

Fig. 8. Average time (seconds): chart for Table 2.

from Set C. The calculated average distances are shown on Table 3 and 4 and the respective chars for each table shown on Fig. 9 and Fig. 10. We can see that BMT_{h1_b} is the best heuristic in time and quality and is our most powerful version because its graph construction tool (Bifrost) is capable of creating much larger graphs. BMT_{h3} is a heuristic that, despite being simple, manages to be the second best and deliver results in an accessible time. Another important detail is that the number of anchors is relevant for the good execution of the heuristics BMT_{h1} and BMT_{h1_b} and the greater the number of anchors, the better the answer will be and therefore we will process less of the sequence. For heuristics BMT_{h2} and BMT_{h3}, anchors are not used, but it is important to note that a sequence with many anchors is a sequence very similar to the graph and this indicates that the BMT_{h2} and BMT_{h3} heuristics will obtain better answers.

We perform another tests with sequences of length between 1000 and 10000 from Set C and we use De Bruijn graphs built by Set A. The calculated average distances are shown on Table 5 and the average running times of each heuristic shown on Table 6, with the respective charts for each table shown of Fig. 11 and 12. In these new tests we get several sequences with length between 1000 and 10000; and the value of k varying between 5, 10 and 20. In these new tests we can verify a more interesting competitiveness in terms of time and quality. The heuristics were very close in values and heuristics BMT_{h2} and BMT_{h3} showed their efficiency in achieving results close to the other heuristics.

Table 3. Average distances and accuracy: tests with length of long reads between 2381 and 6225.

k	Qty. k-mers in G_k	BMT$_d$	Average distances			
			BMT$_{h1_b}$	BMT$_{h1}$	BMT$_{h2}$	BMT$_{h3}$
10	78661	1746,4	3046,8	5623,0	5435,6	4722,7
15	86214	2416,3	5197,5	6255,8	6216,3	5022,4
			Accuracy			
			1,7	3,2	3,1	2,7
			2,2	2,6	2,6	2,1

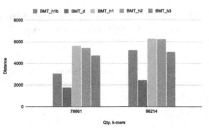

Fig. 9. Average distances: chart for Table 3.

Table 4. Average time (seconds): tests with length of long reads between 2381 and 6225.

k	Qty. k-mers in G_k	BMT$_{h1_b}$	BMT$_{h1}$	BMT$_{h2}$	BMT$_{h3}$
10	78661	1125,0	2250,0	1508,4	2160,6
15	86214	1365,0	3160,3	1882,5	4560,0

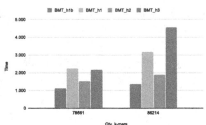

Fig. 10. Average time (seconds): chart for Table 4.

Here the number of anchors is between 0 and 9234. For the small k 5 we have the largest number of anchors and this gives us a very mapped sequence. For k 10 we have the amount of anchors being around 50% of the sequence length and this gives us a partially mapped sequence. For k 20 we have a special case that consists of having a few anchors and the result is very close to the BMT$_d$ and this happens because our heuristics return a walk p that spells a small sequence and when calculating the accuracy with the original sequence we have a high edit distance and this is close to the distance returned by BMT$_d$.

4.3   Tests to Obtain only Distances - Heuristic 1

A relevant test is to want to find only the mapping distance (and not the mapping) and in this section we perform this test. To run the tests of this section, we use De Bruijn graphs with a varying amount of k-mers built by Set A and we take sequences of length between 2381 and 6225 from Set C. The calculated average distances are shown on Table 7 and the average running times of each heuristic are shown on Table 8, with the respective charts for each table shown on Fig. 13 and 14. We can see that for the version that only looks for the distance, it is possible to have a great time gain with heuristics compared to BMT$_d$ because we take advantage of anchors to not process the entire sequence, on the other hand, we have a loss of accuracy with the heuristics. The anchors in these tests increase as the number of k-mers in the graph increases, with their number varying between 23 and 6000 anchors.

Table 5. Average distances and accuracy: tests with length of long reads between 1000 and 10000.

k	Qty. k-mers in G_k	BMT_d	BMT_{h1_b}	BMT_{h1}	BMT_{h2}	BMT_{h3}
		Average distances				
5	1017	8,3	9,9	11,5	54,7	26,8
10	11375	2363,5	5173,2	5334,4	5841,8	5684,6
20	10243	5278,5	5743,5	5383,8	6158,5	5850,6
		Accuracy				
		1,2	1,4	6,6	3,3	
		2,2	2,3	2,5	2,41	
		1,1	1,1	1,2	1,1	

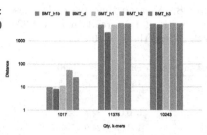

Fig. 11. Average distances: chart for Table 5.

Table 6. Average time (seconds): tests with length of long reads between 1000 and 10000.

k	Qty. k-mers in G_k	BMT_{h1_b}	BMT_{h1}	BMT_{h2}	BMT_{h3}
5	1017	5,6	6,1	6,4	6,4
10	11375	242,4	263,5	276,7	276,7
20	10243	226,6	246,3	258,6	258,6

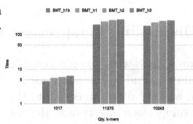

Fig. 12. Average time (seconds): chart for Table 6.

Table 7. Average distances and accuracy: tests with length of long reads between 2381 and 6225 and the $k = 10$.

Qty. k-mers in G_k	BMT_d	BMT_{h1_d}	$\mathrm{BMT}_{h1_{db}}$	BMT_{h1_d}	$\mathrm{BMT}_{h1_{db}}$
	Average distances			Accuracy	
4577	1537,5	3147,0	3181,0	2,1	2,1
9119	1453,3	3184,3	3098,3	2,2	2,2
11375	1427,0	3142,3	3028,0	2,2	2,2
22485	1201,7	3111,3	2835,0	2,6	2,4
43842	995,3	2850,5	2558,0	2,8	2,6
84683	662,7	1663,3	1550,0	2,5	2,4
557522	314,5	552,3	477,3	1,7	1,5

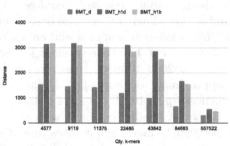

Fig. 13. Average distances: chart for Table 7.

Table 8. Average time (seconds): tests with length of long reads between 2381 and 6225 and the $k = 10$.

Qty. k-mers in G_k	BMT_d	BMT_{h1_d}	$BMT_{h1_{db}}$
4577	73,7	5,0	3,5
9119	222,5	7,7	5,7
11375	370,0	32,5	24,7
22485	1632,3	24,0	13,3
43842	13324,0	261,7	177,7
84683	89152,0	66,0	41,7
557522	151787,3	45,0	29,7

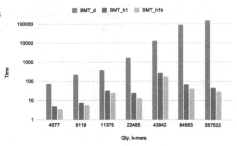

Fig. 14. Average time (seconds): chart for Table 8.

5 Discussion, Perspectives and Conclusions

This work deals with two versions of De Bruijn Graph Sequence Problem – BSMP: one aims to find a minimum cost mapping between a sequence and a Bruijn graph, and the other aims to find the distance between them. For each version, we develop exact algorithms that is a simple adaptations of Rautiainen and Marschall [12] algorithm for simple sequence graphs. The developed algorithms are De Bruijn Mapping Tool – BMT that returns the mapping and BMT_d that returns only the distance between them. However, BMT is not capable of working with large graphs because it requires a lot of memory and BMT_d takes a lot of running time. Therefore, we also design heuristics that overcome these difficulties and find a low-cost mapping and an approximate distance.

BMT can not handle sequences longer than 1000 elements or graphs with more than 2000 10-mers. However, our best heuristic for finding the mapping of approximate distance, BMT_{h1_b} can handle graphs with 86214 15-mers and sequences up to 10000 elements in less than 22 min.

BMT_d can handle sequences with up to 7000 elements and graphs with with up 560,000 10-mers, but it takes more than 40 h. On the other hand, our best heuristic for the approximated distance, $BMT_{h1_{db}}$, spends only 29 s.

From this work, several variations should be considered to improve the performance and quality of practical solutions.

Firstly, concerning the graph mapping problem, we not only propose the BMT_{h1_b} heuristic but also introduce two other heuristics, BMT_{h2} and BMT_{h3}, that employ the seed-and-extend strategy. Although BMT_{h2} and BMT_{h3} exhibit lower performance than BMT_{h1_b}, the concepts developed in these heuristics can be incorporated into BMT_{h1_b}, resulting in a new and more efficient heuristic version.

Hirschberg [5] reduces the quadratic space used to find an alignment for a pair of sequences using linear space by using the divide-and-conquer paradigm. Therefore, secondly, in the context of the mapping version, these ideas could be adapted to reduce the space and extend the scope of this work.

Finally, another promising approach to enhance the practical results of both versions is the parallelization of the algorithms. This approach can significantly reduce the execution time and increase the scalability of the algorithms.

References

1. Amir, A., et al.: Pattern matching in hypertext. J. Algor. **35**, 82–99 (1997)
2. Limasset, A., et al.: Read mapping on de bruijn graphs. BMC Bioinf. **17**(1), 1–12 (2016)
3. Jain, C., et al.: On the complexity of sequence-to-graph alignment. J. Comput. Biol. **27**, 640–654 (2019)
4. Gibney, D., Thankachan, S., Aluru, S.: On the hardness of sequence alignment on De Bruijn graphs. J. Comput. Biol. **29**, 1377–1396 (2022)
5. Hirschberg, D.S.: A linear space algorithm for computing maximal common subsequences. Commun. ACM **18**(6), 341–343 (1975)
6. Garrison, E., et al.: Variation graph toolkit improves read mapping by representing genetic variation in the reference. Nat. Biotechnol. **36**, 875–879 (2018)
7. Myers, E.W.: The fragment assembly string graph. Bioinformatics (2005)
8. Navarro, G.: Improved approximate pattern matching on hypertext. Theor. Comput. Sci. **237**, 455–463 (1998)
9. Holley, G., Melsted, P.: Bifrost: highly parallel construction and indexing of colored and compacted de bruijn graphs. Genome Biol. **21**, 1–20 (2020)
10. Li, H., Homer, N.: A survey of sequence alignment algorithms for next-generation sequencing. Brief Bioinf. **11**, 473–483 (2010)
11. Park, K., Kim, D.K.: String matching in hypertext. In: Galil, Z., Ukkonen, E. (eds.) CPM 1995. LNCS, vol. 937, pp. 318–329. Springer, Heidelberg (1995). https://doi.org/10.1007/3-540-60044-2_51
12. Rautiainen, M., Marschall, T.: Aligning sequences to general graphs in o $(v + me)$ time. In: bioRxiv, pp. 216–127 (2017)
13. De Bruijn, N.G.: A combinatorial problem. In: Proceedings of Koninklijke Nederlandse Academie van Wetenschappen, vol. 49, pp. 758–764 (1946)
14. Pevzner, P.A., et al.: An eulerian path approach to dna fragment assembly. Proc. Natl. Acad. Sci. **98**, 9748–9753 (2001)
15. Akutsu, T.: A linear time pattern matching algorithm between a string and a tree. In: Annual Symposium on Combinatorial Pattern Matching, pp. 1–10 (1993)
16. Manber, U., Wu, S.: Approximate string matching with arbitrary costs for text and hypertext. In: Advances in Structural and Syntactic Pattern Recognition, pp. 22–33. World Scientific (1992)

Computational Grid Optimization for the 3D Higher-Order Parabolic Equation

Mikhail S. Lytaev$^{(\boxtimes)}$ (iD)

St. Petersburg Federal Research Center of the Russian Academy of Sciences,
14-th Linia, V.I., No. 39, Saint Petersburg 199178, Russia
mikelytaev@gmail.com

Abstract. This work is devoted to the wave propagation modeling in an essentially three-dimensional medium. Finite-difference Padé approximations of the three-dimensional one-way Helmholtz equation are considered. An algorithm for automatic mesh generation based on minimizing the dispersion error is proposed. The mesh is optimized in such a way as to minimize the computational complexity of the numerical scheme. It is shown that reference propagation constant affects the performance of the numerical scheme and a formula for its optimal value was derived. Approximations of the transversal operator of the second and fourth order of accuracy, the alternating-direction implicit (ADI) splitting method were considered. The optimal meshes were analyzed for various configurations of the numerical scheme, which allowed to quantify its possibilities and limitations. Automating the numerical scheme setup allows to prevent modeling errors and overspending of the computational resources.

Keywords: wave propagation · parabolic equation · mesh optimization · alternating-direction implicit · Padé approximation · Finite-difference

1 Introduction

The need for computer modeling of the wave field spatial distribution arises in various fields of mathematical physics: acoustics, radiophysics, geophysics, optics and quantum mechanics. Despite the different nature of the underlying physical phenomena, corresponding mathematical models are, in a certain sense, universal [22]. Accordingly, the numerical methods used to solve them can be reused in various applications.

One of such universal methods of the wave propagation theory is the parabolic equation (PE) method. It is usually used to compute the wave field in inhomogeneous waveguides. It was originally developed in 1946 by Leontovich and Fock [11] to tackle the tropospheric radio wave propagation problem. Then the PE method found wide application in computational sonar problems [9]. Various modifications and effective numerical schemes appeared, which were then used in optics [3] and seismology [5]. There are also a number of theoretical papers [2,21], where, in particular, the connection between the PE and the Helmholtz equation is revealed [6,7]. Owing to these studies, in this paper terms "parabolic equation" and "one-way Helmholtz equation" are used as synonyms. Basically, the PE method is used in a two-dimensional environment, but recently there has been increasing interest in its application in essentially three-dimensional problems. In [12,19,24] it is proposed to use the PE method to compute the radio wave field in tunnels. In [8,15,16], the PE method is used to compute the radio wave propagation in dense urban conditions. There are more and more works devoted to modeling the acoustic field in a three-dimensional inhomogeneous underwater environment [10,13,20].

The main problems with the numerical solving of the three-dimensional PE are the low computation speed and the huge memory requirements. In part, this problem can be tackled by applying the higher-order approximations and the transverse operator splitting using the alternating direction implicit [18] (ADI) method. Meanwhile, the issue of the automatic selection of the computational grid and other artificial parameters in an optimal way is relevant. Indeed, using a grid that is too dense will lead to overspending of the computational resources, and computing on an insufficiently dense grid will yield an incorrect results. Currently, there is no general theory of choosing the optimal computational parameters of a numerical scheme. They are usually selected manually by an expert based on some empirical considerations.

Previously, the optimization problem of the finite-difference PE approximation was solved for the two-dimensional case in a homogeneous [17] and inhomogeneous medium [14]. The aim of this paper is to develop a method for optimizing a finite-difference numerical scheme for the three-dimensional PE and analyze optimal grids under various configurations. In this paper, by optimization we mean reducing the required computing time and memory without increasing the computing resources. It should also be mentioned work [23], where it is proposed to jointly use the Padé approximation of the propagation operator along the longitudinal coordinate and the 4th order approximation of the transversal operator. The analysis of the scheme accuracy depending on the approximation order and the propagation angle was also carried out in [23].

The paper is organized as follows. In the next section, the mathematical formulation of the problem is posed and the one-way Helmholtz equation in the spectral domain is derived. Section 3 is devoted to the numerical scheme under consideration. In Sect. 4, the discrete dispersion relations are derived, on the basis of which the algorithm for optimizing the computational grid is constructed in Sect. 5. Section 6 presents and analyzes optimization results for various configurations.

2   3D PE

Consider the following three-dimensional scalar Helmholtz equation defined in the Cartesian coordinate system

$$\frac{\partial^2 \psi}{\partial x^2} + \frac{\partial^2 \psi}{\partial y^2} + \frac{\partial^2 \psi}{\partial z^2} + k^2 \psi = 0, \tag{1}$$

where $\psi(x, y, z)$ is the wave field distribution to be determined, $k = 2\pi f / c$ is the wavenumber, f is the radiation frequency, c is the wave propagation speed.

The wave propagation process is generated by the initial condition

$$\psi(0, y, z) = \psi_0(y, z)$$

where $\psi_0(y, z)$ in known function, which corresponds to the radiation source.

Function $\psi(x, y, z)$ may be subject to additional boundary and radiation conditions, which, however, do not matter for the present study.

It is further assumed that the wave propagation process occurs mainly in the positive direction of the x axis.

We introduce into consideration the two-dimensional Fourier transform of function ψ with respect to variables y and z

$$\tilde{\psi}(x, k_y, k_z) = \frac{1}{2\pi} \int\limits_{-\infty}^{+\infty} \int\limits_{-\infty}^{+\infty} \psi(x, y, z) e^{-ik_z z - ik_y y} dy dz,$$

and inverse Fourier transform

$$\psi(x, y, z) = \frac{1}{2\pi} \int\limits_{-\infty}^{+\infty} \int\limits_{-\infty}^{+\infty} \tilde{\psi}(x, k_y, k_z) e^{ik_z z + ik_y y} dk_y dk_z.$$

Note that the Fourier transform in this case has the physical meaning of decomposing the wave field into the plane waves with transversal wavenumbers k_y and k_z.

Applying the above transformation to Eq. (1), we obtain the following equation

$$\frac{\partial^2 \tilde{\psi}}{\partial x^2} - k_y^2 \tilde{\psi} - k_z^2 \tilde{\psi} + k^2 \tilde{\psi} = 0. \tag{2}$$

Equation (2) may be rewritten as follows

$$\left[\frac{\partial}{\partial x} - i\sqrt{-k_y^2 - k_z^2 + k^2} \right] \left[\frac{\partial}{\partial x} + i\sqrt{-k_y^2 - k_z^2 + k^2} \right] \tilde{\psi} = 0.$$

The latter equation has the physical meaning of decomposition into waves propagating in the positive and negative directions along the x axis. Next, we are only interested in waves propagating in the positive direction, so we consider the following equation

$$\left[\frac{\partial}{\partial x} - i\sqrt{-k_y^2 - k_z^2 + k^2} \right] \tilde{\psi} = 0. \tag{3}$$

3   Numerical Solution

The numerical solution is sought on a uniform grid with steps Δx, Δy and Δz. It is usually assumed that $\Delta y = \Delta z$. The following notation is further used

$$\psi_{i,j}^n = \psi\left(n\Delta x, i\Delta y, j\Delta z\right).$$

The number of grid nodes along each coordinate is denoted respectively as n_x, n_y and n_z.

3.1   Padé Approximation of the Propagator

Let's use the following replacement

$$u(x, y, z) = e^{-i\beta x}\psi(x, y, z), \tag{4}$$

where β is the reference propagation constant, which sense will be clarified in the next sections.

The step-by-step solution can be written as follows

$$\tilde{u}\left(x + \Delta x, k_y, k_z\right) = \exp\left(i\beta\Delta x\left(\sqrt{1 + \xi} - 1\right)\right)\tilde{u}\left(x, k_y, k_z\right), \tag{5}$$

where

$$\xi = -\frac{k_y^2}{\beta^2} - \frac{k_z^2}{\beta^2} + \frac{k^2}{\beta^2} - 1. \tag{6}$$

Following [4], we apply the Padé approximation [1] of order $[m/n]$ in the vicinity of $\xi = 0$ to the propagation operator (5)

$$\exp\left(ik\Delta x\left(\sqrt{1 + \xi} - 1\right)\right) \approx \frac{1 + \sum_{l=1}^m \tilde{a}_l\xi^l}{1 + \sum_{l=1}^n \tilde{b}_l\xi^l} = \prod_{l=1}^p \frac{1 + a_l\xi}{1 + b_l\xi}, \tag{7}$$

where a_l and b_l are the Padé approximation coefficients.

Now the action of propagation operator (5) in the spectral domain can be written using auxiliary functions v_l as follows

$$\begin{cases} (1 + b_1\xi)\,\tilde{v}_1^n = (1 + a_1\xi)\,\tilde{u}^{n-1} \\ (1 + b_l\xi)\,\tilde{v}_l^n = (1 + a_l\xi)\,\tilde{v}_{l-1}^n \qquad l = 2\ldots p-1 \\ \ldots \\ (1 + b_p\xi)\,\tilde{u}^n = (1 + a_p\xi)\,\tilde{v}_{p-1}^n. \end{cases} \tag{8}$$

Applying the inverse Fourier transform, we obtain a system of two-dimensional differential equations in the spatial domain (y, z)

$$\begin{cases} (1 + b_1 L)\,v_1^n = (1 + a_1 L)\,u^{n-1} \\ (1 + b_l L)\,v_l^n = (1 + a_l L)\,v_{l-1}^n \qquad l = 2,\ldots,p-1 \\ \ldots \\ (1 + b_p L)\,u^n = (1 + a_p L)\,v_{p-1}^n, \end{cases} \tag{9}$$

with transversal operator

$$Lu = \frac{1}{\beta^2}\frac{\partial^2 u}{\partial y^2} + \frac{1}{\beta^2}\frac{\partial^2 u}{\partial z^2} + \left(\frac{k^2}{\beta^2} - 1\right)u. \tag{10}$$

3.2   Approximation of the Transversal Operator

Next, we need to construct a numerical approximation of the transversal operator (10). The second derivatives will be approximated by the following 4th order 3-point scheme

$$\frac{\partial^2 u}{\partial z^2} \approx D_{\Delta z}u = \frac{1}{\Delta z^2}\delta_z^2\left(1 + \alpha\delta_z^2\right)^{-1}u,$$

where $\alpha = 0$ for the 2nd order scheme and $\alpha = 1/12$ for the 4th order one. Second difference operator is defined as follows

$$\delta_{\Delta z}^2 = u\left(z - \Delta z\right) - 2u\left(z\right) + u\left(z + \Delta z\right).$$

The approximation of the second derivative along y is written similarly.

Now the approximation of operator L can be written as follows

$$Lu \approx L_d u = \frac{1}{\beta^2}D_{\Delta y}u + \frac{1}{\beta^2}D_{\Delta z} + \left(\frac{k^2}{\beta^2} - 1\right)u. \tag{11}$$

Setting $\Delta y, \Delta z \to 0$, one can achieve an arbitrarily accurate approximation. However, substitution such an approximation into each line of system (9) yield a system of linear algebraic equations with dimension $n_y n_z \times n_y n_z$. Sparsity matrix of such a system depicted at Fig. 1. Given its sparsity, the specified system can be solved in $O\left((n_y n_z)^2\right)$ operations.

The solution of the above mentioned system can be too time and memory consuming for practical problems, so an approximate approach of splitting operator L into two operators that are applied sequentially has been proposed [18]

$$L_d^{ADI}u = \left[\frac{1}{\beta^2}D_{\Delta y} + \frac{1}{2}\left(\frac{k^2}{\beta^2} - 1\right)\right]\left[\frac{1}{\beta^2}D_{\Delta z} + \frac{1}{2}\left(\frac{k^2}{\beta^2} - 1\right)\right]u. \tag{12}$$

This approach is called an Alternating-direction implicit (ADI) method [24] and allows to get an approximate solution faster, namely in $O\left(n_y n_z\right)$ operations. Further, it will be shown that the splitting error increases with the growth of the propagation angle and, in fact, this approximation is not applicable at large propagation angles.

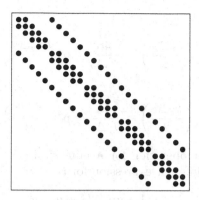

Fig. 1. Sparsity matrix.

4   Dispersion Relations

Consider a three-dimensional plane wave

$$\phi\left(x, y, z\right) = \exp\left(-ik_x x - ik_y y - ik_z z\right), \qquad (13)$$

where

$$k_x = k \cos\theta, \qquad (14)$$

$$k_y = k \cos\varphi \sin\theta,$$

$$k_z = k \sin\varphi \sin\theta,$$

θ is the angle between the positive direction of the x axis and the direction of the plane wave (further denoted as propagation angle), φ is the angle between the y axis and the projection of the plane wave direction onto the yz plane. Further we assume that $\varphi \in [0, 2\pi]$, $\theta \in [0, \theta_{max}]$, $\theta_{max} \in [0, \pi/2]$ is the maximum propagation angle for a particular problem, selected based on geometric considerations [14].

Substituting plane wave (13) into numerical scheme (9), (11), we obtain the following expression for the discrete longitudinal wavenumber [3,24]

$$\tilde{k}_x\left(\varDelta x, \varDelta y, \varDelta z, a_1 \ldots a_p, b_1 \ldots b_p, \theta, \varphi\right) = k + \frac{\ln \prod_{l=1}^{p} t_l}{i \varDelta x},$$

where

$$t_l = \frac{1 + a_l\left(\xi_d^y + \xi_d^z\right)}{1 + b_l\left(\xi_d^y + \xi_d^z\right)},$$

$$\xi_d^y = -\frac{1}{\beta^2 \Delta y^2} \sin^2\left(\frac{k_y \Delta y}{2}\right) - \frac{4\alpha}{\beta^2 \Delta y^2} \sin^4\left(\frac{k_y \Delta y}{2}\right) + \frac{1}{2}\left(\frac{k^2}{\beta^2} - 1\right),$$

$$\xi_d^z = -\frac{1}{\beta^2 \Delta z^2} \sin^2\left(\frac{k_z \Delta z}{2}\right) - \frac{4\alpha}{\beta^2 \Delta z^2} \sin^4\left(\frac{k_z \Delta z}{2}\right) + \frac{1}{2}\left(\frac{k^2}{\beta^2} - 1\right).$$

Performing a similar operation for a numerical scheme with splitting (9), (12), we get a slightly different expression for t_l

$$t_l = \frac{(1 + a_l \xi_d^y)(1 + a_l \xi_d^z)}{(1 + b_l \xi_d^y)(1 + b_l \xi_d^z)}.$$

The following rough estimate

$$|[1 + a_l(\xi_d^y + \xi_d^z)] - (1 + a_l\xi_d^y)(1 + a_l\xi_d^z)| = |a_l^2 \xi_d^y \xi_d^z|$$

indicates that the splitting-related error grows with increasing k_y and k_z. At the same time, setting $\Delta y, \Delta z \to 0$ will not reduce the error. Thus, ADI is a small-angle approximation and is inapplicable at large propagation angles regardless of the approximation order and the mesh density. Approach to overcome this issue was made in [3], where an iterative ADI method was proposed.

5   Optimization Algorithm

It is further assumed that maximum propagation angle θ_{max}, as well as the acceptable error ε at the distance x_{max} from the propagation staring point are given.

5.1   Optimizing of the Reference Propagation Constant

Previously in (4) we introduced artificial parameter β, called the reference propagation constant. The most common choice of its value is $\beta = k$. Although the specific value of this parameter does not affect the derivation and validity of the numerical scheme, we will show further that it can be chosen in an optimal way.

Consider the error of rational approximation (7)

$$R(\xi) = |\exp\left(ik\Delta x\left(\sqrt{1 + \xi} - 1\right)\right) - \prod_{l=1}^{p} \frac{1 + a_l \xi}{1 + b_l \xi}|.$$

Figure 2 demonstrates the dependence of R on ξ when $\Delta x = 25\,\mathrm{m}$, Padé order is [6/7]. In can be seen that since Padé approximation is local, the minimum error is localized in the vicinity of point $\xi = 0$ and monotonically increases with distance from the specified point. A similar behavior is observed for other

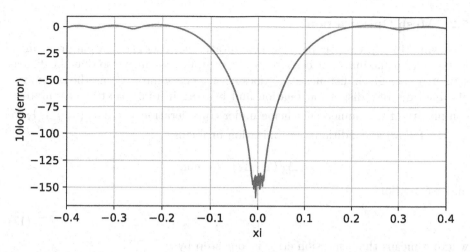

Fig. 2. The dependence of rational approximation error R on ξ when $\Delta x = 25\,\text{m}$, Padé order is [6/7].

values of Δx and approximation orders. Keeping in mind formulas (6) and (14), variable ξ can be expressed via propagation angle θ and propagation constant β as follows

$$\xi = -\frac{k^2}{\beta^2} \sin^2 \theta + \frac{k^2}{\beta^2} - 1.$$

Then the set of its possible values will take the form

$$\xi \in \left[-\frac{k^2}{\beta^2} \sin^2 \theta_{max} + \frac{k^2}{\beta^2} - 1, \frac{k^2}{\beta^2} - 1 \right]. \tag{15}$$

For example, if one select the standard value $\beta = k$, then according to (15), the values $\xi \in [-\sin^2 \theta_{max}, 0]$, i.e. will always be negative. So the Padé approximation at $\xi > 0$ turns out to be unused. Considering this observation, it would be reasonable to choose such a value of β, at which the range of values of ξ most fully falls into the neighborhood of point $\xi = 0$. To do this, we write the following equality

$$-\left(-\frac{k^2}{\beta^2} \sin^2 \theta_{max} + \frac{k^2}{\beta^2} - 1 \right) = \frac{k^2}{\beta^2} - 1,$$

from which we van easily get the following optimal value of the propagation constant

$$\beta = \frac{2\pi f}{c} \sqrt{\frac{2 - \sin^2 \theta_{max}}{2}}. \tag{16}$$

5.2 Mesh Optimization

Following [14,17], we formulate the computational grid optimization problem. It is required to maximize the cell sizes of the computational grid so that the dispersion error at a given distance x_{max} does not exceed some ε. Using the previously obtained discrete dispersion relation and bearing in mind that the asymptotic complexity of the numerical scheme under consideration is $O\left(n_x \left(n_y n_z\right)^2\right)$, we get the following conditional optimization problem

$$\Delta x \left(\Delta y \Delta z\right)^2 \to \max$$

under condition

$$n_x \tau < \varepsilon, \tag{17}$$

where τ means the dispersion error at one step by x

$$\tau = \max_{\theta \in [0,\theta_{max}], \varphi \in [0,2\pi]} |\tilde{k}_x - k \cos \theta|,$$

$n_x = \lceil x_{max}/\Delta x \rceil$ is the number of required steps along x axis. This algorithm takes into account the total accumulation of the dispersion error with each step along x axis.

Given the small dimension of this optimization problem and the fact that the steps along the transverse coordinates can be set equal ($\Delta y = \Delta z$), the problem is solved effectively by simply iterating over the reasonable values of cell sizes.

6 Optimization Results

This section presents the results of the proposed optimization algorithm under various conditions. In all examples we set $k = 2\pi$, $\varepsilon = 10^{-2}$.

6.1 Reference Propagation Constant Impact

First, let's evaluate how the value of parameter β affects the cell sizes. We will compare the standard value of β, equal to the wavenumber k, and the value obtained using proposed formula (16). Table 1 demonstrates the comparison of the optimal cell sizes for various values of θ_{max} and x_{max}. The gain is calculated as the ratio of asymptotic complexities

$$Gain = \frac{\Delta x_2 \left(\Delta y_2 \Delta z_2\right)^2}{\Delta x_1 \left(\Delta y_1 \Delta z_1\right)^2},$$

in other words, it shows how many times the proposed method is faster than the standard one. It is clearly seen that the proposed optimal value of β allows to reduce the computing time by 4–6 times. In addition, it follows from the results that with increasing θ_{max}, an increasingly dense computational grid is required. A decrease in longitudinal step Δx with an increase in θ_{max} leads to an increase in n_x, which makes condition (17) unfeasible at large propagation angles. The proposed method of optimizing β allows to increase the maximum allowable angle by about $10°$.

Figure 3 demonstrates the dependence of the discrete dispersion relation error on angle θ when $\Delta x = 7$ m, $\Delta y = \Delta z = 0.09$ m, Padé order is [6/7] and $\theta_{max} = 30°$. It can be seen that with the same computational parameters, standard value $\beta = k$ allows to account only angles up to $22°$, while the proposed method can give precise results at angles up to $30°$.

Table 1. Comparison of the optimal cell sizes. In all examples Padé order is [6/7], 4th order approximation is used for the transversal operator, splitting is not used. "-" means that a reasonable grid cannot be constructed for the given parameters.

$\theta_{max}(°)$	x_{max} (m)	$\beta = k$		Optimal β		Gain
		Δx_1 (m)	$\Delta y_1 = \Delta z_1$ (m)	Δx_2 (m)	$\Delta y_2 = \Delta z_2$ (m)	
3	10000	370	4.3	700	5.2	4.0
5	1000	130	2.8	245	3.4	4.1
10	1000	32.5	0.7	65.5	0.8	3.6
20	1000	8.2	0.16	15.5	0.19	3.76
30	1000	3.7	0.08	7.0	0.09	3.88
45	1000	1.6	0.034	3.02	0.04	3.61
60	100	1.0	0.03	1.6	0.04	6.17
70	100	-	-	1.0	0.025	-
80	10	-	-	-	-	-

6.2   Impact of the Operator Splitting

Next, let's consider how the splitting of operator L using the ADI method affects the accuracy of the numerical scheme. Table 2 presents the optimal values of the grid cell sizes for the ADI method and approximation without splitting. There are practically no differences in the required mesh, however, the proposed optimization method indicates that meshes for the ADI method that satisfy any feasible precision requirements do not exist when $\theta_{max} > 10°$. This is due to the splitting error, which increases with increasing propagation angle.

Figure 4 depicts the two dimensional distribution of the discrete dispersion error. It can be seen that when using the scheme without splitting, the minimum error is observed when $k_y, k_z = 0$ and monotonously increases in all directions as moving from this point. The ADI scheme gives a much larger error, while the location of areas with minimal error depends on the value of β.

6.3   Comparison of the 2nd and 4th Order Schemes

Now we will quantitatively estimate what performance gain is provided by using the 4th order accuracy scheme for approximating the derivatives in transverse

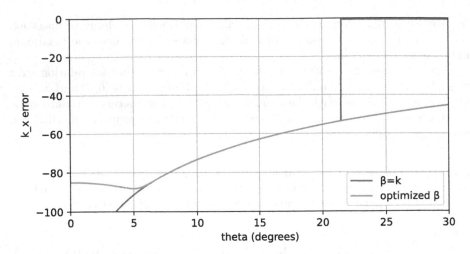

Fig. 3. Dependence of the discrete dispersion relation error $(10 \log |\tilde{k}_x - k_x|)$ on angle θ when $\Delta x = 7$ m, $\Delta y = \Delta z = 0.09$ m, Padé order is $[6/7]$, $\theta_{max} = 30°$. 4th order approximation is used for the transversal operator, splitting is not used.

Table 2. Comparison of the optimal cell sizes. In all examples Padé order is $[6/7]$, 4th order approximation is used for the transversal operator, value of β is computed by formula (16). "-" means that a reasonable grid cannot be constructed for the given parameters.

$\theta_{max}(°)$	x_{max} (m)	Splitting (ADI)		No splitting	
		Δx (m)	Δz (m)	Δx (m)	Δz (m)
3	10000	700	5.2	700	5.2
5	1000	245	3.4	245	3.4
10	1000	65.5	0.9	65.5	0.82
20	1000	-	-	15.5	0.19
30	1000	-	-	7.0	0.09

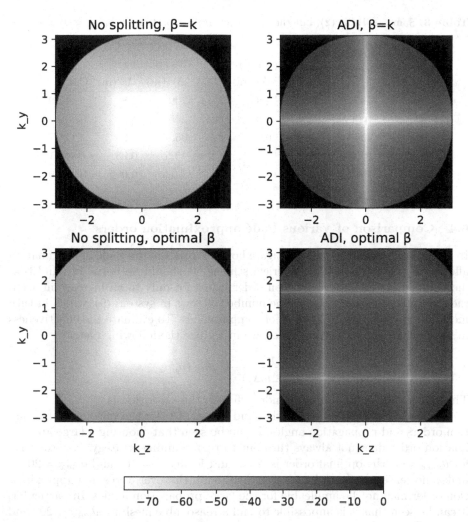

Fig. 4. Two dimensional distribution of the discrete dispersion error ($10 \log |\tilde{k}_x - k_x|$). In all examples $\Delta x = 3.7$ m, $\Delta z = 0.08$ m, $\theta_{max} = 30°$, Padé order is [6/7], 4th order approximation is used for the transversal operator.

operator L. Source data of the Table 3 is analogous to Table 2, but the optimal grid is computed for the 2nd order accuracy scheme ($\alpha = 0$). Comparing the both tables, it is clearly seen that the 4th order scheme allows using a more sparse grid along y and z axes, while the difference between the methods grows as the propagation angle increases. The gain in this case is considered between the 2nd and 4th order schemes. Density reduction is especially important for a non-splitting scheme, given its asymptotic complexity.

Table 3. Same as Table (2), but the 2nd order approximation order ($\alpha = 0$) was used instead.

$\theta_{max}(°)$	x_{max} (m)	Splitting (ADI)			No splitting		
		Δx (m)	Δz (m)	Gain	Δx (m)	Δz (m)	Gain
3	10000	700	2.8	3.44	700	2.8	11.9
5	1000	245	1.9	3.2	245	1.9	10.6
10	1000	65.5	0.3	8.05	65.5	0.25	115.7
20	1000	-	-	-	15.5	0.03	1411.1
30	1000	-	-	-	7.0	0.009	10451.9

6.4   Comparison of Various Padé approximation orders

In the last example, we will investigate how the order of the Padé approximation affects the efficiency of the numerical scheme. It should be borne in mind that increasing the Padé approximation order leads not only to an increase in accuracy, but also to an increase in the number of rows in system (9), which in turn means an increase in the amount of computations. To evaluate the effectiveness in view of the approximation order, we introduce the following metric

$$V = \frac{p}{\Delta x \left(\Delta y \Delta z\right)^2} \sim p n_x \left(n_y n_z\right)^2.$$

The smaller the value of V, the more efficient the algorithm is.

Table 4 shows the optimal meshes and values of V for the various approximation orders and propagation angles. It can be seen that choosing a large approximation order does not always turn out to be a winning strategy. For example, for $\theta_{max} = 3°$ the optimal order is [2/3], and for $\theta_{max} = 10°$ and $\theta_{max} = 20°$ it makes no sense to take order greater than [5/6]. However, too small approximation order may not be applicable for the large propagation angles. In particular, it can be seen that it is impossible to find a reasonable mesh for $\theta_{max} = 20°$ and order [1/1].

Table 4. Comparison of the optimal cell sizes. In all examples the 4th order approximation is used for the transversal operator, value of β is computed by formula (16). "-" means that a reasonable grid cannot be constructed for the given parameters.

$\theta_{max}(°)$	x_{max} (m)	Order	Δx (m)	$\Delta y = \Delta z$ (m)	V(lower is better)
3	10000	[1/1]	130	1.9	6.0E−4
		[2/3]	730	5.2	5.62E−6
		[5/6]	700	5.2	1.17E−05
		[6/7]	700	5.2	1.36E−5
		[7/8]	700	5.2	1.56E−5
10	1000	[1/1]	0.8	0.16	1907
		[2/3]	47.5	0.64	0.37
		[5/6]	65.5	0.82	0.2
		[6/7]	65.5	0.82	0.23
		[7/8]	65.5	0.82	0.27
20	1000	[1/1]	-	-	-
		[2/3]	5.8	0.13	1811.0
		[5/6]	16.0	0.19	287.7
		[6/7]	16.0	0.19	335.7
		[7/8]	16.0	0.19	383.7

7   Conclusion

From a theoretical point of view, the proposed mesh optimization method provides a rigorous quantitative approach to evaluating various configurations of the finite-difference approximation. In particular, it gives an opportunity to clearly justify the optimal choice of the reference propagation constant. The method allows to evaluate the accuracy of the scheme as a whole, not just its separate steps.

From a practical point of view, the proposed method makes it possible to reduce the influence of the human factor on the modeling process, since artificial computational parameters are selected automatically. It gives an opportunity to eliminate the modeling errors due to an incorrectly selected computational grid, and also eliminates the overspending of the computational resources due to the choice of an unreasonably dense computational grid. In addition, being automated and not requiring expert intervention, numerical schemes can be more deeply integrated into complex software systems.

In this study, the case of constant velocity c was considered, but it can also be generalized to an inhomogeneous medium. In further research, it is planned to consider the optimization problem in relation to specific subject areas: radiophysics, computational underwater acoustics, seismology, optics.

Acknowledgments. This study was supported by the Russian Science Foundation grant No. 21-71-00039.

References

1. Baker, G.A., Graves-Morris, P.: Padé Approximants, vol. 59. Cambridge University Press (1996)
2. Bamberger, A., Engquist, B., Halpern, L., Joly, P.: Higher order paraxial wave equation approximations in heterogeneous media. SIAM J. Appl. Math. **48**(1), 129–154 (1988)
3. Bekker, E.V., Sewell, P., Benson, T.M., Vukovic, A.: Wide-angle alternating-direction implicit finite-difference beam propagation method. J. Light. Technol. **27**(14), 2595–2604 (2009)
4. Collins, M.D.: A split-step Padé solution for the parabolic equation method. J. Acoust. Soc. Am. **93**(4), 1736–1742 (1993)
5. Collins, M.D., Siegmann, W.L.: Parabolic equation techniques for seismology, Seismo-acoustics, and arctic acoustics. J. Theor. Comput. Acoust. **29**(02), 2130003 (2021)
6. Fishman, L., de Hoop, M.V., Van Stralen, M.J.N.: Exact constructions of square-root Helmholtz operator symbols: the focusing quadratic profile. J. Math. Phys. **41**(7), 4881–4938 (2000)
7. Fishman, L., McCoy, J.J.: Derivation and application of extended parabolic wave theories. I. factorized Helmholtz equation. J. Math. Phys. **25**(2), 285–296 (1984)
8. Janaswamy, R.: Path loss predictions in the presence of buildings on flat terrain: a 3-D vector parabolic equation approach. IEEE Trans. Antennas Propag. **51**(8), 1716–1728 (2003)
9. Jensen, F.B., Kuperman, W.A., Porter, M.B., Schmidt, H.: Computational Ocean Acoustics. Springer, New York (2014). https://doi.org/10.1007/978-1-4419-8678-8
10. Kozitskiy, S.: Coupled-mode parabolic equations for the modeling of sound propagation in a shallow-water waveguide with weak elastic bottom. J. Mar. Sci. Eng. **10**(10), 1355 (2022)
11. Leontovich, M.A., Fock, V.A.: Solution of the problem of propagation of electromagnetic waves along the Earth's surface by the method of parabolic equation. J. Phys. USSR **10**(1), 13–23 (1946)
12. Li, Y.S., Bian, Y.Q., He, Z., Chen, R.S.: EM pulse propagation modeling for tunnels by three-dimensional ADI-TDPE method. IEEE Access **8**, 85027–85037 (2020)
13. Lin, Y.T., Porter, M.B., Sturm, F., Isakson, M.J., Chiu, C.S.: Introduction to the special issue on three-dimensional underwater acoustics. J. Acoust. Soc. Am. **146**(3), 1855–1857 (2019)
14. Lytaev, M.: Mesh optimization for the acoustic parabolic equation. J. Mar. Sci. Eng. **11**(3), 496 (2023)
15. Lytaev, M., Borisov, E., Vladyko, A.: V2I propagation loss predictions in simplified urban environment: a two-way parabolic equation approach. Electronics **9**(12), 2011 (2020)
16. Lytaev, M.S.: Higher-order 3D parabolic equation for radio wave propagation modeling in a street canyon. In: 2019 IEEE Conference of Russian Young Researchers in Electrical and Electronic Engineering (EIConRus), pp. 873–876. IEEE (2019)

17. Lytaev, M.S.: Automated selection of the computational parameters for the higher-order parabolic equation numerical methods. In: International Conference on Computational Science and Its Applications 2020 (12249), pp. 296–311 (2020)
18. Marchuk, G.I.: Splitting and alternating direction methods. Handb. Numer. Anal. **1**, 197–462 (1990)
19. Martelly, R., Janaswamy, R.: An ADI-PE approach for modeling radio transmission loss in tunnels. IEEE Trans. Antennas Propag. **57**(6), 1759–1770 (2009)
20. Petrov, P., Katsnelson, B., Li, Z.: Modeling techniques for underwater acoustic scattering and propagation (including 3D effects). J. Mar. Sci. Eng. **10**(9), 1192 (2022)
21. Petrov, P.S., Ehrhardt, M., Trofimov, M.: On decomposition of the fundamental solution of the Helmholtz equation over solutions of iterative parabolic equations. Asymptot. Anal. **126**(3–4), 215–228 (2022)
22. Samarskii, A.A., Mikhailov, A.P.: Principles of Mathematical Modelling: Ideas, Methods, Examples. Taylor and Francis, Oxford (2002)
23. Wu, X., Li, Z., Liang, Z., Long, Y.: Higher-order FD-Padé scheme for 3D parabolic equation in radio-wave propagation. IEEE Antennas Wireless Propag. Lett. (2023)
24. Zhang, X., Sarris, C.D.: Error analysis and comparative study of numerical methods for the parabolic equation applied to tunnel propagation modeling. IEEE Trans. Antennas Propag. **63**(7), 3025–3034 (2015)

Sensitivity Analysis of Markovian Exact Reproduction Numbers

María Gamboa$^{(\boxtimes)}$ (iD) and Maria Jesus Lopez-Herrero (iD)

Faculty of Statistical Studies, Complutense University of Madrid, Madrid, Spain
{mgamboa,lherrero}@ucm.es

Abstract. In this investigation a sensitivity analysis is presented by computing the partial derivatives and elasticities of several summary statistics with respect to parameters of the exact reproduction numbers, R_{e0} and R_p, for the stochastic SVIS model with an external source of infection and imperfect vaccine. These epidemic quantifiers are significant improvements over the basic reproductive number, R_0, to study the potential transmission of an epidemic under a stochastic approach. Our research provides theoretical and algorithmic results for understanding the impact of vaccination strategies on the spread of epidemics. We provide efficient tools to evaluate the importance of each model parameters in the propagation of the pathogen which have significant implications for public health policies aimed at controlling and preventing infectious disease outbreaks. We illustrate our methodology in the context of the transmission of the diphtheria virus.

Keywords: Stochastic epidemic model · Basic reproduction number · Perturbation problem · Imperfect vaccine

1 Introduction

Reproduction numbers are fundamental measures used to quantify the potential transmission of an epidemic in public health practice. There are several quantities that can be classified as reproduction numbers but the basic reproductive number, R_0, is probably the most widely used descriptor of disease spread and plays a privileged role in epidemiology under a deterministic approach. It represents the average number of secondary infections that result from a single infected individual over the course of his/her infectious period in a fully susceptible population. In simpler terms, R_0 measures how contagious a disease is and it is used to assess the potential for an epidemic or pandemic to occur. For example, for an SIS model high values of R_0 are associated with epidemics that persist for long time. In contrast, short epidemics are identified by lower values of the basic reproduction number [1].

Supported by the Government of Spain, Department of Science, Innovation and Universities; European Commision project: PID2021-125871NB-I00.

In a compartmental deterministic framework where population size is, as a premise infinite, the probability that two specific individuals have contact equals zero. However, in real-world situations, this behaviour is not true at all.

Moreover, the deterministic approach takes into account only average values and neglects that the agent itself diminishes the availability of susceptible individuals [2,3]. This has a bad consequence in the computation of R_0 because there is an overestimation of the number of contacts and secondary infections produced by the typical individual as authors discuss in [3]. Contacts of infectious individuals to whom have been previously infected should be eliminated [4,5]. Consequently, it seems relevant to explore alternative measures to R_0.

In a Markovian framework, these alternative measures are the exact reproduction number, R_{e0} and the population reproduction number, R_p. Both descriptors were described in 2013, by Artalejo and Lopez-Herrero, in [1], for stochastic SIS and SIR epidemic models. The authors described R_{e0} as a random variable that counts the exact number of secondary cases, produced by a typical infective individual during its entire period of infectiousness. R_p is a random variable that counts the number of infections produced by the whole infectious group no matter who is the spreader, prior the first recovery occurs. The main feature of the exact reproduction numbers is that they do not take into account contacts to previously infected individuals.

In [6], we extended the above mentioned work by including vaccination as strategy for controlling disease transmission in non-isolated populations. More precisely, we studied both exact reproduction numbers for a stochastic SVIS model with an external source of infection and imperfect vaccine.

In the present investigation our interest is in complementing the work in [6] by providing a local sensitivity analysis for both exact reproduction numbers.

In general a sensitivity analysis is a technique used to study perturbation effects of parameters that define a mathematical model on outputs of this model [7]. Recently, this methodology has been applied to various subjects of study as demography, ecology [8] and epidemiology [9]. In the context of stochastic epidemic models, this methodology can help us to identify which parameters have the greatest impact on the probabilistic behaviour of measures related to the spread of a pathogen. There is a vast literature that addresses this problem, for example in [10], author uses matrix calculus to obtain sensibilities and elasticities for moments of the random variable time until absorption, time spent in transitory states and number of visits to transitory states before the absorption in a continuous-time Markov chain. In [11], authors determine the most influential parameters in the spread of malaria by computing sensitivity indices of the basic reproduction number. In [12], authors analyze the perturbation problem through matrix calculus in a LD-QBD process and provide algorithms to compute elasticities related to the random variable maximum visits to a state before absorption. To supplement information, we refer the interested reader to the following works for further investigation on the topic [13–15].

The remainder of the present paper is organized as follows. In Sect. 2, we give a description of the stochastic SVIS model with an external source of infection and imperfect vaccine, and introduce the exact reproduction numbers R_{e0} and R_p. In Sects. 3 and 4, a local sensitivity analysis is conducted via derivatives and elasticities for the exact reproduction numbers. Finally, in Sect. 5 and for diphtheria outbreaks, we illustrate theoretical and algorithmic derivations provided in previous sections by presenting numerical results related to disease spread, followed by some conclusions.

2   Quantifying the Potential Transmission in a Stochastic SVIS Model with an External Source of Infection and Imperfect Vaccine

The stochastic SVIS model with an external source of infection and imperfect vaccine was introduced in [6]. There we consider a constant and moderate size population, N, that is afflicted by a disease that does not confers immunity. Individuals in the population are well mixed and the topological structure of the contact network established by the individuals of the host population is not important to describe the expansion of the epidemic. Population is not closed and in the sense that, the pathogen can be transmitted by direct contact with an infected individual within or outside of the population. The internal and external transmission rates are β and ξ, respectively. Each infected individual recovers from the disease at rate γ. Prior the start of the epidemic and to assure herd immunity, a percentage of the population is vaccinated to be protected from the disease. However, this vaccine is not perfect and it fails with probability h.

We define the random variables, $V(t)$, $I(t)$ and $S(t)$ that count the number of vaccinated, infected and susceptible individuals at any time $t \geq 0$, respectively. As we are considering a constant size population, the number of susceptible individuals can be calculated as $S(t) = N - V(t) - I(t)$. According to above hypotheses, the evolution of the epidemic process is modeled as the following bi-dimensional Markov chain,

$$X = \{(V(t), I(t)), t \geq 0\}.$$

The state space of the Markov chain, X, is $S = \{(v, i) : 0 \leq v \leq v_0, 0 \leq i \leq N - v\}$ and includes $(v_0 + 1)(N + 1 - v_0/2)$ states.

The exact reproduction number, R_{e0}, quantifies the potential transmission of an epidemic and it is described as the number of infections produced by a marked individual during its entire infectious period. To quantify the global potential transmission of an epidemic, we introduce the exact population number, R_p, that counts infections produced by the entire infectious population previously to the first recovery occurs. Both random measures are directly related to the recovery time of infectious individuals. Throughout this interval of time population contains at least one infected individual. Consequently, the CTMC, X, evolves in the following subset of S, which is decomposed in levels according to the number of vaccine-protected individuals

$$\widehat{S} = \bigcup_{v=0}^{v_0} \widehat{L}(v) = \bigcup_{v=0}^{v_0} \{(v, i) : 1 \leq i \leq N - v\}.$$

The perturbation analysis will be conducted for performance measures of the exact reproduction numbers, R_{e0} and R_p. In that sense, we introduce factorial moments of both variables. Factorial moments of the exact reproduction number, R_{e0}, conditioned to a generic state $(v, i) \in \widehat{S}$ are defined as follows

$$
m_{v,i}^k = \begin{cases} 1, & \text{if } k = 0, \\ E\left[R_{e0}\left(R_{e0} - 1\right) \cdots \left(R_{e0} - k + 1\right) | (V(0) = v, I(0) = i)\right], & \text{if } k > 0. \end{cases}
$$

Factorial moments of the population reproduction number conditioned to a generic state $(v, i) \in \widehat{S}$ is defined as follows

$$
M_{v,i}^k = \begin{cases} 1, & \text{if } k = 0, \\ E\left[R_p\left(R_p - 1\right) \cdots \left(R_p - k + 1\right) | (V(0) = v, I(0) = i)\right], & \text{if } k > 0. \end{cases}
$$

3 Sensitivity Analysis of the Factorial Moments of R_{e0}

The sensitivity analysis is relevant in the modeling of epidemics, particularly when the model parameters are estimated from a given data set. This methodology allows researchers to assess the robustness of their model, ensuring that it provides accurate and reliable insights into the spread and control of infectious diseases. In that sense, our interest is to quantify how small variations in each model parameter can affect in mathematical epidemic model output and to evaluate the importance and the influence of each model parameter in the expansion of an epidemic.

The perturbation problem will be approached through derivatives and elasticities of expected values and standard deviations of the exact reproduction numbers, that provide information about model parameters.

The elasticity of a general random variable, Y, respect to a model parameter, θ, is defined as

$$
\varepsilon_Y = \frac{(\partial Y / \partial \theta)}{(Y / \theta)}. \tag{1}
$$

To address this study we rely on matrix calculus and we start by computing first derivative of conditional factorial moments of order k of R_{e0}, $m_{v,i}^k$, for any $(v, i) \in \widehat{S}$ and $k \geq 1$, with respect to the whole set of model parameters $\theta = (\theta_1, \theta_2, \theta_3, \theta_4)^T = (\beta, \xi, \gamma, h)^T$, where T denotes matrix transposition.

The first partial derivative of the factorial moments of order $k \geq 0$, regarding parameter θ_r, with $r \in \{1, 2, 3, 4\}$ is denoted by $\frac{\partial m_{v,i}^k}{\partial \theta_r}$, and gives the exchange rate of $m_{v,i}^k$, for changing values of θ_r, when the rest of the parameters are constant. We compute them as follows.

We recall that Equation (7) in [6], involves factorial moments of order k, $m_{v,i}^k$, has the following expression for any $(v, i) \in \widehat{S}$ and are computed, starting from boundary conditions $m_{v,i}^0 = 1$, by applying Algorithm 1 in [6].

$$m_{v,i}^k = (1 - \delta_{v,0}) \left(\frac{\beta_{v,i}}{q_{v,i}} m_{v-1,i+1}^k + k \frac{\beta_v^*}{q_{v,i}} m_{v-1,i+1}^{k-1} \right) + \frac{\gamma_{i-1}}{q_{v,i}} m_{v,i-1}^k$$

$$+ (1 - \delta_{i,N-v}) \left(\frac{\alpha_{v,i}}{q_{v,i}} m_{v,i+1}^k + k \frac{\alpha_{v,i}^*}{q_{v,i}} m_{v,i+1}^{k-1} \right), \tag{2}$$

where $\delta_{a,b}$ denotes the Dirac's delta function (defined as 1 when $i = j$, and 0 otherwise) and coefficients, for any $(v,i) \in \widehat{S}$, are $\alpha_{v,i} = \left(\frac{\beta i}{N} + \xi \right) (N - v - i)$, $\alpha_{v,i}^* = \frac{\beta}{N}(N - v - i)$, $\beta_{v,i} = h \left(\frac{\beta i}{N} + \xi \right) v$, $\beta_v^* = h \frac{\beta}{N} v$ and $\gamma_i = \gamma i$.

In what follows we omit the corresponding Dirac's delta terms to ease notation.

Taking derivatives on (2) respect to each single parameter of the model and keeping the others constant, we obtain the following expression that involves both factorial moments and its derivatives, conditioned to a generic state $(v,i) \in \widehat{S}$, for any $k > 0$.

$$- \gamma_{i-1} \frac{\partial m_{v,i-1}^k}{\partial \theta_r} + q_{v,i} \frac{\partial m_{v,i}^k}{\partial \theta_r} - \alpha_{v,i} \frac{\partial m_{v,i+1}^k}{\partial \theta_r} = \beta_{v,i} \frac{\partial m_{v-1,i+1}^k}{\partial \theta_r} \tag{3}$$

$$+ k \beta_v^* \frac{\partial m_{v-1,i+1}^{k-1}}{\partial \theta_r} + k \alpha_{v,i}^* \frac{\partial m_{v,i+1}^{k-1}}{\partial \theta_r} + \frac{\partial \beta_{v,i}}{\partial \theta_r} m_{v-1,i+1}^k + k \frac{\partial \beta_v^*}{\partial \theta_r} m_{v-1,i+1}^{k-1}$$

$$+ k \frac{\partial \alpha_{v,i}^*}{\partial \theta_r} m_{v,i+1}^{k-1} + \frac{\partial \gamma_{i-1}}{\partial \theta_r} m_{v,i-1}^k - \frac{\partial q_{v,i}}{\partial \theta_r} m_{v,i}^k + \frac{\partial \alpha_{v,i}}{\partial \theta_r} m_{v,i+1}^k.$$

We continue introducing the following notation for the derivatives of conditional moments of order $k \geq 0$ respect to each parameter θ_j, with $r \in \{1, 2, 3, 4\}$

$$\frac{\partial m_{v,i}^k}{\partial \theta_r} = A_{v,i}^k(\theta_r)$$

and we define $\rho_{v,i}^k(\theta_r)$ as

$$\rho_{v,i}^k(\theta_r) = \frac{\partial \beta_{v,i}}{\partial \theta_r} m_{v-1,i+1}^k + k \frac{\partial \beta_v^*}{\partial \theta_r} m_{v-1,i+1}^{k-1} + k \frac{\partial \alpha_{v,i}^*}{\partial \theta_r} m_{v,i+1}^{k-1}$$

$$+ \frac{\partial \gamma_{i-1}}{\partial \theta_r} m_{v,i-1}^k - \frac{\partial q_{v,i}}{\partial \theta_r} m_{v,i}^k + \frac{\partial \alpha_{v,i}}{\partial \theta_r} m_{v,i+1}^k.$$

Hence, for any $(v,i) \in \widehat{S}$, Eq. (3) and boundary conditions can be expressed as follows

$$-\gamma_{i-1} A_{v,i-1}^k(\theta_r) + q_{v,i} A_{v,i}^k(\theta_r) - \alpha_{v,i} A_{v,i+1}^k(\theta_r) = \tag{4}$$

$$\beta_{v,i} A_{v-1,i+1}^k(\theta_r) + k \beta_v^* A_{v-1,i+1}^{k-1}(\theta_r) + k \alpha_{v,i}^* A_{v,i+1}^{k-1}(\theta_r) + \rho_{v,i}^k(\theta_r),$$

$$A_{v,i}^0(\theta_r) = 0. \tag{5}$$

Taking derivatives of rates $\alpha_{v,i}^*$, $\alpha_{v,i}$, β_v^*, $\beta_{v,i}$, γ_{i-1} and $q_{v,i}$ regarding each model parameter, $\theta_r \in \{\beta, \xi, \gamma, h\}$, we obtain that

$$\rho_{v,i}^k(\theta_r) = \begin{cases} \frac{N-v-i}{N}(km_{v,i+1}^{k-1} + im_{v,i+1}^k - im_{v,i}^k) \\ + \frac{hv}{N}(km_{v-1,i+1}^{k-1} + im_{v-1,i+1}^k - im_{v,i}^k), & \text{if } \theta_j = \beta, \\ hv(m_{v-1,i+1}^k - m_{v,i}^k) + (N - v - i)(m_{v,i+1}^k - m_{v,i}^k), & \text{if } \theta_j = \xi, \\ (i-1)(m_{v,i-1}^k - m_{v,i}^k), & \text{if } \theta_j = \gamma, \\ v(\frac{\beta i}{N} + \xi)(m_{v-1,i+1}^k - m_{v,i}^k) + k\frac{\beta v}{N}m_{v-1,i+1}^{k-1}, & \text{if } \theta_j = h. \end{cases}$$

We obtain the related derivatives by solving the system of Eqs. (3). These equations can be expressed in matrix form and they can be solved by applying an inverse matrix method in a recursively way for each parameter, θ_r and taking into account the boundary conditions (5). This result is summarized in Theorem 1.

Theorem 1. *Given a fixed initial number of vaccinated individuals, v_0 and for each model parameter, $\theta_r \in \{\beta, \xi, \gamma, h\}$ derivatives in the set $\{A_{v,i}^k(\theta_r) : (v,i) \in \widehat{S}\}$ are recursively computed from the following equations for any $k \geq 0$ and any level $0 \leq v \leq v_0$ as follows*

$$\mathbf{A}_{\mathbf{v}}^0(\theta_{\mathbf{r}}) = \mathbf{0}_{N-v}, \ for\ 0 \leq v \leq v_0, \tag{6}$$

$$\mathbf{R}_{\mathbf{v}}\mathbf{A}_{\mathbf{v}}^{\mathbf{k}}(\theta_{\mathbf{r}}) = (1 - \delta_{v,0})(\mathbf{D}_{\beta,v}\widehat{\mathbf{A}}_{\mathbf{v}-\mathbf{1}}^k(\theta_r) + k\mathbf{D}_{\beta,v}^*\widehat{\mathbf{A}}_{\mathbf{v}-\mathbf{1}}^{k-1}(\theta_r)) + k\mathbf{D}_{\alpha,v}^*\widetilde{\mathbf{A}}_{\mathbf{v}}^{k-1}(\theta_r)$$
$$+ (1 - \delta_{v,0})(\mathbf{D}_{\beta,v}'\widehat{\mathbf{m}}_{\mathbf{v}-\mathbf{1}}^k + k(\mathbf{D}_{\beta,v}^*)'\widehat{\mathbf{m}}_{\mathbf{v}-\mathbf{1}}^{k-1})$$
$$+ k(\mathbf{D}_{\alpha,v}^*)'\widetilde{\mathbf{m}}_{\mathbf{v}}^{k-1} - \mathbf{R}_{\mathbf{v}}'\mathbf{m}_{\mathbf{v}}^k, \tag{7}$$

where matrices appearing in Eqs. (6) and (7) are described as the following $\mathbf{R}_{\mathbf{v}}$ and its gradient matrix $\mathbf{R}_{\mathbf{v}}'$ are tridiagonal square matrices of dimension $N - v$ with non-null entries given by

$$\mathbf{R}_{\mathbf{v}}(i,j) = \begin{cases} -\gamma_{i-1}, & \text{if } j = i - 1 \text{ and } 2 \leq i \leq N - v, \\ q_{v,i}, & \text{if } j = i \text{ and } 1 \leq i \leq N - v, \\ -\alpha_{v,i}, & \text{if } j = i + 1 \text{ and } 1 \leq i \leq N - v - 1, \end{cases}$$

$$\mathbf{R}_{\mathbf{v}}'(i,j) = \begin{cases} -\frac{\partial\gamma_{i-1}}{\partial\theta_r}, & \text{if } j = i - 1 \text{ y } 2 \leq i \leq N - v, \\ \frac{\partial q_{v,i}}{\partial\theta_r}, & \text{if } j = i \text{ and } 1 \leq i \leq N - v, \\ -\frac{\partial\alpha_{v,i}}{\partial\theta_r}, & \text{if } j = i + 1 \text{ and } 1 \leq i \leq N - v - 1. \end{cases}$$

$\mathbf{D}_{\beta,\mathbf{v}}$, $\mathbf{D}_{\beta,\mathbf{v}}^*$ $\mathbf{D}_{\alpha,\mathbf{v}}$ *and their respective gradient matrices* $\mathbf{D}_{\beta,\mathbf{v}}'$, $(\mathbf{D}_{\beta,\mathbf{v}}^*)'$ *and* $(\mathbf{D}_{\alpha,\mathbf{v}}^*)'$ *are diagonal matrices of dimension* $(N - v)$*, with non-null diagonal elements given by* $\mathbf{D}_{\beta,v}(i,i) = \beta_{v,i}$, $\mathbf{D}_{\beta,v}^*(i,i) = \beta_{v,i}^*$, $\mathbf{D}_{\alpha,v}^*(i,i) = \alpha_{v,i}^*$, $\mathbf{D}_{\beta,\mathbf{v}}'(i,i) = \frac{\partial\beta_{v,i}}{\partial\theta_r}$, $\mathbf{D}_{\beta,\mathbf{v}}^{*}{}'(i,i) = \frac{\partial\beta_{v,i}^*}{\partial\theta_r}$, $\mathbf{D}_{\alpha,\mathbf{v}}^{*}{}'(i,i) = \frac{\partial\alpha_{v,i}^*}{\partial\theta_r}$*, for* $1 \leq i \leq N - v$.

The rest of vectors are defined as follows: $\mathbf{A}_v^k = (A_{v,1}^k, ..., A_{v,N-v}^k)^T$, $\widetilde{\mathbf{A}}_v^k = (A_{v,2}^k, ..., A_{v,N-v}^k, 0)^T$, $\widehat{\mathbf{A}}_v^k = (A_{v,2}^k, ..., A_{v,N-v}^k)^T$, $\mathbf{m}_v^k = (m_{v,1}^k, ..., m_{v,N-v}^k)^T$, $\widetilde{\mathbf{m}}_v^k = (m_{v,2}^k, ..., m_{v,N-v}^k, 0)^T$, $\widehat{\mathbf{m}}_v^k = (m_{v,2}^k, ..., m_{v,N-v}^k)^T$, *and* $\mathbf{0}_{N-v}$ *is a all-zeros vector of dimension* $N - v$.

Algorithm 1 shows how to proceed to compute the related derivatives in an ordered and efficient way, starting from $k = 0$ in natural order and for $0 \le v \le v_0$.

Algorithm 1. The derivatives of the moments of order $k \ge 0$, $m_{v,i}^k$ can be determined numerically according to the following scheme

---

Input: α, β, γ, h, k_{max}, θ_r, $m_{v,i}^k$ for any $(v, i) \in \widehat{S}$ and $0 \le k \le k_{max}$

Step 1: Set $A_{N-v}^0 = 0_{N-v}$ for $0 \le v \le N - v$.

Step 2: Set $k = 1$ and $v = 0$

> Step 2a: Compute

$$\mathbf{A}_{N-v}^1(\theta_r) = \mathbf{R}_v^{-1}((\mathbf{D}_{\alpha,v}^*)'(\theta_r)\widetilde{\mathbf{m}}_v^{k-1} - \mathbf{R}_v')$$

> Step 2b: Set $v = v + 1$ and compute

$$\mathbf{A}_{N-v}^1(\theta_r) = \mathbf{R}_v^{-1}(\mathbf{D}_{\beta,v}\widehat{\mathbf{A}}_{v-1}^k(\theta_r) + (\mathbf{D}_{\beta,v}')(\theta_r)\widehat{\mathbf{m}}_{v-1}^1 (\mathbf{D}_{\beta,v}^*)'(\theta_r)\widehat{\mathbf{m}}_{v-1}^0) + (\mathbf{D}_{\alpha,v}^*)'(\theta_r)\widetilde{\mathbf{m}}_v^0 - \mathbf{R}_v'(\theta_r)).$$

> Step 2c: If $v < v_0$ go to Step 2b.

Step 3: Set $k = k + 1$ and $v = 0$

> Step 3a: Compute

$$\mathbf{A}_{N-v}^k(\theta_r) = \mathbf{R}_v^{-1}(k\mathbf{D}_{\alpha,v}^*\widetilde{\mathbf{A}}_v^{k-1}(\theta_r) + k(\mathbf{D}_{\alpha,v}^*)'(\theta_r)\widetilde{\mathbf{m}}_v^{k-1} - \mathbf{R}_v'(\theta_r)\mathbf{m}_v^k).$$

> Step 3b: Set $v = v + 1$ and compute

$$\mathbf{A}_{N-v}^1(\theta_r) = \quad \mathbf{R}_v^{-1}(\mathbf{D}_{\beta,v}\widehat{\mathbf{A}}_{v-1}^k(\theta_r) + k\mathbf{D}_{\beta,v}^*\widehat{\mathbf{A}}_{v-1}^{k-1}(\theta_r) + k\mathbf{D}_{\alpha,v}^*\widetilde{\mathbf{A}}_v^{k-1}(\theta_r) + \mathbf{D}_{\beta,v}'(\theta_r)\widehat{\mathbf{m}}_{v-1}^k$$
$$+ k(\mathbf{D}_{\beta,v}^*)'(\theta_r)\widehat{\mathbf{m}}_{v-1}^{k-1}) + k(\mathbf{D}_{\alpha,v}^*)'(\theta_r)\widetilde{\mathbf{m}}_v^{k-1} - \mathbf{R}_v'(\theta_r)\mathbf{m}_v^k).$$

> Step 3c: If $v < v_0$ go to Step 3b.
> Step 3d: If $k < k_{max}$ go to Step 3.

Output: $A_{v,i}^k(\theta_r)$ for any $(v, i) \in \widehat{S}$ and $0 \le k \le k_{max}$

When conducting sensitivity analysis in conditional moments, it is not sufficient to rely on a single derivative. Instead, we must solve Eq. (7) once for each parameter. This is particularly relevant for models with a large number of parameters, where an approach to differentiating matrix-valued functions of vector arguments is needed. Matrix calculus allows us to collect partial derivatives with respect to a vector into vectors and matrices of derivatives, which simplifies the process of solving systems of differential equations. A helpful resource for reviewing the notation and properties of matrix calculus can be found in [18]. Furthermore, from Eq. (7) in Theorem 1 and applying the mentioned methodology we derive the following expression

$$\frac{d\mathbf{m_v^k}}{d\theta'} = -(\mathbf{R_v^{-1}}(\mathbf{D}_{\beta,v}\widehat{\mathbf{m}}_{\mathbf{v-1}}^{\mathbf{k}} + \mathbf{D}_{\beta,v}^{*}\widehat{\mathbf{m}}_{\mathbf{v-1}}^{\mathbf{k-1}} + k\mathbf{D}_{\alpha v}^{*}\widetilde{\mathbf{m}}_{\mathbf{v-1}}^{\mathbf{k-1}})' \otimes \mathbf{R_v^{-1}})\frac{dvec\mathbf{R_v}}{d\theta'}$$

$$+ \mathbf{R_v^{-1}}(\mathbf{D}_{\beta,v}\widehat{\mathbf{A}}_{\mathbf{v-1}}^{\mathbf{k}}(\theta) + \mathbf{D}_{\beta,v}^{*}\widehat{\mathbf{A}}_{\mathbf{v-1}}^{\mathbf{k-1}}(\theta) + k\mathbf{D}_{\alpha,v}^{*}\widetilde{\mathbf{A}}_{\mathbf{v}}^{\mathbf{k-1}}(\theta)) \qquad (8)$$

$$+ ((\widehat{\mathbf{m}}_{\mathbf{v-1}}^{\mathbf{k}} \otimes \mathbf{R_v^{-1}})\frac{dvec\mathbf{D}_{\beta,\mathbf{v}}}{d\theta'} + (\widehat{\mathbf{m}}_{\mathbf{v-1}}^{\mathbf{k-1}} \otimes \mathbf{R_v^{-1}})\frac{dvec\mathbf{D}_{\beta,\mathbf{v}}^{*}}{d\theta'}$$

$$+ k(\widehat{\mathbf{m}}_{\mathbf{v}}^{\mathbf{k-1}} \otimes \mathbf{R_v^{-1}})\frac{dvec\mathbf{D}_{\beta,\mathbf{v}}^{*}}{d\theta'},$$

and initial conditions $\frac{\partial \mathbf{m_v^0}}{\partial\theta'} = \mathbf{0}_{(N-v)\times 4}$, for any $0 \leq v \leq v_0$ and $k \geq 1$, where $\frac{d\mathbf{m_v^k}}{d\theta'}$ is the Jacobian matrix with entries given by $\frac{dm_{v,i}^k}{d\theta_r}$, $\otimes$ represents Kronecker product and $vec(A)$ is the column-wise vectorization of the matrix A.

Following we derive explicit expressions for the expected and standard deviation elasticises of R_{e0} that are needed to obtain the numerical results in Sect. 5.

For a given state $(v,i) \in \widehat{S}$, derivatives of conditioned expected values and standard deviations respect to any model parameter, θ_r, denoted by $\frac{\partial E[R_{e0}]}{\partial\theta_r}$ and $\frac{\partial Sd[R_{e0}]}{\partial\theta_r}$ respectively, can be computed as follows

$$\frac{\partial E[R_{e0}]}{\partial\theta_r} = \frac{\partial m_{v,i}^1}{\partial\theta_r} = A_{v,i}^1(\theta_r), \qquad (9)$$

$$\frac{\partial Sd[R_{e0}]}{\partial\theta_r} = \frac{\partial(m_{v,i}^2 + m_{v,i}^1 - (m_{v,i}^1)^2)^{\frac{1}{2}}}{\partial\theta_r}$$

$$= \frac{A_{v,i}^2(\theta_r) + A_{v,i}^1(\theta_j) - 2m_{v,i}^1 A_{v,i}^1(\theta_r)}{2Sd[R_{e0}]}. \qquad (10)$$

Applying elasticity definition (1) and Expressions (9) and (10), the elasticities for the mean and standard deviation of R_{e0}, conditioned to any state $(v,i) \in \widehat{S}$, respect to each model parameter θ_r are given by

$$\varepsilon_{E[R_{e0}]} = \frac{\partial E[R_{e0}]/\partial\theta_r}{E[R_{e0}]/\theta_r} = \frac{A_{v,i}^1(\theta_r)}{m_{v,i}^1/\theta_r},$$

$$\varepsilon_{Sd[R_{e0}]} = \frac{\partial Sd[R_{e0}]/\partial\theta_r}{Sd[R_{e0}]/\theta_r} = \frac{\theta_r(A_{v,i}^2(\theta_r) + A_{v,i}^1(\theta_r) - 2m_{v,i}^1 A_{v,i}^1(\theta_r))}{2Sd^2[R_{e0}]}.$$

4 Sensitivity Analysis of the Factorial Moments of R_p

In this section we derive a sensitivity analysis for the random variable, R_p.

We apply an analogous methodology as in the previous section so we omit the procedure and only we give the results obtained.

We recall that in [6], we obtained the following equations involving R_p-Factorial moments of order $k \geq 1$, for any $(v,i) \in \widehat{S}$

$$q_{v,i}M_{v,i}^k = \alpha_{v,i}\left(kM_{v,i+1}^{k-1} + M_{v,i+1}^k\right) + \beta_{v,i}\left(kM_{v-1,i+1}^{k-1} + M_{v-1,i+1}^k\right), \quad (11)$$

with boundary conditions

$$M_{v,i}^0 = 1.$$

These factorial moments are necessary to obtained the related derivatives and it can be done with the help of Theorem 2 in [6].

We introduce the following notation for the first derivatives of the R_p-Factorial moments order k, respect to each parameter θ_r, $\frac{\partial M_{v,i}^k}{\partial \theta_r}$, and $\widetilde{\rho}_{v,i}^k(\theta_r)$

$$\frac{\partial M_{v,i}^k}{\partial \theta_r} = \mathbb{A}_{v,i}^k(\theta_r),$$

$$\widetilde{\rho}_{v,i}^k(\theta_r) = -\frac{\partial q_{v,i}}{\theta_r} M_{v,i}^k + \frac{\partial \alpha_{v,i}}{\theta_r}[k M_{v,i+1}^{k-1} + M_{v,i+1}^k]$$

$$+ \frac{\partial \beta_{v,i}}{\partial \theta_r}[k M_{v-1,i+1}^{k-1} + M_{v-1,i+1}^k].$$

Taking derivatives on Eq. (11), respect to each parameter θ_r and applying the above notation, we obtain the following equations for any $k \geq 0$ and any $(v,i) \in \widehat{S}$

$$q_{v,i}\mathbb{A}_{v,i}^k(\theta_r) - \alpha_{v,i}\mathbb{A}_{v,i+1}^k(\theta_r) = \alpha_{v,i}k\mathbb{A}_{v,i+1}^{k-1}(\theta_r) + \beta_{v,i}[k\mathbb{A}_{v-1,i+1}^{k-1}(\theta_r)$$

$$+ \mathbb{A}_{v-1,i+1}^k(\theta_r)] + \widetilde{\rho}_{v,i}^k(\theta_r), \tag{12}$$

with boundary conditions

$$\mathbb{A}_{v,i}^0(\theta_r) = 0, \tag{13}$$

and

$$\widetilde{\rho}_{v,i}^k(\theta_r) = \begin{cases} \frac{(N-v-i)i}{N}[k M_{v,i+1}^{k-1} + M_{v,i+1}^k - M_{v,i}^k] \\ +\frac{hvi}{N}[k M_{v-1,i+1}^{k-1} + M_{v-1,i+1}^k - M_{v,i}^k], & \text{if } \theta_r = \beta, \\ (N-v-i)[k M_{v,i+1}^{k-1} + M_{v,i+1}^k - M_{v,i}^k] \\ +hv[k M_{v-1,i+1}^{k-1} + M_{v-1,i+1}^k - M_{v,i}^k], & \text{if } \theta_r = \xi, \\ -i M_{v,i}^k, & \text{if } \theta_r = \gamma, \\ (\frac{\beta i}{N} + \xi)v[k M_{v-1,i+1}^{k-1} + M_{v-1,i+1}^k - M_{v,i}^k], & \text{if } \theta_r = h. \end{cases}$$

At any level $0 \leq v \leq v_0$, Eqs. (12) can be solved by applying matrix techniques for $k > 0$ and $1 \leq i \leq N - v$, and derivatives of factorial moments of order $k \geq 0$ of the conditioned variables of R_p are obtained with the help of Theorem 2.

Theorem 2. *Given a fixed initial number of vaccinated individuals, v_0 and for each model parameter, $\theta_r \in \{\beta, \xi, \gamma, h\}$ derivatives in the set $\{\mathbb{A}_{v,i}^k(\theta_r) : (v,i) \in \widehat{S}\}$ are recursively computed from the following equations for any $k \geq 0$ and any level $0 \leq v \leq v_0$ as follows*

$$\mathbf{A}_v^0(\theta_r) = \mathbf{0}_{N-v}, \tag{14}$$

$$\mathbf{H}_v \mathbf{A}_v^k(\theta_r) = k\mathbf{L}_v \widehat{\mathbf{A}}_v^{k-1}(\theta_r) + \mathbf{D}_v[k\widetilde{\mathbf{A}}_{v-1}^{k-1}(\theta_r) + \widetilde{\mathbf{A}}_{v-1}^k(\theta)] - \mathbf{H}_v'(\theta_r)\mathbf{M}_v^k$$

$$+ \mathbf{D}'_\mathbf{v}(\theta_r)[\widetilde{\mathbf{M}}_{v-1}^{k-1} + \widetilde{\mathbf{M}}_{v-1}^k] + k\mathbf{L}'_\mathbf{v}(\theta_r)\widehat{\mathbf{M}}_v^{k-1}, \tag{15}$$

where $\mathbf{A}_v^k = (\mathbb{A}_{v,1}^k, ..., \mathbb{A}_{v,N-v}^k)^T$, $\widetilde{\mathbf{A}}_{v-1}^k = (\mathbb{A}_{v-1,2}^k, ..., \mathbb{A}_{v-1,N-v+1}^k)^T$,
$\widehat{\mathbf{A}}_v^{k-1} = (\mathbb{A}_{v,2}^{k-1}, ..., \mathbb{A}_{v,N-v}^{k-1}, 0)^T$, $\widetilde{\mathbf{M}}_{v-1}^{k-1} = (M_{v-1,2}^{k-1}, ..., M_{v-1,N-v+1}^{k-1})^T$,
$\widehat{\mathbf{M}}_v^{k-1} = (M_{v,2}^{k-1}, ..., M_{v,N-v}^{k-1}, 0)^T$. $\mathbf{H_v}$ *and its gradient matrix* $\mathbf{H}'_\mathbf{v}$ *are squared bi-diagonal matrices of dimension* $(N - v)$, *with non-null entries given by*

$$\mathbf{H_v}(i,j) = \begin{cases} q_{v,i}, & \text{if } j = i \text{ and } 1 \leq i \leq N - v, \\ -\alpha_{v,i}, & \text{if } j = i + 1 \text{ and } 1 \leq i \leq N - v - 1, \end{cases}$$

$$\mathbf{H}'_\mathbf{v}(i,j) = \begin{cases} \frac{\partial q_{v,i}}{\partial \theta_r}, & \text{if } j = i \text{ and } 1 \leq i \leq N - v, \\ -\frac{\partial \alpha_{v,i}}{\partial \theta_r}, & \text{if } j = i + 1 \text{ and } 1 \leq i \leq N - v - 1. \end{cases}$$

$\mathbf{D_v}$, $\mathbf{L_v}$ *and their respective gradient matrices,* $\mathbf{D}'_\mathbf{v}$ *and* $\mathbf{L}'_\mathbf{v}$ *are diagonal matrices of dimension* $(N - v)$, *with non-null diagonal elements given by* $\mathbf{D_v}(i,i) = \beta_{v,i}$, $\mathbf{D}'_\mathbf{v}(i,i) = \frac{\partial \beta_{v,i}}{\partial \theta_r}$, $\mathbf{L_v}(i,i) = \alpha_{v,i}$, $\mathbf{L}'_\mathbf{v}(i,i) = \frac{\partial \alpha_{v,i}}{\partial \theta_r}$.

We compute factorial moments of the related random variable with the help of Algorithm 2.

Algorithm 2. The derivatives of the moments of order $k \geq 0$, $M_{v,i}^k$, can be determined numerically according to the following scheme

---

Input: α, β, γ, h, k_{max}, θ_r, $M_{v,i}^k$ *for any* $(v,i) \in \widehat{S}$ *and* $0 \leq k \leq k_{max}$
Step 1: Set $A_{N-v}^0 = 0_{N-v}$ for $0 \leq v \leq N - v$.
Step 2: Set $k = 1$ and $v = 0$
    Step 2a: Compute

$$\mathbf{A}_{\mathbf{N-v}}^1(\theta_r) = \mathbf{H_v}^{-1}(\mathbf{L}'_\mathbf{v}(\theta_r)\widehat{\mathbf{M}}_\mathbf{v}^0 - \mathbf{H_v}'(\theta_r)\mathbf{M}_\mathbf{v}^1)$$

    Step 2b: Set $v = v + 1$ and compute

$$\mathbf{A}_{\mathbf{N-v}}^1(\theta_r) = \mathbf{H_v}^{-1}(\mathbf{D_v}\widetilde{\mathbf{A}}_{\mathbf{v-1}}^1(\theta_r) + \mathbf{D_v}'(\theta_r)(\widetilde{\mathbf{M}}_{\mathbf{v-1}}^0 + \widetilde{\mathbf{M}}_{\mathbf{v-1}}^1) + \mathbf{L}'_v(\theta_r)\widehat{\mathbf{M}}_\mathbf{v}^0 - \mathbf{H}'_\mathbf{v}(\theta_r)\mathbf{M}_\mathbf{v}^1).$$

    Step 2c: If $v < v_0$ go to Step 2b.
Step 3: Set $k = k + 1$ and $v = 0$
    Step 3a: Compute

$$\mathbf{A}_{\mathbf{N-v}}^k(\theta_r) = \mathbf{H_v}^{-1}(k\mathbf{L_v}\widehat{\mathbf{A}}_\mathbf{v}^{k-1}(\theta_r) + k\mathbf{L_v}'(\theta_r)\widehat{\mathbf{M}}_\mathbf{0}^{k-1} - \mathbf{H_v}'(\theta_r)\mathbf{M_0}^k).$$

    Step 3b: Set $v = v + 1$ and compute

$$\mathbf{A}_{\mathbf{N-v}}^1(\theta_r) = \quad \mathbf{H_v}^{-1}(k\mathbf{L_v}(\widehat{\mathbf{A}}_\mathbf{v}^{k-1}(\theta_r) + \mathbf{D_v}(k\widetilde{\mathbf{A}}_{\mathbf{v-1}}^{k-1}(\theta_r) + \widetilde{\mathbf{A}}_{\mathbf{v-1}}^k(\theta_r)) + \mathbf{D}'_v(\theta_r)(\widetilde{\mathbf{M}}_{\mathbf{v-1}}^{k-1}$$
$$+ \widetilde{\mathbf{M}}_{\mathbf{v-1}}^k) + k\mathbf{L}'_v(\theta_r)\widehat{\mathbf{M}}_\mathbf{v}^{k-1} - \mathbf{H_v}'(\theta_r)\mathbf{M_v}^k).$$

    Step 3c: If $v < v_0$ go to Step 3b.
    Step 3d: If $k < k_{max}$ go to Step 3.
Output: $A_{v,i}^k(\theta_r)$ *for any* $(v,i) \in \widehat{S}$ *and* $0 \leq k \leq k_{max}$

Applying some basic rules and properties of calculating differentials, we obtain the following expression that involves more than one partial derivative

$$\frac{d\mathbf{M_v^k}}{d\theta'} = -(\mathbf{H_v^{-1}}(\mathbf{D_v}(k\widehat{\mathbf{M}}_{v-1}^{k-1} + \widehat{\mathbf{M}}_{v-1}^k) + k\widetilde{\mathbf{D}}_v\widetilde{\mathbf{M}}_v^{k-1})' \otimes \mathbf{H_v^{-1}})\frac{\partial vec\mathbf{H_v}}{\partial\theta'} \quad (16)$$
$$+ \mathbf{H_v^{-1}}(\mathbf{D_v}(k\widetilde{\mathbf{A}}_{v-1}^{k-1}(\theta) + \widetilde{\mathbf{A}}_{v-1}^k(\theta)) + k\widetilde{\mathbf{D}}_v\widetilde{\mathbf{A}}_v^{k-1}(\theta))$$
$$+ ((k\widehat{\mathbf{M}}_{v-1}^{k-1} + \widehat{\mathbf{M}}_{v-1}^k)' \otimes (\mathbf{H_v})^{-1})\frac{\partial vec\mathbf{D_v}}{\partial\theta'} + ((k\widetilde{\mathbf{M}}_v^{k-1})' \otimes \mathbf{H_v^{-1}})\frac{\partial vec\mathbf{D_v}}{\partial\theta'},$$

and initial conditions $\frac{\partial \mathbf{M_v^0}}{\partial\theta'} = \mathbf{0}_{(N-v)\times 4}$, for any $0 \le v \le v_0$ and $k \ge 1$.

For a given state $(v, i) \in \hat{\mathcal{S}}$, first derivatives of conditioned expected values and standard deviations of R_p, respect to any parameter, θ_r, can be calculated as follows

$$\frac{\partial E[R_p]}{\partial\theta_r} = \frac{\partial M_{v,i}^1}{\partial\theta_r} = \mathbb{A}_{v,i}^1(\theta_r),$$
$$\frac{\partial Sd[R_p]}{\partial\theta_r} = \frac{\partial(M_{v,i}^2 + M_{v,i}^1 - (M_{v,i}^1)^2)^{\frac{1}{2}}}{\partial\theta_r} = \frac{\mathbb{A}_{v,i}^2(\theta_r) + \mathbb{A}_{v,i}^1(\theta_r) - 2M_{v,i}^1\mathbb{A}_{v,i}^1(\theta_r)}{2Sd[R_p]}.$$

For any $0 \le v \le v_0$ and $1 \le i \le N - v$, elasticities for the conditioned mean and standard deviation, for each parameter θ_r, are given by

$$\varepsilon_{E[R_p]} = \frac{\partial E[R_p]/\partial\theta_r}{E[R_p]/\theta_r} = \frac{\mathbb{A}_{v,i}^1(\theta_r)}{M_{v,i}^1/\theta_r},$$

$$\varepsilon_{Sd[R_p]} = \frac{\partial Sd[R_p]/\partial\theta_r}{Sd[R_p]/\theta_r} = \frac{\theta_r(\mathbb{A}_{v,i}^2(\theta_r) + \mathbb{A}_{v,i}^1(\theta_r) - 2M_{v,i}^1\mathbb{A}_{v,i}^1(\theta_r))}{2Sd^2[R_p]}.$$

5   Numerical Analysis

The aim of this section is to study the relative importance of the model parameters for transmission of diphtheria virus. Diphtheria is a highly infectious bacterial disease caused by the bacterium Corynebacterium diphtheriae. It primarily affects the respiratory system but can also affect other organs. The disease is characterized by the formation of a thick gray or white membrane in the throat, which can lead to severe breathing difficulties and even death. The transmission of diphtheria occurs through direct contact with an infected person's respiratory secretions or by touching contaminated objects. Diphtheria remains a significant public health concern, particularly in areas with low vaccination coverage and poor living conditions.

For all experiments we consider a population of $N = 100$ individuals where prior the start of epidemic a percentage of the population, $v_0 \in \{20, 60, 90\}$ has received a vaccine to prevent infection. The epidemic is detected as soon as the first case of infection is produced and in consequence, the initial state of the Markov chain describing the evolution of the infectious process is $(V(0), I(0)) = (v_0, 1)$. We fix the time unit to be the expected infectious time of an infected individual, therefore we take $\gamma = 1.0$. The internal rate of transmission is $\beta = 10.0$, that is taken by considering a basic reproduction number $R_0 = \frac{\beta}{\gamma} = 10.0$ and a vaccine failure probability, $h = 0.03$, according to the information presented in [16,17]. Infections produced from an external source of infection occur at rate $\xi = 0.01$, indicating that most of infections occur within the population and to guarantee the reintroduction of the disease when there are not infected individuals in the community.

In Table 1, we present values for mean and standard deviation of R_{e0} and R_p, under different coverage values to enhance understanding of the numerical results appearing in Table 2. We can see that increasing vaccine coverage conducts to a decrease in the number of infections produced by the index case and the entire infected population. We recall that these values are obtained applying theoretical and algorithm results in [6]. Our goal is to study if elasticities for a given parameter present a similar behaviour when increasing vaccine coverage and to find the most significant model parameters in the potential transmission of the pathogen.

Table 2 presents elasticities of the expected and standard deviation of the random variables, R_{e0} and R_p. Elasticities were computed numerically by appealing theoretical and algorithmic results in Sect. 3 and 4. To interpreter the elasticity values respect to each model parameter we keep all other parameter fixed. Regardless vaccine coverage sign patterns for elasticities of $E[R_{e0}]$ and $E[R_p]$ in Table 2 indicate that the most influential parameters are the external rate transmission β and the recovery rate γ but have opposite effect. In particular increasing β or decreasing γ by a 1% increases the expected number of secondary infections produced by the index case by a 0.3%, a 0.5% and a 0.9% when considering vaccine coverage of 20, 60 and 90, respectively. For the random variable R_p, these quantities are always between 0.85% and 0.92%. For the exact reproduction number, R_{e0}, when considering low vaccine coverage the external transmission rate is more sensitive than the vaccine failure probability h and have opposite effects. Increasing h by a 1% increases the expected number of secondary infections produced by the index case by a 0.007% and decreasing ξ by a 1% increases these infections by a 0.01%. In contrast, when prior the start of epidemic the percentage of the vaccinated individuals is larger the parameter h is more sensitive than the external contact rate ξ. In particular when increasing h by a 1% increases the expected number of secondary infections produced by the index case by a 0.24% and decreasing ξ only by a 0.004%. Regarding the elasticities of the number of infections produced by all the entire population for the parameter ξ and γ we notice the same behaviour as R_{e0} but they do not have an opposite effect. In addition, changes in parameters have larger effect on both random variables when vaccine coverage is larger. The stochastic uncertainty of the exact reproduction numbers, is more affected by perturbations in β or γ.

Table 1. Expected and standard deviation values for $N = 100$

Coverage	$E[R_{e0}]$	$\sigma(R_{e0})$	$E[R_p]$	$\sigma(R_p)$
$v_0 = 20$	4.20352	2.94801	7.42982	1.18173
$v_0 = 60$	2.98428	2.60305	3.86460	1.43269
$v_0 = 90$	1.11003	1.38102	1.15562	0.97599

Table 2. R_{e0}-Elasticities versus vaccine coverage for $N = 100$

Coverage	Parameter	$E[R_{e0}]$	$\sigma(R_{e0})$	$E[R_p]$	$\sigma(R_p)$
	β	+0.33949	-0.00082	+0.86997	+30.3866
$v_0 = 20$	ξ	−0.01657	−0.01378	+0.02402	+0.36422
	h	+ 0.00782	+ 0.00790	+0.00812	+0.16152
	γ	−0.32291	+0.02105	−0.89437	−13.2925
	β	+0.55173	+0.21260	+0.85942	+5.68674
$v_0 = 60$	ξ	−0.01322	−0.01335	+0.03485	+0.10997
	h	+0.04304	+0.03995	+0.04727	+0.19232
	γ	−0.53850	−0.17349	−0.89428	−2.75651
	β	+ 0.92055	+0.75071	+ 0.85362	+1.27075
$v_0 = 90$	ξ	−0.00432	-0.00409	+0.05748	+0.05036
	h	+0.24911	+0.24025	+0.24301	+ 0.29031
	γ	−0.91622	−0.66947	−0.91110	−0.88260

6   Conclussions and Future Work

In this investigation we analyzed the influence of parameter variation on the exact reproduction numbers R_{e0} and R_p by performing a local sensitivity analysis for a stochastic SVIS model with an external source of infection and imperfect vaccine. To measure the potential transmission of an epidemic, under a stochastic framework and for moderate size populations, the exact reproduction numbers are preferable to the deterministic quantifier R_0. In that context, the basic reproduction number overestimates the average number of secondary infections produced by the index case while R_{e0} and R_p provide exact measures of the disease spread.

We performed the sensitivity analysis via derivatives and elasticises. These quantities are obtained with the help of the Algorithm 1 and 2 which were implemented in R software environment.

Regarding the CPU times for Algorithms 1 and 2, we obtain that these quantities are similar but a bit larger for the computation of the derivatives of factorial moments of order k of R_{e0}. These times depend on the population size and when considering larger populations we obtain larger execution times. In particular, the average times to execute Algorithm 1 for a population of

$N = 100$, 500 and 1000 individuals are 0.22, 12.2 and 78.07, respectively and for Algorithm 2 these times are 0.21, 10.03 and 60.23.

Results can be used to help institution authorities to identify the most effective prevention control health strategies such as revaccination campaigns, social distancing measures or contact tracing efforts. The methodology can be applied to other epidemic models and descriptors of disease propagation and we are considering to extend the analysis to epidemic models with latency period or recovery, involving vaccines that wane the effect along time.

References

1. Artalejo, J.R., Lopez-Herrero, M.J.: On the exact measure of disease spread in stochastic epidemic models. Bull. Math. Biol. **75**, 1031–1050 (2013). https://doi.org/10.1007/s11538-013-9836-3
2. Diekmann, O., Heesterbeek, J.A.P.: Mathematical Epidemiology of Infectious Diseases: Model Building, Analysis and Interpretation. John Wiley and Sons (2000)
3. Diekmann, O., Heesterbeek, H., Britton, T.: Mathematical Tools for Understanding Infectious Disease Dynamics. Princeton University Press (2012). https://doi.org/10.1515/9781400845620
4. Diekmann, O., de Jong, M.C.M., Metz, J.A.J.: A deterministic epidemic model taking account of repeated contacts between the same individuals. J. Appl. Probab. **35**(2), 448–462 (1998). https://doi.org/10.1239/jap/1032192860
5. Ball, F., Nåsell, I.: The shape of the size distribution of an epidemic in a finite population. Math. Biosci. **123**(2), 167–181 (1994). https://doi.org/10.1016/0025-5564(94)90010-8
6. Gamboa, M., Lopez-Herrero, M.J.: Measuring infection transmission in a stochastic SIV model with infection reintroduction and imperfect vaccine. Acta. Biotheor. **68**(4), 395–420 (2020). https://doi.org/10.1007/s10441-019-09373-9
7. Saltelli, A., Tarantola, S., Campolongo, F., Ratto, M.: Sensitivity Analysis in Practice: A Guide to Assessing Scientific Models. Wiley, New York (2004)
8. Caswell, H.: Perturbation analysis of continuous-time absorbing Markov chains. Numer. Linear Algebra Appl. **18**(6), 901–917 (2011). https://doi.org/10.1002/nla.791
9. Hautphenne, S., Krings, G., Delvenne, J.C., Blondel, V.D.: Sensitivity analysis of a branching process evolving on a network with application in epidemiology. J. Complex Netw. **3**(4), 606–641 (2015). https://doi.org/10.1093/comnet/cnv001
10. Caswell, H.: Sensitivity Analysis: Matrix Methods in Demography and Ecology. DRM, Springer, Cham (2019). https://doi.org/10.1007/978-3-030-10534-1
11. Samsuzzoha, M.D., Singh, M., Lucy, D.: Uncertainty and sensitivity analysis of the basic reproduction number of a vaccinated epidemic model of influenza. Appl. Math. Model. **37**(3), 903–915 (2013)
12. Gómez-Corral, A., López-García, M.: Perturbation analysis in finite LD-QBD processes and applications to epidemic models. Numer. Linear Algebra Appl. **25**(5), e2160 (2018). https://doi.org/10.1002/nla.2160
13. Avrachenkov, K.E., Filar, J., Haviv, M.: Singular perturbations of Markov chains and decision processes. In: Handbook of Markov Decision Processes 2002, pp. 113–150. Springer, Boston (2002). https://doi.org/10.1007/978-1-4615-0805-2_4
14. Seneta, E.: Sensitivity of finite Markov chains under perturbation. Statist. Probab. Lett. **17**, 163–168 (1993). https://doi.org/10.1016/0167-7152(93)90011-7

15. Li, W., Jiang, L., Ching, W.K., Cui, L.B.: On perturbation bounds for the joint stationary distribution of multivariate Markov chain models. East Asian J. Appl. Math. **3**, 1–17 (2013). https://doi.org/10.42018/eajam.291112.090113a

16. Matsuyama, R., et al.: Uncertainty and sensitivity analysis of the basic reproduction number of diphtheria: a case study of a Rohingya refugee camp in Bangladesh, November–December 2017. PeerJ **6**, e4583 (2018). https://doi.org/10.7717/peerj.4583

17. World Health Organization: Diphtheria vaccine: WHO position paper. Weekly Epidemiolog. Rec. **92**(31), 417–36 (2017)

18. Magnus, J.R., Neudecker, H.: Matrix differential calculus with applications to simple, Hadamard, and Kronecker products. J. Math. Psychol. **29**(4), 474–492 (1985). https://doi.org/10.1016/0022-2496(85)90006-9

Invariant Polarization Signatures for Recognition of Hydrometeors by Airborne Weather Radars

Anatoliy Popov[1]([✉]) [iD], Eduard Tserne[1] [iD], Valerii Volosyuk[1] [iD], Simeon Zhyla[1] [iD],
Vladimir Pavlikov[1] [iD], Nikolay Ruzhentsev[1] [iD], Kostiantyn Dergachov[1] [iD],
Olena Havrylenko[1] [iD], Oleksandr Shmatko[1] [iD], Yuliya Averyanova[2] [iD],
Ivan Ostroumov[2] [iD], Nataliia Kuzmenko[2] [iD], Olga Sushchenko[2] [iD],
Maksym Zaliskyi[2] [iD], Oleksandr Solomentsev[2] [iD], Borys Kuznetsov[3] [iD],
and Tatyana Nikitina[4] [iD]

[1] National Aerospace University "Kharkiv Aviation Institute", Kharkiv, Ukraine
a.v.popov@khai.edu
[2] National Aviation University, Kyiv, Ukraine
[3] State Institution "Institute of Technical Problems of Magnetism of the National Academy of
Sciences of Ukraine", Kharkiv, Ukraine
[4] Kharkiv National Automobile and Highway University, Kharkiv, Ukraine

Abstract. Hydrometeors, such as thunderclouds, hail, and snow, pose a threat
to the safety of civil aviation flights. For their timely detection, airborne weather
radars with dual polarization of radiation, two-channel reception of reflected signals, and signal processing by artificial intelligence methods are used, which makes
it possible to distinguish signatures for the detection and recognition of dangerous
hydrometeors for flights. The dependence of the characteristics of the reflected
signal on a variety of microphysical and macrophysical parameters requires an
expansion of the signature space to improve the reliability of detection. This article proposes invariant polarization signatures of hydrometeors, which are defined
on the basis of the coherent decomposition of eigenvalues and eigenvectors of the
polarization backscattering matrix. Based on the data of experimental studies, it is
shown that the polarization parameters of the radar target's eigenbasis allow distinguishing the degree of ordering of hydrometeor particles (a characteristic feature
of thunderstorm core in clouds) and the parameters of the invariant polarization
transfer functions of hydrometeors make it possible to estimate the phase state of
the hydrometeor, the presence of ice particles in it, hail, etc. even when the radar
observes some mixture of hydrometeors of various types. The obtained results
will improve the efficiency of the application of artificial intelligence methods in
airborne meteorological radars.

Keywords: Weather Radar · Polarization Signature · Backscattering Matrix
Decomposition

O. Gervasi et al. (Eds.): ICCSA 2023, LNCS 13956, pp. 201–217, 2023.
https://doi.org/10.1007/978-3-031-36805-9_14

1 Introduction

Flight safety today still depends on weather conditions. Airborne weather radars installed on civil aircrafts mainly use dual polarization of signals [1] and let generally estimate the danger of weather conditions and avoid risk areas during flight [2], providing information to avionic-specific equipment, such as Electronic Flight Bag (EFB) [3]. At the same time, they do not always ensure timely detection of possible icing zones [4], thunderstorm cores [5], a lightning hazard [6], or a hail area [7]. Airborne weather radars are constantly being improved [8–10], they become multifunctional [11], and apply the most modern technologies [12]. The use of artificial intelligence methods [1] increases the probability of detecting dangerous hydrometeors [13], enhances the accuracy of estimation of their parameters [14], and improves weather predictions [15, 16]. However, methods for information extraction about hydrometeors from a radar signal remain traditional [17], mainly integral estimates are used, such as reflectivity (Z) and differential reflectivity (ZDR), differential phase (DP) [18], linear depolarization ratio (LDR) and eigenvalues [19]. This reduces the efficiency of using machine learning methods and neural networks [13, 14], and also does not solve the problem of separation of hydrometeors mixtures [20].

In this paper, we propose an approach to extraction of polarimetric information about hydrometeors, based on the coherent concept of polarimetry [21] and the theory of polarization transfer functions, which showed good results in the experiment in detecting ground objects by their electrical properties [22, 23], but have not been studied for hydrometeors.

2 Microphysical Parameters of Hydrometeors

The polarization of the reflected by hydrometeors signals essentially depends on the microphysical parameters. Hydrometeors that scatter an electromagnetic wave (EMW) in the radio range (fogs, clouds, and precipitation) are assemblies of condensed water particles suspended or falling in the atmosphere in various phase states [24]. Thunderclouds, which have areas of volumetric electric charges that cause drops to stick together in strong electrostatic fields, pose a particular danger to flights. The presence of a charge on drops in thunderclouds leads to their greater flattening compared to drops in clouds of other shapes [6].

Precipitation is usually understood as hydrometeors that are observed near the earth's surface. The main causes of precipitation are two mechanisms known as the processes of formation of warm and cold rain [5]. When warm rains are formed, the initial growth of droplets in clouds happens due to the condensation of water vapor, and the further transition from cloudy drops to raindrops is caused by the coagulation of small droplets. Droplets growth leads to enlargement in their fall velocity until the steady fall velocity reaches its maximum value (about 9 m/s). A further increase in size leads to spontaneous destruction of large unstable drops. The process of formation of cold rains is initiated by the absorption of water on ice crystals, which leads to their growth, causing the drop of large crystals below the level of the zero isotherm and their melting with the formation of hailstones and water drops [7].

The characteristics of the reflected radar signal are affected not only by macroparameters of the hydrometeor, such as type, height, and linear dimensions but also by microparameters characterizing the properties of hydrometeors in the local (specific) volume: concentration, distribution of particles by size, orientation, shape and phase state, permittivity, the particles fall velocity. Microphysical parameters determine the integral parameters: water content, precipitation intensity, radar reflectivity, etc. [24].

The particle distribution of hydrometeors by size determines the power of the reflected signal [25]. The smallest raindrops have a size of tens of micrometers, the maximum droplet size can reach 6–7 mm, the maximum size of hailstones can reach 60 mm, and powder particles is 10–12 mm, the maximum size of snowflakes is 15–20 mm, generally the diameters of snowflakes are in the range from 2 to 5.5 mm [26]. With the same intensity, thunderstorm rain contains larger droplets than a downpour and incessant rain.

To describe the distribution of hydrometeor particles by size, such analytical functions as the gamma function, exponential and logarithmically normal distributions, and power functions are most often used [27].

The shape of hydrometeor particles depends both on their phase state and size and differs from spherical. Liquid drops with a radius of more than 1 mm have the shape of an oblate spheroid with a flattened base [24]. Their shape is described by the ratio $m = b/a$ of the particle size in the symmetry plane b to its size along the symmetry axis a: $m > 1$ for oblate spheroids and $m < 1$ for prolate spheroids. For hail particles, the ratio of the minimum and maximum sizes m ranges from 0.3 to 1.0, with the most common values being 0.75...0.8 [27]. Unlike drops, the shape of hailstones is practically independent of size. The particles of ice pellets have a shape close to spheroidal or conical, and the ratio m varies between 0.5... 0.9 and, on average, increases with an increase of particles volume. The crystals observed in the upper part of the clouds at low temperatures are the most anisotropic in their shape. The sizes of lamellar crystals vary from 20 μm to 10 mm in diameter and from 10 to 90 μm in thickness. The sizes of columnar crystals range from 20 μm to 3 mm in length and from 10 to 40 μm in thickness.

The depolarization of the reflected radar signal depends on the orientation of the hydrometeor particles in space. Depending on the inclination of the particles to the plane of the irradiating electromagnetic wave, the effective scatterers' length changes along directions orthogonal to the polarized signal components. This causes depolarization of the incident field. The orientation of a particle is determined by the tilt angle β (the angle between the projection of the particle's symmetry axis onto the wavefront plane and the vertical) and the orientation angle γ (the angle between the particle's symmetry axis and the wavefront plane) (see Fig. 1).

The tilt angle β of raindrops does not depend on the internal properties of the drop, and it's a function of external impacts (wind speed, ascending and descending air currents). The distribution of drops over the tilt angles has a rather narrow maximum near the vertical direction, the width of which at the level of 0.5 is, on average, 10...20°, the mean value depends on the horizontal component of the wind speed. Correlation between the parameters of the tilt angle distribution and the drop sizes is not observed [24].

Hail particles have a much less ordering of orientations; their average orientation is commonly close to vertical or horizontal. Ice crystals are oriented, as a rule, randomly

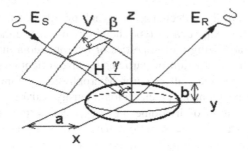

Fig. 1. Geometry of scattering on a hydrometeor particle.

in a horizontal plane. In the presence of a powerful electric field in thunderclouds, small crystals of all shapes tend to orient themselves with a high degree of an order along the direction of the electric field, which does not always coincide with the horizontal or vertical.

3 Radar Characteristics of Hydrometeors

A plane EMW falling on a single hydrometeor particle at an angle γ, excites a field inside it, which generates a scattered field. Let $\mathbf{E}_S$ be the electric field of the incident wave, $\vec{K}_1$ be a unit vector in the direction of incident wave propagation, and $\vec{K}_2$ be a unit vector directed from the coordinate origin to the observation point (see Fig. 1).

In the far field, the electric field of the scattered wave can be represented as

$$e_R(t) = \mathbf{E}_R \cdot \exp(j\omega \cdot t), \ \mathbf{E}_R = f\left(\vec{K}_1, \vec{K}_2\right) \cdot r^{-2} \cdot \exp(-j \cdot k \cdot r), \tag{1}$$

where $f\left(\vec{K}_1, \vec{K}_2\right)$ is the vector function specifying the scattering amplitude and the polarization of the scattered wave; r is the distance from the coordinate origin to the observation point; k is the EMW propagation constant in free space.

The amplitude of the incident wave in (1) is assumed to be a unit value. The scattering amplitude vector $f\left(\vec{K}_1, \vec{K}_2\right)$ is theoretically obtained from the solution of a boundary value problem on the surface of a hydrometeor particle [24].

It is known [17] that a complex polarization backscattering matrix (PBM) $\dot{\mathbf{S}}$ of size 2×2 gives a complete picture of the depolarizing properties of an object and relates the intensity of the emitted $\dot{\mathbf{E}}_S$ and the reflected from the object $\dot{\mathbf{E}}_R$ signals as

$$\dot{\mathbf{E}}_R = \dot{\mathbf{S}} \cdot \dot{\mathbf{E}}_S. \tag{2}$$

PBM describes the reflecting properties of an object at orthogonal polarizations at a given sensing frequency, and the squares of the modules of its elements correspond to the radar cross section (RCS) of the object

$$\sigma_{ij} = \left|\dot{S}_{ij}\right|^2 = \dot{S}_{ij}\dot{S}_{ij}^*.$$

Under the condition of propagation medium reciprocity, the PBM for the monostatic case is always symmetric [21]. In the "horizontal-vertical" $\{HV\}$ polarization basis (PB), the PBM of a spheroidal particle with semi-axes a and b (see Fig. 1) can be written as:

$$\dot{\mathbf{S}} = \mathbf{Q}^{-1} \cdot \dot{\mathbf{S}}_0 \cdot \mathbf{Q}, \tag{3}$$

where $\mathbf{Q}$ is the unitary transformation matrix of the linear PB $\{HV\}$ into the PB $\{\xi\eta\}$, associated with the projections of the ξ and η axes of the particle onto the plane of the wavefront

$$\mathbf{Q} = \begin{bmatrix} \cos\beta & \sin\beta \\ -\sin\beta & \cos\beta \end{bmatrix},$$

$\dot{\mathbf{S}}_0$ is the diagonal matrix whose elements $\dot{f}_\xi$, and $\dot{f}_\eta$ correspond to the reflection coefficients $f\left(\vec{K}_1, -\vec{K}_1\right)$ in (1) in the polarization basis $\{\xi\eta\}$.

PBM (3) can be rewritten as [24]:

$$\dot{\mathbf{S}} = \dot{\sigma}_0 \cdot \begin{bmatrix} 1 - \dot{v} \cdot \cos 2\beta & \dot{v} \cdot \sin 2\beta \\ \dot{v} \cdot \sin 2\beta & 1 + \dot{v} \cdot \cos 2\beta \end{bmatrix}, \tag{4}$$

where $\dot{\sigma}_0|_{\gamma=0} = (\dot{f}_\xi + \dot{f}_\eta)/2$ is the average amplitude of the reflected signal if $\gamma = 0°$ (the axis of symmetry of the particle lies in the plane of the wavefront); $\dot{v}|_{\gamma=0} = (\dot{f}_\xi - \dot{f}_\eta)/(\dot{f}_\xi + \dot{f}_\eta)$ is the particle anisotropy coefficient.

Thus, the polarization backscattering matrix contains information about shape, orientation angles, and dielectric properties of reflecting particles.

The pulse volume of the radar contains N particles randomly located in space. The mean distance between the particles is much greater than the wavelength of the incident radiation and the mean particle size. Under such conditions, each particle of the assembly is an independent reflector, and the contribution of multiple scattering inside the volume can be considered negligible. Then the PBM of the considered volume of the hydrometeor can be written as the sum of N PBMs of all single independent reflectors that make up this volume [28]:

$$\dot{\mathbf{S}} = \sum_{i=1}^{N} e^{j\phi_i} \cdot \dot{\mathbf{S}}_i, \tag{5}$$

where ϕ is the random phase shift of signals reflected from different particles; it can take values from 0 to 2π with equal probability.

Taking into account the relative position of the radar and scattering particles, the signal from the impulse volume containing N hydrometeor particles is determined at the antenna input by the ratio:

$$\dot{\mathbf{E}}_\Sigma = \sum_{i=1}^{N} \frac{e^{jkR_i}}{jkR_i} \cdot \dot{\mathbf{S}}_i \dot{\mathbf{E}}_S,$$

where R_i is the distance from the i-nth particle to the antenna phase center; it is a random value that changes rapidly due to the particle motion. Therefore, the scattered field $\dot{\mathbf{E}}_\Sigma$ will also be a rapidly fluctuating random value.

When averaging over the range R within the radar pulse volume, which occurs in the radar receiver

$$\langle \dot{E}_{\Sigma} \rangle_R = \sum_{i=1}^{N} \left\langle \frac{e^{jkR_i}}{jkR_i} \right\rangle \cdot \dot{S}_i \dot{E}_S,$$

at the output of the receiver we get a signal

$$\left| \langle E_{\Sigma} \rangle \right| \sim N \cdot \left| \langle S_i \rangle \right| \cdot \dot{E}_S \qquad (6)$$

proportional to the reflection coefficient from some mean hydrometeor particle, but this averaging takes place with account of the distribution of particles in size, orientation in space, shape, and other microphysical parameters.

Therefore, in radar meteorology, to study the shape, orientation, and phase state of hydrometeor particles and quantitative estimates of precipitation, a number of integral radar signatures are used.

Radar reflectivity (normalized RCS) for horizontally and vertically polarized waves Z_H and Z_V depends significantly on the type of hydrometeors, the concentration, and the size of particles in the pulse volume (large particles create the main power of the reflected signal [29]), and changes when particles pass from one phase state to other. The differential reflectivity $Z_{DR} = 10 \cdot \lg(Z_H / Z_V)$ is used as a measure of the average ratio between the axes of the hydrometeor particles in the volume. One of the areas of practical use of Z_{DR} is the recognition of hail zones in powerful cumulus clouds [6].

The depolarization of the sensing signal is affected by the shape of the hydrometeor particles, the phase state, the permittivity, and the tilt angle with respect to the EMW polarization plane. To estimate the degree of EMW depolarization, linear depolarization ratios are used in H- and V-sensing [29]

$$LDR_H = 10 \cdot \lg\left(\left|\dot{S}_{HV}\right|^2 \Big/ \left|\dot{S}_{HH}\right|^2\right), \quad LDR_V = 10 \cdot \lg\left(\left|\dot{S}_{VH}\right|^2 \Big/ \left|\dot{S}_{VV}\right|^2\right),$$

and a number of other radar parameters.

The discussed radar characteristics of hydrometeors are determined directly from the results of measurements of the polarization backscattering matrix (3) in the orthogonally linear polarization basis {HV} (the horizontal and vertical). They are used both for classifying hydrometeors and for their recognition by artificial intelligence methods as signatures, for example, in [1, 7, 13, 14].

4 Invariant Polarization Signatures of Radar Targets

The coherent approach [21] to the study of signals reflected by a radar target involves the use of full polarization information [30] obtained by modern radars [8, 9].

The complex amplitudes $\dot{E}_H$ and $\dot{E}_V$ of the orthogonally polarized components (6) form the polarization vector

$$\vec{\mathbf{E}} = \begin{bmatrix} E_H \cdot e^{j\psi_H} \\ E_V \cdot e^{j\psi_V} \end{bmatrix}. \qquad (7)$$

While propagating, the electric field vector rotates with a periodically changing velocity, describing an ellipse in space. A complete revolution occurs during the period of the carrier frequency ω. The initial position of the vector $\vec{\mathbf{E}}$ inside the ellipse at the time $t = 0$ determines the phase of the elliptically polarized wave. The $\vec{\mathbf{E}}$ vector's direction of rotation is determined by the value of the phase difference $\delta = \psi_H - \psi_V$. For a quantitative description of an electromagnetic wave polarization, the geometric parameters of the polarization ellipse (Fig. 2) [21] are used. They are the ellipticity $\varphi\varphi$

$$\varphi = arctg\left(\frac{b}{a}\right), \varphi \in \left[-\frac{\pi}{4}, \frac{\pi}{4}\right], \tag{8}$$

where b and a are the minor and major semiaxes of an ellipse, and the orientation angle θ, that is the angle between the axis $\vec{n}_X$ and the major semi-axis of the ellipse; the orientation angle lies within the limits $\theta \in [0, \pi]$.

Signal parameters φ and θ can be determined out of the measurement results

$$tg(2\theta) = \frac{2|E_H| \cdot |E_V| \cdot \cos(\delta)}{|E_H|^2 - |E_V|^2}, \quad \sin(2\varphi) = \frac{2|E_H| \cdot |E_V| \cdot \sin(\delta)}{|E_H|^2 + |E_V|^2}. \tag{9}$$

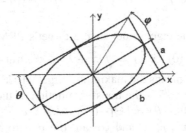

Fig. 2. Polarization ellipse parameters.

The measured polarization backscattering matrix $\dot{\mathbf{S}}$ (5) can be reduced to the diagonal form

$$\dot{\mathbf{S}}_E = \dot{\mathbf{Q}}^T_{\{\varphi_E, \theta_E\}} \cdot \dot{\mathbf{S}} \cdot \dot{\mathbf{Q}}_{\{\varphi_E, \theta_E\}}, \quad \dot{\mathbf{S}}_E = \begin{bmatrix} \dot{\lambda}_1 & 0 \\ 0 & \dot{\lambda}_2 \end{bmatrix}, \tag{10}$$

where $\dot{\lambda}_1, \dot{\lambda}_2$ are eigenvalues; $\dot{\mathbf{Q}}_{\{\varphi_E, \theta_E\}}$ is the PBM eigenvectors (5).

In the polarimetry theory [21] eigenvectors are interpreted as polarizations of the object, which form the target's polarization eigenbasis $\zeta_E = \{\varphi_E, \theta_E\}$, in which the signal reflection coefficients $\dot{\lambda}_1$ and $\dot{\lambda}_2$ will be maximum.

An approach alternative to (7) is the definition of an electromagnetic wave using a double complex plane [22, 23]

$$\ddot{E}(t) = E \cdot e^{-ij\varphi} e^{i\theta} e^{j\left(\omega t + \psi - 2\pi Z/\lambda\right)}, \tag{11}$$

where i is the spatial imaginary unit (the $(1, i)$ plane coincides with the electromagnetic wavefront plane); j is the temporal imaginary unit (direction of $(0, j)$ coincides with the direction of electromagnetic wave propagation along the Z axis); E, ω, ψ and λ are the amplitude, frequency, phase, and wavelength; φ and θ are the angles of ellipticity (8) and orientation (9) of the electromagnetic wave.

When the signal $\ddot{E}_S$ is reflected by the target, the amplitude of the reflected signal $\ddot{E}_R$, its phase, and polarization changes, which in [22] is proposed to be represented in the formulation of the double complex plane in the form:

$$E_R \cdot e^{-ij\varphi_R} e^{i\theta_R} e^{j\psi_R} = \ddot{S}(\bullet) \times \left(E_S \cdot e^{-ij\varphi_S} e^{i\theta_S} e^{j\psi_S} \right), \tag{12}$$

where $\ddot{S}$ is the operator of transformation of the electromagnetic wave parameters that takes place when the wave is reflected from a target; $\times$ is the symbol for operator multiplication.

It is shown in [23] that the operator $\ddot{S}$ can be represented based on eigenvalues and eigenvectors $\vec{\lambda}$ (10) of the polarization backscattering matrix of the target as a consecutive transformation of the amplitude $\Lambda(\vec{\lambda})$, phase $e^{j\psi_T}$, orientation $\ddot{\Theta}(\theta_T)$, and ellipticity $\ddot{\Phi}(\varphi_T, \theta_E)$:

$$\ddot{S}\left(\vec{\lambda}, \ddot{\zeta}_E\right) = \Lambda(\vec{\lambda}) \cdot e^{j\psi_T} \cdot \ddot{\Theta}(\theta_T) \cdot \ddot{\Phi}(\varphi_T, \theta_E), \tag{13}$$

where $\vec{\lambda} = [\dot{\lambda}_1, \dot{\lambda}_2]$ are the eigenvalues of the target's PBM; $\ddot{\zeta}_E = \zeta(\varphi_E, \theta_E)$ is the target's eigenpolarization (10); $\Lambda(\vec{\lambda}) = \sqrt{\lambda_1^2 + \lambda_2^2}$ is the transfer function of the target in amplitude ($\lambda_1^2 + \lambda_2^2$ here means the maximum target's RCS); $e^{j\psi_T}$ is the signal phase transfer function; $\ddot{\Theta}(\theta_T) = e^{i\theta_T}$ is the transfer function of the orientation angle of the signal polarization vector; $\ddot{\Phi}(\varphi, \theta) = \left\{ \ddot{\Theta}[-(\theta + \pi/4)] \times e^{-ij\varphi} \right\} \cdot \ddot{\Theta}(\theta + \pi/4)$ is the signal ellipticity transfer function; φ_T, θ_T and ψ_T are the transformations of the ellipticity, orientation, and phase of the signal parameters induced by the target. Parameters φ_T, θ_T and ψ_T are of interest in the problems of recognizing objects by their polarization properties since they depend only on the electrophysical and geometric characteristics of the reflecting object and do not depend on the type of sensing and received polarization, i.e. are invariant characteristics of the target.

In [31], a method for determining the parameters (13) was proposed. Based on the results of the target's polarization backscattering matrix (5) measurements with a four-channel full radar polarimeter in an orthogonal polarization basis, $\{H, V\}$ for example, the known relations can be used to find the eigenvalues $\vec{\lambda} = [\dot{\lambda}_1, \dot{\lambda}_2]$ and eigenvectors $\dot{Q}_{\{\varphi_E, \theta_E\}}$ PBM $\dot{S}|_{HV}$.

Their ratio is calculated from the eigenvalues ($\dot{\lambda}_1 > \dot{\lambda}_2$):

$$\gamma_T = \arctan\left(\frac{|\lambda_2|}{|\lambda_1|}\right), \quad \dot{p}_T = \frac{\dot{\lambda}_2}{\dot{\lambda}_1}, \quad \Delta\psi_T = \arctan\left(\frac{\operatorname{Im} \dot{p}_T}{\operatorname{Re} \dot{p}_T}\right),$$

which are used to calculate the parameters of the operator (13):

$$\varphi_T = \tfrac{1}{2} \arcsin\{\sin(2\gamma_T) \cdot \sin(\Delta\psi_T)\}, \quad \theta_T = \arctan\left\{\frac{\sin(2\gamma_T) \cdot \cos(\Delta\psi_T)}{\cos(2\gamma_T) + \cos(2\varphi_T)}\right\} \tag{14}$$

In this paper, we studied the possibility of using parameters (14) and parameters of the eigenbasis (10) φ_E, θ_E as signatures for recognizing the types of hydrometeors by polarimetric radar data.

5 Experimental Equipment

For the experimental research of reflections from hydrometeors, an experimental quadrature-polarimetric (Quad-Pol) X-band radar measuring system was used, built of standard airborne radars blocks with an improved antenna system. Our radar system operates in a pulse mode and contains one polarizing-isotropic reflector antenna (see Fig. 3) with an orthomode converter and an emitted pulses polarization switch, which allows emitting sensing pulses of vertical and horizontal polarization in turn. Reflected signals are received on the same reflector antenna. The orthomode converter separates the vertically polarized and horizontally polarized components of the reflected signal, which enter the two-channel receiver through the receive-transmit circulators. To expand the dynamic range of the receiver, the gain coefficients of the intermediate frequency amplifiers are digitally changing depending on the distance. High-speed analog-to-digital converters convert a fragment of an intermediate frequency signal specified by distance. This allows restoring the amplitude and phase of the received signals synchronously in two polarization-orthogonal channels. Thus, two successively emitted pulses with a time interval of 2.5 ms make it possible to measure the full polarization backscattering matrix. The radar has a built-in system for calibrating receivers with microwave pulses, which allows controlling the receiving channels' parameters during measurements. To improve the accuracy of measurements, an external active-passive calibration system is also used, which allows taking into account the errors of the transmitter, antenna, and non-identity of the receiving channels.

Main specifications of the Quad-Pol radar measuring system:

– transmitter power (in pulse) is 1 kW;
– working frequency is 9,37 GHz;
– pulse duration is 0,5 μs;
– receiver sensitivity is not less than 120 dB/mW;
– pulse repetition rate is 400 Hz;
– range of change of the emitted signal orientation angle is 0° to 90°;
– polarization modulator limit frequency is 10 kHz;
– antenna beamwidth (by zeros) is 3°;
– antenna cross-polarization level is not worse than 36 dB;
– polarizing separator decoupling degree is not worse than 38 dB;
– polarization basis setting error is not more than 0,1°.

During the experiments, the radar was installed on the roof of a high-rise building. The antenna position control system provided space scanning within the 270° in azimuth and 0...45° in elevation. Measurements of the polarization characteristics of hydrometeors were made at distances from 1 to 20 km in a movable window d = 2 km (see Fig. 3) with a fixed antenna to eliminate the effects of additional signal modulation due to antenna movement. Meteorological conditions were recorded according to the airport weather service.

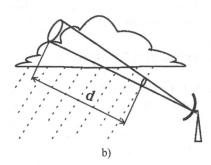

a)   b)

Fig. 3. Quad-Pol radar (a) and experiment geometry (b).

6 Experimental Results

From the database obtained in field experiments the records of reflected by hydrometeors signals with approximately the same normalized RCS were selected for analysis, which complicates hydrometeors recognition task by energy characteristics.

Experimental studies of reflected by hydrometeors of various types (rain, hail, snow, thunderclouds, etc.) signals have shown that it is rather difficult to isolate a specific type of hydrometeor in a "pure" form during measurements. Figure 4 shows a radar image fragment of rain with an intensity of up to 10 mm/h when sensing with an elevation angle of 7.5°. At a distance of up to 1.5 km, the reflected signal is mainly formed by raindrops, over 2 km - mainly by a rain cloud. Figure 5 shows a radar rain image with a hail band (the size of ice particles, according to ground control data, reached 5 mm) at a distance of 1.5 km to 2.5 km. At short distances (up to 1.3 km), the reflected signal is formed by water particles in the liquid state. Therefore, mixes of hydrometeors of different types are present in almost any real data, which, as noted in [20], creates the problem of detecting dangerous for flight hydrometeors.

The RCS of hydrometeors fluctuates over a wide range (up to 60 dB), and the amplitude histograms of the reflected by different hydrometeors signals overlap. For example, Fig. 6 shows the experimentally obtained PBM S_{HH} and S_{HV} elements histograms of four hydrometeors (rain, hail, snow, thunderclouds). That means that it is rather difficult to determine the type of hydrometeors according to such traditional in radar meteorology signal parameters as reflectivity at different polarizations (Z_H, Z_V) when the hydrometeors intensities or water contents are close values.

The wide-range fluctuations of amplitudes of signals in polarization-orthogonal channels of the radar receiver are caused by fluctuation of polarization of the reflected signals.

Changes in signal polarization can be clearly seen in a polarimetric diagram [32] (Fig. 7), where each possible value of the ellipticity and orientation corresponds to a point in polar coordinates. Plotting of two-dimensional histograms of signals' ellipticity and orientation in the polarimetric diagram allows us to "see" the most probable signal polarization values areas. For example, Fig. 7-b shows histograms of the ellipticity and

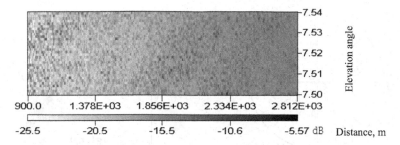

Fig. 4. Radar rain image, PBM element S_{VV}.

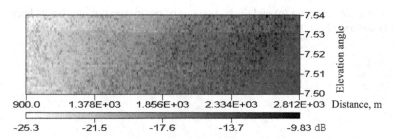

Fig. 5. Radar hail image, PBM element S_{VV}.

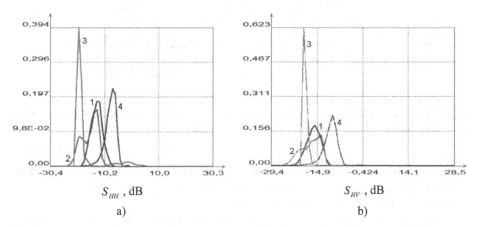

a)   b)

Fig. 6. Histograms of PBM elements S_{HH} (a), S_{HV} (b) of four types of hydrometeors (1 is a rain, 2 is a hail, 3 is a snow, 4 is a thunderclouds).

orientation of the signals reflected by rain and hail when they are sensed by a horizontally polarized signal. Figure 7 shows that backscattering changes both the ellipticity of the signal and its orientation. Moreover, the angle of the backscattered signal orientation rotation can reach 45°.

As orientation angles of hydrometeor particles are random, the projections of the reflected electric field vector according to (3) will have significant fluctuations, which

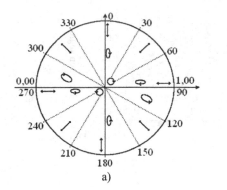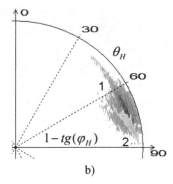

a)   b)

Fig. 7. Polarimetric diagram (a) and the histograms of polarization of the signals backscattered by rain (1) and hail (2) in the polarimetric diagram (b).

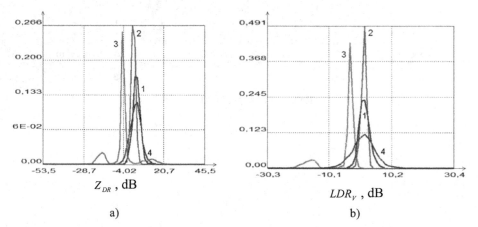

a)   b)

Fig. 8. Histograms of differential reflectivity (a) and linear depolarization ratio (b) for various types of hydrometeors: rain (1), hail (2), snow (3), thunderstorm (4).

is observed in the histograms of traditional relative radar characteristics, namely differential reflectivity Z_{DR} and linear depolarization ratios LDR. An example of these radar characteristics histograms is shown in Fig. 8.

A feature of the invariant polarization signatures discussed in Sect. 4 is that these signatures separate the sources of fluctuations in the reflected signal parameters. The parameters of the target's polarization eigenbasis φ_E, θ_E (eigenvectors (10)) show the changes in the signal associated with the target's orientation relative to the radar, and the parameters of polarization transformation by the target φ_T and θ_T describe the changes in the polarization of the signal backscattered by the target oriented in the radar coordinate system. Therefore, invariant polarization signatures have lower dispersion and are more compactly located in the polarimetric diagram.

Figure 9 shows the histograms of the polarization eigenbasis parameters plotted in the polarimetric diagram for the four studied types of hydrometeors. Analysis of the polarimetric diagrams shows that depending on the hydrometeor type the position of the distribution mode for the object's eigenpolarizations shifts. If for the thunderclouds the mode of the eigenorientation θ_E is located near the orientation angle of 100°, for the rain of medium intensity it is about 110°, then for solid-phase hydrometeors it noticeably shifts towards larger angles: for hail it is approximately 130°, for dry snow it is almost 145°. With a relatively small dispersion of θ_E these objects become distinguishable.

The obtained result is quite understandable from the point of view of the microphysics of hydrometeors (see Sect. 2). There is a belief that in thunderclouds the water droplets are more flattened and more orderly oriented due to the presence of electrostatic electricity, which leads to a more pronounced "mean orientation" of the observed average droplet (6). Hail particles have much less orientation order, while snowflakes and ice crystals are oriented, as a rule, chaotically. So the signature θ_E can be used as an indicator for the degree of particles ordering in a hydrometeor.

The polarization transformation parameters φ_T and θ_T (14) turned out to be interesting for practical use. Studies [22, 23] have shown that they are sensitive to the target's electrophysical properties – dielectric permittivity and conductivity. Calculation of these parameters for hydrometeors showed that the polarization transformation parameters φ_T and θ_T clearly/strictly distinguish the phase state of the hydrometeor and group these objects into the classes "liquid water" and "solid" state (snow, ice).

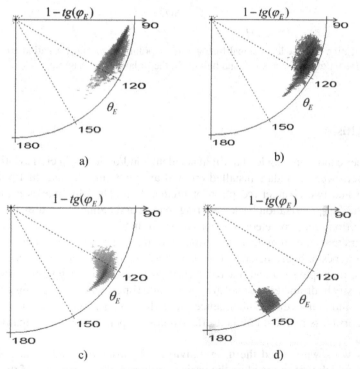

Fig. 9. Location of two-dimensional histograms of eigenellipticity φ_E and eigenorientation θ_E in the polarimetric diagram for various types of hydrometeors: storm (a), rain (b), hail (c), snow (d).

Figure 10 shows location of the polarization transformation φ_T and θ_T histograms of rain, thunderclouds (almost identical to rain), snow, and hail in the polarimetric diagram. To build the polarization transformation φ_T and θ_T histograms of hail we used the sample, which was shown in Fig. 5. Approximately half of the sample contain readouts of signals reflected from the hydrometeor in the liquid phase, therefore, in Fig. 10, the histogram of the "hail" object has a pronounced bimodal nature; part of the samples refers to the hydrometeor in the liquid state and it is almost identical to the rain in its position in the polarimetric diagram, and the second mode is shifted noticeably closer to the area occupied by snow. Thus, the polarization transformation parameters φ_T and θ_T can be used as indicators of the hydrometeor phase state.

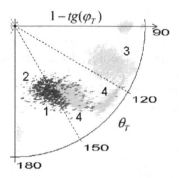

Fig. 10. Location of two-dimensional histograms of polarization transformation φ_T and θ_T of rain (1), thundercloud (2), snow (3), and hail (4) in the polarimetric diagram.

7   Conclusion

Bad weather conditions can lead to flight accidents and/or delays in civil aviation flights [33]. Modern weather radars installed on civil aviation aircrafts use dual polarization of sensing and two-channel reception of reflected signals. This makes it possible to measure the full polarization backscattering matrix and define signatures for detection and recognition of hydrometeors dangerous for flights.

Hydrometeors are complex non-stationary radar targets that may contain a mixture of different types of hydrometeors. The characteristics of the reflected signal depend on a variety of microphysical and macrophysical parameters. The signatures traditionally used to classify hydrometeors do not always provide timely and reliable danger detection. The use of modern artificial intelligence methods increases the probability of correct hydrometeors classification, but their effectiveness depends on the informativity of the initial data.

In this work we studied the informativity of hydrometeors invariant polarization signatures, which were derived on the basis of coherent decomposition of the polarization backscattering matrix, extracting its eigenvalues and eigenvectors, followed by the detailed treatment of decomposition results. This allowed us to identify new signatures that provide additional information about hydrometeors.

On the basis of our own experimental data we have shown that invariant polarization signatures based on the decomposition of the eigenvalues and eigenvectors of the polarization backscattering matrix make it possible to get the hydrometeor particles' degree of order, which is a characteristic feature of thunderstorm cores in clouds, and the phase state of the hydrometeor, the presence of ice particles in it, hail particles, etc.

No doubt, the obtained results are preliminary and require subsequent large-scale experimental studies. But the already available data suggest that expansion of the signature space for the artificial intelligence methods will increase the reliability of detecting hydrometeors dangerous for flights and, accordingly, will enhance the safety of civil aviation flights.

References

1. Chandrasekar, V.: AI in weather radars. In: 2020 IEEE Radar Conference (RadarConf20), pp. 1–3. IEEE, Florence, Italy (2020)
2. Cuccoli, F., Lupidi, A., Facheris, L., Baldini, L.: Polarimetric radar for civil aircrafts to support pilots' decision in bad weather conditions. In: 2015 IEEE International Geoscience and Remote Sensing Symposium (IGARSS), pp. 2327–2330. IEEE, Milan, Italy (2015)
3. D'Amico, M., et al.: The X-WALD project: towards a cleaner sky. In: 2014 44th European Microwave Conference, pp. 1888–1891. IEEE, Rome, Italy (2014)
4. Shrestha, Y., Zhang, Y., Fusselman, J., McFarquhar, G.M., Blake, W., Harrah, S.D.: Potential application of PARADOX (Polarimetric Airborne Radar Operating at X-band) to High Ice Water Content (HIWC) monitoring. In: 2022 IEEE Radar Conference (RadarConf22), pp. 1–6. IEEE, New York City, NY, USA (2022)
5. Nagel, D.: Detection of rain areas with airborne radar. In: 2017 18th International Radar Symposium (IRS), pp. 1–7. IEEE, Prague, Czech Republic (2017)
6. Wu, S., Si, J., Hu, D., Guo, Z., Zhang, Y., Zhao, Q.: Analysis of echo characteristics of dual-polarization Doppler weather radar in lightning weather. In: 2019 International Conference on Meteorology Observations (ICMO), pp. 1–4. IEEE, Chengdu, China (2019)
7. Schmidt, M., Trömel, S., Ryzhkov, A.V., Simmer, C.: Severe hail detection: hydrometeor classification for Polarimetric C-band radars using fuzzy-logic and T-matrix scattering simulations. In: 2018 19th International Radar Symposium (IRS), pp. 1–7. IEEE, Bonn, Germany (2018)
8. Yeary, M., Cheong, B.L., Kurdzo, J.M., Yu, T.-Y., Palmer, R.: A brief overview of weather radar technologies and instrumentation. IEEE Instrum. Meas. Mag. 17(5), 10–15 (2014)
9. Berizzi, F., et al.: The X-WALD project: first measurements in Europe with an avionic polarimetric weather radar. In: 2017 IEEE Radar Conference (RadarConf), pp. 0487–0491. IEEE, Seattle, WA, USA (2017)
10. Ren, Z., Wu, D., Gao, M., Shen, M., Zhu, D.: Clutter suppression for airborne weather radar using 3D-STAP. In: 2020 IEEE 5th International Conference on Signal and Image Processing (ICSIP), pp. 468–473. IEEE, Nanjing, China (2020)
11. Kunstmann, F., Klarer, D., Puchinger A., Beer, S.: Weather detection with an AESA-based airborne sense and avoid radar. In: 2020 IEEE Radar Conference (RadarConf20), pp. 1–6. IEEE, Florence, Italy (2020)
12. Vivekanandan, J., Karboski, A., Loew, E.: Airborne Polarimetric doppler weather radar: antenna aperture and beam forming architecture. In: 2019 IEEE International Symposium on Phased Array System & Technology (PAST), pp. 1–6. IEEE, Waltham, MA, USA (2019)

13. Yu, Q., Wu, D., Zhu, D., Qian, J.: CNN-based weather signal detection algorithm for airborne weather radar. In: 2020 IEEE 5th International Conference on Signal and Image Processing (ICSIP), pp. 660–664. IEEE, Nanjing, China (2020)
14. Wang, L., Chen, H.: Machine learning for polarimetric radar quantitative precipitation estimation. In: 2023 United States National Committee of URSI National Radio Science Meeting (USNC-URSI NRSM), pp. 298–299. IEEE, Boulder, CO, USA (2023)
15. Zhang, J., Chen, H., Han, L.: An investigation of a probabilistic nowcast system for dual-polarization radar applications. In: IGARSS 2020 - 2020 IEEE International Geoscience and Remote Sensing Symposium, pp. 5294–5297. IEEE, Waikoloa, HI, USA (2020)
16. Yao, S, Chen, H., Thompson, E.J., Cifelli, R.: An improved deep learning model for high-impact weather Nowcasting. IEEE J. Sel. Top. Appl. Earth Obs. Remote Sens. **15**, 7400–7413 (2022)
17. Yanovsky, F.: Retrieving information about remote objects from received signals. In: 2022 IEEE 2nd Ukrainian Microwave Week (UkrMW), pp. 512–517. IEEE, Kharkiv, Ukraine (2022)
18. Biswas, S.K., Cifelli, R., Chandrasekar, V.: Quantitative precipitation estimation using X-band radar for orographic rainfall in the San Francisco bay area. IEEE Trans. Geosci. Remote Sens., 1 (2022)
19. Galletti, M., Gekat, F., Goelz, P., Zrnic, D.S.: Eigenvalue signal processing for phased-array weather radar polarimetry: removing the bias induced by antenna coherent cross-channel coupling. In: 2013 IEEE International Symposium on Phased Array Systems and Technology, pp. 502–509. IEEE, Waltham, MA, USA (2013)
20. Pejcic, V., Simmer, C., Trömel, S.: Polarimetric radar-based methods for evaluation of hydrometeor mixtures in numerical weather prediction models. In: 2021 21st International Radar Symposium (IRS), pp. 1–10. IEEE, Berlin, Germany (2021)
21. Boerner, W.-M., Yan, W.-L., Xi, A.-Q., Yamaguchi, Y.: On the basic principles of radar polarimetry: the target characteristic polarization state theory of Kennaugh, Huynen's polarization fork concept, and its extension to the partially polarized case. Proc. IEEE **79**(10), 1538–1550 (1991)
22. Popov, A., Bortsova, M.: Detection of metal objects against mountain ranges using polarization transfer functions. In: 2018 IEEE 17th International Conference on Mathematical Methods in Electromagnetic Theory (MMET), pp. 290–293. IEEE, Kyiv, Ukraine (2018)
23. Popov, A., Bortsova, M.: Experimental research of polarization transfer functions of mobile ground objects. In: 2019 IEEE 2nd Ukraine Conference on Electrical and Computer Engineering (UKRCON), pp. 119–122. IEEE, Lviv, Ukraine (2019)
24. Oguchi, T.: Electromagnetic wave propagation and scattering in rain and other hydrometeors. Proc. IEEE **71**(9), 1029–1078 (1983)
25. Zrnic, D., Ryzhkov, A., Fulton, R.: Classification and measurement of precipitation using a dual-polarization radar. In: IEEE 1999 International Geoscience and Remote Sensing Symposium. IGARSS 1999, pp. 711–713. IEEE, Hamburg, Germany (1999)
26. El-Magd, A., Chandrasekar, V., Bringi, V.N., Strapp, W.: Multiparameter radar and in situ aircraft observation of graupel and hail. IEEE Trans. Geosci. Remote Sens. **38**(1), 570–578 (2000)
27. Straka, J.M., Zrnić, D.S., Ryzhkov, A.V.: Bulk hydrometeor classification and quantification using polarimetric radar data: synthesis of relations. J. Appl. Meteorol. Climatol. **39**, 1341–1372 (2000)
28. Mishchenko, M.I.: Electromagnetic scattering by nonspherical particles: a tutorial review. J. Quant. Spectrosc. Radiat. Transfer **110**(11), 808–832 (2009)
29. Wolf, D.A., Russchenberg, W.J., Ligthart, L.P.: Radar reflection from clouds: gigahertz backscatter cross sections and Doppler spectra. IEEE Trans. Antennas Propag. **48**(2), 254–259 (2000)

30. Chen, S.: Polarimetric coherence pattern: a visualization and characterization tool for PolSAR data investigation. IEEE Trans. Geosci. Remote Sens. **56**(1), 286–297 (2018)
31. Popov, A., Bortsova, M.: Polarization transfer functions of remote sensing objects. In: 9th International Kharkiv Symposium on Physics and Engineering of Microwaves, Millimeter and Submillimeter Waves (MSMW 2016), pp. 1–4. IEEE, Kharkiv, Ukraine (2016)
32. Popov, A.V., Pogrebnyak, O.: Informativity of polarimetric radar invariants. In: SPIE's 48th Annual Meeting on Optical Science and Technology, Earth Observing Systems VIII, vol. 5151, pp. 74–84. San Diego, California, United States (2003)
33. Ostroumov, I., et al.: A probability estimation of aircraft departures and arrivals delays. In: Gervasi, O., et al. (eds.) ICCSA 2021. LNCS, vol. 12950, pp. 363–377. Springer, Cham (2021). https://doi.org/10.1007/978-3-030-86960-1_26

Extended Pairwise Sequence Alignment

Eloi Araujo[1]([✉])[iD], Fábio V. Martinez[1][iD], Luiz C. Rozante[2][iD],
and Nalvo F. Almeida[1][iD]

[1] Faculdade de Computação, Universidade Federal de Mato Grosso do Sul,
Campo Grande, MS, Brazil
{francisco.araujo,fabio.martinez,nalvo.almeida}@ufms.br
[2] Centro de Matemática Computação e Cognição, Universidade Federal do ABC,
Santo André, SP, Brazil
luiz.rozante@ufabc.edu.br

Abstract. A pairwise sequence alignment is a structure describing a set
of editing operations that transforms one given sequence into another
given sequence. We consider insertion, deletion, and substitution of symbols as editing operations. Given a fixed function assigning a weight for
each editing operation, the weight of an alignment A is the sum of the
editing operations described by A. Needleman and Wunsch proposed an
algorithm for finding a pairwise sequence alignment of minimum editing
weight. However, a sequence of editing operations that transforms one
sequence into another cannot always be represented by an alignment. We
present a more general structure that allows us to represent any sequence
of editing operations that transforms one sequence into another. We also
show how to find a minimum weight sequence of editing operations to
transform one sequence into another in quadratic time, even if they cannot be represented by an alignment. Additionally, we show that there
exists no algorithm to solve the problem with subquadratic running time,
unless SETH is false. This approach may be used to explain non-trivial
evolutionary models in Molecular Biology, where the triangle inequality does not hold for the distance between the sequences, such as those
involving adaptive and back mutations.

Keywords: edit distance · alignment distance · pairwise sequence
alignment · extended pairwise sequence alignment

1 Introduction

Sequence comparison is a useful tool for solving problems in several areas such as
computational biology, text processing, and pattern recognition. A scoring function is a measure to determine the degree of similarity or dissimilarity between
two sequences and can be defined by editing operations that transform one given
sequence into another given sequence. Typically, the editing operations considered are insertion, deletion, and substitution of symbols. A well-known scoring
function to sequences s and t is the *Levenshtein distance* [13], also called *edit*

© The Author(s), under exclusive license to Springer Nature Switzerland AG 2023
O. Gervasi et al. (Eds.): ICCSA 2023, LNCS 13956, pp. 218–230, 2023.
https://doi.org/10.1007/978-3-031-36805-9_15

distance, defined as the minimum number of editing operations that transform s into t. Thus, the edit distance is a way to quantifying the dissimilarity of two strings and, as a consequence, it is used in several applications where the data can be represented by strings.

The pairwise sequence alignment is a structure that allows us to visualize editing operations that transform one sequence into another. It can be obtained putting one sequence above the other in such way that edited symbols are in the same column. In other words, an alignment of sequences s and t is a structure that allows us to identify exactly one editing operation in each symbol of s that ends up turning s into t.

Occasionally, some editing operations are considered more likely to occur than others and thus one can compare the given sequences s and t by computing the *weighted edit distance*, that is, minimizing the sum of weights of the editing operations necessary to transform s into t through a sequence of editing operations given by an alignment. The weighted edit distance is useful, for instance, in applications such as spelling correction systems [6]. The weights of editing operations are given by a scoring matrix γ, where $\gamma_{a \to b}, \gamma_{a \to \sqcup}$ and $\gamma_{\sqcup \to a}$ are the weights to replace a with b, and delete and insert a, respectively, for any pair of symbols a and b. Levenshtein distance is a particular case of weighted edit distance considering editing operations with weights $\gamma_{a \to b} = 0$ if $a = b$ and $\gamma_{a \to b} = 1$ if $a \neq b$. Needleman and Wunsch [18] proposed an algorithm to determine a pairwise sequence alignment of minimum weight using Levenshtein distance in quadratic time, which is also easily extended to solve the weighted edit distance problem with the same running time.

Other scoring functions have been described based on alignments and individual editing operations. Barton *et al.* [5] used the edit distance in genome assembly and showed that adding the flexibility of bounding the number of gaps inserted in an alignment strengthens the classical pairwise sequence alignment scheme. Another typical scoring function is the so called *normalized edit distance* [17], where the number of editing operations is taken into account when computing the distance between two sequences. Examples of applications of the normalized edit distance are the text reading from street view images [23] and software verification [8]. The *generalized normalized edit distance* of two sequences proposed by [25] is a function that takes into account the weighted edit distance and the lengths of involved sequences. This distance was applied in a handwritten digit recognition study. Another variation is the *contextual normalized edit distance*, where the weight of each editing operation is divided by the length of the string on which the editing operation takes place. It was introduced by [11] and authors showed that this variation is useful in many applications with classification purposes. Consequently, alignments based on editing operations have been a standard way to compare two or even more sequences with a myriad of applications in important topics such as computational biology [1, 3, 7, 12, 14, 15, 18, 19, 22].

A pairwise sequence alignment represents a set of editing operations where each symbol of s and t is edited once. However, not every set of editing operations can be represented by an alignment, even if it represents one whose sum of weights of the editing operations is minimum. For example, suppose that $\{a, b, c\}$ is an alphabet with three symbols, and $s = a$ and $t = b$ are sequences from the alphabet. There exist only three classical ways to align s and t:

$$\begin{bmatrix} a \\ b \end{bmatrix}, \qquad \begin{bmatrix} \sqcup & a \\ b & \sqcup \end{bmatrix}, \qquad \text{and} \qquad \begin{bmatrix} a & \sqcup \\ \sqcup & b \end{bmatrix}.$$

If the weighted editing operations are given by the matrix γ in Fig. 1, we have that the weight of the first alignment is 5, and the weight of both second and third alignments are $2 + 2 = 4$. Hence, the second and third are alignments of sequences $s = a$ and $t = b$ with minimum weight.

γ	a	b	c	$\sqcup$
a	0	5	1	2
b	5	3	1	1
c	3	1	0	2
$\sqcup$	2	2	2	

Fig. 1. Instance of a scoring matrix γ. The row i and column j represents the weight for editing the symbol i to j.

Notice that none of the alignments above represents the following transformation: "*edit symbol* a *to symbol* c *and then edit symbol* c *to symbol* b". The sum of weights of the editing operations in such transformation is 2, which is smaller than any of those presented before. We can represent this transformation as follows:

$$\begin{bmatrix} a \\ c \\ b \end{bmatrix}.$$

Nevertheless, notice that this structure is not a classical alignment, as shown previously.

Araujo et al. [2] present the *extended alignment problem* that takes into account a set of editing operations regardless of the existence of a usual corresponding alignment to represent them. It is a generalization of the concept of alignment in such way that it can represent a set of sequences of editing operations to transform one given sequence into another given sequence. Consequently, this framework assumes that a single symbol can be edited many times.

Although general substitution models for biological sequences assume each detected mutation as a unique evolutionary event, sometimes it is useful to consider a mutation as a result of a sequence of intermediary steps. In these cases, the classical alignment structure cannot capture such events. It has been shown, for instance, that back mutations ("edit a to b and then b to a") can change the rate of compensatory molecular evolution, where mutations located at two sites, either within a gene or on different genes, are correlated in the sense that they are individually deleterious but harmless when appropriately combined [16].

Adaptive mutation is another important example of an evolutionary setting that can be explained by such intermediary events. In this case, mutations may arise as an immediate and direct response to selective pressure or even by DNA repair. By suffering a sequence of such pressures, intermediary mutation events may occur [10, 20].

This paper is dedicated to the development of a method for finding the sequence of editing operations to transform one given sequence into another given sequence, where the total sum of the single transformation weights is minimum. We use an extended alignment to represent such sequence of operations. We propose a straightforward and efficient algorithm to find an optimal extended pairwise sequence alignment and show that there exists no subquadratic algorithm to perform this task, unless SETH is false.

We organize this paper as follows. Section 2 formalizes the basic concepts necessary for the development of the main results. Section 3 describes how to find a sequence of editing operations of an extended pairwise alignment with minimum weight, presents the running time of the proposed algorithm, and an additional discussion on the complexity of the problem as well. Finally, Sect. 4 concludes showing final remarks.

2   Preliminaries

Let Σ be a finite set of symbols called *alphabet*. We denote a sequence s over Σ by $s(1) \cdots s(n)$, where each $s(j) \in \Sigma$, and we say that $n = |s|$ is its *length*. The set of all sequences over Σ is denoted by Σ^*. A symbol $\sqcup \notin \Sigma$, called *space*, represents insertions and deletions of symbols.

A real-valued *scoring matrix*, whose rows and columns are indexed by symbols of $\Sigma_\sqcup = \Sigma \cup \{\sqcup\}$, stores the weights of editing operations. Given $a, b \in \Sigma_\sqcup$ and a scoring matrix γ, we denote by $\gamma_{a \to b}$ the entry in row a and column b of γ. The value of $\gamma_{a \to b}$ is the weight of editing operation of substitution if $a, b \in \Sigma$, insertion if $a = \sqcup$, and deletion if $b = \sqcup$. The entry $\gamma_{\sqcup \to \sqcup}$ is not defined. See Fig. 1 for an example of scoring matrix.

Given two sequences s and t, a *classical alignment* of s, t is a pair $[s', t']$ of sequences in $\Sigma_\sqcup^*$, where s' and t' are obtained by inserting spaces into s and t, $|s'| = |t'|$, and there is no index j such that $s'(j) = t'(j) = \sqcup$. It is easy to show that if $n = \max\{|s|, |t|\}$, then the *length* $|s'|$ of alignment $[s', t']$ is $O(n)$. The A_γ-score of a classical alignment $[s', t']$ is given by

$$A_\gamma([s', t']) = \sum_{j=1}^{|s'|} \gamma_{s'(j) \to t'(j)} .$$

We define $\text{optA}_\gamma(s, t)$ as the A_γ-score of a classical alignment of s, t with minimum A_γ-score. A classical alignment A of s, t whose A_γ-score is equal to $\text{optA}_\gamma(s, t)$ is called an A_γ-*optimal alignment* of s, t.

Problem Minimum Alignment Score (**MAS**): *Given two sequences* s, t *in* Σ^*, *find an* A_γ-*optimal alignment of* s, t, *where* γ *is a fixed scoring matrix.*

MAS is the Levenshtein problem if $\gamma_{a \to b} = 0$ when $a = b$, and $\gamma_{a \to b} = 1$ otherwise, and thus γ is a metric on Σ.

An *extended alignment* of s, t is a n-tuple $[c_1, \ldots, c_n]$, where each c_j is a column that represents a sequence of editing operations of a symbol. Precisely, each c_j is a finite sequence with $m_j = |c_j| \geq 1$ symbols in $\Sigma_\sqcup$, $c_j(1) \neq \sqcup$ or $c_j(m_j) \neq \sqcup$, and it doesn't have consecutive symbols $\sqcup$; the sequence s is obtained by removing symbols $\sqcup$ from $c_1(1) \cdots c_n(1)$, and sequence t is obtained by removing symbols $\sqcup$ from $c_1(m_1) \cdots c_n(m_n)$. For example, the 8-tuple $A = [a, abcd, b\sqcup, \sqcup d, ca, \sqcup dabc, \sqcup abc, dab]$ is an extended alignment of the sequences $aabcd, addaccb$. Notice that each c_j is a sequence of $m_j - 1$ editing operations. The graphical representation

$$
A = \begin{bmatrix} & a & & & & \sqcup & & \\ & b & b & \sqcup & c & d & \sqcup & d \\ a & c & \sqcup & d & a & a & a & a \\ & d & & & & b & b & b \\ & & & & & c & & c \end{bmatrix}
$$

of the extended alignment A of sequences $aabcd, addaccb$ shows the editing operations that are represented by A.

The E_γ-score of a column c_j is the sum of the editing operations represented in c_j, i.e.,

$$
E_\gamma(c_j) = \sum_{i=1}^{m_j - 1} \gamma_{c_j(i) \to c_j(i+1)},
$$

and the E_γ-score of an extended alignment $[c_1, \ldots, c_n]$ is

$$
E_\gamma([c_1, \ldots, c_n]) = \sum_{j=1}^{n} E_\gamma(c_j).
$$

We define $optE_\gamma(s, t)$ as a minimum E_γ-score among all extended alignments of seqeunces s, t. An extended alignment A of s, t whose E_γ-score is equal to $optE_\gamma(s, t)$ is called an E_γ-*optimal alignment* of s, t.

Problem Minimum Edit Score (**MES**): *Given two sequences* s, t *in* Σ^*, *find an* E_γ-*optimal alignment of* s, t, *where* γ *is a fixed scoring matrix.*

We simply say 'alignment' instead of 'classical' or 'extended alignment' if the type of the alignment is obvious from the context.

A scoring matrix γ can be seen as a digraph $D(\gamma)$ with cost on its arcs, where the set of vertices is $V(D) = \Sigma_\sqcup$, the set of arcs is $E(D) = \Sigma_\sqcup \times \Sigma_\sqcup \setminus \{(\sqcup, \sqcup)\}$, and the cost of an arc $(a, b) \in E(D)$ is given by $cost_\gamma(a, b) = \gamma_{a \to b}$. See Fig. 2.

A sequence of arcs $P = (x_1, x_2), (x_2, x_3), \ldots, (x_{n-1}, x_n)$, for $x_i \in V(D)$, is a *walk* from x_1 to x_n, with *length* $|P| = n - 1$ and *cost* given by $cost_\gamma(P) =$

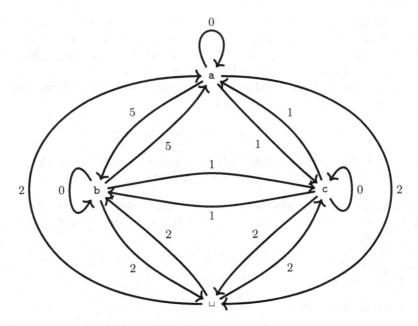

Fig. 2. Digraph $D(\gamma)$ with cost on its arcs given by γ, where γ is the matrix presented in Fig. 1.

$\sum_{i=1}^{n-1} \text{cost}_\gamma(x_i, x_{i+1})$. If $x_1 = x_n$, we say that P is a cycle, and if P is a cycle and $\text{cost}_\gamma(P) < 0$, we say that P is a *negative cycle*. An *optimal walk* from x_1 to x_n in $D(\gamma)$ is a minimum cost walk from x_1 to x_n in $D(\gamma)$ and we denote its cost by $\mathcal{P}_\gamma(x_1, x_n)$. When P and Q are walks from a to c and from c to b, respectively, we denote by PQ the walk from a to b obtained by concatenation of arcs in P and then in Q and we notice that $\text{cost}_\gamma(PQ) = \text{cost}_\gamma(P) + \text{cost}_\gamma(Q)$.

We can easily check that there exists no negative cycle in $D(\gamma)$ if and only if $\text{optE}_\gamma(s,t)$ is well-defined for any $s, t \in \Sigma^*$. Thus, we assume that $D(\gamma)$ does not have a negative cycle as a subgraph.

Finally, we say that a classical alignment $[s', t']$ *induces* an extended alignment $[s'(1)\ t'(1), \ldots, s'(n)\ t'(n)]$. Any classical alignment induces an extended alignment with same E_γ-score. This means that

$$A_\gamma([s', t']) = E_\gamma([s'(1)\ t'(1), \ldots, s'(n)\ t'(n)]), \tag{1}$$

for any $s, t \in \Sigma^*$. Hence, we have that

$$\text{optE}_\gamma(s, t) \leq \text{optA}_\gamma(s, t). \tag{2}$$

3   Computing Optimal Extended Alignments

In this section, we show how to compute an E_γ-optimal alignment for two given sequences. The main procedure is the preprocessing of the scoring matrix γ in order to obtain a second scoring matrix δ such that $\text{optE}_\gamma(s,t) = \text{optA}_\delta(s,t)$. Since we know efficient algorithms to solve Problem **MAS** [18], we must find matrix δ. Furthermore, we show an algorithm to obtain an E_γ-optimal alignment of sequences s,t from an A_δ-optimal alignment of s,t.

A scoring matrix δ is defined from the scoring matrix γ as follows. For each pair of symbols $a, b \in \Sigma_\sqcup$, we have that

$$\delta_{a \to b} = \mathcal{P}_\gamma(a,b), \qquad (3)$$

where $\mathcal{P}_\gamma(a,b)$ is a minimum cost walk from a to b in the digraph $D(\gamma)$.

The scoring matrix δ has the following properties.

Lemma 1. *Let Σ be an alphabet, γ be a scoring matrix such that the digraph $D(\gamma)$ has no negative cycle, and δ be a scoring matrix defined according to Eq. (3). Then,*

1. $\delta_{a \to a} = 0$, and
2. $\delta_{a \to b} \leq \delta_{a \to c} + \delta_{c \to b}$,

for any symbols $a, b, c \in \Sigma_\sqcup$.

Proof. First, suppose that $a \in \Sigma_\sqcup$. A walk with length zero has cost equal to zero and thus $\mathcal{P}_\gamma(a,a) \leq 0$. On the other hand, since $D(\gamma)$ has no negative cycles, $\mathcal{P}_\gamma(a,a) \geq 0$. Therefore, we conclude that $\mathcal{P}_\gamma(a,a) = 0$, which implies from Eq. (3) that $\delta_{a \to a} = \mathcal{P}_\gamma(a,a) = 0$.

Let $a, b, c \in \Sigma_\sqcup$ and suppose that P_1 and P_2 are optimal walks from a to c and from c to b, respectively. By Eq. (3), we have that $\text{cost}_\gamma(P_1) = \mathcal{P}_\gamma(a,c)$ and $\text{cost}_\gamma(P_2) = \mathcal{P}_\gamma(c,b)$. It follows that $\text{cost}_\gamma(P_1) = \mathcal{P}_\gamma(a,c) = \delta_{a \to c}$ and $\text{cost}_\gamma(P_2) = \mathcal{P}_\gamma(c,b) = \delta_{c \to b}$. Since P_1 and P_2 are walks from a to c and from c to b, $P_1 P_2$ is a walk from a to b and $\text{cost}_\gamma(P_1 P_2) = \text{cost}_\gamma(P_1) + \text{cost}_\gamma(P_2)$. Hence, since $\mathcal{P}_\gamma(a,b) \leq \text{cost}_\gamma(P_1 P_2)$ and by Eq. (3) we have $\delta_{a \to b} = \mathcal{P}_\gamma(a,b)$, it follows that

$$\delta_{a \to b} = \mathcal{P}_\gamma(a,b) \leq \text{cost}_\gamma(P_1 P_2) = \text{cost}_\gamma(P_1) + \text{cost}_\gamma(P_2) = \delta_{a \to c} + \delta_{c \to b}.$$

$\square$

Lemma 2. *Let Σ be an alphabet, γ be a scoring matrix such that $D(\gamma)$ has no negative cycles, δ be a scoring matrix defined from γ according to Eq. (3), and sequences $s, t \in \Sigma^*$. Then, there exists an E_δ-optimal alignment $[c_1, \ldots, c_n]$ that is induced by an A_δ-optimal alignment of s, t, i.e., $|c_j| = 2$ for each j.*

Proof. Let $A' = [c'_1, \ldots, c'_n]$ be an E_δ-optimal alignment and $A = [c_1, \ldots, c_n]$ be the extended alignment of s, t induced by the classical alignment

$$[(c'_1(1)c'_2(1) \cdots c'_n(1), c'_1(m_1)c'_2(m_2) \cdots c'_n(m_n))],$$

i.e., $c_j = c'_j(1)c'_j(m_j)$ for each j.

In order to prove this lemma, since $E_\delta(A') = \mathrm{optE}_\delta(s,t)$, it is enough to show that $E_\delta(A) \leq E_\delta(A')$ and to do this, it is enough to prove that $E_\delta(c_j) \leq E_\delta(c'_j)$ for an arbitrary $j \in \{1, 2, \ldots, n\}$. We consider two cases: $m_j = 1$ and $m_j > 1$.

Suppose that $m_j = 1$ and $c'_j = \mathtt{a}$. Trivially, we have that $E_\delta(c'_j) = 0$. Furthermore, since $D(\gamma)$ has no negative cycles, we have from Lemma 1 that $\delta_{\mathtt{a}\to\mathtt{a}} = 0$. Thus, $E_\delta(c_j = \mathtt{aa}) = \delta_{\mathtt{a}\to\mathtt{a}} = 0 = E_\delta(c'_j)$.

Now, suppose that $m_j > 1$. Since $D(\gamma)$ has no negative cycles, it follows from Lemma 1 that

$$
\begin{aligned}
E_\delta(c_j) = E_\delta(c'_j(1)c'_j(m_j)) &= \delta_{c'_j(1)\to c'_j(m_j)} \\
&\leq \delta_{c'_j(1)\to c'_j(2)} + \delta_{c'_j(2)\to c'_j(m_j)} \\
&\leq \delta_{c'_j(1)\to c'_j(2)} + \delta_{c'_j(2)\to c'_j(3)} + \delta_{c'_j(3)\to c'_j(m_j)} \leq \cdots \\
&\leq \sum_{i=1}^{m_j-1} \delta_{c'_j(i)\to c'_j(i+1)} = E_\delta(c'_j).
\end{aligned}
$$

$\square$

Now we can show the main results of this paper. Given two sequences s, t, we show that $\mathrm{optE}_\gamma(s,t) = \mathrm{optA}_\delta(s,t)$ and present a straightforward algorithm for finding an E_γ-optimal alignment of s, t.

Theorem 3. *Let Σ be an alphabet, γ be a scoring matrix such that $D(\gamma)$ has no negative cycles, δ be a scoring matrix defined from γ according to Eq. (3), and $s, t \in \Sigma^*$. Then, $\mathrm{optE}_\gamma(s,t) = \mathrm{optA}_\delta(s,t)$. Furthermore, let $[s', t']$ be an A_δ-optimal alignment of s, t, $|[s', t']| = n$. Then, we also have that*

$$
C = [\mathcal{C}_\gamma(s'(1), t'(1)), \ldots, \mathcal{C}_\gamma(s'(n), t'(n))]
$$

is an E_γ-optimal alignment of s, t, where $\mathcal{C}_\gamma(x, y)$ is an optimal walk from x to y in $D(\gamma)$.

Proof. From Lemma 2, there exists an E_δ-optimal extended alignment A of s, t, that is the alignment induced by a classical alignment A' of s, t. Since, by Eq. (1), $E_\delta(A) = A_\delta(A')$, it follows that

$$
\mathrm{optE}_\delta(s,t) = E_\delta(A) = A_\delta(A') \geq \mathrm{optA}_\delta(s,t).
$$

Moreover, by Eq. (2), we have that $\mathrm{optE}_\delta(s,t) \leq \mathrm{optA}_\delta(s,t)$. Therefore, $\mathrm{optE}_\delta(s,t) = \mathrm{optA}_\delta(s,t)$. Since $[s', t']$ is an A_δ-optimal alignment of s, t, it follows that $A = [s'(1)t'(1), \ldots, s'(n)t'(n)]$ is an E_δ-optimal alignment of s, t.

Now, suppose that $B = [c_1, \ldots, c_r]$ is an E_γ-optimal alignment of s, t. Since $E_\gamma(c_j)$ is the cost of a walk from $c_j(1)$ to $c_j(m_j)$ in $D(\gamma)$ and $\mathcal{P}_\gamma(c_j(1), c_j(m_j))$ is a cost of an optimal walk from $c_j(1)$ to $c_j(m_j)$ in $D(\gamma)$ for an arbitrary integer j, we have that $E_\gamma(c_j) \geq \mathcal{P}_\gamma(c_j(1), c_j(m_j))$. The E_δ-score of extended alignment $[c_1(1)c_1(m_1), \ldots, c_r(1)c_r(m_r)]$ of s, t is $\sum_j \delta_{c_j(1)\to c_j(m_j)}$ and, by Eq. (3), $\mathcal{P}_\gamma(c_j(1), c_j(m_j)) = \delta_{c_j(1)\to c_j(m_j)}$. It follows that

$$\text{optE}_\gamma(s,t) = \text{E}_\gamma(B) = \sum_j \text{E}_\gamma(c_j) \geq \sum_j \mathcal{P}_\gamma(c_j(1), c_j(m_j)) = \sum_j \delta_{c_j(1) \to c_j(m_j)}$$
$$= \text{E}_\delta\left([c_1(1)c_1(m_1), \ldots, c_r(1)c_r(m_r)]\right)$$
$$\geq \text{optE}_\delta(s,t). \tag{4}$$

On the other hand, the extended alignment C obtained from the alignment A replacing each column $s'(j)t'(j)$ by a sequence of symbols $\mathcal{C}_\gamma(s'(j), t'(j))$, is an extended alignment of s, t whose E_γ-score is also $\text{E}_\delta([s'(1)t'(1), \ldots, s'(n)t'(n)]$. Since $[s'(1)t'(1), \ldots, s'(n)t'(n)]$ is an E_δ-optimal alignment of s, t, it follows that

$$\text{optE}_\delta(s,t) = \text{E}_\delta([s'(1)t'(1), \ldots, s'(n)t'(n)]$$
$$= \text{E}_\gamma(C = [\mathcal{C}_\gamma(s'(1), t'(1)), \ldots, \mathcal{C}_\gamma(s'(n), t'(n))]) \geq \text{optE}_\gamma(s,t). \tag{5}$$

From $\text{optE}_\delta(s,t) = \text{optA}_\delta(s,t)$ and Eqs. (4) and (5), we conclude that $\text{optE}_\gamma(s,t) = \text{optA}_\delta(s,t)$. We also conclude by construction that C is an E_γ-optimal alignment of s, t. $\qquad\square$

As a consequence of Theorem 3, we can compute $\text{optE}_\gamma(s,t)$ using an algorithm that obtains $\text{optA}_\delta(s,t)$, spending additional time only for computing the scoring matrix δ.

As an example, suppose that

γ	a	b	c	d	⊔
a	2	1	3	4	7
b	3	3	−1	1	1
c	2	4	0	5	8
d	9	7	8	0	2
⊔	3	7	50	6	

is a scoring matrix and $s = \text{addd}$ and $t = \text{acddaaa}$ are given sequences. We want to find a minimum weight sequence of editing operations that transforms s into t. Figure 3 shows the subgraph of $D(\gamma)$ containing the arcs (x, y) that are in optimal walks in $D(\gamma)$ and a minimal walks connecting each pair of vertices.

Using Eq. (3) and an algorithm to solve Problem **MAS**, we obtain

	a	b	c	d	⊔
a	0	1	0	2	2
b	1	0	−1	1	1
c	2	3	0	4	4
d	5	6	5	0	2
⊔	3	4	3	5	0

and

$$\begin{bmatrix} \text{a} & \text{⊔} & \text{d} & \text{d} & \text{d} & \text{⊔} \\ \text{a} & \text{c} & \text{d} & \text{d} & \text{a} & \text{a} \end{bmatrix},$$

which are a scoring matrix δ and an A_δ-optimal alignment of $\text{addd}, \text{acddaaa}$, respectively. Thus, $\text{optA}_\delta(\text{addd}, \text{acddaaa}) = 11$. Finally, using Theorem 3, we obtain an E_γ-optimal alignment

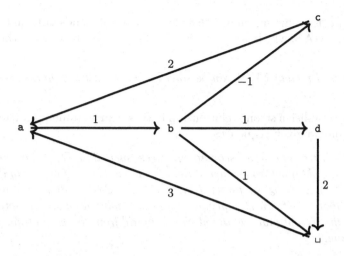

	a	b	c	d	⊔
a	a	a → b	a → b → c	a → b → c	a → b → c
b	b → c → a	b	b → c	b → d	b → ⊔
c	c → a	c → a → b	c	c → a → b → d	c → a → b → ⊔
d	d → ⊔ → a	d → ⊔ → a → b	d → ⊔ → a → c	d	d → ⊔
⊔	⊔ → a	⊔ → a → b	⊔ → a → b → c	⊔ → a → b → d	

Fig. 3. A subgraph of $D(\gamma)$ containing the edges (x, y) that are optimal walks in $D(\gamma)$. The table below shows a minimal walk connecting vertices which are useful for construct the extended alignment.

$$A = \begin{bmatrix} a & \begin{matrix} ⊔ \\ a \\ b \\ c \end{matrix} & d & d & \begin{matrix} d \\ ⊔ \\ a \end{matrix} & \begin{matrix} ⊔ \\ a \end{matrix} \end{bmatrix}$$

such that $\mathrm{E}_\gamma(A) = 11$.

3.1 Running Time and Complexity

In order to compute matrix δ, it is enough to solve the well-known *all-pairs shortest paths problem* for the digraph $D(\gamma)$. Since $D(\gamma)$ does not have negative cycles, we can use Floyd-Warshall algorithm [9, 24], whose time and space complexities are $\Theta(|\Sigma|^3)$, i.e., depend only on the size of the alphabet Σ. Since alphabet Σ does not belong to the instance of **MES**, the preprocessing running time is $\Theta(1)$. In addition, Floyd-Warshall algorithm can also compute a useful structure to obtain optimal walks in $D(\gamma)$ without spending extra time. This structure can be used for obtaining the pairwise extended sequence alignment, again without spending extra time.

Therefore, the running time of the whole process depends only on the running time to solve **MAS**, which is quadratic [21]. This allows us to claim the following result.

Theorem 4. *Problem* **MES** *can be solved in* $O(n^2)$ *time, where* n *is the length of an instance* s, t.

Now we establish a strong relationship between an alignment and an extended alignment of two given sequences.

Lemma 5. *Let* γ *and* δ *be scoring matrices such that* $D(\gamma)$ *has no negative cycles and* δ *is obtained from* γ *using Eq. (3). Then,* $\delta = \gamma$ *if and only if* $\gamma_{a \to a} = 0$ *and* $\gamma_{a \to b} \le \gamma_{a \to c} + \gamma_{c \to b}$, *for each* $a, b, c \in \Sigma$. *Besides that, for any pair of sequences, there exists an* E_γ-*optimal alignment induced by an* A_δ-*optimal alignment, and the* A_δ-*optimal alignment can be found from the* E_γ-*optimal alignment in* $O(n)$ *time.*

Proof. Suppose that $\gamma = \delta$. We have $\delta_{a \to a} = 0$ and $\delta_{a \to b} \le \delta_{a \to c} + \delta_{c \to b}$ for each $a, b, c \in \Sigma$ from Lemma 1, which implies that $\gamma_{a \to a} = 0$ and $\gamma_{a \to b} \le \gamma_{a \to c} + \gamma_{c \to b}$ for each $a, b, c \in \Sigma$.

Conversely, suppose that $\gamma_{a \to a} = 0$ and $\gamma_{a \to b} \le \gamma_{a \to c} + \gamma_{c \to b}$ for each $a, b, c \in \Sigma$ and, by contradiction, $\gamma_{a \to a} \ne \delta_{a \to a}$ or $\gamma_{a \to b} \ne \delta_{a \to b}$ for each $a, b \in \Sigma$. Since $\delta_{a \to a} = 0$ from Lemma 1 we have that $\delta_{a \to a} = 0 = \gamma_{a \to a}$. Thus, we assume that $\gamma_{a \to b} \ne \delta_{a \to b}$. Since $\gamma_{a \to b}$ is the cost of edge (a, b) and $\delta_{a \to b}$ is the cost of minimum cost walk from a to b, $\gamma_{a \to b}$ cannot be smaller than $\delta_{a \to b}$ which implies, since $\gamma_{a \to b} \ne \delta_{a \to b}$, that $\gamma_{a \to b} > \delta_{a \to b}$. Let $(a = x_1, x_2), (x_2, x_3), \ldots, (x_{m-1}, x_m = b)$ an walk with minimum cost, i.e., $\delta_{a \to b} = \gamma_{x_1 \to x_2} + \gamma_{x_2 \to x_3} + \ldots + \gamma_{x_{m-1} \to x_m}$. Since $\gamma_{a \to b} \le \gamma_{a \to c} + \gamma_{c \to b}$ for each $a, b, c \in \Sigma$, it follows that

$$\delta_{a \to b} = \gamma_{a \to x_2} + \gamma_{x_2 \to x_3} + \ldots + \gamma_{x_{m-1} \to b}$$
$$\ge \gamma_{a \to x_3} + \ldots + \gamma_{x_{m-1} \to b} \ge \gamma_{a \to b},$$

contradicting $\gamma_{a \to b} > \delta_{a \to b}$. Therefore, $\gamma_{a \to a} = \delta_{a \to a}$ and $\gamma_{a \to b} = \delta_{a \to b}$ for each $a, b \in \Sigma$.

Since $\gamma = \delta$ and δ is obtained from Eq. (3), it follows from Lemma 2, that there exists an E_γ-optimal alignment $A = [s'(1)t'(1), \ldots, s'(m)t'(m)]$ that is induced by an A_γ-optimal alignment $[s'(1) \ldots s'(m), \ldots, t'(1)t'(m)]$ of s, t whose length is $m = O(n)$ and that clearly can be found from A in $O(n)$ time. $\square$

Finally, we present a discussion on the complexity of **MES**. Backurs and Indik [4] showed that the Levenshtein problem cannot be computed in $O(n^{2-\varepsilon})$ time, for some constant $\varepsilon > 0$, unless the Strong Exponential Time Hypothesis (SETH) if false. In this case, the scoring matrix γ is a metric on Σ, which implies that $\gamma_{a \to a} = 0$ and $\gamma_{a \to b} \le \gamma_{a \to c} + \gamma_{c \to b}$, for each $a, b, c \in \Sigma$. Thus, from Lemma 5, we have that an A_γ-optimal alignment can be found from an E_γ-optimal alignment spending $O(n)$ extra time. Therefore, if there exists an algorithm A to solve **MES** in $O(n^{2-\varepsilon})$ time, for some $\varepsilon > 0$, then algorithm A could be used to solve **MAS** in $O(n^{2-\varepsilon}) + O(n)$ time, and therefore SETH is false. Thus, we can state the following.

Theorem 6. *There exists no strongly subquadratic algorithm to solve* **MES**, *unless SETH is false.*

4 Conclusion

In this paper we present a more general structure to represent any sequence of editing operations that transforms one given sequence into another given sequence, the so called extended pairwise sequence alignment. We show a straightforward and efficient algorithm to find an optimal extended pairwise sequence alignment and prove that there exists no strongly subquadratic algorithm to solve it, unless SETH is false.

This approach has potential to explain non-trivial evolutionary models in Molecular Biology, in applications such as those involving adaptive and back mutations. Theoretically, this proposed setting can be used especially when the triangle inequality does not hold for the distance between the sequences.

Experiments on simulated and real data for the extended pairwise sequence alignment, in comparison to the classical pairwise sequence alignment, can enrich this work and will be considered in our future steps.

Acknowledgments. The authors thank José Augusto Ramos Soares, Said Sadique Adi, and Vagner Pedrotti for valuable discussions on this topic.

References

1. Altschul, S.F., Gish, W., Miller, W., Myers, E.W., Lipman, D.J.: Basic local alignment search tool. J. Mol. Biol. **215**(3), 403–410 (1990)
2. Araujo, E., Martinez, F.V., Higa, C.H.A., Soares, J.: Matrices inducing generalized metric on sequences. Discrete Appl. Math. (2023, to appear)
3. Araujo, E., Rozante, L.C., Rubert, D.P., Martinez, F.V.: Algorithms for normalized multiple sequence alignments. In: Proceedings of ISAAC. LIPIcs, vol. 212, pp. 40:1–40:16 (2021)
4. Backurs, A., Indyk, P.: Edit distance cannot be computed in strongly subquadratic time (unless SETH is false). In: Proceedings of STOC, pp. 51–58 (2015)
5. Barton, C., Flouri, T., Iliopoulos, C.S., Pissis, S.P.: Global and local sequence alignment with a bounded number of gaps. Theor. Comput. Sci. **582**, 1–16 (2015)
6. Chaurasiya, R.K., Londhe, N.D., Ghosh, S.: A novel weighted edit distance-based spelling correction approach for improving the reliability of Devanagari script-based P300 speller system. IEEE Access **4**, 8184–8198 (2016)
7. Chenna, R., et al.: Multiple sequence alignment with the Clustal series of programs. Nucleic Acids Res. **31**(13), 3497–3500 (2003)
8. Fisman, D., Grogin, J., Margalit, O., Weiss, G.: The Normalized Edit Distance with Uniform Operation Costs is a Metric. arXiv:2201.06115 (2022)
9. Floyd, R.: Algorithm 97: shortest path. Commun. ACM **5**(6), 345 (1962)
10. Foster, P.: Adaptive mutation in Escherichia coli. J. Bacteriol. **186**(15), 4846–4852 (2004)
11. de la Higuera, C., Micó, L.: A contextual normalised edit distance. In: Proceedings of ICDEW, pp. 354–361. IEEE (2008)

12. Karplus, K., Barrett, C., Hughey, R.: Hidden Markov models for detecting remote protein homologies. Bioinformatics **14**(10), 846–856 (1998)
13. Levenshtein, V.: Binary codes capable of correcting deletions, insertions and reversals. Sov. Phys. Doklady **10**(8), 707–710 (1966)
14. Lipman, D.J., Altschul, S.F., Kececioglu, J.D.: A tool for multiple sequence alignment. PNAS **86**(12), 4412–4415 (1989)
15. Lipman, D.J., Pearson, W.R.: Rapid and sensitive protein similarity searches. Science **227**(4693), 1435–1441 (1985)
16. Ichinose, M., Iizuka, M., Kusumi, J., Takefu, M.: Models of compensatory molecular evolution: effects of back mutation. J. Theor. Biol. **323**(0), 1–10 (2013)
17. Marzal, A., Vidal, E.: Computation of normalized edit distance and applications. IEEE T. Pattern Anal. **15**(9), 926–932 (1993)
18. Needleman, S.B., Wunsch, C.D.: A general method applicable to the search for similarities in the amino acid sequence of two proteins. J. Mol. Biol. **48**(3), 443–453 (1970)
19. Notredame, C., Higgins, D.G., Heringa, J.: T-Coffee: a novel method for fast and accurate multiple sequence alignment. J. Mol. Biol. **302**(1), 205–217 (2000)
20. Rosenberg, S.: Evolving responsively: adaptive mutation. Nat. Rev. Genet. **2**, 504–515 (2001)
21. Setubal, J.C., Meidanis, J.: Introduction to Computational Molecular Biology. PWS Pub. (1997)
22. Smith, T.F., Waterman, M.S.: Identification of common molecular subsequences. J. Mol. Biol. **147**(1), 195–197 (1981)
23. Sun, Y., et al.: ICDAR 2019 competition on large-scale street view text with partial labeling-RRC-LSVT. In: Proceedings of ICDAR, pp. 1557–1562. IEEE (2019)
24. Warshall, S.: A theorem on Boolean matrices. J. ACM **9**(1), 11–12 (1962)
25. Yujian, L., Bo, L.: A normalized Levenshtein distance metric. IEEE T. Pattern Anal. **29**(6), 1091–1095 (2007)

Exploring Machine Learning Algorithms and Numerical Representations Strategies to Develop Sequence-Based Predictive Models for Protein Networks

David Medina-Ortiz[1]([⊠]), Pedro Salinas[2], Gabriel Cabas-Moras[1], Fabio Durán-Verdugo[2], Álvaro Olivera-Nappa[3], and Roberto Uribe-Paredes[1]

[1] Departamento de Ingeniería en Computación, Universidad de Magallanes, Av. Pdte. Manuel Bulnes, 01855 Punta Arenas, Chile
david.medina@umag.cl

[2] Escuela de Ingeniería en Bioinformática, Universidad de Talca, Av. Lircay S/N, Talca, Chile

[3] Departamento de Ingeniería Química, Biotecnología y Materiales, Universidad de Chile, Beauche 851, Santiago, Chile

Abstract. Predicting the affinity between two proteins is one of the most relevant challenges in bioinformatics and one of the most useful for biotechnological and pharmaceutical applications. Current prediction methods use the structural information of the interaction complexes. However, predicting the structure of proteins requires enormous computational costs. Machine learning methods emerge as an alternative to this bioinformatics challenge. There are predictive methods for protein affinity based on structural information. However, for linear information, there are no development guidelines for elaborating predictive models, being necessary to explore several alternatives for processing and developing predictive models. This work explores different options for building predictive protein interaction models via deep learning architectures and classical machine learning algorithms, evaluating numerical representation methods and transformation techniques to represent structural complexes using linear information. Six types of predictive tasks related to the affinity and mutational variant evaluations and their effect on the interaction complex were explored. We show that classical machine learning and convolutional network-based methods perform better than graph convolutional network methods for studying mutational variants. In contrast, graph-based methods perform better on affinity problems or association constants, using only the linear information of the protein sequences. Finally, we show an illustrative use case, expose how to use the developed models, discuss the limitations of the explored methods and comment on future development strategies for improving the studied processes.

Keywords: Protein networks · machine learning algorithms · protein language models · protein discovery · deep learning architectures

© The Author(s), under exclusive license to Springer Nature Switzerland AG 2023
O. Gervasi et al. (Eds.): ICCSA 2023, LNCS 13956, pp. 231–244, 2023.
https://doi.org/10.1007/978-3-031-36805-9_16

1   Introduction

Protein interaction networks allow understanding and identifying relationship patterns between proteins used in biotechnology, bioinformatics, drug discovery, and drug repurposing [8,21,31]. The affinity between proteins and ligands could be improved by combining bioinformatic approaches with protein engineering techniques, like directed evolution or rational design, benefiting pharmaceutical and industrial applications [13,30]. Furthermore, measuring changes in the stability of interaction complexes, evaluating biochemical constants such as dissociation, and recording rates of relatedness between two proteins foster information enrichment and facilitate the development of more complex methodologies benefiting the protein engineering applications [7,30].

Protein interaction network databases provide information on proteins and their interactors. Intact [14] and STRING [25] are two databases that present information on protein-protein interactions based on likelihood estimated using the number of reports in the literature. The use of a likelihood value is an ambiguous method when evaluating the level of affinity between two proteins. In addition, Intact and STRING do not have negative information, i.e., it cannot be assumed that if two proteins are not registered as interacting, they do not present interactions. As alternatives, databases such as PDBbind [27] and Pip [2] provide quantitative values that allow evaluating the interaction affinity between two proteins. Databases such as PROXiMATE [12] and SKEMPI [11] give knowledge on the changes in stability produced by mutations on the interaction complexes, evaluating different biochemical constants and the effects of association and dissociation.

Computational methods have been developed for constructing interaction predictive systems between two proteins using the information reported in biological databases. Classical approaches are based on molecular dynamics to study the affinity between proteins, employing tools like Autodock vina [6], InterEvDock [29], and ZDock [23]. The application of molecular dynamics methods implies a high computational cost and having the three-dimensional structures of the proteins to be evaluated, not applying to a study of latent space navigation and landscape reconstruction. Thanks to the constant growth of data reported in the literature, predictive systems via machine learning techniques have acquired a more significant role in recent years [5].

Commonly, machine learning methods use structural information to train predictive models, applying both interaction complexes [28], 3D-voxel box strategies, and using data from techniques such as molecular docking or dynamics obtained from molecular simulations [1,9]. In general, the methods apply deep learning architectures based on convolutional neural networks (CNN) [10,32], recurrent neural networks (RNN) [20,33], or long short-term memory (LSTM) [15,26].

Constructing interaction affinity predictive systems using only linear information is a current problem, and there are no established solutions or development guides with straightforward methods for elaborating these predictive systems. One of the significant challenges during the training of predictive models via linear information of protein sequences consists of the numerical representation of protein sequence. Methods such as amino acid encodings based on physicochemical properties have been proposed [17]. In addition, the use of Fourier transforms for spatial transformations has been explored, allowing elaborate representations that emulate the structural behaviors of proteins [3,17,24]. Recently, representation learning methods based on Natural Language Processing (NLP) techniques have been studied, giving birth to different pre-trained models and computational tools such as bio-embedding [4], TAPE [22], or ECNet [16]. However, there is yet to be a clear alternative for employing these methods. On other hands, to represent the complex structure in protein interactions problems is commonly to apply concatenation strategies not being explored transformations and combinations strategies through techniques such as Principal Component Analysis.

This work explores different machine learning strategies for developing predictive models for protein-protein interaction using linear sequences. First, different coding methods are implemented to represent protein sequences numerically. Then, CNN and graph convolutional networks (GCN) architectures are designed for training predictive models, and classical supervised learning algorithms such as Random Forest (RF) and support vector machine (SVM) are trained. Alternatively, post-processing strategies for the linear representation of structural complexes via applying principal component analysis (PCA) or nonlinear combinations are analyzed. Each model is evaluated using metrics such as mean squared error (MSE) and R^2 score. The evaluated strategies are compared to determine common strategies to develop guidelines to build predictive models.

The evaluation of the methodologies was developed by studying six datasets collected from databases such as PROXiMATE or SKEMPI, demonstrating that classical machine learning methods and models via CNN outperform GCN models in problems related to changes in kinetic constants in mutational change evaluation. At the same time, predictive systems based on GCN architectures perform better in affinity problems or association constants between proteins, acquiring better learning of hidden patterns than CNN or classical machine learning methods. Finally, we show a use case of predictive model development via CNN and how the model is used to obtain predictions. Finally, we discuss the presented methods' limitations, future work, and possible development applications.

2 Methods

This section will describe the different methodologies developed to meet the objectives of this work, considering the stages of data collection, data processing, numerical representation strategies, training, and validation of predictive models.

2.1 Collecting and Processing Datasets

The PROXiMATE and SKEMPI databases were used to search affinity values in protein-protein interactions, protein complex with point mutations or mutational variants and the effects caused by mutational changes in terms of kinetic constants, affinity, and other properties commonly applied in biochemical studies for the study of interactions in protein complexes. All records were downloaded manually using the download options available on each database. Then, the datasets were built using the downloaded records, and processed by a classical cleanup of removal of unreported records and statistical methods to detect outliers in the reported responses and the lengths of the protein sequences, to facilitate the application of numerical representation strategies.

2.2 Numerical Representation Strategies of Protein Sequences

For the numerical representations of protein sequences, three strategies were employed. The first was based on amino acid encodings using physicochemical properties reported in [17]. The second consisted of applying spatial transformations employing FFT following the basis reported in [3,17,24], which indicates that any set represented by codings based on amino acidic properties can be transformed via FFT. As a requirement for the application of FFT, the sequences encoded via physicochemical properties were manipulated so that they all had the same length by applying *zero-padding*, resulting in numerical vectors of maximum size 1024 after the application of FFT. The third strategy was the application of pre-trained protein language models. For this purpose, the glove, one-hot, bepler, and fasttext models, enabled in the bio-embedding tool [4], were used. When applying these models, it is unnecessary to manipulate sequence sizes or use *zero-padding*. However, as a requirement, a maximum length of amino acids per sequence, which consists of 1024, is required, thus agreeing with the application of the methods based on amino acid coding. This work did not explore strategies such as one hot encoding or sequence description, since we wanted to analyze the effect of amino acid encodings v/s representations based on NLP learning models.

2.3 Building Datasets to Train Predictive Models

The following strategy was developed to generate input datasets for predictive model training. First, interaction sequences were concatenated according to literature reports before the numerical representation strategy was applied. Then, transformation methods were implemented to explore the effect of linear and nonlinear combinations of the initial inputs using PCA and kernel-PCA methods, resulting in three matrices for each representation strategy: i) simple concatenation, ii) application of PCA after concatenation, and iii) application of kernel-PCA post concatenation. These matrices were employed as input for training predictive models based on CNN architectures and classical supervised learning algorithms. In the case of datasets for the development of predictive models based on graph architectures, datasets were constructed to represent interactions and edge weights (this value being the model response and the desired value to predict). Matrices with the unique protein sequences existing in the dataset are numerically represented by all the numerical representation strategies explored in this work.

2.4   Implementation Strategies of Preprocessing and Predictive Models and Execution Process

The data preprocessing strategies were implemented using Python v3.8 programming language and employing classic dataset management modules such as Pandas or Numpy. In the case of predictive model training, the scikit-learn library was used for the application of classical machine learning algorithms. The predictive models built via convolutional neural network architectures were implemented using the TensorFlow framework. For the predictive models based on graph convolutional network architectures, the Torch framework was used. The optimization of the training and data processing runs was done using GPUs and configuring the libraries for their use. A machine processed all model training runs with Linux operating system, Arch distribution, with the following characteristics: i) Processor: AMD Ryzen 7 6800H, 3.2 GHz up to 4.7 GHz, ii) Core numbers: Octa Core, iii) Memory: 16 GB DDR5-SDRAM 4800 MHz (2×8 GB) 2 Slot, iv) Storage: 512 GB SSD NVMe, PCI Express 4.0 M.2, Graphic card: NVIDIA GeForce RTX 3060 (6 GB GDDR6). A conda environment with all the requirements is enabled to facilitate the replication of the experiments and the evaluation of the generated implementation. The source code is available for non-commercial use, licensed under the GPL-3.0 license at the following URL https://github.com/ProteinEngineering-PESB2/protein-interactions-models to facilitate the replication of the experiments and the evaluation of the generated implementation.

3   Results and Discussions

This section describes the main results obtained and discusses the methodologies evaluated, contemplating both the evaluation of the machine learning algorithms and the strategies for the numerical representation of protein sequences assessed in this work. Finally, a use case is presented to demonstrate how to apply the methodologies for developing predictive models of interaction affinity in protein complexes.

3.1   Exploring Datasets and Numerical Representation Strategies

A total of six protein interaction datasets were built in this work (See Table 1). Three of the datasets contain protein-protein affinity information, and three have information on mutational changes and their effect on interaction complexes estimated in responses such as free energy difference (PROXiMATE-dg dataset) and kinetic constants (PROXiMATE-kd and SKEMPI-koff, PROXiMATE-kon and SKEMPI-kon datasets). Datasets from databases such as intact or STRING were discarded because they present only positive interactions, not contemplating knowledge of negative interactions, implying that the construction of classification models in the lack of negative responses would not make sense. In addition, it was desired to explore the existence of generalities in applying numerical representation methods and predictive model development strategies, so it was preferred to explore varied datasets with reported and experimentally validated responses. All sequences were coded independently using the selected representation strategies, and data sets were generated by concatenating both proteins according to the interaction reported in the data sets used. Once the sequences were represented numerically, two additional strategies were applied to process or describe interactions from a linear point of view (only using the information of the protein sequences that interact with each other). In the first strategy, dimensionality reduction methods were applied via Principal component analysis (PCA) as a transformation strategy and development of descriptors via linear combinations of the initial points of each vector. Similarly, the second strategy applied kernel-PCA methods to ensure spatial transformations in nonlinear combinations. Thus, for each data set, three ways of representing the interaction were devised (concatenation, linear combinations, and nonlinear combinations), generating 60 alternatives to train for each dataset.

Table 1. Description of the datasets employed in this work

#	Dataset	Number of examples	Task	Reference
1	PROXiMATE-dg	2496	Evaluation of free energy differences	[12]
2	PROXiMATE-kd	2495	Estimation of kinetic constants	[12]
3	PROXiMATE-kon	561	Estimation of kinetic constants	[12]
4	SKEMPI-kon	855	Estimation of kinetic constants	[11]
5	SKEMPI-koff	860	Estimation of kinetic constants	[11]
6	SKEMPI-affinity	3180	Prediction of affinity between protein sequences	[11]

3.2 Training Predictive Models via Classic Machine Learning Algorithms and Deep Learning Architectures

Each dataset was trained by applying classical predictive model training algorithms such as support vector machine, KNN, decision tree, Bagging, Random Forest, AdaBoost, and Gradient tree boost, each with default hyperparameters following a classic training pipeline [18,19]. Besides, deep learning architectures based on convolutional neural networks were explored, summarized in Table 2. Finally, in the case of models trained via GCN methods, a two-block architecture was designed combining GCN and batch normalization layers, activated by a ReLU activation function and a learning layer based on linear methods, which varied the number of hidden layers between 5 and 30. Combining the three strategies explored, we have 17 predictive model development methods. Considering the 60 processed datasets, a total of 1020 trained models were evaluated in this work.

All generated models were evaluated applying classical performance metrics like MSE and R^2 score. Figure 1 shows the MSE (Mean squared error) distribution for all tasks evaluated in the three predictive model training strategies. The

Table 2. CNN architectures designed for exploring predictive models in protein-protein network tasks

Architecture	Pattern extraction configuration	Learning configuration	Optimization	Loss Function
A	A block of three Conv1D layers with MaxPooling activated by ReLU function	Two dense layers activated by tanh and linear functions	Adam	MSE
B	A block of three Conv1D layers with MaxPooling and dropout, activated by ReLU function	Two dense layers activated by tanh and linear functions	Adam	MSE
C	Pattern extraction blocks of two Conv1D and one MaxPooling, activated with ReLU function	One dense layer activated by linear function	Adam	MSE
D	Pattern extraction blocks of two Conv1D, one MaxPooling, and one droput, activated with ReLU function	One dense layer activated by linear function	Adam	MSE

results obtained by the classical machine learning application present a better performance than those obtained by the GCN and CNN architectures. However, when analyzing the best performances individually for each task, differences are observed between the method or strategy that achieves the best performance. Table 3 summarizes the best models for each dataset explored with each methodology evaluated.

Developing predictive models by applying pre-trained models for protein sequence representation achieves better performance when applying classical machine learning algorithms. However, using protein language model strategies in CNN or GCN architectures only achieves better results than using descriptors based on physicochemical properties. In the case of amino acid coding methods, better performance results were observed when combined with FFT for signal space representations and transformed into variance maximization spaces using techniques such as PCA or kernel-PCA, which was observed in the different tasks, both for classical machine learning and CNN methods. In the case of predictive models based on GCN architectures, there are significant differences in tasks such as affinity estimation compared to classical machine learning and CNN methods, achieving R^2 score performances above 0.8.

When evaluating the explored methods in terms of tasks and strategies, no marked results allow for generating a guide of recommendations for constructing predictive models. However, some considerations can be generalized. In the case of estimating and predicting association rates, CNN or classical machine learning methods achieve better performance than GCN. In this work, differences were found between the results concerning the prediction models of changes in association rate constants since SKEMPI-Kon and PROXiMATE-Kon datasets present the exact type of measurements with different measurement strategies and with other records, not being feasible to unify them for the training of a single model. However, it can be seen that as the number of records increases,

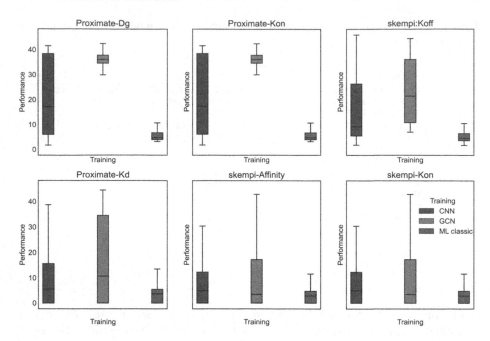

Fig. 1. Performances obtained for the predictive models in the six evaluated tasks for the three development strategies used to build predictive models. The methods explored in this work are summarized in performance distributions using boxplot visualization. The GCN and CNN methods present higher MSE distributions than the classical machine learning methods. Regarding distribution, CNN methods do not show significant differences compared to GCN methods. However, there tends to be a better performance in CNN methods. When analyzing the best versions of the models in each task, it is observed that there is no tendency for a specific process. However, in the cases of mutation evaluation and its effect on the interaction complex, CNN methods show better results than GCN methods. On the other hand, in protein interaction affinity methods, predictive models based on GCN achieve better performance and greater generalization of learning

deep learning methods are favored in terms of performance compared to classical machine learning methods, which is related to the generalization of behaviors, and the number of records in the dataset plays a crucial role in the training stages via deep learning methods. The GCN methods achieved the best performances with the same architecture in the affinity cases. However, the characterization or representation strategies of the nodes varied between amino acid encoders via physicochemical properties and numerical representations via pre-trained models.

The performances achieved by these models are similar, so employing GCN-based strategies for training this type of model allows the learning of the existing relationships between positive and negative interactions. However, further studies are required to discover and interpret these patterns from a biological point

Table 3. Summary of the best models for the explored tasks, evaluating the three strategies employed to develop predictive models

Task	Training strategy	Description	R2 performance
Proximiate-Dg	ML classic	OneHot as pretrained model and Random Forest as supervised learning algorithm	0.92
	CNN methods	**Hydropathy as encoder combined with PCA representations and using A architecture**	**0.94**
	GCN methods	Alpha structure combined with FFT transformation and 15 hidden layers in the created architecture	0.31
PROXiMATE-Kon	**ML classic**	**Bepler as pretrained model and Decision tree as supervised learning algorithm**	**0.72**
	CNN methods	Alpha structure as encoder combined with FFT representations and kernel-PCA as transformation and using D architecture	0.41
	GCN methods	Secondary structure as encoder and 15 hidden layers in the created architecture	0.01
SKEMPI-Koff	**ML classic**	**Alpha structure property as encoder combined with PCA transformation and Random Forest as supervised learning**	**0.85**
	CNN methods	Volume as encoder combined with FFT representations and PCA transformations and using D architecture	0.76
	GCN methods	Beta structure as encoder and 10 hidden layers in the created architecture	0.76
PROXiMATE-Kd	ML classic	Glove as pretrained model and Decision tree as supervised learning algorithm	0.76
	CNN methods	Bepler as pretrained models and architecture A to train the predictive model	0.26
	GCN methods	**Bepler as pretrained model and 20 hidden layers in the created architecture**	**0.88**
SKEMPI-Affinity	ML classic	Encoder Hydrophobicity combined with FFT applications and AdaBoost as supervised learning algorithm	0.05
	CNN methods	Fasttext as pretrained model and architecture A to train the predictive model	0.01
	GCN methods	**Secondary structure as encoder and 20 hidden layers in the created architecture**	**0.87**
SKEMPI-Kon	ML classic	Bepler pretrained models and KNN as supervised learning algorithm,	0.64
	CNN methods	**Secondary structure as encoder combined with FFT applications and kernel-PCA transformation and using the architecture C**	**0.72**
	GCN methods	Energetic as encoder strategy and 30 hidden layers in the created architecture	0.01

of view. Finally, in the case of mutation-related tasks, classical machine learning and CNN methods perform better than NGS methods in the case of tasks related to PROXiMATE-Dg, PROXiMATE-Kon, and PROXiMATE-Kd. However, the representation strategy needs clear patterns, which require evaluation and exploration to design the best models.

The effect of epochs was analyzed for the GCN methods in two models with the highest performance and a predictive model with the worst performance compared to the rest of the models developed. The different representation strategies are analyzed, and the epochs needed to present no significant changes in learning are compared. Figure 2 A shows the learning progress regarding epochs and the decrease in error for the loss function used in the GCN methods, and Fig. 2 B shows a zoom between the epochs 10 and 40 for the tasks SKEMPI-

Affinity and PROXiMATE-Kd. The predictive models for estimating protein interaction affinity (SKEMPI-affinity) and association constants (PROXiMATE-Kd) achieve learning and lower the prediction error in a minimum number of epochs, whereas the models for estimating interaction complex stability changes (PROXiMATE-Dg) exhibit higher instability in their learning, presenting perturbations during the process for all three types of protein representations. However, from epoch 70 onwards, a stabilization of the error is observed, except for the NLP-based methods, which continue to present variations during the process. With this information, it can be mentioned that FFT and NLP-based representations generate a positive synergy for affinity estimation problems and the use of predictive model training via GCN architectures, promoting better performance compared to classical methods and GCN architectures, which was also observed in Table 3. In the case of SKEMPI-Affinity and PROXiMATE-Kd the predictive models based on FFT and NLP representations achieve better performances in early training epochs.

3.3   Using the Explored Strategies to Build a Predictive Model

The development of the predictive model for predicting thermal stability changes in interaction complexes using the PROXiMATE-Kd dataset illustrates the methodologies proposed in this work. First, the design of architecture A of the CNN methods (See Table 2 for more details) is based on three pattern extraction blocks composed of conv1D and pooling layers, followed by a flattening layer and two learning layers. The pattern extraction layers are activated by the ReLU functions, while the learning layers are activated by tanh and linear functions. With the architecture designed, the next step consists of preparing the data sets. We work with the representation based on amino acid encodings via physicochemical properties for this. Specifically, the hydropathy property of those reported in [17] is used, and all the proteins in the dataset are encoded. The interaction network is assembled, and the interaction matrix is created, concatenating the protein representations indicated by the network. Once the network is made, a linear transformation is applied using PCA techniques. This transformation allows the two proteins to be "mixed" into a single representation via the linear combination developed by PCA to create its components. Then, the model is trained following a classical training pipeline [19], and performance metrics are obtained. Next, the results are reported, and the model is exported. The presented combination achieved the highest performance in the thermal stability evaluation problem, with a 0.94 R^2 score in the testing stage and a 0.96 R^2 score in the validation stage. Finally, the model can be used to explore new evaluations and stability changes to discover mutational variants with improved affinity. To do this, the mutational landscape of the protein of interest must be generated and encoded with the selected strategy. Then, the PCA transformation and the predictive model must be applied to predict the effects on the association constant (Kd), which can be validated using bioinformatics techniques such as simulations and molecular dynamics.

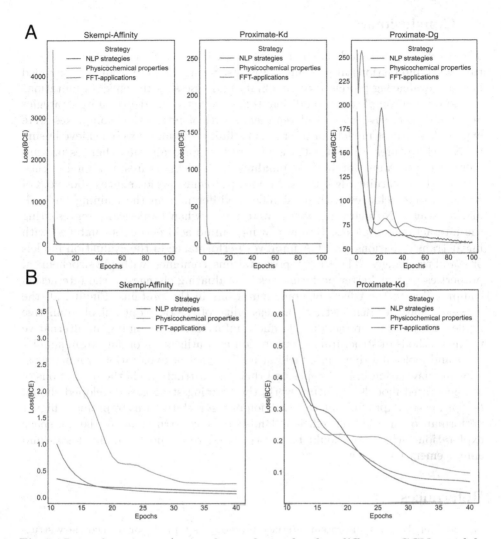

Fig. 2. Loss function v/s number of epochs for different GCN models employing varied numerical representation strategies to represent the protein sequences. A. Visualization of loss function for protein-protein affinity models (left), association constant estimation models (center), and stability estimation of structural complexes (right). Both affinity and association models achieve better performances in fewer epochs, exhibiting stability with a minimum of 10 runs, independent of the type of representations. In the case of the thermal stability predictive systems, more significant learning disruptions are observed, not achieving stability until 70 epochs of execution, and in the NLP representations, no stability of the learning process is achieved during all the epochs executed, this may be related to the low performance of the stability model, in comparison with the affinity estimation models. B. Zoom to the evaluation of learning between epochs 10 and 40. Significant improvement is observed at epochs 30 for PROXiMATE-Kd and 20 for SKEMPI-Affinity to benefit the models trained using amino acid coding and subsequent FFT transformation

4   Conclusions

This work explored methods of training predictive models for problems related to affinity interactions in protein complexes. Six tasks were evaluated, divided between evaluating protein-protein affinity and assessing the effect of mutations on interaction complexes. In addition, three predictive model training strategies and nine alternative numerical representations of interaction complexes were explored. The best models for interaction affinity evaluation were achieved using GCN architectures. In contrast, the best results for evaluating changes in complex structures were obtained by building CNN architectures or applying classical machine learning algorithms. In both problems, performances above 0.8 of R^2 score were achieved with no significant differences in the training and validation stages. No marked patterns were found when numerically representing the interaction complexes. However, using amino acid encoders combined with linear transformations via PCA improves performance in the evaluation models of stability changes. The FFT representations combined with physicochemical properties present better performances in evaluating changes in the interaction complex due to the effects of point mutations in the proteins. Finally, all the exposed strategies demonstrate the feasibility of the development of predictive models for protein interactions via linear information, becoming an alternative to the methods of structural representation and utilization of data from simulations and molecular dynamics, facilitating the efficient exploration of mutations, allowing navigation in landscapes and their reconstruction via the predictions of the generated models. In future work, the training strategies developed should be optimized, improving the construction of the architectures to promote higher performance. In addition, efficient landscape reconstruction and latent space exploration techniques should be incorporated to support protein design and enhancement techniques.

References

1. Bouvier, B.: Protein-protein interface topology as a predictor of secondary structure and molecular function using convolutional deep learning. J. Chem. Inf. Model. **61**(7), 3292–3303 (2021)
2. Bunkute, E., Cummins, C., Crofts, F.J., Bunce, G., Nabney, I.T., Flower, D.R.: PIP-DB: the protein isoelectric point database. Bioinformatics **31**(2), 295–296 (2015)
3. Cadet, F., et al.: A machine learning approach for reliable prediction of amino acid interactions and its application in the directed evolution of enantioselective enzymes. Sci. Rep. **8**(1), 16757 (2018)
4. Dallago, C., et al.: Learned embeddings from deep learning to visualize and predict protein sets. Current Protoc. **1**(5), e113 (2021)
5. Das, S., Chakrabarti, S.: Classification and prediction of protein-protein interaction interface using machine learning algorithm. Sci. Rep. **11**(1), 1–12 (2021)
6. Gaillard, T.: Evaluation of AutoDock and AutoDock vina on the CASF-2013 benchmark. J. Chem. Inf. Model. **58**(8), 1697–1706 (2018)

7. Gapsys, V., et al.: Large scale relative protein ligand binding affinities using non-equilibrium alchemy. Chem. Sci. **11**(4), 1140–1152 (2020)
8. Gil, C., Martinez, A.: Is drug repurposing really the future of drug discovery or is new innovation truly the way forward? Expert Opin. Drug Discov. **16**(8), 829–831 (2021)
9. Gupta, P., Mohanty, D.: SMMPPI: a machine learning-based approach for prediction of modulators of protein-protein interactions and its application for identification of novel inhibitors for RBD: hACE2 interactions in SARS-CoV-2. Briefings Bioinf. **22**(5), bbab111 (2021)
10. Huang, L., et al.: LGFC-CNN: prediction of lncRNA-protein interactions by using multiple types of features through deep learning. Genes **12**(11), 1689 (2021)
11. Jankauskaitė, J., Jiménez-García, B., Dapkūnas, J., Fernández-Recio, J., Moal, I.H.: SKEMPI 2.0: an updated benchmark of changes in protein-protein binding energy, kinetics and thermodynamics upon mutation. Bioinformatics **35**(3), 462–469 (2019)
12. Jemimah, S., Yugandhar, K., Michael Gromiha, M.: Proximate: a database of mutant protein-protein complex thermodynamics and kinetics. Bioinformatics **33**(17), 2787–2788 (2017)
13. Kairys, V., Baranauskiene, L., Kazlauskiene, M., Matulis, D., Kazlauskas, E.: Binding affinity in drug design: experimental and computational techniques. Expert Opin. Drug Discov. **14**(8), 755–768 (2019)
14. Kerrien, S., et al.: The intact molecular interaction database in 2012. Nucleic Acids Res. **40**(D1), D841–D846 (2012)
15. Liu, J., Gong, X.: Attention mechanism enhanced LSTM with residual architecture and its application for protein-protein interaction residue pairs prediction. BMC Bioinf. **20**, 1–11 (2019)
16. Luo, Y., et al.: ECNet is an evolutionary context-integrated deep learning framework for protein engineering. Nat. Commun. **12**(1), 1–14 (2021)
17. Medina-Ortiz, D.: Generalized property-based encoders and digital signal processing facilitate predictive tasks in protein engineering. Frontiers Mol. Biosci. **9** (2022)
18. Medina-Ortiz, D., Contreras, S., Quiroz, C., Asenjo, J.A., Olivera-Nappa, Á.: Dmakit: a user-friendly web platform for bringing state-of-the-art data analysis techniques to non-specific users. Inf. Syst. **93**, 101557 (2020)
19. Medina-Ortiz, D., Contreras, S., Quiroz, C., Olivera-Nappa, Á.: Development of supervised learning predictive models for highly non-linear biological, biomedical, and general datasets. Front. Mol. Biosci. **7**, 13 (2020)
20. Mewara, B., Lalwani, S.: Sequence-based prediction of protein-protein interaction using auto-feature engineering of RNN-based model. Res. Biomed. Eng., 1–14 (2023)
21. Parvathaneni, V., Kulkarni, N.S., Muth, A., Gupta, V.: Drug repurposing: a promising tool to accelerate the drug discovery process. Drug Discov. Today **24**(10), 2076–2085 (2019)
22. Rao, R., et al.: Evaluating protein transfer learning with tape. In: Advances in Neural Information Processing Systems, vol. 32 (2019)
23. Sable, R., Jois, S.: Surfing the protein-protein interaction surface using docking methods: application to the design of PPI inhibitors. Molecules **20**(6), 11569–11603 (2015)
24. Siedhoff, N.E., Illig, A.M., Schwaneberg, U., Davari, M.D.: Pypef-an integrated framework for data-driven protein engineering. J. Chem. Inf. Model. **61**(7), 3463–3476 (2021)

25. Szklarczyk, D., et al.: The string database in 2021: customizable protein-protein networks, and functional characterization of user-uploaded gene/measurement sets. Nucleic Acids Res. **49**(D1), D605–D612 (2021)
26. Tsukiyama, S., Hasan, M.M., Fujii, S., Kurata, H.: LSTM-PHV: prediction of human-virus protein-protein interactions by LSTM with Word2Vec. Briefings Bioinf. **22**(6), bbab228 (2021)
27. Wang, R., Fang, X., Lu, Y., Yang, C.Y., Wang, S.: The PDBbind database: methodologies and updates. J. Med. Chem. **48**(12), 4111–4119 (2005)
28. Yang, F., Fan, K., Song, D., Lin, H.: Graph-based prediction of protein-protein interactions with attributed signed graph embedding. BMC Bioinf. **21**(1), 1–16 (2020)
29. Yu, J., Vavrusa, M., Andreani, J., Rey, J., Tufféry, P., Guerois, R.: InterEvDock: a docking server to predict the structure of protein-protein interactions using evolutionary information. Nucleic Acids Res. **44**(W1), W542–W549 (2016)
30. Yun, S., Lee, S., Park, J.P., Choo, J., Lee, E.: Modification of phage display technique for improved screening of high-affinity binding peptides. J. Biotechnol. **289**, 88–92 (2019)
31. Zeng, M., Zhang, F., Wu, F.X., Li, Y., Wang, J., Li, M.: Protein-protein interaction site prediction through combining local and global features with deep neural networks. Bioinformatics **36**(4), 1114–1120 (2020)
32. Zhang, H., et al.: Deep residual convolutional neural network for protein-protein interaction extraction. IEEE Access **7**, 89354–89365 (2019)
33. Zhao, L., Wang, J., Hu, Y., Cheng, L.: Conjoint feature representation of go and protein sequence for PPI prediction based on an inception RNN attention network. Mol. Ther. Nucleic Acids **22**, 198–208 (2020)

A Constructive Algorithm for the Split Delivery Vehicle Routing Problem (SDVRP)

Francisco Jones⬤, Rodrigo Astudillo, Benjamín Acosta, Alexis Olmedo⬤, Alejandro Córdova, and Gustavo Gatica$^{(\boxtimes)}$⬤

Faculty of Engineering - CIS, Universidad Andres Bello, Santiago, Chile
ggatica@unab.cl

Abstract. Vehicle routing is a classic of operations research. The objective is to contribute with heuristic knowledge emphasizing the complexity of the divided delivery vehicle problem. A homogeneous vehicle fleet is considered, where the demand of all clients must be covered, being able to visit clients more than once. The preliminary results are encouraging because they allow the identification of several lines of research regarding implementing practical solutions for last-mile logistics problems. Furthermore, when comparing the response times of the heuristics (0.043 s.) with the LocalSolver application (1 s and 5 s), managing to solve large instances, constantly navigating in the space of feasible solutions.

Keywords: Vehicle Routing Problem · Split Delivery Vehicle Routing · Problem · Heuristic · Representation Problem

1 Introduction

Minimizing costs is a priority for companies, especially regarding operations associated with shipping goods to many clients. However, to achieve the goal of cost reduction, additional constraints must be considered [3]. Therefore, in recent years, there has been an increasing trend to generalize classical problems, such as the Traveling Salesman Problem (TSP), to incorporate more variables and parameters to address real-world scenarios [15].

This trend has led to vehicle routing issues that consider several factors. Some focus on time windows, such as the Capacitated Vehicle Routing Problem with Time Windows (CVRPTW) [15]. Others focus on vehicle capacity, such as the Capable Vehicle Routing Problem (CVRP) [5]. In addition, there is the split-delivery vehicle routing problem (SD-VRP), which aims to perform split deliveries as long as there is remaining demand to be met and vehicle capacity allows it [3].

The goal is to find the optimal route to visit each client with specific demand requirements to minimize the cost of travel along the route. Efficient utilization of space within a vehicle reduces volume and weight, leading to significant cost savings in the industry. Dror and Trudeau [9] showed that by implementing split deliveries and fully utilizing the capacity of a vehicle, the number of delivery vehicles needed can be reduced while still meeting total demand. Among the various variants of the original Vehicle Routing

Problem (VRP), the Split Delivery Vehicle Routing Problem (SD-VRP) is particularly challenging, with NP-Hard complexity [8]. This means that finding an optimal solution requires significant processing time. It should be noted that the SD-VRP is a deterministic model since its input parameters and initial conditions are known and do not involve randomness in data processing [3].

The SD-VRP originates as a generalization of the original VRP, allowing multiple visits to a client by splitting their demand, which is then delivered by different vehicles along separate routes. The goal is to meet client demand and maximize the capacity of each vehicle. Dror and Trudeau proposed this generalization, offering a new demand-driven perspective to demonstrate potential savings in travel distances and the number of cars needed to meet established demand [8].

Various approaches have been proposed in the academic literature to address the SDVRP. These approaches include genetic algorithms, tabu searches, ant colony algorithms, and combinatorial optimization methods. These approaches have proven effective in resolving SDVRP instances and have provided quality solutions in a reasonable amount of time.

To effectively solve SD-VRP from a software development perspective, the goal is to develop a heuristic solution capable of delivering solutions within a feasible zone for SD-VRP.

In conclusion, the split delivery vehicle routing problem presents complex challenges for minimizing costs and optimizing business delivery operations. However, by considering split deliveries and efficient use of vehicle capacities, significant cost savings can be achieved. This document aims to develop a heuristic solution that addresses SD-VRP from a software development perspective, providing feasible solutions to navigate the problem's constraints. This will be compared with a standard application known as a local solver to compare results, especially computational time.

1.1 SDVRP

As demonstrated by Dror and Trudeau [9], the application of split delivery, utilizing the total capacity of a vehicle, effectively reduces the number of delivery vehicles required to fulfill the entire demand. This approach ensures efficient coverage of clients while optimizing resource utilization.

It is important to note that the Split Delivery Vehicle Routing Problem (SD-VRP) is characterized as a deterministic model. This deterministic nature arises from the known input parameters and initial conditions, which do not introduce random values during the data processing stage. These characteristic guarantees consistency and predictability throughout the problem-solving process.

Dror and Trudeau [8] provide a fresh perspective from the demand side, illustrating the potential travel savings and reduced vehicle requirements associated with this delivery approach. In addition, their research highlights the benefits of considering split delivery strategies to optimize travel costs and enhance overall operational efficiency.

In formulating the mathematical model for the SD-VRP [3], the following variables should be taken into consideration:

- C_{ij} : is the cost of the edge (i, j).

- $X_{ij}^v \in \{0, 1\}$: is a binary variable that takes the value 1 if vehicle v travels directly from i to j, and 0 otherwise.
- $Y_{iv} \geq 0$: is the amount of demand i delivered by vehicle v.

Function Objective

$$Min \sum_{i=0}^{n} \sum_{j=0}^{n} \sum_{v=1}^{m} C_{ij} X_{ij}^v \tag{1}$$

Constraints

$$\sum_{i=0}^{n} \sum_{v=1}^{m} X_{ij}^v \geq 1, j \; 0, \ldots, n \tag{2}$$

$$\sum_{i=0}^{n} X_{ip}^v - \sum_{j=0}^{n} X_{pj}^v = 0 \; p = 0, \ldots, n; v = 1, \ldots, m \tag{3}$$

$$\sum_{i \in S} \sum_{j \in S} X_{ij}^v \leq |S| - 1 \; v = 1, \ldots, m; S \subseteq V - \{0\} \tag{4}$$

$$y_{iv} \leq d_i \sum_{j=0}^{n} X_{ij}^v \; i = 1, \ldots, n; \; v = 1, \ldots, m \tag{5}$$

$$\sum_{v=1}^{m} y_{iv} = d_i \; i = 1, \ldots, n \tag{6}$$

$$\sum_{i=1}^{m} y_{iv} \leq d_i \; v = 1, \ldots, m \tag{7}$$

$$x_{ij}^v \in \{0, 1\} i = 0, \ldots, n; \; j = 0, \ldots, n; \; v 1, \ldots, m \tag{8}$$

$$y_{iv} \geq 0 \; i = 1, \ldots, n; \; v = 1, \ldots, m \tag{9}$$

Constraint (3) ensures that each client is visited at least once, (4) seeks the conservation of flow, and the vehicle must follow the route without stopping at a single client. (5) eliminates the subtours, avoiding the creation of island routes; this means not considering the depot within the route but only generating routes with clients. (6) ensures that client i is served by truck v only if v passes through i. (7) seeks to satisfy the total demand of each client. Finally, (8) ensures that the quantity delivered by each truck does not exceed its capacity.

An SDVRP is defined [3] as a pairwise undirected Graph $G = (V, E)$. Where a set of vertices $V = \{0, 1, \ldots, n\}$, which contemplates from 0 to the nth value, where 0 represents the deposit, and the other vertices represent the clients, Each Client $i \in V - \{0\}$ is associated with a demand d_i.

The set of Edges where an edge $(,) \in$ has a cost. $C_{ij} > 0$. An unbounded fleet of vehicles with capacity $Q > 0$ each and a lower bound of vehicles sufficient to satisfy d_t is given by $\sum_{i=1}^{n} \frac{d_i}{Q}$.

2 Literature Review

The concept of routing problems can be traced back to the Travelling Salesman Problem (TSP) [7]. This problem emerged from the need to find the shortest route when visiting a specific number of cities, starting and ending at the same origin city, with known distances between cities. The TSP sparked significant interest in the field of mathematics and optimization. In 1950, the RAND Corporation organized a contest challenging participant to find an optimal tour for visiting the capitals of the United States. In 1954, three mathematical optimization specialists achieved the first exact solution [7] for this instance involving 49 cities, guaranteeing the optimal value.

Considering the problem proposed in the 50s, where many cities need to be visited, and the goal is to find the optimal travel value, finding a feasible solution by sequentially visiting cities may seem straightforward. However, the challenge lies in selecting the method or strategy for choosing the cities due to the numerous possible routes. This is why the TSP, its variant VRP, and its different generalizations are classified as NP-Hard. In [11], a TSP and a VRP exemplify two different methods of visiting the same number of clients. The TSP focuses on optimizing a single route without considering vehicles or constraints such as capacity. On the other hand, the Vehicle Routing Problem (VRP) feels like a limited and homogeneous fleet of vehicles with a maximum capacity to meet client demand, aiming to optimize the routes generated [11].

The Split Delivery Vehicle Routing Problem (SDVRP) introduces specific conditions that must be met for a solution to be considered optimal or feasible, depending on the problem-solving perspective.

Based on the premise of the SDVRP, the following conditions must be satisfied:

Only one depot is considered: The demand to be distributed and the vehicles allocated for this task originate from a single depot.

Each client must be visited at least once: For a client to be considered service, the delivery vehicle must pass by the client's location at least once. This problem allows for multiple visits if the client's complete demand still needs to be met.

Homogeneous load is assumed: The demands in terms of volume and value are equal for all clients, disregarding individual variations. Therefore, they occupy the same space within the vehicles.

Each vehicle must adhere to its capacity without exceeding it Fig. 1 illustrates how the SDVRP can be solved through a split distribution of the demand among the vehicles if there is pending demand that can be fully satisfied and the delivery vehicles do not exceed their maximum capacity while traveling these routes [8].

Various techniques and mathematical methods have recently been proposed as new approaches to solving routing problems. Split partitioning has received attention and has been tackled through different solutions. For instance, Belenguer implemented an algorithm based on cutting planes [6]. Arquetti, on the other hand, has proposed several resolution methods, including the three-phase tabu search and a branch-and-price-and-cut focused algorithm [2, 4]. Jin has put forward an optimal solution algorithm [10]. Alemán utilized the local search method to create an adaptive memory algorithm [1]. Wilcker and Cavalier recently developed a constructive procedure specifically for the SD-VRP [16].

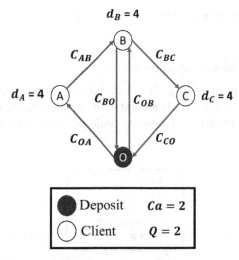

Fig. 1. Own illustration of an example for SD-VRP

3 Methodology

The methodology employed in this study comprised four main tasks, each aimed at minimizing the complexity of the process. These tasks are described below:

1. **Analysis and interpretation:** To comprehend the problem at hand, it was necessary to analyze both its definition and the corresponding mathematical model. This involved abstracting the figurative elements and devising a solution that operates within a feasible framework.
2. **Solution development:** The initial step involved developing a Python script based on the fundamental principles of abstract data structures. Three criteria were implemented, and an optimization algorithm was applied to enhance the obtained results.
3. **Validation:** After completing the development of the Python script, various tests were conducted using different instances, thereby expanding the dataset pertaining to the clients. During the validation stage, these solution paths were examined and evaluated against the problem's constraints and requirements to determine their feasibility as solutions for the SD-VRP.
4. **Comparative analysis:** Once feasible solutions were identified, a similar algorithmic proposal was studied, focusing on creating an approach rooted in mathematical programming modeling. This approach allowed for multiple iterations as the processing time increased. A quantitative comparative analysis was conducted, considering variables that accurately represented the obtained results.

3.1 Variable Storage Design

To ensure the proposed representation, careful consideration was given to the internal structure of arrays. Therefore, in this initial stage, the internal structure for storing information was defined in a structured manner, facilitating its management within the arrays.

3.2 Storage of Variables I (Client/depot)

By establishing the repository (Fig. 2) and compiling a list of clients, a simple linked list containing all the clients (Fig. 3) present in the given instance was generated based on the data read. Additionally, the repository could be stored in a separate node, isolated from the client list.

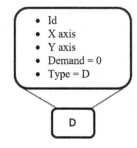

Fig. 2. Illustration of a node (reservoir).

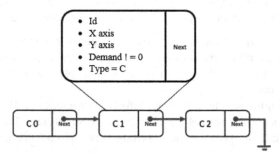

Fig. 3. Simple linked list (clients)

3.3 Variable Storage II (Vehicle)

In the second design phase, our objective is to create a storage system that effectively manages the information used in the support structures (Fig. 4). This design aims to capture and store crucial details related to vehicles, including the total number of clients within a route, total demand of the course, the average direction of the road and total distance to be traveled within the same way.

3.4 Solution Design

The solution design considers the coordinates of both the warehouse and the clients to establish a visitation order. The warehouse's coordinates serve as the reference point

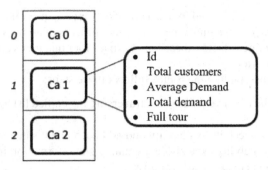

Fig. 4. Variable storage II (vehicle), prepared by the company.

(OX, OY) within a 2D plane, and the design divides the plane into four quadrants as follows:

- Quadrant 1: The X-coordinate of the client is greater than that of the warehouse, and the Y-coordinate of the client is greater than that of the warehouse.
- Quadrant 2: The X-coordinate of the client is greater than that of the warehouse, but the Y-coordinate of the client is less than that of the warehouse.
- Quadrant 3: The X-coordinate of the client is less than that of the warehouse, and the Y-coordinate of the client is also less than that of the warehouse.
- Quadrant 4: The X-coordinate of the client is less than that of the warehouse, but the Y-coordinate of the client is greater than that of the warehouse.

In addition to organizing the clients by quadrants, ordering criteria are applied to determine the visitation sequence within each quadrant. The ordering criteria are as follows:

- Criterion A: Clients within a quadrant are sorted based on their proximity to the axis intersecting the quadrant in a clockwise direction. For example, in quadrant 1, the X-axis is crossed, so the clients are ordered based on their proximity to this axis, considering the value of the Y-axis. The same logic applies to the other quadrants, with the ordering based on the proximity to the corresponding axis.
- Criterion B: This criterion follows a counterclockwise path. In quadrant 1, for instance, the counterclockwise path intersects the Y-axis, so the clients are ordered based on their proximity to this axis, considering the value of the X-axis. The same principle applies to the other quadrants, with the ordering determined by the proximity to the corresponding axis.
- Criterion C: Unlike the previous criteria, this criterion calculates the distance between the warehouse and each client while considering the defined quadrants. The length is calculated using Euclidean space, and the clients are ordered from the most minor to the most considerable distance.

Simple linked lists are created for each criterion for each quadrant, storing the clients in the respective order. To facilitate the subsequent process of assigning clients to routes associated with specific vehicles, these lists from all four quadrants are combined into a single index per criterion.

The process of assembling the routes follows these steps:

- Iterate through the list of vehicles while traversing the unified list based on the chosen criterion.
- For each vehicle, check its availability and add each client's demands to the vehicle as long as the availability exceeds the demand. The information in the node storing the vehicle's data is updated accordingly.
- As client demands are associated with a particular vehicle, the clients are inserted into a circular linked list, representing the structure that will store the solution routes (Fig. 5). It is important to note that both the first and last nodes in this list correspond to the warehouse.
- In cases where a client's demand exceeds the vehicle's availability, the market is divided into two parts. The first part equals the remaining availability to be added to the vehicle. At the same time, the total demand of the client is updated to reflect the remaining value, representing the remaining unsatisfied demand that will be addressed by the next vehicle. Once the maximum capacity of a vehicle is reached, this process is repeated with the next vehicle in the list.
- This process is repeated for each vehicle in the list, updating the data for each vehicle (number of clients to deliver, average demand, total demand, and total distance to each client) and the list containing the solution routes.

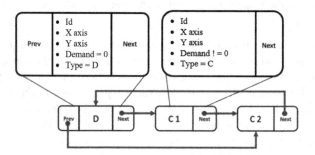

Fig. 5. Circular linked list (solution routes).

3.5 Rectification of Routes

To enhance the results and prevent arcs from intersecting within the same routes, an additional measure was implemented alongside the proposed structure. A heuristic known as 2-OPT was employed for this purpose. By utilizing an arc matrix, this heuristic examines the angles and rectifies them by changing the visiting order of clients within each individual route. It is important to note that these rectifications are applied to each course separately to avoid merging clients from different routes. This approach reduces the processing time of the algorithm and minimizes the number of clients to be processed.

The 2-OPT algorithm, as described and implemented in the document (Slootbeek, Average-Case Analysis of the), employs nested loops within another loop, resulting in an efficiency of order $\theta(n2)$ [14].

The rectification of initial solutions generated by the proposed structures significantly improves the routes by preventing trucks from traversing intersections in a similar manner.

3.6 Comparative Analysis

To conduct a comprehensive comparative analysis, it is crucial to have a clear understanding of the algorithm against which the heuristic solution is being compared.

In the research process, a comparative analysis is performed by exploring other existing algorithms that can address routing problems with similar approaches. Various programming language APIs, such as Java, C++, and Python, are considered, which provide solutions for routing problems like CVRP (Capacitated Vehicle Routing Problem), CVRPTW (Vehicle Routing Problem with Time Windows), TSP (Travelling Salesman Problem), SDVRP (Split Delivery Vehicle Routing Problem), and others [12].

The selected algorithm for this analysis can deliver feasible solutions that closely approximate an exact solution. As stated in its documentation, the algorithm is based on mathematical programming models, utilizing decision variables, constraints, and objectives [13]. Specifically, for the SDVRP, the algorithm defines an objective function expression, establishes constraints associated with the process, and utilizes floating-point decision variables within a range of possibilities. Furthermore, the algorithm allows for runtime configuration and performs multiple iterations to optimize the path by progressively reducing the improvement range to zero.

The chosen algorithm is tested with execution times of 1 and 5 s. These times are selected because the developed heuristic can generate three feasible solutions in a fraction of a second (less than 1 s) for the same instance. It is important to note that the type of solution chosen is a viable solution and not an exact solution that guarantees finding the minimum path.

4 Results

The developed model was applied to a randomly generated sample for the 20-client experiment (Fig. 6).

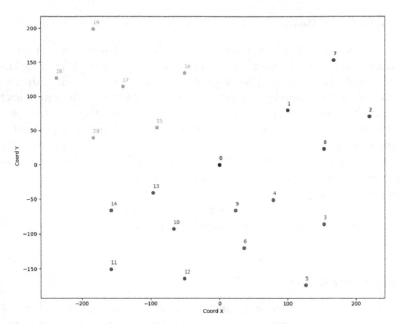

Fig. 6. Sample distribution in the plane

The models are developed based on various criteria, yielding the following results (Figs. 7, 8, 9 and Tables 1, 2, 3):

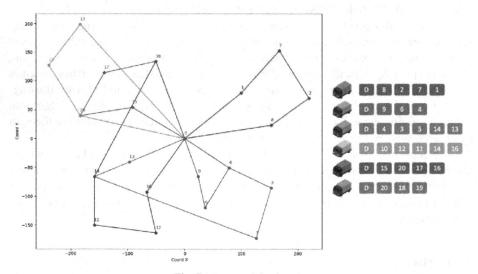

Fig. 7. Routes Criterion A.

Table 1. Information on each vehicle Criterion A

INFORMATION TRUCKS				
ID_TRUCKS	NUM_CUST	AVG_DEMAND	CAPACITY_ACHIEVED	TOTAL_TRAVEL
0	4	10	40	560.7515172
1	3	13.33	40	300.7292421
2	5	8	40	742.2734389
3	5	8	40	750.2377217
4	4	10	40	521.5598685
5	3	3	9	651.535338

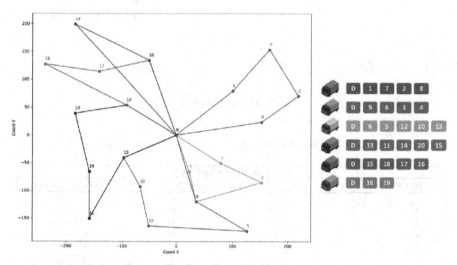

Fig. 8. Routes Criterion B

Table 2. Information on each vehicle Criterion B

INFORMATION TRUCKS				
ID_TRUCKS	NUM_CUST	AVG_DEMAND	CAPACITY_ACHIEVED	TOTAL_TRAVEL
0	4	10	40	560.7515172
1	4	10	40	422.6431497
2	5	8	40	645.484488
3	5	8	40	622.6179426
4	4	10	40	603.153697
5	2	4.5	9	562.0926964

In order to evaluate the program's efficiency, multiple instances are created with varying numbers of clients while maintaining the same format. These instances are designed not only to assess efficiency but also to test the program's performance against increasingly larger examples.

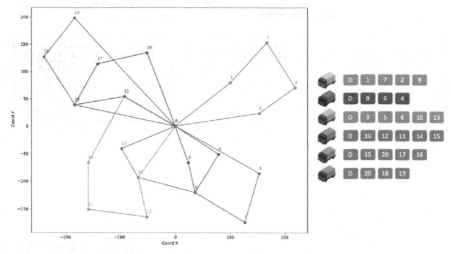

Fig. 9. Routes Criterion C

Table 3. Information for each vehicle in the 2-Opt route (Criterion C).

INFORMATION TRUCKS				
ID_TRUCKS	NUM_CUST	AVG_DEMAND	CAPACITY_ACHIEVED	TOTAL_TRAVEL
0	4	10	40	560.7515172
1	3	13.33	40	300.7292421
2	5	8	40	643.0658405
3	5	8	40	622.9965454
4	4	10	40	521.5598685
5	3	3	9	651.535338

Table 4 presents the instances that were tested, where the number of clients was incrementally increased to assess the efficiency of the heuristic in tackling more substantial examples. The third column indicates the number of trucks proposed by each model, while the fourth column demonstrates a significant decrease in this value. This reduction is achieved through the exploration of a lower limit for the number of vehicles required to fulfill the total demand.

Table 5 displays the total travel costs for each tested instance, both before and after implementing the 2-Opt algorithm.

4.1 Results of the Computational Experiment

The evaluation of the results for this computational experiment involves a comprehensive analysis of various factors, including execution time, number of iterations, covered demand, and total runtime. Additionally, the solution paths generated by the algorithm are taken into consideration. However, it is important to note that while the algorithm

Table 4. Comparison table

INSTANCE	N° OF CLIENTS	N° OF TRUCKS PROPOSED	MAXIMUM CAPACITY	N° TRUCS USED	DEMAND COVERED
1	10	5	25	4	81
2	20	13	30	12	352
3	30	20	35	13	432
4	40	26	40	17	677
5	50	35	52	27	1383
6	65	48	61	27	1600
7	80	60	75	33	2411
8	100	75	99	41	4046
9	120	98	130	51	6551

Table 5. Comparison 2-opt.

INSTANCE	TOTAL TRAVEL			2-Opt TOTAL TRAVEL		
	Criterion A	Criterion B	Criterion C	Criterion A	Criterion B	Criterion C
1	3861.95	3416.72	4024.10	3394.48	3189.46	3441.29
2	8334.78	8689.83	8577.33	8245.78	8321.43	8320.10
3	7677.18	7838.23	7896.29	7251.46	7019.82	7284.82
4	11391.02	11689.08	11720.76	10736.46	10539.30	10953.92
5	16537.99	15641.03	16859.40	15540.50	14561.34	15744.29
6	16591.50	16539.01	15666.16	15277.48	15649.08	14692.18
7	19486.90	19523.02	19614.87	18132.37	18263.63	17751.27
8	24990.24	22943.65	24546.60	22845.47	21013.63	21687.43
9	31271.47	29127.80	30462.75	28351.67	26859.26	26990.03

successfully minimizes the total path cost for this instance, to classify the resulting solution as exact, it is necessary to consider the concept of divided partitioning, which is not directly derived from the solution paths.

Table 6. Localsolver vs. proposed heuristics comparison.

	Local solver 1	Local solver 5	Proposed model
Time (sec)	1	5	0.043
Number of iterations	1675	80000	N/A
Covered demand (UN)	22500	22500	22500
Total travel	404	375	495.81

5 Conclusion

The proposed heuristic solution effectively addresses the constraints imposed by the mathematical model and satisfies the necessary conditions for feasible solutions. In particular, the algorithm demonstrates the ability to resolve large instances in less than one second of execution time (0.043 s) (Table 6).

Regarding the solutions generated based on different criteria, it is impossible to identify a consistent pattern that consistently delivers the optimal path. Multiple instances were generated with the same number of clients but different coordinate values and demands, and no single criteria consistently produced the lowest route. Therefore, finding a near-optimal feasible solution will depend on the specific instance values and not just the number of clients.

In terms of comparative analysis, the solutions provided by the LocalSolver algorithm are promising. However, it fails to fully implement the concept of split delivery in its solutions, which is a key aspect of the SD-VRP relaxation of the original VRP. The algorithm only allows one visit per client, without making the type of installment deliveries required.

Considering the concepts discussed and comparing them with the heuristics proposed earlier in this conclusion, it can be concluded that heuristics offer a reasonable solution for this type of routing problem. It effectively meets all the requirements and conditions described during problem definition.

References

1. Aleman, R.E., Zhang, X., Hill, R.R.: An adaptive memory algorithm for the split-delivery vehicle routing problem. J. Heurist. **16**, 441–473 (2010)
2. Archetti, C., Speranza, M.G.: A tabu search algorithm for the split delivery vehicle routing problem (2011)
3. Archetti, C., Speranza, M.G.: Vehicle routing problems with split deliveries. Int. Trans. Oper. Res. **19**(1–2), 3–22 (2012)
4. Archetti, C., Bianchessi, N., Speranza, M.G.: A column generation approach for the split delivery vehicle routing problem. Networks **58**, 241–254 (2011)
5. Archetti, C., Feillet, D., Speranza, M.G.: The complexity of the VRP and SDVRP (2011)
6. Belenguer, J.M., Martinez, M.C., Mota, E.: A lower bound for the split delivery vehicle routing problem. Oper. Res. **48**, 801–810 (2000)

7. Chvátal, V., Cook, W., Dantzig, G.B., Fulkerson, D.R., Johnson, S.M.: Solution of a large-scale traveling-salesman problem. In: Jünger, M., Liebling, Thomas M., Naddef, Denis, Nemhauser, George L., Pulleyblank, William R., Reinelt, Gerhard, Rinaldi, Giovanni, Wolsey, Laurence A. (eds.) 50 Years of Integer Programming 1958-2008, pp. 7–28. Springer, Heidelberg (2010). https://doi.org/10.1007/978-3-540-68279-0_1
8. Dror, M., Trudeau, P.: Savings by split delivery routing. Transp. Sci. **23**(2), 141–145 (1989). https://doi.org/10.1287/trsc.23.2.141
9. Dror, M., Trudeau, Pierre: Split delivery routing: split delivery. Naval Res. Logist. (NRL) **37**(3), 383–402 (1990). https://doi.org/10.1002/nav.3800370304
10. Jin, M., Liu, K., Bowden, R.O.: A two-stage algorithm with valid inequalities for the split delivery vehicle routing problem. Int. J. Prod. Econ. (2007)
11. Lin, T.-H., Sheng-Hung, C., Lin, I.-C.: A decision system for routing problems and rescheduling issues using unmanned aerial vehicles (2022)
12. LocalSolver. Retrieved from Example Tour - Split Delivery Vehicle Routing Problem: https://www.localsolver.com/docs/last/exampletour/split-delivery-vehicle-routing-problem-sdvrp.html
13. LocalSolver. Mathematical modeling features (2023). https://www.localsolver.com/docs/last/modelingfeatures/mathematicalmodelingfeatures.html
14. Slootbeek, J.J.A.: Average-Case Analysis of the 2-opt Heuristic for the TSP (2017)
15. Velazquez, E.: Application of the Vehicle Routing Problem (VRP) to a distribution problem. University of the Americas Puebla (2005)
16. Wilck IV, J., Cavalier, T.: Una construcción heurística para el vehículo de reparto dividido problema de enrutamiento. Am. J. Oper. Res. (2012)

High Performance Computing
and Networks

Energy Consumption Monitoring System (kWh) and Load Control Through Messaging Applications

José L. Simancas-Garcìa[1], Farid A. Meléndez Pertuz[1(✉)], Eckner Chaljub[1],
Bernardo Troncozo[1], César A. R. Cárdenas[2], Vanesa Landero Nájera[3],
and Carlos Andrés Collazos Morales[4(✉)]

[1] Department of Computer Science and Electronics, Universidad de la Costa, Barranquilla,
Colombia
fmelende1@cuc.edu.co

[2] Department of Aerospace Engineering, Virginia Polytechnic Institute and State University,
Blacksburg, VA, USA

[3] Universidad Politécnica de Apodaca, Nuevo León, México

[4] Universidad Manuela Beltrán, Bogotá, Colombia
carlos.collazos@docentes.umb.edu.co

Abstract. In the city of Barranquilla (Colombia), the company that provides residential energy services uses analog meters to mea- sure energy consumption. These meters are not user friendly and keeping track of energy consumption based on their reading is a tedious task. In addition, it is not generally known how this energy consumption is calculated in money, especially considering that the calculation changes depending on the socioeconomic status of the user. For this reason, most users do not know how much they have consumed, nor the economic cost of the service, until they receive the bill. There are solutions that use the IoT and that offer the user a more accessible and easy way to keep track of energy consumption, but they do not offer an ac- curate representation of the monetary value of energy consumption, since they do not take into account the Colombian con- text. In this work, a solution that takes this into account is expo- sed. The PZEM-004T multiparameter meter and the PZCT-02 current sensor were used to measure energy consumption in a home. These are connected to a microcontroller with a Wi-Fi module, the NodeMCU ESP8266, which communicates with a Telegram application messaging bot for data visualization and user interaction. Through the messaging bot of the Telegram application, the user can set alarms, check in real time the estimate of their energy consumption and its monetary value, make adjustments to the parameters used to calculate the energy value, as well as exercise control of some of the loads that demand more power in the home. The result obtained by the developed system deviated by -1.37% with respect to the energy service provider's bill.

Keywords: Energy monitoring · Load control · Telegram · Messaging BOT

O. Gervasi et al. (Eds.): ICCSA 2023, LNCS 13956, pp. 263–276, 2023.
https://doi.org/10.1007/978-3-031-36805-9_18

1 Introduction

Using energy intelligently by reducing its consumption without decreasing the quality of life is a sign of energy efficiency. The consumption of energy is constant, applicable to commerce, industry, mining, means of transport, housing, etc. [1]. There are two types of energy, renewable energy sources such as wind, hydroelectric, oceanic and solar, which use resources that do not affect the environment. On the other hand, non-renewable energy sources are those that are consumed and depleted when transformed and exploited into useful energy. The most widely used sources are: oil, natural gas and carbon.

Energy consumption speaks of well-being and social growth, but the use of fossil resources brings with it a very high price to pay because the consumption of these resources generates a direct impact on the environment, "global warming". Such is the importance of achieving a rational consumption of energy, that the CIGEPI, of the Superintendence of Industry and Commerce of Colombia, publishes a technological bulletin for the measurement and management through the use of innovative techniques at a global level for this purpose [2]. Contributing to energy efficiency through responsible and well-informed decision-making are key actions for reducing dependence on energy purchases, building large and expensive production, transmission and distribution systems, reducing pressure on natural resources and, why not, making savings on consumers' pockets. In other words, responsible practices contribute to the reduction of greenhouse gases, which in the end is profitable and healthy.

The work carried out in this article makes extensive use of the so-called chatbots. Chat-bots or messenger bots are computer programs that process natural language as input and generate a response back to the user [11]. There are currently two kinds of bots: those that are operated by rule-driven engines or by artificial intelligence (AI). The difference is that the first responds to specific commands and the second uses machine learning to provide indicated answers and not pre-planned commands by the creator. In 2015 Telegram opened its bot API for developers to create their own bots offering a number of services. Shortly after, other big ones like Facebook followed, and since then the use of bots in messaging applications has grown exponentially.

The interaction between user and bot is mainly done through a text interface. It is well known that there are bots that recognize spoken language such as Siri, Alexa, and Google Home among others. These types of bots are based on technologies similar to that of voice assistants, which transform the voice into text so that the program can work with it. The advantage of using a text-based interface is that the user can express his intention using natural language. However, for the developer to transform the natural language into a code that the program can understand, it is very difficult, considering the countless possibilities that exist. This brings the difficulty for the user that not all their queries can be answered. For this reason, elements such as buttons, quick-replies, carousels, web-views, among others were introduced, so that the bot could show certain types of data to the user and the user could reply to the bot with just one touch [10]. The bot turns out to be, in simple words, the interface between the user and the hardware as shown in Fig. 1.

Fig. 1. Interaction between users – hardware through bot.

2   Related Works

It is essential to promote processes educational practices that allow the implementation of responsible consumption practices, such as: washing clothes with full charge and with cold water, disconnecting electrical appliances that are not operational; being perhaps at night the most critical hours; plan-char minimally, changing habits when selecting devices with category A or B, are basic practices that transform the place where they are implemented into sustainable areas. There is a wide variety of instruments for measuring electricity consumption, but some innovative applications and systems propose models that integrate measurement, control application, use of industrial communication networks, cost projections and integration into robust data transmission systems, among others [3].

These processes have as a fundamental parameter or main variable the energy consumption of households and buildings in general, and are projected as a tool for optimizing energy consumption [4]. Before the widespread diffusion of the IoT, monitoring systems were carried out that were directly connected to a PC to which the measured data was directly projected, using protocols such as USB, although the acquisition and deployment devices were connected via Wi-Fi [3]. With the advent of IoT and cloud computing-based applications, energy monitoring systems migrated to this field [5]. In [6] an energy monitoring system is presented with a similar objective to that developed in this article, in which the energy consumption of the users is calculated and the tariff that they would have to pay during the month consumed is presented to them. For this purpose, they make use of the current sensor ASC712 that works with Hall effect, the microcontroller Atmega328, and develop a mobile application that must be installed on the smartphone to be able to visualize the information that is received via Bluetooth. Thus, the user must first pair his mobile phone with the monitoring device in order to have access to the energy consumption data. The calculation of the consumption and the tariff is made by the implementation of algorithms that are programmed in the microcontroller. The mobile application is for visualization purposes only.

In [7] a system is exposed which seeks to encourage good practices of energy consumption in households by monitoring this. For this purpose, the main wiring of the home is divided into three zones which are individually monitored using two sensors, the SCT-013–000 for currents between 1 - 100A and the ACS712-20A for currents below 20A. This system does not consider the variations of the supply voltage, considering it constant, just as it only allows the local visualization of the information. In [8] the aim is to implement a monitoring system of energy consumption for households and at the same time to promote good consumption practices that allow people to know the negative effects on the environment. This process is carried out through simulations where are indicated what are the benefits that are obtained by controlling the consumption of energy. This system is able to send information such as: voltage, current, power, and additionally the values of temperature and humidity that could serve for control of heaters or air conditioners based on the area of influence, however, does not provide information on the monetary value of energy consumption. On the other hand [9] implements a load control system through Telegram for the control of different devices in a dwelling.

The project uses an ESP8266 NodeMCU, an ACS712 current sensor and three relays as actuators. This work performs control functions through a messenger bot and uses an ACS712 current sensor to confirm the current flow to the device to which it is connected, but not with the intention of monitoring the energy consumption. In [10] we present the development of a residential energy monitoring system based also on the ACS712 current sensor, which, by means of an ESP8266 NodeMCU and an Arduino Uno module, sends the data to a Web server using the HTTP protocol and to a mobile application developed to be installed on the user's smartphone. It is an IoT solution supported by the technology of Google Cloud and Database whose communication is supported by the IoT Gateway Thingspeak. The mobile application of the user not only allows the monitoring and monitoring of energy consumption, but also has the possibility of carrying out load control.

3   Design of the System

The overall design of the system is dealt with in three stages, which are described below.

3.1   Stage 1. Design of Basic Functions

In this stage the structure of the NodeMCU programming was carried out, besides the connections in the physical part of the prototype were established. It was possible to establish the implementation of basic functions of the project, including communication with the Pzem-004t analyzer, the parameters for calculating the energy values, communication with the NTP and protection of sensitive information in the EEPROM. In the physical part, the connections of the module PZEM-004t, current sensor PCZT-02 and NodeMCU were realized, as well as the installation of the assembly of these to the home electrical network. At this stage only one sensor operated in the prototype, the collected and processed data were transmitted via serial communication and could be analyzed with the help of Arduino IDE software, where the first quality estimates of the measurements were analyzed and established. The architecture of stage 1 can be seen in Fig. 2.

3.2   Stage 2. Design of the Monitoring System

In stage 2 it was possible to implement messaging bots that allowed to perform different processes among them to establish the connection with the NodeMCU. This action makes it easier to send a data or signal to the microcontroller, which receives, processes and implements an action according to the instruction, and additionally stores the data in the EEPROM to preserve the established configuration. Another of the characteristics of stage 2 is the implementation of alerts (exceeding the established threshold), the sending

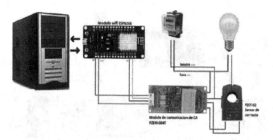

Fig. 2. Architecture of the basic functions stage.

of daily messages with the value for consumption of the last 24 h, as well as the ability of the bot to identify the types of characters received (text or number) and answer if the type of character is valid or invalid.

It was possible to structure the state machine that would allow access to the different instruction blocks or options of the prototype, among the most important are: States, Monitoring and Configuration. The structure of the status machine allows to see the information in an orderly way and to access the options via direct commands or routes established in the options tree, as can be seen in Fig. 3.

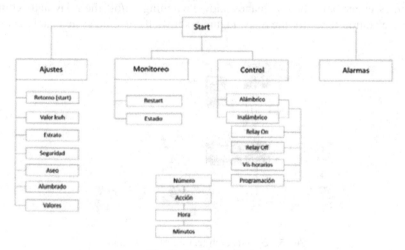

Fig. 3. Tree of options.

When one of the commands is selected, the parameters of the measurement delivered by the current sensor are displayed and it is possible to set configurations through messages containing the novelties or values processed by the microcontroller. Figure 4 shows the architecture of the monitoring stage.

3.3 Stage 3. Implementation of Load Control

For stage 3, load control was implemented. Two alternatives were implemented for this control. The first consists of a relay connected to the NodeMCU through one of the output

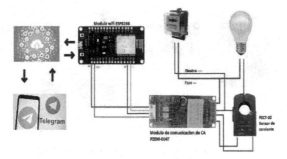

Fig. 4. Architecture of the monitoring stage.

pins and the second system through the ESP8266 Relay. The control of both systems is done through Telegram by commands to the messenger bot. The commands allow switching on/off the relay and setting of On-Off activation times for the relay. Figure 5 shows the overall system architecture. For stage 3, load control was implemented. Two alternatives were implemented for this control. The first consists of a relay connected to the NodeMCU through one of the output pins and the second system through the ESP8266 Relay. The control of both systems is done through Telegram by commands to the messenger bot. The commands allow switching on/off the relay and setting of On-Off activation times for the relay. Figure 5 shows the overall system architecture.

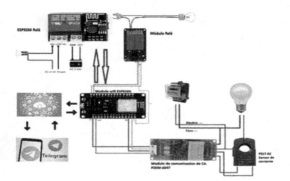

Fig. 5. General architecture of the system.

4   Implementation of the System

4.1   Calculation of the Value of Energy Consumption

In Colombia, payment for the consumption of residential public services, such as energy, is based on a system of charges for differential rates. These rates are associated to the socioeconomic stratum to which the residential property belongs. In this way, housing belonging to socio-economic strata, considered to be of lower resources, may receive subsidies and other assistance from the state. The tariffs of the domestic public service of electric energy in Colombia are established through Resolution CREG 079 of 1997, in Table 1 of tariff charges, it is possible to appreciate the system of calculation to be considered by the CREG (Commission of Regulation of Energy and Gas of Colombia) to establish the invoicing values. For its part, Table 2 shows the socioeconomic strata in Colombia and the subsidies corresponding to each of them.

Table 1. Tariff charges of the energy service in Colombia.

Tariff	=	Value
Tariff strata 1, 2 and 3	=	CU – Subsidy Tariff
Strata 4 and Officer	=	CU
Tariff strata 5, 6 and industrial	=	CU + Contribution

Table 2. Strata and subsidies for the charging of the energy service in Colombia.

Strata	Subsidies
1	50%
2	40%
3	15%
4	0%
5,6	Industry, 20% contribution

Figure 6 shows the flow diagram for the calculation of the estimation of the value of the energy bill. The values of Toilet, Lighting and Security are fixed values charged by the company that supplies the energy service.

4.2 Assembly

The functioning of the developed system was checked and validated, installing it in the main connection of electric power supply of a residence in the city of Barranquilla, stratum 5. Figure 7 shows the picture of the installed system and the names of its listed parts:

1. Current sensor PCZT-002.
2. Main impact (neutral).
3. Main task (1st phase).
4. Main task (2nd phase).
5. Multifunction meter PZEM-004T.
6. Microcontroller Node MCU ESP8266.

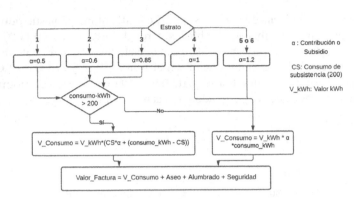

Fig. 6. Flow diagram for the calculation of the estimation of the value of the energy bill.

Fig. 7. Installed system and its parts listed.

5 Results

Before exposing the results obtained, we show the answers associated with the implementation of the parameters, technical specifications, operating characteristics and control processes from a computer with internet access, through the Telegram bot and directed to the NodeMCU. Next, in Fig. 8 (Selection Start, Access to the bot) it is observed how it is possible to access the initial menu of the options tree and the submenus that are in it.

Fig. 8. Access to Telegram bot with/Start.

One of the sub-menus is that of Settings through which you can access the tab of attributes or configuration values, where it is possible to enter the values of stratum, toilet, security, illumination and value of Kwh. This can be seen in Fig. 9. It is noteworthy that the values obtained for the different results were collected during the months in which this project was developed, and therefore the value per kWh used by the prototype to calculate the estimation of the cost of energy consumption may vary between the different results, since this value changes month to month.

Fig. 9. Values required to calculate the energy bill.

The implementation of the Telegram App allowed, through the bot, to weave the bridge between the user and the prototype, and thus, in a simple way to access the features of programming, data request and control of the associated devices. Later it will be appreciated how the final implementation of the prototype allowed the day-to-day verifications of the costs per consumption, i.e. the total invoiced at the date of consultation. Another function of the prototype is to alert when the consumption in weights exceeds a threshold programmed by the user. To set this threshold, the user sends the command /Alarms, to which the bot responds and the user enters the desired threshold, as shown in Fig. 10 and Fig. 11.

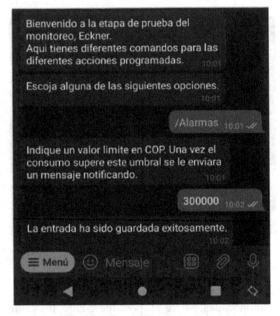

Fig. 10. Threshold programming.

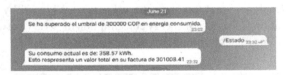

Fig. 11. Threshold crossing message.

By means of the command /Status located in the submenu´ Monitoring, as can be seen in Fig. 12, the consumption and an approximation of the invoiced value are evidenced, based on what was measured by the prototype. This value will be contrasted with that invoiced by the company providing the service in Barranquilla (Colombia) to calculate the variation or deviation of the measurements of the equipment under test.

The prototype sends a daily message with the measured consumption and its approximate value every 24 hours, as shown in Fig. 13.

Figure 14 shows the values collected during 8 days, the days the measurements were made and the differences in consumption of one day with respect to the previous one.

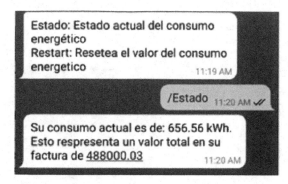

Fig. 12. Request of State (Partial Invoiced Value).

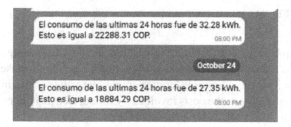

Fig. 13. Daily message of measured consumption.

The collected values were saved in a photographic record for later comparison with the measurement delivered by the prototype. It should be noted that the meter readings were taken visually on an analogue device and rounded to the most visible unit, so that errors of a few tenths of kWh will occur. The time difference between the respective measurements and photos is only a few minutes and does not significantly affect the result. The figure checks the precision of the prototype.

Subtracting the value of day 10 with that of day 17 of the results obtained through Telegram, we get 258.98 kWh. This gives a difference from the total measured by the meter of −3.02 kWh, which represents deviation from −1.15 % with respect to the accumulated household meter. It is clarified that the dates of the measurements are known, but the exact time of the measurements is not known; it is to be expected that there will be a variation in the final result, which will be taken into account when evaluating all the data collected.

The estimated value on December 9, 2021 obtained by the prototype reaches a value of $655,523.63 (six hundred and fifty-five thousand five hundred and twenty-three pesos with 63 cents), i.e. a consumption of 839.32 kWh; while the value invoiced by the provider reaches a value of $681350.0 (six hundred and eighty-one thousand three hundred and fifty pesos), the value payable, month of consumption November for a consumption of 851 kWh. Consumption in kilowatts obtaining a difference of - 11.68kWh with that of the prototype. For a greater fidelity of the estimation made by the prototype, an attempt was made to restart the accumulated and take the consumption

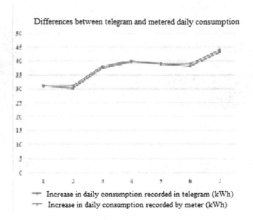

Fig. 14. Request of State (total value invoiced November).

measure at the same time as the service provider carried out the readings. In the first case the difference was a couple of hours and in the second case the proposed was achieved.

Finally, Table 3 invoicing and difference shows the value of the invoice, the value accumulated by the analyzer, the costs invoiced by the service provider and by the meter, as well as the final difference of both measurements.

Table 3. Invoicing by energetic meter and difference with measure of the prototype.

Billed accountant	851.00 kWh	$681,350.00
Prototype measurement	839.32 kWh	$655,523.63
Difference	11.68 kWh	$25,826.37

The difference could well be associated with the time difference of the reset time of the sensor PZEM-004T and the time of the reading of the service provider, as well as with the associated losses in the measurement systems, which could be the object of study later. The deviation between the measurement of the prototype with respect to that of the counter is -1.37 %, which is consistent with the interpretation made of the values in Table 3. The main reason for the difference between the calculated values and the actual value is the change in cost per kWh. The reference value taken is 575.39 COPs and between November and December the value increased to 592.79 COPs. The incremental difference of the reference kWh values is multiplied by 1.2 because the residence where the device is installed belongs to stratum 5.

$$1,2 \times (592,79 - 575,39) \times 839,32 = 17,52 \tag{1}$$

$$655523,63 + 17525 = 673048,63 \, COP \tag{2}$$

This results in a difference of 8.265.37 COP between the invoice and the prototype estimate.

As for the control part, in order to be able to operate the different commands, first choose the relay with which you want to interact. If a relay is not selected, the bot will respond with an error message.

To program the routines, you must send the command /prog routines to which the BOT will respond asking the routine to modify, the action to perform and the time. To activate the routine, the command /vis times must be sent where the times of the routines will appear and if they are activated (A) or deactivated (D).

6 Conclusions

For The installation of the prototype at the main power outlet of the home for the measurement of energy consumption became successful and quickly. Mainly because the installation of the sensors was made easier, because they are non-invasive sensors. In the same way the creation of the messaging bot in the Telegram application for sending commands and receiving messages from the prototype was done successfully. The results in the monitoring part showed the precision of the prototype to measure energy consumption, having a difference of 11.68 kWh, which represents an error of -1.37%, with respect to the home meter. The difference of 25,826 COP between the estimated cost and the cost on the invoice lies primarily in the difference in the kWh value. Little can be done here, since the estimates are made with the kWh value of the previous invoice and there is no way to check the new kWh value until the new invoice is received. The aim was to show the accumulated energy consumption and the estimation of the value to be paid in real time as well as to send alarm messages through the Telegram application. The control of the status of the wire and wireless relays was achieved using the Telegram application. In addition, it was achieved the establishment of up to three times to automatically put the respective relay in the programmed state. It is noteworthy that the command tree was made with the intention of being intuitive for the user, however, the monitoring commands can be executed in any order, unlike the control part where you must first choose the relay to control before executing the different commands. As aspects to be improved and to extend the functions of this project, it would be interesting to implement a function that allows adding and removing devices in the control part. Also the implementation of routines where the user can add the available devices and program an action, making the project more dynamic and similar to the systems found today on the market. Moreover, as mentioned earlier, this project does not show the history of consumption. One could implement the use of a server where this data is sent, as was done by other projects mentioned in the background section, or establish a range of days that allows the information to be stored in the EEPROM of the microcontroller, or also the use of external memories.

References

1. Lee, J.-W., Kim, Y.-L.: Energy saving of a university building using a motion detection sensor and room management system. Sustainability 12(22) (2020)
2. CIGEPI, Medición y gestión inteligente de consumo eléctrico. Boletín Tecnológico. Superintendendencia de Industria y Comercio (2016)

3. Josue J.G., Pina, J., Ventim-Neves, M.: Home electric energy monitoring system: De- sign and prototyping. IFIP Advances in Information and Communication Technology, vol. 349 (2011)
4. Jorge, A., Guerreiro, J., Pereira, P., Martins, J., Gomes, L.: Energy consumption monitoring system for large complexes. In: Camarinha-Matos, L.M., Pereira, P., Ribeiro, L. (eds.) Emerging Trends in Technological Innovation. DoCEIS 2010. IFIP Advances in Information and Communication Technology, vol 314. Springer, Berlin, Heidelberg (2010). https://doi. org/10.1007/978-3-642-11628-5_46
5. Bharathi R., Madhusree, M., Kumari, P.: Power consumption monitoring system using iot. Int. J. Comput. Appli. **173**(5), 23–25 (2017)
6. Serapio-Carmona A., Diaz-Rangel I., García Lozano, R,Z.:Sistema de monitoreo de consumo eléctrico con interfaz para teléfono inteligente. Res. Comput. Sci. **148**(10), 279–289 (2019)
7. De La Hoz J., G. B., K., B.,. Dispositivo de monitoreo de consumo para el ahorro de energ´ıa en el hogar. Computer and Electronic Sciences: Theory and Applications 2 (1), pp-18 (2021)
8. Guamán, P,F.J., Cabrera-Mejia, J.B.: Sistema de monitoreo remoto del consumo energético para hogares en la ciudad de Cuenca, basado en principios de IoT y servicios en la nube. Polo del Conocimiento: Revista científico - Profesional **5**(1), pp. 443–458. (2020)
9. Segura-Garrido, J.J.: Control y monitorización de una vivienda mediante Arduino y telegram. Ph.D. thesis, Universitat Politècnica de València, España, grado en Ingenier´ıa Elèctrica. Junio (2019)
10. Hariharan R.S., Agarwal R., K. M., Gaffar, H.A.: Energy consumption monitoring in smart home system. IOP Conf. Series: Mater. Sci. Eng., 1–10 (2021)
11. Rashid, K., Das, A.: Introduction to Chatbots. In Build Better Chatbots: A Complete Guide to Getting Started with Chatbots, 1st Edición. Apress, Berkeley, CA, Bangalore, Karnataka, India (2017)

Developing Ultrahigh-Resolution E3SM Land Model for GPU Systems

Peter Schwartz⬝, Dali Wang(✉)⬝, Fengming Yuan⬝, and Peter Thornton⬝

Environmental Sciences Division, Oak Ridge National Laboratory, Oak Ridge, TN 37830, USA
{schwartzpd,wangd,yuanf,thorntonpe}@ornl.gov

Abstract. Designing and refactoring complex scientific code, such as the E3SM land model (ELM), for new computing architectures is challenging. This paper presents design strategies and technical approaches to develop a data-oriented, GPU-ready ELM model using compiler directives (OpenACC/OpenMP). We first analyze the datatypes and processes in the original ELM code. Then we present design considerations for ultrahigh-resolution ELM (uELM) development for massive GPU systems. These techniques include the global data-oriented simulation workflow, domain partition, code porting and data copy, memory reduction, parallel loop restructure and flattening, and race condition detection. We implemented the first version of uELM using OpenACC targeting the NVidia GPUs in the Summit supercomputer at Oak Ridge National Laboratory. During the implementation, we developed a software tool (named SPEL) to facilitate code generation, verification, and performance tuning using these techniques. The first uELM implementation for Nvidia GPUs on Summit delivered promising results: 1) over 98% of the ELM code was automatically generated and tuned by scripts. Most ELM modules had better computational performances than the original ELM code for CPUs. The GPU-ready uELM is more scalable than the CPU code on fully-loaded Summit nodes. Example profiling results from several modules are also presented to illustrate the performance improvements and race condition detection. The lessons learned and toolkit developed in the study are also suitable for further uELM deployment using OpenMP on the first US exascale computer, Frontier, equipped with AMD CPUs and GPUs.

Keywords: Exascale Energy Earth System Model · E3SM Land Model · Ultrahigh-Resolution ELM · OpenACC · Compiler Directives

This research was supported as part of the Energy Exascale Earth System Model (E3SM) project, funded by the U.S. Department of Energy, Office of Science, Office of Biological and Environmental Research. This research used resources of the Oak Ridge Leadership Computing Facility and Experimental Computing Laboratory at the Oak Ridge National Laboratory, which are supported by the Office of Science of the U.S. Department of Energy under Contract No. DE-AC05-00OR22725.
P. Schwartz and D. Wang—These authors contributed equally.

1 Introduction

State-of-the-art Earth system models (ESM) provide critical information on climate changes and advance our understanding of the interactions among natural and human systems and the Earth's climate. Energy Exascale Earth System Model (E3SM) is a fully coupled ESM that uses code optimized for the US Department of Energy's (DOE) advanced computers to address the most critical Earth system science questions [3]. Inside the E3SM framework, the E3SM Land Model (ELM) simulates the interactions among terrestrial land surfaces and other Earth system components. ELM were used to understand hydrologic cycles, biogeophysics, and ecosystem dynamics of terrestrial ecosystems [2].

We are in the process of developing large-scale, ultrahigh-resolution ELM (uELM) simulation targeting the coming exascale computers [11] for high fidelity land simulation at continental and global scales. One major challenge is to develop an efficient ELM code suitable for the accelerators (e.g., GPUs) within the hybrid computing architecture of these Exascale computers. We have developed a function unit test framework that takes the code into pieces, and completed several individual ELM module development [6]. This study systematically presents the data structures and data flow of uELM, and summarize the technical experience gained in the uELM development to support unprecedented ultrahigh resolution simulations (1 km × 1 km) using GPU systems.

We first analyze the dataflow and computational characteristics of the ELM code, then present our strategies to develop a GPU-ready uELM, and demonstrate our first uELM implementation on a pre-exascale computer using a code porting toolkit and OpenACC. At last, we demonstrated several performance results of the first uELM implementation using a synthesized dataset.

2 Terrestrial Ecosystem Data-Oriented ELM Simulation

2.1 ELM Datatypes and Globally Accessible Variables

Highly-customized landscape datatypes (gridcell, topographic unit, land cover, soil column, and vegetation) are used to represent the heterogeneity of the Earth's surface and subsurface [16]. The gridcells are geospatially explicit datatypes, the subgrid components within gridcells (topographic unit, landunit, columns, and vegetation) were spatially implicit and configured with gridded surface properties dataset.

As shown in Table 1, eleven groups of landscape datatypes (over 2000 global arrays) are designed to store the state and flux variables at gridcells and their subgrid components. The physical properties datatypes contain association information among subgrid components so that the energy, water, and CNP variables can be tracked, aggregated, and distributed among gridcells and their subgrid components. Beside the landscape datatypes, customized ELM process datatypes are also used to represent the biogeophysical and biogeochemical processes in the terrestrial ecosystems. Examples of these ELM process datatypes are Aerosol_type, Canopystate_type, Lake_type, Photosynthesis_type, Soil_type,

Table 1. Eleven groups of ELM landscape datatypes and total number of public (globally accessible) variables in each group.

Landscape datatype	# variables	Associated grid components
cnstate_type	125	patch, column
column_energy_state,	850	column
column_water_state,		
column_carbon_state,		
column_nitrogen_state,		
column_phosphorus_state,		
column_energy_flux,		
column_water_flux,		
column_carbon_flux,		
column_nitrogen_flux,		
column_phosphorus_flux		
column_physical_properties	27	column, and association with other subgrid components
gridcell_energy_state,	170	gridcell
gridcell_water_state,		
gridcell_carbon_state,		
gridcell_nitrogen_state,		
gridcell_phosphorus_state,		
gridcell_energy_flux,		
gridcell_water_flux,		
gridcell_carbon_flux,		
gridcell_nitrogen_flux,		
gridcell_phosphorus_flux		
gridcell_physical_properties_type	33	gridcell, and association with other subgrid components
landunit_energy_state,	6	landunit
landunit_water_state,		
landunit_energy_flux		
landunit_physical_properties	22	landunit, and association with other subgrid components
topounit_atmospheric_state,	35	topounit
topounit_atmospheric_flux,		
topounit_energy_state		
vegetation_energy_state,	930	Vegetation (patch)
vegetation_water_state,		
vegetation_carbon_state,		
vegetation_nitrogen_state,		
vegetation_phosphorus_state,		
vegetation_energy_flux,		
vegetation_water_flux,		
vegetation_carbon_flux,		
vegetation_nitrogen_flux,		
vegetation_phosphorus_flux		
vegetation_properties_type	120	vegetation
vegetation_physical_properties	16	vegetation, and association with other subgrid components

and Urban_type. In total, these ELM process datatypes contained more than 1000 global arrays associated with gridcells and their subgrid components. All the ELM datatypes (functions and variables) are initialized and allocated as static, globally accessible objects on each computing (e.g., MPI) process after domain partitioning.

2.2   Domain Decomposition and Gridcell Aggregation

At the beginning of a simulation, ELM scans through the computational domain and assigned unique id to each land gridcell, then distributes these land gridcells to individual MPI processes using a round-robin scheme to achieve a balanced workload [4]. ELM uses special datatypes (Table 2) to define the computational domain on each MPI process. The gridcells on individual MPI processes are aggregated together as clumps. Each clump stores the procesor_id (MPI rank) and the total number of subgrid components with their starting and ending positions. Each MPI process allocates contiguous memory blocks (arrays) to hold the ELM variables across all the gridcells and associated subgrid components. All the ELM variables are allocated and initialized as globally accessible arrays. The maximum number of subgrid components are allocated within each gridcell, a group of filters are generated at each timestep to track the active subgrid components inside gridcells.

Table 2. Customized datatypes to define computational domain

int, npes	The number of MPI processes
int, clump_pproc	Max number of clumps per MPI process
int, nclumps	The number of clumps on individual process
clump_type	Owner, size of gridcells(subgrid components), begin and end indexes of these gridcell(subgrid components) in each clump
processor_type	nclumps, clump_id, size of gridcells (subgrid components), begin and end indexes of these gridcells(subgrid components) in each mpi_process
bounds_type*	Data_type to store the size and the begin and end indexes of gridcells (subgrid components) in clumps or processes

*Bounds_type is used to store the total number of gridcell components, as well as the start and end indexes of these gridcell components in either clumps or MPI processes.

2.3   Terrestrial Ecosystem Processes in ELM

ELM simulates key biogeochemical and biogeophysical processes in the terrestrial ecosystems, and their interactions with atmosphere. The general flow of an ELM simulation starts with the water and energy budget calculation and carbon-nitrogen balance check at each gridcell. ELM simulates phenomena of hydrology, radiation, lakes, soil, aerosols, temperature, ecosystem dynamics, dust, and albedo (Table 3). At each timestep, ELM also updates vegetation structure and checked the mass and energy balance. Over 1000 subroutines are developed to represent these biogeochemical and biogeophysical processes in the terrestrial ecosystems.

Table 3. ELM processes and execution sequence

Vertical decomposition, Dynamic Subgrid, CNP and Water Balance check	Determine decomposition vertical profile, update subgrid weights with dynamic landcover, and check mass balance
Canopy Hydrology and Temperature	Canopy Hydrology, and determine leaf temperature and surface fluxes based on ground temperature from previous time step
Surface and Urban Radiation	Surface Radiation Calculation
Flux Calculation (BareGround, Canopy, Urban, Lake)	Calculate energy fluxes in gridcell components (bareground, canopy, urban, and lake)
Dust Emission and DryDep	Dust mobilization and dry deposition
LakeTemperature and Hydrology	Lake temperature and hydrology
SoilTemperature and Fluxes	Set soil/snow temperatures including ground temperature and update surface fluxes for new ground temperature
HydrologyNoDrainage	Vertical (column) soil and surface hydrology
LakeHydrology	Lake hydrology
AerosolMasses	Calculate column-integrated aerosol masses
SoilErosion	Update sediment fluxes from land unit
EcosystemDynNoLeaching	Ecosystem dynamics: Uses CN, or static parameterizations
HydrologyDrainage	Calculate soil/snow hydrology with drainage (subsurface runoff)
EcosystemDynLeaching	Ecosystem dynamics: with leaching
SurfaceAlbedo and UrbanAlbedo	Determine albedos for next time step
subgridAve, Vegstructupdate, AnnualUpdate, Water and CNP balance check	Performance averaging among subgrid components, Update vegetation, WaterCPN balance check
Lnd2atm, lnd2grc	Interaction with atm and glacier
Hist_htapes_wrapup, restFile_write	HistoryRestart files (output)

2.4   ELM Simulation with Computational Loops

In our study, ELM is configured for land-only mode (i.e., driven by atmospheric forcing derived from observed datasets to predict ecosystem responses under past climatic scenarios). Several datasets have been developed to drive the land-only ELM simulation [5, 8, 9, 14]. The land surface has been a critical interface through which climate change impacts humans and ecosystems and how humans and ecosystems can affect global environmental change. The land surface is configured with surface properties datasets. The ELM simulations have several phases: the first phase is spin-up simulation to find the equilibrium states of terrestrial systems (may take a long period), the second phase is to simulate terrestrial ecosystems' responses to the historical atmospheric forcing (e.g., 1850 - present), and the third phase is to predict the ecosystem responses to future climatic scenarios.

The ELM simulations take half-hourly or hourly timesteps. At each timestep, ELM loops over each clump (aggregated gridcells and their active subgrid components) to calculate the changes of terrestrial ecosystem states and fluxes (more than 3000 global arrays) through the ELM processes (Table 3). The majority of computation over gridcells, their subgrid components, as well as the nutrient elements (that is carbon, nitrogen, and phosphorus (CNP)) are independent, with exception of several functions inside ecosystem dynamics, such as carbon-nitrogen allocation and soil litter decomposition [13]. In these cases, the CNP functions are limited by the carbon-nitrogen ratio and carbon-phosphorus ratio. The computational complexity of ELM come from the accessing, tracking, calculating, updating, and conservation-law checking (mass and energy) of these large number of state and flux variables (global arrays) within the ELM datatypes across the entire computational domain. To ensure mass and energy conservation, water, energy, and CNP states are aggregated and thoroughly checked in each gridcell at every timestep. At the end, ELM generates rich simulation results: by default, each monthly history output contains more than 550 variables representing the terrestrial ecosystem's geophysical, and biogeochemical processes (such as water, energy, carbon, nitrogen, and phosphorus cycles) at every land gridcell.

In summary, ELM is a gridcell independent, data-centric terrestrial ecosystem simulation that contains massive computational loops over gridcells and their subgrid components (Fig. 1). ELM has more than 1000 subroutines, none of which are computationally intensive.

3   GPU-ready uELM Development on Summit

We first present design considerations for the GPU-ready uELM development, then we describe the first uELM implementation on a pre-exascale computer with Nvidia GPUs.

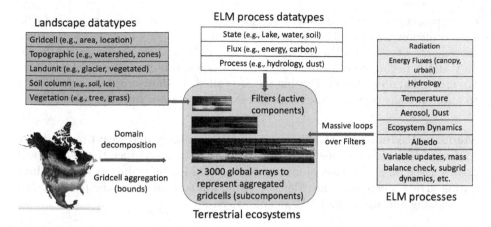

Fig. 1. Data-centric ELM simulation with numerous computational loops

3.1 uELM Design Considerations

ELM has been an integral part of E3SM simulations. We want uELM to maintain the maximum compatibility with the current E3SM framework and software engineering practices, including ELM datatypes and subroutines, data exchange with other E3SM components via a coupler, parallel IO, and model setup/configuration with the Common Infrastructure for Modeling the Earth.

Domain Partition. uELM is designed to support simulations over extremely large computational domains. For example, at a 1km by 1km resolution, the North America region contains around 22.5 million of land gridcells, that is approximately 230 times larger than the current global high resolution ELM simulation at a 0.5 by 0.5 °C resolution. Current implementation of uELM still support static domain decomposition with balanced workloads using a round-robin scheme. The size of subdomain (number of gridcells) are calculated to ensure all ELM inputs, datatypes (with global arrays), and code kernels present in GPU memory for many timesteps to achieve better performance. For example, each 16GB NVidia V100 GPU is used for uELM simulations over a subdomain of around 6000 gridcells. Technically, to increase the parallel execution performance on GPU, each clump in uELM contains 1 gridcell and each uELM subdomain contained around 6000 clumps. Approximately 700 computing nodes of Summit (4200 GPUs) will be needed for the uELM simulation over the entire North America region (22.5 millions of land gridcells).

Code Porting and Data Copy. As ELM contained more than 1000 computationally non-intensive subroutines, compiler directives (OpenACC or OpenMP) are selected for code porting [6], instead of the GPU-ready math libraries [1] or a new programming language [15]. To better handle these highly customized ELM datatypes, we use unstructured data regions to store these global arrays in GPU shared memory, and applied deepcopy function extensively to expedite the data movements between CPUs and GPUs. All global variables are copied to device only at the beginning of simulation, but for each subroutine, the local variables are created and deleted every time they're called. Python scripts are developed to automatically generate the enter and exit data clauses for each subroutine.

Memory Reduction. To efficiently use GPU memory and save time on host-to-device data transfers, we use scripts to systematically reduce the size of local arrays based on active filters for most of the uELM subroutines as well as eliminating arrays where possible. Memory reduction also increases the performance of accessing and updating ELM global arrays.

Parallel Loop Reconstruction and Flattening. Considering that the majority of ELM computation over gridcells(subgrid components) and nutrient elements (carbon, nitrogen, and phosphorus (CNP)) are independent, we reconstruct and flatten parallel loops inside uELM to improve performance. We also assign a large number of clumps (each containing one gridcell) onto each GPU for efficient parallel loop execution. For ELM functions with many internal loop structures and nested function calls, we reconstruct these routines to "flatten" their internal loops at column and patch levels, and group them under different parallel loop constructs. The technique has also been applied to many GPU-ready modules, including EcosystemDynNoLeaching [6], UrbanFlux, LakeFlux and LakeTemperature.

Variable Summation and Race Condition. Race conditions in the parallel constructs need to be inspected in the ELM water, energy, and mass aggregation and balance checking process, as lower level (such as patch) variables are summed into higher-level (column or gridcell) variables. Reduction clauses are used to increase the model performance with the same results. However, these parallel loop reconstructions require changes in loop logic that could not easily be inspected automated. Technically, we scan every uELM parallel do loop and detect race conditions based on following criteria:

1. a variable (an array or scalar) found on both sides of an assignment
2. the gridcell component that the variable is associated with was NOT the same gridcell component that was being looped over.
3. the variable had less indices than the number of loop variables (e.g., $a(c) = a(c) + b(c,j)$ where both c and j are looped over.)
4. a new value depends on a prior values (e.g., $a(c,j) = a(c,j-1) + other\_ops$)

If the first and one of the other three criteria are met (true), a do loop is flagged for manual inspection of race conditions by outputting the subroutine name and line number of the outermost loop.

3.2   uELM Code Generation and Performance Tuning on Summit

The computational platform used in the study is the Summit leadership computing system at the Oak Ridge National Laboratory. Summit has 4,608 computing nodes, most of them contain two 22-core IBM POWER9 CPUs, six 16-GB NVIDIA Volta GPUs, and 512 GB of shared memory.

We have developed a python toolkit, called SPEL [7], to port the all ELM module onto Nvidia GPUs using OpenACC. SPEL is used to generate 98% of the uELM code automatically. For the complete of the paper, the general workflow of code generation with SPEL is summarized in Fig. 2.

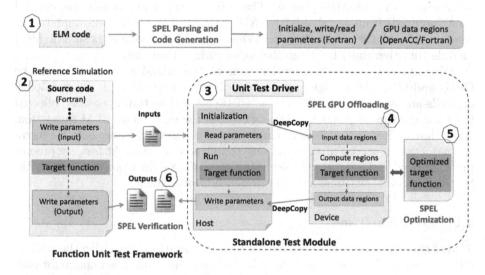

Fig. 2. uELM code porting workflow and SPEL functions

The SPEL workflow within a Functional Unit Testing framework [10,12] contains six steps: 1) SPEL parses the ELM code and generates a complete list of ELM function parameters. For an individual ELM function, SPEL marks the active parameters generates Fortran modules to read and write, initialize, and offload parameters. 2) SPEL inserts the write modules before and after a target ELM function to collect the input and output parameters from a reference ELM simulation. 3) SPEL constructs a unit test driver for standalone ELM module test. The driver initializes and reads function parameters, executes the target ELM module, and saves the output. 4) SPEL generates GPU-ready ELM test modules with OpenACC directives. 5) SPEL optimizes the GPU-ready test module (e.g., memory reduction, parallel loop, and data clauses). And 6) SPEL verifies code correctness at multiple stages of the ELM module testing (CPU, GPU, and GPU-optimized).

After the standalone ELM models testing and performance tuning, we then conduct end2end code integration and overall performance tuning with SPEL's tuning function again.

4 Numerical Experiments and Performance Evaluation

In this study, we use synthesized data from 42 AmeriFlux sites in the United States (https://ameriflux.lbl.gov/) to drive the uELM spin-up simulation for performance evaluation. On each Summit computing node, we launch 6 MPI processes, each managing one CPU core and one GPU. Around 6000 gridcells are assigned to each MPI process. The surface properties dataset are derived (downsampled) from a global $0.5 \times 0.5\,°C$ dataset. The GPU code validation is conducted by bit4bit comparison with the original CPU code at both individual module (function unit) level and the entire end2end simulation.

We present the overall execution time of the uELM simulation using the CPUs and GPUs of a single, fully-loaded Summit node (that is around 36000 gridcells are assigned to 6 GPUs or 42 CPU cores). The timing data is collected from a single timestep (on January 1st) within the end-to-end ELM simulation. After that we focus on technical details of performance improvements via memory reduction, loop restructure and race condition detection. At last, we present profiling results of several modules using Nvidia's Nsight Compute and Nsight Systems to reveal machine-level performance improvements.

4.1 Execution Time

Table 4 shows the execution time of GPU implementation along with the original CPU version of ELM on a single fully-loaded Summit node. The domain for each GPU is 5954 gridcells (142 sets of these 42 AmeriFlux sites) and the domain for each CPU core is 840 gridcells (20 sets of these 42 AmerFlux sites). Better performance had been achieved with most of ELM functions, except soilFlux and ecosystemDynLeaching that still have more rooms for improvements.

4.2 Memory Reduction

Table 5 lists examples of memory reduction within several individual uELM modules, On average, we achieved over 95% of reduction rate. The forcing data and uELM datatypes, including all the global variables, take 11 GB GPU memory when 6000 gridcells (approximate 1.8 MB data per gridcell) is assigned to each GPU. The total memory utilization after the memory reduction is around 14.4 GB, safely under the total 16 GB memory capability of the Nvidia V100.

Memory reduction improved code performance significantly as majority of ELM kernels are not compute bound. Herein, we present the timing results of major code sections inside an ELM module (LakeTemperature) to illustrate the speedup through memory reduction (Table 6). The most significant speedup occurred in the Initialization section where device copies of local variables

Table 4. Execution time of ELM functions in an single timestep end-to-end simulation using a single fully-loaded Summit node

Function names	GPU (millisecond)	CPU (millisecond)
DecompVertProfiles	3.81	25.30
dynSubgrid	27.96	35.17
ColBalanceCheck	14.68	2.01
Biogeophys setup	11.81	1.08
Radiation	1.40	1.07
CanopyTemp	0.95	1.36
CanopyFluxes	5.52	142
UrbanFluxes	3.08	4.18
LakeFluxes	0.82	5.45
LakeTemps	13.82	9.00
Dust	2.87	8.07
SoilFluxp2c	58.78	3.42
Hydro-Aerosol	18.70	18.54
EcosystemDynNoLeaching	66.25	99.10
EcosystemDynLeaching	110.50	23.16

Table 5. Examples of memory reduction within individual uELM modules

Module	Before reduction	After reduction	Percentage
LakeTemperature	50 arrays * 704 cols	45 arrays * 32 cols	4%
SoilLittVertTransp	15 arrays * 704 cols	6 arrays * 42 cols	2%
UrbanFluxes	73 arrays * 200 landunits	43 arrays * 21 landunits	6%
HydrologyNoDrainage	63 arrays * 704 cols	63 arrays * 40 cols	5%
CanopyFluxes	63 arrays * 1376 pfts	59 arrays * (0 or 4) pfts	< 1%
UrbanRadiation	21 array * 200 landunits	No arrays, all scalars	< 1%

are created and initialized to certain values. Memory reduction increases the percentage of computing time from 23% to 38%. Profiling individual kernels with Nsight™Compute confirm that the uncoalesced global accesses decreased or even disappeared, allowing better GPU utilization. For example, after memory reduction, kernels in the TriDiag Section require 4–8x less sectors and have less wasted cycles. These kernels also have a higher SM usage of approximately 25% (increased from 2% SM usage prior to memory reduction). Further performance improvements are also possible through fine-tuned pipelining and transpose of global and local arrays to accommodate new loop order.

Table 6. Timing results of major code sections in LakeTemperature

Code sections	Before reduction (millisecond)	Data reduction (millisecond)	Speedup
Initialize	20.8	6.82	3.05
Diffusion	0.36	0.20	1.76
SoilThermProp_Lake	1.23	0.48	2.57
EnergyCheck	0.14	0.13	1.12
Interface	0.32	0.13	2.43
TriDiag	0.58	0.17	3.45
PhaseChange_Lake	0.68	0.50	1.36
Mixing1stStage	1.12	1.11	1.00
MixingFinal	1.13	1.22	0.92
Diagnostic	0.77	0.22	3.53

4.3 Advanced Performance Improvements and Race Condition Detection

Many ELM subroutines contain nested loop structures and nested function calls that yielded poor performance with the routine directive, and so we use SPEL to further reconstruct many of these subroutines. We remove the external gridcell loop so that the internal loops can be as large as possible and accelerated with OpenACC parallel constructs. ELM subroutines also contain many summation operations that aggregate states and fluxes from lower-level gridcell components into higher-level gridcell components. To achieve better performance, we reorder the loops and increased the number loops to ensure the outer loops are independent, then we use gangs and workers for the outer loops (collapsed) and vectors for the innermost loop with OpenACC reduction clause. Further parallelism is also enhanced by reconstructing the parallel loop over similar operations among CNP cycles and history buffer (output) calculation. Good examples of these loop reconstruction can be found in a previous paper [6].

Race condition cases are detected in many ELM modules by SPEL. For illustration purposes, we present the race condition detection in three ELM modules (Table 7). Among 144 parallel loops in three modules, 46 cases (approximately 30%) are flagged by SPEL for manual investigation. Only 2 of these 46 flagged cases (LakeTemperature:L386 and LakeTemperature:L666) are not confirmed as a race condition as they either involve a scalar variable (sabg_nir) that is made private or a special array index is used for a multi-dimensional array (e.g. zx).

Table 7. Examples of race conditions within several uELM modules

Modules	Loops*	Race condition flagged by SPEL ** (subroutine:line_number [variables involved])
LakeTemperature	14 (40)	LakeTemperature:L386 ['sabg_nir', 'sabg_nir']
		LakeTemperature:L616 ['temp', 'temp', 'ocvts(fc)']
		LakeTemperature:L666 ['zx(fc,j)']
		phasechange_lake:L1693 ['qflx_snomelt(c)']
		phasechange_lake:L1752 ['qflx_snofrz_col(c)']
		LakeTemperature:L906 ['icesum']
		LakeTemperature:L1156 ['temp', 'lakeresist(c)']
		LakeTemperature:L1295 ['sum1']
Hydrology-NoDrainage	29 (90)	buildsnowfilter:L2891 ['snow_tot', 'nosnow_tot']
		snowwater:L343 ['qout(fc)']
		compute_effecrootfrac_and_verttransink:L1221 ['num_filterc']
		soilwater_zengdecker2009:L452 ['smp1', 'vwc_zwt(fc)']
		snowcompaction:L709 ['ddz1_fresh', 'ddz1', 'ddz3', 'ddz3', 'burden(fc)']
		combinesnowlayers:L1130 ['sum1', 'sum2', 'sum3', 'sum4']
		dividesnowlayers:L2001 ['dztot(fc)', 'snwicetot(fc)', 'snwliqtot(fc)']
		HydrologyNoDrainage:L553 ['sum1', 'sum2', 'sum3']
UrbanFluxes	2 (14)	UrbanFluxes:L441['fwet_roof', 'fwet_road_imperv', 'taf_numer(fl)', 'taf_denom(fl)', 'qaf_numer(fl)', 'qaf_denom(fl)', 'eflx_wasteheat(l)', 'zeta', 'zeta', 'iter']
		UrbanFluxes:L879['eflx_scale', 'qflx_scale']

* The first number showed the number of loops were flagged by SPEL for further investigation of race conditions. The second number showed the total number of loops in the module that were checked by SPEL
** For illustration purposes, we only listed up to 8 examples of race conditions in each module.

5 Conclusions

The paper reviewed the ELM software, presented design strategies and technical approaches to develop a data-oriented, GPU-ready uELM using compiler directives. We also described a software tool (SPEL) to code porting and the first implementation of uELM using OpenACC on the Summit supercomputer. The lessons learned and toolkit (SPEL) developed in the study will be used for the uELM deployment using OpenMP on the first US exascale computer, Frontier, equipped with AMD CPUs and GPUs.

References

1. Bertagna, L., et al.: A performance-portable nonhydrostatic atmospheric dycore for the energy exascale earth system model running at cloud-resolving resolutions. In: SC20: International Conference for High Performance Computing, Networking, Storage and Analysis, pp. 1–14. IEEE (2020)

2. Burrows, S., et al.: The doe e3sm v1. 1 biogeochemistry configuration: Description and simulated ecosystem-climate responses to historical changes in forcing. J. Adv. Modeling Earth Syst. **12**(9), e2019MS001766 (2020)

3. Golaz, J.C., et al.: The doe e3sm coupled model version 1: overview and evaluation at standard resolution. J. Adv. Model. Earth Syst. **11**(7), 2089–2129 (2019)

4. Hoffman, F.M., Vertenstein, M., Kitabata, H., White, J.B., III.: Vectorizing the community land model. Int. J. High Performance Comput. Appl. **19**(3), 247–260 (2005)

5. Qian, T., Dai, A., Trenberth, K.E., Oleson, K.W.: Simulation of global land surface conditions from 1948 to 2004. part i: Forcing data and evaluations. J. Hydrometeorol. **7**(5), 953–975 (2006)

6. Schwartz, P., Wang, D., Yuan, F., Thornton, P.: Developing an elm ecosystem dynamics model on gpu with openacc. In: Computational Science-ICCS 2022: 22nd International Conference, London, UK, June 21–23, 2022, Proceedings, Part II. pp. 291–303. Springer (2022). DOI: https://doi.org/10.1007/978-3-031-08754-7_38

7. Schwartz, P., Wang, D., Yuan, F., Thornton, P.: Spel: Software tool for porting e3sm land model with openacc in a function unit test framework. In: Accelerator Programming-WACCPD 2022: 9th Workshop on Accelerator Programming Using Directives, Dallas, USA, Nov 18, 2022, Proceedings. pp. 1–14. Springer (2022)

8. Thornton, P.E., Shrestha, R., Thornton, M., Kao, S.C., Wei, Y., Wilson, B.E.: Gridded daily weather data for north america with comprehensive uncertainty quantification. Sci. Data **8**(1), 1–17 (2021)

9. Viovy, N.: Cruncep version 7-atmospheric forcing data for the community land model. Research Data Archive at the National Center for Atmospheric Research, Computational and Information Systems Laboratory 10 (2018)

10. Wang, D., et al.: Scientific functional testing platform for environmental models: An application to community land model. In: International Workshop on Software Engineering for High Performance Computing in Science, 37th International Conference on Software Engineering (2015)

11. Wang, D., Schwartz, P., Yuan, F., Thornton, P., Zheng, W.: Towards ultra-high-resolution e3sm land modeling on exascale computers. Comput. Sci. Eng. **01**, 1–14 (2022)

12. Wang, D., et al.: A functional test platform for the community land model. Environ. Model. Softw **55**, 25–31 (2014)

13. Xu, Y., Wang, D., Janjusic, T., Wu, W., Pei, Y., Yao, Z.: A web-based visual analytic framework for understanding large-scale environmental models: a use case for the community land model. Procedia Comput. Sci. **108**, 1731–1740 (2017)

14. Yoshimura, K., Kanamitsu, M.: Incremental correction for the dynamical downscaling of ensemble mean atmospheric fields. Mon. Weather Rev. **141**(9), 3087–3101 (2013)

15. Zhang, S., et al.: Optimizing high-resolution community earth system model on a heterogeneous many-core supercomputing platform. Geosci.ent Model Develop. **13**(10), 4809–4829 (2020)

16. Zheng, W., Wang, D., Song, F.: Xscan: an integrated tool for understanding open source community-based scientific code. In: International Conference on Computational Science, pp. 226–237. Springer (2019)

A Reliability-Based Task Scheduling Method for Wireless Distributed Systems

Sonali Bodkhe[1]([✉]) and Anjali Mahajan[2]

[1] Department of Computer Science, Sant Gadge Baba Amravati University, Amravati, Maharashtra, India
sendtowiser@gmail.com
[2] Government Polytechnic, Nagpur, Maharashtra, India

Abstract. Parallel computing and distributed computing are the popular terminologies of scheduling. With advancement in technology, systems have become much more compact and fast and need of parallelization plays a major role for this compaction. Wireless computing is also a common concept associated with each new development. Scheduling of tasks has always been a challenging area and is an NP-complete problem. Moreover, when it comes to wireless distributed computing, reliable scheduling plays an important role in order to complete a task in a wireless distributed system. This work proposes an algorithm to dynamically schedule tasks on heterogeneous processors within a wireless distributed computing system. A lot of heuristics, meta-heuristics & genetics have been used earlier with scheduling strategies. However, most of them haven't taken reliability into account before scheduling. Here a heuristic that deals with reliable scheduling is considered. The scheduler also works within an environment which has dynamically changing resources and adapts itself to changing system resources. The testing was carried out with up to 200 tasks being scheduled while testing in a real time wireless distributed environment. Experiments have shown that the algorithm outperforms the other strategies and can achieve a better reliability along with no increase in make-span, in spite of wireless nodes.

Keywords: Distributed Computing · Scheduling · Reliability · Wireless Distributed Systems (WDS)

1 Introduction

One of the basic steps to exploit the capabilities of heterogeneous distributed computing systems is scheduling which is an NP-complete problem. In such cases meta-heuristic is the best choice. The use of heuristics in the initial stages of a meta-heuristic can be effective for improving the solutions obtained by meta-heuristics. Make-span is an important factor to evaluate the efficiency of scheduling algorithms. Task scheduling can be classified in to various types as shown in Fig. 1.

The process of scheduling can be carried out for wired as well as wireless systems. When a set of identical processors connected in the system have the same computational

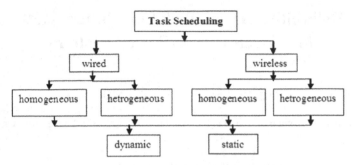

Fig. 1. Classification of task scheduling

speed and processor, the distributed systems are termed as homogeneous distributed computing systems.

When several processors with different computational speeds are interconnected through high speed links together to solve a problem with varying computational requirements, the distributed system is termed as an heterogeneous distributed computing system.

Real time scheduling in multiprocessor systems has gained increased attention over past years and is becoming common these days [1]. However, most of the work carried out targets "under loaded" systems, i.e., systems where the total task utilization demand 'U', is always less than the total available processing capacity of the system, which can be stated as 'm' for an m-processor system. The majority of research on multiprocessor systems focuses on developing scheduling algorithms by trying to understand their schedulability, utilization bounds, i.e., utilization bounds of tasks, below which all task deadlines are met. The limit of this approach is that it is possible to determine the worst-case execution-time behaviors of applications and hence determine the total task utilization demands. After the task utilization demand is known, task schedulability, i.e., the ability of processors to meet all task deadlines can be ensured. For some applications (e.g., [2–4]), it is difficult to determine worst-case execution-time as a priori, since it may depend on the run-time demands like the execution time overruns and unpredictable task arrival patterns, causing short term and/or permanent overloads. Whenever overloads occur, such applications require graceful timeliness degradation, thus fulfilling as many deadlines of importance tasks as possible, irrespective of the urgency of tasks.

Heterogeneous systems are dependable computing platforms. Many a times heterogeneous distributed computing (HDC) systems can achieve higher performance with lesser cost than single super-systems on account of resource optimization. Besides performance, fairness is also a very important requirement for the scheduling approaches.

However, in these systems, processors and networks are not free from failure and thus tend to increase the criticality of the running applications. In order to deal with failures, a reliable scheduling algorithm is an important requirement. Unfortunately, most scheduling algorithms applied for scheduling tasks in HDC systems do not sufficiently consider inter-dependent reliability requirements of tasks [5–9].

Reliability of a wireless distributed system is an important parameter in real time scheduling of tasks [10–12]. The failures occurring in a distributed system can result in anything from minute errors to disastrous halts. When a reliable distributed system is designed it should as fault tolerant as possible. The proposed work focuses on finding a solution at the software level to wireless core-computing with due attention to the factor of concern i.e. power utilization along with scheduling and reliability. On the lines of scheduling with heuristics, a strategy for the same is applied to wireless distributed systems wherein WDSs are more prone to instability.

The work aims in proposing a reliable task scheduling strategy so that a job submitted can be reliably and successfully completed [13–17]. It also focuses on the power factor of a wireless node along with reliability. Make-span is another parameter that has been worked upon, such that, both reliability and make-span can be reduced.

2 Methodology/Experimental

The basic scheduling methodology considered so far in earlier researches, takes into account the basic scheduling model of Fig. 2 in a heterogeneous cluster environment, wherein a *global scheduler* works in collaboration with a Resource Manager. It is assumed that all parallel jobs are submitted to the global scheduler in the form of a Directed Acyclic Graph. A *schedule queue (SQ)* for arriving jobs is maintained by the scheduler, which is responsible for scheduling real-time tasks of each job in SQ. It places an accepted job in a *dispatch queue (DQ)* and from here, tasks of each accepted job are sent to designated machines, also called *processing elements (PEs)*, for execution. The scheduler also executes in parallel with PEs, each of which maintains a *local queue (LQ)* to which real-time tasks are transmitted from *DQ*. [7, 18].

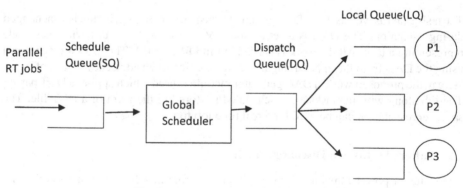

Fig. 2. A Basic Task Scheduling Model

However, keeping tasks in queue doesn't fulfill the reliability concept since the tasks are in a waiting state and also the amount of computations done by the earlier task might no longer retain the reliability of that wireless system to the same extent for other tasks in the queue. Hence, the local queues have been eliminated as in Fig. 3. According to the proposed strategy, a SQ contains all the tasks in a job defined in terms of dependency levels here. The proposed scheduling algorithm is applied to these levels and one task at a time is assigned to each scheduler [7].

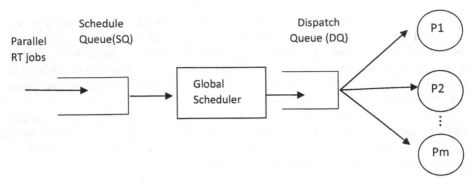

Fig. 3. A Proposed Task Scheduling Model

The input to the algorithm is a job which is modeled through a directed acyclic graph (*DAG*). $G = \{V, E\}$, where $V = \{v_1, v_2,..., v_n\}$ represents a set of real-time tasks and E represents a set of directed edges among the real-time tasks. $M_{ij} = (v_i, v_j) \in E$ denotes a message transmitted from task v_i to v_j, and $|m_{ij}|$ is the volume of data transmitted between these tasks. A heterogeneous cluster is represented by a set $P = \{p_1, p_2,......, p_m\}$ of processors, where p_i is a processor with local memory. Machines in the heterogeneous cluster are connected with one other by a high-speed network. A machine communicates with other machines through message passing, and time between two tasks assigned to the same machine is assumed to be zero [20, 21].

2.1 Generation of DAG

The task graph as well as the WDS is assumed to be static, meaning, it remains unchanged during execution. The DAG is a set of nodes $V = \{u_1, u_2, ..., u_n\}$ with each node representing a task. All the work is carried out in OPEN-MPI. The tasks are generated using the DAG from the upper triangular representation of an adjacency matrix of tasks. Here in the proposed work, a DAG generator module is used which applies a DOT parser. The job along with the tasks to be scheduled is stored in the form of a DOT file. The same representation can be used for a real time job too.

2.2 Battery Status and Discharge Power

The status of power remaining plays an important role in scheduling of tasks that are being shifted. The amount of power remaining with a wireless node determines its acceptability for extra tasks. This power is considered in the calculation of the discharge rate for allotted tasks.

Discharge power= 1-remaining power

2.3 Reliability of the System

Reliability is defined to be the probability that the system will not fail during the time that it is executing the tasks. The failure rate helps in determining the reliability of the system to complete a particular task. The higher the reliability cost, the less reliable the system is.

The reliability of task execution of each process on each processor is given as in Eq. 1

$$R_{ij} = dp_j t_i(j) + f_j c_i t_j(i) + \sum_{p \in Pred(i)} \sum_{k=1}^{M} g_{kj} w_{pi} d_{kj} \tag{1}$$

Rate of power discharge + computation time + data transfer rate.
Where,
dp_{ij} = discharged power by task$_i$ on processor$_j$ = 1 − (value / 100).
t_{ij} = Computation time of task$_i$ on processor$_j$
f_j = failure rate of processor$_j$
c_i = criticality of task$_i$
g_{kj} = communication link failure rate of kth task on j^{th} processor
w = weight matrix
d = time delay to send unit length data from Pk to Pj
n = no. of tasks
m = no. of processors
R = Reliability matrix

Most of the earlier work focuses on one or two parameters only. If reliability is the issue to be dealt, scheduling is not stressed upon, if scheduling is the issue to be dealt, reliability is ignored. Also amount of power associated with a wireless node has a crucial role to play. The current work focuses on all parameters. The estimation of the failure rate of a wired and wireless system listed below:

Failure rate for.

1. **Wireless node = 8% = 0.08**
2. **Wired node = 4% = 0.04**

To maximize system reliability, it is needed to minimize the Reliability Cost. Thus Reliability Cost is used as the indicator of how reliable a given system is when a group of tasks are scheduled and executed on to it. The lower the reliability cost is, the higher the reliability is. The Overall Reliability cost is given as

$$RC = \sum_{j=1}^{M} R_j \tag{2}$$

where, Rj is the reliability cost of task ui on processor Pj

2.4 Phases of Task Scheduling in WDS

As shown in Fig. 4, task scheduling is carried out in 3 phases:

1. System Analysis
2. Scheduling

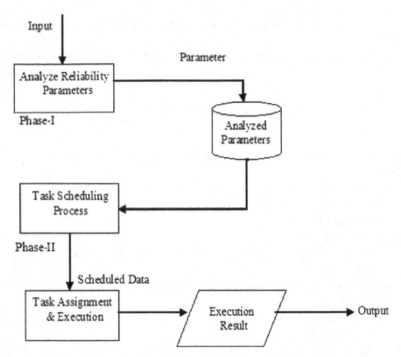

Fig. 4. Phases of task scheduling in Wireless Distributed Systems.

3. Task Assignment & execution

The first phase is the *System Analysis* phase. The input to this phase is a DAG. Depending on the number of active hosts, which is stored in a *hostfile*, this phase evaluates the various parameters necessary to compute the reliability and scheduling of the submitted job. The output of this phase is stored in a file.

The second phase is the *Task Scheduling* phase. The input to this phase is a DAG which is given as input to ASAP/ALAP. These algorithms produce as output, the various levels and the dependency among the tasks at each level. Depending on the availability of existing and active processors/systems, tasks are then scheduled/ assigned to various processors in the wireless systems by combining the reliability using RBTSA and discharge power factors.

The third phase is the *Task Assignment & Execution* phase. This phase counts the number of tasks in each level, sends each task to the identified processor for execution and evaluates the total execution time for the submitted job. The algorithms for the 3 phases are given below:

Phase-1

Compute System Analysis()

1. Read the DAG file.
2. Identify active hosts/systems and processors.
3. Evaluate the communication link failure.
4. Evaluate computation time of n tasks on m processors.
5. Evaluate communication delay for each processor.
6. Evaluate the failure rate of each processor.
7. Display the parameters computed from steps 2 to 6.
8. Store the parameters in step 7 into a file for next phase.

Phase-2

Reliability Based Distributed Task Scheduling Algorithm-RBDTSA

Compute Task Scheduling ()

   Takes as input the various analyzed parameters & DAG.

1. Schedule ASAP or ALAP on the input DAG and compute dependency levels.
2. Execute fragmentation on the output of ASAP/ALAP.
   a. Read the number of active processors.
   b. Depending on the number of active processors, split the created level, keeping only as many processes in the split as the number of active processors.
3. Read various parameters of system analysis.
4. Compute discharge power Dp_k for each active processor k.
5. Compute reliability cost RC matrix using Dp_k.
6. Send task to the identified processor on the basis of reliability cost matrix in 5.
7. Schedule tasks according to processors identified in step 6.

Phase-3

Compute Assignment-Execution ()

1. Depending on the number of active processors, the scheduling strategy, count the number of tasks assigned to each processor after fragmentation.
2. Send these tasks to each slave for execution.
3. Read the HM, MI, DT values for each task and send them to the respective processor.
4. Depending on DT & MI, the corresponding task will execute. Record the execution time of each slave.
5. Calculate the total execution time of the submitted job.
6. Display ET as output.

   The output of testing and execution are discussed in the next section.

3 Results

The WDS was tested with 06 machines-03 wired, 03 wireless so that heterogeneity could be included. The configuration included is listed below.

System configuration:

Machine Configuration						
	M1	M2	M3	M4	M5	M6
Cores	4	4	2	4	4	4
Speed per Processor (GHz)	3.2	3.07	2.2	3.2	3.2	3.2
RAM (GB)	2	2	1	2	2	2

Number of Machines = 6 Total processors = 22.
Number of Slaves = 21 Master = 1 No of nodes in graph = 10

The testing has been carried out on graphs with 10, 20, 30, 40, 50, 100, 150 & 200 nodes (tasks). However, the results have been discussed only on the basis of a graph with 10 nodes. The first phase produces values for parameters like computation time, communication delay, link failure rate, failure rate, etc. After the first phase, the task scheduling is carried out. In this phase the ASAP/ALAP are used to find the dependency levels among tasks and fragmentation is carried to limit the tasks in each level to the number of processors. At the same time, the reliability of each task on each processor is also evaluated. The matrices of evaluated parameter values have not been included here since 22 processors were used, which resulted in large matrix size. A sample graph is shown in Fig. 5 and its task dependency using ASAP/ALAP is given below. The output of fragmentation is also listed for an overview.

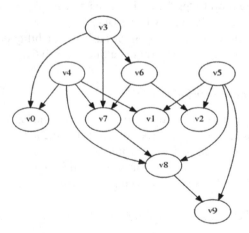

Fig. 5. An input DAG of 10 tasks

ASAP Time Matrix:

nVertex	nTask	Scheduled Time
0	1	2
1	2	2
2	3	3
3	4	1
4	5	1
5	6	1
6	7	2
7	8	3
8	9	4
9	10	5

ALAP Time Matrix:

nVertex	nTask	Scheduled Time
0	1	5
1	2	5
2	3	5
3	4	1
4	5	2
5	6	3
6	7	2
7	8	3
8	9	4
9	10	5

Output of fragmentation:

Fragmented Time Matrix:

Level	Task(s)	No. of Processors
1	4 5 6	3
2	1 2 7	3
3	3 8	2
4	9	1
5	10	1

The total time required to evaluate various parameters for reliability cost calculation for various graphs is given in the Table 1 and its graphical representation in Fig. 6

As shown in Fig. 7 and Table 2 it can be seen that the reliability cost of the proposed scheduling strategy is lower as compared to the other scheduler implemented. Also, it can be clearly stated from the shape of the representation that as the number of tasks increase the graph would form a conical structure wherein the reliability cost of random scheduler is more prone to increase indicating less reliable scheduling. Figure 8 gives the bar graph representation of Table 2.

The makespan values of the two algorithms have also been compared in Table 3 and indicate that makespan of proposed RBDTS algorithm for scheduling a DAG is better as compared to RS. The reliability values of existing implemented methods can also be compared as shown in Table 4. However there are wide variations in the way reliability is referred in the existing and proposed techniques. Most of the existing methods use

System Analysis time graph

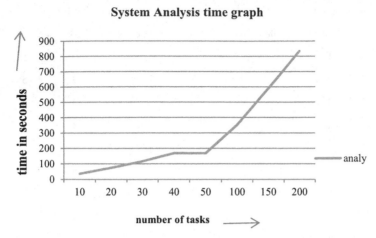

Fig. 6. Plot of time required for system analysis for varying nodes/tasks

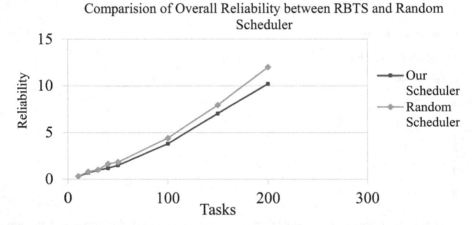

Fig. 7. Comparison of Overall Reliability between the RBTS and Random Scheduler (line graph)

simulation and have assumed values. Also a large number of methods are first assigning tasks and then evaluating reliability whereas the proposed method first evaluates reliability of processors and then assigns tasks Fig. 9.

It can be clearly seen that the overall reliability values for different set of tasks higher as compared to the two implemented methods (RBDTS, RS). The higher the reliability, the less reliable the system is. Thus it can be clearly said that the proposed method is a reliable method for task scheduling. A graphical comparison of the reliability values of Table 4 is shown in Fig. 10.

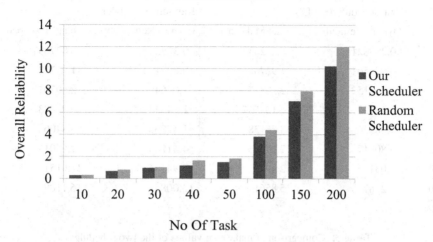

Fig. 8. Comparison of Overall Reliability between the RBTS and Random Scheduler (bar graph)

Table 1. System Analysis

Task	Time (sec)
10	36.2988
20	74.347
30	116.704
40	169.099
50	168.824
100	352.258
150	588.1
200	834.502

Table 2. Comparison of Scheduling

Task	Our Scheduler(RBTS)		Random Scheduler	
	Overall Reliability	Total Makespan	Overall Reliability	Total Makespan
10	0.283821	0.912037	0.317246	0.877697
20	0.677561	1.9276	0.801174	1.93772
30	0.962152	2.38857	1.0264	2.60701
40	1.18722	4.103537	1.64644	6.93073
50	1.48946	3.86138	1.82865	3.8406
100	3.80217	7.47043	4.41203	7.65011
150	7.03167	12.4979	7.94194	11.6151
200	10.2187	15.8561	12.008	16.1109

Table 3. Comparison of makespan values of the two schedulers

Task	Our Scheduler (RBDTS)	Random Scheduler
	Total Makespan	Total Makespan
10	0.912037	0.877697
20	1.9276	1.93772
30	2.38857	2.60701
40	4.103537	6.93073
50	3.86138	3.8406
100	7.47043	7.65011
150	12.4979	11.6151
200	15.8561	16.1109

The earlier implementations have used ASAP, ALAP for scheduling and compared the values of these standard methods with their proposed method-RCD. In the proposed work, RS and RBDTS have been implemented. RS uses a random scheduling strategy whereas RBDTS is the proposed reliable task scheduling method. It can be clearly stated that RBDTS algorithm when applied for task scheduling, gives a more reliable task schedule since the overall reliability values of RBDTS over a range of tasks is significantly less as compared to other methods thus indicating that the wireless distributed system is more reliable Fig. 11.

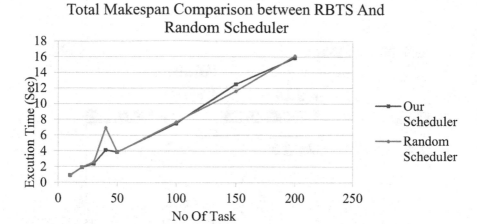

Fig. 9. Comparison of make-span of Random & Our Scheduler (RBDTS)

Table 4. Comparison of reliability values of existing and proposed implementation

No. of Tasks Reliability evaluation methods		10	30	50	70	90
Existing	**ASAP**	10.04	29.14	46.58	64.21	79.56
	ALAP	8.95	23.17	35.58	45.75	54.58
	RCD	0.83	2.5	4.18	5.82	7.44
	RS	0.31725	1.0264	1.82865	---	---
Proposed	**RBDTS**	0.28382	0.96215	1.48946	2.05524	2.60572

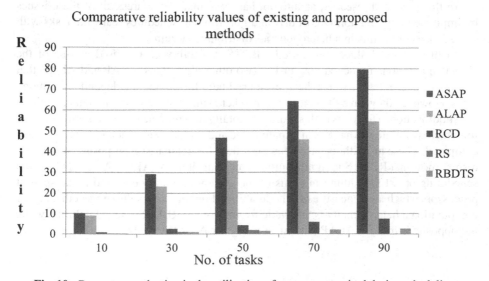

Fig. 10. Percentage reduction in the utilization of resources required during scheduling

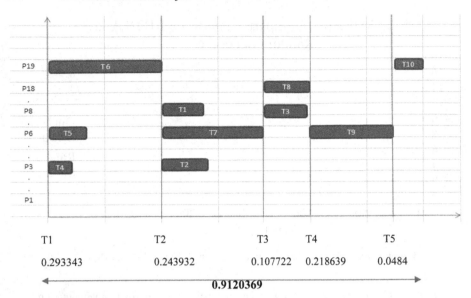

T1	T2	T3	T4	T5
0.293343	0.243932	0.107722	0.218639	0.0484

0.9120369

Fig. 11. Total Makespan in terms of task allocation & execution sequence.

4 Discussion

From the above sections, it can be concluded that till recent years, most research work in the area of real-time task scheduling in distributed systems was based on the following considerations:

1. It did not consider reliability issues prior to scheduling.
2. It only considered homogeneous systems, or assumed independent tasks.
3. Power discharged wasn't an issue, since wired networks were considered.

In this proposed research, an attempt has been made to address all of these issues by implementing a reliability cost driven algorithm that schedules real-time tasks with precedence constraints in a heterogeneous distributed system.

In the proposed algorithm, called RBDTS, reliability cost is used as one of the objective functions for scheduling tasks. Two other algorithms, ASAP and ALAP, that do not consider reliability cost, have been used here for finding the dependency among tasks. However, they haven't been mentioned here since they have implemented without any modification. The focus in this work was totally on a reliable task scheduling method for which two strategies have been implemented and explained and their results have been compared. These algorithms have been used here for comparison purposes. Simulation results show that RBDTS is significantly better than either ASAP, ALAP, RCD, random scheduling or list scheduling in terms of the system reliability cost and make-span of processors which are a measure of schedulability. Further, the results suggest that higher computational heterogeneity is favorable for improving RBDTS's schedulability, while the opposite is true for ALAP (and most likely for ASAP as well).

5 Conclusion

The proposed algorithm evaluates system reliability and accordingly generates a schedule for the tasks of a particular program/job submitted in the distributed system. Here a dynamic wireless distributed system has been assumed so as to justify the real purpose of scheduling. Also, two algorithms of a normal distributed system are tested by executing in wireless distributed systems.

However, the newly proposed algorithm could not be compared since strategies related to reliable scheduling in wireless distributed systems are unavailable. The methods applied earlier to a normal distributed system and their results are compared here with the two new approaches used for comparison.

In conclusion, the main features of the design proposed in the current research work can be summarized as:

- The proposed strategy considers parameters of normal as well as wireless distributed systems.
- 02 existing algorithms of a normal heterogeneous system have been used for scheduling and the results for reliability can be compared using 2 existing strategies for this proposed algorithm in the wireless distributed system.
- The newly designed algorithm aims to give a better scheduling strategy after being tested for existing algorithms.
- Scheduling using ASAP gives better results as compared to ALAP in WDS in terms of reliability cost.

Data Availability Statement. The task graphs, processor timings and other statistics used to support the findings of this study are available from the corresponding author upon request. (email-sonali.mahure@gmail.com).

References

1. Carpenter, J., Funk, S., Holman, P., Srinivasan, A., Anderson, J., Baruah, S.: A categorization of real-time multiprocessor scheduling problems and algorithms. In: Handbook on Scheduling Algorithms, Methods, and Models. Chapman Hall, CRC, Boca (2004)
2. Raymond Clark, E., et al.: An adaptive, distributed airborne tracking sysem: Process the right tracks at the right time. Presented at the (1999). https://doi.org/10.1007/BFb0097917
3. Tan, T.G., Hsu, W.: Scheduling multimedia applications under overload and nondeterministic conditions. IEEE RTSS, 0, 178 (1997)
4. Vallidis, N.M.: Whisper: a spread spectrum approach to occlusion in acoustic tracking. PhD thesis at the University of North Carolina at Chapel Hill (2002)
5. Beaumont, O., Legrand, A., Robert, Y., ENS Lyon, L. Carter., Ferrante, J.: Bandwidth-Centric Allocation of Independent Tasks on Heterogeneous Platforms. In: Proceedings International Parallel and Distributed Processing Symposium (2002)
6. Doğan, A., Özgüner, F.: Reliable matching and scheduling of precedence-constrained tasks in heterogeneous distributed computing. In: Proceedings of the International Conference on Parallel Processing, pp. 307–314 (2000)
7. Kebbal, D., Talbi, E.G., Geib, J.M.: Building and scheduling parallel adaptive applications in heterogeneous environments. In: Proceedings of the IEEE International Workshop Cluster Computing, pp.195–201 (1999)

8. Radulescu, A., van Gemund, A.J.C.: Fast and effective task scheduling in heterogeneous systems. In: Proceedings of the Euromicro Conference on Real-Time Systems, pp. 229–238 (2000)

9. Tang, X.Y., Chanson, S.T.: Optimizing static job scheduling in a network of heterogeneous computers. In: Proceedings of the International Conference on Parallel Processing, pp. 373–382 (2000)

10. Kalogeraki, V., Melliar-Smith, P.M., Moser, L.E.: Dynamic scheduling for soft real-time distributed object systems. In: Proceedings of the IEEE International Symposium on Object-Oriented Real-Time Distributed Computing, pp.114–116 (2000)

11. Lundqvist, T., Stenstrom, P.: Timing anomalies in dynamically scheduled micromachines. In: Proceedings of the IEEE Real-Time Systems Symposium, pp.12–21 (1999)

12. Palis, A.: Online Real-Time Job Scheduling with Rate of Progress Guarantees. In: Proceedings of the 6th International Symposium on Parallel Architectures, Algorithms, and Networks, Manila, Philippines, pp. 65–70 (2002)

13. Beaumont, O., Boudet, V., Robert, Y.: Realistic Model and an Efficient Heuristic for Scheduling with Heterogeneous Processors. In: Proceedings of the 11th Heterogeneous Compting Workshop (2002)

14. Doğan, A., Özgüner, F.: Reliable matching and scheduling of precedence-constrained tasks in heterogeneous distributed computing. In: Proceedings of the International Conference on Parallel Processing (ICPP), Toronto, Canada, August 21–24, pp 307–316 (2000)

15. Braun, T.D., Siegel, H.J., Maciejewski, A.A.: Static Mapping Heuristics for Tasks with Dependencies, Priorities, Deadlines, and Multiple Versions in Heterogeneous Environments. In: Proceedings of the International Parallel and Distributed Processing Symposium (2002)

16. Qin, X.: Hong Jiang, A dynamic and reliability-driven scheduling algorithm for parallel realtime jobs on heterogeneous clusters. J. Parallel Distrib. Comput. **65**(8), 885–900 (2005)

17. Raj, J.S., Vasudevan, V.: Intelligent Reliable Schedule with Budget Constraints in Grid Computing. Res. J. Appl. Sci., Eng. Technol. **7**(4), 650–655 (2014)

18. Kalogeraki, V., Melliar-Smith, P.M., Moser, L.E.: Dynamic scheduling for soft real-time distributed object systems. In: Proceedings of the IEEE International Symposium on Object-Oriented Real-Time Distributed Computing, pp.114–121 (2000)

19. Bodkhe, S.T., Mahajan, A.R.: Reliability Aware Task Scheduling In: Wireless Hetrogeneous Systems, published in International Journal of Computer Applications, ISSN: 0975–8887, Vol. 140 – No.8, April 2016, pp. 20–26 (2016)

20. Zomayya, A.Y., Ward, C., Macey, B.S.: Genetic scheduling for parallel processor systems: comparative studies and performance issues. IEEE Trans Parallel Distrib Syst **10**(8), 795–812 (1999)

21. Dai, Y.-S., Levitin, G., Trivedi, K.S.: Performance and reliability of tree-structured grid services considering data dependence and failure correlation. IEEE Trans. Comput. **56**(7), 925–936 (2007)

Information Systems and Technologies

Maize (Corn) Leaf Disease Detection System Using Convolutional Neural Network (CNN)

Joy Oluwabukola Olayiwola[1,2(✉)] and Jeremiah Ademola Adejoju[2]

[1] Department of Electrical and Information Engineering, Covenant University, Ota, Nigeria
Joy.olayiwolapgs@stu.cu.edu.ng
[2] Department of Computer Engineering, The Federal Polytechnic Ilaro, Ilaro, Ogun State, Nigeria

Abstract. Crop disease prevention is essential for global food security, and early detection of crop illnesses is a critical component of disease protection. Manual approaches require specialist knowledge, which takes longer time depending on the perimeter of the field or farmland, incurs more money, and can still be inaccurate, hence AI is touted as the ideal answer. In this study, three common maize leaf diseases (Leaf Blight, Common Rust, and Leaf Spot) and their healthy counterparts were classified using a deep learning - convolutional neural network (CNN) based model, Keras on TensorFlow. The CNN model does not require any preprocessing or explicit feature extraction, and it takes a 224×224 pixel images of corn leaf of any class at random as input. The four classes were correctly identified with an accuracy of 98.56%. These and other performance metrics have values that allow for the development and deployment of programs that help farmers and plant pathologists diagnose sickness and administer suitable remedies more quickly and correctly. Consequently, farmers who identify plant disease manually can save time and reduce their concerns about incorrect detection.

Keywords: Convolutional Neural Network (CNN) · Keras · TensorFlow · Maize leaf · Disease detection

1 Introduction

According to [1], Maize also known as corn, is a grain cereal that was first made fit for domestic life and human consumption around 10,000 years ago, by native people in southern Mexico. According to [2], maize output has surpassed that of wheat and rice, making it a staple crop all throughout the world. In addition, he added, it is used to make corn ethanol, animal feed, and a few other maize products, such corn starch and corn syrup, besides being consumed by people. Dent corn, flint corn, flour corn, pod corn, popcorn, and sweet corn are the six primary varieties of maize that are now grown [3].

Maize is cultivated more frequently than any other grain each year, because of its vast cultivation across the world, uses for maize include making cornmeal, oil, alcoholic drinks such bourbon whiskey, feedstock for the chemical sector, and alcoholic beverages through fermentation and distillation. Moreover, ethanol and other biofuels are produced using it. [4].

© The Author(s), under exclusive license to Springer Nature Switzerland AG 2023
O. Gervasi et al. (Eds.): ICCSA 2023, LNCS 13956, pp. 309–321, 2023.
https://doi.org/10.1007/978-3-031-36805-9_21

Plant diseases are unfavorable factors that drastically lower crop output and quality. There is little to no question that pests, diseases, and other unfavorable elements in crops may significantly reduce agricultural output. Therefore, detection and identification of crop leaf disease is highly important if we are concerned about improving the quality of crop cultivation.

Zea mays L., sometimes known as maize, occupies a special place in global agriculture as a source of food, feed, and other industrially significant goods. Over 100 million hectares of land are used to grow maize in poor nations, and roughly 70% of the world's total maize output comes from low- and lower-middle-income nations [5]. It offers food and money to more than 300 million households in sub-Saharan Africa [6, 7]. From research it was known that being a staple meal, a raw material for breweries, and a component of livestock feed, maize is in great demand in Nigeria. It is used to make corn syrup, corn oil, custard, corn flour, and corn flakes in the confectionery and food industries, even golden morn and so on, some of which includes baby foods for healthy growth. Nigerians consume maize in a variety of ways. In order to make pap, it is ground, fermented, and regionally processed. In the Southwest, Ogi, Akamu, and Koko are some of the regional names for this pap. As a staple cuisine, corn on the cob is also cooked or grilled.

In 2018, 7.5% of the world's maize crop, or around 75 million tons, was produced in Africa. The greatest producer in Africa, Nigeria, produces about 33 million tons of maize annually, followed by South Africa, Egypt, and Ethiopia. Maize accounts for around 24 percent of cropland in Africa, with an average output of about 2 tons/hectare/year [8].

According to [8] recent research, about sixty percent of the maize produced in Nigeria is used to manufacture poultry feeds. Maize is reported to be responsible for 50–70% of feeds for poultry farming in Nigeria, this was disclosed in a statement by the chairman of the Poultry Association of Nigeria (PAN) in 2020. The association also attributed the high cost of egg and other poultry products in the country recently to an increase in the price of maize. Beverage companies utilize another twenty-five percent. In comparison, about 15% percent is consumed locally in homes. Nigeria's agricultural sector accounts for a sizable portion of the country's GDP. Agriculture's share of the overall GDP between January and March 2021 was 22.35 percent, up almost one percentage point from the corresponding period in 2020. 5.88 percent of Nigeria's agricultural GDP is accounted for by maize alone. [8].

Leaf blight, gray spot and rust are the most prevalent disease that causes substantial economical loses to maize crop, thus, it is essential to have a system that can detect maize disease through the leafs at an early stage.

2   Literature Review

One of the most important crops, maize, often known as corn, is remarkably adaptable to a variety of environmental conditions [9]. The maize disease can affect many different sections, including the panicle, leaf, or stem. But only leaf-related diseases are taken into account in this area. Agriculture is now using computer vision technologies, and there has been a lot of development in recent years in the exploration of picture segmentation based on the location of the crop and the sickness, which has been a huge help to agriculture.

[10] This section reviews the previous works on classifying maize leaf disease using different algorithms.

In their paper, [11] utilized an image supplied by a system user as an input, and the uploaded image was analyzed using CNN Classifier. The K closest neighbors (KNN) method is then used to choose the best mix of elements to validate the illness. The K closest neighbors (KNN) method is a simple algorithm that maintains all available examples and classifies new cases using a similarity metric (e.g., distance functions). This technology is used to determine and anticipate an automated system for the user to properly detect maize leaf diseases. To validate the illness, the CNN classifier (Convolutional Neural Network) technique is utilized to extract features from photos, and the KNN algorithm is used to store all known instances and classify new cases based on a similarity measure.

Furthermore, [12] suggested a unique DenseNet architecture-based approach for recognizing and classifying three maize leaf diseases. In selecting appropriate hyper parameter values, the authors employed a grid search to discover optimal values. Unfortunately, this poses a plague of dimensionality, which is a project restriction. DenseNet employs much less parameters than the other CNN architectures tested in their experiment. The experiment findings indicated that the DenseNet utilized in the experiment obtained an accuracy of 98:06% while using less parameters and training time.

To identify maize leaf disease, some researchers developed a convolutional neural network (CNN) optimized by a Multi-Activation Function (MAF) module, with the goal of improving the accuracy of standard artificial intelligence approaches. Because they were unable to get adequate dataset, they used image pre-processing methods to extend and supplement the illness samples. To expedite the training, transfer learning and the warm-up approach were applied. As a consequence, three types of maize illnesses (maculopathy, rust, and blight) were reliably and effectively recognized. In the validation set, their method's accuracy reached 97.41%, and they performed a baseline test to validate its efficacy. Secondly, they chose three groups of CNNs based on their performance. They then performed ablation trials on five CNNs. The findings revealed that adding the MAF module increased the performance of CNNs. Furthermore, the multiplexing of Sigmoid, ReLU, and Mish performed best on ResNet50, as the accuracy could be enhanced by 2.33%, demonstrating that their proposal is suitable for agricultural output [13].

In the study, [14] suggested an upgraded ResNet50 maize disease diagnosis model to address the issue of disease identification accuracy and speed in real-time spraying operations in maize fields. First, the Adam algorithm is used to optimize the model. It then adopts an exit strategy and a Rectified Linear Activation Unit (ReLU) incentive function, modifies the learning strategy using an inclined triangle learning rate, and increases Ridge Regression (L2 regularization) to reduce overfitting. Second, three 3x3 tiny convolution kernels were added to the ResNet50 model's initial convolution kernel. Last but not least, the training set to verification set ratio was 3:1. In an experimental comparison, [14] suggested's maize disease recognition model outperformed other models in terms of accuracy. Their achievement was great because unlike Sumita et al., whose model achieved an average accuracy of 98:40%, but reduced to 88:66% when deployed, their model accuracy in the dataset is 98.52%, and 97.826% in the farmland. Also, the average identification speed is 204 ms, which offers technical assistance for the investigation of maize field spraying equipment while also meeting the accuracy and speed needs of maize field spraying operations.

Nevertheless, [15] used datasets from Kaggle on three major leaf disease: big spot, gray leaf spot and rust. VGG and ResNet were used to build a two-channel CNN. Using maize leaf illnesses as study objectives, a data collection on maize leaf diseases was created and preprocessed using the composition and features of AlexNet, VGG, and ResNet, respectively. According to their study, the grouping findings on those three categories of maize leaf diseases reveal that the two-channel CNN model outperforms the single AlexNet model.

Public dataset from Plant Village and some taken by Smartphones in natural environment which accumulates to a total of 7,701 images were used by [16]. To reduce the computation efforts, all the images were resized to 224×224 pixels before training the model. Separately, certain data augmentation techniques were used to the picture to improve the model's generalization capabilities and prevent it from overfitting. Their model consists of three steps. Stage one gathers information from small parts of an image and encodes it into tokens, stage two is the main computational network that conducts self-attention, and stage three maps the classification token into four classes to finish the final classification. The model's total accuracy was 97.87%.

A network-based maize leaf disease detection approach based on wavelet threshold-guided bilateral filtering, multi-channel ResNet, and attenuation factor (WG-MARNet) is suggested. The difficulties of noise, interference from the backdrop, and low detection accuracy of maize leaf disease photos are solved using this approach. Firstly, the capacity to feature extract and the environmental interference resistance of the input picture were improved using the Wavelet threshold guided bilateral filtering (WT-GBF) processing layer based on the WG-MARNet model. WT-GBF was used to decompose the input image into its high- and low-frequency components and decrease image noise. Secondly, by utilizing the multiscale feature fusion approach, the feature representation was improved and the danger of overfitting was reduced. Then, an attenuation factor is added to high- and low-frequency multi-channel to enhance performance instability during deep network training. After comparing convergence and correctness, PRelu and Adabound are employed in place of the ReLU activation function and the Adam optimizer. The experiment's findings showed that the approach had an average identification accuracy of 97.96% and a detection time of 0.278 s for a single image [10].

3 Methods and Materials

To develop the CNN-based maize leaf detection model, data were collected, trained, evaluated and made available in a format deploy-able for real life application. The flow chart in Fig. 1 shows the overview of the system.

The remaining section of the work is divided as follows:

- Datasets collection & analysis
- System Specification
- The CNN Model Architecture
- Model development
- Summary

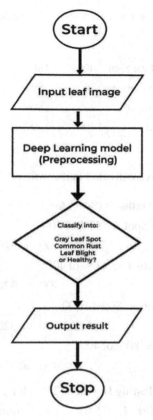

Fig. 1. Flow chart of overall system

3.1 Dataset Collection and Analysis

For every research work, gathering and processing as many data as possible is primary because datasets contribute vital action. For the purpose of this research work, a maize leaf disease dataset was collect from Kaggle which include leaf blight, gray spot, rust and healthy containing 4,109 images [17].

Due to limited training system resources, a subset of the collected dataset was made to reduce the total number of data from 4,109 images that was collected to 1,600 images in total with 400 for each class respectively. See Table 1 below for analysis.

Table 1. Subset of the datasets collected from Kaggle

s/n	Type	Amount	Training	Testing
1	Gray Leaf Spot	400	80%	20%
2	Common Rust	400	80%	20%
3	Leaf Blight	400	80%	20%
4	Healthy	400	80%	20%

The sample in each label were divided in the ratio 80:20 of training to the testing.

Training Datasets (80%) for :

Gray Leaf Spot $= 80\%$ of 400

$$400 = 320 \, \text{samples}$$

Common Rust $= 80\%$ of 400

$$400 = 320 \, \text{samples}$$

Leaf Blight $= 80\%$ of 400

$$400 = 320 \, \text{samples}$$

Healthy $= 80\%$ of 400

$$400 = 320 \, \text{samples}$$

Testing Datasets(20%) for :

Gray Leaf Spot $=$ total$-$train

$$= 400 - 320 = 80$$

Common Rust $=$ total$-$train

$$= 400 - 320 = 80$$

Leaf Blight $=$ total$-$train

$$= 400 - 320 = 80$$

Healthy $=$ total$-$train

$$= 400 - 320 = 80$$

The total train dataset is 1200 while the total test datasets is 320

Furthermore, the data in each folder are separated into sub-folder labeled train and test with ratio 80:20 respectively as illustrated in Table 1. Also, Fig. 2 showed example of datasets collected.

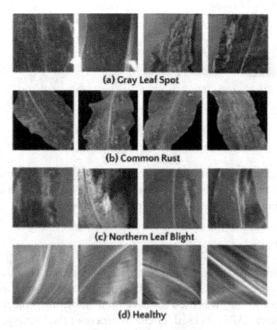

(a) Gray Leaf Spot

(b) Common Rust

(c) Northern Leaf Blight

(d) Healthy

Fig. 2. Dataset sample

Table 2. Summary of the system employed

S/N	NAME	TYPE/SPEC
1	System Model	Lenovo T460 - ThinkPad
2	CPU	Intel i5-6300U (4) @ 3.000GHz
3	GPU (Graphics)	Intel Skylake GT2 [HD Graphics 520]
4	RAM	8 GB
5	HDD	500 GB
6	Operating System	Linux Mint 21.1 × 86_64
7	Virtual Machine	Google Colab

3.2 System Specification Model

TensorFlow, the software used to create machine learning models, and Python's Keras are tightly linked neural network Application Programming Interfaces (APIs). A neural network may be easily defined using Keras' models, and TensorFlow will then construct the network. [18]. Google created the high-level, deep learning API called Keras for using neural networks. It is used to make neural network implementation simple and is built in Python. Moreover, it allows different neural network computing backends [19]. The Keras API was developed with people, not machines, in mind. Keras adheres to best practices for reducing cognitive load by providing consistent & straightforward APIs,

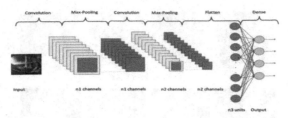

Fig. 3. Keras (TensorFlow) Architecture Model

minimizing the number of user interactions required for typical use cases, and providing clear & responsive error signals. It also has a ton of documentation and development instructions [20]. Figure 3 shows Keras architectural model.

3.3 Model Development

This model was developed on a virtual machine, the popular Google Colab was used due to the system's resources. Table 2 described the system information employed. The Google TensorFLow library was used for development of this project, a process called transfer learning. Keras API was used for enhancement of the training. The inputs to the CNN are 224 × 224 image sizes for each classes of the disease. The details of the model and the dimensions of each layer are shown in Table 3.

Table 3. Model summary

Model: "Sequential"		
Layer (type)	Output Shape	Parameters (params) #
conv2d (Conv2D)	(None, 222, 222, 32)	896
conv2d_1 (Conv2D)	(None, 220, 220, 64)	18496
max_pooling2d (MaxPooling2D)	(None, 110, 110, 64)	0
dropout (Dropout)	(None, 110, 110, 64)	0
flatten (Flatten)	(None, 774400)	0
dense (Dense)	(None, 128)	99123328
dropout_1 (Dropout)	(None, 128)	0
dense_1 (Dense)	(None, 4)	516
Total params: 99,143,236 ‖ Trainable params: 99,143,236 ‖ Non-trainable params: 0		

3.4 Summary of Methodology

The summary of the methodology presented in this section is explained in chronological form of the above sub-sections. Accordingly, a flow chart overview of the system was shown. Datasets was collected from Kaggle and no preprocessing was performed on them as the model used accepts RGB images as input. To avoid over-fitting, the datasets were augmented and re-sized to 224 x 224 which is the Keras input image size. The datasets were then trained using the Keras, a Tensorflow machine learning model. The results for training, validation, and evaluation were recorded, explained, and presented in the subsequent chapter.

4 Result and Discussion

4.1 Result

The final training accuracy is 0.9859 and the test loss is 0.0830, while the validation accuracy is 0.8031 and the test loss is 0.6843. The results and discussion of results in this section are arranged in chronological order as presented below.

4.2 Results Obtained After Training

The results obtained from the model fitting for 20 epochs with a batch size of 64 using Adam optimizer is shown in Table 4. The figure also shows the training accuracy and loss, and the validatiom accuracy and loss after every epoch.

Table 4. Model fitting

EPOCH [20 = = = 20]	TRAINING LOSS	TRAINING ACCURACY	VALIDATION LOSS	VALIDATION ACCURACY
Epoch 1/20	8.4309	0.4258	0.9721	0.5531
Epoch 2/20	0.8091	0.6445	0.6507	0.7281
Epoch 3/20	0.6399	0.7117	0.6111	0.6938
Epoch 4/20	0.5711	0.7406	0.5768	0.7281
Epoch 5/20	0.5211	0.7680	0.4965	0.7750
Epoch 6/20	0.4745	0.7828	0.4797	0.8062
Epoch 7/20	0.4239	0.8148	0.4509	0.7937
Epoch 8/20	0.3812	0.8320	0.5331	0.7688
Epoch 9/20	0.3029	0.8680	0.4489	0.7875
Epoch 10/20	0.2426	0.9250	0.4811	0.8156
Epoch 11/20	0.2380	0.9062	0.7147	0.7875
Epoch 12/20	0.2735	0.9055	0.5249	0.8125
Epoch 13/20	0.1761	0.9320	0.5466	0.8031

(continued)

Table 4. (*continued*)

EPOCH [20 == == 20]	TRAINING LOSS	TRAINING ACCURACY	VALIDATION LOSS	VALIDATION ACCURACY
Epoch 14/20	0.1335	0.9539	0.5993	0.7844
Epoch 15/20	0.1477	0.9523	0.5450	0.8062
Epoch 16/20	0.1062	0.9734	0.5195	0.8125
Epoch 17/20	0.0874	0.9766	0.6439	0.8188
Epoch 18/20	0.0663	0.9867	0.6604	0.8313
Epoch 19/20	0.0720	0.9758	0.6161	0.8375
Epoch 20/20	0.0830	0.9859	0.6843	0.8031

The training and loss percentage accuracy, and corresponding confusion matrix for the model are shown in Fig. 4, 5 and 6 and Table 5 shows the classification report for maize (corn) leaf disease detection system.

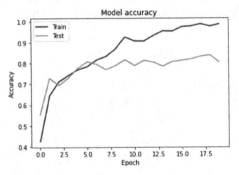

Fig. 4. Model accuracy graph for Maize (Corn) Leaf Disease Detection System

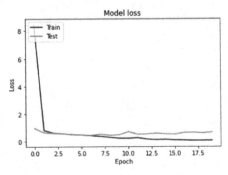

Fig. 5. Model loss graph for Maize (Corn) Leaf Disease Detection System

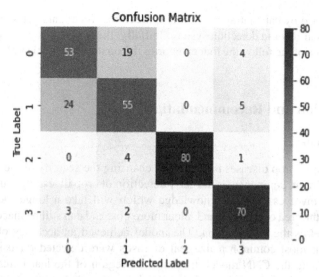

Fig. 6. Confusion Matrix for Maize (Corn) Leaf Disease Detection System

Table 5. Classification report for Maize (Corn) Leaf Disease Detection System

Labels	Precision	Recall	F1-score	Support
0	0.50	0.73	0.59	55
1	0.79	0.64	0.71	98
2	0.99	1.00	0.99	79
3	0.94	0.85	0.89	88
accuracy			0.80	320
macro avg	0.80	0.81	0.80	320
weighted avg	0.83	0.80	0.81	320

4.3 Discussion of Result for Datasets

Considering the fact that only three common classes of disease were considered in this work and with a forth class being the healthy ones, datasets were collected from Kaggle which includes; leaf blight, gray spot, rust and healthy containing of 4,109 images. Chronologically, each classes contains 1,146 images, 1,306 images, 574 images, and 1,162 images from which a subset of the datasets was extracted reducing the total amount of data from 4,109 images to 1,600 images, 400 for each class respectively due to limited training system resources. Before training, the datasets were re-sized and augmented to avoid over-fitting and improve accuracy.

The training uses 20 epoch and 64 batch size. Input images of size 224 ×224 are fed to the network. Based on the result presented above, the model achieved an overall accuracy of 98.58%. As illustrated in the classification report in Table 5, the trained model is assessed by calculating its accuracy, precision, recall, and F1-score values for maize (corn) leaf disease detection system. Initially, these results may be explained by indicating which of the following four categories the on the test model predictions belong into:

5   Conclusion and Recommendation

5.1   Conclusion

The prevention of crop diseases is crucial for ensuring the security of the world's food supply, and its main component is the early detection of crop illnesses. Manual methods of doing this involves expertise knowledge which will take a longer detection time depending on the area of the farmland, incur more cost and can still be inaccurate, hence AI is presented as the best solution. The model achieved an accuracy of 98.59%. In this study, four most common maize leaf diseases were detected for using Keras on Tensorflow. Using the CNN model, the transited region of the leaf is readily divided and analyzed, and the best results are immediately produced. As a consequence, farmers who identify plant diseases by hand can save time and reduce the likelihood of making a mistaken identification.

5.2   Recommendations

This model can be further worked on and improved in the following ways:

i. Live images should be strictly used as the datasets and maybe with a few.
ii. Deploying the model to a plant watering drone to be able get a real-time plant monitoring system where disease can be detected during irrigation process.
iii. The model can be improved to a detect as many maize diseases as possible
iv. Step by step solution to the detected disease can be included to the model to suggest what action is to be taken after a disease is detected.
v. Bayesian hyper-parameter optimization can be used to improve the model's accuracy by tweaking some hyper-parameter and fine-tuning the model.

References

1. Doebley, J., Stec, A., Hubbard, L.: The evolution of apical dominance in maize. Nature **386**(6624), 485–488 (1997). https://doi.org/10.1038/386485A0
2. Joshua, Z.P., Mariam, I.S., Goje, E.A., Suleiman, M.M., Dallhatu, R.Y.: Formulation and evaluation of maize (Zea mays) flour fortified with carrot (Daucus carota) powder. Sci. World J. **16**(3), 390–396 (2021)
3. Corn articles - Encyclopedia of Life. https://eol.org/pages/1115259/articles. Accessed 03 Apr 2023
4. Shi, M., Zhang, S., Lu, H., Zhao, X., Wang, X., Cao, Z.: Phenotyping multiple maize ear traits from a single image: Kernels per ear, rows per ear, and kernels per row. Comput. Electron. Agric. **193**, 106681 (2022). https://doi.org/10.1016/J.COMPAG.2021.106681

5. Shiferaw, B., Prasanna, B.M., Hellin, J., Bänziger, M.: Crops that feed the world 6. Past successes and future challenges to the role played by maize in global food security. Food Secur. **3**(3), 307–327 (2011). https://doi.org/10.1007/S12571-011-0140-5/TABLES/3
6. Tefera, T.: Post-harvest losses in African maize in the face of increasing food shortage. Food Secur. **4**(2), 267–277 (2012). https://doi.org/10.1007/S12571-012-0182-3
7. Yarnell, A.: Feeding Africa. Chem. Eng. News **86**(4), 74 (2008). https://doi.org/10.1021/cen-v086n004.p074
8. "Maize Farming in Nigeria: Exciting Facts You Should Know|Babban Gona. https://bab bangona.com/maize-farming-in-nigeria-exciting-facts-you-should-know/. Accessed 03 Apr 2023
9. Panigrahi, K.P., Das, H., Sahoo, A.K., Moharana, S.C.: Maize leaf disease detection and classification using machine learning algorithms. Adv. Intell. Syst. Comput. **1119**, 659–669 (2020). https://doi.org/10.1007/978-981-15-2414-1_66/COVER
10. Li, Z., et al.: Maize leaf disease identification based on WG-MARNet. PLoS ONE **17**(4), e0267650 (2022). https://doi.org/10.1371/JOURNAL.PONE.0267650
11. Didbhai, S., Nandgaonkar, S., Narkar, S.: Detection of maize leaf disease using CNN, vol. 7 (2019). Accessed 09 Apr 2023. www.ijirmps.org
12. Waheed, A., Goyal, M., Gupta, D., Khanna, A., Hassanien, A.E., Pandey, H.M.: An optimized dense convolutional neural network model for disease recognition and classification in corn leaf. Comput. Electron. Agric. **175** (2020). https://doi.org/10.1016/J.COMPAG.2020.105456
13. Zhang, Y., Wa, S., Liu, Y., Zhou, X., Sun, P., Ma, Q.: High-accuracy detection of maize leaf diseases cnn based on multi-pathway activation function module. Remote Sens. **13**(21), 4218 (2021). https://doi.org/10.3390/RS13214218
14. Wang, G., Yu, H., Sui, Y.: Research on maize disease recognition method based on improved ResNet50. Mob. Inf. Syst. **2021** (2021). https://doi.org/10.1155/2021/9110866
15. Wu, Y.: Identification of maize leaf diseases based on convolutional neural network. J. Phys. Conf. Ser. **1748**(3), 032004 (2021). https://doi.org/10.1088/1742-6596/1748/3/032004
16. Qian, X., Zhang, C., Chen, L., Li, K.: Deep learning-based identification of maize leaf diseases is improved by an attention mechanism: self-attention. Front. Plant Sci. **13**, 1154 (2022). https://doi.org/10.3389/FPLS.2022.864486/BIBTEX
17. Corn or Maize Leaf Disease Dataset | Kaggle. https://www.kaggle.com/datasets/smaranjit ghose/corn-or-maize-leaf-disease-dataset. Accessed 03 Apr 2023
18. What is a Keras model and how to use it to make predictions- ActiveState. https://www.act ivestate.com/resources/quick-reads/what-is-a-keras-model/. Accessed 03 Apr 2023
19. What is Keras and Why it so Popular in 2021 | Simplilearn. https://www.simplilearn.com/tut orials/deep-learning-tutorial/what-is-keras. Accessed 03 Apr 2023
20. Python Tensorflow - tf.keras.layers.Conv2D() Function - GeeksforGeeks. https://www.gee ksforgeeks.org/python-tensorflow-tf-keras-layers-conv2d-function/. Accessed 03 Apr 2023

An Empirical Study on the Effectiveness of Bi-LSTM-Based Industry Rotation Strategies in Thai Equity Portfolios

Thanason Eiamyingsakul⬤, Sansiri Tarnpradab⬤, and Unchalisa Taetragool$^{(\boxtimes)}$⬤

Department of Computer Engineering, Faculty of Engineering, King Mongkut's University of Technology Thonburi, Bangkok, Thailand
thanason.eiam@mail.kmutt.com, {sansiri.tarn, unchalisa.tae}@kmutt.ac.th

Abstract. Portfolio optimization poses a significant challenge due to asset price volatility caused by various economic factors. Portfolio optimization typically aims to achieve a high risk-adjusted return through asset allocation. However, high-volatility assets such as equities can lead to significant losses in the event of crises, such as trade wars. An industry rotation strategy can reduce portfolio risk by investing in industry indexes. This research aims to develop industry rotation strategies for Thailand by analyzing previous consecutive months of economic variables with the goal of maximizing the portfolio's Sharpe ratio in the following period. Two strategies are proposed in this paper, one with cash and the other without, both of which include eight Thai industry indexes in their portfolios. Both strategies are developed using Bidirectional Long Short-term Memory (Bi-LSTM) models, which generate the allocation ratio based on historical economic variable data. The models then optimize the allocation ratio by using a modified loss function to maximize the Sharpe ratio. In addition to the Sharpe ratio, the return on investment and the Calmar ratio are used to assess the performance of the strategies. The results showed that our strategies outperformed the baseline buy-and-hold SET50 and equal-weight strategies.

Keywords: Asset Allocation · Bidirectional Long Short-time Memory · Deep Learning · Investment Strategies · Portfolio Optimization · Sector Rotation

1 Introduction

Portfolio optimization is a method of determining the asset distribution or asset ratio that gives the best performance based on certain objectives, such as the portfolio's return on investment. Given numerous economic factors such as interest rates, market sentiment, or political events, a constant fluctuation in asset prices could be expected, thus making portfolio optimization a challenging problem.

In 1996, Stovall presented an investment strategy according to economic timing in his book. His strategy, so-called "sector rotation" or "industry rotation", suggested investing in stocks based on industry sector behavior and economic cycle phases. Sector rotation

O. Gervasi et al. (Eds.): ICCSA 2023, LNCS 13956, pp. 322–333, 2023.
https://doi.org/10.1007/978-3-031-36805-9_22

usually divides the equity market into phases, then constructs portfolios according to the historical performance of market sectors in those phases, which are usually identified directly from macroeconomic indicators. For example, Fidelity Investments, one of the largest financial corporations, divided the equity market into four phases and utilized the historical performance calculation to suggest an investment strategy accordingly [2].

Many research studies, however, did not consider business cycle phases when performing sector rotation. For instance, Conover et al. conducted sector rotation experiments under monetary conditions [4], to which they classified industries as cyclical or noncyclical and rearranged the portfolio in response to changes in Federal Reserve policy. Tangjitprom [5], on the other hand, used a momentum strategy in sector rotation. He implemented the strategy by utilizing Thailand's industry sectors via The Stock Exchange of Thailand (SET) industry indexes. The strategy focused on the momentum of those indexes by capturing each index's return over months. The return indexes for those months were then calculated, and the highest return index was invested by holding for a period.

Machine learning has been extensively applied due to its proven success in a wide strand of research. To perform sector rotation in particular, many efforts have been made using machine learning, as evidenced in several studies. For example, Raffinot and Benoit applied Random Forest and Boosting algorithms to predict economic turning points in the United States and the Eurozone [6]. In comparison with the buy-and-hold benchmark strategy, they used a dynamic asset allocation strategy during different phases. The result showed that the proposed strategy outperformed the buy-and-hold strategy, particularly in terms of risk-adjusted return. Deep learning models, among other techniques, have also been used to optimize portfolios in sector rotation strategies. Karatas and Hirsa used deep learning models to predict asset prices in eight major U.S. industry sectors [7]. They decided to invest in the top four industries with the highest return. In addition, the study was tested in multiple lookback windows and was evaluated using investment return, Sharpe ratio, and Calmar ratio. The results indicated that all tested models outperformed the equal-weight portfolio benchmark. Zhang et al. also presented portfolio optimization using deep learning models to determine the optimal portfolio with the best Sharpe ratio among four U.S. indexes [8]. They used LSTM with 51 days of four indexes as the model's input to optimize the allocation ratio of those four assets. According to the results, LSTM was demonstrated to outperform all other strategies.

Previous research on sector rotation that uses machine learning can be divided into two categories: those using business cycle prediction and those focusing on portfolio optimization. The studies that used business cycle prediction sought to optimize the static proportion of assets at various stages of the business cycle. However, it has been observed that no sector behaves consistently in the same way during specific phases [3]. Furthermore, these phases are frequently identified by National Bureau of Economic Research (NBER) committees, which can be subject to delays and human biases. On the other hand, some study has adopted an alternative strategy by predicting asset prices and choosing the top performers for investments from the prediction [5, 7]; some paper has employed optimized ratios throughout all business cycles [8]. This study implements an industry rotation strategy for Thailand's economy by proposing a dynamic sector rotation strategy that adjusts asset allocation to the various market conditions in Thailand. A deep learning model is used to implement the sector rotation strategy because it can capture the nonlinearity effect of many economic factors and learn the complex relationships between them [1]. In contrast to the United States, where many exchange-traded funds (ETFs) track sector indexes and allow investors to buy and sell them to implement sector rotation strategies, Thailand has no ETFs that track industry indexes. This study assumes that investors can trade stocks that closely track those indexes, and the cost of trading is not factored in.

2 Methodology

2.1 Data Aggregation

This study relies solely on economic variables derived from publicly available data. The goal of this study is not to improve model performance through the selection of economic variables. The dataset used consists of macroeconomic data and industry indexes.

Macroeconomic Data. Six of Thailand's macroeconomic time-series variables are collected from the Office of the National Economics and Social Development Council (NESDC) [13], the Bank of Thailand (BOT) [14], the Office of Industrial Economics (OIE) [15] and National Statistical Office of Thailand (NSO) [16]. The time-series variables in this dataset present monthly and quarterly data from October 2006 to November 2021. Table 1 provides information about this dataset.

Table 1. Macroeconomic variables used in this paper.

Macroeconomic variables	Frequency	Symbol abbreviation	Source
Industrial Production Index	Monthly	INDPRO	OIE
Unemployment Rate	Monthly	UNEMPLOY	NSO
Retail Sales Index	Monthly	RETAIL	BOT
Private Final Consumption Expenditure	Quarterly	PFCE	NESDC
Real Gross Domestic Product	Quarterly	Real GDP	NESDC
Gross Domestic Product	Quarterly	GDP	NESDC

Industry Indexes. An industry index is a capitalization-weighted index calculated from the prices of the common stocks in Thailand with the same fundamentals [12]. The Stock Exchange of Thailand (SET) categorizes listed companies into eight industry groups as shown in Table 2. All eight SET industry group indexes will then be used in this study. The dataset compiles the closed value of those indexes in each month from October 2006 to November 2021.

Table 2. SET Industry Group Index

Industry group	Symbol abbreviation
Agro & Food Industry	AGRO
Consumer Products	CONSUMP
Financials	FINCIAL
Industrials	INDUS
Property & Construction	PROPCON
Resources	RESOURC
Services	SERVICE
Technology	TECH

2.2 Data Preprocessing

Firstly, three quarterly macroeconomic variables in the dataset are interpolated to monthly data using Cubic spline interpolation, which has been shown in [10, 11] to be efficient when used with economic data. Secondly, missing data is handled because many macroeconomic data are not available in real-time. For example, to make a prediction for February, Thailand's GDP data from October to January of the previous year is required; however, since NESDC normally releases the GDP of the fourth quarter in February of the following year, such timing constraint thereby brings about a scenario where portions of data are unavailable. After testing different methods for data preparation, it was discovered that our model performs best when the monthly interpolated macroeconomic data is forward shifted based on the missing time since the most recent data is then used to make predictions. In this study, the data from NESDC, PFCE, GDP, and Real GDP are shifted by four months, the data from INDPRO and UNEMPLOY are shifted by one month, and the data from RETAIL are shifted by two months. Figure 1 depicts an example of shifted macroeconomic data used in the February 2017 prediction.

	...	Aug 16	Sep 16	Oct 16	Nov 16	Dec 16	Jan 17	Feb 17
INDPRO	...	Jul 16	Aug 16	Sep 16	Oct 16	Nov 16	Dec 16	▼
UNEMPLOY	...	Jul 16	Aug 16	Sep 16	Oct 16	Nov 16	Dec 16	
RETAIL	...	Jun 16	Jul 16	Aug 16	Sep 16	Oct 16	Nov 16	Prediction
PFCE	...	Apr 16	May 16	Jun 16	Jul 16	Aug 16	Sep 16	
Real GDP	...	Apr 16	May 16	Jun 16	Jul 16	Aug 16	Sep 16	▲
GDP	...	Apr 16	May 16	Jun 16	Jul 16	Aug 16	Sep 16	

Input data

Fig. 1. An example of shifted macroeconomic data used in the February 2017 prediction.

Thirdly, the first difference or percent change of all variables in the dataset is then computed and used as a feature to capture the growth rate and make the data stationary.

Finally, the prepared data is transformed for use in Bi-LSTM models. To train the models, monthly growth rate data from the six macroeconomic variables and eight industry indexes for m consecutive months are used as inputs (X). The next k months growth rates of the eight industry indexes are used as holding period data (Y) to compute the portfolio's Sharpe ratio from the portfolio allocation (Z) returned by the Bi-LSTM models. Figure 2 depicts the overall model framework with a 12-month holding period ($k = 12$). The inputs to the Bi-LSTM models are denoted as $x_1, x_2, \ldots, x_n$, where n is the number of input data points, which is calculated by multiplying 14 input attributes by m consecutive months ($n = 14 \times m$). The output vector of the Bi-LSTM's last layer is represented as $z_1, z_2, \ldots, z_a$ where a is the number of assets in the portfolio. $y_{h,k}$ represents the investment return on asset h during the next k-th month of the holding period. The goal of the models is to maximize the Sharpe ratio of the portfolio by optimizing portfolio allocation. Two portfolio allocation strategies are investigated in this study: (1) with-cash and (2) no-cash, provided that both include eight industry indexes in their portfolios. The holding period data (Y) for the cash strategies contain a cash growth rate of zero over the next k months.

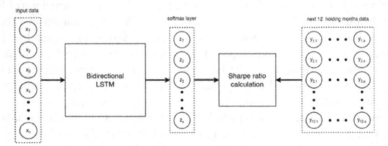

Fig. 2. Overall model framework with a 12-month holding period.

2.3 Model

According to the results of a previous study [9], LSTM performed the best in portfolio optimization. The current study investigates Bi-LSTM models, an improved LSTM variant. Bi-LSTMs use two sets of LSTMs to process data in both forward and reverse directions. It enables the model to predict using both past and future context, making it well-suited to the task of using time series data as input. Figure 3 depicts the overall architecture of Bi-LSTM.

As shown in Fig. 2, the Bi-LSTM model's output will be the asset ratio in the portfolio, which is the ratio of the eight assets in the no-cash portfolio and the nine assets in the with-cash portfolio. Our Bi-LSTM models are built in the following layers.

1. Input layer to receive input data.
2. Bi-LSTM layer with n_BiLSTM nodes and a dropout rate of 0.50.
3. Flatten layer that transforms the output to a one-dimensional vector.
4. The first dense layer with n_Dense nodes, ReLU as the activation function, He uniform as the weight initializer.

5. Dropout layer with 0.50 dropout rate.
6. The second dense layer with eight or nine nodes for the no-cash and the with-cash models, respectively; *softmax* calculated by Eq. (1) is used as the activation function and He uniform is used as the weight initializer.

$$Softmax(z_i) = \frac{e^{z_i}}{\sum_{j=1}^{n} e^{z_j}} \tag{1}$$

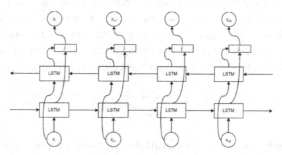

Fig. 3. An architecture of Bi-LSTM.

The goal of this research is to use the Bi-LSTM models to optimize the portfolio's Sharpe ratio. The Adam algorithm is used as the model's optimizer. As in [9], the Sharpe ratio is calculated directly in the loss function of the model using the portfolio output from the softmax layer. The model will then be able to predict the assets ratio for the subsequent k-month holding period that maximizes the Sharpe ratio, using information from the previous m months. However, since this study aims to maximize the Sharpe ratio while Bi-LSTM minimizes the loss function, the loss function is modified to minimize the exponential of the negative of the Sharpe ratio, as shown in Eq. (2).

$$Loss = e^{(-sharperatio)} \tag{2}$$

2.4 Evaluation Metrics

In addition to the Sharpe ratio, which is used in the loss function, the performance of the baselines and our predicted strategies is also evaluated using the rate of return and the Calmar ratio.

Return on Investment. Return on investment is the profit or loss on an investment over time. In this study, the return on investment each year is calculated as the value increased from the portfolio's initial value divided by the portfolio's initial value (Eq. (3)).

$$Return\ on\ investment = \frac{portfolio's\ value\ at\ the\ end - portfolio's\ value\ at\ initial}{portfolio's\ value\ at\ initial} \tag{3}$$

Sharpe Ratio. The Sharpe ratio measures the portfolio's return in relation to its risk. It is calculated by dividing the difference between the expected return and the risk-free rate by the volatility, as shown in Eq. (4).

$$Sharpe\ ratio = \frac{R_p - R_f}{\sigma(R_p)} \tag{4}$$

where R_p is the expected return of the portfolio, R_f is the risk-free return, and $\sigma(R_p)$ is the standard deviation of R_p. The risk-free return (R_f) is the return on an investment that is guaranteed to return to the investor with no possibility of loss, such as a government bond. In this study, R_f is set to zero because no risk-free investment is made. Monthly returns can be calculated by multiplying the growth rate of the assets over the next k months by their weights based on the portfolio allocation from the model's output. The return of the portfolio (R_k) at the k-th month is calculated by Eq. (5).

$$R_k = \sum_{i=1}^{a} w_i \cdot r_{i,k} \tag{5}$$

where a is the number of assets in the portfolio, w_i is the proportion of asset i from the model's output, and $r_{i,k}$ is the growth rate of asset i at month k-th. R_p is the average of R_k over k months. The Sharpe ratio of the portfolio can then be rewritten as shown in Eq. (6).

$$Sharpe\ ratio = \frac{R_p}{\sqrt{\frac{1}{N}\sum_n (R_k - R_p)^2}} \tag{6}$$

During the model testing phase, however, the Sharpe ratio will be calculated annually using Eq. (4).

Calmar Ratio. Calmar ratio is a risk-adjusted return metric similar to the Sharpe ratio, except that it uses maximum drawdown as the denominator rather than the standard deviation. The maximum drawdown metric computes the loss in portfolio value between the highest peak and lowest trough prior to the new peak. It evaluates the downside risk and shows investors the maximum possible portfolio drawdown. Eq. (7) illustrates the Calmar ratio calculation.

$$Calmar\ ratio = \frac{average\ yearly\ return}{Maximum\ drawdown} \tag{7}$$

2.5 Experimental Setup

The pre-processed dataset is divided into training and testing data with January 2016 as the dividing date. The training data ranges from October 2006 to December 2015, while the testing data ranges from January 2016 to November 2021. Our experiments begin with the training phase, in which the data is divided into the training set and the validating set by 67% and 33%, respectively. Using the values shown in Table 3, hyperparameters are tested to find the set of values that produced the best results.

Table 3. Set of parameters used in creating Bi-LSTM models.

Parameter	Value
Input time horizontal (m)	6, 12, 18, 24, 30, 36
Holding period after getting the allocation ratio (n)	3, 6, 12
Number of nodes in Bi-LSTM layer (n_BiLSTM)	256, 512, 1024
Number of nodes in the first Dense layer (n_Dense)	128, 256, 512

In each experiment, the Bi-LSTM model with each hyperparameter combination is built and run for thirty rounds. The average value of the Sharpe ratio in the loss function is used to assess the model's performance in each experiment. The combination with the highest Sharpe ratio using the validation set is chosen. Then, the model is tested in the testing phase by using the previous m consecutive months as input, and holding assets based on the model's output ratio for the next k months. During the testing phase, backtesting is conducted using the model for twelve different time intervals to make sure that our models do not accidentally perform well at any particular time as shown in Fig. 4. Each interval contains data for a period of five years. The first interval runs from January 2016 to December 2020. For the remaining intervals, each will be advanced by one month. For example, the second interval runs from February 2016 to January 2021, and the twelfth interval runs from December 2016 to November 2021.

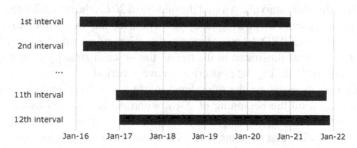

Fig. 4. Twelve intervals used in testing phase.

Since this study focuses on Thailand's industry rotation, the SET50 index, which is a stock price index used to show the price movement of the 50 largest common stocks in terms of market capitalization, and the equal weight allocation are used as baselines in this study.

3   Results and Discussion

Results from the training phase show that the best hyperparameter combination for the with-cash strategy is $m = 24$, $k = 3$, $n_{BiLSTM} = 1024$, and $n_{Dense} = 512$, with an average Sharpe ratio of 1.9647. The best combination for the no-cash strategy is $m = 24$,

$k = 3$, $n_{BiLSTM} = 512$, and $n_{Dense} = 256$, with an average Sharpe ratio of 1.886. The testing phase then uses twelve intervals to test each model. As shown in Table 4, the three evaluation metrics are calculated and compared to baselines. The results show that, apart from the with-cash model's average annual return for the period starting in November 2016, both proposed strategies outperformed the baselines across all three metrics and all time periods. Furthermore, our proposed strategies outperformed the baselines for all average metrics values derived from twelve intervals.

In terms of average yearly return, the no-cash strategy outperformed the with-cash strategy for all interval average values. These findings suggest that the no-cash strategy can provide us with a higher return on investment year after year. In terms of the Sharpe ratio, however, the with-cash strategy outperformed the no-cash strategy which demonstrates that the with-cash strategy can reduce portfolio volatility. Therefore, while the no-cash strategy outperforms in terms of return, the with-cash strategy outperforms in terms of risk. Regarding the Calmar ratio, it can be observed that the with-cash strategy performed better than the no-cash strategy. The results demonstrated that the with-cash strategy significantly reduced the maximum drawdown, which occurred during the market crash at the beginning of 2020 due to fear of COVID-19, with the average values of all intervals being 17.74% compared to 34.15%, 38.09%, and 37.47% of the no-cash, equal weight, and SET50 strategies, respectively.

To investigate the movement of the portfolios' return for each strategy, Fig. 5 presents the cumulative return from our proposed strategies during the testing phase along with the baselines for four out of twelve intervals beginning in January, April, July, and October 2016. The figure demonstrates a similar pattern in the movement of our proposed strategies from the four intervals. Around the middle of 2017, the no-cash strategy begins to outperform the baselines with a higher upside. Then, it behaves similarly to the SET50, including during the COVID-19 crisis in the early 2020s, when values dropped by more than 30%. However, as illustrated in the figure, the no-cash strategy outperformed the baselines significantly during the post-crisis recovery period.

The with-cash strategy, on the other hand, performs quite differently than the no-cash strategy. Up until the beginning of 2018, when the market fell as a result of the US-China trade war [12], it performed worse than other strategies. By overweighting cash by roughly 67% during that year, the with-cash strategy was able to lower the downside and outperform the equal weight strategy while still trailing the other two. During the COVID-19 market crash, however, the with-cash strategy significantly outperformed other strategies by allocating the portfolio to an average cash level of about 70%. Figure 6 displays the cumulative return from November 2016 to October 2021, which is the only period where, as we mentioned earlier, the with-cash strategy underperformed the baselines in terms of average yearly return. The findings reveal that the with-cash strategy underperformed in terms of upside return in the first half of 2019 and following the COVID-19 crash compared to the intervals in Fig. 5, as it chose to overweight in cash instead of other indexes. The results in Table 4 also indicate the inconsistency of the deep learning model in the with-cash strategy, where it has a higher standard deviation of Sharp ratio in twelve testing intervals at 0.3632 in comparison to the no-cash, equal weight, and SET50, which are 0.0836, 0.0515, and 0.0722, respectively.

Table 4. Results from the testing phase compared with the baselines.

| Metric | Strategy | Date of beginning testing | | | | | | | | | | | | Avg |
		Jan 2016	Feb 2016	Mar 2016	Apr 2016	May 2016	Jun 2016	Jul 2016	Aug 2016	Sep 2016	Oct 2016	Nov 2016	Dec 2016	
Average return (yearly)	With-cash	0.067	0.044	0.056	0.073	0.047	0.068	0.068	0.023	0.045	0.061	0.020	0.051	0.052
	No-cash	0.072	0.076	0.082	0.104	0.095	0.093	0.082	0.047	0.053	0.074	0.058	0.045	**0.074**
	Equal weight	0.032	0.030	0.029	0.037	0.025	0.018	0.018	0.003	0.012	0.022	0.030	0.003	0.021
	SET50	0.023	0.026	0.029	0.046	0.036	0.030	0.029	0.008	0.018	0.023	0.023	0.006	0.025
Sharpe Ratio (yearly)	With-cash	1.151	0.494	0.818	0.606	0.713	0.984	1.566	0.336	0.450	0.940	0.212	0.914	**0.765**
	No-cash	0.625	0.617	0.469	0.372	0.495	0.562	0.530	0.391	0.383	0.482	0.405	0.470	0.483
	Equal weight	0.236	0.217	0.193	0.178	0.173	0.156	0.145	0.024	0.087	0.120	0.147	0.031	0.138
	SET50	0.219	0.218	0.203	0.194	0.215	0.219	0.200	0.071	0.126	0.149	0.142	0.084	0.170
Calmar Ratio	With-cash	0.450	0.230	0.290	0.491	0.244	0.350	0.459	0.120	0.231	0.415	0.106	0.262	**0.304**
	No-cash	0.211	0.220	0.243	0.306	0.275	0.275	0.242	0.137	0.157	0.217	0.167	0.133	0.215
	Equal weight	0.083	0.079	0.077	0.097	0.065	0.046	0.048	0.008	0.032	0.057	0.079	0.008	0.055
	SET50	0.061	0.069	0.078	0.122	0.096	0.080	0.076	0.021	0.047	0.063	0.061	0.017	0.066

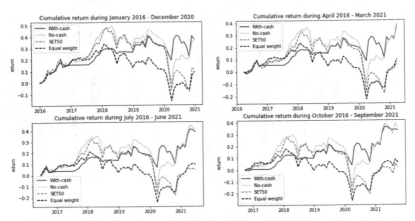

Fig. 5. Cumulative returns of all strategies in four intervals which are intervals beginning in January 2016 (top-left), April 2016 (top-right), July 2016 (bottom-left), and September (bottom-right).

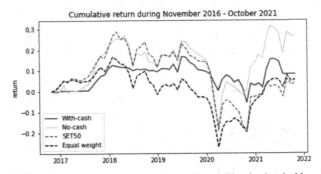

Fig. 6. Cumulative returns of all strategies in the interval beginning in November 2016

4 Conclusion

In this paper, we have proposed two strategies for Thailand's industry rotation: with-cash and no-cash. Both strategies' portfolios include eight of Thailand's industry indexes, but the with-cash strategy includes cash. We constructed the Bi-LSTM model for each strategy, which take historical data of economic variables for consecutive m months as input and give the allocation ratio as the model's output. The ratio will be used to hold the assets for the next n months. The models optimize the allocation ratio directly with a modified loss function that maximizes the Sharpe ratio. The models were trained and tested in twelve different intervals. The results showed that our proposed strategies outperformed the baselines, which are SET50 and the equal weight strategies. The with-cash strategy showed it could reduce the drawdown when the market dropped by overweighting cash during that period. However, the deep learning model in the with-cash strategy shows inconsistency when testing with different intervals. One direction of future works could be using the other assets instead of indexes that we can actually trade and including the trading cost in the calculation.

References

1. Goulet Coulombe, P., Leroux, M., Stevanovic, D., Surprenant, S.: How is machine learning useful for macroeconomic forecasting? J. Appl. Economet. **37**(5), 920–964 (2022)
2. Fidelity Investment O2010). http://personal.fidelity.com/products/pdf/a-tactical-handbook-of-sector-rotations.pdf (Accessed 2 March 2022)
3. Stangl, J., Jacobsen, B., Visaltanachoti, N.: Sector Rotation over the Business Cycle. Presented at the 20th Australasian Finance and Banking Conference, The University of South Wales, 13 December, pp. 1–34 (2007)
4. Conover, C.M., Jensen, G.R., Johnson, R.R., Mercer, J.M.: Sector rotation and monetary conditions. J. Investing. **17**(1), 34–46 (2008)
5. Tangjitprom, T.: Industry rotation using momentum strategy: evidence from the stock exchange of Thailand. RMUTT Global Bus. Econ. Rev. **11**(2), 41–58 (2016)
6. Raffinot, T., Benoît, S.: Investing through economic cycles with ensemble machine learning algorithms. Working paper (2016). https://doi.org/10.2139/ssrn.2785583
7. Karatas, T., Hirsa, A.: Two-Stage Sector Rotation Methodology Using Machine Learning and Deep Learning Techniques. arXiv preprint arXiv:2108.02838 (2021)
8. Zhang, Z., Zohren, S., Roberts, S.: Deep learning for portfolio optimization. J. Financ. Data Sci. **2**(4), 8–20 (2020)
9. The Stock Exchange of Thailand (2021). https://www.set.or.th/th/products/index/setindex_p2.htm (Accessed 23 February 2022)
10. The Stock Exchange of Thailand (2019). https://classic.set.or.th/en/about/annual/2018/index.html (Accessed 23 February 2022)
11. Ajao, I., Ibraheem, A., Ayoola, F.: Cubic spline interpolation: a robust method of dis-aggregating annual data to quarterly series. J. Phys. Sci. Environ. Safety **2**(1), 1–8 (2012)
12. Ilyasov, R.H.: About the method of analysis of economic correlations by differentiation of spline models. Mod. Appl. Sci. **8**(5), 197 (2014)
13. The National Economic and Social Development Council (NESDC). National Accounts. https://www.nesdc.go.th/nesdb_en/main.php?filename=national_account (Retrieved 9 January 2023)
14. Bank of Thailand (BOT). Retail Sales Index. https://www.bot.or.th/App/BTWS_STAT/statistics/ReportPage.aspx?reportID=830&language=eng. (Retrieved January 9 2023)
15. National Statistical Office Thailand (NSO). The Labor Force Survey. http://www.nso.go.th/sites/2014en/Pages/Statistical%20Themes/Population-Society/Labour/Labour-Force.aspx
16. The Office of Industrial Economics. Industrial Indices. https://www.oie.go.th/view/1/industrial_indices/EN-US. (Retrieved 9 January 2023)

Prediction of Urban Population-Facilities Interactions with Graph Neural Network

Margarita Mishina[1,2(✉)] (iD), Stanislav Sobolevsky[1,3,4] (iD), Elizaveta Kovtun[6] (iD),
Alexander Khrulkov[1,2] (iD), Alexander Belyi[1] (iD), Semen Budennyy[5,6] (iD),
and Sergey Mityagin[2] (iD)

[1] Department of Mathematics and Statistics, Faculty of Science, Masaryk University,
Kotlarska 2, Brno 61137, Czech Republic
marg.mished@gmail.com
[2] ITMO University, Birzhevaya line, 14, Saint-Petersburg, Russia
[3] Center for Urban Science and Progress, New York University, 370 Jay Street,
Brooklyn 11201, NY, USA
[4] Institute of Law and Technology, Faculty of Law, Masaryk University, Veveri 70,
Brno 61180, Czech Republic
[5] Artificial Intelligence Research Institute (AIRI), Moscow, Russia
[6] Sber AI Lab, Moscow, Russia

Abstract. The urban population interacts with service facilities on a daily basis. The information on population-facilities interactions is considered when analyzing the current city organization and revealing gaps in infrastructure at the neighborhood level. However, often this information is limited to several observation areas. The paper presents a new graph-based deep learning approach to reconstruct population-facilities interactions. In the proposed approach, graph attention neural networks learn latent nodes' representation and discover interpretable dependencies in a graph of interactions based on observed data of one part of the city. A novel normalization technique is used to balance doubly-constrained flows between two locations. The experiments show that the proposed approach outperforms classic models in a bipartite graph of population-facilities interactions.

Keywords: urban mobility · graph neural network · flows prediction

1 Introduction

Today, the spatial development of urban infrastructure aims to ensure the normal functioning of a city and the ability to meet the urgent needs of citizens and tourists. Urban infrastructure covers engineered systems, municipal utilities, and various service facilities (kindergartens, schools, polyclinics, and others) [16]. The quality of urban infrastructure, in particular the service facilities system, is determined not only by the number of its elements located in a city but also by the spatial correspondence of their location to the places of citizens'

O. Gervasi et al. (Eds.): ICCSA 2023, LNCS 13956, pp. 334–348, 2023.
https://doi.org/10.1007/978-3-031-36805-9_23

concentration (in the areas of residence, leisure, work, and others). The latter reflects the peculiarity of population-facilities interactions prevailing in a city - where and how long citizens must travel to get a specific service.

Given the growing impact of service facilities on citizens' daily life, the issue of spatial population-facilities interactions is of keen interest among government, developers, and researchers [30]. Recent studies consider this issue to examine spatial inequality, which implies the inability of the population living in some parts of a city to access required facilities within a moderate distance [5,9,13]. The solution to this problem lies in facility distribution optimization based on knowledge about population density and population movements between locations of primary activities and preferable facilities in a city [13,15]. One may notice that information about population density in cities is available in the census data of many countries. However, information about intra-city movements is limited with several observation areas and needs modeling in most cases.

Over the last decades, the scientific community has been working on examining the aspects of human mobility and understanding the patterns of preferences the urban population would have for some objects over others [8,17,27]. A breakthrough has been made in this field of study due to publishing in open access a large amount of location-embedded information about people's movement in an urban environment (from census data, mobile phone records, GPS trackers, social networks, and other data sources). Since then, various laws and mathematical models have been derived to formalize people's movement in a city by abstracting it into a straightforward set of regularities applicable to a territory of interest where observed data is unavailable [6].

Among the models that have been proposed, the gravity model [33] and the radiation model [29] have been most commonly used to approximate aggregated population flows between origins and destinations. The models represent two leading schools of thought that explain human mobility patterns differently. The gravity model and its derivatives assume that flows between origin and destination decline as the distance between them increases. Meanwhile, the radiation model and similar ones postulate that the probability of commuting between origin and destination is inversely proportional to the number of opportunities in between (i.e., the number of alternative destinations). Both models are distinguished due to their simplicity and clear interpretability, though they commonly tend to simplify the complex structure of human mobility flows [6]. This limitation can be partly solved via the constrained versions of the models and the calibration of its free parameters based on observed data.

Recently machine learning approaches have been proposed to address the shortcomings of traditional models and improve the ability to reconstruct mobility flows. In [26], the authors train an XGBoost model and a densely connected feed-forward neural network (FNN) to predict migration flows considering a set of externalities. Similarly, the Deep Gravity model introduced in [28] adopts FNN to reconstruct the number of trips between regions of interest. The studies find that the neural network approach outperforms the state-of-the-art models and offers promising results. The recombination of locations' features in a non-linear way allows to capture more complex dependencies and provides higher generalization capability. This observation seems to indicate that there is room for further development and improvements.

Considering information on urban population-facilities interactions, the organization of available knowledge in the form of graphs emerges quite naturally. Nodes of a graph could be associated with urban objects, while graph edges are inherently connected with linking routes. When there is a necessity to learn intrinsic patterns of such data structure, Graph Neural Networks (GNNs) take the stage. The benefits that come from leveraging GNNs are tracked in a variety of fields: crystallography [12], fake news detection [7], pose estimation [11]. Similar to the case of the revolutionization of the natural language processing domain with an attention-based mechanism, the incorporation of attention idea into GNNs has led to significant performance enhancements in many tasks. So, there are Graph Attention Networks (GATs) [31] that include self-attentional layers, which implicitly learn the importance of neighboring nodes. This peculiarity is frequently crucial in a range of applied areas, such as recommendation systems [32] or travel time estimation [14]. Noteworthy, graph prediction problems can be broadly divided into three groups: graph-level, node-level, and edge-level tasks. In this work, we focus on the reconstruction of population flows. Thus, the edge-level view, namely edge regression problem formulation, comes to our attention.

To confirm the assumption that GNNs can improve the accuracy of reconstruction population flows between two locations in a city, we designed a new graph-based deep learning approach to modeling population-facilities interactions. The study addresses the inductive problem of predicting the number of people interacting with facilities considering observed demand associated with places of residence, facilities capacity, and travel distance.

The peculiarity of the task is that the population flows between two locations in a city are often doubly constrained, which means that the sum of prediction for all out-going and in-going edges must not exceed the fixed values associated with nodes (namely, the number of people demand facility and facility capacity). The traditional mobility models comply with the constraints using an iterative balancing procedure, which can not be adopted for the neural network models due to the back-propagation mechanism. Previously, this side of the issue has yet to be considered [25,26,28]. To fill the gap, we introduce a one-step normalization technique that substitutes the iterative balancing procedure while using neural networks to predict doubly-constrained population flows.

The study shows that the proposed approach outperforms the doubly constrained gravity model and the model that uses only FNN. The experiments demonstrate that spatial dependencies in a network of interactions learned by GNNs contribute to the accuracy increase in the edge-level prediction task.

2   Materials and Methods

This section is organized the following way: first describes the data used for the experiments (as well as the process of its collection and preparation), then the following subsection clarifies which version of the Gravity Model we use as a baseline, and finally, the last subsection presents the proposed approach.

2.1   Data

The proposed approach operates on a direct bipartite graph in which each edge represents the interaction between two kinds of nodes that stand for places of population activities and facilities. While modeling population-facilities interactions, using smaller location units as urban objects is advantageous instead of grid cells. This makes it possible to reconstruct the interactions on the small distance that constitutes a significant part of the intra-city population movements, although it requires more accurate data. Nodes' features of a graph include the information about origins (places of activities) and destinations (facilities) that may impact the interaction between them, in particular, the population demands concentrated in places of activities (i.e., the number of people who demand a facility) and capacities of facilities. An edge between two nodes represents a population-facility interaction – the number of people concentrated in location i that get the facility's service j per specified unit of time. Each edge is associated with the travel distance between the origin and destination that it connects.

In the study, we perform experiments with the data of the population's daily interactions with kindergartens (as one of the essential social services for a substantial part of the population) in Saint Petersburg, Russia (Fig. 1). According to city-planning regulations, kindergartens are usually located in residential neighborhoods; therefore, we considered residential buildings to be places of primary activity. The graph of interactions consisted of 21 463 origin nodes, 1 278 destination nodes, and 27 429 714 edges (21 463 · 1 278) from which only 21 742 denoted actual interactions. The nodes' features represented the demand in each residential building and the capacity of each facility. The edge attributes included the number of people interacting with the facility and the travel distance in meters.

The residential buildings and kindergartens' locations were collected from different mapping services (OpenStreetMap [3], GoogleMaps [2], and 2GIS [1]) and merged into one dataset. The same mapping services helped determine each kindergarten's capacity via its standardized building type[1], which could be clearly distinguished on a map or satellite imagery.

The number of people with a demand for kindergartens was specified based on Russian census data [4]. The target group was considered to be people with children aged from 3 to 6 years. Since Russian census data provide the relevant information only for municipal units, the total number of people in the target

---

[1] In Russian regions, social facilities, such as kindergartens, are usually built on standard projects determining maximum capacity.

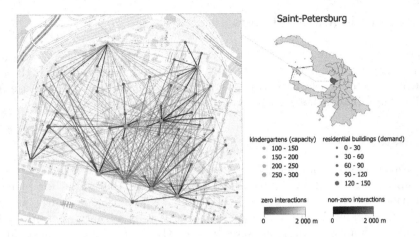

Fig. 1. A part of the bipartite graph representing the population's daily interactions with kindergartens (Saint-Petersburg).

group was distributed between residential buildings in the corresponding municipal unit, as described in the study [20].

Travel distances between residential buildings and kindergartens were measured as the shortest paths on the city road network consisting of driveways and walkways. The city road network was obtained from OpenStreetMap and pre-processed to eliminate topological errors [23]. Identifying the shortest paths between a large number of objects on a road network is often computationally expensive and, therefore, might be simplified to calculating Euclidian distances. However, one should keep in mind that only road network distances consider the urban environment's barriers that impede citizens' movement and thus provide more precise measurements, which can be crucial in some cases.

Unlike other urban data described above, data on actual population-facilities interactions is not publicly available. However, this is the information that stakeholders (represented by the government and some types of corporations) usually own. To conduct the experiments without real data, we modeled the population-facilities interactions based on the two statements. Given that kindergartens is a critical daily-use social infrastructure for a significant part of the urban population, we assumed the following:

1. All citizens prefer applying to the nearest kindergarten to meet the demand.
2. The system of interactions is in balance so that the maximum number of people is distributed between all facilities within available capacities.

We formed the proposed assumptions as an optimization function to distribute the citizens between available facilities. The system of linear inequalities implied the double constraints on the sum of out-going and in-going flows. The constraints reflect that the total number of interactions originating from the residential building i must not exceed the demand O_i (assuming that a citizen can apply to only one facility), and the total number of interactions with the facility j must not be greater than its capacity D_j (not to cause facility's overloading).

$$\text{maximize} \sum_{i=1}^{m} \sum_{j=1}^{n} \frac{y_{ij}}{d_{ij}}$$

$$\sum_{j=1}^{n} y_{ij} \leq O_i, i = 1..m \tag{1}$$

$$\sum_{i=1}^{m} y_{ij} \leq D_j, j = 1..n$$

where m and n denote the numbers of residential buildings and facilities respectively; O_i is the demand accumulated in the building i (origin); D_j is a capacity of facility j (destination); y_{ij} indicates the number of people living in the building i that get a service of the facility j traveling the distance d_{ij}.

Solving this system via integer linear programming, we obtained information on population-facilities interactions throughout the city. One may notice that the data obtained this way can differ from the real one. However, they provide a solid opportunity to investigate the performance of the proposed approach, which might encourage further research with more accurate data.

2.2   Gravity Model

The Gravity Model broadly applies to model spatial interactions in many domains. In most studies on human mobility, the Gravity Model is considered a fundamental baseline. The basic idea of the model is that the number of interactions between two locations is directly proportional to their sizes (in terms of population and other quantitative characteristics) and inversely proportional to the distance between them. In addition, the singly- and doubly-constrained model versions fix the total number of people originating from a location i or/and arriving at a location j. The choice of a model version depends on the amount of information available. In the current study, the demand accumulated in a residential building and the capacity of a facility naturally constrain the sum of out-going and in-going flows in the system of spatial interactions (Eq. 1). Therefore, we employ the Doubly-Constrained Gravity Model (DCGM) as a primary baseline.

$$\widehat{y}_{i,j} = A_i B_j O_i D_j f(d_{ij})$$

$$A_i = \frac{1}{\sum_j B_j D_j f(d_{ij})}; B_j = \frac{1}{\sum_i A_i O_i f(d_{ij})} \tag{2}$$

where $\widehat{y}_{i,j}$ denotes the predicted number of interactions between building i and facility j; $f(d_{ij})$ indicates a distance decay function which commonly modeled with a power-law d_{ij}^{β} or an exponential form $\exp(\beta d_{ij})$, β stands for a free parameter; A_i is a vector of the origin balancing factors; B_j is a vector of the destination balancing factors.

Most often, DCGM implements three steps: model calibration, estimation of interactions probabilities, and balancing the origin-destination (OD) matrix. The calibration aims to tune a free model parameter β based on observed data, more commonly via Poisson regression and Generalized Linear Modeling frameworks [18,24]. In the second step, the probability of interactions between each pair of locations is computed by Eq. 2 with the adjusted parameter β and unit vectors A_i, B_j. Finally, the obtained OD matrix is balanced by calibrating vectors A_i, B_j with the Iterative Proportional Fitting procedure [10].

The current study performed the experiments with the R package TDLM[1], which implements all three steps of DCGM [21]. Applying the gravity model to the dataset described in the previous section, we spotted a poor generalization ability of the model in this particular case which can be justified by a large size of interactions network [19]. To overcome this obstacle, we additionally tested the local version of the gravity model introduced in [22], which implies applying the model not to the whole graph but to the interactions within a truncation radius r. We slightly modified the model suggesting its iterative application to the graph with the increase of the truncation radius by Δr and recalculation of the residual fixed sum of in-going (out-going) flows on each step (Fig. 2).

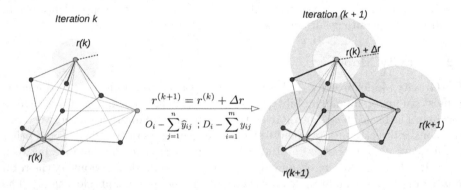

Fig. 2. The application of the Local Doubly-Constrained Gravity Model (LDCGM) to the interactions network. On each iteration k, LDCGM is applied to the edges with the distances $r^k \leq d_{ij} < r^k + \Delta r$; then for each node in a graph, the demand O_i and the capacity D_j recalculated by subtracting the sum of predicted in-going (out-going) flows so that on the next iteration, only residual values (that have not been distributed within the truncation radius) are included in calculations. The first iteration starts from the state $r^{(0)} = 0$ and $r^{(1)} = r^{(0)} + \Delta r$, and the last iteration finishes when the longest edge in a graph is reached, or the demands (capacities) are fully distributed.

---

[1] https://epivec.github.io/TDLM/.

2.3   The Proposed Approach

The neural network approach performs non-linear recombination of nodes' and edges' features in a graph, which detects intrinsic patterns and improves model performance. Still, the advantage of neural network models is often accompanied by high computational complexity. The large size of a densely connected network further complicates model training and prediction.

The densely connected network of spatial interactions might include millions of edges. However, the edges are heavily zero-inflated – most do not represent any actual interaction (flow) between pair of locations. This peculiarity makes the dataset large and imbalanced; both can adversely affect the training process. To address this problem, we employed the undersampling technique to prepare the training dataset. The technique suggests decreasing the number of negative (zero) edges to $n_p f$, where n_p denotes the number of positive (non-zero) edges and f indicates a hyperparameter adjusting the ratio between positive and negative edges. Compared to the study [26], which describes a similar undersampling technique, we additionally clarify that the negative edges should be sampled with the same distance distribution as the positive edges. This clarification might be crucial if the positive edges have long-tail distance distribution.

In contrast to the training process, testing must be performed on all edges of a densely connected network to avoid adjusting model predictions on knowledge about actual interactions. Given the size of the interactions network, the prediction on a full graph would have required a substantial amount of computational resources. To tackle this issue, we employed a local approach to the model prediction described in the previous section (Fig. 2), considering the step of the truncation radius Δr to be a hyperparameter.

The following subsection describes a four-step model architecture to predict population-facilities interactions in a city (Fig. 3). The model implements a novel doubly-constrained normalization technique that substitutes the iterative balancing procedure that can not be used in the back-propagation mechanism of neural networks.

Model Architecture. First, two-layer multi-head GAT operates on a directed bipartite graph to learn the latent nodes' representations considering the relative importance of the neighbors' features. Each GAT layer performs two convolutions with different message-passing directions (from origin to destination and destination to origin) to learn representations of nodes of each type in the directed graph. Multi-head attention mechanism executes five independent transformations. As recommended in the paper [31], the first layer of GAT concatenates new nodes' embeddings, while the second layer averages them. On each layer, GAT employs 128 neurons, 5 attention heads, the LeakyRelu activation function, a dropout technique (with a probability equal to 0.3), and layer normalization.

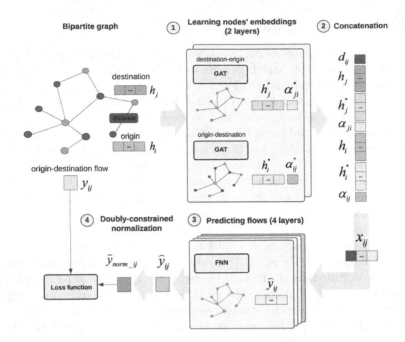

Fig. 3. Model architecture of the proposed approach. A directed bipartite graph is treated as input to the multi-head GAT, which learns attention coefficients and nodes' embeddings. For every edge, an input vector is obtained by concatenating the travel distance between nodes d_{ij}, their input features h_i, h_j, learned embeddings h_i'', h_j'' and the averages of attention coefficients $\overline{\alpha}_{ij}''$, $\overline{\alpha}_{ji}''$. Edges' input vectors are fed to the FNN to predict the number of interactions which are subsequently normalized with respect to the sum of nodes' in-going and out-going flows

The nodes' input features for learning nodes' embeddings include the information about origins and destinations that impact the interaction between them, specifically, the node's type (origin or destination) and either the population demands (for origin nodes) or capacity (for destination nodes).

$$
h_i' = \overset{K=5}{\underset{k=1}{\Big\|}} LeakyReLU \left(\sum_{j \in \mathcal{N}(i)} \alpha_{ij}'^k W'^k h_j \right)
$$
$$
h_i'' = LeakyReLU \left(\frac{1}{K} \sum_{k=1}^{K=5} \sum_{j \in \mathcal{N}(i)} \alpha_{ij}''^k W''^k h_j' \right)
\tag{3}
$$

where h_j is an input feature vector of node j, $\alpha_{ij}'^k$ and $\alpha_{ij}''^k$ are attention coefficients computed by the k-th attention head for nodes i and j; W'_k and W''_k are the linear transformation's weight matrices; $\mathcal{N}(i)$ is the neighborhood of node i; h_i' and h_i'' are embeddings on the first and the second layers respectively.

Second, for every edge in a graph, the input vector x_{ij} is formed by concatenating the travel distance between nodes that it connects d_{ij}, their input feature vectors h_i, h_j, learned embeddings h_i'', h_j'' and the averages of attention coefficients $\overline{\alpha}_{ij}''$, $\overline{\alpha}_{ji}''$.

$$x_{ij} = \left(d_{ij}, h_i, h_j, h_i'', h_j'', \overline{\alpha}_{ij}'', \overline{\alpha}_{ji}''\right) \qquad (4)$$

As a third step, the obtained vectors are fed to FNN. The architecture of FNN includes three hidden linear layers of dimensions 128 with the LeakyRelu function, dropout technique (with a probability equal to 0.3), and layer normalization. The last one-dimensional layer makes final predictions $\hat{y}_{ij}$. In the last layer, ReLU function limits the output $\hat{y}_{ij}$ with the interval $[0, \infty)$ as the number of interactions assumes non-negative values.

Finally, the predicted values $\hat{y}_{ij}$ are normalized to comply with the double constraints on the sum of out-going and in-going flows:

$$\hat{y}_{norm_{ij}} = \min\left(\frac{\hat{y}_{ij}O_i}{\sum\limits_{j\in\mathcal{N}(i)}\hat{y}_{ij}}, \frac{\hat{y}_{ij}D_j}{\sum\limits_{i\in\mathcal{N}(j)}\hat{y}_{ij}}\right) \qquad (5)$$

The loss function for the model is Weighted Mean Square Error (WMSE). The weight $\log(d_{ij})$ assigns higher importance to prediction errors for edges of greater distance, which are a minority in the training dataset with long-tail distance distribution.

$$Loss = \frac{1}{N}\sum_{i=1}^{m}\sum_{j=1}^{n}\left((y_{ij} - \hat{y}_{norm_{ij}})^2 \log(d_{ij})\right) \qquad (6)$$

where N is the number of predictions (equal to the number of edges in the training dataset represented actual and undersampled zero interactions); y_{ij} indicates the observed number of interactions, while $\hat{y}_{norm_{ij}}$ denotes the normalized predicted number of interactions for edge ij; d_{ij} is the travel distance between nodes i and j.

3 Results and Discussion

The described models were evaluated with a cross-validation technique on subgraphs obtained by splitting the dataset into parts related to the central, southern, northern, and eastern parts of the city. The cross-validation was repeated four times, with each subgraph used exactly once as the test data. In each subgraph, nodes' features comprised a node type (residential building or facility) and either capacity or demand associated with a node. The edge attributes contained the distance and the number of interactions (as a target value) between the nodes. Table 1 represents the number of elements (nodes and edges) included in each subgraph.

Table 1. The size of subgraph for each part of the city.

Part of the city	Origins	Destination	Edges
Central	5456	381	2 078 736 (5 731)*
Southern	6490	250	1 622 500 (6 599)
Northern	6092	413	2 515 996 (6 365)
Eastern	2901	231	670 131 (3 047)

*The value in the brackets is the number of (actual) non-zero interactions.

DCGM was calibrated and tested with power law (pow) and exponential (exp) distance decay functions by the R package TDLM. In a series of experiments, we observed a poor generalization ability of traditional DCGM on an extensive network of interactions. Specifically, DCGM tended to underestimate the number of interactions heavily. To minimize this downside of the traditional model, we additionally tested the local version of DCGM (LDCGM) with fitted hyperparameters β and Δr and found a better performance. However, both models appeared to share the identical problem - in the large system of interactions, it is practically impossible to reach a convergence during the iterative balancing of OD matrices which means that either the sum of out-going flows or in-going flows will exceed the fixed values.

The proposed graph-based deep learning approach significantly improved performance on each out-of-sample data compared to both DCGM and LDCGM models. Moreover, the suggested normalization technique (used to substitute the iterative balancing procedure) managed to consider the double constraints on the sum of in-going and out-going flows in OD matrix. To reduce the computational complexity of the neural network model, we employed the undersampling technique for model training and the local approach for predicting. Two hyperparameters f and Δr were fitted based on training data.

Further, we noticed that minor feature engineering positively impacts prediction accuracy. We extended nodes' feature vectors with information on the average distance of out-going (in-going) edges and the total demand (capacity) of connected nodes. The additional engineered features included in convolutions brought a noticeable increase in accuracy metrics.

Finally, to confirm our assumptions that GNNs embeddings could improve the accuracy of reconstruction population flows, we evaluated the interactions predicted only by FNN. The architecture of FNN was the same as described in the proposed approach, except that the input layer consisted of edge vectors obtained by concatenation only nodes' input features and travel distance between them. The experiments showed that four-layer FNN outperformed DCGM and

LDCGM models, although the accuracy of predictions was considerably lower than using the graph-based deep learning approach that adopts GAT.

To evaluate the models' performance, we computed metrics most commonly used in the regression tasks – MAE, MSE, and R-squared. Table 2 represents out-of-sample model performance for the eastern part of the city. The results for the rest parts of the city are placed in the Supplementary Materials.

Table 2. Performance on out-of-sample data for eastern part.

Models	MAE	MSE	R-squared
DCGM (pow)	14.456	468.490	0.114
DCGM (exp)	14.472	469.144	0.112
LDCGM (pow)	6.215	209.031	0.417
LDCGM (exp)	5.828	193.848	0.469
FNN	6.677	148.136	0.653
GAT + FNN (ours)	5.003	121.045	0.698
GAT ext. features + FNN (ours)	**4.719**	**113.341**	**0.719**

pow/exp - power law/exponential distance decay function.
ext. features - extended nodes' features included in convolutions.

4   Conclusion

The paper presents a new graph-based deep learning approach to modeling the population-facilities interactions. The proposed approach shows a significantly better performance in predicting doubly-constrained mobility flows than the classic Gravity Model used as a baseline. The one-step normalization technique effectively substitutes the iterative balancing procedure of OD matrix and complies with double constraints on in-going and out-going flows that often take place in the task formulation considered. The results obtained with partly modeled data provide reasonable grounds to exert efforts in collecting factual information on population-facilities interactions prevailing in a city and further research.

The experiments demonstrate that GAT significantly contributes to increased accuracy in edge regression tasks due to the attention mechanism that learns the relative importance of the neighbor's features. Moreover, based on the model's performance on out-of-sample data, GAT indicates transferability across graphs related to different parts of the city. This observation makes one think about the ability of GNNs to be transferred across graphs associated with the different cities to reconstruct population-facilities interactions. Moving forward, the transferability property of GNNs could be broadly applied to solve the problem of the incomplete availability of observed data in a city by replacing them with accurate predictions.

5 Supplementary Materials

The results of the models' evaluation for central, southern, northern, and eastern parts of the city that were obtained independently by k-fold cross-validation technique (the number of folds k is equal to 4).

Table 3. Performance on out-of-sample data.

Models	MAE	MSE	R-squared
Central part			
DCGM (pow)	14.333	489.973	0.109
DCGM (exp)	14.098	478.502	0.127
LDCGM (pow)	6.383	208.078	0.377
LDCGM (exp)	6.162	197.455	0.411
NN	6.952	173.660	0.614
GAT + FNN (ours)	6.270	167.531	0.647
GAT ext. features + FNN (ours)	**5.418**	**151.024**	**0.669**
Northern part			
DCGM (pow)	5.774	86.26	0.028
DCGM (exp)	5.791	86.06	0.030
LDCGM (pow)	2.748	37.178	0.305
LDCGM (exp)	2.625	34.435	0.366
NN	3.312	34.332	0.524
GAT + FNN (ours)	**2.253**	29.995	0.531
GAT ext. features + FNN (ours)	2.333	**28.045**	**0.592**
Southern part			
DCGM (pow)	12.336	350.747	0.134
DCGM (exp)	0.158	339.042	12.122
LDCGM (pow)	4.677	115.026	0.520
LDCGM (exp)	4.471	107.402	0.555
NN	5.66	102.783	0.690
GAT + FNN (ours)	**4.318**	**97.125**	0.694
GAT ext. features + FNN (ours)	4.829	97.240	**0.695**
Eastern part			
DCGM (pow)	14.456	468.490	0.114
DCGM (exp)	14.472	469.144	0.112
LDCGM (pow)	6.215	209.031	0.417
LDCGM (exp)	5.828	193.848	0.469
FNN	6.677	148.136	0.653
GAT + FNN (ours)	5.003	121.045	0.698
GAT ext. features + FNN (ours)	**4.719**	**113.341**	**0.719**

pow/exp - power law/exponential distance decay function.

ext. features - extended nodes' features included in convolutions.

Acknowledgments. This research is financially supported by the Russian Science Foundation, Agreement 17-71-30029 (https://rscf.ru/en/project/17-71-30029/), with co-financing of Bank Saint-Petersburg.

References

1. 2GIS. City information service. www.2gis.ru
2. Google Maps. Satellite image. https://www.google.com.sg/maps/
3. Map data from OpenStreetMap. https://www.openstreetmap.org/copyright
4. Rosstat. https://rosstat.gov.ru/
5. Ashik, F.R., Mim, S.A., Neema, M.N.: Towards vertical spatial equity of urban facilities: An integration of spatial and aspatial accessibility. J. Urban Manag. **9**(1), 77–92 (2020)
6. Barbosa, H., et al.: Human mobility: Models and applications. Phys. Rep. **734**, 1–74 (2018)
7. Benamira, A., Devillers, B., Lesot, E., Ray, A.K., Saadi, M., Malliaros, F.D.: Semi-supervised learning and graph neural networks for fake news detection. In: Proceedings of the 2019 IEEE/ACM International Conference on Advances in Social Networks Analysis and Mining, pp. 568–569 (2019)
8. Calabrese, F., Di Lorenzo, G., Ratti, C.: Human mobility prediction based on individual and collective geographical preferences. In: 13th International IEEE Conference On Intelligent Transportation Systems, pp. 312–317. IEEE (2010)
9. Dadashpoor, H., Rostami, F., Alizadeh, B.: Is inequality in the distribution of urban facilities inequitable? exploring a method for identifying spatial inequity in an iranian city. Cities **52**, 159–172 (2016)
10. Deming, W.E., Stephan, F.F.: On a least squares adjustment of a sampled frequency table when the expected marginal totals are known. Ann. Math. Stat. **11**(4), 427–444 (1940)
11. Doosti, B., Naha, S., Mirbagheri, M., Crandall, D.J.: Hope-net: A graph-based model for hand-object pose estimation. In: Proceedings of the IEEE/CVF Conference On Computer Vision And Pattern Recognition, pp. 6608–6617 (2020)
12. Eremin, R.A., Humonen, I.S., Zolotarev, P.N., Medrish, I.V., Zhukov, L.E., Budennyy, S.A.: Hybrid dft/data-driven approach for searching for new quasicrystal approximants in sc-x (x= rh, pd, ir, pt) systems. Crystal Growth Design **22**(7), 4570–4581 (2022)
13. Fan, C., Jiang, X., Lee, R., Mostafavi, A.: Equality of access and resilience in urban population-facility networks. npj Urban Sustainability **2**(1), 9 (2022)
14. Fang, X., Huang, J., Wang, F., Zeng, L., Liang, H., Wang, H.: Constgat: Contextual spatial-temporal graph attention network for travel time estimation at baidu maps. In: Proceedings of the 26th ACM SIGKDD International Conference on Knowledge Discovery & Data Mining, pp. 2697–2705 (2020)
15. Farahani, R.Z., Fallah, S., Ruiz, R., Hosseini, S., Asgari, N.: Or models in urban service facility location: A critical review of applications and future developments. Eur. J. Oper. Res. **276**(1), 1–27 (2019)
16. Ferrer, A.L.C., Thome, A.M.T., Scavarda, A.J.: Sustainable urban infrastructure: A review. Resour. Conserv. Recycl. **128**, 360–372 (2018)
17. Grauwin, S., et al.: Identifying and modeling the structural discontinuities of human interactions. Sci. Rep. **7**(1), 46677 (2017)

18. Griffith, D.A., Fischer, M.M.: Constrained variants of the gravity model and spatial dependence: model specification and estimation issues. Springer (2016). https://doi.org/10.1007/978-3-319-30196-9_3
19. Hsu, C., Fan, C., Mostafavi, A.: Limitations of gravity models in predicting fine-scale spatial-temporal urban mobility networks. arXiv preprint arXiv:2109.03873 (2021)
20. Kontsevik, G., Sokol, A., Bogomolov, Y., Evstigneev, V.P., Mityagin, S.A.: Modeling the citizens' settlement in residential buildings. Procedia Comput. Sci. **212**, 51–63 (2022)
21. Lenormand, M., Bassolas, A., Ramasco, J.J.: Systematic comparison of trip distribution laws and models. J. Transp. Geogr. **51**, 158–169 (2016)
22. Li, Z., Ren, T., Ma, X., Liu, S., Zhang, Y., Zhou, T.: Identifying influential spreaders by gravity model. Sci. Rep. **9**(1), 8387 (2019)
23. Mishina, M., Khrulkov, A., Solovieva, V., Tupikina, L., Mityagin, S.: Method of intermodal accessibility graph construction. Proc. Comput. Sci. **212**, 42–50 (2022)
24. Oshan, T.M.: A primer for working with the spatial interaction modeling (spint) module in the python spatial analysis library (pysal). Region **3**(2), R11–R23 (2016)
25. Peregrino, A.A., Pradhan, S., Liu, Z., Ferreira, N., Miranda, F.: Transportation scenario planning with graph neural networks. arXiv preprint arXiv:2110.13202 (2021)
26. Robinson, C., Dilkina, B.: A machine learning approach to modeling human migration. In: Proceedings of the 1st ACM SIGCAS Conference on Computing and Sustainable Societies, pp. 1–8 (2018)
27. Schläpfer, M., et al.: The universal visitation law of human mobility. Nature **593**(7860), 522–527 (2021)
28. Simini, F., Barlacchi, G., Luca, M., Pappalardo, L.: A deep gravity model for mobility flows generation. Nat. Commun. **12**(1), 6576 (2021)
29. Simini, F., González, M.C., Maritan, A., Barabási, A.L.: A universal model for mobility and migration patterns. Nature **484**(7392), 96–100 (2012)
30. Temeljotov Salaj, A., Lindkvist, C.M.: Urban facility management. Facilities **39**(7/8), 525–537 (2021)
31. Veličković, P., Cucurull, G., Casanova, A., Romero, A., Lio, P., Bengio, Y.: Graph attention networks. arXiv preprint arXiv:1710.10903 (2017)
32. Wang, X., He, X., Cao, Y., Liu, M., Chua, T.S.: Kgat: Knowledge graph attention network for recommendation. In: Proceedings of the 25th ACM SIGKDD International Conference On Knowledge Discovery & Data Mining, pp. 950–958 (2019)
33. Zipf, G.K.: The p 1 p 2/d hypothesis: on the intercity movement of persons. Am. Sociol. Rev. **11**(6), 677–686 (1946)

JurisBERT: A New Approach that Converts a Classification Corpus into an STS One

Charles F. O. Viegas[1], Bruno C. Costa[1], and Renato P. Ishii[2]

[1] Alfaneo, Goias, 405, 79020-100 Campo Grande, MS, Brazil
{charles.viegas,bruno.catais}@alfaneo.ai
[2] Federal University of Mato Grosso do Sul, Campo Grande, MS, Brazil
renato.ishii@ufms.br
https://alfaneo.ai, https://www.facom.ufms.br/

Abstract. We propose in this work a new approach that aims to transform a classification corpus into an STS (Semantic Textual Similarity) one. In that sense, we use BERT (Bidirectional Encoder Representations from Transformers) to validate our hypothesis, i.e., a multi-level classification dataset can be converted into an STS dataset which improves the fine-tuning step and evidences the proposed corpus. Also, in our approach, we trained from scratching a BERT model considering the legal texts, called JurisBert which reveals a considered improvement in fastness and precision, and it requires less computational resources than other approaches. JurisBERT uses the concept of sub-language, i.e., a model pre-trained in a language (Brazilian Portuguese) passes through refining (fine-tuning) to better attend to a specific domain, in our case, the legal field. JurisBERT uses 24k pairs of ementas with degrees of similarity varying from 0 to 3. We got this data from search mechanisms available on the court websites to validate the model with real-world data. Our experiments showed JurisBERT is better than other models such as multilingual BERT and BERTimbau with 3.30% better precision (F_1), 5 times reduced training time, and using accessible hardware, i.e., low-cost GPGPU architecture. The source code is available at https://github.com/alfaneo-ai/brazilian-legal-text-dataset and the model is here: https://huggingface.co/alfaneo.

Keywords: Semantic Textual Similarity · Retrieving Legal Precedents · Sentence Embedding · Bert

1 Introduction

Searching legal precedents is very important for legal professionals. They use it as a means for either supporting and strengthening their points or exposing opposing arguments. In Brazil, data from the *Conselho Nacional de Justiça*[1] [6]

---

[1] The Conselho Nacional de Justiça is a public institution that aims to help the Brazilian judiciary. It maintains administrative and procedural control and transparency.

© The Author(s), under exclusive license to Springer Nature Switzerland AG 2023
O. Gervasi et al. (Eds.): ICCSA 2023, LNCS 13956, pp. 349–365, 2023.
https://doi.org/10.1007/978-3-031-36805-9_24

shows a significant growth of legal proceedings, confirming that the Brazilian Judiciary System is overly congested, with a big amount of workload, and with an annual influx of millions of proceedings. In this scenario, an approach for efficiently retrieving precedents is very relevant for the Brazilian legal area.

In this context, several information-retrieving applications are using methods for evaluating semantic similarities, a process that is in the Natural Language Processing (NLP) field and involves determining the similarity between two text segments. Recently, models based on Transformers [27] networks and big unlabeled datasets (ex: BERT [8] and RoBERTa [17]) are raising the bar in a lot of NLP tasks, including evaluating the semantic textual similarity. Among some proposed approaches that stand out is Sentence BERT (sBERT) [24], which puts forward a change in the pre-trained BERT network and uses Siamese and triple network structure. This is used to derive semantically relevant sentence embedding, which can be compared by cosine similarity. This approach combines sentence embedding with indexing techniques such as FAISS [12]. It can quickly deal with outstanding amounts of data without losing the precision of transformers models.

However, most of the studies on transformers models are focused on the English language. This presents a challenge to bring technological advances to other languages, like Brazilian Portuguese. Even with popular models, such as BERT [8], having multi-language versions, models trained specifically with Brazilian Portuguese beat them, as shown by BERTimbau [26]. Besides, several works have revealed better results when pre-trained with domain-specialized corpus [3,21]. The BERTLaw study [19] shows that pre-training BERT with legal field specialized vocabulary has better results than using BERT Base. It exposes significant differences in unit vectors and that the intersection between both vocabularies is lower than half of the total vocabulary of each model separated. These differences directly affect the interpretation of a text segment by each model.

In order to validate our approach, we propose a methodology divided into 3 steps: 1) pre-training BERT for Masked Language Modeling (MLM) starting from scratch and using legal field-specific texts, containing laws, decisions, and court votes, besides several legal treatises of the Brazilian law; 2) experiments with the sBERT network using as base pre-trained BERT networks, multilingual BERT (mBERT) and BERTimbau; and 3) fine-tuning sBERT models over dataset generated by our proposed approach, which was prepared for evaluating the effectiveness of experiments and the similarities between the ementas of acordãos, these concepts will be explained at the Sect. 5. The dataset developed in our research has 24k pairs of ementas with a degree of similarity ranging between 0 and 3 got from court websites.[2].

JurisBERT got 3.30% F_1 more than BERTimbau with lower hardware cost for pre-training, confirming the hypothesis that a pre-trained BERT model for a specific domain has superior performance. We also noticed that sBERT with BERTimbau outperforms mBERT, validating that models with specific lan-

---

[2] STF, STJ, TJRJ, TJMS.

guages do better than the multilingual ones. Also, we could not find other public works of domain-specialized corpus for evaluating text similarity in the Brazilian legal field. In that case, we believe that our research is the first to provide this data publicly and that our contributions will help the development of new studies in this field.

We organized this paper in the following sections: in Sect. 2, we present the main concepts used in the other sections; in Sect. 3, we discuss other similar techniques that inspired us; in Sect. 4, we describe the steps of pre-training and dataset construction; in Sect. 5, we cover the fine-tuning of the models and discuss the results; finally, in Sect. 6, we present the main contributions of our research and point out future works.

2   Background

2.1   Legal Precedent Retrieval

Legal precedents are used to substantiate arguments by attorneys and judges. They use it to reinforce the justification of their decisions [29]. In Brazil, after the Constitution of 1998, precedents became more important since they started to have binding force over decisions made by the Brazilian Supreme Court [13]. For that reason, Brazilian courts have to provide public access to all its decisions over judged proceedings (except the ones that are classified as confidential). However, as the number of proceedings is big and keeps growing every year, more efficient solutions to retrieve precedents are in very high demand.

Worldwide, the retrieval of legal precedents is a very popular theme in the literature, especially the techniques for exploring semantic retrieval. They assist the better understanding of concepts related to contexts and the treatment of linguistic phenomenons, which affects the quality of the retrieval.

In Brazil, the main document used as precedent is named acordão. It shows the decisions made by the judging court. Even though it does not have a standard format, most of the time it has the following sections: identification of the concerned parties, the judge who wrote the opinion, the discussed objects, the given facts, the court votes, and the ementa, which is similar to the syllabus in the United States law. In Fig. 1 we show an example of ementa. We can see a standard in the writing. In the superior part, the text is written in capital letters and in entry, while in the other parts, the text is written in enumerated paragraphs.

Empirically, we see a lot of legal professionals using only the ementa section of the acordão to decide which precedents to choose. This probably happens because the ementa summarizes the decision and can be enough to understand the whole acordão. Besides, it is very common to find in lawsuits the full transcription of the ementa used to reference the precedent. Such observations helped us make the choice to use the ementa as the source material for similarity comparison, which is the goal of our study.

AGRAVO INTERNO – ART. 1.030, § 2°, CPC – ACÓRDÃO
ESTADUAL QUE COINCIDE COM A ORIENTAÇÃO FIRMADA
PELO SUPERIOR TRIBUNAL DE JUSTIÇA EM SEDE DE RECURSO
REPRESENTATIVO DE CONTROVÉRSIA – LIMITAÇÃO DOS
JUROS REMUNERATÓRIOS À TAXA MÉDIA DO MERCADO
SOMENTE SE VERIFICADA ABUSIVIDADE – CAPITALIZAÇÃO
MENSAL DOS JUROS PERMITIDA – EMBARGOS
PROTELATÓRIOS – MULTA APLICADA – RECURSO IMPROVIDO.
1–As questões de direito enfrentadas e decididas nos recursos
representativos da controvérsia guardam plena identidade ao
posicionamento do Tribunal de Origem, pois somente será aplicável a
limitação dos juros à taxa média do mercado em caso de comprovada
desvantagem ao consumidor, demonstrando abusividade do fornecedor. 2–
A capitalização mensal de juros é permitida nos contratos bancários desde
que expressamente pactuada e celebrada após após 31.3.2000, ou que haja
previsão de taxa de juros anual superior ao décuplo da mensal. 3–Recurso
improvido.

Fig. 1. Example of a `ementa` written in Brazilian Portuguese. This text is used to compare similarities.

2.2   Semantic Textual Similarity (STS)

To make precedent-retrieving systems is necessary to use semantic similarity comparison techniques. In NLP, is proposed to use the STS task, which can be considered a regression task, to calculate the *score* that represents the similarity between two sentences. Given a collection of sentences and two sentences, the *score* will have higher values when the similarity is higher and lower values when the similarity is lower. In this area, the *International Workshop on Semantic Evaluation* (SemEval) [1] stands out promoting a series of research on the NLP field to advance the semantic analysis and the creation of high-quality datasets.

In Brazil, the first collection of public data that included semantic similarity between sentences in Portuguese was the ASSIN [9]. Years later, the ASSIN 2 [22] suggested a new data collection based on the SICK-BR [23] collection. However, neither of those collections specializes in legal texts.

2.3   BERT

BERT or *Bidirectional Encoder Representations from Transformers* is a language model used to pre-train deep bidirectional representations from unlabeled texts. It uses a bidirectional approach to model the context to the left and right of the entered sequence tokens. As a result, the pre-trained BERT model is adjusted with only one additional out layer to make models for NLP downstream tasks.

In Fig. 2 we show the relations between BERT versions with pre-training and fine-tuning. The pre-trained version is the base for the fine-tuning versions that are adjusted to perform downstream tasks (ex: STS, Entity Named Recognition, Text classification, etc.). The pre-training uses unlabeled data, while the fine-tuning uses labeled ones.

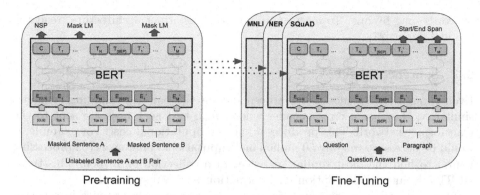

Fig. 2. BERT training process [8].

In the original BERT paper, there are two goals during pre-training: Masked Language Modeling (MLM) and Next Sentence Prediction (NSP). Within MLM, the number of random tokens in the input sequence is replaced by the special tokens [MASK] that are predicted using cross-entropy loss, 15% of the input tokens are evenly selected for possible replacements, of these tokens, 80% are in fact replaced by the token [MASK], 10% are unchanged and the remaining 10% are replaced by another random token of the vocabulary. In NSP, is used a binary classification loss to predict if two text segments follow one another in the original text. Positive examples are made with consecutive sentences and negative ones by paring text segments of different documents, both are created in equal proportions.

2.4   Transformers

The BERT architecture is based on the encoder part of the transformers [27] network architecture, which is considered a neural network of encoder-decoder type. The transformer network does not use either Recurrent Neural Networks structures or Convolution ones. Its main characteristics are being capable of reading sequential entries (from the left to the right or from the right to the left) in a single time. This characteristic allows for considering contexts from the right and the left. Also, it promotes better parallelization and requires less training time.

The transformer network is composed of an encoder that receives as input a sequence of words and transforms it into a vector sequence (internal representation). Next, a decoder, out of the internal representation, makes a sequence of words, one by one. To learn more about transformer architecture, read the original paper [27].

2.5   Sentence BERT

Even though BERT models have been raising the bar in evaluating semantic similarity, they use a cross-encoder where both text sentences are sent to the transformer network. This produces a huge computational cost. For example, it would be necessary roughly 50 million in computational inferences (65 processing hours) to find the most similar sentences in a collection of 10, 000. This turns BERT into an unviable option for information retrieval systems.

A way to address this type of problem is to map each sentence in a vector space, where semantic similar ones lay close together. For this, fixed sentence embeddings can be gotten by sending individual sentences to the BERT network. The most used technique gets the fixed vector embeddings from the average of values generated in the output layer of BERT (known as BERT embeddings) or using the output of the first token (or [CLS] token), though both techniques have lower performances than older ones like GloVe embeddings [20].

To fix this problem, sBERT was developed. It uses Siamese network architecture, which means using two identical networks with shared weights. As shown in Fig. 3, sBERT allows for deriving fixed-size vectors that, using a similarity measurement (ex: cosine similarity and Manhattan distance), can calculate the similarity between two sentences. To make sure that the generated embeddings have fixed sizes, there is a pooling[3] operation on the BERT output.

The sBERT model is computationally efficient. In the previously discussed example, the authors say that sBERT can reduce the computational cost to find the most similar pair of sentences, from 65 hours to approximately 5 seconds.

3   Related Works

The sBERT is basically a sentence embedding technique, a field with several studies and methods proposed. Unsupervised methods based on encoder-decoder techniques look to be dominating recent research. Skip-Thought [16] proposes a model with encoder-decoder architecture that uses neighbor sentences to codify the embedding. However, this model needs a corpus made with continuous texts for training. The Universal Sentence Encoder [4] suggests a general model that uses the encoder part of the transformer network, it utilizes the attention mechanism to compute the words that are sensitive to the context, that way, getting the sentence embedding from the average of the internal state of the codified tokens. It is also suggested that transferring knowledge at the level of sentences is more efficient than at the level of words. More recently, PromptBERT [11] applies prompts to reduce biases found in the internal state of the tokens for making the original BERT layers more effective.

---

[3] It is an operation that reduces the dimensionality of data by applying an aggregation of type max average.

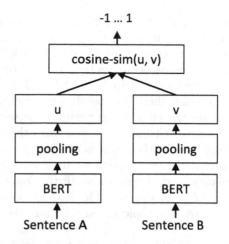

Fig. 3. sBERT architecture [24].

In [30], the authors conclude transformers model pre-trained with domain-specific contexts performs better than general models. This suggests that the best approach is merging both general and domain-specific models, by continuing pre-training using the last checkpoint of the general model in the domain-specific corpus. The corpus size was compared and concluded that it makes little difference between themselves.

Other works propose approaches that aim to transpose barriers from human annotation, which motivated us to develop our method that converts a classification dataset to STS to eliminate the annotation step. Meshram and Anand Kumar [18] propose a deep contextual long semantic textual similarity network. Deep contextual mechanisms for collecting high-level semantic knowledge are used in the LSTM network, and such a model performs better than human annotation. Keskar et al. [14] propose a unified span-extraction approach that allows combinations of question-answering and text classification datasets in intermediate-task training that outperform using only one or the other. Banerjee et al. [2] provide an unsupervised modeling approach that allows for a more flexible representation of text embeddings, transforming such a problem into an optimization problem over the spherical manifold. Results show improvements in document classification, document clustering, and semantic textual similarity benchmark tests.

4   JurisBERT

In this work, JurisBERT is the model trained from scratch using the BERT model and considering the legal texts. Our proposed approach aims to transform a classification corpus into an STS one. To validate our hypothesis, a multi-level classification dataset was converted into an STS dataset which improves the fine-tuning step and evidences the proposed corpus. The JurisBERT is a specific model for semantic textual similarity of the ementas of acordãos with an sBERT network. Our study puts forward pre-training BERT with Brazilian legal field domain-specific texts. For this, we constructed two corpora (for training and fine-tuning), discussed in more detail in Sects. 4.1 and 5. For evaluating the experiments we have two steps: first, we iterate over each model with all the analyzed ementas to create the embedding vectors[4]. Second, we calculate the degree of similarity between each pair of embeddings through the method of cosine similarity (as suggested by the authors of sBERT [5,24]). The score got from the cosine similarity can only have values between 0 and 1, the closer to 1, the higher the similarity, and the closer to 0, the lower the similarity. We stabilized a threshold number to optimize the division into two groups. That way, the score values over the threshold are similar and the ones under are not similar.

These two models chosen for comparison were pre-trained with general domain texts and with a much larger corpus than JurisBERT. The mBERT was pre-trained with 104 different languages, provided by the authors of BERT. BERTimbau, in turn, was pre-trained in Brazilian Portuguese with data from BrWac [28], which is a corpus got from Brazilian websites. We made two variations of pre-training: one from scratch, called JurisBERT, and the other, coming from the BERTimbau checkpoint, we apply further pre-training with legal texts called BERTimbau further. The goal is to determine if there are significant differences between both methods.

All BERT models are based on the $BERT_{BASE}$ architecture ($L = 12$, $H = 768$, $A = 12$, Total parameters $= 110M$). We chose this architecture because, even though it is not the most performative, it has a lightweight model that is more suitable for our hardware.

4.1   Pre-training Corpus

To pre-train JurisBERT, we had to create our own corpus, because we could not find one done with the amount of data and variety needed. Then, the first step was developing web scrappers to read and retrieve public documents from many sources, for example, court websites, public agencies, and universities. During the construction of this corpus, we aimed for the primary sources of the legal field, such as laws, precedents, treatises, analogies, general principles of law, and equity [7]. So, among the retrieved documents are laws and federal decrees, súmulas[5], decisions, acordãos and court votes, besides treatises of different legal fields. In Fig. 4, we show a chart with the participation of each type of legal source. The predominating of laws happens because of the plentifulness of this kind of document on governmental websites.

---

[4] It is a dense vector of floating points that aims to capture the semantic of the text in the vector space.

[5] The súmulas summarizes the dominant precedent of a given court.

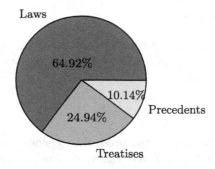

Fig. 4. Participation of each type of legal source in the pre-training corpus.

After retrieving the documents, we pre-processed them to remove special characters, excesses of spaces, and blank lines, though we maintained the accentuation and the letter casing because the networks we used are case-sensitive. Also, we split the documents into paragraphs and dispose of the ones with less than 10 tokens and the duplicated ones. We made this choice, intending to make the paragraphs more similar to the average size of the *ementa*. The result we got was 1.5 million of sentences(paragraphs), 99% of those with less than 384 tokens, as shown in Fig. 5, repeating a proportion like the one in the corpus of the *fine-tuning*, detailed in Sect. 5. After the pre-processing, the corpus reached 410 MB of raw text, a significantly lower number than the ones of BERTimbau (17 GB) and RoBERTa (160 GB). Then, we divided the corpus into two parts: training (95%) and evaluation (5%).

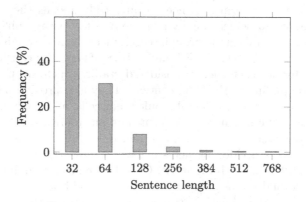

Fig. 5. Frequency of each sentence length.

4.2   Vocabulary Generation

For training JurisBERT, we generated an uncased vocabulary of 30k units of sub-words using the training corpus. The chosen tokenizer was WordPiece [25] of the huggingface library.

4.3   Pre-training

We used only the MLM goal in the pre-training since recent papers [17] have suggested that the NSP goal is not effective. During training, we optimized JurisBERT with Adam [15] using the following parameters: $\beta_1 = 0.9$, $\beta_2 = 0.999$, $\epsilon = 1e - 6$ e L_2 weight decay of 0.01. The learning rate in the first $10,000$ steps with the apex of $1e - 4$ and linear decay. We also used a *dropout* of 0.1 in all levels, alongside GELU's [10] activation function. The model was pre-trained with 20 epochs ($220k$ steps, 5 times smaller than the BERTimbau), with a batch size of 128 and sequences with a maximum length of 384 tokens. We used two **NVIDIA GeForce RTX 3080** with 12 GB **GDDR6X** each. The training time of models JurisBERT and BERTimbau further was 7 and 21 days, respectively.

5   Evaluating Semantic Textual Similarity

We evaluated the performance of the models after their fine-tuning. This step is essential to confirm our hypothesis, in other words, if the dataset generated by fine-tuning step provides better results in STS, this proves that our approach is adequate to construct qualifiers STS datasets. For this, we also needed to develop our own dataset composed of many paired sentences showing whether they were similar. The term sentence, in our study, means the content of the ementa of an acordão, which usually is made of a few paragraphs.

We constructed our dataset through search mechanisms available on the websites of the courts: STF, STJ, TJRJ, and TJMS. There, the courts provide one or more acordãos for each theme considered stable, which means that it has a standard understanding in the legal context. They also provide notorious cases such as racial quotas, the use of embryonic stem cells, and party infidelity.

In particular, STF's search mechanism has an interesting characteristic to define degrees of similarity, it is organized hierarchically at three levels of grouping. The first level is divided by fields of law: Administrative, Civil, Constitutional, Electoral, Criminal, Retirement, Civil Procedural, Criminal Procedural, and Tax. The second themes, for example, in the field of Administrative Law, the divided themes are Public Job Applications, Pharmaceutical Assistance Programs, Liability of Public Administration, and Public Sector Employees. The third and final level is divided by legal discussions, for example, in the Public Sector Employees theme we got the following discussions: Teacher's Special Retirement, Public Employee Payment Discount for Striking, Vested Right of Probationary Period, Judgment Deadline for Legality of Retirement.

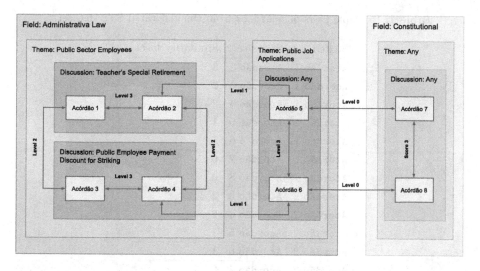

Fig. 6. Example of the method used to define the similarity levels during STS dataset generation.

So, to STF's search mechanism, we applied a scale of similarity between acordãos considering the group hierarchy, because acordãos inside the same discussion is more similar than acordãos of different themes and fields. Thus, we automatically annotated acordãos of the same discussion with a similarity of 3, acordãos of different discussion but of the same theme with a similarity of 2, acordãos of different themes but of the same field with similarity of 1 and acordãos of different fields with similarity of 0 as shown in Fig. 6.

Applying this strategy with STF, we got a total of 24,926 pairs of acordãos applying a combination two by two. Table 1 shows an example of acordãos pairs generated using the same examples shown in Fig. 6.

We dedicate 80% of generated pairs to training and 20% to evaluation and the other search mechanisms (STJ, TJRJ, and TJMS) got only a single level of grouping, we only used those for testing and comparing models. The strategy used for automatically annotating these searches was considering acordãos of the same group as similarity of 1 and the rest as similarity of 0. Therefore, we generated 19,027 pairs from the STJ, 8,626 from the TJRJ, and 6,305 from the TJMS.

5.1   Fine-tuning

In the beginning, we had defined the maximum sequence length after analyzing the corpus; it showed that 91.33% of the ementa texts had lengths lower than 384 tokens. However, we trained models with low epochs varying only in the maximum sequence length to validate this hypothesis. As shown in Table 2, the value 384 had better results.

Table 1. Example pairs of acordãos from the generated STS dataset.

Sentence 1	Sentence 2	Similarity level
Acordão 1	Acordão 2	3
Acordão 1	Acordão 3	2
Acordão 1	Acordão 4	2
Acordão 1	Acordão 5	1
Acordão 1	Acordão 6	1
Acordão 1	Acordão 7	0
Acordão 1	Acordão 8	0
Acordão 2	Acordão 3	2
Acordão 2	Acordão 4	2
Acordão 2	Acordão 5	1
Acordão 2	Acordão 6	1
Acordão 2	Acordão 7	0
Acordão 2	Acordão 8	0
Acordão 3	Acordão 4	3
Acordão 3	Acordão 5	1
Acordão 3	Acordão 6	1
Acordão 3	Acordão 7	0
Acordão 3	Acordão 8	0
Acordão 4	Acordão 5	1
Acordão 4	Acordão 6	1
Acordão 4	Acordão 7	0
Acordão 4	Acordão 8	0
Acordão 5	Acordão 6	3
Acordão 5	Acordão 7	0
Acordão 5	Acordão 8	0
Acordão 6	Acordão 7	0
Acordão 6	Acordão 8	0
Acordão 7	Acordão 8	3

After having defined the maximum sequence length, we made the fine-tuning training with 3 epochs, hyper-parameters, batch size, and maximum sequence length of 8 and 384, respectively. The cosine similarity loss was used. The training took roughly 3 hours using the same hardware as described in Sect. 4.3. To measure and compare our experiments, we considered only the checkpoint of the models that got the best performance during the training epochs.

Table 2. Experiments varying the maximum sequence length.

Sequence length	$F_1(\%)$
64	71.30
128	76.72
256	81.93
384	**83.27**
512	82.70

5.2 Discussions

We evaluated the models with $F_1(\%)$ metric, as shown in Table 3. In general, we can see that all the models that went through fine-tuning performed better than the ones that did not. These results suggest that our approach to constructing the dataset and making the fine-tuning was, in fact, effective. Afterward, these results demonstrated that our proposed approach could be useful in other areas not only in the law field. We believe that the multi-level characteristic from the classification dataset was crucial to infer the distance degrees for the sentence pairs.

Also, we can notice that models pre-trained with specific texts of a sub-language, in other words, texts specialized in a specific domain, performed better than the others. Models BERTimbau and JurisBERT showed better general results. This means there are advantages in training from scratch and in doing more training on pre-existing models. Our training approach proved effective even with a corpus size 42 times smaller and with 5 times fewer pre-training steps than other methods.

In that regard, we can say that our work addresses an important problem in NLP, dealing with domain-specific topics (healthcare, law, and others). These have plenty of data pulverized through different mediums, but few of those are annotated for a specific task. Even without fine-tuning, our approach proved to be a viable option, beating even fine-tuned mBERT and BERTimbau. These results infer it is also possible to have good performances in other downstream tasks.

Our pre-training had a hardware cost lower than the other models, the training time was lower and the graphics card used was inferior to those used in BERTimbau and mBERT. The P100 graphics card, by NVIDIA, is more expensive than the RTX used in our study. So, we showed it is technically and financially viable to replicate these experiments in other sub-language domains, considering the accessible price of current RTX models. For instance, the price of a graphic card used in our study is about $1,000$ dollars.

Table 3. Comparing $F_1(\%)$ results.

Model	TJMS	TJRJ	STJ	Mean
No Fine-tuning				
mBERT	65.05	63.78	30.39	53.08
BERTimbau	71.20	63.88	35.55	56.88
BERTimbau further	75.48	64.06	41.75	60.43
JurisBERT (ours)	**80.25**	**73.21**	**52.00**	**68.49**
Fine-tuning approaches				
mBERT	69.51	64.21	39.49	57.73
BERTimbau	81.77	71.34	50.75	67.95
BERTimbau further	84.39	73.46	47.37	68.41
JurisBERT (ours)	**85.16**	**77.65**	**50.95**	**71.25**

6   Conclusion

This work's main contribution is a new approach that transforms a classification corpus into an STS one. We use BERT to validate our hypothesis, i.e., a multi-level classification dataset can be converted into an STS dataset which improves the fine-tuning step and evidences the proposed corpus.

Moreover, we contribute to creating a corpus for unsupervised pre-training, including many laws, treatises, and decisions of several branches of Brazilian law. Similarly, the pre-training from scratching is 5 times faster than other approaches in training time, and it can be deployed in a low-cost environment considering a usual graphics card, i.e., with a price of less than $1,000$. Using our dataset alongside the data from acordãos contributes to many other NLP tasks like clustering and topic modeling. Further, the source code of the web scrappers and parsers we used in the construction of the datasets is available in a public repository[6].

Finally, JurisBERT got 3.30% F_1 more than BERTimbau with lower hardware cost for pre-training, confirming the hypothesis that a pre-trained BERT model for a specific domain has superior performance. We also noticed that sBERT with BERTimbau outperforms mBERT, validating that models with specific languages do better than the multilingual ones. Also, we could not find other public works of domain-specialized corpus for evaluating text similarity in the Brazilian legal field. In that case, we believe that our research is the first to provide this data publicly and that our contributions will help the development of new studies in this field.

---

[6] Proposed dataset and web scrappers are available here: https://github.com/alfaneo-ai/brazilian-legal-text-dataset, and the models, here: https://huggingface.co/alfaneo.

Acknowledgments. We thank the support of the UFMS (Universidade Federal de Mato Grosso do Sul), FUNDECT, and Finep. We also thank the support of the INCT of the Future Internet for Smart Cities funded by CNPq, proc. 465446/2014-0, Coordenação de Aperfeiçoamento de Pessoal de Nível Superior - Brasil (CAPES) - Finance Code 001, and FAPESP, proc. 2014/50937-1 and 2015/24485-9.

Any opinions, findings, and conclusions or recommendations expressed in this material are those of the authors and do not necessarily reflect the views of FUNDECT, Finep, FAPESP, CAPES, and CNPq.

References

1. Agirre, E., Cer, D., Diab, M., Gonzalez-Agirre, A.: SemEval-2012 task 6: A pilot on semantic textual similarity. In: *SEM 2012: The First Joint Conference on Lexical and Computational Semantics - Volume 1: Proceedings of the main conference and the shared task, and Volume 2: Proceedings of the Sixth International Workshop on Semantic Evaluation (SemEval 2012), pp. 385–393. Association for Computational Linguistics, Montréal, Canada (7–8 Jun 2012), https://aclanthology.org/S12-1051

2. Banerjee, S., Mishra, B., Jawanpuria, P., Shrivastava, M.: Generalised spherical text embedding (2022)

3. Beltagy, I., Lo, K., Cohan, A.: Scibert: A pretrained language model for scientific text. In: EMNLP (2019)

4. Cer, D., et al.: Universal sentence encoder for English. In: Proceedings of the 2018 Conference on Empirical Methods in Natural Language Processing: System Demonstrations. pp. 169–174. Association for Computational Linguistics, Brussels, Belgium (Nov 2018). https://doi.org/10.18653/v1/D18-2029, https://aclanthology.org/D18-2029

5. Choi, H., Kim, J., Joe, S., Gwon, Y.: Evaluation of bert and albert sentence embedding performance on downstream nlp tasks (2021). https://doi.org/10.48550/ARXIV.2101.10642, https://arxiv.org/abs/2101.10642

6. CNJ: Justiça em números 2020: ano-base 2019. Tech. rep., Conselho Nacional de Justiça (2020), https://www.cnj.jus.br/pesquisas-judiciarias/justica-em-numeros/

7. Cunha, A.S.: Introdução ao estudo do direito. Saraiva (2012)

8. Devlin, J., Chang, M., Lee, K., Toutanova, K.: BERT: pre-training of deep bidirectional transformers for language understanding. CoRR abs/1810.04805 (2018). http://arxiv.org/abs/1810.04805

9. Fonseca, E.R., Borges dos Santos, L., Criscuolo, M., Aluísio, S.M.: Visão geral da avaliação de similaridade semântica e inferência textual. Linguamática 8(2), 3–13 (Dez 2016). https://linguamatica.com/index.php/linguamatica/article/view/v8n2-1

10. Hendrycks, D., Gimpel, K.: Gaussian error linear units (gelus) (2016). https://doi.org/10.48550/ARXIV.1606.08415, https://arxiv.org/abs/1606.08415

11. Jiang, T., et al.: Promptbert: Improving bert sentence embeddings with prompts (2022). https://doi.org/10.48550/ARXIV.2201.04337, https://arxiv.org/abs/2201.04337

12. Johnson, J., Douze, M., Jégou, H.: Billion-scale similarity search with gpus (2017). https://doi.org/10.48550/ARXIV.1702.08734, https://arxiv.org/abs/1702.08734

13. Júnior, H.: Curso de direito processual civil, vol. I. Editora Forense (2019)

14. Keskar, N.S., McCann, B., Xiong, C., Socher, R.: Unifying question answering, text classification, and regression via span extraction (2019)

15. Kingma, D.P., Ba, J.: Adam: A method for stochastic optimization (2014). https://doi.org/10.48550/ARXIV.1412.6980, https://arxiv.org/abs/1412.6980

16. Kiros, R., Zhu, Y., Salakhutdinov, R., Zemel, R.S., Torralba, A., Urtasun, R., Fidler, S.: Skip-thought vectors (2015). https://doi.org/10.48550/ARXIV.1506.06726, https://arxiv.org/abs/1506.06726

17. Liu, Y., et al.: Roberta: A robustly optimized bert pretraining approach (2019). https://doi.org/10.48550/ARXIV.1907.11692, https://arxiv.org/abs/1907.11692

18. Meshram, S., Anand Kumar, M.: Long short-term memory network for learning sentences similarity using deep contextual embeddings. International Journal of Information Technology, pp. 1633–1641 (2021)

19. Nguyen, H.T., Nguyen, L.M.: Sublanguage: A Serious Issue Affects Pretrained Models in Legal Domain. arXiv e-prints arXiv:2104.07782 (Apr 2021)

20. Pennington, J., Socher, R., Manning, C.: GloVe: Global vectors for word representation. In: Proceedings of the 2014 Conference on Empirical Methods in Natural Language Processing (EMNLP), pp. 1532–1543. Association for Computational Linguistics, Doha, Qatar (Oct 2014). https://doi.org/10.3115/v1/D14-1162, https://aclanthology.org/D14-1162

21. Rasmy, L., Xiang, Y., Xie, Z., Tao, C., Zhi, D.: Med-bert: pre-trained contextualized embeddings on large-scale structured electronic health records for disease prediction (2020). https://doi.org/10.48550/ARXIV.2005.12833, https://arxiv.org/abs/2005.12833

22. Real, L., Fonseca, E., Gonçalo Oliveira, H.: The assin 2 shared task: A quick overview. In: Quaresma, P., Vieira, R., Aluísio, S., Moniz, H., Batista, F., Gonçalves, T. (eds.) Computational Processing of the Portuguese Language, pp. 406–412. Springer International Publishing, Cham (2020)

23. Real, L., et al.: SICK-BR: A Portuguese Corpus for Inference: 13th International Conference, PROPOR 2018, Canela, Brazil, September 24–26, 2018, Proceedings, pp. 303–312. Springer, Cham (01 2018). https://doi.org/10.1007/978-3-319-99722-3_31

24. Reimers, N., Gurevych, I.: Sentence-bert: Sentence embeddings using siamese bert-networks (2019). https://doi.org/10.48550/ARXIV.1908.10084, https://arxiv.org/abs/1908.10084

25. Song, X., Salcianu, A., Song, Y., Dopson, D., Zhou, D.: Fast wordpiece tokenization (2020). https://doi.org/10.48550/ARXIV.2012.15524, https://arxiv.org/abs/2012.15524

26. Souza, F., Nogueira, R., Lotufo, R.: Bertimbau: Pretrained bert models for brazilian portuguese. In: Intelligent Systems: 9th Brazilian Conference, BRACIS 2020, Rio Grande, Brazil, October 20–23, 2020, Proceedings, Part I. p. 403–417. Springer-Verlag, Berlin, Heidelberg (2020). https://doi.org/10.1007/978-3-030-61377-8_28

27. Vaswani, A., et al.: Attention is all you need (2017)

28. Wagner Filho, J.A., Wilkens, R., Idiart, M., Villavicencio, A.: The brwac corpus: A new open resource for brazilian portuguese. In: Proceedings of the Eleventh International Conference on Language Resources and Evaluation (LREC 2018) (2018)

29. Weber, R.: Intelligent jurisprudence research: A new concept. In: Proceedings of the 7th International Conference on Artificial Intelligence and Law. p. 164–172. ICAIL '99, Association for Computing Machinery, New York, NY, USA (1999). https://doi.org/10.1145/323706.323791, https://doi.org/10.1145/323706.323791

30. Zhang, G., Lillis, D., Nulty, P.: Can Domain Pre-training Help Interdisciplinary Researchers from Data Annotation Poverty? A Case Study of Legal Argument Mining with BERT-based Transformers. In: Proceedings of the Workshop on Natural Language Processing for Digital Humanities (NLP4DH), pp. 121–130. Association for Computational Linguistics (2021), https://rootroo.com/downloads/nlp4dh_proceedings_draft.pdf

Computational Music: Analysis of Music Forms

Jing Zhao[1], KokSheik Wong[1(✉)], Vishnu Monn Baskaran[1],
Kiki Adhinugraha[3], and David Taniar[2]

[1] Monash University Malaysia, Bandar Sunway, SL 47500, Malaysia
{jing.zhao,wong.koksheik,vishnu.monn}@monash.edu
[2] Monash University, Clayton, VIC 3800, Australia
david.taniar@monash.edu
[3] La Trobe University, Bundoora, VIC 3086, Australia
k.adhinugraha@latrobe.edu.au

Abstract. With the development of computational science, many fields, including computational linguistics (sequence processing) and computational vision (image processing), have enabled various applications and automation with satisfactory results. However, the development of Computational Music Analysis (CMA) is still in its infancy. The main factor hindering the development of CMA is the complex form found in music pieces, which can be studied and analyzed in many different ways. Considering the advantages of Deep Learning (DL), this paper envisions a methodology for using DL to promote the development of Music Form Analysis (MFA). First, we review some common music forms and emphasize the significance and complexity of music forms. Next, we overview the CMA in two different processing ways, i.e., sequence-based processing and image-based processing. We then revisit the aims of CMA and propose the analysis principles that need to be satisfied for achieving the new aims during music analysis, including MFA. Subsequently, we use the fugue form as an example to verify the feasibility and potential of our envisioned methodology. The results validate the potential of using DL to obtain better MFA results. Finally, the problems and challenges of applying DL in MFA are identified and concluded into two categories, namely, the music and the non-music category, for future studies.

Keywords: Music form · Computational music analysis · Deep learning · Computational science

1 Introduction

Music is an ancient yet common information carrier used from generation to generation. As the soul and essence of music, *music form* (MF) organizes individual musical notes together to form layered and expressive sound. Hence, many studies, applications, and analyses of music are inseparable from MF. These include music education, musicology, and music appreciation, which uses MF directly. In addition, other applications emerge from utilizing the derived information from MF, such as music composition [20,68], music emotion classification [51], genre classification [17], thumbnail generation [46], making chord and downbeat estimation [27], music recommendation [58], to name a few. Furthermore, music has also been used for health and information security purposes in recent years. For example, music has been adopted in psychology [37], Covid-19 treatment [39], heart disease treatment [16], neurology [25,60], and cryptography [38,43]. Therefore, MF has become the development cornerstone that provides a basis and important music characteristics for in-depth research in many fields.

Popular music form usually lacks richness with just a few variations (e.g., key, rhythm, chord) [70]. In contrast, classical music is of complex forms, and it is informative with deep content. In fact, the notion of MF is more applicable to the case of complex classical music [18], which has different forms such as *theme and variation, fugue, sonata,* etc. Interestingly, research also shows that classical music is closely related to human physiological responses, such as changes in mood, heartbeat, etc. [70]. Therefore, regardless of research significance or traditional MF definition in musicology, classical music form is worthy of attention.

While some domains have advanced significantly using deep learning models (e.g., classification for MS-COCO @ 65.4% of mean average precision [65] using CNN model, and IMDB Review data set @ 96.21% of accuracy [55] using XLNet model), we envision that music form analysis (MFA), which is an important sub-field in computational music analysis (CMA), can also benefit from the data and computationally driven approaches (e.g., deep learning models). Therefore, being the first article that envisions the analysis of the complex and informative classical music form based on the development of the data-driven approach, we set to explore a few interesting questions, including:

Q1: What is music form, and why is it complex yet important to achieve advanced results?

Q2: What is CMA?

Q3: Why is the development of CMA slow, and how can the CMA develop better?

Q4: What is a data-driven approach, and how can it work for MFA?

The rest of the article is structured as follows. Section 2 addresses the first question (Q1). Specifically, we overview the classical music forms and emphasize the significance of MF in music and other fields as well as the complexity of MF. Such discussions are conducted from two processed ways, namely, sequence-based processing and image-based processing. In Sect. 3, we review and clarify the eventual aims of the whole CMA field. We also stipulate the principle to which the results from the sub-field of CMA (e.g., MFA) should conform for a deeper study. Such discussion address question Q2 and Q3. Since many computational science studies have benefited from the development of data-driven approach, we introduce a data-driven approach for MFA in Sect. 4.1 and Sect. 4.2, which addresses question Q4. To demonstrate the feasibility of applying the DL methodology to MFA, we conduct an initial experiment for fugue form analysis and present the results of the case study in Sect. 4.3. Finally, Sect. 5 identifies the challenges of MFA and concludes this paper.

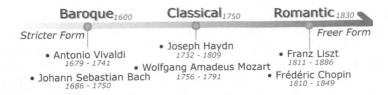

Fig. 1. Three eras of classical music and some representative composers.

2   Music Form

In this section, we first overview some common music forms in classical music and its three eras. Subsequently, we systematically highlight the significance of *music form* in music and other domains and analyze its complexity.

Typically, the term *music form* (MF) refers to the classical music form rather than the popular music form [18]. The first reason is that the form of popular music is relatively simple, with merely a few variations (e.g., key, rhythm, chord) [70]. Secondly, the components of different pop music are similar, including verse, chorus, bridge, etc. Under this situation, although the simple form satisfies the aesthetics of the general public, the music it presents lacks richness and depth. Therefore, complex classical music is often considered in the form analysis under traditional musicology. Furthermore, interestingly, research shows that classical music, which contains deep content while being expressive, is closely related to human physiological responses, such as changes in mood, heartbeat, etc. [70]. Therefore, regardless of research significance or the traditional definition of MF in musicology, classical music form is worthy of attention.

Classical music can typically be divided into three eras, namely, *Baroque, Classical, Romantic*, as shown in Fig. 1. Furthermore, the music in the *Baroque* era has a relatively strict form. As time passes, the meaning of the music form is weakened to a certain extent, noticeably in the *Romantic* era [66]. In other words, the composition of music becomes relatively more free. The common classical music forms include *fugue, theme and variation, sonata*, to name a few. We will discuss these music forms based on their most prevalent era.

2.1   Fugue

The *fugue* form prevailed in the Baroque period (the 1600 s)). It is polyphonic with a strictly ordered counterpoint form [59,61]. In other words, the complexity and richness of this music are attributed to stacking voices. For most cases, a *fugue* contains four voices, namely, *Soprano, Alto, Tenor*, and *Bass* [19], as shown in Fig. 2. In addition, Fig. 2 also shows the annotation of the *Subject* (S) and *Counter-Subject* (CS), which are the main components in the *fugue* form. Generally speaking, S is the main melody, and all other melodies are composed around S.

Technically, S and CS have different characteristics from the perspective of music composition. First, S will start at the beginning of the *fugue* music

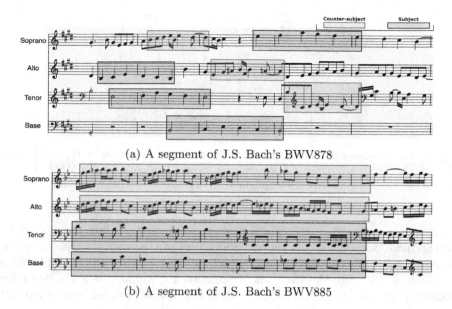

(a) A segment of J.S. Bach's BWV878

(b) A segment of J.S. Bach's BWV885

Fig. 2. Two segments showing the *fugue* form with four voices.

Fig. 3. An example of the *sonata* form's *exposition* part (Mozart K545).

independently (i.e., in a single voice). In addition, different S can appear in different voices and overlap in the temporal dimension, such as the two examples shown in Fig. 2. Such overlapping feature is the common composition technique in the *fugue* form, viz., *stretto* [59]. This technique is most used at the end of the music to add a sense of compactness to the music [59]. For CS, it is often accompanied by S, and sometimes, CS will continue following S (see Fig. 2) [41, 56]. Additionally, in the whole *fugue* form, the S and CS are repeated melody segments with artful variations. The common variations are tonal, duration, pitch interval, note augmentation or diminution [26,31,53].

2.2 Sonata

Sonata form becomes noticeable since the Classical era [4,57]. Such form is large-scale with three main parts at the *structure level*, namely, *exposition*, *develop-*

Fig. 4. The segments of a *theme* melody and the third *variation* (*VIII*) melody in Mozart's KV265 music (*theme and variation* form). The notes in the *VIII* that are similar to the *theme* melody are highlighted in orange. (Color figure online)

ment, and *recapitulation* [2,7]. These three parts shape the whole piece of music. Furthermore, sometimes, the *sub-structure level* of the sonata's *exposition* and *recapitulation* parts can still be divided further. Figure 3 shows an example of the *sonata* form with two themes in the *exposition*. By adding a new theme or key transition, the *sonata* form can express more conflict and tension in emotion [48].

2.3   Theme and Variation Music

The *theme and variation* (*TV*) form is another important music form in the classical era [52]. At the *structure level* (i.e., highest level), the TV form consists of a *theme* segment (*T*) at the beginning of the music and a series of *variation* segments (*V*). Different *V* segments innovate the *T* segment from different aspects [48]. In other words, the *V* segments will be composed based on *T* with some changes, such as notes number change, key variation, etc., so that the *V* segments are similar to *T* to a certain extent. An example of the *T* and a *V* segment is shown in Fig. 4. Here, the notes in the third *V* segment (labeled as *VIII*) that are similar to the *T* melody are highlighted. Furthermore, in the segment labeled *VIII*, the main change in the treble part ($\flat$) is notes diminution and adding more transition notes, while the main change in the bass part ($\mathcal{9}$) is a variation of octave number with a similar contour. However, in the *TV* form, the keys of most *V* segments are the same as the key of the corresponding *T* segment. These are illustrated in Fig. 9. The same argument applies to the number of bars in the segments. Hence, the TV form is more concise in comparison to the *sonata* form [13].

2.4   Other Forms

In addition to the above three common yet complex music forms, there are other music forms. For example, the *binary* form and the *ternary* form include two and three sections/themes, respectively [23]. Among these sections/themes, they may involve key transitions (e.g., a major key transition to the dominant key) [23]. The typical example of the *binary* form is J.S. Bach BWV996, which contains only two sections. Interestingly, after expanding these basic forms, such as adding more repetitions of the sections/themes, the *Rondo* form is constructed. Alternatively, when adding more repetitions and variations, the *theme and variation* form is constructed. Hence, the *binary* and *ternary* forms are arguably the simplest and most basic forms.

2.5 Significance and Complexity

After understanding some common music forms, we try answering the question: *"What is music form, and why is it complex yet important to achieve advanced results?"*. Specifically, the main music elements are notes [32], which can exist objectively and independently without any form. After structuring notes into a series of segments, a layered and expressive music piece is formed. Hence, *music form* (MF) is the soul of music, and music cannot exist without a form. Due to the importance and indispensability of MF in music, the study of MF benefits many research fields, including music education, musicology, and music appreciation. Some derivative fields rely on MF information as well, and its roles are broadly summarized below:

1. Providing new research methodology (e.g., different rules for notes combination in different music forms) for the field of arrhythmia research [16] and cryptography [38], etc.
2. Adding emotional value to music [51], and in a way participating in the treatment of Covid-19 disease [39].
3. Serving as the basic features for genre classification tasks [17], music attribute calculation [27], music recommendation algorithm [58], structured music composition [20,68] to low the threshold of composition for non-professionals [34], neurological treatment (movement disorders [25], aphasia [60], and psychiatric [11]).
4. Serving as a key feature of music visualization [46], which is further enhanced for music education and appreciation [6,12,22], music summarization and retrieval (e.g., cover song retrieval [21], music thumbnail [46]), music cryptography [43], and other fields.
5. Contributing to treating personality disorder patients as a social bond [37].

Although MF enables many applications, it is difficult to analyze because of its complexity, thus inhibiting it from unleashing its full potential. Specifically, MF is not a simple mechanical combination of segments. It manages the melody from two music perspectives of structure (i.e., the rhythm and pitch structures) [32]. The rhythm and pitch are responsible, respectively, for the rhythmic and pitch relationship (i.e., tonality and harmony) among notes. Although these two structures are relatively independent and can be discussed separately [32], without any of such two structures, the music becomes monotonous and poor in emotions and content, thus losing the meaning of MFA. Hence, the informative classical music form always involves these two perspectives of structure.

The other factor contributing to the complexity of MF is the rich and robust relationships of music. The relationships within the music form can be roughly

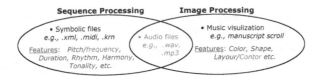

Fig. 5. Two common music processing ways and available features.

divided into two categories, internal relations (i.e., relationships of notes within a segment) and external relations (i.e., relationships among segments). Such rich relationships are the premise of music being expressive and capable of carrying in-depth content, but unfortunately, the rich relationships also complicate the MFA task.

3   Computational Music Analysis

This section reviews computational music analysis (CMA), contrasting it with computational vision and linguistics. We clarify the new aims of CMA and promote its development, focusing on two principles obeyed by the CMA results.

As a product of human beings, music has established a close connection with people from multiple dimensions (e.g., business, culture, and life) in multiple ways (audio, image, and symbolic files) [10,50]. In the early years, music analysis was performed manually by humans. Thanks to the recent advancement in computational power and machine learning capabilities, CMA has received some attention and emerges as a rising field. Typically, CMA can be considered a sequence processing task (e,g., symbolic files), or an image processing (e.g., manuscript scroll) task, as shown in Fig. 5. Unlike the symbolic file and manuscript scroll, which fall clearly in the respective categories, music presented in the audio form is more interesting. Specifically, when managing the music audio as a sequential signal, CMA can be treated as computational linguistics (sequence processing). On the other hand, when visualizing the music audio as a spectrogram, it can be treated as computational vision (image processing).

However, although CMA may adopt the existing information processing methodologies designed for other computational sciences, such as sequence-based computational linguistics [42] and image-based computational vision [44,62], CMA is still an emerging interdisciplinary field because of the uniqueness of music.

Like text for natural languages, music has a context with a temporal structure. However, unlike text for natural languages that assume general features in language sequences (e.g., collocations, logical vocabulary, negative words), there are no general features in the sequence of music. On the other hand, from the perspective of images, the basic elements are color and shape. Such basic elements can be used to distinguish content in different images (e.g., recognizing document layout [63,71] via the basic spatial elements). Although a music manuscript scroll also contains black-and-white colors and note shapes, the melodic content of the notation is recorded by the position of the note (relative to the 5-lines) and the shape of the notes together, but not the colors and shapes themselves. Hence, despite the similarities, it is not straightforward to directly adopt methodologies designed for other matured fields to perform CMA due to the aforementioned intrinsic differences.

3.1   Aims and Principles

It is generally perceived that CMA mainly aims to produce interesting music results or to assist human analysts [3], hence CMA's results should conform to human cognition of music. Based on such perception and aim, the CMA results pay less attention to whether they can be reused in other fields, such as MIR, which seriously hinders the development of CMA and reduces the value of CMA results. Hence, with technological improvement and the rising trend of inter-disciplinary research, it is necessary and timely to re-visit the perception and aim of CMA [45].

Referring to other matured fields in computational science and putting aside technological limitations and complexity, we conjecture that CMA can have a higher purpose, namely, understanding music more intelligently and profession-ally and even replacing human analysis in the future.

However, to achieve these purposes, the current principle adopted (viz., whether the results meet the human cognition of music) to obtain CMA results is insufficient. Based on our analysis, the CMA's results should satisfy two prin-ciples: 1) conforming to human cognition of music, and 2) being reusable in other research investigations.

Firstly, conforming to the human cognition of music can ensure that the CMA's results are trustworthy and authoritative from the music perspective. However, it is impossible to conform absolutely to the cognition principle, as argued by Marsden et al. [45]. Hence, for different studies, the researcher needs to decide on the level to which this principle is conformed.

Secondly, the principle stipulating that computers can understand and pro-cess CMA results ensures the usability of the results. This leads to two issues; one is the form of the result, and the other is the objectivity of the result. For the former issue, the form of the result needs to be catered to the computer instead of only conforming to the form of human vision or hearing. For the latter issue, although absolute neutrality or objectivity is also unrealistic [3] and CMA usu-ally relies on some preliminary human knowledge [45], the result of CMA cannot depend excessively on prior knowledge of human cognition of music. Results involving too much subjective knowledge will include prejudice, thus affecting the subsequent application and reducing the value and authority of the CMA results. When the two aforementioned principles are satisfied simultaneously, CMA can provide more authoritative and reusable results.

In fact, no clear indicators can measure whether the results of CMA are in line with human cognition of music or whether the results of CMA are objec-tive enough [45]. However, it is necessary to follow the guidance of the above principles for highlighting the value of CMA (including MFA) for further study in many fields.

4 Envisioned Methodology

Based on the above analysis, the MFA methods have two processing ways (i.e., sequence and image). So far, for image processing (e.g., the visualization of audio files), some methods analyze the structure by manually labelling [15,49], searching for mechanically repeated melody segments [14,67], or detecting short segments and merging them to meet the length of the music form level [9,35]. Even when using deep learning (DL) techniques to detect the components of MF, such as Deep Belief Network [8] or Convolutional Neural Network [30], the results of music segmentation are subpar (i.e., 40%-50% of accuracy).

Relatively speaking, sequence-based methods have received less attention than image-based methods. Nonetheless, sequence-based methods have focused on the analysis of complex classical music forms, such as *fugue* form [28,29], *sonata* form [2,7]. Their main research idea is to find repetitive segments through a dynamic programming algorithm. Then, they use the Viterbi algorithm and Hidden Markov Model (HMM) to calculate the structure of the MF (i.e., the label of detected segments). Indeed, these methods contribute more in the MFA fields, but they have lower robustness and more limitations. For example, the *fugue* form analysis methods proposed by Giraud et al. [28,29] require three assumptions, including: (as1) the length of S, and (as2) the position of CS, and (as3) using the voice-separated symbolic files to simplify the parallel issues (e.g., multiple voices) in the *fugue*.

In short, there is still much room for improvement in both sequence-based and image-based MFA methods to serve the newly identified purpose. Therefore, considering that DL technology has been widely used in recent years and has achieved commanding results in many fields, we explore whether DL can break through the status quo of MFA for complex music forms.

4.1 Feature Engineering

In the DL era, common feature engineering includes handcraft and non-handcraft techniques. As the name implies, handcraft feature engineering artificially selects music features and embeds them in neural network models. In contrast, non-handcrafted feature engineering automatically extracts music features directly by using some machine-learning techniques. However, although the non-handcrafted feature engineering techniques are automatic with fewer answer leak risks, their performance is not always better than that of handcrafted feature engineering techniques [54]. Therefore, handcraft feature selection is still common in the field of music analysis. The common features used in handcraft feature engineering for CMA are shown in Fig. 5.

Fig. 6. An example showing the data description with *SeqHead* proposed for the MTBert model. The notes that are highlighted are the ground truth *subject* melody.

4.2 Deep Learning

The neural network model of deep learning simulates the biological nervous system in the human brain [1]. A large number of units in neural networks and brain neurons have similar functions. They can amplify some basic features to multiple layers, thus capturing more details [40]. In recent years, the neural network has already become a powerful computing approach thanks to the availability of data in large volumes. This ability enables DL to obtain state-of-art results (e.g., MF-COCO @ 65.4% of mean average precision [65] using CNN model, and IMDB Review data set @ 96.21% of accuracy [55] using XLNet model). The popular deep learning models include RNN, BERT, and CNN, to name a few. We will introduce them from the perspective of sequence processing (RNN, BERT) and image processing (CNN).

Specifically, for sequence processing, compared to the RNN-based model that learns sequentially and is unable to handle long-term relationships between contexts [5,33], BERT is better at processing information in the temporal dimension with rich long-term relationships. The advantage of the transformer-based model (e.g., BERT model [24]) is attributed to the position encoding and the self-attention mechanism. Such two mechanisms enable the model to permute the position of the input sequences to learn the relationship among contexts. In addition, they can better deal with contextual information with long-term relationships [69]. In short, a large-scale transformer-based model has a high capability to learn context and long-term relationships and has stronger interdisciplinary adaptability [36].

On the other hand, the CNN model is typically utilized to learn from images, which contain spatial information. This is due to the fixed-size kernel of CNN, which performs convolution operations on multiple layers. In other words, for an image, its local feature is meaningful, and the relationship among long-distanced elements is not strong. Therefore, the CNN model can capture many local features [5]. However, the local features of the musical image (e.g., manuscript scroll) may be meaningless or unimportant. For example, there may be a large amount of transitional melody in two *subjects* in a *fugue* form. In this case, the limited kernel size will lose or ignore some important information in the long-term relationship. Therefore, CNN is better at capturing short-term context relationships [64], but is not so attractive for long-term context relationships.

Inspired by the BERT model's ability to handle contextual information with long-term relationships, we conduct preliminary experiments using a proposed BERT-based model to explore the feasibility of applying DL for the purposes of MFA.

4.3   Case Study: Fugue Form Analysis

In this case study, we try weakening the assumptions (i.e., as1, as2 and as3 in Sect. 4) as a means to fulfill the second principle (viz., regarding reusability in Sect. 3.1). Note that, in the same MF, there is no clear relationship and general features between different pieces of music. To enhance the connection among the different *fugue* music files, which in turn, helps the DL model to learn, we propose a general feature to describe each piece of music, namely *SeqHead*. As shown in Fig. 6, *SeqHead* contains the first S occurrence of a *fugue* that starts independently. The length of *SeqHead* refers to Giraud et al. [28]'s statistical results (d_I), that is, $L_m + max(d_I), d_I \in [-8, 6]$, where L_m is the length of the first voice before the second voice, and d_I is the difference between L_m and the correct length of S in J.S. Bach's Well-Tempered Clavier (WTC) book I data set with 24 symbolic voice-separated fugue files [28]. After extracting *SeqHead* for each music piece, the music will be separated into segments with a length of 64 notes and the *SeqHead* of each music piece is concatenated to every segment of the same music.

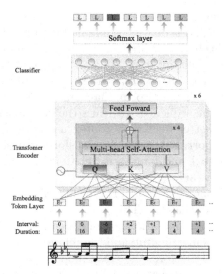

Fig. 7. The overall architecture of the MTBert model.

Next, we design a BERT-based model called *Music Tiny BERT model (MTBert)* for *fugue* form analysis, viz., extracting the S and CS in a given *fugue* form. An overview of the architecture of the proposed MTBert is shown in Fig. 7. Meanwhile, based on our designed data description method, we use

LSTM as the baseline model for comparison. Both models are trained and validated using WTC book I data set.

Table 1 shows the results of the note-level binary classification (i.e., S/non-S and CS/non-CS) obtained for BWV869 in the WTC data set using LSTM and MTBert. In the case of detecting S, the performance of LSTM is 73.3% for F1 score with high recall (91.7%). In the case of detecting CS, despite attaining 100% recall, LSTM predicts many False Positive errors causing extremely low precision. Hence, LSTM is non-reliable and infeasible to detect CS. On the other hand, using the same setup (*SeqHead*) and assumption (voice-separated input files) with as LSTM, MTBert can detect S with high precision (97.0%) and recall (90.6%). Furthermore, without making any assumption on CS, MTBert can detect more than 50% of the notes in CS with more balance recall and precision than LSTM. Note that such performances are better than those reported by Giraud et al. [28] who focus more on occurrence detection[1] based on the assumptions of as1 for S, as2 for CS, and as3 for the input files. However, under enough assumption, Giraud et al.'s [28] method cannot detect any occurrences of CS in BWV869. Although Giraud et al. [28] can detect all occurrences of S, there are still many errors in terms of length.

Table 1. The evaluation of MTBert and the baseline model of BWV869

	S			CS		
	Recall	Precision	F1 score	Recall	Precision	F1 score
LSTM	91.7%	61.1%	73.3%	100.0%	16.3%	28.0%
MTBert	97.0%	90.6%	93.7%	56.4%	74.8%	64.3%

Since the current techniques for computational *fugue* form are very limited, it is impossible to achieve significant improvement overnight. However, our method could at least demonstrate that it is possible to improve the performance using DL method under fewer assumptions, in comparison to the results obtained by non-DL methods. Furthermore, unlike the detection of occurrence allowing errors of length, MTBert's results are clear with zero-tolerance in length so that the results can be reused directly for other tasks. Hence, such outcomes follow the principle (i.e., the second principle involving objectivity and reusability in Sect. 3.1) of CMA analysis. Overall, the results of our case study, which is the first of its kind, can verify the feasibility of the application of DL on MFA and the potential of reaching the new purpose of MFA using DL.

---

[1] The mismatch in lengths for S and CS would not affect the results on the detected occurrences.

5 Problems and Challenges

Despite the promising outcome report above, applying DL on MFA still faces some challenges. We divide the challenges into two broad categories, namely, the music category and the non-music category. Here, the music category refers to the challenge caused by the complexity of the MF itself and the features of processing different music carriers (viz., sequence-based and image-based processing). On the other hand, the non-music category refers to the challenge of using DL on the complex MFA task.

5.1 Music Category

Under the music category, there are four subchallenges. The first subchallenge is the nonexistence of a general characteristic in different MFs. In other words, for the features shown in Fig. 5, they are utilized only to record the music notes instead of any other information regarding the MF. For example, no melody contour (pitch interval combination), fixed pitch/rhythm/harmony combination, color, or shape can represent or reflect the characteristics of a certain MF. This subchallenge is the reason why some researchers believe that there are no general features for creating a general method that can accommodate all music forms [47,67].

The second subchallenge is that some variation features of the MF's components (i.e., rhythm and pitch) cannot be computed directly. For example, in the *fugue* form shown in Fig. 2, the S or CS repeats with some variations, such as notes diminution (rhythm perspective), key variation (pitch perspective), etc.

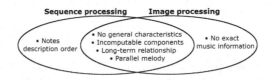

Fig. 8. Some challenges in the music category.

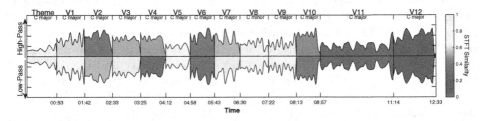

Fig. 9. Visualization of a *theme and variation* form (Mozart's KV265). *V* refers to the *variation* and the color shows the level of similarity between every *V* segments and the *theme* from the high-pass part and the low-pass part. These two parts can be understood simply as the treble part and the bass part.

Therefore, these changes take place in different music perspectives, and they cannot be quantified directly from the available features shown in Fig. 5.

The third subchallenge is that the internal relationships of music (i.e., the connection of different segments) are strong and long-term. A typical example is that every *variation* segment in *theme and variation* form is based on the *theme* segment, so there are strong relationships among the *variation* and *theme* segments. Figure 9 is a visualization of a *theme and variation* form in Mozart KV265. In this figure, the time distance between the last *variation* segment and the *theme* segment is around 11 min. This duration is too long for both the sequence processing and image processing approaches.

The last subchallenge is the parallel melody in music. A typical example is shown in the segments of the *fugue* in Fig. 2. As highlighted in green boxes, the components of this form (i.e., S and CS) can appear simultaneously. Hence, the boundary of music form components will overlap. Similarly, the *chords* in music with multiple notes at an instant also involve the problem of melody parallelism.

In addition to the four subchallenges mentioned above, analyzing MF using sequence or image-based methods also has a challenge each. For the sequence processing method, the order of the notes will be sensitive. Hence, the order to process the inseparable notes in parallel melody needs to be addressed. For the image processing method, even if one visualizes the image from the audio files or the manuscript scroll score, no exact music notes information can be used. Hence, the results of MFA are prone to bias.

5.2   Non-music Category

Under the non-music category, the vague definition of MF is an obstacle for training DL models. In other words, there is no clear definition of the corresponding segments in the higher/lower-levels within a piece of music. Hence, different definitions of the boundaries lead to different training results. Normally, when the segments in the music cannot be aggregated further, it is considered to be the highest-level music form, and comparatively, the highest level of form is less controversial.

Furthermore, due to the complexity of the music form, an approach needs to be designed for every specific music form [47, 67]. This leads to a situation where there are many datasets of classical music, but only a limited number of them could be used for MFA. In other words, the usable dataset for every specific music form will be limited. Moreover, using the DL technique on a small-scale dataset is prone to suffer from the overfitting problem, i.e., learning features with low generalizability.

In short, the MFA task becomes very challenging due to the complexity of the music form. Although DL has achieved good results in various fields, the application in MFA tasks still faces some fundamental challenges, which need to be addressed.

6 Conclusion and Outlook

Music Form Analysis (MFA) is one of the most important sub-fields in Computational Music Analysis (CMA). Two typical ways of MFA are sequenced-based methods and image-based methods. Inspired by many fields in computational science that have attained commanding results through deep learning techniques (DL), this paper envisions a methodology to apply DL techniques in MFA. We first conjecture that, in the future, CMA will attain more consistent and reliable results, thus replacing human analysis and stimulating the development of related fields. To achieve this higher goal, this paper stipulates two principles that need to be followed by subfields' results in CMA, namely, (i) conforming to the human cognition of music, and (ii) being reusable in other research investigations. These principles ensure that the results are trustworthy and reusable, which serve as the foundation for future exploration in other fields related to music.

Based on these two principles, we conduct a preliminary verification of our vision, proposing a BERT-based model (MTBert) for the *fugue* form's symbolic files (sequence processing). The results show that although the DL-based method still has some limitations, it can achieve better performance than the non-DL approach, which is an excitation for the future application of DL methods in MFA. Meanwhile, we also suggest combining the feature of the key transition in MF with DL for further complex MFA.

Finally, we systematically identify and address the challenges of MFA, and conclude them into two broad categories: music and non-music. The music category refers to the challenges caused by the particularity and complexity of MF as well as the features used for processing different music carriers. In contracts, the non-music category refers to two challenges of using DL on the complex MFA task, namely, the vague definition and complexity of the music form. When these challenges are addressed, the development of many fields related to music form can be further promoted, such as music education, music composition, music emotion/genre classification, making chord and downbeat estimation, psychology, Covid-19 treatment, heart disease treatment, etc.

References

1. Abiodun, O.I., Jantan, A., Omolara, A.E., Dada, K.V., Mohamed, N.A., Arshad, H.: State-of-the-art in artificial neural network applications: a survey. Heliyon **4**(11), e00938 (2018)
2. Allegraud, P., et al.: Learning sonata form structure on mozart's string quartets. Trans. Int. Society Music Inform. Retrieval (TISMIR) **2**(1), 82–96 (2019)
3. Anagnostopoulou, C., Buteau, C.: Can computational music analysis be both musical and computational? J. Math. Music **4**(2), 75–83 (2010)
4. Arnold, J.M.: The role of chromaticism in Chopin's sonata forms: a Schenkerian view. Northwestern University (1992)
5. Basiri, M.E., Nemati, S., Abdar, M., Cambria, E., Acharya, U.R.: Abcdm: an attention-based bidirectional cnn-rnn deep model for sentiment analysis. Futur. Gener. Comput. Syst. **115**, 279–294 (2021)

6. Bergstrom, T., Karahalios, K., Hart, J.C.: Isochords: visualizing structure in music. In: Proceedings of Graphics Interface 2007, pp. 297–304 (2007)
7. Bigo, L., Giraud, M., Groult, R., Guiomard-Kagan, N., Levé, F.: Sketching sonata form structure in selected classical string quartets. In: ISMIR 2017-International Society for Music Information Retrieval Conference (2017)
8. Buccoli, M., Zanoni, M., Sarti, A., Tubaro, S., Andreoletti, D.: Unsupervised feature learning for music structural analysis. In: 2016 24th European Signal Processing Conference (EUSIPCO), pp. 993–997. IEEE (2016)
9. Buisson, M., Mcfee, B., Essid, S., Crayencour, H.C.: Learning multi-level representations for hierarchical music structure analysis. In: International Society for Music Information Retrieval (ISMIR) (2022)
10. Burgoyne, J.A., Fujinaga, I., Downie, J.S.: Music information retrieval. A new companion to digital humanities, pp. 213–228 (2015)
11. Carr, C., Odell-Miller, H., Priebe, S.: A systematic review of music therapy practice and outcomes with acute adult psychiatric in-patients. PLoS ONE 8(8), e70252 (2013)
12. Chan, W.Y., Qu, H., Mak, W.H.: Visualizing the semantic structure in classical music works. IEEE Trans. Visual Comput. Graphics 16(1), 161–173 (2009)
13. Chawin, D., Rom, U.B.: Sliding-window pitch-class histograms as a means of modeling musical form. Trans. Int. Society for Music Inform. Retrieval 4(1), (2021)
14. Chen, P., Zhao, L., Xin, Z., Qiang, Y., Zhang, M., Li, T.: A scheme of midi music emotion classification based on fuzzy theme extraction and neural network. In: 2016 12th International Conference on Computational Intelligence and Security (CIS), pp. 323–326. IEEE (2016)
15. Cheng, T., Smith, J.B., Goto, M.: Music structure boundary detection and labelling by a deconvolution of path-enhanced self-similarity matrix. In: 2018 IEEE International Conference on Acoustics, Speech and Signal Processing (ICASSP), pp. 106–110. IEEE (2018)
16. Chew, E.: Cosmos: Computational shaping and modeling of musical structures. Front. Psychol. 13 (2022). https://doi.org/10.3389/fpsyg.2022.527539
17. Chillara, S., Kavitha, A., Neginhal, S.A., Haldia, S., Vidyullatha, K.: Music genre classification using machine learning algorithms: a comparison. Int. Res. J. Eng. Technol. 6(5), 851–858 (2019)
18. Clercq, T.d.: Embracing ambiguity in the analysis of form in pop/rock music, 1982–1991. Music Theory Online 23(3), (2017)
19. Corazza, G.E., Agnoli, S., Martello, S.: Counterpoint as a principle of creativity: extracting divergent modifiers from'the art of fugue'by johann sebastian bach. Musica Docta 4, 93–105 (2014)
20. Dai, S., Jin, Z., Gomes, C., Dannenberg, R.B.: Controllable deep melody generation via hierarchical music structure representation. arXiv preprint arXiv:2109.00663 (2021)
21. De Prisco, R., et al: Music plagiarism at a glance: metrics of similarity and visualizations. In: 2017 21st International Conference Information Visualisation (IV), pp. 410–415. IEEE (2017)
22. De Prisco, R., Malandrino, D., Pirozzi, D., Zaccagnino, G., Zaccagnino, R.: Understanding the structure of musical compositions: is visualization an effective approach? Inf. Vis. 16(2), 139–152 (2017)
23. Dent, E.J.: Binary and ternary form. Music Lett. 17(4), 309–321 (1936)
24. Devlin, J., Chang, M.W., Lee, K., Toutanova, K.: Bert: Pre-training of deep bidirectional transformers for language understanding. arXiv preprint arXiv:1810.04805 (2018)

25. Devlin, K., Alshaikh, J.T., Pantelyat, A.: Music therapy and music-based interventions for movement disorders. Curr. Neurol. Neurosci. Rep. **19**, 1–13 (2019)
26. Dirst, M., Weigend, A.S.: On completing js bach's last fugue. Time Series Prediction: Forecasting the Future and Understanding the Past, pp. 151–177 (1994)
27. Fuentes, M., McFee, B., Crayencour, H.C., Essid, S., Bello, J.P.: A music structure informed downbeat tracking system using skip-chain conditional random fields and deep learning. In: ICASSP 2019–2019 IEEE International Conference on Acoustics, Speech and Signal Processing (ICASSP). pp. 481–485. IEEE (2019)
28. Giraud, M., Groult, R., Leguy, E., Levé, F.: Computational fugue analysis. Comput. Music. J. **39**(2), 77–96 (2015)
29. Giraud, M., Groult, R., Levé, F.: Subject and counter-subject detection for analysis of the well-tempered clavier fugues. In: Aramaki, M., Barthet, M., Kronland-Martinet, R., Ystad, S. (eds.) CMMR 2012. LNCS, vol. 7900, pp. 422–438. Springer, Heidelberg (2013). https://doi.org/10.1007/978-3-642-41248-6_24
30. Hernandez-Olivan, C., Beltran, J.R., Diaz-Guerra, D.: Music boundary detection using convolutional neural networks: a comparative analysis of combined input features. Int. J. Interact. Multimedia Artif. Intell. **7**(2), 78 (2021). https://doi.org/10.9781/ijimai.2021.10.005
31. Huang, C.Z.A., Cooijmans, T., Roberts, A., Courville, A., Eck, D.: Counterpoint by convolution. arXiv preprint arXiv:1903.07227 (2019)
32. Jackendoff, R., Lerdahl, F.: The capacity for music: what is it, and what's special about it? Cognition **100**(1), 33–72 (2006)
33. Jain, A., Zamir, A.R., Savarese, S., Saxena, A.: Structural-rnn: Deep learning on spatio-temporal graphs. In: Proceedings of The IEEE Conference On Computer Vision And Pattern Recognition, pp. 5308–5317 (2016)
34. Jin, C., Tie, Y., Bai, Y., Lv, X., Liu, S.: A style-specific music composition neural network. Neural Process. Lett. **52**, 1893–1912 (2020)
35. Jun, S., Hwang, E.: Music segmentation and summarization based on self-similarity matrix. In: Proceedings of the 7th International Conference on Ubiquitous Information Management and Communication, p. 4. No. 82 in ICUIMC '13, Association for Computing Machinery, New York, NY, USA (2013)
36. Kao, W.T., Lee, H.Y.: Is bert a cross-disciplinary knowledge learner? a surprising finding of pre-trained models' transferability. arXiv preprint arXiv:2103.07162 (2021)
37. Kenner, J., Baker, F.A., Treloyn, S.: Perspectives on musical competence for people with borderline personality disorder in group music therapy. Nord. J. Music. Ther. **29**(3), 271–287 (2020)
38. Kumar, C., Dutta, S., Chakborty, S.: Musical cryptography using genetic algorithm. In: 2014 International Conference on Circuits, Power and Computing Technologies [ICCPCT-2014], pp. 1742–1747. IEEE (2014)
39. Lawes, M.: Creating a covid-19 guided imagery and music (gim) self-help resource for those with mild to moderate symptoms of the disease. Approaches: An Interdisciplinary Journal of Music Therapy, pp. 1–17 (2020)
40. LeCun, Y., Bengio, Y., Hinton, G.: Deep learning. Nature **521**(7553), 436–444 (2015)
41. Lewin, D.: Notes on the opening of the f# minor fugue from wtci. J. Music Theor. **42**(2), 235–239 (1998)
42. Manning, C.D.: Computational linguistics and deep learning. Comput. Linguist. **41**(4), 701–707 (2015)

43. Marandi, Y.M.H., Sajedi, H., Pirasteh, S.: A novel method to musicalize shape and visualize music and a novel technique in music cryptography. Multimedia Tools Appl. **80**, 7451–7477 (2021)
44. Marr, D.: Vision: A computational investigation into the human representation and processing of visual information. MIT press (2010)
45. Marsden, Alan: Music analysis by computer: ontology and epistemology. In: Computational Music Analysis, pp. 3–28. Springer, Cham (2016). https://doi.org/10.1007/978-3-319-25931-4_1
46. Mauch, M., Levy, M.: Structural change on multiple time scales as a correlate of musical complexity, pp. 489–494 (01 2011)
47. Meredith, D.: Music analysis and point-set compression. J. New Music Res. **44**(3), 245–270 (2015)
48. Miller, R.I.M.: Unity and contrast: A study of Ludwig van Beethoven's use of variation form in his symphonies, string quartets and piano sonatas. University of Glasgow (United Kingdom) (2003)
49. Müller, M.: Music Structure Analysis, pp. 167–236. Springer International Publishing, Cham (2015)
50. North, A.C., Hargreaves, D.J., Hargreaves, J.J.: Uses of music in everyday life. Music. Percept. **22**(1), 41–77 (2004)
51. Panda, R., Malheiro, R.M., Paiva, R.P.: Audio features for music emotion recognition: a survey. IEEE Trans. Affective Comput, 99, 1–1 (2020)
52. Pang, T.H.: The variation technique in selected piano works of Haydn, Mozart, Beethoven and Schubert: A performance project. University of Maryland, College Park (1998)
53. Paulus, J., Müller, M., Klapuri, A.: Audio-based music structure analysis. In: Proceedings of the 11th International Society for Music Information Retrieval Conference, ISMIR 2010, pp. 625–636 (01 2010)
54. Pereira, R.M., Costa, Y.M., Aguiar, R.L., Britto, A.S., Oliveira, L.E., Silla, C.N.: Representation learning vs. handcrafted features for music genre classification. In: 2019 International Joint Conference on Neural Networks (IJCNN), pp. 1–8. IEEE (2019)
55. Pipalia, K., Bhadja, R., Shukla, M.: Comparative analysis of different transformer based architectures used in sentiment analysis. In: 2020 9th International Conference System Modeling and Advancement in Research Trends (SMART), pp. 411–415. IEEE (2020)
56. Prout, E.: Fugue. Library Reprints (1891)
57. Ratner, L.: Harmonic aspects of classic form. J. Am. Musicol. Soc. **2**(3), 159–168 (1949)
58. Roy, S., Biswas, M., De, D.: imusic: a session-sensitive clustered classical music recommender system using contextual representation learning. Multimedia Tools Appl. **79**, 24119–24155 (2020)
59. Sheldon, D.A.: The stretto principle: some thoughts on fugue as form. J. Musicol. **8**(4), 553–568 (1990)
60. Shi, E.R., Zhang, Q.: A domain-general perspective on the role of the basal ganglia in language and music: Benefits of music therapy for the treatment of aphasia. Brain Lang. **206**, 104811 (2020)
61. Sutton, E.: Virginia Woolf and Classical Music: Politics, Aesthetics. Edinburgh University Press, Form (2013)
62. Tavares, J.M.R., Jorge, R.M.N., et al.: Topics in Medical Image Processing and Computational Vision. Springer (2013). https://doi.org/10.1007/978-94-007-0726-9

63. Umer, S., Mondal, R., Pandey, H.M., Rout, R.K.: Deep features based convolutional neural network model for text and non-text region segmentation from document images. Appl. Soft Comput. **113**, 107917 (2021)
64. Verma, P.K., Agrawal, P., Madaan, V., Prodan, R.: Mcred: multi-modal message credibility for fake news detection using bert and cnn. Journal of Ambient Intelligence and Humanized Computing, pp. 1–13 (2022). DOI: https://doi.org/10.1007/s12652-022-04338-2
65. Wang, W., et al.: Internimage: Exploring large-scale vision foundation models with deformable convolutions. arXiv preprint arXiv:2211.05778 (2022)
66. Webster, J.: Schubert's sonata form and brahms's first maturity. Nineteenth-Century Music, pp. 18–35 (1978)
67. Wen, R., Chen, K., Xu, K., Zhang, Y., Wu, J.: Music main melody extraction by an interval pattern recognition algorithm. In: 2019 Chinese Control Conference (CCC), pp. 7728–7733. IEEE (2019)
68. Wu, J., Liu, X., Hu, X., Zhu, J.: Popmnet: generating structured pop music melodies using neural networks. Artif. Intell. **286**, 103303 (2020)
69. Wu, X., Lv, S., Zang, L., Han, J., Hu, S.: Conditional BERT contextual augmentation. In: Rodrigues, J.M.F., et al. (eds.) ICCS 2019. LNCS, vol. 11539, pp. 84–95. Springer, Cham (2019). https://doi.org/10.1007/978-3-030-22747-0_7
70. Young, J.O.: How classical music is better than popular music. Philosophy **91**(4), 523–540 (2016)
71. Zhong, X., Tang, J., Yepes, A.J.: Publaynet: largest dataset ever for document layout analysis. In: 2019 International Conference on Document Analysis and Recognition (ICDAR), pp. 1015–1022. IEEE (2019)

Learning by Small Loss Approach Multi-label to Deal with Noisy Labels

Vitor Sousa(✉) , Amanda Lucas Pereira , Manoela Kohler ,
and Marco Pacheco

Pontifícia Universidade Católica Do Rio de Janeiro, Rio de Janeiro, RJ, Brazil
vitorbds@aluno.puc-rio.br
https://puc-rio.ai/

Abstract. Noisy data samples is a common problem for deep learning models applied to real-world applications. In this context, noisy samples refer to samples with incorrect labels, which can potentially degenerate the robustness of a model. Several works account for this issue in multi-class scenarios. However, despite a number of possible applications, multi-label noise remains an under-explored research field. In this work, two novel approaches to handle noise in this scenario are presented. First, we propose a new multi-label version of the Small Loss Approach (SLA), formerly multi-class, to handle multi-label noise. Second, we apply the multi-label SLA to a novel model, *Learning by SLA Multi-label*, based on Co-teaching. The proposed model achieves a performance gain of 15% in the benchmark UcMerced when compared to its baseline Co-teaching and a standard model (without any noise-handling technique). In addition, the model is also evaluated in a real-world scenario of underwater equipment imagery classification, yielding a relative improvement of 9% in F1-Score.

Keywords: Deep Learning · Noisy Samples · Noisy Labels

1 Introduction

Fully-supervised deep learning models have a large number of applications in Computer Vision, solving a variety of multi-label classification problems [1,5,7,34]. However, a large amount of carefully annotated samples is required to train such models, which can limit the performance obtained for some scenarios. Depending on the problem at hand, it may be difficult to obtain an equally representative number of labeled samples for each class. For real-world industry applications, labels can pose an even greater challenge, since it commonly demands a group of highly specialized personnel to be able to provide a set of accurate labels.

Common approaches to mitigate the problem of labels' availability are: the use of crowdsourcing [31], web queries [22] and the reliance on non-specialists in

Supported by organization Conselho Nacional de Desenvolvimento Científico e Tecnológico (CNPq).

the process of labeling the set. Such solutions, although they may help increase the number of available samples, can potentially yield a high presence of noisy labels [12,21]. In this context, *noisy labels* refer to the fact that some samples from the set are incorrectly labeled, which can degenerate the robustness of the deep learning model [12].

Several works have been developed in order to solve the problem of label noise in multi-class scenarios [12,15,29,35]. Benchmark datasets to compare the performance of models are available in the literature [32], and a variety of approaches to handle this type of noise can be found, each with its own advantages [12,15,21]. On the other hand, the development of models that are able to account for multi-label noise remains a less explored field [3], where both evaluation protocols and benchmark datasets are still at early stage, being investigated in works such as [3,14,28].

Most multi-class models supposedly can be directly adjusted to fit multi-label scenarios [3], as in [15,20,29]. However, we identified that the most common strategy from state-of-the-art (SOTA) methods for multi-class noisy labels – which relies mainly on Small Loss Approach (SLA) [12], used in several works [26,29,35,36] –, presents two major problems when directly applied to a multi-label scenario: (1) the possibility of noise being present only in some of the classes whilst others may be clean for the same sample; and (2) the SLA excludes samples with any level of noise from the training process.

Therefore, to alleviate the problem of label noise in multi-label scenarios, a novel multi-label version of the SLA is proposed (SLAM, as in SLA Multi-label), on which we mitigate the problems mentioned above. Furthermore, we also propose a new model, "Learning by SLA Multi-label", based on Co-teaching [12], where we replace the former SLA with its new multi-label version. The model is eveluted in a noisy version of the multi-label benchmark UcMerced [4, 33], where we synthetically injected 25% multi-label noise in mixed form [3]. We share the noisy version of the benchmark along with a clean test set in [https://github.com/ICA-PUC/Uc MercedNoiseDataset] for reproducibility and also for future works that wish to assess the results of new models with comparison to ours under fair conditions.

We compare the results obtained by our model to the model Co-teaching (adapted to multi-class), and also to a standard baseline, where no noise-handling method is used during the training procedure. Our model reduced the present noise from 25% to 5%, yielding an improvement in the F1-score measured over the test set by 15%. In addition, we evaluate our model on a real-world industry problem of underwater equipment imagery classification, where the model tries to identify event(s) of interest given a frame from an underwater inspection video. Specialists from an oil&gas company observed the presence of noise in the set, so the methods developed in this work were applied. We share the results obtained for a controlled setting, where the same amount and type of multi-label noise mentioned above is injected. We note that the latter is a private set so images cannot be disclosed, as requested by the data owners, therefore the figures presented as for this application are fictional.

The main contributions of our work are the following:

1. We propose a new multi-label version of the Small Loss Approach (SLA) (formerly multi-class). This modification can be either applied to the development of new models, or in the adaptation of multi-class models to multi-label scenarios.
2. We propose a novel model that handles multi-label noise
3. We disclose a new public noisy version of the multi-label benchmark Uc Merced for reproducibility and comparison for future works under fair conditions
4. We evaluate the proposed model in a real-world industry application

This paper is organized as follows: in Sect. 2, we outline the main existent multi-label and multi-class models to deal with noise labels, going into detail for the SLA and the Co-teaching model; then, in Sect. 3, we describe the several modifications made in SLA to be suitable to multi-label and present our proposed model *Learning by Small Loss Aproach Multi-label*. In Sect. 4, we provide the experimental setup and a description for each dataset. In Sect. 5, the results of our model *Learning by Small Loss Aproach Multi-label* are presented and discussed. Finally, in Sect. 6 we present the conclusion and outline future works.

2   Related Work

2.1   Deep Learning Models for Multi-class Noise

The use of deep learning models to deal with multi-class noisy labels is a well explored issue in the literature, with a variety of works addressing the problem [12,15,36]. One common approach to deal with noisy label is based on the Transition Matrix [21,24,27]. However, in some cases, where the number of classes is large, the estimation of the Transition Matrix may be a challenging task [12]. In addition, some authors propose using a loss function robust to noisy labels [11,20,30], such as the design of a regularization term to prevent the memorization of noisy labels [20].

Another popular approach focuses on the selection of *clean samples* from the group of available data points, discarding the remainder during training [17,23]. Clean samples refer to data points with correct labels, whilst corrupted labels present some level of noise. Current state-of-the-art (SOTA) methods such as Co-teaching [12], Co-teaching+ [36], JoCoR [29] and JoCoR-SLR [35], use the small loss strategy [12] – which we refer to as Small Loss Approach (SLA) – to perform the samples selection, outperforming standard models in benchmarks with noisy samples as in [21].

This strategy is based on the value of the loss function to determine the clean samples. Once the clean samples are elected, these methods differ in the strategy adopted to leverage information from the clean set in order to improve the model's performance.

2.2   Deep Learning Models for Multi-label Noise

In contrast to the multi-class scenario, where there are a variety of established methods and benchmark datasets [32], multi-label classification with noisy labels remains relatively unexplored in literature. Although there are papers with multi-label applications, the approaches and datasets used are mostly divergent and the topic deserves more attention [3].

Some papers focus on *multi-task learning* where the network tries to simultaneously learn to clean and correctly classify the samples [28]. There is also an intersection of the field with the study of models that handle noise by a *partial multi-label learning* approach, where the labels for each sample are considered as "candidates" rather than assuming they are correct [14]. The main difference is that partial multi-label learning does not assume that noise can occur for all labels, only the relevant ones.

On the recent work [3], the authors propose adapting the models [29], ElR [20] and SAT [15] from the multi-class noise scenario to fit a multi-label application which handles noisy labels. The main modifications comprise exchanging the former categorical cross entropy loss and softmax activation function at the final layer of the network for a binary cross entropy and a sigmoid function.

Other works as [13,16] use a strategy based on teacher-student network, where the teacher supervises the training process of the student. The supervision is based on training the teacher on a clean subset, so it can clean the noisy labels for the student.

2.3   Small Loss Approach

Small Loss Approach (SLA) [12] is a technique widely used by SOTA models for multi-class noise [29,35,36]. It consists of selecting clean (correct) samples from the dataset and discarding the ones with corrupted labels. Based on the assumption that models trained with fewer noisy samples perform better, only the clean set is used for training.

During the training process, the samples that present the lowest loss value over the batch of images are chosen for the clean set. Generally, this process is done at every iteration for each epoch. Once the clean instances are selected, training can be performed through different strategies aiming to fully exploit the clean set.

This technique is based on observation that Deep learning models tends to learn easy instances first, and gradually adapt to hard instance over the epochs [12]. Hence, it is expected that mislabeled samples to be memorized at more advanced time during training.

2.4   Co-teaching

On the paper that introduces the method Co-teaching [12], the authors propose using two networks trained simultaneously with SLA to deal with noisy labels.

Since the SLA method is based on the fact that networks memorize easier patterns – which may correspond to clean labels– earlier in the training process [2]. Therefore, each network should be able to identify different errors from the labels, making the learning process more robust to noise.

During training, each network receives as input the entire mini-batch containing both noisy and clean samples. Then, through SLA, each net selects which of the presented samples are clean and should be backpropagated through its peer network. After each net performs their selection of clean samples, the chosen ones are used for learning whilst the others are discarded for the given mini-batch.

The networks share architecture but do not share parameters. The reason to train both networks simultaneously is based on the fact that two networks can identify different types of errors from the noisy labels, since they have different learning abilities [29], i.e. different starting weights. Therefore, when the networks exchange the selected clean samples in each mini-batch, error should be mutually reduced by their peer.

3   Learning by Small Loss Approach Multi-label

The model Learning by Small Loss Approach Multi-label is based on SLA, which is used on models for Single Noise Labels. However, there are two major problems in directly adapting the SLA to the Multi-Label Noise scenario. Therefore, we make several changes in SLA in order to address such problems, and this modified version of SLA we refer to as *Small Loss Approach Multi-Label* (SLAM).

The first problem is that, for multi-label data, given one sample, some classes can present noise whilst others do not (Fig. 1). In Fig. 1(A), we see a version of the image with clean labels, while in Fig. 1(B) and Fig. 1(C), we see two versions of noise labels for the same sample image. In this example, the classes Baresoil, Buildings, Car and Pavement are correctly for both scenarios (Fig. 1(B) and Fig. 1(C)). On the other hand, we note there is noise for the class Grass, since it is absent on the labels in Fig. 1(B); and mislabeled as Airplane in Fig. 1(C). Therefore, a multi-labeled sample image can contain both correct and incorrect labels.

Based on the different manners that noise can be present for a multi-label sample as described above, the first proposed modification is to perform SLA analysis *by class* instead of *by sample*. Since some classes may be noisy while others remain clean (Fig. 1), we modify SLA to be applied separately for each class. Therefore, the SLA is performed in the following manner: calculate the cost for each class independently using the same loss function; select as *clean* the *small loss instances over all classes*. In this manner, it is possible to identify the noise by class for each image, allowing the model to keep the cleans classes of an image during training while discarding the noisy ones.

The second problem is that the former SLA excludes samples with noise from the training stage. This can be an issue due to the fact that the discarded samples may contain important features of a class to which it belongs. Hence, excluding such samples from training, deep Learning models can be deprived from learning important features that could potentially improve the generalization of the

Clean Sample

Bare-soil; Buildings; Cars; Pavement; Grass

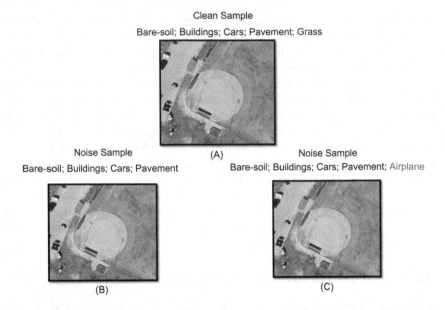

Noise Sample   (A)   Noise Sample

Bare-soil; Buildings; Cars; Pavement   Bare-soil; Buildings; Cars; Pavement; Airplane

(B)   (C)

Fig. 1. (A) Example of clean sample of multi-label. (B) Example of noise sample where the class Grass was not annotated. (C) Example of noise sample where the class Grass was mislabel for Airplane class

model. To address this problem, we first observe that, for each one-hot encoded class, there are only two options: the class is either present in the image – **1** – or the class is not present in the image – **0**. So, once the class is identified as a noise label, we simply invert the label signal from **1** to **0** or from **0** to **1** to turn the noise label into a clean label.

3.1   Small Loss Approach Multi-Label(SLAM)

Given a dataset $D = (x_i, y_i)_{i=1}^z$ where x_i is the i-th sample of D and y_i is the multi-label class vector $y_i = [c_i^1, c_i^2, ..., c_i^M]$ with $c_i \in [0, 1]$ and **0** indicating the absence of a class and **1** indicating presence, for a number of classes M. Given $P_{model}(y|x_i; \theta)$ a model that produces a prediction over the classes labels vector y for a input sample x_i with parameters θ. Finally, the vector of the cross entropy loss $CE_M{}^i$ for sample x_i is given by:

$$CE_M(x_i) = -y_i \odot \log(P_{model}(y|x_i; \theta)) \tag{1}$$

where $\odot$ is an element-wise multiplier operator and log is also applied element-wise. So $CE_M(x_i)$ is the loss vector for all classes of instance x_i, being $CE_M(x_i) = [l_i^1, .., l_i^M]$, where l_i is loss for the i-th class. Then, CE_M for a batch of size B from the dataset D can be concatenated and be represented as matrix MC with B lines and M columns, MC_{BM}:

$$MC_{BM} = \begin{bmatrix} l_{11}\ l_{12}\ l_{13}\ \dots\ l_{1M} \\ l_{21}\ l_{22}\ l_{23}\ \dots\ l_{2M} \\ \dots\dots\dots\dots\dots\dots \\ l_{B1}\ l_{B2}\ l_{B3}\ \dots\ l_{BM} \end{bmatrix} \qquad (2)$$

In SLAM, we calculate the k maximum values for each column from MC_{BM}, where each column represents one class of y. k is an integer value, estimated by a function of the noise present in the specific class. This parameter can either be a fixed value or adjusted over the epochs. The vector of indexes $Y(m)$ of the k maximum values for the column m of MC_{BM} is given by:

$$Y(m) = arg\ max_k(MC_{1:B,m}) \qquad (3)$$

Therefore, we have $Y(m) = [id_m^1, id_m^2, id_m^k]$, where id_m is the index of matrix MC_{BM} for class m. The operator $arg\ max_k$ return the index of the k max values of the input vector. Then, $MC_{1:B,m}$ is a vector equal to all lines of column m of MC_{BM}.

The indexes of $Y(m)$ are equivalent to the index of the samples x in batch B, where the class label m will be inverted. We calculate $Y(m)$ for all M classes. Finally, we assign the new labels for each class m for the samples from batch B where the indexes are those from $Y(m)$. To assign the new label for class m of sample x with index id_m from $Y(m)$, we simply invert the label, i.e. if the label is **1** it will be **0** or if it is **0** it will be **1**.

3.2   The Proposed Approach

In this section, we propose a novel deep learning model to deal with multi-noise labels, *Learning by SLA Multi-label*, built upon the model Co-teaching [12], adding the SLAM.

In Fig. 2, the training flow is illustrated. Following [12], we use peer networks that are trained simultaneously over the same mini-batch, where each network will identify the noise samples of the batch individually, assigning new labels by the method SLAM. Then, the mini-batch with corrected labels assigned by each network is used to train its peer. With the assigned labels, each network calculates the loss function considering these new labels, and proceeds to the back-propagation with the optimizer.

The model procedure is detailed in Algorithm 1. The SLAM procedure is applied after some epochs defined experimentally as a hyperparameter $start_{epoch}$ in step 5 of Algorithm 1. In order to define the k maximum values used in Eq. 5 for each epoch, we use the function $R(t)$ adapted from [12]:

$$R(t) = min[\frac{\tau t}{T_k}, \tau] \qquad (4)$$

where the minimum value between $\frac{\tau t}{T_{max}}$ and τ is returned. T_k is an integer value, hyperparameter of model; τ is the estimated noise from the dataset; and t is the training epoch. The k value is given by multiplying the $R(t)$ by the batch size, i.e. $k = R(t) * batchsize$. k is linearly increased until it reaches the value τ (the estimated noise).

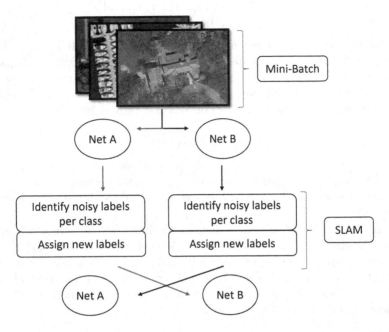

Fig. 2. Two networks, A and B, are trained simultaneously over the same mini-batch. The Network A will assign the new labels for network B, also B for A .

4   Experimental Details

In this section, the experiments are described. First, a thorough explanation of the method used to introduce noise for each dataset is provided. Then, the metric used to evaluate the performance of each model is introduced. Next, the benchmark and the real-world dataset of subsea equipment used to evaluate the model are presented. Finally, the experimental setup used for each set is explained.

4.1   Introduced Noise

To evaluate the robustness of our model, synthetically injected multi-label noise in mixed form is adopted, as in [3]. The noise was injected class-wise, and could be either additive or subtractive. Additive noise refers to adding a class that does not exist in the image, whereas subtractive noise excludes a class that appears in that sample.

Algorithm 1. Learning by SLA Multi-label Algorithm

Require: Network $w_f(\theta_1)$ and Network $w_g(\theta_2)$, learning rate η, fixed τ , epoch T_k, T_{max}, Noise Dataset $D = (x_i, y_i)_{i=1}^z$, number of class M, function $R(t)$, iteration I_{max}, $batch_{size}$, $start_{epoch}$:

1: **for** $t = 1, 2..., T_{max}$ **do**
2:     `Shuffle training set D`
3:     **for** $n = 1, 2..., I_{max}$ **do**
4:         `Fetch mini-batch` D_n `from D`
5:         **if** $t > start_{epoch}$ **then**
6:             `Create a copy` $D_n^{w_g}$ `from` Dn
7:             `Create a copy` $D_n^{w_f}$ `from` Dn
8:             `Calculate` $CE_M(x) \forall x \in D_n$ `with` w_g
9:             `Calculate` $CE_M(x) \forall x \in D_n$ `with` w_f
10:          `Obtain matrix` $MC_{BM}^{w_g}$ `from vectors` $CE_M(x)$ `of step 8`
11:          `Obtain matrix` $MC_{BM}^{w_f}$ `from vectors` $CE_M(x)$ `of step 9`
12:          `Calculate` $Y(m)^{w_g}$ `with Eq.5` $\forall\ m \in\ [1, .., M]$ `using` $MC_{BM}^{w_g}$ `and` k
13:          `Calculate` $Y(m)^{w_f}$ `with Eq.5` $\forall\ m \in\ [1, .., M]$ `using` $MC_{BM}^{w_f}$ `and` k
14:          **for** $m = 1, 2..., M$ **do**
15:             `Update Label` $y_i[m]$ $\forall\ i \in Y(m)^{w_g}$ `of sample` x_i `in` $D_n^{w_g}$
16:             `Update Label` $y_i[m]$ $\forall\ i \in Y(m)^{w_f}$ `of sample` x_i `in` $D_n^{w_f}$
                                      ▷ Update Label is done by $logical_{not}$ operator.
                                      ▷ $logical_{not}$ $0 \rightarrow 1; 1 \rightarrow 0$
17:          **end for**
18:         **end if**
19:         **if** $t > start_{epoch}$ **then**
20:             `Update` $\theta_1 = \theta_1 - \triangledown L(w_g, D_n^{w_f})$
21:             `Update` $\theta_2 = \theta_2 - \triangledown L(w_f, D_n^{w_g})$
22:         **else**
23:             `Update` $\theta_1 = \theta_1 - \triangledown L(w_g, D_n)$
24:             `Update` $\theta_2 = \theta_2 - \triangledown L(w_f, D_n)$
25:         **end if**
26:         `Update:` $R(t) = min[\frac{\tau t}{T_k}, \tau]$
27:         `Update:` $k = R(t) * batch_{size}$
28:     **end for**
29: **end for**

For both datasets, UcMerced and the Subsea Equipment, noise is added in the following manner: (1) given a class of interest, we randomly select 25% out of the total samples from the training set; (2) if the sample contains the class, we remove it (subtractive noise); if it does not, we add the class to its labels (additive noise).

We disclose the public noise version produced by adding the mixed noise to the dataset UcMerced, for future works that want compare the results in fair condition with our model.

The performance of the models are evaluated by comparison of the F1-Score measured over the test set per epoch as in the protocol used by [12,29,35,36]. The test set only contains clean samples, therefore the performance of the model is analyzed without the influence of noise.

4.2 Accuracy SLA Multi-label

The proposed method SLAM has its performance evaluated using the metric *Accuracy SLA Multi-Label*. This metric measures the accuracy of the labels assigned by SLAM for each class, at the end of every training epoch. The Accuracy SLA Multi-Label for class m is given by:

$$\text{Accuracy SLA Multi-Label(m)} = \frac{\# \text{ of correctly assigned labels}}{\# \text{ total of labels}} \tag{5}$$

It is important to highlight that the Accuracy SLA Multi-Label measures both class absence and class presence. So, the number of correctly assigned labels takes into account both presence and absence of corrected assignments performed by SLAM. The total of labels is equivalent to the number of samples from the set.

4.3 Dataset UCMerced Multi-label

We create a noisy version of the dataset UcMerced [4], which is a multi-label version of the former dataset [33]. This dataset contains 17 classes, depicting aerial satellite image scenarios of both urban and countryside regions. The classes include objects like cars, boats and airplanes, and also natural land-cover classes such as water, trees and buildings.

Following the protocol proposed by the authors from [12,29,35,36], first, the dataset is partitioned into train and test sets. For this dataset, this comprises of a training set of 1700 images and a test set of 217 images. Then, noise is introduced only in the training set while the test set remains clean. This version of the dataset is available at https://github.com/ICA9-PUC/UcMercedNoiseDataset.

4.4 Dataset Subsea Equipment

The Dataset Subsea Equipment is being elaborated in order to develop a deep learning model to assist specialists at underwater inspections of subsea equipment used for oil and gas extraction. It currently contains over 30,000 images with more than 39 potential classes per images, and it is a multi-label dataset. In this context, such potential classes refer to either structures (e.g. pipeline accessories) or events (e.g. a pipeline crossing).

The motivation behind testing our model in this set of data was built upon the notice of the presence of noise from underwater inspections specialists. Therefore, the experiments presented in this work were performed with a subset from this set of data, part of the much larger set mentioned above, as a proof-of-concept, following the experimental setup described in Sect. 4.1.

The subset used for our experiments contain a total of 1327 images with 12 classes. The samples were all carefully revised in order to assure clean labels. Then, the set was partitioned into training and test sets, each with 664 and 664 images, respectively. As in the UCMerced Dataset (Sect. 4.3), noise is added only to training set whilst the test set is kept clean, following the protocol from [12, 29, 35, 36].

The classes present at this set are the following: Anode, Anode Debris, Pipeline Buoy, Pipeline, Marine Life, Flange, Rope, Text, Chain, ROV, End Fitting, Pipeline Crossing. As the images are private, a fictional example queried from a search engine is presented in Fig. 3.

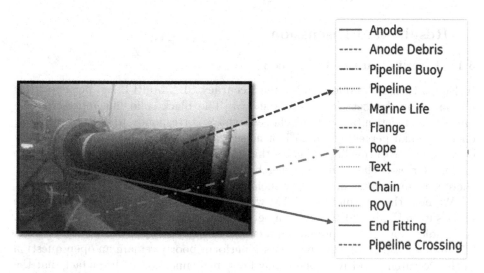

Fig. 3. Fictional example of an image from the dataset Subsea Equipment. This sample image depicts three different classes: Pipeline, Rope and End Fitting

4.5 Experimental Setup

We use peer networks $w_f(\theta_1)$ and $w_g(\theta_2)$ with VGG16 as the architecture [25], with pre-trained weights on ImageNet [9], and only the final 4 layers are optimized. To enable multiple predictions, we use a binary cross entropy loss, and exchange softmax by sigmoid layers. All input images to $(224, 224)$ and the default pre-processing of Tensorflow version 2.4 for VGG-16 is applied, using the function `vgg16.preprocess_input`. Model's performance is measured by f1-score [6] over test data, and the Accuracy SLA Multi-Label. The optimizer was the Adam [18] and the model was implemented using Tensorflow 2.4 and the experiments were carried out using the NVIDIA® Tesla® V100.

We compare our model with the standard VGG-16 network under same condition for multi-label. In addition, we compare our model with a Co-teaching model directly adapted for multi-label, i.e. using the conventional SLA for multi-class as pointed out in work [3]. The comparison of our model with this model is important to illustrate the performance gains obtained using SLAM instead of SLA, once this is the main difference between our model and Co-teaching model.

For the experiments with UcMerced, the learning rate η was set to 0.00025, and the network is trained for a total of epochs $T_{max} = 50$. The hyperparameter T_k was set to 40, the SLAM $start_{epoch}$ was 1, the estimated noise τ was 0.25, and a $batch_{size}$ 64. For UcMerced, the number of classes M was 17. For the experiments with Subsea Equipment, the learning rate η was 0.001, the total of epochs T_{max} was 200, $T_k = 30$, the SLAM $start_{epoch}$ was 5, the estimated noise τ was 0.25, the $batch_{size}$ 32. The number of classes M was 12.

5   Results and Discussion

5.1   Results Dataset UcMerced

In Fig. 4, the results obtained for the Accuracy SLA Multi-Label per epoch for all classes in dataset UcMerced is shown. The black solid line represents the initial clean percentage for all classes, which corresponds to a value of 75%, once an equal percentage of 25% of noise was introduced for each class. Every curve superior to this line indicates that the SLAM process is reducing the noise present for each class. On the other hand, a curve below that line reveals that there was an increase of noise for such class.

We note that the method SLAM was able to reduce the noise for most of the classes from UcMerced, achieving a percentage of 95% of clean samples for a few. Also, solely four classes present an increase of noisy samples during the process. The understanding of why such classes perform poorly remain an open question in this research. Intuitively, there may be some connection with the fact that the data is highly unbalanced. Nonetheless, this behaviour is not repeated on the results obtained for the Subsea Equipment dataset, so further experiments are required in order to reach a solid conclusion.

In Fig. 5, we compare our model (blue line) with a standard model (orange line) trained under the same conditions. Our model improved the F1-Score in 15%, showing that reducing noise per class-instance can significantly improve the results. As expected, this suggests that models trained on data with less noise tend to perform better.

We also compare our model with the model Co-teaching, directly adjusted from multi-class to the multi-label scenario (green line). First, we observe that the model Co-teaching can improve the performance when compared to the standard model (orange line). This illustrates that, indeed, the direct adaptation of SLA models to multi-class is possible as mentioned in [20]. However, the performance gains are only 2%, whereas when we replace the former SLA in Co-teaching by SLAM the performance improves significantly (blue line). It is important to highlight here that our model essentially replaces the SLA used in

Co-teaching with SLAM, so this result proves the benefit of replacing SLA by SLAM in Co-teaching model. We also show in Table 1, using ANOVA TEST [8], that the models belongs to different distributions. In the Table, STD refer to the standard model.

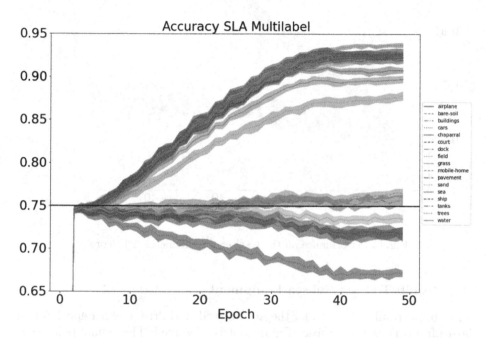

Fig. 4. Accuracy SLA Multi-Label for all classes in the dataset UcMerced. The curves over this line point a reduction in label noise, whilst below indicates an increase in noise during the SLAM process.

Table 1. ANOVA Test for the experiments. In the table, "STD" refer to the standard model.

Model 1	Model 2	Model 3	Dataset	Epoch	p-value	Distribution
SLAM	Co-teaching	STD	UcMerced	45	2^{-23}	Different
SLAM	Co-teaching	STD	Subsea	150	7^{-13}	Different

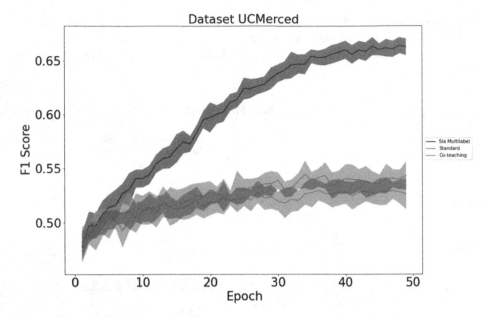

Fig. 5. Performance on the test set for the metric F1-Score

5.2   Results Dataset Subsea Equipment

In Fig. 6, the results obtained for the Accuracy SLA Multi-Label per epoch for all classes from the dataset Subsea Equipment is presented. The results point that SLAM was able to reduce the noise present at all classes, achieving a percentage of 90% clean samples for some classes. Contrary to the experiments from the SAR scenario, none of the classes had noise increase.

In epoch 25, we have an interesting observation, where we note a local peak performance to all classes in the Accuracy SLA Multi-Label. This local peak coincides with the performance peak observed for the F-1 score to our model (blue line in Fig. 7). Intuitively, fixing the labels assigned at this epoch would lead to an improvement in performance for the model. However, adding a hyper-parameter to control this process would be extremely dataset-dependent, since such behavior was not observed in the experiments with UcMerced. Therefore, this hyperparameter may be hard to tune for real-world industry applications.

Despite that, an in-depth understanding of this phenomenon poses an interesting option for future works. Once in [12] we also observe a peak of Label Precision [12] around epoch 25 of SLA in single label for the datasets MNIST [10], CIFAR-10 and CIFAR-100 [19], the peak of performance in the Test accuracy [12] occurs at the same point. Understanding this process could enable an improvement at both the SLA and SLAM, thereby future models could be developed.

In Fig. 7, we compare our model with a standard model trained under same conditions. We note that our model improved the F1-Score in 8%, being a considerable improvement for a real-world industry application. We also present the comparison with the model Co-teaching, and as in the experiments with the UcMerced dataset, Co-teaching (green line) presented results that are superior to the ones from the standard model, but within a small margin of 2%. On the other hand, the performance gain that SLAM brings are solid, enabling the application of such method to real problems. We show in Table 1, using Analysis of Variance (ANOVA Test) [8], that the three models that were assessed (standard, Co-teaching and SLAM) belong to different distributions.

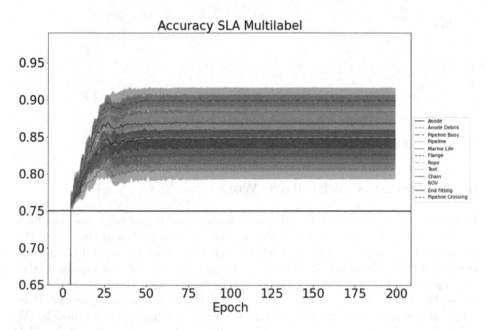

Fig. 6. Accuracy SLA Multi-Label for all classes in the dataset Subsea Equipment. The solid black line represents the initial amount of clean samples from the training set. The curves over this line point a reduction in label noise, whilst below indicates an increase in noise during the SLAM process.

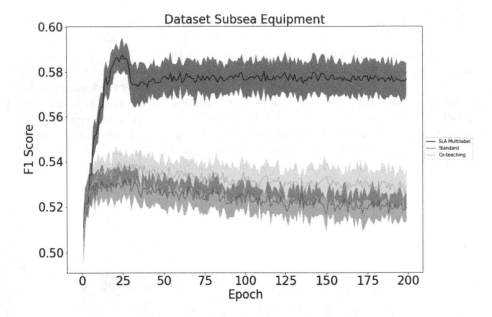

Fig. 7. Performance on the test set for the metric F1-Score

6   Conclusions and Future Work

In this work, we identified two major problems in directly adjusting the SLA (used by SOTA methods to deal with noisy label in multi-class problems) to the multi-label scenario. To address such problems, we propose several changes in the former SLA (for multi-class) in order to make it more suitable for multi-label applications. This new method we propose as Small Loss Approach Multi-label (SLAM). SLAM allows adapting formerly multi-class methods appropriately to multi-label scenarios, or it can be used to develop new methods and models. We also propose a new model, Learning by Small Loss Approach Multi-label, which is an adaptation of the model Co-teaching – used in multi-class noisy scenarios – to multi-label. The major difference of our model to the model Co-teaching is the replacement of SLA with the novel SLAM.

We evaluate our model in benchmark dataset UcMerced, and also provide the results obtained for a real-world industry application of Subsea Equipment, where we apply the model to underwater inspection videos. Our model significantly improved the results obtained for both datasets, with a performance gain in the F1-score of 15% for dataset Ucmerced and 9% for Subsea Equipment application in comparison to the standard model and also to the original Co-teaching (adapted to the multi-label scenario with its former SLA). The gain in performance illustrates the robustness of our model for dealing with noisy labels in multi-label scenarios, which emboldens its application in sets of data from either academia or industry problems.

Acknowledgements. The authors would like to thank Conselho Nacional de Desenvolvimento Científico e Tecnológico (CNPq), Coordenação de Aperfeiçoamento de Pessoal de Nível Superior (Capes) and Pontifícia Universidade Católica do Rio de Janeiro (PUC-Rio) for their financial support.

References

1. Ahmadi, Z., Kramer, S.: A label compression method for online multi-label classification. Pattern Recogn. Lett. **111**, 64–71 (2018)
2. Arpit, D., et al.: A closer look at memorization in deep networks. In: International conference on machine learning, pp. 233–242. PMLR (2017)
3. Burgert, T., Ravanbakhsh, M., Demir, B.: On the effects of different types of label noise in multi-label remote sensing image classification. IEEE Trans. Geosci. Remote Sens. **60**, 1–13 (2022)
4. Chaudhuri, B., Demir, B., Chaudhuri, S., Bruzzone, L.: Multilabel remote sensing image retrieval using a semisupervised graph-theoretic method. IEEE Trans. Geosci. Remote Sens. **56**(2), 1144–1158 (2017)
5. Chen, Z.M., Wei, X.S., Wang, P., Guo, Y.: Multi-label image recognition with graph convolutional networks. In: Proceedings of the IEEE/CVF Conference On Computer Vision And Pattern Recognition, pp. 5177–5186 (2019)
6. Chicco, D., Jurman, G.: The advantages of the matthews correlation coefficient (mcc) over f1 score and accuracy in binary classification evaluation. BMC Genom. **21**(1), 1–13 (2020)
7. Coulibaly, S., Kamsu-Foguem, B., Kamissoko, D., Traore, D.: Deep convolution neural network sharing for the multi-label images classification. Mach. Learn. Appl. **10**, 100422 (2022)
8. Cuevas, A., Febrero, M., Fraiman, R.: An anova test for functional data. Comput. Stat. Data Anal. **47**(1), 111–122 (2004)
9. Deng, J., Dong, W., Socher, R., Li, L.J., Li, K., Fei-Fei, L.: Imagenet: A large-scale hierarchical image database. In: 2009 IEEE Conference On Computer Vision And Pattern Recognition, pp. 248–255. IEEE (2009)
10. Deng, L.: The mnist database of handwritten digit images for machine learning research [best of the web]. IEEE Signal Process. Mag. **29**(6), 141–142 (2012)
11. Ghosh, A., Kumar, H., Sastry, P.S.: Robust loss functions under label noise for deep neural networks. In: Proceedings of the AAAI Conference On Artificial Intelligence, vol. 31 (2017)
12. Han, B., et al.: Co-teaching: Robust training of deep neural networks with extremely noisy labels. In: Advances in Neural Information Processing Systems, vol. 31 (2018)
13. Hu, M., Han, H., Shan, S., Chen, X.: Multi-label learning from noisy labels with non-linear feature transformation. In: Computer Vision-ACCV 2018: 14th Asian Conference on Computer Vision, Perth, Australia, December 2–6, 2018, Revised Selected Papers, Part V 14. pp. 404–419. Springer (2019)
14. Hu, M., Han, H., Shan, S., Chen, X.: Weakly supervised image classification through noise regularization. In: Proceedings of the IEEE/CVF Conference on Computer Vision and Pattern Recognition, pp. 11517–11525 (2019)
15. Huang, L., Zhang, C., Zhang, H.: Self-adaptive training: bridging the supervised and self-supervised learning. arXiv preprint arXiv:2101.08732 (2021)

16. Inoue, N., Simo-Serra, E., Yamasaki, T., Ishikawa, H.: Multi-label fashion image classification with minimal human supervision. In: Proceedings of the IEEE International Conference on Computer Vision Workshops, pp. 2261–2267 (2017)
17. Jiang, L., Zhou, Z., Leung, T., Li, L.J., Fei-Fei, L.: Mentornet: Learning data-driven curriculum for very deep neural networks on corrupted labels. In: International Conference On Machine Learning, pp. 2304–2313. PMLR (2018)
18. Kingma, D.P., Ba, J.: Adam: A method for stochastic optimization. arXiv preprint arXiv:1412.6980 (2014)
19. Krizhevsky, A., Hinton, G., et al.: Learning multiple layers of features from tiny images (2009)
20. Liu, S., Niles-Weed, J., Razavian, N., Fernandez-Granda, C.: Early-learning regularization prevents memorization of noisy labels. Adv. Neural. Inf. Process. Syst. **33**, 20331–20342 (2020)
21. Liu, T., Tao, D.: Classification with noisy labels by importance reweighting. IEEE Trans. Pattern Anal. Mach. Intell. **38**(3), 447–461 (2015)
22. Liu, W., Jiang, Y.G., Luo, J., Chang, S.F.: Noise resistant graph ranking for improved web image search. In: CVPR 2011, pp. 849–856. IEEE (2011)
23. Malach, E., Shalev-Shwartz, S.: Decoupling "when to update" from "how to update". In: Advances in Neural Information Processing Systems, vol. 30 (2017)
24. Sanderson, T., Scott, C.: Class proportion estimation with application to multiclass anomaly rejection. In: Artificial Intelligence and Statistics, pp. 850–858. PMLR (2014)
25. Simonyan, K., Zisserman, A.: Very deep convolutional networks for large-scale image recognition. arXiv preprint arXiv:1409.1556 (2014)
26. Song, H., Kim, M., Lee, J.G.: Selfie: Refurbishing unclean samples for robust deep learning. In: International Conference on Machine Learning, pp. 5907–5915. PMLR (2019)
27. Van Rooyen, B., Williamson, R.C.: A theory of learning with corrupted labels. J. Mach. Learn. Res. **18**(1), 8501–8550 (2017)
28. Veit, A., Alldrin, N., Chechik, G., Krasin, I., Gupta, A., Belongie, S.: Learning from noisy large-scale datasets with minimal supervision. In: Proceedings of the IEEE Conference On Computer Vision And Pattern Recognition, pp. 839–847 (2017)
29. Wei, H., Feng, L., Chen, X., An, B.: Combating noisy labels by agreement: A joint training method with co-regularization. In: Proceedings of the IEEE/CVF Conference on Computer Vision and Pattern Recognition, pp. 13726–13735 (2020)
30. Wei, T., Shi, J.X., Tu, W.W., Li, Y.F.: Robust long-tailed learning under label noise. arXiv preprint arXiv:2108.11569 (2021)
31. Welinder, P., Branson, S., Perona, P., Belongie, S.: The multidimensional wisdom of crowds. In: Advances in Neural Information Processing Systems, vol. 23 (2010)
32. Xiao, T., Xia, T., Yang, Y., Huang, C., Wang, X.: Learning from massive noisy labeled data for image classification. In: CVPR (2015)
33. Yang, Y., Newsam, S.: Bag-of-visual-words and spatial extensions for land-use classification. In: Proceedings of the 18th SIGSPATIAL International Conference on Advances in Geographic Information Systems, pp. 270–279 (2010)
34. Yao, L., Poblenz, E., Dagunts, D., Covington, B., Bernard, D., Lyman, K.: Learning to diagnose from scratch by exploiting dependencies among labels. arXiv preprint arXiv:1710.10501 (2017)

35. Yao, Y., Sun, Z., Zhang, C., Shen, F., Wu, Q., Zhang, J., Tang, Z.: Jo-src: A contrastive approach for combating noisy labels. In: Proceedings of the IEEE/CVF Conference on Computer Vision and Pattern Recognition, pp. 5192–5201 (2021)
36. Yu, X., Han, B., Yao, J., Niu, G., Tsang, I., Sugiyama, M.: How does disagreement help generalization against label corruption? In: International Conference on Machine Learning, pp. 7164–7173. PMLR (2019)

Predicting Multiple Domain Queue Waiting Time via Machine Learning

Carolina Loureiro[1], Pedro José Pereira[1,2(✉)], Paulo Cortez[2],
Pedro Guimarães[1,2], Carlos Moreira[3], and André Pinho[3]

[1] EPMQ-IT Engineering Maturity and Quality Lab, CCG ZGDV Institute,
Guimarães, Portugal
{carolina.loureiro,pedro.pereira}@ccg.pt
[2] ALGORITMI Centre/LASI, Department of Information Systems,
University of Minho, Guimarães, Portugal
pcortez@dsi.uminho.pt
[3] Qevo–Queue Evolution Lda., Lisboa, Portugal

Abstract. This paper describes an implementation of the Cross-Industry Standard Process for Data Mining (CRISP-DM) methodology for a demonstrative case of human queue waiting time prediction. We collaborated with a multiple domain (e.g., bank, pharmacies) ticket management service software development company, aiming to study a Machine Learning (ML) approach to estimate queue waiting time. A large multiple domain database was analyzed, which included millions of records related with two time periods (one year, for the modeling experiments; and two year, for a deployment simulation). The data was first preprocessed (including data cleaning and feature engineering tasks) and then modeled by exploring five state-of-the-art ML regression algorithms and four input attribute selections (including newly engineered features). Furthermore, the ML approaches were compared with the estimation method currently adopted by the analyzed company. The computational experiments assumed two main validation procedures, a standard cross-validation and a Rolling Window scheme. Overall, competitive and quality results were obtained by an Automated ML (AutoML) algorithm fed with newly engineered features. Indeed, the proposed AutoML model produces a small error (from 5 to 7 min), while requiring a reasonable computational effort. Finally, an eXplainable Artificial Intelligence (XAI) approach was applied to a trained AutoML model, demonstrating the extraction of useful explanatory knowledge for this domain.

Keywords: CRISP-DM · Automated Machine Learning · Regression

1 Introduction

Nowadays, human queues are still required in several service sectors (e.g., health, banks). Waiting in these queues is often stressful and exhausting, leading to unsatisfied and frustrated citizens. Therefore, providing a beforehand accurate

O. Gervasi et al. (Eds.): ICCSA 2023, LNCS 13956, pp. 404–421, 2023.
https://doi.org/10.1007/978-3-031-36805-9_27

estimation of citizens waiting time in queues would reduce such frustration, since it allows them to optimize their schedule, avoiding spending an excessive time waiting. Furthermore, this estimation enhances a better resource management by the responsible entities, allowing to avoid excessively long queues. However, an imprecise estimation could produce the opposite effect. If the queue waiting time is overestimated, citizens could loose their turn in the queue, while an underestimation would still force them to wait in the physical queue.

This paper addresses a multiple domain queue waiting time estimation task by adopting a Machine Learning (ML) approach. This research work was developed in collaboration with a Portuguese software development company that operates in the ticket management sector and has several customer companies from multiple domains (e.g., banking). Over the past years, the company collected and stored a large amount of data that holds valuable knowledge related with human queues. Hence, there is a potential in using Data Mining (DM) and ML [21] to extract valuable predictive knowledge that improves the queue waiting time estimation task. Currently, the analyzed company addresses this estimation by using a rather rigid formula that was based on their business expertise. In this work, adopted the popular Cross-Industry Standard Process for Data Mining (CRISP-DM) methodology [20], which provides a framework for developing successful DM projects. In effect, CRISP-DM has been widely used on multiple DM research studies (e.g., [4,16]).

The CRISP-DM methodology is composed by a total of six phases, namely business understanding, data understanding, data preparation, modeling, evaluation and deployment. In this paper, we describe the adopted CRISP-DM execution regarding all these phases. The company business goal is to accurately predict the queue waiting time of a specific ticket, which we addressed as a ML supervised regression task. The sample of data used in this study was collected from the company database server and it is corresponds to millions of tickets withdrawn from 58 stores related with five distinct domains (i.e., banking, insurance companies, pharmacies, public and private services). An initial one-year dataset (from January to December of 2022) was first analyzed and preprocessed, which included data cleaning (e.g., outlier removal), feature engineering and data scaling processes. Then, concerning the modeling stage, five state-of-the-art ML algorithms were adapted and compared: Decision Trees (DT), Random Forest (RF), Gradient Boosted Trees (GBT), deep Artificial Neural Networks (ANN) and an Automated Machine Learning (AutoML). Furthermore, in this phase we defined four input set scenarios (A, B, C and D), which include distinct input feature selections and new engineered attributes that feed the ML models. The ML algorithms and input set scenarios were evaluated under two modes of a robust cross-validation procedure, using both predictive performance and computational effort measures. The performance was evaluated in terms of four popular regression metrics: Mean Absolute Error (MAE), Normalized MAE (NMAE), Root Mean Squared Error (RMSE) and the Area under the Regression Error Characteristic (AREC) curve [4,6]. As for the computational effort, it was measured in terms of training and prediction times. After analyzing the cross-validation results, we selected the best ML model (AutoML method and scenario C, which includes newly engineered attributes). Then, an additional Rolling Window (RW) robust validation procedure [19] was executed, using a larger two-year time period dataset, collected from January 2021 and December 2022. The goal was to realistically simulate the ML model deployment phase performance, further comparing it with the company currently adopted queue time estimation method. Finally, we applied the SHapley Additive exPlanations (SHAP) method [13] to a trained RW model, aiming to demonstrate the extraction of eXplainable Artificial Intelligence (XAI) knowledge.

This paper is organized as follows. The related work is presented in Sect. 2. Next, Sect. 3 details the adopted DM approach in terms of the CRISP-DM methodology phases. Finally, Sect. 4 discusses the main conclusions and presents future steps.

2   Related Work

Accurately estimating beforehand human waiting time in a queue is crucial tool for ticket management systems, providing benefits for both citizens and organizations. Waiting time estimation is a challenging task, since it can be affected by a wide range of phenomena (e.g., sudden increase of customers, employee attendance slowness) that often are not directly measured by ticket management systems. Recently, several research studies have addressed this task, assuming traditional approaches, such as: Average Predictions (AP) [18]; Queuing Theory [17]; and DM/ML approaches [7]. In this work, we detail the ML based approaches, since they are more related with our CRISP-DM approach.

In 2018, a study was carried out in Portugal regarding the use ML algorithms to predict waiting times in queues, assuming a categorical format, thus a multi-class classification task (e.g., "very high", "low") [7]. To validate the results, the authors used a dataset from an emergency department of a Portuguese hospital, containing 4 years of data and around 673.000 records. Only one ML algorithm was used (RF). Interesting results were obtained for the most frequent time interval categories (e.g., "low"), although poor quality results were achieved for the infrequent classes.

In 2019, Sanit-in et al. [18] compared 3 different approaches to estimate queue waiting times: Queuing Theory [17], AP and ML. However, similarly to [7], instead of estimating the exact waiting time, the authors grouped the values into multi-class intervals (e.g., "very short", "short", "medium", "long" and "very long"). In order to validate their results, two datasets related to the queuing sector in Thailand were used. The first (1,348 records) was related with a medical care service, while the second (3,480 rows) was related to a post office store. In terms of used input features, the authors selected (among others): the queue identification number; the day of the week, hour and corresponding period of the day when the ticket was withdrawn; and the number of tickets taken and served per minute. For both datasets, the ML best results were achieve by the RF algorithm, with an overall accuracy of 86% and 82%, respectively.

In a different context, in 2019, Kyritsis et al. [11] performed a study that aimed to present the benefits of using ML for predicting queue waiting times in banks, assuming a regression approach. The ML algorithm used was an ANN and it was tested using a four week dataset with around 52,000 records related to 3 banks in Nigeria. The ANN outperformed both AP and Queuing Theory estimation systems.

More recently, in 2020, Kuo et al. [10] studied a real-time prediction of queue waiting time in an hospital emergency department in Hong Kong. In terms of ML, 4 regression algorithms were compared: Linear Regression (LR), used as baseline; ANN; Support Vector Machines (SVM) and Gradient Boost Machines (GBM). The used dataset had nearly 13,000 records and two combinations of attributes were used: using attributes including patient triage category (non-urgent, semi-urgent and urgent), arrival time and number of doctors in the emergency room; and using the same attributes but complemented with information about the patients in the queue. Additionally, the authors applied outlier detection and removal techniques and feature selection, using a LR feature importance measure. In terms of results, the GBM achieved the better predictive metrics for both attribute combinations.

Finally, in 2023, Benevento et al. [3] analyzed the use of ML to predict, in real time, the waiting time in emergency department queues, aiming to improve the department resource management. The datasets used refer to two hospitals in Italy and each contained approximately 500,000 records. The ML regression algorithms used were: Lasso, RF, SVM, ANN and an Ensemble Method (EM). The attributes used include information regarding the patient age, mode of arrival at the emergency room, wristband color after triage, an average estimation of patient arrivals by wristband color, the number of patients in the queue, grouped by wristband color, among others. The results revealed that the ensemble (EM) provided the best predictive performance, achieving a MAE of approximately 30 min.

When compared with our study, the related works are focused in different and single queuing domains, mostly related with health institutions. In particular, emergency services were targeted in [3,7,10,18], while bank queues were considered in [11] and a post office store data was modeled in [18]. In contrast, our research targets a single global ML model for several stores from multiple domains (e.g., banks, pharmacies). This is a more complex task, since it can only use more general queuing attributes that are common to all analyzed domains. Thus, it is not feasible to employ very specific features, such as the wristband color from the emergency services. Aiming to improve the waiting time estimation performance, in this work we use both the company ticket management attributes and newly proposed engineered attributes, computed using the company queuing data. Additionally, in our study we explore much larger dataset, with more than 2 million records, when compared with the ones used by the related works (e.g., 673,000 in [7] and 500,000 in [3]). Furthermore, similarly to [3,10,11], we addressed the queue waiting time predictions as a pure regression task, instead of a classification of time intervals, which is less informative and that was performed in [7, 18]. Moreover, we explore a recently proposed AutoML tool, which automatically selects the best predictive model among seven distinct ML algorithms. None of the related ML works have employed an AutoML. Finally, we employ two robust validation schemes to measure the predictive performance of the ML models, a standard cross-validation (under two modes) and a RW, comparing the ML results with the method currently adopted by the analyzed company. In particular, we note that the RW performs a realistic simulation of usage of the predictive models in a real environment, since it simulates several training and test iterations over time [19].

3   CRISP-DM Methodology

This section details the developed work in each of the CRISP-DM methodology phases for the multiple domain queue waiting time prediction task.

3.1   Business Understanding

Currently, the company under study uses their own solution to estimate multiple domain queue waiting time, which is quite complex and involves multiple steps. First, they remove outliers from the data and compute the average service time for each costumer, store and counter for the next day, using only data from homologous days. This step is performed daily, during the night, in order to avoid a computational system overload. Next, when there is a ticket withdrawing request, their solution queries the database to get the number of counters open to a specific service, the open counters status (e.g., servicing, paused) and the number of citizens in the queue and being serviced. Then, they simulate the allocation of all citizens to counters, order by their priority, resulting in multiple queues (one by counter). Lastly, it sums the average service times relative to the ticket being printed queue, returning it as their waiting time estimation.

The goal of this project was set in terms of predicting the queue waiting time by using supervised ML regression algorithms. Moreover, we considered the improvement of the current estimation method (termed here as "Company") as a success criteria, measured in terms of the Mean Absolute Error (MAE) computed over a test set. This criteria was validated by the company. Additionally, the ML model inference time (when producing a prediction) must be equal or less than 10 milliseconds, in order to ensure an acceptable ticket withdrawing time. Concerning the software, we adopted the Python programming language. In particular, due to the vast volume of data, we adopted the Spark computational environment for data preprocessing operations and MLlib, which is the Spark ML library, for the modeling phase, as well as H2O (for AutoML) and TensorFlow (for the deep ANN).

3.2   Data Understanding and Preparation

Two datasets were collected from the company database server using a Structured Query Language (SQL). At an initial CRISP-DM execution stage, the company provided us a sample that included 1,238,748 records and 52 attributes. The raw data was related with tickets withdrawn from a set of 58 stores, associated with five different ticket management sectors (banking, insurance companies, pharmacies, public and private services), from January 2022 to December 2022. We used this one-year dataset when executing the first five CRISP-DM stages, which includes the cross-validation ML comparison experiments that were held during the CRISP-DM modeling stage. Then, in a later research stage, we had access to a larger two-year company sample, with a total of 2,087,771 records from January 2021 to December 2022 and related with the same 58 stores. This second dataset was used only for the CRISP-DM deployment simulation experiments.

Using the one-year raw data, we first executed the CRISP-DM data understanding and preparation stages. The latter stage was performed in collaboration with the business experts. The preprocessing aimed to enhance the quality of the data used to feed the ML models and it included several operations: data cleaning, outlier removal, creation of new data attributes (feature engineering) and data transformations.

First, we discarded all null valued attributes (e.g., with no citizen information). We also ignored data variables that could only be computed after the ticket being printed (e.g., service duration, counter and user that served the citizen), thus unfeasible to be used in a real-time prediction. The remaining 23 data attributes are presented in Table 1 and were considered for the CRISP-DM modeling phase, under distinct input set combinations, as shown in Column **Scenarios** and detailed in Sect. 3.3.

In terms of outlier removal, several records presented queue waited times above 20 h, which reflects errors in the costumers data gathering process. Together with the company experts, a maximum threshold value of 8 h was set for the waited time, allowing to remove all records that did not fulfill this time limit. Additionally, the priority attribute (isPriority from Table 1), which is computed when the counter user calls the citizen, revealed several inconsistencies and led to the removal of several records. Then, we detected around 57% of null values in the company estimation of queue waited time (CompanyEstimation attribute). Since these null values do not affect the ML models, we decided to maintain them and adopt two evaluation modes. In the first mode ("All"), we compute the regression metrics using all the test records. In the second ("Sampled"), we compute the same performance metrics using only the records that have the company estimation, in order to ensure a fair comparison with the company solution (see Sect. 3.4). Finally, 1.5% of waited time values were null and we have calculated them by subtracting the printing hour to the calling hour attribute.

Aiming to further improve the ML results, the next step of the data preparation stage included the creation of 9 new attributes, as presented in Table 2. The first 8 new attributes concern with the average and standard deviation values of waiting times and service duration, in seconds, for both the previous and current days, for a given store, service and priority. Finally, the 9th attribute is

Table 1. List of analyzed data attributes.

Context	Name	Description	Scenarios
Location	storeId	Identifier of the store where the ticket was withdrawn	A,B,C,D
	entityId	Identifier of the store entity	
	peopleInFront	Number of people in front for a given store and service	
	serviceId	Identifier of the service	
	storeProfileStoreId	Identifier of the in-store profile set up	
	entityQueueId	Identifier of the entity queue	
	partnerId	Identifier of the partner	A, C
Printing device	inputChannelId	Identifier of where the ticket request was made	A,B,C,D
	outputChannelId	Identifier of the channel where the ticket will be printed	
	deviceId	Identifier of the device where the ticket was withdrawn	A, C
Ticket info	printingHour	Time of ticket request	A,B,C,D
	isPriority	If the ticker has priority	
	isFastLane	If the ticket has a fast lane priority	
	isForward	If the ticket is forwarded from other service/store	A, C
	ticketLanguageId	Ticket language identifier	
	ticketOutputId	Ticket format identifier	
	ticketTypeId	Ticket type identifier	
	ticketNumber	Ticket number	
	originalServiceId	If forward, the initial service ID	
	originalStoreId	If forward, the initial store ID	
	subId	Number of times that a ticket was forward	
Target	CompanyEstimation	Company waiting time estimation (in seconds)	–
	waitedTime	Queue waiting time (in seconds)	–

Table 2. List of newly computed attributes.

Name	Description
AvgPrev_waitedTime	Average waiting time for previous day
AvgCurr_waitedTime	Average waiting time for current day
AvgPrev_duration	Average service duration for previous day
AvgCurr_duration	Average service duration for current day
StdPrev_waitedTime	Standard deviation of waiting times for previous day
StdDevCurr_waitedTime	Standard deviation of waiting times for current day
StdPrev_duration	Standard deviation of service duration for previous day
StdDevCurr_duration	Standard deviation of service duration for current day
LastSimilarWaitedTime	Waited time of the last similar ticket

the waiting time of the last similar ticket withdrawn, with this similarity being defined as the same store, service and priority.

All input data attributes are numeric and have different scales (e.g., week day ranges from 0 to 6; store ID ranges from 8 to 537), which often results in different ML algorithms impacts due only to scale differences [15]. Therefore, in the last data preparation step, we performed the scale normalization to all input attributes by applying a standard scaling (also known as z-scores) [8], which transforms each attribute to have a mean of zero and standard deviation equal to 1.

3.3 Modeling

The first task of CRISP-DM modeling stage concerns with the selection of modeling techniques. After analyzing the related studies, in terms of ML algorithm, the most popular choice were RF [3,7,18] and ANN [3,10,11] and therefore we tested them. Furthermore, we tested two other tree-based algorithms, Decision Trees (DT) and Gradient-Boosted Trees (GBT), and an Automated ML (AutoML) algorithm, as provide by the H2O tool [12].

All ML algorithms were implemented by using the Python programming language. In particular, we used the pyspark package for all tree-based methods, with all the default hyperparameters. In terms of defaults: RF uses a total of 20 trees, each one with a maximum depth of 5, and one third as feature subset strategy, i.e., each tree node considers one third of the total of features for split; DT uses maximum depth of 5; and GBT uses a maximum of 20 iterations, maximum depth of 5, all features for subset strategy and squared error as loss function.

As for the ANN implementation, since pyspark does not have an ANN implementation for regression tasks, we used the popular TensorFlow package [1]. The implemented ANN architecture, similarly to the ones used in [2,14], uses a triangular shape deep Multilayer Perceptron (MLP). Assuming the input layer size I, the H hidden layers with size L, and a single output neuron, each subsequent layer size is smaller in a way that $I > L_1 > L_2 > ... > L_H > 1$. After some preliminary experiments, assuming only the first iteration of the 10-fold cross-validation procedure (as detailed in the last paragraph of this section), we defined the following ANN setup. The ANN model includes a total of $H = 5$ hidden layers, with the following layer structure: $(I, 25, 20, 15, 10, 5, 1)$. In each layer, the ReLu activation function was used. Furthermore, in order to avoid overfitting, we added: a dropout applied on the 2nd and 4th hidden layers, with a dropout ratio of 0.2 and 0.1, respectively, as in [14]; an inverse time decay to Adam optimizer, with an initial learning rate of 0.0001, a decay rate of 1 and a decay step of 30 epochs, similarly to [5]; and an early stopping monitoring of the Mean Squared Error (MSE) on the validation data, with a patience of 20 epochs, similar to [14]. Lastly, we trained our ANN with a batch size of 1000, for a maximum of 100 epochs, using the MSE as loss function.

Finally, concerning the AutoML algorithm, we selected the H2O tool based on recent AutoML benchmarking studies [6,15]. In terms of implementation, we used the h2o python package, assuming the default parameters in terms of the searched ML algorithms, which were: Generalized Linear Model (GLM), RF, Extremely Randomized Trees (XRT), Gradient Boosting Machine (GBM), XGBoost, a Deep Learning Neural Network (DLNN) and two Stacked Ensembles. Regarding the stopping metric, we selected MSE, which is also used to sort the learderboard on the validation data. Additionally, we set a maximum runtime limitation of 30 min for the model and hyperparameter selection process.

During the CRISP-DM modeling phase, we also designed multiple input selection scenarios, allowing us to test different hypotheses regarding the influence of attributes on the queue waiting time prediction. In particular, we compared 4 attribute combination scenarios: A) use of all 21 input attributes presented in Table 1 (from storeID to subId); B) use of domain knowledge selected attributes (as advised in [21]), which corresponds to the 11 input variables listed in Table 1 and that were signaled as relevant by the domain experts; C) combination of scenario A) with the 9 new engineered attributes shown in Table 2 (e.g., mean and standard deviation values of waiting times), thus resulting in a set with 30 input features; and D) combination of scenario B) with the 9 created attributes, leading to 20 numeric inputs.

In order to evaluate the performance of the distinct input scenario and ML algorithm combinations, we executed the standard 10-fold cross-validation [8] using the whole one-year data (from 2022). The 10-fold procedure randomly divides the dataset into 10 equal sized data partitions. In the first iteration, the data included in 9 of the folds is used to train a ML model, which is then tested using the remaining data. This procedure is repeated up to 10 times, with each 10-fold iteration assuming a distinct fold as the external (unseen) test data. Regarding the two ML algorithms that require validation data (ANN and AutoML), the training data is further randomly split into fit (with 90%) and validation (with the remaining 10%) sets.

3.4   Evaluation

During this step, we performed the evaluation of all ML algorithms and input selection scenarios using two different modes. The first mode, termed here as "All", computes the performance metrics for each of the 10-fold test set partitions by using the entire test data. The second "Sampled" mode filters first the records with null values for the company queue waiting time estimation from the 10-fold test sets, keeping only the test examples for which there is a company method estimation value. Thus, the "Sampled" mode ensures a fair performance comparison between the ML algorithms and the estimation system currently used by the company.

In this work, ML algorithms are evaluated in terms of two relevant problem domain dimensions: the computational cost and predictive performance. For the former, we compute both the algorithm training time, in seconds, and the prediction time (i.e., the time to perform a single estimation), measured in microseconds. Regarding the latter, we selected four popular regression metrics [4,6]: Mean Absolute Error (MAE), Normalized NMAE (NMAE), Root Mean Squared Error (RMSE) and Area under the Regression Error Characteristic curve (AREC). Although multiple metrics are presented, the company agreed that a major focus should be given to the MAE measure and to the prediction time.

Table 3 presents the median 10-fold cross-validation predictive and computational measures obtained for all ML algorithms and input set scenarios, assuming the "All" evaluation mode. The predictive performance statistical significance is measured by adopting the nonparametric Wilcoxon test [9] over the 10-fold results. Regarding the predictive metrics, the results clearly show that the H2O is the best ML algorithm, regardless of the scenario, returning MAE values that are inferior to 11 min for all scenarios. In particular, the best MAE value (6.48 min) was achieved for H2O and scenario C. The second best ML performance is provided by GBT, with a median MAE of nearly 1 min more, and then ANN, DT and RF, respectively. On the other hand, in terms of training time, H2O has the highest values in all scenarios, requiring the allowed 30 min execution time for the model and hyperparameter selection. Although it is the slowest ML model it terms of training, H2O is the fastest one in terms of the predictive time, regardless the scenario, with the maximum inference time of 7.69 microseconds for scenario D. This time is much lower than the company 10 millisecond limit for a real-time ticket management time estimation. Regarding the computational cost of the remaining algorithms, DT is the fastest during the training process, followed by RF, GBT and ANN. In terms of time taken for each prediction, H2O is the best option, followed by DT, RF, GBT and ANN, which take almost 10 times more to perform predictions. As for the scenarios, all models achieve a better predictive performance when using the new 9 attributes calculated during the data preparation phase (scenarios C and D). In particular, H2O, GBT and ANN achieve a better predictive performance on scenario C, while DT and RF obtain their best predictive results on scenario D.

Table 4 displays a comparison of predictive metrics for all ML models across each scenario, in terms of median 10-fold cross validation measures, for the "Sampled" evaluation mode. Since the ML train and predictive time are the same as in mode "All" and we do not have access to the estimation time of the company solution, these values were not considered on this evaluation mode. In terms the predictive performance, the obtained results are similar to the ones obtained for the "All" mode. In effect, H2O also achieves the best predictive in all scenarios, with the best MAE value of 5.20 min for scenario C. In terms of MAE, the best performing ML algorithm is H2O, followed by GBT, DT, ANN and RF, respectively. Concerning the scenarios, H2O, ANN and GBT achieve a better predictive performance when using the features from scenario C, while the remaining ML models improved their performance when using the attributes from scenario D. In this evaluation mode, all the predictive results improved, when compared with the "All" mode, with the highest MAE value (10.52 min) being obtained by RF when using the attributes from scenario B.

A summary of the best ML algorithm predictive results (H2O), obtained for all scenario and evaluation modes, is presented in Table 5. In particular, we highlight the scenario C results, for which H2O obtained MAE values below 7 min for the "All" and "Sampled" modes. In case of the latter mode, we compare all explored scenarios with the company current estimation system. Clearly, the best results are provided by H20 regardless of the input set scenario. In effect, for scenario C, the company system achieves a median MAE value of 9.86 min, while the H2O method only required 5.20 min. Thus, an impressive 53% MAE improvement was obtained by the H2O algorithm. Following this results, we

Table 3. Comparative results for evaluation mode "All" (median cross-validation values; best values in **bold**).

Scenario	ML Model	MAE (min.)	RMSE (min.)	AREC (%)	Train Time (s)	Prediction Time (μs)
A	DT	12.20	23.54	67.58	9.09	10.04
	RF	12.07	23.29	67.47	12.46	11.23
	GBT	10.94	21.82	70.50	30.32	10.18
	H2O	**10.22***	**20.48***	**72.24***	1798.15	5.56
	ANN	11.01	22.80	70.64	624.58	106.86
B	DT	12.02	23.75	68.08	6.61	9.23
	RF	12.05	23.43	67.58	9.48	9.01
	GBT	11.16	22.46	69.96	26.57	9.50
	H2O	**10.76***	**21.41***	**70.94***	1796.78	6.33
	ANN	11.26	23.38	70.01	570.77	89.00
C	DT	8.90	18.40	75.08	11.06	10.37
	RF	9.12	17.67	73.91	14.67	10.53
	GBT	7.71	16.87	78.34	33.53	11.47
	H2O	**6.48***	**14.20***	**81.06***	1799.54	7.37
	ANN	7.74	16.58	77.97	586.48	110.11
D	DT	8.86	18.41	75.44	8.41	9.22
	RF	8.93	17.67	74.57	11.28	9.46
	GBT	7.84	17.25	78.14	29.58	9.79
	H2O	**6.84***	**14.96***	**80.20***	1798.87	7.69
	ANN	8.56	17.84	76.31	645.73	90.81

⋆ – Statistically significant under a paired comparison with all other methods.

selected for the next CRISP-DM stage the H2O algorithm and the input set scenario C as the best predictive ML approach to be further compared with the company based method.

3.5   Deployment

In terms of deployment, we did not implement the DM approach on the company environment yet. Nevertheless, we performed a realistic simulation of its implementation potential performance by employing a RW validation scheme [19]. During this stage execution, we had access to a larger sample of two-year data, relative to the same 58 stores. The two-year dataset includes around 2 millions of records collected from January 2021 and December 2022. Using this larger sample, we first executed the same data preprocessing that was previously applied to the one-year data (described in Sect. 3.2), selecting then the input variables associated with scenario C, which led to best predictive results shown in Sect. 3.4.

Next, the RW simulation was executed over the two-year preprocessed data. The RW approach mimics what would occur in a real-world environment, since it assumes that data is time-ordered, thus the ML model is always trained using historical data and produces predictions for more recent unseen data. Moreover, it performs several training and testing iterations over time.

Table 4. Comparative results for evaluation mode "Sampled" (median cross-validation values; best values in **bold**).

Scenario	ML Model	MAE (min.)	RMSE (min.)	AREC (%)
A	DT	9.23	15.98	72.67
	RF	9.94	15.73	69.64
	GBT	9.03	14.93	72.59
	H2O	**7.97***	14.38*	75.90*
	NN	9.18	15.53	73.19
B	DT	9.83	15.99	70.55
	RF	10.52	15.86	68.23
	GBT	9.27	15.23	71.86
	H2O	**8.45***	14.51*	73.90*
	NN	10.11	16.27	69.99
C	DT	7.56	12.41	76.60
	RF	7.83	11.55	75.34
	GBT	6.15	10.55	80.82
	H2O	**5.20***	9.30*	83.66*
	NN	6.21	11.16	80.80
D	DT	7.36	11.74	77.08
	RF	7.78	11.63	75.38
	GBT	6.39	10.79	79.93
	H2O	**5.52***	9.48*	82.62*
	NN	7.26	12.63	77.79

$\star$ – Statistically significant under a paired comparison with all other methods.

Table 5. Overall H2O and company method predictive results (median cross-validation values; best values in **bold**).

Mode	Scenario	MAE (min.)	NMAE (%)	RMSE (min.)	AREC (%)
"All"	A	10.22	2.15	20.48	72.24
	B	10.76	2.26	21.41	70.94
	C	**6.48**	**1.37**	**14.20**	**81.06**
	D	6.84	1.44	14.96	80.202
"Sampled"	A	7.97	3.14	14.38	75.90
	B	8.46	3.32	14.51	73.90
	C	**5.20***	**2.00***	**9.30***	**83.66***
	D	5.53	2.11	9.48	82.62
	Company	9.86	3.96	19.88	72.34

$\star$ – Statistically significant under a paired comparison with the Company method.

The RW training time window was set to one year and the testing and sliding windows were set to two weeks. In the first RW iteration, one year of the oldest records were used to train the ML algorithm, except for the last week data that was used as a validation subset for H2O model selection purposes. Then, the subsequent two weeks of data were used as the external (unseen) data, for predictive testing purposes. In the second RW iteration, we update the training data by advancing the testing period 2 weeks in time, thus discarding the oldest two weeks of data. The next two subsequent weeks of data are now used for test purposes. And so on. In total, this procedure produces in 26 iterations, advancing 2 weeks of data in each iteration, resulting in a total of 1 year of predictions. In order to reduce the computational effort, the H2O algorithm selection is only executed during the first RW iteration, assuming the last week of the available training data as the validation subset, allowing to select the best ML algorithm and its hyperparameters. Once this model is selected, in the remaining RW iterations (from 2 to 26), we just retrain the selected ML using the newer training data. In terms of the H2O setup, we used the same as in the previous experimentation (Sect. 3.3).

Table 6 presents the obtained RW results. In terms of mode "All", H2O obtained only a slight increase on the median MAE value (0.40 min) when compared with the previous experiments, which demonstrates a consistency of the H2O Scenario C model performance. Moreover, the H2O algorithm outperformed the current company estimation system by 4.7 min (improvement of 53%) in the "Sampled" evaluation mode, which suggests a strong potential predictive value for the company ticket management system.

Table 6. Overall results for the simulation system (median RW values; best values in **bold**).

Mode	Estimator	MAE (min.)	NMAE (%)	RMSE (min.)	AREC (%)
"All"	H2O	6.88	1.49	14.81	80.06
"Sampled"	H2O	**5.37***	**2.48***	**9.76***	**83.15***
	Company	10.07	4.60	19.11	72.53

⋆ – Statistically significant under a paired comparison with the Company method.

A further predictive analysis is provided in Fig. 1, which shows the median REC curves for all RW iterations (colored curve), associated with the respective Wilcoxon 95% confidence intervals (colored area), for both the systems tested. Particularly, the REC curve shows the model accuracy ($y - axis$), measured in terms of correct predictions for a given absolute error tolerance ($x - axis$). For instance, for a 5 min tolerance, H2O has an accuracy of nearly 70%. In this graph, we limited the absolute deviation to 30 min, after which we consider that the predictions have low value for the company. When comparing both algorithms results, the company estimation system has a better accuracy (40%) for a very small error tolerance (less than 2 min), which is quite low. As for the

ML approach, it achieves a better accuracy for the remaining absolute error values of the curve. Moreover, in the H2O (blue) curve, the Wilcoxon confidence intervals are practically unnoticed in Fig. 1 (cyan shadowed area), denoting a small variation of model accuracy for all absolute errors over the 26 RW iterations, which increases the confidence and reliability of the model. On the other hand, the company system presents a greater variation of results, denoted by the gray shadowed area, particularly for absolute deviations between 5 and 20 min. These results reflect a higher level of uncertainty associated to the model in the mentioned tolerance interval.

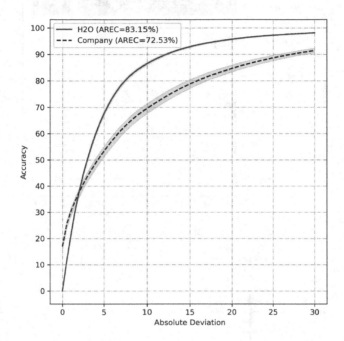

Fig. 1. Median REC curves with Wilcoxon 95% confidence intervals for RW. (Color figure online)

For demonstration purposes, we analyzed the ML model selected by the H2O algorithm in the first RW iteration, which was XGBoost, with a total of 50 trees. Although it had a training time of 30 min in the first iteration, which corresponds to the established limit, its retraining on the remaining iterations was very fast. Specifically, the median training time for those iterations was around 25 s. The H2O tool includes an XAI module based on the SHAP method [13]. Using such XAI, the top of Fig. 2 presents the 5 most relevant inputs extracted from the XGBoost model on the last RW iteration. The waiting time of the last similar ticket is the predominant attribute, with a relative importance superior to 70%. In second place appears the number of people in front in the queue, with less than 10%, followed by the averaged waited time in the current day (4%), the number of times that a ticket was forwarded (subID, 4%), hour of the day (2%) and the ticket type ID (2%). Overall, these results demonstrate the importance of data preparation stage, since 2 of the newly engineered input variables are among the 4 top relevant inputs of the model. As for the bottom XAI graph of Fig. 2, it shows the overall impact of an input in the predicted responses. For instance, any decrease of the top three inputs (e.g., waiting time) produces also an average decrease on the estimated time (as shown by the blue colored dots).

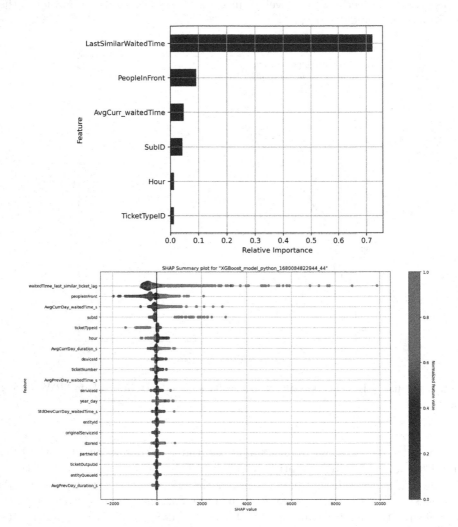

Fig. 2. Input importance for H2O best model on the last iteration of RW (top) and overall impact of an input in the predicted responses (bottom).

4   Conclusions

In this paper, we demonstrate the execution of the CRISP-DM methodology to predict a challenging task: multiple domain queue waiting times for printed tickets of physical stores. Working in collaboration with a ticket management software company, we have analyzed millions of records, aiming to compare a ML approach with the current estimation method adopted by the company. Using a one-year dataset (related with the year of 2022), the data was first analyzed and preprocessed. Then, five ML regression algorithms and four input selection scenarios were compared, using a robust cross-validation procedure and several predictive and computational measures. The best modeling results were obtained by an AutoML algorithm fed with newly engineered attributes (scenario C). In the deployment phase, we applied a RW procedure to realistically simulate the predictive performance of the selected ML approach. The RW experiments were executed over a larger two-year dataset (collected from January 2021 to December 2022), assuming a total of 26 training and testing iterations over time (one year of predictions). Overall results, competitive results were obtained by the AutoML method, both in the evaluation and deployment phases, show a high level of consistency and outperforming the current company estimation system. Furthermore, the selected AutoML tool requires a reasonable computational effort and very fast inference times, thus being feasible for real-time responses. Finally, we used a XAI approach to demonstrate the extraction of explanatory knowledge from a trained predictive model.

The obtained results were shown to the ticket management software company, which provided a positive feedback. Indeed, in future work, we intend to implement our approach in the company real-world environment and further assess the quality of its predictions. Furthermore, we plan to create additional engineered features (e.g., average waiting time for specific time periods) and also include external features (e.g., meteorology data) in the next CRISP-DM iterations.

Acknowledgments. This work has been supported by FCT - Fundação para a Ciência e Tecnologia within the R&D Units Project Scope: UIDB/00319/2020 and the project "QOMPASS .: Solução de Gestão de Serviços de Atendimento multi-entidade, multi-serviço e multi-idioma" within the Project Scope NORTE-01-0247-FEDER-038462.

References

1. Abadi, M., et al.: TensorFlow: Large-scale machine learning on heterogeneous systems (2015). https://www.tensorflow.org/, software available from tensorflow.org
2. Azevedo, J., et al.: Predicting yarn breaks in textile fabrics: A machine learning approach. In: Cristani, M., Toro, C., Zanni-Merk, C., Howlett, R.J., Jain, L.C. (eds.) Knowledge-Based and Intelligent Information & Engineering Systems: Proceedings of the 26th International Conference KES-2022, Verona, Italy and Virtual Event, 7–9 September 2022. Procedia Computer Science, vol. 207, pp. 2301–2310. Elsevier (2022). https://doi.org/10.1016/j.procs.2022.09.289

3. Benevento, E., Aloini, D., Squicciarini, N.: Towards a real-time prediction of waiting times in emergency departments: A comparative analysis of machine learning techniques. Int. J. Forecast. **39**(1), 192–208 (2023). https://doi.org/10.1016/j.ijforecast.2021.10.006
4. Caetano, N., Cortez, P., Laureano, R.M.S.: Using data mining for prediction of hospital length of stay: An application of the CRISP-DM methodology. In: Cordeiro, J., Hammoudi, S., Maciaszek, L.A., Camp, O., Filipe, J. (eds.) Enterprise Information Systems - 16th International Conference, ICEIS 2014, Lisbon, Portugal, April 27–30, 2014, Revised Selected Papers. LNBIP, vol. 227, pp. 149–166. Springer (2014). https://doi.org/10.1007/978-3-319-22348-3_9
5. Core, T.: Overfit and Underfit. https://www.tensorflow.org/tutorials/keras/overfit_and_underfit. (Accessed 28 Mar 2023)
6. Ferreira, L., Pilastri, A.L., Martins, C.M., Pires, P.M., Cortez, P.: A comparison of automl tools for machine learning, deep learning and xgboost. In: International Joint Conference on Neural Networks, IJCNN 2021, Shenzhen, China, 18–22 July 2021, pp. 1–8. IEEE (2021). https://doi.org/10.1109/IJCNN52387.2021.9534091
7. Gonçalves, F., Pereira, R., Ferreira, J., Vasconcelos, J.B., Melo, F., Velez, I.: Predictive Analysis in Healthcare: Emergency Wait Time Prediction. In: Novais, P., et al. (eds.) ISAmI2018 2018. AISC, vol. 806, pp. 138–145. Springer, Cham (2019). https://doi.org/10.1007/978-3-030-01746-0_16
8. Hastie, T., Tibshirani, R., Friedman, J.: The Elements of Statistical Learning. SSS, Springer, New York (2009). https://doi.org/10.1007/978-0-387-84858-7
9. Hollander, M., Wolfe, D.A., Chicken, E.: Nonparametric statistical methods. John Wiley & Sons, NJ, USA (2013)
10. Kuo, Y., et al.: An integrated approach of machine learning and systems thinking for waiting time prediction in an emergency department. Int. J. Med. Inform. **139**, 104143 (2020). https://doi.org/10.1016/j.ijmedinf.2020.104143
11. Kyritsis, A.I., Deriaz, M.: A machine learning approach to waiting time prediction in queueing scenarios. In: Second International Conference on Artificial Intelligence for Industries, AI4I 2019, Laguna Hills, CA, USA, 25–27 September 2019. pp. 17–21. IEEE (2019). https://doi.org/10.1109/AI4I46381.2019.00013
12. LeDell, E., Poirier, S.: H2O AutoML: Scalable automatic machine learning. In: 7th ICML Workshop on Automated Machine Learning (AutoML) (July 2020). https://www.automl.org/wp-content/uploads/2020/07/AutoML_2020_paper_61.pdf
13. Lundberg, S.M., Lee, S.: A unified approach to interpreting model predictions. In: Guyon, I., von Luxburg, U., Bengio, S., Wallach, H.M., Fergus, R., Vishwanathan, S.V.N., Garnett, R. (eds.) Advances in Neural Information Processing Systems 30: Annual Conference on Neural Information Processing Systems 2017, 4–9 December 2017, Long Beach, CA, USA, pp. 4765–4774 (2017)
14. Matos, L.M., Cortez, P., Mendes, R., Moreau, A.: Using deep learning for mobile marketing user conversion prediction. In: International Joint Conference on Neural Networks, IJCNN 2019 Budapest, Hungary, 14–19 July 2019, pp. 1–8. IEEE (2019). https://doi.org/10.1109/IJCNN.2019.8851888
15. Pereira, P.J., Gonçalves, C., Nunes, L.L., Cortez, P., Pilastri, A.: AI4CITY - An Automated Machine Learning Platform for Smart Cities. In: SAC 2023: The 38th ACM/SIGAPP Symposium on Applied Computing, Tallinn, Estonia,27–31 March 2023, pp. 886–889. ACM (2023). https://doi.org/10.1145/3555776.3578740
16. Ribeiro, R., Pilastri, A.L., Moura, C., Rodrigues, F., Rocha, R., Cortez, P.: Predicting the tear strength of woven fabrics via automated machine learning: An application of the CRISP-DM methodology. In: Filipe, J., Smialek, M., Brodsky, A., Hammoudi, S. (eds.) Proceedings of the 22nd International Conference on Enterprise

Information Systems, ICEIS 2020, Prague, Czech Republic, 5–7 May 2020, vol. 1, pp. 548–555. SCITEPRESS (2020). https://doi.org/10.5220/0009411205480555

17. Saaty, T.L.: Elements of queueing theory: with applications, vol. 34203. McGraw-Hill New York (1961)
18. Sanit-in, Y., Saikaew, K.R.: Prediction of waiting time in one stop service. Int. J. Mach. Learn. Comput. **9**(3), 322–327 (2019)
19. Tashman, L.J.: Out-of-sample tests of forecasting accuracy: an analysis and review. Int. J. Forecast. **16**(4), 437–450 (2000)
20. Wirth, R., Hipp, J.: Crisp-dm: Towards a standard process model for data mining. In: Proceedings of the 4th International Conference on the Practical Applications Of Knowledge Discovery And Data Mining, Manchester, vol. 1, pp. 29–39 (2000)
21. Witten, I.H., Frank, E., Hall, M.A., Pal, C.J.: Data mining: practical machine learning tools and techniques, 4th edn. Morgan Kaufmann (2016)

Evaluation of Time Series Causal Detection Methods on the Influence of Pacific and Atlantic Ocean over Northeastern Brazil Precipitation

Juliano E. C. Cruz[1,2]($\boxtimes$), Mary T. Kayano[3], Alan J. P. Calheiros[3],
Sâmia R. Garcia[4], and Marcos G. Quiles[4]

[1] Applied Computing Postgraduate Program, National Institute for Space
Research (INPE), São José dos Campos, Brazil
`juliano.cruz@inpe.br`
[2] Research and Technology Department, EMBRAER S.A.,
São José dos Campos, Brazil
[3] National Institute for Space Research (INPE), São José dos Campos, Brazil
[4] Federal University of São Paulo (UNIFESP), São José dos Campos, Brazil

Abstract. The detection of causation in natural systems or phenomena has been a fundamental task of science for a long time. In recent decades, data-driven approaches have emerged to perform this task automatically. Some of them are specialized in time series. However, there is no clarity in literature what methods perform better in what scenarios. Thus this paper presents an evaluation of causality detection methods for time series using a well-known and extensively studied case study: the influence of El Niño-Southern Oscillation and Intertropical Convergence Zone on precipitation in Northeastern Brazil. We employed multiple approaches and two datasets to evaluate the methods, and found that the SELVAR and SLARAC methods delivered the best performance.

Keywords: causality · time series · ENSO · precipitation

1 Introduction

Understanding the causes behind an observed phenomena is among the great goals of science. There are basically two paths to investigate causes: by using observational data, either in raw format or through models, or employing interventionist experiments under well-controlled conditions [23]. In order to discover the cause behind symptoms or behaviors, medicine and social sciences predominantly employ randomized controlled experiments [19], but for most

This study was nanced in part by the Coordenac ao de Aperfeicoamento de Pessoal de Nvel Superior - Brasil (CAPES) - Finance Code 001.

Supplementary Information The online version contains supplementary material available at https://doi.org/10.1007/978-3-031-36805-9_28.

Earth science fields, it is done by employing computer simulation, which can be very expensive, time-consuming, and may be strongly based on assumptions and knowledge from specialists [23]. In the past few decades, there has been a significant rise in the availability of time series data, originating from both observational data and models. This trend, coupled with the rapid growth in computational power, has resulted in the creation of new opportunities to leverage data-driven approaches.

Causal detection methods and applications have been a subject of research for quite some time [8]. However, with the introduction of a more comprehensive and consolidated causal framework [19,20], there has been a surge in the number of studies published, including those that focus on time series data [5,9,17]. Time series has an additional feature and challenge: time order indexation. Regarding climate time series, there are also several studies targeting different parts of the globe, i.e. Arctic [23], Europe [26], India [3], Atlantic Ocean [26], Pacific Ocean [24] etc. and using different types of meteorological variables. However, it is really hard to foresee which methods may work or not only based on time series aspects such as frequency, shape, noise etc. Most published papers only target specific climatic scenarios or systems and they do not extrapolate results for general usage. Therefore, the best way to evaluate the causal detection methods is to employ them in a case study of interest.

Although there are several studies done in the last decades that connect the Northeastern Brazil (NEB) precipitation variation to ENSO and to Tropical Atlantic phenomena [11,13,18], none of them employ causal detection methods. In that region, severe impacts on the precipitation behavior have been registered since the sixteenth century and due to its characteristics, it has a high seasonal climate predictability [18]. One explanation for the phenomenon is that extreme changes in sea surface temperature (SST) in the tropical Pacific, the El Niño-Southern Oscillation (ENSO), influence precipitation anomalies through changes in the Walker circulation [1]. But it accounts for only part of the rainfall variability. For example, from the 46 strong or moderate El Niño events between 1849 and 1992, only 21 were associated with droughts in north of Northeastern Brazil (NEB) [13,18]. The other ones can be explained by an anomalous northern position of the Intertropical Convergence Zone (ITCZ) over the Atlantic, caused by a warmer tropical North Atlantic [18].

The NEB precipitation anomalies have a well-understood behavior, therefore they are an excellent case study for evaluating the performance of data-driven causal detection methods. Thus, the objective of this study is to evaluate causal detection methods for time series on the relationship of NEB precipitation with ENSO and with Tropical Atlantic SST. Three experiments were performed. The first one aims to test whether the methods are capable of detecting the already known causality between the raw (but linear detrended) time series. The second one tests how the causal detection methods behave when filtering is applied on the time series. The third experiment checks how stable the best methods found in the prior experiments are when varying the time series length and their start and end over time.

2 Data

Seven types of monthly time series are used, where the time span ranges from 1950 to 2016. Three precipitation time series are from the region of interest, Northern NEB. One precipitation time series (SRUNK) is from east of Southern Ural Mountains region. Two time series are related to the causative phenomena: Oceanic Niño Index (ONI) and the Tropical North Atlantic (TNAtl) SST. The last one is a synthetic random series, which does not affect or is caused by any of Earth system time series.

All the precipitation time series were extracted from GPCC (NOAA Global Precipitation Climatology Centre) repository, which has 0.5°x0.5° resolution. A polygon in the north part of Northeastern Brazil was used after two papers [10,13] also used the same area for precipitation anomaly prediction. The polygon is located between 3°-8°S and 36°-41°W. As already said, three time series from this region were used: the polygon precipitation average, the precipitation of the cells with the highest (4°-4.5°S and 40.5°-41°W) and the lowest (7.5°-8°S and 36°-36.5°W) correlation with SST of the TNAtl region and with ONI. The latter two time series were chosen, because it is quite normal in large areas to exist local variability, then the extremes (most correlated and less correlated) were picked in order to see how the detection methods would behave. The correlation with SST of the TNAtl region and with ONI were performed after a Morlet wavelet filtering considering the range from 2 to 7 year frequency [6,30].

SRUNK is an average from the polygon located between 52°-55°N and 60°-70°E, which is south of the Russian Ural District, east of the Ural Mountains, and in Northern Kazakhstan. It was chosen mainly because Lin and Qian [16] showed that ENSO has little or no influence over this area.

ONI and a region on the TNAtl are used as time series related to the causative phenomena. ONI, Oceanic Niño Index, is an index used to monitor ENSO, which can be used to know if the phenomenon is on El Niño or La Niña phase and its severity. It is calculated using a 3-month running mean on the SST of the region Niño 3.4 [7]. The polygon of Tropical North Atlantic SST is between 6°-22°N and 15°-60°W and was extracted from ERSST (Extended Reconstructed Sea Surface Temperature) dataset, which has 2°x2° resolution.

Prior studies [14,25,26] calculate time series anomalies and other studies [2,4,27] besides that, also apply filters in order to remove unwanted frequencies when trying to establish relationships among meteorological variables. Therefore, another set of time series was also employed in this study, which was created by applying a transformation on the prior dataset presented. Besides wide usage, the objective is also to check whether a less noisy time series can contribute to a better performance in causal detection. The process applied on precipitation data was sequentially the following: month-wise z-score calculation, linear trend removal, and finally, wavelet filtering.

3 Methods

There are two main groups of methods that were employed in this study. The ones that use hypothesis significance test (Granger, FullCI, PC, PCMCI, and

PCMCI+) and the ones (QRBS, SLARAC, LASAR, SELVAR) that output scalar results between 0 and positive infinity, which is used to infer the causal link likelihood [31].

3.1   Statistical Hypothesis Methods

Granger causality is a statistical concept of causality based on prediction, where its mathematical formulation is based on linear regression modeling of stochastic processes [8]. According to this method, for detecting causation of X on Y, Y_{t+1} has to be better predicted using X_{t-a} and Y_{t-b}, where $a, b \geq 0$, than with only Y_{t-b}. There is two principles that must exist in order to claim a Granger causality exists: the cause happens before the effect; and the cause series has unique information about the future behaviors of the effect series that would not be available otherwise [5,8].

FullCI, acronym for Full Conditional Independence, is one of the most direct methods known for causal link detection [21]. In its original formulation, the Granger causality between time series X and Y is based on the use of a linear or non-linear model which may include possible confounders for Y. A causal connection $X \rightarrow Y$, is evaluated by quantifying whether the inclusion of the history of variable X in the model significantly reduces the forecast error about Y. Thus, FullCI can be interpreted as a Granger version that uses specific time windows [21].

PC, is an algorithm that was originally formulated for general random variables without assuming temporal order and was named after its creators Peter and Clark [28]. In the structural discovery phase, this method generates an undirected graphical model in which connections are driven using a set of rules. The version for time series uses the temporal ordering information, which naturally creates an orientation rule for the links [21].

PCMCI is the junction of the PC method [28] with MCI, acronym for Momentary Conditional Independence [24]. PCMCI is a method that was proposed later than PC and presents an approach that solves some limitations of the latter algorithm [24]. The PC version used in PCMCI differs from the canonical one, because only thesubset with the highest yield is used, instead of testing all possible combinations. It employs some approaches in order to have fewer tests, which theoretically does not take away the capacity to remove spurious connections [21]. An extended version, PCMCI+, was later proposed in [22]. In addition to the features of prior version, it can also detect contemporaneous links.

Three conditional independence tests are used in this study are: Partial Correlation, GPDC (Gaussian Process Distance Correlation), and CMI (Conditional Mutual Information). The first test is linear and the other ones, non-linear. Except for Granger, all the other methods used Partial Correlation. GPDC and CMI were just used with PCMCI and PCMCI+. Partial correlation is a very fast algorithm. On the other hand, GPDC and CMI are very costly and they can be more than one hundred times slower then the former.

3.2   Scalar Output Methods

Although being able to handle linear and non-linear causal-effect problems, all the four methods in this group use internally linear approaches. Furthermore, they do not make any data normalization or hypothesis testing, as Weichwald *et al.* [31] claims it considerably decreases the accuracy.

QRBS is the abbreviation for Quantiles of Ridge regressed Bootstrap Samples [31]. The general idea is to regress present values on past ones and then, verify the coefficients in other to decide whether one variable cause (according to Grange [8]) another variable. The method employs ridge regression [12] of time-deltas $X_t - X_{t-1}$ on the preceding values X_{t-1}. All the samples used are generated with bootstrap, that is, random sampling with replacement.

SLARAC stands for Subsampled Linear Auto-Regression Absolute Coefficients and was proposed by Weichwald *et al.* [31]. It also uses the concept of regression applied to past values and inspection of the coefficients in order to determine whether one variable causes (according to Grange) another. SLARAC fits a vector autoregression model on bootstrap samples, each time choosing a random number of lags to include. It sums all coefficient values obtained for every lag and in the end, it selects the highest score as result.

LASAR stands for LASSO Auto-Regression and was also proposed by Weichwald *et al.* [31]. As QRBS and SLARAC, it also relies in regression analysis in order to infer causation [8] between two variables, and different from the other approaches as it uses LASSO [29]. LASAR also uses bootstrap samples.

SELVAR or Selective Auto-Regressive model, detects causality with a hill-climbing procedure based on the leave-one-out residual sum of squares and at the final step, it scores the selected causal links with the absolute values of the regression coefficients [31].

4   Results

First, charts with lag correlations are shown in order to have a baseline for the rest of the paper. Then, the causal detection methods itself are evaluated in Sect. 4.2. The performance ranking regarding the previous experiments is subsequently presented in Sect. 4.3. Finally, a temporal stability experiment is done, which aims to find out if the best methods identified in Sect. 4.3 have the same behavior in smaller time windows as it does in full-length time series.

4.1   Correlation

The lag correlations among the precipitation time series and ONI and TNAtl SST were calculated for both time series set, raw and filtered. The results for raw time series are shown in Fig. 1. As expected, the correlation of ONI with SRUNK precipitation average is low. The Northern NEB precipitations also have low correlation. Regarding the Atlantic, Fig. 1(b) , the correlation have higher values in magnitude compared to chart (a). SRUNK precipitation has a

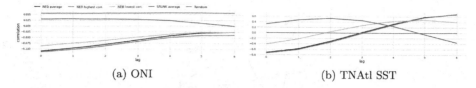

(a) ONI   (b) TNAtl SST

Fig. 1. Precipitation time series correlation with Pacific and Atlantic. One time lag unit represents one month.

significant correlation, reaching its peak at lag 2. The SRUNK precipitation kept with low correlation, a fact already expected [16].

The results for the filtered times series set can be seen in Fig. 2. The wavelet filtering improved drastically the correlation values for ONI when compared to raw data correlation results. On the other hand, Fig. 2(b) did not keep the behavior saw in raw data chart, and it has lower peak values. Finally, all the random time series correlations for all lags stayed between 0.06 and 0, and had imperceptible tiny oscillations.

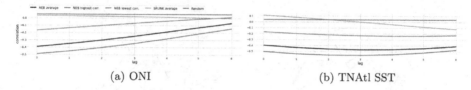

(a) ONI   (b) TNAtl SST

Fig. 2. Filtered time series correlation with Pacific and Atlantic. One time lag unit represents one month.

4.2   Raw and Filtered Dataset

Most studies used as reference in this paper use p-value as 0.05 [21,22,24], which is also adopted here.

The famous quote says "correlation does not imply causation", which means in this context that causal detection methods must be capable of detecting causality having or not a significant correlation for true causal links and not detecting causality between time series despite there is significant correlation. Thus, the perfect result for either datasets would be the one that only ONI and TNAtl SST causes the NEB precipitations (average, highest correlation, and lowest correlation time series) and obviously, no other link is detected. That is exactly what is shown in Fig. 3.

Even though five of six real links were detected, the results of Granger using the raw dataset, Fig. 4(a), had plenty of spurious causal links with most of them

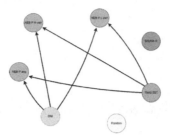

Fig. 3. The perfect result, where only the time series (ONI and TNAtl SST) related to the causative phenomena have a causality link with NEB precipitation time series.

being bidirectional. Except for the random time series, all the rest is being caused at least by another node. Most of the links had detection for all time lags, which most of them have p-value lower than 0.01. When the filtered dataset were used, Fig. 4(b), all the expected links were detect, but more spurious links were detected and the lag amount detected also raised. Like the raw dataset, most of the p-value are under 0.01.

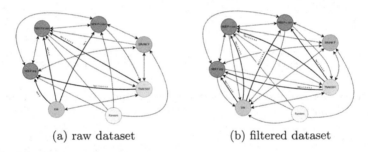

(a) raw dataset   (b) filtered dataset

Fig. 4. Granger results. Solid lines are real relationships and dashed lines spurious ones. Due to the large amount of links, lag information for spurious links were suppressed, but they are shown in Appendix.

The results for PC and FullCI, which employed partial correlation, can be seen in Fig. 5. Using the raw dataset, the PC algorithm detected the causation from the TNAtl SST in the SRUNK and Northern NEB average precipitation, in time lag 4 and 1 respectively. The other detections are among precipitation time series. No link was detected when the filtered dataset was used, which explains why it was suppressed from Fig. 5.

The FullCI results for raw time series, Fig. 5(b), show that besides the detection about the TNAtl and the NEB precipitations, the other ones are spurious: i.e. precipitation causing SST variation and especially the random time series causing the NEB precipitations. Using the filtered dataset, Fig. 5(c), the amount of true links increased (there are five out of six), however the spurious ones and the detected lag amount also increased considerably. Most of links are bidirectional.

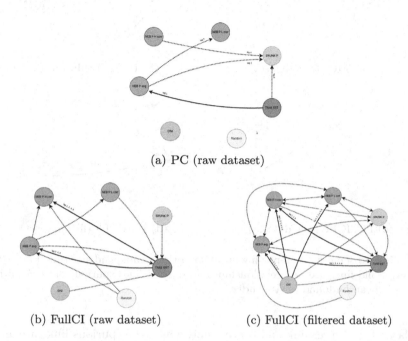

(a) PC (raw dataset)

(b) FullCI (raw dataset)   (c) FullCI (filtered dataset)

Fig. 5. Results of methods employing linear conditional independence test (Partial Correlation). PC result with filtered dataset was suppressed due to no link detection. Solid lines are real relationships and dashed lines spurious ones. Additional information can be found in Appendix.

The results for PCMCI and PCMCI+ employing linear conditional independence test are shown in Fig. 6. PCMCI succeed in detecting most of the expected links but the price paid was to also detect a lot of spurious links. When using filtered dataset, PCMCI detected all true links, but had much more spurious links and detected lags than the raw dataset results and had much more bidirectional links and much lower p-values. On the other hand, PCMCI+ had very few spurious links, but also very few true links. All links had p-value lower than 0.01.

When the non-linear conditional tests were employed, Fig. 7 and Fig. 8, no significant improvement was seen compared to Partial Correlation. Except for Fig. 7(c), which has four spurious links and PCMCI+ results had no links.

PCMCI with GPDC and CMI keeps detecting the correct links and had a slightly increase in the amount of spurious links, which most of them are bidirectional. Compared to filtered dataset, Fig. 7(b), PCMCI with GPDC using

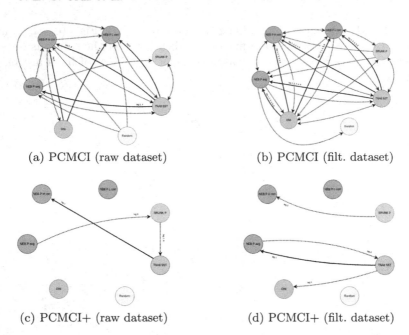

(a) PCMCI (raw dataset)   (b) PCMCI (filt. dataset)

(c) PCMCI+ (raw dataset)   (d) PCMCI+ (filt. dataset)

Fig. 6. Results of methods employing linear conditional independence test (Partial Correlation). Solid lines are real relationships and dashed lines spurious ones. Additional information can be found in Appendix.

raw dataset has lower link and lag amount, where the spurious links are among precipitation nodes themselves or caused by the random time series, precipitations and TNAtl SST. When the p-value threshold is decreased to 0.01, shown in Appendix, the spurious links among precipitation nodes are still present, and so the precipitation causing TNAtl SST.

Employing CMI, as shown in Fig. 8, PCMCI also detected a lot of spurious links, i.e. precipitation causing ONI and TNAtl SST, and the random time series causing and being caused by precipitation nodes. Decreasing the p-value to lower than 0.01 does not help either to improve the accuracy.

One general conclusion regarding the method results that employ statistical test is that the method accuracy do not get much better when the threshold is decreased to 0.01 or lower. Most of link detection already have a very low p-value. When the filtered dataset was used, it considerably increased the occurrence of causal connections.

QRBS, SELVAR, SLARAC and LASAR have a scalar output and there is no preestablished threshold for these methods, then there are infinity thresholds that can be placed among data points. Thus, the approach employed is: if there is linear separability between classes (causal and non-causal), then it is established a threshold for each maximum lag value that could separate all the causal links from the non-causal links, with the lowest false positive rate possible. Figure 9 show

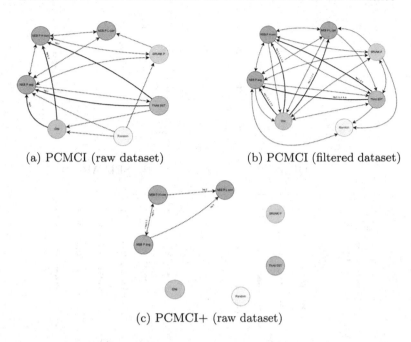

(a) PCMCI (raw dataset)   (b) PCMCI (filtered dataset)

(c) PCMCI+ (raw dataset)

Fig. 7. Results of methods employing non-linear conditional independence tests GPDC. PCMCI+ result with filtered dataset was suppressed due to no link detection. Solid lines are real relationships and dashed lines spurious ones. Additional information can be found in Appendix.

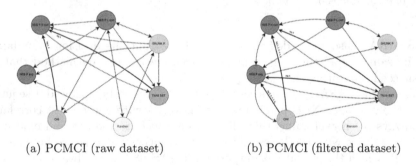

(a) PCMCI (raw dataset)   (b) PCMCI (filtered dataset)

Fig. 8. Results of methods employing non-linear conditional independence test CMI. PCMCI+ results were suppressed due to no link detection. Solid lines are real relationships and dashed lines spurious ones. Additional information can be found in Appendix.

the filtered dataset results and them clearly do not show any linear separability between classes, not allowing then, to establish a threshold.

Strip plots of scalar method outputs using the raw dataset are shown in Fig. 10, where most results had a linear separation between classes. SELVAR, Fig. 10(b), is the method that had the best separation between classes. QRBS

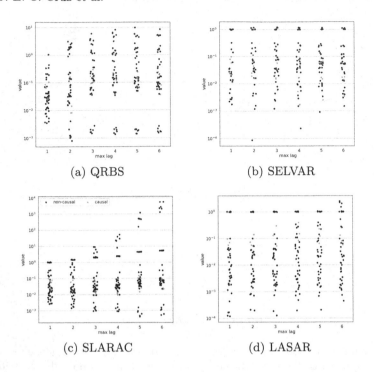

(a) QRBS   (b) SELVAR

(c) SLARAC   (d) LASAR

Fig. 9. Strip plots of the scalar output methods for filtered data, where y-axis is related to the causal detection and x-axis is the maximum time lag used for each execution, where one lag unit is one month.

and SLARAC also succeeded to separate classes but the decision boundary is not the same for all time lags. Finally, LASAR was the only method that did not succeed separating the classes properly.

Except for LASAR, the causal link outputs (blue dots) followed a sequence where the Northern NEB precipitation time series with the highest correlation had always the higher value, then the average precipitation one and finally, the NEB time series with the lowest correlation. Another pattern also happened in SELVAR, which the causal link outputs for TNAtl SST were always higher than the ones for ONI. In the four strip plots in Fig. 10, there is a red dot which sometimes appear near to an isolated blue dot on the boundary of the classes. It is correspondent to SRUNK average precipitation, which sometimes refers to the link with ONI, other times from TNAtl.

In general, they had much better performance and accuracy than the previous methods using both datasets. QRBS, SELVAR, and SLARAC correctly detected the causal effect of ONI and TNAtl SST on the Northern NEB precipitations. However, QRSB and LASAR detected the causal link from ONI to SRUNK precipitation.

The significant correlation values between SRUNK precipitation and TNAtl SST, shown in Fig. 1(b), was also detected by QRBS, SELVAR, and SLARAC.

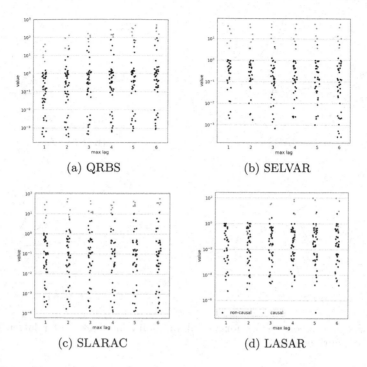

           (a) QRBS   (b) SELVAR

          (c) SLARAC   (d) LASAR

Fig. 10. Strip plots of the scalar output methods for raw dataset, where y-axis is related to the causal detection and x-axis is the maximum time lag used for each execution, where one lag unit is one month.

That fact is obviously not conclusive at all, but it may indicate a possible connection between them [15]. Another possibility is that there are other variables (confounders) that were not taken into account in this study that influence both variables creating a false impression of causal link.

4.3   Detection Comparison

Table 1 consolidates the result and allows a better comparison. The metrics for comparison are the True Positive rate, which is the percentage of correct links detected, and the False Positive rate which is the amount of spurious links detected divided by the total amount of possible spurious links. Even though some methods detect unitary time lags, the comparison will be done by the percentage of correct or incorrect links, because there is a group of methods that uses range of lags instead of unitary ones, thus making impossible a lag-wise comparison. The best methods are SELVAR and SLARAC with raw dataset, which detected all the expected links and just one spurious link each. QRBS also detected all expected links but detected two spurious ones, which one of them is the relationship $ONI \rightarrow SRUNK$. The most recent method from the statistical group, PCMCI+, had a very poor result for either datasets and

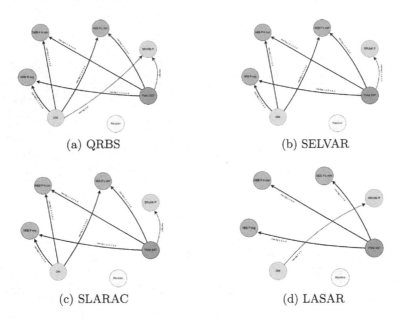

(a) QRBS   (b) SELVAR

(c) SLARAC   (d) LASAR

Fig. 11. Scalar method results for raw data. Solid lines are real relationships and dashed lines spurious ones.

conditional independence test types. In general, most of results with non-linear independence tests did not even detect a link.

In average, the results obtained using the filtered dataset increased the spurious link amount and lags detected. What was supposed to improve performance due to the theoretical removal of unnecessary information, produced the opposite effect. Analyzing each method individually, they performed better when employing partial correlation than non-linear tests.

4.4   Temporal Stability

This section presents some experiments that check the temporal stability of the best methods found in Table 1. The first one is regard growing time window, starting with 12 months and with a 6 month step, and has the objective to check the minimum window length and the method sensitivity over time. The second one employs temporal sliding windows, with 20 and 40 year length and also with a 6 month step, and has the objective to check if there are significant oscillations in the causal output with a fixed window size over time. The analysis is done for TNAtl and ONI causing NEB precipitations, TNAtl causing SRUNK average precipitation, and the main (the highest and the second highest) non-causal links, as well the average for the rest of non-causal links. Due to the best results, the dataset used was the raw one.

The growing window experiment, Fig. 12, shows that SELVAR outputs had several discontinuities while SLARAC did not. The time series in SELVAR that

Table 1. Method ranking according to True Positive and False Positive rate.

Method	Dataset	TP rate	FP rate
SELVAR	raw	100%	2.8%
SLARAC	raw	100%	2.8%
QRBS	raw	100%	5.6%
PCMCI + ParCorr	filtered	100%	63.9%
Granger	filtered	100%	66.7%
PCMCI + GPDC	filtered	100%	77.8%
PCMCI + ParCorr	raw	83.3%	33.3%
Granger	raw	83.3%	52.8%
FullCI + ParCorr	filtered	83.3%	55.6%
PCMCI + GPDC	raw	66.7%	44.4%
LASAR	raw	50%	2.8%
PCMCI + CMI	filtered	50%	36.1%
FullCI + ParCorr	raw	33.3%	22.2%
PCMCI + CMI	raw	33.3%	44.4%
PCMCIPlus + ParCorr	raw	16.7%	8.3%
PCMCIPlus + ParCorr	filtered	16.7%	8.3%
PC + ParCorr	raw	16.7%	11.1%
PC + ParCorr	filtered	0%	0%
PCMCIPlus + CMI	raw	0%	0%
PCMCIPlus + CMI	filtered	0%	0%
PCMCIPlus + GPDC	filtered	0%	0%
PCMCIPlus + GPDC	raw	0%	11.1%

had discontinuities are: *ONI → NEB P H corr.*, *ONI → NEB P avg.*, *ONI → NEB P L corr.*, *TNAtl SST → SRUNK avg.*, and *TNAtl SST → NEB P L corr.* Another point to note in SELVAR is that the highest (non-causal 1st H value) and the second highest (non-causal 2nd H value) value for non-causal links in max lag 1 are almost always higher than the *TNAtl SST → SRUNK avg.* link, while on the other max lags that behavior did not happen after 12-year length. The behavior seen in SLARAC outputs are totally different. After 10-year length almost all max lags got stabilized. The only one that have some oscillations was in max lag 1, where ONI links do not go so straight. Analyzing all max lags, it is possible to see that ONI outputs become higher than TNAtl ones and as the max lag get higher, the non-causal average value tends to stay more time near to 1.

The second experiment uses sliding windows, which lengths – 20 and 40 years – were chosen, because it is when SLARAC and SELVAR start to get stabilized. SELVAR had plenty of discontinuities before the length of 35 years. As shown in Fig. 13(a), with a sliding window of 20-year length it still has a lot of discontinuities, but most of them vanishes after 1980. Except for *TNAtl SST → SRUNK avg.* and its discontinuities in max lag with 1, after 1980 the separability of causal and non-causal has the same aspect what was seen with full-length time series, Fig. 12(a).

The SLARAC results for the 20-year sliding window show almost the same behavior of the full-length time series: ONI links get higher than TNAtl links

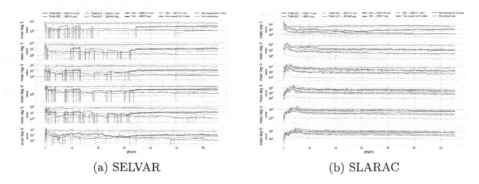

(a) SELVAR   (b) SLARAC

Fig. 12. Results using raw data and growing window with 12 months of initial length and 6 months of incremental step.

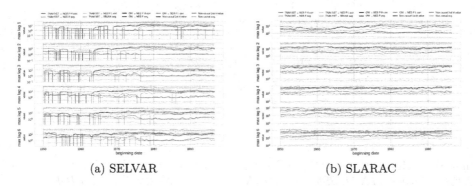

(a) SELVAR   (b) SLARAC

Fig. 13. Results using raw data and sliding window with 20 year length.

over the max lags, all the outputs are sort of stable except for max lag 1, and *TNAtl SST → SRUNK avg.* is higher than the other non-causal time-series in max lag 2. The differences are: *TNAtl SST → SRUNK avg.* get detached from the non-causal class after 1987 in max lag 1, and most of times in max lag 4, 5, and 6 *TNAtl SST → NEB P L corr.* stays inside or very near to the non-causal class.

When a 40-year length sliding window was used, Fig. 14, the outputs in SELVAR got much less discontinuities when comparing to the 20-year window, a fact already expected. The only time series that still experienced discontinuities were *TNAtl SST → SRUNK avg.* in max lag 1 and *TNAtl SST → NEB P L corr.* in all max lags. On the other hand, SLARAC had pretty much the same behavior of the prior sliding window experiment.

A point of attention regarding the prior charts – Fig. 12, 13, and 14 – is that *TNAtl SST → SRUNK avg.*, *TNAtl SST → NEB P L corr.*, and *ONI → NEB P L corr.*, had several issues in the growing window or sliding window experiments, what may suggest that their causal link may not be so strong as the other ones or not that consistent over time.

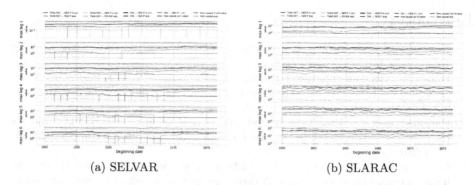

(a) SELVAR   (b) SLARAC

Fig. 14. Results using raw data and sliding window with 40 year length.

5   Conclusion

Several studies have employed causal detection methods in climate time series, but none of them in the connection of ENSO and ITCZ to the Northeastern Brazil precipitation. Moreover, it is not clear on the literature what scenarios each method performs better. Then, the goal of this study was to evaluate the performance of time series causal detection methods on the aforementioned phenomena. Nine methods were used, but only two had a satisfactory performance: SLARAC and SELVAR. Moreover, the employment of filtered time series also degraded the detection performance of the methods.

There are two facts that must be highlighted about the top three methods – SELVAR, SLARAC, and QRBS. First, besides the good performance, they were even able to detect causation properly even when the correlation was very low. That is the case of the link from ONI to NEB precipitation time series. Second, they detected causation of TNAtl SST on SRUNK precipitation which they have a significant correlation for the first lags. It is definetly not conclusive, however, it may suggest the existence of a real connection or it may be simply just the result of a confounder variable that was not considered in this study.

The temporal stability experiments did not show any other significant oscillation, besides the already expect discontinuities in SELVAR. Nevertheless, the discontinuities of *TNAtl SST → SRUNK avg.* and *ONI → NEB P L corr.* in SELVAR and the fact *TNAtl SST → NEB P L corr.* most of the time (SLARAC with max lag 4, 5, and 6) stayed within or quite near to the non-causal cluster, may suggest that their causal link strength may not be as strong as the other ones.

The employment of SLARAC and SELVAR had good results indeed, but there are some caveats to be considered. It is not possible to know the exact time lag of a causal connection detection. The second point is that the window length is a very important parameter, which the longest, normally the better and the more stable. Another critical parameter is the threshold for causal and non-causal separability. In scenarios where there is no ground truth for finding the best threshold, some experiments should be firstly conducted in order to define the value range of causal and non-causal samples.

References

1. Ambrizzi, T., de Souza, E.B., Pulwarty, R.S.: The hadley and walker regional circulations and associated ENSO impacts on south american seasonal rainfall. In: Diaz, H.F., Bradley, R.S. (eds.) The Hadley Circulation: Present, Past and Future. AGCR, vol. 21, pp. 203–235. Springer, Dordrecht (2004). https://doi.org/10.1007/978-1-4020-2944-8_8
2. Canedo-Rosso, C., Uvo, C.B., Berndtsson, R.: Precipitation variability and its relation to climate anomalies in the bolivian altiplano. Int. J. Climatol. **39**(4), 2096–2107 (2019)
3. Di Capua, G., et al.: Tropical and mid-latitude teleconnections interacting with the indian summer monsoon rainfall: A theory-guided causal effect network approach. Earth Syst. Dynam. **11**, 17–34 (2020)
4. Du, X., Hendy, I., Hinnov, L., Brown, E., Zhu, J., Poulsen, C.J.: High-resolution interannual precipitation reconstruction of southern california: Implications for holocene enso evolution. Earth Planet. Sci. Lett. **554**, 116670 (2021)
5. Eichler, M.: Causal inference in time series analysis. Wiley Online Library (2012)
6. Garcia, S.R., Kayano, M.T.: Some evidence on the relationship between the south american monsoon and the atlantic itcz. Theoret. Appl. Climatol. **99**(1), 29–38 (2010)
7. Glantz, M.H., Ramirez, I.J.: Reviewing the oceanic niño index (oni) to enhance societal readiness for el niño's impacts. Int. J. Disaster Risk Sci. **11**, 394–403 (2020)
8. Granger, C.W.: Investigating causal relations by econometric models and cross-spectral methods. Econometrica: J. Econom. Soc., 424–438 (1969)
9. Guo, R., Cheng, L., Li, J., Hahn, P.R., Liu, H.: A survey of learning causality with data: Problems and methods. arXiv preprint arXiv:1809.09337 (2018)
10. Hastenrath, S.: Prediction of northeast brazil rainfall anomalies. J. Clim. **3**(8), 893–904 (1990)
11. Hastenrath, S.: Circulation and teleconnection mechanisms of northeast brazil droughts. Prog. Oceanogr. **70**(2–4), 407–415 (2005)
12. Hoerl, A.E., Kennard, R.W.: Ridge regression: Biased estimation for nonorthogonal problems. Technometrics **12**(1), 55–67 (1970)
13. Kane, R.: Prediction of droughts in north-east brazil: Role of enso and use of periodicities. Int. J. Climatol. **17**(6), 655–665 (1997)
14. Kretschmer, M., Coumou, D., Donges, J.F., Runge, J.: Using causal effect networks to analyze different arctic drivers of midlatitude winter circulation. J. Clim. **29**(11), 4069–4081 (2016)
15. Lim, Y.K.: The east atlantic/west russia (ea/wr) teleconnection in the north atlantic: climate impact and relation to rossby wave propagation. Clim. Dyn. **44**(11–12), 3211–3222 (2014)
16. Lin, J., Qian, T.: A new picture of the global impacts of el nino-southern oscillation. Sci. Rep. **9**(1), 1–7 (2019)
17. Malinsky, D., Danks, D.: Causal discovery algorithms: A practical guide. Philos Compass **13**(1), e12470 (2018)
18. Marengo, J.A., Torres, R.R., Alves, L.M.: Drought in northeast brazil-past, present, and future. Theoret. Appl. Climatol. **129**(3–4), 1189–1200 (2017)
19. Pearl, J.: Causality: models, reasoning and inference, vol. 29. Springer (2000)
20. Pearl, J., et al.: Causal inference in statistics: An overview. Stat. Surv. **3**, 96–146 (2009)

21. Runge, J.: Causal network reconstruction from time series: From theoretical assumptions to practical estimation. Chaos Interdis. J. Nonlinear Sci. **28**(7), 310 (2018)
22. Runge, J.: Discovering contemporaneous and lagged causal relations in autocorrelated nonlinear time series datasets. In: Proceedings of the 36th Conference on Uncertainty in Artificial Intelligence, vol. 124, pp. 1388–1397. PLMR (2020)
23. Runge, J., et al.: Inferring causation from time series in earth system sciences. Nat. Commun. **10**(1), 2553 (2019)
24. Runge, J., Nowack, P., Kretschmer, M., Flaxman, S., Sejdinovic, D.: Detecting and quantifying causal associations in large nonlinear time series datasets. Sci. Adv. **5**(11), 4996 (2019)
25. Runge, J., et al.: Identifying causal gateways and mediators in complex spatio-temporal systems. Nat. Commun. **6**, 8502 (2015)
26. Runge, J., Petoukhov, V., Kurths, J.: Quantifying the strength and delay of climatic interactions: The ambiguities of cross correlation and a novel measure based on graphical models. J. Clim. **27**(2), 720–739 (2014)
27. Shaman, J.: The seasonal effects of enso on european precipitation: Observational analysis. J. Clim. **27**(17), 6423–6438 (2014)
28. Spirtes, P., Glymour, C.: An algorithm for fast recovery of sparse causal graphs. Soc. Sci. Comput. Rev. **9**(1), 62–72 (1991)
29. Tibshirani, R.: Regression shrinkage and selection via the lasso. J. Roy. Stat. Soc.: Ser. B (Methodol.) **58**(1), 267–288 (1996)
30. Torrence, C., Compo, G.P.: A practical guide to wavelet analysis. Bull. Am. Meteor. Soc. **79**(1), 61–78 (1998)
31. Weichwald, S., Jakobsen, M.E., Mogensen, P.B., Petersen, L., Thams, N., Varando, G.: Causal structure learning from time series: Large regression coefficients may predict causal links better in practice than small p-values. In: NeurIPS 2019 Competition and Demonstration Track, pp. 27–36. PMLR (2020)

An Approach for Team Formation Using Modified Grey Wolf Optimizer

Sandip T. Shingade and Rajdeep Niyogi[✉]

Indian Institute of Technology Roorkee, Roorkee 247667, India
{stukaram,rajdeep.niyogi}@cs.iitr.ac.in

Abstract. The team formation problem is to find a subset of agents, referred to as a team, from a given set of agents such that the team satisfies some desirable property. The computational complexity of this problem is known to be NP-hard. In this paper, we suggest a modified grey wolf optimization approach to find a team with minimum communication cost. The proposed algorithm is evaluated with two real-world data sets, namely the ACM data set and the Academia Stack exchange data set. The experimental results show that the algorithm outperforms some existing approaches with respect to some parameters.

Keywords: Team formation · GWO · JAYA · IGWO

1 Introduction

Team formation is a vital task in many applications, such as hiring experts in the industry, working on project groups, and product development. Team formation is required in mission-oriented applications. For instance, in order to rescue people affected by an accident, a rescue team would typically consist of different types of agents, with distinct skills, such as policemen, ambulances and doctors, and cranes. The team should perform the rescue act and medical treatment with efficient collaboration using their expertise and within a specific deadline as per the severity and emergency of the accident. The team members should communicate among themselves and a team with minimum communication cost is desirable.

Given a set of agents, description of agents and tasks, the computational complexity to find a subset of the agents (team) with minimal cost for a task is known to be NP-hard. In this paper, we suggest a metaheuristic approach to finding a team with minimal communication cost. The approach is a modified grey wolf optimization technique.

The rest of the paper is organized as follows. In Sect. 2, we describe related work for team formation problems. In Sect. 3 we provide some motivations for using metaheuristic-based approaches. Some preliminary notions are given in Sect. 4. The proposed approach is discussed in Sect. 5. Experimental results are given in Sect. 6. Conclusions are drawn in Sect. 7.

© The Author(s), under exclusive license to Springer Nature Switzerland AG 2023
O. Gervasi et al. (Eds.): ICCSA 2023, LNCS 13956, pp. 440–452, 2023.
https://doi.org/10.1007/978-3-031-36805-9_29

2   Related Work

An effective team with a distance diameter and minimum spanning tree as a communication framework is suggested in [1]. In [6,7] the authors identify the distance for each team member with and without a team leader effectively and collaboratively in a social network. The expert team formation where the agents are connected using a social network is studied in [8,9].

A new approach based on a genetic algorithm for finding multiple teams to fulfill the requirements of multiple projects with socially connected people is proposed in [2]. A sociometric matrix has been used for calculating the positive relationship between people. In [11], the authors suggest a genetic algorithm-based approach for group formation in collaborative learning, considering multiple student characteristics to achieve groups. They experimented with college students considering three characteristics: an estimate of student knowledge levels, student communicative skills, and student leadership skills. The results obtained show that groups formed with the proposed method produced better outcomes than those formed with traditional methods like random assignment and self-organization.

In [5], the authors utilize the particle swarm optimization (PSO) algorithm for solving a team formation problem by minimizing the communication cost among the agents. The authors applied a new swap operator within PSO to ensure the consistency of the capabilities and the skills to perform the required project. They also applied the algorithm to different experiments with standard PSO by considering different numbers of agents and skills.

In [3], the authors proposed the Improved African Buffalo Optimization algorithm (IABO) where a new concept of swap sequence was applied to improve the performance by generating better team members that cover all the required skills. An improved JAYA algorithm with a modified swap operator is introduced by in [4]. They also compared the results with GA and PSO, ABO, and standard JAYA improved JAYA algorithm with a modified swap operator. All these papers apply modified swap operations and compare them with standard heuristic team formation algorithms.

In [13], the authors focus on a simple and new JAYA algorithm for solving constrained and unconstrained optimization problems. This algorithm is based on the concept that the solution obtained for a given problem should move toward the best solution and avoid the worst solution. It requires only the standard control parameters and does not require any algorithm-specific control parameters [12]. A self-adaptive multi-population-based JAYA (SAMP-JAYA) algorithm for solving the constrained and unconstrained numerical and engineering optimization problems is proposed by [13]. The search mechanism of the JAYA algorithm is upgraded by using the multi-population search scheme. The algorithm is compared and evaluated with the other latest algorithms, and JAYA showed better performance.

Most of works used only one heuristic approach with methodologies such as MSO or GA. If the algorithm changes the parameters and applies an objective function, it always gives better results. In [14], the authors reduced the data by applying state space reduction techniques for horizontal and vertical reduction. Further improvements on the earlier heuristic approaches based on MSO, GA can be obtained using GWO (Grey Wolf Optimizer) [10].

3 Metaheuristic-Based Approach for Team Formation

The motivation for using a metaheuristic-based approach is due to the following reasons: The metaheuristic-based approach is a simple evolutionary notion of studying animal behaviour. It appears like a black box testing only focusing on final optimized results. These techniques also provide a random solution without calculating derivation search space to find an optimal solution. This first derivative decides the direction, and the second derivative minimizes or maximizes optimization results. It also works on avoiding stagnation for a local solution and extensively searches for the entire solution; however, there is no metaheuristic approach to best solve all optimization problems [10].

3.1 Grey Wolf Optimization

A metaheuristic optimization technique called GWO [10] was developed as a result of studying how grey wolves hunt in the wild. GWO is a population-based method that begins with an initial population of wolves, which stand in for potential solutions to an optimization problem. There are four groups of wolves in the population: alpha, beta, delta, and omega. In a pack, the alpha wolf is the best one and the omega wolf is the worst. In order for the algorithm to function, the population's distribution of wolves is updated after each iteration. Based on the locations of the alpha, beta, and delta wolves, each wolf's position is updated.

3.2 JAYA Algorithm

A population-based metaheuristic approach called JAYA algorithm was sugggested in [12]. Since it does not require parameters to be set, unlike other metaheuristic algorithms, it is a simple approach that was created primarily for continuous optimization problems. The algorithm was developed with the intention of handling both constrained and unconstrained optimization functions. This algorithm blends features of evolutionary algorithms with swarm-based intelligence. The search process looks for the best solutions available in an effort to increase the likelihood of success and looks to prevent failure by avoiding the worst options. This method has several advantages over other population-based algorithms, including being straightforward to use and not requiring any algorithm-specific settings (i.e., the population size, and a maximum number of iterations). The objective function of JAYA algorithm is given below.

$$X_{j,k}^{t+1} = X_{j,k}^t + r_{1,j}^t[(X_{j,\text{best}}^t) - |(X_{j,k}^t)|] - r_{2,j}^t[(X_{j,\text{worst}}^t) - |(X_{j,k}^t)|]$$

Fig. 1. JAYA objective function.

4   Preliminaries

4.1   Team Formation with Minimum Communication Cost

The Team Formation (TF) problem is a combinatorial optimization problem that involves grouping individuals into teams based on their skills, preferences, and other characteristics. The goal is to form teams that are both effective and efficient, and meet specific constraints or objectives.

Definition 1 (Team Formation). *Given: a set of agents, skills of agents, and tasks. An agent has a set of skills (abilities). A task is defined by a set of skills. Team formation problem is to find a subset of agents whose combined skills (union of the skills of the individual agents) is a superset of the skills required for the task.*

Definition 2 (Communication Graph). *A communication graph $G = (V, E)$ is an undirected weighted graph where the set of vertices are the agents and an edge (u, v) is given a weight w, $0 \leq w \leq 1$, where low weight means that the agents can communicate easily.*

Definition 3 (Communication Cost (CC) of two agents). *Let the agents A_i, A_j have skills S_i, S_j respectively. The communication cost of the agents is given as:*

$$CC_{i,j} = 1 - |(S_i \cap S_j)|/|(S_i \cup S_j)| \tag{1}$$

Figure 2 shows the communication cost among the agents. The skills of the agents are given in Table 1.

Table 1. Skills of the agents

Agent	Agent Skills		
A_1	agent computing	distributed data mining	intrusion detection
A_2	speech acts	agent computing	-
A_3	security	social dynamics	multi agent systems
A_4	agent computing	model checking	verification
A_5	machine learning	multi agent systems	advice exchange

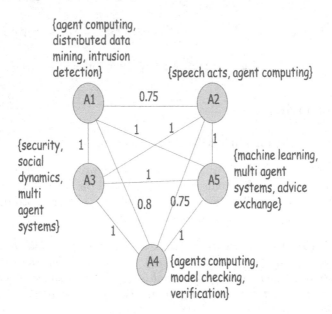

Fig. 2. ACM database example of team formation in social networks.

Definition 4 (Total Communication Cost of a team (TC)). *Let a team comprise of the agents $A_1, \ldots, A_m$, $m > 1$. Let the communication graph for the team be $G = (V, E)$, where $V = \{A_1, \ldots, A_m\}$, and $CC_{i,j}$ is the weight of the edge (A_i, A_j). Then TC is the sum of the weights of all the edges in G.*

A task requires the following skills: {*agent computing, multi-agent systems, model checking, machine learning* }. Some of the possible teams are: $T_1 = \{A_1, A_3, A_4, A_5\}$. The communication cost of the team is the sum of the weights of the edges connecting the team members. The edges are: (A_1, A_3), (A_1, A_4), (A_1, A_5),(A_3, A_4), (A_3, A_5), and (A_4, A_5). The weights of the edges are 1, 0.8, 1, 1, 1, and 1 respectively. Therefore the communication cost of the team is equal to 5.8. Similarly, for $T_2 = \{A_2, A_3, A_4, A_5\}$, $T_3 = \{A_1, A_4, A_5\}$, $T_4 = \{A_4, A_5\}$, the communication costs are 5.75, 2.8, and 1.0 respectively.

The goal of the proposed metaheuristic algorithm is to find the team with minimum communication cost. For the above example, the team T_4 is thus selected.

5 Proposed Improved Grey Wolf Optimization (IGWO) Algorithm

The pseudocode of our metaheuristic approach based on GWO that we refer to as IGWO, Improved Grey wolf optimization is shown in Fig. 3 and the flowchart is given in Fig. 4. We now give a detailed illustration of our algorithm using an example scenario taken from the Stack exchange dataset.

Algorithm: Improved Grey Wolf Optimization Algorithm (IGWO)

Input: P- Number of wolves in the population, MaxIter-Maximum
number of iterations, S- Number of skills
Output: The best solution found (alpha)

1. Initialize the positions of alpha, beta, and delta wolves randomly
    within the search space
2. Initialize the iteration counter c := 0
3. for (i = 1; i <= S; i++)
4.   for (j = 1; j <= P; j++)
5.   Generate the initial population randomly x_{ij}^c
6.   end for
7. end for
8. Evaluate the fitness function for the population $f(x)^c$ of
    bestAlpha solution
9. do
10.   for (i = 1; i <= S; i++)
11.   for (j = 1; j <= P; j++)
12.   Apply crossover on the best solution $x_{alp\,ha}^c$ and current
               solution x_{ck}^c
13.   Select the best offspring solution x_{best}^c and update the
               solution
14.   if $f(x_{ij}^{c+1})$ <= $f(x_{alp\,ha}^c)$ then
15. $x_{alp\,ha}^c = x_{ij}^{c+1}$
16.   else
17. $x_{alp\,ha}^c = x_{alp\,ha}^c$
18.   end if
19.   end for
20.   end for
21.   Increment the iteration counter $c = c + 1$
22.   Update the position of search agents alpha, beta and gama to
       determine optimized best alpha solution
23. While (c < MaxIter)
24. Get the best solution alpha

Fig. 3. Algorithm: Improved Grey Wolf Optimization Algorithm (IGWO).

Initialization step:

– We take an initial population of size 100 and the maximum number of iterations is 25.
– Each agent's id and its skills are represented as key : [value] pair. For example,
  160429 : [writing, writing-style, peer-review] where 160429 is the agent id and
  [writing, writing-style, peer-review] are the skills.
– We consider a task and the number of skills required to fulfill the task.
  We identify the agents for each skill. For example, the four skills that
  are required to complete a task are   [**computer science, graduate-
  admissions, graduate-school, research process**]. The agents for each
  skill are: computer science: [14842, 149199, 139056, 173659,.....] graduate-
  admissions: [11702, 16206, 14251, 14844,......] graduate-school: [16766, 21628,

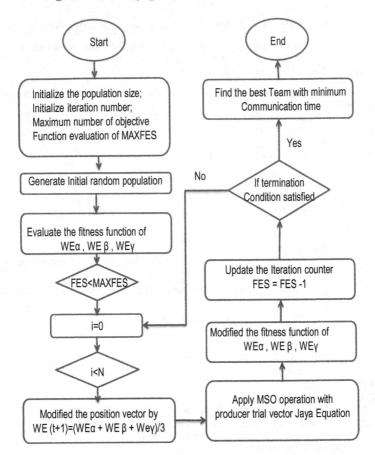

Fig. 4. Flow chart of IGWO algorithm for minimization communication time.

151956, 11849, 25785,....] research-process: [184, 534, 43201, 48875, 11498, 16270,...]

Evaluation step:

- Generate a random population of the given list of agents as shown in Table 2. We consider a population size of 100 and each solution (team) has four agents (team size).
- Find the communication cost between any two agents according to Definition 4. Determine the communication cost of each team according to Definition 4, shown in Table 3. The team for population number 83 has minimum communication cost 0.63.

- Determine the best search agent (alpha), second best agent (beta) and third best agent (delta). The alpha solution is **0.66** at position 61. The beta solution

Table 2. Random population/teams of the given list of agents

Population No.	Solution			
1	161227	32336	161676	13455
2	145368	13491	14515	54913
3	36965	17778	161676	186739
–	–	–	–	–
–	–	–	–	–
99	173150	77220	38259	170157
100	37428	154770	58514	5580

Table 3. Total communication cost of a team

Population No.	Solution				TC
1	107149	140092	169846	40326	0.95
2	12076	44002	127021	34316	0.98
3	61014	173938	9359	180514	1.03
–	–	–	–	–	
–	–	–	–	–	
83	47634	42379	123167	11264	**0.63**
–	–	–	–	–	
–	–	–	–	–	
99	156469	184696	155922	86273	1.06
100	162140	88080	6054	76265	1.04

is **0.73** at position 45. The delta solution is **0.74** at position 48. This is obtained from Table 3.

- Apply a swap operation that works as follows. Consider the *jth* column of any two populations numbered, say P_1 and P_2; $swap(P_1, P_2, j)$ means the agents at position j corresponding to these populations are interchanged. Accordingly the total communication cost of the teams would change.
- Apply the objective function of JAYA algorithm (Fig. 1).
- Update the positions of each search agent. The Alpha solution Instance value is **0.63** at position 83. The Beta solution Instance value is **0.66** at position 66. The Delta solution Instance value is **0.69** at position 92.

Output step:

- The team obtained for the given task is 47634, 42379, 123167, 11264 with a final cost of **0.63**.

6   Experimental Results

For the implementations we used Python with Jypytor notebook with i7 core CPU having 16 GB RAM. We have compared the performance of IGWO with other algorithms JAYA, GWO, and modified JAYA. We have used two real-world data sets namely Academia stack exchange data set and ACM data set for the evaluations.

ACM Dataset. To evaluate our technique, we used the real-world ACM dataset. We collect data on author collaboration based on the agent's research expertise and construct a table for this data, that has 3856 lines of data.

Stack Exchange Dataset. To evaluate our approach, we employed another real-world Academia stack exchange dataset. We collect data with author cooperation skills in this data produced table that has 5730 lines of data, and if another author cites with his article, we state that they will connect with data. We also consider it related if any author shares their content with another author. We will look at the most crucial abilities, such as computer science, graduate entrance, graduate school, research procedure, conferences, and journal articles.

6.1   Parameter Setting

For all experiments we consider a population size of 100. We do five trials in succession with a variety of skills, 2 with 5 iterations, 3 with 10 iterations, 4 with 15 iterations, 5 with 20 iterations, and 6 with 25 iterations.

Table 4. Communication cost for ACM dataset.

Exp No	No of skill	Iterations	JAYA	IJMSO	GWO	IGWO
1	2	5	0.02	0.02	0.02	**0.02**
2	3	10	0.08	0.07	0.07	**0.06**
3	4	15	0.17	0.16	0.22	**0.18**
4	5	20	0.19	0.21	0.23	**0.18**
5	6	25	0.43	0.42	0.41	**0.33**

Table 5. Communication cost for academia stackexchange dataset.

Exp No	No of skill	Iterations	JAYA	IJMSO	GWO	**IGWO**
1	2	5	0.1	0.1	0.1	**0.1**
2	3	10	0.32	0.32	0.32	**0.3**
3	4	15	0.74	0.7	0.66	**0.66**
4	5	20	1.16	1.2	1.24	**1.13**
5	6	25	1.64	1.7	1.87	**1.55**

In all the simulations, IGWO algorithm outperformed JAYA, IJMSO, and GWO algorithms on both the datasets in terms of communication cost, as demonstrated in Tables 4 and 5. The IGWO technique yielded communication cost parameters of 0.02 and 0.1 for experiment 1, 0.06 and 0.3 for experiment 2, 0.18 and 0.66 for experiment 3, 0.18 and 1.13 for experiment 4, and 0.33 and 1.55 for experiment 5. For the other three techniques, the communication cost parameter values ranged from 0.02 to 0.42 for the ACM dataset and from 0.1 to 1.55 for academia stackexchange dataset.

Table 6. Communication cost for ACM dataset (Sample Mean).

Exp No	No of skill	Iterations	JAYA	IJMSO	GWO	IGWO
1	2	5	0.0608	0.0656	0.0644	**0.0583**
2	3	10	0.1732	0.1755	0.1682	**0.1841**
3	4	15	0.3657	0.3913	0.4028	**0.3816**
4	5	20	0.6484	0.6554	0.668	**0.6683**
5	6	25	1.1113	1.1114	1.1166	**1.196**

Table 7. Communication cost for academia stackexchange dataset (Sample Mean).

Exp No	No of skill	Iterations	JAYA	IJMSO	GWO	**IGWO**
1	2	5	0.1493	0.1583	0.1521	**0.1506**
2	3	10	0.4945	0.5006	0.4891	**0.5106**
3	4	15	1.0252	0.1074	1.0267	**0.9961**
4	5	20	1.6476	1.6576	1.6394	**1.6393**
5	6	25	2.4332	2.4442	2.4501	**2.4339**

In all simulations utilising Sample Mean, the IGWO algorithm technique outperformed the other three algorithms (JAYA, IJMSO, and GWO) in terms of the communication cost parameter, as demonstrated in Table 6 and 7. The communication cost parameter of the IGWO algorithm was 0.0583 and 0.1506 in experiment 1, 0.1841 and 0.5106 in experiment 2, 0.3816 and 0.9961 in experiment 3, 0.6683 and 1.6393 in experiment 4, and 1.196 and 2.4339 in experiment 5. During the same experiments, the communication cost parameter values for the other three algorithms ranged from 0.0608 to 1.1116 for the ACM dataset, and from 0.1493 to 2.4501 for the academia stackexchange dataset.

In all simulations utilising Standard deviatiaon, the IGWO algorithm technique outperformed the other three algorithms (JAYA, IJMSO, and GWO) in terms of the communication cost parameter, as demonstrated in Table 8 and Table 9. The communication cost parameter of the IGWO algorithm was 0.0318 and 0.045 in experiment 1, 0.0823 and 0.1199 in experiment 2, 0.1564 and 0.1744 in experiment 3, 0.2364 and 0.2073 in experiment 4, and 0.4364 and 0.2863 in

Table 8. Communication cost for ACM dataset (Std. Deviation).

Exp. No.	No. of skill	Iterations	JAYA	IJMSO	GWO	IGWO
1	2	5	0.0361	0.0328	0.0363	**0.0318**
2	3	10	0.085	0.0813	0.0671	**0.0823**
3	4	15	0.1151	0.1395	0.1324	**0.1564**
4	5	20	0.2134	0.2234	0.2074	**0.2364**
5	6	25	0.415	0.455	0.3751	**0.4364**

Table 9. Communication cost for academia stackexchange dataset (Std. Deviation).

Exp. No.	No. of skill	Iterations	JAYA	IJMSO	GWO	**IGWO**
1	2	5	0.0468	0.0534	0.0437	**0.045**
2	3	10	0.1124	0.1155	0.1081	**0.1199**
3	4	15	0.1737	0.1854	0.1796	**0.1744**
4	5	20	0.2295	0.2195	0.2244	**0.2073**
5	6	25	0.2847	0.2888	0.3142	**0.2863**

experiment 5. During the same experiments, the communication cost parameter values for the other three algorithms ranged from 0.0328 to 0.0328 for the ACM dataset, and from 0.0468 to 0.3142 for the academia stackexchange dataset.

Table 10. Computing time for ACM dataset.

Exp. No.	No. of skill	Iterations	JAYA	IJMSO	GWO	**IGWO**
1	2	5	0.02332	0.076825	0.010185	**3.6970048**
2	3	10	0.050389	0.355808	0.022542	**7.3005062**
3	4	15	0.096243	0.657781	0.061759	**10.7778158**
4	5	20	0.296295	0.306295	0.189573	**14.8616639**
5	6	25	2.266233	2.356233	1.461107	**21.3694483**

According to the experimental table data, IGWO algorithm required more computation time than the other three algorithms (JAYA, IJMSO, and GWO) for all tests in both the datasets, as demonstrated in Tables 10 and 11. IGWO algorithm required time around 3.697 to 21.369 s for ACM dataset and 3.737 to 27.976 s for academia stackexchange dataset. The computation time for the other three algorithms ranged from 0.023 to 1.461 s for ACM dataset and from 0.029 to 8.6 s for academia stackexchange dataset. IGWO is more complex than the other three algorithms and so it performs more computations to arrive at an optimal solution that is better than that obtained by the other three algorithms. For example, when the communication cost of IGWO is 0.33, the minimum cost

Table 11. Computing time for academia stackexchange dataset

Exp No	No of skill	Iterations	JAYA	IJMSO	GWO	IGWO
1	2	5	0.028943	0.071224	0.107659	**3.7368715**
2	3	10	0.037418	0.240848	0.010023	**7.3201007**
3	4	15	0.061079	0.461732	0.019232	**10.8939794**
4	5	20	0.221946	0.251246	0.11478	**14.6149771**
5	6	25	11.08188	12.13188	8.600857	**27.9755678**

obtained by the other algorithms is 0.41 (Table 4); similarly when when the communication cost of IGWO is 1.55, the minimum cost obtained by the other algorithms is 1.64 (Table 5).

7   Conclusion

In this paper, we proposed an improved grey wolf optimization technique to find a team with minimal communication cost. For the evaluation of the algorithm, we used two real-world data sets (Stack exchange data set, ACM data set). The output of our suggested algorithm shows a significant improvement in communication cost compared to state-of-the-art algorithms. As part of future work, we would like to develop metaheuristic approaches for team formation with multiple objectives.

Acknowledgement. The second author was in part supported by a research grant from Google.

References

1. Anagnostopoulos, A., Becchetti L., Castillo, C., Gionis, A., Leonardi, S.: Online team formation in social networks. In: Proceedings of the 21st international conference on World Wide Web, pp. 839–848 (2012)
2. Baghel, V.S., Bhavanim S.D.: Multiple team formation using an evolutionary approach. In: 2018 Eleventh International Conference on Contemporary Computing (IC3), pp. 1–6. IEEE (2018)
3. El-Ashmawi, W.H.: An improved african buffalo optimization algorithm for collaborative team formation in social network. Int. J. Inf. Technol. Comput. Sci. **10**, 16–29 (2018)
4. El-Ashmawi, W.H., Ali, A.F., Slowik, A.: An improved jaya algorithm with a modified swap operator for solving team formation problem. Soft. Comput. **24**(21), 16627–16641 (2020)
5. El-Ashmawi, W.H., Ali, A.F., Tawhid, M.A.: An improved particle swarm optimization with a new swap operator for team formation problem. J. Indust. Eng. Internat. **15**(1), 53–71 (2019)

6. Kargar, M., An, A.: Discovering top-k teams of experts with/without a leader in social networks. In: Proceedings of the 20th Acm International Conference On Information And Knowledge Management, pp. 985–994 (2011)
7. Kargar, M., Zihayat, M., An, A.: Finding affordable and collaborative teams from a network of experts. In Proceedings of the 2013 SIAM International Conference On Data Mining, pp. 587–595. SIAM (2013)
8. Lappas, T., Liu, K., Terzi, E.: Finding a team of experts in social networks. In: Proceedings of the 15th ACM SIGKDD International Conference On Knowledge Discovery and Data Mining, pp. 467–476 (2009)
9. Li, C.-T., Shan, M.-K.: Team formation for generalized tasks in expertise social networks. In: 2010 IEEE second International Conference on Social Computing, pp. 9–16. IEEE (2010)
10. Mirjalili, S., Mirjalili, S.M., Lewis, A.: Grey wolf optimizer. Adv. Eng. Softw. **69**, 46–61 (2014)
11. Moreno, J., Ovalle, D.A., Vicari, R.M.: A genetic algorithm approach for group formation in collaborative learning considering multiple student characteristics. Comput. Educ. **58**(1), 560–569 (2012)
12. Rao, R.: Jaya: A simple and new optimization algorithm for solving constrained and unconstrained optimization problems. Int. J. Ind. Eng. Comput. **7**(1), 19–34 (2016)
13. Rao, R.V., Saroj, A.: A self-adaptive multi-population based jaya algorithm for engineering optimization. Swarm Evolut. Comput. **37**, 1–26 (2017)
14. Rehman, M.Z., et al.: A novel state space reduction algorithm for team formation in social networks. PLoS ONE **16**(12), e0259786 (2021)

FastCELF++: A Novel and Fast Heuristic for Influence Maximization in Complex Networks

Vitor Elisiário do Carmo, Vinícius da Fonseca Vieira, Rafael Sachetto Oliveira,
and Carolina Ribeiro Xavier[✉]

Universidade Federal de São João del Rei, São João del Rei, Brazil
carolinaxavier@ufsj.edu.br

Abstract. Social networks reflect the relationships and interactions between individuals and have played a significant role in the spread of information, in which the communication of ideas and sharing of opinions happen all the time. There are various examples of how social networks can affect the behavior of individuals, like viral marketing, the spread of memes, and the propagation of fake news. This dynamic of information diffusion has motivated the research of several approaches to identify the prominent influencers in a network. The Influence Maximization Problem consists of identifying a subset S, called a seed set, of at most k elements to achieve the maximum (expected) propagation through a diffusion model, with S as the initial influencers on a network. It demonstrated that the influence maximization problem is an NP-hard optimization problem. Therefore, it is unfeasible to identify the subset S that ensures the most extensive diffusion due to its complexity. The most typical approach to this problem is using approximate algorithms, highlighting the Cost-Effective Lazy Forward (CELF), about 700 times faster than the greedy strategy proposed by Kemp et al., and CELF++, which presents a runtime gain of between 35 to 55% over CELF. This work modifies the two above-mentioned state-of-the-art algorithms, CELF and CELF++, replacing Monte Carlo simulations with functions to calculate the diffusion estimations (metamodels) for selecting a set of seeds. The adoption of well-known methods in the literature with metamodels can identify orders of magnitude faster, more influential individuals and, in some cases, even outperform the results of these methods in terms of propagation.

Keywords: Influence maximization · social networks · CELF · CELF++ · optimization

1 Introduction

The dynamics of information diffusion in networks have motivated the study of several approaches to identify the prominent influencers in a social network since the diffusion of such information can affect society and bring significant

O. Gervasi et al. (Eds.): ICCSA 2023, LNCS 13956, pp. 453–470, 2023.
https://doi.org/10.1007/978-3-031-36805-9_30

consequences, both good and bad. Considering viral marketing, for example, a company pays people to promote its products and services online to reach an audience that is often unaware of its brand. The company wants to make an advertising campaign as profitable as possible, and the choice of who will advertise it may directly impact the success of this campaign. Ideally, those selected to carry out the outreach are highly influential people.

This problem may be posed as Influence Maximization Problem (IMP) and has applications in several domains, in addition to those previously mentioned, such as personalized recommendations [16], classification of news feeds [7], selection of influential profiles in *Twitter* [1], and real-time ad targeting [13].

It has already demonstrated that the IMP is an NP-hard optimization problem [9]; therefore, due to its complexity, it is not feasible to find the subset S that guarantees the maximum diffusion in viable computational time. Thus, heuristic approaches are widely used, such as the greedy strategy (GK) proposed by [9].

In one of the most notable works on the subject, Leskovec *et al.* [10] propose the *Cost-Effective Lazy Forward* (CELF), around 700 times faster than the GK, for exploiting the property of propagation function submodularity for diffusion models. This algorithm selects a node with the greatest marginal gain in each iteration. The marginal gain of a selected node in each iteration must be greater than the previous ones. This algorithm manages to reduce the number of calls in the influence propagation evaluation.

Goyal *et al.* [6] propose CELF++, which tries to improve the CELF strategy by performing the influence propagation calculation for two steps of the algorithm simultaneously, but at an exceptionally high execution time. However, their experiments have shown gains in runtime between 35 to 55% on CELF.

Inspired by the two well-known algorithms, *Cost-Effective Lazy Forward* (CELF) [10] and CELF++ [6], this work presents a modification of them, using two metamodels named *Expected Diffusion Value* (EDV) [5] and *Local Influence Estimation* (LIE) [8] to replace the Monte Carlo simulations, aiming to reduce the computational cost and the execution time of the classical algorithms.

The results found by the experiments performed considering the methodology presented in this work show that the main methods in the literature combined with meta-models can identify the potential set of the most influential individuals in a much lower execution time than the original methods and even outperform the results of those methods in terms of the number of influenced individuals.

2 Background

2.1 Heuristics for the Solution of the IMP

One of the most effective heuristics for the estimation of influential nodes in networks for the Influence Maximization Problem (IMP) is the *DegreeDiscount*, proposed by Chen *et al.* [3] and designed originally for the Information Cascade (IC) model. For a specific diffusion probability p, *DegreeDiscount* tries to perform a deeper analysis of the local structure of the vertices. The general idea of the algorithm is that nodes with high degrees are good seeds for the IMP, but the edges that connect to it will not take into account for the calculation of the degrees of its neighbors, i.e., after considering a node as a seed, the evaluation of the next nodes will discount the edges that connect them to the nodes already in the seed set.

In addition to greedy strategies, it is possible to find in the literature several approaches that try to find suitable solutions for IMP through meta-heuristics. For example, Jiang et al. [8] propose an approach based on *Simulated Annealing* for the IMP, with the difference of replacing Monte Carlo simulations by a very efficient objective function, called Expected Diffusion Value (EDV). EDV obtains a diffusion estimate by performing a simple calculation that considers the diffusion probability and the number of neighbors within a hop of the evaluated nodes. Following the same approach, Gong et al. [5] use a Discrete Particle Swarm algorithm combined with an objective function called *Local Influence Estimation* (LIE), which extends the EDV to consider the neighborhood of two-hop distances making it more sensitive to the obtained estimate. In order to simplify the reading, the term "metamodel" will be further used to refer to the diffusion estimation functions, such as EDV and LIE.

2.2 Calculation of the Propagation Estimate

According to [3,4] it is computationally difficult to calculate the exact value of σ, the number of active nodes, for an IC model, thus making it necessary to estimate this value. One way to calculate this estimate is to average the number of vertices activated over several IC runs. Let $\mathcal{A}$ be the set of active vertices at the end of an IC execution. As IC is a probabilistic model, it can obtain different active vertices set at each execution. So $|\mathcal{A}|$ is a random variable, with an expected value $\sigma_{IC}(S)$. Knowing this, one way to achieve greater precision on $\sigma_{IC}(S)$ is to extract the mean result of all runs of the IC. This type of estimate is known as the Monte Carlo Method, a tool to estimate values through sampling and simulation [14]. More generally, the diffusion estimate of a S set in a m diffusion model is obtained by the Eq. 1:

$$\sigma_m(S) = \frac{1}{\mathcal{R}} \sum_{i}^{\mathcal{R}} |\mathcal{A}_i|, \tag{1}$$

where r is the number of executions of the model m and $\mathcal{A}_i$ is the set of nodes activated in the diffusion process in the i^{-th} execution. Traditionally, it is necessary to carry out a large number of simulations to obtain a good accuracy in the estimate and usually the value of $\mathcal{R} = 10000$ [3,6,10].

2.3 Expected Diffusion Value (EDV)

The Expected Diffusion Value (EDV) is a local approximation method proposed by Jiang et al. [8] for the influence propagation in the IC model, and aims at an approximation of the diffusion calculated by Monte Carlo simulations.

Furthermore, in the same work where EDV is proposes, it is used as an objective function for a method based on *Simulated Annealing* (SAEDV) adapted for the IMP and has shown to be able to obtain good results with millions of iterations. Let G be a graph $G = (V, E)$ and S a set $S \subseteq V$ of size k. The EDV is calculated by the Eq. 2

$$EDV(S) = k + \sum_{i \in N_S^{(1)} \setminus S} (1 - (1 - p)^{\tau(i)}), \tag{2}$$

where $N_S^{(1)}$ represents the direct neighbors of S, $i \in N_S^{(1)} \setminus S$ represents the neighbor vertices of i that are not part of S, p is the activation probability in the IC model and $\tau(i)$ represents the number of edges between the vertex i and the initial set of vertices S. When the vertex i has a high degree and many neighbors that do not belong to S, its contribution to the EDV is greater, because the chance of i activating some new vertex is greater and the term $(1 - (1-)p)^{\tau(i)})$, as observed in Eq. 2.

2.4   Local Influence Estimation (LIE)

Local Influence Estimation (LIE) [5] is also a local approximation method for influence propagation under the IC, but unlike the EDV which only considers the neighborhood one hop away from the vertex set, this method also covers the neighborhood two hops away. Like EDV, LIE was designed to be used as an objective function in a particle swarm optimization method, which achieved good results with an acceptable runtime under the IC, as proved by Tang *et al.* [17]. LIE can be described as an estimation function by Eq. 3

$$LIE(S) = k + (1 + \frac{1}{|N_S^{(1)} \setminus S|} \sum_{u \in N_S^{(2)} \setminus S} p_u^* d_u^*) \sum_{i \in N_S^{(1)} \setminus S} (1 - \prod_{(i,j) \in E, j \in S} (1 - p_{i,j}))), \tag{3}$$

where $N_S^{(1)}$ and $N_S^{(2)}$ represent the neighborhood of S at one and two hops away, respectively, p_u^* is the activation probability of a node u, which corresponds to the propagation probability p in the IC model or to the $\frac{1}{d_i^{(in)}}$ for the *Weighted Cascade* template, d_u^* represents the number of edges between the 1 and 2 jump neighborhoods of the u vertex.

2.5   Rank-Biased Overlap (RBO)

The *Rank-Biased Overlap* (RBO) is a coefficient that calculates the similarity of two ordered sets proposed by Webber *et al.* [18] to work with ordinal and undefined rankings. Since it is a measure based on ordering and intersection, this method is suitable to analyze the formation of the seeds' sets for each criterion and its order. RBO respects a numerical range between 0 and 1, where larger values imply a more significant similarity between the lists. The principle of RBO is that elements with different ratings have different weights, giving higher weights to those with higher ratings. For example, the RBO coefficient of two lists S and T is calculated by Eq. 4:

$$RBO(S, T, w) = (1 - w) \sum_{d=1}^{\eta} w^{d-1} A(S, T, d), \tag{4}$$

where η is the number of elements in the ranking list and the parameter w determines how steep the decline in weights is - the smaller the w, the more weighted the metric. In Eq. 4, $A(S, T, d)$ is the overlap value between two ranking lists S and T up to position d in *ranking*, calculated by Eq. 5.

$$A(S, T, d) = \frac{|S_{1:d} \cap T_{1:d}|}{|S_{1:d} \cup T_{1:d}|}, \tag{5}$$

where $S_{1:d}$ are the elements present in positions from 1 to d of list S, and $T_{1:d}$ indicates the same elements of list T.

3 Proposed Methods

The diffusion estimate of CELF and CELF++, as initially described, is calculated by Monte Carlo simulations, in which a high number of repetitions are necessary to obtain satisfactory results. Typically 10,000 repetitions are used. In this work, we address this aspect to explore for improvement.

The main idea is straightforward, although very effective: to replace Monte Carlo simulations with a metamodel. The modified CELF and CELF++ methods were now FastCELF and FASTCELF++, respectively. The EDV and LIE metamodels replace the Monte Carlo simulations in each proposed algorithm in this work. Thus, we have four heuristics to be investigated: FastCELF EDV, FASTCELF++ EDV, FastCELF LIE and FASTCELF++ LIE.

3.1 Calculating Diffusion Estimates with Metamodels

Equation 1 presents the calculation of $\sigma_m(S)$, which corresponds to the diffusion estimate of a set S for a model m through Monte Carlo simulations. Knowing that calculating σ is the most computationally expensive part of the original algorithms and aiming to maintain the same structure, we propose to replace σ with a function γ.

The generic representation of the propagation estimate of a set by a metamodel is $\gamma_{\bar{m}}(S, p)$, where S is the set of seeds, $\bar{m}$ is a metamodel, and p is the propagation probability. Thus, the propagation estimates calculated by the EDV and LIE metamodels are written according to the respective Eqs. 6 and 7:

$$\gamma_{EDV}(S, p) = EDV(S) \tag{6}$$

$$\gamma_{LIE}(S, p) = LIE(S) \tag{7}$$

which are equivalent to the Eqs. 2 and 3 presented in Sect. 2.

3.2 FastCELF

A pseudo-code for FastCELF is presented in the Algorithm 1. It is essential to highlight that the suggested modifications in this work can be found in lines 4 and 15, where $\sigma_m(\{u\})$ is replaced by $\gamma(\{u\}, p)$, with γ being any metamodel and p the diffusion probability. As the metamodels considered in this work require the parameter p to calculate the diffusion estimate, it is also a parameter for FastCELF.

Algorithm 1. FastCELF

```
1: function FASTCELF(G, k, γ, p)
2:     S ← ∅, Q ← ∅
3:     for each u ∈ V do
4:         u.mg ← γ({u}, p)
5:         u.flag ← 0
6:         Q ← Q ∪ {u}
7:     end for
8:     heapify(Q)                                    ▷ based on u.mg
9:     while |S| < k do
10:        u ← Q[0]
11:        if u.flag = |S| then
12:            S ← S ∪ {u}
13:            Q ← Q − {u}
14:        else
15:            u.mg ← γ(S ∪ {u}, p) − γ(S, p)
16:            u.flag ← |S|
17:        end if
18:        heapify(Q)                                ▷ based on u.mg
19:    end while
20:    return S
21: end function
```

3.3 FASTCELF++

Similarly to FastCELF, FastCELF++ is also parameterized by p, that represents the propagation probability considered for the metamodels. In the pseudo-code illustrated by Algorithm 2, the modifications regarding CELF++ can be found in lines 5, 6, 22 and 24, corresponding to the calls to the function σ. As in FastCELF, $\sigma_m(\{u\})$ is replaced by $\gamma(\{u\}, p)$, which is a single metamodel call, instead of the traditional Monte Carlo simulations. $\Delta_u^\gamma(cur\_best, p)$ corresponds to the marginal gain of u with respect to the set cur_best, calculated by the metamodel γ with diffusion probability p. In line 22 of Algorithm 2, for example, the term $u.mg1 \leftarrow \Delta_u^\gamma(S, p)$ could be rewritten analogously to line 15 of Algorithm 1, that is:

$$u.mg1 \leftarrow \Delta_u^\gamma(S, p) \equiv u.mg1 \leftarrow \gamma(S \cup \{u\}, p) - \gamma(S, p)$$

Algorithm 2. FastCELF++

```
 1: function FASTCELF++(G, k, γ, p)
 2:     S ← ∅, Q ← ∅
 3:     last_seed ← NULL, cur_best ← NULL
 4:     for each u ∈ V do
 5:         u.mg1 ← γ({u}, p)
 6:         u.mg2 ← Δ_u^γ(cur_best, p)
 7:         u.prev_best ← cur_best
 8:         u.flag ← 0
 9:         Q ← Q ∪ {u}
10:     end for
11:     heapify(Q)                                    ▷ based on u.mg1
12:     while |S| < k do
13:         u ← Q[0]
14:         if u.flag = |S| then
15:             S ← S ∪ {u}
16:             last_seed ← u
17:             cur_best ← NULL
18:             Q ← Q − {u}
19:         else if u.prev_best = last_seed and u.flag = |S| − 1 then
20:             u.mg1 ← u.mg2
21:         else
22:             u.mg1 ← Δ_u^γ(S, p)
23:             u.prev_best ← cur_best
24:             u.mg2 ← Δ_u^γ(S ∪ {cur_best}, p)
25:         end if
26:         u.flag = |S|
27:         update cur_best
28:         heapify(Q)                                ▷ based on u.mg1
29:     end while
30:     return S
31: end function
```

3.4 Complexity Analysis

The CELF and CELF++ algorithms have an identical time complexity for the IC model, $\mathcal{O}(k\mathcal{R}\mathcal{N}\mathcal{M})$ [2,12], where k is the number of seeds to be selected, $\mathcal{R}$ is the number of Monte Carlo simulations, and $\mathcal{N}$ and $\mathcal{M}$ correspond to the number of vertices and edges of the network, respectively. The worst-case scenario of the IC model occurs when all vertices of the network are activated during the cascade process since all edges are visited in this case, so its complexity is $\mathcal{O}(\mathcal{M})$.

The EDV presented in Sect. 2 has time complexity $\mathcal{O}(k\bar{D})$, with $\bar{D}$ as the average degree of the network. Since it covers a larger neighborhood, the worst-case scenario of LIE, presented in Sect. 2, regarding time complexity is $\mathcal{O}(k\bar{D}^2)$, where $\bar{D}$ is the average degree of the network.

The outer loop of FastCELF (Algorithm 1) in lines 3–7 has time complexity $\mathcal{O}(\mathcal{N}\gamma_{\bar{m}})$, where $\mathcal{O}(\gamma_{\bar{m}})$ is the complexity of the metamodel $\bar{m}$. The loop of lines

9–19 is executed $\mathcal{O}(k\mathcal{N})$ times, since the condition of line 11 can take up to $\mathcal{O}(\mathcal{N})$ iterations to occur. The calculation of the marginal gain in line 15 has complexity $2\mathcal{O}(\gamma_{\bar{m}})$. So the resulting complexity of FastCELF for any metamodel $\bar{m}$ is $\mathcal{O}(\mathcal{N}\gamma_{\bar{m}}) + 2\mathcal{O}(k\mathcal{N}\gamma_{\bar{m}}) \equiv \mathcal{O}(k\mathcal{N}\gamma_{\bar{m}})$.

In FastCELF++ (Algorithm 2) the main difference is in the number of calls of the estimative, calculated by the metamodel $\gamma_{\bar{m}}$. In the loop of lines 4–10, lines 5 and 6 have one and two calls to $\gamma_{\bar{m}}$, respectively, executed $\mathcal{O}(\mathcal{N})$ times, resulting at a complexity of $3\mathcal{O}(\mathcal{N}\gamma_{\bar{m}})$. In the second loop (lines 12–29) there are four calls to $\gamma_{\bar{m}}$, two on line 22 and two on line 24. Analogous to Algorithm 1, the loop is executed $\mathcal{O}(k\mathcal{N})$ times. As a result, the FastCELF++ complexity for any $\bar{m}$ metamodel is $3\mathcal{O}(\mathcal{N}\gamma_{\bar{m}}) + 4\mathcal{O}(k\mathcal{N}\gamma_{\bar{m}}) \equiv \mathcal{O}(k\mathcal{N}\gamma_{\bar{m}})$. For comparison purposes, Table 1 summarizes the complexities described.

Table 1. Time complexity of algorithms: k is number of seeds to be selected, $\mathcal{R}$ is number of Monte Carlo simulations, $\mathcal{N}$ is number of vertices, $\mathcal{M}$ is the number of edges and $\gamma_{\bar{m}}$ represents any metamodel.

Algorithm	Time Complexity
Algorithm: CELF	$\mathcal{O}(k\mathcal{R}\mathcal{N}\mathcal{M})$
Algorithm: CELF++	$\mathcal{O}(k\mathcal{R}\mathcal{N}\mathcal{M})$
Algorithm 1: FastCELF	$\mathcal{O}(k\mathcal{N}\gamma_{\bar{m}})$
Algorithm 2: FastCELF++	$\mathcal{O}(k\mathcal{N}\gamma_{\bar{m}})$

Considering the EDV and LIE metamodels, described in Sect. 2, it is possible to replace $\gamma_{\bar{m}}$ by their respective complexities. Substituting the EDV complexity we have $\mathcal{O}(k\mathcal{N}k\bar{D}) \equiv \mathcal{O}(k^2\mathcal{N}\bar{D})$. For LIE, the resulting complexity is $\mathcal{O}(k\mathcal{N}k\bar{D}^2) \equiv \mathcal{O}(k^2\mathcal{N}\bar{D}^2)$. Although the proposed methods have quadratic complexity in k, the value of this term tends to be much smaller than $\mathcal{N}$ and D. Table 2 presents the time complexities of the heuristics with the metamodels presented in Sect. 2.

Table 2. Time complexity of algorithms with metamodels: k is the number of seeds to be selected, $\mathcal{N}$ is the number of vertices and $\bar{D}$ is the average degree of the network.

Algorithm	Time Complexity
Algorithm 1: FastCELF with EDV	$\mathcal{O}(k^2\mathcal{N}\bar{D})$
Algorithm 2: FastCELF++ with EDV	$\mathcal{O}(k^2\mathcal{N}\bar{D})$
Algorithm 1: FastCELF with LIE	$\mathcal{O}(k^2\mathcal{N}\bar{D}^2)$
Algorithm 2: FastCELF++ withcom LIE	$\mathcal{O}(k^2\mathcal{N}\bar{D}^2)$

4 Data and Experiments

4.1 Networks

The methodology proposed in this work was evaluated considering a varied set of real networks, ranging from different categories and contexts, like social networks, communication, co-authorship and collaboration networks. Table 3 describes the characteristics of this dataset. Each network was pre-processed in order to extract its giant component. Therefore, the values presented in Table 3 refer to the giant component of their respective networks.

Table 3. Characteristics of used networks: number of nodes ($|V|$); number of edges ($|E|$); medium degree ($\hat{k}$); average *clustering* coefficient ($\hat{c}$).

Network	Type	$|V|$	$|E|$	$\hat{k}$	$\hat{l}$	Category
netscience[†]	non-directed	379	914	4.82	0.741	Co-authoring
email[†]	non-targeted	1134	5451	9.62	0.220	Communication
soc-hamsterster[*]	non-targeted	2000	16097	16.09	0.539	Social
CA-GrQc[*]	non-targeted	4158	13422	6.45	0.556	Collaboration
CA-HepTh[*]	non-targeted	8638	25998	5.74	0.481	Collaboration
fb-pages-company[†]	non-targeted	14113	52310	7.38	0.239	Social
fb-pages-sport[†]	non-targeted	13866	86858	12.52	0.276	Social
CA-AstroPh[*]	non-targeted	17903	196972	22.00	0.632	Collaboration
CA-CondMat[*]	non-targeted	21363	91286	8.54	0.641	Collaboration
soc-epinions[*]	targeted	75877	508836	13.41	0.137	Social
soc-slashdot0902[*]	targeted	82168	870161	21.18	0.060	Social

The networks tagged with $*$ were collected from the database $SNAP^1$ [11] while the networks tagged with † were collected from the *Network Repository*[2] [15].

4.2 Experiments

In order to establish fair conditions for the experiments, a familiar environment was defined. The seed sets k range from 5 to 50, with increments of 5 for the calculation of influence propagation. To calculate the similarity between the pairs of seed sets, the maximum size of the sets was 50. *Independent Cascade* (IC) was adopted as the diffusion model. The activation probability p for both the IC and the metamodels was set to 0.01. In order to obtain a good approximation of the influence propagation by the IC, the number of Monte Carlo simulations adopted in this work was 10000 [3,6,10].

---

[1] http://snap.stanford.edu/data/index.html.
[2] http://networkrepository.com/.

The proposed algorithms FastCELF and FastCELF++ were evaluated using both EDV and LIE. Thus, this work has four novel methods capable of achieving competitive results in diffusion quality and executing in considerably lower time than the original algorithms. For comparison purposes, the DegreeDiscount algorithm was evaluated with the original algorithms, CELF and CELF++ and the proposed heuristics.

Each heuristic was used to select 50 seeds from each network and simulate the IC model with multiples of five seeds. Next, the similarities of the seeds were checked pairwise using a heatmap with the RBO to compare the sets, and finally, the diffusion process with the seeds was started. It was noteworthy that, in this diffusion process, Monte Carlo simulations are used for all methods, including the proposed ones, and the results were plotted as a line chart.

The final evaluation of the efficiency of all methods was done by the diffusion process (IC model), which uses Monte Carlo simulations to obtain good accuracy, as it is a stochastic process. So, the following figures show the results for the original way for simulation, with seeds selected by each method.

5   Results and Discussion

The execution times of the original algorithms for seed selection, CELF and CELF++, together with their respective modified versions, are presented in Fig. 1. The proposed methods (FastCELF and FastCELF++), when used together with EDV, were much faster, taking less than 5 s in the "slashdot0902" network, the largest network in the base, to select the seeds. The execution time was less than 1 s for the four heuristics in the smallest network. On the other hand, the relative inefficiency of CELF and CELF++ is notorious in a network with a few hundred vertices, taking about 2 min and 3 min, respectively. The execution time increases with the size of the networks, taking each of the two algorithms approximately 23 h to finish executing in the "fb-pages-company" network. For this network, it was impractical to execute both original CELF and CELF++.

The modified FastCELF and FastCELF++ versions that use LIE as an estimating function take slightly longer than the EDV versions in the experiments performed. It happens because the LIE considers a larger neighborhood than the EDV to calculate its estimate. However, even being less efficient in runtime, the modified versions considering LIE are still much faster than the original algorithms. Among the proposed methods, FastCELF++ LIE was the most time-consuming in the "fb-pages-company" network, taking 30 s to finish its execution, a substantial gain compared to 23 h for the original methods.

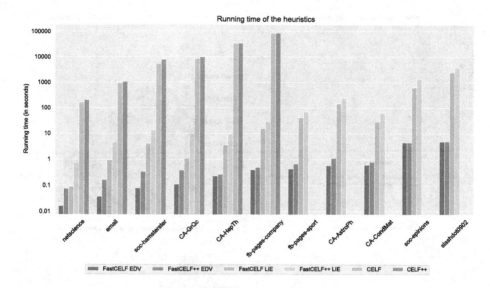

Fig. 1. Algorithm execution time for seed selection.

In terms of influence propagation, the results of experiments show that the proposed algorithms are competitive and outperform the original versions in all networks in experiments scenarios, even by a small margin. The Fig. 2 shows the results for netscience, email and soc-hamsterster.

Regarding the "email" network, the correlations between the seeds sets are high to very high, CELF and CELF++ chose the same set in the same order. One can see that all algorithms perform identically, varying the mean for their reached numbers in less than one unit.

In the "soc-hamsterster" network , the correlations are high, but even so it can be seen that the same three algorithms, *DegreeDiscount*, FastCELF++ LIE, FastCELF++ EDV show pairs of higher correlation. In this case FastCELF++ LIE outperforms *DegreeDiscount* by a small margin.

The first line of Fig. 3 shows the results of propagation considering the proposed heuristics and the correlation between their seeds' sets for the "CA-GrQc" network. *DegreeDiscount*, FastCELF++ LIE, FastCELF++ EDV methods, in that order, present the best results and outperform by far the CELF and CELF++ algorithms. Seed correlations show that high similarities reflect the performance of heuristics. CELF and CELF++ are similar to FastCELF algorithms that adopt EDV and LIE.

Diffusion results for "CA-HepTh" network can be seen in second line of Fig. 3. One can see that that FastCELF++ and *DegreeDiscount* outperformed other algorithms.

It is possible to observe in third line of Fig. 3 that for the "fb-pages-company" network, all algorithms work in a very similar way, which can be corroborated by

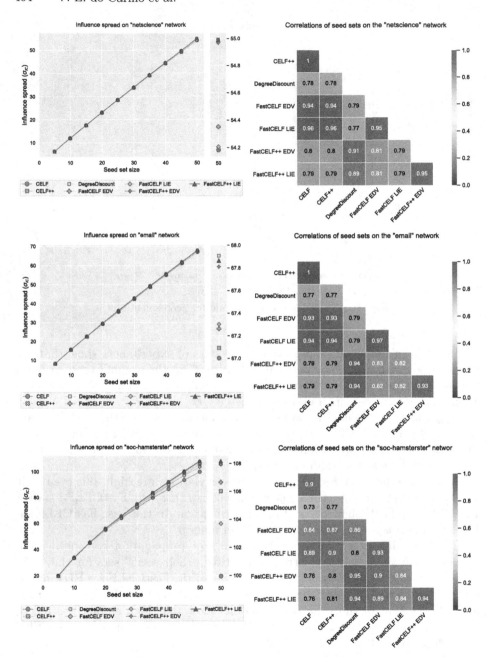

Fig. 2. Influence propagation and correlations of seed sets selected by heuristics

the correlation between their selected seed sets. A small margin can be observed for the Algorithms *DegreeDiscount*, FastCELF++EDV and FastCELF++LIE.

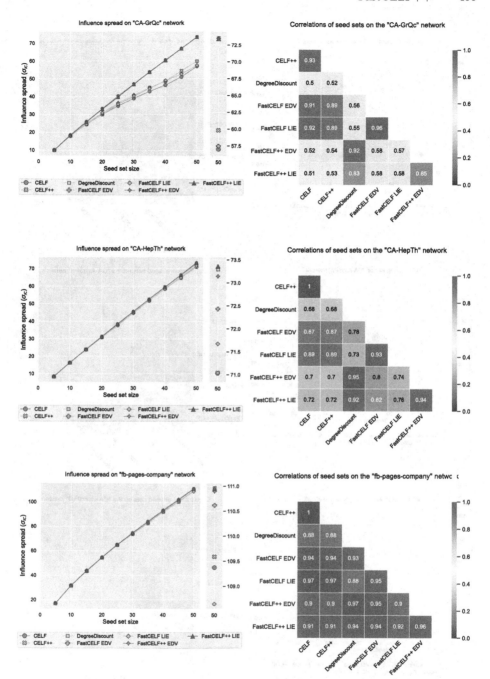

Fig. 3. Influence propagation and correlations of seed sets selected by heuristics.

For the network "fb-pages-sports", "CA-AstroPh" and "CA-condMat" the algorithms CELF and CELF++ can not be executed. The reason for that is the

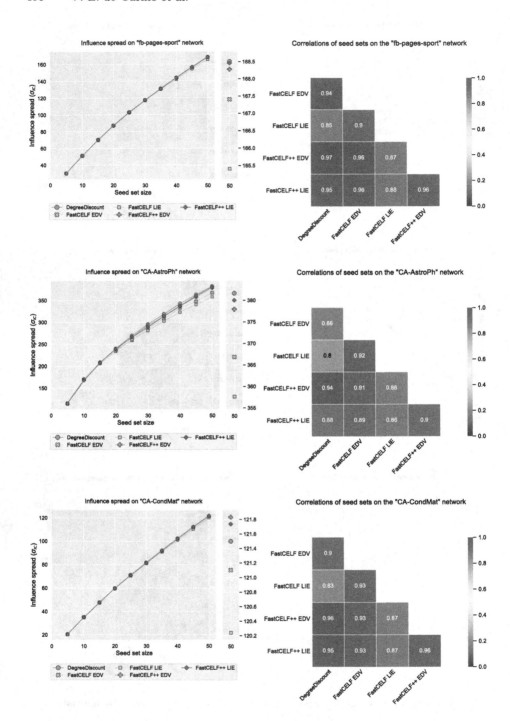

Fig. 4. Influence propagation and correlations of seed sets selected by heuristics.

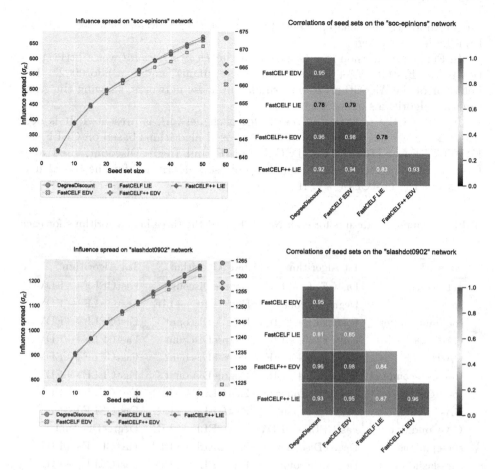

Fig. 5. Influence propagation and correlations of seed sets selected by heuristics

high computational time cost for these networks, which have more than 86000, 196000 and 91000 edges.

In Fig. 4, in first line, one can see that for the "fb-pages-sports" network, all algorithms work in a very similar way, which can be confirmed by the correlation between their selected seed sets. A small margin can be observed for the Algorithms *DegreeDiscount*, FastCELF++EDV and FastCELF++LIE.

In Fig. 4, in second line, one can see that for the "CA-AstroPh" there are a margin between Algorithms *DegreeDiscount*, FastCELF++EDV and FastCELF++LIE and the variations of FastCELF. The correlation between the selected seed sets of these algorithms is high.

In Fig. 4, in the last line, one can see that for the "CA-CondMat" network, all algorithms are almost identical, varying from 120.2 to 121.8, a small margin can be observed for the Algorithms FastCELF++EDV and FastCELF++LIE.

Furthermore, the heatmap presented the correlation between these seed sets, all from high to very high.

In Fig. 5 the diffusion results show that the *DegreeDiscount* was a little superior to the FastCELF++ networks for "soc-epinions" and "slashdot0902". The behavior of the Algorithms is very similar in these networks, showing the same rank for algorithms in two situations.

In Table 4 the summary of results for each network is presented. It is necessary to notice the superiority of the proposed algorithms based on CELF++, FASTCELF++EDV and FASTCELF++LIE and DegreeDiscount, used as a baseline. The best choice between the proposed algorithms for the tested networks was the FastCELF++LIE.

Table 4. Summary Results for each Networks and the three best algorithms for each one.

Network	1st Algorithm	2nd Algorithm	3rd Algorithm
netscience	FastCELF++LIE	DegreeDiscount	FastCELF++EDV
email	DegreeDiscount	FastCELF++LIE	FastCELF++EDV
soc-hamsterster	FastCELF++LIE	DegreeDiscount	FastCELF++EDV
CA-GrQc	FastCELF++LIE	DegreeDiscount	FastCELF++EDV
CA-HepTh	FastCELF++LIE	DegreeDiscount	FastCELF++EDV
fb-pages-company	FastCELF++LIE	DegreeDiscount	FastCELF++EDV
fb-pages-sport	DegreeDiscount	FastCELF++LIE	FastCELF++EDV
CA-AstroPh	DegreeDiscount	FastCELF++LIE	FastCELF++EDV
CA-CondMat	FastCELF++EDV	FastCELF++LIE	DegreeDiscount
soc-epinions	DegreeDiscount	FastCELF++EDV	FastCELF++LIE
soc-slashdot0902	DegreeDiscount	FastCELF++EDV	FastCELF++LIE

6   Conclusions and Future Works

The Influence Maximization Problem (IMP) in Complex Networks is an NP-hard problem. Therefore, it is necessary to use approximate strategies to guarantee a satisfactory solution with a possible execution time.

Many studies try to overcome the results achieved by the best-known greedy strategies in the literature. However, seed selection is the most critical task for the IMP problem, as it is directly related to the performance of diffusion models; therefore, creating new intelligent methods or improving existing strategies becomes essential.

Overall, the implemented heuristics proved to be comparable to *DegreeDiscount*, the FastCELF++, in different networks overcome in influence propagation, as using LIE or EDV. Therefore, the feasibility of replacing Monte Carlo simulations in the CELF and CELF++ algorithms with metamodels was shown, thus achieving a gain in propagation quality. The methodology developed was sufficient to achieve the objectives proposed in this work. The correlations between pairs of seed sets with the RBO helped to understand the diffusion results and showed the similarity between the seeds selected by the classical methods and the seeds selected by the presented heuristics. Metamodels can quickly estimate the influence propagation and still maintain qualitatively comparable results to Monte Carlo simulations; as one can see in the RBO heatmaps, the seeds sets are very close. The developed methods have good efficiency and proved to be computationally scalable.

The results of this work are expected to contribute to the area, pointing to better strategies that present good performance, efficiency and speedup for the IMP problem.

Some directions can still be explored from this work: (1)The use of other diffusion models, as threshold model; (2) A sequence of the research carried out in this work is the variation of the activation probability p, indicating whether the metamodels are sensitive to this parameter; and, (3) One can develop a new metamodel that is quantitatively comparable to the propagation function calculation.

Acknowledgments. The authors thank CNPq and FAPEMIG for funding their projects.

References

1. Bakshy, E., Hofman, J.M., Mason, W.A., Watts, D.J.: Everyone's an influencer: quantifying influence on twitter. In: Proceedings of the Fourth ACM International Conference On Web Search and Data Mining, pp. 65–74 (2011)
2. Banerjee, S., Jenamani, M., Pratihar, D.K.: A survey on influence maximization in a social network. Knowl. Inf. Syst. **62**(9), 3417–3455 (2020). https://doi.org/10.1007/s10115-020-01461-4
3. Chen, W., Wang, Y., Yang, S.: Efficient influence maximization in social networks. In: Proceedings of the 15th ACM SIGKDD International Conference On Knowledge Discovery And Data Mining, pp. 199–208. ACM (2009)
4. Chen, W., Yuan, Y., Zhang, L.: Scalable influence maximization in social networks under the linear threshold model. In: 2010 IEEE International Conference On Data Mining, pp. 88–97. IEEE (2010)
5. Gong, M., Yan, J., Shen, B., Ma, L., Cai, Q.: Influence maximization in social networks based on discrete particle swarm optimization. Inf. Sci. **367**, 600–614 (2016)
6. Goyal, A., Lu, W., Lakshmanan, L.V.: Celf++ optimizing the greedy algorithm for influence maximization in social networks. In: Proceedings of the 20th International Conference Companion On World Wide Web, pp. 47–48 (2011)
7. Ienco, D., Bonchi, F., Castillo, C.: The meme ranking problem: Maximizing microblogging virality. In: 2010 IEEE International Conference on Data Mining Workshops, pp. 328–335. IEEE (2010)
8. Jiang, Q., Song, G., Gao, C., Wang, Y., Si, W., Xie, K.: Simulated annealing based influence maximization in social networks. In: Twenty-fifth AAAI Conference On Artificial Intelligence (2011)

9. Kempe, D., Kleinberg, J., Tardos, É.: Maximizing the spread of influence through a social network. In: Proceedings of the ninth ACM SIGKDD International Conference on Knowledge Discovery And Data Mining, pp. 137–146. ACM (2003)

10. Leskovec, J., Krause, A., Guestrin, C., Faloutsos, C., VanBriesen, J., Glance, N.: Cost-effective outbreak detection in networks. In: Proceedings of the 13th ACM SIGKDD International Conference on Knowledge Discovery and Data Mining, pp. 420–429. ACM (2007)

11. Leskovec, J., Krevl, A.: SNAP Datasets: Stanford large network dataset collection. http://snap.stanford.edu/data (Jun 2014)

12. Li, Y., Fan, J., Wang, Y., Tan, K.L.: Influence maximization on social graphs: a survey. IEEE Trans. Knowl. Data Eng. 30(10), 1852–1872 (2018)

13. Li, Y., Zhang, D., Tan, K.L.: Real-time targeted influence maximization for online advertisements (2015)

14. Mitzenmacher, M., Upfal, E.: Probability and computing: Randomization and probabilistic techniques in algorithms and data analysis. Cambridge University Press (2017)

15. Rossi, R.A., Ahmed, N.K.: The network data repository with interactive graph analytics and visualization. In: AAAI (2015). http://networkrepository.com

16. Song, X., Tseng, B.L., Lin, C.Y., Sun, M.T.: Personalized recommendation driven by information flow. In: Proceedings of the 29th Annual International ACM SIGIR Conference On Research And Development in Information Retrieval, pp. 509–516 (2006)

17. Tang, J., et al.: Maximizing the spread of influence via the collective intelligence of discrete bat algorithm. Knowl.-Based Syst. 160, 88–103 (2018)

18. Webber, W., Moffat, A., Zobel, J.: A similarity measure for indefinite rankings. ACM Trans. Inform. Syst. (TOIS) 28(4), 1–38 (2010)

Enhancing Amazigh Speech Recognition System with MFDWC-SVM

Fadwa Abakarim[✉] and Abdenbi Abenaou

Research Team of Applied Mathematics and Intelligent Systems Engineering, National School of Applied Sciences, Ibn Zohr University, 80000 Agadir, Morocco
fadwa.abakarim@gmail.com

Abstract. In this research, a new Automatic Speech Recognition (ASR) system is introduced for the Amazigh language, more precisely Tachelhit, spoken in the High Atlas and the South-West of Morocco. The implementation of this system is a challenging task because the availability of Amazigh speech databases is limited, so the first step is to create a database and then to develop the system. Our database contains 33 letters and 10 digits (0 to 9). 120 speakers participated in the recording of the speech corpus: 80 adults (40 males and 40 females) and 40 children (20 boys and 20 girls). Among them, 60 are native speakers and the other 60 are speaking the language for the first time. After creating the database, we used Short-Time Energy (STE) to remove silence and compress the length of the input speech signals. Next, the features are extracted by a combination of two well-known approaches: the Mel-Frequency Cepstral Coefficients (MFCC) and the Discrete Wavelet Transform (DWT). The result is the Mel-Frequency Discrete Wavelet Coefficients (MFDWC) method. Finally, the classification step is conducted using Support Vector Machine (SVM) model. The experimental results prove that the system performs well by achieving an accuracy of 94.42% for the recognition of 10 digits, 90.82% for the recognition of 33 letters and 92.22% for the recognition of 33 letters and 10 digits.

Keywords: Automatic Speech Recognition · Amazigh Language · Short-Time Energy · Support Vector Machine · Mel-Frequency Cepstral Coefficients · Discrete Wavelet Transform · Mel-Frequency Discrete Wavelet Coefficients

1 Introduction

Speech is a type of communication used by humans to interact with each other. In the same context, there is also human-machine interaction, where a machine detects and recognizes the spoken words. This is called Automatic Speech Recognition (ASR).

Several languages have been used for the achievement of a speech recognition system such as Hindi [1], Arabic [2], French [3] and English [4]. However, it is rare to find an Amazigh-Tachelhit speech recognition system, and our goal is to develop one. This sort of system can be used in various applications, including learning new languages, controlling devices and translation.

O. Gervasi et al. (Eds.): ICCSA 2023, LNCS 13956, pp. 471–488, 2023.
https://doi.org/10.1007/978-3-031-36805-9_31

The Amazigh language is a vital component of Moroccan culture, with around half of the population speaking it as their first language. Although the Royal Institute of Amazigh Culture (IRCAM) has facilitated its integration into various areas, the language still suffers in Information and Communication Technologies (ICT) because of the lack of Natural Language Processing (NLP) compared to other languages [5]. Therefore, several researchers are focused on the development of Amazigh speech recognition systems.

Most ASR systems are developed using free software such as HTK [6], CMU Sphinx [7], ISIP [8] and AVCSR [9]. Of these, HTK and CMU Sphinx are commonly used by researchers to build Amazigh speech recognition systems.

El Ouahabi et al. [10] presented an Amazigh ASR system able to identify 43 isolated words, including 33 letters and 10 digits. The MFCC was used for feature extraction and the Hidden Markov Model Toolkit (HTK) for system development. The database contained 19500 audio files: 16500 for letters and 3000 for digits. The number of speakers was 80, including 40 males and 40 females. The system achieved a high recognition rate of 91.31% using Hidden Markov Models (HMMs) with 3 states and 32 Gaussian Mixture Models (GMMs).

Telmem and Ghanou [11] realized an Amazigh ASR system using CMU Sphinx-4. The database contained 2970 audio files of 33 letters recorded by 9 speakers. The system achieved a high accuracy of 88.00% using 3 HMMs and 2 GMMs.

Satori and Elhaoussi [12] developed an Amazigh ASR system using CMU Sphinx tools. The features were extracted using an MFCC approach. The database contained 25800 audio files of 33 letters and 10 digits. The number of speakers was 60, including 30 males and 30 females. The system achieved an improved performance of 89.07% using 5 HMMs and 16 GMMs.

El Ouahabi et al. [13] created an Amazigh ASR system using CMU Sphinx-4. The features were extracted by the MFCC approach. The database used in this study contained 46750 audio files of 187 isolated words. The number of speakers was 50, including 25 males and 25 females. The results show that the combination of 6 and 8 GMMs with 2000, 3000 and 4000 tied states (senones) gives the best recognition rate of 91.80%.

Telmem and Ghanou [14] proposed an Amazigh ASR system using CMU Sphinx-4. The database contained 11220 audio files of 33 letters recorded by 34 speakers. A high recognition rate of 90.00% was obtained using 3 HMMs and 128 GMMs.

The Moroccan Amazigh language has three regional variants: Tachelhit in the High Atlas and the South-West, Tamazight in the Central and the South-East and Tarifit in North regions. Most of the Amazigh ASR research is conducted on Tarifit [12, 13, 15]. Therefore, in this research, we focus on the Amazigh language spoken in the city of Agadir and its surroundings, which is Tachelhit. Moreover, the MFCC approach and the open-source toolkits based on HMMs: CMU Sphinx 4 and HTK, are commonly used for the development of Amazigh ASR systems.

In this study, a new Amazigh ASR system is created, based on a combination of two well-known feature extraction methods, MFCC and DWT. This combination produces the MFDWC method. The classification process is realized using SVM. A self-created database is used to train and test the system performance. It contains 43 isolated words (33 letters and 10 digits) recorded by 120 speakers.

The structure of the article is as follows: A concise summary of the Amazigh language is given in Sect. 2. Section 3 introduces the self-created database. Section 4 describes the applied methods used to create the proposed system. The experimental results are presented in Sect. 5. Finally, Sect. 6 concludes the paper.

2 Amazigh Language

The Amazigh language, also known as Tamazight or Berber, is a subcategory of the Afro-Asiatic language family and consists of two parts: the Berber languages of the North and the South. They are spoken in several countries, from Morocco, which has a population of around 50% Amazigh speakers, to Egypt, through Algeria with 25%, Libya, Mauritania, Mali, Tunisia, and Niger [5].

In Morocco, the Amazigh language is classified into three main regional dialects: Tachelhit in the High Atlas and the South-West, Tarifit in the North and Tamazight in Central and South-East Morocco [16].

In 2001, the Royal Institute of Amazigh Culture (IRCAM) was founded to standardize the Amazigh language and integrate it into various fields. As such, it has become a national language and since 2003 it has been introduced in administration and the media. It is taught in the educational system as an essential subject in elementary school, and as a course in the faculty of letters and humanities [17].

The Tifinaghe-IRCAM alphabet system, developed by IRCAM, is written from left to right and is built on the basis of a graphic system that shows phonological tendencies. However, it does not preserve all the phonetic realizations produced, but only the functional ones. This system contains [5, 18, 19]:

27 consonants including: the alveolars (Ⴚ, Ⴒ, ✱, ✖), the dentals (ⵔ, ⵕ, ⵏ, ⴹ, ✝, Ⴅ, Ⴈ, l), the labials (ⵀ, ⵞ, ⵛ), the labiovelars (ⵔⵯ, ✗ⵯ), the laryngeal (ⵠ), the palatals (ⵊ, ⵛ), the pharyngeals (ⵅ, ⵇ), the uvulars (✕, ⵣ, Ⴣ) and the velars (ⵔ, ✗).

2 semi-consonants: ⵞand ⵥ.

4 vowels: neutral vowel (or schwa) ⵦwhich has a distinctive position in Amazigh phonology, and three full vowels ⵥ, ₒ, ⵦ.

Tifinaghe does not have a specific set of punctuation marks. Instead, IRCAM suggests using international symbols such as " " (space), ".", ",", ";", " ?", " !" and "..." as punctuation marks. For numerals, in Morocco, the standard ones are used (0, 1, 2, 3, 4, 5, 6, 7, 8, 9) which are recommended for Tifinaghe writing [18, 19].

Tables 1 and 2 show the 33 characters of the Amazigh alphabet and the 10 Amazigh digits along with their transcriptions in Arabic and English and their syllables.

Table 1. The 33 Amazigh characters with their transcriptions in Arabic and English and their syllables [12, 15].

Tifinaghe-IRCAM	Arabic Transcription	Arabic correspondence	English Transcription	Syllables
ⴰ	يا	ا	YA	CV
ⴱ	ياب	ب	YAB	CVC
ⴳ	ياك	-	YAG	CVC
ⴳⵯ	ياك	-	YAGG	CVC
ⴷ	ياد	د	YAD	CVC
ⴹ	ياض	ض	YADD	CVCC
ⴻ	ياي	ي	YEY	CVC
ⴼ	ياف	ف	YAF	CVC
ⴽ	ياك	ك	YAK	CVC
ⴽⵯ	ياكك	-	YAKK	CVCC
ⵀ	ياه	ه	YAH	CVC
ⵃ	ياح	ح	YAHH	CVC
ⵄ	ياع	ع	YAAA	CVC
ⵅ	ياخ	خ	YAKH	CVC
ⵇ	ياق	ق	YAQQ	CVC
ⵉ	يي	ي	YI	CV
ⵊ	ياج	ج	YAJ	CVC
ⵍ	يال	ل	YAL	CVC
ⵎ	يام	م	YAM	CVC
ⵏ	يان	ن	YAN	CVC
ⵓ	يو	و	YO	CV
ⵔ	يار	ر	YAR	CVC
ⵕ	يار	-	YARR	CVC
ⵖ	ياغ	غ	YAGH	CVC
ⵙ	ياس	س	YAS	CVC
ⵚ	ياص	ص	YASS	CVC
ⵛ	ياش	ش	YASH	CVC
ⵜ	يات	ت	YAT	CVC
ⵟ	ياط	ط	YATT	CVC
ⵡ	ياو	و	YAW	CVC
ⵢ	ياي	ى	YAY	CVC
ⵣ	ياز	ز	YAZ	CVC
ⵥ	ياز	-	YAZZ	CVCC

Table 2. The 10 Amazigh digits with their transcriptions in Arabic and English and their syllables [12, 15].

Tifinaghe-IRCAM	Arabic Transcription	Arabic correspondence	English Transcription	Syllables
₀ᴄᵌ₀	أميا	صفر	AMYA	VC-CV
ᵌ₀I	يان	واحد	YEN	CVC
⊙ᵌI	سين	اثنان	SIN	CVC
ᴋQ₀E	كراض	ثلاثة	KRAD	VC-CVC
ᴋᴋ:✳	كوز	أربعة	KOZ	CVC
⊙ᴄᴄ:⊙	سموس	خمسة	SMMUS	CC-CVC
⊙Eᵌ⊘	سضيص	ستة	SDES	CCVC
⊙₀	سا	سبعة	SA	CV
+₀ᴄ	تام	ثمانية	TAM	CVC
+✳₀	تزا	تسعة	TZA	CC-CV

3 Amazigh Speech Database

For intelligent systems in the field of signal processing, a database is always needed for training and testing. However, a common problem that researchers may encounter during implementation of their work is the lack of input data that can be processed to train and test the system. This work will focus on the realization of a speech recognition system.

Speech databases are available in several different languages, such as Mandarin Chinese, English, Javanese, Nepali, Korean and French, to serve researchers [20]. However, the availability of Amazigh speech databases is limited. Therefore, this gives us the opportunity and motivation to create our own database. Furthermore, it will be available to all researchers and could be used to perform various tasks, including speaker recognition, gender recognition, and keyword recognition.

The database consists of 33 letters (see Table 1) and 10 digits (see Table 2) of the Amazigh language, collected from 120 speakers. Among them, 60 are native Amazigh-Tachelhit and the other 60 are speaking the language for the first time.

The advantage of our database is that the speakers are of various ages. There are 80 adults from 19 to 55 years old, and in addition, there are 40 children from the ages of 7 to 13. Tables 3 and 4 show more details.

The audio files were recorded using Audacity software [21] in a normal environment. The recording has a resolution of 16 bits and a sampling rate of 16 kHz. Each speaker was asked to record each word with 10 repetitions, for a total of 51600 audio recordings in ".wav" format. More details are provided in Table 5. In addition, to simplify the recording process, all speakers were asked to record 10 repetitions of each word in a single voice file (see Fig. 1). Then, it was necessary to manually segment the result files and save each word as an audio file (see Fig. 2). In the end, each word had 10 audio files for each speaker.

Table 3. Gender and age of adult speakers.

Age Category	Gender		
	Male	Female	Total
19–29	20	20	40
30–40	10	10	20
41–55	10	10	20
Total	40	40	80

Table 4. Gender and age of child speakers.

Age Category	Gender		
	Male	Female	Total
7–9	10	10	20
10–13	10	10	20
Total	20	20	40

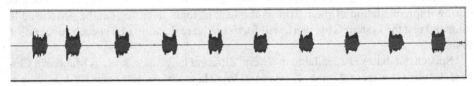

Fig. 1. Voice recording of the digit "Amya" with 10 repetitions from a female speaker before cutting.

Fig. 2. Single voice recording of the digit "Amya" from a female speaker after cutting.

Table 5. Database technical parameters.

Parameter	Value
Corpus	Amazigh 33 letters and 10 digits
Accent	Moroccan Amazigh-Tachelhit
Number of speakers	120
Origin of speakers	Morocco, the city of Agadir and its surroundings
Age of speakers	7–55 years old
Gender of speakers	60 males and 60 females
Native speakers' number	60
Non-native speakers' number	60
Words' number	43 (33 letters and 10 digits)
Number of repetitions per word	10
Number of tokens per speaker	430 (43 words × 10 repetitions)
Total number of audio files	51600 (43 words × 10 repetitions × 120 speakers)
Each audio file duration	Between 1 and 3 s
Number of bits	16 bits
Sampling rate	16 kHz
Audio data file format	.wav
Channels	1 (Mono)
The recording software	Audacity

4 Applied Methods

In our study, the achievement of an Amazigh speech recognition system consists of three steps:

First, pre-processing. After collecting the database, it was observed that the input speech signals contained silence at the beginning and end of each spoken word. Therefore, we used Short-Time Energy (STE) to remove the silence and compress the length of the speech signals.

Second, feature extraction, in which we combined two well-known feature extraction methods, MFCC and DWT. The result is MFDWC, which provides good time-frequency localization and is robust in noisy environments.

Finally, the classification, which affects the system performance and the final decision. Therefore, we chose one of the most used models for classification problems and pattern recognition, the SVM model.

4.1 Pre-processing

To create a fast and efficient ASR system, the input speech signals should be pre-processed to compress them and preserve their quality by removing irrelevant information. In this study, we used the Short-Time Energy (STE) approach to detect and remove the unvoiced parts of the input signal, producing a fully voiced signal.

The speech signal amplitude varies over time, and typically, the voiced segments have a higher amplitude than unvoiced speech segments. STE can be used to represent these amplitude variations. It is a measure of the energy in a voice signal over a short period of time [22].

The short-time energy can be defined as follows [22]:

$$E_n = \sum_{m=-\infty}^{\infty} [x(m)w(n-m)]^2 \tag{1}$$

The choice of window function can significantly affect the characteristics of the short-time energy representation. For the proposed system, we opted for the Hamming window because it provides higher out-of-band attenuation compared to the rectangular window. This means that it reduces the amplitude of frequencies that are not within the window.

$$w(n) = (1 - \alpha) - \alpha \cos\left[\frac{2\pi n}{N-1}\right] \tag{2}$$

The value of α is between 0 and 1. We used $\alpha = 0.46$, which gives:

$$w(n) = \begin{cases} 0.54 - 0.46 \cos\left[\frac{2\pi n}{N-1}\right], & 0 \leq n \leq N-1 \\ 0, & otherwise \end{cases} \tag{3}$$

where
  n represents the current sample, while N represents the total number of samples.
  Figure 3 presents the process of STE.
  Figure 4 shows the speech signal of the Amazigh digit "Amya" before and after applying STE.

4.2 Feature Extraction

Feature extraction is a major phase in signal processing, as it transforms the input data into more valuable information that can be used for classification.

The quality of the extracted features has a direct impact on the classification performance. Indeed, they must be sufficiently discriminating to ensure a good separation between the different classes of signals. Moreover, they should be robust to noise and other disturbances to provide a good generalization of the classification.

In speech recognition, The Mel-Frequency Cepstral Coefficients (MFCC) are the most commonly used features, and their extraction involves an important step known as the Discrete Cosine Transform (DCT). However, the DCT basis vectors have similar time and frequency resolution, and they cover all frequency bands. This means that noise in one frequency band can affect all of the coefficients, which can be problematic in noisy

Speech Signal

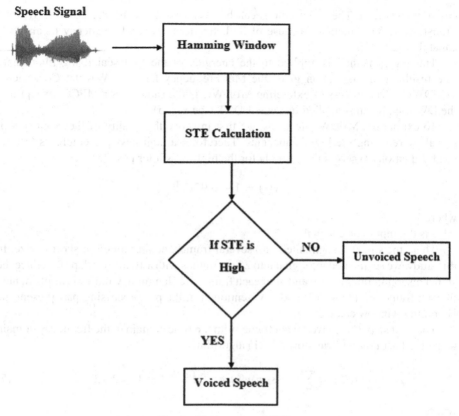

Fig. 3. The process of STE.

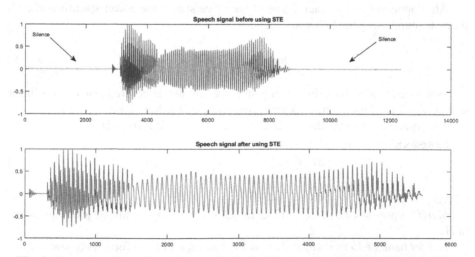

Fig. 4. Removing silence from the speech signal of the Amazigh digit "Amya" using STE.

environments [23]. These limitations can be overcome by using the Discrete Wavelet Transform (DWT) method because of its better temporal and frequency localization capability [23, 24].

The DWT method is applied to the energies of the Mel scaled log filter bank. The result of this operation gives the Mel-Frequency Discrete Wavelet Coefficients (MFDWC). The process of extracting MFDWC is the same as for MFCC, except that the DWT approach is applied instead of DCT (see Fig. 5).

To extract the MFDWC features, we first improve the quality of the input speech signal by reducing the low frequencies. Therefore, a high-pass pre-emphasis filter is used. Equation (4) shows the formula for the high-pass filter [25, 26]:

$$y(s) = 1 - 0.97s^{-1} \tag{4}$$

where

s is the input voice signal.

Then, the signal is segmented into several frames, neither long nor short in size. In this study, we segmented the signal into 25 ms frames with a 10 ms overlap. To reduce the signal discontinuities before and after each frame, the Hamming window is implemented in each frame. Equations (2) and (3) mentioned in the pre-processing part present the Hamming window calculation.

The next step is to convert each frame from the time domain to the frequency domain using the Fast Fourier Transform (FFT) algorithm.

$$s_i(k) = \sum_{n=1}^{N} s_i(n)w(n)e^{-2j\pi kn/N}, 1 \le k \le N/2 \tag{5}$$

where

$s_i(n)$ is the speech signal after framing and i is the frame index.

After applying FFT to each frame of the voice signal, the power spectrum of each frame is found using the following equation:

$$p_i(k) = \frac{1}{N}|s_i(k)|^2 \tag{6}$$

Psychophysical studies show that human ears do not detect frequencies on a linear scale [27]. Thus, the filter bank is processed based on the Mel scale.

The formula to convert the linear scale to the Mel scale is the following:

$$Mel(f) = 1125 * \ln\left(1 + \frac{f}{700}\right) \tag{7}$$

where

$Mel(f)$ represents the perceived Mel frequency and f represents the given frequency in Hz.

A filter bank of 25 triangular filters is used, obtained by the formula below:

$$b_m(k) = \begin{cases} \frac{k-f(mel-1)}{f(mel)-f(mel-1)}, & f(mel-1) \le k \le f(mel) \\ \frac{f(mel+1)-k}{f(mel+1)-f(mel)}, & f(mel) \le k \le f(mel+1) \\ 0, & otherwise \end{cases} \tag{8}$$

where

$f(mel)$ is the frequency in the Mel scale.

To calculate the energy of Mel filter bank, we multiply each filter bank defined in Eq. (8) by the power spectrum defined in Eq. (6), as shown in Eq. (9):

$$\tilde{e}_m = \sum_{k=0}^{K/2} p_i(k)b_m(k) \tag{9}$$

Finally, we apply the DWT approach to the logarithm of the Mel filter bank energies. This gives as a result the Mel-Frequency Discrete Wavelet Coefficients (MFDWC).

$$\tilde{c}_n = DWT(\log(\tilde{e}_m)) \tag{10}$$

The wavelet transform creates a set of basic functions called "child wavelets" using a prototype function known as "mother wavelets". The choice of the mother wavelet is crucial in achieving good temporal and frequency resolution. After trying several families of wavelets to get a good performance, we chose the "Daubechies4", which produces a result of 16 MFDWC features.

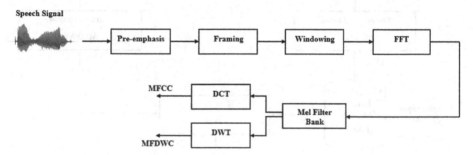

Fig. 5. The extraction process of MFCC and MFDWC features.

4.3 Classification

After feature extraction comes the classification step. The choice of a classification model is essential in achieving good performance. In this study, we used a powerful and commonly used classifier in the speech recognition field, the SVM model [24, 28–30].

SVM performs complex transformations of the data according to the selected kernel function. This transformation aims at maximizing the separation boundaries between data points based on defined labels or classes.

In our study, we do multiclass classification and SVM does not support this. SVM supports binary classification and separation of data points into two classes. Therefore, we decompose the multiclass classification problem into several binary classification problems, and this is what the one-versus-one and the one-versus-all approaches use. In the one-versus-one approach, the decomposition is set to a binary classifier for each pair of classes (N classes require $N(N-1)/2$ models). In the one-versus-all approach, the decomposition is set to a binary classifier for each class (N classes require N models).

Although the one-versus-one approach uses a high number of binary SVMs $(N(N-1)/2)$, it requires less training data and is less sensitive to unbalanced datasets. On the other hand, the one-versus-all method generates a relatively lower number of binary SVMs (N), but it needs a large dataset to train each binary SVM. Therefore, in this research, we chose the one-versus-one approach and used LIBSVM because it is more practical. In addition, as a kernel function, we used the Radial Basis Function (RBF).

Figure 6 presents the three steps involved in implementing the proposed system.

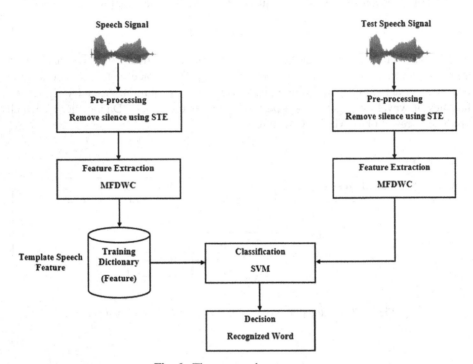

Fig. 6. The proposed system steps.

5   Experimental Results and Discussion

One of the most rarely used languages in technology is the Amazigh language. It is rare to find recognition systems based on the Amazigh language including speaker recognition, speech recognition and voice pathology recognition. The goal is to create an Amazigh-Tachelhit ASR system, using MFDWC for feature extraction and SVM for classification. Our database consists of 51600 audio files of 33 letters and 10 digits, 70% is used for training and 30% for testing (see Table 6). Moreover, to evaluate the system performance, different speakers are used in the testing process than the ones used in the training process.

Table 6. The training and test datasets used in this study.

Data	Training data	Test data	Total
Letters	27720	11880	39600
Digits	8400	3600	12000
Total	36120	15480	51600

To test the effectiveness of the system, three experiments were conducted. The first involved training and testing the system using only Amazigh digits, while the second used exclusively Amazigh letters and the third a combination of letters and digits (see Table 7).

Table 7. The various experiments conducted to test the proposed system effectiveness.

Experiments	Training dataset	Test dataset
Experiment 1: 10 digits (0 to 9)	8400	3600
Experiment 2: 33 letters	27720	11880
Experiment 3: 10 digits + 33 letters	36120	15480

The experiments were performed using MATLAB 2019 on a 64-bit operating system equipped with 8 GB of RAM and an Intel Core i7 processor.

Table 8 shows the recognition rates obtained from the first experiment. The test dataset of this experiment consisted of 3600 audio files. A total recognition rate of 94.42% was obtained. We can see that the digits that are well recognized by the system are: YEN (ⵢ ⴰ ⵏ) and KRAD (ⴽ ⵔⴰ ⴹ), with accuracies of 97.50% and 98.06% respectively. On the other hand, the digits that are poorly recognized by the system are: KOZ (ⴽ ⴽ ⵓ ⵣ) and SA (ⵙⴰ), with recognition rates of 92.22% and 90.56% respectively.

Table 9 shows the recognition rates from the second experiment. The test dataset of this experiment consisted of 11880 audio files. A total recognition rate of 90.82% was obtained. We can see that the letters that are well recognized by the system are: YAD (ⴷ) and YAT (ⵜ), with recognition rates of 96.39% and 96.94% respectively. On the other hand, the letters that are poorly recognized by the system are: YA (ⴰ) and YI (ⵉ), with recognition rates of 84.72% and 85.00% respectively.

Table 8. The recognition rates of 10 Amazigh digits using the MFDWC method and the SVM classifier.

Digits	Recognition rate (%)
AMYA	97.22
YEN	97.50
SIN	92.50
KRAD	98.06
KOZ	92.22
SMMUS	92.78
SDES	94.17
SA	90.56
TAM	96.67
TZA	92.50
Total recognition rate (%)	**94.42**

Table 9. The recognition rates of 33 Amazigh letters using the MFDWC method and the SVM classifier.

Letters	Recognition rate (%)
YA	84.72
YAB	86.94
YAG	93.06
YAGG	91.39
YAD	96.39
YADD	95.83
YEY	90.00
YAF	91.94
YAK	93.33
YAKK	93.06
YAH	92.50
YAHH	92.22
YAAA	86.39
YAKH	88.61
YAQQ	93.06
YI	85.00
YAJ	94.17
YAL	93.61

(*continued*)

Table 9. (*continued*)

Letters	Recognition rate (%)
YAM	93.06
YAN	92.22
YO	86.11
YAR	91.39
YARR	89.17
YAGH	91.67
YAS	87.22
YASS	87.78
YASH	87.50
YAT	96.94
YATT	95.83
YAW	93.61
YAY	91.11
YAZ	85.83
YAZZ	85.28
Total recognition rate (%)	**90.82**

Tables 8 and 9 show that the total recognition rate of the 33 letters is the least accurate compared to the total recognition rate of the 10 digits. In addition, we can observe that words containing the letters "Z" or "S" are the most misrecognized.

Table 10 shows the overall recognition rate from the third experiment, which is 92.22%. The test dataset of this experiment consisted of 15480 audio files including 33 letters and 10 digits.

Table 10. Overall recognition rate of the global data (Amazigh 10 digits and 33 letters) using the MFDWC method and the SVM classifier.

Global data	Recognition rate (%)
10 digits + 33 letters	92.22

Although we used different speakers in the testing process than those used in the training process, the system performed well, achieving more than 92.00%. Many conditions affect system performance and cause recognition results to differ from system to system, depending on the number of speech files used in the training and test datasets. These conditions include: the quality of the audio files, the environment in which they are recorded, whether it is a noisy or normal environment, the number, age, gender and accent of the speakers, as well as the methods used to train and test the system.

Table 11 shows the results obtained by other systems and our system.

Table 11. The recognition rates obtained by other systems and our system.

State of the art	Proposed System	Amazigh Corpus	Number of speakers	Number of training voice recordings	Number of test voice recordings	Recognition rate (%)
[11]	System based on CMU Sphinx tools	33 letters	9	2640	330	88.00
[12]	System based on CMU Sphinx tools	33 letters + 10 digits	60	18060	7740	89.07
[14]	System based on CMU Sphinx tools	33 letters	34	9900	1320	90.00
Current study	System based on MFDWC and SVM	33 letters + 10 digits	120	36120	15480	92.22

6 Conclusion

In this work, our goal was to focus on a new language, one less documented and less explored by researchers, which is the Amazigh language, Tachelhit. Therefore, a new speech recognition system has been proposed for the Amazigh-Tachelhit language. The database used in this system is a self-created database. It is collected from 120 speakers: 60 are native speakers and the other 60 are not. 30% of the database is used for testing and 70% for training. The system is based on a combination of two widely used feature extraction methods, MFCC and DWT, to form a new method called MFDWC. The SVM model is used for classification, and the one-versus-one approach is used to handle the multiclass classification problem. To test the effectiveness of the system, we used different speakers in the testing process to those used in the training process. The system performed well, with an overall rate of 92.22%. According to the experimental results, the total recognition rate of the 33 Amazigh letters is less accurate than that of the 10 Amazigh digits. In addition, words containing the letters "Z" or "S" are the least recognized. The proposed system can be used in various applications, including language learning, translation and dictation.

References

1. Patil, U.G., Shirbahadurkar, S.D., Paithane, A.N.: Automatic speech recognition of isolated words in Hindi language using MFCC. In: Proceedings of the 2016 International Conference on Computing, Analytics and Security Trends (CAST), pp. 433–438. IEEE (2016). https://doi.org/10.1109/CAST.2016.7915008
2. Satori, H., Harti, M., Chenfour, N.: Introduction to Arabic speech recognition using CMUSphinx system. arXiv Preprint (2007). arXiv:0704.2083
3. Youcef, B.C., Elemine, Y.M., Islam, B., Farid, B.: Speech recognition system based on OLLO French Corpus by using MFCCs. In: Chadli, M., Bououden, S., Zelinka, I. (eds.) Recent Advances in Electrical Engineering and Control Applications. LNEE, vol. 411, pp. 326–331. Springer, Cham (2017). https://doi.org/10.1007/978-3-319-48929-2_25
4. Naithani, K., Thakkar, V.M., Semwal, A.: English language speech recognition using MFCC and HMM. In: Proceedings of the 2018 International Conference on Research in Intelligent and Computing in Engineering (RICE), pp. 1–7. IEEE (2018). https://doi.org/10.1109/RICE.2018.8509046
5. Nejme, F.Z., Boulaknadel, S., Aboutajdine, D.: Analyse automatique de la morphologie nominale Amazighe. In: Proceedings of the 2013 Actes de la conférence du Traitement Automatique du Langage Naturel (TALN), pp. 5–18 (2013)
6. Young, S.J., Young, S.: The HTK Hidden Markov Model Toolkit : Design and Philosophy. Cambridge University Engineering Department (1993)
7. Lamere, P., et al.: The CMU Sphinx-4 speech recognition system. In: Proceedings of the 2003 IEEE International Conference on Acoustics, Speech and Signal Processing (ICASSP), pp. 2–5. IEEE (2003)
8. Ordowski, M., Deshmukh, N., Ganapathiraju, A., Hamaker, J., Picone, J.: A public domain speech-to-text system. In: Proceedings of the 1999 European Conference on Speech Communication and Technology. (1999)
9. Liu, X., Zhao, Y., Pi, X., Liang, L., Nefian, A.V.: Audio-visual continuous speech recognition using a coupled hidden Markov model. In: Proceedings of the 2002 International Conference on Spoken Language Processing (ICSLP) (2002)
10. El Ouahabi, S., Atounti, M., Bellouki, M.: Optimal parameters selected for automatic recognition of spoken Amazigh digits and letters using Hidden Markov Model Toolkit. Int. J. Speech Technol. 23(4), 861–871 (2020). https://doi.org/10.1007/s10772-020-09762-3
11. Telmem, M., Ghanou, Y.: Amazigh speech recognition system based on CMUSphinx. In: Ben Ahmed, M., Boudhir, A.A. (eds.) SCAMS 2017. LNNS, vol. 37, pp. 397–410. Springer, Cham (2018). https://doi.org/10.1007/978-3-319-74500-8_37
12. Satori, H., ElHaoussi, F.: Investigation Amazigh speech recognition using CMU tools. Int. J. Speech Technol. 17(3), 235–243 (2014). https://doi.org/10.1007/s10772-014-9223-y
13. El Ouahabi, S., Atounti, M., Bellouki, M.: Toward an automatic speech recognition system for amazigh-tarifit language. Int. J. Speech Technol. 22(2), 421–432 (2019). https://doi.org/10.1007/s10772-019-09617-6
14. Telmem, M., Ghanou, Y.: Estimation of the optimal HMM parameters for amazigh speech recognition system using CMU-Sphinx. Procedia Comput. Sci. 127, 92–101 (2018). https://doi.org/10.1016/j.procs.2018.01.102

15. El Ouahabi, S., Atounti, M., Bellouki, M.: Amazigh isolated-word speech recognition system using hidden Markov model toolkit (HTK). In: Proceedings of the 2016 International Conference on Information Technology for Organizations Development (IT4OD), pp. 1–7. IEEE (2016). https://doi.org/10.1109/IT4OD.2016.7479305

16. Ouakrim, O.: Fonética y fonología del Bereber. Survey: University of Autònoma de Barcelona (1995)

17. Boulaknadel, S., Talha, M.: Analyse syntactico-sémantique de la langue amazighe (2013)

18. Ataa Allah, F., Boulaknadel, S.: Natural language processing for Amazigh language: challenges and future directions. In: Proceedings of the 2012 workshop on Language Technology for Normalisation of Less-Resourced Languages (SALTMIL8/AfLaT2012) (2012)

19. Ataa Allah, F., Boulaknadel, S.: Convertisseur pour la langue amazighe: script arabe-latin–tifinaghe. In: Proceedings of the 2011 Symposium International sur le Traitement Automatique de la Culture Amazighe, pp. 3–10 (2011)

20. Open Speech and Language Resources. https://www.openslr.org/resources.php. Accessed 20 Jan 2023

21. Audacity software. https://www.audacityteam.org/. Accessed 17 Dec 2022

22. Bachu, R.G., Kopparthi, S., Adapa, B., Barkana, B.D.: Separation of voiced and unvoiced using zero crossing rate and energy of the speech signal. In: Proceedings of the 2008 American Society for Engineering Education (ASEE), pp. 1–7 (2008)

23. Tufekci, Z., Gowdy, J.N.: Feature extraction using discrete wavelet transform for speech recognition. In: Proceedings of the 2000 IEEE SoutheastCon. 'Preparing for The New Millennium' (Cat. No. 00CH37105), pp. 116–123. IEEE (2000). https://doi.org/10.1109/secon.2000.845444

24. Cutajar, M., Gatt, E., Grech, I., Casha, O., Micallef, J.: Comparative study of automatic speech recognition techniques. In: Proceedings of the 2013 IET Signal Processing, vol. 7, no. 1, pp. 25–46 (2013). https://doi.org/10.1049/iet-spr.2012.0151

25. Hammami, N., Lawal, I.A., Bedda, M., Farah, N.: Recognition of Arabic speech sound error in children. Int. J. Speech Technol. 23(3), 705–711 (2020). https://doi.org/10.1007/s10772-020-09746-3

26. Pandit, P., Makwana, P., Bhatt, S.: Automatic speech recognition of continuous speech signal of Gujarati language using machine learning. In: Sahni, M., Merigó, J.M., Jha, B.K., Verma, R. (eds.) Mathematical Modeling, Computational Intelligence Techniques and Renewable Energy. AISC, vol. 1287, pp. 147–159. Springer, Singapore (2021). https://doi.org/10.1007/978-981-15-9953-8_13

27. Senthil Raja, G., Dandapat, S.: Speaker recognition under stressed condition. Int. J. Speech Technol. 13, 141–161 (2010). https://doi.org/10.1007/s10772-010-9075-z

28. Padmanabhan, J., Johnson Premkumar, M.J.: Machine learning in automatic speech recognition: a survey. IETE Tech. Rev. 32(4), 240–251 (2015). https://doi.org/10.1080/02564602.2015.1010611

29. Ghai, W., Singh, N.: Literature review on automatic speech recognition. Int. J. Comput. Appl. 41(8), 42–50 (2012). https://doi.org/10.5120/5565-7646

30. Ali, H., Jianwei, A., Iqbal, K.: Automatic speech recognition of Urdu digits with optimal classification approach. Int. J. Comput. Appl. 118(9), 1–5 (2015). https://doi.org/10.5120/20770-3275

Bibliometric Analysis of Robotic Process Automation Domain: Key Topics, Challenges and Solutions

Tiong Yew Tang[✉] 🆔 and Ha Jin Hwang 🆔

Sunway Business School, Sunway University, Subang Jaya, Selangor 47500, Malaysia
{tiongyewt,hjhwang}@sunway.edu.my

Abstract. In the era of Industry Revolution 4.0, organizations around the world are continuously looking for new technological breakthroughs that can enhance business process efficiency and reduce the cost of operations. Robotic Process Automation (RPA) has effectively addressed these issues in many different business sectors. RPA is a software application that automates Graphical User Interface (GUI) tasks that were previously performed by human users. However, the current literature in this research is lacking comprehensive bibliometric literature review which can be used to identify the future trend and the latest issues in the RPA research domain. To address these gaps, the objective of this study is to identify the current issues and future trends in the RPA domain. Firstly, a performance analysis of the dataset is performed to understand the future trend of the research domain. Then, the science mapping co-word examination bibliometric data analysis is performed on the selected dataset to identify current issues in this research domain. This work also addresses these issues with a practical evaluation framework for business organizations to effectively exploit the advantages provided by the RPA implementation.

Keywords: Industry Revolution 4.0 · Robotic Process Automation · RPA · Intelligent Process Automation · IPA · Bibliometric Literature Review

1 Introduction

1.1 Background

In the era of Industry Revolution 4.0, business organizations are constantly looking for technological breakthroughs that foster their business growth and reduce operating costs. Such technological breakthroughs also contribute to a country's economic development [1, 2]. Especially during the post-Covid-19 era, organizations need to sustain business in the Volatility, Uncertainty, Complexity and Ambiguity (VUCA) [3] environment whereby it is hard to predict future events for sustaining business.

RPA enables the completion of repetitive tasks more rapidly while freeing up time for human resources for other important tasks that require a higher level of human intelligence [4]. Also, RPA implementation provides significant cost savings, high scalability, efficiency, productivity and improved service quality for business operations to gain a competitive advantage [5]. Hence, RPA gain traction in this research domain in recent years and we will discuss this in the following sections.

Despite such high importance, many business organizations, particularly small or medium-sized enterprises (SMEs) lack an in-depth understanding of major RPA components (e.g. issues, software tools, business impact, new topics and methodologies), particularly before implementing RPA projects [6]. Many times, organizations attempt to implement RPA but remain unsuccessful because of the lack of understanding of RPA methodology in synchronizing the human user policy with RPA policy, which results in loss of data [7]. Therefore, this research provides an overview to understand the future trends and current issues in the RPA research domain.

2 Literature Summary

In the RPA domain, there are a few bibliometric studies have been done in the past, however, the current literature lacks comprehensive bibliometric data analysis to identify the current issues and future research trends. For instance, one of the attempts made by Afriliana and Ramadhan [8] focused on the digital transformation perspectives of the RPA research domain. Their study offers practices and success criteria for professionals and businesses on how to use RPA to improve their digital workforce. However, one of the major limitations of the study was that it included publications between the years 2017 and 2021 only. Moreover, their work did not identify the current issues and key topics in the RPA research domain.

Another bibliometric study was done by Atanasovski and Toceva [9] on disruptive technologies for accounting. Their findings encourage adaptation and alignment to technological developments by showing that academics and scientific researchers work in the same general direction as practitioners. The study focuses on the predefined categories of accounting disruptive technologies which are RPA, big data, data analytics, cloud computing, artificial intelligence and blockchain, however, their work did not identify the latest issues or keywords in the articles. Also, their work focuses on publications between 2016 to 2020 only.

Besides the above bibliometric studies, a systematic literature review has been conducted by D. Pramod [10] in the RPA domain using PRISMA methodology [11]. Their study shows that RPA has been widely employed in banking and associated industries, with less widespread usage in the healthcare and industrial sectors. A research agenda has been developed by speculating on future paths, but there are still many more opportunities in other disciplines that need to be exploited by leveraging technology. For instance, conducting special focus workshops on healthcare and industrial sectors can create more awareness of these domains. However, their literature review lacks a science mapping method to identify current issues discussed in the RPA research domain.

Another systematic literature review done by Ivančić et al. [12] on RPA Robotic process automation focuses on the categorization of the article documents. Their study offers a summary of RPA concepts and practical applications, as well as the advantages of its adoption in various industries. However, the author's analysis bias also may be accidentally introduced into the review process because it is not done with machine learning analysis of the articles. Machine learning analysis does not depend on humans to analyze data and is more objective in analyzing data. Also, the years of publication selected is only between 2016 and 2018.

Another systematic literature review is done by Schlund and Schmidt [13] on RPA in Industrial Engineering. Their results highlight the need for the manufacturing and industrial engineering sectors to catch up on research to fully use RPA's potential for future applications. The study classifies five types of the contribution of RPA mainly process planning, planning and scheduling, authoring tasks, robot programming and incident management. However, such pre-defined classifications conducted by the authors themselves may have human biases.

This research was conducted by Rogers and Zvarikova [14] on algorithmic governance powered by RPA for sustainable smart manufacturing with a quantitative literature review using Web of Science, Scopus and ProQuest tools. The methodology selected is Preferred Reporting Items for Systematic Reviews and Meta-analysis (PRISMA) and the total number of final selected articles is just 21. However, in this work, the article selection process may be accidentally introduced with human biases.

Hence, to overcome the weaknesses of all the discussed bibliometric studies/reviews, the current study first incorporates publications over a longer period i.e., from the year 1985 until 2022. Second, the current study incorporates more keyword synonyms in the initial search, which results in retrieving a greater number of related publications to encompass the widest possible range of RPA literature. Third, the current study incorporates text mining and co-word examination to identify the latest key topics and issues discussed in the RPA research domain. Following that, we aim to suggest practical solutions for each identified current issue in the RPA domain. And lastly, we use machine methods with science mapping features to remove human biases in data analysis. Using science mapping, we aim to foreground the transition in the RPA research trends over time and determine future research directions.

3 Methodology

Referring to Fig. 1. on the research methodology, this work gathers bibliometric data on RPA research for its literature review. This work implements the Scientific Procedures and Rationales for Systematic Literature Reviews (SPAR-4-SLR) protocol, which comprises three major steps which are assembling, arranging, and assessing articles [15]. This work integrates bibliometric analysis methods [16] into SPAR-4-SLR [15] at the assessing phase of the methodology. As illustrated in Fig. 1. The current study adopts standardized and replicable procedures and incorporates two types of bibliometric analysis, (i) Performance analysis, and (ii) mapping text mining and co-word examination at the assessing phase of SPAR-4-SLR. Therefore, bibliometric analysis tools such as VOSViewer [17] or Bibliometrix [18] and be utilized to analyze the selected article data at the assessing phase of SPAR-4-SLR.

To begin with, we chose Scopus which is the largest database of peer-reviewed publications [19]. This ensured the selection of the high-quality and widest range of literature for our analysis. Next, we searched the keyword "Robotic Process Automation" along with several other terms with the same meaning, which are: "software robots", "intelligent process automation", and "software-based intelligent process automation" in the article titles, abstracts and keywords of documents. Searching with similar terms together resulted in retrieving comparatively a greater number of related publications, thus encompassing the widest possible range of RPA literature. This initial search which was performed on the date of 13th January 2023 revealed 929 documents.

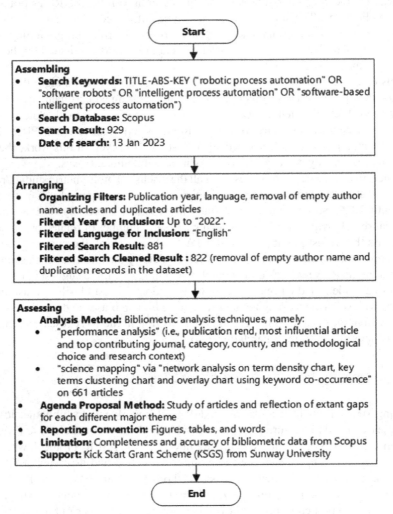

Fig. 1. Scientific Procedures and Rationales for Systematic Literature Reviews (SPAR-4-SLR) Protocol [15]

Following the initial search, we included all publication years from the beginning of the RPA research domain (i.e., 1985) until 2022. Since we aimed to analyze the RPA research domain, therefore, our selection criteria are selected to specifically capture all the articles to analyze the latest research trend. Further, we chose articles written in the English language to read and understand the content. After these inclusions, the final number of articles appeared to be 881.

After completing the initial search, we started the data-cleaning process. For that, we exported the CSV file from the Scopus database containing all the bibliometric information of all articles. Before processing further, we first cleaned this system-generated raw file for duplicated records or missing information. This step eliminated documents which were missing the author name and duplicated titles, making our final sample reach 822 articles. After this, the cleaned file was used first in the Bibliometrix [18] bibliometric analysis R software for the performance analysis, and then in VOSviewer [17] software for text mining and co-word examination.

Performance analysis describes how well a research topic is performing over some time [16]. We performed an in-depth performance analysis using the Bibliometrix [18] bibliometric analysis R software and visualized the RPA publication growth from 1985 to 2022. Then, we focus on the latest era and present the documents by subject areas over the last 10 years as well to forecast the future research trend.

Another type of bibliometric analysis that we conducted is the text mining and co-word examination. This is defined as research analysis that concentrates on the textual content of the publications and investigates the past, present, or potential links between key topics in a research field [16]. We conducted this analysis using VOSviewer [17] software and foregrounded the most frequent author keywords and their categorization; such as current issues in intelligent process automation, natural language processing, cognitive automation, deep learning and sustainability. Hence, this science mapping method will identify the current issues in the RPA research domain.

Referring to Fig. 1, the first phase of SPAR-4-SLR is assembled. To assemble in this study is to determine the search terms related to RPA from the preliminary evaluation of pertinent literature to compile the corpus of papers on RPA [15]. Then, the next phase of SPAR-4-SLR is arranged. Arranging refers to the arrangement and cleaning up of literature. The third phase is defined as assessing. The term assessing of SPAR-4-SLR refers to evaluating and summarizing research articles. Therefore, these three phases are the main phases for the SPAR-4-SLR methodology to analyze the published articles on the RPA research domain.

3.1 Article Selection

The research methodology of this work is to select a set of RPA domain articles from a reputable research indexing database and then utilize bibliometric software to generate data visualization to identify the current issues and trends in this research domain. The bibliometric research methodology approach had been widely accepted and discussed for literature review study [16]. The detailed steps to conduct the article selection research methodology for this work as below:

Table 1. Article Selection Settings

Selection Criteria	Description
Database	Scopus index database only
Search Section	Title, abstract and keyword only
Keyword Searched	TITLE-ABS-KEY ("robotic process automation" OR "software robots" OR "intelligent process automation" OR "software-based intelligent process automation") AND (EXCLUDE(PUBYEAR,2023)) AND (LIMIT-TO (LANGUAGE, "English"))
Years	Until 2022
Language	English language articles only
Download File	Comma Separated Values (CSV) format
Data Cleaning	Remove empty author name records and remove duplicated records

Referring to Table 1, this study selects the published articles only written in the English language from the earliest article document dated 1985 until 2022 from the Scopus index database. The search keywords are selected based on the title and abstract sections of the article. However, this work excluded the published articles for the year 2023 because the time of writing the journal is during the year 2023 and the 2023 articles data are still in the accumulating process. Hence, only 881 published articles are selected from the Scopus index article database and it is based on the keywords and filtering criteria in Table 1. However, after cleaning the missing author name records and 825 published articles remained in the dataset. The remaining 822 records are checked for duplication and 3 duplication records are found and these records are cleaned.

3.2 Bibliometric Visualization Software Settings

This study selected the co-word examination bibliometric data visualization methodology [16] because this methodology can effectively identify current issues in the research domain. Next, this step is to download the selected articles from the Scopus index database website generated Comma Separated Value (CSV) file with the article search criteria in Table 1. The none selected articles will not be included in the CSV. Then, import the download CSV file to VOSViewer bibliometric software [17].

The next step is to proceed with the VOSViewer software [17] according to Table 2 to generate the co-word examination [16] bibliometric data visualization charts. The final step is to conduct a co-word examination bibliometric analysis and proceed with report writing on the obtained results. Furthermore, the Bibliometrix [18] software tool for bibliometric analysis will also be used in the performance analysis to generate descriptive statistic information and bibliometric information of the selected dataset.

Table 2. VOSViewer [17] Settings

VOSViewer Setting	Description
Software version	1.6.18
Choose the type of data	Create a map based on bibliographic data
Choose data source	Read data from bibliographic database files
Select files	Scopus
Type of Analysis	Co-occurrence
Unit of Analysis	Author keywords
Counting method	Full counting
Choose threshold	The minimum number of occurrences of a term is 3
Choose a number of terms	The number of terms to be selected is 139

4 Performance Analysis

A bibliometric analysis method called performance analysis describes how well a research topic is performing [16]. This section discusses the performance analysis of the selected article documents from the Scopus index database based on the search criteria in Table 1. The objective of this section is to understand the context of the dataset by using data visualization before interpreting the bibliometric information in the following section.

4.1 Overall Publication Documents Over Time

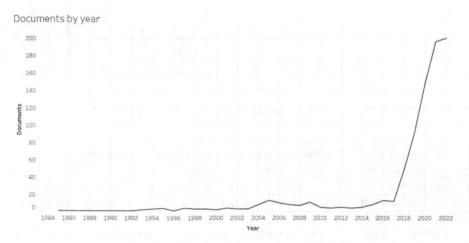

Fig. 2. Overall Publication Documents Count Over Time Chart

The Fig. 2. Line chart illustrates this research domain key terms such as "software robots", "intelligent process automation" or "software-based intelligent process automation" being introduced as early as 1985 to 2022. However, this research domain did not gain much attention in its early years. Then, recently this research domain started to gain exponential growth in terms of research article publication total count around the year 2017 until 2022. These phenomena show the recent RPA technology interest and acceptance in both research and business communities.

Initially, the research field is defined as software robotic for software-based automation research. Then, the term Robotic Process Automation (RPA) was first coined by Blue Prism for the business service's lexicon started in 2012 [20]. However, the actual growth of the RPA research domain research article published in the year 2017 is only visible after 5 years from the initial definition of the RPA term. In summary, this RPA research domain is still on its uptrend growth in terms of article publication.

4.2 Publication Documents by Subject Area Over the Last 10 Years

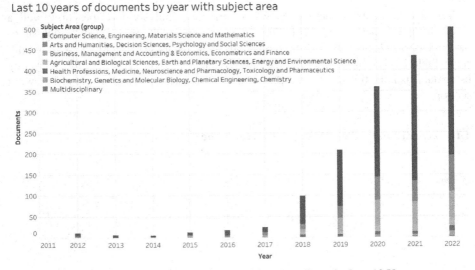

Fig. 3. Publication Documents by Subject Area Over the Last 10 Years

Referring to Fig. 3. The bar chart explains the different research subject areas and categorized them into the stacked bar chart over the last 10 years. The last 10 years of data are selected based on Table 1 search criteria for data visualization because the significant changes can be observable visually on the chart. The subject areas are grouped for ease of data visualization.

The Fig. 3. Bar chart shows the computer science and engineering research subject areas are the leading areas in this research domain throughout the last 10 years. The chart shows the significant upward growth trend of these disciplines in this research domain. The reason is artificial intelligence, machine learning and software robot automation in

RPA are related closely to computer science and engineering disciplines. These disciplines are part of the Industry Revolution 4.0 [21] agenda to promote business process automation and digitization of organizations.

Next, business domain research subject areas such as management and accounting, economics, and finance research ranked the second highest research contribution in this RPA research domain. Some of the reasons that this research domain gained interest from the business industry are reduced personnel expenses, improved operational effectiveness, accuracy, and availability of services around-the-clock [22]. Therefore, Fig. 3. Bar chart shows the business domain publication contribution leads in second place in this article dataset for the last 10 years.

Furthermore, psychology and social sciences subject areas are also gaining progress as the third highest contributor in this research domain. If the project did not implement change management when introducing RPA to the users then users' acceptance of business process automation will be low [23]. Some of the factors users accept RPA software robot's integration positively are social influence, work relevance and demonstrating results to the stakeholders [24]. Therefore, psychology and social sciences subject areas are important factors in the RPA domain.

Moreover, Fig. 3. Chart shows recently during the years 2020 and 2022, a new emergence of a multidisciplinary section is shown in the chart. This is motivated by the research community's interest in multidiscipline publication in the RPA research domain that triggered the new multidiscipline phenomenon that started to gain attention recently. In short, the RPA research trend is growing and vibrant in different subject areas and is supported by diverse disciplines of research communities.

5 Science Mapping

5.1 Co-word Examination Bibliometric Analysis

Science mapping is an examination that reveals and presents a visual depiction of the information that is currently available and how it is connected to other knowledge in a certain subject [16]. The co-word examination bibliometric analysis [16] is defined as research analysis work that concentrates on the textual content of the publication itself and investigates the past, present, or potential links between subjects in a research field. Some examples of co-word examination applications in research are [25–29]. The co-word examination bibliometric analysis is a method used in this work to identify the current issues that arise in the research domain with the bibliometric data visualization software tools.

In contrast to citation analysis, co-citation analysis, and bibliographic coupling [16], which use either cited or citing publications as a basis for their analyses, this work only focuses on co-word examination bibliometric to analyze the potential links between author's text keywords in the "article titles", "keywords" and "abstracts" sections. This work selected co-word examination bibliometric analysis because this method can identify the current issues and related keywords in the RPA research domain effectively.

Referring to Fig. 4 and 5, key terms clustering visualization chart, the bigger term label size display is used to identify which terms in this research domain have the highest frequency of occurrence across the selected article dataset. The bigger size key term

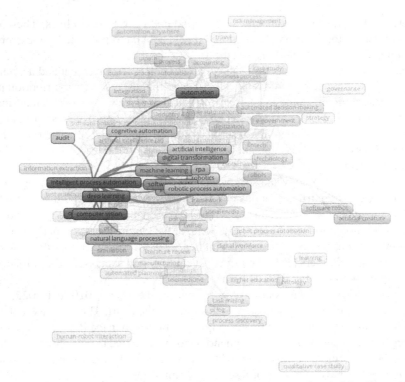

Fig. 4. Natural Language Processing + Intelligent Process Automation and Intelligent Process Automation + Cognitive Automation Clustering Visualization Chart

labels indicate the higher term frequency used across all the selected articles dataset. On the other hand, the smaller size key term labels indicate the low term frequency used in the dataset. The term density data visualization effectively shows the related common words used in the title, keywords and abstract across the selected article dataset.

Referring to Fig. 4 and 5. All are based on the experiment settings in Table 2, The VOSviewer software [17] network visualization feature identified 13 different clusters discussed in the selected article dataset. In summary, the thin line connection between these keywords in different clusters indicates there are only a few investigations on these areas from the different clusters and potentially it may lead to promising multidisciplinary research in these clusters. We will discuss more details on the relationship between each of these keywords in the next section.

5.2   Overlay Visualization Analysis on Current Issues

The generated overlay co-word examination bibliometric data visualization chart will be discussed in this section. The latest emerging topics of interest are labelled with a yellow label and the old topics are labelled with a dark blue label in the chart. The objective of this section is to select the current issues in the RPA research domain that is colored in yellow/green (current issues) in the different cluster for analysis and discussion. The

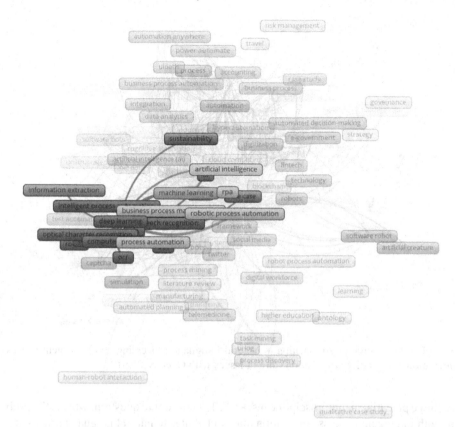

Fig. 5. Deep Learning + Sustainability Clustering Visualization Chart

selected current issues (yellow/green label) with little investigation work (thin line of connection between labels) from different clusters (different colors of labels) may lead to potential high-value multidisciplinary research.

The Fig. 6. Overlay chart shows the current issues in the RPA research domain. Our study investigates the current state of research in intelligent process automation and identifies any urgent situations arising from a lack of responsiveness to the needs of natural language processing. To achieve this, VOSViewer software computes the occurrence of keyword terms in the author's keywords of selected articles. Figure 6. Provides an overview of the terms and their interconnectivity, with term size representing the frequency of occurrence and the thickness of connecting lines reflecting the frequency of co-occurrence between two terms [30].

In Fig. 6., it could be seen that one of the most recently emerging terms that authors have used is 'intelligent process automation'. Furthermore, the term 'intelligent process automation' has a thin connecting line with the term 'natural language processing'. This means that fewer authors are recently giving focused on these different research cluster's topics which are intelligent process automation and natural language processing that

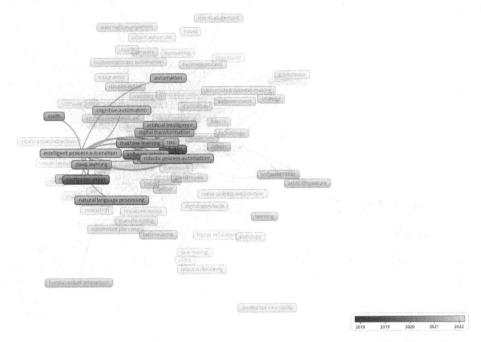

Fig. 6. Intelligent Process Automation + Natural Language Processing and Intelligent Process Automation + Cognitive Automation Current Issues with Overlay Chart

have huge potential in multidiscipline research. This raises the question: what is the problem with intelligent process automation that contributes to natural language processing, particularly in the context of RPA? To answer this, there are wide technical capability gaps that exist in intelligent process automation [31] and natural language processing [32], which enable the implementation success of RPA projects for automating difficult business processes that require human intelligence to process the natural language text information. For example, intelligent process automation applications of RPA projects such as using natural language processing [32] automate the daily business transaction to each manual task to improve the efficiency of the business transaction. If businesses would not respond timely and delay the new opportunity of implementing natural language processing into their intelligent process automation for their RPA project, their prospective users may lose many opportunities to automate the unstructured text data business processes for operation cost saving.

Furthermore, the term 'intelligent process automation' has a thin connecting line with the term 'cognitive automation'. This means that fewer researchers are recently giving few attentions to these different research cluster's topics which are intelligent process automation and cognitive automation that may have huge multidisciplinary research opportunities. Cognitive automation is defined as machine learning facilitated business process automation (BPA) [33]. This raises the question: what is the problem with intelligent process automation that contributes to cognitive automation, particularly in the context of RPA? To answer this, there are wide technical capability gaps that exist in intelligent process automation [31] and cognitive automation [34], which enable successful RPA project implementation for automating business process tasks that require human intelligence to discover the possible business processes that need automation. For example, intelligent process automation applications of RPA projects such as cognitive automation [34] structure data, drive existing business models and create value between legacy industries. If a business could not engage timely and missed the new opportunity of implementing cognitive automation into their intelligent process automation for their RPA project, their prospective stakeholders may suffer from a lack of opportunity to automate the business process that is not able to be detected by human users.

In Fig. 7., the term 'Deep Learning' has a thin connecting line with the term 'Sustainability'. This means that few researchers are recently giving focused on these separated topics which are deep learning and sustainability of RPA technologies that may lead to possible multidisciplinary research outcomes. This raises the question: what is the problem with deep learning that contributes to the sustainability of RPA technologies? To address this, there are research discussions on deep learning in the RPA domain [35] and its sustainability adoption implementation in business, which indicate the success of the RPA project. For example, in this research [36] RPA adoption in businesses and its impact on user adoption and software application sustainability in the domain of the services industry. Deep learning capability will increase the application adoption sustainability. If businesses could not adopt timely and missed the opportunity of implementing deep learning into their RPA project, their prospective stakeholders may not view the RPA project as sustainable for their business.

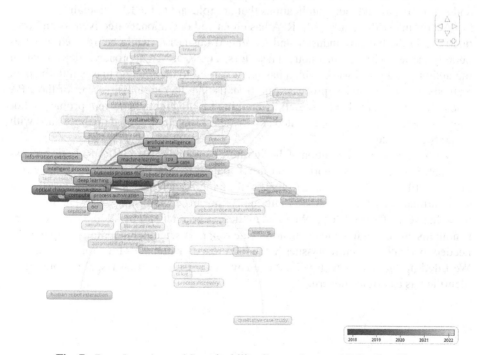

Fig. 7. Deep Learning and Sustainability Current Issues with Overlay Chart

6 Discussions

This section discusses the contribution of this work towards the research gaps in the literature. This work addressed the author analysis bias that may be introduced accidentally during the literature review process. The methodology utilized bibliometric analysis literature review methodology in this work utilizes machine learning clustering algorithms to analyze the selected dataset without introducing human error or biases in the process.

Firstly, this bibliometric study [8] focused on the RPA research domain's viewpoints on digital transformation. We address the research gaps with a bibliometric analysis from the year 1985 to 2022 with more years of selection for a comprehensive understanding of the research domain. Additionally, this effort included new keyword synonyms with related search parameters, increasing the number of relevant articles that could be retrieved for the study's completion. In this study, we were able to pinpoint the change in the research from software robots to RPA in the articles, and as a result, we were able to provide a more comprehensive picture of the whole research area. Additionally, the co-word analysis is used to pinpoint the most recent hot themes and difficulties the RPA research sector is facing.

Secondly, this article [9] is research on disruptive technology in accounting that uses bibliometric analysis. To successfully find the newest keywords in the RPA study area without being constrained by the author's predetermined categories of keywords, this work employs a co-word analysis to fill this research gap. Additionally, the publications between 2016 and 2020 are the subject of this investigation. These research gaps will be filled over a longer period using search parameters that include additional keywords and synonyms to find more publications that are relevant to the RPA domain.

According to this study [10], RPA has enhanced operational effectiveness and productivity in the banking industry and its related businesses while being used less frequently in the healthcare and industrial sectors. The PRISMA approach is dependent on the author's analytical work, which has the potential to incorporate biases into the data analysis during the review process. Additionally, the literature assessment of the RPA research area does not have a scientific mapping tool to highlight current problems. For every issue that this study highlighted as a present problem, we filled up these gaps with workable remedies.

With a thorough examination of the literature, this study [12] on RPA Robotic process automation focuses on categorizing the article papers (SLR). Because the review method does not utilize machine learning to analyze the papers, analytical bias might nevertheless unintentionally enter the process. Additionally, the chosen publishing years are limited to those between 2016 and 2018. We filled in these research holes by adding new keyword synonyms and extending the publication date range. A scientific mapping component is needed to identify the current issues in the RPA research domain's literature assessment. We filled up these gaps with workable answers for every current issue that our study identified as a current concern.

Using the systematic literature review (SLR) technique, another study of the literature on RPA in industrial engineering was conducted [13]. Four categories of RPA contributions are categorized by the systematic literature review research, including process planning, planning and scheduling, writing tasks, robot programming, and incident management. However, as the authors themselves carry out this pre-determined categorization, biases may unintentionally enter the review process. With a bibliometric literature review approach, this study fills the research gap that might be caused by human biases or errors and replaces them with machine learning techniques.

7 Practical Implications

The practical implication of this study for a business organization is to provide a practical solution before venturing into RPA implementation. The business organization will be benefited from the higher success rate of RPA implementation of risks and benefits are carefully taken into consideration when venturing into RPA implementation. Below is the list of practical implications for adopting RPA into businesses:

- Natural language processing will enable wider business process automation.
- Cognitive automation will provide more efficient business process automation.
- Deep learning with sustainability consideration will allow long-term benefits.

8 Conclusions

This work investigates the bibliometric literature review for 36 years from 1985 until 2022. This study identified that this research domain gained traction over the last 10 years and recently in the year 2017 it showed exponential growth in research article contributions. Also, there is a new emergence in multidisciplinary RPA research in recent years between 2020 and 2022. One of the reasons for many emerging RPA multidiscipline research is gaining attention is because RPA involves a wide range of disciplines such as computer science, business, management, accounting, human resources, customer relationship management, engineering, chemistry, health sciences, social science, decision science, etc. Therefore, the research article publication contribution in this research domain is still on its upward trend.

In summary, the key factor for successful RPA project implementation is to adopt more of the latest technologically advanced tools that automate business processes that is previously done by humans (e.g. natural language processing). Therefore, human expertise can be focused on other important tasks to save operation costs to enable widespread RPA adoption and acceptance from the project's stakeholders. Hence, the RPA project can be viewed as a sustainable long-term solution and a competitive advantage for businesses in the challenging VUCA market environment.

9 Limitations and Future Works

This work covered a wide range of different research subject areas across the RPA research domain. This study aims to understand the overview of the RPA research domain in terms of co-word examination bibliometric literature review and to understand the current challenges faced in this research domain. However, this study has not utilized advanced machine learning techniques such as deep learning for RPA bibliometric literature review. Hence, future work will be focusing on advanced machine learning techniques to discover hidden data patterns and hence will enable more in-depth study of the research domain.

Acknowledgement. This work was supported in part by Sunway University and Sunway Business School under Kick Start Grant Scheme (KSGS) NO: GRTIN-KSGS-DBA[S]-02-2022. This work is also part of the Sustainable Business Research Cluster and Research Centre for Human-Machine Collaboration (HUMAC) at Sunway University. We also wish to thank those who have supported this research.

References

1. Kedziora, D., Kiviranta, H.-M.: Digital business value creation with robotic process automation (rpa) in northern and central europe. Management (2018). https://doi.org/10.26493/1854-4231.13.161-174
2. Ahmed, S., Hossain, M.F.: The impact of robotics in the growth and economic development. Bus. Manag. Rev. **10**(5) (2019)
3. Linstone, H.A.: Leaders: The strategies for taking charge. Technol. Forecast. Soc. Change **29**(2) (1986). https://doi.org/10.1016/0040-1625(86)90067-3
4. Dahiyat, A.: Robotic process automation and audit quality. Corp. Gov. Organ. Behav. Rev. **6**(1), 160–167 (2022). https://doi.org/10.22495/cgobrv6i1p12
5. Manuraji, I., Vitharanage, D., Bandara, W., Syed, R., Toman, D.: An empirically supported conceptualisation of robotic process automation(RPA) benefits (2020)
6. Johansson, J., Thomsen, M., Åkesson, M.: Public value creation and robotic process automation: normative, descriptive and prescriptive issues in municipal administration. Transform. Gov. People, Process Policy, no. ahead-of-print (2022)
7. Boulton, C.: What is RPA? A revolution in business process automation. Comput, Hong Kong (2017)
8. Afriliana, N., Ramadhan, A.: The trends and roles of robotic process automation technology in digital transformation: a literature. J. Syst. Manag. Sci. **12**(3), 51–73 (2022)
9. Atanasovski, A., Toceva, T.: Research trends in disruptive technologies for accounting of the future--A bibliometric analysis.. Account. Manag. Inf. Syst. si Inform. Gestiune **21**(2) (2022)
10. Pramod, D.: Robotic process automation for industry: adoption status, benefits, challenges and research agenda. Benchmarking **29**(5) (2022). https://doi.org/10.1108/BIJ-01-2021-0033
11. Moher, D.et al.: Preferred reporting items for systematic reviews and meta-analyses: The PRISMA statement. PLoS Med. **6**(7) (2009). https://doi.org/10.1371/journal.pmed.1000097
12. Ivančić, L., Suša Vugec, D., Bosilj, V.: Robotic process automation: systematic literature review. In: Di, C., et al. (eds.) BPM 2019. LNBIP, vol. 361, pp. 280–295. Springer, Cham (2019). https://doi.org/10.1007/978-3-030-30429-4_19
13. Schlund, S., Schmidt, M.: Robotic Process automation in industrial engineering: challenges and future perspectives. In: Trzcielinski, S., Mrugalska, B., Karwowski, W., Rossi, E., Di Nicolantonio, M. (eds.) AHFE 2021. LNNS, vol. 274, pp. 320–327. Springer, Cham (2021). https://doi.org/10.1007/978-3-030-80462-6_40
14. Rogers, S., Zvarikova, K.: Big data-driven algorithmic governance in sustainable smart manufacturing: robotic process and cognitive automation technologies. Anal. Metaphys. **20**, 130–144 (2021)

15. Paul, J., Lim, W.M., O'Cass, A., Hao, A.W., Bresciani, S.: Scientific procedures and rationales for systematic literature reviews (SPAR-4-SLR). Int. J. Consum. Stud. (2021). https://doi.org/10.1111/ijcs.12695

16. Donthu, N., Kumar, S., Mukherjee, D., Pandey, N., Lim, W.M.: How to conduct a bibliometric analysis: An overview and guidelines. J. Bus. Res. 133 (2021). https://doi.org/10.1016/j.jbusres.2021.04.070

17. Perianes-Rodriguez, A., Waltman, L., van Eck, N.J.: Constructing bibliometric networks: A comparison between full and fractional counting. J. Informetr. 10(4) (2016). https://doi.org/10.1016/j.joi.2016.10.006

18. Aria, M., Cuccurullo, C.: Bibliometrix: An R-tool for comprehensive science mapping analysis. J. Informetr. 11(4) (2017). https://doi.org/10.1016/j.joi.2017.08.007

19. Schotten, M., Meester, W.J.N., Steiginga, S., Ross, C.A., et al.: A brief history of Scopus: The world's largest abstract and citation database of scientific literature. Res. Analyt. 31–58 (2017)

20. Lacity, M., Willcocks, L., Hindel, J., Khan, S.: Robotic process automation: benchmarking the client experience. Electron. Mark. (November 2017) (2018)

21. Ribeiro, J., Lima, R., Eckhardt, T., Paiva, S.: Robotic process automation and artificial intelligence in Industry 4.0 - a literature review. Proc. Comput. Sci. 181 (2021). https://doi.org/10.1016/j.procs.2021.01.104

22. Vijai, C., Suriyalakshmi, S.M., Elayaraja, M.: The future of robotic process automation (rpa) in the banking sector for better customer experience. Shanlax Int. J. Commer. 8(2), 61–65 (2020). https://doi.org/10.34293/commerce.v8i2.1709

23. Fernandez, D., Aman, A.: The challenges of implementing robotic process automation in global business services. Int. J. Bus. Soc. 22(3) (2021). https://doi.org/10.33736/ijbs.4301.2021

24. Wewerka, J., Reichert, M.: Towards quantifying the effects of robotic process automation. In: Proceedings - IEEE International Enterprise Distributed Object Computing Workshop, EDOCW, vol. 2020, pp. 11–19 (2020). https://doi.org/10.1109/EDOCW49879.2020.00015

25. Liu, Y., Mai, F., MacDonald, C.: a big-data approach to understanding the thematic landscape of the field of business ethics, 1982–2016. J. Bus. Ethics 160(1), 127–150 (2018). https://doi.org/10.1007/s10551-018-3806-5

26. Baker, H.K., Kumar, S., Pandey, N.: A bibliometric analysis of managerial finance: a retrospective. Manag. Financ. 46(11) (2020). https://doi.org/10.1108/MF-06-2019-0277

27. Burton, B., Kumar, S., Pandey, N.: Twenty-five years of the european journal of finance (EJF): a retrospective analysis. Eur. J. Financ. 26(18) (2020). https://doi.org/10.1080/1351847X.2020.1754873

28. Emich, K.J., Kumar, S., Lu, L., Norder, K., Pandey, N.: Mapping 50 years of small group research through small group research. Small Gr. Res. 51(6) (2020). https://doi.org/10.1177/1046496420934541

29. Donthu, N., Gremler, D.D., Kumar, S., Pattnaik, D.: Mapping of journal of service research themes: a 22-year review. J. Ser. Res. 25(2) (2022). https://doi.org/10.1177/1094670520977672

30. Van Eck, N.J., Waltman, L.: Visualizing bibliometric networks. Meas. Sch. impact Methods Pract., 285–320 (2014)

31. Chakraborti, T., et al.: From robotic process automation to intelligent process automation. In: Asatiani, A., et al. (eds.) BPM 2020. LNBIP, vol. 393, pp. 215–228. Springer, Cham (2020). https://doi.org/10.1007/978-3-030-58779-6_15

32. Ionescu, L.: Robotic process automation, deep learning, and natural language processing in algorithmic data-driven accounting information systems. Anal. Metaphys. 19 (2020). https://doi.org/10.22381/AM1920206

33. Engel, C., Ebel, P., Leimeister, J.M.: Cognitive automation. Electron. Mark, 1–12 (2021). https://doi.org/10.1007/s12525-021-00519-7
34. Helm, C., Herberger, T.A., Gerold, N.: Application of cognitive automation to structuring data, driving existing business models, and creating value between legacy industries. Int. J. Innov. Technol. Manag. **19**(02), 2250003 (2022)
35. Massarenti, N., Lazzarinetti, G.: A Deep Learning based Methodology for Information Extraction from Documents in Robotic Process Automation (2021)
36. Srinivasan, S., Latha, R.: The Role of RPA and its impact on the user adoption and software application sustainability in the services industry. Int. J. Adv. Sci. Technol. **29**(6), 2389–2407 (2020)

A Software Architecture Based on the Blockchain-Database Hybrid for Electronic Health Records

Tiago Leoratto[1], Diego Roberto Colombo Dias[2],
Alexandre Fonseca Brandão[3], Rogério Luiz Iope[4],
José Remo Ferreira Brega[4], and Marcelo de Paiva Guimarães[1,5]

[1] Centro Univertiário Campo Limpo Paulista (Unifaccamp),
Campo Limpo Paulista, Brazil
[2] Federal University de São João del Rei (UFSJ), São João del Rei, Brazil
[3] University of Campinas (Unicamp), Campinas, Brazil
[4] Universidade Estadual Paulista (Unesp), São Paulo, Brazil
{rogerio.iope,remo.brega}@unesp.br
[5] Universidade Federal de São Paulo (UNIFESP- EPPEN), São Paulo, Brazil
marcelo.paiva@unifesp.br

Abstract. Blockchain applications are regarded as a disruptive technology in the health area for working in a decentralized manner, with inherited features such as immutability, privacy, scalability, and security, and with users managing their data. We present a software architecture based on blockchain and a document-oriented database to manage and store electronic health records (EHRs). This software architecture was designed and implemented to manage EHRs of patients in the process of motor function recovery and assist the research on virtual reality and neurofunctional recovery (BRAINN_VR) at the Brazilian Institute of Neuroscience and Neurotechnology (BRAINN). This solution allows BRAINN_VR researchers to analyze data while respecting the patient's privacy. We evaluate the network performance of our solution to validate EHR insertions using four scenarios with varying data block size, network latency, and jitter. The consensus performance reached shows the feasibility of our architecture. Our software architecture has the potential to provide seamless interaction between multi-institutional research laboratories, health institutions, and patients.

Keywords: blockchain · eletronic health records · software architecture

1 Introduction

People seek various medical facilities throughout their lives to receive treatment, answered by diverse professionals, hospitals, and clinics. These multiple events generate information in various formats that make up one's lifetime medical

O. Gervasi et al. (Eds.): ICCSA 2023, LNCS 13956, pp. 507–519, 2023.
https://doi.org/10.1007/978-3-031-36805-9_33

record. When a medical history is organized and provides instant access to accurate and up-to-date information, it can improve the overall quality of health services, creating benefits such as error prevention, security, and easy information access. Electronic health records (EHRs) can offer medical record availability, and their services are widely recognized in the literature [4]. However, their full potential has rarely been achieved because they depend on the success of technological factors such as usability, regulation, infrastructure, training, and interoperability [11,13].

This study focuses on one of the critical factors of EHRs, namely, the software architecture (component-and-connector structures) that defines the software elements (components) by delineating their features and the interactions (connectors) between the structural parts [7]. These interactions create the desired EHR software behavior that requires consideration of all stakeholders (e.g., patients, researchers, and health professionals) and software characteristics (e.g., scalability, interoperability, performance, reusability, and security). These prerogatives affect software development principles such as standards, data modeling, software maintenance, rules of thumb, and empirical practices, all of which are fundamental for decision making toward a specific direction and evaluating the EHR's success. While EHR factors such as usability and performance can be evaluated early during the system adoption phase, many other essential aspects are hidden by the underlying software, making them challenging to create and evaluate, such as the software architecture that is the foundation for solid software to meet all requirements.

In recent years, blockchain-based EHRs have aroused interest in the health sector [1,10,14,21,25,26] for their capability to provide the underlying software architecture. With the adoption of such EHRs, patients can manage their data [15]. Moreover, medical records can be added and shared but not changed or deleted. Blockchain-based EHRs aim to allow all interested people who previously did not know or trust one another to share data in a secure and tamper-proof way.

Adopting blockchain to EHR creates a distributed data storage system with security access and validation that replaces centralized systems. However, only authorized entities with explicit permission, such as doctors, hospitals, and other health insurers, can access patient records to serve their purpose. There is a trend toward merging blockchain and databases (blockchain-database hybrid), with one feature incorporated by the other and vice versa [23]. For example, concurrency control techniques are being used to increase the performance of blockchains, and, at the same time, blockchain security features are being incorporated into the blockchain-database hybrid [23]. Examples of this approach are BigchainDB [19], Blockchain Relational Database (BRD), and ChainifyDB. These blockchain databases combine the key benefits of distributed databases (i.e., high throughput, low latency - latency is the amount of time a network packet takes to travel from the sender to its destination -, and rich querying) and traditional blockchains (i.e., decentralized control, immutability, and creation and movement of digital assets) with an emphasis on scale. An asset in this work is a tangible (patient,

patient data, patient responsible, admin, medical record and institution) or intangible (access) resource owned by the entity (i.e., patient, institution, laboratory). For example, patient and institutional data.

Any blockchain software requires a consensus protocol to validate the data entries, the most famous of which is Proof of Work (PoW) because of its integration with Bitcoin [3,6]. A consensus is a mechanism used to achieve the necessary agreement on a single data value among the nodes. PoW offers the most robust protocol based on brute force, demanding high computer performance to validate the data. Another protocol is Byzantine fault tolerance (BFT), in which each node needs two-thirds of the votes from all nodes to perform a data commit [3,9].

This paper describes a software architecture to provide medical record availability to multi-institutional research laboratories and patients. More specifically, we developed a software architecture based on a permissioned blockchain (private) using BigchainDB to manage and store EHRs using eighth assets. Permissioned blockchain has an identity provider that controls the identity of the entities. This study describes how our software architecture provided a feasible environment for our healthcare and research context. We also evaluated the network performance to validate the transactions by using four scenarios with varying EHR sizes, network latency, and jitter - it is a variance in latency when a data packet is transmitted and when it is received; the variance is caused by network congestion or route changes -. The significant contributions presented in this paper are:

- The software architecture designed and implemented allows to manage EHRs of patients in the process of motor function recovery and assists the research on virtual reality and neurofunctional recovery (BRAINN_VR) at the Brazilian Institute of Neuroscience and Neurotechnology (BRAINN). This solution allows BRAINN_VR researchers to analyze data while respecting the patient's privacy; and
- Evaluation of the performance of this software architecture using network parameters considering real network adversities that of a real environment. Network adversities are issues that can cause delays in the transmission of data. We simulated a network between five universities in different Brazilian regions (north, northeast, midwest, southeast, and south).

The solution was developed to manage and store EHRs with inherited blockchain features such as data availability, immutability, privacy, scalability, security, and users' data management. This solution can provide seamless interaction between multi-institutional research laboratories, health institutions, and patients. Our research aims to develop new body-tracking devices and interfaces for virtual and augmented reality to assist patients during motor function rehabilitation. In BRAINN_VR project, we collected kinematic data and analyzed them to identify patterns and correlations.

The remainder of this paper is organized as follows. Section 2 presents related work. Section 3 describes our software architecture and the transactions comprising an actor sender, an actor recipient, and an amount of health data. Section 4 presents the method used to evaluate our solution, which applied different parameters (data block size, network latency, and jitter), and a scenario with five Brazilian regions in our evaluation. Section 5 describes the tests and discusses the results. Finally, Sect. 6 presents the concluding results and future work.

2 Related Work

EHR is one the most popular subject espouse to apply blockchain in the healthcare area [1,2,10,14,16,20,21,25,26] for their capability to provide the underlying software architecture. Moreover, blockchain-based EHRs adoption allows patients to manage their data [15,16]. However, few studies present empirical results to substantiate their claims.

MedRec developed by Azaria, Ekblaw, Vieira, and Lippman [5] is based on Ethereum's blockchain to create a system that represents the ownership and viewing permissions of data shared by members of a peer-to-peer network. MedRec uses smart contracts to create the representation of medical records that are stored within specific computer nodes. Smart contracts permit trusted transactions and agreements to execute autonomously when certain conditions are met without the need for a central authority. SQLite database was used to implement their prototype. The contracts keep metadata about the record ownership, permissions, and data integrity. This study does not present performance analysis; however, the validation is based on the PoW algorithm, in which miners compete in solving a computational hard puzzle [12]. This algorithm requires a long processing time and high energy consumption of the computers. MedRec is a working prototype focused on evaluating the technology and implementation of blockchain prior to any real use.

Roehrs et al. [22] described the prototype and evaluation of the OmniPHR architecture model based on their blockchain and openEHR interoperability standard. This studies focus on EHR and Personal Health Record (PHR)[1] which is an emerging trend in healthcare context. The data follow a proprietary or an open standard and then is converted using a middleware. OmniPHR focus on creating a distributed architecture that is scalable, elastic, and interoperable. They list some studies that deal with implementing blockchain technology into EHR. The authors evaluated the network performance considering a scenario with ten super peers and thousands of competing sessions transacting operations on health records simultaneously, but without taking care of network adversities related to communication performance.

MedHypChain [17] is an architecture based on permissioned blockchain Hyperledger for a data-sharing system for healing the COVID-19 situation. The authors analyzed their solution's latency, execution time, and throughput, considering peers up to 10,000 transactions. The performance evaluation was done using the Hyperledger caliper tool. However, they do not consider network adversities related to communication performance. Their study also presented a comparison between diverse blockchain-based healthcare systems. They presented

---

[1] https://www.iso.org/obp/ui/#iso:std:iso:tr:18638:ed-1:v1:en:term:3.20.

a study case in which medical service is implemented based on MedHypChain. This service stores data of patients using sensors. According to the authors, MedHypeChain can handle up to 20 nodes for 1000 concurrent transactions and four nodes for 10,000 concurrent transactions.

The review paper by Kuo, Kim, and Ohno-Machado [18] presented benefits, pitfalls, and applications in healthcare domains. They covered key challenges, including issues like confidentially, scalability, and transaction performance. According to the authors, when using the PoW algorithm, Bitcoin reaches about 3.3 transactions per second on average due to the required computation workload. They highlighted that this is an important issue when creating a real-time healthcare application based on blockchain. The authors suggested the adoption of BigchainDB as a plausible solution to deal with speed, as we did in our study.

Many studies have described how EHR can be based on blockchain technologies. However, unlike related work that uses blockchain platforms like Ethereum, Hyperledger, or Chord algorithm, our work use BigchainDB. Moreover, none of the previous research compared the network performance considering realistic network inferences or designed to create EHRs for patients in the process of motor function recovery that can be accessed and managed by healthcare services and research laboratories.

The Brazilian Ministry of Health incentives the computerization of medical records. Our work advances the creation of patient records, treating the entire process as assets with their respective owners. Patients, medical and research institutions will reach a consensus via a vote-based protocol and data stored in a document-driven database.

3   Software Architecture for Electronic Health Records

In our software architecture for EHR, the actors are the entities that send, receive, and/or treat the messages. They are as follows:

- Patients: anyone who receives healthcare services;
- Health institutions: anyone or any facility that provides healthcare (e.g., laboratories, medical facilities, nurses, etc.); and
- Research laboratories: university facilities that provide the infrastructure to store and validate transactions and receive permission to access all data for conducting research anonymously.

Patients and health institutions use a web application on a webserver to interact with the EHR system inside the blockchain. Their privileges are taken care of by services offered by the certificate authority (research lab) that assigns a public and private key to each user. Our EHR solution uses BigchainDB to deploy a blockchain-like decentralized application using off-the-shelf technologies. Each blockchain node uses a local MongoDB (https://www.mongodb.com/) database and the Tendermint protocol (https://tendermint.com/) to communicate and reach a consensus between the nodes. BigchainDB uses the BFT protocol to ensure the system continues to work, even if up to a third of the blockchain nodes fail. Figure 1 depicts the actors interacting with the developed blockchain-database hybrid, the architecture of which is provided by the research laboratories of Brazilian universities (Federal University of São Paulo (UNIFESP), University of Campinas (Unicamp), São Paulo State University (Unesp), and Federal University of São João del–Rei (UFSJ)). Other nodes can be added to increase capacity and throughput. This software architecture just focused on private blockchains instead of public blockchains due to data security and privacy issues, as well as due to the specific domain of healthcare targeted by BRAINN_VR project. Private blockchains address emergencies, giving access to EHRs to health professionals not previously authorized.

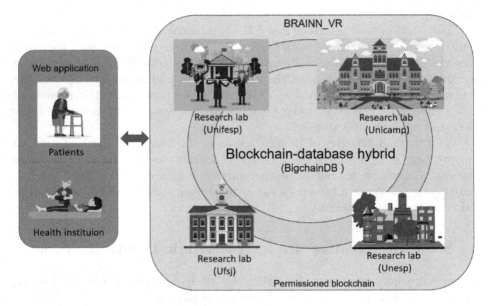

Fig. 1. Actors interacting in the EHR based on the blockchain-database hybrid.

The software architecture has eight types of assets that are created with distinct features but work in an integrated way. Figure 2 shows the relationship between the assets. The black arrows show the common data between the assets used to bond them together. The green arrows indicate the provided private key used to create the asset - if the private key is not public key pair, the asset is not created. The red arrow depicts a medical record transferring to a patient, becoming the asset owner. An attachment (e.g., video, sound, and image) can be part of a medical record. Just medical record assets can be transferred. The assets depicted in Fig. 2 are:

- Patient: it has an identifier (CPF - a Brazilian individual taxpayer registry identification) used to perform searches. Its public keys are also stored to perform transactions and encryption;

- Patient Data: contains information such as name, date of birth, and gender, among others. The patient only creates this asset, and when it needs to be updated, the patient must create a new asset of this type with the new information;
- Patient responsible: the patient can link other people to be co-responsible for his/her information. An example is the father and mother of a child, a patient with a child, or a patient with a disability;
- Institution: contains information about a health or research institution that uses the system. It also keeps its public keys;
- Medical record: holds the patient's EHR;
- Access: created after the creation of the patient EHR and when the patient wants to give someone else access to their record. It stores the EHR identifier and all public keys that have access to the EHR;
- Attachment: stores the notes of the files linked to the patient's EHR. These notes can be made through a file system or using some mechanism within the files or some mechanism within the database; and
- Admin: it is linked to all created assets. This asset is created only at blockchain setup time. It stores the public keys of the nodes configured to perform consensus.

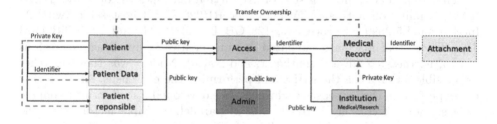

Fig. 2. Types of assets and relationship.

Transactions register the movement of assets between the actors (e.g., patients, therapists, nurses). BigchainDB provides an application programming interface to make transactions and register, issue, create, or transfer assets. Every transaction comprises an actor sender, an actor recipient, and an amount of medical data. The owners manage assets and can give access to other actors. The following steps are executed during the asset creation process: initially, an actor creates an asset and sends it to the blockchain (1), which asks the Tendermint (2) to reach a consensus using the BFT protocol. After the consensus, the current block is confirmed (3). Now the asset is sent to MongoDB (4). Then, the block is confirmed (5). The applications then receive the message that the asset was successfully created (6). This architecture guarantees the data's security and immutability to all actors.

The Medical Record asset is characteristic of multiple owners and is encrypted. When the asset is created and transferred to the patient, the system checks if there are other responsible parties (co-responsible parties); if so, they must be registered in the asset as owners. Before the institution submits the asset to the blockchain, a session key is randomly generated and used to encrypt the asset symmetrically. Afterward, the session key is encrypted asymmetrically using the patient's public keys, co-responsible parties, institutions, and administrators.

Regarding multimedia files, we design their storage in a file system with only its pointer appearing in the database. This approach helps minimize indexing and searching problems in the database. In the model implemented, it is possible to create an attachment asset. We store the medical record's identifier and the pointer to the file in a file system or database table.

4   Evaluation

The transaction performance of medical records among health institutions, research laboratories, and patients is crucial to ensuring the adoption of blockchain-based EHRs. We evaluated the network performance to validate the task of creating and validating EHRs using four setups with varying data block size, network latency, and jitter (packet delivery). In these scenarios, consensus occurs by validating two-thirds of the blockchain nodes (BFT algorithm).

The laboratory setup consisted of five virtual machines (8 cores and 24 GB RAM) running on a Huawei FusionServer RH2288H V3 host server with 2x Intel Xeon E5-2690 v3 processors, 128 GB DDR4 RAM, and 2×2 TB hard disk. The virtual machines simulated five universities in five Brazilian regions (north, northeast, midwest, southeast, and south). Node 1 was the dispatcher responsible for creating the EHRs and performing the consensus. All the other nodes performed the consensus exclusively. We developed a shell script to handle 32 executions of creating EHRs to run in parallel. Multiple factors (i.e., the distance of a link, state of intermediate routers, and jitter amount) may cause packet delay on network links, affecting the data throughput between connected nodes. When the latency is very high, the throughput of a connection cannot be considered reliable. Generally, a network can be regarded as reliable when jitter is on the order of 10% of the average round trip time that is the amount of time it takes for a network packet to travel from a starting point to a destination and back again to the starting point.

We used the NetEm tool (https://www.linux.org/docs/man8/tc-netem. html) to emulate the network adversities in these regions. The simulation parameters were based on the report from the Brazilian Network Information Center [8], which allowed the definition of the threshold values to indicate the operational limits of the experiment. Table 1 depicts the scenarios that combine the major adversities related to the latency and jitter of data networks. These parameters hardly appear in isolation in the real environment. For each simulation, we created 20,000 EHRs and varied the packet sizes (i.e., 15, 20, 40, and 80 Kb). Each EHR creates the following three transactions: CreateEHR, which creates the EHR; CreateAcess, which defines the privileges of the created EHR to the patient, co-responsible parties, institution, and administrators; and Transfer-toPatient, which associates the EHR with the patient's property. A total of 20,000 EHRs requested 60,000 transactions.

Table 1. Test scenarios with varying latency and jitter for the creation of 20,000 EHRs.

Setup 1					
	Node 1(north)	Node 2 (northeast)	Node 3 (midwest)	Node 4 (southeast)	Node 5(south)
Node 1 (north)	latency (0 ms) jitter (0 ms)	latency (0 ms) jitter (0 ms)	latency (0 ms) jitter (0 ms)	latency (0 ms) jitter (0 ms)	latency (0 ms) jitter (0 ms)
Setup 2					
Node1 (north)	latency (50 ms) jitter (6 ms)	latency (55 ms) jitter (6 ms)	latency (65 ms) jitter (7 ms)	latency (60 ms) jitter (6 ms)	latency (77 ms) jitter (8 ms)
Setup 3					
Node1 (north)	latency (50 ms) jitter (4 ms)	latency (55 ms) jitter (4 ms)	latency (65 ms) jitter (5 ms)	latency (60 ms) jitter (4 ms)	latency (77 ms) jitter (6 ms)
Setup 4					
Node1 (north)	latency (50 ms) jitter (2 ms)	latency (55 ms) jitter (2 ms)	latency (65 ms) jitter (4 ms)	latency (60 ms) jitter (2 ms)	latency (77 ms) jitter (5 ms)

5 Discussion

An effective software architecture to manage and store EHRs with inherited blockchain features should allow the building of applications tailored to the network. From the EHRs point of view, data block size, network latency, and jitter are quality parameters of the network. From the EHRs user's point of view, they experience the cumulative effect of these parameters. The software architecture supported a high volume of transactions (60,000) even with different setups. The combination of network latency and EHR size influenced the consensus time. Setup 3 was the worst scenario, averaging 41 EHRs per minute. Setup 1 was the best, with an average of 47 EHRs per minute. Blockchain network performance also depends on the consensus mechanism chosen. We chose the BFT algorithm in our scenarios, and the four fastest nodes were enough to reach the consensus.

Given our context, the main features of the architecture developed are as follows:

- It provides fast transaction validation using the resources of the research facilities;
- The database solution adopted inherits the features of modern distributed databases, such as linear scaling in throughput and capacity with the number of nodes, efficient querying, and full support to NoSQL query language, and a private blockchain;
- Patients can administer and own their health data, that is known as Personal Health Record (PHR), which is an emerging trend in healthcare context;
- It facilitates auditing because data are stored chronologically and cannot be deleted;

- It provides access to the patient's medical records regardless of where the care was performed;
- It integrates into a solution the useful features from blockchain and databases; and
- Research laboratories can have access to medical records without compromising the identity of patients.

Our performance evaluation did not cover the execution of business rules that health information systems have and users' interaction with the interface. Instead, we limited the tests to execute transactions using scripts. The test scenarios were defined to stress the EHR system shared by research laboratories without generating errors or crashes, such as time out.

Swan [24] identified the following technical challenges related to the blockchain implementation: (1) throughput, (2) latency, (3)size and bandwidth, (4) security, (5) wasted resources, (6) usability, and (7) versioning, hard forks, and multiple chains. We could find that our practical experience faced these challenges. We tailored the software architecture to our problem, but creating a facto standard requires more research in the future. Moreover, it must comply with legislation that changes significantly from country to country (for example, Brazilian General Data Protection (LGPD) in Brazil, Health Insurance Portability and Accountability Ac (HIPAA) in the USA, and General Data Protection Regulation (GDPR) in Europe).

Therefore, we surmise that our software architecture is a promising solution to be used in many healthcare and research contexts, similar to the one presented in this study, with little or no effort can be benefited from all the features (e.g., scalability, performance, security, and easy information access). Consequently, it can improve the overall quality of health services, develop new treatments and cures, and enable precision medicine.

6 Conclusions

EHRs must integrate data from multiple players, creating challenging security, privacy, and governance requirements. A significant challenge for EHRs is collecting patient information, even from the same patient, and carrying it from one care facility to another with a reliable software architecture that provides scalability, cost-effectiveness, and capacity to adapt new functionality with minimum changes.

This paper presented software architecture whose main aim is to assist the rehabilitation of patients in the process of motor function recovery. This software architecture is part of the research on virtual reality and neurofunctional recovery (BRAINN_VR) at the Brazilian Institute of Neuroscience and Neurotechnology (BRAINN). Patients benefit from medical history being accessible and credible, and healthcare can learn by analyzing patterns and correlations of treatments. This architecture was designed for application in research projects linked to the BRAINN VR initiative, with e-health solutions for telemonitoring and virtual reality for neurofunctional recovery. We developed the software architecture based on a permissioned blockchain using BigchainDB to manage and store EHRs. The architecture was created considering the requirements of stakeholders and software characteristics, such as scalability, interoperability, performance flexibility, reusability, and security. Moreover, the solution developed is feasible to assist healthcare and research. Network performance was also evaluated to validate the EHR insertions using four scenarios with varying data block size, network latency, and jitter. It took 0.38 s on average to create one EHR.

This study evaluated the EHRs software architecture; then, others studies are needed to evaluate other key factors such as usability, regulation, infrastructure, and training. In future research, we plan to improve the software architecture by adding new features, such as data integration with healthcare professionals' tools, some of which have already been developed.

References

1. Abu-elezz, I., Hassan, A., Nazeemudeen, A., Househ, M., Abd-alrazaq, A.: The benefits and threats of blockchain technology in healthcare: A scoping review. Int. J. Med. Inform. **142**, 104246 (Oct 2020). https://doi.org/10.1016/j.ijmedinf.2020. 104246, https://www.sciencedirect.com/science/article/pii/S1386505620301544
2. Agbo, C.C., Mahmoud, Q.H., Eklund, J.M.: Blockchain Technology in Healthcare: A Systematic Review. Healthcare **7**(2), 56 (Jun 2019). https://doi.org/10.3390/ healthcare7020056, https://www.mdpi.com/2227-9032/7/2/56, number: 2 Publisher: Multidisciplinary Digital Publishing Institute
3. Alsunaidi, S.J., Alhaidari, F.A.: A Survey of Consensus Algorithms for Blockchain Technology. In: 2019 International Conference on Computer and Information Sciences (ICCIS), pp. 1–6 (Apr 2019). https://doi.org/10.1109/ICCISci.2019.8716424
4. Amatayakul, M.K.: Electronic Health Records: A Practical Guide for Professionals and Organizations. Ahima, Chicago, Ill., 5th 2013 update ed. edition edn. (Apr 2013)
5. Azaria, A., Ekblaw, A., Vieira, T., Lippman, A.: MedRec: Using Blockchain for Medical Data Access and Permission Management. In: 2016 2nd International Conference on Open and Big Data (OBD), pp. 25–30. IEEE, Vienna, Austria (Aug 2016). https://doi.org/10.1109/OBD.2016.11, http://ieeexplore.ieee. org/document/7573685/
6. Bashir, I.: Mastering Blockchain: A deep dive into distributed ledgers, consensus protocols, smart contracts, DApps, cryptocurrencies, Ethereum, and more, 3rd Edition. Packt Publishing (Aug 2020)
7. Bass, L., Clements, P., Kazman, R.: Software Architecture in Practice. Addison-Wesley Professional, fourth edn. (2021)
8. Ceptro.br, Nic.br: Covid-19 Impacto na qualidade da internet no Brasil. Tech. rep., CEPTRO.BR/NIC.br (May 2021), https://www.ceptro.br/assets/publicacoes/ pdf/2021.01.05-relatorio-covid.pdf
9. Chondros, N., Kokordelis, K., Roussopoulos, M.: On the Practicality of Practical Byzantine Fault Tolerance. In: Narasimhan, P., Triantafillou, P. (eds.) Middleware 2012, pp. 436–455. Lecture Notes in Computer Science, Springer, Berlin, Heidelberg (2012). DOI: https://doi.org/10.1007/978-3-642-35170-9_22

10. Dimitrov, D.V.: Blockchain Applications for Healthcare Data Management. Healthcare Inform. Res. **25**(1), 51–56 (Jan 2019). https://doi.org/10.4258/hir. 2019.25.1.51, https://www.ncbi.nlm.nih.gov/pmc/articles/PMC6372466/

11. Fennelly, O., et al.: Successfully implementing a national electronic health record: a rapid umbrella review. International Journal of Medical Informatics 144, 104281 (Dec 2020). https://doi.org/10.1016/j.ijmedinf.2020.104281, https://www. sciencedirect.com/science/article/pii/S1386505620310650

12. Gervais, A., Karame, G.O., Wüst, K., Glykantzis, V., Ritzdorf, H., Capkun, S.: On the security and performance of proof of work blockchains. In: Proceedings of the 2016 ACM SIGSAC Conference on Computer and Communications Security. p. 3–16. CCS '16, Association for Computing Machinery, New York, NY, USA (2016). https://doi.org/10.1145/2976749.2978341

13. Gesulga, J.M., Berjame, A., Moquiala, K.S., Galido, A.: Barriers to electronic health record system implementation and information systems resources: a structured review. Procedia Comput. Sci. **124**, 544–551 (Jan 2017). https://doi. org/10.1016/j.procs.2017.12.188https://www.sciencedirect.com/science/article/ pii/S1877050917329563

14. Hölbl, M., Kompara, M., Kamišalić, A., Nemec Zlatolas, L.: A Systematic Review of the Use of Blockchain in Healthcare. Symmetry 10(10), 470 (Oct 2018). https://doi.org/10.3390/sym10100470, https://www.mdpi.com/2073-8994/ 10/10/470 number: 10 Publisher: Multidisciplinary Digital Publishing Institute

15. Karafiloski, E., Mishev, A.: Blockchain solutions for big data challenges: A literature review. In: IEEE EUROCON 2017–17th International Conference on Smart Technologies, pp. 763–768 (Jul 2017). https://doi.org/10.1109/EUROCON.2017. 8011213

16. Kassab, M., et al.: Exploring research in blockchain for healthcare and a roadmap for the future. IEEE Trans. Emerg. Top. Comput. **9**(4), 1835–1852 (2021). https:// doi.org/10.1109/TETC.2019.2936881

17. Kumar, M., Chand, S.: Medhypchain: A patient-centered interoperability hyperledger-based medical healthcare system: Regulation in covid-19 pandemic. J. Netw. Comput. Appl. **179**, 102975 (2021). https://doi.org/10.1016/j.jnca.2021. 102975, https://www.sciencedirect.com/science/article/pii/S1084804521000023

18. Kuo, T.T., Kim, H.E., Ohno-Machado, L.: Blockchain distributed ledger technologies for biomedical and health care applications. J. Am. Med. Inform. Assoc.: JAMIA 24(6), 1211–1220 (November 2017). https://doi.org/10.1093/ jamia/ocx068, https://europepmc.org/articles/PMC6080687

19. Mconaghy, T., et al.: BigchainDB: a scalable blockchain database. Whitepaper **1**(1), 65 (2016)

20. McGhin, T., Choo, K.K.R., Liu, C.Z., He, D.: Blockchain in healthcare applications: Research challenges and opportunities. J. Netw. Comput. Appl. **135**, 62–75 (2019). https://doi.org/10.1016/j.jnca.2019.02.027, https://www.sciencedirect. com/science/article/pii/S1084804519300864

21. Omar, A.A., Bhuiyan, M.Z.A., Basu, A., Kiyomoto, S., Rahman, M.S.: Privacy-friendly platform for healthcare data in cloud based on blockchain environment. Future Gen. Comput. Syst. **95**, 511–521 (2019). https://doi.org/ 10.1016/j.future.2018.12.044, https://www.sciencedirect.com/science/article/pii/ S0167739X18314201

22. Roehrs, A., da Costa, C.A., da Rosa Righi, R., da Silva, V.F., Goldim, J.R., Schmidt, D.C.: Analyzing the performance of a blockchain-based personal health record implementation. J. Biomed. Inform. **92**, 103140 (2019). https://doi.org/10.1016/j.jbi.2019.103140, https://www.sciencedirect.com/science/article/pii/S1532046419300589
23. Ruan, P., et al.: Blockchains vs. Distributed Databases: Dichotomy and Fusion. In: ACM SIGMOD p. 14 (2021)
24. Swan, M.: Blockchain : blueprint for a new economy. O'Reilly Media, Sebastopol, Calif. (2015) http://shop.oreilly.com/product/0636920037040.do
25. Wang, J., et a.: A blockchain-based eHealthcare system interoperating with WBANs. Future Generation Computer Systems **110**, 675–685 (2020). https://doi.org/10.1016/j.future.2019.09.049, https://www.sciencedirect.com/science/article/pii/S0167739X19321247
26. Zhang, P., Schmidt, D.C., White, J., Lenz, G.: Blockchain Technology Use Cases in Healthcare - Chapter One. In: Raj, P., Deka, G.C. (eds.) Advances in Computers, Blockchain Technology: Platforms, Tools and Use Cases, vol. 111, pp. 1–41. Elsevier (Jan 2018). https://doi.org/10.1016/bs.adcom.2018.03.006, https://www.sciencedirect.com/science/article/pii/S0065245818300196

Convolutional Neural Networks and Ensembles for Visually Impaired Aid

Fabricio Breve$^{(\boxtimes)}$ (iD)

São Paulo State University, Rio Claro, SP 13506-900, Brazil
fabricio.breve@unesp.br
https://www.fabriciobreve.com

Abstract. Recent surveys show that smartphone-based computer vision tools for visually impaired individuals often rely on outdated computer vision algorithms. Deep-learning approaches have been explored, but many require high-end or specialized hardware that is not practical for users. Therefore, developing deep learning systems that can make inferences using only the smartphone is desirable. This paper presents a comprehensive study of 25 different convolutional neural network (CNN) architectures to tackle the challenge of identifying obstacles in images captured by a smartphone positioned at chest height for visually impaired individuals. A transfer learning approach is employed, with the CNN models initialized with weights pre-trained on the vast ImageNet dataset. The study employs k-fold cross-validation with $k = 10$ and five repetitions to ensure the robustness of the results. Various configurations are explored for each CNN architecture, including different optimizers (Adam and RMSprop), freezing or fine-tuning convolutional layer weights, and different learning rates for convolutional and dense layers. Moreover, CNN ensembles are investigated, where multiple instances of the same or different CNN architectures are combined to enhance the overall performance. The highest accuracy achieved by an individual CNN is 94.56% using EfficientNetB4, surpassing the previous best result of 92.11%. With the use of ensembles, the accuracy is further improved to 96.55% using multiple instances of EfficientNetB4, EfficientNetB0, and MobileNet. Overall, the study contributes to the development of advanced deep-learning models that can enhance the mobility and independence of visually impaired individuals.

Keywords: Convolutional Neural Networks · Deep Learning · Computer Vision · Visually Impaired Aid

1 Introduction

According to the World Health Organization, approximately 2.2 billion people suffer from some form of visual impairment, including at least 1 billion with moderate or severe distance vision impairment [40]. The prevalence of distance vision impairment is significantly higher in low- and middle-income areas compared to high-income regions [34]. This population faces numerous

O. Gervasi et al. (Eds.): ICCSA 2023, LNCS 13956, pp. 520–534, 2023.
https://doi.org/10.1007/978-3-031-36805-9_34

difficulties in their daily routines, mostly linked to mobility and navigation. White canes and guide dogs are currently the most commonly utilized tools to aid visually impaired (VI) individuals [15]. With advancements in computer vision and related technologies, numerous navigation systems have been proposed [1,3,4,11,15–17,20,21,24,25,29,39]. However, many of these systems have limitations [15], such as requiring costly, bulky, and/or custom equipment [11,25–27,29,39] or being too computationally intensive to run on portable devices and requiring a network connection to a more powerful remote server [16,23].

A systematic literature review conducted by Budrionis et al. [3] found that smartphone-based computer vision tools for the VI often employ outdated image and video processing techniques. Another systematic review, conducted by Mandia et al. [24], discovered that researchers have started to adopt deep learning approaches [6,22,32] and that these techniques have grown with the advent of increased computational power in machines. However, carrying high-powered computational devices for vision-based assistive solutions is not practical for users. Hence, a deep learning system that can make inferences using only an edge device such as a smartphone is desirable. Ideally, this system should not require network connectivity or additional accessories.

In a prior study, Breve et al. [2] proposed a framework that leverages Convolutional Neural Networks (CNNs), transfer learning, and semi-supervised learning (SSL). The focus of the framework was to minimize computational costs and make it feasible for implementation on smartphones without requiring additional hardware. The framework uses a smartphone camera to capture images of the user's path and immediately classifies them, providing real-time feedback to the user. A dataset was created to train the classifiers, encompassing various indoor and outdoor environments with different lighting, flooring, and obstacles. The effectiveness of various CNN architectures was evaluated by fine-tuning pre-trained weights from the ImageNet dataset [28]. A prototype of the framework running on a smartphone was recently presented [31].

In this study, previous works are significantly expanded upon with the following key contributions:

1. Eight additional CNN models were added to the study, based on the cutting-edge EfficientNet architecture [37], bringing the total number of networks evaluated to 25.
2. The K-Fold Cross Validation process was repeated five times, providing more robust results.
3. Image pre-processing functions were introduced to enhance image preparation for each network type, resulting in improved accuracy in most cases.
4. Ensembles of CNNs were employed to boost the overall accuracy by leveraging the strengths of multiple CNN architectures.

The rest of the paper is structured as follows: Sect. 2 shows some related work on visually impaired aid (VIA). Section 3 presents the VIA dataset. Section 4 displays the CNN architectures employed in this paper. Section 5 presents experimental results and analysis comparing the performance of these models on the

VIA dataset. Section 6 shows simulations with CNN ensembles, which enhance the accuracy of individual models. Finally, the conclusions are summarized in Sect. 7.

2   Related Work

Several endeavors have been undertaken to integrate computer vision into aiding visually challenged individuals. Mandia et al. [24] conducted a review of current vision-based assistive solutions for VI individuals. The review primarily focuses on camera-based systems and summarizes the sensors, image processing algorithms, and communication protocols used. The use of acoustic output devices, RFID, and GPS in addition to cameras is also discussed. The evolution from traditional image processing techniques to deep learning for assistance for the VI is highlighted. The paper concludes that the literature does not fully optimize deep learning models for edge devices.

Budrionis et al. [3] provides an overview of recent research prototypes of electronic travel aids (ETA) that use smartphones to assist VI people in orientation, navigation, and wayfinding. The authors systematically review scientific achievements in the field and compare various smartphone-based ETA prototypes. The meta-analysis found a few attempts to use state-of-the-art computer vision methods based on deep neural networks. The study contrasts these findings with a survey of blind expert users to reveal a major mismatch between user needs and academic development in the field. The authors conclude that the development of affordable smartphone-based ETAs is crucial for VI people in low-income countries and highlight the need for further research to address the identified gaps.

Islam et al. [15] reviews the development of walking assistants for VI individuals and highlights the recent advancements, including their benefits and limitations. The authors aim to provide a comprehensive overview of the current state of walking assistants and suggest areas for future development in sensors, computer vision, and smartphone-based technology.

Kuriakose et al. [20] propose an EfficientNet-Lite based scene recognition model for use in a smartphone application that supports navigation for the blind and VI. The model is trained and tested using a custom dataset of indoor and outdoor scenes. A proof of concept prototype app was developed on the Android platform.

Bai et al. [1] present a wearable assistive device for VI people to help them navigate and recognize objects in indoor and outdoor environments. The device consists of a RGB-D camera, an inertial measurement unit, a smartphone, and an audio module. It uses a CNN-based object recognition system for perception and navigation. The system provides semantic information about the surroundings and interacts with the user through audio.

Jiang et al. [16] proposed a wearable system that uses stereo vision. The system leverages binocular vision sensors to capture images and selects the best images based on stereo image quality assessment. The selected images are then sent to the cloud for processing using a CNN and it returns information to the user to assist with decision-making.

Paul et al. [17] proposes a system consisting of a camera, GPS, infrared and light sensors connected to a microprocessor (Raspberry Pi) to process and relay information about the user's surroundings. The camera captures images, while the microprocessor uses image processing techniques to analyze the images and identify objects and obstacles. The control unit then relays this information to the user through audio output. The authors did not specify which processing techniques they used, stating only that they have used the OpenCV library.

Hoang et al. [11] developed a system that employs a Kinect camera mounted on a belt to capture and analyze the surroundings. The system detects obstacles and conveys this information to the user via audio feedback. A laptop computer must be carried in a backpack to process the captured information using the Point Cloud Library.

In 2013, Tapu et al. [38] introduced a real-time obstacle detection and classification system that utilized video from a smartphone camera. They created a framework consisting of tracking, motion estimation, and clustering methods. Four years later, Tapu et al. [39] introduced a more advanced framework based on CNNs for detecting, tracking, and recognizing objects in outdoor settings. However, this system requires the use of a laptop computer, carried in a backpack, as the processing unit.

Lin et al. [23] proposed a guiding system that utilizes a smartphone. The system incorporates CNNs for object recognition but relies on a desktop server with a GPU and Compute Unified Device Architecture (CUDA) to handle the computational intensive object recognition task. Although the system has an offline mode, it only offers recognition for faces and stairs.

Kumar and Meher [19] introduced an object recognition system that employs a mixture of CNN (Convolutional Neural Network) and RNN (Recurrent Neural Network). It can identify everyday indoor objects and their hues and generates auditory responses to the user. Saffoury et al. [29] put forward a system that uses a smartphone and laser pointer. The system makes use of laser triangulation to establish a collision avoidance protocol, and also delivers auditory feedback to the user.

Poggi and Mattoccia [25] developed a wearable device that consists of glasses with a custom RGBD sensor and FPGA onboard processing, a glove with micromotors for tactile feedback, a pocket battery, a bone-conductive headset, and a smartphone. The system employs deep learning techniques to categorize detected obstacles semantically. Previously, Poggi et al. [26] introduced a similar system for recognizing crosswalks.

Rizzo et al. [27] propose a fusion framework for combining signals from a stereo camera and infrared sensor for obstacle detection using a multi-scale CNN, with plans to implement the framework into a wearable vest.

Islam and Sadi [14] applied a CNN to detect path holes and obtained impressive results. However, it should be noted that they utilized a separate dataset for "path hole" images and another for "non-path hole" images, with the latter consisting of road images taken with a wider angle. This raises the possibility that the network may have learned differences in style that are not relevant to the task at hand, thereby simplifying its job.

3 Dataset

The VIA dataset[1] includes 342 images separated into two categories: 175 "clear-path" and 167 "non-clear path". The images were taken with a smartphone camera and resized to 750×1000 pixels. The smartphone was positioned at chest height and inclined at an angle of 30° to 60° to capture several meters of the path ahead, including areas beyond the reach of a standard white cane.

Despite its small size, the dataset covers various indoor and outdoor environments with different floor types, including dry and wet, light conditions with both natural and artificial lighting, and obstacles like stairs, trees, holes, animals, and traffic cones. See Fig. 1 for examples of images in the proposed dataset.

4 CNN Architectures

This section showcases the CNN architectures explored in this study. It also outlines the layers added to complete the models and classify the VIA dataset images.

Table 1 displays the 25 evaluated architectures, along with some of their characteristics and references from literature.

The original CNN architectures were used with their existing structures and weights for ImageNet classification [28], except for the dense classification layers which were removed. Instead, an average global pooling layer was added, followed by a dense layer with 128 neurons and ReLU (Rectified Linear Unit) activation, then followed by a softmax classification layer. Figure 2 illustrates this proposed architecture, where x represents the CNN's horizontal and vertical input size (image size), and w, y, and z represent the size of the CNN's output in the last convolutional layer, which depends on the original CNN architecture and is specified in Table 1. The table also displays the number of trainable parameters in each CNN structure, including both the original layers and the added dense layers for VIA dataset classification."

5 CNN Comparison

This section presents the results of computer simulations that compared various CNN models applied to the VIA dataset. The simulations were carried out using Python and TensorFlow on three desktop computers equipped with NVIDIA GeForce GPU boards: GTX 970, GTX 1080, and RTX 2060 SUPER, respectively.

---

[1] Available at: https://github.com/fbreve/via-dataset.

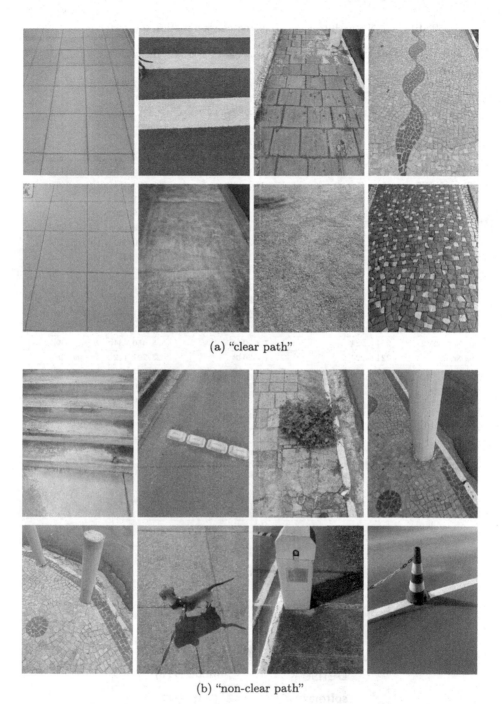

(a) "clear path"

(b) "non-clear path"

Fig. 1. Examples of images from the VIA dataset: (a) "clear path" category; and (b) "non-clear path" category.

Table 1. CNN architectures, selected characteristics, and references.

Model	Input Image Resolution	Output of Last Conv. Layer	Trainable Parameters	Reference
DenseNet121	224×224	$7 \times 7 \times 1024$	$7,085,314$	[13]
DenseNet169	224×224	$7 \times 7 \times 1664$	$12,697,858$	[13]
DenseNet201	224×224	$7 \times 7 \times 1920$	$18,339,074$	[13]
EfficientNetB0	224×224	$7 \times 7 \times 1280$	$4,171,774$	[37]
EfficientNetB1	240×240	$8 \times 8 \times 1280$	$6,677,410$	[37]
EfficientNetB2	260×260	$9 \times 9 \times 1408$	$7,881,604$	[37]
EfficientNetB3	300×300	$10 \times 10 \times 1536$	$10,893,226$	[37]
EfficientNetB4	380×380	$12 \times 12 \times 1792$	$17,778,378$	[37]
EfficientNetB5	456×456	$15 \times 15 \times 2048$	$28,603,314$	[37]
EfficientNetB6	528×528	$17 \times 17 \times 2304$	$41,031,002$	[37]
EfficientNetB7	600×600	$19 \times 19 \times 2560$	$64,115,026$	[37]
InceptionResNetV2	299×299	$8 \times 8 \times 1536$	$54,473,186$	[35]
InceptionV3	299×299	$8 \times 8 \times 2048$	$22,030,882$	[36]
MobileNet	224×224	$7 \times 7 \times 1024$	$3,338,434$	[12]
MobileNetV2	224×224	$7 \times 7 \times 1280$	$2,388,098$	[30]
NASNetMobile	224×224	$7 \times 7 \times 1056$	$4,368,532$	[41]
ResNet101	224×224	$7 \times 7 \times 2048$	$42,815,362$	[8]
ResNet101V2	224×224	$7 \times 7 \times 2048$	$42,791,426$	[9]
ResNet152	224×224	$7 \times 7 \times 2048$	$58,482,050$	[8]
ResNet152V2	224×224	$7 \times 7 \times 2048$	$58,450,434$	[9]
ResNet50	224×224	$7 \times 7 \times 2048$	$23,797,122$	[8]
ResNet50V2	224×224	$7 \times 7 \times 2048$	$23,781,890$	[9]
VGG16	224×224	$7 \times 7 \times 512$	$14,780,610$	[33]
VGG19	224×224	$7 \times 7 \times 512$	$20,090,306$	[33]
Xception	299×299	$10 \times 10 \times 2048$	$21,069,482$	[5]

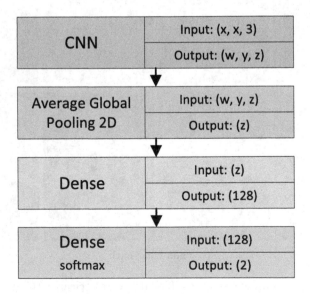

Fig. 2. Diagram of the proposed CNN networks.

The images were prepared for each CNN architecture by resizing them to the CNN input size and normalizing their range, with no other pre-processing applied. The networks were initialized with pre-trained weights from the Imagenet dataset [28], which has millions of images and hundreds of classes, and is a commonly used source for transfer learning. These pre-trained weights are available in Tensorflow. For the dense layers, the He uniform variance scaling initializer [7] was used.

The training phase involved six different scenarios with varying optimizers, learning rates, and frozen layers. The optimizers evaluated were RMSprop [10] and Adam [18]. In two of the scenarios, only the dense layer weights were trainable, while the convolutional layer weights remained frozen. In the other four scenarios, all layers were trainable, with two scenarios using the same adaptive learning rates for all layers and the other two using different fixed learning rates for the convolutional and dense layers. These scenarios are summarized in Table 2.

Table 2. The various scenarios in which each CNN was tested.

Config.	Fine-Tuning	Different Learning Rates	Optimizer
A	No	No	RMSprop
B	No	No	Adam
C	Yes	No	RMSprop
D	Yes	No	Adam
E	Yes	Yes	RMSprop
F	Yes	Yes	Adam

Configurations A and B were designed to preserve the weights trained on the large Imagenet dataset, while avoiding damaging them with the changes made using the smaller VIA dataset. In these scenarios, the CNNs acted as feature extractors for the dense layers, with an adaptive learning rate that varied from 10^{-3} to 10^{-5}. Configurations C and D explored the benefit of fine-tuning the weights in the convolutional layers for the target dataset, with an adaptive learning rate that varied from 10^{-3} to 10^{-5} applied to all layers. The learning rate was adjusted by a factor of 0.5 whenever the validation accuracy did not increase in the last two epochs. Configurations E and F explored the idea that the dense layers needed to be trained from scratch, while the convolutional layers received minor adjustments based on the weights learned from the Imagenet dataset. In these scenarios, the learning rate was fixed at 10^{-5} for the convolutional layers and 10^{-3} for the dense layers.

All models were trained for up to 50 epochs, with an early stopping criterion set to interrupt the training phase if the loss on the validation set did not decrease during the last 10 epochs. In most scenarios, the batch size was set to 16. However, for the scenarios involving EfficientNetB3 to EfficientNetB7, the batch size was reduced to accommodate the memory constraints of the available GPUs with up to 8GB of RAM. The specific batch sizes for these exceptions can be found in Table 3.

Table 3. Batch sizes used for each method and configuration, based on the GPU memory constraints. For methods not listed in the table, the batch size was uniformly set to 16 for all configurations.

Method	Conf. A	Conf. B	Conf. C	Conf. D	Conf. E	Conf. F
EfficientNetB3	16	16	16	16	16 – 8	16
EfficientNetB4	16	16	4	8	4	8
EfficientNetB5	16	16	2	4	2	4
EfficientNetB6	16	16	2	2	2	2
EfficientNetB7	16	16	1	1	1	1

Table 4 shows the classification accuracy obtained through transfer learning with the 25 different CNN architectures. The results were obtained using K-Fold Cross Validation with $k = 10$ and repeated 5 times, so each value in the table represents the average of 50 executions. In all scenarios, 20% of the training instances were randomly selected as the validation subset to guide the learning rate adjustments and to determine the stopping criterion.

MobileNet was found to be the best architecture in three out of the six configurations and had the best average performance considering all configurations. Its success is noteworthy as MobileNet was specifically designed to operate on mobile devices with limited processing power, which are the target devices for this framework. EfficientNetB0, EfficientNetB4, and InceptionV3 were the best-performing architectures in the remaining configurations. The highest accuracy overall was achieved by EfficientNetB4 with configuration D (0.9456), closely followed by EfficientNetB0 with configuration C (0.9427). This suggests that fine-tuning the convolutional layers can improve accuracy for some networks. However, in general, most architectures saw a decrease in accuracy when fine-tuned, as indicated by the best performing configurations being A and B in average. Configurations E and F did not yield exceptional results, with their best results being worse than those achieved with other configurations. Nonetheless, their average performance was better than that achieved with configurations C and D. Regarding optimizers, Adam and RMSprop produced similar results, with Adam showing a slight advantage by achieving an average accuracy of 0.8490 (configurations B, D, and F) compared to 0.8453 of RMSprop (configurations A, C, and E).

Table 4. Comparison of 25 different CNN-based models applied to the VIA datasets with the six proposed configurations. The best results in each column are highlighted in bold and the best results in each row are highlighted in italics.

Method	Conf. A	Conf. B	Conf. C	Conf. D	Conf. E	Conf. F	Average
MobileNet	*0.9158*	**0.9152**	0.9299	0.9257	0.8729	**0.9105**	**0.9117**
Xception	0.8749	0.8755	*0.9374*	0.9252	0.8934	0.9029	0.9016
EfficientNetB0	0.8877	0.8876	**0.9427**	*0.9274*	0.8724	0.8819	0.9000
EfficientNetB3	0.8901	0.8889	*0.9404*	0.9291	0.8727	0.8761	0.8995
EfficientNetB2	0.8725	0.8660	0.9391	*0.9426*	0.8672	0.8679	0.8926
EfficientNetB4	0.8813	0.8807	0.9304	*0.9456*	0.8414	0.8632	0.8904
EfficientNetB1	0.8908	0.8855	*0.9369*	0.9341	0.8482	0.8463	0.8903
DenseNet201	0.8841	*0.8847*	*0.8847*	0.8807	0.8696	0.8809	0.8808
InceptionResNetV2	0.8650	0.8644	0.8954	*0.9217*	0.8632	0.8668	0.8794
InceptionV3	0.8691	0.8657	0.8611	*0.8965*	**0.8936**	0.8807	0.8778
DenseNet169	0.8789	0.8766	0.8779	*0.8854*	0.8679	0.8713	0.8763
DenseNet121	0.8730	0.8671	0.8867	*0.8912*	0.8715	0.8680	0.8763
ResNet50	*0.8947*	0.8901	0.8139	0.8392	0.8801	0.8761	0.8657
ResNet101	*0.8925*	0.8919	0.8130	0.7919	0.8731	0.8626	0.8542
EfficientNetB5	0.8953	0.8947	0.8760	*0.9233*	0.6398	0.8327	0.8436
MobileNetV2	*0.8924*	0.8912	0.8324	0.7954	0.8116	0.8042	0.8378
ResNet152	0.8755	0.8754	0.7418	0.7724	*0.8819*	0.8638	0.8351
ResNet50V2	0.8539	0.8581	0.7273	0.8263	0.8516	*0.8587*	0.8293
EfficientNetB6	0.8719	0.8690	0.8514	*0.8738*	0.7383	0.7516	0.8260
ResNet101V2	*0.8807*	0.8790	0.6184	0.7256	0.8778	0.8779	0.8099
ResNet152V2	*0.9106*	0.9077	0.5942	0.6663	0.8890	0.8885	0.8094
VGG19	0.8263	0.8118	0.7916	0.6707	*0.8746*	0.8680	0.8072
VGG16	0.8263	0.8175	0.7877	0.6316	*0.8759*	0.8543	0.7989
NASNetMobile	0.8560	*0.8578*	0.6671	0.6997	0.7092	0.7050	0.7491
EfficientNetB7	*0.8731*	0.8714	0.5248	0.4999	0.5242	0.5230	0.6361
Average	*0.8773*	0.8749	0.8241	0.8289	0.8344	0.8433	0.8472

6   CNN Ensembles

This section presents the computer simulations involving ensembles of multiple instances of CNN models, including ensembles of single and multiple instances of different architectures. In all ensemble experiments, the output of the last dense layer, just before the softmax activation function, was used. This resulted in two continuous values for each image, which represent the probability of each class. The ensemble output was then computed by taking the average of its members' output. The same folds used in the previous section were employed, and the results in this section represent the average of 50 executions, obtained through

K-Fold Cross Validation with $k = 10$ repeated 5 times. Ensemble outputs were computed for each fold individually and then averaged.

The first ensemble experiment involved creating ensembles using only instances of the same CNN model. For each configuration, the architecture that provided the best individual results in Table 4 was selected. Specifically, MobileNet was used for configurations A, B, and F, EfficientNetB0 for configuration C, EfficientNetB4 for configuration D, and InceptionV3 for configuration E. One to ten instances were created and initialized with different seeds, and the accuracy achieved with each ensemble was recorded in Table 5. Across all tested scenarios, ensembles achieved higher accuracies than a single instance, with the best results typically obtained using six instances. While all configurations benefited from the use of ensembles, configuration D achieved the best results overall. Specifically, the highest accuracy achieved was 0.9602, obtained using six and ten instances of EfficientNetB4 with configuration D.

The second ensemble experiment was similar to the first, but ensembles were formed using one to ten instances of the best architecture in each configuration. Configurations were added to the ensembles one by one according to their performance in Table 4, with configurations D, C, A, B, F, and E added in that specific order. The accuracy achieved with each ensemble is presented in Table 6, with the best overall accuracy of 0.9655 obtained using six instances from each of the three best configurations: EfficientNetB4 with configuration D, EfficientNetB0 with configuration C, and MobileNet with configuration A.

Table 5. Comparison of ensembles of single CNN-based models applied to the VIA datasets with the six proposed configurations. The best results in each column are highlighted in bold and the best results in each row are highlighted in italics.

Instances	Conf. A	Conf. B	Conf. C	Conf. D	Conf. E	Conf. F	Average
1	0.9158	0.9152	0.9427	*0.9456*	0.8936	0.9105	0.9206
2	0.9187	0.9135	0.9451	*0.9502*	0.9065	0.9170	0.9252
3	0.9170	0.9176	0.9445	*0.9532*	0.9112	0.9193	0.9271
4	0.9164	0.9158	0.9485	*0.9562*	0.9176	0.9182	0.9288
5	0.9187	0.9182	0.9491	*0.9585*	0.9171	**0.9217**	0.9306
6	0.9176	**0.9199**	**0.9549**	***0.9602***	0.9182	0.9199	**0.9318**
7	**0.9211**	0.9182	0.9543	*0.9579*	**0.9211**	0.9164	0.9315
8	0.9164	0.9158	0.9509	*0.9596*	0.9194	0.9158	0.9297
9	0.9182	0.9176	0.9538	*0.9596*	0.9200	0.9193	0.9314
10	0.9188	0.9159	0.9526	***0.9602***	0.9194	0.9176	0.9308
Average	0.9179	0.9168	0.9496	*0.9561*	0.9144	0.9176	0.9287

Table 6. Comparison of ensembles of multiple CNN-based models applied to the VIA datasets using the one to six of the proposed configurations. The best results in each column are highlighted in bold and the best results in each row are highlighted in italics.

Instances of each conf.	Conf.D	Conf.DC	Conf.DCA	Conf.DCAB	Conf. DCABF	All Conf.	Average
1	0.9456	0.9532	*0.9567*	0.9550	0.9503	0.9491	0.9517
2	0.9502	0.9491	*0.9544*	0.9538	0.9486	0.9521	0.9514
3	0.9532	0.9544	*0.9597*	0.9545	0.9509	0.9539	0.9544
4	0.9562	0.9555	*0.9614*	0.9527	0.9515	0.9556	0.9555
5	0.9585	0.9567	*0.9620*	0.9544	0.9544	**0.9573**	0.9572
6	**0.9602**	**0.9579**	*0.9655*	0.9562	0.9538	0.9556	**0.9582**
7	0.9579	0.9544	*0.9643*	**0.9574**	0.9544	0.9550	0.9572
8	0.9596	0.9532	*0.9626*	0.9562	0.9526	**0.9573**	0.9569
9	0.9596	0.9555	*0.9637*	0.9568	0.9568	0.9550	0.9579
10	**0.9602**	0.9561	*0.9626*	0.9556	**0.9579**	0.9550	0.9579
Average	0.9561	0.9546	*0.9613*	0.9553	0.9531	0.9546	0.9558

7 Conclusions

This paper explores the application of 25 different CNN architectures to identify obstacles in the path of visually impaired individuals. K-Fold Cross Validation was utilized with $k = 10$ and five repetitions to provide robust results. The architectures have low computational costs during inference, executing in milliseconds on current smartphones, allowing them to be implemented without relying on external equipment or remote servers. The CNN architectures were pre-trained on large datasets and evaluated first as feature extractors with pre-trained weights, then with fine-tuned weights for the proposed task. Fine-tuning an EfficientNetB4 network achieved the highest accuracy of 0.9456.

CNN ensembles were examined, comprising multiple instances of the single best architecture in each configuration, as well as instances of the best architectures in each configuration. In the first scenario, an ensemble of six instances was utilized, resulting in an accuracy improvement to 0.9602 for the fine-tuned EfficientNetB4. In the second scenario, the six instances of EfficientNetB4 were combined with six instances of EfficientNetB0, which were also fine-tuned to the proposed task, and six instances of MobileNet, which were used as a feature extractor. This approach resulted in a further accuracy increase to 0.9655.

The numerous computer simulations conducted in this study yielded promising results for some CNN architectures and investigated the use of different optimizers (Adam and RMSprop), learning strategies (single learning rate versus different rates for convolution and dense layers), and pre-trained weights (fixed versus fine-tuned). The study also demonstrated that ensembles could enhance accuracy by utilizing multiple instances of the same architecture and configuration or multiple instances of different architectures and configurations.

Future work includes expanding the proposed dataset by acquiring more images and exploring other approaches and modifications to the current framework to further enhance classification accuracy. Recently, a smartphone prototype application was developed to test real-world scenarios [31]. Furthermore, the findings presented in this paper can guide future research on related datasets as numerous CNN architectures were tested and compared.

Acknowledgements. This study was financed in part by the Coordenação de Aperfeiçoamento de Pessoal de Nível Superior - Brasil (CAPES) and by the São Paulo Research Foundation - FAPESP (grant #2016/05669-4).

References

1. Bai, J., Liu, Z., Lin, Y., Li, Y., Lian, S., Liu, D.: Wearable travel aid for environment perception and navigation of visually impaired people. Electronics **8**(6), 697 (2019)
2. Breve, F., Fischer, C.N.: Visually impaired aid using convolutional neural networks, transfer learning, and particle competition and cooperation. In: 2020 International Joint Conference on Neural Networks (IJCNN), pp. 1–8 (2020). https://doi.org/10.1109/IJCNN48605.2020.9207606
3. Budrionis, A., Plikynas, D., Daniušis, P., Indrulionis, A.: Smartphone-based computer vision travelling aids for blind and visually impaired individuals: A systematic review. Assistive Technology **34**(2), 178–194 (2022). https://doi.org/10.1080/10400435.2020.1743381,https://doi.org/10.1080/10400435.2020.1743381, pMID: 32207640
4. Cardillo, E., Caddemi, A.: Insight on electronic travel aids for visually impaired people: a review on the electromagnetic technology. Electronics **8**(11), 1281 (2019)
5. Chollet, F.: Xception: Deep learning with depthwise separable convolutions. In: 2017 IEEE Conference on Computer Vision and Pattern Recognition (CVPR), pp. 1800–1807 (July 2017). https://doi.org/10.1109/CVPR.2017.195
6. Goodfellow, I., Bengio, Y., Courville, A.: Deep learning. MIT press (2016)
7. He, K., Zhang, X., Ren, S., Sun, J.: Delving deep into rectifiers: Surpassing human-level performance on imagenet classification. In: Proceedings of the IEEE International Conference On Computer Vision, pp. 1026–1034 (2015)
8. He, K., Zhang, X., Ren, S., Sun, J.: Deep residual learning for image recognition. In: The IEEE Conference on Computer Vision and Pattern Recognition (CVPR), pp. 770–778 (June 2016)
9. He, K., Zhang, X., Ren, S., Sun, J.: Identity mappings in deep residual networks. In: Leibe, B., Matas, J., Sebe, N., Welling, M. (eds.) ECCV 2016. LNCS, vol. 9908, pp. 630–645. Springer, Cham (2016). https://doi.org/10.1007/978-3-319-46493-0_38
10. Hinton, G., Srivastava, N., Swersky, K.: Neural networks for machine learning lecture 6a overview of mini-batch gradient descent (2012)
11. Hoang, V.-N., Nguyen, T.-H., Le, T.-L., Tran, T.-H., Vuong, T.-P., Vuillerme, N.: Obstacle detection and warning system for visually impaired people based on electrode matrix and mobile Kinect. Vietnam J. Comput. Sci. **4**(2), 71–83 (2016). https://doi.org/10.1007/s40595-016-0075-z
12. Howard, A.G., et al.: Mobilenets: Efficient convolutional neural networks for mobile vision applications. arXiv preprint arXiv:1704.04861 (2017)
13. Huang, G., Liu, Z., van der Maaten, L., Weinberger, K.Q.: Densely connected convolutional networks. In: The IEEE Conference on Computer Vision and Pattern Recognition (CVPR), pp. 4700–4708 (July 2017)

14. Islam, M.M., Sadi, M.S.: Path hole detection to assist the visually impaired people in navigation. In: 2018 4th International Conference on Electrical Engineering and Information Communication Technology (iCEEiCT), pp. 268–273 (Sep 2018). https://doi.org/10.1109/CEEICT.2018.8628134

15. Islam, M.M., Sheikh Sadi, M., Zamli, K.Z., Ahmed, M.M.: Developing walking assistants for visually impaired people: a review. IEEE Sens. J. **19**(8), 2814–2828 (2019). https://doi.org/10.1109/JSEN.2018.2890423

16. Jiang, B., Yang, J., Lv, Z., Song, H.: Wearable vision assistance system based on binocular sensors for visually impaired users. IEEE Internet Things J. **6**(2), 1375–1383 (2019). https://doi.org/10.1109/JIOT.2018.2842229

17. Joe Louis Paul, I., Sasirekha, S., Mohanavalli, S., Jayashree, C., Moohana Priya, P., Monika, K.: Smart eye for visually impaired-an aid to help the blind people. In: 2019 International Conference on Computational Intelligence in Data Science (ICCIDS), pp. 1–5 (2019). DOI: https://doi.org/10.1109/ICCIDS.2019.8862066

18. Kingma, D.P., Ba, J.: Adam: A method for stochastic optimization (2014)

19. Kumar, R., Meher, S.: A novel method for visually impaired using object recognition. In: 2015 International Conference on Communications and Signal Processing (ICCSP), pp. 0772–0776 (April 2015). https://doi.org/10.1109/ICCSP.2015.7322596

20. Kuriakose, B., Shrestha, R., Sandnes, F.E.: Scenerecog: A deep learning scene recognition model for assisting blind and visually impaired navigate using smartphones. In: 2021 IEEE International Conference on Systems, Man, and Cybernetics (SMC), pp. 2464–2470 (2021). https://doi.org/10.1109/SMC52423.2021.9658913

21. Lakde, C.K., Prasad, P.S.: Review paper on navigation system for visually impaired people. Int. J. Adv. Res. Comput. Commun. Eng. **4**(1), (2015)

22. LeCun, Y., Bengio, Y., Hinton, G.: Deep learning. Nature **521**(7553), 436 (2015)

23. Lin, B.S., Lee, C.C., Chiang, P.Y.: Simple smartphone-based guiding system for visually impaired people. Sensors **17**(6), 1371 (2017)

24. Mandia, S., Kumar, A., Verma, K., Deegwal, J.K.: Vision-based assistive systems for visually impaired people: a review. In: Tiwari, M., Ismail, Y., Verma, K., Garg, A.K. (eds.) Optical and Wireless Technologies, pp. 163–172. Springer Nature Singapore, Singapore (2023)

25. Poggi, M., Mattoccia, S.: A wearable mobility aid for the visually impaired based on embedded 3d vision and deep learning. In: 2016 IEEE Symposium on Computers and Communication (ISCC), pp. 208–213. IEEE (2016)

26. Poggi, M., Nanni, L., Mattoccia, S.: Crosswalk recognition through point-cloud processing and deep-learning suited to a wearable mobility aid for the visually impaired. In: International Conference on Image Analysis and Processing, pp. 282–289. Springer (2015)

27. Rizzo, J.R., Pan, Y., Hudson, T., Wong, E.K., Fang, Y.: Sensor fusion for ecologically valid obstacle identification: Building a comprehensive assistive technology platform for the visually impaired. In: 2017 7th International Conference on Modeling, Simulation, and Applied Optimization (ICMSAO), pp. 1–5. IEEE (2017)

28. Russakovsky, O., et al.: ImageNet large scale visual recognition challenge. Int. J. Comput. Vision **115**(3), 211–252 (2015). https://doi.org/10.1007/s11263-015-0816-y

29. Saffoury, R., et al.: Blind path obstacle detector using smartphone camera and line laser emitter. In: 2016 1st International Conference on Technology and Innovation in Sports, Health and Wellbeing (TISHW), pp. 1–7. IEEE (2016)

30. Sandler, M., Howard, A., Zhu, M., Zhmoginov, A., Chen, L.C.: Mobilenetv 2: Inverted residuals and linear bottlenecks. In: The IEEE Conference on Computer Vision and Pattern Recognition (CVPR), pp. 4510–4520 (June 2018)
31. Sanga, G.M., Polo, J.M.G., Passerini, J.A.R.: Auxílio a deficientes visuais utilizando redes neurais convolucionais (2022)
32. Schmidhuber, J.: Deep learning in neural networks: an overview. Neural Netw. **61**, 85–117 (2015)
33. Simonyan, K., Zisserman, A.: Very Deep Convolutional Networks For Large-scale Image Recognition, pp. 1–14. Computational and Biological Learning Society (2015)
34. Steinmetz, J.D., et al.: Causes of blindness and vision impairment in 2020 and trends over 30 years, and prevalence of avoidable blindness in relation to vision 2020: the right to sight: an analysis for the global burden of disease study. Lancet Glob. Health **9**(2), e144–e160 (2021)
35. Szegedy, C., Ioffe, S., Vanhoucke, V., Alemi, A.A.: Inception-v4, inception-resnet and the impact of residual connections on learning. In: Thirty-first AAAI Conference On Artificial Intelligence (2017)
36. Szegedy, C., Vanhoucke, V., Ioffe, S., Shlens, J., Wojna, Z.: Rethinking the inception architecture for computer vision. In: The IEEE Conference on Computer Vision and Pattern Recognition (CVPR), pp. 2818–2826 (June 2016)
37. Tan, M., Le, Q.: EfficientNet: Rethinking model scaling for convolutional neural networks. In: Chaudhuri, K., Salakhutdinov, R. (eds.) Proceedings of the 36th International Conference on Machine Learning. Proceedings of Machine Learning Research, vol. 97, pp. 6105–6114. PMLR (09–15 Jun 2019), https://proceedings.mlr.press/v97/tan19a.html
38. Tapu, R., Mocanu, B., Bursuc, A., Zaharia, T.: A smartphone-based obstacle detection and classification system for assisting visually impaired people. In: The IEEE International Conference on Computer Vision (ICCV) Workshops (June 2013)
39. Tapu, R., Mocanu, B., Zaharia, T.: Deep-see: joint object detection, tracking and recognition with application to visually impaired navigational assistance. Sensors **17**(11), 2473 (2017)
40. World Health Organization: Vision impairment and blindness (Oct 2022), https://www.who.int/news-room/fact-sheets/detail/blindness-and-visual-impairment Accessed: 2023-01-30
41. Zoph, B., Vasudevan, V., Shlens, J., Le, Q.V.: Learning transferable architectures for scalable image recognition. In: The IEEE Conference on Computer Vision and Pattern Recognition (CVPR), pp. 8697–8710 (June 2018)

Artificial Bee Colony Algorithm for Feature Selection in Fraud Detection Process

Gabriel Covello Furlanetto[1], Vitoria Zanon Gomes[2], and Fabricio Aparecido Breve[1(✉)]

[1] Department of Statistics, Applied Mathematics and Computer Science, Universidade Estadual Paulista (UNESP), Avenida 24A, 1515 - Jardim Bela Vista, RioClaro-Sp 13506 -900, Brazil
{gabriel.furlanetto,fabricio.breve}@unesp.br
[2] Department of Computer Science and Statistics, Universidade Estadual Paulista (UNESP), Rua Cristóvão Colombo, 2265 - Jardim Nazareth, São José do Rio Preto-SP 15054-000, Brazil
vitoria.zanon@unesp.br

Abstract. More and more, nowadays, better performance and quality of current classifiers are required when the topic is fraud detection. In this context, processes such as feature selection help to increase the quality of the results obtained by the existing classifiers in the literature, since the high dimensionality of current datasets and redundant information significantly affect the performance of these techniques. This work proposes a wrapper method of feature selection using the ABC algorithm combined with Logistic Regression classification, seeking to obtain better results for fraud detection. Through the tests performed and the results obtained, it is observed that the reduction in the number of features can reduce the database complexity and achieve a higher accuracy in classification when compared to the set classification when using all its attributes. It is also notable the effectiveness of the method as it reaches the proposed objective with as much as quality as other well-known methods while also contributing to optimizing parameters of other feature selection algorithms.

Keywords: Artificial Bee Colony · Feature Selection · Fraud Detection · Machine Learning

1 Introduction

Fraud detection is no longer an option for companies nowadays [15]. With the growing increase in banking operations via smartphones and the internet, also driven by the pandemic reported in the year 2019, fraud multiplied, making the

This study was financed in part by the Coordenação de Aperfeiçoamento de Pessoal de Nível Superior - Brasil (CAPES) under grant number 88887.686064/2022-00 and the Sao Paulo Research Foundation - FAPESP (grant #2016/05669-4).

investment, in efficient fraud detection systems, vital for the survival of companies and, principally for financial institutions, since these malicious activities not only cause harm but also cause distrust on the part of customers.

At the same time, the use of Machine Learning techniques for this purpose has been growing gradually in the literature, and it is possible to find several approaches, ranging from supervised learning through classical algorithms to the hybridization of techniques seeking better performance in unbalanced datasets [4].

However, despite the remarkable role of these techniques, the information itself, to be classified, can affect the performance of the algorithm. Datasets that gather information about financial transactions, tend to have a huge amount of attributes, often irrelevant, redundant, or highly correlated [17], making the classifier expend time looking for patterns and correlations that will not bring significant gain, only consuming time and computational resources. To solve this problem, the process known as Feature Selection is used.

The present work explores the Feature Selection process in order, not only, to reduce the complexity of the supplied attributes delivered to the classifier, but also to improve classifier performance by reducing attributes. For this, the Artificial Bee Colony (ABC) algorithm or Bee Swarm Algorithm (as found in the literature) was used, to perform the attribute selection, taking into account its simplicity, jointly with the classifier through Logistic Regression in a scenario of detection of frauds.

Furthermore, as another contribution, this work does not use the ABC algorithm only as a tool for feature selection, but also to find the optimal parameter and feed other algorithms whose goal is the same, such as K-best and RFE, for example. Unlike other works found in the literature that evaluate results using only one classifier algorithm this work also proposed test scenarios in which the performance of three different classification algorithms (Logistic Regression, Random Forest, and Gradient Boosting) are evaluated with the optimal features. As a result, it is clear that ABC is stable as a feature selection tool and as a good option to define the optimal parameter for K-best.

For this purpose, this article was divided as follows: in Sect. 3 the attribute selection method is detailed. In Sect. 4, a generic approach to particle swarm algorithms is made, followed by the explanation of the ABC algorithm, which is the subject of this article. Works related to the proposed one are presented in Sect. 2. In Sect. 5, the implementation of the proposed method is described. After implementation, the tests scenarios and their results are described in Sect. 6, and finally, in Sect. 7 final considerations are made about the work.

2   Related Works

When searching the literature, other works with the same application of attribute selection with ABC can be find. Among them, Pavithra and Thangadurai [17], implement the ABC together with the Support Vector Machine (SVM) classifier to perform feature selection in the fraud detection scenario. In this work, the tests were performed with a dataset with a relatively low number of attributes, but positive results were obtained in relation to the classification without selection of attributes. Despite the little dimensionality of the test cases, this work supports the efficiency of ABC in fraud detection cases.

Meanwhile, in the work of Hancer, Xue, Karaboga, and Zhang [9], ABC is used as a filtering method. The objective function of the algorithm seeks to evaluate the proximity relationship between the attributes and, therefore, the objective of the algorithm becomes to determine a set of attributes where their proximity is as close as possible using the kNN classifier. In this work, the tests were performed with several datasets available for free in the machine learning repository of the University of California (UCI), and the results obtained validated the effectiveness of ABC as a filter method, which results in a better performance in the selection process.

Palanisamy and Kanmani [16], in turn, use ABC with a different approach in the onlooker bee phase. Food sources are represented by the attributes of the dataset, and therefore each employed bee becomes responsible for an attribute. Onlooker bees, then, are responsible for selecting the best sources, joining them together, and then evaluating the possible solution through a classifier. Good results were obtained when compared to other bioinspired algorithms, such as ACO, for feature selection. This approach is valid when used in datasets with high data dimensionality since through the work of the onlooker bees, a large reduction in the cost involved in the classification could be observed.

Finally, Agrawal and Chandra [1] use ABC for feature selection in medical image classification processes. Considering the number of factors to be observed in an exam to perform a diagnosis, a high range of attributes is involved in the classification, detracting from the performance of the classifier. For the tests, the kNN and SVM classifiers (with linear and Gaussian kernel) were used. The authors concluded that ABC was successful in its objective, even though biases and unbalanced data interfered remarkably in the final solution.

3   Feature Selection

Feature Selection consists of the selection of features of a dataset, seeking to maximize the performance of classifiers by using only selected attributes for the classification process, leading to a reduction in the complexity of the dataset, in addition to optimizing the accuracy of the method [17]. This selection can be made through several methods, which are divided into two categories:

- **Filter methods:** The methods of this category work without considering the classifier to be used. In them, the attributes of the dataset are analyzed individually and collectively, and the statistical data extracted from these analyses help the method to define which are the most relevant characteristics for a good result of classification. This type of method is widely used due to its simplicity of implementation and little use of computational resources [17] [7].

– **Wrapper methods:** In this class of methods, the classifier acts as a kind of black box, being part of an objective function used to evaluate the various possible combinations of attributes. The main problem of this approach is in dealing with sets of data with high dimensionality, since the computational performance decreases significantly, although it does not make its use unfeasible [7].

Machine learning algorithms and optimization algorithms are widely used for this purpose. In this work, the optimization algorithms based on population will be highlighted, with the selection of attributes by wrapping methods.

4   Population-Based Algorithms

Population-based algorithms are a subgroup within the class of bioinspired algorithms. As the name suggests, its performance is based on the behavior of species that live in society. Examples include the Genetic Algorithm [14] and algorithms based on swarm intelligence, such as Particle Swarm Optimization (PSO) [6], Ant Colony Optimization (ACO) [5], and Artificial Bee Colony Algorithm (ABC) [11]. Among those mentioned, ABC stands out for its simplicity, robustness, and ease of implementation. Besides, it still needs fewer input parameters to execute, in comparison with the others and it can be easily combined with other algorithms to obtain better performance.

4.1   Artificial Bee Colony Algorithm (ABC)

The ABC algorithm simulates the work of honey bees throughout the foraging process, that is, the search for food for the members of the hive [12].

Biological Behavior: The worker bees are responsible for all the maintenance of the hive, including the search for food. To this end, the workers are divided into three groups: Employees, Onlookers, and Scouts [12].

Scout bees, as the name suggests, are responsible for randomly looking for food sources in the vicinity of the hive. When they meet, they become employed bees. After choosing the food source, the bees assess its quality through factors such as the distance from the hive and the difficulty in extracting the nectar, and return to the hive with a sample of the food found [12]. Upon returning, the employed bees pass the information about the source and the sample of the nectar to the onlooker bees, who will summarize and evaluate the information brought by the employees, in a way to decide which source should be exploited [2].

The Algorithm: In the Bee Swarm Algorithm, food sources represent possible solutions to the problem to be solved, and their several characteristics to be analyzed by the bees are replaced by only one: an objective function. The bee's work is performed by routines executed iteratively until a stopping condition is reached, and then the best solution found is returned. This work can be described by the sequence of steps of the algorithm:

1. **Population initialization:** The population of n scout bees is randomly initialized, making these bees employed;
2. **Phase 1 - Employed bees:** The score for each of the current food sources is calculated, as well as the probability of them being chosen by an onlooker bee, considering their quality in relation to the others ;
3. **Phase 2 - Onlooker bees:** The n onlooker bees will choose, taking into account the previously calculated probability, food sources to be exploited, that is, which will undergo small modifications to try to improve your score. If it is possible to improve any of the solutions, this new solution is saved;
4. **Phase 3 - Verification of Stagnation (scout bees):** If any food source has reached its stagnation limit, that is, it is at a pre-defined of unimproved iterations, this source is abandoned, and the bee responsible for it becomes an explorer again, randomly choosing a new food source to evaluate;
5. At the end of the iteration, the best score is saved;
6. If the stop condition is met, the execution ends. Otherwise, it continues from item 2.

The sequence of steps described can also be seen, in the form of a flowchart, in Fig. 1. In it, the order of execution of the algorithm can be seen.

5   Methodology

In the proposed work, to improve the classification of possible frauds, through Machine Learning, the first step performed was the definition of the dataset that would be used to validate the model.

Through a search on the Kaggle website, the Credit Card Transactions Fraud Detection Dataset was found[1], a complete dataset with a good description of its attributes, generated through simulation, in a synthetic way[2], bringing data from fictitious customers and with good documentation. Thus, it was chosen for this work, since its objective is not only to validate the proposed method, but also to use it in the fraud detection application.

With the definition of the dataset, ABC was implemented using the Python programming language, since it is widely used in the research segment, moreover, it has a large number of libraries aimed for data processing, Machine Learning, and statistics. For this, a class called Bee was created, where its attributes are the information related to each bee, such as which food source is under its responsibility, the quality of the source, and the stagnation of the same.

The solution, in this case, is in the form of a list of indexes, whose length can vary from 1 to N, where N is the number of attributes of the dataset that

---

[1] https://www.kaggle.com/kartik2112/fraud-detection.
[2] https://www.github.com/namebrandon/Sparkov_Data_Generation.

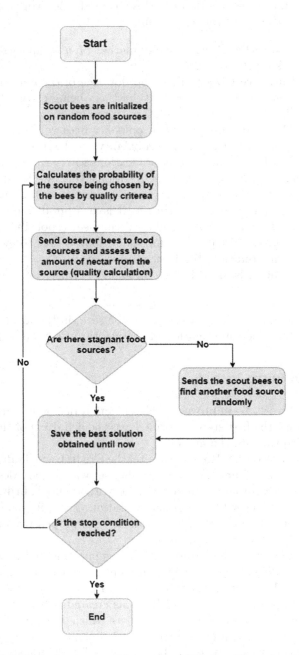

Fig. 1. Flowchart exemplifying the ABC algorithm execution.

you want to work with. The indexes in a solution are not repeated, to avoid information redundancy. Still in ABC, to evaluate the quality of the food source of each bee, the objective function was developed.

5.1 Objective Function

The objective function used performs the training and testing process, through Logistic Regression, Gradient Boosting, or Random Forest, of the dataset considering the selected attributes as a possible solution. After the classification, the F1-score accuracy measure is used as a way to attest the quality of the solution that was evaluated. The objective of ABC, becomes, then, to search for a set of attributes that reduce the final error and maximize the F1-score of the classifier.

After the implementation of the ABC algorithm, which allows the selection of attributes, Logistic Regression, Gradient Boosting, and Random Forest algorithms were used to carry out the classification.

5.2 Logistic Regression

Logistic Regression [13] is a statistical method that allows predicting the behavior of a variable, usually binary, based on the value of others, whether discrete or continuous. As a classifier, it allows determining the class value of an item, according to the values of the input attributes, through a set of weights, determined in the training phase of the algorithm. These weights make up the so-called logistic function, which acts as a kind of objective function within the classifier.

In Eq. 1,an example of a logistic function can be seen:

$$f(x) = e^{(b0+b1x1+...+bnxn)}/(1 + e^{(b0+b1x1+...+bnxn)}) \tag{1}$$

, where $b0, b1, ...bn$ would be the n+1 weights defined through the analysis of training data.

5.3 Gradient Boosting

The Gradient Boosting algorithm [8] is part of a class of machine learning algorithms that can be used for problems of predictive modeling of classification or regression.

Its development is based on decision tree models. For this, such trees are added one by one to the set and adjusted to correct the prediction errors of the previous models, a technique known as boosting. In this way, the "gradient reinforcement" occurs, since its loss is minimized as the model is adjusted, similar to a neural network.

5.4 Random Forest

Random Forest [10] was built on the decision tree algorithm and seeks to increase its accuracy and solve its limitations. It consists of a set of decision trees and can also be used in classification and regression problems.

Thus, when we talk about classification, which is the subject of this work, the prediction employing the random trees algorithm is made based on the class label selected by most of the trees of decision generated to compose the algorithm in highlight.

It can be seen, therefore, that the use of these three algorithms as a classification method is due to their simplicity and because they are better suited to the analysis scenario, since the inputs can be classified only in two ways as possible cheats or as a normal operation, being then a scenario with a binary output variable.

Finally, to increase the performance of the proposed algorithm, considering that datasets referring to fraud are usually unbalanced because malicious activities occur less frequently in relation to normal transactions, the dataset balancing treatment was realized.

In this case, since it is a very large set and is difficult to process in a common computer, it was decided to use the balancing edge by undersampling. For this, from the number of records in the training dataset in which the known classification was fraud, that is, a minority dataset within the base, the number of records of common operations can be reduced, without any indication of malicious activity, so that the base of training and tests of the algorithm kept balanced.

After the method was implemented, and any adjustments were made, tests were carried out in an attempt to demonstrate its effectiveness in preventing and combating fraud. Thus, the results obtained are presented in Sect. 6.

5.5 Algorithm Complexity

Considering the implemented algorithm, through its serial execution, its computational complexity order can be obtained from the time of each execution in relation to the input size data, as shown in Fig. 2.

Through it, we can perceive that the context to be solved by the algorithm consists on a optimization problem of variable, of NP-complete, with a complexity of the order $O(n) = (2^n)$.

6 Results and Discussion

As mentioned before, a set of Kaggle with synthetic fraud data was used for this article. This dataset is composed of the attributes presented in Table 1. Thus, after processing such attributes, to transform them into input for the developed algorithm, as described in 5, 3 scenarios of tests were proposed. In all of them, 100 repetitions of the algorithm were performed to remove the averages and

Input size x Execution time

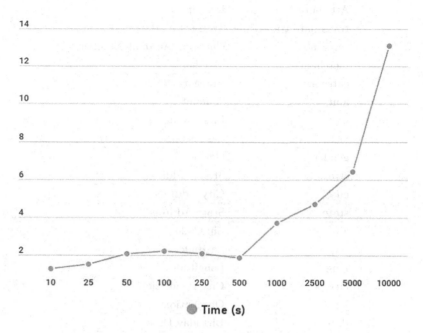

Fig. 2. Complexity analysis of implemented algorithm using runtime for different input sizes

deviations from the results. It should also be noted that all tests were performed on a notebook with a 64-bit Windows 10 operating system, 16.0 GB RAM, Intel(R) Core(TM) i7-1165G7, 2.80GHz, of 11th generation.

Each of the proposed scenarios is described below:

– **Scenario 1:** In the first test scenario, the Bee Swarm Algorithm is used in an isolated way to perform the selection of atributtes (Feature Selection). Then, Logistic Regression, Random Forest, and Gradient Boosting algorithms are applied to perform the classification on the data set and extract the results for analysis.
– **Scenario 2:** In the second test scenario, the Logistic Regression, Random Forest, and Gradient Boosting algorithms are applied over the complete data set, without going through a selection of attributes, and then the execution metrics are extracted.
– **Scenario 3:** In the third scenario, ABC is applied to the dataset, to extract the amount of best attributes. This quantity of best attributes will be used as

Table 1. Dataset attributes description for the algorithm tests

Attribute Name	Description
trans_date_trans_time	Transaction date and hour
cc_num	Checking Account Number
merchant	Merchant
category	Category
amt	Amount
first	First Name
last	Last Name
gender	Gender
street	Street Address
city	City Address
state	State Address
zip	Zip Code
lat	Latitude
long	Longitude
city_pop	City Population
job	Occupation
dob	Birthday Date
trans_num	Transaction Number
unix_time	System time
merch_lat	Latitude Merchant
merch_long	Longitude Merchant
is_fraud	Fraud Flag

input to the K-best[3], RFE,[4] and Feature Importance[5], all feature selection per wrap algorithms. They in turn will perform the selection of attributes in the dataset. After this procedure, for each of the attribute selection methods, the

---

[3] K-best: Algorithm that classifies resources by their ranking scores and then selects the top k resources with the highest score. In this scenario, ABC is used to provide the input number k for the algorithm [18].

[4] Recursive Feature Elimination (RFE): Recursive Feature Elimination (RFE): Algorithm that performs selection by recursively removing the attributes and building a model on those that remain. It uses the precision of the model to identify which attributes (or a combination of them) to keep (strong attributes) and which to discard (weak attributes) [3].

[5] Feature Importance: As a third selection method, it was chosen to use the N most relevant attributes for the algorithm, whose importance is calculated using the Extra Trees-Classifier algorithm, that is, the most important attributes are calculated and, in the sequence, from the bee algorithm it is obtained how many will remain for training and testing of the model.

three classification models (Logistic Regression, Random Forest, and Gradient Boosting) are applied for extraction of the evaluation metrics.

In addition to the 100 executions for each of the proposed scenarios, it was used as parameters for the ABC algorithm, the maximum number of 100 iterations, 10 bees, and a stagnation limit equals 5 food sources in all runs.

From the proposed scenarios, from this point onwards, the results obtained and their analysis will be displayed from now on.

In Tables 2 and 3, it is possible to observe the data collected from the training scenarios with 100 iterations of the ABC, when pertinent (Scenarios 1 and 3), and from the tests with the same amount. In the results, two different situations can be observed:

- In the first, for the Gradient Boosting and Random Forest classifiers, the use of the ABC algorithm practically does not change the accuracy and the F1-Score (measures related to the algorithm's hit rates) of the results. The biggest difference is presented when there is a direct application of the algorithm to select attributes (Scenario 1), in which the results end up getting worse by approximately 1%.
- In the second, with the Logistic Regression classification model, there is an increase in performance, both for the accuracy and the F1-Score, for Scenarios 1 and 3 with respect to Scenario 2 (no attribute selection).

The same information, referring to the test data, is presented in the graphs of Figs. 3 and 4.

Table 2. 100 iterations training

Test Scenario	Classifier	Feature SelectionAlgorithm	Accuracy Average	F1-Score Average	Accuracy Standard Deviation	F1-Score Standard Deviation
Scenario 1	Gradient Boosting	ABC	97,2425%	97,1355%	3,7057%	4,1919%
Scenario 2	Gradient Boosting	N/A	98,6867%	98,6744%	0,0000%	0,0000%
Scenario 3	Gradient Boosting	Feature Importance	98,4318%	98,4169%	0,1578%	0,1562%
Scenario 3	Gradient Boosting	Kbest	98,1872%	98,1643%	0,5567%	0,5793%
Scenario 3	Gradient Boosting	RFE	98,6458%	98,6321%	0,0990%	0,1008%
Scenario 1	Random Forest	ABC	99,8902%	99,8930%	0,8925%	0,8634%
Scenario 2	Random Forest	N/A	99,9996%	99,9996%	0,0019%	0,0019%
Scenario 3	Random Forest	Feature Importance	99,9998%	99,9998%	0,0013%	0,0013%
Scenario 3	Random Forest	Kbest	99,9997%	99,9997%	0,0016%	0,0016%
Scenario 3	Random Forest	RFE	99,9996%	99,9996%	0,0019%	0,0019%
Scenario 1	Logistic Regression	ABC	93,4635%	93,4943%	7,6677%	6,1883%
Scenario 2	Logistic Regression	N/A	83,9646%	82,2239%	0,0000%	0,0000%
Scenario 3	Logistic Regression	Feature Importance	85,3035%	83,7628%	3,7050%	4,1998%
Scenario 3	Logistic Regression	Kbest	95,8987%	95,7574%	0,0747%	0,0778%
Scenario 3	Logistic Regression	RFE	89,8953%	88,7512%	0,0803%	0,1794%

In addition, it is noted that, in Scenario 3, when applying the bees algorithm to generate the number of attributes reverted to feed both the K-best and the RFE, there is greater stability of results, with a lower standard deviation, again for both metrics (Accuracy and F1-Score), if compared with Scenario 1 and with the use to feed the Feature Importance algorithm, although both the latter also presented better performance than the exclusive execution of the classifiers.

Table 3. 100 iterations test

Test Scenario	Classifier	Feature SelectionAlgorithm	Accuracy Average	F1-Score Average	Accuracy Standard Deviation	F1-Score Standard Deviation
Scenario 1	Gradient Boosting	ABC	97,1201%	97,0496%	3,8576%	4,3000%
Scenario 2	Gradient Boosting	N/A	98,4680%	98,4704%	0,0000%	0,0000%
Scenario 3	Gradient Boosting	Feature Importance	98,0604%	98,0645%	0,2122%	0,2091%
Scenario 3	Gradient Boosting	Kbest	97,8501%	97,8493%	0,4374%	0,4475%
Scenario 3	Gradient Boosting	RFE	98,4130%	98,4150%	0,0978%	0,0976%
Scenario 1	Random Forest	ABC	98,1452%	98,1729%	2,3717%	2,2374%
Scenario 2	Random Forest	N/A	99,0548%	99,0592%	0,0431%	0,0430%
Scenario 3	Random Forest	Feature Importance	98,8308%	98,8373%	0,2011%	0,1993%
Scenario 3	Random Forest	Kbest	98,6661%	98,6737%	0,2880%	0,2872%
Scenario 3	Random Forest	RFE	98,9808%	98,9954%	0,1456%	0,1436%
Scenario 1	Logistic Regression	ABC	93,8819%	94,0002%	7,6516%	6,1605%
Scenario 2	Logistic Regression	N/A	84,1252%	82,6835%	0,0000%	0,0000%
Scenario 3	Logistic Regression	Feature Importance	85,5011%	84,2290%	3,7847%	4,2124%
Scenario 3	Logistic Regression	Kbest	96,2842%	96,2183%	0,0874%	0,0890%
Scenario 3	Logistic Regression	RFE	90,2016%	89,2765%	0,1649%	0,2679%

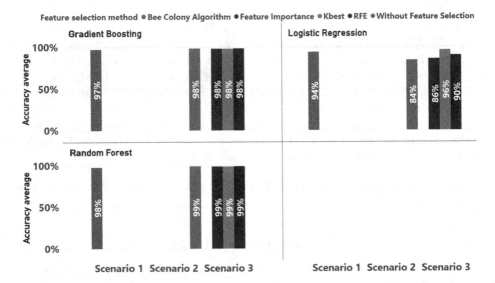

Fig. 3. Accuracy comparison in different scenarios.

In Tables 4 and 5, the results related to the training and testing confusion matrices are presented, respectively for the executions of the scenarios with 100 iterations. In them, the indexes of the matrices are designated in the column headers (Ex: **Avg 00** is referring to the confusion matrix in the position where the returned result should be 0 (expected result) and the predicted result actually materialized as 0). From these two tables, one can notice the low rate of false positives and false negatives, when compared with true positives and true negatives, mainly for the Gradient Boosting and Random Forest classification algorithms.

Finally, for the scenario in which there was the selection of attributes through the bee algorithm, the execution times of the algorithm and the average of the best score returned by the objective function of the same. These results can be seen in Table 6.

Table 4. Confusion Matrix for training with 100 iterations

Test Scenario	Classifier	Feature Selection Method	Avg 00	Avg 01	Avg 10	Avg 11
Scenario 1	Gradient Boosting	ABC	5201	217	73	5017
Scenario 2	Gradient Boosting	N/A	5234	98	40	5136
Scenario 3	Gradient Boosting	Feature Importance	5222	113	52	5121
Scenario 3	Gradient Boosting	Kbest	5214	131	60	5103
Scenario 3	Gradient Boosting	RFE	5235	103	39	5131
Scenario 1	Random Forest	ABC	5266	4	8	5230
Scenario 2	Random Forest	N/A	5274	0	0	5234
Scenario 3	Random Forest	Feature Importance	5274	0	0	5234
Scenario 3	Random Forest	Kbest	5274	0	0	5234
Scenario 3	Random Forest	RFE	5274	0	0	5234
Scenario 1	Logistic Regression	ABC	5062	475	212	4759
Scenario 2	Logistic Regression	N/A	4926	1337	348	3897
Scenario 3	Logistic Regression	Feature Importance	4954	1224	320	4010
Scenario 3	Logistic Regression	Kbest	5214	371	60	4863
Scenario 3	Logistic Regression	RFE	5257	1045	17	4189

Table 5. Confusion Matrix for training with 100 iterations

Test Scenario	Classifier	Feature Selection Method	Avg 00	Avg 01	Avg 10	Avg 11
Scenario 1	Gradient Boosting	ABC	2197	95	35	2177
Scenario 2	Gradient Boosting	N/A	2214	51	18	2221
Scenario 3	Gradient Boosting	Feature Importance	2204	59	28	2213
Scenario 3	Gradient Boosting	Kbest	2203	68	29	2204
Scenario 3	Gradient Boosting	RFE	2213	53	19	2219
Scenario 1	Random Forest	ABC	2194	45	38	2227
Scenario 2	Random Forest	N/A	2220	31	12	2241
Scenario 3	Random Forest	Feature Importance	2213	34	19	2238
Scenario 3	Random Forest	Kbest	2209	37	23	2235
Scenario 3	Random Forest	RFE	2217	30	15	2242
Scenario 1	Logistic Regression	ABC	2146	190	86	2082
Scenario 2	Logistic Regression	N/A	2082	565	150	1707
Scenario 3	Logistic Regression	Feature Importance	2095	516	137	1756
Scenario 3	Logistic Regression	Kbest	2208	143	24	2129
Scenario 3	Logistic Regression	RFE	2225	435	7	1838

Table 6. 100 iterations ABC test results

Test Scenario	ABC Iterations	Best Score Average	Average Time	Best Score Standard Deviation	Time Standard Deviation
Scenario 1	100	0,0351	14,0794	0,0061	3,7044

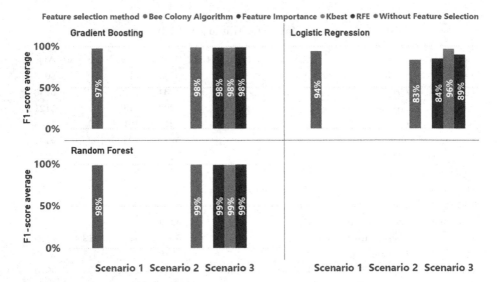

Fig. 4. F1-Score comparison in different scenarios.

7   Conclusion

This article presented a new feature selection technique based on the ABC algorithm. The results show that the reduction in the number of attributes can not only reduce the complexity of the database, for further training and testing of the classifier, but it can also achieve a higher accuracy of classification than the obtained when using the complete set of data. The results obtained corroborate the quality of ABC as a wrapper method for feature selection, validating the hypothesis that the algorithm could reduce the cost and increase the quality of the results obtained in a fraud detection process, so significant nowadays. Not only that, but its results are comparable to other state-of-art methods, a fact that encourages its use for such tasks. It is worth mentioning that ABC can be also used to optimize the parameters from other feature selection methods, a secondary task that heavily influences the quality of the result.

References

1. Agrawal, V., Chandra, S.: Feature selection using artificial bee colony algorithm for medical image classification. In: 2015 Eighth International Conference on Contemporary Computing (IC3), pp. 171–176. IEEE (2015)
2. Bansal, J.C., Sharma, H., Jadon, S.S.: Artificial bee colony algorithm: a survey. Int. J. Adv. Intell. Paradigms **5**(1–2), 123–159 (2013)
3. Chen, X.w., Jeong, J.C.: Enhanced recursive feature elimination. In: Sixth International Conference on Machine Learning and Applications (ICMLA 2007), pp. 429–435 (2007). https://doi.org/10.1109/ICMLA.2007.35

4. Darwish, S.M.: An intelligent credit card fraud detection approach based on semantic fusion of two classifiers. Soft. Comput. **24**(2), 1243–1253 (2020)
5. Dorigo, M., Di Caro, G., Gambardella, L.M.: Ant algorithms for discrete optimization. Artif. Life **5**(2), 137–172 (1999)
6. Eberhart, R., Kennedy, J.: Particle swarm optimization. In: Proceedings of the IEEE International Conference On Neural Networks. vol. 4, pp. 1942–1948. Citeseer (1995)
7. El Aboudi, N., Benhlima, L.: Review on wrapper feature selection approaches. In: 2016 International Conference on Engineering & MIS (ICEMIS), pp. 1–5. IEEE (2016)
8. Friedman, J.H.: Greedy function approximation: a gradient boosting machine. Annals of statistics, pp. 1189–1232 (2001)
9. Hancer, E., Xue, B., Karaboga, D., Zhang, M.: A binary abc algorithm based on advanced similarity scheme for feature selection. Appl. Soft Comput. **36**, 334–348 (2015)
10. Ho, T.K.: Random decision forests. In: Proceedings of 3rd International Conference On Document Analysis and Recognition. vol. 1, pp. 278–282. IEEE (1995)
11. Karaboga, D.: An idea based on honey bee swarm for numerical optimization. Tech. rep., Technical report-tr06, Erciyes university, engineering faculty, computer engineering department (2005)
12. Karaboga, D., Akay, B.: A comparative study of artificial bee colony algorithm. Appl. Math. Comput. **214**(1), 108–132 (2009)
13. Kleinbaum, D.G., Dietz, K., Gail, M., Klein, M., Klein, M.: Logistic Regression. Springer, New York (2002)
14. Lanzi, P.L.: Fast feature selection with genetic algorithms: a filter approach. In: Proceedings of 1997 IEEE International Conference on Evolutionary Computation (ICEC'97), pp. 537–540. IEEE (1997)
15. Liu, O., Ma, J., Poon, P.-L., Zhang, J.: On an ant colony-based approach for business fraud detection. In: Huang, D.-S., Jo, K.-H., Lee, H.-H., Kang, H.-J., Bevilacqua, V. (eds.) ICIC 2009. LNCS, vol. 5754, pp. 1104–1111. Springer, Heidelberg (2009). https://doi.org/10.1007/978-3-642-04070-2_116
16. Palanisamy, S., Kanmani, S.: Artificial bee colony approach for optimizing feature selection. Int. J. Comput. Sci. Issues (IJCSI) **9**(3), 432 (2012)
17. Pavithra, T., Thangadurai, D.K.: Fraud detection of credit cards using abc methodology based on svm algorithm (2019)
18. Yang, Y., Pedersen, J.O.: A comparative study on feature selection in text categorization. In: Icml. vol. 97, pp. 412–420. Nashville, TN, USA (1997)

Automatic Features Extraction from the Optic Cup and Disc Segmentation for Glaucoma Classification

Marcus Oliveira[1], Cleverson Vieira[1], Ana Paula De Filippo[3],
Michel Carlo Rodrigues Leles[1], Diego Dias[1(✉)], Marcelo Guimarães[2],
Elisa Tuler[1], and Leonardo Rocha[1]

[1] Universidade Federal de São João del Rei (UFSJ), São João del Rei, Brazil
{mleles,diegodias,etuler,lcrocha}@ufsj.edu.br
[2] Universidade Federal de São Paulo (UNIFESP), São Paulo, Brazil
marcelo.paiva@unifesp.br
[3] Centro de Estudos e Pesquisas Oculistas Associados (CEPOA), Rio de Janeiro, Brazil

Abstract. Glaucoma is a disease that progressively affects the optic nerve, the leading cause of blindness worldwide. One of the most assertive strategies to make the diagnosis is Optical Coherence Tomography (OCT) which identifies anomalies in the anatomy of the optic nerve. OCT is a high-cost exam, so some works in the literature have been using computationally expensive deep neural networks to analyze images on retinal fundus images to diagnose glaucoma. As an alternative to these approaches, in this work, we propose a low-cost computational method for extracting characteristics of the optic nerve anatomy (i.e., optic cup and disc segmentation) through the processing of retinal fundus images, which is used in conjunction with lower computational cost classification algorithms (i.e., support vector machine (SVM)), is capable of performing accurate diagnoses. The most dominant attributes were identified using shapely adaptive explanations (SHAP) and local interpretable model-agnostic explanations (LIME) analysis. More specifically, the more precise the extraction of features, the greater the accuracy of the classifier.

Keywords: Data Mining · Automatic Glaucoma Classification · Feature Extraction

1 Introduction

Glaucoma is a difficult-to-diagnose eye disease and the leading cause of irreversible blindness worldwide. According to [20], glaucoma affects the optic nerve progressively. It is commonly detected by three approaches: detection of increased intraocular pressure, identification of the normal field of vision, and

This work was partially funded by CNPq, CAPES and Fapemig.

assessment of optic nerve damage by calculating the cup-to-disc ratio (CDR). The first approach is the most commonly used in ophthalmic offices because it is easy to perform the evaluation. However, false negative diagnoses are common because the intraocular pressure can remain unchanged at all stages of the disease. The second approach is dependent on complementary exams to evaluate the visual field. On the other hand, the third approach is usually more effective and precise in the diagnosis, performed by fundoscopy, that is, evaluation of detailed images of the optic nerve, identifying possible alterations in its anatomy, more precisely by the vertical increase of the optic disc cup. The optic nerve head evaluation is one of the most clinically effective screening techniques for glaucoma. In this evaluation, some measurements are proposed as clinical conditions for glaucoma screening, such as the vertical cup-to-disc ratio (CDR), disc diameter, rim area, and inferior-superior to nasal-temporal (ISNT) [21] rule. In order to obtain accurate measurements, it is necessary to submit the patient to an examination known as optical coherence tomography (OCT) [23], which in turn has a high cost.

Some machine learning models are being used in various fields of research [3,4,6]. In this way, as an alternative to the OCT exam, we observed some work proposals that use ophthalmologic images of the retinal fundus as a data source for algorithms based on neural networks, which can automatically analyze the anatomical characteristics of the optic nerve and make a possible diagnosis of the eye evaluated [22]. Despite being very assertive, these proposals are limited by some issues, among them: 1) they need a large number of previously classified samples for training; 2) they have a high computational cost, requiring, for example, ophthalmological offices to be equipped with processing servers; and 3) they make predictions with little or no explainability. This last one is the most important since the ophthalmologist needs to understand why the diagnosis was presented to his patient.

This paper proposes an alternative solution to the three existing approaches. Our proposal aims to extract from ophthalmic images the anatomical features of the optic nerve and the segmentation of the optic cup and disc. This information should then be used by computationally less expensive automatic classification algorithms, in which their predictions can be explainable from the extracted and analyzed features. In simplified form, the solution segments the disc and optic cup by processing retinal fundus images and comprises four steps. In the first step, we scan the eye image to locate the optic nerve region (region of interest). In the second step, we process the image by applying the contrast-limited adaptive histogram-limited equalization (CLAHE) algorithm from the scikit-image library [24] for a local contrast enhancement of the images. This algorithm works by dividing the image into rectangular sections and computing the histogram for each section. The intensity values of the pixels are redistributed to improve the contrast and enhance the details of the images. In the third step, we segment the optical disk (delimiting its edges). Our algorithm loads the enhanced/equalized image, binarizes it, removes noise (edge pixels), extracts the points referring to the largest contour of the image using the method findContour, from the

OpenCV library [1], and draws a rectangle marking the extremities of the contour found. This way, the segmentation of the optical disk is performed. In the fourth stage, the cutout region (excavated) segmentation is performed using the same principle of segmentation of the optic disc but with other values of threshold seeking greater emphasis on the internal region, with greater luminosity, also removing noise. The central space in the optic nerve (excavated region), determined by the absence of nerve fibers, is used to extract the anatomical characteristics of the optic nerve, such as CDR, disc diameter, border area and border area and ISNT rule [27].

We evaluated our solution on a dataset with different previously diagnosed images by analyzing the quality of the extracted features in conjunction with the support vector machine (SVM) classification algorithm. The most dominant features were identified using shapely adaptive explanations (SHAP) and local interpretable model-agnostic explanations (LIME) analysis. In our results, we observed that the more accurate the feature extraction is, the higher the accuracy of the classifier will be. On the other hand, the worse the quality of the images, the more difficult our strategy is to extract the features correctly. That points us in the direction of further research to improve some steps of the proposal and its comparison with various databases with images of different quality and thus establish the limits of our solution.

2   Theoretical Framework

Glaucoma can be characterized by a change in the structure of the optic nerve, more specifically in the optic disc, which is the area in which the optic nerve connects to the eye. The optic disc can be divided into two parts: (1) the optic cup, which is in the center of the optic disc as a bright circular area and; (2) the peripheral region around the cup, which is the neuroretinal rim. The optic disc changes visually when the optic nerve fibers are damaged due to glaucoma; this leads to enlargement of the cup region called cupping and is an indicator for detecting suspected glaucoma [20].

There are some quantitative strategies to evaluate the structure of the optic nerve. One is the vertical CDR, which corresponds to the vertical cup diameter (VCD) ratio to the vertical disc diameter (VDD). Figure 1 depicts the metric – (a), where the VCD is indicated by the letter v and the VDD is indicated by the letter V. The CDR measures the widening of the cup relative to the disc (thinning of the neuroretinal rim). The greater the CDR, the greater the risk for glaucoma [12, 27].

Another quantitative strategy used to differentiate the normal optic nerve from the glaucomatous optic is the ISNT rule. In normal eyes, the inferior (I) disc edge thickness is greater than the superior (S) edge thickness which is greater than the nasal (N) edge thickness, which is greater than the temporal (T) [12]. Figure 1 (b) represents a clinical evaluation of the ISNT (inferior, superior, nasal, temporal) rule for a normal optic nerve, and Fig. 1 (c) shows a clinical evaluation of a glaucomatous optic nerve (right figure).

Analysis of blood vessel characteristics at the optic nerve head is also a useful quantitative tool for diagnosing and clinically managing glaucoma. The blood vessel ratio (BVR) is a measure that assesses the density of the blood vessels in the retina. In individuals with glaucoma, the progressive loss of nerve fibers leads to reduced blood vessel density, which results in a lower BVR [5]. Figure 1 (d) represents a glaucomatous optic nerve with less dense blood vessels.

 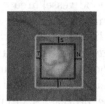  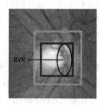

(a) Detail of the optic nerve [10]

(b) ISNT rule I >S >N >T - Normal eye [10]

(c) ISNT rule I >S >N >T - Glaucomatous eye [10]

(d) Blood Vessel Density (BVR) - Glaucomatous eye [10]

Fig. 1. Examples of optic nerves

3   Related Work

This section presents the set of works most related to our proposal. There are different works aimed at solving the glaucoma detection problem [2,11,18], which can be divided into two approaches: (1) deep learning neural networks; and (2) image processing. We discuss the main proposals of each of them below.

Several papers focus on using deep learning-based approaches [11]. In [25], an ensemble network was proposed for optical disk and optical cup segmentation. The ensemble network consists of eight networks, such as Mask-RCNN, M-Net, etc. Different data augmentation methods were used for each network, such as blurring and multi-scale detail manipulation. Each network learns different aspects of the data, and then a voting algorithm is designed to combine the results of these models. In [22], an investigation is performed into the applicability of pre-trained convolutional neural networks (CNNs) for glaucoma diagnosis by extracting features from high-level abstractions of retinal fundus images. The proposed system has been validated on high-resolution fundus (HRF), a publicly available database. The results show that among other pre-trained CNNs, the VGG16 network is best suited for glaucoma diagnosis. In [15], the optic disc and optic cup are segmented using a modified U-Net architecture employing the pre-trained SEResNet50 for a glaucoma diagnosis based on the CDR. These methods, however, need a large amount of training data that may not be readily available and would require large amounts of graphics processing unit (GPU) memory to train while taking more prediction time [11].

Another classification methodology is by the use of image processing [11]. In [16], a technique based on the neuroretinal kidney (NRR) Otsu segmentation is proposed where the disease is confirmed by calculating the CDR, rim-to-disc ratio (RDR), ISNT ratio, using SVM as a classifier in identifying glaucoma. In [9], the damage caused during glaucoma to the retinal nerve fiber layer is detected using computer-aided detection (CAD) and Gabor filtering. In [17], a series of features such as CDR ratio, the ratio of optic nerve head displacement distance to optic disc diameter, and the ratio of blood vessel area on the ISNT were used to classify the available retinal fundus images as normal and glaucoma images using a neural network classifier. In [8], based on line profile analysis, the cup-to-disc ratio is measured in retinal images. In [18], an automatic segmentation technique based on mathematical morphology has been used to diagnose glaucoma. In [7], a technique involves extracting and removing blood vessels using a hat transform and an internal painting process. A circular Hough transform is applied to the detected edges to obtain a coarse boundary of the optic disc. Then, the probable points of the optic disc are fed to a curve-fitting algorithm that uses a higher-order polynomial to draw the final boundary of the optic disc. Although these methods show good diagnostic accuracy, with the added advantage of not requiring much training data compared to deep learning models [11], they still have a high computational cost associated with feature extraction.

4   Proposed Solution

Our goal is to provide mechanisms that allow the extraction of features that can serve as medical support in diagnosing glaucoma. As previously mentioned, the attributes of fundus images must be extracted using minimal computational resources, which is our proposal's focus. In a simplified way, our proposal can be defined in the following steps:

1. Find the region of interest (optic nerve region) and perform its isolation/cutting;
2. Apply the CLAHE algorithm from the scikit-image library, resulting in the standardization and improvement of contrast and, consequently, the enhancement of image details;
3. Perform segmentation of the optical disk (delimitation of its edges) by detecting the most prominent contour of the normalized/equalized image using the OpenCV library;
4. Perform the segmentation of the optic disc's canopy (delimiting its edges) using the same principle as for the segmentation of the optic disc but with a different threshold value;
5. With the segmentations performed (edges defined), the attributes referring to the vertical and horizontal ratios of the disk cup, generating the CDRV and CDRH attributes, respectively, are calculated;
6. By analyzing the image of the optic nerve, we also extract the information on whether the eye in question is right or left by storing it in an attribute that we define as Eye;

7. The integrity of the optic nerve ISNT pattern is checked by comparing the Inferior, Superior, Nasal, and Temporal quadrants. The values are stored in the attributes IgtS (Inferior greater than Superior), IgtN (Inferior greater than Nasal), IgtT (Inferior greater than Temporal), SgtN (Superior greater than Nasal), SgtT (Superior greater than Temporal) and NgtT (Nasal greater than Temporal), with values of true or false; and

8. The density of the blood vessels related to the BVR is extracted by dividing the optic disc into quadrants (left and right). A count of pixels in the red hue is performed and compared to the area of the optical disk. The calculated value is stored in an attribute named BVR.

First, all attributes are extracted from a database containing previously classified images and adequately tabulated. This data is used to train a classical classifier, the SVM [13], which will generate a classification model. Then, for each eye image not yet analyzed, the same steps described above are performed to define the attributes of this new eye, which in turn must be classified by the generated model.

In the following subsections, the main steps mentioned above will be detailed.

4.1 Optic Nerve Isolation

Isolation of the optic nerve is performed using the following process:

1. The original image is reduced to one-fifth of its height, keeping the dimensions proportional to the width;
2. The reduced image is subjected to a CLAHE technique for enhancement of local image contrast and detail enhancement; and
3. The nerve is isolated by an algorithm that, starting from the center of this reduced image (cx, cy), searches for the brightest point in an area delimited by a rectangle of vertices $[(cx - N, cy - N), (cx + N, cy + N)]$, where N is $1/12$ of the height of the reduced image. It is then checked whether the sum of the color channels (R, G, and B) of the brightest point obtained in the bounded area is greater than 700. If so, the coordinates (cx, cy) are defined to the selected point, and the isolated optic nerve is defined in a rectangle with vertices $[(cx - 75, cy - 75), (cx + 75, cy + 75)]$ of the original image, resulting in an image of 150×150 pixels. Otherwise, the value of N is increased by $1/12$ of the reduced image's height and repeated until an isolated optic nerve is reached. Figure 2 (a) represents the isolated optic nerve using the algorithm.

4.2 Optical Disc Segmentation

From the image of the isolated optic nerve, the process of segmenting the optic disc (delimiting the ends) is started:

1. The CLAHE is applied, as shown in Fig. 2 (b);

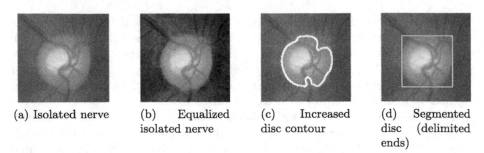

(a) Isolated nerve   (b)   Equalized   (c)   Increased   (d)   Segmented
                          isolated nerve   disc contour   disc   (delimited
                                                                          ends)

Fig. 2. Isolation of the Optic Nerve and Segmentation (Delimitation of the Extremities) of the Optic Disc [10]

2. Next, the proposed algorithm performs the binarization of the equalized image and, through the findContours method from the OpenCV library, searches for and returns the largest contour in the image;
3. This contour is then drawn on the image of the isolated nerve, and its points are used to delimit the ends of the optic disc (Fig. 2 (c)); and
4. A rectangle is drawn at the endpoints of the contour and the optic disc is defined as in Fig. 2 (d).

4.3   Disc Cup Segmentation

The disk canopy is segmented (defining its edges) following the same principle as the disk segmentation, with the following change:

1. The algorithm performs binarization of the equalized image using another threshold value, seeking greater emphasis on the internal region, with higher brightness, and through the method findContours, from the OpenCV library, search and return the largest contour of the image;
2. This contour is then drawn on the image of the isolated nerve, and its points are used to delimit the extremities of the disk cup, as in Fig. 3 (a); and
3. A rectangle is drawn at the endpoints of the contour and the canopy of the optical disc is defined as in Fig. 3 (b).

4.4   Setting the Eye Direction

To define whether the eye is Right or Left, the following steps are followed:

1. The enhanced/equalized optic nerve image is split vertically;
2. Each of the parts (right and left) is scanned pixel by pixel, counting the brightest pixels in the red and green channels;
3. The total number of pixels found is compared, and the direction of the eye is set on the part containing the greatest number of counted pixels; and
4. The Eye attribute is then set to 0 for the left eye and 1 for the right eye.

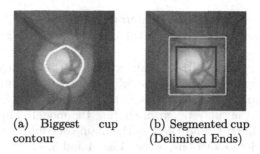

(a) Biggest cup contour

(b) Segmented cup (Delimited Ends)

Fig. 3. Segmentation (edge delimitation) of the optical disc Cup [10]

5 Proposal Evaluation

5.1 Environment

To evaluate our proposal, we considered the ORIGA image bank [26], provided by [10], composed of 650 fundus images of the eye, being 482 healthy and 168 glaucomatous. All steps of our experimentation (feature extraction and instance classification) were performed in the following environment: computer with Intel(R) Core (TM) i5-6500 CPU @ 3.20 GHz, 8 GB RAM, 480 GB SSD, and Linux Ubuntu 20.04 operating system. Ten-fold cross-validation was used as a technique for separating training and test data. SVM was used to classify the images using the following parameters: cost = 9, kernel = poly, degree = 8, gamma = scale, coefficient = 0.5. 650 images were processed in 437.27 s, representing an average processing time of approximately 0.67 s for each image.

5.2 Results

From the effectiveness point of view, we considered the metrics Accuracy, Recall, Precision, and F1-Score, commonly used to evaluate classification algorithms. After the cross-validation process (ten folds) considering only the tabulated attributes, Vertical CDR and Eye Direction, provided along with the dataset, and considering all the attributes extracted in the new proposal (Eye, Vertical CDR, Horizontal CDR, IgtS, IgtN, IgtT, SgtN, SgtT, NgtT, BVR), we found the values according to Table 1.

Table 1. Results obtained from tabulated attributes supplied with the dataset vs. results of the new proposal

Attributes	Accuracy	Recall	Precision	F1-Score
Supplied with the dataset	0.7430	0.0297	0.5555	0.6458
New Proposal	0.9153	0.7321	0.9248	0.8172

From the point of view of model interpretability, two (2) explainability techniques were analyzed, SHAP [14] (global analysis), and LIME [19] (local analysis).

Based on game theory, SHAP assigns each attribute an importance value for a specific prediction in the [14] model. The idea of this method is that the attributes of an instance are "players," and the "final score" is related to the performance of all the "players" in predicting the model. This method showed the attributes SgtT, IgtT, and BVR as the main contributors (with the highest weight) to the model predictions, as per Figs. 4 and 5.

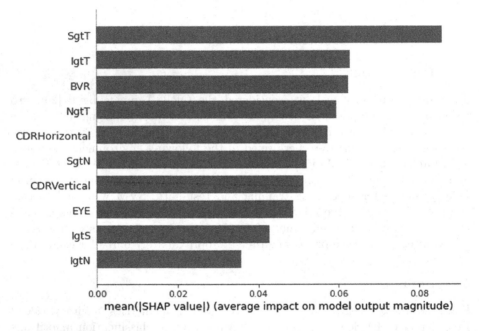

Fig. 4. SHAP values chart for attributes in descending order of importance

LIME, on the other hand, interprets individual instance predictions based on the local approximation of the model around a given prediction [19]. This method showed, for the second instance of the model, for example, the attributes NgtT, SgtT, and SgtN as the main contributors (of most significant weight) to the prediction, as per Figs. 6 and 7.

Analyzing the explanations generated by the SHAP and LIME methods, we found that the attributes with the most significant contribution to the model prediction were attributes extracted by the proposal of this paper.

We manually inspected some misclassified images and found that the feature extraction needed to be performed correctly. We show some examples in Fig. 8.

As the dataset used (ORIGA) has an image database with the official markings defined (quantitative characteristics duly annotated), a comparison process

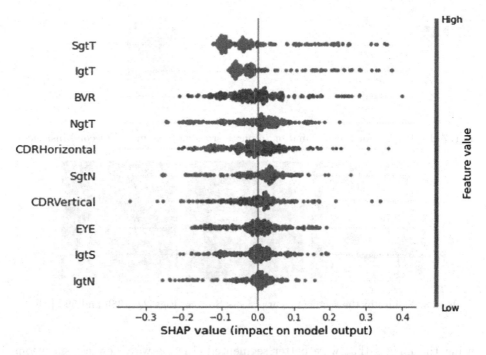

Fig. 5. SHAP values chart with the contribution of each attribute for all database instances

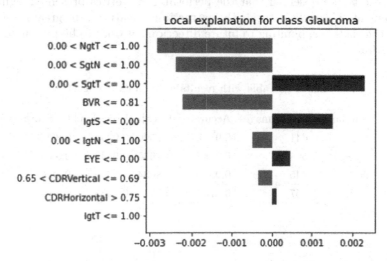

Fig. 6. LIME plot of the contribution of each attribute to the prediction of the second instance of the model

by cosine similarity was done between the official segmentation data (optical disk location and disk cup) and the data obtained by the segmentation method proposed in this paper, being possible to make the classification of the images

Fig. 7. LIME plot for the explanation of one instance of the model (second instance)

Fig. 8. Failure in the segmentation process Source: Figs. 224, 335 and 594 [10]

using the images that were better segmented. In this way, new classifications were made with varying similarity indices. The results can be seen in Table 2. In our results, we observed that the performance metrics presented significant improvement. The more accurate the extraction of features, the greater the accuracy of the classifier, pointing to future directions of work to be presented in the next section.

Table 2. Table with results with similarity level

Similarity	Total Images	Accuracy	Recall	Precision	F1-Score
80%	641	0.9157	0.7500	0.9044	0.8200
85%	504	0.9246	0.7615	0.9339	0.8389
90%	445	0.9325	0.8034	0.9306	0.8623
95%	257	0.9766	0.9218	0.9833	0.9516

6 Conclusion and Future Works

Glaucoma is a disease that progressively affects the optic nerve, the leading cause of irreversible blindness worldwide. One of the most assertive strategies to make the diagnosis is the OCT, which identifies anomalies in the optic nerve anatomy. OCT is a high-cost test, so some work in the literature has been using computationally expensive deep neural networks to analyze fundoscopy (retinal fundus) images for glaucoma diagnosis. As an alternative to these approaches, in this work, we proposed and implemented a low-cost computational method to extract features of the optic nerve anatomy (i.e., optic cup and disc segmentation) by processing retinal fundus images, which is used in conjunction with low computational cost classification algorithms (i.e., SVM), being able to perform an accurate diagnosis. More specifically, the more accurate the feature extraction, the higher the accuracy of the classifier.

As future work, we point out the need to improve the image normalization process and the segmentation steps of the optical disc and the disc cup for an improvement in the segmentation process. We also point out the need to perform new experiments with other publicly available datasets and thus be able to perform a broader evaluation of the solution proposed in this article.

References

1. Bradski, G.: The OpenCV library. Dr. Dobb's J. Softw. Tools (2000)
2. Camara, J., Neto, A., Pires, I.M., Villasana, M.V., Zdravevski, E., Cunha, A.: Literature review on artificial intelligence methods for glaucoma screening, segmentation, and classification. J. Imaging 8(2), 19 (2022). https://doi.org/10.3390/jimaging8020019, https://www.mdpi.com/2313-433X/8/2/19
3. D'Angelo, G., Palmieri, F., Robustelli, A., Castiglione, A.: Effective classification of android malware families through dynamic features and neural networks. Connect. Sci. **33**(3), 786–801 (2021). https://doi.org/10.1080/09540091.2021.1889977
4. D'Angelo, G., Rampone, S.: Diagnosis of aerospace structure defects by a HPC implemented soft computing algorithm. In: 2014 IEEE Metrology for Aerospace (MetroAeroSpace), pp. 408–412 (2014). https://doi.org/10.1109/MetroAeroSpace.2014.6865959
5. Deepika, E., Maheswari, S.: Earlier glaucoma detection using blood vessel segmentation and classification. In: 2018 2nd International Conference on Inventive Systems and Control (ICISC), pp. 484–490 (2018). https://doi.org/10.1109/ICISC.2018.8399120
6. D'Angelo, G., Castiglione, A., Palmieri, F.: A cluster-based multidimensional approach for detecting attacks on connected vehicles. IEEE Internet Things J. **8**(16), 12518–12527 (2021). https://doi.org/10.1109/JIOT.2020.3032935
7. Gopalakrishnan, A., Almazroa, A., Raahemifar, K., Lakshminarayanan, V.: Optic disc segmentation using circular Hough transform and curve fitting. In: 2015 2nd International Conference on Opto-Electronics and Applied Optics (IEM OPTRONIX), pp. 1–4. IEEE (2015). https://doi.org/10.1109/OPTRONIX.2015.7345530
8. Hatanaka, Y., et al.: Automatic measurement of cup to disc ratio based on line profile analysis in retinal images. In: 2011 Annual International Conference of the IEEE Engineering in Medicine and Biology Society, pp. 3387–3390. IEEE (2011). https://doi.org/10.1109/IEMBS.2011.6090917
9. Hayashi, Y., et al.: Detection of retinal nerve fiber layer defects in retinal fundus images using Gabor filtering. In: Giger, M.L., Karssemeijer, N. (eds.) Medical Imaging 2007: Computer-Aided Diagnosis, vol. 6514, p. 65142Z. International Society for Optics and Photonics, SPIE (2007). https://doi.org/10.1117/12.710181

10. Kaggle Inc.: Glaucoma detection (2022). https://www.kaggle.com/datasets/sshikamaru/glaucoma-detection
11. Krishnan, R., Sekhar, V., Sidharth, J., Gautham, S., Gopakumar, G.: Glaucoma detection from retinal fundus images. In: 2020 International Conference on Communication and Signal Processing (ICCSP), pp. 0628–0631. IEEE (2020). https://doi.org/10.1109/ICCSP48568.2020.9182388
12. Kumar, B.N., Chauhan, R.P., Dahiya, N.: Detection of glaucoma using image processing techniques: a review. In: 2016 International Conference on Microelectronics, Computing and Communications (MicroCom), pp. 1–6. IEEE (2016). https://doi.org/10.1109/MicroCom.2016.7522515
13. Lin, K.C., Liu, T.Y., Chen, P.H., Lin, C.T.: Use support vector machine (SVM) to estimate gas concentration in mixture condition. In: 2017 International Conference on Applied System Innovation (ICASI), pp. 744–746. IEEE (2017). https://doi.org/10.1109/ICASI.2017.7988537
14. Lundberg, S.M., Lee, S.I.: A unified approach to interpreting model predictions. In: Guyon, I., et al. (eds.) Advances in Neural Information Processing Systems, vol. 30, pp. 4765–4774. Curran Associates, Inc. (2017). http://papers.nips.cc/paper/7062-a-unified-approach-to-interpreting-model-predictions.pdf
15. Maadi, F., Faraji, N., Bibalan, M.H.: A robust glaucoma screening method for fundus images using deep learning technique. In: 2020 27th National and 5th International Iranian Conference on Biomedical Engineering (ICBME), pp. 289–293. IEEE (2020). https://doi.org/10.1109/ICBME51989.2020.9319434
16. Naga Kiran, D., Kanchana, V.: Recognistion of Glaucoma using OTSU segmentation method (2019)
17. Nayak, J., Acharya, U.R., Bhat, P., Shetty, N., Lim, T.C.: Automated diagnosis of Glaucoma using digital fundus images. J. Med. Syst. **33**, 337–46 (2009). https://doi.org/10.1007/s10916-008-9195-z
18. Pal, S., Chatterjee, S.: Mathematical morphology aided optic disk segmentation from retinal images. In: 2017 3rd International Conference on Condition Assessment Techniques in Electrical Systems (CATCON), pp. 380–385. IEEE (2017). https://doi.org/10.1109/CATCON.2017.8280249
19. Ribeiro, M.T., Singh, S., Guestrin, C.: "Why should I trust you?": explaining the predictions of any classifier. In: Proceedings of the 22nd ACM SIGKDD International Conference on Knowledge Discovery and Data Mining, San Francisco, CA, USA, 13–17 August 2016, pp. 1135–1144 (2016)
20. Sarhan, M.H., et al.: Machine learning techniques for ophthalmic data processing: a review. IEEE J. Biomed. Health Inform. **24**(12), 3338–3350 (2020). https://doi.org/10.1109/JBHI.2020.3012134
21. Stefan, A.M., Paraschiv, E.A., Ovreiu, S., Ovreiu, E.: A review of glaucoma detection from digital fundus images using machine learning techniques (2020). https://doi.org/10.1109/EHB50910.2020.9280218
22. Sushil, M., Gnanaprakasam, S., Rajan, L., Devi, N.: Performance comparison of pre-trained deep neural networks for automated glaucoma detection, January 2019. https://doi.org/10.1007/978-3-030-00665-5-62
23. Vessani, R.M.: Comparação entre diversas técnicas de imagem para diagnóstico do glaucoma, Faculdade de Medicina, Universidade de São Paulo (2008). https://doi.org/10.11606/T.5.2008.tde-02062008-112610
24. Van der Walt, S., et al.: Scikit-image: image processing in Python. PeerJ **2**, e453 (2014)
25. Yin, P., et al.: Optic disc and cup segmentation using ensemble deep neural networks (2018)

26. Zhang, Z., et al.: ORIGA(-light): an online retinal fundus image database for glaucoma analysis and research. In: Conference Proceedings : ... Annual International Conference of the IEEE Engineering in Medicine and Biology Society. IEEE Engineering in Medicine and Biology Society. Conference 2010, p. 3065-8, August 2010. https://doi.org/10.1109/IEMBS.2010.5626137

27. Zhao, R., Chen, X., Liu, X., Chen, Z., Guo, F., Li, S.: Direct cup-to-disc ratio estimation for glaucoma screening via semi-supervised learning. IEEE J. Biomed. Health Inform. **24**(4), 1104–1113 (2020). https://doi.org/10.1109/JBHI.2019.2934477

Implementation of eXplainable Artificial Intelligence
Case Study on the Assessment of Movements to Support Neuromotor Rehabilitation

Luiz Felipe de Camargo[1]([✉]), Diego Roberto Colombo Dias[2],
and José Remo Ferreira Brega[1]

[1] Universidade Estadual Paulista "Júlio de Mesquita Filho", Bauru, SP, Brazil
{luiz.felipe,remo.brega}@unesp.br
[2] Universidade Federal de São João del-Rei, São João del-Rei, Brazil
diegodias@ufsj.edu.br

Abstract. Solutions based on Artificial Intelligence are being used to solve problems in various domains. However, many people feel uncomfortable with this type of solution because they must understand how it works. In the face of this, the so-called eXplainable Artificial Intelligence arises, seeking not only to provide the answers produced by Artificial Intelligence but also to offer aspects of explainability, detailing the decision process and generating confidence. In this context, a literature review on eXplainable Artificial Intelligence has presented a brief comparative study between the most popular libraries for this implementation and a deepening of the theme of explainability evaluation and the comprehension process. A proposal for the implementation and evaluation of eXplainable Artificial Intelligence in the context of movement classification to support neuromotor rehabilitation was built from the results obtained. The first experiments performed showed to be promising. The proposal is expected to be relevant for addressing a growing theme in a context, the health area, that demands explicability and transparency in decisions.

Keywords: artificial intelligence · explainable artificial intelligence · implementation · rehabilitation · motion assessment

1 Introduction

Artificial Intelligence (AI) can perform the most diverse activities, almost always superior and more reliable than human beings. However, the world press spreads information that often leads the population to fear this type of technology, imagining that there will be a significant reduction in the number of jobs available. This dissemination of incorrect information about the use of AI hampers the adoption of this type of technology, ignoring that there will not necessarily be a reduction in jobs. However, a change like the work to be performed, often going from hard work, with significant physical wear and tear, to equipment control work, based on intellectual effort and requiring greater prior training [1].

The process of using AI almost always consists of inputting data into a computational model in order to train it to solve a particular problem. This model learns the patterns from this training data and can identify and predict them in other masses of data, identifying situations and making recommendations. However, the internal structure of the model, which leads to learning and making decisions, is often complex and challenging to understand, especially for the average user [14].

This complexity, added to the stance of media on the subject, generates great fear and discomfort for average users, creating barriers to adopting this type of technology. Life-threatening situations, such as using AI for medical diagnosis, tend to be even more frightening. That is the current situation of this technology, AI can make decisions superior many times to humans, but it cannot explain and justify its decision.

In this scenario, the concept of eXplainable Artificial Intelligence (XAI) arises, seeking to make AI more accessible, producing, in addition to the expected result, mechanisms that aid in understanding the results and the path taken to them. The first initiative to develop XAI came from the Defense Advanced Research Projects Agency (DARPA), an American governmental research agency focused on defense projects, where the foundations of the Internet were also developed. However, several other initiatives exploring XAI have emerged in recent years, including from giants such as Google [14,16].

The main objective of this article is to present a Systematic Literature Review (SLR) that seeks to explore the research field of XAI implementation and thereby obtain information about the implementation and application of XAI techniques to improve the understanding of users of the operation of AI methods. From the review, develop a proposal for implementing XAI in evaluating the movement to support neuromotor rehabilitation.

2   Background

2.1   Artificial Intelligence

The term was coined in the 1950s s by professor and researcher John McCarthy. He defined it as: "the science and engineering of making intelligent machines, especially intelligent computer programs" [9].

Several researchers in the area discuss the definition of AI, and with this, a definition considered quite enlightening is the one by authors Rich and Knight: "AI is the study of how to make computers perform tasks that, so far, men do better" [12]. Author Laurière adds: "every problem for which no algorithmic solution is known is an AI problem" [6].

2.2   eXplainable Artificial Intelligence

XAI is a strand of AI that aims to explain its purpose and provide results. This explanation should include its purpose and decision process, widely recognized as a crucial feature for the practical implementation of AI models [2]. Discussions about XAI are becoming increasingly present in the technology world.

When the model is considered complete, without the need to improve it through explainability, and it is not necessary to question its functioning, understanding the problem can be considered complete. If this is the situation, the recommendation would be not to use machine learning since it should be used when it is impossible to define an algorithm with specific rules to address the problem [8].

3   Systematic Literature Review

This Section presents the methods and data about the review process performed in this study, describing mainly the RSL method.

3.1   Review Objectives and Research Questions

The executed review aims to get an overview of the implementation of XAI techniques and, through this, to deeply understand the research field.

After several prior discussions and research, the main research question was: How does one implement XAI? This main question can be expanded into the following questions: What are the existing XAI solutions (techniques, methods, or frameworks)? What are the main areas that XAI serves? How does XAI integrate with existing AI platforms? What visual capabilities are used by these XAI solutions? How is the XAI research area evolving?

3.2   Search Strategy

For the present work, the search string used was: (explainable AND ("artificial intelligence" OR "machine learning" OR "deep learning")) AND (framework OR technique) AND (trust OR interpretability). The initial searches were performed using search strings in ACM Digital Library, IEEE Digital Library, ISI Web of Science, Science@Direct and Scopus.

3.3   Inclusion and Exclusion Criteria

For the present review, the following criteria were defined:

- Inclusion - "Affinity of the study to the desired topics" and "Presents a practical application";
- Exclusion - "Study is not available in full in the English language", "Study has no access granted to the institution", "Lack of affinity of the study with the desired topics", "It is not an article", "It does not deal with implementation, being limited only to XAI concepts", "Review or survey on the subject" and "It deals with a tool already analyzed".

3.4 Data Extraction

For the present study, the following data composed the extraction form:

- Name of the technique, method, or framework;
- What is the objective?;
- AI technique developed with explainability or further explanation?;
- Which methods or AI platforms are supported?;
- What is the visualization technique employed?; and
- Has there been an evaluation or validation study with users?

3.5 Analysis and Discussion of Results

An overview of the review and its steps can be seen in Fig. 1.

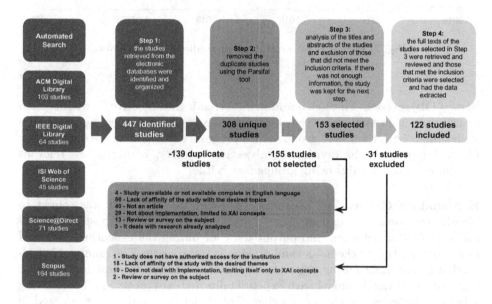

Fig. 1. Review steps.

Year of Studies. Figure 2 shows the increase in the number of studies dealing with the subject of the present review over the past five years, demonstrating the growing relevance of the subject, considering that the year 2021 was not fully analyzed.

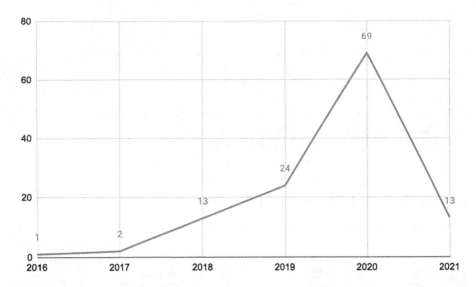

Fig. 2. Evolution of the amount of studies over the years.

Study Objectives. Through question 2, "What is the objective?", we sought to identify the main motivation that led to the development of each study. Studies with similar objectives were grouped into categories to organize the data better. Figure 3 represents the division by objective category, with the less relevant categories (1 study only) being grouped as "Other".

Explanation Generation Moment. Through question 3, it was sought to identify the moment of explanation generation, which can be a posterior explanation, using model input and output data, or during the execution of the AI model, integrating to the model and making it transparent. The number of studies that demonstrated using posterior explanation (63) and the number of studies that combined the AI model with explainability (60) are pretty similar, showing a balance between the two approaches. This balance can also be visualized in Fig. 4.

Artificial Intelligence Models. Question 4 sought to identify the families of AI models with which the developed explainability technique is compatible. The most diverse AI models were cited in the studies; thus they were grouped into broader families, which aggregate several more specific models.

In Fig. 5 the cited AI model families can be compared.

The use of neural networks stands out, cited in 64 studies, currently widely used models and tend to be complex, especially in the so-called deep neural networks, which have several layers, thus increasing the need for explainability. The tools that propose to be model-agnostic were identified in 22 studies.

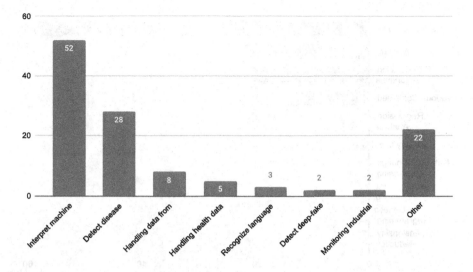

Fig. 3. Categories of study objectives.

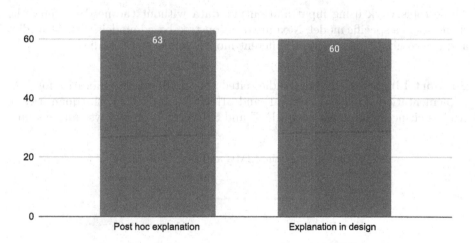

Fig. 4. Studies separated by a moment of explainability generation.

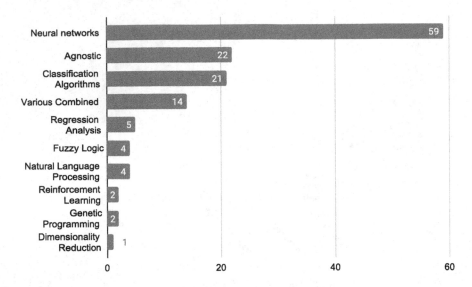

Fig. 5. Families of AI models.

These tools work using input and output data without the need to know the structure of a specific model. Next are decision-tree-based models with 14 studies and the combination of several different models, cited in 11 studies..

Support Libraries. Several studies cited the use of existing libraries for XAI implementation, such as LIME [11] and SHAP [7]. In Table 1, the quantities of studies citing involvement with LIME and SHAP in various ways can be seen.

Table 1. Using the LIME and SHAP libraries.

Frameworks	Studies	%
Uses Lime	16	13,11
Uses SHAP	11	9,01
Compare with Lime	8	6,55
Compare with SHAP	3	2,46
Uses Lime and SHAP	2	1,64
Compare with Lime and SHAP	1	0,81
Total	41	33,60

It can be observed that the relevant quantity (41 studies, 33.60%) of researchers that use somehow the two most relevant libraries in the implementation of XAI to obtain a speed gain by using already implemented solutions instead of choosing to perform the full development without any support. Model-independent methods, such as SHAP and LIME, are widely used, as they offer explainability in the most diverse situations, be it for processing tabular data, text, and images, including deep learning models [2].

3.6   Information Visualization

Through question 5, it was sought to identify which visualization technique was used. To help identify the techniques, a taxonomy created by [5] was used, which classifies visualization techniques into the following families:

- Comparing categories
- Assessing hierarchies and part-to-whole relationships
- Show changes over time;
- Plotting connections and relationships; and
- Mapping geo-spatial data.

Besides the categories based on the taxonomy presented, two other categories were created: "Others", indicating differentiated techniques, often created together with the tool and which are not classified within the taxonomy; and "Does not use directly", where the studies that do not use Information Visualization in the process of generating explainability were allocated.

Once the categories were defined, the studies were distributed as follows, according to Fig. 6.

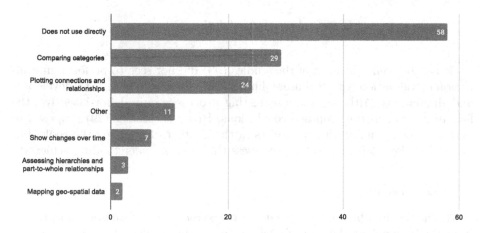

Fig. 6. Families of Visualization techniques.

It can be observed that most of the studies (58) do not directly use visualization techniques during the explanation generation process, among the studies that do use visual techniques, techniques that seek to compare categories (29) and demonstrate connections and relationships (24) can be highlighted.

3.7   Evaluation or Validation with Users

According to question 6, we tried to identify if the analyzed study described the execution of an evaluation or validation process of the proposed explainability technique with users through tests, interviews, or evaluation forms, thus seeking to guarantee the positive results of the proposal regarding ease of understanding and use. In Fig. 7, the results of this question can be observed.

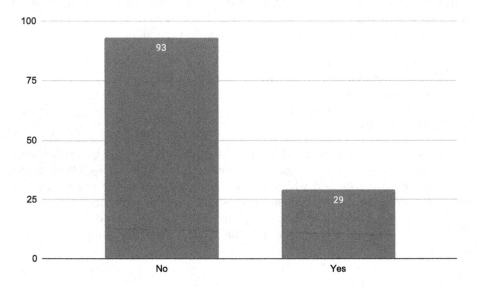

Fig. 7. Evaluation or validation with users.

It can be seen that most of the studies (93) did not seek to perform an evaluation or validation with real users, limiting themselves to tests with developers and simulations. Although the user testing process is quite labor-intensive, the lack of it weakens the proposed conclusions. However, studies (29) proposed to perform tests, usually with specialists in the context of applying the tools, but also with a lay audience, seeking to assess the level of understanding achieved.

3.8   Discussion

Next, the results obtained are discussed to extract new information and trends from them, exposing the review's relevance and limitations. In order to obtain information that composes an answer to the main research question presented, "How does one implement XAI?", the secondary research questions will be addressed, presenting information obtained that represents an answer for each of them.

What Are the Existing eXplainable Artificial Intelligence Solutions (techniques, Methods or Frameworks)? It was possible to ascertain many techniques based on libraries such as LIME and SHAP, but with different approaches and methods. The use of libraries for support indicates an interesting starting point for the continuation of the current project, seeking to understand how a working standard can be defined in the research area, which is still very recent.

What Are the Main Areas that eXplainable Artificial Intelligence Serves? A good part of the analyzed studies demonstrates its objective, such as improving interpretability issues, without depending on a closed context, showing that XAI tends to evolve as a tool to be applied in the most diverse areas. A point of emphasis is the application of XAI in Healthcare, especially disease detection, since this area deals with data and prudent decisions to be made, highlighting the importance of explainability in decisions made in an automated way. Several other areas were cited in the other studies, showing that the application of XAI has been expanding to other fields.

How Does eXplainable Artificial Intelligence Integrate with Existing Artificial Intelligence Platforms? Regarding integrating XAI tools into AI solutions, the two ways of integration (explainability generated during the AI process and explainability afterward) were equally cited, indicating that both approaches are relevant, presenting advantages and disadvantages but being appropriate depending on the situation to be addressed.

What Visual Resources Are Used by These eXplainable Artificial Intelligence Solutions? Analyzing the use of visual resources and Information Visualization, most studies do not directly use these resources. In the analyzed articles, graphs are often presented to expose the results, but graphical tools are not used during the explanation process.

How Is the Research Area of eXplainable Artificial Intelligence Evolving? Through the information of the studies' publication years, it can be seen that they deal with a new area, still in expansion, which has been gaining strength over the years. However, it was found that many studies need to present the evaluation of techniques and tools with real users, restricting themselves to simulated tests. That shows that there is room for evolution, even though the evaluation process with users is a complex process that demands considerable effort.

Relevance and Limitations of the Study. The present study is relevant because of the number of studies analyzed (122), obtained after several previous searches with various search strings to perform a comprehensive search that returned studies relevant to the topic in question. As a limitation, we can cite the restriction of the automated search method used, with no recourse to manual searches or other search forms. Another limitation is the need for clear information in many studies, not informing the names of the tools developed, among other missing or unclear information.

4   Proposal

In this section, the XAI application proposal that composes this work is presented, initially presenting the context where the proposal is inserted, then detailing the AI solutions that are being studied for use, and finally, the proposal for continuity addressing XAI implementation.

4.1   Scenario

The scenario where explainability will be applied is the estimation and evaluation of movements obtained through body tracking to use data in rehabilitating patients, especially those who have suffered a stroke. The authors [13] have been working in this context with the Brazilian Institute for Neuroscience and Neurotechnology - CEPID BRAINN, using AI in motion classification, but still without involving aspects of XAI. Thus, one of the goals of this work is to add this approach to collaborate in the development of the solution and add explainability at various points, providing new information for different audiences, including users of the solution, domain experts, AI developers, thus obtaining very comprehensive aspects of explainability, with several possibilities.

4.2   Tool Structure

Several authors sought to apply AI in motion estimation, classification, and evaluation. In the work of [3], the Pose Trainer tool was proposed, using convolutional neural networks and heuristic techniques to detect a user's pose and then evaluate the vector geometry of the pose. Pose Trainer runs on four common exercises and supports any Windows or Linux computer with a GPU. [4] developed Pose Tutor, an AI-based explainable pose recognition and correction system. This system uses several AI models to estimate the pose, classify the motion and indicate by explainability tools the points to be corrected in the pose. For pose estimation, the tool uses the TransPose model, based on a neural network solution with Transformers [18]. Pose Tutor shows good results given pose data from Yoga, Pilates, and Kung Fu.

Based on these two studies, we propose creating a tool that can estimate poses in rehabilitation exercises and indicate through explainability the points to be corrected in the pose, to improve the estimation, thus improving the quality of the exercise. As a proof of concept, we initially sought to implement separately two AI solutions, one for pose estimation and the other for evaluation of the positions of key points, with explainability.

4.3   Pose Estimation

For the pose estimation studies, experiments were performed with the solutions proposed by [18] and [10]. Since the goal is to estimate using videos, it was decided to continue the study using the VideoPose3D solution by [10]. It does pose estimation on video data through the Detectron2 library, which uses a convolutional neural network model for several visual recognition tasks, among them pose estimation [17]. Both solutions, VideoPose3D and Detectron2, were developed and are maintained by the Meta Research team.

In Figs. 8 and 9, results of the VideoPose3D application on two selected videos can be seen, thus obtaining the joint position estimation, pose, and 3D reconstruction of the pose.

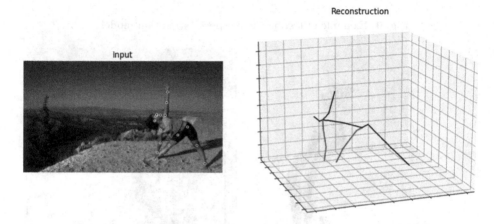

Fig. 8. Example of testing the 3D pose estimation model.

4.4   Motion Evaluation

Studies were started on measuring the angles of the joints detected in a pose to use this information to evaluate the movement quality and develop the motion evaluation solution. Tests were conducted with a prototype based on OpenCV and MediaPipe technologies, used respectively for computer vision, and detection and tracking in video inputs [15].

The proof of concept created allows the input of video information, and after pose estimation, it provides the value of the flexion angle of the trunk of an individual, as can be seen in Figs. 10 and 11.

4.5   Use of Explainability

Considering the use of explainability as a tool to support the end user of the application, as in the examples presented in the works of [3] and [4], the goal

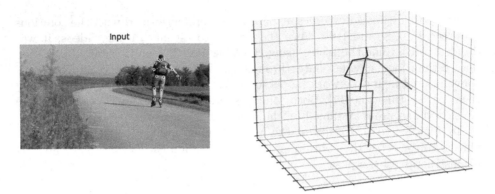

Fig. 9. Example of testing the 3D pose estimation model.

Fig. 10. Example of angle evaluation model test.

of the proposal is to use explainability as a tool to evaluate the movements presented in rehabilitation activities, allowing the evaluation of the movement, comparing it with the proposal of the health professional.

For the development and implementation of this solution, the solutions of pose estimation and angle evaluations will be combined with aspects of explainability, seeking to obtain visual feedback with the evaluation of the executed movement. Figures 12 and 13 depict tests performed with the concept tests presented in a video showing footage of a rehabilitation session.

Fig. 11. Example of angle evaluation model test.

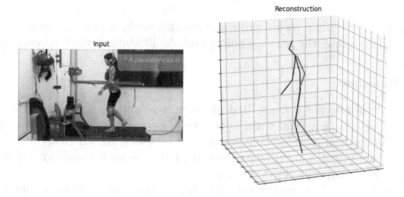

Fig. 12. Application of the proof of concept of pose estimation in rehabilitation imaging.

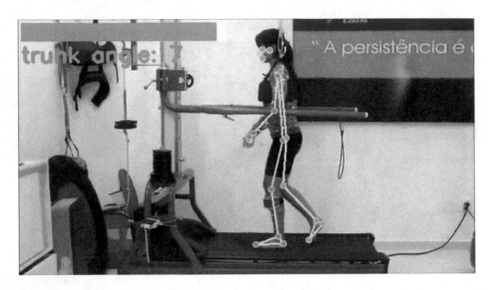

Fig. 13. Application of the proof of concept of angle evaluation in rehabilitation imaging.

5 Conclusion

In the present section, seeking to conclude this work, a brief discussion will be presented regarding the relevant points and the limitations of the present study.

5.1 Relevance

This study is relevant because it deals with a new area, XAI, which has been gaining strength in recent years, along with discussions about the fair use of AI in classification and decision processes. Collaborating with this relevance is the case study in the health area, one area that most demand an increase in confidence in computer-aided decisions.

Another point that contributes to the relevance of this work is its consistency, performing a literature review and proposing a case study for implementing XAI.

5.2 Limitations

Since XAI is a new field of research, there is the limitation that the implementation process needs to be better defined in the available literature, requiring a deepening of this theme and empirically seeking positive results.

The possibilities of the application of XAI are enormous. However, we focused efforts on the case study involving the evaluation of movements to aid neuromotor rehabilitation without seeking new areas for the development of practical applications.

Acknowledgements. This study was financed in part by the Coordenação de Aperfeiçoamento de Pessoal de Nível Superior - Brasil (CAPES).

References

1. Abuselidze, G., Mamaladze, L.: The impact of artificial intelligence on employment before and during pandemic: a comparative analysis. J. Phys. Conf. Ser. **1840**(1), 012040 (2021). https://doi.org/10.1088/1742-6596/1840/1/012040. https://iopscience.iop.org/article/10.1088/1742-6596/1840/1/012040
2. Barredo Arrieta, A., et al.: Explainable artificial intelligence (XAI): concepts, taxonomies, opportunities and challenges toward responsible AI. Inf. Fus. **58**, 82–115 (2020). https://doi.org/10.1016/j.inffus.2019.12.012. https://www.sciencedirect.com/science/article/pii/S1566253519308103
3. Chen, S., Yang, R.R.: Pose trainer: Correcting exercise posture using pose estimation. arXiv; Computer Vision and Pattern Recognition, June 2020. http://arxiv.org/abs/2006.11718
4. Dittakavi, B., et al.: Pose tutor: an explainable system for pose correction in the wild. In: Proceedings of the 2019 IEEE/CVF Conference on Computer Vision and Pattern Recognition (CVPR), pp. 3539–3548. IEEE, June 2022. https://doi.org/10.1109/CVPRW56347.2022.00398
5. Kirk, A.: Data Visualization: A Successful Design Process; A Structured Design Approach to Equip You with the Knowledge of how to Successfully Accomplish Any Data Visualization Challenge Efficiently and Effectively. Packt Publishing (2012)
6. Lauriere, J.L.: Problem-Solving and Artificial Intelligence. Prentice Hall (1990)
7. Lundberg, S.M., Lee, S.I.: A unified approach to interpreting model predictions. arXiv 1(Section 2), 1–10 (2017)
8. Masís, S.: Interpretable Machine Learning with Python: Learn to Build Interpretable High-Performance Models with Hands-on Real-world Examples. Packt Publishing (2021)
9. Mccarthy, J.: What is artificial intelligence? (2007). http://www-formal.stanford.edu/jmc/
10. Pavllo, D., Feichtenhofer, C., Grangier, D., Auli, M.: 3d human pose estimation in video with temporal convolutions and semi-supervised training. In: Proceedings of the 2019 IEEE/CVF Conference on Computer Vision and Pattern Recognition (CVPR), pp. 7745–7754. IEEE (June 2019). https://doi.org/10.1109/CVPR.2019.00794
11. Ribeiro, M.T., Singh, S., Guestrin, C.: "why should i trust you?" explaining the predictions of any classifier. In: Proceedings of the ACM SIGKDD International Conference on Knowledge Discovery and Data Mining, 13–17-August, pp. 1135–1144 (2016). https://doi.org/10.1145/2939672.2939778
12. Rich, E., Knight, K.: Inteligencia Artificial. McGraw-Hill (1994)
13. Rodrigues, L.G.S., et al.: Classification of human movements with motion capture data in a motor rehabilitation context. In: Anais do XXIII Simpósio de Realidade Virtual e Aumentada, pp. 55–62. SBC, Porto Alegre, RS, Brasil (2021). https://sol.sbc.org.br/index.php/svr/article/view/17519
14. Sarkar, T.: Google's new "explainable AI" (XAI) service - towards data science (2019). https://towardsdatascience.com/googles-new-explainable-ai-xai-service-83a7bc823773

15. Editorial Team: Detecting bad posture with machine learning, January 2023. https://towardsai.net/p/machine-learning/detecting-bad-posture-with-machine-learning
16. Turek, M.: Explainable Artificial Intelligence (2018). https://www.darpa.mil/program/explainable-artificial-intelligence
17. Wu, Y., Kirillov, A., Massa, F., Lo, W.Y., Girshick, R.: Detectron2 (2019)
18. Yang, S., Quan, Z., Nie, M., Yang, W.: TransPose: keypoint localization via transformer. In: Proceedings of the IEEE International Conference on Computer Vision, pp. 11782–11792, December 2020. http://arxiv.org/abs/2012.14214

A Novel Natural Language Processing Strategy to Improve Digital Accounting Classification Approach for Supplier Invoices ERP Transaction Process

Wei Wen Chi[ID], Tiong Yew Tang[✉][ID], Narishah Mohamed Salleh[ID], and Ha Jin Hwang[ID]

Sunway Business School, Sunway University, 47500 Subang Jaya, Selangor, Malaysia
{tiongyewt,narishahm,hjhwang}@sunway.edu.my

Abstract. Natural language processing (NLP) is a developing field that offers increasing potential to simplify accounting-related tasks. This research studies a novel NLP approach to classify invoice categories based on the invoice text description. The preprocessing steps can be divided into three parts, namely text cleaning, semantic enrichment using the labels as an information source, and text augmentation. A total of 12 different training datasets were prepared based on the raw invoice data, each reflecting an output of a unique combination of the preprocessing steps. Each training dataset was then sent for modelling with one traditional classifier and two deep learning classifiers, namely Linear Support Vector Machine (LSVM), Bi-directional Long Short-Term Memory (Bi-LSTM) and Bidirectional Encoder Representations from Transformers (BERT). Overall, the best approach yielded an improvement of up to 6.7 percentage points (ppts) for accuracy and 20 ppts for macro F1 score. Noise and overfitting were successfully reduced when only English text was retained for modelling. Using label data to semantically enrich invoice text descriptions improved the model's generalizability. The lexical synonym substitution approach proved more effective in preserving semantics compared to the word embedding approach for short text augmentations. BERT outperformed Bi-LSTM and LSVM and performance improved further with an increase in training data, confirming the superiority of deep learning classifier performance compared to traditional classifiers. Multi-class balancing by lexical-based data augmentation improved the model generalizability, evidenced by a high macro F1 score. This novel discovery contributes to the area of automating invoice text classification, which up until today has remained largely a manual task in practice. The classification approach is well suited to be integrated with other artificial intelligence solutions like Optical Character Recognition (OCR) and Robotic Process Automation (RPA) to form a completely automated invoice processing system. Since invoice classification is a repetitive and non-value-added process, the combination of this novel text classification method with RPA can reduce overhead costs by approximately 90%.

Keywords: Deep Learning · Natural Language Processing · Machine Learning · Invoice · Robotic Process Automation · RPA · Intelligent Process Automation · IPA

O. Gervasi et al. (Eds.): ICCSA 2023, LNCS 13956, pp. 581–598, 2023.
https://doi.org/10.1007/978-3-031-36805-9_38

1 Introduction

1.1 Background

The amount of unstructured enterprise data is increasing at an alarming rate of up to 65% per year, but the problem with unstructured data is that it lacks structure, making analysis and extraction of insights complex and costly [1]. The advent of data management, processing, and analysis solutions such as Hadoop and Google Colab have enabled the use of unstructured data. Unstructured data has the potential to lift enterprises above their competitors in customer engagement, operational excellence, and product leadership if used effectively [2].

Textual data is unstructured and requires structuring, so its analysis is equivalent to textual data analysis. Holsti's 1970 study described the manual classification of genuine and fake suicide texts, which led to the recommendation that machines be used due to the resource-intensive nature of manual classification. NLP is the process of transforming textual input into usable and actionable information. NLP imposes structure on textual data, allowing computers to understand it, and is critical to the text conversion process [1, 3]. Even though NLP is still a relatively new pitch in terms of applications, businesses have already used it with some success [4].

NLP can automatically extract essential risk results, reducing auditor workload and shortening the review process from half a year to a month while achieving capacity freedom [5]. Deloitte and EY used natural language processing (NLP) to automate the review of large numbers of contracts, detect changes in control provisions, extract critical accounting information from current merger and acquisition agreements, and evaluate existing leases to determine the impact on lease accounting rules [6]. NLP and deep learning are gaining research traction, but they have yet to be adopted in the finance organization.

To summarize, unstructured data presents a significant challenge for enterprises; however, the emergence of data management, processing, and analysis solutions, as well as NLP, has enabled enterprises to extract valuable insights from unstructured data, giving them a competitive advantage.

1.2 Objective

The purpose of this study is to investigate the practical applications of NLP in automating daily business tasks and lowering operational costs. NLP techniques and tools can assist machines in reading unstructured data, allowing businesses to scale their big data processing efforts while freeing up human capacity for more intelligent tasks [7]. The accounting domain's lack of automation is also a motivator, with many repetitive tasks that could be automated using NLP to avoid human error. Prior research has focused on sentiment analysis in external financial reports, but despite the presence of unstructured data in these processes, little emphasis has been placed on NLP processing for internal accounting processes such as invoice classification and bank reconciliations [8]. Deloitte and EY's successful implementation of NLP and RPA serves as a reminder of the significant benefits of a well-implemented NLP technique.

1.3 Research Approach

The research focuses on the accounting domain and aims to develop a practical and innovative method for categorizing based on Chart of Account (COA) for invoices based on their text descriptions. Short text issues and class imbalance issues, on the other hand, pose challenges in invoice classification. Traditional machine learning methods struggle to extract important features from a large feature space in short text classification, and a lack of data makes deep learning models difficult to use [9, 10]. Furthermore, most short-text vocabularies are informal and field-specific, resulting in misspellings, abbreviations, and typos. The multi-class classification of unbalanced data complicates the classification problem even more, and optimizing experiments are required to find the best classifier configurations [11].

The study suggests a new way to balance class distribution and add meaning to short text data. If this approach works, it can be used in many ways to classify text in the finance and accounting fields. The study's contribution is the creation of a novel approach to invoice text classification that has the potential to help organizations reduce overhead costs for repetitive accounting tasks. The research also aims to provide a useful technique for data augmentation that preserves semantic information while producing cutting-edge results.

The next section discusses the related work for key components of this novel approach. Section 3 discusses the methodology employed for the novel experiment. Section 4 shows the results and discussion of the experiment. Section 5 discusses the conclusion. Lastly, Sect. 6 presents the research limitations and future works are presented.

2 Literature Summary

The literature review focuses on methods and techniques for classifying text in the accounting domain, such as semantic enrichment, text data augmentation, and learning models.

2.1 Semantic Enrichment

The article discusses various methods for preserving or improving a document's semantic meaning, particularly in cases of short text like social media [12]. One common way to give more semantic information is to use extra sources like the internet or texts from previous conversations. Researchers have come up with models like Dual Latent Dirichlet Allocation (DLDA) and label embedding to deal with differences in meaning and make it easier to understand the meaning. The article talks about a new way to combine original text with augmented label data to improve semantic information and make data less sparse [13, 14]. Aside from label embedding, this method is novel and has received little attention.

2.2 Text Data Augmentation

The Data Augmentation (DA) Technique is a process that makes training data bigger without collecting more data. It does this by making different versions of real datasets. There are different techniques, including Easy Data Augmentation (EDA), which enhances original content by simple operations such as synonym substitution, arbitrary insertion, swapping, and deletion [15]. Other augmentation methods include TABAS, adversarial embeddings, and generative model-based augmentation [17]. Word embeddings convert text into numbers, and different embedding methods exist. Most research employs word embeddings to train LSTM or BERT models, but no augmentation study has been conducted in the context of invoice data, either to increase training data or to manage class imbalance [18, 19]. Some studies have shown that augmentation techniques can improve sentiment detection and text classification [17, 20].

2.3 Learning Models

The article compares traditional and deep-learning text categorization models. Traditional machine learning methods, such as Support Vector Machines (SVM), are effective in text analysis, but they are being supplanted by deep learning models such as bidirectional long short-term memory (Bi-LSTM) and bidirectional encoder representations from Transformers (BERT) [21]. Bi-LSTM can manage long context memories more efficiently than recurrent neural networks (RNNs), and BERT is a cutting-edge model that can learn bidirectionally from unlabeled text and capture context [21, 22]. Despite its benefits, BERT has limitations due to its large scale and high latency, making it unsuitable for some real-time scenarios. No study has used bi-LSTM or BERT to classify invoice text, and traditional methods such as LSVM are still effective as a baseline for comparison [23].

3   Methodology

The Cross-Industry Standard Process for Data Mining (CRISP-DM) framework was used in this section, and it will proceed in the following order: business understanding, data understanding, data preparation, modelling, and evaluation. Amani and Fadlalla [24] mentioned the use of this paradigm in data mining implementations. According to Sharda et al. (2018) [25], text mining initiatives necessitate more involved preprocessing steps than a typical data mining project. The next section explains in detail the steps and procedures:

3.1   Business Understanding

The business understanding of processing supplier invoices from capturing the information in the ERP system to classifying it to the correct chart of accounts and translating it into the financial profit and loss definition is explained. The next step is to describe the current process flow before suggesting a text classification automation approach.

The current procedure involves the accounts staff receiving a supplier invoice and entering it into the ERP system before making payment. The staff summarizes the invoice details in the invoice description, identifies the associated account code, enters it, and saves the data into the ERP system. The invoice classification process flow is shown in Fig. 1, which includes several human-dependent steps, as depicted in Fig. 2.

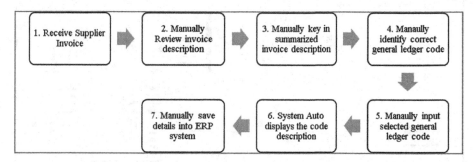

Fig. 1. "As-Is" Invoice Classification Process Flow

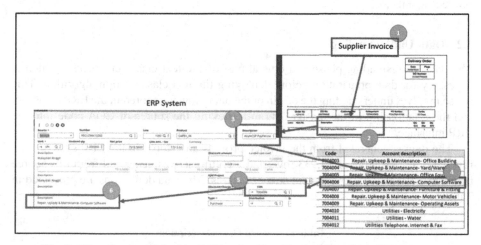

Fig. 2. Visualization of the "As-Is" Invoice Classification Steps in the ERP system.

The ERP interface and its relevant fields for entering supplier invoice information are displayed in Fig. 2. The labelled fields are required to be stored in the database for reporting purposes, which is crucial for financial reporting analysis by the finance team. Therefore, comprehending the process flow and relevant steps of the ERP User Interface can help identify areas for automation improvement.

Steps 2 through 6 have the potential to be automated, with steps 2–3 and 5–6 using RPA technology. Step 4 involves the automatic classification of the account code based on the invoice text description obtained, which will be explained in the following sections outlining the methodology for the text classifier scope. Figure 3 shows the proposed process steps for the invoice classification which will be done by RPA.

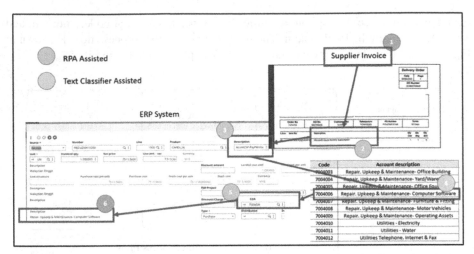

Fig. 3. "To-Be" Invoice Classification Process Steps which will be handled by RPA and a new assisted algorithm.

3.2 Data Understanding

The data understanding phase is a crucial part of the text classifier process, which is necessary for data preparation before deploying the text classification algorithm. This phase involves understanding the origin of the data, how it is stored in the ERP database, and the relationship of the master data in retrieving the source of COA code into the ERP interface.

The data is generated from the invoice process and stored in the ERP system. The raw dataset, consisting of 13,933 rows and 2 columns, was generated from this source between 2019 and 2021, with a total of 77 classes. The data definitions are presented in Table 1.

Table 1. Invoice Data Description

Data	Data Type	Description
Description	String	The invoice text description
Label	String	The general ledger code description

Initial data observations revealed the presence of uppercase letters, special characters, digits, and reference numbers, which should be removed as they are noise and negatively impact the modelling process. Stop words were also found and should be removed. Homogeneous class labels with slight differences, named entities, abbreviations, and misspellings were also detected. Invoices descriptions appearing for multiple classes will be removed from the dataset. The data is imbalanced due to the multi-class nature of the dataset, as shown in Fig. 4, which will help prioritize text classification automation development.

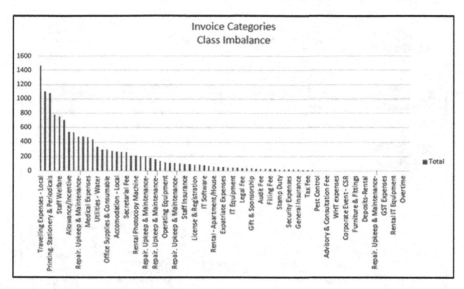

Fig. 4. The Invoice Categories Class Imbalance

From the data preparation phase up to the evaluation phase, the scope is based on the overall framework displayed in Fig. 5. Briefly, the major steps taken in these phases include text cleaning, sentiment enrichment, text augmentation, text categorization and classification, and finally evaluation. Most of the operational steps were performed using Python.

3.3 Data Preparation

The data preparation process involves text cleaning, semantic enrichment, and text augmentation of the original raw dataset named 'D1'. After text cleaning, the dataset 'D2' is split into train and test datasets and then used for semantic enrichment to produce the 'D3' dataset. 'D3_train' is further augmented using WordNet, GloVe, and BERT to create three training datasets of incremental sizes. At the end of the process, there will be 12 unique sets of training data and 3 unique sets of test data, which are paired accordingly. The details of the train-test pairing sets are presented in Table 2 while Table 3 summarizes the techniques applied sequentially.

The total number of datasets produced from this phase will be 12 datasets. Each data set contains a training set, a validation set and a test set. See Fig. 6.

The "Text Representation and Classification" phase falls under "Modeling." Here, each dataset is subjected to three classifiers, resulting in a total of 36 outputs. The "Evaluation" step concludes the CRISP-DM framework's evaluation phase, where the 36 results are evaluated. Python is the primary analysis tool employed in this study. To utilize their available graphics processing unit (GPU), the Python codes were executed on Google Colab and Kaggle.

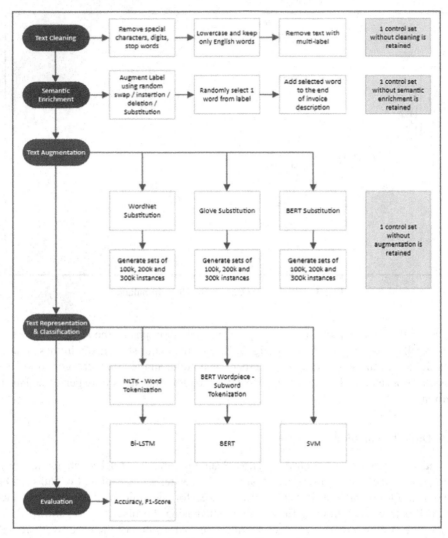

Fig. 5. The Overview Framework

3.4 Experimental Design

In this modelling phase, the three classifiers involved are LSVM, Bi-LSTM and BERT. The total result outputs from this phase will be 36 outputs. Table 4 Summarized the setting for the experiments:

In this phase, the 36 outputs produced will be evaluated using the accuracy and macro F1-score. The macro F1 scores are the average F1 scores for all classes. This score does not consider the weightage of each class and is a good indicator of whether the F1 scores are balanced across all the classes without accounting for weightage. A high score will indicate that the model generally is not biased towards any class. The weighted average F1 scores are also F1 scores but already accounted for the weightage.

Table 2. Train-Test Pairing Datasets

Set	Training Set	Testing Set
D01	D1_train	D1_test
D02	D2_train	D2_test
D03	D3_train	D3_test
D04	D3_WNtrain100k	D3_test
D05	D3_GLtrain100k	D3_test
D06	D3_BTtrain100k	D3_test
D07	D3_WNtrain200k	D3_test
D08	D3_GLtrain200k	D3_test
D09	D3_BTtrain200k	D3_test
D10	D3_WNtrain300k	D3_test
D11	D3_GLtrain300k	D3_test
D12	D3_BTtrain300k	D3_test

Table 3. Summary of Data Preparation Process

Technique	Summary of the process
1.0 Text Cleaning	It is the process of removing special characters, digits, stop words, and single characters to keep only English words. Entirely blank rows and multi-labelled instances are removed, except when a minority label has only one sample, in which case it is reclassed to the majority label. The dataset is split into train-validation-test sets
2.0 Semantic Enrichment	A new label column is generated with augmented text using random swap, deletion, or insertion, and then tokenized. One random word is selected from the tokens, and a new column is generated by concatenating it with the original description text to create semantically enriched synthetic instances, and a new dataset is generated by appending it to the "D2" train set to create a "D3" train set with double the training data. The "D3" train set is split into train validation, and the test set of "D2" is used to test the model trained with the "D3" train set
3.0 Text Augmentation	This is to examine the impact of larger training data sets on classification performance. The required number of augmented samples is determined to reach approximately 300,000 samples with equal distribution for WordNet, GloVe, and BERT substitution. The "D3" train dataset is loaded, and instances are augmented iteratively to achieve approximately 300,000 samples for each substitution

Text Cleaning	Semantic Enrichment	Increase Train Volume		Dataset Code
None				D01
	None			D02
		None		D03
Yes	Yes	100000	WN	D04
			GLV	D05
			BERT	D06
		200000	WN	D07
			GLV	D08
			BERT	D09
		300000	WN	D10
			GLV	D11
			BERT	D12

Fig. 6. Total Datasets Produced from Data Preparation Phase

This score is closer to the overall accuracy score. 80% was used as a benchmark for good classification performance.

4 Results

The detailed results from the modelling stage are collated in Fig. 7 based on Accuracy and F1-Score:

Figure 8 displays the visualization chart to compare Accuracy and Macro F1 scores by Dataset Codes and Classifier.

The results show that the top three accuracy scores were from datasets D04, D07 and D10, all of which were WordNet-augmented datasets trained with the BERT classifier. The top three Macro-F1 scores were driven by datasets D10, D11 and D12, all of which were characterized by a dataset of 300,000 instances generated by WordNet, GloVe and BERT augmenters respectively, and trained with the BERT classifier. The BERT classifier achieved above 80% accuracy for all datasets and is the best classifier. The results also show BERT having the lowest Macro F1 scores for non-augmentation datasets but becoming the best performer for all the augmented datasets. For pre-augment observations, dataset D03, which was semantically enriched but without augmentation, significantly improved classifier performance across all three classifiers compared to dataset D02 which was not semantically enriched. The D03 dataset also performed better than some of the augmented datasets. The biggest improvement in accuracy scores can be seen in the Bi-LSTM experiment with an improvement of 6.7 percentage points (ppts) while the biggest improvement in Macro F1 scores can be observed in the BERT experiment with an improvement of up to 20 ppts. Overall, the deep learning classifiers BERT and Bi-LSTM performed better than LSVM.

Table 4. Summary of Experiment's Configuration

No	LSVM	Bi-LTSM	BERT
1	Default Setting	The training and testing set is loaded, labelled as X_train, X_test, y_train, and y_test	Split Train set into training and validation set (15% of Train set)
2	Training set and test data uploaded	The train set text is tokenized using NLTK library word-based tokenization	The Train, Validation and Test sets are loaded, and labels are encoded
3	12 Experiments	Convert the train and test description into a sequence using a token	Replace Train, Validation and Test Sets with the encoded labels
4		Pad all the sequences so all vectors are of the same length. Create and Embedded the layer	Load BERT Tokenizer. The Tokenizer is based on pre-trained 'Bert Base Uncased'. Encode Training, Validation and Testing Sets
5		Build and Compile the LSTM model. The learning rate is set to 0.01	Load Pretrained Model. Load Data loaders, Optimizer and Scheduler. The learning rate is set at 1e-5 and batch size 16 to cater for lower memory processing
6			Define evaluation function Run the Training Loop. Manual early stopping is done when the validation loss increases 3 times from the last lowest validation loss measure
7			Run the full evaluation

Reference Codes:

a. Full LSVM codes at https://github.com/cwwdaniel/invoice-text-classification/blob/main/lsvm

b. Full Bi-LSTM codes at https://github.com/cwwdaniel/invoice-text-classification/blob/main/bi-lstm

c. Full BERT codes at https://github.com/cwwdaniel/invoice-text-classification/blob/main/bert

Text Cleaning	Semantic Enrichment	Increase Train Volume		Dataset Code	LSVM Accuracy	Bi-LSTM Accuracy	BERT Accuracy	LSVM Macro F1-Score	Bi-LSTM Macro F1-Score	BERT Macro F1-Score
None				D01	77.9%	78.3%	81.1%	67.0%	61.0%	61.0%
	None			D02	84.4%	83.2%	84.1%	75.0%	68.0%	63.0%
		None		D03	84.6%	85.7%	86.4%	76.0%	78.0%	73.0%
Yes	Yes	100000	WN	D04	81.4%	83.8%	86.7%	72.0%	78.0%	75.0%
			GLV	D05	79.6%	81.3%	84.2%	67.0%	71.0%	77.0%
			BERT	D06	78.5%	80.2%	82.8%	67.0%	68.0%	75.0%
		200000	WN	D07	82.9%	84.7%	86.9%	74.0%	76.0%	78.0%
			GLV	D08	80.6%	83.8%	86.1%	69.0%	74.0%	78.0%
			BERT	D09	79.3%	83.1%	85.0%	69.0%	71.0%	76.0%
		300000	WN	D10	82.7%	85.0%	87.7%	74.0%	75.0%	81.0%
			GLV	D11	80.4%	81.8%	86.6%	68.0%	70.0%	79.0%
			BERT	D12	80.0%	78.5%	86.6%	70.0%	66.0%	79.0%

Fig. 7. Model Output Results. Top performers are highlighted in green. (Color figure online)

Figure 9 and Fig. 10 display the visualization chart to compare Accuracy and Macro F1scores by Augment Volume and Classifier or Augmenter.

Figure 9 shows that the BERT classifier consistently achieved accuracy scores of more than 80% on average at different augmentation volumes in an increasing trend. Bi-LSTM and LSVM trended inconsistently with the increase of synthetic data, ultimately trending downwards or flat at the 300,000-instance dataset. Macro F1 scores trended upwards for the BERT classifier, and just slightly short of 80% at 300,000 augmented instances. A significant improvement was observed in BERT classifier Macro-F1 results with the 100,000-instance dataset over the non-augmented results. It is also observed in Fig. 10 that the WordNet augmenter has the best performance among the augmenters, also increasing in performance as the augmented volume increases. The GloVe and BERT augmenter performance had similar trends where the non-augmented results were superior to the augmented dataset results.

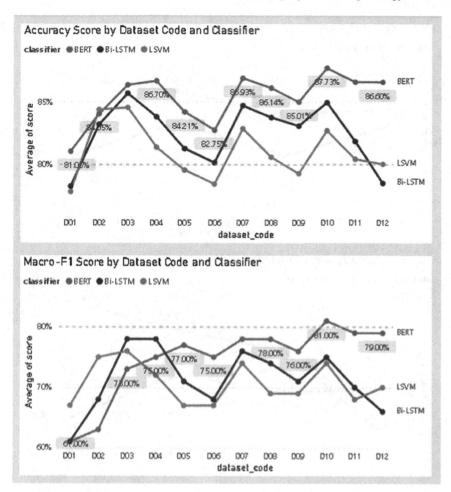

Fig. 8. Accuracy & Macro F1 scores by Dataset Code and Classifier

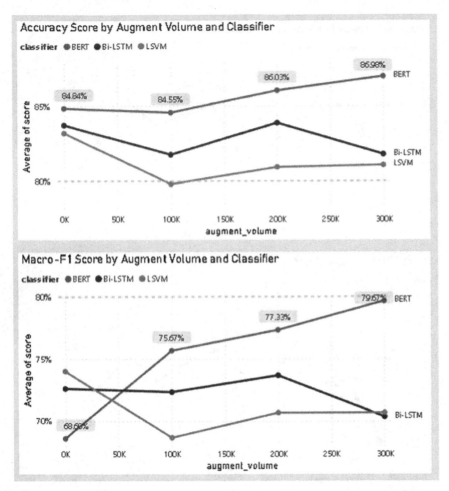

Fig. 9. Accuracy & Macro F1 scores for different levels of augmentation volume by Classifier

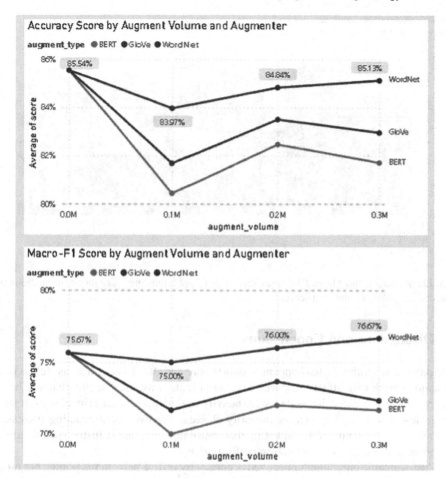

Fig. 10. Accuracy & Macro F1 scores for different levels of augmentation volume by Augmenter

Figure 11 displays the visualization chart to compare the augmenter-classifier combination Accuracy and Macro-F1 scores in descending order.

The data shows that the BERT method consistently achieves accuracy scores of more than 80% for each augmenter-classifier. The top performer is the BERT-WordNet augmenter-classifier. The BERT classifier and WordNet augmenter were frequently found in the top five augmenter-classifiers in terms of performance, indicating the significance of these two techniques on the performance of the classification task. Consistently It is observed that the larger difference in performance for augmenter-classifiers was in the Macro F1 scores rather than the accuracy.

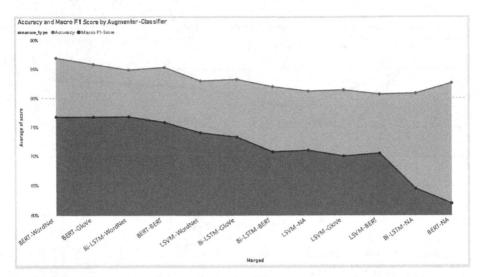

Fig. 11. Accuracy and Macro F1 Scores for the different augmenter-classifier combinations by descending order of combined scores.

5 Discussions and Conclusions

The passage talks about what happens to data before and after it is cleaned, as well as how semantic enrichment affects how well text classification works. The pre-cleaning baseline results revealed that the models were heavily biased towards majority classes, resulting in lower macro-F1 scores for minority classes. However, post-cleaning increased overall accuracy by up to 7%, indicating that removing noise and industry-specific terms from raw text improves classification performance.

Post-semantic enrichment improved accuracy by up to 2 percentage points, but more importantly, it greatly improved macro F1 scores for minority classes. This shows that additional semantic information from labels helps reduce data sparsity and improve text classification performance. The results support the idea that it helps classification performance to get additional semantic information from labels.

The objective of the research was to improve how invoices are classified by text by using semantic enrichment and data augmentation strategies. The results showed that minority classes were more likely to be misclassified than majority classes. However, once the data was cleaned up, the accuracy of classification went up to more than 80%. It was found that using BERT as a classifier and the WordNet synonym augmentation as a data enlargement were both good ways to classify short texts. The findings of this study have several implications for corporate practice, one of which is the reduction of overhead costs associated with routine and repetitive accounting procedures. The unique method of short-text semantic enrichment that was utilized in this investigation is an approach that has the potential to add to the expanding body of research that focuses on semantically enhancing short-text data. In conclusion, the findings of the study demonstrated that an effective augmentation strategy that maintains semantic information can produce state-of-the-art outcomes and can make a significant contribution to the research community.

6 Limitations and Future Works

In this study, only one traditional learner was used to compare against deep learning models. It is recommended that more traditional learners be compared against the deep learning model for more concrete findings on the question of the effectiveness of traditional versus deep learning models.

Acknowledgement. This work was supported in part by Sunway University and Sunway Business School under Kick Start Grant Scheme (KSGS) NO: GRTIN-KSGS-DBA[S]-02-2022. This work is also part of the Sustainable Business Research Cluster and Research Centre for Human-Machine Collaboration (HUMAC) at Sunway University. We also wish to thank those who have supported this research.

References

1. Sharda, R., Delen, D., Turban, E., Aronson, J. E., Liang, T.-P., King, D.: Business Intelligence, Analytics, and Data Science: A Managerial Perspective (Fourth). Pearson (2018)
2. Taylor, C. Structured vs Unstructured Data. Datamation. https://www.datamation.com/big-data/structured-vs-unstructured-data/. Accessed 21 May 2021
3. Guo, L., Shi, F., Tu, J: Textual analysis and machine learning: crack unstructured data in finance and accounting. J. Finance Data Sci. 2(3), 153–170 (2016)
4. Zhou, Y., Cui, S., Wang, Y.: Machine learning based embedded code multi-label classification. IEEE Access 9, 150187–150200 (2021)
5. Zhang, Y., Xiong, F., Xie, Y., Fan, X., Gu, H.: The impact of artificial intelligence and blockchain on the accounting profession. IEEE Access 8, 110461–110477 (2020)
6. Li, L., Feng, Y., Lv, Y., Cong, X., Fu, X., Qi, J.: Automatically detecting peer-to-peer lending intermediary risk - top management team profile textual features perspective. IEEE Access 7, 72551–72560 (2019)
7. Baviskar, D., Ahirrao, S., Potdar, V., Kotecha, K.: Efficient automated processing of the unstructured documents using artificial intelligence: a systematic literature review and future directions. IEEE Access 9, 72894–72936 (2021)
8. Korhonen, T., Selos, E., Laine, T., Suomala, P.: Exploring the programmability of management accounting work for increasing automation: an interventionist case study. Acc. Audit. Accountability J. 34(2), 253–280 (2021)
9. Samant, S.S., Bhanu Murthy, N.L., Malapati, A.: Improving term weighting schemes for short text classification in vector space model. IEEE Access 7, 166578–166592 (2019)
10. Balakrishnan, V., Shi, Z., Law, C.L., Lim, R., Teh, L.L., Fan, Y.: A deep learning approach in predicting products' sentiment ratings: a comparative analysis. J. Supercomput. 78(5), 7206–7226 (2021). https://doi.org/10.1007/s11227-021-04169-6
11. Garcia-Mendez, S., Fernandez-Gavilanes, M., Juncal-Martinez, J., Gonzalez-Castano, F.J., Seara, O.B.: Identifying banking transaction descriptions via support vector machine short-text classification based on a specialized labelled corpus. IEEE Access 8, 61642–61655 (2020)
12. Mehanna, Y.S., Mahmuddin, M.B.: A semantic conceptualization using tagged bag-of-concepts for sentiment analysis. IEEE Access 9, 118736–118756 (2021)
13. Subedi, B., Sathishkumar, V.E., Maheshwari, V., Kumar, M.S., Jayagopal, P., Allayear, S.M.: Feature learning-based generative adversarial network data augmentation for class-based few-shot learning. Math. Probl. Eng. 2022, 1–20 (2022)

14. Xiang, R., Chersoni, E., Lu, Q., Huang, C.R., Li, W., Long, Y.: Lexical data augmentation for sentiment analysis. J. Am. Soc. Inf. Sci. **72**(11), 1432–1447 (2021)
15. Wan, C., Wang, Y., Liu, Y., Ji, J., Feng, G.: Composite feature extraction and selection for text classification. IEEE Access **7**, 35208–35219 (2019)
16. Wang, J., Li, Y., Shan, J., Bao, J., Zong, C., Zhao, L.: Large-scale text classification using scope-based convolutional neural network: a deep learning approach. IEEE Access **7**, 171548–171558 (2019)
17. Luo, J., Bouazizi, M., Ohtsuki, T.: Data augmentation for sentiment analysis using sentence compression-based SeqGAN with data screening. IEEE Access **9**, 99922–99931 (2021)
18. Liu, C.-L., Fink, G.A., Govindaraju, V., Jin, L.: Special issue on deep learning for document analysis and recognition. Int. J. Doc. Anal. Recogn. (IJDAR) **21**(3), 159–160 (2018). https://doi.org/10.1007/s10032-018-0310-5
19. Somayajula, S.A., Song, L., Xie, P.: A multi-level optimization framework for end-to-end text augmentation. Trans. Assoc. Comput. Linguist. **10**, 343–358 (2022)
20. Tan, K.L., Lee, C.P., Lim, K.M., Anbananthen, K.S.M.: Sentiment analysis with ensemble hybrid deep learning model. IEEE Access **10**, 103694–103704 (2022)
21. Yan, C., Chen, Y., Zhou, L.: Differentiated fashion recommendation using knowledge graph and data augmentation. IEEE Access **7**, 102239–102248 (2019)
22. Lee, S., Liu, L., Choi, W.: Iterative translation-based data augmentation method for text classification tasks. IEEE Access **9**, 160437–160445 (2021)
23. El-Alami, F.-Z., El Alaoui, S.O., En Nahnahi, N.: Contextual semantic embeddings based on fine-tuned AraBERT model for Arabic text multi-class categorization. J. King Saud Univ.-Comput. Inf. Sci. **34**(10), 8422–8428 (2022)
24. Amani, F.A., Fadlalla, A.M.: Data mining applications in accounting: a review of the literature and organizing framework. Int. J. Acc. Inf. Syst. **24**, 32–58 (2017)
25. Sharda, R., Delen, D., Turban, E.: Business Intelligence, Analytics, and Data Science: A Managerial Perspective. Pearson (2017)

Knowledge Management Model: A Process View

Luciano Straccia[(✉)], María F. Pollo-Cattaneo, and Adriana Maulini

Departamento de Ingeniería en Sistemas de Información, Grupo GEMIS, Universidad Tecnológica Nacional, Facultad Regional Buenos Aires, Buenos Aires, Argentina
`lstraccia@frba.utn.edu.ar`

Abstract. Knowledge is an indispensable resource for organizations to perform their tasks successfully and to innovate. Knowledge management is an integrated field of multiple disciplines that seek to exploit knowledge more efficiently. This paper analyzes the activities (and stages) of knowledge management. For this purpose, a survey of more than 2000 papers and thesis is presented, in which the proposed activities are analyzed. A knowledge management model is then presented that considers various perspectives: the individual perspective (associated with learning), repositories perspective (storage and retrieval), the team's perspective (sharing and dissemination) and the identification and creation and acquisition of knowledge. The knowledge management model proposed included these activities: learning, retrieval, representation & structuring, socialization, dissemination, identification, creation and acquisition.

Keywords: Knowledge Management · Process · Activities

1 Introduction

This article identifies the essential activities required for a Knowledge Management Model. It presents a theoretical framework on knowledge (Sect. 2) and knowledge management (Sect. 3). Section 4 provides a comparative analysis of various recognized knowledge management models, many of which were developed 20 to 30 years ago. The goal of this paper is to analyze recently proposed knowledge management models in the academic literature to obtain a more detailed understanding of the activities necessary for effective knowledge management and to propose a comprehensive knowledge management model. To accomplish this, a literature review was conducted following the methodology outlined in Sect. 5. The subsequent sections offer an analysis of the findings and suggest a knowledge management model. Finally, Sect. 10 presents the complete Knowledge Management Model.

2 Knowledge

Ackoff [1] propose a DIKW Hierarchy, in which each concept adds value to the previous one: data, information, knowledge and wisdom. Data is a simple observation of the state [2], a raw, simple and discrete fact [3]. Information can be defined as a function of

O. Gervasi et al. (Eds.): ICCSA 2023, LNCS 13956, pp. 599–616, 2023.
https://doi.org/10.1007/978-3-031-36805-9_39

data that makes sense of data in a context and return information; knowledge can be defined as a function of information that makes sense of information incorporating the insights [4]. The term "insight" represents the tacit implications behind Information Accordingly. The DIKW model was extended by Hey in to DIKIW by introducing a layer of Intelligence between Knowledge and Wisdom elements [5].

According to Davenport [2] the knowledge is a "mixture of structured experiences, values and non-contextual information that provides a framework for evaluating new experiences and information". Wiig [6] affirms that knowledge is the "integration and relationship of isolated information to develop new meanings". Martinez Marin and Rios Rosas [7] present four epistemological schools on knowledge: rationalism (knowledge has its origin in reason, it affirms that a knowledge is only really such when it possesses logical necessity and universal validity), empiricism (the only cause of human knowledge is experience), phenomenology (knowledge is the result of experience, of participation in the object of study) and hermeneutics (maintains that there is no objective, transparent or disinterested knowledge about the world is mediated by a series of prejudices, expectations and presuppositions).

3 Knowledge Management

Knowledge management (KM) is defined as "a managerial approach or emerging discipline that seeks in a structured and systematic way to take advantage of the knowledge generated to achieve the organization's objectives and optimize the decision-making process" [8]. Knowledge "is the most important strategic resource, and the ability to generate, acquire, codify, transfer, apply, and reuse it has become a substantial competence for obtaining a sustainable competitive advantage" [9].

KM is an integrated field of multiple disciplines that allows the development of initiatives in organizations [10]. According to [11], KM "from the social psychology of organizations lies in a process of social influence of collaborative groups around the transfer of implicit knowledge towards the safeguarding of tacit knowledge in order to take advantage of the experience and skills of talents and leaders in the face of environmental contingencies, or the risks and threats of the context".

KM can be analyzed from different views. A view is a representation of the system from the perspective of a specific set of related concerns, which suppresses details to provide a simplified model that has only the elements related to the concerns of the viewpoint [12, 13]. There are five KM views: 1) people, 2) organizational aspects, 3) activities and processes, 4) technology and representation, and 5) measurement [14].

This paper analyzes the activity and process dimension of knowledge management according to the method detailed in Sect. 5 [14].

4 Background

Straccia et al. [15] makes a comparison between knowledge management models, looking for similarities and differential contributions and identifying phases required for any knowledge management methodology. The work considers the models of Nonaka and Takeuchi, Wiig, Sveiby, Earl, Kerschberg, Bustelo and Amarilla, Mc Elroy, the CEN

Guide of Good Practices in Knowledge Management, Pons, KMC and K-TSACA and incorporates new models found in the Association for Computing Machinery ACM, the Institute of Electrical and Electronic Engineers IEEE, Directory of Open Access Journals DOAJ and Science Direct. After the analysis and terminology standardization process, the following phases have been found: identification, creation, acquisition, sharing, application, refinement, and validation. These phases can be considered in any knowledge management methodology.

Maulini et al. [16, 17] present a knowledge management model that proposes, in addition to the different stages, a first stage of preparing of the organization for the application of the model and a stage transversal to the whole model and of continuous execution: maintenance.

Among the works found in the search presented in this paper, [18] analyzes the knowledge management models of Wiig, Nonaka and Takeuchi, Kerschberg, Riesco, Paniagua and Lopez and Angulo and Negrón, compares the different stages and proposes 5 activities for knowledge management: creation or capture, structuring, storage, transfer and transformation and use. [19] analyzes similarities and differences between the phases of the knowledge management processes over the models of Wiig, Nonaka and Takeuchi, Davenport and Prusak, Meyer and Zack, Gupta and Govindarajan, Alavi and Leidner, Gold, Malhotra and Segars, King, Chung and Haney Evans, Dalkir and Bidiam, proposing a summary of 4 fundamental activities: generation, storage, transfer and application.

Nonaka and Takeuchi [20] proposed a knowledge management model known as "knowledge spiral" in which they present four fundamental activities: internalization, socialization, externalization and combination. In each of these activities the authors propose different ways of conversion between tacit knowledge (that which is difficult to express, formalize and share, very personal and subjective, derived from experience) and explicit knowledge (that which can be easily expressed and formalized, and is therefore acquired through formal methods of study).

Internalization implies the conversion of explicit knowledge into tactical knowledge, where a person acquires the knowledge, learns, and internalizes the knowledge, so these are operations that occur in the individual himself and must consider aspects of behavior and learning; these aspects will be discussed in Sect. 6.

Externalization implies the conversion of tacit knowledge into explicit knowledge and the fundamental aspect is the storage of knowledge in appropriate devices, giving rise to a repository perspective, which is dealt with in Sect. 7. Socialization is a process that involves thinking the organization collectively where diverse actors are sharing their knowledge; this collective organizational view is dealt with in Sect. 8.

5 Methods

A review of the literature in the Latin American (La Referencia, Redalyc, Scielo, SEDICI and SNRD) and English (ACM, DBLP, IEEE, Springer) bibliography was carried out using the sources and criteria specified in Tables 1 and 2. In La Referencia, Scielo and IEEE the keyword was used only in Document Title. In ACM was found in Abstract. For the others source was applied for all text.

Table 1. Search criterial

Criterial	Detail
Keywords in Latin American bibliography	"gestion del conocimiento"
Keywords in English bibliography	"knowledge management"
Period	2019–2021

Table 2. Specific search criterial

Criterial		Detail
Publication Type	La Referencia, SEDICI and SNRD	Master Thesis, Doctoral Thesis and Articles
Publication Type	Scielo, ACM, DBLP and Springer	Article
Publication Type	IEEE	Conference and Journals
Discipline	Redalyc	Computation, Engineering, Administration, Accounting and Information Sciences
Discipline	Springer	Business and Management

In the search, 2012 papers were found. From them, was selected which propose tasks or activities for knowledge management: 110 papers were selected.

Next, the terms found in the different activities were obtained. From the results, a detailed analysis of the terms and the meaning that each author gives to that term was carried out, understanding that the same term can have different meanings and that different terms can be used with similar meanings. Contributions from other disciplines outside knowledge management and management were included, including visions associated with psychology and education.

6   The Individual Perspective: Learning

To Alavi and Leidner [21] the knowledge transfer process occurs in several levels: between individuals, from individuals to explicit sources, from individuals to groups and from the group to the organization. The capacity to absorb knowledge is based on several dimensions: acquisition (which involves obtaining external knowledge, essential to the organization's operations), assimilation (is related to the ability to process, interpret and understand the acquired knowledge) and transformation (concerns the combination of already existing knowledge with the assimilated external knowledge). This definition of transformation corresponds to the one proposed by [22]: "the ability to internalize knowledge, by combining one's previous knowledge with the new acquired knowledge". The activities defined by the mentioned authors are part of the learning process according to the theories of the educational field. The following is an analysis of different terms found in the literature search that can be related to the individual's perspective: internalization, learning, association, discovery and other terms such as acquisition or transfer when used with this perspective.

6.1 Individual and Organizational Learning

[23] includes individual learning as a stage of knowledge transfer. For the authors, transfer includes individual learning and organizational learning. [24] also refers to organizational learning without specifying concrete activities.

The term organizational learning is usually attributed to Peter Senge. For Peter Senge, intelligent organizations are those capable of effectively exploiting collective knowledge and increasing their capacity to adapt in a competitive environment [25, 26]. Team learning is part of the conditions required (which Senge calls disciplines) for the creation of these intelligent organizations, also known as organizational learning, which refers to "the ability to dialogue, recognize the obstacles to learning, develop the ability to discuss, solve problems, make decisions and transform by generating knowledge" [25]. For [27], based on Senge's notions, it is the "process through which people and organizations increase their capacity to produce and generate the results they want to generate". Also, for [28], the team must use the available knowledge to generate collective learning.

The concept of organizational learning began to be used in the 1960s with the publication of Cangelosi and Dill [29], when the authors proposed to observe learning processes within organizations to explain their capacity to adapt to a new market and social contexts.

Organizational learning is not so much a concrete activity of the organization and much less of knowledge management, but a set of notions, ideas and activities that lead to a way of managing organizations.

6.2 Internalization and Learning

Although authors such as [30] believe that knowledge is created through dynamic interaction between individuals and/or between individuals and the environment, they ignore the individual characteristic of learning and that interaction alone is not a producer of knowledge.

The concept of internalization is embraced from psychology, with debates about its interpretation [31], especially based on Vygotsky's ideas. For Vygotsky, internalization is not a transfer of information from the outside to the inside of the individual, but a process of inter-functional reorganization. Internalization is understood "as a process of transformation, of interfunctional reorganization, which results in the mastery of the sign and the formation of the internal plane of consciousness" [31]. Internalization is not an institutional action, but a process in the individual, analyzable from psychology and other disciplines that have the individual as a subject of study.

On the other hand, learning is "a process of relatively permanent change in a person's behavior generated by experience" [32] and implies a behavioral change or a change in behavioral capacity that lasts over time [33].

According to Santana, learning "is a relatively permanent change in behavior that is achieved through practice and with the reciprocal interaction of individuals and their environment" [34]. Like the notions of internalization, learning is neither an institutional action nor an organizational process and therefore cannot be included in an organizational knowledge management process. Knowledge management processes must generate institutional conditions for internalization and learning.

6.3 Assimilation, Acquisition and Discover

Some authors present a stage called assimilation. For [35] this stage "relates to the routines, habits, and processes that allow firms to examine, understand, and make sense of external information; while the transformation dimension relates to firms' capability to develop, refine, combine, and integrate a set of external and internal knowledge".

Assimilation is a concept mainly developed by Piaget and "consists in the integration of external elements into the structure of the organism, whether they are already finished or in the process of formation. The process of assimilation affects behavior and organic life; no behavior, even new for the individual, constitutes an absolute beginning. It is always grafted on previous schemes and consists in assimilating new elements to structures already built, innate or acquired reflexes" [36].

For [37], knowledge acquisition is the identification and elicitation of data, the interpretation of this data, and the structuring and interlinking of this data [38]. In addition, knowledge acquisition can be defined as the development or creation of skills, insights, and relationships [39]. Knowledge is acquired through the combination of interactive and individual learning. [40] incorporate a stage called "discover" to refer to learning activities: "learners discover knowledge from practice or experience, or from data synthesis".

6.4 Summary About the Individual Perspective

From the concepts defined throughout this section, it can be stated that learning, internalization and other aspects mentioned are specific to the individual and cannot be defined as part of an organizational process of knowledge management. The obtaining of information by individuals for the realization of internalization and learning and organizational practices can be the subject of an analysis of the knowledge management process. These activities are presented in the Knowledge Management Model in Sect. 10. Therefore, in the next section, information storage and information retrieval by individuals is analyzed (Sect. 7), while socialization is analyzed next (Sect. 8).

7 Repositories Perspective: Storage and Retrieval

7.1 Storage and Retrieval

Persistence is the ability of a software to maintain the state beyond its execution and to allow subsequent executions to use the data generated in previous executions. The data generated during the operation of the software is stored for later retrieval. Persistence includes the following elements: persistence medium (the physical medium where data is stored), structure (storage format), database or repository (the files where storage occurs), metadata (information about the data) and two processes relating persistence to its use: mechanisms to alter the repository by adding new data or updating it and mechanisms to retrieve the stored data. Persistence is sometimes also referred to as "persistent storage".

Most of the articles analyzed in this work present the storage stage, although they omit to make explicit reference to data retrieval and updating. Other authors define it with other terms: [28] calls it relating and defines it as "systematization of explicit knowledge in a knowledge platform" understanding as a result of the task the explicit knowledge in the knowledge management system.

It can be stated that the work that involves human activity is precisely the retrieval and updating of data, while the actual storage (or persistence) is a technical activity of computer tools.

Some authors refer to retrieval [41, 42] and consider it as a single stage called "knowledge storage and retrieval", while [43] identify two broad types of information retrieval: pull model and push model. Alavi and Leidner [21] say about pull and push model that: "two broad types of information retrieval are the pull model, which involves search and retrieval of information based on specific user queries, and the push model, where information is automatically retrieved and delivered to the potential user based on some predetermined criteria".

Some authors call it "coding" [19, 23, 44]. For example, [19] denotes coding as "creating models, documenting knowledge in manuals and books (more linked to storage) and coding in databases even though it does not specify more detail" based on concept "coding" from Wiig [6]. [45] includes within the storage phase the classification of information. These definitions lead to reflect on two aspects: the creation of models (in Sect. 7.2) and the classification of information (in Sect. 7.3).

7.2 Representation

A knowledge representation model "is a particular way of representing knowledge by using the knowledge and reasoning mechanism" [46]. The knowledge "must be represented in a way that allows information systems to actively process knowledge, rather than only to represent it, and thus to enable knowledge-based reasoning" [47]. For the SUNY Center [48], the knowledge representation is "structure used to store knowledge in a manner that relates items of knowledge to one another, and that permits an inference engine to manipulate the knowledge and its relationships."

Although many papers refer to storage, few articles mention the representation or modeling of knowledge representation. [49, 50] mention a stage called "codify" that refers to the representation or m-modeling of knowledge objects. [51] say that "appropriate models for representing knowledge objects in the organizational knowledge management system (OKMS) should be developed" and [52]: "knowledge representation may be in the form of publication, which is joint authoring, structuring, contextualizing and release of knowledge elements supported by workflows".

7.3 Structuring

These activities are called by different terms, being the most used: structuring, categorization and classification. All of them seek to optimize the way in which information and knowledge is stored (after the explicitness processes) so that its retrieval is more efficient and the information obtained is more likely to be useful.

Structuring is a term used by [18] that include classifying, describing and indexing data, information and knowledge, using standardized metadata. For [53] identification, classification and categorization are activities that seek to index and organize information, making it more accessible and offering optimal ways for its consultation. [54] call "combining and integrating knowledge" the quest to reduce redundancy, increase consistency and optimize efficiency by eliminating excessive volume. [55] presents a process of "conversion-oriented knowledge management" that refer to those processes oriented towards making existing knowledge useful. [56] proposes to include in the storage stage, as a first action, a classification subprocess that allows filtering whether the knowledge is relevant to the organization. For [57] it includes knowledge debugging.

Alvarez et al. [58] proposes information grouping activities at the time of its acquisition. He also proposes classification and indexing in knowledge organization activities. [28] proposes a cataloging activity. [45] includes within storage a sub-activity of classification of information and knowledge. [59] proposes that according to the classification and prioritization of knowledge, a unique identifier (code) is assigned to easily administer and manage knowledge. [52] calls "classification" the stage with this definition: "taxonomies, also called classification or categorization schemes, are considered to be knowledge organization systems that serve to group objects together based on a particular characteristic". Similarly, [60] proposes organizing data with tags. [61] proposes categorizing knowledge into five categories: "short term knowledge, basic organizational knowledge, written knowledge, spatial knowledge and digitized knowledge".

7.4 Summary About the Repositories Perspective

As described in this section, storage can be performed with an appropriate structure and representation. However, no reference is made to whether these activities must be performed prior to knowledge explicitness in storage (and by the knowledge worker) or if knowledge can be made explicit in an unstructured way and then, through specific techniques, its structuring can be performed. This allows categorizing knowledge as structured (that on which representation and structuring was previously performed) and unstructured. And to define that the conversion of unstructured knowledge into structured knowledge can be done by the worker who owns the knowledge or by a knowledge manager. These activities are presented in the Knowledge Management Model in Sect. 10.

8 The Team's Perspective: Sharing and Dissemination

Knowledge sharing between different actors in the organization is called by different terms depending on the work. [28] calls it expressing where "the learner and the knowledge expert perform knowledge exchange by constructing new ideas and expressing what they have learned". [62] call it sharing but say that "his element could be named as knowledge dissemination"; [45] identified this stage as dissemination, too. [63] calls it as "socializing or sharing" and [64] includes socialization of knowledge as part of the acquisition stage. For [65] socialization is the process of sharing traditional knowledge through observation, imitation, practice and participation in a formal and informal community. Socializing implies "getting the target audience to appropriate a concept, understand it, assume it and mobilize actions and decisions. Thus, communicating to mobilize requires considering the opinions and points of view of those directly involved" [66].

According to [67]: "from social psychology, Arnett (…) proposes three types of objectives for socialization, of general scope to different societies and cultures: 1) impulse control, 2) preparation for occupying social roles and 3) internalization of meaning" These ideas can also be applicable to the organizational sphere as objectives of socialization.

As expressed above, [64] includes a socialization stage. However, it also defines a dissemination stage after storage. It is understood that this stage is associated with what other authors call "divulger" or "difundir", which seeks to maximize the scope of knowledge socialization. [68, 69] use the compound term "disseminar/compartilhar". For [66] diffusion, as propagation and dissemination of knowledge, is a possible socialization strategy.

Then, there are two ways of knowledge sharing: among knowledge workers through interpersonal communication strategies and from the work of the knowledge manager who summarizes, generates communications and disseminates among teams. These activities are presented in the Knowledge Management Model in Sect. 10.

9   Identification, Creation and Acquisition

9.1   Identification

According to [70] the identification phase aims to identify the intellectual capital that exists in the organization, the key processes and the critical knowledge held by experts. The creation of knowledge maps is proposed in this phase. [71] calls it knowledge audit. [54] includes in the knowledge access activity the search for the person who possesses the specific or necessary knowledge for a given situation. It is an activity that is preferably performed prior to the identification of a knowledge need, with the objective of having identified the possible sources of knowledge for a more efficient access when its use is required.

As stated by [72] the knowledge identification is a response to problems of knowledge location. [70] say that this stage aims to identify the intellectual capital that exists in the organization, the key processes and the critical knowledge possessed by the experts. To [59] "knowledge is identified through the area of human management in the organization, they are one of the most important and strategic areas, since they identify the skills, the competencies of key collaborators for the organization, in order to exploit such knowledge and skills for the benefit of customers and the organization".

Figueroa Ocoro calls "identification or capture" [73] to the classification of knowledge and information possessed by employees with respect to their skills, experiences, strengths, practices and criticality, since not all knowledge is important to the institution to be classified. [74] calls it "identification and acquisition" [57] introduces the concept of knowledge assets. [24] calls it "search".

In agreement with [70, 75] states that the first step in knowledge management is the identification of the organization's key processes.

According to the sources surveyed, identification includes: determine the key processes, determine existing knowledge and its location, determine the knowledge needed, and identifying knowledge sources and their networks.

Knowledge sources can be internal or external. Although most of the works surveyed deal with the internal sources of the organization, external sources are also a concern of the literature and many articles that were found. [71] states that among these knowledge sources are workers, customers, suppliers, shareholders and competition as knowledge creators.

The processes of obtaining knowledge, both from internal and external sources, are discussed in the next sections.

9.2 Creation

According to [60] the knowledge creation depends on the method of generating new knowledge through the repositioning and integration of present knowledge to achieve goals such as the introduction of a new product or service development, or management enhancement in an organization. [76] says that this process refers to the ideas and actions undertaken towards the generation of new ideas or objects. To [77] the knowledge creation is the process of generating new knowledge for which the existing knowledge is a prerequisite and "it is described as the development of know-how, unique expertise and new activities within an organization".

Melo proposes, once the knowledge has been used, to apply it in other contexts or areas of the organization [78]. In this way, its applicability in different contexts could be evaluated and new knowledge could be generated. [18] includes an activity called "transformation and use" that includes not only the use of knowledge but also the transformation aspect as "the generation of new concepts, processes, models, methodology or anything that generates value". [54] includes it in the access to knowledge activity.

The mentioned articles refer to the creation of knowledge from previously existing co-knowledge in the organization.

9.3 Acquisition

From the works found and analyzed, it is not possible to identify a univocal use of terms for the activities associated with seeking and obtaining knowledge, both from internal and external sources, and the generation of new knowledge from previously existing knowledge. This section presents some of the concepts and terms found.

To Probst et al. [79], acquisition has to do with renewing the organization's knowledge by obtaining external knowledge. With a similar concept, [22] calls acquisition the transfer of knowledge from one organization to another, including an assimilation activity that allows the understanding of external knowledge in the company. [54] distinguishes the concepts of creation, when it comes from internal sources, and provision of knowledge when it comes from external sources. For [54], acquisition includes activities related to the search, identification and access to new knowledge.

To [49] the acquisition, which mainly to gather and identify the valuable information in the organization. [55] says that "the acquisition of knowledge requires more than simply the sharing and collaboration of experiences, but also requires the organization to be able identify its importance or lack there-of". [76] refers to the process that covers the activities of the accessibility and collecting knowledge, including recognize, obtain, and amass knowledge (internal or external). For [81] the term acquisition implies the aptitude to recognize and attain new knowledge, which is crucial for effective organizational processes [82]. Primarily, employees acquire new knowledge from internal corporate sources such as colleagues and team members. To [35] the acquisition dimension of absorptive capacity is related "to routines for identifying and acquiring knowledge that resides outside of the firms' boundary". [62] say that "the formal inner knowledge of the firm, how to capture and get use of external knowledge and the link between both".

Given the impossibility to identify specific terms for the relationship with knowledge from internal and external sources, this paper chooses to call it acquisition (a term mostly used, and which differs from the creation proposed in the previous section) differentiating the origin: acquisition from internal sources and acquisition from external sources. The acquisition of knowledge from external sources can also be assimilated to the concept of "surveillance", which is discussed in the next section.

9.4 Surveillance

The causes that originate the incorporation of knowledge can be linked to the needs of the organization's own members regarding specific knowledge (which requires the search and identification of who possesses such knowledge) or through mechanisms of continuous search for new knowledge. The first case is covered in Sect. 7 with the concept of "retrieval"; the second can be related to the concept of surveillance.

Surveillance can be defined as "the systematic and organized effort by the company to observe, capture, analyze, accurately disseminate and retrieve information on the facts of the environment that are relevant to it because they may imply an opportunity or threat to it, in order to be able to make strategic decisions with less risk and anticipate changes" [83]. For [84] it is "the capture, analysis, dissemination and exploitation of information useful to the organization".

Zaintek [83] identifies four types of watch: technological, competitive, commercial and environmental. [85] classifies surveillance into 3 categories: technological, talent and knowledge. In the process described in this paper, the object of surveillance is knowledge, so it seems desirable to call this activity knowledge surveillance. However, this term is hardly used: a Google search on the term yields few searches. [86] incorporates this term as part of knowledge management processes, although it does not present its characteristics or details.

9.5 Summary

This section describes all the activities associated with the search and acquisition of knowledge. For this purpose, the following activities are performed: identification, creation and acquisition. The acquisition of knowledge from external sources is convenient to be done through knowledge surveillance. These activities are presented in the Knowledge Management Model in Sect. 10.

10 Knowledge Management Model

This article identifies the essential activities required for a Knowledge Management Model, incorporating the different concepts found and presented in previous section and considering the perspective of knowledge management as a discipline, but also to recognize the contributions that the field of education can contribute to it.

Learning and internalization is not a transfer of information from the outside to the inside of the individual, but an individual process that occurs in the mind of the learner as a process of inter-functional reorganization and generates change in a person's behavior generated by experience. Organizations must have the appropriate tools to be able to access the necessary resources to carry out such learning (with access to repositories and external sources) facilitating the tasks of knowledge acquisition and retrieval (see the individual perspective in Fig. 1). This learner is called knowledge worker, as it was called by Peter Drucker.

To achieve organizational learning, the learning individual must be socialized in the organization: for this purpose, socialization strategies can be carried out in the interpersonal exchange (for which spaces that allow it must be created) or through the work of a knowledge manager that summarizes knowledge, generates communications and disseminates them among work teams, and can also be disseminated outside the organization or to other remote teams (see the team's perspective in Fig. 2).

Except for socialization, the remaining proposed activities require considering a repositories perspective (see Fig. 3) for knowledge persistence. The representation and structuring are necessary activities for the optimization of knowledge persistence in order to maximize its exploitation. These activities can be performed previously to the knowledge explicitness in the storage (and by the knowledge worker) or it can be made explicit in an unstructured way and then, through of specific techniques, knowledge manager performs its structuring. Thus, knowledge can be persisted as unstructured knowledge or structured knowledge.

The fundamental objective of any knowledge management process is the application of existing knowledge and to achieve this, maximize the knowledge that is possessed. For this reason, activities related to obtaining new knowledge are very important. As presented in this work, the sources of knowledge can be both internal sources and external sources and for this, various activities must be carried out. Identification is one of the fundamental activities and includes: determine the key processes, determine existing knowledge and its location, determine the knowledge needed, and identifying knowledge sources and their networks. Once the sources are identified, it is possible to obtain knowledge from them. In the model presented, the knowledge gaining from external sources is called acquisition, and it can be carried out directly by the knowledge worker or by the knowledge manager, proposing knowledge surveillance activities. Obtaining knowledge from internal sources has been called retrieval from the repository perspective and a knowledge creation process is proposed through the repositioning and integration of present knowledge to achieve goals. This perspective of obtaining knowledge is presented in Fig. 4.

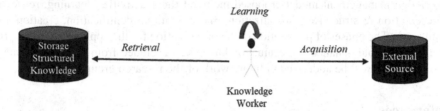

Fig. 1. Knowledge Management Model: The Individual Perspective

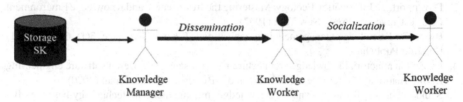

Fig. 2. Knowledge Management Model: the Team's Perspective

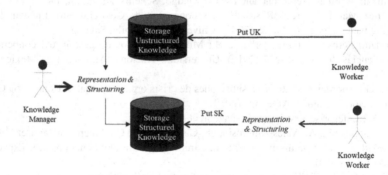

Fig. 3. Knowledge Management Model: Repositories Perspective

Fig. 4. Knowledge Management Model: Identification, Creation and Acquisition

11 Conclusions

Knowledge is an indispensable resource for organizations to perform their tasks successfully and innovate. Knowledge management is an integrated field of multiple disciplines that seek to exploit knowledge more efficiently. This paper analyzes activities in the knowledge management literature and presents a knowledge management model. The knowledge management model proposed included these activities: learning, retrieval, representation & structuring, socialization, dissemination, identification, creation and acquisition. The phases of preparation of the organization for the application of the proposed model, maintenance and evaluation have been excluded from the present paper; these activities will be addressed in future work of the research group.

References

1. Ackoff, R.: From data to wisdom. J. Appl. Syst. Anal. **16**, 3–9 (1989)
2. Davenport, T.: Information Ecology: Mastering the Information and Knowledge Environment. Oxford University Press, New York (1997)
3. Bhatt, G.: Knowledge management in organisations. J. Knowl. Manage. **5**(1), 68–75 (2001). Emerald Publishing
4. Li, Z.: On a factorial knowledge architecture for data science-powered software engineering. In: International Conference on Software and e-Business, Osaka, Japan (2020)
5. Saukkonen, J.: Towards dynamic knowledge management in technology-based SMEs. University of Jyväskylä, Finlandia (2020)
6. Wiig, K.: Knowledge Management Foundations: thinking about thinking - how people and organizations create, represent, and use knowledge, Schema, Arlington, TX (1993)
7. Martinez Marín, A., Ríos Rosas, F.: Los conceptos de Conocimiento, Epistemología y Paradigma. Cinta de Moebio **25** (2006). Universidad de Chile, Santiago
8. Avendaño Pérez, V., Flores Urbáez, M.: Modelos teóricos de gestión del conocimiento. Entreciencias **4**(10), 201–227 (2016). Universidad Nacional Autónoma de México, León (2016)
9. Gelaf, G.: Abordajes creativos en situaciones de crisis organizacionales, Contaduría General de la Nación, Tucumán, Argentina (2010)
10. Wiig, K.: Enterprise Knowledge Management (2007)
11. Sánchez-Sánchez, A., Valés-Ambrosio, O., García-Lirios, C., Amemiya-Ramirez, M: Confiabilidad y validez de un instrumento que mide la gestión del conocimiento. Espacios en blanco **30**(1) (2020)
12. IEEE Std 610.12, IEEE Standard Glossary of Software Engineering Terminology (1990)
13. Alhir, S.: Understanding the Model Driven Architecture. Methods & Tools. Fall (2003)
14. Straccia, L., Pollo-Cattaneo, M., Maulini, A.: Visões da Gestão do Conhecimento para a construção de um modelo integral, In: Proceeding in Congresso Brasileiro de Gestão do Conhecimento, São Paulo, Brasil, pp. 19–22 (2022)
15. Straccia, L., Maulini Buño, A., Ramacciotti, C., Pollo-Cattáneo, M.: Fases propuestas para el diseño y construcción de un modelo de Gestión del Conocimiento. In: Serna, E. (ed.) Desarrollo e Innovación en Ingeniería, Instituto Antioqueño de Investigación, Medellín (2021)
16. Maulini, A., Straccia, L., Pollo-Cattaneo, M.: Una aproximación a un modelo de gestión de conocimiento aplicable a las pequeñas y medianas fábricas de software. In: Serna, E. (ed.) Desarrollo e Innovación en Ingeniería, Instituto Antioqueño de Investigación (2018)

17. Maulini, A., Straccia, L., Pollo-Cattaneo, M.F.: Un modelo de gestión de conocimiento aplicable a las pequeñas y medianas fábricas de software. In: Serna, E. (ed.) Desarrollo e Innovación en Ingeniería, Instituto Antioqueño de Investigación, Medellín (2019)
18. Gomez Gutierrez, Y.: Propuesta de un modelo de gestión del conocimiento para la biblioteca de la Universidad Externado de Colombia, Área de Servicios. Universidad Externado de Colombia, Bogotá (2019)
19. Brotons Martinez, M.: La gestión del conocimiento para la innovación en hoteles: la influencia de las prácticas de Recursos Humanos. Universidad de Alicante (2021)
20. Nonaka, I., Takeuchi, H.: The Knowledge-Creating Company: How Japanese Companies Create the Dynamics of Innovation. Oxford University Press, Oxford (1995)
21. Alavi, M., Leidner, D.: Knowledge management and knowledge management systems: conceptual foundations and research issues. MIS Q. **25**, 107–136 (2001)
22. Campos, R., Teixeira, M., Carmo, L., de Assis, L.: Gestão do conhecimento: um estudo em franquias de escolas de idiomas. E&GEconomia e Gestão **18** (2018). Belo Horizonte
23. Cruz-Rodriguez, J., Bautista-Rodriguez, S.: Modelo de Gestión del Conocimiento Ambiental en la Agroindustria. Revista Lasallista de Investigación **18**(1) (2021). Caldas
24. Calvanti, G., Brito, L., Castro, A., Brunni Cartaxo de, S., Arthur, W.: Knowledge management in public administration of education, science and technology in Northeast Brazil. Revista de Gestão e Avaliação Educacional **9**(18) (2021). Santa María
25. Velez Evans, M.I.: Aprender significa "perfeccionarse siguiendo un camino": el proceso de toma de decisiones estratégicas y el aprendizaje organizacional. Semestre Económico **10**(19) (2007). Medellín
26. Senge, P.: La quinta disciplina: cómo impulsar el aprendizaje en la organización inteligente. Granica, Barcelona (1992)
27. Gonzalez Vargas, A.: Aprendizaje organizacional sistémico: una mirada al impacto del talento humano en la productividad organizacional. Universidad de la Sabana, Chia (2005)
28. Rivero Suarez, A.: Modelo de gestión del conocimiento basado en el enfoque ágil para mejorar la producción en las empresas. Universidad Federico Villarreal, Lima (2019)
29. Cangelosi, V., Dill, W.: Organizational learning: observations toward a theory. Adm. Sci. Q. **10**(2), 175–203 (1965)
30. Nonaka, I., Ryoko, T., Akiya, N.: A firm as knowledge-creating entity: a new perspective on the theory of the firm. Ind. Corp. Change **9**(1) (2000)
31. Wyszengrad, M.: ¿Cómo entender el concepto internalización? Reconstruyendo el debate en la psicología histórico-cultural. In: XIII Congreso Internacional de Investigación y Práctica Profesional en Psicología, Universidad de Buenos Aires, Buenos Aires (2021)
32. Feldman, R.: Psicología: con aplicaciones en países de habla hispana. 6ta Edición, Mc-Graw Hill, México (2005)
33. Ecured, Aprendizaje. Cuba. Accedido el 10 de marzo de 2023
34. Santana, M.: La enseñanza de las matemáticas y las NTIC. Una estrategia de formación permanente, Universidad Rovira i Virgili (2007)
35. Dabic, M., Vlacic, E., Ramanathan, U., Egri, C.: Evolving absorptive capacity. IEEE Trans. Eng. Manage. **67**(3), 783–793 (2020)
36. Zuluaga, J.: El punto de vista de Piaget: Una fundamentación a nuestro quehacer pedagógico. Universidad Autónoma de Manizales, Facultad de Odontología
37. Abdullah Al Saifi, S.: Toward a theoretical model of learning organization and knowledge management processes. Int. J. Knowl. Manage. **15**(2), 55–80 (2019)
38. Scheuermann, A.: Theory-based knowledge acquisition for ontology development. Unpublished doctoral dissertation, University of Hohenheim, Stuttgart, Germany (2016)
39. Thuy Pham, N., Swierczek, F.: Facilitators of organisational learning in design. Learn. Organ. **13**(2), 186–201 (2006)

40. Silamut, A., Petsangsri, S.: Self-directed learning with knowledge management model to enhance digital literacy abilities. Educ. Inf. Technol. **25**(6), 4797–4815 (2020)
41. Tang, X.: Research on higher education human resource departments knowledge management of teachers in the era of Big Data. In: International Conference on Big Data and Informatization Education (2020)
42. Andrade Barros Ouriques, R., Wnuk, K., Gorschek, T., Berntsson-Svensson, R.: Knowledge management strategies and processes in agile software development. Int. J. Softw. Eng. Knowl. Eng. **29**(3) (2019)
43. Passos, D.: Cultura organizacional, gestão do conhecimento, satisfação e desempenho no trabalho: um estudo empírico com técnicos administrativos no setor educacional público do Brasil, Politécnico do Porto (2021)
44. Lu, W., Harncharnchai, A., Saeheaw, T.: Social media strategy for Batik SMEs using customer knowledge management. In: Joint International Conference on Digital Arts, Media and Technology (2021)
45. Aldana Lamprea, D.: Modelo de gestión del conocimiento para la integración al sistema de licenciamiento urbanístico de la curaduría urbana número tres de Bogotá. Universidad EAN, Bogotá (2019)
46. Ling, C., Noor, N., Mohd, F.: Knowledge representation model for crime analysis. Procedia Comput. Sci. **116**, 484–491 (2017)
47. Portmann, E., Kaltenrieder, P., Pedrycz, W.: Knowledge representation through graphs, Procedia Comput. Sci. **62**, 245–248 (2015)
48. Gartner Group, The Gartner Glossary of Information Technology Acronyms and Terms, Technical report, Gartner Group (2004)
49. Al-Maawali, Z., Saqib, M.: Knowledge management: a case study of Ceed Oman company, issues and solutions. In: 17th International Conference on ICT and Knowledge Engineering (2019)
50. Tounkara. T.: A framework to analyze knowledge management system adoption through the lens of organizational culture. Artif. Intell. Eng. Des. Anal. Manuf. **33**(2), 226–237 (2019)
51. Voitenko, O., Achkasov, I., Timinsky, A.: Competence-based knowledge management in project oriented organisations in bi-adaptive context. In: IEEE 14th International Conference on Computer Sciences and Information Technologies, vol. 3, pp. 111–115 (2019)
52. Kruesi, L., Burstein, F., Tanner, K.: A knowledge management system framework for an open biomedical repository. J. Knowl. Manage. **24**(10) (2020)
53. Pastrana Cruz, A.: Proyecto piloto para la implementación del sistema de gestión del conocimiento para el área de Help Desk. Universidad EAN, Bogotá (2020)
54. Ugalde Vasquez, A.: El papel de los sistemas de contabilidad y control de gestión, los equipos de alta dirección y la gestión del conocimiento en la efectividad empresarial, Universidad de Sevilla (2021)
55. Dabic, M., Kiessling, T.: The performance implications of knowledge management and strategic alignment of MNC subsidiaries. J. Knowl. Manage. **23**(8), 1477–1501 (2019)
56. Justiniano Advincula, L.: Comportamiento de equipos de trabajo y gestión del conocimiento en las oficinas dependientes del vicerrectorado académico de la Universidad Nacional Agraria de la Selva. Universidad Nacional de la Selva, Tingo María, Perú (2020)
57. Hernandez Prieto, E., Sanchez Reyes, Y.: Diseño de un modelo de gestión del conocimiento para el Departamento de Comunicaciones del Ejército Nacional de Colombia, Universidad EAN (2021)
58. Alvares, L., et al.: Interfaces disciplinares selecionadas da gestão do conhecimento: características, contribuições e reflexões. Questão **26**(2), 132–160 (2020)
59. Galindo Acevedo, L., Alvarez Pacheco, E.: Propuesta de un modelo de gestión del conocimiento enfocado en el proceso del grupo de servicios administrativos del Ministerio de Minas y Energía. Universidad Externado de Colombia, Bogotá (2019)

60. Akbar Haddadi Harandi, A., Bokharaei Nia, M., Valmohammadi, C.: The impact of social technologies on knowledge management processes. Kybernetes **48**(8) (2019)
61. Schuh, G., Kelzenberg, C., de Lange, J., Boshof, J.: Development and application of a systematic knowledge management process model for the tooling industry. In: Proceedings 3rd International Conference on Information System and Data Mining (2019)
62. Mehrez, A., Aladel, L.: Modelling Sustainability, Cloud computing and knowledge transmission in education in developing countries. In: Proceedings 3rd International Conference on Networking, Information Systems & Security, pp. 1–9 (2020)
63. Sinisterra-Núñez, A., Osorio-Bayter, L., Gabalán-Coello, J., Vásquez-Rizo, F.: Ruta de aprendizaje de gestión del conocimiento en fundaciones empresariales. In: Económicas CUC, Bogotá (2019)
64. Reguera, M.L.: Centros de Servicios Compartidos de segunda generación: Aporte a la cadena global de valor de la firma, Universidad Nacional de Mar del Plata (2020)
65. Shibata, T., Takeuchi, H.: Japan Moving Toward a More Advanced Knowledge Economy: Advanced Knowledge-Creating Companies. The World Bank, Washington DC (2006)
66. INEE: La importancia de comunicar, socializar y movilizar. Instituto Nacional para la Evaluación de la Educación, INEE, México (2019)
67. Simkin, H., Becerra, G.: El proceso de socialización. Apuntes para su exploración en el campo psicosocial. Ciencia, Docencia y Tecnología **24**(47), 119–142 (2013). Universidad Nacional de Entre Ríos, Concepción del Uruguay
68. Martins, D., Pelógia, I., Moro Cabero, M.: Proposição de um modelo de gestão do conhecimento voltado às características da memória organizacional. Encontros Bibli **25**, 1–21 (2020). Universidade Federal de Santa Catarina, Brasil
69. Bem, R., Rossi, T.: Information and Communication Technology tools to support the knowledge management process. In: Revista Digital de Biblioteconomía e Ciencia da Informação, 19, Campinas, San Pablo (2021)
70. Ramirez Macías, A., Romo Moncayo, E.: Propuesta de un modelo de gestión del conocimiento para el área de gestión documental de la Bolsa de Valores de Colombia, Universidad Externado de Colombia, Bogotá (2019)
71. Zamora Valencia, C.: Gestión del conocimiento en la capacitación empresarial: una visión desde el rol del consultor, Universidad Externado de Colombia (2019)
72. Latifa Oufkir, I.: Performance measurement for knowledge management project: model development and empirical validation. J. Knowl. Manage. **23**(7), 1403–1428 (2019)
73. Figueroa Ocoro, L.: La gestión del conocimiento, una herramienta para la innovación en el proceso de la gestión académica de la Institución Educativa Diocesana Jesús Adolescente Del Distrito De Buenaventura. Universidad ICESI, Santiago de Cali (2019)
74. Satya, D., Sastramihardja, H.: University knowledge management model. In: 7th International Conference on Advance Informatics: Concepts, Theory and Applications, pp. 1–6 (2020)
75. Straccia, L.: La importancia de socializar el conocimiento en las organizaciones. La Gran Capital (2022)
76. Shehabat, I.: The Role of Knowledge Management in Organizational Performance and Gaining Sustainable Competitive Advantage (2020)
77. Raudeliuniene, J., Albats, E., Kordab, M.: Impact of information technologies and social networks on knowledge management processes in Middle Eastern audit and consulting companies. J. Knowl. Manage. **25**(4), 871–898 (2021)
78. Melo, C.: A gestão do conhecimento e o processo de inovação de medicamento. Fundação Oswaldo Cruz (2019)
79. Probst, G., Raub, S., Romhardt, K: Administre el conocimiento. Pearson, México (2001)
80. Farooq Sahibzada, U., Cai, J., Fawad Latif, K., Farooq Sahibzada, H.: Fueling knowledge management processes in Chinese higher education institutes. J. Enterprise Inf. Manage. **33**, 1395–1417 (2020). Emerald Publishing

81. Shahzad, M., Qu, Y., Ullah Zafar, A., Ur Rehman, S., Islam, T.: Exploring the influence of knowledge management process on corporate sustainable performance through green innovation. J. Knowl. Manage. **24**(9) (2020). Emerald Publishing

82. Attia, A., Salama, I.: Knowledge management capability and supply chain management practices in the Saudi food industry. Bus. Process Manage. **24**(2), 459–477 (2018)

83. Zaintek: Guía de Vigilancia Tecnológica: Sistema de información estratégica en las pymes, Diputación Foral de Bizkaia (2003)

84. Asociación Española de Normalización y Certificación, AENOR (2014)

85. Parisi, D.: https://www.linkedin.com/posts/darioparisi78_designthinking-innovaci%C3% B3n-talento-activity-6805197863736356864-01dE/. Accessed 15 Mar 2023

86. Arango Moreno, S.: Propuesta de estrategias técnicas para desarrollar procesos operacionales de gestión del conocimiento. Universidad EAFIT, Medellín (2016)

eXplainable Artificial Intelligence - A Study of Sentiments About Vaccination in Brazil

Luiz Felipe de Camargo(✉), Juliana da Costa Feitosa, Eloísa Bonatti,
Giovana Ballminut Simioni, and José Remo Ferreira Brega

Universidade Estadual Paulista "Júlio de Mesquita Filho", Bauru, SP, Brazil
{luiz.felipe,juliana.feitosa,eloisa.bonatti,giovanna.simioni,
remo.brega}@unesp.br

Abstract. Sentiment analysis in social networks is a focus in several studies on Machine Learning, this happens because the scope and speed with which opinions and emotions about events, controversial issues and products and services are treated on the Internet make it attractive to analyze this medium to obtain relevant information and of interest. Based on this context, this paper presents a sentiment analysis on social networks, focusing on Twitter, about the COVID-19 vaccination campaign in Brazil, using Machine Learning techniques, more specifically, logistic regression, and subsequently the eXplainable Artificial Intelligence (XAI) with the methods LIME, SHAP and Eli5 to interpret the model output. Although there are several applications in the field of sentiment analysis, this study focuses on using real Twitter data, extracted according to the desired context, for five months, processing, analyzing and preparing them for training, and on the explainability of the results obtained during the analysis. The results obtained show that the sample population was mostly in favor of vaccination for issues such as health and the collective good of the population, while those who were against wondered about compulsion and the power of freedom of choice, and expressed fear of being part of an experiment, given the design time of vaccine development.

Keywords: explicable artificial intelligence · explainability · sentiment analysis · machine learning · vaccination · COVID-19

1 Introduction

With the immense popularization of AI, concerns about the privacy of user data, the compromise of characteristic traits of human subjectivity, and the ethics behind algorithms with discriminatory biases have gained momentum. Furthermore, there are many controversies about how AI may affect democracy and political pluralism, through various sources of fake news, ideological radicalization, or even mass surveillance [1].

O. Gervasi et al. (Eds.): ICCSA 2023, LNCS 13956, pp. 617–634, 2023.
https://doi.org/10.1007/978-3-031-36805-9_40

The concerns that permeate this topic are intensified and based on the fact that the inner workings of Machine Learning algorithms are a complete mystery to average technology users, and often even to advanced users and the developers themselves [2].

In the context of this study, social network algorithms can facilitate the dissemination of fake news and through the recommendation algorithm, these news and opinions are boosted, affecting the choices of population about important facts, such as the Covid-19 vaccination. The use of eXplainable Artificial Intelligence (XAI) grants the possibility to explain in an accessible way to non-technical users, Machine Learning models and find what are the main patterns that the model detects in the trained data, mainly with the help of local models that are applied to individual examples, analyzing specific situations, as for example, the posts on Twitter regarding the Covid-19 vaccination in Brazil.

This paper presents a Machine Learning training model and the subsequent application of interpretive methods on the model outputs, aiming to analyze the sentiment of the Brazilian population regarding vaccination and what are the posting patterns of users who are in favor and against immunization, in an attempt to find patterns and understand the results of the predictions.

2   Existing Solutions

The authors [11] conducted a study of data taken from Twitter during the 2014 World Cup period, in order to analyze the sentiment of population towards the Brazilian team and the event held in the country. The extraction of the tweets was done through the API provided by the platform itself and there was a separation in two parts of neutral or positive words, and the other part of negative words in relation to the cup. After a series of treatments of the base, the data classification used the AI technique, Naive Bayes classification, which learned to predict whether a tweet was positive or negative based on the words that were written, from a training with the labeled base, reaching an accuracy of 73%, representing a good accuracy.

The study by [7] sought to implement an explainable artificial intelligence method to make the process behind decisions well understood. The work, uses some popular Machine Learning algorithms, such as logistic regression, random forest, extra-trees, and others, to measure the influence of various factors in soccer match results, and through the SHAP interpretation technique answers the proposed question that is "How to identify the main most significant factors behind a victory, draw or defeat of a team?", to reach the goal the researcher used metrics and factors that had numerical value and implemented some predictive models, through methods that worked with qualitative variables allowing the evaluation of the data. The result was the finding of patterns in the analysis of the predictive models, related to goal opportunities, total passes, pass corrections, ball possession, and ball recovery time, as proposed in the goal. Some of the problems encountered were the low information in a very new field of research, and a lack of validation of the results found through interpretation.

3 Development

3.1 Data Extraction

The extraction of the data was the first step to continue the others, in which the Twitter API was used. First it was necessary to create an account, activate the developer mode and submit a series of answers to evaluate the possibility of making the tokens available. With the tokens available, through Jupyter Notebook, and using Python, the tweepy library was imported, which as defined on the documentation site is an easy-to-use Python library to access the Twitter API. Then code was used to authenticate the four access keys needed to start accessing, through the application and the library, the first tweets on the timeline, i.e. the first public posts on the home page. After that, the available JSON format of any tweet was analyzed, and it was then possible to create an empty dictionary in Python that could store all the attributes of each tweet that would be added to the dataset.

After these steps, some parameters were assigned to work with the search method of the Application Programming Interface, until reaching the number of two thousand tweets per sample, from the months of August, September, October, November, and December 2021. The extractions were always made at the beginning of each month, between the 8th and 12th. The search method worked with a query of the following Portuguese words: vacina (en: vaccine), vacinação (en: vaccination), imunização (en: immunization), Janssen, Johnson, Pfizer, Astrazeneca, Coronavac, Sputnik V, Covaxin, Butantan, vacinasim (en: vaccineyes), vacinanão (en: vaccineno), vacinei (en: vaccinated) e vacinar (en: vaccinate), i.e., all words in the same semantic field as vaccine plus the name of the vaccines and some of their manufacturers. Furthermore, retweets were filtered, to prevent the same tweet from being stored more than once. It was also added as a parameter to search only information with the language in Portuguese and not limited to 140 characters, but the 280 currently available.

3.2 Data Processing

After extracting the data on Twitter, with the use of filters by words of interest, they were saved in .csv (Comma Separated Value) format, that is, a text type file with table structured formatting. In this type of file, the data are organized by rows and columns, where each column represents a factor and each row represents an example of the factor. Figure 1 illustrates this format with the project data set. Each row in this file corresponds to a tweet extracted from Twitter, and each column represents each of the attributes that this data has.

Choice of Attributes. The use of the Twitter API brings by default a diversity of data, but not all of them were used in this experiment. In the attribute selection stage, each column of the table was analyzed and those that would bring little value to the core of this project were discarded. After a thorough

created_at,id,id_str,full_text,truncated,entities,source,in_reply_to_status_id,in_reply_to_status_id_str,in_reply_to_user_id,in_reply_to_user_id_str,in_reply_to_screen_name,user,geo,coordinates
,place,contributors,is_quote_status,retweet_count,favorite_count,favorited,retweeted,possibly_sensitive,possibly_sensitive_appealable,lang
Fri Nov 12 19:01:34 +0000 2021,1459234934686732289,1459234934686732289,"@TovendolRJ Precisei submeter meu filho de 15 anos a essa vacina.
Exigência internacional de viagem.

Ou seja, fui obrigado a vacinar ele.",False,"{'hashtags': [], 'symbols': [], 'user_mentions': [{'screen_name': 'TovendolRJ', 'name': 'TovendolRJ', 'id': 319609049, 'id_str': '319609049', 'indices'
: [0, 11]}], 'urls': []}","<a href=""http://twitter.com/download/android"" rel=""nofollow"">Twitter for Android</a>",1,459231737477795880e18,1459231737477795844,319609049.0,319609049,TovendolRJ
,"{'id': 233388371, 'id_str': '233388371', 'name': 'Pedro Malta', 'screen_name': 'Pedro@Malta', 'location': 'Rio de Janeiro, Brasil', 'description': 'Ora et labora.\n\nBrasileiro, Carioca e
Flamenguista.', 'url': None, 'entities': {'description': {'urls': [{}]}, 'protected': False, 'followers_count': 13431, 'friends_count': 11252, 'listed_count': 2, 'created_at': 'Mon Jan 03 03:05:27
+0000 2011', 'favourites_count': 69557, 'utc_offset': None, 'time_zone': None, 'geo_enabled': True, 'verified': False, 'statuses_count': 24069, 'lang': None, 'contributors_enabled': False,
'is_translator': False, 'is_translation_enabled': False, 'profile_background_color': 'C0DEED', 'profile_background_image_url': 'http://abs.twimg.com/images/themes/theme1/bg.png',
'profile_background_image_url_https': 'https://abs.twimg.com/images/themes/theme1/bg.png', 'profile_background_tile': False, 'profile_image_url': 'http://pbs.twimg.com/profile_images
/1434776058927194117/YKy87zEa_normal.jpg', 'profile_image_url_https': 'https://pbs.twimg.com/profile_images/1434776058927194117/YKy87zEa_normal.jpg', 'profile_banner_url': 'https://pbs.twimg.com
/profile_banners/233388371/1626444689', 'profile_link_color': '1DA1F2', 'profile_sidebar_border_color': 'C0DEED', 'profile_sidebar_fill_color': 'DDEEF6', 'profile_text_color': '333333',
'profile_use_background_image': True, 'has_extended_profile': True, 'default_profile': True, 'default_profile_image': False, 'following': False, 'follow_request_sent': False, 'notifications':
False, 'translator_type': 'none', 'withheld_in_countries': []}",,,False,0,0,False,False,,,pt
Fri Nov 12 18:56:46 +0000 2021,1459233729143095382,1459233729143095382,"Que nota?
Vacinar pra não pegar covid
Pera: a vacina não impede o contágio, eh pra n ter sintomas
Pera _ eh pra não morrer
Pera_
Vacinas salvam vidas 🙄
Bobinho, https://t.co/dxZBVfbH5I",False,"{'hashtags': [], 'symbols': [], 'user_mentions': [], 'urls': [], 'media': [{'id': 1459233692858126340, 'id_str': '1459233692858126340', 'indices': [165,
188], 'media_url': 'http://pbs.twimg.com/ext_tw_video_thumb/1459233692858126340/pu/img/UOwSkfyojRDaQjIT.jpg', 'media_url_https': 'https://pbs.twimg.com/ext_tw_video_thumb/1459233692858126340/pu
/img/UOwSkfyojRDaQjIT.jpg', 'url': 'https://t.co/dxZBVfbH5I', 'display_url': 'pic.twitter.com/dxZBVfbH5I', 'expanded_url': 'https://twitter.com/lufiqueiredo7/status/1459233729143095382/video/1',

Fig. 1. Example of data in .csv format.

evaluation, it was decided that the attributes of the table that would remain for labeling and analysis would be:

- **created_at**: field where the date of the tweet creation is located;
- **full_text**: the text of the tweet in its entirety with the mentions, links, and emojis;
- **source**: field with the link that directs to the tweet and shows on what type of device the text was posted;
- **user**: field where there are all kinds of data that the user may have, from the saved name, network alias, bio description, to how many users follow him and profile picture of the profile that triggered the tweet. This column was saved specifically so that in the data structuring process, it was possible to retrieve the information of user location;
- **retweet_count**: the number of times the text in question has been shared by people other than the author himself; and
- **favorite_count**: number of times the text was liked by other users;

Data Structuring. The data extracted from Twitter has a characteristic of semi-structured data. That is, data is stored in the form of a structured table, but it has some internal characteristics that differ from the standardization of data from other attributes. The "user" column, unlike the others, does not bring direct text data. It brings a set of data in an attribute and value format separated by a comma, in Fig. 2 the structure can be observed.

Analyzing each of the information that the "user" column offers, you can see that some of it is already present in other columns and others are almost always empty. Therefore, the decision was made that of all the information available within this column, the only one to be used would be the "location" one. The location information of the user who wrote the tweet helped to know the nature of the data. Some hypotheses are created when the subject of vaccination in Brazil is mentioned, and many of them are linked to politics and, consequently, to voting areas and political support and its location around the country. The idea in saving this information was to verify if there is any pattern in the distribution of positive and negative texts about immunization.

In [22]: dados_semiestruturados.user[1]

Out[22]: "{'id': 1076097405836279808, 'id_str': '1076097405836279808', 'name': 'nomedesanto', 'screen_name': 'davisaantos', '1
ocation': 'sp • br', 'description': 'já peço desculpas pela bagunça', 'url': 'https://t.co/Ki5OtmSbQT', 'entities':
{'url': {'urls': [{'url': 'https://t.co/Ki5OtmSbQT', 'expanded_url': 'http://www.instagram.com/davisaantos', 'display
_url': 'instagram.com/davisaantos', 'indices': [0, 23]}]}, 'description': {'urls': []}}, 'protected': False, 'followe
rs_count': 155, 'friends_count': 302, 'listed_count': 0, 'created_at': 'Fri Dec 21 12:49:49 +0000 2018', 'favourites_
count': 33494, 'utc_offset': None, 'time_zone': None, 'geo_enabled': True, 'verified': False, 'statuses_count': 1132
6, 'lang': None, 'contributors_enabled': False, 'is_translator': False, 'is_translation_enabled': False, 'profile_bac
kground_color': '000000', 'profile_background_image_url': 'http://abs.twimg.com/images/themes/theme1/bg.png', 'profil
e_background_image_url_https': 'https://abs.twimg.com/images/themes/theme1/bg.png', 'profile_background_tile': False,
'profile_image_url': 'http://pbs.twimg.com/profile_images/1433634200230498305/6reMBdDq_normal.jpg', 'profile_image_ur
l_https': 'https://pbs.twimg.com/profile_images/1433634200230498305/6reMBdDq_normal.jpg', 'profile_banner_url': 'http
s://pbs.twimg.com/profile_banners/1076097405836279808/1627950860', 'profile_link_color': '000000', 'profile_sidebar_b
order_color': '000000', 'profile_sidebar_fill_color': '000000', 'profile_text_color': '000000', 'profile_use_backgrou
nd_image': False, 'has_extended_profile': True, 'default_profile': False, 'default_profile_image': False, 'followin
g': False, 'follow_request_sent': False, 'notifications': False, 'translator_type': 'none', 'withheld_in_countries':
[]}"

Fig. 2. Viewing the first row of the "user" column in the data frame.

Studying a little bit about the location field on Twitter, it can be observed that it is a non-mandatory open input. Because it is an open field, structuring an analysis of this attribute becomes a little more complex because there is the possibility of people writing the same location in different ways and, in addition, not all users fill out the complete information with the city/state formatting, some of them put only the state or only the city, or put a name like "São Paulo", making it impossible to identify whether it was the city or the state. Because of the difficulty of dealing with an open field, a strategy was established: separate only by state, eliminate the classification by cities, and exclude the information of those who filled in information that was not consistent with what was requested in the field and put some catchphrase that did not actually correspond to the location. This standardization happened in all cases where there was a correct filling in of an existing location in Brazil. By matching the 26 Brazilian states plus the Federal District, the "user" column in the table was replaced by a column labeled "location" and the respective states of the tweets that filled in this field.

Characteristics of the Preprocessed Table. The data extracted from Twitter went through all the synthetic processing described above and in the end a fully structured data frame was created that served as the basis for labeling the data and generating discoveries and insights about them. These attributes were used in the data visualizations and also in labeling the tweets. The final data frame looks like Fig. 3.

Data Labeling. A new column called "vaccine" was included and, line by line, the texts in the "full_text" column were analyzed and classified as either favorable or against the vaccination campaign against COVID-19 in the country. The tweets that were judged favorable were labeled "accept" and those against "reject". There was also a third class of tweets, those that were discarded from the sample for being off-topic about the vaccination. The criteria for the classification of the tweets in favor of and against the COVID-19 vaccination in Brazil followed the very guidelines posted on the official campaign website, the slogan "Vaccine for all is our priority" [9] was the statement that guided the rules for the labeling. Thus, all tweets that in some way cited the benefits of vaccination,

created_at	full_text	source	location	retweet_count	favorite_count
9/9/2021	A Prefeitura de M:	Sem informação	Alagoas	0	0
9/9/2021	Mais vacinas para	Twitter for iPhone	Alagoas	1	12
9/8/2021	@prefeiturabelem	Twitter for iPhone	Alagoas	0	0
9/8/2021	@EdmilsonPSOL	Twitter for iPhone	Alagoas	0	0
9/8/2021	⚠ #VacinaçãoCo	Twitter for iPhone	Alagoas	0	1
9/8/2021	Pessoal, os adoles	Twitter for iPhone	Alagoas	0	0
9/8/2021	@jdoriajr Vc deve	Twitter for iPhone	Alagoas	0	0
9/9/2021	@Pedrox Engraça(	Twitter Web App	Alagoas	0	5
9/8/2021	Ananindeua vai va	Twitter Web App	Alagoas	0	0

Fig. 3. Final data frame with the structured data.

or simply reported that they were going to get vaccinated, were classified as positive.

There were also tweets that were probably written in a tone of irony, that is, they used a figure of speech to say the opposite of what they wanted to express, but, because only the context of the tweet was used in the training, we had to classify even those that were probably ironic, as if they were literally what the user wanted to say.

The tweets that were classified as contrary to vaccination are those that preach the opposite of the statement "Vaccine for all is our priority" [9], that is, all those that somehow posted against vaccination for 100% of the Brazilian population.

It is also worth noting that despite making use of the interest word filter in the API to bring only data from the thematic axis, there were cases in which, despite the tweet presenting the word of interest it did not necessarily deal with the vaccination campaign in Brazil and this made it necessary to discard it from the sample.

Vaccination topics were always among the most commented on Twitter and because the microblog provides users with a Trend Topics page highlighting these most popular topics, many people and even brands misused both the vaccination hashtags and vaccination keywords to highlight their often off-topic content. All of these examples were removed from the sample for follow-up training.

Sample Data. The visualization of the sample data is very important to guide the understanding of the results after the training and the application of the explainability techniques. The original sample of ten thousand extracted tweets, divided into classes is represented in Fig. 4.

For data training and descriptive analysis, the only tweets that will be used are those that were classified as "accept" and "reject". It was important to observe the distribution per month of the labels among the three possible labels: "accept", "reject" and "ignore".

One notable feature to relate to the labels is which device was used to publish the rated text. This data is taken from the "source" field, and it is interesting to note that the massive majority of them are made by mobile devices and that

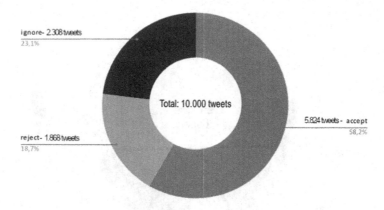

Fig. 4. Distribution of labeling.

almost 50% of the sample is made by Android devices. The graph in Fig. 5 shows this percentage distribution of devices within the sample of valid tweets.

Other information is taken from the "location" column, that is, the location of the user who posted the tweet on the network. Of the seven thousand six hundred and ninety-two valid tweets in the sample, only three thousand two hundred and eighty-nine of them had valid information, susceptible to structuring, to present value to location of the user. In Fig. 6, there is a graphical representation of the percentage of each of the 26 Brazilian states in the number of tweets, which had location filled in the sample.

Another form of representation, done by percentages, was to show the label representations in each state, using the political map of the country, as seen in Fig. 7. From these graphs, it is important to highlight three pieces of information: All Brazilian states had a higher number of texts in favor of the vaccination campaign than those against it.

Analyzing the data, the favorable tweets accounted for 63.12% of the sum of all retweets in the sample and the remaining 38.88%, were on the contrary tweets. Regarding favorites, 78.39% of the sum of all favorites in the sample were on positive tweets to the campaign and 21.61% were on opposing tweets. Analyzing the data and the graphical representations, one can notice that tweets that are in agreement with the vaccination campaign in Brazil were much more liked and shared than those that were against the campaign.

3.3   Model Training

For this experiment the Python language was used with the libraries pandas, seaborn, matploid and NumPy for the data manipulation steps and the scikit-learn library for training. Jupyter Notebooks were used as the training environment. Data import was done via the "read.csv" method of the pandas library. The feasible labeled data from all months was concatenated by means of the

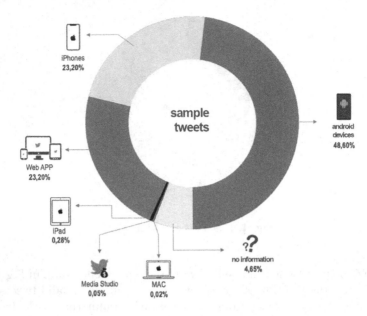

Fig. 5. Distribution of devices used to tweet about vaccination in the sample.

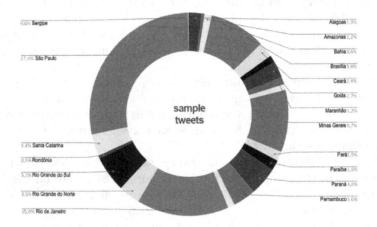

Fig. 6. Representativeness of each state in the number of tweets in the sample.

"concat" method into a single data frame with the name "data" to start the first preprocessing steps.

The training base has already undergone some modifications with the processes of attribute selection, data structuring and sample labeling. All these maneuvers have been described in detail in the previous topics. At this point, the processing will be focused on preparing the database for training itself and will be divided into two steps: normalization and text transformation. The normalization step is a set of rules that organizes the data to reduce redundancy between

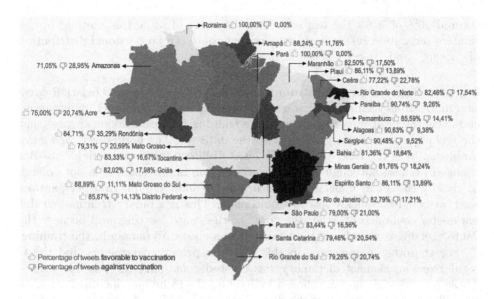

Fig. 7. Brazilian political map with label percentages by state.

them and increase completeness. For this purpose, the following resources were used:

1. Clean up the text using regular expressions to remove line breaks, mentions using the at sign character, and hyperlinks beginning with "https".
2. Using the Unidecode method: This method is used to make words uniform by removing accents from character strings.
3. Removal of stop words, these are those linking words that are present in the sentence to contextualize and link the words of interest.

A method, from scikit-learn, called TfidfVectorizer, was used to apply the bag-of-words technique and translate the text to numerical value. TF-IDF (Term Frequency - Inverse Document Frequency) is a numerical statistic that aims to indicate how important a word or token is for a document in a corpus [4]. About the parameters, "min_df " is used to remove terms that appear infrequently, in this case, if it is equal to 2, the vectorizer will ignore terms that appear in less than 2 tweets. The "max_df " is used to remove terms that appear very frequently in tweets, so in this case, if "max_df " is 0.9, the terms that appear in more than 90% of the tweets will also be ignored.

Test and Training Set. The train_test_split method from scikit-learn was used to split the test and training set in the present work. The method receives the texts (X) and the labels (y) after vectorization as parameters, and it is also necessary to define the size of the test set by the parameter test_size, which in this case was 0.2, i.e., 80% of the preprocessed sample data remained for the training set and 20% of it for the test set. The advantage of using this method over a random separation is that it guarantees that there is a proportional distribution of "accept" and "reject" labels on the subsets.

Logistic Regression Adjustment. For this study, the linear LogisticRegression model from scikit-learn was used. The definition of the model hyperparameters was the most important step in the training because it alone ensures that the technique used has a good fit with the data set. The best solver for binary problems, as is the case in this study, was liblinear. The class weight was not changed because, although there is concentration in one class, it is not enough to classify the set as unbalanced and in need of intervention. Another parameter that could be quickly set was multi_class. This is a binary training, so this parameter could accept either the "ovr" or the "auto" setting, and because the "auto" setting is already set by default, it was chosen to remain in the training.

For the other parameters, in this case the penalty parameters and the C regularizer, an element dictionary was created containing the possible values. These possible options were chosen by reading the technique documentation on the scikit-learn website. Once the dictionary was established, the GridSearchCV method was chosen, to make the combinations of each parameter and result in the best possible combo. The GridSearchCV method passes the parameters of this function and the parameter dictionary already defined. Next to the dictionary, the cross-validation technique is employed to help in the search for a more efficient generalization of the predictive models [6].

For penalty, the possibilities "l1", "l2" and "elasticnet" were set, and for C the possibilities "0.001", "0.001", "0.01", "0.1", "1", "10", "100", "1000", "10000" in the variable parametric_grid that served as the dictionary of possibilities. After running the method, it was concluded that the best parameters are C equal to "10" and penalty "l2". Once all the parameters were chosen, all that was needed was to apply the LogisticRegression method.

In summary, with $C = 10$, penalty $=$ "l2", solver $=$ "liblinear" and multi_class $=$ "auto" the classifier was trained and fitted to the data with the "fit(X_train, y_train)" snippet. Once this was done, the predictions were estimated and saved in "predLR" and thus, the model was trained with fit to the data. After finishing the training, we proceeded to the step of analyzing the metrics.

3.4   Training Metrics Analysis

Confusion Matrix. The confusion matrix method from scikit-learn was used to generate the confusion matrix in the present work. By default, for this method, the set of labels from the test set (y_test) and the regression predictor (predLR) are passed. The heatmap method from the seaborn library was also used to have a nicer visual representation, Fig. 8 shows the result.

As can be seen, there were 1104 true positive predictions, 202 predictions that were classified as positive but were false, 61 predictions that were classified as negative but were positive, and 172 predictions that were classified as negative and were.

```
cm = confusion_matrix(y_test, predLR)
sn.heatmap(cm, annot=True, fmt='d')
plt.xlabel('Predicted')
plt.ylabel('Truth')
```

Text(33.0, 0.5, 'Truth')

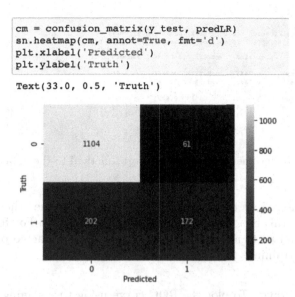

Fig. 8. Result in confusion matrix of job training.

Accuracy. Accuracy represents the total percentage of model hits, and the ratio is the sum of true positives (TP) and true negatives (TN) divided by the total. For the trained model, the accuracy was 82.91%. An interesting point to note is that this measure is especially useful and represents the reality in data sets with balanced classes, that is, with equivalent proportions of positive and negative classes to vaccination, which is not the case in this work.

In this training, the predominant class is the class of examples positive to vaccination. As can be seen in the Sample Data section, more than 75% of the sample is composed of the class of positive examples and only less than 25% of it is composed of negative examples. Precisely because of the unbalance of the classes of the model in question, it is necessary to evaluate it in other ways. Searching the literature, metrics such as precision, recall, and the F1-score measure (also called F1-measure or simply F1) came up, together they cover these imposed needs [10].

Precision, Recall and F-1 Score. To analyze these metrics in the training of this paper, the classification_report method from scikit-learn was used. This method takes as parameters the labels from the separate test set and the predictions using the trained model. It returns the precision, recall, F1-score and support, which is the total of positive and negative examples per class. In Fig. 9 you can see the application of the method and the results obtained.

As can be seen, on average, all three metrics performed well and this means that the data had a good fit with the training. The overall accuracy was 81.93% for a recall of 82.91% and an F1-score of 81.41%, excellent rates. Something to point out is the recall of the negative examples (contrary to vaccination) of

```
#print da precisão, recall e F1 por classe
print(classification_report(y_test, predLR, digits=4))
print("AUC: {:.4f}\n".format(roc_auc_score(y_test,y_prob[:,1],labels=clfLR.classes_)))
```

	precision	recall	f1-score	support
accept	0.8453	0.9476	0.8936	1165
reject	0.7382	0.4599	0.5667	374
accuracy			0.8291	1539
macro avg	0.7918	0.7038	0.7301	1539
weighted avg	0.8193	0.8291	0.8141	1539

AUC: 0.8479

Fig. 9. Applying the "classification_report" method to the data training.

the "reject" class. Since the training performed well for the other class and the overall average, this is not something to worry about now. For future work, an alternative would be to add more negative examples, extracted or synthetic, to the sample for training.

ROC/AOC Curve. To plot the ROC curve using the training in this paper, the roc_curve method from scikit-learn was used. The method receives the labels from the test set and the probabilities of the target category. The AUC index was obtained by running roc_auc_score, also from scikit-learn. Running these methods on the study data returned the graph in Fig. 10. As can be seen, the AUC of the training was 0.85, which is a good index by the defined standards.

Generalization Capability. In this experiment, the scikit-learn function cross_value_score was used to perform this process. In detail, the logistic regression training determined in the other steps (clfLR), the training sets X_train and y_train also used in the initial training, the cv that corresponds to the number of total splits and the scoring method used to gauge the accuracy of the initial set were passed as parameters.

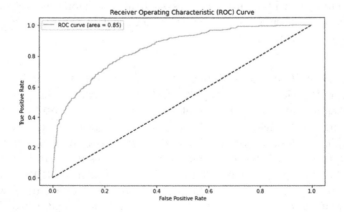

Fig. 10. Viewing the ROC/AUC curve with data from this training.

A differentiator for this step is the use of method StratifiedKFold of scikit-learn to determine the splitting of the cross-validation method splits. Setting a value of integer type for the cv index will cause the folds to be split directly, i.e. if there is 1000 data in the sample and cv is equal to 5, the first 200 will be part of the first fold, from 200 to 400 will be the second fold, and so on. This division can hinder training because there may be folds without the presence of both classes (tweets against and for vaccination), so StratifiedKFold was used. This method ensures that not only do you have both classes in all splits, but it also ensures that you have the same proportion of classes in all subsets.

In this context, analyzing the data, the accuracy range is between 82.86% and 86.82%, with an average accuracy of 84.84%. These data are well compatible with the score of 84.78% obtained in the initial training of the data, so the training has not been overfitted.

4   Applying Explainability Techniques

The first step in the interpretation was to use the word cloud method applied in three different sets, all with tweets within the sample of valid tweets, the first application was done in the general sample, with the data in favor and against the immunization, after that the data in favor and against were separated, and the method was applied in each one of them, generating the plots in Fig. 11.

It was possible to analyze that the three word clouds have highlighted the words "vaccine", "vaccinate" and "vaccination" that were among the words for which the extraction search was done, however, checking in more detail, the word cloud plot with favorable tweets highlighted "vacinas salvam vidas" (en: vaccines save lives), "feliz" (en: happy), "saúde" (en: health), "viva o sus" (en: long live sus) and even political messages against the president as "fora bolsonaro" (en: out bolsonaro). In the word cloud of the opposing tweets, "criança" (en: child), "experimental", "passaporte" (en: passport), "liberdade" (en: freedom) and "obrigatória" (en: obligatory) stood out, in addition to the political slant of "bolsonaro". Regarding the types of vaccines, in the cloud of positive tweets, it was possible to see the highlighting of "pfizer" and "butantan", while in the

Fig. 11. Word clouds of the tweets - general, pro-vaccination, and anti-vaccination.

cloud of negative tweets the highlighting was for "butantan" and "coronavac". The general word cloud, brought a mix of all these words.

In sequence, the local XAI method was used, i.e., that interprets predictions of an individual instance known as LIME, which receives as parameters the index of the text string to be explained, the regressor model, in this case the logistic regression model and the labels "accept" and "reject". Some of the results obtained, are exemplified in Fig. 12 for positives and Fig. 13 for negatives, thus showing in a clear visual way which variables impacted the value of the individual predictions [8].

Fig. 12. Example of the LIME method in a positive prediction.

The SHAP method was also used for global predictions. In the method, we passed as parameters the classifier that saved the regression training, the texts used in the training (X_train), and the name of the table column that saved the texts via the [5] "feature_names" method. The plot of the overall result can be seen in Fig. 14.

It can be seen that the main features that weighed for the positive ratings were, from most significant to least, "vacinasim" (en: vaccineyes), "vacinação" (en: vaccination), "Brasil" and "vacinar" (en: vaccinate), while the main features for the negative predictions were, from most significant to least, "experimental", "quer" (en: wants), "não" (en: no), "obrigar" (en: force) and "covid". It is important to note that since the model has many value words, the last line of the graph was left as an overlap of several features, and therefore looked confusing. Also, the word "want" was found in many tweets talking about "querer obrigar a vacinação" (en: want to force vaccination), so it had a high prominence.

Finally, the interpretation model, also global, eli5 was used, which receives as parameters the classifier that saved the regression training (clfLR) and the vectorization of the texts used in the training by means of "vectorizer.get_feature_names()" [3]. The result can be found in Fig. 15.

The graphical representation plotted was the ordered list from the most relevant to the least relevant features, with their respective Feature Importance value, for the "reject" data in green and the "accept" data in red.

Fig. 13. Example of the LIME method in a negative prediction.

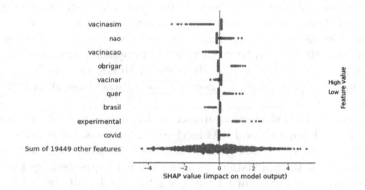

Fig. 14. Example of the global SHAP method.

y=reject top features

Weight?	Feature
+7.371	experimental
+7.294	nao vacinei
+6.701	obrigar
+6.048	obrigado vacinar
+5.321	obrigatoriedade
+5.165	vender
+4.679	vacina experimental
+4.625	impor
+4.625	pressao
+4.334	vacinar pq
+4.298	vacinar criancas
+4.176	nao
+4.120	filha
+4.008	eficaz
+3.954	serve
+3.920	nao impede
+3.902	pareceres
... 6992 more positive ...	
... 12014 more negative ...	
-4.045	vacinacao
-4.543	coletivo
-8.397	vacinasim

Fig. 15. Example of the eli5 method.

5   Conclusion

As can be observed through the sample data, in the period mentioned, more than 75% of valid tweets were in favor of vaccination, but almost 25% of them were against it, and this portion is quite significant given the kind of information disseminated. Vaccination for the entire population is something scientifically based and Brazil itself has had a very strong culture of vaccination coming from many years, so it is not natural that almost a quarter of the Brazilian population feels averse to the idea of being vaccinated.

Another important point to report regarding the tweets is the unequal distribution among the states. Almost 30% of the triggered texts came from the state of São Paulo, another 15% came from Rio de Janeiro, and another almost 10% came from Minas Gerais, that is, the other 23 states plus the Federal District divided among themselves the other 45% of the tweets. Still talking about spatial distribution of the analyzed texts, one can conclude that there was not a significantly unequal distribution between positive and favorable texts by region, because all of them, without exception, had more favorable opinions to vaccination, to the detriment of the opposing ones, and the percentage division hovered on average from 80% of positive texts to 20% of opposing texts, with a variation of 10% up and down, with a small decrease in Rondônia, which was the only state in which the percentage of favorable tweets was lower than 70%, staying at 64.71%.

Using the word cloud plotting divided in favorable, against and total word clouds, and the global and local XAI methods, it was concluded that the sample with positive posts were mostly based on issues related to the well-being and collective health of the population, besides showing happy feelings for receiving the vaccine doses and grateful for the good functioning of the Unified Health System that was responsible for the vaccination campaign. Still in this favorable context, one can find many tweets with a political slant against the current government, which at first refused to purchase the vaccines and several times discouraged their use.

In the sample of counter tweets, using these same techniques, what stood out the most was the fear of getting immunized with a vaccine that was developed very quickly, creating the wrong idea that they were experimental and that their effect was not proven yet, or that they would bring negative side effects in the long term. Another point that was emphasized was the fear and denial of vaccinating children and adolescents, who were seen as a group with a low risk of contamination in detriment of the possible side effects. Finally, one of the points that were present in almost all texts was the issue of mandatory, passport vaccination, and thus the supposed loss of freedom of choice not to be immunized and the pressure suffered by regulatory agencies and the general population.

Talking a bit about the differences found in the application of the XAI methods, one can observe that the local models brought more clarity about specific tweets, helping to understand in that context which words had more weight and helped in decision of the model. It is worth noting that in the negative models, the local XAI predictions (LIME) coincided with the global XAI predictions (eli5 and SHAP) because the arguments against vaccination always used the same principles, which were the compulsion, the time of the vaccine manufacturing and the side effects, thus making these features always have a very high value in the interpretability. While in the positive predictions, the features chosen by the local XAI were more informative, as the positive tweets had multiple arguments.

5.1 Future Work

For future work, it is possible to explore a more intensive approach at each step of the process. For the data extraction step, an idea would be to segment the extraction by filtering separately for positive and negative words to vaccination, with the idea of ensuring a greater homogeneity in the representativeness of the classes in the dataset. Still talking about the data, other pre-processing techniques can be explored such as the use of regular expressions to transform words with the same root. All these words have the same weight in the construction of a sentence, but because they are written differently, they end up being vectorized separately and understood as different words by the parser. The explainability methods also open room for improvement in future projects. In this work LIME, SHAP, and Eli5 were used, two global techniques and one local one. An idea would be to apply new methods to have other angles of vision regarding the understanding of the models tested, such as the use of the PDP (Partial Dependence Plot) that shows the marginal effect of one or more variables on the predictions of the model.

Acknowledgements. This study was financed in part by the Coordenação de Aperfeiçoamento de Pessoal de Nível Superior - Brasil (CAPES).

References

1. Alves, M.A.S., Andrade, O.M.d.: Da "caixa-preta" à "caixa de vidro": o uso da explainable artificial intelligence (xai) para reduzir a opacidade e enfrentar o enviesamento em modelos algorítmicos. Direito Público 18(100), January 2022. https://doi.org/10.11117/rdp.v18i100.5973. https://www.portaldeperiodicos.idp. edu.br/direitopublico/article/view/5973
2. Cortiz, D.: Inteligência artificial: conceitos fundamentais. Vainzof, Rony; Gutierrez, Adriei. Inteligência artificial: sociedade, economia e Estado. São Paulo: Thomson Reuters, pp. 45–60 (2021)
3. Korobov, M.: Overview - eli5 0.11.0 documentation (2017). https://eli5. readthedocs.io/en/latest/overview.html
4. Leskovec, J., Rajaraman, A., Ullman, J.D.: Mining of Massive Datasets, 2nd edn. Cambridge University Press, USA (2014)
5. Lundberg, S.M., Lee, S.I.: A unified approach to interpreting model predictions. In: Proceedings of the 31st International Conference on Neural Information Processing Systems, NIPS 2017, pp. 4768–4777. Curran Associates Inc., Red Hook, NY, USA (2017)
6. Malik, F.: What is grid search? February 2020. https://medium.com/ fintechexplained/what-is-grid-search-c01fe886ef0a
7. Marques, B.O.: Inteligência artificial explicável para análise de partidas de futebol. Master's thesis, Universidade Federal do Rio Grande do Sul (2020)

8. Ribeiro, M.T., Singh, S., Guestrin, C.: "why should i trust you?" explaining the predictions of any classifier. In: Proceedings of the ACM SIGKDD International Conference on Knowledge Discovery and Data Mining, 13–17-August, pp. 1135–1144 (2016). https://doi.org/10.1145/2939672.2939778
9. da Saúde, M.: Vacinas. https://www.gov.br/saude/pt-br/coronavirus/vacinas
10. Schumacher, N.M.: Estudo comparativo de modelos de aprendizado de máquina para detecção de email spam, May 2021. https://bdm.unb.br/handle/10483/27588
11. Seron, W., Zorzal, E., Quiles, M.G., Basgalupp, M.P., Breve, F.A.: #Worldcup2014 on Twitter. In: Gervasi, O., et al. (eds.) ICCSA 2015. LNCS, vol. 9155, pp. 447–458. Springer, Cham (2015). https://doi.org/10.1007/978-3-319-21404-7_33

Integrating Counterfactual Evaluations into Traditional Interactive Recommendation Frameworks

Yan Andrade[1], Nícollas Silva[2], Adriano Pereira[2], Elisa Tuler[1],
Cleverson Vieira[1], Marcelo Guimarães[3], Diego Dias[1(✉)], and Leonardo Rocha[1]

[1] DCOMP/UFSJ, São João del-Rei, MG, Brazil
yrandrade123@aluno.ufsj.edu.br, {etuler,diegodias,lcrocha}@ufsj.edu.br
[2] DCC/UFMG, Belo Horizonte, MG, Brazil
{ncsilvaa,adrianoc}@dcc.ufmg.br
[3] UNIFESP, Osasco, SP, Brazil

Abstract. Online recommendation task has been recognized as a Multi-Armed Bandit (MAB) problem. Despite the recent advances, there still needs to be more consensus on the best practices to evaluate such bandit solutions. Recently, we observed two complementary frameworks that allow us to evaluate bandit solutions more accurately: *iRec* and OBP. The first has a complete set of datasets, metrics, and MAB models implemented, allowing only offline evaluations of these solutions. However, the second is limited to a few bandit solutions with more current metrics and methodologies, such as counterfactuals. In this work, we propose and evaluate an integration between these two frameworks, demonstrating the potential and richness of analyzes that can be carried out from this combination.

1 Introduction

Several Web applications have invested in recommendation systems (RSs) to guide the entire user experience from their first interactions as a sequential decision model [15]. In this case, the system should recommend one or more items upon each user interaction, receive the user's feedback, and update its knowledge for the next recommendation [12]. The idea is to learn with each interaction to increase the knowledge of the system and maximize user satisfaction in the long run. Current works have addressed this challenge as a Multi-Armed Bandit (MAB) problem, where items are modeled as arms to be selected, and the user experience is represented by the accumulated reward [7].

Despite the recent advances, there needs to be more consensus on best practices for evaluating an interactive RS. Traditionally, evaluations of new algorithms are performed offline using a pre-selected dataset related to item recommendations and their respective ratings by users. This set is divided into training, used to train the recommenders, and testing for evaluation. The algorithms'

This work was partially funded by CNPq, CAPES, FINEP and Fapemig.

O. Gervasi et al. (Eds.): ICCSA 2023, LNCS 13956, pp. 635–647, 2023.
https://doi.org/10.1007/978-3-031-36805-9_41

performance is measured through metrics such as precision and recall. For this scenario, we highlight the *iRec* [8], a framework to evaluate interactive RSs providing a fair comparison between different RSs with several evaluation methodologies widely tested and used in the literature. However, offline evaluations suffer from data bias, as all recorded user evaluations were collected based on items recommended by a previously implemented policy, which may result in an inaccurate reflection of the users' real preferences [13].

RSs can also be evaluated by online methodologies, such as A/B [3] tests to avoid this bias. However, these methodologies require more time and effort to obtain results. To overcome these limitations, researchers have turned to counterfactual evaluation approaches [5]. In this case, from pre-existing data, as in offline evaluation, for which we know the recommendation policy used in the recommendations, we estimate what the performance of a new strategy would be like if it was used to replace the source policy (estimators). Thus, counterfactual evaluation simulates a hypothetical situation where the user received a different recommendation and compares the probability of taking the desired action in these two situations, similar to an offline A/B test [5]. In this scenario, we have the Open Bandit Pipeline (OBP), a framework that provides a complete and standardized experimental evaluation procedure using a counterfactual methodology. Since most public data collections do not present the used recommendation policy, the OBP also includes modules for creating synthetic data.

It is clear that, in order to perform comprehensive evaluations of interactive RSs, it is necessary to take into account both the traditional methodologies provided by the *iRec* and the counterfactual ones offered by the OBP, supporting different types of analysis allowing the precise and objective comparison of results. Thus, in this paper, we propose an integration between the *iRec* [8] and the OBP [5], resulting in a tool that performs both offline assessments (with the main metrics) and online assessments (with different estimators)[1]. We evaluated our proposal through an experiment considering four collections (three traditional and one synthetic), five different RSs, three traditional evaluation metrics, and three counterfactual estimators. Through this experiment, we were able to evaluate not only the algorithms' performance but also the impact of external factors such as user context and the recommender's interaction with the user over time.

The remainder of the paper is organized as follows. Section 2 presents the theoretical framework of the work. The tools proposed and developed in this work are presented in Sect. 3. In Sect. 4, we present the experiments and discuss their results. Finally, the conclusions and future work are presented in Sect. 5.

2   Theoretical Framework

Collaborative filtering (CF), MAB, and counterfactual evaluation approaches are machine learning techniques used in various contexts. Succinctly defined,

---

[1] Available at https://github.com/YanAndrade61/iRec-OBP.

CF is an approach that uses the similarity of preferences, tastes, and choices among users over time; MAB is an optimization technique that seeks to find the best trade-off between exploration and exploitation in a set of options; and the counterfactuals address what the model would predict if changed the action input. They enable to recognize and evaluate a machine learning model in terms of how it reacts to input (feature) changes. This section briefly introduces each of these techniques.

2.1 Collaborative Filtering

CF model-based approaches have been achieving the best results in the recommendation. In this context, users and items are represented by multiple aspects. Each user $u \in U$ has a probability of being interested in each aspect $z \in Z$. Therefore, users with similar preferences participate in the same interest groups. Similarly, each item $i \in I$ will likely attract users in each aspect $z \in Z$. Thus, model-based approaches define the probability of interest of u over i by the combination of these interests:

$$P(i|u) = \sum_{z \in Z} P(i|z) \cdot P(z|u) \tag{1}$$

The term $P(i|z)$ does not depend on the target user and represents how relevant an item i is to group z. The term $P(z|u)$ is the user's personalization, also known as the user model $\theta_u = \theta_{uz} : \theta_{uz} = P(z|u) \wedge z \in Z$. In recent years, both have been addressed by latent factor models [1]. These methods factorize the classification matrix $M^{m \times n}$ into the product of two low-rank matrices $P \in \mathbb{R}^{m \times z}$ and $Q \in \mathbb{R}^{z \times n}$. While the matrix $P^{m \times z}$ contains the user model θ_u, representing the multiple interests of each user u in groups z, the matrix $Q^{z \times n}$ represents the relevance of item i to groups z. In this approach, the recommendation is redefined as the association of user and item factors: $s(i, u) = p_u^\top \cdot q_i$

2.2 Multi-armed Bandits

Although effective, CF approaches are inefficient and must be retrained at each system update. They cannot handle online scenarios, where the model has to learn from the data provided in sequential order and update itself at each iteration [9,14]. Recent advances in RSs have been related to the theory of reinforcement learning, modeling the online learning problem as a MAB problem to handle the recommendation task in this context. The MAB is a sequential decision model that continuously chooses an action a from a set of actions $\mathcal{A}$ – a.k.a. arms. Selecting an action $a \in \mathcal{A}$ at a point t in time results in a particular reward $R(a_t) \in \mathbb{R}$, which can be summarized as an actual number. Although the reward is not known until the arm is selected, the main goal in the bandit model is to maximize the expected rewards returned $\sum R(a_t)$.

In case the system has sufficient knowledge about the domain, the best option is to select the action that provides the maximum possible reward at all times [6,14]. However, this knowledge is uncertain and often unknown. Therefore, the MAB model always has to decide between two options. The first, more conservative option is to select the arms with the highest past rewards – an exploitation approach. In contrast, another option is investing in different arms to gain more information about the domain and make even better future decisions – an exploration approach. Such options characterize the dilemma of exploitation-exploration (i.e., exp-exp) and require that the model be able to exploit the maximum available knowledge while also exploring the solution space to acquire even more knowledge about the domain [14]. Thus, different MAB methods have been proposed in the literature to consider the dilemma exp-exp [9]. They generally include the traditional MAB methods, such as ϵ-$Greedy$ [14], Upper Confidence Bounds (UCB) [14] and Thompson Sampling (TS) [2].

2.3   CF-Based Multi-armed Bandits

In MAB representations for RSs, the items to be recommended are modeled as the arms. Selecting an arm is equivalent to recommending an item, and the reward is the feedback from the user (e.g., satisfaction) [6]. The feedback is saved continuously in a $\mathcal{H}(t)$ set. An item is recommended according to a prediction rule π, defined as a function that exploits current information about the user: $i(t) \equiv \pi(\mathcal{H}(t))$. The optimal strategy should maximize rewards on T interactions:

$$i^*(\cdot) = \sum_{i(\cdot)}^{T} \mathbb{E}\left[r_{u,i(t)}|t\right] \tag{2}$$

The prediction rule π is based on combining the CF classes and the MAB models from the literature [10,14]. As in traditional CF scenarios, model-based approaches achieve better recommendations and propose a probabilistic matrix formulation via PMF (Probabilistic Matrix Factorization), modeling the distribution of rewards by the latent factors of users and items similar to model-based [10,11,14] methods. The expected reward is modeled as the product of the user's latent factors p_u with the item factors q_i. Such modeling reformulates the objective function as follows:

$$i^*(\cdot) = \sum_{i(\cdot)}^{T} \mathbb{E}\left[r_{u,i(t)}|t\right] = \sum_{i(\cdot)}^{T} \mathbb{E}\left[p_u^\top q_{i(t)}|t\right] \tag{3}$$

Current efforts focus on optimizing this objective function, balancing the dilemma of *exp-exp*. Traditional MAB approaches, such as ϵ-$Greedy$, UCB and TS, are being adapted to consider this objective function as a prediction rule [2,10,14]. Table 1 summarizes the main features of each MAB approach. The difference between the algorithms is in how they control the exp-exp dilemma. The *silon-Greedy* exploits the prediction rule with probability $(1 - \epsilon)$ and the UCB and TS first measure an uncertainty Σ around the available information about users and items.

Table 1. Models used as a basis by CF-based MAB algorithms

	ϵ-Greedy	UCB	Thompson Sampling
Prediction Rule	- Estimate $p_{u,t}$ based on $\mathcal{H}(t)$ - With probability $(1 - \epsilon)$: $- i^*(t) = \underset{i \in I}{} (p_{u,t}^\top \cdot q_i)$ - Otherwise: $-$ randomly $i^*(t)$ select - Get the reward $r_{u,i}$ - Update $\mathcal{H}(t)$ based on $r_{u,i}$	- Estimate $p_{u,t}$ based on $\mathcal{H}(t)$ - Estimate $\Sigma_{u,i}$ com $\mathcal{H}(t)$ e $\{q_i : i \in I\}$ - Select the item: $- i^*(t) = \underset{i \in I}{} (p_{u,i}^\top q_i + \Sigma_{u,i})$ - Get the reward $r_{u,i}$ - Update $\mathcal{H}(t)$ based on $r_{u,i}$	- Estimate $\mu_{u,t}$ based on $\mathcal{H}(t)$ - Estimate $\Sigma_{u,t}$ based on $\mathcal{H}(t)$ - Sample $\tilde{p}_u$ of $\mathcal{N}(p_{u,t}\vert\mu_{u,t}, \Sigma_{u,t})$ - Select the item: $- i^*(t) = \underset{i \in I}{} (\tilde{p}_{u,t}^\top \cdot \tilde{q}_i)$ - Get the reward $r_{u,i}$ - Update $\mathcal{H}(t)$ based on $r_{u,i}$

2.4 Counterfactual

Although several approaches exist to solve the problem, there still needs to be a consensus on the best way to evaluate these algorithms. Traditional metrics have served as a basis for comparing the efficiency of each one, but recent studies have shown how selection bias and exposure bias [4], existing in collections, impact the evaluation result. Both occur when the data used to train the system needs to be representative of the population as a whole, resulting in an inaccurate reflection of user preferences that leads to a biased selection of the exposed items. That happens in offline datasets because all recorded user evaluations were collected based on items recommended by a previously implemented policy (i.e., the model in production at the time of user interaction). Counterfactual estimators allow using existing log data to estimate how some new target recommendation policy (i.e., a new approach) would have performed if it had been used instead of the policy that recorded the data. It allows for an Off-Policy Evaluation (OPE) like an unbiased offline A/B test. There are several counterfactual estimators proposed in the literature [3]. Direct method (DM) uses a model to complete missing rewards and uses the rewards of the selected items. Inverse propensity score (IPS) assigns importance weights to the current policy based on the original recommender values used to generate the dataset collection. Clipped IPS (CIPS) adapts the original IPS, limiting large weights with a λ parameter. Self-Normalized IPS (SNIPS) rescales the original IPS value by summing all importance weights. Doubly robust (DR) combines DM with IPS to reduce variance and work well with small samples. OBP has all these estimators implemented internally.

3 Tools for MAB Models

The tool proposed in this work aims to integrate two classical frameworks: iRec and OBP, obtaining a complete environment for analysis of interactive RSs, allowing from data processing to experiments execution and comprehensive evaluation, encompassing both offline and online aspects.

3.1   iRec

iRec[2] is a framework proposed to enable the use of interactive models, in particular those based on MAB models, in the recommendation domain. As we can see in Fig. 1, the iRec is composed of three main components that cover the whole experimentation process: (1) the construction of an Environment; (2) the definition of a Recommendation Agent; and (3) the definition of an Experimental Evaluation. In the Environment component, we configure the entire data structure to be processed by the framework. In it, we load the desired databases and define all the data preparation modules to be applied to them, such as the pre-filtering and splitting strategies for the training and test sets. The iRec has 17 public datasets for various application scenarios, such as movies, music, points of interest, products, and clothing. In turn, the Recommendation Agent component selects the model that will be used to define the best item(s) for each user in each iteration. In other words, this component implements the RS used in the recommendation. Finally, the component Experimental Evaluation integrates the models proposed in the Recommendation Agent over the data specified in the first component - Environment. First, we define the interaction between these two components through an Evaluation Policy module. In it, we configure an environment in which an item (or a set of items) is recommended in each algorithm iteration (one trial). For a predetermined time (number of tries), the Recommendation Agent performs the recommendations within the Environment, receiving a positive or negative reward and updating its knowledge. All logs (i.e., records of the actions performed by the Recommendation Agent and rewards provided by the users, according to the data in the test suite) are stored. Finally, the Experimental Evaluation analyzes these logs, applies the recommendation evaluation metrics, and performs the necessary statistical tests to perform a proper evaluation of the performance of the RSs implemented in the Recommendation Agent.

3.2   Open Bandit Pipeline - OBP

OBP [5] is a library that includes some modules to implement preprocessing of data collections and various recommendation methods. Unlike iRec, this library attempts to deal with the bias of existing databases for the recommendation scenario. Currently, the datasets used during the recommendation model's training phase are logs from a given recommender containing information about user interactions and items. However, the recommendation process changes how users interact with the system through clicks, ratings, etc. Thus, using this user interaction data, we are ignoring the intervening nature of recommendations. As a result, we are not evaluating whether users would click or buy more due to our new recommendations but rather to what extent the new recommendations fit the recorded data. It is precisely this problem that OBP tries to minimize through a Counterfactual evaluation policy. We present a library overview in

---

[2] Available at https://github.com/irec-org.

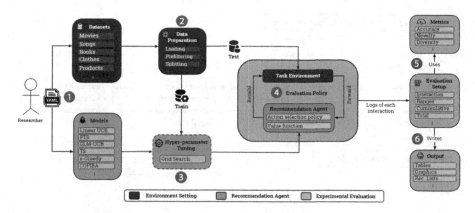

Fig. 1. An overview of the iRec framework [8]

Fig. 2. We can see the whole structure and its main modules. In short, we divided the library into four main modules: (i) the data module, which provides mechanisms to work on data collections, from the data loading step, and basic preprocessing steps to methods to generate synthetic data, among others; (ii) the policy module that provides interfaces for implementing new bandits methods and new evaluation policies, besides already having several relevant evaluation models and policies from the literature, both for the online and offline scenario; (iii) the simulation module that provides functions to perform offline simulation of bandits models. Through it, it is possible to compare and evaluate the performance of MAB algorithms; and (iv) the evaluation policy module that has generic abstract interfaces, ideal for custom implementations, in which users can add new estimators, besides having classical and advanced estimators already implemented (Sect. 2.2).

3.3   Integration Tool

As previously mentioned, there is no consensus on evaluating interactive recommendation models. Applying frameworks such as iRec and OBP is essential for this scenario. Even though they are already beneficial individually, there is more potential in combining them. iRec offers implementations of the main recommenders known in the literature, with modules for offline simulation and evaluation using traditional metrics. In turn, OBP provides an environment for evaluation using the main counterfactual estimators by generating synthetic data with a base recommender and calculating the probabilities of each item in the interactions. Thus, it is possible to simulate the synthetic data generated by OBP on iRec recommenders and evaluate performance online (using OBP) and offline (using iRec))[3].

In this sense, we propose a tool that integrates the two frameworks iRec and OBP (Fig. 3), to perform a complete analysis of recommenders implemented as a

---

[3] Available at https://github.com/YanAndrade61/iRec-OBP.

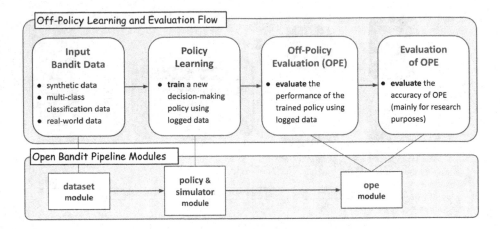

Fig. 2. OBP library overview [5]

MAB model. This tool provides a standardized methodology for the implementation of data preprocessing, the selection of learning methods, and a complete evaluation employing traditional metrics and counterfactual estimators (Off-Policy Evaluation - OPE). The unification process between the frameworks is separated into three main modules: (1) the data construction (OBP); (2) the simulation of the recommenders (iRec); (3) and the experimental evaluation (OBP and iRec). In addition, our tool also aims at maintaining the practicality of new implementations existing in each of the tools.

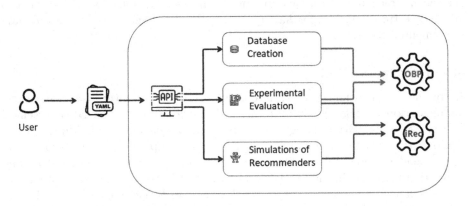

Fig. 3. Integration API between iRec and OBP

The first module uses OBP and consists of preparing the data to run the experiments, including creating, organizing, and parameterizing the synthetic data in a format suitable for analysis. We included two new parameters to the dataset construction step beyond those already provided by OBP to improve the flexibility and adaptability of the tool. The first parameter allows it to indicate the number of distinct users that will be simulated in the analysis, allowing the creation of datasets with different sizes. The second parameter allows it to define the context vector of each user and additional information used by the models to make more precise recommendations. With the addition of these parameters, it is possible to simulate more complex and realistic scenarios in evaluating recommenders in MAB models. The separation of data into training and testing is carried out using iRec, with different possibilities.

In the second module, the prepared data is used to train and test the recommender models implemented by iRec, which offers several recommendation algorithms, from classical approaches to more recent algorithms based on deep learning. The highly customizable framework offers an intuitive API that facilitates integration with other software. By using iRec in this second module, it is possible to evaluate different recommender models based on MAB.

Finally, the third module evaluates the implemented recommendation algorithms based on the logs generated in the previous module. To this end, we used MAB performance evaluation techniques, divided into two groups: (1) the traditional metrics, such as precision and recall, performed by iRec; and (2) the counterfactual estimators, such as DM, IPS, and DR, performed by OBP.

The configurations for using the tool are composed of several *yaml* files responsible for defining all the module parameters. *Yaml* is a human-readable data serialization language commonly used for configuration files. This way, a researcher can define the dataset parameters, the policy used in its creation, the simulation's recommenders, all the offline and online evaluation metrics, and more. Configuration 1 depicts an example of its use.

syntheticData.yaml

```
SyntheticData:
n_actions: 1000           users_context_file: path
dim_context: 23           random_state: 12345
reward_type: continuos    obp_parameters: None
reward_function: Linear   splitting:
min_reward: 1               strategy: temporal
max_reward: 5               train_size: 0.8
n_users: 943                test_consumes: 5
```

experimentalSetup.yaml   **evaluationSetup.yaml**

```
ExperimentalSetup:            EvaluationSetup:
  irec_parameters_file: path    irec_parameters_file: "path"
  input_file: path              ope_estimators: [IPW,DM,DR]
  output_file: path             regression_model:
```

Configuration 1. Synthetic Data, Experimental Setup and Evaluation Setup

We defined the specifications for the generated data in Configuration 1 (Synthetic Data). It is possible to specify the number of actions (n_actions), the dimension of the user context (dim_context), the type of generated reward (reward_type), the policy that will be implemented (reward_function), and the limits of the generated returns, in case it is continuous. In addition, it is possible to define the number of users (n_users) and provide a file with the contexts of each user (user_context_file) or let the system generate the contexts. It is also possible to define a randomness index (random_state) and include extra parameters available through OBP (obp_parameters). Finally, it is possible to select the data splitting strategy.

Configuration 2 (Experimental Setup) follows the pattern used by iRec and its configuration file of the recommendation agent module (irec_parameters_file). It adds two parameters for the path of the input and output files that will be used. In this sense, Configuration 3 (Evaluation Setup) maintains the format used by iRec in the experimental evaluation module to define the metrics that will be used (irec_parameters_file), along with the counterfactual estimators for analysis (ope_estimators) and the regression model (regression_model), if the DM or DR estimators are used.

4   Experiments

This section presents an experimental evaluation demonstrating the potential and richness of analyses that can be performed when we combine the two main evaluation frameworks for interactive recommenders. While iRec provides a huge amount of MAB models, offline evaluation metrics, and data collections – in addition to a whole framework of statistical comparisons, OBP offers the possibility of creating synthetic and unbiased data collections – in addition from estimators to counterfactual assessments. Using our integration tool of these two frameworks, we divided our experiments between the traditional and the counterfactual evaluation, comparing the obtained results.

4.1   Traditional Evaluation

In our experiments, we first selected three datasets made available by iRec: Netflix (movies), Good Books (books), and Yahoo Music (music). We compared the performance of the following algorithms, previously described in Sect. 2.1 and made available in iRec: e-Greedy, UCB, TS, Linear e-Greedy, and Linear UCB, considering three metrics implemented by iRec: Hits: the number of recommendations that matched the user's history (relevance); ILD: measured by the Pearson correlation of the item attribute vectors among the recommended items list (diversity); and Users Coverage: represented by the percentage of distinct users who have a relationship with the recommended items (coverage).

Table 2. Performance of bandit models in the offline scenario. Results were compared using the Wilcoxon test with a p-value of 0.05. The symbol ▲ indicates statistical gains, and the symbol • represents ties

Dataset	Yahoo Music			Netflix			Good Books		
Metric	Hits			Hits			Hits		
T	10	50	100	10	50	100	10	50	100
e-Greedy	1.460	7.424	13.360	1.320	5.390	9.936	0.800	3.072	5.633
UCB	1.358	7.330	13.277	1.284	5.440	9.915	0.764	2.984	5.493
TS	1.907	8.356	14.720	1.882	7.498	12.959	1.361	4.528	7.216
Linear e-Greedy	0.011	0.316	1.059	0.158	2.303	6.037	0.060	0.815	2.543
Linear UCB	**3.157▲**	**15.514▲**	**25.361▲**	**1.980▲**	**12.076▲**	**22.361▲**	**1.586▲**	**6.848▲**	**12.593▲**
Metric	ILD			ILD			ILD		
T	10	50	100	10	50	100	10	50	100
e-Greedy	**0.461•**	0.462	0.465	0.401	0.416	0.421	0.489	0.494	0.495
UCB	**0.465•**	0.463	0.465	0.404	0.416	0.421	**0.490▲**	**0.495▲**	**0.495▲**
TS	0.431	0.452	0.459	0.336	0.373	0.387	0.467	0.487	0.492
Linear e-Greedy	**0.466▲**	**0.478▲**	**0.488▲**	**0.481▲**	**0.482▲**	**0.481▲**	0.487	0.488	0.488
Linear UCB	0.387	0.418	0.436	0.375	0.387	0.394	0.428	0.469	0.476
Metric	UsersCoverage			UsersCoverage			UsersCoverage		
T	10	50	100	10	50	100	10	50	100
e-Greedy	0.684	0.960	0.985	0.545	0.857	0.954	0.499	0.853	0.932
UCB	0.664	0.960	0.986	0.544	0.872	0.949	0.483	0.842	0.930
TS	0.748	0.960	0.986	**0.631▲**	0.895	0.957	**0.636▲**	**0.893▲**	**0.944▲**
Linear e-Greedy	0.005	0.038	0.075	0.078	0.129	0.244	0.037	0.181	0.306
Linear UCB	**0.806▲**	**0.967▲**	**0.990▲**	0.588	**0.920▲**	**0.963▲**	0.489	0.819	0.915

Table 2, automatically generated by iRec, shows the experimental results generated with the configurations described earlier. It is important to note that none obtained the best results for all evaluated metrics, demonstrating the importance of using different evaluation metrics appropriate to the recommendation scenario. RSs should be able to provide relevant, diverse, and novel items, meeting the consumption needs of most users. Regarding relevance (hits), the superiority of Linear UCB is clear, regardless of the recommended list size. Considering diversity, Linear e-Greedy presents the best results for the Yahoo Music and Netflix collections, while UCB was superior for the Good Books collection. However, contrary to the perspective of relevance, the superiority of these algorithms is not so disparate from the perspective of diversity, reinforcing the need for statistical tests like the one used by iRec (i.e., Wilcoxon). From the coverage perspective, we again observe the superiority of Linear UCB. However, in this case, we have TS with a performance very close to Linear UCB, even reaching statistical superiority in the Good Books collection.

4.2 Counterfactual Evaluation

Counterfactual evaluation allows an RSs evaluation without the bias of selection and exposure. Based on pre-existing collections, it estimates how the performance of a new strategy would be if it were used in place of the original policy through estimators. Current counterfactual estimators require knowing the recommendation policy used in production to create the dataset, which is unavailable for offline datasets. In this sense, we created a synthetic recommendation dataset using OBP to produce ratings from 1 to 5, following the same pattern as the traditional MovieLens 100k (100 thousand ratings for the same number of users). Each context contains the user ID and its characteristics (e.g., gender, age, and occupation). A linear policy makes recommendations. In this case, we evaluated the same RSs from the previous experiment, which was only possible after integrating iRec with OBP. We configured them to make 100 recommendations for each user. Three distinct estimators were used to evaluate each RS, provided by OBP and described in Sect. 2.2 (i.e., IPS, DM, and DR).

Table 3 shows the results. The first and second columns refer to the estimated mean value of the policy and the confidence interval made by the selected metrics for each recommender. The original policy (linear) used to create the dataset influenced the DM, and IPS has a higher variance than the other methods. DR is the fairest and most consistent value. The third column shows the relative value of the policy – how much this new policy improved the original policy. Values greater than one mean that the policy would perform better if it replaced the original one. When evaluating the results, we observed that the Linear UCB and UCB strategies perform best, reinforcing the results obtained in the traditional evaluation. However, TS highlighted previously had a lower-than-expected performance in the counterfactual evaluation, being unable, in some cases, to even outperform the original recommender (linear). This fact demonstrates how TS, to some extent, benefits from the pre-existing bias in pre-existing datasets.

Table 3. Counterfactual estimators for bandit models on synthetic data. DR is the most unbiased and consistent estimator to ensure reliable evaluation. The best results are in bold text.

Dataset	Synthetic Dataset								
Measure	Estimated policy value			95.0% CI (lower) – 95.0% CI (upper)			Relative policy value		
Estimators	IPS	DM	DR	IPS	DM	DR	IPS	DM	DR
e-Greedy	6.244	4.468	4.495	2.854–10.154	4.458–4.477	4.432–4.596	1.901	1.36	1.368
UCB	8.318	4.484	4.438	3.821–13.279	4.474–4.492	4.397–4.473	**2.532**	1.365	1.351
TS	3.248	4.303	4.312	1.511–5.274	4.294–4.312	4.273–4.367	0.988	1.31	1.312
Linear e-Greedy	2.874	3.973	3.916	1.086–5.133	3.945–4.0	3.828–3.981	0.875	1.209	1.192
Linear UCB	3.35	4.893	4.89	1.192–5.952	4.89–4.895	4.864–4.918	1.02	**1.489**	**1.488**

5   Conclusion and Future Works

This work filled a gap in the literature regarding the evaluation of interactive RSs based on MAB approaches by integrating two of the most important evaluation frameworks: iRec and OBP. The first one is focused on offline evaluations, providing a complete set of collections, metrics, and RSs. The second one offers methodologies and metrics focused on counterfactual evaluations. Our integration allows any bandit solution to be evaluated offline and from a counterfactual perspective, including synthetic collections free from the bias of pre-selected collections. We evaluated the integration by considering four collections (three selected and one synthetic), six evaluation metrics (three offline and three counterfactual), and four state-of-the-art MAB algorithms. Our first observation is that evaluating the results regarding only one metric in the short, medium, or long term is not enough to assert that one model is better than another. Another important observation in our results concerns how much some algorithms "benefit" from the data bias, leading to erroneous conclusions about their performance. In these cases, the effectiveness of a model is more associated with how well it can approach the recommendations made by the recommender that originated the collection than effectively satisfying the user. We intend to conduct an even broader evaluation in future work, considering many other MAB models, metrics, and data collections.

References

1. Bobadilla, J., Ortega, F., Hernando, A., Gutiérrez, A.: Recommender systems survey. Knowl.-Based Syst. **46**, 109–132 (2013)
2. Chapelle, O., Li, L.: An empirical evaluation of thompson sampling. In: Advances in Neural Information Processing Systems, pp. 2249–2257 (2011)
3. Liu, Y., Yen, J.N., Yuan, B., Shi, R., Yan, P., Lin, C.J.: Practical counterfactual policy learning for top-k recommendations. In: ACM SIGKDD, pp. 1141–1151 (2022)
4. Pan, W., Cui, S., Wen, H., Chen, K., Zhang, C., Wang, F.: Correcting the user feedback-loop bias for recommendation systems. arXiv preprint arXiv:2109.06037 (2021)
5. Saito, Y., Aihara, S., Matsutani, M., Narita, Y.: Open bandit dataset and pipeline: towards realistic and reproducible off-policy evaluation. arXiv preprint arXiv:2008.07146 (2020)
6. Sanz-Cruzado, J., Castells, P., López, E.: A simple multi-armed nearest-neighbor bandit for interactive recommendation. In: RecSys, pp. 358–362 (2019)
7. Shams, S., Anderson, D., Leith, D.: Cluster-based bandits: fast cold-start for recommender system new users (2021)
8. Silva, T., Silva, N., Werneck, H., Mito, C., Pereira, A.C., Rocha, L.: irec: an interactive recommendation framework. In: SIGIR, pp. 3165–3175 (2022)
9. Sutton, R.S., Barto, A.G.: Reinforcement Learning: An Introduction. MIT press, Cambridge (2018)
10. Wang, H., Wu, Q., Wang, H.: Factorization bandits for interactive recommendation. In: Thirty-First AAAI Conference on Artificial Intelligence (2017)
11. Wang, Q., et al.: Online interactive collaborative filtering using multi-armed bandit with dependent arms. IEEE Trans. Knowl. Data Eng. **31**(8), 1569–1580 (2018)
12. Wu, Q., Iyer, N., Wang, H.: Learning contextual bandits in a non-stationary environment. In: SIGIR, pp. 495–504 (2018)
13. Yang, Y., Xia, X., Lo, D., Grundy, J.: A survey on deep learning for software engineering. ACM Comput. Surv. (CSUR) **54**(10s), 1–73 (2022)
14. Zhao, X., Zhang, W., Wang, J.: Interactive collaborative filtering. In: Proceedings of the 22nd ACM International Conference on Information & Knowledge Management, pp. 1411–1420 (2013)
15. Zhou, S., et al.: Interactive recommender system via knowledge graph-enhanced reinforcement learning. In: SIGIR, pp. 179–188 (2020)

Comparative Analysis of Community Detection and Transformer-Based Approaches for Topic Clustering of Scientific Papers

Daniel Bretsko[1]([envelope]) [ID], Alexander Belyi[1] [ID], and Stanislav Sobolevsky[1,2,3] [ID]

[1] Department of Mathematics and Statistics, Faculty of Science, Masaryk University, Kotlarska 2, Brno 61137, Czech Republic
bretsko@math.muni.cz
[2] Center for Urban Science and Progress, New York University, 370 Jay Street, Brooklyn 11201, NY, USA
[3] Institute of Law and Technology, Faculty of Law, Masaryk University, Veveri 70, Brno 61180, Czech Republic

Abstract. We are solving the topic clustering problem, where we need to categorize papers with initially available subjects into more consistent and higher-level topics. We approach the task from two perspectives, one is the traditional network science, where we perform community detection on a subject network with the use of *Combo* algorithm, and the second is the transformer-based *top2vec* algorithm which uses sentence-transformer to embed the content of the papers. The comparison between the two approaches was conducted using a dataset of scientific papers on computer science and mathematics collected from the SCOPUS database, and different coherence scores were used as a measure of performance. The results showed that the community detection *Combo* algorithm was able to achieve a similar coherence score to the transformer-based *top2vec*. The findings suggest that community detection may be a viable alternative for topic clustering when one has predefined topics, especially when a high coherence score and fast processing time are desired. The paper also discusses the potential advantages and limitations of using *Combo* for topic clustering and the potential for future work in this area.

Keywords: Network analysis · NLP · Topic clustering · Community detection · Sentence-transformers

1 Introduction

Topic modeling is often used in natural language processing (NLP) and text mining to group documents or texts that are similar in content. In most cases, topic classification is built exclusively based on the document content. However, in some cases, initial topic attachments may already be provided along with

O. Gervasi et al. (Eds.): ICCSA 2023, LNCS 13956, pp. 648–660, 2023.
https://doi.org/10.1007/978-3-031-36805-9_42

the documents. But such initial classification may not be satisfactory for the particular applied purposes due to its granularity, heterogeneity, and, often, lack of clarity on the criteria of how it was defined. At the same time, it may still carry helpful information not to be discarded. Topic clustering can help reduce the number of provided topics and create a higher-level balanced document category representation that can be useful for arranging and grouping the documents or for supervised learning tasks in NLP. The main difference from the more general topic modeling is that in topic clustering, a certain classification attached to the documents is already given and can be used to derive higher-level topics or clusters rather than building them solely based on the content of the documents. It also enables the application of a broader spectrum of techniques, including traditional network science tools.

Different algorithms and approaches are available for topic clustering and topic modeling, each with its strengths and limitations. Some papers describe the approach with classical clustering methods applied to transformer-network embeddings [8,24] or probabilistic and frequency models [21], but without access to external data, they cannot leverage network science approaches that in our case showed great results in terms of coherence. There are also papers employing community detection for topic clustering [5], especially on the basis of social networks [2,16], but they lack the comparison with current state-of-the-art transformer-based models as well as the state-of-the-art *Combo* [19] algorithm for community detection.

To fill these gaps, we compare approaches from network science and modern deep learning applied to the problem of topic clustering. We use two state-of-the-art techniques from each discipline: *Combo* [19] algorithm for community detection in networks, and *top2vec* [4] algorithm, which utilizes *Sentence-BERT* [17] transformer model. We evaluated two methods using a dataset of 10,000 scientific papers related to computer science and mathematics collected from the SCOPUS database. The results are compared using coherence scores [18] as the measure of performance. To ensure the robustness of our results, we use several coherence score algorithms.

2   Topic Modeling

2.1   Problem Setup

The text data for this study was collected from ten thousand *SCOPUS* scientific papers on computer science and mathematics domains. They contain information about the papers' *titles, abstracts,* and *subjects* they belong to. There are three hundred unique subjects, and each paper may belong to several subjects. Our task is to assign each document to one of several subjects, providing a higher-level document classification of desired granularity. To create such a classification based on given data, we employ *Combo* [19] algorithm for community detection in networks, and *top2vec* [4] algorithm, which utilizes *Sentence-BERT* [17] transformer model.

Combo is a state-of-the-art optimization algorithm for community detection in complex networks, which is perfectly suitable for analyzing small to medium size networks, particularly in research tasks that require the quality of resulting partitioning to be as high as possible and was successfully evaluated on partitioning human mobility and interaction networks [6,9,20,23]. The algorithm uses three types of operations to find the best partitions: merging two communities, splitting a community into two, and moving nodes between two distinct communities. After selecting an initial partition made of a single community, the following steps are iterated as long as any gain in terms of the modularity score can be obtained: (1) for each source community, the best possible redistribution of every source nodes into each destination community (either existing or new) is calculated; this also allows for the possibility that the source community entirely merges with the destination; (2) the best merger/split/recombination is performed.

Top2Vec algorithm is a popular and reliable [3,5,7,11] method for performing topic modeling and semantic search, which jointly embeds topic, document, and word vectors in such a way that their proximity represents semantic similarity. Firstly, the *Sentence-BERT* is utilized to create jointly embedded document and word vectors, ensuring that documents are placed close to other similar documents and to the most distinguishing words. Subsequently, the *UMAP* [13] algorithm is applied to reduce the dimensionality of the document vectors, as the high-dimensional document vectors can be sparse. The *HDBSCAN* [12] clustering technique is then employed to find dense areas in the documents and detect anomalies. For each dense area, *top2vec* calculates the topic vector, which is the centroid of the document vectors belonging to the area in the original dimension. Finally, the n-closest word vectors to the topic vector are determined and ordered by proximity, with the closest word vectors serving as the topic words.

2.2   Preprocessing

Text preprocessing was performed with *spaCy* [10] and *Gensim* [15] libraries and regex to clean and prepare the data for both approaches. First, we preprocess the given *subjects* by lowercasing and manual editing. Second, we preprocess the 'title' + 'abstract' concatenation by getting rid of unexpected URLs, extending the contractions, lowercasing the text, and lemmatizing it while deleting the stop words and leaving just nouns(NOUN), proper nouns(PROPN), and adjectives(ADJ), as they are sufficient for text analysis in this case and well-suited as topic cluster keywords. After that, we perform bigram and trigram detection for better keywords and key phrases. Worth noting that developers of *top2vec* point out that it does not require stop-word elimination or lemmatizing for good topic modeling, but during the experiments, we observed that it gave much better coherence score results as well as more human-interpretable keywords and key phrases for cluster description.

2.3   Evaluation Metrics

For the evaluation of our clusters of subjects, we use two different measures of topic coherence [1,18]. The coherence score is a widely used metric for evaluating the quality of topic models [5,24]. It calculates the score of a single topic by measuring the degree of semantic similarity between high-scoring words (keywords) in the topic. These measurements help distinguish between topics that are semantically interpretable and topics that are artifacts of statistical inference. Two types of coherence measures used in our experiments are:

- C_{uci} measure is based on a sliding window and the point-wise mutual information (PMI) of all word pairs of the given top words.
- C_v measure is based on a sliding window, one-set segmentation of the top words, and an indirect confirmation measure that uses normalized point-wise mutual information (NPMI) and the cosine similarity.

While both measures have shown a high correlation with human assessments of topic quality, the correlation of C_v was stronger [18]. As our coherence scores depend on the amount of describing keywords and key phrases for each topic, we will use different amounts of them to describe both algorithms' performance. We have chosen 5, 10, 15, and 20 keywords per topic because fewer amounts do not give a good representation of a topic, and for more than 20 keywords, the scores do not change.

2.4   Modeling

Top2Vec. We use our dataset to obtain embedding for each document in 384-dimensional space (which will also be used to obtain keywords for clusters found by *Combo*) with the use of the *all-MiniLM-L6-v2* sentence transformer model, which is a smaller version of *all-MiniLM* [22]. Next, we create embedding for each unique subject by averaging the embeddings of documents that belong to that subject. After that, we follow the steps described in Sect. 2.1. We reduce the dimensionality of 384-dimensional vectors with the *UMAP* algorithm to perform *HDBSCAN* clustering. We tried several dimensions and found that clustering of 2-dimensional vectors gave the best coherence scores. And we also used them for visualization. Then we find a centroid for each cluster by averaging the embeddings of the subjects that belong to that centroid (in the original 384-dimensional space). We also embed the words in the dictionary to find the closest keywords to the clusters' centroid. We tweak the hyperparameters of HDBSCAN to conduct the comparison of the results for different numbers of clusters. All other hyperparameters were chosen in a way to maximize coherence scores.

Combo. For our community-detection-based topic clustering, we create a graph where subjects correspond to nodes connected by weighted edges, where the weights are the counts of how often papers belong to both topics. On that graph, we run the *Combo* algorithm using *PyCombo* library, which provides the cluster assignment for each node. After we find the partitions, we follow the same steps as for **Top2Vec** 2.4, but instead of clustering with the *HDBSCAN* algorithm, we use our received communities as a clustering result and then proceed to build the clusters' centroids on their basis. Worth noting that Combo is capable of automatically finding the optimal amount of communities, but for research purposes, we tweaked the *modularity resolution* hyperparameter to receive results with different numbers of found clusters. We ran the algorithm 10 times with different random seeds and selected the result with the highest modularity. All other hyperparameters were chosen in a way to maximize coherence scores.

3   Results

To provide a comprehensive comparison and show the capabilities of both approaches, we conducted the experiments with:

- different numbers of clusters (by tweaking the hyperparameters);
- different numbers of keywords describing the newly-created clusters (for coherence scores pipelines);
- different coherence scores.

To evaluate performance, we measured the execution time of both algorithms and compared coherence scores. After choosing the best number of clusters for each algorithm, we create a 2-D representation of clustering and show wordclouds to facilitate human-interpretable evaluation (qualitative analysis).

3.1   Performance Speed

We measured the performance of both *top2vec* and *Combo* for creating clusters. Since we used preprocessed text and *all-MiniLM-L6-v2* embeddings to analyze both approaches, for the community detection approach, we only measured the performance of *Combo* for the already created subjects-graph, and for *top2vec* only the *UMAP* and *HDBSCAN* steps, where they receive ready-to-use embedding from *all-MiniLM-L6-v2* model. We obtained the following results:

- *Combo*: 334 ms ± 71.9 ms per loop (mean ± std. dev. of 7 runs);
- *UMAP+HDBSCAN*: 1.16 s ± 13.3 ms per loop (mean ± std. dev. of 7 runs).

As we can see, *Combo* is 3 times faster than the *UMAP+HDBSCAN* combination. Worth noting that both approaches have their own preprocessing steps, like creating a graph before applying *Combo* or calculating embeddings for *top2vec*. And those steps are the most time-consuming parts of the pipeline. However, creating a graph takes fractions of a second, while calculating embeddings takes more than 20 min for our dataset.

3.2 Scores Plots and Evaluation

In Fig. 1, we present the results of both algorithms in terms of different coherence scores. Since coherence scores depend on the number of keywords selected for cluster description, we evaluate our results for 5, 10, 15, and 20 keywords. We also adjust the parameters of clustering algorithms to obtain different numbers of clusters.

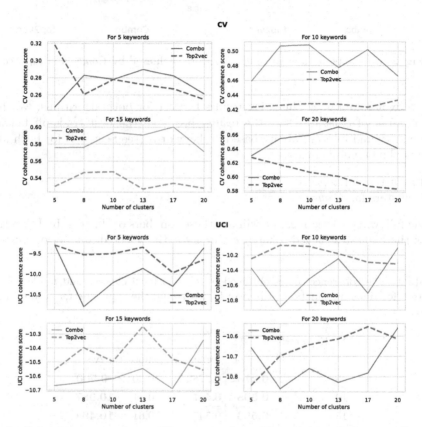

Fig. 1. Coherence scores for a different number of keywords and clusters. *Combo*'s results are represented with solid lines, while *top2vec*'s with dashed lines

It could be seen from Fig. 1 that *Combo* outperforms *top2vec* in terms of C_v coherence (in 96% of the cases), while in terms of C_{UCI} coherence *top2vec* has an advantage over the *Combo* (in 75% of the cases). However, for 20 clusters, Combo demonstrates consistent advantage in all cases. To explore the distribution of scores, in Fig. 2, we show obtained coherence scores in box-plots. As one can see, neither approach shows clear superiority in both topic coherences, so we can conclude that on the quantitative level, they perform similarly.

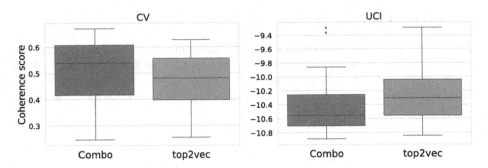

Fig. 2. Box-plots of different coherence scores achieved by *Combo* and *top2vec*

To explore obtained clustering results further for both algorithms, we chose the number of clusters where the results provided the best trade-off between granularity and interpretability based on keywords (see Sect. 3.4) for both algorithms. These numbers are:

- 10 clusters for *top2vec*;
- 9 clusters for *Combo*.

In the following subsections, we will use these numbers of clusters. In Table 1, we show the highest achieved coherence scores for the selected number of clusters.

Table 1. The coherence scores obtained by *Combo* for 9 clusters and *top2vec* for 10 clusters for different numbers of keywords describing the topic (better results are in **bold**)

No Keywords	C_v		C_{uci}	
	Combo	top2vec	Combo	top2vec
5	**0.2782**	0.2780	−10.20	**−9.500**
10	**0.508**	0.427	−10.51	**−10.087**
15	**0.593**	0.547	−10.61	**−10.494**
20	**0.659**	0.606	−10.75	**−10.642**

3.3   2-D Clustering Plot

To visualize the clustering results of both methods and see how different subjects are located relative to each other, we reduce the embedding dimensionality to two dimensions using *UMAP* and show 2-D plots in Figs. 3 and 4. As described in previous sections, for both algorithms, we found the closest keywords for each cluster's centroid. These keywords are used to describe obtained clusters and calculate coherence scores, but we also use the best keyword as the name of each cluster.

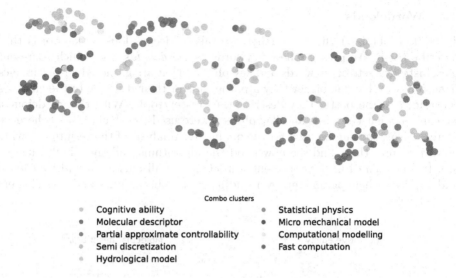

Combo clusters

- Cognitive ability
- Molecular descriptor
- Partial approximate controllability
- Semi discretization
- Hydrological model

- Statistical physics
- Micro mechanical model
- Computational modelling
- Fast computation

Fig. 3. *Combo* topic clustering result with top-1 keywords as a name

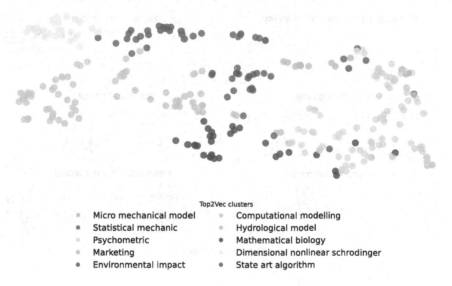

Top2Vec clusters

- Micro mechanical model
- Statistical mechanic
- Psychometric
- Marketing
- Environmental impact

- Computational modelling
- Hydrological model
- Mathematical biology
- Dimensional nonlinear schrodinger
- State art algorithm

Fig. 4. *top2vec* topic clustering result with top-1 keywords as a name

Since *Combo* uses network topology to find meaningful clusters, while *top2vec* uses subjects' embeddings, 2-D visualization better reflects clusters obtained by *top2vec*.

3.4   Wordclouds

To explore obtained clusters further, we take a deeper look at keywords that describe them. We present these keywords as *wordclouds* [14], which represent our clusters as sets of keywords and key phrases that are gathered within images in such a way that the bigger they are, the shorter their distance to the cluster's centroid, and the better they describe the cluster/topic. With the wordclouds, we can see what keywords and key phrases were used to calculate the coherence scores. Also, they can be used for the qualitative analysis of the results, allowing us to interpret them and see how good the algorithms and their built clusters are. In Fig. 5 and Fig. 6, we present wordclouds of all clusters found by *Combo* and *top2vec* when parameters were adjusted to obtain nine and ten clusters respectively.

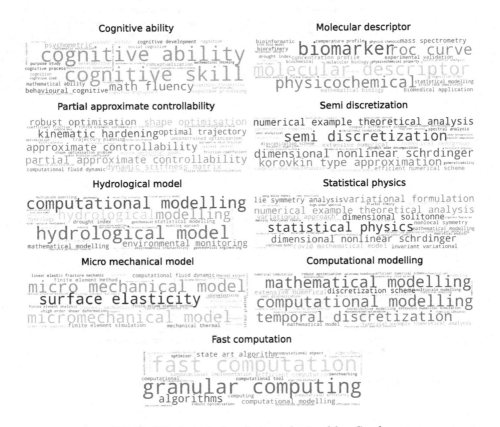

Fig. 5. Wordclouds for clusters obtained by *Combo*

Even though all papers were related to computer science and mathematics, *Combo* clearly distinguished various subtopics related to these fields. We can also observe that even if topics concentrate more on physics or cognitive skills, each of them contains keywords related to computer science and mathematics like 'mathematical modeling', 'computational modeling', 'statistical modeling', 'modeling', 'computation', etc., which gives us the sanity-check on created clusters for community detection approach.

Fig. 6. Wordclouds for clusters obtained by *top2vec*

Top2Vec was also able to find interpretable clusters. Topics like 'Micro mechanical model', 'Hydrological model', and 'Computational modeling' were found by both *Combo* and *top2vec*. Topics like 'Dimensional nonlinear Schrodinger' and 'Psychometric' represent topics similar to 'Semi discretization' and 'Cognitive ability' found by *Combo* but with different topic names (top-1 keywords). 'Mathematical biology' topic is very close to *Combo*'s 'Molecular descriptor', and 'Environmental impact' and 'Hydrological model' look like two separate topics made from *Combo*'s 'Hydrological model', while *top2vec*'s 'Marketing' and 'Statistical mechanic', and *Combo*'s 'Partial approximate controllability' and 'Statistical physics' are unique for each algorithm.

Based on build wordclouds and their analysis, we conclude that both community detection and transformer-network approaches have found well-interpretable clusters of topics.

4 Discussion

Based on the previous results, we can conclude that for both methods, we were able to achieve comparable coherence scores and receive well-interpretable topics. We can notice that *Combo* performed better in C_v coherence metric and *top2vec* was superior in C_{UCI}, so we concluded that both algorithms perform on the same level in terms of coherence on a given dataset.

The additional advantage of *Combo* is the processing speed. To receive the output for preprocessed 10,000 documents, *top2vec* needs 10–20 min, while *Combo* finds community partitions in seconds. However, to create a graph for our community detection approach, we needed additional information about the documents' topics, where several topics (in our case subjects) are provided for each document. On the contrary, *top2vec* works with the documents' text and does not require any prior information about topics.

Yet, this limitation of the community-detection method might be mitigated when it is possible to create a meaningful graph structure from available information (like a documents co-citation graph). Also, worth noting that by itself *Combo* does not find any keywords, as it gives us the community partitions. So, for additional analysis of received clusters, other tools are needed (as in our approach, *Sentence-BERT* was used to get embeddings for keywords), which is not the case for *top2vec*, as it was designed as a topic modeling algorithm, which does not depend on any predefined topics. On the other hand, *Combo* only requires some graph structure and does not depend on any kind of corpora preprocessing, while *top2vec* needs to get the embedding for the text to use it as an input for *UMAP* and *HDBSCAN*. So, in cases where the aim is to get a higher level representation of already given topics, *Combo* is preferable in the means of processing time and results reliability.

5 Conclusions and Future Work

Based on the findings of this study, it can be concluded that the community detection approach with *Combo* algorithm can be successfully applied to topic modeling through clustering some initial topics provided for the considered documents. The results of such purely network-based topic clustering in terms of processing time could outperform deep topic classification performed from scratch by one of the best algorithms for topic modeling *top2vec* while retaining comparable and often better topic coherence with well-interpretable describing keywords. This suggests that network methods can still be practical tools for topic modeling along with newer state-of-the-art transformer-based techniques, performing deep analysis of the documents' content. It also calls for further research on integrating network and transformed-based approaches for identifying more coherent topics in big text datasets whenever some initial topic classification or network links between documents are provided. For instance, future research could explore the use of *Combo* in topic modeling using word-based or citation-based graphs, where the graph is built based on words or citations. This could provide insights into how the algorithm performs without predefined topics. One may also consider a question and methodology for finding communities of papers and subjects based on both – their network connections as well as content embeddings, which could inform the development of more effective topic-modeling and topic-clustering algorithms.

Acknowledgement. This research was supported by the MUNI Award in Science and Humanities (MASH Belarus) of the Grant Agency of Masaryk University under the Digital City project (MUNI/J/0008/2021). The work of Stanislav Sobolevsky was also partially supported by ERDF "CyberSecurity, CyberCrime and Critical Information Infrastructures Center of Excellence" (No. CZ.02.1.01/0.0/0.0/16_019/0000822).

References

1. Aletras, N., Stevenson, M.: Evaluating topic coherence using distributional semantics. In: Proceedings of the 10th International Conference on Computational Semantics (IWCS 2013)-Long Papers, pp. 13–22 (2013)
2. Amati, G., et al.: Topic modeling by community detection algorithms. In: Proceedings of the 2021 Workshop on Open Challenges in Online Social Networks, pp. 15–20 (2021)
3. Anello, E.: Topic modeling approaches: Top2Vec vs BERTopic, January 2023. www.kdnuggets.com/2023/01/topic-modeling-approaches-top2vec-bertopic.html
4. Angelov, D.: Top2Vec: distributed representations of topics. arXiv preprint arXiv:2008.09470 (2020)
5. Austin, E., Zaïane, O.R., Largeron, C.: Community topic: topic model inference by consecutive word community discovery. In: Proceedings of the 29th International Conference on Computational Linguistics, pp. 971–983. International Committee on Computational Linguistics, Gyeongju, Republic of Korea, October 2022. https://www.aclanthology.org/2022.coling-1.81
6. Belyi, A., et al.: Global multi-layer network of human mobility. Int. J. Geogr. Inf. Sci. **31**(7), 1381–1402 (2017)
7. Egger, R., Yu, J.: A topic modeling comparison between LDA, NMF, Top2Vec, and BERTopic to demystify twitter posts. Front. Sociol. **7**, 1–16 (2022)
8. George, L., Sumathy, P.: An integrated clustering and Bert framework for improved topic modeling (2022)
9. Grauwin, S., et al.: Identifying and modeling the structural discontinuities of human interactions. Sci. Rep. **7**(1), 46677 (2017)
10. Honnibal, M., Montani, I.: spaCy 2: natural language understanding with Bloom embeddings, convolutional neural networks and incremental parsing (2017)
11. Mavuduru, A.: How to perform topic modeling with Top2Vec, November 2021. https://towardsdatascience.com/how-to-perform-topic-modeling-with-top2vec-1ae9bb4e89dc
12. McInnes, L., Healy, J., Astels, S.: HDBSCAN: hierarchical density based clustering. J. Open Source Softw. **2**(11), 205 (2017)
13. McInnes, L., Healy, J., Melville, J.: UMAP: uniform manifold approximation and projection for dimension reduction. arXiv preprint arXiv:1802.03426 (2018)
14. Oesper, L., Merico, D., Isserlin, R., Bader, G.D.: WordCloud: a cytoscape plugin to create a visual semantic summary of networks. Source Code Biol. Med. **6**(1), 7 (2011)

15. Rehurek, R., Sojka, P.: Gensim-Python framework for vector space modelling. NLP Centre, Faculty of Informatics, Masaryk University, Brno, Czech Republic 3(2) (2011)
16. Reihanian, A., Minaei-Bidgoli, B., Alizadeh, H.: Topic-oriented community detection of rating-based social networks. J. King Saud Univ. Comput. Inf. Sci. **28**(3), 303–310 (2016)
17. Reimers, N., Gurevych, I.: Sentence-BERT: sentence embeddings using Siamese BERT-networks. arXiv preprint arXiv:1908.10084 (2019)
18. Röder, M., Both, A., Hinneburg, A.: Exploring the space of topic coherence measures. In: Proceedings of the 8th ACM International Conference on Web Search and Data Mining, pp. 399–408 (2015)
19. Sobolevsky, S., Campari, R., Belyi, A., Ratti, C.: General optimization technique for high-quality community detection in complex networks. Phys. Rev. E **90**(1), 012811 (2014)
20. Sobolevsky, S., Kats, P., Malinchik, S., Hoffman, M., Kettler, B., Kontokosta, C.: Twitter connections shaping New York city (2018)
21. Tagarelli, A., Karypis, G.: A segment-based approach to clustering multi-topic documents. Knowl. Inf. Syst. **34**, 563–595 (2013)
22. Wang, W., Wei, F., Dong, L., Bao, H., Yang, N., Zhou, M.: MiniLM: deep self-attention distillation for task-agnostic compression of pre-trained transformers (2020). arXiv: 10.48550/ARXIV.2002.10957
23. Xu, Y., Li, J., Belyi, A., Park, S.: Characterizing destination networks through mobility traces of international tourists-a case study using a nationwide mobile positioning dataset. Tour. Manage. **82**, 104195 (2021)
24. Zhang, Z., Fang, M., Chen, L., Namazi-Rad, M.R.: Is neural topic modelling better than clustering? An empirical study on clustering with contextual embeddings for topics. arXiv preprint arXiv:2204.09874 (2022)

Interactive Information Visualization Models:
A Systematic Literature Review

MacArthur Ortega-Bustamante[1,2], Waldo Hasperué[2], Diego H. Peluffo-Ordóñez[3,4],
Daisy Imbaquingo[1,2], Hind Raki[3,4(✉)], Yahya Aalaila[3,4], Mouad Elhamdi[3,4],
and Lorena Guachi-Guachi[4,5]

[1] Facultad de Ingeniería en Ciencias Aplicadas, Universidad Técnica del Norte, Ibarra, Ecuador
{mc.ortega,deimbaquingo}@utn.edu.ec
[2] III-LIDI, Facultad de Informática, Universidad Nacional de la Plata, La Plata, Argentina
cosme.ortegab@info.unlp.edu.ar, whasperue@lidi.info.unlp.edu.ar
[3] College of Computing, Mohammed VI Polytechnic University, Ben Guerir, Morocco
{peluffo.diego,hind.raki,yahya.aalaila,mouad.elhamdi}@um6p.ma
[4] SDAS Research Group, 43150 Ben Guerir, Morocco
lorena.guachi@sdas-group.com, loguachigu@uide.edu.ec
[5] Department of Mechatronics, Universidad Internacional del Ecuador, Av. Simon Bolivar,
170411 Quito, Ecuador
https://sdas-group.com/

Abstract. Interactive information visualization models aim to make dimensionality reduction (DR) accessible to non-expert users through interactive visualization frameworks. This systematic literature review explores the role of DR and information visualization (IV) techniques in interactive models (IM). We search relevant bibliographic databases, including IEEE Xplore, Springer Link, and Web of Science, for publications from the last five years. We identify 1448 scientific articles, which we then narrow down to 52 after screening and selection. This study addresses three research questions, revealing that the number of articles focused on interactive DR-oriented models has been in the minority in the last five years. However, related topics such as IV techniques or RD methods have increased. Trends are identified in the development of interactive models, as well as in IV techniques and RD methods. For example, researchers are increasingly proposing new DR methods or modifying existing ones rather than relying solely on established techniques. Furthermore, scatter plots have emerged as the predominant option for IV in interactive models, with limited options for customizing the display of raw data and details in application windows. Overall, this review provides insights into the current state of interactive IV models for DR and highlights areas for further research.

Keywords: information visualization · dimensionality reduction · interactive models

© The Author(s), under exclusive license to Springer Nature Switzerland AG 2023
O. Gervasi et al. (Eds.): ICCSA 2023, LNCS 13956, pp. 661–676, 2023.
https://doi.org/10.1007/978-3-031-36805-9_43

1 Introduction

Developing tools that enable users to explore data and discover underlying patterns becomes increasingly important, with stored data exponential growth, where dimensionality reduction (DR) and information visualization (IV) techniques play a critical role. Moreover, interactive models (IM) have been developed to make dimensionality reduction more accessible to non-expert users by providing a generalized interactive visualization framework [1, 2]. The inception of interactive dimensionality reduction using a linear mixture of DR methods is attributed to study presented in [3]. These models can be classified into various types: geometric approximation or homotopy, color-based, Geo-Desic approximation and similarity-based [2]. Modern DR approaches use improved versions of stochastic neighbor embedding [4]. Similarly, IV techniques are classified into two groups: a) navigation strategies (Zoom and Pan, Overview + Detail, Focus + Context) and b) visual interaction strategies (Selecting, Linking, Filtering, and Rearranging and Remapping) [5]. Additionally, DR methods can be classified into linear and nonlinear techniques [6].

This work conducts a systematic literature review (SLR) to obtain the latest information on technologies used for IV with a focus on DR, by addressing three research questions. We perform a search in three relevant bibliographic databases (IEEE Xplore, Springer Link, Web of Science) covering the period between 2016 and 2022. We adapt the search strings to each database based on the supported format. Our search yields 1448 scientific articles, which we then narrow down to 52 publications through a selection process. We concluded that there was a remarkable increase in articles treating either IV techniques or DR methods, while the number of articles focusing on interactive models for DR is relatively low. Among various trends in IM, IV and DR, authors tend to propose new or modified DR formulations instead of using established ones. Additionally, the degree of customization in how data and details are displayed in application windows is another trend in this area.

The rest of the article is organized as follows. Section 2 presents the methodology used to conduct the systematic literature review. In Sect. 3, we present our key results. Section 4 provides a discussion of the findings and highlights the contributions and limitations of the present work. Finally, in Sect. 5, we draw conclusions and suggest future research directions, emphasizing the potential of interactive models for dimensionality reduction.

2 Methodology

We select the methodology proposed by [7–9] to conduct this SLR. The review protocol is illustrated in Fig. 1 and comprises four stages: (i) defining research questions, (ii) conducting a literature search, (iii) selecting relevant articles, and (iv) extracting and synthesizing data.

2.1 Research Questions

Our review process on interactive IV for DR uses three established research questions (RQ) as its guidelines, as summarized in Table 1. In addition, we consider three scientific databases that are accessible at our institution (Technical University of the North, Ibarra), namely IEEE Xplore Digital Library [10], Springer Link [11], and Web of Science [12].

Table 1. Research Questions (RQ).

Number	Research Question	Objectives
RQ1	Which interactive IV models have been developed specifically for DR purposes?	Identify IMs that allow for parameter or method selection in controlling DR
RQ2	Which information visualization techniques are commonly used to represent DR?	Identify IV techniques that display DR and offer interactivity beyond basic rotation and zooming
RQ3	What are the most widely adopted methods of DR in IV?	Identify DR methods used in IV that are aligned with the IMs identified in RQ1

2.2 Literature Search

We use ("data visualization" AND "dimensionality reduction") as our baseline search string. Although, for each database search string, we consider each platform's distinct criteria and search functionalities. As a result, we found 1448 documents, with 464 from Web of Science, 639 from Springer Link, and 345 from IEEE Xplore.

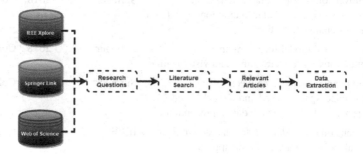

Fig. 1. SLR protocol diagram.

2.3 Selection of Articles

Three phases are set for the selection of articles. In the first phase, we apply inclusion and exclusion criteria. The inclusion criteria are Computer Science related scientific articles and reviews, published between 2016 and 2022 in English. The exclusion criteria are (i) duplicate works, (ii) technical reports, (iii) book chapters, (iv) theses, and (v) studies published in other fields.

In the second phase, we apply criteria related to search strings to highlight the most pertinent literature and respond to the proposed RQs. Then, we order the documents according to the publication, and we initially review the title, abstract, and keywords. Finally, in the third phase, we examine the Introduction and Conclusion sections to confirm their relevance and connection to the three established RQs. Table 2 presents the total number of documents retrieved after the three-phase review process.

Table 2. Selection of Articles for the SLR

Database	Phase I	Phase II	Phase III
IEEE Xplore	345	46	17
Springer Link	639	28	15
Web of Science	464	34	20
Total	*1.448*	108	52

Table 3 presents key details of the 52 scientific articles ultimately selected through our review process. These details include titles, databases, publication years, and countries of publication.

Table 3. Selected Articles for the SLR

Code	Title	Database	Year	Country
A1	A novel color-based data visualization approach using a circular interaction model and dimensionality reduction	Springer	2018	Colombia
A2	Angle-based model for interactive dimensionality reduction and data visualization	Springer	2018	Colombia
A3	Comparative analysis between embedded-spaces-based and Kernel-based approaches for interactive data representation	Springer	2018	Colombia
A4	Dimensionality reduction for interactive data visualization via a Geo-Desic approach	IEEE	2016	Colombia
A5	Generalized Low-Computational Cost Laplacian Eigenmaps	Springer	2018	Colombia
A6	Generalized Spectral Dimensionality Reduction Based on Kernel Representations and Principal Component Analysis	Springer	2021	Ecuador
A7	Interactive data visualization using dimensionality reduction and dissimilarity-based representations	Springer	2017	Colombia

(continued)

Table 3. (*continued*)

Code	Title	Database	Year	Country
A8	Interactive Data Visualization Using Dimensionality Reduction and Similarity-Based Representations	Springer	2017	Ecuador
A9	Interactive Visualization Interfaces for Big Data Analysis Using Combination of Dimensionality Reduction Methods: A Brief Review	Springer	2020	Ecuador
A10	Interactive visualization methodology of high-dimensional data with a color-based model for dimensionality reduction	IEEE	2016	Colombia
A11	Introducing the Concept of Interaction Model for Interactive Dimensionality Reduction and Data Visualization	Springer	2020	Ecuador
A12	Inverse Data Visualization Framework (IDVF): Towards a prior-knowledge-driven data visualization	Springer	2020	Ecuador
A13	Data visualization using interactive dimensionality reduction and improved color-based interaction model	Springer	2017	Ecuador
A14	Semantic-aware visual abstraction of large-scale social media data with geo-tags	IEEE	2019	China
A15	Visual Interaction with Dimensionality Reduction: A Structured Literature Analysis	IEEE	2016	Germany
A16	Improved interactive color visualization approach for hyperspectral images	Web of Science	2021	China
A17	Explaining dimensionality reduction results using Shapley values	Web of Science	2021	Brazil
A18	ExplorerTree: A Focus + Context Exploration Approach for 2D Embeddings	Web of Science	2021	Brazil
A19	What you see is what you can change: Human-centered machine learning by interactive visualization	Web of Science	2017	Germany
A20	Supporting Analysis of Dimensionality Reduction Results with Contrastive Learning	IEEE	2020	EE. UU
A21	Scaled radial axes for interactive visual feature selection: A case study for analyzing chronic conditions	Web of Science	2018	Spain
A22	Feature selection based on star coordinates plots associated with eigenvalue problems	Web of Science	2021	Spain

(*continued*)

Table 3. (*continued*)

Code	Title	Database	Year	Country
A23	Designing Progressive and Interactive Analytics Processes for High-Dimensional Data Analysis	IEEE	2017	UK
A24	Hinted Star Coordinates for Mixed Data	Web of Science	2019	Germany
A25	Adaptable Radial Axes Plots for Improved Multivariate Data Visualization	Web of Science	2017	Spain
A26	Cluster aware Star Coordinates	Web of Science	2018	China
A27	SADIRE: a context-preserving sampling technique for dimensionality reduction visualizations	Web of Science	2020	Brazil
A28	DimLift: Interactive Hierarchical Data Exploration through Dimensional Bundling	IEEE	2021	EE. UU
A29	Dimensionality reduction for data visualization and linear classification, and the trade-off between robustness and classification accuracy	IEEE	2020	Germany
A30	Immersive Visualization of Abstract Information: An Evaluation on Dimensionally-Reduced Data Scatterplots	IEEE	2018	Brazil
A31	ChemVA: Interactive Visual Analysis of Chemical Compound Similarity in Virtual Screening	IEEE	2020	Argentina
A32	Focus + context exploration of hierarchical embeddings	Web of Science	2019	Netherlands
A33	PolarViz: a discriminating visualization and visual analytics tool for high-dimensional data	Web of Science	2019	Singapore
A34	SeekAView: An Intelligent Dimensionality Reduction Strategy for Navigating High-Dimensional Data Spaces	IEEE	2016	EE. UU
A35	Glyphboard: Visual Exploration of High-Dimensional Data Combining Glyphs with Dimensionality Reduction	IEEE	2020	Germany
A36	A Graphical User Interface for Fast Evaluation and Testing of Machine Learning Models Performance	IEEE	2019	Mexico
A37	Temporal MDS Plots for Analysis of Multivariate Data	IEEE	2016	Germany
A38	SolarView: Low Distortion Radial Embedding with a Focus	IEEE	2019	Netherlands

(*continued*)

Table 3. (*continued*)

Code	Title	Database	Year	Country
A39	NetScatter: Visual analytics of multivariate time series with a hybrid of dynamic and static variable relationships	IEEE	2021	EE. UU
A40	Gaussian Cubes: Real-Time Modeling for Visual Exploration of Large Multidimensional Datasets	IEEE	2017	EE. UU
A41	Random forest similarity maps: A scalable visual representation for global and local interpretation	Web of Science	2021	Canada
A42	CoeViz: A web-based integrative platform for interactive visualization of large similarity and distance matrices	Web of Science	2018	EE. UU
A43	Scalable Visual Exploration of 3D Shape Databases via Feature Synthesis and Selection	Springer	2022	China
A44	Focused multidimensional scaling: Interactive visualization for exploration of high-dimensional data	Web of Science	2019	Finlandia
A45	Multi-level Massive Data Visualization: Methodology and Use Cases	Web of Science	2018	Lithuania
A46	A general framework for visualization of sound collections in musical interfaces	Web of Science	2021	UK
A47	Interactive browsing of large image repositories	Springer	2019	UK
A48	Interactive Dimensionality Reduction for Comparative Analysis	Web of Science	2022	EE. UU
A49	Attribute-based Explanations of Non-Linear Embeddings of High-Dimensional Data	Web of Science	2021	Germany
A50	SemanticAxis: exploring multi-attribute data by semantic construction and ranking analysis	Web of Science	2021	China
A51	Projective Latent Interventions for Understanding and Fine-tuning Classifiers	Springer	2020	UK
A52	Recommendations Based on Collective Intelligence – Case of Customer Segmentation	Springer	2019	Polonia

2.4 Data Extraction

After a thorough screening process, we extracted data from the articles according to the objectives of the RQs, where several studies addressed more than one research question. We review interactive IV models developed for DR methods in the last five years to identify the most frequently used DR methods in those models and information visualization techniques.

3 Results

In this section, we present the 52 articles (refer to Table 3) that offer insights into the research questions in Table 1. The first question, RQ1, serves as the main inquiry, with RQ2 and RQ3 as sub-questions. Thus, we follow a hierarchical order in presenting the articles, starting with those that answer the main question, followed by those that address the sub-questions.

Interactive Models
An interactive model is defined as a mixture of DR techniques with a generalized interactive IV framework [2, 3] and is intended to bring DR closer to non-expert users [4]. This definition allows for various IMs approaches to be considered. For example, in the work of [4], a literature review shows several types of IM by geometric approximation or homotopy, color-based, Geo-Desic approximation, and similarity-based. The paper published by [13] proposes a geometric IM based on a chromatic circle that distributes three DR methods at 120°. To interact with this model, users can drag a small circle from the edge toward the center using the cursor. The work published by [14] proposes a geometric IM based on the angles of a triangle, where each vertex represents a DR method. These models differ from the IM in [15], which uses the latitude and longitude coordinates of the map of the Earth to mix four DR methods. On the other hand, [16] and [17] propose color-based IM methods where a chromatic triangle represents three DR methods for each corner: CMD, LE, and LLE. Selecting a point within the triangle area initiates DR mixing. Within the same field, [17] develops an interface that interacts with the weights of the DR mixture through horizontal bars, each with one of the RGB colors. In a similar fashion, the model in [18] uses a vertical bar equalizer corresponding to five available DR methods (CMDS, LE, LLE, SNE and t-SNE). Choosing a value in any of the bars initiates a DR mixture. Finally, the result is processed with a similarity-based approximation and displayed in a scatter plot.

The interactive model (IDVF) proposed by [19] allows users to move the points that result from the DR directly on the scatter plot. After that, the reverse process obtains the DR mixture that best fits the new location of the points. However, other types of IM approaches exist, as proposed in [20], which creates a Visual Interaction SLA with DR. This study identifies four types of IM processes for DR: iPCA, Cluster Separation, StarSPI-RE, and Persistent Homology. On the other hand, the work of [21] proposes a framework for expert users like visualization technicians or data operators. This model integrates Machine Learning and Visual Analytics. Moreover, [22] addresses high-dimensional data analysts, and [23] introduces a graphical tool to evaluate machine learning algorithms' performance in classification tasks quickly. Users can access customization options for the data set's characteristics, DR method size, and training batch size. The tool then generates a plot displaying the model's results and accuracy. In [24], an interactive system allows for dataset selection, projection, and clustering. Also, the system updates the scatter plots and generates heat maps of each cluster as the view changes. Finally, [25] proposes a methodology for IV of multilevel data at scale which improves visual data analysis especially for complex data sets.

Information Visualization Techniques and Dimensionality Reduction Methods Used in Interactive Models

This section outlines the most recurrent IV techniques and DR methods in the selected papers. Works by [1, 2, 13–18, 26–29] utilize the Zoom and Pan strategy through an unmodified scatter plot in either 3D or 2D formats. These works share some similarities in their use of DR methods, which include LE, CMDS, and LLE, with minor variations such as t-SNE [13], RBF [15], SNE [4], or KPCA [19]. Additionally, the selected articles offer clear instances of various IV strategies. For example, [30] presents a Focus + Context interactive exploration tool (SolarView), where the user can click on any entity to focus on it or use the search bar. Meanwhile, [19] proposes a Linking and Selecting interactive model (IDVF) that performs the reverse process of DR mixing (CMDS and KPCA) by allowing the user to move the resulting DR points directly on the 2D scatter plot.

The Filtering strategy reduces the amount of visualized data and focuses on relevant features [5]. For example, [23] introduces a graphical tool to evaluate ML algorithms' performance in classification tasks quickly. The tool offers customization options for the data set's characteristics, DR method size (Linear, Polynomial, RBF, Sigmoid, Cosine), and training batch size. By combining multiple navigation strategies, researchers have developed novel techniques to visualize high-dimensional data. For example, [31] and [32] combine Zoom and Pan and Focus + Context by adding a new context to the data displayed on the scatter plot. In addition, [33] allows the user to explore the scatter plot in a VR environment. PCA is used as the DR method in [33] and [34].

Several works have employed the combination of Overview + Detail for displaying geotagged social media data in multiple windows, including [22, 34], and [35]. In terms of DR, [34] uses t-SNE, while both [22] and [35] use PCA. Rearranging and Remapping is the ability to customize the application [5], as shown in [36], the display changes by reducing the pixels on the screen using DR at varying reduction levels. In addition, [37] maps the data into glyphs that are encoded using DR (PCA, t-SNE and MDS). Several papers adopt more than one navigation and visual interaction strategy. For example, [38] and [39] combine Zoom and Pan, Focus + Context, Selecting, and Filtering. Similarly, [40–42] use Focus + Context, Selecting, and Linking. Moreover, [43] and [44] use Focus + Context, Selecting, and Filtering strategies. In [45], an IV technique based on astronomical coordinates combines Zoom and Pan, Focus + Context, Linking, and Filtering strategies. The user can interact with a bar chart to compare data or remove some features from the plot based on PCA. In addition, The IV technique in [31] is based on radial axes which modify axials by including weights and constraints in the optimization problem, enabling the ordering of attributes using PCA and LDA. The work in [25] proposes a methodology for the interactive visualization of multilevel data at scale. This methodology uses DR techniques such as LLE, PCA, Isomap, and MDS. Meanwhile, [46] proposes a general framework for a modular combination of segmentation, analysis, and projection to two-dimensional spaces using UMAP.

The IV techniques of Zoom and Pan, Overview + Detail, Selecting, Linking, and Filtering are employed in [47] and [48], while [49] and [50] also use Filtering. Similarly,

[51] uses Focus + Context, Selecting and Linking, as well as [52] and [53], which also employ Filtering. Also, the work of [54] presents the Hue Sphere ImageBrowser, an interface for interactively browsing large image repositories, which employs the Zoom and Pan, Selecting, and Filtering strategies. In contrast, [55] proposes SemanticAxis, which creates semantic vectors in a two-dimensional space through interactive means. This technique uses Overview + Detail, Linking, and Filtering strategies. The work in [56] proposes Gaussian Cubes to aid the exploration of large datasets in real-time. In addition, [57] improves Hyperspectral Imaging (HSI) analysis and visualization tools. The work [58] proposes a new IV interface for clusters using celestial coordinate axes. The user can manipulate the points' values and move the axes with an assistance system. Likewise, [59] develops an IV application for long molecule assemblies. Using a Hexagon view, the features are represented by colors and opacity. A difference view compares multiple DR projections and evaluates their reliability. This approach uses t-SNE for DR. Finally, [60] proposes an IV technique that computes one-dimensional temporal MDS plots for time-evolving multivariate data through a sliding window. In [20], a Visual Interaction SLA with DR is developed, including four interactive model processes: iPCA, Cluster Separation, StarSPIRE, and Persistent Homology. These processes utilize various IV techniques, such as scatter plots and Word Maps, and DR methods like PCA, t-SNE, HLLE, or Isomap. Meanwhile, [21] proposes a framework that integrates Machine Learning and Visual Analytics (VA), with a visual interface acting as a mediator between the analyst and the Machine Learning algorithm. Furthermore, the interface allows changes in the observed visualization, restarting the cycle. This framework provides four IV examples: iPCA, Regression, ForceSPIRE, and Baobab-View, which employ IV techniques such as scatter plots and Word Maps, and DR methods like PCA and t-SNE.

4 Discussion

Most articles do not explicitly refer to interactive IV models for DR [1, 2], however, several articles combine the DR and IV domains (see Fig. 2). Also, PCA is the most used DR method, accounting for 16% of the articles reviewed, t-SNE comes in a close second with 14%. However, the "Others" category in Fig. 3, represents methods mentioned or used only once in the SLR, accounting for 20%. These methods are often modifications of existing techniques, but once analyzed together, there is a trend in proposing new DR methods instead of relying solely on existing techniques.

Multiple IV strategies are employed in the selected articles, including navigation and/or visual interaction (see Fig. 4). Zoom and Pan is the most used navigation technique, due to the widespread use of scatter plots in various rendering libraries. On the other hand, Overview + Detail is the least used strategy suggesting a trend toward concealing raw data in the displayed views. Furthermore, Filtering is the most used visual interaction strategy whereas Rearranging and Remapping are the least used. Hence, there is an upward trend in providing filtering tools to the users in the interactive view context, rather than offering customization options to create new types of views.

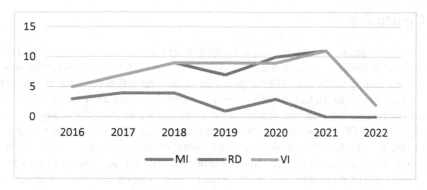

Fig. 2. Number of articles found between 2016 and 2022 in the SLR.

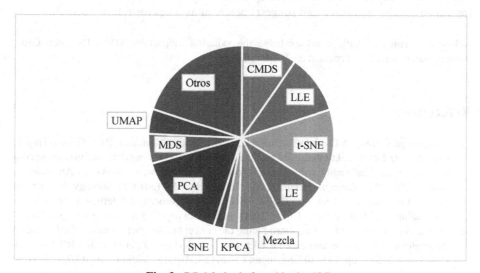

Fig. 3. DR Methods found in the SLR.

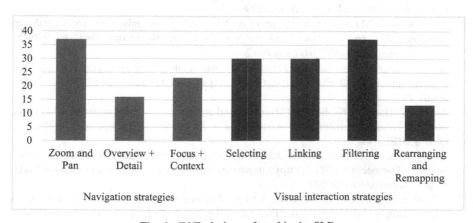

Fig. 4. IV Techniques found in the SLR.

5 Conclusions

A significant number of articles and reviews concentrate on information visualization techniques for dimensionality reduction, while fewer articles address interactive models for dimensionality reduction. This disparity does not imply that research in interactive models is nonexistent. In fact, there has been an increase in the number of articles focusing on interactive information visualization techniques and dimensionality reduction methods since 2020. Our systematic literature review highlights relevant trends and patterns in the use of interactive models for dimensionality reduction. Some studies went for proposing new dimensionality reduction methods instead of using existing ones, with the widespread use of the scatter plot as the primary visualization technique. Furthermore, there is a growing trend toward concealing raw data in the views presented to end-users. Overall, this study provides valuable insights into current research on interactive models for dimensionality reduction and suggests potential avenues for future research.

Acknowledgements. Authors acknowledge the valuable support by SDAS Research Group (https://sdas-group.com/, accessed on 26 Mars 2023).

References

1. Umaquinga-Criollo, A.C., Peluffo-Ordóñez, D.H., Rosero-Montalvo, P.D., Godoy-Trujillo, P.E., Benítez-Pereira, H.: Interactive visualization interfaces for big data analysis using combination of dimensionality reduction methods: a brief review. In: Basantes-Andrade, A., Naranjo-Toro, M., Zambrano Vizuete, M., Botto-Tobar, M. (eds.) Technology, Sustainability and Educational Innovation (TSIE). TSIE 2019. Advances in Intelligent Systems and Computing, vol 1110. Springer, Cham (2020). https://doi.org/10.1007/978-3-030-37221-7-17
2. Ortega-Bustamante, M.C., et al.: Introducing the concept of interaction model for interactive dimensionality reduction and data visualization. In: Gervasi, O., et al. (eds.) ICCSA 2020. LNCS, vol. 12250, pp. 193–203. Springer, Cham (2020). https://doi.org/10.1007/978-3-030-58802-1_14
3. Peluffo-Ordóñez, D.H., et al.: Geometrical homotopy for data visualization. In: ESANN (2015). http://hdl.handle.net/2078.1/168996
4. Lee, J.A., et al.: Multi-scale similarities in stochastic neighbour embedding: reducing dimensionality while preserving both local and global structure. Neurocomputing **169**, 246–261 (2015). https://doi.org/10.1016/j.neucom.2014.12.095
5. Steed, C.A.: Interactive data visualization. In: Data Analytics for Intelligent Transportation Systems, pp. 165–190. Elsevier Inc. (2017). https://doi.org/10.1016/B978-0-12-809715-1.00007-9
6. Ayesha, S., Hanif, M.K., Talib, R.: Overview and comparative study of dimensionality reduction techniques for high dimensional data. Inf. Fus. **59**, 44–58 (2020). https://doi.org/10.1016/j.inffus.2020.01.005
7. Kitchenham, B., Charters, S.: Guidelines for performing Systematic Literature Reviews in Software Engineering (2007). https://userpages.uni-koblenz.de/~laemmel/esecourse/slides/slr.pdf. Accessed 07 Dec 2021
8. Fernandez, A., Insfran, E., Abrahão, S.: Usability evaluation methods for the web: A systematic mapping study. Inf. Softw. Technol. **53**(8), 789–817 (2011). https://doi.org/10.1016/J.INFSOF.2011.02.007

9. Genero Bocco, M., Cruz Lemus, J.A., Piattini Velthuis, M.: Métodos de Investigación en Ingeniería del Software. http://190.57.147.202:90/xmlui/handle/123456789/2525. Accessed 07 Dec 2021

10. Institute of Electrical and Electronic Engineers: Institute of Electrical and Electronic Engineers (2021). https://ieeexplore.ieee.org/Xplore/home.jsp. Accessed 08 Dec 2021

11. Springer Link: Springer Link (2021). https://link.springer.com/. Accessed 08 Dec 2021

12. Web of Science: Web of Science Core Collection (2021). https://www.webofscience.com/wos/woscc/basic-search. Accessed 08 Dec 2021

13. Salazar-Castro, J.A., et al.: A novel color-based data visualization approach using a circular interaction model and dimensionality reduction. In: Huang, T., Lv, J., Sun, C., Tuzikov, A.V. (eds.) ISNN 2018. LNCS, vol. 10878, pp. 557–567. Springer, Cham (2018). https://doi.org/10.1007/978-3-319-92537-0_64

14. Basante-Villota, C.K., et al.: Angle-based model for interactive dimensionality reduction and data visualization. In: Hernández Heredia, Y., Milián Núñez, V., Ruiz Shulcloper, J. (eds.) IWAIPR 2018. LNCS, vol. 11047, pp. 149–157. Springer, Cham (2018). https://doi.org/10.1007/978-3-030-01132-1_17

15. Salazar-Castro, J.A., et al.: Dimensionality reduction for interactive data visualization via a Geo-Desic approach. In: 2016 IEEE Latin American Conference on Computational Intelligence (LA-CCI), November 2016, pp. 1–6 (2016). https://doi.org/10.1109/LA-CCI.2016.7885740

16. Pena-Unigarro, D.F., et al.: Interactive visualization methodology of high-dimensional data with a color-based model for dimensionality reduction. In: 2016 21st Symposium on Signal Processing, Images and Artificial Vision, STSIVA 2016, pp. 1–7 (2016). https://doi.org/10.1109/STSIVA.2016.7743318

17. Rosero-Montalvo, P.D., Peña-Unigarro, D.F., Peluffo, D.H., Castro-Silva, J.A., Umaquinga, A., Rosero-Rosero, E.A.: Data visualization using interactive dimensionality reduction and improved color-based interaction model. In: Ferrández Vicente, J.M., Álvarez-Sánchez, J.R., de la Paz López, F., Toledo Moreo, J., Adeli, H. (eds.) IWINAC 2017. LNCS, vol. 10338, pp. 289–298. Springer, Cham (2017). https://doi.org/10.1007/978-3-319-59773-7_30

18. Rosero-Montalvo, P., et al.: Interactive data visualization using dimensionality reduction and similarity-based representations. In: Beltrán-Castañón, C., Nyström, I., Famili, F. (eds.) Progress in Pattern Recognition, Image Analysis, Computer Vision, and Applications. CIARP 2016. Lecture Notes in Computer Science, vol. 10125. Springer, Cham (2017). https://doi.org/10.1007/978-3-319-52277-7-41

19. Vélez-Falconí, M., González-Vergara, J., Peluffo-Ordóñez, D.H.: Inverse data visualization framework (IDVF): towards a prior-knowledge-driven data visualization. In: Florez, H., Misra, S. (eds.) ICAI 2020. CCIS, vol. 1277, pp. 266–280. Springer, Cham (2020). https://doi.org/10.1007/978-3-030-61702-8_19

20. Sacha, D., et al.: Visual interaction with dimensionality reduction: a structured literature analysis. IEEE Trans. Vis. Comput. Graph 23(1), 241–250 (2017). https://doi.org/10.1109/TVCG.2016.2598495

21. Sacha, D., et al.: What you see is what you can change: human-centered machine learning by interactive visualization. Neurocomputing 268, 164–175 (2017). https://doi.org/10.1016/j.neucom.2017.01.105

22. Turkay, C., Kaya, E., Balcisoy, S., Hauser, H.: Designing progressive and interactive analytics processes for high-dimensional data analysis. IEEE Trans. Vis. Comput. Graph 23(1), 131–140 (2017). https://doi.org/10.1109/TVCG.2016.2598470

23. Rosasn-Arias, L., Sanchezn-Perez, G., Toscano-Medina, L.K., Perez-Meana, H.M., Portillo-Portillo, J.: A graphical user interface for fast evaluation and testing of machine learning models performance. In: 2019 7th International Workshop on Biometrics and Forensics (IWBF), May 2019, pp. 1–5 (2019). https://doi.org/10.1109/IWBF.2019.8739238

24. Fujiwara, T., Kwon, O.H., Ma, K.L.: Supporting analysis of dimensionality reduction results with contrastive learning. IEEE Trans. Vis. Comput. Graph. **26**(1), 45–55 (2020). https://doi.org/10.1109/TVCG.2019.2934251

25. Liutvinavičiene, J., Kurasova, O.: Multi-level massive data visualization: methodology and use cases. Baltic J. Mod. Comput. **6**(4) (2018). https://doi.org/10.22364/bjmc.2018.6.4.01

26. Basante-Villota, C.K., Ortega-Castillo, C.M., Peña-Unigarro, D.F., Revelo-Fuelagán, J.E., Salazar-Castro, J.A., Peluffo-Ordóñez, D.H.: Comparative analysis between embedded-spaces-based and kernel-based approaches for interactive data representation. In: Serrano C., J.E., Martínez-Santos, J.C. (eds.) CCC 2018. CCIS, vol. 885, pp. 28–38. Springer, Cham (2018). https://doi.org/10.1007/978-3-319-98998-3_3

27. Salazar-Castro, J.A., et al.: Generalized low-computational cost Laplacian eigenmaps. In: Yin, H., Camacho, D., Novais, P., Tallón-Ballesteros, A. (eds.) Intelligent Data Engineering and Automated Learning – IDEAL 2018. IDEAL 2018. Lecture Notes in Computer Science, vol. 11314, pp. 661–669. Springer, Cham (2018). https://doi.org/10.1007/978-3-030-03493-1_69

28. Ortega-Bustamante, M.C., Hasperué, W., Peluffo-Ordóñez, D.H., González-Vergara, J., Marín-Gaviño, J., Velez-Falconi, M.: Generalized spectral dimensionality reduction based on kernel representations and principal component analysis. In: Gervasi, O., et al. (eds.) ICCSA 2021. LNCS, vol. 12952, pp. 512–523. Springer, Cham (2021). https://doi.org/10.1007/978-3-030-86973-1_36

29. Peña-Unigarro, D.F., et al.: Interactive data visualization using dimensionality reduction and dissimilarity-based representations. In: Yin, H., et al. (eds.) IDEAL 2017. LNCS, vol. 10585, pp. 461–469. Springer, Cham (2017). https://doi.org/10.1007/978-3-319-68935-7_50

30. Castermans, T., et al.: SolarView: low distortion radial embedding with a focus. IEEE Trans. Vis. Comput. Graph. **25**(10), 2969–2982 (2019). https://doi.org/10.1109/TVCG.2018.2865361

31. Sanchez, A., Soguero-Ruiz, C., Mora-Jiménez, I., Rivas-Flores, F.J., Lehmann, D.J., Rubio-Sánchez, M.: Scaled radial axes for interactive visual feature selection: a case study for analyzing chronic conditions. Exp. Syst. Appl. **100**, 182–196 (2018). https://doi.org/10.1016/j.eswa.2018.01.054

32. Becker, M., Lippel, J., Zielke, T.: Dimensionality reduction for data visualization and linear classification, and the trade-off between robustness and classification accuracy. In: Proceedings of the International Conference on Pattern Recognition, pp. 6478–6485 (2020). https://doi.org/10.1109/ICPR48806.2021.9412865

33. Wagner Filho, J.A., Rey, M.F., Freitas, C.M.D.S., Nedel, L.: Immersive visualization of abstract information: an evaluation on dimensionally-reduced data scatterplots. In: 25th IEEE Conference on Virtual Reality and 3D User Interfaces, VR 2018 - Proceedings, August 2018, pp. 483–490 (2018). https://doi.org/10.1109/VR.2018.8447558

34. Zhou, Z., Zhang, X., Zhou, X., Liu, Y.: Semantic-aware visual abstraction of large-scale social media data with geo-tags. IEEE Access **7**, 114851–114861 (2019). https://doi.org/10.1109/ACCESS.2019.2935471

35. Krause, J., Dasgupta, A., Fekete, J.-D., Bertini, E.: SeekAView: an intelligent dimensionality reduction strategy for navigating high-dimensional data spaces. In: 2016 IEEE 6th Symposium on Large Data Analysis and Visualization (LDAV), October 2016, vol. 35, no. 11, pp. 11–19 (2016). https://doi.org/10.1109/LDAV.2016.7874305

36. Marcilio-Jr, W.E., Eler, D.M.: SADIRE: a context-preserving sampling technique for dimensionality reduction visualizations. J. Vis. **23**(6), 999–1013 (2020). https://doi.org/10.1007/s12650-020-00685-4

37. Kammer, D., et al.: Glyphboard: visual exploration of high-dimensional data combining glyphs with dimensionality reduction. IEEE Trans. Vis. Comput. Graph. **26**(4), 1661–1671 (2020). https://doi.org/10.1109/TVCG.2020.2969060

38. Marcílio-Jr, W.E., Eler, D.M.: Explaining dimensionality reduction results using Shapley values. Exp. Syst. Appl. **178**, 115020 (2021). https://doi.org/10.1016/j.eswa.2021.115020
39. Nguyen, B.D.Q., Hewett, R., Dang, T.: NetScatter: visual analytics of multivariate time series with a hybrid of dynamic and static variable relationships. In: 2021 IEEE 14th Pacific Visualization Symposium (PacificVis), April 2021, vol. 2021-April, pp. 52–60 (2021). https://doi.org/10.1109/PacificVis52677.2021.00015
40. Höllt, T., Vilanova, A., Pezzotti, N., Lelieveldt, B.P.F., Hauser, H.: Focus+context exploration of hierarchical embeddings. Comput. Graph. Forum **38**(3), 569–579 (2019). https://doi.org/10.1111/cgf.13711
41. Wang, Y.C., Zhang, Q., Lin, F., Goh, C.K., Seah, H.S.: PolarViz: a discriminating visualization and visual analytics tool for high-dimensional data. Vis. Comput. **35**(11), 1567–1582 (2018). https://doi.org/10.1007/s00371-018-1558-y
42. Marcílio-Jr, W.E., Eler, D.M., Paulovich, F.v., Rodrigues-Jr, J.F., Artero, A.O.: ExplorerTree: a focus+context exploration approach for 2d embeddings. Big Data Res. **25**, 100239 (2021). https://doi.org/10.1016/j.bdr.2021.100239
43. Garrison, L., Muller, J., Schreiber, S., Oeltze-Jafra, S., Hauser, H., Bruckner, S.: DimLift: interactive hierarchical data exploration through dimensional bundling. IEEE Trans. Vis. Comput. Graph. **27**(6), 2908–2922 (2021). https://doi.org/10.1109/TVCG.2021.3057519
44. Matute, J., Linsen, L.: Hinted star coordinates for mixed data. Comput. Graph. Forum **39**, 117–133 (2019). https://doi.org/10.1111/cgf.13666
45. Sanchez, A., Raya, L., Mohedano-Munoz, M.A., Rubio-Sánchez, M.: Feature selection based on star coordinates plots associated with eigenvalue problems. Vis. Comput. **37**(2), 203–216 (2020). https://doi.org/10.1007/s00371-020-01793-w
46. Roma, G., Xambó, A., Green, O., Tremblay, P.A.: A general framework for visualization of sound collections in musical interfaces. Appl. Sci. (Switzerland) **11**(24) (2021). https://doi.org/10.3390/app112411926
47. Baker, F.N., Porollo, A.: CoeViz: a web-based integrative platform for interactive visualization of large similarity and distance matrices. Data (Basel) **3**(1), 4 (2018). https://doi.org/10.3390/data3010004
48. Pondel, M., Korczak, J.: Recommendations based on collective intelligence – case of customer segmentation. In: Ziemba, E. (ed.) AITM/ISM -2018. LNBIP, vol. 346, pp. 73–92. Springer, Cham (2019). https://doi.org/10.1007/978-3-030-15154-6_5
49. Chen, X., Zeng, G., Kosinka, J., Telea, A.: Scalable visual exploration of 3d shape databases via feature synthesis and selection. In: Computer Vision, Imaging and Computer Graphics Theory and Applications. VISIGRAPP 2020. Communications in Computer and Information Science, vol. 1474, pp. 153–182. Springer, Cham (2022). https://doi.org/10.1007/978-3-030-94893-1_7
50. Sohns, J.-T., Schmitt, M., Jirasek, F., Hasse, H., Leitte, H.: Attribute-based explanations of non-linear embeddings of high-dimensional data, July 2021. http://arxiv.org/abs/2108.08706
51. Mazumdar, D., Neto, M.P., Paulovich, F.v.: Random forest similarity maps: a scalable visual representation for global and local interpretation. Electronics (Switzerland) **10**(22), 2862 (2021). https://doi.org/10.3390/electronics10222862
52. Urpa, L.M., Anders, S.: Focused multidimensional scaling: interactive visualization for exploration of high-dimensional data. BMC Bioinform. **20**(1), 221 (2019). https://doi.org/10.1186/s12859-019-2780-y
53. Fujiwara, T., Wei, X., Zhao, J., Ma, K.L.: Interactive dimensionality reduction for comparative analysis. IEEE Trans. Vis. Comput. Graph. **28**(1), 758–768 (2022). https://doi.org/10.1109/TVCG.2021.3114807
54. Schaefer, G.: Interactive browsing of large image repositories. In: Patnaik, S., Jain, V. (eds.) Recent Developments in Intelligent Computing, Communication and Devices. AISC, vol. 752, pp. 1–7. Springer, Singapore (2019). https://doi.org/10.1007/978-981-10-8944-2_1

55. Li, Z., Zhang, C., Zhang, Y., Zhang, J.: SemanticAxis: exploring multi-attribute data by semantic construction and ranking analysis. J. Vis. **24**(5), 1065–1081 (2021). https://doi.org/10.1007/s12650-020-00733-z

56. Wang, Z., Ferreira, N., Wei, Y., Bhaskar, A.S., Scheidegger, C.: Gaussian cubes: real-time modeling for visual exploration of large multidimensional datasets. IEEE Trans. Vis. Comput. Graph. **23**(1), 681–690 (2017). https://doi.org/10.1109/TVCG.2016.2598694

57. Yu, H., Li, S.: Improved interactive color visualization approach for hyperspectral images. Inf. Vis. **21**(2), 153–165 (2022). https://doi.org/10.1177/14738716211048142

58. Feng, K., Wang, Y., Zhao, Y., Fu, C.W., Cheng, Z., Chen, B.: Cluster aware Star Coordinates. J. Vis. Lang. Comput. **44**, 28–38 (2018). https://doi.org/10.1016/j.jvlc.2017.11.003

59. Sabando, M.V., et al.: ChemVA: interactive visual analysis of chemical compound similarity in virtual screening August 2020. http://arxiv.org/abs/2008.13150

60. Jäckle, D., Fischer, F., Schreck, T., Keim, D.A.: Temporal MDS plots for analysis of multivariate data. IEEE Trans. Vis. Comput. Graph. **22**(1), 141–150 (2016). https://doi.org/10.1109/TVCG.2015.2467553

A Framework to Assist Instructors Help Novice Programmers to Better Comprehend Source Code – A Decoding Perspective

Pakiso J. Khomokhoana$^{(\boxtimes)}$ and Liezel Nel

Department of Computer Science and Informatics, University of the Free State, Bloemfontein, South Africa
{khomokhoanap,nell}@ufs.ac.za

Abstract. The Decoding the Disciplines paradigm posits that each discipline has unique mental operations – often invisible to instructors due to their own expert blind spots. If the nature of these operations is not made explicit to students, they are likely to develop learning bottlenecks that could prevent them from mastering key disciplinary practices – such as the ability to reliably work through the chain of reasoning necessary for efficient source code comprehension (SCC). This study seeks to assist instructors to help novice programmers reliably think and work their way through a long chain of reasoning to efficiently comprehend a piece of source code. We followed a narrative approach where data was collected through decoding interviews with five expert programming instructors. Several SCC strategies were identified, but only the seven key ones were used to devise a step-by-step framework for efficient SCC. Our findings aim to create awareness among instructors regarding the explicit mental operations required for efficient SCC.

Keywords: Source code comprehension · expert programming instructors · decoding the disciplines · decoding interview · computer science education · bottleneck · CS1

1 Introduction

Source code comprehension (SCC) refers to an ability to read, interpret, and understand existing source code [10, 17, 62]. Despite SCC being a critical disciplinary skill [29, 44, 48], many Computer Science (CS) students are still unable to reliably think and work their way through a long chain of reasoning to efficiently comprehend a piece of source code [20, 26]. This student-learning bottleneck can be attributed to students' fragile knowledge of basic programming concepts [5]. A bottleneck refers to specific places where the learning of many students gets interrupted [31]. This interruption happens when students are not sure how to approach a given problem and as a result, apply improper strategies [38].

The severity of a bottleneck can be further intensified when instructors are unable to accurately portray disciplinary ways of thinking to students [31]. This may occur due to instructors' expert blind spots, which typically occur when vital operations have become so natural to disciplinary experts that they tend to omit crucial mental steps when explaining concepts and procedures to others [36]. Decoding the Disciplines (DtDs) is a paradigm that focuses on increasing student learning by bridging the gap between the thinking of novice and expert programmers [32]. The seven-step DtDs paradigm can be used to initially expose the nature of such hidden operations (linked to a specific bottleneck) and to create awareness among instructors regarding steps/operations they typically omit when teaching their students. In subsequent steps of this paradigm, instructors are guided to devise ways of helping students master these operations and hence overcome specific learning bottlenecks [31, 38].

Bottlenecks are typically identified in Step 1 of the DtDs paradigm, while Step 2 focuses on exploring explicit mental steps that disciplinary experts follow to accomplish a task identified as a bottleneck [31, 38]. In executing Step 2, several artefacts and/or techniques (e.g., decoding interviews, rubrics, metaphors/analogies, mind maps, reflective writing, and non-verbal modelling) can be used to uncover the explicit steps followed by experts [31, 32]. However, decoding interviews are cited as the most rigorous and effective technique in this regard [38]. A decoding interview is a special type of interview where disciplinary experts are intellectually guided to reveal explicit steps they follow to get through a predetermined learning bottleneck [30, 38]. As a first step in dealing with a previously defined discipline-specific learning bottleneck (see 2nd sentence of this Section), this study focuses on Step 2 of the DtDs paradigm to answer the following two questions:

- What are the explicit mental strategies that CS experts employ while comprehending source code?
- How can knowledge of these strategies be applied in the formulation of a step-by-step framework that could ultimately contribute towards ways of assisting novice programmers to overcome their "inability to reliably think and work their way through a long chain of reasoning to efficiently comprehend a piece of source code"? (A bottleneck established in [20]).

The rest of this paper is structured as follows: Sect. 2 presents an overview of previously identified SCC strategies relevant to the specific learning bottleneck under investigation. It also provides a discussion comparing strategies used by both novice and expert programmers while comprehending source code. In Sect. 3, detail is provided regarding the selection of the decoding interview participants, interview panel, and validation issues. Section 4 provides the study findings, while Sect. 5 presents a proposed step-by-step framework for efficient SCC. The conclusions, recommendations for future work, and contribution of this study are presented in Sect. 6.

2   Related Work

2.1   Source Code Comprehension Strategies

Literature defines various generic SCC strategies namely, top-down, bottom-up, and variations that either combine these two strategies or incorporate elements thereof [27, 41, 60]. Novice programmers and expert programmers have been shown to favour different strategies, with bottom-down mostly observed with novices [35]. Although the basic steps involved in each of these generic SCC strategies are well documented, more specific details are needed to truly understand the explicit mental operations required for efficient SCC. Previously, researchers used observations [51] and think-alouds [26] to gather more information on specific strategies employed during SCC.

In evaluating ways by which students answered code-based Multiple-Choice Questions (MCQs), Fitzgerald et al. [11] identified 19 strategies used by novice programmers. These range from reading the question; previewing the code (e.g., by identifying data structures and their initialisation); understanding new concepts (semantic); pattern recognition (e.g., temporally self-referential, outside knowledge and seeking higher levels of meaning from the code); walkthroughs; strategising; thoroughness; starting over; coming back to the question later; posing questions; and doodling. Although this list includes several good SCC strategies, as also identified by other researchers (e.g., [26]), the novices did not always execute these strategies in an optimum way. However, Fitzgerald et al.'s [11] strategies are much more specific than the generic SCC strategies alluded to in the previous paragraph. Although students and experts do not necessarily follow the same SCC strategies, these generic strategies could serve as a starting point to identify more explicit details on the exact mental operations required for effective SCC.

In Fitzgerald et al.'s [11] study, the novices used the reading the question and previewing strategies to acquaint themselves with some elements of the code-based questions they were answering. This type of self-orientation is a strategy used by people to familiarise themselves with the elements of the problem to be tackled [16]. Simon et al. [52] emphasise the importance of reading programs or pieces of code to comprehend them. In this regard, Moore et al. [34] even suggest reading through question specifications or a piece of source code twice. To further enhance comprehension of a task, strategies such as highlighting, underlining, and colouring some words or text can also be used [43, 46]. These important words or pieces of text could be regarded as key for a programmer's comprehension of either the problem description or code in question. However, the use of keywords is one SCC strategy that has not been observed with Fitzgerald et al.'s [11] novices.

Littman et al. [27] observe that programmers use either systematic (line-by-line) source code reading or control/data-flow abstractions to better comprehend the behaviour of a given program or piece of code. For novice programmers to fully comprehend code behaviour, they need to have a global understanding of the piece of source code in question. Global understanding entails gaining an overall understanding of the problem to be solved or the question to be answered before trying to understand the minute details of the task. This understanding already starts to develop in the previewing SCC strategies suggested by Fitzgerald et al. [11]. Comprehension can also be enhanced through pattern recognition where similar or related code elements are organised into categories [22].

Similar to solving many real-world problems, the solving of SCC problems also requires the application of logical reasoning processes [4]. The logical reasoning processes are also a huge challenge to students in comprehending code [19]. In SCC problems, test cases can, for example, be used to check the logic of both basic and advanced conditions [58]. To evaluate these test cases, a programmer typically conducts a walkthrough of the given source code. Walkthroughs are defined as "simply reading the code carefully in the order it would be executed (except for branch points, where all branches are considered serially), to careful simulation, where the [programmer] attempts to mimic as closely as possible the actions of the [computer/compiler] that executes the code" [18] (p. 12). Other ways in which programmers can apply logical reasoning, is by strategising about how they would solve a given problem if they had to write code from scratch or by asking themselves specific questions (i.e., posing questions) that could help with their comprehension of a given piece of code. The thoroughness strategy, where an answer is re-checked to confirm the correctness thereof, can be applied in answering any type of question. Frederick [12] (p. 35) states that people should have "the ability or disposition to resist reporting the response that first comes to mind" – thereby suggesting that, regardless of the type of question, an answer to a question should always be evaluated to confirm its correctness thereof.

Given the relative simplicity (e.g., in terms of instructions and code fragments used) of the code-based questions used in Fitzgerald et al.'s [11] study, the starting over and coming back to the question later strategies could be regarded as typical novice strategies that one would not necessarily expect to observe with expert programmers.

From this discussion, it is evident that although various SCC strategies have previously been identified, some of these strategies seem to be more novice-specific. For comprehensive literature coverage, a discussion of similarities and differences between novices and experts during SCC could be necessary.

2.2 Comparing Novice and Expert Programmers

In the initial stages of SCC, both experienced and novice programmers follow similar overall strategies, but their strategies differ later on [18]. Experienced programmers use their experience, syntactic knowledge, and knowledge of a problem domain, while novice programmers read source code line-by-line [23, 53]. Experienced programmers focus only on reading source code relating to a particular task at hand, while novice programmers focus on all elements of the code [27, 56]. Experienced programmers further use a semantic approach, while novice programmers are driven by how a program works syntactically rather than what a program does semantically [1, 54]. Experienced programmers get more affected by violations of the rules of discourse in a piece of code than novice programmers [55, 57]. Both experienced and novice programmers pay the least attention to the keywords in the source code's text [9].

Experienced programmers outdo novices in situations where they must recall meaningful source codes. However, both do equally well when they must recall source codes that are not well-designed [47]. Experienced programmers link parts of the source code to the problem domain, which is unusual for novice programmers [41]. It is easier for experienced programmers to realise when they must change or adapt their comprehension strategy – especially as a result of discovering an anomaly in the source code or when the requested task has some inherent special needs [59]. Experts have, however, been observed to revert to a line-by-line strategy in cases where they were not familiar with a programming system [21].

The next section presents the research design and procedure that was followed to identify strategies that expert programming instructors follow during SCC.

3 Research Design and Methods

A narrative research approach based on Plowright's [42] Frameworks for an Integrated Methodology (FraIM) was adhered to in this study. The data source management strategy was a case study. Data were mainly collected through face-to-face decoding interviews [31] (as a means of asking questions), while observations were used as a supplementary strategy. The study population consisted of CS instructors from a selected South African university. From this population, five instructors were purposefully selected [7] based on their experience in teaching programming courses. Two of the participants (P1 and P4) had more than 14 years of experience in this regard, while P2 and P3 had between five and nine years of similar experience. Except for P5, all the other participants worked as industry programmers for at least four years, and they were all, to some extent, still involved in private programming consultancy work. This sample can also be regarded as convenient [40] since the selected participants were close to the researcher and therefore easily reachable. Ethical clearance for this study was obtained from the selected institution and all ethical considerations were adhered to throughout the study investigations.

3.1 Decoding Interviews

Decoding interviews are considered intellectually very demanding [31], where a single interviewer can easily get lost in the details. Pace [38] recommends the involvement of at least two interviewers, as two minds are in a better position to control the interview process. Both interviewers should be able to verbalise their thinking, challenge the interviewees' explanations, and summarise the interviewees' thinking back to them at an abstract level [50]. As members of the same discipline are more likely to share common expert blind spots, Pace [38] also suggests using a second interviewer from outside the discipline in question. Such an interviewer is more likely to notice when mental steps are not well explained. Since we could not find a readily available individual with the relevant decoding-interview experience from outside the CS discipline, we instead selected a non-teaching CS researcher who had some decoding-interview experience as the second interviewer. The decision was also influenced by the context of this research activity. Given the highly discipline-specific nature of SCC, someone from outside the discipline might not necessarily be able to follow the reasoning of the interviewees and could find it difficult to instantly think of appropriate and relevant probing questions to ask.

Separate decoding interviews were conducted with each of the five selected participants. The principal researcher (first author) acted as the main interviewer, while the second interviewer (as described in the above paragraph) played a supporting role. The proceedings of each interview were audio recorded with the permission of the participant. Where relevant, observations were also recorded by the principal researcher. The main purpose of the decoding interviews was to uncover the explicit mental strategies and steps followed by participants during an SCC task. In the first part of the decoding interview, each participant was asked to explain the steps they would follow when requested to predict the output of any piece of source code provided on a piece of paper. The participants' responses to this general question allowed the interviewers a first glance at some of the basic SCC strategies utilised by expert programmers.

To uncover more explicit details regarding the nature of the shared strategies, the participants were each presented with an SCC task and asked to illustrate how they would implement their SCC strategy (as explained in the first part of the interview) to solve the given problem. The question selected for this activity was sourced from the original set of 12 MCQs used in Lister et al.'s [26] study. The selected question (Question 6 – see Fig. 1) was identified as the second most challenging question in the Lister et al. [26] study. This question was particularly selected as it covers a wider range of concepts (e.g., Boolean variables, for loops, array indices, and the use of a return statement to terminate the for loop) than the most challenging question (Question 12, which mainly focuses on arrays). In answering the selected question, the missing piece of code had to be identified from the five given options. (Note: The correct answer is Option B). The only change made to the question was to convert the original Java code into C# (which was the language mainly used by participants in their teaching). The code line numbers as indicated in Fig. 1 were only added in aid of the discussion in this paper.

3.2 Data Analysis

An adapted version of Creswell and Creswell's [8] narrative Data Analysis Framework guided the transcription of the audio recordings (made during the decoding interviews), as well as the analysis of the resultant narrative data. Considering the open-endedness of the decoding interview proceedings, a fuzzy-validation strategy [39] was employed to clean the data. This strategy allows some corrections to the data if there is a close match or known answer. The resulting transcripts were validated by each participant as part of member checking [25]. Inherently, it is well-accepted that in dealing with narrative inquiries, the researcher is regarded as the instrument [40]. As such, we had to immerse ourselves in the data to be fully familiar with its breadth and depth [3]. This was achieved through several counts of listening and re-listening to the audio recordings, coupled with intensive reading and re-reading of the transcripts.

After immersing ourselves in the data, we decided on a coding plan that would help with the analysis of the data to address the research questions. The five validated transcripts were imported into NVivo 12 software and codes were created based on the strategies identified in the data. Subsequently, words and/or short phrases [45] containing indications of the relevant strategies or steps were extracted (under the guidance of the theoretical guidelines from literature) from the imported transcripts onto the various nodes (forming codes) created on NVivo. As coding gives rise to recurring themes [45], the extraction and movement of the relevant text gave birth to such themes. For each theme, NVivo generated the frequency of occurrence, hence making it easier to put the data back together to make new meaning in relation to fully answering the research questions of the study [24].

3.3 Validation

After completion of the data analysis, an initial step-by-step framework for efficient SCC was compiled. To enhance the validity of the framework, we deemed it necessary to have this framework evaluated and validated by an informed audience. The validation was deemed necessary to enhance the trustworthiness [49] of this study's findings. In this regard, two separate validation activities were conducted. First, the second decoding interviewer reviewed the initial framework to confirm that the identified strategies and steps were a true representation of the data gathered during the decoding interview; and to check all the statements for clarity and ambiguity. Second, a validation meeting was arranged with five participants (one junior lecturer, a postdoctoral student, and three professors) from the CS department. One of the professors earlier participated in the decoding interviews (as described in Sect. 3.1). The purpose of this meeting was to further check for possible ambiguities in the proposed steps/strategies. To validate the implementability and usefulness of the framework, participants were requested to follow the framework steps (as closely as possible) while answering two SCC questions. After an explanation of the framework, participants worked on solving the first problem under the guidance of the principal researcher. For the second question, each participant independently followed the framework steps to answer the question. This was followed by an open discussion where participants shared their experiences in using the framework to answer the two questions. Some issues regarding the wording of some of the steps came to light and recommendations for possible changes and additions were discussed.

```
The following method isSorted should return true if the array is sorted in ascending
order. Otherwise, the method should return false:

1. public static bool isSorted (int[] x)
2. {
3.    //missing source code goes here
4. }

Which of the following is the missing source code from the method isSorted?
a)   5. bool b = true;
     6. for (int i = 0; i < x.Length - 1; i++)
     7. {
     8.    if (x[i] > x[i + 1])
     9.        b = false;
     10.   else
     11.       b = true;
     12. }
     13. return b;

b)   14. for (int i = 0; i < x.Length - 1; i++)
     15. {
     16.   if (x[i] > x[i + 1])
     17.        return false;
     18. }
     19. return true;

c)   20. bool b = false;
     21. for (int i = 0; i < x.Length - 1; i++)
     22. {
     23.   if (x[i] > x[i + 1])
     24.       b = false;
     25. }
     26. return b;

d)   27. bool b = false;
     28. for (int i = 0; i < x.Length - 1; i++)
     29. {
     30.   if (x[i] > x[i + 1])
     31.       b = true;
     32. }
     33. return b;

e)   34. for (int i = 0; i < x.Length - 1; i++)
     35. {
     36.   if (x[i] > x[i + 1])
     37.        return true;
     38. }
     39. return false;
```

Fig. 1. Source code question used in the decoding interview

Based on the feedback received during this validation meeting, a few minor changes were made to the initial framework. The findings of this study are presented in Sect. 4.

4 Results and Interpretation

Based on the analysis of the decoding-interview transcripts, several SCC strategies were observed with our participants. However, only strategies with four or more occurrences are presented except for the keyword identification strategy (two occurrences). Though not commonly mentioned by the participants, this strategy was frequently observed during the decoding interview when participants were tackling the given task.

4.1 Self-orientation

During self-orientation, programmers typically read the question and perform a lot of code previewing on related aspects as suggested by Fitzgerald et al. [11]. Application of this strategy was identified in all our participants, with a total of 18 occurrences. Participant 4 (P4) employed the strategy the most, with eight occurrences.

As part of his self-orientation, P4 shared very specific details about how he typically starts to comprehend a piece of code and provided reasons for his actions. Linking to the importance of reading the question description and code statement [52], P4 also provided some insight regarding the reading intensity he would employ in the process:

> *"Whenever I read code, I browse through it very quickly, not looking at detail. I try to get the basic idea and then I browse through it again. So, I do not read once from top to bottom and then I am done – never! I read through a piece of code more than once – three, four, five times ... Some of the details will go slow, and some of them will be quick depending on my familiarity with that specific code fragment. ... I will go and look at it globally. Again, I will make sure that my conceptual understanding of what it is supposed to be, is in order."*

From this excerpt, it is apparent that P4 read the source code more than once (i.e., reread – [34]) to ensure that he attained the correct understanding. Expert programmers tend to read code at least twice (even if they understood it at first) just to confirm their original understanding [52]. To confirm the importance of rereading code, P4 was asked if he ever reads a piece of code just once, even if it is very simple. In response, he said: *"No, it depends on the length. If it is two lines of code, yes, then I might read it more than once by looking at it once. I mean, your brain can cognitively observe a thing more than once, while visually looking at it once."* This response could serve as an indication that experts understand that there is some coordination between seeing something and processing it in the brain, as reading is cognitive in nature [37].

4.2 Walkthroughs

Adopting the definition of code walkthrough by Jeffries [18] (see Sect. 2.1), sixteen occurrences of this strategy were identified. P4 employed walkthroughs the most, with seven occurrences.

There were several instances where participants modelled this strategy through their mental actions, as suggested by Hertz and Jump [15]. P2 in particular, said:

"I will do a trace table. And I will draw and say, this is where I am tracing the code. I will carry on to another trace table. If I have the code on a piece of paper, I will go and write – in line 1, this is what is happening, and this is my variable. In line 2, this is what is happening. In line 3, we are making a function call to that method. And then I will jump to that method and associate it with lines and write out a picture of what is happening."

In this instance, P2 was observed physically drawing a trace table and putting in arbitrary labels for the respective input and output values of variables. She was actually trying to make her SCC steps or processes as visible as possible [6] and also modelling what was happening in her mind [15].

Concerning situations where the use of test cases might not be specifically feasible, other participants indicated that they would not use test cases as suggested by Srikant and Aggarwal [58], because it would be time-consuming to consider all cases available in each scenario. In this regard, P2 said: *"Let us say I have an array of 100 elements, I am not going to sit in class and draw 100 things on my trace table, so I will do a few."* However, P2 would be careful in selecting a limited set of test cases that would at least cover the *"worst, average, and best cases"*, thereby accommodating testing boundary or error conditions as specified by Fitzgerald et al. [11].

4.3 Strategic Thinking

Strategic thinking involves the use of high-level and critical thinking as well as logical reasoning in both understanding and solving a problem, thereby approaching this problem from a variety of angles or differing perspectives [14]. Activities performed as part of the strategising and posing questions strategies, as suggested by Fitzgerald et al. [11], require high-level reasoning [26]. These strategies, therefore, challenge programmers to tap into their strategic skills. Fifteen occurrences were identified where this strategy was used. P4 employed the strategy the most, with seven occurrences. It is impossible not to use logical/strategic reasoning processes in problem-solving [4]. P4 used an example of a repetition structure to explain his reasoning while dealing with such a structure: *"If I read code, let us say there is a while loop. The first things I look for are: Are the three elements there? (Do not look at the code, look if those three elements are there.) Is there a condition? Is the condition initialised? Is there a place somewhere in the loop where the conditions will be changed? If those three elements are not there, the while loop is not going to work."* As can be seen from this excerpt, P4's strategic reasoning allowed him to understand that it would be useless to read the code further [27, 56] if the conditions under which such a repetition structure would operate are not met. It is also evident in the excerpt that P4 would be very careful to heavily rely on code functionality than other aspects such as code syntax.

4.4 Revisit Previous Stages

In executing the revisit previous stages strategy, a programmer moves back and forth between different parts of the question (problem specification and/or code). This strategy is typically performed to ensure a complete understanding of concepts and to integrate various aspects contained in the question to be answered and/or the problem to be solved. Five occurrences of this strategy were identified among the participants in this study. P3 employed the strategy the most, with three occurrences.

As an indication that P2 would check previous occurrences of a certain variable if a need arises, she said: *"And you can always refer back if you forget that there was this variable."* Similarly, P3 said: *"If it is something I cannot fit into my working memory and reliably remember what happened earlier in the program, I have to continually refer back to the previous part of the program just to familiarise myself again."* It can be deduced from P3's excerpt that this strategy is not applied all the time. Instead, participants (as experts) employ the notion of the capacity of the working memory [33], to say there is no need to revisit previous stages if information needed can be recalled from the working memory. This resonates with Wiedenbeck et al. [61] that expert programmers use little working memory during SCC.

4.5 Data Structure Identification

The identification of data structures entails locating a place where a variable/constant or an object is first encountered (i.e., declared), and identifying the value originally assigned to it (i.e., instantiation or initialisation). The identification occurs mostly during the previewing strategies (e.g., identifying data structures, the initialisation of data structures, and control structures) of Fitzgerald et al. [11]. If a data structure is unfamiliar to a programmer, they could resort to using the *understanding new concept (semantic) strategy*, thereby suggesting that previewing the code and understanding new concepts (e.g., semantic) may be usable in the identification of data structures. Four occurrences of this strategy were identified in the participants of this study. P3 employed the strategy the most, with three occurrences. P2 indicated that, although she would do it faster than students might do it (as a result of experience gathered over many years), she would still identify the data structures involved in a given piece of code. This is a very valid statement since identifying and understanding data structures is a challenge often experienced by novice programmers [28]. In this regard, P2 said: *"I do not have to look line-by-line and explain to myself what is happening. I can follow it much quicker than a student might. So, there might be things that I skip, but I would still look at the variables."* P2's revelation that she would skip some steps could point to an expert blind spot – causing her not to share the same steps she would personally follow while teaching her students. This action could have a negative impact on the SCC's understanding of her students [2].

4.6 Deduction of Meaning from Context

Deduction of meaning from context entails understanding the meaning of certain challenging concepts from reading associated statements or pieces of text. This could form part of Fitzgerald et al.'s [11] understanding of new concepts (semantic) strategy. To deduce meaning from the problem context, expert programmers follow various courses of action. Three of our participants (though four occurrences) shared what they would do if they came across challenging concepts. P4 employed this strategy the most, with two occurrences. He shared the following in this regard: *"So I carry on, and the context of the global view might clarify that little piece that I do not understand. It happens quite often that if I understand something globally, it will lead me to the details that I do not understand, and it becomes easier. It is all a matter of context. It is easier to understand difficult parts if I have the context to which they belong."* It, therefore, becomes evident that failing to understand how a specific concept is used does not necessarily block the understanding of experts in terms of how that concept works. As established by Fitzgerald et al. [11] and observed with P4, experts do not have a problem proceeding with subsequent steps, because they believe that such steps may give them some idea(s) that could help to improve their understanding of difficult or unclear concepts.

4.7 Keyword Identification

A keyword is a word/concept that provides preliminary ideas on the significance of such words/concepts in the task to be tackled, hence pre-empting a person to remember it throughout the task. As indicated by Powell et al. [43], different ways can be used to identify keywords while comprehending source code. Two occurrences of using keywords were identified in two of the participants. In this regard, P2 said: *"What will catch my attention are the keywords. If I have syntax highlighting, it is a lot easier to identify the keywords."* This suggests that while using an integrated development environment (IDE) such as Microsoft Visual Studio that provides this colour functionality, P2 would take advantage of the built-in syntax highlighting [29, 46] to identify important words in the code.

Another participant, P4, took advantage of the keywords contained in the problem specifications by earmarking them as his main focus. He explicitly indicated that the other words were just there to link all the ideas together: *"The first thing to do is to make sure that I understand the question. You have helped me a bit by boldfacing some words. So, I will read the question, focusing only on the boldfaced words. Then I will read it again, and I will boldface in my mind some other words such as array, method, and sorted. So, these are the words that immediately come to mind. The other words glue everything together."* In this regard, it should be noted that, in the question presented to participants (see Fig. 1), words that referred to specific coding concepts were formatted in a different typeface – merely to distinguish it from the normal sentence text. P4 took advantage of our formatting strategy by using these words to mentally prepare himself for his SCC endeavour and to enhance his understanding of what was required of him in answering the question. In contrast to Crosby and Stelovsky [9], our expert participants focused more on the keywords. These words are scaffolds that help in making links to known information or previously seen/solved problems [13].

5 Framework for Efficient SCC

By using strategies identified in Sect. 4 together with insights gained from literature, observations made of expert participants during the decoding interviews, feedback received from the validation meeting, and the authors' collective experience as programming instructors, a proposed step-by-step framework for efficient SCC (see Table 1) was formulated. As an example, Step 1 was formulated by using the relevant aspects of the five SCC strategies (self-orientation, keyword identification, strategic thinking, and revisiting previous stages; and Step 2 was constituted from the necessary elements of the two strategies namely, self-orientation and revisiting previous stages. As each strategy has various dimensions in its implementation, some strategies have been used in the formulation of more than one step. Typically, strategic thinking has been used in the formulation of seven steps, while self-orientation in six steps. This framework contains 10 key steps linked to each of the relevant mental strategies used by the experts in executing each of these steps (as discussed in Sect. 4). However, within some of the main steps, several sub-steps can be performed. In using this framework, it is recommended that users put a tick mark (✓) against each step/sub-step they use, and a cross mark (✗) against any step/sub-step they do not use. The additional resource(s) mentioned in Step 1 could include official study material, resources from the Internet, or an expert (e.g., instructor, tutor, student assistant). It is also suggested that users of this framework should be encouraged to revisit previous steps whenever they get stuck.

Table 1. Step-by-step framework for answering a source code comprehension question

Strategies Applied	Steps	Description
• Self-orientation • Keyword identification • Strategic thinking • Revisit previous stages	1. Understand the problem	Read through the question statement/requirements at least twice (until you understand what you have to do). • Highlight/mark important words and/or phrases and make sure you understand their meaning or implication. • If there are any words and/or phrases that you do not understand, consult any additional resource(s)* for clarification. • If I were to write the code to solve the problem, how would I do it?
• Self-orientation • Revisit previous stages	2. Scan through the code (not recognising syntax)	Preview all the given code by scanning through it at least twice (to get a global overview). • Do not look at detailed syntax.
• Self-orientation • Data structure identification • Strategic thinking • Walkthroughs	3. Scan through the code (recognising syntax)	Scan through the code line-by-line. • Identify all the data structures. • Identify all the control structures (e.g., *Sequence, Iteration, Selection*). • Identify any methods/functions/properties. • Make sure that you understand the syntax and meaning (e.g., *semantics*) of each individual code fragment/statement. • Mark any code syntax and/or code fragments/statements that you do not understand. • Mark code fragments/statements that are similar or repeated.
• Self-orientation	4. Seek clarification	If there is code syntax that you do not understand, consult any additional resource(s) for clarification.
• Deduction of meaning from context	5. Use context	If there are still code fragments/statements that you do not understand, consider the context in which the fragment/statement is used. (Note: A more global view of the context in which the code fragment/statement is used might help to clarify your misunderstanding).
• Self-orientation • Strategic thinking • Revisit previous stages	6. Confirm your understanding	Scan through all the code again (as many times as necessary) to make sure that you fully understand how everything fits together. • Repeat Step 3, Step 4 and/or Step 5 if necessary. • Draw a diagram to visualise your understanding of the program logic (if applicable).
• Strategic thinking	7. Scan through the code (not recognising syntax)	If the question requires you to select the correct code fragment/statement(s) from multiple options: • Identify the option(s) that look(s) more correct. (Consider these first in Step 8). • Identify options that could possibly be incorrect. (Only consider these *possibly incorrect* options if none of the *more correct* options turn out to be a valid/correct answer). • Explain to yourself why you think some option(s) could be more correct than others.
• Self-orientation • Strategic thinking • Walkthroughs	8. Deal with multiple choice questions	Trace through the code by executing (from the top) each line according to the rules of the programming language. • Whenever a new variable/constant/object is created, write down its name and the initial value(s) (if applicable) on a piece of paper. (*Suggestion: Start a trace table*). • Record any changes to the value(s) of the variables/objects on your piece of paper. • Make any applicable drawings, notes or annotations that could help you keep track of or follow the program logic. (**Do not try to keep it all in your head!**)
• Strategic thinking • Revisit previous stages	9. Trace and execute the code	Write down your answer. • If it is not a valid answer, repeat Step 8 using one of the other answer options.
• Strategic thinking • Walkthroughs • Revisit previous stages • Thoroughness	10. Report your result	Repeat Step 8 to confirm the correctness of your final answer. • Use your own test case values (if not provided).

6 Conclusions and Future Work

The gap that exists between the ways in which novice and expert programmers comprehend source code continues to be a challenge. A better understanding of those mental operations that have become invisible to instructors (because they perform them automatically), could be valuable in enhancing novice programmer thinking. This can be achieved by uncovering the explicit nature of the mental strategies followed by experts during SCC. By focusing on Step 2 of the DtDs framework, this study utilised decoding interviews to systematically deconstruct mental operations performed by expert programmers while comprehending a piece of source code. Thematic analysis of the data collected during the decoding interviews revealed several strategies that expert programmers typically employ during SCC. However, this paper reports only on the seven key of those strategies. Given the nature of the source code question used as an example and the previous experience in programming subjects, it is worth noting that most of the strategies described by Fitzgerald et al. [11] and in this paper are very imperative-oriented. What also became apparent, is that each expert approaches SCC differently. At any stage during the SCC process, experts' prior knowledge or experience can trigger them to use specific strategies. Experts also find it easy to switch to a completely different strategy based on what they are currently thinking and the information or details they are encountering.

The SCC strategies identified in this study, combined with existing knowledge (from literature and based on the authors' experience), were used to develop a proposed step-by-step framework for efficient SCC. This framework is set to create awareness among instructors regarding the explicit mental operations required for efficient SCC. Knowledge of the nature of these mental operations could help instructors to better understand their expert blind spots. Furthermore, as a practical contribution within the realm of the DtDs philosophy [31], this framework could also serve as a starting point for devising explicit strategies to model these mental operations to students and to help them master each of the identified strategies. It is also believed that the framework has the potential to make a theoretical contribution to the field of CS education as a source of further research on efficient SCC strategies. This framework could also stimulate further research regarding the application and refinement of the framework itself.

The distinct decoding interview approach followed in this study – where multiple experts were observed and questioned (regarding their mental actions) while performing an actual discipline-specific task – could be regarded as an extension of the traditional decoding-interview approach. In disciplines where it is possible to observe actual tasks in real-time, a similar decoding-interview strategy could be used to uncover even more explicit details regarding the mental operations required to overcome discipline-specific student learning bottlenecks. This study also serves as further proof that the DtDs paradigm can be used in the investigation of classroom practices as suggested by Middendorf and Pace [31]. Consequently, such a research approach should hold particular appeal for instructors working in CS education as well as computing education and other related disciplines.

References

1. Adelson, B.: Structure and Strategy in the Semantically-Rich Domains. Harvard University, Cambridge (1983)
2. Ambrose, A.S., Bridges, W.M., DiPietro, M., Lovett, C.M., Norman, K.M.: How learning works: Seven research-based principles for smart teaching. John Wiley & Sons (2010). https://doi.org/10.1002/mop.21454
3. Braun, V., Clarke, V.: Using thematic analysis in psychology. Qual. Res. Psychol. 3(2), 77–101 (2006). https://doi.org/10.1191/1478088706qp063oa
4. Butler, M., Morgan, M.: Learning challenges faced by novice programming students studying high level and low feedback concepts. In: Atkinson, R., McBeath, C., Swee Kit, A.S., Cheers, C. (Eds.) Proceedings of Ascilite Singapore 2007 ICT: Providing Choices for Learners and Learning, pp. 99–107. Nanyang Technological University (2007)
5. Cheah, C.S.: Factors contributing to the difficulties in teaching and learning of computer programming: A literature review. Contemp. Educ. Technol. 12(2), 1–14 (2020). https://doi.org/10.30935/cedtech/8247
6. Chou, C.Y., Sun, P.F.: An educational tool for visualizing students' program tracing processes. Comput. Appl. Eng. Educ. 21(3), 432–438 (2013). https://doi.org/10.1002/cae.20488
7. Cooper, D., Schindler, P.: Business Research Methods, 12th edn. McGraw-Hill Education (2013)
8. Creswell, J.W., Creswell, J.D.: Research Design: Qualitative, Quantitative, and Mixed Methods Approaches, 5th edn. Sage (2017)
9. Crosby, M.E., Stelovsky, J.: How do we read algorithms?: A case study. Computer 23(1), 25–35 (1990). https://doi.org/10.1109/2.48797
10. Fellah, A., Bandi, A., Yousef, M.: Moving towards program comprehension in software development: A case study. In: Proceedings of the 4th International Conference on Computing Methodologies and Communication, ICCMC 2020, pp. 660–665 (2020). https://doi.org/10.1109/ICCMC48092.2020.ICCMC-000122
11. Fitzgerald, S., Simon, B., Thomas, L.: Strategies that students use to trace code: An analysis based in grounded theory. In: Proceedings of the First International Workshop on Computing Education Research, pp. 69–80 (2005). https://doi.org/10.1145/1089786.1089793
12. Frederick, S.: Cognitive reflection and decision making. J. Econ. Perspect. 19(4), 25–42 (2005). https://doi.org/10.1257/089533005775196732
13. Gaspar, A., Langevin, S.: Restoring "coding with intention" in introductory programming courses. In: SIGITE'07 - Proceedings of the 2007 ACM Information Technology Education Conference, March 2016, pp. 91–98 (2007). https://doi.org/10.1145/1324302.1324323
14. Grundy, T.: Demystifying strategic thinking: lessons from leading CEOs. Kogan Page Publishers (2014)
15. Hertz, M., Jump, M.: Trace-based teaching in early programming courses. In: Proceedings of the 44th ACM Technical Symposium on Computer Science Education, pp. 561–566 (2013). https://doi.org/10.1145/2445196.2445364
16. Illeris, K.: Learning, identity and self-orientation in youth. Nord. J. Youth Res. 11(4), 357–373 (2003). https://doi.org/10.4324/9781315620565-6
17. Izu, C., et al.: Fostering program comprehension in novice programmers - learning activities and learning trajectories. In: Annual Conference on Innovation and Technology in Computer Science Education, ITiCSE, December, pp. 27–52 (2019). https://doi.org/10.1145/3344429.3372501
18. Jeffries, R.: A comparison of the debugging behavior of expert and novice programmers. In: Proceedings of AERA Annual Meeting, pp. 1–17 (1982)

19. Karahasanović, A., Thomas, R.C.: Difficulties experienced by students in maintaining object-oriented systems: An empirical study. Proc. Ninth Australas. Conf. Comput. Educ. **66**, 81–87 (2007)

20. Khomokhoana, P.J., Nel, L.: Decoding Source Code Comprehension: Bottlenecks Experienced by Senior Computer Science Students. In: Tait, B., Kroeze, J., Gruner, S. (eds.) SACLA 2019. CCIS, vol. 1136, pp. 17–32. Springer, Cham (2020). https://doi.org/10.1007/978-3-030-35629-3_2

21. Ko, A.J., Uttl, B.: Individual differences in program comprehension strategies in unfamiliar programming systems. In: Proceedings of the 11th IEEE International Workshop on Program Comprehension (2003). https://doi.org/10.1109/WPC.2003.1199201

22. Kpalma, K., Ronsin, J.: An overview of advances of pattern recognition systems in computer vision. In: Obinata, G., Dutta, A. (Eds.) Vision Systems: Segmentation and Pattern Recognition, pp. 357–382. IntechOpen (2007). https://doi.org/10.5772/4960

23. Letovsky, S., Soloway, E.: Delocalized plans and program comprehension. IEEE Softw. **3**(3), 41–49 (1986). https://doi.org/10.1109/MS.1986.233414

24. Lewins, A., Silver, C.: Using Software in Qualitative Research: A Step-by-Step Guide. Sage Publications (2007)

25. Lincoln, Y.S., Guba, E.G.: Naturalistic inquiry. Sage Publications (1985)

26. Lister, R., et al.: A multi-national study of reading and tracing skills in novice programmers. In: SIGCSE Bulletin (Association for Computing Machinery, Special Interest Group on Computer Science Education), vol. 36, no. 4 (2004). https://doi.org/10.1145/1041624.104 1673

27. Littman, D.C., Pinto, J., Letovsky, S., Soloway, E.: Mental models and software maintenance. J. Syst. Softw. **7**(4), 341–355 (1987). https://doi.org/10.1016/0164-1212(87)90033-1

28. Litvinov, S., Mingazov, M., Myachikov, V., Ivanov, V., Palamarchuk, Y., Sozonov, P., Succi, G.: A tool for visualizing the execution of programs and stack traces especially suited for novice programmers. In: Proceedings of the 12th International Conference on Evaluation of Novel Approaches to Software Engineering, pp. 235–240. https://doi.org/10.5220/000633 6902350240

29. Medvidova, M., Porubän, J.: Program comprehension and quality experiments in programming education. In: OpenAccess Series in Informatics, vol. 102, no. 14, pp. 14:1–14:0. Schloss Dagstuhl – Leibniz-Zentrum für Informatik, Dagstuhl Publishing, Germany (2022). https://doi.org/10.4230/OASIcs.ICPEC.2022.14

30. Middendorf, J., Baer, A.: Bottlenecks of information literacy. In: Gibson, C., Mader, S. (Eds.), Building Teaching and Learning Communities: Creating Shared Meaning and Purpose, pp. 51–68. ACRL Publications (2019)

31. Middendorf, J.K., Pace, D.: Decoding the disciplines: A model for helping students learn disciplinary ways of thinking. New Dir. Teach. Learn. **2004**(98), 1–12 (2004). https://doi.org/10.1002/tl.142

32. Middendorf, J., Shopkow, L.: Overcoming Student Learning Bottlenecks: Decode Your Disciplinary Critical Thinking. Stylus Publishing, LLC (2018)

33. Miller, G.A.: The magical number seven, plus or minus two: Some limits on our capacity for processing information. Psychol. Rev. **101**(2), 343–352 (1956). https://doi.org/10.1037/h00 43158

34. Moore, D., Zabrucky, K., Commander, N.E.: Metacomprehension and comprehension performance in younger and older adults. Educ. Gerontol. **23**(5), 467–475 (1997). https://doi.org/10.1080/0360126970230506

35. Mosemann, R., Wiedenbeck, S.: Navigation and comprehension of programs by novice programmers. In: Proceedings of the 9th International Workshop on Program Comprehension, pp. 79–88 (2001). https://doi.org/10.1109/WPC.2001.921716

36. Nathan, M.J., Petrosino, A.: Expert blind spot among preservice teachers. Am. Educ. Res. J. **40**(4), 905–928 (2003). https://doi.org/10.3102/00028312040004905
37. O'Brien, M.P., Buckley, J.: Inference-based and expectation-based processing in program comprehension. In: Proceedings of the 9th International Workshop on Program Comprehension (2001). https://doi.org/10.1109/WPC.2001.921715
38. Pace, D.: The Decoding the Disciplines Paradigm: Seven Steps to Increased Student Learning. Indiana University Press (2017)
39. Parcell, E.S., Rafferty, K.A.: Interviews, recording and transcribing. In: Allen, M. (Ed.), The SAGE Encyclopedia of Communication Research Methods. Sage Publications, Inc. (2017). https://doi.org/10.4135/9781483381411.n275
40. Patton, M.Q.: Qualitative Research & Evaluation Methods: Integrating Theory and Practice, 4th edn. Sage Publications (2015)
41. Pennington, N.: Comprehension strategies in programming. In: Olson, G.M., Sheppard, S., Soloway, E. (eds.) Empirical Studies of Programmers: Second Workshop, pp. 100–113. Ablex Publishing Corporation (1987)
42. Plowright, D.: Using Mixed Methods: Frameworks for an Integrated Methodology. Sage Publications (2011)
43. Powell, N., Moore, D., Gray, J., Finlay, J., Reaney, J.: Dyslexia and learning computer programming. ACM SIGCSE Bull. **36**(3), 242 (2004). https://doi.org/10.1145/1026487.1008072
44. Rus, V., Akhuseyinoglu, K., Chapagain, J., Tamang, L., & Brusilovsky, P.: Prompting for free self-explanations promotes better code comprehension. In: CEUR Workshop Proceedings, p. 3051 (2021)
45. Saldaña, J.: The Coding Manual for Qualitative Researchers. Sage Publications (2016)
46. Sarkar, A.: The impact of syntax colouring on program comprehension. In: Proceedings of the 26th Annual Conference of the Psychology of Programming Interest Group, pp. 49–58 (2015)
47. Schmidt, A.L.: Effects of experience and comprehension on reading time. Int. J. Man-Mach. Stud. 399–409 (1986)
48. Schröer, M., Koschke, R.: Recording, visualising and understanding developer programming behaviour. In: Proceedings - 2021 IEEE International Conference on Software Analysis, Evolution and Reengineering, SANER 2021, pp. 561–566 (2021). https://doi.org/10.1109/SANER50967.2021.00066
49. Schwandt, T.A., Lincoln, Y.S., Guba, E.G.: Judging interpretations: But is it rigorous? Trustworthiness and authenticity in naturalistic evaluation. N. Dir. Eval. **2007**(114), 11–25 (2007). https://doi.org/10.1002/ev.223
50. Shopkow, L., Diaz, A., Middendorf, J., Pace, D., Díaz, A., Middendorf, J., Pace, D.: The History learning project "decodes" a discipline: The union of teaching and epistemology. In: McKinney, K. (Ed.) Scholarship of Teaching and Learning in and Across the Disciplines. Indiana University Press (2013)
51. Siegmund, J., Kástner, C., Apel, S., Brechmann, A., Saake, G.: Experience from measuring program comprehension - Toward a general framework. In: Kowalewski, S., Rumpe, B. (Eds.) Software Engineering 2013 - Fachtagung des GI-Fachbereichs Softwaretechnik. GI-Edition - Lecture Notes in Informatics (LNI), vol. P-213, pp. 239–257. Gesellschaft für Informatik e.V (2013)
52. Simon, B., Lopez, M., Sutton, K., Clear, T.: Surely we must learn to read before we learn to write! In: Proceedings of the Conferences in Research and Practice in Information Technology Series, pp. 165–170 (2009)
53. Soloway, E.: Learning to program = learning to construct mechanisms and explanations. Commun. ACM **29**(9), 850–858 (1986). https://doi.org/10.1145/6592.6594

54. Soloway, E., Adelson, B., Ehrlich, K.: Knowledge and processes in the comprehension of computer programs. In: Chi, M.T.H., Glasser, R., Farr, M.J. (eds.) The Nature of Expertise, pp. 129–152. Lawrence Erlbaum Associates (1988)
55. Soloway, E., Ehrlich, K.: Empirical studies of programming knowledge. IEEE Trans. Softw. Eng. **SE-10**(5), 595–609 (1984)
56. Soloway, E., Lampert, R., Letovsky, S., Littman, D., Pinto, J.: Designing documentation to compensate for delocalized plans. Commun. ACM **31**(11), 1259–1267 (1988). https://doi.org/10.1145/50087.50088
57. Soloway, E., Lochhead, J., Clement, J.: Does computer programming enhance problem solving ability? Some positive evidence on Algebra word problems. In: Sediel, R.J., Anderson, R.E., Hunter, B. (Eds.) Computer Literacy, pp. 171–201. Academic Press, Inc. (1982). https://doi.org/10.1016/b978-0-12-634960-3.50023-3
58. Srikant, S., Aggarwal, V.: A system to grade computer programming skills using machine learning. In: Proceedings of the 20th ACM SIGKDD International Conference on Knowledge Discovery and Data Mining, pp. 1887–1896 (2014). https://doi.org/10.1145/2623330.2623377
59. Storey, M.A.D., Wong, K., Müller, H.A.: How do program understanding tools affect how programmers understand programs? Sci. Comput. Program. **36**(2), 183–207 (2000). https://doi.org/10.1016/S0167-6423(99)00036-2
60. Von Mayrhauser, A., Vans, A.M.: Industrial experience with an integrated code comprehension model. Softw. Eng. J. **10**(5), 171–182 (1995). https://doi.org/10.1049/sej.1995.0023
61. Wiedenbeck, S., Fix, V., Scholtz, J.: Characteristics of the mental representations of novice and expert programmers: an empirical study. Int. J. Man Mach. Stud. **39**(5), 793–812 (1993). https://doi.org/10.1006/imms.1993.1084
62. Xie, B., Nelson, G.L., Ko, A.J.: An explicit strategy to scaffold novice program tracing. In: Proceedings of the 49th ACM Technical Symposium on Computer Science Education, pp. 344–349 (2018). https://doi.org/10.1145/3159450.3159527

From Selecting Best Algorithm to Explaining Why It is: A General Review, Formal Problem Statement and Guidelines Towards to an Empirical Generalization

Vanesa Landero Nájera[1]([⊠]), Joaquín Pérez Ortega[2],
Carlos Andrés Collazos Morales[3], and Sandra Silvia Roblero Aguilar[4]

[1] Universidad Politécnica de Apodaca, El Barretal, Nuevo León, México
vlandero@upapnl.edu.mx
[2] Centro Nacional de Investigación y Desarrollo Tecnológico (CENIDET), Departamento de Ciencias Computacionales, AP 5-164, Cuernavaca 62490, México
jperez@cenidet.edu.mx
[3] Universidad Manuela Beltrán, Bogotá, Colombia
[4] Instituto Tecnológico de Tlalnepantla, Ciudad de México, México

Abstract. It has been observed on solution algorithms for problems as sorting, forecasting, classification, clustering, constraint satisfaction, decision, optimization from several disciplines (computational complexity theory, data mining, artificial intelligence, machine learning, operations research) that algorithm performance is better in certain problem instances than other. This paper describes how has been the way for trying to reach the empirical generalization for this phenomenon existing in the experimental relation problem – algorithm. For each understanding level, research questions, problem description were formulated, using the same Rice's nomenclature and supplementing it; as well as, influence indexes and analysis approaches were described. A diagram about this long trajectory and a reflection is performed, highlighting contributions and scope. It shows that up to now the problem of explaining formally why an algorithm is the best for solving an instance set had remained open. A formal problem statement for describing this phenomenon and a general framework were proposed as a guide for working in adequate way toward generation of theories; which could contribute to build generalized indexes and self-adaptive algorithms to give the best solution to problems.

1 Introduction

There exist many approximation algorithms have been proposed to give solution to problems as constraint satisfaction, decision, optimization, forecasting, classification, clustering, sorting; from different application domains, to name a few: computational complexity theory, operations research, data mining, machine learning, artificial intelligence, bioinformatics. It is observed from the experimental relation problem-algorithm that algorithm performance is the best in a problem instances set and worst in another [1–5]. According to this phenomenon observed by specialized literature, the related works

O. Gervasi et al. (Eds.): ICCSA 2023, LNCS 13956, pp. 694–712, 2023.
https://doi.org/10.1007/978-3-031-36805-9_45

in the majority of cases have focused in: predicting of algorithm performance (runtime) [6] or tuning parameter in an automatic way [7–12], or predicting the instances hardness [13], or building hyperheuristics [14, 15], or selecting the algorithm more appropriated in solving a problem instance [16–23]. However, these fall on predictive understanding level without obtaining formally a deeper understanding of why this phenomenon occurs [24, 25]. Cohen described in his book [26] a general diagram about empirical generalization for the analysis of behavior of an observed phenomenon. It evolves through three levels: description (D), prediction (P) and explanatory (E). The understanding and generalization were considered. It would be interesting to know how has been the way performed by reviewed literature through these levels. The focus and main contributions of this paper are next. A review of state of art and a diagram of understanding levels were performed. A formal research question is stated for each level where the specialized literature, as a sample of an extended population of related works is located with relevant indexes and applied analysis approaches. A reflection about this sample of trajectory is performed (there is not a results quantitative comparison due to diversity to before mentioned) highlighting only advantages, disadvantages and contributions. It is noteworthy that the algorithm selection problem ASP is formally formulated in predictive level and worked by several works. However, it would be interesting to know beyond this problem and understand better the phenomenon. A formal problem statement for describing it in the explanatory level is proposed, using and supplementing the Rice's nomenclature. Finally, a general framework is presented as a guide to continue the way towards the empirical generalization; where found theories can permit build generalized indexes and self-adaptive algorithms that solve efficiently real problems.

2 A General Review: Understanding Levels, Influence Indexes and Analysis Approaches

In this section a few works will be mentioned (some other in Sect. 3) with the sole purpose of exemplifying the understanding levels and the principal analysis approach applied. The Rice's formal nomenclature is highlighted, slightly modified and supplemented for describing questionings and kind of relevant information.

2.1 Formal Nomenclature

$P = \{x_1, x_2, ..., x_m\}$ a set instances of problem domain P, the space for analysis.
$F =$ the problem features or indexes space generated by a description process to P.
$A = \{a_1, a_2, ..., a_n\}$ a set of n algorithms.
$Y =$ the performance space, it represents the mapping of each algorithm to a set of performance metrics.
$C = \{C_1, C_2, ..., C_n\}$ a partition of P, where $|A|=|C|$.
$W = \{(a_q \in A, C_q \in C) \mid Y_{aq,x} > Y_{\alpha,x} \; \forall \alpha \in (A - \{a_q\}), \forall x \in C_q\}$, is a set of domains, ordered pairs (a_q, C_q), where each dominant algorithm $a_q \in A$ is associated with one element C_q of partition C, because this gives the best solution to partition C_q, considering set Y.
$L =$ the algorithm features or indexes space generated by a description process (Operative or/and searching behaviour) applied to A.

2.2 Descriptive Understanding Level (D): The Phenomenon is Observed

The interest has been to describe the algorithm performance. Therefore,

1. What is the performance of algorithm $a_q \in A$ to solve the problem P?

The performance can be measured, depending on application domain, by means time functions, for computing the run time or quality functions, for measuring the found solution quality; as well as other functions for obtaining iterations number, evaluations number, prediction accuracy, classification accuracy, between others. Once the performance metrics set is identified $y \in Y$, a set of algorithms A is run over a set of problem instances P and their performances are compared in some way. One classical example for the comparison is by means some statistical analysis (statistical tests The Sign, Wilcoxon and Friedman tests, among others) or tabular analysis or graphical analysis [27]. However, the average efficiency is compared without considering its dispersion. Reeves [28] commented that a heuristic with good averaged performance, but with high dispersion, has a very high risk to show a poor or low performance in many instances. It is suggested as alternative to formulate for each algorithm, a utility function adjusted to a gamma distribution, whose parameters permit to compare the heuristics on a range of risk value. Another related work identified different performances of algorithms on problem instances different sets, where each set have one or several similar features in the context of the problem structure description; for example, particularly the performance of different algorithms was projected on a wide range of instances specifications of the Constraint Satisfaction Problem (CSP) [24]. The instances are characterized by the parameters $< w, x, y, z >$, which describe in a simplified way the structure of the problem. The process consists in generating instances sets, so that, the instances in a same set have the similar values of their relevant parameters. A map is built, which shows the algorithm with the best average performance for each set of instances. In another similar work, the relation between the performance of a backtracking algorithm and instances generated randomly of Constraint Satisfaction Problem (CSP) was modeled by two standard families of functions of continuous probability distribution, when this algorithm solves them [29]. It is to say, the resoluble instances can be modeled by the Weibull distribution and not resoluble instances by the lognormal distribution. Other papers suggest somehow characterize problem descriptive structure (meta-features), showing that the performance of algorithms on characterized instances is better than those are not characterized [30]. In the same way, other related works make changes in any of the four fundamental aspects of algorithm internal logic structure for improving the algorithms performance. It is, to redesign the methodology for: tuning parameter, generating initial solution, searching and obtaining solutions, and stopping the algorithm execution (divergence or convergence). Some related works are [31–33]. Although it is observed that the new proposal has a better performance in most instances of the problem with respect to the existing algorithms, there is always a set of instances where each existing algorithm was better at solving them. This phenomenon observed by the reviewed literature and No Free Lunch theorems [2] could be described by means of a dominions partition of the algorithms A. It is, a set W of pairs in the form (a_q, C_q), where one algorithm a_q correspond better to an instances subset C_q of specific problem P (see nomenclature for a major compression).

2.3 Predictive Understanding Level (P)

The phenomenon was observed in the before level (described by means the set W), an interesting question in the predictive understanding level arises:

2. What is the mechanism to learn W (dominions partition, pairs (a_q, C_q)) in order to predict algorithm $a_q \in A$ that will give the best solution for an instance $x \in P$ with features $f(x) \in F$?

One formal problem statement in this level, similar to above questioning, is the algorithm selection problem ASP [34] which includes a selection mapping (a mechanism for learning set W and predicting). Miles describes a generalization of this problem through different research disciplines [35], its solution is important. It is stated as:

For a given problem instance $x \in P$, with features $f(x) \in F$, find the selection mapping $S(f(x))$ into algorithm space A, such that the selected algorithm $\alpha \in A$ maximizes the performance mapping $y(\alpha(x)) \in Y$.

The consulted literature that has worked in a similar way to the above have obtained the knowledge in terms of prediction (selection mapping) in various guidelines. It is to say, depending of kind of features or indexes with predictive value (space of the problem (F) and the algorithm (L)) as well as the approach applied (a mechanism for learning set W and predicting). Some approaches will be described of a general manner and exemplary; for more detail and formal description about these and other as regression analysis, functions of probability distribution and other related works can be found in [6, 14, 35–41].

Functions of Rules. Some related works have proposed rules by means functions to select the more appropriate algorithm. The majority of these functions are simple rules about problem structural features that is being solved, or about history of performance in past experimentations or about the computational environment. As well as, the human experience could contribute to definition of these rules. Some related works [42, 43] were exemplified by [14]. Another work is [4], where a setup time dominance matrix was developed considering results from graphical and statistical analysis; it is used for selecting the algorithm for a problem particular instance size.

Montecarlo Approach. Some works are based in a short execution of an algorithm on an instance to obtain a representative sample of statistical data; which can predict the algorithm general behaviour on this instance. In the work Knuth [44], a sample is taken by means of the exploration of a way from the root of the tree to a leaf drawn up by Chronological Backtracking algorithms. The way is randomly chosen. The statistics of interest are the cost of processing a node and the number of children of the node. If the number of children of level i is d_i then: $(1) + (d_1) + (d_1 \times d_2) + \ldots + (d_1 \times \ldots \times d_n)$ is considered an approximation of the number nodes of the tree. If the cost of processing of each node in the level i is c_i, then $c_1 + c_2 (d_1) + c_3 (d_1 \times d_2) + \ldots + c_n + 1 (d_1 \times \ldots \times d_n)$ is considered an approximation of the cost of processing all the tree nodes. Purdom [45] allows the exploration of more than a path, and receives as input the number of children that will explore themselves from each visited node. The method proposed in [46] for algorithms of Backward movement with Propagation of Restrictions, allows the complete exploration of the tree until certain level of depth, and from there, the number of nodes is calculated by applying a sampling similar to the one of Purdom. This technique is applied to algorithms of Backward movement with Propagation of Restrictions and Tabu Search algorithms in [47] and algorithms of Ramification and Demarcation in [48]. Another related work was [49], where the algorithm selection problem is focused on minimization problem of execution total time, which is solved with a Reinforced Learning algorithm (RL). The well-known Q-learning algorithm is adapted for this case in a way that combines both Monte-Carlo and Temporal Difference methods. Two classical problems were focused: selecting and ordering. A function that predicts the best algorithm for a new instance using its problem size is determined by means of training. It combines several recursive algorithms to improve its performance: the actual problem is divided in subproblems in each recursive step, and the most adequate algorithm in size is used for each of them; it is extended to backtracking algorithms to SAT problem in [3].

Algorithm Portfolio. The strategy of running several algorithms in parallel, potentially with different algorithms being assigned different amounts of CPU time, or when some stop criterion is satisfied [50]. The performance of all algorithms is measured by means some function, so too, it is characterized and adjusted to a model (model-based portfolio). For example, a probability distribution model [36]. The framework employs three core components: a portfolio of algorithms (SAT solvers); a generative model, which is fit to data on those algorithms' past performance, then used to predict their future performance; and a policy for action selection, which repeatedly chooses algorithms based on those predictions. The models of solver behaviour are two latent class models: a multinomial mixture model of the outcomes of solver-duration pairs, and a mixture model DCM (Dirichlet compound multinomial) that additionally captures the burstiness of those outcomes. Another example is [21], where a multiple evolutionary algorithm portfolio to solve multiobjective optimization problems is proposed for solving benchmark functions: bi-objective, tri-objective, five-objective. Two principal parts are included for each population generation. The first part, for each multiobjective evolutionary algorithm (MOEA), its score is computed. The second part, a bootstrap probability distribution is built and predicted performance is obtained at a common future point and selects the algorithm more appropriated to generate the next population and so on. The algorithms switch automatically as a function of the computational budget. Another guideline of approach is to consider instances features to build the model (feature-based portfolio). Classical examples, a supervised learning model was built by decision tree algorithm in [18], a regression model including parameter control information to select the best in [7]; other recent related works [51–53].

Machine Learning (Supervised Learning). The objective is to learn patterns identified from data with predictive value by means a supervised learning model and use it to make predictions about unseen data. In the majority cases, the relevant information was highlighted by means mathematical or statistical indexes. Some examples. For solving classification problems, in terms of problem description, proportion of symbolic attributes, the mean correlation coefficient for any two continuous attributes, mean mutual information, mean of the mutual information for each discrete attribute and target class, class entropy, median entropy of attribute, median of entropies of all attributes [54]; a k-Nearest Neighbour algorithm was applied. For clustering problems, the mean and deviation standard of eigenvectors from image histograms [17]; the algorithm Support Vector Machine was applied. For sorting problems, the size of input permutation and presortedness measures [19]; a decision tree algorithm was applied. For optimization problems, in the problem Bin-Packing in one dimension, the weight's dispersion and the relation between the weights and container capacity; a decision tree algorithm was applied [20]. For problem Quasigroup with Holes (QWH), the number of holes in rows and columns, as well as, in terms of algorithm operative behaviour were the variance of uncolored cells number in the QWH instance across rows and across columns, the ratio of the number of uncolored cells and the number of columns or rows, the minimum depth of all leaves of the search tree; Neural Networks were applied [55]. For MIP problem, some of problem description were number of variables and constraints, features of graphs (variable, variable-constraint), as well as, features about algorithm operative behaviour, it is, the CPLEX with default settings is ran by 5 s runs for obtain indexes about pre-solving features, cut usage and probing result; also, during the searching, the behaviour is characterized by the tour length of local minima, the tour quality improvement per search step, number of search steps to reach a local minimum, distance between two local minima, probability of edges appearing in any local minimum encountered [6, 8]. For decision problem SAT, the number of clauses and variables, the clause and variable node degree statistics, as well as information about problem space, algorithm operative behaviour and searching behaviour; it is, the SAPS and GSAT algorithms were ran in two seconds of each run for obtaining mean and variation coefficient of the number of unsatisfied clauses in each local minimum and other indexes related to confidence of variables and the probability of unconstrained variables; as well as, indexes represent information about number of steps to the best local minimum, the average improvement to best in a run and the fraction of improvement due to first local minimum [6, 8]; the Random Forest algorithm was applied. There are other works where the information about parameter tuning was considered to build a model and select the best algorithm, some interesting works are: applying Bayesian Networks [9, 10], Decision trees [11, 57]. Finally, other related works and supervised learning algorithms that were applied: Case-Base reasoning [10]; k-nearest neighbour [21, 57], Random Forest [22, 56], and Neural Networks [57–60].

Hyper-Heuristic. A hyper-heuristic is an automated methodology for selecting or generating heuristics to solve hard computational search problems [15, 38]. It is to say, produce an adequate combination of available low-level heuristics in order to effectively solve a given instance by means a built high-level algorithm that can select and apply an appropriate low-level heuristic or metaheuristic at each decision step. One classical example to solve the SQRP problem [14]; the goal of SQRP is locating information in a network based on a query formed by keywords, within the shortest path. Each query traverses the network, moving from the initiating node to a neighbouring node and then to a neighbour of a neighbour and so forth, until it locates the requested resource. A hyper-heuristic algorithm is proposed to automatically select, among basic-heuristics, the most promising to adjust a parameter control of an Ant Colony Optimization algorithm for routing messages. The basic-heuristics are different ways to adjust the time to live (TTL) parameter during the execution of the algorithm. The search process for the next node is based on the pheromone table and information about the distances, the successes of past queries and number of documents which are the closest nodes that can satisfy the query. The selection process of basic-heuristics is based on data structures that store information of prior consultations about hyper-heuristic visibility states, which allows the hyper-heuristic know if is necessary to add more TTL, because the number of resources found are few and decreases the lifetime. Another recent work [61].

2.4 Explanatory Understanding Level

In above level a predictive knowledge (model) is learned from hidden patterns existing in relation problem-algorithm; it is to say, a mapping is found, a W set learned by means some approach (mechanism) applied to a data set with predictive value. The obtained model is used to select the best algorithm. In this level, delving deeper into the knowledge learned, the following question arises.

3. What is the mechanism to understand why for each pair $(a_q, C_q) \in W$, a problem instance subset C_q correspond better to an algorithm a_q than other instances $(C_q)^c$ in a specific problem domain?

Some related works have performed graphical or statistical analysis or data exploratory analysis, or developing some visual tool, mechanisms to interpret according their own knowledge the results and obtain explanations about algorithm performance: [62–68]. There are other related works [25, 50, 57, 69–71] have reached explicative knowledge by means these approaches in conjunction with other: Transition Phase, Markov Chains Model, Supervised Learning, Causal Analysis. For more detail and other works can be found in [24, 50, 72–78].

Transition Phase Analysis. The algorithm performance is analysed by means graphical analysis of a relevant index that in the majority of the cases is about the problem structure description. So that a particular value of this index (phase boundary) the algorithm performance has a strong fluctuation of its value, either a decrease or an increase. This change is known as transition point. This boundary is a type of phase transition and it must be preserved under mappings between problems. For more detail and formal description about this approach can be found in [79]. A conjecture about this approach was suggested by [72]: *All NP-complete problems have at least one order parameter and the hard to solve problems are around a critical value of this order parameter. This critical value (a phase transition) separates one region from another, such as overconstrained and underconstrained regions of the problem space. In such cases, the phase transition occurs at the point where the solution probability changes abruptly from almost zero to almost 1.* A very known application of this approach has been for SAT decision problem, where explanations about the performance of several SAT solvers were obtained; a relation between an index of the problem structure description (c/v) and the algorithm runtime was found [72, 80]. It is to say, a phase transition was observed from $p(c, v)$ when the index c/v crosses a critical value of about 4.26, where v is held constant; instances with many clauses are overconstrained and almost always unsatisfiable, so too, instances with few clauses are underconstrained and almost always satisfiable. For several SAT solvers, when all tested values of v are fixed, even for the SAT solvers that perform best on these instances, the phase transition point occurs between these extremes when $p(c, v)$ is exactly 0.5. Other examples, for optimization problems, the Quasigroup Completion Problem (QCP) shows for random instances that there is a peak in terms of problem hardness over a range of values for an index that represent the ratio of the number of uncoloured cells to the total number of cells [55]. So too, for the Quasigroup with Holes Problem (QWH), its problem instances hardness is marked significantly by structural properties. It is, a pattern representing a balance of the number holes in each row and column of instances. Later other related works identified interesting observations about these discoveries, which is necessary to explore more features performing a more deeply analysis [13, 37].

Markov Chains Model. The algorithm behaviour is characterized in terms of search trajectory to understand why algorithm dynamics are so effective on problem instances and deduce how these dynamics might be modified to yield further improvements in performance. For example, a Markov model is developed for studying the run-time behaviour of Tabu Search algorithm when it solves the job-shop scheduling problem (JSP) [69]. It is to say, the cost of locating both optimal and sub-optimal solutions to a wide range of problem instances. The performance was analysed (graphical statistical analysis) using different methods for constructing the initial solution and different tabu tenure sizes. Explanations are described in Sect. 3.

Machine Learning (Supervised and Unsupervised Learning). Patterns are recognized from data, by means a supervised learning model. Relations between dependent variables are identified and analysed; key variables with respect some independent variables of interest are explained. A set of algorithms has been applied to carry out the above, some related works are K-means, Self-organizing maps [81], Decision trees [58, 82]. The kind of information utilized is about the problem description. One example, the rules generated in [58] indicated that cluster ratio seemed be a boundary for phase transition, it is around of 0.05; as well as, the fraction of distinct distances around 1.4% as a phase transition parameter [58].

Causal Analysis. This approach consists, in general terms, of identifying the principal causes of the behaviour of some phenomenon, representing them in the form of relations cause-effect in a causal model. A causal model consists of a Directed Acyclic Graph (DAG) over a set $V = \{V_1, \ldots, V_n\}$ of vertices, representing variables of interest, and a set E of directed edges, or arrows, that connect these vertices. These graphs can be causally interpreted if they have the properties: Causal Markov condition, Minimality condition, Faithfulness condition. These properties make the connection between causality and probability [74]. Causal modelling has four phases. The first phase is structure learning, where its objective is to find the principal structure of causal relations between several relevant indexes and a data set; it is to say, a causal graph G is found that represents the causal structure $G = (V, E)$; there exist several algorithms of structure learning, one of them is PC algorithm (Peter&Clark). The second phase is estimation of the found causal relations; one of algorithms that perform it is Counting algorithm [83]. The third phase is the interpretation of causal model; the causal relations with higher magnitudes are analysed and interpreted. The fourth phase is the causal model validation. Some examples of related works performed this kind of analysis can be found in [70, 71, 84–86].

3 A Trajectory Diagram and General Discussion

The Fig. 1 shows a diagram of trajectory achieved (TA) by some works related in the analysis of the experimental relation between problem and algorithm. It is according to: the grade of the contribution to the science, the understanding level (Descriptive (D), Predictive (P), Explanatory (E)); the kind of information (problem (F), algorithm behaviour (L) indexes, algorithm performance (Y)); and principal approaches to perform the analysis in each understanding level. Focusing on recent works, firstly on predictive level and later on explanatory level; it can be seen in the figure, considering problem information (F), some related works included only one feature or index that characterizes the problem structure description (*). For example, the problem size feature has been considered for building a model, using the regression analysis approach, and relating it with the algorithm performance [87]. However, it is well known that it is not enough, there exists the necessity to explore more features or indexes [13, 82]. In this context, the research results of some related works [19, 54, 58, 59, 88] build formal models, using machine learning, to select the most appropriate algorithm to solve better a problem instance, where it considers several features or indexes of the problem structure (*) which adjust better to this selected algorithm; other works, included specifically indexes about problem solutions space (+), also known as problem landscape features [56, 60] to establish a relation between these features (+) and algorithm performance. Some similar to this type of information was included along with problem structure (*) years ago by work [16]; the feature-based algorithm portfolio approach with regression was used. Now, in the context of considering only algorithm information (L) for building an algorithm [52], in the portfolio approach or in the hyper-heuristic approach [14, 61] or tunning parameter [9], learning configurations (♦) with the machine learning approach for giving the best solution to a problem instance. Also, this approach was used by [55], where the algorithm operative behaviour (Δ) was learned in a model to predict the best solver to a SAT problem instance. The principal advantage, in terms only of (L), is the independence to problem description, which can be applied to any problem. There were works that included both, problem (F) and algorithm (L) information. The problem structure description (*) was mainly used in conjunction with information about algorithm configuration (♦) [7, 10, 11, 51] or algorithm searching behaviour (∇) [22], or with all of the above and algorithm operative behaviour (Δ) [6]. The information about the problem space (+) was mainly used in conjunction with information about algorithm searching behaviour (∇), again with the approaches portfolio with regression and machine learning [53, 60], for giving the most adequate algorithm. However, there is still the general question from the explanatory understanding level "why an algorithm is best for a certain set of instances of a problem and why not in another". The problem structure index (*) in the form (c/v ratio) within transition phase approach for SAT problem [72, 80], has helped to indicate when the instances are hard or easy for SAT solvers; so too, for TSP problem [58], a decision tree defined rules with indexes calculated from distances: between cities, normalized nearest neighbour; ratio of cluster and outliers for identifying hard or easy instances to heuristics. Another recent work, the problem structure index (*), proportional to number of variable interactions (k/n) was used in conjunction with problem space features (+) relating to autocorrelation of random walks for multi-objective optimization problems [82]; it is found by means statistical analysis (regression) that if the index increases then the landscape ruggedness too (knowledge found also in single-objective optimization problems). So too, the problem structure index (*), correlation between objective functions (p) impacts to algorithm performance. The problem space features (+) were included by a decision tree for indicating what algorithm performs better in one instance (Global Simple Evolutionary Multi-Objective Optimizer and Iterative Pareto local search algorithms). As future work, the information about the algorithm internal logic structure will be considered for a better design of algorithms Evolutionary Multi-Objective (EMO).

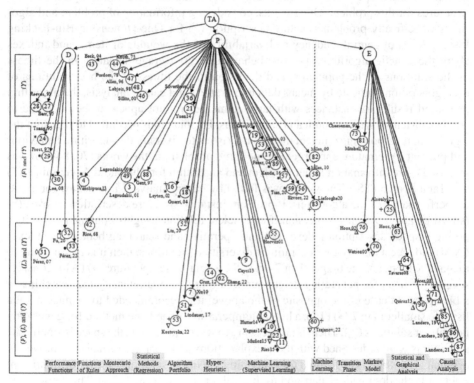

Fig. 1. Trajectory of consulted specialized literature

Another similar recent work [25], includes constraints to problem, it found, by means of the Instance Space Analysis methodology (ISA), two indexes about problem space (+). The isolation of non-dominate set and the correlation between constraints and objectives permitted explanations about the algorithm performance. The algorithm CCMO is more appropriated to converge on an isolated optima and the algorithm PPS when there is a large optimal set and there is the necessity to generate more diversity. So too, if there is negative correlation between constraints and objectives then most of analyzed CMOEA algorithms will fail to give high quality solutions. However, the analysis is looked only from the side of the problem. Other works viewed the instances hardness from the algorithm's viewpoint, it is analyzed, the algorithm internal logic structure and indexes that characterize the operative behaviour (Δ) [75]. In [69], the searching behaviour (∇) is modelled by a Markov process and indicated that the method for generating initial solution not impact the algorithm performance (•) and a small tabu list (♦) is recommend to avoid recession in the searching of algorithm Tabu for TSP problem instances. In [63], the metrics autocorrelation length and fitness distance correlation characterized the searching behaviour (∇) to encodings of bit-flip mutation, crossover (one point, uniform) and different heuristics ($\square$) for genetic algorithms applied to five solution representations for Multidimensional Knapsack problem; it is observed that adding heuristics and local improvement to binary representation, so too use a log-normal mutation operator to weight-coding representation are the best logical internal structures for this problem. Other works, considering information of problem and algorithm; specifically problem structure description (*) for One-Dimension Bin-Packing [89], indexes of central tendency and variability of the weights of items, and indexes about the genetic algorithm operative behaviour (Δ), average deviation in the fitness of the solutions of the population and deviation in the fitness of the best solutions of each generation, indicate by means data exploratory and causal analysis, the algorithm had good results for instances with large items but do not appear to be adequate to address instances with medium and small items. Explanations permitted to redesign the algorithm, incorporating efficient random heuristics to diversify the algorithm behaviour and prevent a premature converge. For the same problem, in the works [70, 84–86] was included more information about problem and algorithm for Threshold Accepting (AT) and Tabu Search (TS). Knowledge was found by causal analysis; it is to say, for a better performance of the algorithms, if problem instance structure description indexes (*) (statistics about weights dispersion, frequencies, relation weights-container capacity), problem space description indexes (+) and operative and searching behaviour indexes (Δ,∇) indicate a facility for generating a diversity of solutions, then it is recommend to manage a Tabu list size bigger than 7 (♦) (TS), a smaller temperature (♦) (AT), consider several methods for generating neighbour solutions ($\square$) and intensify the searching in a big space. In case of the opposite of the above, it is recommended to manage a Tabu list size smaller than 7 (♦) (TS), a bigger temperature (♦) and one method for generating neighbour solutions ($\square$). There is no necessity to work much when the space is small. The algorithms were redesigned with these explanations and their performance improved to original algorithms. The method for generating the initial solution (•) was not significant to identify the dominations partition for both algorithms (TS) and (TA). This knowledge was similar for the problem TSP and Tabu Search algorithm [69]. Finally, this reviewing indicates there is no work that analyses all kind of information; problem and algorithm indexes in conjunction with the algorithm logic structure. In the majority of cases, it is seen as a black-box. However, it is important to open the box and identify logical parts relevant to the connection of the algorithm and problem during the solution process [27]. There is still hidden knowledge significant to understand the phenomenon and give an answer to questioning in the explanatory understanding level.

4   Setting the Problem Statement

It is necessary to break ground with a starting point, something very essential, simple, and important in the way for the phenomenon comprehension in the explanatory understanding level. A formal formulation that considers all significant information from problem (structure, solutions space), algorithm (operative and searching behaviour) and algorithm logical internal structure; beyond to algorithm selection problem ASP. There is no work has made this before. The next problem statement is fixed.

> For a set of algorithms A, with logical internal structure each one, applied to a set of problem instances P, with problem indexes F, algorithm indexes L, the algorithms performance space Y, the set of algorithms domination partitions W, according to Y, and an ordered pair $(a_q, C_q) \in W$; find the Explanation Mapping $E(a_q, P, A, F, L, Y, W)$ that discovers an explanation formal model M, such that M, represents the latent knowledge from relations between problem and algorithm indexes and provides solid foundations to explain, why certain problem instances, being the partition C_q correspond better to algorithm a_q with certain logical internal structure, according to performance space Y, and why other partitions $(C_q)^c$ do not correspond to algorithm a_q with certain logical internal structure.

5   A Framework General Proposal and Guidelines

Figure 2 illustrates a general framework proposed for starting in an adequate way and giving a solution to above problem, firstly for a specific domain through next phases and after of a repetitive process, build the theoretical bases towards generalization. It is based from the recommendations and contributions by reviewed literature, as well as, from previous works results [84–86]. The validation is recommended to be performed in Phase V and Phase VII, but it can be left to the researcher's choice in conjunction with other specific details. So too, it is recommended that the results (successful or failed) of these phases and all of its concerning information must be registered [27] for identifying the explored ways and continuing with the unexplored.

Phase I. Identification of problem and algorithms. A kind of problem and algorithms of interest are fixed as study objects. It can be that one algorithm only be changed, keeping everything else fixed. It will depend of the explored and unexplored ways.

Phase II. Designing of experiments. The principal goal of the designing of experiments must be revealing [27]. It must offer, in general terms, insights of why one algorithm is the best to solve a problem instances subset and why not in other; more formally to solve the problem formal statement described in the last section. For it, is necessary to obtain a sample of instances representative to problem. It is recommended obtain real instances and to generate random instances representative of problem space [25, 27]. The set P is defined. So too, is necessary analyze all factors involved in the solution process between problem-algorithm [27] (the environmental and programming factors would be controlled). It was observed in the Sect. 3 that it is important to include information about structure (*) and space (+) of problem, operative (Δ) and searching (∇) behavior of algorithm [27]; mathematical or statistical indexes of above and performance metrics are defined. So too, the algorithm internal logical structure is important to analyze [27, 82]. According to all above and gain insight into the effect of specific factors on an algorithm, it is recommended test two codes that are identical except for the singled-out one part of their internal logical structure within a well-designed experiment (it must be registered); such as a factorial design of experiments that permits an analysis scenario of the smallest detail in algorithm logical in conjunction with the other problem and algorithm factors [27]. The set A and one algorithm of interest a_q are fixed.

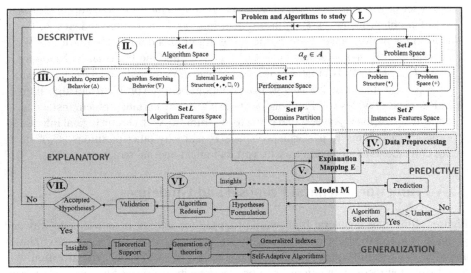

Fig. 2. Proposed General Framework (a connection between understanding levels towards an empirical generalization)

Phase III. Characterization of problem and algorithms. A process of description, by means indexes [84–86, 91] is applied before execution to set P for characterizing the structure (*) and space (+) of the problem; a set F is obtained. During the execution, mathematical or statistical indexes are applied to algorithms for characterizing the operative (Δ) and searching behavior (∇), as well as, the performance metrics are applied to measure the performance. The sets F, L, Y, W are obtained.

Phase IV. Preprocessing of data. It is recommended to perform a step of data preprocessing (elimination of missing values, balancing datasets, discretization) that could improve the quality of the data [30, 90, 92]. Also is recommended the elimination of redundant data and identification of significant features (selection) [71].

Phase V. Explanation Mapping. Perform a mechanism that permits an explanation mapping. It is recommended an analysis approach that generate a **M** model that represents the latent knowledge of relevant relations from preprocessed dataset. Also, this model must be very clear and easy to interpret how the problem and algorithm indexes are relating; the explanations obtained would help to researchers in this area to understand the performance and behaviour of algorithm in its operation and searching process, and identify internal logical design aspects that are relating with the problem structure and solutions space; how these relations influence to find the best solution. So too, the model must permit to predict the algorithm performance. It is important a validation of prediction process (this is not included in figure to avoid confusion) with test instances. If the results are superior to a stablished umbral then it will continue with the Phase VI (it is good to predict, it is expected to be good to explain); otherwise return to Phase I, modifying samples, sets, design of experiments or indexes and continue again with Phase II and so on. The promising analysis approaches are Machine Learning (Decision Tree, Bayesian Net), Markov Model, Causal Analysis; all these conjugating with a visual analysis.

Phase VI. Formulation of Hypotheses and Algorithm Redesign. The explanations from model **M** are insights to formulate hypothesis and redesign the algorithms.

Phase VII. Validation of Hypothesis and Feed-Back. The redesigned algorithms are run over the set **P**, as well as it is recommended over another set **P'** (**P** $\neq$ **P'**) representative of problem domain; if there is a significant improving of the redesign over those sets (**P** and **P'**), then the hypotheses will be accepted, considered as found knowledge and return to Phase I; modifying samples, sets or indexes for continuing again with Phase II and so on. As well as, depending of the obtained advances, it can be chosen to apply another problem domain and other algorithms.

Finally, theoretical support is obtained from a refining process orderly and repetitive of Phase I to Phase VII through other problem domains and algorithms. Theories can be found for generalizing indexes about problem, algorithm and performance metrics; as well as, permitting the building of Self-Adaptive algorithms. It is to say, the automatic redesign of algorithms, during execution time; adapt the algorithm logical structure, operational and search behavior of algorithm to: structure and solutions space of problem, and to difficulties presented during execution to give the best optimal solution to real problems in a broad range of disciplines.

References

1. Papadimitriou, C., Steiglitz, K.: Combinatorial Optimization, Algorithms and Complexity. Prentice Hall(1982)
2. Wolpert, D., Macready, W.: No free lunch theorems for optimizations. IEEE Trans. Evol. Comput. 1(1), 67–82 (1996)
3. Lagoudakis, M., Littman, M.: Learning to select branching rules in the dpll procedure for satisfiability. Electron. Notes Discr. Math. 9, 344–359 (2001)
4. Vanchipura, R., Sridharan, R.: Development and analysis of constructive heuristic algorithms for flow shop scheduling problems with sequence-dependent setup times. Int. J. Adv. Manuf. Technol. 67, 1337–1353 (2013)
5. Kerschke, P., Hoos, H.H., Neumann, F., Trautmann, H.: Automated algorithm selection: Survey and perspectives. Evol. Comput. 27(1), 3–45 (2019)
6. Hutter, F., Xu, L., Hoos, H., Leyton-Brown, K.: Algorithm runtime prediction: Methods & evaluation. Artif. Intell. 206, 79–111 (2014)
7. Xu, L., Hoos, H., Leyton-Brown, K.: Hydra: Automatically configuring algorithms for portfolio-based selection. In: Proceedings of the 25th National Conference on Artificial Intelligence (AAAI'10), pp. 210–216 (2010)

8. Hutter, F., Hoos, H.H., Leyton-Brown, K.: Sequential model-based optimization for general algorithm configuration. In: Coello, C.A.C. (ed.) LION 2011. LNCS, vol. 6683, pp. 507–523. Springer, Heidelberg (2011). https://doi.org/10.1007/978-3-642-25566-3_40

9. Cayci, A., Menasalvas, E., Saygin, Y., Eibe, S.: Self-configuring data mining for ubiquitous computing. Inf. Sci. **246**, 83–99 (2013)

10. Yeguas, E., Luzón, M., Pavón, R., Laza, R., Arroyo, G., Díaz, F.: Automatic parameter tuning for evolutionary algorithms using a bayesian case-based reasoning system. Appl. Soft Comput. **18**, 185–195 (2014)

11. Ries, J., Beullens, P.: A semi-automated design of instance-based fuzzy parameter tuning for metaheuristics based on decision tree induction. J. Oper. Res. Soc. **66**(5), 782–793 (2015)

12. Schede, E., et al.: A survey of methods for automated algorithm configuration. J. Artif. Intell. Res. **75**, 425–487 (2022)

13. Leyton-Brown, K., Hoos, H., Hutter, F., Xu, L.: Understanding the empirical hardness of NP-complete problems. Magaz. Commun. ACM **57**(5), 98–107 (2014)

14. Cruz, L., Gómez, C., Pérez, J., Landero, V., Quiroz, M., Ochoa, A.: Algorithm Selection: From Meta-Learning to Hyper-Heuristics, INTECH Open Access Publisher (2012)

15. Drake, J.H., Kheiri, A., Özcan, E., Burke, E.K.: Recent advances in selection hyper-heuristics. Eur. J. Oper. Res. **285**(2), 405–428 (2020)

16. Leyton-Brown, K., Nudelman, E., Shoham, Y.: Learning the empirical hardness of optimization problems: The case of combinatorial auctions. In: Van Hentenryck, P. (ed.) CP 2002. LNCS, vol. 2470, pp. 556–572. Springer, Heidelberg (2002). https://doi.org/10.1007/3-540-46135-3_37

17. Yong, X., Feng, D., Rongchun, Z.: Optimal selection of image segmentation algorithms based on performance prediction. In: Proceedings of the Pan-Sydney Area Workshop on Visual Information Processing, Australian Computer Society, Inc., pp. 105–108 (2003)

18. Guerri, A., Milano, M.: Learning techniques for automatic algorithm portfolio selection. In: Burke, V.A. (ed.) Proceedings of the 16th Biennial European Conference on Artificial Intelligence, pp. 475–479. IOS Press, Spain (2004)

19. Guo, H., Hsu, W.H.: A learning-based algorithm selection meta-reasoner for the real-time MPE problem. In: Webb, G.I., Yu, X. (eds.) AI 2004. LNCS (LNAI), vol. 3339, pp. 307–318. Springer, Heidelberg (2004). https://doi.org/10.1007/978-3-540-30549-1_28

20. Perez O., J., et al.: A machine learning approach for modeling algorithm performance predictors. In: Torra, V., Narukawa, Y. (eds.) MDAI 2004. LNCS (LNAI), vol. 3131, pp. 70–80. Springer, Heidelberg (2004). https://doi.org/10.1007/978-3-540-27774-3_8

21. Yuen, S., Zhang, X.: Multiobjective evolutionary algorithm portfolio: Choosing suitable algorithm for multiobjective optimization problem. In: 2014 IEEE Congress on Evolutionary Computation (CEC), Beijing, China, pp. 1967–1973 (2014)

22. Munoz, M., Kirley, M., Halgamuge, S.: Exploratory landscape analysis of continuous space optimization problems using information content. Evolution. Comput. IEEE Trans. **19**(1), 74–87 (2015)

23. Müller, D., Müller, M.G., Kress, D., Pesch, E.: An algorithm selection approach for the flexible job shop scheduling problem: Choosing constraint programming solvers through machine learning. Eur. J. Oper. Res. **302**(3), 874–891 (2022)

24. Tsang, E., Borrett, J., Kwan, A.: An attempt to map the performance of a range of algorithm and heuristic combinations. In: Hallam, J. et al. (ed.) Hybrid Problems, Hybrid Solutions. Proceedings of the AISB-95, vol. 27, pp. 203–216. IOS Press, Amsterdam (1995)

25. Alsouly, H., Kirley, M., Muñoz, M.A.: An instance space analysis of constrained multi-objective optimization problems. IEEE Trans. Evolution. Comput. (2022)

26. Cohen, P.: Empirical Methods for Artificial Intelligence. The MIT Press Cambridge, London, England (1995)

27. Barr, R., Golden, B., Kelly, J., Resende, M., Stewart, W.: Designing and reporting on computational experiments with heuristic methods. J. Heurist. **1**(1), 9–32 (1995)
28. Reeves, C.: Modern Heuristic Techniques for Combinatorial Problems. Blackwell Scientific Publishing, England (1993)
29. Frost, D., Rish, I., Vila, L.: Summarizing CSP hardness with continuous probability distributions. In: Proceedings of the 14th National Conference on AI, American Association for Artificial Intelligence, pp. 327–333 (1997)
30. Lee, J., Giraud, C.: Predicting algorithm accuracy with a small set of effective meta-features. In Machine Learning and Applications, In: Eleventh International Conference on IEEE, pp. 808–812 (2008)
31. Pérez O, J., Pazos R, R., Cruz R, L., Reyes S, G., Basave T, R., Fraire H, H.: Improving the efficiency and efficacy of the K-means clustering algorithm through a new convergence condition. In: Gervasi, O., Gavrilova, M.L. (eds.) ICCSA 2007. LNCS, vol. 4707, pp. 674–682. Springer, Heidelberg (2007). https://doi.org/10.1007/978-3-540-74484-9_58
32. Fu, H., Xu, Y., Chen, S., Liu, J.: Improving WalkSAT for random 3-SAT problems. J. Univ. Comput. Sci. **26**(2), 220–243 (2020)
33. Pérez-Ortega, J., et al.: Hybrid fuzzy C-means clustering algorithm oriented to big data realms. Axioms **11**(8), 377 (2022)
34. Rice, J.: The algorithm selection problem. Adv. Comput. **15**, 65–118 (1976)
35. Smith-Miles, K.: Cross-disciplinary perspectives on meta-learning for algorithm selection. ACM Comput. Surv. **41**(1), 1–25 (2009)
36. Silverthorn, B., Miikkulainen, R.: Latent class models for algorithm portfolio methods. In: Proceedings of the Twenty-Fourth AAAI Conference on Artificial Intelligence, Georgia (2010)
37. Xu, L., Hoos, H., Leyton-Brown, K.: Predicting Satisfiability at the Phase Transition. In AAAI (2012)
38. Burke, E., et al.: Hyper-heuristics: A survey of the state of the art. J. Oper. Res. Soc. **64**(12), 1695–1724 (2013)
39. Li, B., Hoi, S.: Online portfolio selection: A survey. ACM Comp. Surveys (CSUR) **46**(3), 35 (2014)
40. Yuen, S.Y., Zhang, X.: On composing an algorithm portfolio. Memet. Comput. **7**(3), 203–214 (2015). https://doi.org/10.1007/s12293-015-0159-9
41. Karimi-Mamaghan, M., Mohammadi, M., Meyer, P., Karimi-Mamaghan, A.M., Talbi, E.G.: Machine learning at the service of meta-heuristics for solving combinatorial optimization problems: A state-of-the-art. Eur. J. Oper. Res. **296**(2), 393–422 (2022)
42. Rice, J.: On the construction of poly-algorithms for automatic numerical analysis. In: Klerer, M., Reinfelds, J. (eds.) Interactive System for Experimental Applied Mathematics, pp. 301–313. Academic Press, MA (1968)
43. Beck, J.C., Freuder, E.C.: Simple rules for low-knowledge algorithm selection. In: Régin, J.-C., Rueher, M. (eds.) CPAIOR 2004. LNCS, vol. 3011, pp. 50–64. Springer, Heidelberg (2004). https://doi.org/10.1007/978-3-540-24664-0_4
44. Knuth, D.: Estimating the efficiency of backtrack programs. Math. Comput. **29**(129), 122–136 (1975)
45. Purdom, P.: Tree size by partial backtracking. SIAM J. Comput. **7**(4), 481–491 (1978)
46. Sillito, J.: Improvements to and estimating the cost of backtracking algorithms for constraint satisfaction problems. M.Sc. thesis, Department of Computing Science, University of Alberta, Department of Computing Science, Edmonton, Alberta (2000)
47. Allen, J.A., Minton, S.: Selecting the right heuristic algorithm: Runtime performance predictors. In: McCalla, G. (ed.) AI 1996. LNCS, vol. 1081, pp. 41–53. Springer, Heidelberg (1996). https://doi.org/10.1007/3-540-61291-2_40

48. Lobjois, L., Lemaître, M.: Branch and bound algorithm selection by performance prediction. In: Proceedings of the 15th National Conference on Artificial Intelligence (AAAI-98), Madison, Winsconsin, pp. 353–358 (1998)
49. Lagoudakis, M., Littman, M.: Algorithm selection using reinforcement learning. In: Kaufmann, M. (ed.), International Conference on Machine Learning (ICML 2000), pp. 511–518 (2000)
50. Huberman, B., Hogg, T.: Phase transitions in artificial intelligence systems. Artif. Intell. **33**(2), 155–171 (1987)
51. Lindauer, M., Hoos, H., Leyton-Brown, K., Schaub, T.: Automatic construction of parallel portfolios via algorithm configuration. Artif. Intell. **244**, 272–290 (2017)
52. Liu, S., Tang, K., Yao, X.: Generative adversarial construction of parallel portfolios. IEEE Trans. Cybernet. **52**(2), 784–795 (2020)
53. Kostovska, A., et al.: Per-run algorithm selection with warm-starting using trajectory-based features. In: Parallel Problem Solving from Nature–PPSN XVII: 17th International Conference, Proceedings, Part I, pp. 46–60. Springer, Cham (2022). https://doi.org/10.1007/978-3-031-14714-2_4
54. Soares, C., Pinto, J.: Ranking learning algorithms: Using IBL and meta-learning on accuracy and time results. J. Mach. Learn. **50**(3), 251–277 (2003)
55. Horvitz, E, Ruan, Y.: A Bayesian approach to tackling hard computational problems. In: Proceedings of the 17th Conference in Uncertainty in Artificial Intelligence, pp. 235–244. Morgan Kaufmann Publishers Inc., San Francisco (2001)
56. Skvorc, U., Eftimov, T., Korošec, P.: Transfer learning analysis of multi-class classification for landscape-aware algorithm selection. Mathematics **10**(3), 432 (2022)
57. Kanda, J., De Carvalho, A., Hruschka, E., Soares, C., Brazdil, P.: Meta-learning to select the best meta-heuristic for the traveling salesman problem: A comparison of meta-features. Neurocomputing **205**, 393–406 (2016)
58. Smith-Miles, K., van Hemert, J., Lim, X.Y.: Understanding TSP difficulty by learning from evolved instances. In: Blum, C., Battiti, R. (eds.) LION 2010. LNCS, vol. 6073, pp. 266–280. Springer, Heidelberg (2010). https://doi.org/10.1007/978-3-642-13800-3_29
59. Tian, Y., Peng, S., Zhang, X., Rodemann, T., Tan, K.C., Jin, Y.: A recommender system for metaheuristic algorithms for continuous optimization based on deep recurrent neural networks. IEEE Trans. Artif. Intell. **1**(1), 5–18 (2020)
60. Trajanov, R., Dimeski, S., Popovski, M., Korošec, P., Eftimov, T.: Explainable landscape analysis in automated algorithm performance prediction. In: Jiménez Laredo, J.L., Hidalgo, J.I., Babaagba, K.O. (eds.) EvoApplications 2022. LNCS, vol. 13224, pp. 207–222. Springer, Cham (2022). https://doi.org/10.1007/978-3-031-02462-7_14
61. Zhang, Y., Bai, R., Qu, R., Tu, C., Jin, J.: A deep reinforcement learning based hyper-heuristic for combinatorial optimisation with uncertainties. Eur. J. Oper. Res. **300**(2), 418–427 (2022)
62. Hoos, H.H., Smyth, K., Stützle, T.: Search space features underlying the performance of stochastic local search algorithms for MAX-SAT. In: Yao, X., et al. (eds.) PPSN 2004. LNCS, vol. 3242, pp. 51–60. Springer, Heidelberg (2004). https://doi.org/10.1007/978-3-540-302 17-9_6
63. Tavares, J., Pereira, F., Costa, E.: Multidimensional knapsack problem: A fitness landscape analysis. IEEE Trans. Syst. Man Cybern. B Cybern. **38**(3), 604–616 (2008)
64. Le, M., Ong, Y., Jin, Y.: Lamarckian memetic algorithms: local optimum and connectivity structure analysis. Memet. Comput. **1**, 175–190 (2009)
65. Taghavi, T., Pimentel, A., Sabeghi, M.: VMODEX: A novel visualization tool for rapid analysis of heuristic-based multi-objective design space exploration of heterogeneous MPSoC arquitectures. Simul. Model. Pract. Theory **22**, 166–196 (2011)

66. Cruz, L., Gómez, C., Castillo, N., Quiroz, M., Ortíz, C., Hernández, P.: A visualization tool for heuristic algorithms analysis. In: Uden, L., Herrera, F., Bajo, J., Corchado, J. (eds.) 7th International Conference on Knowledge Management in Organizations: Service and Cloud Computing, Advances in Intelligent Systems and Computing, vol. 172, pp. 515–524. Springer, Heidelberg (2013). https://doi.org/10.1007/978-3-642-30867-3_46

67. Lopez, T.T., Schaefer, E., Domiguez-Diaz, D., Dominguez-Carrillo, G.: Structural effects in algorithm performance: A framework and a case study on graph coloring. In: Computing Conference, 2017, pp. 101–112. IEEE (2017)

68. Kerschke, P., Trautmann, H.: Comprehensive feature-based landscape analysis of continuous and constrained optimization problems using the R-package flacco. In: Bauer, N., Ickstadt, K., Lübke, K., Szepannek, G., Trautmann, H., Vichi, M. (eds.) Applications in Statistical Computing. SCDAKO, pp. 93–123. Springer, Cham (2019). https://doi.org/10.1007/978-3-030-25147-5_7

69. Watson, J., Darrell, W., Adele, E.: Linking search space structure, run-time dynamics, and problem difficulty: A step toward demystifying Tabu search. J. Artif. Intell. Res. **24**, 221–261 (2005)

70. Pérez, J., Cruz, L., Pazos, R., Landero, V., Pérez, V.: Application of causal models for the selection and redesign of heuristic algorithms for solving the bin-packing problem. Polish J. Environ. Stud. **17**(4C, Hard) 25–30 (2008)

71. Pérez, J., et al.: A causal approach for explaining why a heuristic algorithm outperforms another in solving an instance set of the bin packing problem. In: An, A., Matwin, S., Raś, Z.W., Ślęzak, D. (eds.) ISMIS 2008. LNCS (LNAI), vol. 4994, pp. 591–598. Springer, Heidelberg (2008). https://doi.org/10.1007/978-3-540-68123-6_64

72. Cheeseman, P., Kanefsky, B., Taylor, W.: Where the really hard problems are. In: The 12th IJCAI 91, pp. 331–337 (1991)

73. Thiebaux, S., Slaney, J., Kilby, P.: Estimating the hardness of optimization. In: ECAI, Berlin, pp. 123–130 (2000)

74. Spirtes, P., Glymour, C.: Causation, prediction, and search. MIT Press (2001)

75. Hoos, H.: A mixture-model for the behaviour of SLS algorithms for SAT. In: AAAI/IAAI, pp. 661–667 (2002)

76. Zhang, W.: Phase transitions and backbones of the asymmetric traveling salesman problem. J. Artif. Intell. Res. **21**, 471–497 (2004)

77. Watson, J.: An introduction to fitness landscape analysis and cost models for local search. In: Gendreau, M., Potvin, J. (eds.) Handbook of Metaheuristics, International Series in Operations Research & Management Science, vol. 146, pp. 599–623. Springer, Boston (2010). https://doi.org/10.1007/978-1-4419-1665-5_20

78. Gao, W., Nallaperuma, S., Neumann, F.: Feature-based diversity optimization for problem instance classification. Evol. Comput. **29**(1), 107–128 (2021)

79. Hogg, T., Huberman, B., Williams, C.: Phase transitions and the search problem. Artif. Intell. **81**(1), 1–15 (1996)

80. Mitchell, D., Selman, B., Levesque, H.: Hard and easy distributions of SAT problems. Proc. Conf. Artif. Intell. **92**, 459–465 (1992)

81. Smith-Miles, K.A., James, R.J.W., Giffin, J.W., Tu, Y.: A knowledge discovery approach to understanding relationships between scheduling problem structure and heuristic performance. In: Stützle, T. (ed.) LION 2009. LNCS, vol. 5851, pp. 89–103. Springer, Heidelberg (2009). https://doi.org/10.1007/978-3-642-11169-3_7

82. Liefooghe, A., Daolio, F., Verel, S., Derbel, B., Aguirre, H., Tanaka, K.: Landscape-aware performance prediction for evolutionary multiobjective optimization. IEEE Trans. Evol. Comput. **24**(6), 1063–1077 (2019)

83. Korb, K.: Bayesian Artificial Intelligence. Chapman and Hall, London (2004)

84. Landero, V., Pérez, J., Cruz, L., Turrubiates, T., Ríos, D.: Effects in the algorithm performance from problem structure, searching behavior and temperature: A causal study case for threshold accepting and bin-packing. In: Misra, S., et al. (eds.) ICCSA 2019. LNCS, vol. 11619, pp. 152–166. Springer, Cham (2019). https://doi.org/10.1007/978-3-030-24289-3_13

85. Landero, V., Ríos, D., Pérez, J., Cruz, L., Collazos-Morales, C.: Characterizing and analyzing the relation between bin-packing problem and Tabu search algorithm. In: Gervasi, O., et al. (eds.) ICCSA 2020. LNCS, vol. 12249, pp. 149–164. Springer, Cham (2020). https://doi.org/10.1007/978-3-030-58799-4_11

86. Landero, V., Ríos, D., Pérez, O.J., Collazos-Morales, C.A.: A composite function for understanding bin-packing problem and Tabu search: Towards self-adaptive algorithms. In: Gervasi, O., et al. (eds.) ICCSA 2021. LNCS, vol. 12949, pp. 592–608. Springer, Cham (2021). https://doi.org/10.1007/978-3-030-86653-2_43

87. Gent, I., Macintyre, E., Prosser, P., Walsh, T.: The scaling of search cost. In: AAAI'97, pp. 315–320. Mit Press, Rhode Island (1997)

88. Pérez, J., Pazos, R.A., Frausto, J., Rodríguez, G., Romero, D., Cruz, L.: A statistical approach for algorithm selection. In: Ribeiro, C.C., Martins, S.L. (eds.) WEA 2004. LNCS, vol. 3059, pp. 417–431. Springer, Heidelberg (2004). https://doi.org/10.1007/978-3-540-24838-5_31

89. Quiroz, M., Cruz, L., Torrez, J., Gómez, C.: Improving the performance of heuristic algorithms based on exploratory data analysis. In: Castillo, O., Melin, P., Kacprzyk, J. (eds.) Recent Advances on Hybrid Intelligent Systems, Studies in Computational Intelligence, vol. 452, pp. 361–375. Springer, Heidelberg (2013). https://doi.org/10.1007/978-3-642-33021-6_29

90. Cruz R., L., Pérez, J., Landero N., V., del Angel, E.S., Álvarez, V.M., Peréz, V.: An ordered preprocessing scheme for data mining. In: Zhang, C., W. Guesgen, H., Yeap, W.-K. (eds.) PRICAI 2004. LNCS (LNAI), vol. 3157, pp. 1007–1008. Springer, Heidelberg (2004). https://doi.org/10.1007/978-3-540-28633-2_137

91. Gómez, S., et al.: Ant colony system with characterization-based heuristics for a bottled-products distribution logistics system. J. Comput. Appl. Math. **259**, 965–977 (2014)

92. Xu, L., Hutter, F., Hoos, H., Leyton-Brown, K.: SATzilla: Portfolio-based algorithm selection for SAT. J. Artif. Intell. Res. **32**, 565–606 (2008)

A Machine Learning Methodology for Optimal Big Data Processing in Advanced Smart City Environments

Alfredo Cuzzocrea[1,2]([✉]), Luigi Canadè[1], Riccardo Nicolicchia[3], and Luca Roldo[3]

[1] iDEA Lab, University of Calabria, Rende, Italy
alfredo.cuzzocrea@unical.it
[2] Department of Computer Science, University Paris City, Paris, France
[3] ISIRES, Turin, Italy
{riccardo.nicolicchia,luca.roldo}@isires.org

Abstract. This paper introduces a *Machine Learning methodology for supporting optimal big data processing in advanced smart city environments*. In particular, the proposed work focuses the attention on the issue of efficiently charging *Electric Vehicles* (EVs) in an urban area, given various specific constraints. Our preliminary evaluation and analysis proofs the quality of our heuristics.

Keywords: Network Algorithms · Theory of Computing · Heuristic Algorithms

1 Introduction

Given the growing need and attention given to electric vehicles (EV), in the last decade many researchers have focused their attention on the optimal placement of EV chargers. Many have focused on the placement on large scale networks, to provide optimal placement considering multiple cities. These models consider a set of traffic flows with specific routes and locate charging stations along the routes so that the percentage of traffic flows performing their round trip without running out of charge is maximized, as proposed in [15,22,23,26].

Within the context of optimal location of charging stations for EV, the aim of this paper is exactly that of finding an optimal placement, in terms of location and quantity, of fast and slow charging stations within the parking lots of a urban environment. In particular, this project focuses on the optimal placement of EV charging stations in a urban environment under demand uncertainty conditions, given by variable characteristics of the traffic flows inside the city. Given the complexity of the EV charging station location problem when applied to a real case scenario, some effort has been spent into developing heuristic algorithms. Some related work can be found in [1,4,11]. In particular, the work in [1] was

A. Cuzzocrea—This research has been made in the context of the Excellence Chair in Big Data Management and Analytics at University of Paris City, Paris, France.

analyzed in depth to develop an heuristic algorithm for this paper. Another inspiring line of research has been represented by the emerging *big data call for arms* (e.g., [8,20]).

This paper thus introduces a *Machine Learning methodology for supporting optimal big data processing in advanced smart city environments*. Our preliminary evaluation and analysis proofs the quality of our heuristics. This paper extends the preliminary paper presented in [9].

The model takes as input a map containing a set of buildings and parking lots. The EV users' destination is defined by a specific building, therefore the public parking lots surrounding the buildings are considered as potential location for the charger installation. The model is characterized by the following assumptions:

- Drivers visit two buildings during the day.
- Drivers park their vehicle in a parking lot near the building of interest. Parking lots are considered to be near a building based on a specific distance parameter, that represent an approximate maximum distance that a user is willing to walk.
- EV users are divided in groups, representing traffic flows. Each group is characterized by: the two buildings they visit during the day, the arrival time at the first building, the dwell times in each building and the time they spend travelling from the first building to the second.
- The parameters of each group are deterministic and known with certainty.
- For each group, one single recharging is sufficient to complete the whole path from home to the first building, then to the second one and finally back home.
- The charging behaviour (duration and choice between fast and slow chargers) depends on the state of charge when arriving at the first building. Users of each group can therefore be divided in three different classes, described in Table 1, in which β_i represent the ratio of users of each group belonging to class i. The "Charge state" column represents the charging state of the battery when arriving at the first building and it is divided in three states: *low*, with 1/3 of charge remaining; *middle*, with 2/3 of charge remaining; *high*, with full battery.
- The dwell time in each building is divided in three cases: *short* (θ_1), *medium* (θ_2) and *long* (θ_3) duration.
- Drivers prefer to have the battery fully charged after recharging. Drivers will select the charging mode (*fast/slow*) based on their class (*EV charge state*) and the dwell time in each building. All the possible charging modes selections

Table 1. Classification of Drivers Based on Charge State.

Class	Charge state	Characteristics	Ratio
1	Low	Charge the EV when in the first building	β_1
2	Middle	Can charge the EV when in the first or second building	β_2
3	High	Charge the EV when in the second building	β_3

are listed in Table 2. A combination of class, choice of charging when in the first or second building, dwell time and consequent charging mode is called "type".

Table 2. Type Definition: Charging Modes Selection by Different Classes of Drivers.

Type	Class	Building	Dwell Time	Charging mode
1	1	First	Short, Medium	Fast
2	1	First	Long	Slow
3	2	First	Short	Fast
4	2	First	Medium, Long	Slow
5	2	Second	Short, Medium	Fast
6	2	Second	Long	Slow
7	3	Second	Short	Fast
8	3	Second	Medium, Long	Slow

- The cost of installing a fast or slow charger in a parking lot as well as the purchase cost of a single charger are known with certainty.
- A limited number of chargers can be installed in the whole considered environment. This assumption addresses a budget restriction.
- There is a limitation also on the number of chargers that can be installed in a single parking lot, to set a limit in the physical capacity as well as in the energy consumption of each parking lot.
- There is an upper bound on the number of parking lots that can be equipped with chargers.
- The number of drivers of each group is uncertain and its variation generates multiple possible scenarios.

Based on the listed assumption, the problem is two-stage stochastic programming model. In the first stage parking lots that should be equipped with chargers are determined, as well as the number of fast and slow chargers for each parking. In the second stage, for each scenario, the number of drivers in each group is computed and EVs are assigned to parking lots accordingly. The objective function must take into account both the cost of purchasing and installing the chargers as well as maximizing the coverage of demands, that can be interpreted also as the total income achieved from users charging their vehicles.

For convenience, time is divided in slots, with each slot assumed to be 1 hour long. Let $\mathbb{T}$ (indexed by t) be the set of time-slots, $\mathbb{B}$ (indexed by b) be the set of buildings, $\mathbb{P}$ (indexed by p) be the set of parking lots and $\mathbb{G}$ (indexed by g) be the set of groups. Assume that $\bar{b}_{1,g}, \bar{b}_{2,g} \in \mathbb{B}$ are the first and second buildings visited by EV users of group g, and $\bar{t}_g$ is the time slot at which users of group g arrive at the first building $\bar{b}_{1,g}$. Dwell times, expressed in number of slots, of group g at buildings $\bar{b}_{1,g}$ and $\bar{b}_{2,g}$ are denoted by $d_{1,g}$ and $d_{2,g}$, respectively. The travel time from $\bar{b}_{1,g}$ to $\bar{b}_{2,g}$ is denoted by d'_g. Parameter α represents the maximum distance that a user of every group is willing to walk to reach a building from a parking lot. The fixed costs of equipping a parking lot with fast and slow chargers are represented by F' and F'', respectively, and the cost of purchasing one fast or slow charger is denoted by C' and C''. At most, M parking lots can be equipped with chargers, and a total of M' chargers are installable. Moreover, the number of chargers that can be installed in any parking lot is limited by M''. The number of drivers of each group is uncertain and in this regard, $\mathbb{S}$ (indexed by s) represents the set of possible scenarios. Variable dem_g^s represents the number of drivers of group g under scenario s, while π_s represents the probability of the occurrence of scenario s. The meaning of each described set and parameter is summarized in Table 3.

Table 3. Summary of Sets and Parameters

Name	Description
$\mathbb{T}$	Set of time slots (indexed by t)
$\mathbb{B}$	Set of buildings (indexed by b)
$\mathbb{G}$	Set of groups of EV users (indexed by g)
$\mathbb{P}$	Set of parking lots (indexed by p)
$\mathbb{S}$	Set of scenarios (indexed by s)
π_s	Occurrence prob. of scenario s
$\bar{b}_{i,g}$	i^{th} building visited by users of group g ($i = 1, 2$)
$\bar{t}_g$	Time-slot in which users of group g arrive at first building
$d_{i,g}$	Dwell-time (in time slots) of group g at building $\bar{b}_{i,g}$
d'_g	Time (in time slots) spent by group g to travel from $\bar{b}_{1,g}$ to $\bar{b}_{2,g}$
dem_g^s	Number of drivers of group g under scenario s
α	Maximum walking distance
β_i	Fraction of drivers in a group belonging to class i ($i = 1, 2, 3$)
θ_i	Indicating the duration (in time-slots) of short, medium and long dwell times ($i = 1, 2, 3$)
E'	Income achieved by charging an EV with a fast charger in a unit of time
E''	Income achieved by charging an EV with a slow charger in a unit of time
F'	Fixed cost of equipping a parking lot with fast chargers
F''	Fixed cost of equipping a parking lot with slow chargers
C'	Cost of purchasing a fast charger
C''	Cost of purchasing a slow charger
M	Maximum number of parking lots that can be equipped with chargers
M'	Total number of available chargers
M''	Maximum number of chargers that can be installed in any parking lot

1.1 Map Generation

In order to work, the model needs a set of parking lots, buildings and the distance among them. To do so, an algorithm was built that generates pseudo-random city environments and provides realistic and coherent data to the model. The algorithm takes as input the number of buildings and parking lots to place, the minimum distance among buildings and the desired length of the side of the square map. The algorithm works as follows: (i) Creates a square matrix whose dimensions are those specified by the input settings. This matrix represents a physical map in which each location is identified by the coordinates of the cell. It is assumed that each cell is $10m \times 10m$. Therefore each provided distance is specified in units of 10 m. (*ii*) Places each building, one at the time. The x and y coordinates are randomly chosen, taking however into consideration that no building is already present in that cell or within a certain radius from that cell; the value of the radius is specified in the input settings. (*iii*) Places each parking, in the same fashion of the building placement. Parking lots can be placed within the input radius of a building, but not within an input radius of another parking lot.

In order to check the connectivity between building and parking lots (i.e. which parking lots can be used by EV users to access a building) the map can be translated in a graph, in which parking lots and buildings are nodes and a link between a parking lot and a building is present if the distance among them is lower than the maximum walking distance α. An example with 20 buildings, 10 parking lots, a map side length of 20000 meters, a minimum distance between buildings of 1000meters is shown in Fig. 1. Building indicators have different sizes based on their popularity, which is randomly assigned to buildings when the map is created and whose usage will be described in the next section. The connectivity between parking and buildings is shown in Fig. 2. It is noted that some buildings result inaccessible from any parking lot; groups accessing these buildings will not be considered, for the time they stay in the inaccessible building, in the calculation of the optimal placement of the EV chargers since they will not occupy any present parking lot.

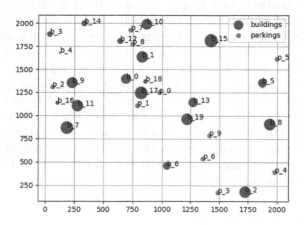

Fig. 1. Urban Environment Map.

1.2   Group Generation

A group is characterized by EV users visiting the same first and second building, have the same dwell time in both the first and second building, arrive at the first building at the same time and take the same time to travel from the first building to the second. Given these characteristics, many groups have to be generated in

Fig. 2. Connectivity between Buildings and Parking Lots.

order to have a realistic flow of EV users. In this problem, group generation is performed by taking random (and different) first and second building, a random arrival time slot, two random dwell times for both the first and second building, and a travel time proportional to the distance between the first and second building. The algorithm also takes care not to generate two identical groups.

1.3   Group Sizing

The number of drivers in each group g, denoted by dem_g^s, is scenario dependent and therefore affected by uncertainty. In each scenario, the number of drivers is assigned to each group using the following procedure: (i) A popularity index q_b, in the range $[0, 1]$, is assigned to each building. (ii) A total amount of population is assigned to each building taking into account the popularity index and the mean (m_{pop}) and variance (σ_{pop}) of one building's population, provided in the input settings. In particular, to each building is assigned an amount of people equal to a realization of $\mathcal{N}(q_b m_{pop}, \sigma_{pop}^2)$. ($iii$) Then, the total population of each building is randomly distributed to all those groups accessing that building, as first or second. Since a group accesses two buildings, its value of dem_g^s will be the result of the sum of this random assignment from the first building and that from the second building.

2   Mathematical Model

Looking at the actual literature, some deterministic approaches in urban environments consider several different factors to make the model more realistic and accurate. The model in [6] considers travelers having two main stops during the day (as was considered also in this paper) and drivers that cannot charge their EV privately. The works in [12] and [13] consider the drivers' spontaneous adjustments and interactions of travel and recharging decision. The model in [21] considers also environmental factors for siting and sizing of EV charging stations. [24] considers real vehicle travel patterns. The study in [14] considers capacitated chargers and flow deviations due to recharging needs.

Turning back to our main problem, in order to properly define constraints and objective function, two subsets are introduced. Subsets $\mathbb{G}'_{i,j,p}$ contain all those groups whose dwell time in their i^{th} building (with $i = 1, 2$) is equals to θ_j (with $\theta_j = 1, 2, 3$)and parking lot p is a possible parking lot when visiting that in building. In particular:

$$\mathbb{G}'_{i,j,p} = \{g \in \mathbb{G} : d(p, \bar{b}_{i,g}) < \alpha \text{ and } d_{i,g} = \theta_j\} \tag{1}$$

where $d(p, \bar{b}_{i,g})$ is the physical distance between parking p and building $\bar{b}_{i,g}$.

Furthermore, subsets $\mathbb{G}''_{t,p,r}$ contain those groups that use the charging mode r (defined in row r in Table 2) and hence may occupy parking lot p in time slot t. All the decision variables of the problem are reported in Table 4.

Table 4. Decision Variables

Name	Description
δ_p	Binary variable that is 1 if parking lot p is equipped with chargers, 0 otherwise
δ'_p	Binary variable that is 1 if parking lot p is equipped with at least one fast charger, 0 otherwise
δ''_p	Binary variable that is 1 if parking lot p is equipped with at least one slow charger, 0 otherwise
γ'_p	Number of fast chargers installed in parking lot p
γ''_p	Number of slow chargers installed in parking lot p
$y^s_{p,g}$	Number of drivers of group g belonging to class 1 and charge their EV in parking lot p during the time they are in the first building under scenario s
$x^s_{p,g}$	Number of drivers of group g belonging to class 2 and charge their EV in parking lot p during the time they are in the first building under scenario s
$x'^s_{p,g}$	Number of drivers of group g belonging to class 2 and charge their EV in parking lot p during the time they are in the second building under scenario s
$w^s_{p,g}$	Number of drivers of group g belonging to class 3 and charge their EV in parking lot p during the time they are in the second building under scenario s

Given the defined parameters and decision variables, the objective function is formulated as follows:

$$\max - \sum_{p \in \mathbb{P}} \left(F' \delta'_p + F'' \delta''_p + C' \gamma'_p + C'' \gamma''_p \right)$$

$$+ \sum_{s \in S} \pi^s \sum_{p \in \mathbb{P}} \left(E' \left[\theta_1 \left(\sum_{p \in G'_{1,1,p}} \left(y^s_{p,g} + x^s_{p,g} \right) + \sum_{p \in G'_{2,1,p}} \left(w^s_{p,g} + x'^s_{p,g} \right) \right) \right. \right.$$

$$+ \theta_2 \left(\sum_{p \in G'_{1,2,p}} y^s_{p,g} + \sum_{p \in G'_{2,2,p}} x'^s_{p,g} \right) \right] + E'' \left[\theta_2 \left(\sum_{p \in G'_{1,2,p}} x^s_{p,g} + \sum_{p \in G'_{2,2,p}} w^s_{p,g} \right) \right. \tag{2}$$

$$\left. \left. + \theta_3 \left(\sum_{p \in G'_{1,3,p}} \left(y^s_{p,g} + x^s_{p,g} \right) + \sum_{p \in G'_{2,3,p}} \left(w^s_{p,g} + x'^s_{p,g} \right) \right) \right] \right)$$

As previously mentioned, the objective function makes a trade-off between minimizing the costs of purchasing and equipping chargers and maximizing the expected coverage demands (earnings obtained by charging their EV). The constraints of the problem are defined in Table 5. Descriptions of constraints are reported in Table 5.

3 Heuristic Model

Two different heuristic models are considered. The first solves the problem presented in the Sect. 1. The second solves an improved version of the former problem because it allows the EV users whose charging mode is slow to park their vehicle in an available fast charger if all the slow ones are occupied. By using this second method, it is possible to obtain a higher value of the objective function.

Both heuristic models are divided into a first and a second stage and operate on the same data generated for the math model. The first stage gives as output the placement of the charging stations (both fast and slow chargers) in the parking lots. The second stage returns the number of EV users that recharge their vehicle in the installed chargers. The drivers are divided according to: (i) the type of used charger; (ii) the dwell time in the building in which they recharge their EV.

Those values are used to evaluate the resulting objective function. Given the variables reported in Table 6, the objective function is evaluated as follow:

$$\max - \sum_{p \in \mathbb{P}} \left(F' \delta'_p + F'' \delta''_p + C' \gamma'_p + C'' \gamma''_p \right)$$

$$+ \sum_{s \in S} \pi^s \left(E' \left[\theta_1 n F_1 + \theta_2 n F_2 + \theta_3 n F_3 \right] \right. \tag{3}$$

$$\left. + E'' \left[\theta_1 n S_1 + \theta_2 n S_2 + \theta_3 n S_3 \right] \right)$$

If the resulting value of the objective function is negative, then the heuristic model does not place any charger at all.

Table 5. Constraints

#	Constraint	Description
1	$\sum_{p \in \mathbb{P}} \delta_p \leq M$	Ensures that at most M parking lots are equipped with chargers
2	$\delta_p' + \delta_p'' \leq 2\delta_p \quad \forall p \in \mathbb{P}$	Ensures that if $\delta_p = 0$, also δ_p' and δ_p'' are zero
3	$\gamma_p' \leq M'' \delta_p' \quad \forall p \in \mathbb{P}$	Ensures that if $\delta_p' = 0$, also $\gamma_p' = 0$
4	$\gamma_p'' \leq M'' \delta_p'' \quad \forall p \in \mathbb{P}$	Ensures that if $\delta_p'' = 0$, also $\gamma_p'' = 0$
5	$\gamma_p' + \gamma_p'' \leq M'' \quad \forall p \in \mathbb{P}$	Restricts the total number of chargers installed in parking lot p
6	$\sum_{p \in \mathbb{P}} (\gamma_p' + \gamma_p'') \leq M'$	Restricts the total number of chargers installed in the network
7	$\sum_{p \in \mathbb{P}: d(p, \bar{b}_{1,g}) \leq \alpha} y_{p,g}^s \leq \beta_1 dem_g^s \quad \forall g \in \mathbb{G}, \forall s \in \mathbb{S}$	Restricts the number of class 1 drivers in each group
8	$\sum_{p \in \mathbb{P}: d(p, \bar{b}_{1,g}) \leq \alpha} x_{p,g}^s + \sum_{p \in \mathbb{P}: d(p, \bar{b}_{2,g}) \leq \alpha} x_{p,g}'^s \leq \beta_2 dem_g^s \quad \forall g \in \mathbb{G}, \forall s \in \mathbb{S}$	Restricts the number of class 2 drivers in each group
9	$\sum_{p \in \mathbb{P}: d(p, \bar{b}_{2,g}) \leq \alpha} w_{p,g}^s \leq \beta_3 dem_g^s \quad \forall g \in \mathbb{G}, \forall s \in \mathbb{S}$	Restricts the number of class 3 drivers in each group
10	$\sum_{g \in \mathbb{G}_{t,p,1}''} y_{p,g}^s + \sum_{g \in \mathbb{G}_{t,p,3}''} x_{p,g}^s + \sum_{g \in \mathbb{G}_{t,p,5}''} x_{p,g}'^s + \sum_{g \in \mathbb{G}_{t,p,7}''} w_{p,g}^s \leq \gamma_p'$ $\forall p \in \mathbb{P} \; \forall t \in \mathbb{T}, \forall s \in \mathbb{S}$	The number of EVs using fast chargers of parking lot p at time t cannot exceed the number of installed fast chargers
11	$\sum_{g \in \mathbb{G}_{t,p,2}''} y_{p,g}^s + \sum_{g \in \mathbb{G}_{t,p,4}''} x_{p,g}^s + \sum_{g \in \mathbb{G}_{t,p,6}''} x_{p,g}'^s + \sum_{g \in \mathbb{G}_{t,p,8}''} w_{p,g}^s \leq \gamma_p''$ $\forall p \in \mathbb{P} \; \forall t \in \mathbb{T}, \forall s \in \mathbb{S}$	The number of EVs using slow chargers of parking lot p at time t cannot exceed the number of installed slow chargers
14	$\delta_p, \delta_p', \delta_p'' \in \{0,1\}, \gamma_p', \gamma_p'' \geq 0, \text{Integer} \quad \forall p \in \mathbb{P}$	Type of variables definition
15	$y_{p,g}^s, x_{p,g}^s \geq 0 \quad \forall g \in \mathbb{G}, \forall p \in \mathbb{P}: d(p, \bar{b}_{1,g}) \leq \alpha, \forall s \in \mathbb{S}$	Type of variables definition
16	$x_{p,g}'^s, w_{p,g}^s \geq 0 \quad \forall g \in \mathbb{G}, \forall p \in \mathbb{P}: d(p, \bar{b}_{2,g}) \leq \alpha, \forall s \in \mathbb{S}$	Type of variables definition

Table 6. Heuristic Variables

Name	Description
nF_1	Number of drivers that recharge their vehicle in a fast charger and whose dwell time is short
nF_2	Number of drivers that recharge their vehicle in a fast charger and whose dwell time is medium
nF_3	Number of drivers that recharge their vehicle in a fast charger and whose dwell time is long
nS_1	Number of drivers that recharge their vehicle in a slow charger and whose dwell time is short
nS_2	Number of drivers that recharge their vehicle in a slow charger and whose dwell time is medium
nS_3	Number of drivers that recharge their vehicle in a slow charger and whose dwell time is long

3.1   First Stage

The first stage of the heuristic model determines the parking lots that should be equipped with chargers and the number of fast and slow chargers for each parking. The variables used are reported in Table 8 and in Algorithm 1 is given the pseudocode. From the fraction of drivers belonging to each class and the cost of purchasing and positioning the chargers, it is computed the number of fast and slow chargers available. Afterward, the maximum number of chargers that can be installed in a parking lot (M") is assigned to the most popular parking lots on the map, firstly fast chargers are positioned and then slow. The outputs of the first stage are two lists, one for slow chargers and the other for fast, where, for each parking lot equipped, it is reported the number of chargers installed (Table 7).

Table 7. Heuristic First Stage Sets

Name	Description
P_{sc}	The set that contains the number of slow chargers for each parking lot
P_{fc}	The set that contains the number of fast chargers for each parking lot

3.2   Second Stage

The second stage of the heuristic model considers the main concepts of [1] and reuse them by adapting them to the different model: (i) Connection Matrix; (ii) Charging Site Degree; (iii) Electric Vehicle Degree.

The sets and parameters to be added to those already present in the mathematical model are given in Table 9 (i can take the value f if it refers to fast chargers, s for slow chargers).

Algorithm 1. Heuristic Model - First Stage

Initialize P_{sc} and P_{fc}
$perc_s = \beta_2/2 + \beta_1/3 + 2\beta_3/3$
$perc_f = \beta_2/2 + 2\beta_1/3 + \beta_3/3$
$price_f = E'/(C' + F')$
$price_s = E''/(C'' + F'')$
$tot\_price = price_s + price_f$
$price_s = price_s/tot\_price$
$price_f = price_f/tot\_price$
$Tot_{charg} = min(M', M \cdot M'')$
$av_i = floor(Tot_{charg} \cdot (perc_i + price_i)/2)$
Sort the set $\mathbb{B}_P$ according to the sum of all the popularity indexes
for $(p \in arg(\mathbb{B}_P))$ **do**
    if $(N_e \geq M)$ **then**
        STOP
    else
        $N_e = N_e + 1$
        if $(av_f \geq M'')$ **then**
            $P_{fc}[p] = M''$
            $av_f = av_f - M''$
        else if $(av_f < M'' \land av_f > 0 \land av_s \geq (M'' - av_f))$ **then**
            $P_{fc}[p] = av_f, P_{sc}[p] = M'' - av_f$
            $av_s = av_s - (M'' - av_f), av_f = 0$
        else if $(av_f = 0 \land av_s \geq M'')$ **then**
            $P_{sc}[p] = M''$
            $av_s = av_s - M''$
        else if $(av_f = 0 \land av_s < M'' \land av_s > 0)$ **then**
            $P_{sc}[p] = av_s$
            $av_s = 0$
        else
            STOP
        end if
    end if
end for
return P_{sc}, P_{fc}

Table 8. Heuristic First Stage Variables

Name	Description
$perc_i$	The percentage of chargers of type i based on the value of $\beta_1, \beta_2, \beta_3$
$price_i$	The percentage of chargers of type i based on the price and on the revenue of the i chargers
av_i	The number of available chargers of type i
$\mathbb{B}_P[p]$	The set of the buildings that can be reached from the parking lot p
N_e	The number of equipped parking lots
Tot_{charg}	The maximum number of chargers that can be placed

Table 9. Heuristic Additional Sets and Parameters

Name	Description
S_i	The set of all the activated charging sites
R_i	The set of all the activated charging sites that are not completely full
O_i	The set of all the occupied chargers per parking lots
K_i	The set of users that arrive in the selected time slot and that need the charging of type i
P_i	The set of all the available charging sites of type i that are not analyzed yet
AR	The set that keeps track of the number of people of the second class that have already recharged their EV in the first building, so they do not need to charge it in the second one
TR_i	The set that contains all the users that must leave for every time slot
$\mathbb{P}_i$	The set of the parking lots containing chargers of type i

The pseudocode of the steps of the second stage is reported in Algorithm 2. Before launching the algorithm, the input structure that contains the groups is modified to divide the people belonging to the groups into subgroups according to the following parameters: (i) the visited building: note that the first and the second building are considered separately; (ii) the arrival time slot to the visited building; (iii) the charging mode needed; (iv) the dwell time inside the building; (v) the cardinality of the considered subgroup; (vi) the class of the considered subgroup; (vii) the ID number of the group.

Then this new set of subgroups is grouped according to other two parameters: (i) the scenario; ii) the time slot of arrival to the building.

Connection Matrix. The Connection Matrix C_i is a matrix ($\mathbb{P}_i$ x $\mathbb{B}$) and its element $C_i(p, b)$ is equal to 1 if the building b can be reached from the parking lot p, 0 otherwise. It happens when the euclidean distance between the building and the parking lot is smaller than the maximum walking distance α.

Charging Site Degree. The Charging Site Degree $CSD(p)$ is the total number of users that can park in the selected parking lot p.

Algorithm 2. Heuristic Model - Second Stage

Initialization
Calculate the Connection Matrices C_i
Initialize the variables in Table 6
for $(s \in \mathbb{S})$ **do**
    Initialize S_i, R_i, TR_i, O_i, AR
    for $(t \in \mathbb{T})$ **do**
        Initialize K_i, P_i
        Calculate EVD_i ▷ considering C_i and $g \in K_i$
        $O_i, S_i, R_i = remove\_users\_function[TR_i, O_i, S_i, R_i]$
(Algorithm 3)   ▷ Delete all the users that should leave in the current time slot
        $K_i = K_i - AR$ ▷ Delete the users already served
        $K_f, S_f, R_f, O_f = solve\_second\_stage\_subproblem\_function$
$[K_f, P_f, S_f, R_f, O_f, EVD_f, C_f]$
(Algorithm 4) ▷ Add the users that arrive in the current time slot who need fast chargers to the available parking lots' chargers
        $K_s, S_s, R_s, O_s = solve\_second\_stage\_subproblem\_function$
$[K_s, P_s, S_s, R_s, O_s, EVD_s, C_s]$ (Algorithm 4)   ▷ Add the users that arrive in the current time slot who need slow chargers to the available parking lots' chargers
        – The following lines are added to obtain the second heuristic model –
        Calculate EVD_{fs} ▷ considering C_f and $g \in K_s$
        $K_s, S_f, R_f, O_f = solve\_second\_stage\_subproblem\_function$
$[K_s, P_f, S_f, R_f, O_f, EVD_{fs}, C_f]$ (Algorithm 4)   ▷ Add the users that arrive in the current time slot that need slow chargers, but that find them all occupied, to the fast chargers
    end for
end for

Algorithm 3. Heuristic Model - $remove\_users\_function[TR_i, O_i, S_i, R_i]$

---

if $(TR_i[t] \neq \emptyset)$ **then**
    for $(item \in TR_i[t])$ **do**
        Assign to p the parking lot where the charging stations become free
        $O_i[p] = O_i[p] - \{item\}$
        if $(p \in S_i \wedge O_i[p] = \emptyset)$ **then**
            $S_i = S_i - \{p\}$
        end if
        if $(p \in R_i \wedge O_i[p] = \emptyset)$ **then**
            $R_i = R_i - \{p\}$
        end if
        if $(p \notin R_i \wedge O_i[p] \neq \emptyset)$ **then**
            $R_i = R_i \cup \{p\}$
        end if
    end for
end if
return O_i, S_i, R_i

$$CSD(p) = \sum_{g \in \mathbb{G}} C_i(p, b) * n \tag{4}$$

where b is the building related to the group g and n is its cardinality.

Electric Vehicle Degree. The Electric Vehicle Degree $EVD(g)$ is the number of parking lots in which the group g can park.

$$EVD(g) = \sum_{p \in \mathbb{P}} C_i(p, b) \tag{5}$$

where b is the building related to the group g.

Algorithm 4. Heuristic Model - *solve_second_stage_subproblem_function* $[K_i, P_i, S_i, R_i, O_i, EVD_i, C_i]$

---

while $(K_i \neq \emptyset \wedge P_i \neq \emptyset)$ do
    Calculate CSD_i
    for $(value \in CSD_i)$ do
        if $(value = 0)$ then
            Assign to p the parking lot value 0
            $P_i = P_i - \{p\}$
        end if
    end for
    $k = argmax(CSD_i(p))$ ▷ Take the parking lot in which more users can park
    Assign to *slots* the number of chargers available in the parking lot k
    $P_i = P_i - \{k\}$
    if $(k \notin S_i)$ then
        $S_i = S_i \cup \{k\}$
    end if
    Initialize $parked\_EV = 0$
    if $(slots - O_i[k] = 0)$ then
        pass   ▷ There are not available slots
    else if $(slots - O_i[k] < CSD_i[k])$ then
        while $(parked\_EV < slots - O_i[k])$ do
            $j = argmin(EVD_i(g))$ ▷ Take the group that can charge its EVs in the smallest
number of parking lots
            Assign to n the cardinality of the group j
            if $(n > slots - O_i[k])$ then
                $n = n - (slots - O_i[k])$ ▷ Update the cardinality of the group j
                $parked\_EV, O_i, TR_i[t], AR, nI_1, nI_2, nI_3 = update\_variable\_function(slots - O_i[k])$ (Algorithm 5)
            else
                $parked\_EV, O_i, TR_i[t], AR, nI_1, nI_2, nI_3 = update\_variable\_function(n)$ (Algorithm 5)
                $K_i = K_i - \{j\}, EVD_i = EVD_i - \{EVD_i[j]\}$
            end if
        end while
    else
        $O_i[k] = O_i[k] + CSD_i[k]$
        if $(k \notin R_i)$ then
            $R_i = R_i \cup \{k\}$
        end if
        Initialize $parked\_group = \emptyset$
        for $(g \in K_i)$ do
            Assign to b the building related to the group g
            if $(C_i[k][b] = 1)$ then
                Assign to n the cardinality of the group g
                $parked\_group = parked\_group \cup g$
                $TR_i[t] = TR_i[t] \cup \{g\}$
                if $(g$ class is 2$)$ then
                      $AR = AR + \{g\}$
                end if
                if (dwell time of g is *short*) then
                    $nI_1 = nI_1 + n$
                else if (dwell time of g is *medium*) then
                    $nI_2 = nI_2 + n$
                else
                    $nI_3 = nI_3 + n$
                end if
            end if
        end for
        for $(g \in parked\_group)$ do
            $K_i = K_i - \{g\}, EVD_i = EVD_i - \{EVD_i[g]\}$
        end for
    end if
end while
return K_i, S_i, R_i, O_i

Algorithm 5. Heuristic Model - *update_variable_function(num)*

$parked\_EV = parked\_EV + num$
$O_i[k] = O_i[k] + num$
$TR_i[t] = TR_i[t] \cup \{j\}$
if (j's class is 2) **then**
  $AR = AR + \{j\}$
end if
if (dwell time of j is *short*) **then**
  $nI_1 = nI_1 + num$
else if (dwell time of j is *medium*) **then**
  $nI_2 = nI_2 + num$
else
  $nI_3 = nI_3 + num$
end if
return $parked\_EV, O_i, TR_i[t], AR, nI_1, nI_2, nI_3$

3.3 Example Result

In order to give a practical example of the obtained results, the heuristic model was launched considering the map in Fig. 1 and the default settings. The heuristic model places 5 fast chargers each in parking lots with ID 0, 1, 2 and 8, while it places 5 slow chargers only in parking lot with ID 7. Comparing the result with what was obtained in the results of the mathematical model with the same settings, the heuristic identifies the same parking lots that need to be equipped. However, it places 5 fast chargers in parking lot with ID 1 instead of 5 slow chargers. In fact, for how the heuristic algorithm is structured, it tends to favor the placement of fast chargers. However, after a number of simulations, it was discovered that this preference suit well cases with a high number of EV users with high diversity (i.e. number of groups), which represents a realistic situation.

3.4 Stability Testing

Both the in sample and out-of-sample stability of the heuristic model were tested. The in sample stability (3a) was tested over 10 different scenario trees, each composed by 50 different scenarios, while the out-of-sample stability (3b) was tested over 10 different scenario trees composed by 200 scenarios. Given the number of repetitions, the settings of the instance were lowered. The results of the in sample ad out-of-sample stability testing are shown in Fig. 3.

It can be stated that the stochastic heuristic model is stable and consistent. The in sample stability presents some fluctuations, but with still in an acceptable amount.

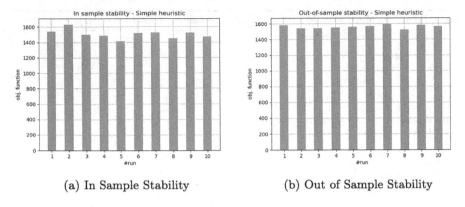

(a) In Sample Stability   (b) Out of Sample Stability

Fig. 3. Sample Stability Heuristic

4   Conclusions and Future Work

Starting from open research challenges of the research community, in this paper we have proposed three innovative heuristic algorithms that solve the optimal charging-station location problem for electric vehicles, whose main benefit consists in achieving good approximate solutions while keeping acceptable computational time. Future work is mainly oriented towards making our algorithms compliant with emerging *big data trends* (e.g., [2,3,5,7,10,16–19,25,27]).

References

1. Adacher, L.: Heuristics for electric vehicle charging station allocation problem. In: 2018 5th International Conference on Mathematics and Computers in Sciences and Industry (MCSI), pp. 72–76. IEEE (2018)
2. Barkwell, K.E., et al.: Big data visualisation and visual analytics for music data mining. In: 22nd International Conference Information Visualisation, IV 2018, Fisciano, Italy, 10–13 July 2018, pp. 235–240. IEEE Computer Society (2018)
3. Bellatreche, L., Cuzzocrea, A., Benkrid, S.: F& A: A methodology for effectively and efficiently designing parallel relational data warehouses on heterogenous database clusters. In: DAWAK 2010, Bilbao, Spain, August/September 2010. Proceedings, pp. 89–104 (2010)
4. Bi, R., Xiao, J., Pelzer, D., Ciechanowicz, D., Eckhoff, D., Knoll, A.C.: A simulation-based heuristic for city-scale electric vehicle charging station placement. In: 20th IEEE International Conference on Intelligent Transportation Systems, ITSC 2017, Yokohama, Japan, 16–19 October 2017, pp. 1–7. IEEE (2017)
5. Camara, R.C., Cuzzocrea, A., Grasso, G.M., Leung, C.K., Powell, S.B., Souza, J., Tang, B.: Fuzzy logic-based data analytics on predicting the effect of hurricanes on the stock market. In: 2018 IEEE International Conference on Fuzzy Systems, FUZZ-IEEE 2018, Rio de Janeiro, Brazil, 8–13 July 2018. pp. 1–8. IEEE (2018)
6. Cavadas, J., de A Correia, G.H., Gouveia, J.: A mip model for locating slow-charging stations for electric vehicles in urban areas accounting for driver tours. Trans. Res. Part E: Logist. Trans. R. **75**, 188–201 (2015)

7. Coronato, A., Cuzzocrea, A.: An innovative risk assessment methodology for medical information systems. IEEE Trans. Knowl. Data Eng. **34**(7), 3095–3110 (2022)
8. Cuzzocrea, A.: Analytics over big data: Exploring the convergence of datawarehousing, OLAP and data-intensive cloud infrastructures. In: COMPSAC 2013, Kyoto, Japan, 22–26 July 2013, pp. 481–483. IEEE Computer Society (2013)
9. Cuzzocrea, A., Canadé, L., Nicolicchia, R., Roldo, L.: Optimal location of charging stations for electric vehicles: A theoretically-sound heuristic approach. In: Proceedings of the 38th ACM/SIGAPP Symposium on Applied Computing, SAC 2023, Tallinn, Estonia, 27–31 March 2023. ACM (2023)
10. Demchenko, Y., De Laat, C., Membrey, P.: Defining architecture components of the big data ecosystem. In: 2014 International Conference On Collaboration Technologies and Systems (CTS), pp. 104–112 (2014)
11. Gatica, G., Ahumada, G., Escobar, J., Linfati, R.: Efficient heuristic algorithms for location of charging stations in electric vehicle routing problems. Stud. Inf. Control **27**, 73–82 (2018)
12. He, F., Yin, Y., Zhou, J.: Deploying public charging stations for electric vehicles on urban road networks. Trans. Res. Part C: Emerging Technol. **60**, 227–240 (2015)
13. He, J., Yang, H., Tang, T., Huang, H.: An optimal charging station location model with the consideration of electric vehicle's driving range. Trans. Res. Part C: Emerg. Technol. **86**, 641–654 (2018)
14. Hosseini, M., MirHassani, S., Hooshmand, F.: Deviation-flow refueling location problem with capacitated facilities: Model and algorithm. Transp. Res. Part D: Transp. Environ. **54**, 269–281 (2017)
15. Kuby, M., Lim, S.: The flow-refueling location problem for alternative-fuel vehicles. Socioecon. Plann. Sci. **39**(2), 125–145 (2005)
16. Leung, C.K., Braun, P., Hoi, C.S.H., Souza, J., Cuzzocrea, A.: Urban analytics of big transportation data for supporting smart cities. In: Ordonez, C., Song, I.-Y., Anderst-Kotsis, G., Tjoa, A.M., Khalil, I. (eds.) DaWaK 2019. LNCS, vol. 11708, pp. 24–33. Springer, Cham (2019). https://doi.org/10.1007/978-3-030-27520-4_3
17. Leung, C.K., Chen, Y., Hoi, C.S.H., Shang, S., Cuzzocrea, A.: Machine learning and OLAP on big COVID-19 data. In: 2020 IEEE International Conference on Big Data (IEEE BigData 2020), Atlanta, GA, USA, 10–13 December 2020, pp. 5118–5127. IEEE (2020)
18. Leung, C.K., Chen, Y., Hoi, C.S.H., Shang, S., Wen, Y., Cuzzocrea, A.: Big data visualization and visual analytics of COVID-19 data. In: 24th International Conference on Information Visualisation, IV 2020, Melbourne, Australia, 7–11 September 2020, pp. 415–420. IEEE (2020)
19. Leung, C.K., Cuzzocrea, A., Mai, J.J., Deng, D., Jiang, F.: Personalized deepinf: Enhanced social influence prediction with deep learning and transfer learning. In: 2019 IEEE International Conference on Big Data (IEEE BigData), Los Angeles, CA, USA, 9–12 December 2019, pp. 2871–2880. IEEE (2019)
20. Li, K., Jiang, H., Yang, L.T., Cuzzocrea, A. (eds.): Big Data - Algorithms, Analytics, and Applications. Chapman and Hall/CRC (2015)
21. Liu, Z., Wen, F., Ledwich, G.: Optimal planning of electric-vehicle charging stations in distribution systems. IEEE Trans. Power Delivery **28**(1), 102–110 (2013)
22. Miralinaghi, M., Keskin, B., Lou, Y., Roshandeh, A.: Capacitated refueling station location problem with traffic deviations over multiple time periods. Netw. Spatial Econom. **17**, 129–151 (2017)
23. MirHassani, S.A., Ebrazi, R.: A flexible reformulation of the refueling station location problem. Transp. Sci. **47**(4), 617–628 (2013)

24. Shahraki, N., Cai, H., Turkay, M., Xu, M.: Optimal locations of electric public charging stations using real world vehicle travel patterns. Transp. Res. Part D: Transp. Environ. **41**, 165–176 (2015)
25. Souza, J., Leung, C.K., Cuzzocrea, A.: An innovative big data predictive analytics framework over hybrid big data sources with an application for disease analytics. In: AINA 2020, Caserta, Italy, 15–17 April, pp. 669–680 (2020)
26. Wang, Y., Shi, J., Wang, R., Liu, Z., Wang, L.: Siting and sizing of fast charging stations in highway network with budget constraint. Appl. Energy **228**, 1255–1271 (2018)
27. White, L., Burger, K., Yearworth, M.: Big data and behavior in operational research: towards a "smart or". In: Behavioral Operational Research, pp. 177–193 (2016)

Structural Node Representation Learning for Detecting Botnet Nodes

Justin Carpenter[1], Janet Layne[1], Edoardo Serra[1], Alfredo Cuzzocrea[2(✉)], and Carmine Gallo[2]

[1] Computer Science Department, Boise State University, Boise, ID, USA
JustinCarpenter836@u.boisestate.edu, {janetlayne, edoardoserra}@boisestate.edu
[2] iDEA LAB, University of Calabria, Rende, Italy
alfredo.cuzzocrea@unical.it

Abstract. Private consumers, small businesses, and even large enterprises are all more at risk from *botnets*. These botnets are known for spearheading *Distributed Denial-Of-Service (DDoS) attacks*, *spamming* large populations of users, and causing critical harm to major organizations. The development of *Internet-of-Things (IoT)* devices led to the use of these devices for *cryptocurrency mining*, in transit data *interception*, and sending *logs* containing private data to the *master botnet*. Different techniques have been developed to identify these botnet activities, but only a few use *Graph Neural Networks (GNNs)* to analyze host activity by representing their communications with a *directed graph*. Although GNNs are intended to extract *structural graph properties*, they risk to cause *overfitting*, which leads to failure when attempting to do so from an unidentified network. In this study, we test the notion that *structural graph patterns* might be used for efficient botnet detection. In this study, we also present SIR-GN, a *structural iterative representation learning methodology for graph nodes*. Our approach is built to work well with untested data, and our model is able to provide a *vector representation* for every node that captures its structural information. Finally, we demonstrate that, when the collection of node representation vectors is incorporated into a *neural network classifier*, our model outperforms the state-of-the-art GNN based algorithms in the detection of bot nodes within unknown networks.

Keywords: Machine Learning · Botnet Detection

1 Introduction

In this paper, we present a method for detecting *botnets*. When developing this technique, we considered the key problems with detecting botnets, such as the rise in devices that are always connected to the network. Due to the constant active connection features of these devices, the exponential growth of IoT devices has increased the chances for cybercriminals to expand and grow these botnets. Wide-range cyberattacks have also become more common, which are challenging to perform without having a lot of devices being connected to the network. *Spam*, *DDoS* attacks, the transmission of *viruses* and

O. Gervasi et al. (Eds.): ICCSA 2023, LNCS 13956, pp. 731–743, 2023.
https://doi.org/10.1007/978-3-031-36805-9_47

malware, password and credential *theft*, and even *cryptocurrency mining* are some of the main cyberattacks that use botnets.

Many effective botnet detection techniques rely on the use of *GNN (Graph Neural Networks)* models to extract patterns that characterize the behavior of the botnet. Although GNNs are capable of acquiring structural information, they still have limitations in relation to the nodes' proximity, which, based on concepts of *similarity*, will allow them to interact with machines that, despite being thought of as reliable, are actually botnet-affiliated machines. As a result, we may assert that botnet identification using the GNN model may be poor if the model was trained on a different network than the network that would be evaluated. Therefore, in this work, we provide the learning technique of the *inferential SIR-GN* graphical representation in order to achieve superior outcomes. Even across very vast networks, it is possible to identify the nodes belonging to the botnet by combining this technique with a *neural network* classification model. Significant benefits of inferential SIR-GN include the preservation of a *graph's structural information*, which can be utilized to identify malicious software even in networks that are completely transparent. For networks when the topology of the training data and the test data is the same, the behavior of the Inferential SIR-GN is almost exactly like that of the GNN model during the *inference* phase. Additionally, it significantly improves when these data topologies are different. Since botnets are constantly developing, we can therefore say with certainty that the Inferential SIR-GN model is a more effective detection strategy than GNN models.

The remaining Sections of this work are structured as follows: Sect. 2 presents the earlier detection techniques, and Sect. 3 describes the datasets that were employed. The Inferential SIR-GN methodology is finally demonstrated in Sect. 4 before being evaluated in Sect. 5. Finally, we give our work's conclusions in Sect. 6.

2 Analysis of State-of-the-Art-Approaches

2.1 The Detection of Botnets

Cybercriminals must first persuade people to install *malware* on their systems in order to gain control over the majority of devices, and the majority of malware used for this purpose is freely available online. We use the *Mirai malware* as an illustration, which preys on Linux-based IoT systems including *routers*, *IP cameras*, and any *home automation* equipment. This botnet was utilized against organizations like *Krebs on Security*, the French *web hosting service OVH*, and even the *DNS provider Dyn*, which is a crucial service for regular internet communications, to cause widespread disruptions and produce internet traffic of up to 1 Tbit/s. The Mirai malware is regarded as the first of its kind, and even though its developers were found and turned over to the police, numerous additional varieties have since emerged, including the *PureMasuta*, *Okiru*, *Satori*, and *Masuta* malware. Figure 1 depicts the conceptual design of a Mirai-based bot that transforms IoT devices into *proxy servers*.

Both the complexity and attacks of botnets are constantly evolving. Fortunately, the methods for identifying botnets have evolved along with the evolution of the networks themselves. It is well known that botnets have the ability to function in a way that tries to *evade* detection. In this instance, a lot of *honeypots* are made to draw in botnets, especially

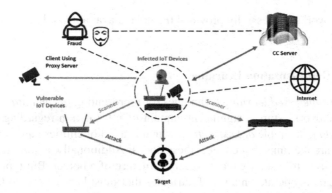

Fig. 1. A Mirai-based bot turning IoT devices into proxy servers

ones that are known to them and that they avoid, as they are able to *bypass* the controls and therefore avoid detection [1]. The *proliferation* of *P2P (Peer-To-Peer)* connections has made it challenging to detect botnets. The difference between a Client-Server mode and P2P mode connection is seen in Fig. 2.

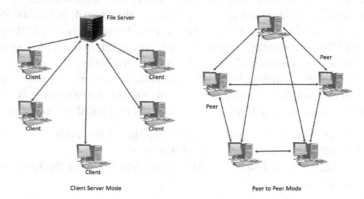

Fig. 2. Client-server and P2P mode connections

In the case of client-server botnets, if the *C&C control node* is located and isolated, the entire botnet can be found and subsequently stopped. Contrary to P2P-type botnets, which are capable of sharing *C&C commands* when discovered and have little knowledge of the other botnets [2], making detection even more difficult. In order to locate the central control node, *BotMiner* [3], for instance, uses *clusters* of nodes with similar communications and *malicious traffic*. Using *fast-flowing server networks*, P2P botnets can change the *addresses* of the C&C server node, enabling *traffic monitoring* between nodes to bypass them [4]. Because of this, the traditional approaches presented in [5] which mostly rely on static properties to characterize network traffic have been rendered worthless. These traditional methods, like *domain names* [6] and *DNS black-lists* [7], also call for a deeper understanding of the network and botnets. Therefore, this type of strategy only works successfully provided the data is available and hasn't been altered by the botnet.

2.2 Graph Representation Learning

The use of *unsupervised learning* techniques for representing *graph data* is growing in popularity. Networks store a significant amount of information regarding relationally *structured data* in a simple *data structure*, which is a list of entities named nodes. And, *edges* which are the links that connect these nodes. Additionally, a graphical representation can be used to instantly recognize the structure of a botnet. But typical *machine learning* programs operate on a set of attributes that must be represented by graphical data structures. The similarity between nodes must be fully extracted using this type of representation. However, the structural position of the node within the network as well as that of its neighbors can serve as the foundation for the concept of similarity. For instance, the highly connected nodes will be close to one another in the feature space when a file is acquired nearby a node. Additionally, it suffices that the structures of surrounding nodes are comparable in order to classify them as similar nodes that represent a node's structural role; and a *path* between them is not necessary.

Numerous representative learning techniques have been used with considerable success in a variety of academic subjects. For instance, the *DeepWalk* method [8], which employs *NLP (Neuro Linguistic Programming)* and is based on the *Word2Vec* algorithm [9, 10] for the *Skip-Gram* model, seeks to anticipate the words in the context starting from a core word in order to optimize all the nearby nodes. In addition, DeepWalk extends the Skip-Gram model by switching from word sequences to graphs. It uses a *randomized path traversal* mechanism to establish this transformation and to provide *insights* about localized network topologies. Here's how the DeepWalk procedure operates:

1. For each node, perform N *"random passes"* starting at that node.
2. Treat each walk as a sequence of node-id strings.
3. Train a Word2Vec model using the Skip-Gram algorithm on the string sequences obtained previously.

This manifests as a node representation learning approach with similar neighbor nodes that is based on *node sharing* and *connectivity*. Due to the necessity of traversing the graph, a major issue arises when the graph is partially connected because there are no links between the nodes. The *Node2vec* algorithm [12] uses random walks around a network beginning at a *target node*, and this methodology is comparable to that used by that algorithm. It removes the connectivity requirement and results in performance upgrades. Each of these techniques is effective at capturing connectivity data between nodes, but they fall short when it comes to maintaining crucial network architecture characteristics for bot machine detection. The most effective techniques for learning representations while maintaining structural information are Graph Neural Networks [13] such as *Graph Convolutional Neural Network, Struct2Vec* [14], *GraphWave* [15] and *Iterative Procedures*. Only the inferential SIR-GN iterative method and neural networks are able to perform inferences that offer predictions for graphs that are entirely different from those used for training. Our botnet detection method's primary goal is to learn the structural representation of inference-capable algorithms. However, other relevant efforts in the areas of *AI* and machine learning are mentioned in [18–30].

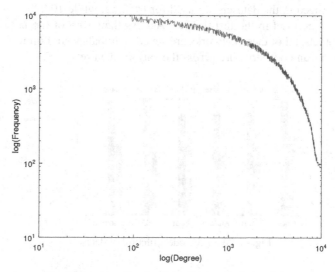

Fig. 3. Log-log distribution of the experimental data

3   Description of Datasets

We have so far discussed two different botnet models, the first of which can be quickly recognized via C&C due to its *centralized* botnet and *star pattern*. The second form, known as P2P, is *decentralized* and has nodes that connect the majority of network nodes in just one or two *hops*. P2P botnet clusters, as we previously noted, are more challenging to identify because there isn't a single core hub. The P2P model is used in the following experiments to show how representation learning applied to the graph can identify *anomalies* that are more difficult to identify when using other techniques. For our purposes, real background traffic data obtained in 2018 related to IPs on a *backbone* monitored by *CAIDA* [31] was employed. Since the monitored traffic is *aggregated*, it is impossible to identify the users who generated it. We chose this background traffic at random on a selection of nodes thought to be part of the botnet in order to take into account the various P2P botnet topologies. In these investigations, we built controlled networks using the P2P topologies De Bruijn [32], Kademlia [33], Chord [34], and Leetchord [35]. Additionally, in order to detect botnet attacks in communication flow, we also use a genuine P2P network [36]. The Log-Log graph, which depicts the degree of distribution within the graphs, is shown in Fig. 3.

As seen in Fig. 3, the *frequency* (number of nodes) decreases as the degree (number of edges) of the nodes increases. This pattern suggests that most nodes have degrees under two and that there aren't many nodes that are well related. Each network has 960 P2P graphs with an average of 144,000 nodes, over 1.5 million edges, and 10,000 botnet nodes within each synthetic graph. The average cluster size in the graphs is 0.007, and each network contains 960 P2P graphs. Based on the existing botnet network, which consists of 144k nodes and 3k botnet nodes, this figure was calculated. 10,000 botnet nodes were utilized in the datasets we used for training, while 10,000, 1,000, and 100 botnet nodes were used in the test dataset. As less than 10% of the network's nodes are part of botnets, all of these networks are severely imbalanced. Figure 4 displays the values for the mean node structure across the various data sets.

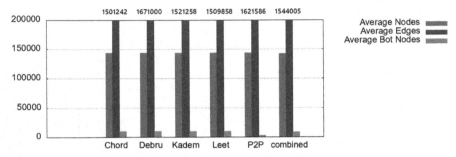

Fig. 4. Average node structure of datasets

4 The Proposed Methodology: Inferential SIR-GN

Our proposed approach is based on the inferential SIR-GN, which is an iterative structural representation learning process with inference capabilities. The symbols we utilize in our methodological explanation are shown in Table 1.

Table 1. Notations used in model description

Notation	Description
nc	The number of clusters chosen for node representation
ngc	The number of clusters chosen for graph representation
k	The depth of exploration, equal to a node's k-hop neighborhood

Layne and Serra provided a detailed description of the Inferential SIR-GN, which is used to extract node representations from directed graphs, in their work [17]. The model is built using the SIR-GN methodology, which was first presented in M. Joaristi and E. Serra [16]. Using this methodology, a node's representation is iteratively updated by first characterizing, then aggregating, its neighbors. Each iteration size of a node representation is determined by a user-selected *nc* hyperparameter. The actual node description, which first starts as the node degree, is clustered into a *nc K-Means* cluster to provide node descriptions. At each iteration, the representation is *normalized* before clustering, thus the distance from each cluster *centroid* is changed into a node probability of being a member of that cluster. The neighbors of a node are then aggregated in its structural description once it has been updated by adding the probability of all the nearby nodes that are part of each cluster for that cluster.

The number of neighbors held by each node in each cluster is represented by the same number of nodes as predicted. Each iteration represents a deeper level of study, and after k iterations, a node description will include information about its k-hop neighborhood structure. The inferential SIR-GN differs from the conventional model in some ways. The structural descriptions of each node are really concatenated into a broader representation, which captures the evolution of the structure and information through a more in-depth examination of the neighborhood. First, it is tied to each interaction. The final representation is compressed into a dimension selected as a hyperparameter in a *Principal Component Analysis (PCA)* to prevent information degradation as a result of the size growth.

For *directed graphs*, a node's initial representation consists of two vectors of dimension nc, one of which represents the node's internal degree and the other its exterior degree. Prior to clustering, these two vectors are concatenated. This vector is then clustered after each iteration, and the nearby nodes are then gathered together. For the next iteration, two intermediate vectors one for neighbors and one for non-neighbors are concatenated together to execute the aggregate in the case of direct data. By pre-training the K-Means algorithm and scaling at each iteration, our suggested model is able to make inferences. This procedure is performed along with the PCA model that will be used to create the final node embedding for each exploration depth where the training is established on saved and used to draw inference random graphs.

In order to make inferences, we repeatedly do normalization using pre-trained models, then clustering, then aggregation, utilizing PCA to create file representations of the end nodes during training. This approach enables the use of the same pre-trained model across several data sources while also decreasing the inference time which Layne and Serra [17] present in great depth and include a thorough algorithm that explains the *time complexity* of the model. Any *classifier* can use the structural representation vectors of SIR-GN nodes to understand the topology of botnets for automatic botnet discovery. A 3-layer neural network is also used in this work to make a final prediction about a node (machine) state as a bot.

5 Experimental Assessment and Analysis

5.1 Setup

We discussed the four basic botnet topologies used to create *synthetic datasets* in Sect. 2 of this article. Where 960 distinct graphs are produced for each topology by using that topology on actual traffic. The graphs size and number are scaled to match a real P2P dataset with 960 graphs of actual botnet attacks. For each set of graphs, representations of the structural nodes are produced using our inferential SIR-GN model. We trained Inferential SIR-GN using a collection of randomly generated graphs, as shown in the technique. Then, we calculated the nodes representation in a way that effectively allowed us to extract each node structural description. This technique produced outstanding results utilizing a relatively small fraction of these representations that had been trained using a classifier.

A neural network (NN) classifier that outperforms all previous models that have been trained similarly can be trained using inferential SIR-GN to train the upstream of any classifier and to transfer learning. Using the ABD-GN model, which is a GNN specifically designed for identifying botnets, we will elaborate on the contrast. We will use the following comparisons to demonstrate how inferential SIR-GN is useful for generalizing invisible data:

1. To begin, we contrast the inferential classifier SIR-GN plus a neural network that was trained on 50 graphs from a dataset (botnet topology) and used to classify 96 graphs from that dataset with the ABD-GN one, which was trained on 80% (768) of the dataset graphs and used to classify a test set of 20% (on the same 96 graphs) from the same topology.
2. Next, we contrast the ABD-GN classifier, which is trained on 768 graphs from a topology and used to classify the test set, with the Inferential SIR-GN plus classifier, which is trained on 50 graphs from a single topology and used to classify the test set of 96 graphs from each of the other topology datasets and real P2P attack data. We will refer to Inferential SIR-GN plus with neural network classifier as isirgn1 in the results report to keep things simple.

5.2 Results

Figure 5 compares the node representations created by Inferential SIR-GN and ABD-GN and displays the results of the NN classifier. We can see that, even though the model was trained to represent nodes using randomly generated graphs and specifically trained on 50 graphs from a dataset, isirgn1 performs very similarly to ABD-GN for all datasets, in contrast to the ABD-GN neural network model, which has been trained on 80% (768) of dataset graphs.

Figure 5 compares the node representations created by Inferential SIR-GN and ABD-GN and displays the results of the NN classifier. We can see that, even though the model was trained to represent nodes using randomly generated graphs and specifically trained on 50 graphs from a dataset, isirgn1 performs very similarly to ABD-GN for all datasets, in contrast to the ABD-GN neural network model, which has been trained on 80% (768) of dataset graphs.

Figure 5 illustrates the outstanding performance of the ABD-GN model for a single topology. The outcomes, however, range from excellent to very poor when these same trained models are tested against an invisible topology, as seen in Table 2. When evaluated on all other synthetic datasets, isirgn1 and ABD-GN perform equally when trained on the Kadem topology. Similar to training on Leet and Chord data, the F1-Score for ABD-GN falls below 10%, with no variance in performance on the other synthetic datasets. It's interesting to note that when Debru data is used to train each model, ABD-GN performs poorly in classification across all other topologies in addition to failing to accurately detect bots in the real-world dataset, whereas isirgn1 works well in this situation.

On test data produced from the same dataset, isirgn1 and ABD-GN behave similarly when trained on real-world datasets. But in the four stealth topologies, isirgn1 also performs well in classification tests whereas ABD-GN significantly underperforms. These

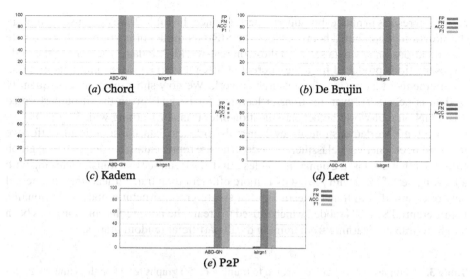

Fig. 5. Botnet detection results

Table 2. F1-Scores of the models trained on one topology and tested on another compared between Inferential SIR-GN (isirgn1) and the base GNN from [37] (ABD-GN)

Trained on Chord						Trained on Debru				
	Chord	*Kadem*	*Debru*	*Leet*	*P2P*	*Chord*	*Kadem*	*Debru*	*Leet*	*P2P*
ABD-GN	99	97.5	99.6	99.4	0	10	2.5	100	0	2.5
isirgn1	99.4	93	100	99	97	93	94	99.5	92.5	97
Trained on Kadem						**Trained on Leet**				
	Chord	*Kadem*	*Debru*	*Leet*	*P2P*	*Chord*	*Kadem*	*Debru*	*Leet*	*P2P*
ABD-GN	97	98	99.5	99	2.5	73	95	100	100	2
isirgn1	99	99	99	99	97.5	99	99.2	94.5	100	98
Trained on P2P										
	Chord		*Kadem*	*Debru*		*Leet*		*P2P*		
ABD-GN	15		22.5	16		17.5		99.5		
isirgn1	93		93	93		93		97.5		

results demonstrate that despite being trained on a much smaller data set, node representations through Inferential SIR-GN, combined with a neural network classifier, outperform even the particular botnet detection approach on stealth data. The results also show that the ABD-GN model can only recognize bots in real-world data when it is given prior information of the structure of a particular botnet.

Then, node representations for a coupled topology were created using inferential SIR-GN. Furthermore, it is clear that utilizing these representations to train a *Random Forest* algorithm results in noticeably superior performance. In Table 2, we demonstrate how, in the situation of combined botnet attacks, the SIR-GN model offers remarkably accurate classifications on any data set, even those on real-world P2P data. Then, using the node representations produced from the inferential SIR-GN model, we examine the training requirements of a classifier for a neural network. We now show that a modest quantity of data is necessary, even for transfer learning for isirgn1, given that it outperformed ABD-GN on real-world botnet classification after transfer learning with 50 graphs.

In Table 3, we demonstrate that even on real-world test data, it is significantly effective to train a neural network classifier for node structure representation using only one graph from a synthetic dataset. Comparing Tables 2 and 3, we can see that transfer learning with a training set of 80% with ABD-GN is more efficient than transfer learning on a neural network trained with transfer learning on a single graph structural node. Additionally, the Inferential SIR-GN model, which is used to create the node representations, has been taught to transfer learning from training data to artificial random graphs.

Table 3. Training on one graph compared to training on 50 graphs tested on the same 96 graphs

Trained on Chord			Trained on Debru		
	1 Graph	*50 Graphs*		*1 Graph*	*50 Graphs*
Chord	99.5	99.5		92.5	92.5
Debru	99.9	100		99.8	99.8
Kadem	94	96		94	93
Leet	92.5	99		92.25	92.25
P2P	98	98		97	97
Trained on Kadem			**Trained on Leet**		
	1 Graph	*50 Graphs*		*1 Graph*	*50 Graphs*
Chord	99	99		99	99
Debru	98.5	99		93	95
Kadem	99.25	99		99	99.25
Leet	99.25	99		99.5	100
P2P	98	97		98	98
Trained on P2P					
	1 Graph		*50 Graphs*		
Chord	93		93		
Debru	93		93		
Kadem	93		93		
Leet	93		93		
P2P	98		98		

6 Conclusions and Future Work

We can draw the conclusion that Inferential SIR-GN can produce vectors to represent the structural data of every node in a network. Additionally, a machine learning technique for botnet identification can be used with the graphical depiction of the nodes. The *inclusion* of a neural network classifier with Inferential SIR-GN enables the identification of botnets, regardless of the topology used for training, which is a noteworthy advantage over models based on prior knowledge of the graph topology. We have also seen how quickly a botnet structure can alter, mostly as a result of the significant rise in P2P connections. The variety of botnet topologies has increased as a result of this circumstance. This means that, in contrast to methods that leverage GNNs, the usage of Inferential SIR-GN in tandem with a neural network classifier will result in a very high botnet detection ability. Due to the difficulty of adaptability, GNN techniques may not be able to identify previously unknown botnet topologies. Another line of research to be followed consists in coupling our framework with emerging *big data trends* (e.g., [38–44]).

Acknowledgement. This work was partially supported by project SERICS (PE00000014) under the MUR National Recovery and Resilience Plan funded by the European Union - NextGenerationEU.

References

1. Zou, C.C., Cunningham, R.: Honeypot-aware advanced botnet construction and maintenance. In: International Conference on Dependable Systems and Networks, pp. 199–208. IEEE (2006)
2. Yan, G., Ha, D.T., Eidenbenz, S.: AntBot: Anti-pollution peer-to-peer botnets. Comput. Netw. **55**(8), 1941–1956 (2011)
3. Gu, G., Perdisci, R., Zhang, J., Lee, W.: Botminer: Clustering Analysis of Network Traffic for Protocol-And Structure-Independent Botnet Detection (2008)
4. Holz, T., Gorecki, C., Freiling, F., Rieck, K.: Detection and mitigation of fast-flux service networks. In: 15th Annual Network and Distributed System Security Symposium (2008)
5. Bartos, K., Sofka, M., Franc, V.: Optimized Invariant Representation of Network Traffic for Detecting Unseen Malware Variants. In: 25th {USENIX} Security Symposium, pp. 807–822 (2016)
6. Perdisci, R., Lee, W.: Method and System for Detecting Malicious and/or Botnet-Related Domain Names. Patent 10,027,688 (2018)
7. Andriesse, D., Rossow, C., Bos, H.: Reliable recon in adversarial peer-to-peer botnets. In: 2015 Internet Measurement Conference, pp. 129–140 (2015)
8. Perozzi, B., Al-Rfou, R., Skiena, S.: Deepwalk: Online learning of social representations. In: 20th ACM SIGKDD International Conference on Knowledge Discovery and Data Mining, pp. 701–710 (2014)
9. Mikolov, T., Chen, K., Corrado, G., Dean, J.: Efficient estimation of word representations in vector space. arXiv preprint arXiv:1301.3781 (2013)
10. Mikolov, T., Sutskever, I., Chen, K., Corrado, G.S., Dean, J.: Distributed representations of words and phrases and their compositionality. In: Advances in Neural Information Processing Systems, pp. 3111–3119 (2013)

11. Tang, J., Qu, M., Wang, M., Zhang, M., Yan, J., Mei, Q.: Line: Large-scale information network embedding. In: 24th International Conference on World Wide Web, pp. 1067–1077 (2015)
12. Grover, A., Leskovec, J.: Node2vec: Scalable Feature Learning for Networks. In: 22nd ACM SIGKDD International Conference on Knowledge Discovery and Data Mining, pp. 855–864 (2016)
13. Scarselli, F., Gori, M., Tsoi, A.C., Hagenbuchner, M., Monfardini, G.: The graph neural network model. IEEE Trans. Neural Netw. **20**(1), 61–80 (2008)
14. Ribeiro, L.F., Saverese, P.H., Figueiredo, D.R.: Struc2vec: Learning node representations from structural identity. In: 23rd ACM SIGKDD International Conference on Knowledge Discovery and Data Mining, pp. 385–394 (2017)
15. Donnat, C., Zitnik, M., Hallac, D., Leskovec, J.: Learning structural node embeddings via diffusion wavelets. In: 24th ACM SIGKDD International Conference on Knowledge Discovery & Data Mining, pp. 1320–1329 (2018)
16. Joaristi, M., Serra, E.: SIR-GN: A fast structural iterative representation learning approach for graph nodes. ACM Trans. Knowl. Discov. Data **15**(6), 1–39 (2021)
17. Layne, J., Serra, E.: INFSIR-GN: Inferential Labeled Node and Graph Representation Learning. arXiv preprint arXiv:1918.10503 (2021)
18. Ceci, M., Cuzzocrea, A., Malerba, D.: Supporting roll-up and drill-down operations over OLAP data cubes with continuous dimensions via density-based hierarchical clustering. In: SEBD. Citeseer, pp. 57–65 (2011)
19. Serra, E., Joaristi, M., Cuzzocrea, A.:, Large-scale sparse structural node representation. In: 2020 IEEE International Conference on Big Data (Big Data), pp. 5247–5253. IEEE (2020)
20. Braun, P., Cuzzocrea, A., Keding, T.D., Leung, C.K., Padzor, A.G., Sayson, D.: Game data mining: clustering and visualization of online game data in cyber-physical worlds. Procedia Comput. Sci. **112**, 2259–2268 (2017)
21. Guzzo, A., Sacca, D., Serra, E.: An effective approach to inverse frequent set mining. In: 2009 9th IEEE International Conference on Data Mining, pp. 806–811. IEEE (2009)
22. Morris, K.J., Egan, S.D., Linsangan, J.L., Leung, C.K., Cuzzocrea, A., Hoi, C.S.: Token-based adaptive time-series prediction by ensembling linear and non-linear estimators: A machine learning approach for predictive analytics on big stock data". In: 2018 17th IEEE International Conference on Machine Learning and Applications, pp. 1486–1491. IEEE (2018)
23. Serra, E., Subrahmanian, V.: A survey of quantitative models of terror group behavior and an analysis of strategic disclosure of behavioral models. IEEE Trans. Comput. Soc. Syst. **1**(1), 66–88 (2014)
24. Bellatreche, L., Cuzzocrea, A., Benkrid, S.: F&A: A methodology for effectively and efficiently designing parallel relational data warehouses on heterogenous database clusters. In: Bach Pedersen, T., Mohania, M.K., Tjoa, A.M. (eds.) DaWaK 2010. LNCS, vol. 6263, pp. 89–104. Springer, Heidelberg (2010). https://doi.org/10.1007/978-3-642-15105-7_8
25. Korzh, O., Joaristi, M., Serra, E.: Convolutional neural network ensemble fine-tuning for extended transfer learning. In: Chin, F.Y.L., Chen, C.L.P., Khan, L., Lee, K., Zhang, L.-J. (eds.) BIGDATA 2018. LNCS, vol. 10968, pp. 110–123. Springer, Cham (2018). https://doi.org/10.1007/978-3-319-94301-5_9
26. Ahn, S., et al.: A fuzzy logic based machine learning tool for supporting big data business analytics in complex artificial intelligence environments. In: 2019 IEEE International Conference on Fuzzy Systems, pp. 1–6. IEEE (2019)
27. Serra, E., Sharma, A., Joaristi, M., Korzh, O.: Unknown landscape identification with CNN transfer learning. In: 2018 IEEE/ACM International Conference on Advances in Social Networks Analysis and Mining, pp. 813–820. IEEE (2018)

28. Serra, E., Shrestha, A., Spezzano, F., Squicciarini, A.: Deeptrust: An automatic framework to detect trustworthy users in opinion-based systems. In: 10th ACM Conference on Data and Application Security and Privacy, pp. 29–38 (2020)

29. Joaristi, M., Serra, E., Spezzano, F.: Inferring bad entities through the panama papers network. In: 2018 IEEE/ACM International Conference on Advances in Social Networks Analysis and Mining, pp. 767–773. IEEE (2018)

30. Joaristi, M., Serra, E., Spezzano, F.: Detecting suspicious entities in offshore leaks networks. Soc. Netw. Anal. Min. **9**(1), 1–15 (2019)

31. CAIDA. The CAIDA UCSD Anonymized Internet Traces-2018. (2018). Accessed 16 Sept. 2017. https://www.caida.org/data/passive/passivedataset.xml

32. Kaashoek, M.F., Karger, D.R.: Koorde: A simple degree-optimal distributed hash table. In: Kaashoek, M.F., Stoica, I. (eds.) IPTPS 2003. LNCS, vol. 2735, pp. 98–107. Springer, Heidelberg (2003). https://doi.org/10.1007/978-3-540-45172-3_9

33. Maymounkov, P., Mazières, D.: Kademlia: A peer-to-peer information system based on the XOR metric. In: Druschel, P., Kaashoek, F., Rowstron, A. (eds.) IPTPS 2002. LNCS, vol. 2429, pp. 53–65. Springer, Heidelberg (2002). https://doi.org/10.1007/3-540-45748-8_5

34. Stoica, I., Morris, R., Karger, D., Kaashoek, M.F., Balakrishnan, H., Chord, A.: A scalable peer-to-peer lookup service for internet applications. Lab. Comput. Sci., Massachusetts Inst. Technol., Tech. Rep. TR-819 (2001)

35. Jelasity, M., Bilicki, V., et al.: Towards automated detection of peer-to-peer botnets: On the limits of local approaches. LEET **9**, 3 (2009)

36. Garcia, S., Grill, M., Stiborek, J., Zunino, A.: An empirical comparison of botnet detection methods. Comput. Secur. **45**, 100–123 (2014)

37. Zhou, J., Xu, Z., Rush, A.M., Yu, M.: Automating botnet detection with graph neural networks. arXiv preprint arXiv:2003.06344 (2020)

38. Coronato, A., Cuzzocrea, A.: An innovative risk assessment methodology for medical information systems. IEEE Trans. Knowl. Data Eng. **34**(7), 3095–3110 (2020)

39. Leung, C.K., Cuzzocrea, A., Mai, J.J., Deng, D., Jiang, F.: Personalized deepinf: Enhanced social influence prediction with deep learning and transfer learning. In: 2019 IEEE International Conference on Big Data, pp. 2871–2880. IEEE (2019)

40. Leung, C.K., Braun, P., Hoi, C.S.H., Souza, J., Cuzzocrea, A.: Urban analytics of big transportation data for supporting smart cities. In: Ordonez, C., Song, I.-Y., Anderst-Kotsis, G., Tjoa, A.M., Khalil, I. (eds.) DaWaK 2019. LNCS, vol. 11708, pp. 24–33. Springer, Cham (2019). https://doi.org/10.1007/978-3-030-27520-4_3

41. Leung, C.K., Chen, Y., Hoi, C.S., Shang, S., Wen, Y., Cuzzocrea, A.: Big data visualization and visual analytics of COVID-19 data. In: 24th International Conference Information Visualisation, pp. 415–420. IEEE (2020)

42. Leung, C.K., Chen, Y., Hoi, C.S., Shang, S., Cuzzocrea, A.: Machine learning and OLAP on big COVID-19 data. In: 2020 IEEE International Conference on Big Data, pp. 5118–5127. IEEE (2020)

43. Barkwell, K.E., et al.: Big data visualisation and visual analytics for music data mining. In: 22nd International Conference on Information Visualisation, pp. 235–240. IEEE (2018)

44. Camara, R.C., et al.: Fuzzy logic-based data analytics on predicting the effect of hurricanes on the stock market. In: International Conference on Fuzzy Systems, pp. 1–8. IEEE (2018)

A Preliminary Result of Implementing a Deep Learning-Based Earthquake Early Warning System in Italy

Abiodun Adebowale[1][✉], Federica Di Michele[2,3], and Bruno Rubino[1]

[1] Department of Information Engineering, Computer Science and Mathematics, University of L'Aquila via Vetoio, loc. Coppito, I, L'Aquila, Italy
`abiodunsaheed.adebowale@student.univaq.it, bruno.rubino@univaq.it`
[2] INGV, via Alfonso Corti 12, Milan, Italy
`federica.dimichele@ingv.it`
[3] GSSI, via M. Iacobucci 2, L'Aquila, Italy
`federica.dimichele@gssi.it`

Abstract. In this paper we present the preliminary results of a study using a deep-learning tool named LSTM (Long Short-Term Memory) network, to classify seismic events as near-source and far-source, with the final purpose of developing efficient earthquake early warning systems. We use a similar approach as in [15], applied to a database, named Instance, containing information about 54,008 earthquakes that occurred in Italy. Although these are preliminary results, the method shows a good ability to detect far-source events with an accuracy of about 67%. For near-source events, the method shows an improvable result with an accuracy of 57%.

Keywords: Earthquake Early Warning system (EEWs) · Long Short-Term Memory (LSTM) · Seismic Events

1 Introduction

It is well known that earthquakes hit without warning, often causing victims and extensive damage to buildings and infrastructures. They cannot be predicted, however, once an earthquake occurs and is detected it is possible to provide some advance notice of ground shaking, from a few seconds to a few minutes depending on the size of the earthquake and the location of the site. This idea has led to the development of *Earthquake Early Warning systems (EEWs)*. Many countries including Mexico, Japan, Turkey, Romania, China, Italy, and Taiwan have all implemented EEWs to identify earthquakes quickly and monitor their development to provide timely alerts in advance.

In the 1990s, the first automated earthquake pre-detection systems were constructed in Calistoga, California. The system automatically activates a citywide siren to inform everyone in the region of an earthquake [20], In 2006, Japan

O. Gervasi et al. (Eds.): ICCSA 2023, LNCS 13956, pp. 744–756, 2023.
https://doi.org/10.1007/978-3-031-36805-9_49

began using its EEWs in real-world situations. In order to alert the public, a warning system was put in place on October 1, 2007. The Urgent Earthquake Detection and Alarm System (UrEDAS) is meant to allow automated braking of bullet trains in case of a dangerous earthquake event [2,3,14]. The ShakeAlert early warning system was built and activated in Vancouver, British Columbia, Canada in 2009. The George Massey Tunnel, which runs under the Fraser River, is a vital piece of transportation infrastructure, and its protection was a top priority. The mechanism is programmed to shut the tunnel entry gates automatically in the case of an impending hazardous seismic event [25]. In 2018, the *ShakeAlertLA* app became the first EEWs to be made accessible to the general public to alert the public of shaking in the Los Angeles area, and in 2019, the state of California implemented a statewide alert distribution system using mobile applications and the Wireless Emergency Alerts (WEA) system, [9,17,23]. ShakeAlert system works as follows: both P (or compressional) and S (or shear) waves are generated during a seismic event. The quickest p-wave triggers sensors in the terrain, sending data to a ShakeAlert processing center to detect the earthquake's location, magnitude, and shaking. USGS issues an alert if the earthquake meets the hazard requirements. ShakeAlert partners may utilize the message to inform individuals to "Drop", "Cover", and "Hold On" or initiate an automated action [12]. Depending on the local faults and the available ground motion data, several EEWs may be necessary to quickly detect a seismic wave [12].

Many interesting results are available in the literature concerning the mathematical tool used for EEWs. Yamada et al. [24] outlined a process for determining whether seismic data are near or far from the point of origin using Fisher's linear discriminant analysis and two Bayesian model class selections to find the best combination of the peak ground-motion parameters. They reported that at 20 seconds, the probability of being in the near-source at 13 stations is computed to be greater than 50%. Kuyuk et al. [16] studied a Japan earthquake 7.3 Mw using a continuous wavelet transform approach to estimate the nearest and farthest stations to the epicenter.

More recently, artificial intelligence techniques such as deep learning have been utilized. The potential use of deep learning algorithms in seismology has been explored for purpose of classification, estimation, and interpretation of many geophysical phenomena such as volcanic eruptions and earthquakes. Several prior studies in seismology utilized Artificial Neural Network (ANN) for capturing pertinent features of seismic data. For example, Bose et al. [6] developed an ANN-based approach to EEWs for finite faults. They developed a shallow neural network model with two layers to estimate the hypocenter location, magnitude, and the progress of the expansion of an ongoing earthquake.

Anggraini et al. [4] developed a deep learning method for classifying p-wave and noise data and using them to estimate earthquake locations for EEWs in Indonesia. Only earthquakes in a cluster near to the station's hypocenter are considered for feature selection in the waveform, thus resulting in a high rate of false alarms. Apraini et al. [5] used Random Forest, a deep-learning method to estimate and classify the magnitude of earthquakes for EEWs. In order to achieve a high level of performance in the specified earthquake parameters, Saad et al. [18] suggested a technique based on a convolutional neural network (CNN) that can extract meaningful characteristics from waveforms. The proposed method achieves classification accuracies of 93.67%, 89.55%, 92.54%, and 89.50%, respectively, for magnitude, origin time, depth, and location.

The aim of this paper is to provide a mechanism for separating near-source and far-source earthquakes in the shortest possible time from the arrival of the p-wave, following the idea first developed by [15]. A database specifically designed for Italy, named Instance [19], is used to test the tools.

With respect to [15] we improved the latency and minimized the computational resources by choosing the right activation functions which reduce the time spent training the model. In more detail, [15] used Softmax activation function which required more epochs (1400) to train, which in turn increases the time required to train the model. In this work, we used Sigmoid activation function since we are dealing with a binary classification problem, hence only 360 epochs are required to fully train the model, which is significantly faster.

2   Materials and Methods

When trying to figure out how to design an intelligent system, it proves relevant to study the structure of the brain and use it as a model to follow. This is the inspiration behind the creation of an ANN, a subset of machine learning which then found a major development in deep-learning algorithms.

The functional unit of the human brain is the neuron. The biological neuron cell has a nucleus and many dendrites and one long axon. The axon's length may range from a few times to tens of thousands of times longer than the cell body. Near its terminus, the axon divides into several branches known as *telodendria*, and at the tips of these branches are minute structures known as synaptic terminals (nerve endings), which are linked to the dendrites or cell bodies of neighboring neurons. In a similar way, an artificial neuron receives information in the form of an input vector, then there is a nucleus with elaborated signals and an output layer. Roughly speaking, an ANN is composed of many neurons connected together. In particular, a neural network contains three kinds of layers, an input layer, one (or more) hidden layers, and an output layer.

To analyze a time series, as in our case, a particular type of Artificial Neural Network called Recurrent Neural Networks (RNNs), can be employed. RNNs use sequential or time-series data as input. They are built to have the ability to recall knowledge from the past and apply it to new situations. They are differentiated by their *memory* since they are built to have the ability to recall knowledge from the past and apply it to new situations. In other words, instead of being independent of the inputs and outputs, RNNs are reliant on the previous parts in the sequence. Depending on the structure of our input and output data, we can categorize sequence modeling as [22]:

- **Many-to-one**: The output is a fixed-size vector, not a sequence, and the incoming data is a sequence. For instance, the classification of seismic wave characteristics, where the inputs are a sequence of ground motion data and the output is a classification label.
- **One-to-many**: The output is a sequence, and the incoming data is in a standard format.
- **Many-to-many**: Both input and output data are streams of sequences. An example is language translation, where a data stream from one language is the input sequence, and a data stream, translated into another language, is the output sequence.

To overcome the limit of vanishing gradient and effectively learn long-term dependencies in sequential data, a new algorithm named Long Short-Term Memory (LSTM) has been introduced in [13].

LSTM is a type of neural network that uses a series of memory cells (also called "blocks") to store information over time. Each cell contains a hidden state vector, h_t, and a memory cell vector, c_t, which are updated at each time step t based on the input, x_t, and the previous state, h_{t-1} and c_{t-1}. The update equations for the memory cell and hidden state vectors are defined in Algorithm 1. where Sigmoid is the sigmoid activation function, tanh is the hyperbolic tangent activation function, $\mathbf{W}$ are weight matrices, and $\mathbf{b}$ are bias vectors. The gates in the above equations (f_t, i_t, and o_t) allow the network to selectively control the flow of information through the memory cells, enabling it to forget old information, store new information, and output relevant information. This makes LSTM particularly useful for tasks that involve long-term dependencies and sequential data. Although the LSTM cell appears just like a conventional cell, it has two separate states: h and c (the letter c stands for "cell"). Short-term and long-term states may be thought of as separate entities representing h and c respectively [10]. A brief representation of the algorithm used is given below.

2.1 Algorithm Behind LSTM

Algorithm 1: The LSTM Algorithm

Input: n, the length of the sequence
for $i = 1$ **to** n **do**
    if $i == 0$ **then**
        $\mathbf{h}^{(t-1)} \leftarrow$ small random number
        $\mathbf{C}^{(t-1)} \leftarrow$ small random number
    else
        $\mathbf{h}^{(t-1)} \leftarrow \mathbf{h}^{(t)}$
        $\mathbf{C}^{(t-1)} \leftarrow \mathbf{C}^{(t)}$
    end
    $SigmoidControllers \leftarrow (\mathbf{f}, \mathbf{i}, \mathbf{o})$
    for $\sigma;$ **in** $SigmoidControllers$ **do**
        $\sigma_t \leftarrow \text{sigmoid}\left(\mathbf{W}_{x\sigma}\mathbf{x}^{(t)} + \mathbf{W}_{h\sigma}\mathbf{h}^{(t-1)} + \mathbf{b}_\sigma\right)$
    end
    $\mathbf{g}_t \leftarrow \tanh\left(\mathbf{W}_{xg}\mathbf{x}^{(t)} + \mathbf{W}_{hg}\mathbf{h}^{(t-1)} + \mathbf{b}_g\right)$
    $\mathbf{C}^{(t)} \leftarrow \left(\mathbf{C}^{(t-1)} \odot \mathbf{f}_t\right) \oplus (\mathbf{i}_t \odot \mathbf{g}_t)$
    $\mathbf{h}^{(t)} \leftarrow \mathbf{o}_t \oplus \tanh\left(\mathbf{C}^{(t)}\right)$
end

In preparing the data and building the deep learning model, the following Python packages were used:

- **ObsPy**: The ObsPy project is an open-source initiative that aims to provide a Python framework for the analysis of seismological data. It offers parsers for the most popular file formats, clients that can connect to data centres, and seismological signal processing algorithms that enable the manipulation of seismological time series. [21]
- **Keras**: Keras is a high-level Deep Learning API that makes it easy to train and execute neural networks. It may be built on top of TensorFlow, Theano, or Microsoft Cognitive Toolkit (previously known as CNTK). TensorFlow has its own version of this API, named **tf.keras**, which supports several advanced TensorFlow features (e.g., the ability to efficiently load data). [10]
- **Tensorflow**: TensorFlow is an advanced library for distributed numerical computing. It makes it feasible to train and operate extremely large neural networks effectively by dividing the computations among possibly hundreds of multi-GPU machines. TensorFlow (TF) was developed at Google and is used in many of the company's large-scale Machine Learning projects. Open source was released in November 2015.

3   Results and Discussion

As mentioned in the introduction, the aim of this work is to adapt the ANN-based approach proposed by [15] in order to apply it to Italy. Most of the data we use comes from the databases of the Istituto Nazionale di Geofisica e Vulcanologia (INGV) and in particular from the database *INSTANCE - The Italian seismic dataset for machine learning*. The recorded waveforms span both weak (HH, EH channels) and strong motion (HN channels), each waveform trace is recorded at 100 Hz, and presented in both counts and ground motion physical units, with the vast majority of the data coming from the Italian National Seismic Network (network code IV) (Fig. 1).[1]

The dataset collected from Italy consisted of $1,159,249$ three-component waveforms representing weak and strong motion data in the north-south, east-west, and up-down directions. Subsequently, the dataset was reduced to $10,863$ three-component waveforms of strong motion data and $6,040$ three-component waveforms after balancing across each magnitude from 3 to 7. Figure 2a illustrates the geographical locations and depths of all seismic events in the database, while Fig. 2b displays the positions of recording stations. Similarly, Figs. 3a and 3b depict the earthquake hypocenters and recording station positions after applying a filter to include only earthquakes within a 50 km epicentral distance in the Italian dataset.

We have processed and filtered this data in a similar fashion as in [15]. We divided the data from the seismographs for near-source and far-source earthquakes by defining a near-source earthquake as an earthquake with a distance

---

[1] http://doi.org/10.13127/instance.

from the epicenter below 17 km. Far-source earthquakes are defined by a distance above 17 km and below 50 km from the epicenter. Both classes are of a minimum magnitude of 3 on the Richter scale. This is an arbitrary choice and other approaches are possible and will be described and analyzed in the future.

Furthermore, the dataset is then balanced across all magnitudes using the SMOTE method [7] (Table 1).

Table 1. Table showing the difference between near- and far-source stations defined by epicentral and hypocentral distances.

Near Source vs Far Source		
Strong-motion Stations (HN)	Epicentral distances (km)	Hypocentral distances (km)
7495191.IV.T1244..HN	15.39	18.086
1736871.IV.STAL..HN	10.85	15.099
10655971.IV.FEMA..HN	5.44	9.674
12697681.IV.T1218..HN	19.317	20.986
4326711.IV.CDCA..HN	41.752	43.789
22823821.ST.RONC..HN	41.756	43.105

Fig. 1. Sample earthquake waveforms from INSTANCE broadband HN channels, selected at random. Three-component traces are inserted into each row at random so that the first row contains near-source events, while the second row contains far-source events. The arrival time of primary and secondary waves are shown with blue and orange marks respectively. (Color figure online)

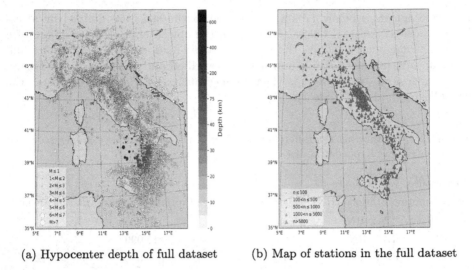

(a) Hypocenter depth of full dataset   (b) Map of stations in the full dataset

Fig. 2. Earthquakes in the dataset are shown on a color-coded map as solid circles of varying depths and the geographical locations of the stations that contributed to all the events.

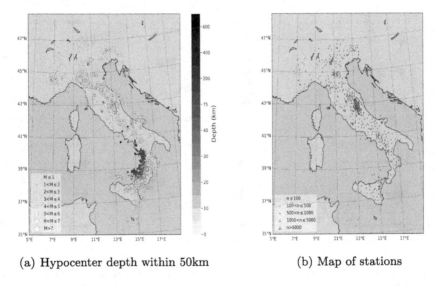

(a) Hypocenter depth within 50km   (b) Map of stations

Fig. 3. Earthquakes in the dataset are shown on a color-coded map as solid circles of varying depths and the geographical locations of the stations that contributed to the filtered events.

Similarly to [15], we selected six fundamental features of any seismological data, namely the time series data extracted from one second of p-wave (which is the three components accelerations (NS, EW, UD)) and the filtered acceleration for each of the components. Since the ground motion from near- and far-sources tends to have different amplitudes, we combined their absolute and cumulative sums. The frequency range of high-frequency vibrations is most prominent at close proximity to the source. The amplitude of high-frequency ground motion decreases more quickly with distance than low-frequency vibration. Since high-frequency vibrations have a stronger correlation with epicentral distance, they may serve as a useful metric for separating stations with close and remote sources [11,24].

Adding the absolute and cumulative sums increased our features from 6 to 12. We also added the geometric mean of the waveforms as in [15], which makes our features a total of 13, with each feature having 100 data points 100 Hz frequency of one second of p-wave data. Therefore, the input matrix for each station is 13 by 100. Figures 4 and 5 show the time series plot of one second of p-wave data of the features and the normalized values respectively. The effects of ground vibrations diminish with increasing distance, as shown in Fig. 4. Indeed the near-source amplitude in blue is much higher than the far-source in red, this is a powerful characteristic of the p-waves that can be used by the LSTM model to detect near and far coming waves.

Looking solely at the overall form of the time series in Fig. 5, it is difficult to tell the different series apart. An earthquake's effects are most pronounced near the epicenter, for instance the near-source motion is stronger around the epicenter and weakens with increasing distance compared to the far-source motion. The final dataset comprises of 6040 three components waveforms of strong motion data and balanced sets across each magnitude from 3 to 7, with each event containing 13 features namely: strong-motion acceleration, filtered acceleration, absolute acceleration, and cumulative absolute acceleration of the three strong-motion components (**NS, EW, UD**), including the geometric mean. Each of the 13 features contains 100 time-series data points. This makes our input shape $6040 \times 13 \times 100$ normalized acceleration data points. Amongst them, 4976 are used to train the model and 1244 to test it.

The first layer of our model is the Sequential model. For neural networks with a single stack of layers linked sequentially, this is the most basic *Keras* model. A Sequential Application Programming Interface is being used here. Next, we added an LSTM layer, consisting of 100 neurons. A dropout layer of 0.2 and finally, since this is a classification problem, we used a Dense output layer consisting of a single neuron activated by a sigmoid activation function to forecast zero or one for each of the problem's two classes (near-source and far-source).

A log loss (binary cross-entropy in *Keras*) is utilized as the loss function since this is a binary classification task. We used the powerful ADAM optimization method. Due to rapid overfitting, the model is only fit for 400 epochs. In order to spread out the training data evenly, we employed a large batch size of 32. Different parameters were used in the hyperparameter tuning, such as using *EarlyStopping* callback to prevent training resource wastage, different activation functions, and varying learning rate, which had little effect on the final output. As a result, we reached the limit of what can be achieved in terms of precision. This demonstrates that we have hit the limits of possible optimization. Our result is similar

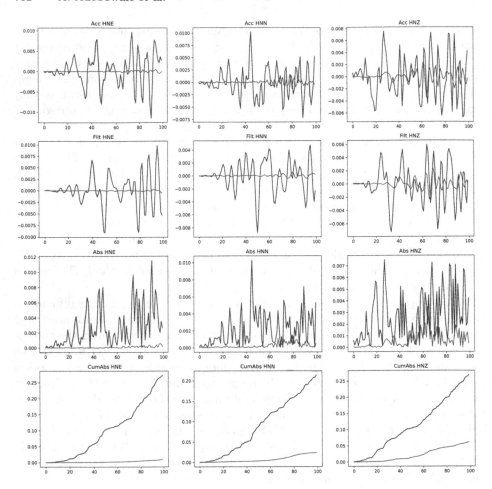

Fig. 4. Features Plot of One Second of p-wave data. The near-source amplitude in blue is much higher than the far-source in red. Evidence from the figures indicates that p-wave is amplitude dependent (Color figure online)

to what was achieved in [15] with a similar dataset but different neural networks tools. There are recordings from 2488 near- and 2488 far-source events included in the training set. Out of 2488 near-source records, 152 do not have the near-source label. The model firstly trained on the training set, reaches an accuracy of 94%. However, 3 events of the far-source data are incorrectly categorized. A total of 97% rate of accuracy is achieved. Only 155 of the 4976 events have the wrong label. Less satisfactory but still acceptable and in line with the available literature are the results achieved by applying the trained model to the test dataset. In more detail, the method has a good ability to detect far-source events with an accuracy of about 67% for the training dataset. Worse is the performance for near-source with an accuracy of 57% (Tables 2 and 3).

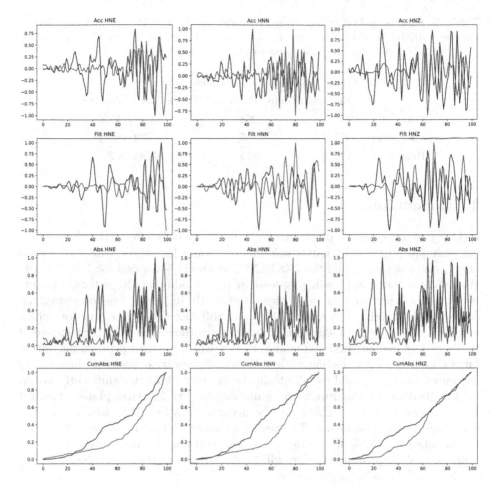

Fig. 5. Normalised Features Plot of One Second of p-wave data

Table 2. Confusion Matrix reporting the result of the LSTM algorithm applied to the training dataset. Accuracy is very good, especially for far-source events where it reaches 99%.

Training Performance of LSTM model on Italian dataset				
	Predicted Right	Predicted Wrong	Total	Accuracy
Near Source	2336	152	2488	94%
Far Source	2485	3	2488	99%
Total Events	4821	155	4976	97%

Table 3. Confusion Matrix reporting the result of the LSTM algorithm applied to the test dataset. Accuracy quite good, especially for far-source events where it reaches 67%, but less satisfactory for near-source events (accuracy 57%)

Test Performance of LSTM model on Italian dataset				
	Predicted Right	Predicted Wrong	Total	Accuracy
Near Source	354	268	622	57%
Far Source	417	205	622	67%
Total Events	771	473	1244	62%

4   Conclusions

In this paper we report preliminary results of a study employing deep learning techniques to classify earthquakes as near- and far-source, only one second after p-wave arrival, using the INSTANCE dataset, developed for Italy in [19]. We used the same approach proposed in [15], modifying the activation function from Softmax to Sigmoid, which significantly improved the computational resources on training the model. [15] used Softmax activation function which required more epochs (1400) to train with Tensorflow, which in turn increased the time required to train the model. In this work, we used sigmoid activation function since we are dealing with a binary classification problem, hence only 360 epochs were required to fully train the model making it significantly faster, as described in [1]. Our results are quite satisfactory for earthquakes classified as far-source, in fact, in this case, the accuracy reaches 67%, which is in line with the available literature. The performance on the near-source, however, is less satisfactory (57% of accuracy) and can certainly be improved. Below are some possible improvements that will be the subject of future studies.

The model can be improved by

– changing the boundary between the near- and far-source, which is fixed at 17 km in this work.
– improving the constraints on the data set.
– increasing the number of events considered, extending the study to the entire Mediterranean area, or including data from numerical simulation. [8]

References

1. Adebowale, A.: A deep learning-based technique to classify near-source and far-source earthquakes. Master's thesis, University of L'Aquila, L'Aquila IT (2022)
2. Agency, J.M.: Overview of the earthquake early warning system (2008). http://www.seisvol.kishou.go.jp/eq/EEW/kaisetsu/eew_naiyou.html
3. Agency, J.M.: What is an earthquake early warning? (2008). https://www.jma.go.jp/jma/en/Activities/eew1.html
4. Anggraini, S., Wijaya, S.: Daryono: Earthquake detection and location for earthquake early warning using deep learning. J. Phys. Conf. Ser. **1951**, 012056 (2021). https://doi.org/10.1088/1742-6596/1951/1/012056

5. Apriani, M., Wijaya, S.: Daryono: Earthquake magnitude estimation based on machine learning: Application to earthquake early warning system. J. Phys. Conf. Ser. **1951**, 012057 (2021). https://doi.org/10.1088/1742-6596/1951/1/012057
6. Böse, M., Wenzel, F., Erdik, M.: Preseis: A neural network-based approach to earthquake early warning for finite faults. Bull. Seismol. Soc. Am. **98** (2008). https://doi.org/10.1785/0120070002
7. Chawla, N., Bowyer, K., Hall, L., Kegelmeyer, W.: Smote: Synthetic minority over-sampling technique. J. Artif. Intell. Res. (JAIR) **16**, 321–357 (2002). https://doi.org/10.1613/jair.953
8. Di Michele, F., et al.: Spectral element numerical simulation of the 2009 l'aquila earthquake on a detailed reconstructed domain. Geophys. J. Int. **230**(1), 29–49 (2022)
9. Government, C.: Wireless emergency alerts (2019). https://earthquake.ca.gov/wireless-emergency-alerts/
10. Géron, A.: Hands-On Machine Learning with Scikit-Learn, Keras, and TensorFlow. O'Reilly, 2nd edn. (2019). ISBN: 978-1-492-03264-9
11. Hanks, T.C., McGuire, R.K.: The character of high-frequency strong ground motion. Bull. Seismol. Soc. Am. **71**(6), 2071–2095 (1981). https://doi.org/10.1785/BSSA0710062071
12. Hazards, E.: Earthquake early warning around the world. https://www.usgs.gov/programs/earthquake-hazards/science/earthquake-early-warning-around-world
13. Hochreiter, S., Schmidhuber, J.: Long short-term memory. Neural Comput. **9**(8), 1735–1780 (1997)
14. Kumagai, J.: A brief history of earthquake warnings (2007). https://archive.ph/20130415005659/http://www.spectrum.ieee.org/print/5156
15. Kuyuk, H., Susumu, O.: Real-time classification of earthquake using deep learning. Procedia Comput. Sci. **140**, 298–305 (2018). https://doi.org/10.1016/j.procs.2018.10.316
16. Kuyuk, H., Talha, K., Yildirim, E., Sümer, Y.: Assessment of near- and far- field earthquake ground motion with wavelet transform. In: Conference: Symposium on Modern Methods in Science (BMYS2010) (2010)
17. Lin II, R.G.: Long-awaited earthquake early warning app for l.a. can now be downloaded (2019). https://www.latimes.com/local/lanow/la-me-ln-earthquake-early-warning-app-20190102-story.html
18. M. Saad, O., Hafez, A., Soliman, M.: Deep learning approach for earthquake parameters classification in earthquake early warning system. IEEE Geoscience and Remote Sensing Letters, pp. 1–5 (2020). https://doi.org/10.1109/LGRS.2020.2998580
19. Michelini, A., Cianetti, S., Gaviano, S., Giunchi, C., Jozinović, D., Lauciani, V.: Instance - the italian seismic dataset for machine learning. Earth Syst. Sci. Data **13**(12), 5509–5544 (2021). https://doi.org/10.5194/essd-13-5509-2021
20. Podger, P.J.: Calistoga to get an earful of nation's first quake siren (2001). https://web.archive.org/web/20140223054531/http://members.napanet.net/
21. Python framework for processing seismological data: Obspy. https://docs.obspy.org/index.html
22. Sebastian, R., Vahid, M.: Python Machine Learning: Machine Learning and Deep Learning with Python, scikit-learn and TensorFlow, 2nd edn. Packt Publishing Ltd., Birmingham (2017). ISBN: 978-1-78712-593-3
23. Snibbe, K.: California's earthquake early warning system is now statewide (2019). https://www.mercurynews.com/2019/10/15/what-you-should-and-should-not-do-during-an-earthquake/

24. Yamada, M., Heaton, T., Beck, J.: Real-time estimation of fault rupture extent using near-source versus far-source classification. Bull. Seismol. Soc. Am. **97**(6), 1890–1910 (2007). https://doi.org/10.1785/0120060243
25. Zaicenco, A., Weir-Jones, I.: Lessons learned from operating an on-site earthquake early warning system. In: 15th Proceedings of World Conference on Earthquake Engineering (2012)

Author Index

O. Gervasi et al. (Eds.): ICCSA 2023, LNCS 13956, pp. 757–760, 2023.
https://doi.org/10.1007/978-3-031-36805-9

Printed in the United States
by Baker & Taylor Publisher Services